THE
X-RATED
VIDEOTAPE
GUIDE

Other books by Robert H. Rimmer

THE X-RATED VIDEOTAPE GUIDE

REVISED AND UPDATED

INCLUDING
*1,300 REVIEWS AND RATINGS
*2,840 SUPPLEMENTAL LISTINGS
*PHOTOS OF THE STARS

ROBERT H. RIMMER

Harmony Books/New York

Published by Harmony Books, a division of Crown Publishers, Inc., 225 Park Avenue South, New York, New York, 10003 and represented in Canada by the Canadian MANDA Group

HARMONY and colophon are trademarks of Crown Publishers, Inc.

Manufactured in the United States of America

Library of Congress Cataloging-in-Publication Data

Rimmer, Robert H.
   The X-rated videotape guide.

   1. Erotic films—Catalogs. 2. Video recordings—
Catalogs. 3. Erotic films—Reviews. 4. Video
recordings—Reviews. I. Title.
PN1995.9.S45R56   1986   016.79143'09'093538   85-27062
ISBN 0-517-56058-5

10 9 8 7 6 5 4 3 2 1

First Revised Edition

Contents

THE REVISED AND UPDATED EDITION OF THIS BOOK . . .

. . . Would not have been possible without the all-out backing and enthusiasm of these key people in the adult-film industry:

David Friedman Entertainment Ventures	Al Bloom Caballero Control	Walter Gernert Video Company of America
Sidney Niekerk Cal Vista Video	Joseph Steinman Essex Video	Norman Arno VCX
Art Morowitz Video-X-Pix	Chuck Vincent Platinum Pictures	Cecil Howard Command Video

or without the perspective on the adult-film industry provided by:

Paul Fishbein

and *The Adult Video News*

and *Adult Video News Confidential* (for video retailers)
P.O. Box 14306, Philadelphia, PA 19115

or

Jared Rutter, Editor
Film World Reports, 8060 Melrose Avenue, Los Angeles, CA 90046

or

Al Goldstein, Publisher
Screw, Milky Way Productions, 116 West 14th Street,
New York, NY 10111

While I never read another review of an adult film until after I have written my own, the above editors and publishers, along with *Adam Film World* (same address as *Film World Reports*), would probably agree with about 75 percent of my CC ratings. Subscription to these periodicals will keep you aware of all the new films, with generally nonhype reporting.

This revised edition would not have been possible without the continuing enthusiasm of Douglas Abrams, my editor, whose organization of these reviews and editorial acumen made this book possible.

Nor would the book have come together in the first edition without the following people, who are either still active in the industry or have moved to other areas of the video business, or have, like Sam Lake, left the earth for a sexier heaven:

Richard Aldrich, Ron Sullivan, Scotty Cox, Bob Sumner, Ted Roter, Jack Genero, Richard Milner, Richard Pacheco, Robert Kane, Bert Anshein, Lindsay Flora, Fred Hirsch, Joseph Periano, David Gussek, Michael Hannan, Jerry Deming, Andre Blay, Jim Duzan, Ray Felder, David Clarke, David Goldin, Bill Wilson, Bruce Swanger, Carol Steer, Richard Stadin, William Gluckman, Russ Meyer, Paula Casey, David Butler, Eric Mart, Sam Lake, Bud Schaffer, Alan Roberts, C. Behr, William Lantto, Dennis Kawicki, Michael McClay, "Sal," Susan Senk, Merril Fine, Alida Gutter, Chris Cummings, Greg Schell, Arthur Morowitz, Vicki Langer, Andre D'Apice, Tom Sinopoli, Saul Saget, Jerry Nieves, Michael Cridole, Joseph Bardo, Susan of Susan's Video, Craig Howard, Linda Crisp, Hank Berger, Eugene Marino, Monica Heath

The following distributors who have continued to work closely with me and who provided the 650 additional tapes from their current catalogues have made this revised and updated edition possible:

Ed Junkins of Ambassador Video
Steve of Baker Video
Anthony Spinelli of Anthony Spinelli Productions
Harry Weinstein of Big Top Video
Barbara Behr of Bizarre Tri-Star
Jack Gallagher of Cal Vista
Kay Parker of Caballero Control
Jim Talmadge and Cindy Walker of Cinderella Distributors
Cecil Howard of Command Video
Alex Tapper of CPLC Video
Lenny Weinstein of I.V.P. Video
Dick Miller of Intropic Video
Kelee Spooner of Dreamland Video
Leslie Dillon and Susan Edwards of Essex Video
John Williams of F.I.V.—Voyeurs Video Club
Ed de Roo and Linda Corso and Mark Arnold of Four-Play Video
George Martin of GM Video
Maria Tobalina of HIFCOA
Norma Resnic of L.A. Video
Susan Fields of New World Video
Jim Chu of Orchids International
Mark Stone of Paradise Visuals
Artie and Jim Mitchell of Mitchell Brothers
Vicki Greenleaf of Media Home Entertainment
Marilyn Chielens of Masterpiece Video
T. Page of Fullerton, CA
Connie Smith and Bob Wolfe of Now Showing Video
Dave Arthur of Standard Video
Pat Ware of VCA (Video Company of America)
Barbara Berkery of Visual Entertainment
Susan Senk of Vestron Video
Bob Marks of Vidco
Bill Falcon of Vista Video
Bob Genoa of VCR
Michael Frydrych of VCX
David Copeland and Colette Connor of Video-X-Pix
Stephen Hirsch of Vivid Video
William Margold, who created himself

A CONTINUOUSLY UPDATED EDITION

The adult-film industry continues to turn out 500 to 1,000 more films annually. If you wish to keep up to date, reviews of new films published by the author are available in a continuously updated edition. For order information write to Challenge Press, P.O. Box 2708, Quincy, MA 02269-2708

Introduction

The Coming Sexvid Explosion

If you've ever watched an X-rated movie, perhaps you've told everyone, "One is enough for me," or, "After watching one, you've seen them all." Nevertheless, you are titillated enough to try again, hoping for a better portrayal of your fantasies, and hopefully you are also smiling at yourself. But win or lose, if you are chuckling a little at such apparent insanity, you have already chosen sides: You're against censorship—well, maybe not all censorship. You're certainly opposed to "kiddie porn," and you probably believe that nonconsentual sex in videotape movies (or any other way) should be outlawed. If you have young children, particularly girls in their early teens, you probably wouldn't want them to catch you watching an X-rated movie—and it's even more likely you wouldn't show such a film to them or share your thoughts about it with them.

Whether you're male or female, you very definitely wouldn't want to be raped, and are offended when you see males displaying aggressive behavior or trying to dominate women (but maybe not quite so upset when you see a woman dominating a man). Still, you probably have fantasized, at least occasionally, forced sex with some person of the opposite sex, whom you are dominating or who is dominating you. But there's a difference: In your fantasies, you probably love the person you are dominating—and you hope that they love you.

If you are laughing, you probably wouldn't censor R-rated movies such as *Straw Dogs* or *Last Tango in Paris*, because watching someone else's rape on film (if it's not too descriptive or gory) holds a certain kind of eroticism for you. But why you feel this way is probably something you don't want to probe too deeply.

If you are crying, or just plain furious, you are either an overly dogmatic feminist, a believer in a Jesus and a God that doesn't condone sexual lust, or a member of Morality in Media (a contributor to Moral Majority) or a similar organization that is running national campaigns to convince you there is no such thing as a victimless crime. Or maybe you may believe that pornographic movies degrade women, make them sex objects, and that the vast, billion-dollar flood of pornography is undermining the family structure.

But perhaps you are more like me and don't quite believe any of these things. When you watch beautiful naked human bodies, male and female, on your television screen you might be just a little bit sad. Because only rarely in the vast storytelling, fairyland of television and movies are our novelists and screenwriters—the people who should be entertaining us and occasionally revealing the truth about life to us—producing stories that are sexually optimistic, stories and pictures that exalt the wonder and joy of human sexuality.

Still, if you think like me, you're optimistic and are even grinning a little. Dick and Jane finally grew up and are writing books and making movies, but they still haven't learned to flush the toilet in the pages of their novels, and virtually never do so in films. Now Dick and Jane are making adult movies. But you can't really be angry with them. They may be calling a spade a shovel, but they are hacking their way through a forest of sexual repressions, too. And, like me, maybe you believe you can show them the light—give them new directions and teach them to pull the chain, at least occasionally. Because I believe that the final battle of the sex revolution, the battle of visual sex, will be won by loving laughter—not censorship.

Whichever side you may be on, the battle lines are drawn. Whether you are for or against personal sexual freedom, during the last half of the 1980s it's going to be increasingly difficult to stay out of the fray. Sex on video cassettes and video discs, made for viewing in the privacy of your own home, is going to make sweeping changes in the manners and mores of the U.S., perhaps more than in any other country in the Western World. Home viewing of sex on television in the next decade is going to set us light-years apart from Islamic cultures and Communistic dictatorships.

The opening guns in the battle were fired several years ago. On December 15, 1979, the *Wall Street Journal* reported, in a brief survey on the rapidly changing video scene: "Pornographic films usually cost more, but they appear to have half the videotape market." The *Journal* did not extrapolate on what that could mean. But think about it: Three million video cassette recorder players (VCRs) had been sold, and are now selling at a rate of 800,000 per year. The lowest VCR prices (around $500) are expected to drop rapidly, especially if video discs gradually invade the hard-core sex market. To lower the selling price even further, VCRs may soon be offered for about $250 without recording capacity. Like video disc machines, they will be able to play various entertainment, but not record it.

In his presentation to the stockholders of Video Corporation of America, a videotape rental company with facilities for transferring films to tape, George Gould, chairman of the company, who did not include sexvids in his projections, predicted that in 1979 most of the major film producers would begin limited videotape release to the VCR market. Gould projected that, in 1980, modest budgets would be made available to produce original movies for direct sale to VCR owners without prior theater showing. This has yet to happen, but is inevitable.

Gould predicted that in 1981, with five million VCRs sold, release of Hollywood and foreign movies to VCRs would take place *before* they would be available via cable or subscription television. Today this prediction is pretty much on target. You can rent most movies (or buy them) a month or two before they are shown on cable or subscription television and within a few weeks after they are released to the general theaters. This was another prediction that came true in late

1981 and 1982, when movies such as *Atlantic City, S.O.B., The Four Seasons, Nine to Five, Ten* and many others were offered on videotape within a month or two after their first release. Theater owners are in direct conflict with major film producers over the release of films to cable and subscription television and to video cassettes. What may develop in the case of major films is a general agreement to withhold them from cable and subscription television for at least six to eight months, and then offer them for viewing on both cable or subscription television as well as on video cassettes.

If you project current purchases into the future, there will be another 12 million VCR owners and 6 million owners of video disc players in the coming three or four years. Alan Hirschfield, chairman of the board of Twentieth Century-Fox (reported in the *Film Journal,* November 1981), estimates that by 1986 there will be 35 million video cassette players and video disc players in consumer hands, with up to 100 million of them worldwide. In 1982, *Los Angeles* magazine pegged the monthly adult video cassette sales volume at approximately 100,000 cassettes per month. That's 1,200,000 cassettes annually, and at average retail prices adds another $100 million to the gross income on adult films in 1982, bringing this figure well into the area of $600 million annually. Based on current purchases, as more and more video cassette players are sold, it is predicted that the owners will probably be buying at least ten million sexvids on cassettes each year by 1990—and this estimate may rise substantially.

Keep in mind that explicit sex is something you can't see on cable or pay television, and you can be sure that the forces of censorship will try to keep it that way. On the other hand, millions of people—whether they will admit it publicly or not—are very interested in watching explicit sexmaking on their own television sets. Inevitably, if the video disc player is going to achieve wide market acceptance (inflation and prices being a factor), all of the best sexvids now available on tape will be made available on discs, with prices running at about $25 or less per disc. When this happens, tape prices for adult films will be forced into the same area. Actually, a few distributors are now pricing some adult films, which run less than an hour and are made from a number of loops packaged together in one film, in the area of $39.50. Keep in mind, too, that when the breakthrough comes, video discs, unlike tapes, can be manufactured as cheaply as phonograph records. Assuming a combined annual market of at least one sexvid per owner (disc or tape), I think it is a safe estimate that by 1990 more than 20 million sexvids will be sold per year—and that estimate may be low. If only a few of the proposals for "reforming" sex on regular network television become a reality, a "frustrated viewer market" of 50 million tapes and discs annually would be a much closer estimate. It is also important to keep in mind that while many of the films listed in this book's filmography may eventually appear in edited versions on cable or subscription television, they will most likely serve to whet the appetites of many viewers to see the unedited versions. Based on an average price of $25 for sexvids by the end of the decade and despite inflation, the production and distribution of sexvids could be a multi-billion dollar industry—and could even represent the biggest segment of the video and film industry in the United States.

The inevitable triumph of home entertainment that you control yourself, either in the form of video discs or tapes, was predicted by the president of RCA. In 1979, he told RCA distributors that by the late 1980s the total market for video discs and video players would exceed $7 billion annually. While the sale of disc players has not taken off as rapidly as expected, nearly three million video discs and five million prerecorded cassettes were sold in 1981, a total sale that *Video Business* magazine estimates at $392.5 million. *Video Business* anticipates that the combined sale of discs and cassettes in 1983 will be over 15 million units with a total sale close to $500 million. My prediction is that by the end of the decade, people in the United States will be spending $2–3 billion annually for home entertainment on cassettes or discs of their own choosing.

A recent Time-Life study of video estimated that, at the moment, the average VCR owner has four videotapes, ranging in cost between $35 and $90. If you merge these figures with the *Wall Street Journal's* estimate that 50 percent of the tapes are sexvids (a more appropriate name than adult or X-rated movies), then already more than two million sexvids have been sold at a price averaging about $75 each. In a so-called sting operation in Los Angeles (March 15, 1980), the *Los Angeles Times* reported that "business records seized in the raids indicated that nine distributors sold about 185,000 sexually oriented videotapes in one month. The average videotape wholesales for about $45, representing a monthly gross of at least $5 million." My guess is that this is only the tip of the iceberg. At retail prices, the sexvid business is already a $200–300 million annual business—and is only in its infancy.

In an article that appeared in *Panorama,* July 1980, entitled "Pornography Unleashed," Howard Polskin tried to anticipate the future. Among other things, he pointed out that the largest collection of sex films in the world, 22,000 of them, is owned by the Institute for the Advanced Study of Human Sexuality. In late 1981, Ted McIlvenna, a Methodist minister who runs the institute, released five videotapes, the first of many to come, called *The Sexual Pleasure Series.* The individual cassettes sell for between $39.50 and $49.50 (see filmography), and all show sexmaking activity between average human beings who are not professional actors or actresses. Nevertheless, even the McIlvenna tapes are still not priced at a mass-market level. But be assured this is coming.

Many people in the developing video disc industry did not believe that sexvids will be offered on discs, at least not in the near future. William H. Fields, publisher of *Video Disc News,* just a few years ago (July 1980) believed "that hard-core porno films will not be pressed on video discs in the near future. Only large, high-technology companies can afford to build the manufacturing facilities needed to press discs, and they have decided not to associate their company images with porno films. When more companies are producing discs under licensing agreements, you will see it happen, but I think that's years away."

Argus Research Corporation, in its report on the emerging video disc market, says, "Adult-oriented discs are likely to be pressed by both RCA and MCA and marketed under independent labels." RCA's executive vice-president, Herbert Schlosser, states in the *Panorama* article, "We won't license it. We won't distribute it. We won't press it, period." But MCA Disco-Vision has already licensed Russell Meyer soft-core films that have previously been distributed in regular theaters, usually with an R-rating. John Reilly, president of MCA Disco-Vision, hedges. "If it's an underground pornographic movie, we don't do it." But he admits he doesn't know what he means by underground.

In the *Panorama* article, the chief legal counsel for the Adult Film Association of America (AFAA), Joseph Rhine, points out: "If some agreement were reached by disc pressers to exclude adult films from the disc market, it would violate antitrust laws."

One sign that sexvids, underground or not, would appear on video discs is an investment proposal offered by Dennis Sobin, who publishes *Tab Reports* and, among many other activities, operates the Red Light Museum in Washington, D.C. Sobin's proposal, dated November 1980, offered an investment opportunity in the world's first erotic video disc, which will be a visual catalog of erotic art, sculpture, books and films with a stereo sound track. The manufacturing cost for a test run of 1,000 discs would be $15,000. The retail price of the Pioneer Laser Disc would be $39.95. Its profit potential was estimated at a minimum of $13,000 with a maximum of over $1 million—"if demand calls for re-pressing the disc as anticipated."

Sidney Niekerk, president of Cal-Vista and also of the Adult Film Association of

America, told the *Film Journal* (March 1982), "As everyone knows, our material accounted for most sales, about 70 percent to 80 percent of video cassettes, when they first appeared on the market. Of course, now with every major distributor offering films on cassettes, our percentage of the market is lower—about 40 percent. But the past record is clear. RCA and MCA had better wake up and talk to us before it is too late." Niekerk reported that he is developing an X-rated disc system with a Japanese firm. The company will offer X-rated and R-rated discs. "The only thing holding up the deal right now," he told the *Film Journal,* "is that I want to guarantee there will be only 'class' X products sold. I told them that if they don't live up to this I'll drop out. There's a lot of garbage on the market, and that is not where Cal-Vista is heading."

Ken Kai, president of Pioneer Video, the first to offer a disc player in a laser format, which is presumably superior to the RCA disc system, claims to have solved the problem of porno films on discs. At a professional meeting in April 1982, he announced that he would press programming of *any* nature on laser video discs. "I have no moral standards about this," he told the gathering. "If they can pay their bills we'll press their programming." Pioneer is a Japanese-controlled company, but because of the very strict censorship in Japan discs cannot be pressed there. But Pioneer has a temporarily deactivated pressing plant in Carson, California. As of the end of 1981, total sales of laser disc players, including Pioneer's, were only 75,000, with two million discs sold. Kai's decision is a hard-headed business decision. If adult films can provide the kind of cash flow that they have for videotape cassettes, they could help save a $500 million investment already made in laser disc technology.

At the moment, you have a choice: you can be an observer of the battle reports, which will be increasingly described in your magazines and newspapers (often with tongue-licking pruriency), or you can be a participant. The cost of participation—actually watching adult sex movies in your home—is less expensive than you might think. You don't have to buy sexvids that cost $75 to $90 (for the better ones). You can rent them. Magazines such as *Video Review* or *Home Video* have numerous advertisers that offer low-cost rental programs that include adult movies. (Full details on the International Home Video Club are given in the filmography.) Many of the men's magazines carry advertisements by distributors that rent adult movies. Vid America and Home Entertainment, two of the big distributors of adult video cassettes, also offer rental services. On the other hand, if you can't afford to buy a VCR but mention your interests to friends, you may be surprised to discover how many of them already own one—along with a couple of sexvids that they would just love to share with you!

Because the technology of video is changing so rapidly, I'm not going to make any attempt to compare the technical differences between the Sony Beta system or one of the many VHS systems, or compare the merits of the many VCRs on the market. All you have to do to get acquainted with the video market is subscribe to one of the new video magazines. They will not only tell you all the pros and cons of the two major tape systems (which are incompatible with each other), but will also tell you about the RCA video disc system, which uses a needle to play the discs and is incompatible with the Magnavox; the North American Philips system, which uses a laser beam; the recently announced General Electric system, which is not compatible with any of the above; and JVC (Japanese Victor Corporation) system, which will use a quarter-inch tape and be compatible with older JVC models.

While the major producers of sexvids are already censoring themselves in an attempt to appeal to and capture the huge at-home female viewer market, it is important to keep in mind that on any video dealer's shelf, or en route to you via United Parcel (for censorship reasons sexvids are rarely mailed through the U.S. Postal System), the actual packages are not any sexier or more titillating than the covers of many paperback books you can buy in any corner store. Moreover, you can't turn the pages of a videotape and read it like you can a book; you must have a video cassette player. As things now stand, unless we elect a new kind of President and a Congress that knows what's good for us—and we believe them—I don't believe that the sale of sexvids can be censored under any present community standard criteria. Actually, the only way sexvids can have any effect on community standards will be if purchasers flaunt them in their apartments or neighborhoods, or show them to underaged children. This may well happen, but for the most part it is rather unlikely, and has about as much probability as young children encountering a "flasher."

On the other hand, there is no denying that the story-line quality and characterization in many of the sexvids produced in the past decade (with the exception of those I have assigned a "Collectors' Choice" rating in the filmography) are boring. Once you have survived the first shock of seeing explicit sex on your television screen, in order to maintain interest you will gradually have to assume a sexologist's perspective. If you do, you may become amazed at the many strange compulsions and hang-ups that human beings have when it comes to expressing their sexuality. And rather than censoring human sexuality, you may become so intrigued that you'll cheer the adult film directors who offer films that try to project more joyous aspects of human sexuality, sexual laughter and wonder. I believe this is not only the key to a healthier society, but ultimately will help to end censorship.

At the moment, there are at least 3,000 adult films available on tape that run 30 minutes or longer. While no one has ever made an exact count, there are probably at least 2,000 "major" films running 60 minutes or longer that have been produced in the past ten years. Most of these have running times from 60 to 90 minutes, with some slightly longer, and the supplemental filmography at the end of this book lists more than 2,000 of them. In the main filmography I have covered 650 additional films, using a unique rating system and giving them a short evaluative review. If you never buy a sexvid and only read these reviews, you will not only get a liberal sex education in abnormal and deviational sex, but you will also discover that quite a few of the films flirt with or actually portray "normal" sexual loving and caring relationships.

Since 1979, a few full-length sexvids have been made directly on tape using video cameras. This is a new development that may quickly kill itself off if the producers/directors resort to producing totally sex-oriented "quickies" with no story line and unimaginative, boring hours of human sucking and fucking. But most current production of adult movies is still based on modern filmmaking techniques, which give the director and editors a creative latitude not available with direct videotaping. You will be surprised, however, if you ever try to make your own at-home sexvids, that with a little ingenuity and not much filmmaking experience, a lone man and woman can immortalize their sexmaking on tape and approximate many of the erotic sequences of the professional adult filmmakers. (See Chapter 5, "Making Your Own Sexvids.")

According to David Friedman, past president and now chairman of the Adult Film Association of America, "There are 894 adult theaters operating in the United States. Despite the burgeoning of the video cassette market these theaters are still the largest source of income for producers and distributors of adult films. Contradicting the fear that video and cable will diminish theater attendance, there has been a marked growth of patronage." The total adult film box office income in 1981 was 17 percent of the entire moving picture industry. Approximately 2.5 million patrons per week pay close to $5 each to see adult films in X-rated theaters. This has meant a box office gross of roughly $10 million a week.

When I talked with adult film theatre owners in 1982 at the Fourteenth Annual

Convention of the AFAA, there seemed to be no fear of diminishing attendance at adult theatres. Jimmie Johnson, vice-president of Pussycat Theaters, the largest adult theater chain in the country, then believed: "Video and cable are helping our theater market because they are introducing people to adult products who may have never seen them before." He was sure that adult theatre attendance was on the way up because "an astonishing 15 percent of adult theaters are cleaner and more attractive, and 83 percent of Pussycat Theater patrons rated them equal to general release movie houses."

Then, in the middle of 1983, adult film producers came face to face with technological future shock. Attendance at adult theatres suddenly started to drop. A combination of burgeoning sales of VCRs and wide availability through most video stores of rental pornos (in most cases you have to ask to see "backroom" selections of adult films) have not only created a huge new market for sexvids, but are gradually diminishing the adult theater audience. By how much has not been revealed. Lower box office receipts do have adult film producers worried. The multimillion dollar box office income not only created big profits, but made it possible to underwrite some adult movies with bigger budgets. For the big budget adult films this budget is still well under the million dollar range, but it makes it possible to expand the film stories beyond the bedroom. Unfortunately, if the producers must depend on sale of video cassettes alone while being undermined by the rental business (which doesn't create much profit for the distributor but can be very lucrative for the local dealer who can rent one film a hundred times), then the potential for better adult films with characterization, story lines, and better acting may never develop.

The same problem is also rapidly emerging with Hollywood's general release commercial film. Momentarily, the new style "tunnel theaters," with as many as ten screens at one location all serving much smaller audiences while depending on popcorn and soft drink sales to survive, are still making it. The younger generation will still spend top dollars to see such first release films as *Star Wars*, *Animal House*, *Porkys*, or *Return of the Jedi*. But a huge and growing audience is being lost to cable television. At the same time, cable television is rapidly losing customers to general release rental movies that allow the VCR owner to program his own movies when he wants to see them, in his own home, at rental costs that run as low as $2 for twenty-four hours. To save money, whether it be for a rental movie or a paperback novel, millions of people are content to wait. Watching a movie at home with drinks, and hors d'oeuvres, in the company of a few friends, is often more fun than being first in line to be packaged like a sardine at the local movie house.

Within the next five years, with a projected market of 35 million VCRs—not to mention disc players and, just as important, new and sharper television screens of up to 45 inches—both general release film producers as well as adult producers will have to learn how to sell movies on tape and discs, just as publishers sell hardcover novels. The adult film producers with lower overhead, particularly in the area of actors' and actresses' salaries, can once again lead the way. To beat the rental market, they'll have to sell direct. What they will need is one big marketing company to handle the sale of their individual products to the viewers. Getting a sale of 100,000 or more video cassette orders of a new sexvid at a rental price of $19.95 plus delivery would allow the adult film producers to go after the direct mail market with larger advertising budgets. Video deals would be encouraged to discount the $19.95 mail order price by a few dollars and not to rent. With this approach, and gross sales on new films running close to two milion dollars, adult film producers who want to survive won't take all their profits and run, but will increase their film budgets for better scripts, better acting, and films that women as well as men will want to see.

Al Goldstein stated in *Screw* that if he owned a porno theater, he'd sell it and invest in parking lots, and predicted, "In fifteen years porno theaters will be dead." Al may be right, but there is another alternative on the horizon. Several adult film producers such as Chuck Vincent see an entirely new future for adult films with strong story lines and character development. In 1982, Chuck set a precedent with his film *Roommates,* which was booked in the so-called art theaters such as the Nickelodeon in Boston, which occasionally shows X-rated films, foreign films or films that appeal to limited audiences.

Dave Friedman, one of the producers and distributors of sexvids, has other worries. He fears "the day a video cassette or video disc of *Deep Throat* is sold without an eyebrow being raised is the day our business will wither on the vine." But Dave underestimates men's and women's preoccupation with their own sexuality. *Playboy* and *Penthouse* have survived for years with basically the same naked women. Of course, with millions of discs and cassettes being purchased for home viewing, there will be millions of other nay-sayers, "upright" citizens who will try to prevent sexmaking of any kind (healthy or unhealthy) from appearing on network or cable television. But they will lose the battle. Tomorrow's children will grow up not only seeing human beings naturally naked when it's convenient to be naked, but making love together in every imaginable way. And they will see it in the privacy of their own homes, in many cases with their parents.

If you have read any or all of my eleven novels, you may wonder why I am chuckling; or why I have written a book about video sex and "porno" (a totally inadequate word) movies. In my novels I have attempted (often to the total exasperation of my editors and critics) to depict human sexuality not only as a joyous, laughing, blending of human flesh, but as the ultimate path to an awareness of the I-am-Thou experience that identifies each of us with the Ultimate Mystery (or whatever we may choose to call it).

After food and shelter, as I have said over and over again, our sexual drives are the lifelong motivation and reason for our achievements—both as individuals and as members of civilized societies. Unlike Freud, who in *Civilization and Its Discontents* attributes human progress to repressed sexuality, I believe that our cultural and technical miracles are a direct reflection of *un*repressed human sexuality. My hero is a Picasso, painting erotic pictures when he was 90, and in his 50s excoriating the war in Spain with his famous painting, *Guernica.*

By contrast, I am fully aware that most sexvids don't celebrate human sexuality. Many of them degrade it and make sexmaking ugly and repulsive. Women are not only sex objects, but the men who screw them don't seem able to carry on much more than a two-syllable conversation. Sex is not loving or caring. It's depicted as a boring piston-and-pump arrangement of two robots, with the male stabbing his penis endlessly into a complacent vagina. Worse, many sexvids depict sick, kinky sex that often balances on the edge of violence.

Recently, feminist authors such as Gabrielle Brown in her book, *The New Celibacy,* try to convince you that sex is overrated, "that the fever for uninhibited orgasmic pleasures which began raging in the 1960s is cooling down . . . growing numbers of people in their twenties and older are now opting for sexual abstinence, even in marriage."

But don't you believe it! In fact, if you finish this book, I may convert you. Remember, I'm a Pollyanna, a Doctor Pangloss! I believe that in the United States, and in many other Western countries, we are on the verge of the next great leap forward in interpersonal relationships. Millions of men and women are discovering a new loving understanding of their sexual and interpersonal needs and behaviors. They're learning that a combination of mental openness and verbal defenselessness, combined with a laughing, caring acceptance of each other, both as potential and actual—totally erotic sexual creatures—and for their entire lifetimes—is the only way to live a fulfilling, self-actualizing life.

Living your life as a laughing, fully sexual person can transform you! It will not only increase your longevity, but will make you handsome and beautiful when you are 80 or 90—and it will keep you out of senior citizen centers or nursing homes. You'll never grow so old that you wonder why you lived so long—you will know! You are alive at 80 or 90 or 100 to love—and be loved. So, the reason I wrote this book is that I believe that the sexvid explosion, which only rarely portrays the wonder of human sexuality, will eventually set the stage for a new kind of visual sex. In the coming years you will see adult films just as explicit as any of the current sexvid offerings—but they will exalt human sexuality and dare to deal with it in a mass medium for the first time as the most amazing facet of our existence as human beings. Eventually, in the process, a frank and uncensored recognition of our sexuality could lay the groundwork for transforming our families, our religions and even our society. How? Simply by utilizing these great new technological wonders—the VCR and the VCR camera and video disc—and using them as a launching platform to create a new kind of sexvid that would make laughing, uninhibited sexuality a fully realized ingredient of our lives.

Before that can happen you have to *believe* that words like *laughing, wondering, joyous* and *playing* are the sine qua non of healthy human sexuality and loving. Many animals, birds, fish and insects give us the impression that they enjoy playful sex, and in some species there is evidence of a caring relationship, at least during the time the female is gestating and raising her young. But only humans both are the product of their sexual drives and have the potential to evaluate them. We can think about our sexual necessities, wonder about our need to give love and sex and receive it, and we can both objectify and subjectify our sexual needs in hundreds of ways, from caring to laughing to lusting, in self-created erotic environments. We may be descended from monkeys, but no monkey or other living creature can do that.

Sadly, while we all have this ability, millions of people are so hung up from their parental and/or religious conditionings that they are shocked by sexual laughter or other display of exuberant sexuality. From an early age, millions of us grew up in homes with locked bedrooms and bathrooms. Most of us never saw our parents naked, or just in bed hugging each other, let alone actually making love. Millions of us, even in two-children families, never saw our siblings naked. We grew up in environments where bodily functions were not discussed and were taken care of in total privacy.

In many respects, our sexual behavior in the 1980s really reflects only a superficial sexual revolution. Nakedness and human sexuality, for most Americans, are still not quite nice—for many it is even sinful, and they are unable to cope with the reality that an erect penis and a moist vagina are joyful facets of human existence.

2

A Quick Look at the
Adult Film Industry

Archeologists have found drawings of human vulvas and penises on the walls of caves in Europe as far back as 30,000 B.C. to 10,000 B.C. Later, during the Neolithic period (9000 B.C. to 7000 B.C.) when the ice age had ended, many clay figurines were found, with protruding breasts and vulvas and chalk phalluses carved by primitive human hands. Organized religion based on fertility worship was slowly evolving. The first visual images of human genitals would be refined into specific gods who would then be worshiped for their sexual prowess. Five hundred years before the birth of Christ, the Greeks were artistically displaying human sexual activities in a completely open manner on vases, lamps and sculpture. A few centuries later, the Romans were also visually portraying their sexual activities, but the playful element of human sexuality was slowly being permeated with a feeling of lasciviousness and human corruption. And finally, the founders of Christianity drew the battle lines of today by identifying the copulation of Adam and Eve as sin, evil, "a fall from Grace."

Since then, even though in all human cultures millions of men and women have never stopped trying to evoke all aspects of their amazing and wondrous need to join with each others' flesh both in words and pictures, their leaders have always tried to stop them, to "legislate your morality and mine." For the most part, the sexual battle of words in the Western World has been won. Within the past 25 years, men and women have been free to express every aspect of human sexuality in print and in other media. With a few exceptions—one of which occurred in India during A.D. 900–1100, when the famous erotic sculptures were carved at the temple in Kailasanath, and another at the Sun Temple at Konorak in fifteenth century China—the battle against the visual portrayal of human sexuality continues virtually unabated.

Visual representations of men and women enjoying each others' bodies permeate the art of the Western World in both painting and sculpture. But as Bradley Smith points out in his book, *20th Century Masters of Erotic Art,* "Artists of earlier generations who painted direct allusions to the sexual life of humans painted for *themselves* and a very limited audience of friends and patrons. The painter's reputation and all his future earnings could be jeopardized by censorship of critics, art dealers who controlled galleries and repressive governments. He could be, and often was, cast out of polite society."

Actually, not until the end of the nineteenth century, with the emergence of photography and moving pictures soon afterward, did the visual portrayal of human sexuality become generally available on a mass level. Then, printing lithographs and making photographic printing plates became cheaper, and millions of people who had never seen a man and woman naked, let alone copulating, could do so. But it was still sub rosa and against the law. By the end of World War I, millions of French postcards had circulated throughout the world offering photographs of buxom ladies in see-through clothing or even naked.

The first stag movies were actually made in 1896. But, today, nearly 100 years later, even though many thousands more stag movies have been made, millions of men and most women have never seen sexmaking on screen. Only in the past ten years has the combination of moviemaking and videotape (and ultimately video discs) laid the groundwork for erotic art for the masses. Far beyond the written word, or the naked but motionless photographs in *Playboy, Penthouse* and various other men's magazines, millions of men and women in the coming decade will hear and watch the sexual behavior of others and see their sexual daydreams come to life—not in a sleazy adult theater but in the privacy of their own homes.

No one knows how many explicit sex films have been made since the first one in 1896—but they're definitely in the tens of thousands. But since *Deep Throat* launched the so-called new wave of porno films there is a ten-year inventory that can (or already has) been transferred to tape. Most of these films are listed in the filmography at the end of the book. Despite the rapid development and transfer to tape of films made during the past ten years, 8-mm porno films, which dominated the market for the past twenty years, are still a very big business. They can be duplicated easily and retailed for as low as $20 for 10–15-minute sequences. Many of these have been transferred to tape and sold, two or three to a one-hour tape, under names such as *Swedish Erotica, Limited Editions, Diamond Collection,* and *Peep Show* (see filmography). There are many leftovers from early adult films that now exist on videotape, offering kinky sex and rape; bondage and discipline sequences are also readily available on videotape. But the really kinky stuff, sodomy and child pornography, e.g., appears only on 8-mm film. Most of it travels underground or under the counter in adult bookstores.

Today, most adult filmmakers do not produce films that transgress a 1980 memorandum from the Los Angeles City Attorney's office. The memorandum pinpointed makers of those films and tapes subject to arrest and prosecution. They included scenes of bestiality and masturbation of animals; so-called snuff films, in which the actress is supposedly murdered in her final orgasm (probably none of these actually exist); and films or tapes showing sex with minors. Although there is a big demand for females to portray teenagers and act as if they were under 16, as far as I've been able to discover there is no "kiddie porn" in *any* of the videotapes listed in the comprehensive filmography at the end of the book.

The police may also try to censor films on tape that show urination (golden showers), defecation (Marquis de Sade style), or films showing pain or sadomasochistic abuse. However, as you will discover in the filmography, there are many bondage-and-discipline films available on videotape. A few tapes even offer "fist fucking," in which an arm, foot or toe is inserted into a vagina; one such sequence appears in the original tapes of *Candystripers,* which were confiscated in a raid by the Los Angeles Police Department in March 1979. If you buy a videotape of *Candystripers* today that scene has been eliminated.

Areas I have labeled "Deviational Kinky" in the filmography (such as anal sex, double insertions, orgies and various combinations of group sex) are no longer subject to police raids. And, of course, in areas such as Los Angeles (considered the porn capital of the United States in terms of dollars and production) as well as San Francisco and New York City, the visual portrayal of "normal" sex, i.e. oral and penile-vaginal sex, and masturbation is no longer shocking.

Before we examine in depth the rapidly changing style of adult films since *Deep Throat*—and particularly the video duplication of these films, now practically simultaneous with the first showing in adult theaters—a background of the industry itself may help to give you some perspective. When I decided to write this book, I was totally unaware of the number of people involved in the industry. Despite its continuing annual Erotic Film Festival of the past five years, the adult film industry tries to maintain a low profile, and is advisedly a little paranoid about investigative reporters like me, who may turn out to be the local police or FBI man in disguise. While there are no accurate statistics, I would guess that more than 10,000 people in the United States earn a good living from the production and distribution of X-rated films. This would include producers, directors, financial backers, actors, actresses, screenwriters, cinematographers, adult film theater owners and employees and retail video dealers.

In her 1974 book, *Blue Money, Pornography and Pornographers, An Intimate Look at the Two Billion Dollar Fantasy Industry,* Carolyn See covered some areas of the newly emerging adult film industry, with separate chapters on Matt Cimber, the last husband of Jayne Mansfield, Linda Lovelace, Marvin Miller (who has long since disappeared, but was then called "King of the Skin Flicks") and many others. Linda Lovelace and Marilyn Chambers have ghostwritten several books, notably Linda's *The Ordeal of Linda Lovelace.* There have been a few other books published about the industry or people in the industry, but most of the books and articles use a *People* Magazine approach—evincing an attitude of more or less horror at the product, accompanied by much of the "How could you do it?" type of reporting combined with supposedly intimate exposures of the actors' and actresses' lives or the lives of people involved in the industry.

If you really want to read more about the actors and actresses in X-rated films and how they supposedly react (Note the word *supposedly.* My feeling is that they are only too happy to cater to your fantasies onstage or offstage—it's good both for their own image and for business.), then you should subscribe to magazines such as *Adam Film World* (the best editorially), *Velvet, High Society, Video X, Cinema X* and of course, *Screw,* which since 1968 has become the tabloid sex newspaper of record. All of these publications devote some of their pages to the idiosyncrasies of X-rated actors, actresses and their directors. Within their pages you'll find long interviews, and (with the exception of *Screw,* which is a black-and-white weekly newspaper) most of them also offer full-color, detailed still photographs as well as reviews of currently released films.

In our so-called advanced sexual society, stars of adult films are beginning to create as much interest in their personal, off-screen lives as did the early motion picture stars. Today, many other men's magazines such as *Gallery, Genesis, Hustler* and occasionally *Playboy* and *Penthouse* offer inside glimpses of the various aspects of the industry and review current adult films.

Much has been written, both true and false, about the financial backers and distributors who have made and are making millions in the porno film business. When Gerard Damiano was asked why he sold his ownership of *Deep Throat* for $25,000, he told reporters he couldn't talk about it. "Do you want me to get both my legs broken?" he demanded.

On Valentine's Day in 1979, Mike Zaffrano, who at 56 was considered one of the kingpins in the porno business, dropped dead in his New York office of a heart attack when the FBI raided his company in what became known as the Miporn investigation. Raids were simultaneously conducted in many other major cities. Thirty-three out of the 58 persons arrested came from California. Zaffrano was only one of the top men involved in pornography. The names of all the key people in the industry were revealed in an article in *Home Video Magazine*

(January 1981), accompanied by their backgrounds and what they did in various parts of the country.

Interestingly, the raids and arrests by the FBI were mostly an attempt to convict the people who were bootlegging or pirating legitimate movies and offering them on video cassettes. They would then force their sale through the video dealers they controlled. Movies such as *Superman II, Star Wars,* and *Close Encounters of the Third Kind,* for example, could make fortunes for those who copied them and offered them for sale on cassettes. All one needs to do is "borrow" the actual film from a theater of a particular exhibitor, make a master tape and then return the film to the theater before the next showing. Another charge leveled was that since these men presumably controlled much of the video cassette distribution of adult films, they were involved in "suppressing" the pirating of their own films, such as *Deep Throat* or *The Devil and Miss Jones.* A few indictments were made, fines paid and that was the end of the matter. No attempt has been made by the FBI to actually stop interstate distribution of adult films or to censor pornography.

I'm sure that books eventually will appear offering lurid details, true or not, of the so-called mob connection with the adult film industry. But how, where and why they function is not the subject of this book. Whether these specific people existed or not, adult films would still be made in profusion. The fact is that the vast majority of the people I have met in the industry comprise most nationalities and ethnic groups. Many of them have a devalued and bored feeling about human sexuality, and only occasionally portray caring sex in the films and tapes they offer—but they are not criminals.

I'm also sure that one day someone will write a book about Dave Friedman, chairman of the board of the Adult Film Association of America. His father was a former editor of the conservative *Birmingham News.* Along with his uncle, his father owned an amusement park and a chain of movie houses. This gave the young David an early exposure to the life of carnival rides, booths, barkers and the theater. In 1956, Dave Friedman formed a company to make what was known then as sex exploitation movies. His experiences touring the country with an amazing attraction that dared to show the birth of a baby—a film called *Mom and Dad*—and his experiences during the 1950s when he made movies such as *The Adventures of Lucky Pierre, Trader Hornee,* the *Erotic Adventures of Zorro* and many others—would make a fascinating motion picture, which I have told Dave should be titled *The Laughing Man.*

One day I am sure someone will write a book about other men in the industry such as Sam Lake, president of Quality X Video Cassettes and Mature Pictures. Sam Lake not only risked all the money he had ever made in lawsuits, but when he first showed *Deep Throat* in the World Theater on Broadway (during those years it grossed $96,000 in one week alone), he also risked going to jail. When I talked to Sam in the first part of 1982, he was in his early 70s. Sam's attitude toward human sexuality is filled with laughter. The key to the ultimate acceptance of adult movies is happy laughter at our own sexual insanities and drives—not shame or shock.

In 1972, when Sam's mother was 80 years old, she asked him what he was doing to make a living. He took her to see *Deep Throat.* Before they walked over a special red carpet he had put out in front of the theater just for her, he told her, "It's as if you owned a toll bridge, Momma, and everyone wants to drive over it. Instead of paying twenty-five cents to get to the other side, here they pay five dollars. If they're so crazy to see a woman playing with a man or a man playing with a woman, why shouldn't I charge them?" When he finally won the lawsuit against the World Theater and himself, Sam announced it on the theater marquee: "Judge Cuts Throat: World Mourns."

In his book, *Erotic Communications, Studies in Sex, Sin, and Censorship,* George N. Gordon has a footnote that parallels my own experience. He addressed the AFAA at its quarterly meeting at the Waldorf Astoria in New York in 1978 at an informal luncheon. "By and large," Gordon reports, "I've found them a surprisingly sincere and intelligent audience and extremely interested in the topic of my talk, which concerned the attitudes of young people today—and tomorrow—toward X-rated films, and the artistic, and even educational potential of such cinema. In many ways, they resemble Hollywood's original filmmakers in the early days of the movies. They are slightly guilty because of their extraordinary financial success, uncertain about the future of their medium, and deeply concerned about public attitudes toward an aspect of culture that much of the public does not understand, but in unspecified ways and without much proof, considers a dangerous form of corruption. Like the other early filmmakers, they, too, consider themselves to be outcasts. Therefore, their drive to band together in their own common interests, as well as their unusual warmth toward a college professor who they perceived as being on their side and who treated them exactly as what they were—his peers—and in terms of common interests, his superiors by far!"

If you can get your hands on a copy of *Sinema* by Kenneth Turan and Stephen F. Zito (Prager, New York, 1975), you'll find a fascinating study of American porno-graphic films and the people who made them during about a twenty-year pe-riod between 1954 and 1974. The feeling I got when I read this book is that most people in the industry sincerely believe they are providing entertainment for which, from time immemorial, there has always been a demand. And like any-one with good business sense, if the demand shifts to more romantic, caring but still explicit sex (which I believe it is in the process of doing), they will shift with it. Whatever their nationalities or whether the actresses and actors do or don't enjoy sexmaking for a living, the truth is that they and the producers, directors, cam-eramen and practically every other person involved in the industry are just as confused in their interpersonal moralities and their sexual values as are you and I.

My first contact with the adult film industry was in the spring of 1980. I attended my first annual three-day Adult Film Convention (the twelfth such convention since the AFAA was formed), which was being held that year at the Sheraton Center Hotel in New York City. The convention was listed on the lobby bulletin board, along with the meeting of the Insurance Actuarial and Statistics Associa-tion, Kinney Shoes, State Liquor Authority, Japan Travel Bureau and the Friendly Sons of St. Patrick. The notation at the bottom simply was the AFAA Meeting, and the presence of the members was completely played down in the hotel environ-ment. At the fourteenth annual convention, held in March of 1982, the members of the AFAA were scarcely noticed among more than 2,000 Sweet Adelines (women who sing barbershop), who were also holding their convention at the hotel.

Lest you think that an AFAA meeting is an occasion for an orgy, let me disillusion you. The AFAA has more than 285 members who include the producers, dis-tributors, theater owners, cable programmers and video cassette manufacturers in the adult film business. It was formed in 1969 in the belief that "we must all hang together, or assuredly we shall all hang separately." Unlike many alternate life-style conventions, meetings of various humanistic psychology groups or seminars in the human potential movement that I have attended, the participants do not come to AFAA meetings for sexual exchange. The three-day meetings have the usual cocktail parties, dinner dances and big luncheons with guest speakers, but if the group of well-dressed men and women have anything in common, it isn't sex—it is bottom-line profits and good living.

A conversation I had with a well-known producer of more than one adult film sums up the middle-class morality of the group. When she learned I was the author of more than one novel with the underlying theme that you could love more than one person without destroying a monogamous marriage, she was more than a little shocked. "If my husband ever got involved with another woman, I'd murder him," she told me grimly. When I suggested that in one of her current films, which concerned movie mogul husbands (whose wives you never see) who were busily fucking young movie starlets on their way up, her laughing response was: "Them's stories, it's not the way most people live. Keep in mind this is a business. It's a way to make a buck." Making a buck is the key, the common denominator.

In their personal lives, most of the people in the adult film industry, whether they actually produce, distribute or act in the pictures, probably have as many hang-ups as most of the people who view their films in the adult theaters, or who see them in their homes on tape. Many of the various workshops at this and later AFAA conventions (held in alternate years in Los Angeles and New York City) are oriented around the adult film theater owners and their continuing community and legal problems. The AFAA has a staff of five attorneys—Arthur Swartz, Robert Eugene Smith, Elliot Ableson, John Weston and Joseph Rhine—who serve on the legal advisory panel for the group. Anne Perry, who is married to Joseph Rhine, is one of the few female producers of adult films. The AFAA also has a national network of lawyers skilled in defusing local arrests and lawsuits against various adult theater owners.

The U.S. Supreme Court's decision to leave the problem of pornography and whether certain films or books comply with the moral standards of thousands of communities throughout the country to local jurisdiction has created a mon-ster—not only for adult filmmakers, but also for magazines such as *Playboy, Hustler* and *Penthouse,* which must publish editions that don't offend the sensibilities of the citizens of Arlington, Texas, or Sandusky, Ohio—and at the same time will attract the more sexually sophisticated buyers in New York City, Los Angeles and San Francisco.

In Texas, for example, most of the towns and some of the major cities do not permit the exhibition of hard-core films. The meaning of what is hard-core in adult films varies from place to place, but essentially it means that there will be no displays of erect penises or open vulvas (with or without erect penises in the act of penetrating them). In one of the workshops at the first AFAA convention I attended, one producer explained in detail how he had developed techniques to produce hard-core and soft-core versions of his films simultaneously, simply by using two cameramen, which he claimed was much less expensive than assem-bling the actors for a second run-through. The soft-core version was produced without the offending genitals. This meant, of course, that the soft-core cam-eraman must somehow shoot the copulating scenes from a different angle, with-out tripping over the hard-core cameraman. At the same time, the male actors somehow or other must maintain an erection. For those who can't, there are female assistants called "fluffers," who are oral sex experts and presumably can bring satiated penises back to erection.

The legal problems facing the members of the AFAA—whether they are the-ater owners, producers or film distributors—are immense and never ceasing. As one of the lawyers pointed out to the members at the fourteenth annual AFAA convention, "There is a tremendous battle going on out there that may terminate your marketplace." Already there are no adult theaters in Atlanta, Jacksonville and Cincinnati. In one way or another, local authorities, either through zoning or other tactics, have eliminated the adult theaters in these cities.

But the biggest battle of the decade—one which AFAA members fear may be won by the so-called Moral Majority—is the cable and subscription television potential of R-rated movies. One of the problems facing the industry is how many versions of an adult film will have to be made to accommodate cable or subscription networks, which funnel their programs through stations in many different areas. Obviously, what may be totally acceptable in New York City will probably not be so in Dubuque, Iowa. Even though individual subscribers may be paying to see R-rated films, and even though they may have lock boxes on their television sets to keep children from watching these films, there are millions of people who don't believe in your First Amendment rights when it comes to watching the sexual behavior of other people on television screens.

If the do-gooders are unable to stop adult films in one way, they will try another. For several years they tried to convince the FBI that adult filmmakers were producing "snuff" movies, in which people were supposedly getting murdered in the act of sexmaking, or who were having a final orgasm at the point of death. The AFAA was so confident that no such movies existed that they offered a $25,000 reward to anyone who would come forth with one. The reward was never claimed.

In 1980, an adult filmmaker was arrested in the state of California for pandering. Basically this was an attempt, still unresolved, to convict filmmakers and the actors and actresses of committing acts of prostitution when they engaged in the making of adult films.

At a recent convention, some film producers griped about certain theater owners who, they insisted, were always complaining about—but who were actually responsible for—the low quality of many of the films. Some of the theaters in the major cities are nothing but "grind houses," one producer insisted. "They must have a new film every two or three days. They cater to the 'raincoat crowd' who don't give a damn about story line or plot but want to see at least ten different girls get fucked in one hour."

The term "raincoat crowd" lumps together quite a few million United States males, young and old, who are either very shy with women, are too fat or too thin, who have physical handicaps or who think they are too ugly. Essentially the theory is that if you took a survey of the male audiences of adult films throughout the United States you would find one common denominator: most of them have very little joyous, fresh contact with females. According to the stereotype, the men arrive at the adult theaters wearing raincoats to give themselves easy access to their genitals while they fantasize—it's not their own hands holding their penises, it's the woman up there on the screen who's nursing them and taking their forlorn little jigger in her mouth and/or her vagina. According to some feminists, the more aggressive viewers may hold a certain amount of female rage, but I doubt it. Most of them would be happy to trade the whole experience for a loving woman who could help to affirm them as men.

In cities such as New York and San Francisco, these poor souls also have access to places like "Show World," which has barred windows opening onto circular stages surrounded by "masturbation booths." There is no cost to enter the booth. Once inside, however, a man has to insert a quarter to get a quick look at a naked female as a metal curtain rises on a barred window. Some of the women are willing to let the viewers try to lap their breasts, vulvas or anuses through the bars—if they are willing to pay an extra dollar or so. The metal curtain drops in about two minutes. It costs another quarter before it goes up again, permitting the sad sexual exchange to continue. Do the men hate the women who are teasing them on with every dirty word they can think of? Probably. Porno movies and fantasies are much better. You can't lick the women on the screen with your tongue, but they don't talk back or humiliate you either.

Some background on the interrelationship of adult film producers, distributors and theater owners gives clues not only to the industry's current profitability, but will also reveal the directions it may take. The owners of adult theaters (incidentally, in many smaller cities they are a husband and wife team) are continually trying to upgrade their audiences and replace the raincoat crowd with young couples, both married and unmarried. It isn't easy. What appeals to one audience either totally shocks the other or bores it to death. The adult film reviewers who cater to the raincoat crowd thoroughly understand this. In a *Screw* review of *Summer School,* a fairly recent adult film, the comment is that the movie "shies away from being hot or erotic . . . and while it does have its moments, it is not pure crotch-teasing material because it is done for the cameras and not for the horny porn-film buff."

Let's now take a look at the profitability of the industry. There are approximately 800 theater owners who cater to the three-million-person audience that passes through their doors each week. About 40 percent of the ticket sales pay for film rental fees. In the April 1980 issue of *Mother Jones,* which is devoted to "Sex, Porn and Male Rage," Carter Stevens, one of the many directors of adult films, assured Henry Schipper that he didn't care what anyone thought about him. "People make porn features for one reason: money—easy money."

Bob Sumner, former head of Mature Pictures, and one of the porn industry's major producers, agrees with him. "It's a very hard business to lose money in," he told Schipper. Sumner went on to say that his company had produced or distributed 37 sex films—all of which made money. Sumner averages a $1.5–2 million gross per picture. "About 60 percent of that goes to the theater owners and the rest is divided by the film companies and distributors," he said. After expenses, according to Schipper, Sumner is left with $300,000–500,000 per picture.

The majority of distributors and producers are located either in New York or Los Angeles. Because the style of the particular directors and the background shots often differ considerably, *Adam Film World,* in its monthly review of new films, actually indicates whether it is an East Coast or a West Coast production. After you've watched a number of sexvids it's easy to decide for yourself whether they were made in New York City or Los Angeles. (Most of the New York producers have New York City backgrounds, and most of the Western producers have either Los Angeles or San Francisco backgrounds.) In the March 1982 *Film Journal* there's an adult film guide listing 82 companies, most of which are involved in the production of adult films. They have names such as A-B Film, Inc., Avarice Films, Inc., Backstreet Film Distribution and Backstreet Productions, Blue Ribbon Video, Cal Vista Video, Citrus Productions, Distripix and Entertainment Ventures, to mention a few. Most of the distributors of adult films such as TVX, VCX, Select, Cal Vista, Quality X or Caballero, whose full names you will find in the filmography, are closely involved with the financial backing and production of films; so are some of the major theater owners, such as the owners of the Pussycat chain. Quite a few of the distributors of adult film tapes actually own one or more adult theaters.

Unlike their Hollywood cousins (who can't produce a commercial film for under two to five million dollars), sexvids rarely have budgets over $300,000. Even today, despite inflation, many are produced with a budget averaging under $75,000. One film producer admitted to me when I told him that his current film was not up to his usual caliber that he had produced it on a long weekend for $17,500.

Production companies market their films directly to the adult theaters, but most of them don't produce or market videotapes from their films. Instead, they sign contracts with the ultimate distributor of the sexvids that will be made from a particular film. The contract gives them a royalty on the sale of each sexvid. Occasionally, if a film has been very successful at the adult film theater box office, or has won an erotic film award, the producer is able to insist on a guaranteed advance—typically, $5,000–10,000—for the rights to offer an adult film on tape. Some producers will sign a contract with several distributors, which accounts for the fact (which you can note in the filmography) that often several companies will offer the same film on tape. This is also true of many films made in the early 1970s, where no copyright ever existed. As a result, anyone could duplicate the tape if they have access to the basic film. Boccaccio 100 (listed in the filmography) is a good example of a small distributor with access to a number of original 16-mm films which, at the moment, no other distributor is offering. Even if the actors or actresses are familiar on some of these older films, they receive no income from the tape sale since when they made the film they signed contracts without any provisions for residuals.

A well-known West Coast producer, Richard Aldrich, laughingly told me that sexvid contracts between producers and distributors are as many and as different as you can think up in a week. Many of the contracts have time and performance limits, and the advances are made against royalties from the sales of the tapes. Thus, producers and distributors have a relationship similar to that of an author and his publisher.

The distributor's wholesale price to a retailer for a sexvid varies, but averages around $50. Included in this price is a royalty paid to the producer—usually about $10 per tape (or more, depending on the popularity of a particular film).

How vital this sexvid royalty has become in the past few years is revealed by one producer who told me, "It's fantastic! I put Blank Blank [the name of the picture is purposely withheld] in the can for $46,000. It's only been in the theaters for two weeks and the distributor has already sold 4,200 sexvids. That's $42,000! Even without theater rentals, I'm in the clear."

Keep in mind these videotapes have a long life. People who don't yet own a VCR or video disc player will be buying tapes listed or reviewed in the filmography of this book for many years to come. Many people in the industry believe that more tape sales will be created if potential buyers can preview them in adult theaters. While you can rent sexvids for approximately $9 to $14 a week or more (see filmography), many male buyers evidently prefer to own them and view them time and time again. Younger men may use them to startle their friends or liven up parties—or hope that by showing them to wives or girlfriends, that they may get them to enjoy sexmaking as much as some of the female stars seem to. Although it is technically illegal to show any videotape (purchased or copied off television) to groups, many tapes are purchased by male clubs and fraternity houses to show to their male members—much as stag films were shown in the 1950s when the ladies weren't around.

Final figures for specific adult film theater grosses are hard to come by. Review after review of many foreign erotic films (particularly from Japan, where almost total sexual censorship still prevails, and even *Playboy* cannot appear unless the genitals are air brushed), reveal that many of these films are not very sexy by the new, far-out U.S. standards. There's a lot of nudity and explicit sex in the Scandinavian and West German films. But often there's not so much concentration on genital thrusting; nor do the films seem so sexually self-conscious as stateside versions. In the Japanese films, there is much soft-core sadism, with naked women being tied up or flagellated. U.S. films sell exceedingly well in Europe, Japan and West Germany, and there is a big black market for them in the Islamic countries—all of which provides additional revenue to the companies that control the video cassettes or particular films.

Deep Throat (two words that have entered the U.S. vocabulary) has grossed, according to various estimates, anywhere from $50 million to $100 million at the box office and still has a long life ahead of it. Box office receipts of the industry in 1978 were $365 million, and in 1980 definitely exceeded $500 million. If you divide the gross into the production of 150 films annually, the average gross on a film that costs an average of about $100,000 to produce would be $1.5 million.

A film you probably never heard of, *Ms. Magnificent,* grossed $22,000 in the first two weeks it was released—in two theaters alone. *Frat House,* another porn flick, grossed $7,993 in three days in one Denver theater, and $11,148 in a theater in San Diego. *Tangerine,* one year after its theater release, had grossed $789,532 at the theater level *without* any sexvid sales.

As sexvid audiences grow—either watching tapes, discs or both—the entire industry will eventually experience some interesting changes and shake-outs. Distributors can make their own tapes by hooking up a battery of video cassette recorders (both in the VHS and Beta formats) to a computer. They can turn out 100 or more tapes an hour from a master tape made from the film, which is usually produced for them, at a relatively small cost for the master, by companies specializing in the transfer of film to tape. But compared with the cost of pressing discs (which can be turned out as fast as phonograph records), producing duplicate tapes is a much more costly business.

I have previously discussed whether or not companies such as RCA and Universal will offer porno discs. My bet is that they will press them for private labels and for distributors who control particular adult films. It's becoming obvious—to RCA in particular—that in order to build a software market they will have to practically give away the disc players. Adult films on discs are a sure way to increase and build a large market for the disc players. By pressing them for private labels both RCA and MCA can maintain a distance. When this happens, you can be sure that prices will tumble because discs, once the original mold is made, are much less costly to produce than tapes—especially if produced in quantity. On the other hand, distributors who control specific adult tapes can produce as few as 25 duplicates and thus maintain small inventories of many different films on tape. Although I am sure that current and highly successful adult X-rated films will eventually appear on discs, avid collectors intrigued with building a library will have to depend on videotape sources.

In July 1980, I attended my first Erotic Film Festival, an important annual gathering of the industry that is a key to the new star system. It was the Fourth Annual Erotic Film Awards and was held at the Hollywood Palladium. Although patterned after the Motion Picture Academy Awards, the proceedings weren't televised—but they soon will be. The AFAA videotaped the entire Fifth Annual Erotic Awards in July of 1981, and has offered it to cable and subscription television.

All the "grandes dames" (the former stars of erotic films) except Linda Lovelace were in attendance at the Hollywood Palladium for the Fourth Annual Erotic Film Awards in 1980. Marilyn Chambers arrived accompanied by Chuck Traynor, Linda's former manager (and, according to Linda, her seducer and hypnotist). Georgina Spelvin, looking mature and slightly heavier, was one of the many presenters, who included new stars such as Samantha Fox, Leslie Bovee, Cindy de Paula, Gloria Leonard, Lisa de Leeuw, Vanessa Del Rio, Seka, Candida Royalle and Desiree Cousteau. And of course John Holmes (Johnny Wadd) led the male contingent, along with Jamie Gillis, John Leslie and Johnny Keyes proving—since there weren't too many other of the newer male stars present—that on the screen at least, the old male actors survive longer than their female peers.

The awarding of the gold Erotica statue, a naked woman clinging to an upright column, was almost as boring and deadly as the Motion Picture Academy's Oscar Awards. Over 600 people paid $60 a plate for their dinner, and the Palladium was jammed to the walls with many who had arrived in Rolls Royces and other expensive foreign cars. The AFAA had promised the Palladium management that there would be no overt sexuality, unlike the year before, when Al Goldstein humorously pretended he was humping Gloria Leonard.

Several low-keyed sexual ballets, film clips from *Babylon Pink, Easy, Ecstasy Girls, Fantasy, Jack and Jill, Pro Ball Cheerleaders* (nominated for best pictures of 1980), together with the singing of the best songs from the erotic films by several stars, were interspersed between the award presentations. The chosen songs were "Leonard's Theme," from *All About Gloria Leonard;* "This Time We Make It," from *Ecstasy Girls;* "One Page of Love," from *Two Sisters;* and "Small Town Girls," from *Small Town Girls.* These songs were actually sung (occasionally out of tune) by Paul Thomas, Cindy de Paula, Samantha Fox and Johnny Keyes. The various pre-

senters, including John Holmes, Leslie Bovee, Jamie Gillis, Turc Lyon, Gerard Damiano, Mark Stevens, John Leslie and Annie Sprinkles, among others, announced
the Best Achievement in Film Editing, the Best Screen Play, the Best Achievement
in Cinematography, the Best Advertising Campaign, the Best Trailer, the Best Production Values, the Best Achievement in Costumes (believe it or not!), the Best
Foreign Film, the Best Musical Score, the Best Original Song, the Best Achievement
in Directing, the Best Performance by an Actor and Actress and the Best Picture of
1980. The winner of the 1980 Erotic Award for Best Picture was *Babylon Pink.*
Samantha Fox came through as Best Actress in *Jack and Jill.* Before the presentations started there were a few picketers wearing "Read the Bible" T-shirts. One of
them was asked if he was against nudity and, if he was, what he thought about
Michelangelo. He replied, "Michelangelo will have to answer to God." Seka, one
of the newer porn stars, arrived chiding the pickets. "We're not dirty people," she
said, and then autographed anything in sight with the words, "Love and Lust."

A business college student interviewed by the *Los Angeles Times* told a reporter: "I'd rather look at these films than the other kind, where the people get
their heads blown off or where there are gang fights and violence."

While he was confessing, a picketer and his wife waved a sign that read "Turn
or Burn!" He told reporters, "These films depict a perversion of the natural way
God created the human body."

Georgina Spelvin and Samantha Fox summed up the fascinating evening,
which admittedly lacked the class of the Academy Awards and was never reported by *Time* or *Newsweek.* When Samantha was asked if she'd display something more than the award she received for Best Actress she replied, defiantly,
"Absolutely not. Remember I'm a lady." (At the Adult Film Convention a few
months earlier, she told my wife that she was the daughter of an English countess—believe it or not!) And Georgina Spelvin, when asked by reporters if there
was a place for acting in porno films, laughed and said: "Acting? Acting is what
you do in between films."

The Fifth Annual Erotic Film Awards, held at the Hollywood Palladium in July
1981, provided an interesting spotlight on the internal problems and bickering
within the industry, particularly on how to behave vis-à-vis the public. Under the
leadership of its new president, Sidney Niekerk (who is also president of Cal-Vista,
Inc.), the AFAA has been trying to give the industry a new image. While sex is the
subject of adult films, the filmmakers, actors, actresses and various people involved in the industry should (from Sidney's point of view and that of many other
industry leaders) try to avoid clashes with the more puritanical citizens in our
society, and not act like sex maniacs at public gatherings. Sidney set the tone for
the new respectability at the AFAA convention at the Universal-Sheraton Hotel in
March 1981, when he insisted that all male members should attend meetings
wearing suit jackets and not arrive in T-shirts and jeans. But keeping Al Goldstein
and actresses such as Carol Connors (and many other female stars who don't
hesitate to display bodily parts to admirers) under control is not easy.

Al arrived at the Erotic Awards the year before in a tank. In 1981, he showed up
in a motorcycle sidecar driven by two Hell's Angels; he wore a suit of medieval
armor. According to Al, Sidney told reporters that Al Goldstein "lent dishonor to
the affair." But Sidney was having even more trouble with Carol Connors, who
appeared in a lacy, see-through gown through which her behind and breasts
were clearly visible—and which revealed without question that she had a full
bush of blonde pubic hair.

It's against Palladium rules for the Erotic Awards Committee to show any explicit
sex scenes from their films, or offer a stage show that goes beyond naked breasts
and Las Vegas-style costumes. But Carol (as well as others) obligingly posed for
photographers with her dress in the air, and several other stars tried to liven up

what was essentially a dull but expensive way for the industry to celebrate its togetherness.

To top off the internal bickering between the adult film producers and the actors and actresses, the Awards Committee split the 1981 top award between *Urban Cowboys* and *Talk Dirty to Me* (see filmography), bypassing *Amanda by Night,* which stars Veronica Hart, and which many thought was a better film.

"Real obscenity," said Al Goldstein from his *Screw* editorial platform (August 3, 1981), "lies not in the honest depiction of sexuality but in the AFAA's slimy, two-faced posturing—accepting the wealth and status of the adult film industry—while at the same time throwing up a blind of respectability and high moral tone to assuage their craven, chickenshit feelings of guilt . . . obviously we have to strip this semantic facade away and reveal them for what they are—peddlars of male and female flesh—entrepreneurs of erotic fantasy. There is nothing wrong with this. I accept this definition for myself and for those in my business. It's no less respectable to traffic in sexual dreams than to make escapist entertainment like *The Raiders of the Lost Ark,* or *Star Wars* or the newest James Bond film. The AFAA would not let porno actresses at the event show a tit or reveal any other provocative charm. For some reason, they want to run AFAA as if it were a meeting of funeral parlor operators instead of show people."

On August 24, 1981, Al Goldstein let David Friedman, chairman of the AFAA and president of TVX (who looks so respectable he could be a vice-president at the Bank of America) reply: "I probably project the most prominent image in the adult film field," Dave wrote. "I tell my family, my bankers, my lodge brothers, my fellow Republicans, my friends from San Marino, Short Hills, Grosse Pointe, Kenilworth and all those other WASP enclaves that 'I'm in the adult movie business, the X-rated movie business, the porno movie business, the dirty movie business, the appellation is yours.' I am quoted and profiled in *Forbes,* the *Wall Street Journal, Newsweek, Time,* the *New York Times, Los Angeles Times, New West, Variety,* etc. . . . but maybe it takes a little more intestinal fortitude to stand up and sell Sodom and gospelize Gomorrah to the people who wouldn't be caught dead reading *Screw* but still might spring for a fin to peek at a sex film. Yes, we set standards for *The Erotica Awards.* It is our show. The public is not admitted. We can run it any way we damn please. We have all seen our performers nude, and in various throes of passion and lubricity. There is not a pubis, penis, pore, pimple or pustule on their lithe lustful bodies we have not seen magnified twelve times life size. We have heard them utter their immoral lines and know all the four letter words, gutter talk and concupiscent catch phrases that are used effectively for shock value. Since seeing our players in the nude is no great novelty and hearing vulgar language is no great theatrical breakthrough, why not among ourselves recognize and honor our people in keeping with the propriety of our fellow show persons in the Academy?"

In addition to splitting the Best Erotic Film award for 1981, *Talk Dirty to Me* won the Best Actor award for John Leslie, for a role he would duplicate in 1982 in *Nothing to Hide.* Samantha Fox was chosen Best Actress (for the second time in a row) for her role in *The Lady Is a Tramp.* Best Supporting Actor and Actress were Richard Pacheco and Georgina Spelvin, for their roles in *Talk Dirty to Me* and *Urban Cowboy,* respectively.

AFAA officials estimate that a Best Picture Award can increase the gross on an adult film at the theater level $100,000 or more—and this does not include increased video cassette sales. Because there was a great deal of disagreement among AFAA members over the 1981 awards and a belief among some that the West Coast producers were controlling what films received the awards, in 1982 a "blue-ribbon committee" of the AFAA decided to appoint an impartial panel of critics, none of whom was associated with the adult film industry. These critics, finally known as "an independent jury," would make the choice from the final five contenders and would submit their ballots directly to a certified public accountant. Only the CPA, Demetri Zafaris, would know the final winners in all the "Best" categories until the envelopes were opened on Award Night, July 8, 1982.

There's no question that the concept of an independent jury did eliminate some of the politicking associated with past awards—but not all. Twenty-two companies producing adult films submitted 184 entries in 15 categories of Best—and 18 of them claimed their films deserved Film Award of the Year honors. The finalists in the 15 categories were submitted to the jury, which was given five choices in each category (determined by the AFAA committee prior to the final ballots). There were no options to choose different films, actors, actresses, directors, etc., for the various Best categories.

Unlike myself, none of the independent jury was in the process of writing a book about adult films, and probably hadn't been exposed to as many adult films as I had. They obviously wouldn't, in the natural course of events, have seen the 25 or more films offered by the producers as the Best in various categories. It was evident to me (for various reasons, probably unknown to the jury) that several films actually produced in 1982 were better or equal to some of the five finally offered to the jury.

Contrasting with the Fifth Annual Erotic Film Awards of 1981, the sixth annual ceremony was much more subdued and almost sexless. As I have mentioned, this "class" approach is part of a deliberate upgrading policy inaugurated by Sidney Niekerk, reelected to a second term as AFAA president. Sidney is also chief of Cal Vista International, which does a gross sale of $60 million.

Instead of the Hollywood Palladium, the 1982 Award ceremony itself took place in the Variety Arts Theatre, one of Los Angeles's oldest legitimate theaters, and was followed by a Victory Dinner at the Hyatt Regency, a few blocks away. More than 1,500 guests, about equally divided between male and female, attended the $75-a-plate affair, which included the ceremony. Many of them followed the invitation and arrived in black tie or summer formal. Al Goldstein made his usual raucous entry in an inflatable Superman suit. He was lowered by a crane to the theater entrance, where a minor porno actress, Linda Schorr, exposed one breast for the waiting cameramen. But all of the well-known adult film stars present refrained from any sexual razzle-dazzle. And a few minutes after his arrival Al Goldstein changed to a handsome gray tux and sat in the theater with his father and mother.

As usual, the sidewalks in front of the theater were picketed by the "Jesus Saves" demonstrators who shouted their threats of hellfire and damnation, particularly at Al Goldstein, who responded: "Show me a little Christian charity." But none of the producers, actors or directors arriving in Rolls and Cadillac limousines contested them. They were simply greeted with the secure smiles of the affluent who had never spent a sleepless night worrying about their immortal souls.

Had the picketers been invited inside the theater to listen to the program, except for a few brief shots of Annette Haven as she appeared in two of the nominated films (naked but not copulating), they might well have wondered if they weren't watching a group of religious leaders who had gathered to compliment each other on their achievements of the past year. Actually, the entertainment, which was interwoven between the actual opening of the award envelopes (all done in true Motion Picture Academy style) was the kind you can see in any nightclub. Replete with a comedian, Charlie Callas, direct from Las Vegas, a dance group called "The Hot Flashes" and a singing trio who sang all the songs.

For the 1982 Erotic Film Awards, the following films were nominated by AFAA members for the Best Picture of 1982: *Nothing to Hide, Neon Nights, Outlaw Ladies, Games Women Play* and *Skintight.* Only one of these films is female-oriented. The rest of them were produced for the 800-theater adult film circuit, primarily a male audience—although females can learn a great deal from them if they will take a wider perspective. Because of the economics of the industry, I believe that for many years to come there will be two types of adult films (see my review of *Neon Nights,* in which I propose—this film being a good example—that there should be two awards for Best Picture: one male-oriented and one couple- or male/female-oriented).

The jury was given no opportunity to make a Best Picture decision on either *The Dancers* or *Roommates* (the latter was produced by Chuck Vincent, who purposely didn't enter it in the competition because he was trying to market it to a more generalized "cross-over" audience). *Roommates,* however, finally received the Erotic Film Award as Best Picture of 1983. *Nothing to Hide* was nominated Best Picture for 1982. If you check my ratings you will discover that I have given it a CC rating, as I have *The Dancers* and *Roommates.* I have given *Neon Nights* a qualified CC rating and explained why. The other three pictures nominated for Best Picture all have some amusing, erotic and clever sequences, but they are basically pedestrian and never really soar sexually. Again, if you read my reviews, you'll understand why I haven't extolled them.

Georgina Spelvin received the Best Actress award for a portrayal of an old maid in *The Dancers.* Her only competition among the nominees for Best Actress was Chelsea Manchester for her role in *Nothing to Hide.* Chelsea is an actress worth watching—as a person she knows where she is coming from, and this showed in her acting. Annette Haven, who is one of the best and most interesting off-screen actresses in the business, as far as I can discover has never received a Best Actress award. In the two pictures (*Wicked Sensations* and *Skintight)* for which she was nominated Best Actress, she does a credible job against the hopeless odds of the story's backgrounds and characters.

Best Actor went to John Leslie again—a deserved accolade—but not for his role in *Wicked Sensations,* for which he won it, but rather for *The Dancers,* for which he was not even nominated (nor were any of the other male actors, Randy West, Richard Pacheco and Joey Civera, all of whom proved, by being totally different-style males, that they can really act).

Why Holly McCall (whom I have never met but love anyway because she lushly defies adult film conventions and is getting pretty plump) was nominated Best Supporting Actress for *Nothing to Hide* is a jury mystery. My guess is that the two ladies on the jury unanimously voted for her scene in which she warns John Leslie not to come on her face. He does anyway and she throws him out of her apartment, telling him how disgusting he is and that she never wants to see him again. My choice was for Jesie St. James, who plays the role of a harassed housewife in *Oriental Hawaii,* the only redeeming part in an otherwise totally male-oriented film. Jesie is a much underrated actress who should have received an award for her role in *Charli,* a film never nominated—this year or last—for anything. I also cheered Merle Michaels for Best Supporting Actress in *Outlaw Ladies,* during which she plays a sequence with Richard Bolla of the girl who is always getting passed by, but who may be more fun to have around than her better-looking competition.

There was a tie between Richard Bolla (who insisted when he accepted the award that his real first name is Robert) and Richard Pacheco for Best Supporting Actor. Actually, in addition to John Leslie (although only Randy West was nominated—for *Country Comfort,* a film I have given a CC rating), Randy West, Richard Pacheco, Richard Bolla and Joey Civera all might well have been nominated for Best Actor. If they had, the jury would have had a tougher decision to make.

Anthony Spinelli won the Best Director for *Nothing to Hide.* I would have given it to him for *The Dancers.* Best Original Screenplay went to Michael Ellis for *The*

Dancers. Best Art and Set Decoration went to Maria Ranoldi for *Pandora's Mirror;* Best Costumes to Sarah Yesko for *Country Comfort.* Best Original Music went to Randy Rivera (along with Best Song) for "Glory Bound" in *Rhinestone Cowgirls.* It proves that even a mediocre picture can have a redeeming feature. ("Glory Bound" should be picked up and sung by Johnny Cash or Kenny Rogers. It's a great country-western song.) Best Cinematography went to Jack Remy for *Nothing to Hide.* I would have chosen *Bad Girls*—an otherwise lackluster film. The Best Editing award was given to Arlo Schifflin for *Outlaw Ladies.* Best Trailer was a tie between Hayes Dupree for *Skintight* and Terence O'Reilly for *The Dancers.* I would have picked James Macreading for *Games Women Play.* Best Advertising Campaign went to Jimmy Johnson for *Nothing to Hide.*

And that brings you up to date on the Adult Film Industry.

3

Plots, Conventions, and Hang-ups of Sexvids

In his book, *Contemporary Erotic Cinema,* William Rotsler lists five basic plots common to most stag films: "Plot 1. A woman alone at home becomes aroused by reading or handling some phallic-shaped object. Masturbation follows. A man arrives—is invited inside, sexual play begins; Plot 2. A farm girl gets excited watching animals copulate. She runs into a farmhand, or a traveling salesman, and sexual play begins; Plot 3. A doctor begins examining a woman and sexual play begins; Plot 4. A burglar finds a girl in bed or rapes her or vice versa; Plot 5. A sunbather or skinny dipper gets caught and seduced."

The films *Deep Throat* and *The Devil and Miss Jones,* produced in 1972, were presumably responsible for a "new wave." The backgrounds for these films were no longer sleazy bedrooms or motel rooms, nor did they depend so much on outdoor settings. Instead, they are filmed in luxurious bedrooms, seductive lodges and expensive mansions with swimming pools. In addition, the actors are people with beautiful bodies who can even act a little and allow the viewers some empathy with their sexuality—and much more frequently there is a plot and some dialogue.

Wayne Losano, in his book, *Sexuality in the Movies,* believes that what distinguishes current adult films from their predecessors "is their tone, and their attitude toward the subject matter." Losano describes a woman in one film who asks a stranger if he wants a blow job; in another film, *The Nurses,* one nurse has sex with a patient in order to get a urine sample; in another film, a nurse screws a patient being given an enema; in *Meatball,* "the hero [Harry Reems] unfailingly gets an erection every hour and reinforcement must be brought in to spell his tiring nurse." Losano concludes, "The effect is to make sex just good clean fun." Losano's essay was published in 1975. In my opinion, as shown by the ratings I have put on the listings of many sexvids in this book, a great number of the films produced in the past five years continue in the stag tradition, i.e., mostly without laughter. Instead, there is much cynical sex, and most of the conversation and action treats human sexuality as a kind of necessary but essentially nasty and dirty business. This, of course, is in keeping with the Christian morality embedded in many of the viewers' minds. Losano insists that a laughing sex film cannot be good pornography, which must depend on evil. I disagree, as you will see if you check the NL (Normal Noncommitted–Laughing Sex) that I have given to a number of films in the Main Filmography.

During the 1970s, in contrast to the image-raising attempts of the AFAA during the past few years, there were many adult films known as One Day Wonders, which dominated much of porno film production. Unlike recent films such as *Babylon Pink, Debbie Does Dallas, Lipps McCain, Beach Blanket Bango* and several Richard Aldrich films which avoid sadism and much kinkiness, the One Day Wonders were produced by one person who was a combination producer, cameraman and director. The films were mass-produced for the raincoat crowd, which, seemingly, is an insatiable market. They're still shown in some adult theaters, usually in the larger cities, and usually in grind houses. The producers of One Day Wonders also specialize in completely stereotyped "sex-loops," which run for approximately 12 minutes and are available in adult stores, where they run on peep-show machines at 25¢ for a two- or three-minute look. After a certain number have been shown they repeat themselves, hence the word "loop." They offer every imaginable sexual act and perversion. A big collection is offered in various men's magazines under the overall title of "Swedish Erotica," available as 8-mm films, which can be run on any home projector without sound. Many of these so-called One Day Wonder productions can be identified by the far-out names of actresses: Ass Pumpin, Passion Ruse, L'il Squeeze, Mary Mendem, Kelly Mint, Misty Winters, Alice Thatch, Ronda More, Veri Knotty, Honeysuckle Devine, Sally Deer, Veronica Melon, etc. (You will find many more of them in the filmography.)

In an interview with Andre Hirschfield that appeared in *Adam Film World* (July 1980), Marcia F., an actress who has appeared in many of the One Day wonder films, tells how the films were made just a few years ago. Here's an excerpt from the article: "Imagine a huge loft where ten different sets are built in a circle with three walls and one open side—all cubicles with different kinds of bedroom set-ups, baby cribs, walls with harnesses, high school locker rooms, dungeons. Chip (the producer) put a crew on a 24-hour day. . . . While one scene is being shot in a bedroom, people are warming up with whips for the dungeon scene. . . . At the end of five days Chip has eight films in the can. . . . Scripts are written on the way over in a cab, but most of them are improvised."

Marcia told Hirschfield that a big budget for films in those days was $6,000–10,000. In the process of shooting, the director allows an extra half foot of film for every foot shot to eliminate mistakes. Actors and actresses ad lib on story lines that they quickly absorb from a few written sentences describing the heavy sex scenes and at least one orgy, bondage-and-discipline or enema scene—the raunchier the better. If they can get two cocks in one cunt they'll do it. If they could stick a cock in someone's ear and film it they would.

Amusingly, since the thrust of *Adam Film World*'s editorial policy is to upgrade adult films and give them a new aura of respectability, Marcia confesses in this interview that an actress such as C. J. Laing is better at this than she is, because "C. J. is into the S&M thing." But Marcia admits that after a few days of work, her "cunt is very sore." And her mouth is so weary from sucking cock and thrusting her tongue in and out of someone's pussy that she spends the next day resting in the tub. Nevertheless, she continues—evidently so as not to disillusion *Adam Film World*'s readers—that "actually it's like a big party. Everybody shows up and gets to see each other, and gets laid and paid. What could be better?"

If you purchase or rent a sexvid of *Untamed*, you'll discover that thematically even a better producer/director such as Harold Lime doesn't hesitate to offer a film that differs from the One Day Wonders only in its use of more glamorous backgrounds. *Untamed* has better editing and cinematography, but it is essentially a plotless One Day Wonder fuck film.

In an interesting book, *The Sex Industry,* by George Csicsery, who produced several films himself way back in the early 1960s, the author reveals how the adult film industry is still hooked to its origins. Along with Gerard Damiano and Alex de Renzy, the Mitchell Brothers were among the first in the sexploitation business. The Mitchell Brothers started making girlie films when they were students at San Francisco State College. Later, in July 1969, they opened their O'Farrell Theater in San Francisco and started showing "beaver" films (endless reels of women masturbating with their fingers or pulling their labia apart to reveal huge on-screen vulvas and deep vaginal tunnels to male audiences).

According to Jim Mitchell, "If the cops hadn't bothered us—business was so good—we probably wouldn't have ever gotten into stories." According to Csicsery, Jim still feels that "the purest form of titillation is the single girl 'automasturbation' film . . . and the beaver film was a lot truer form for getting off on some kind of autoerotic fantasy. When it opened up and you added fucking, you had to show the man and you covered up the girl . . . It disrupted the autoerotic trend of sex films . . . It was boring because all anyone really wanted to see was the close-up penetration shots." Interestingly, at the same time in San Francisco, a producer named Lowell Pickett was too far ahead of his time. Csicsery points out, "Pickett tried to eliminate the external cum shots in which an ejaculating male suddenly withdraws his member from whatever female orifice it happens to be in and has his orgasm outside of the woman's body, preferably spraying her in the face. But a lot of people stopped showing his films because while they were sometimes funnier and more developed dramatically, they violated basic pornographic convention."

Losano, who believes that eroticism disappears with laughter, and Al Goldstein would agree. Here's a *Screw* review of *Dirty Katie,* a 1980 film: "It has difficulty mixing sex with humor. The result is a very funny film in which the humor may drive the audiences to distraction—from sex, that is." Today, new standards of what is obscenity are emerging in the large urban areas. As sexvids penetrate the home market, the One Day Wonder film—either in its cheaply produced version or in its more glamorized version, with the inevitable kinky sadistic scenes—is being replaced by an entirely new kind of sex film. Even without a large home market, but in anticipation of it, the adult film industry is doing everything possible to avoid churning waters and attracting the attention of the guardians of morality and the various women's coalitions against pornography. Adult films with rape, sexual cruelty and so-called kiddie porn quickly bring angry people picketing the films, police raids and occasional legal action in the form of protracted court cases. The final battles against visual sex have yet to be fought, but the forces are gathering. The police will ignore adult theaters until someone begins screaming about a film such as *Little Girls Blue* (the actresses in this film are well over 18, but most of them don't look it), or *Candy Stripers,* which was seized in a raid on distributors in early 1980 because of the fist-fucking scene that has now been eliminated from the sexvid.

Even though new types of films are slowly emerging, in which actors and actresses are doing a much better acting job and all the major producers attempt to maintain a story line from beginning to end, the industry is still plagued with the stereotypes and conventions built into sex films from stag film days and from the early 1970's films, *Deep Throat* and *The Devil and Miss Jones*. Most producers and directors believe that they must play this game or else lose the male audience that has kept them in business from day one. Since there are many more sexvids available today with these conventions more or less intact than without them, it's not only interesting to list them, but watching for them may provide some amusement when viewing sexvids. The following listing includes not only the obvious ones but some that may not be so obvious.

1. The male actor rarely ejaculates inside the female.
2. When he does, he ejaculates on her breast, lips or stomach. Without the friction of his penis and often using her own fingers, the female actress

seems to be climaxing herself while she ecstatically rubs his jism into her flesh.

3. If the male actor is being sucked off, he ejaculates so that not only the female can be seen swallowing his jism or letting it dribble over her face, but in addition her facial expression indicates that it's good to the last drop.

4. Females never feel embarrassed and rarely indicate that they don't know how—or don't enjoy—sucking a male cock. In fact, they often initiate the procedure by grabbing the male and unzipping him.

5. Most actresses, not to be outdone by Linda Lovelace, manage to go down on the entire length of the male penis (the only possible exception being Johnny Wadd's 13½-inch unerected member). Actresses manage to do this for quite a few minutes without gagging.

6. Rarely do actors and actresses say, "I love you" to one another, but via moans and groans and occasionally via speech they tell each other, "It was a great fuck!"

7. There is very little conversation between male and female before or during the act of love in most films produced prior to 1978, but it's becoming much more common in recent films.

8. There is very limited foreplay. The male is usually aroused orally by the female. He may take a quick lap or two of her vulva, but when he enters her she apparently is totally lubricated, waiting and right on the edge of an earth-shaking orgasm—all of which occurs because she enjoyed sucking his penis so much.

9. There is rarely any afterplay or any friendly cuddling. When the male ejaculates, the plot, if there is any, will finally continue until the next fuck scene (the fast forward button on video cassette players is a great convenience in helping the viewer to get past the "ins and outs" and back to the story).

10. Jealousy and most other human emotions (except fear and lust) are rarely expressed in most adult films. In practically all films, two (or more) women work over the hero and share his penis from mouth to mouth, vagina to vagina, or even anus to anus with no apparent jealousy—or worry about sanitation.

11. All sexvids have at least one scene of lesbian sex during which the women enjoy each other—often more than they have enjoyed the hero.

12. A very large percentage of sexvids have one orgy scene (Mazola party) involving at least four or more naked couples screwing together.

13. Practically all sexvids have one scene in which two women work over one man, but rarely are two men ever seen sexmaking with one woman. (*Cosmopolitan's* 1980 sex survey reveals that 23 percent of *Cosmo* girls had sex with more than one partner at a time, and these were male partners.)

14. Anal sex occurs in many sexvids, with the female being penetrated but never the male. Keep in mind that male homosexuality is not a factor in sexvids and is rarely shown, unless the films were specifically produced for gay males.

15. Women rarely get pregnant. If they do (see filmography on *Beach Blanket Bango*) it is treated humorously. Women practically never menstruate, have periods or wear sanitary pads, externally or internally. There's also rarely any discussion of birth control. No condoms are ever used and are rarely seen. Women never admit if they are on the pill.

16. Men past 40 rarely appear naked. If they do they are paunchy, lecherous, can't get it up and are usually cast as simpletons or villains.

17. Sexvids rarely show a woman past 40 naked, let alone sexmaking.

18. Age limits for female lead actresses is between 20 and 30. Georgina Spelvin, who is in her 40s, now appears in supporting roles. Since a great many sexvids are teenage-oriented, both actors and actresses often look

older than the ages they are portraying.

19. Practically all lead roles in sexvids are between unmarrieds or formerly marrieds. If extramarital sex is treated, it is usually from the standpoint of swingers (uncommitted spouse exchange). An amusing exception is *Babylon Pink,* which won the Best Film award in 1980. If a male actor seduces a woman, who is married in the sexvid plot, usually both are totally guiltless. If the husband appears, he is often flaky or some kind of dud.

20. Most males are circumcised. A fascinating exception is John C. Holmes (Johnny Wadd), but you rarely see a scene in which the female plays with his foreskin, moving it over his glans.

21. Many of the 1970 sexvids commence with a genital sexmaking scene that continues through lengthy film credits. This entree is slowly disappearing from films made in the 1980s, but only a few current sexvids actually manage to delay the primal scene as long as ten minutes into the story.

22. Many recent sexvids commence with a real "class" ambiance that equals or exceeds many regular Hollywood productions. But after the first 10 or 15 minutes, complying with most of the conventions listed above, the director frequently loses the plot. In some cases it disappears, never to return.

23. Sexvid stories, with a few unique exceptions (see filmography), rarely revolve around a single male-female or even a two-couple sex relationship. And the male actor must have sex with at least three different females, and often many more, during the course of a particular sexvid.

24. Female stars, such as Vanessa Del Rio, rarely have breasts that hang normally on their chests. You can tell a woman's silicone breasts by their impossible perkiness when the actresses are standing, lying or being touched. It's interesting to watch sexvids for exceptions.

25. A very large percentage of adult films cater to the male fantasy of having a virgin—or a sexually inexperienced woman—who learns all she knows from him. Check out the filmography and see how many films have "teen-age" or "high school" or a "young" reference in the title.

I've previously mentioned that a totally laughing sexvid such as *Alice in Wonderland,* for example, turns off the raincoat crowd and is rarely shown in adult theaters except in a hard-core version. Adult filmmakers are well aware that soft-core is popular with cable and subscription television audiences, including females, but "hard" R or soft-core films are usually only shown late at night on the cable and subscription television stations. Many directors are now shooting two versions of their films: one for the adult theater and videotape audience and one for cable and subscription television.

If you watch many sexvids you may discover that I have missed many more conventions. But they all have one common denominator: they portray the human sexual experience and relationship in ways that may be erotic for some older males, but do not appeal to the many younger-generation males who have discovered that the way to really enjoy a female is to give as much—or more—than one takes. Of course all of these conventions fly in the face of normal human sexuality. On the other hand, like many sex manuals, they give the impression that the "joy of sex" is really based on endless environmental variations—*where* (not in bed) and *how* you do it, but rarely on any mental rapport between the partners. In addition, the female erogenous zone, for most sexvid producers, seems to be the vulva. Most adult filmmakers have not yet learned that although the vulva has lips it can't talk or express emotion. (One French-produced sexvid, *Pussy Talk*—see filmography—takes a shot at it.) Nor have most directors learned that for the viewer (and actually for most males in the act of sexmaking, watching the female's facial expressions can be a most erotic experience.

Listing the conventions that appear in sexvids may seem like carrying coals to

Newcastle. Many critics of sex films believe that without these conventions, which are primarily based on male fantasies and produce a kind of catharsis for males, there would be no purpose to erotic films at all. Their attitude is that men watch erotic films to get a hard-on, and that's all. (This belief may be the biggest convention of all!) Presumably, the man who enjoys porno films and sexvids wants to escape into a world populated by young women who can't wait to suck his cock or spread their legs so he can fuck them to a fare-thee-well while they groan in pleasure. But my feeling is that millions of males are not turned on by this kind of fantasy female; most are much more turned on by mental nakedness coupled with physical nakedness. If the adult filmmakers and producers who are working directly on tape want to avoid drowning in their own jism, they've got to capture this new male market—which is totally interwoven with the female market. The best way to begin is to toss out most of the old conventions—avoid them like the plague—and produce films and sexvids with caring sex and interpersonal relationships, both good and bad.

4

Uncloistering Virtues . . . Or Rating the Sexvids

Today if you see frontal male or female nudity for more than a few seconds in any regular motion picture, chances are that the film will have an X rating. But most producers and directors don't let this happen. An X rating on a film is a commercial kiss of death. The big theater chains with their Cinemas One, Two, Three or Four in suburbia try to avoid battles over visual sex with local morality groups.

In 1973, a movie made from my novel *The Harrad Experiment* offered a scene in a swimming pool where a number of male and female youngsters are shown naked. In those days it carried an R rating (and still does), but even then its distribution in suburban areas was very spotty. In 1980, *The Blue Lagoon* was endorsed by sex educators, but it carried an R rating because of some frontal nudity and teenage lovemaking with which many twelve-year-old girls or boys could identify, but it could not be viewed by teenagers under seventeen unless accompanied by a parent. If you live near a suburban theater showing R-rated movies such as *Saturday Night Fever, Animal House, or Friday the 13th*, which appeared in 1979 and 1980, the chances are you've had many opportunities to "adopt" young people at the door ranging in age from 13 to 16 who are determined to see the picture—and who, according to all statistics, are heavily involved in their own sexuality already. Sadly, despite the fact that there are a million teenage pregnancies annually, the contraceptive message John Travolta offered in the back seat of an automobile in *Saturday Night Fever* was finally excised from the film so that it could get a PG rating.

With the advent of uncensored R-rated movies available from rental sources at low rates, and the coming invasion of the sexvids, chances are that within the next ten years millions of young people will finally get a good sex education via television and in the privacy of their own home. The burning question of who is responsible for sex education—parents or schools—will no longer be an issue. Hundreds of explicit sex education sexvids, carefully developed for children in different age groups, will be widely available. In the next few years parents will face a dilemma: if they don't view these sexvids with their children, their kids may be watching them in the homes of more liberal parents. Inevitably, as several thousand so-called adult films become widely available on tape and disc, teenagers will discover their parents' hidden cache of sexvids and watch them (for better or worse) at home on the family television set when their parents are working or have gone out for the night. Ultimately, teenage sex education films will have to deal not only with the false (and often sick) sexual morality of adult films, but also with the ways interpersonal human sexuality is constantly being portrayed in the mass media, especially advertising—unless, of course, our self-appointed moral guardians win the final battle.

In his essay "A History of Screen Censorship" (see the book *Sexuality in the Movies*), Arthur Lennig traces the history of movie censorship, which is as old as movies themselves. The early concern of those who decided what was visually permissible for us to see, according to Lennig, stemmed from four factors: "(1) Cinema affects a lot of impressionable people; (2) It caters to the lower classes who in particular need strict guidance; (3) It is a medium as yet to be considered an art; and (4) It is too graphic and immediate about life itself. The unwritten rule (which still prevails) is that the closer to life an art form becomes, the more it suffers censorship."

Many of these early beliefs dominate film censorship and film rating systems today. During the first decade or so of commercial moving picture production (approximately 1907 to 1920), movie censorship concerning nudity was pretty relaxed. D. W. Griffith included nude scenes in *Intolerance* (1916), and actresses such as Theda Bara, Gloria Swanson and even an actor such as Valentino (*Blood and Sand*, 1922) were filmed naked. Censorship was accomplished by various state and city organizations that snipped pieces here and there from films. But in 1922, the motion picture industry, trying to keep the heat off and prodded by women's clubs and religious organizations, hired Will Hays. A new code was established that didn't concern itself much about violence on screen but insisted that: "the sanctity of the institution of marriage and the home should be upheld"; "low forms of sexual relationships be avoided"; "adultery must not be explicitly treated or justified or presented attractively"; films should not be presented "to stimulate the lower elements"; and that rape or seduction is not "the proper subject for comedy."

If you watch old movies on late-night television, or you are a film buff now collecting film classics on videotape, you'll understand the story lines better if you are aware of the changing conditions of morality that prevailed in the various periods of movie censorship. You'll also realize how far X-rated films have come in 50 years, and how changes in sexual morality have paved the way for sexvids today. According to Morris L. Ernst, who wrote several books on film censorship, in 1928, when 579 feature films were produced, only 42 escaped some kind of cutting before they were released. In recent years, the Motion Picture Rating Board often precensors films by advising producers in advance of the only rating they will approve on certain potential subject matter, such as best-selling novels that are being turned into movies.

In 1930, prodded by the Legion of Decency, which threatened that its 30 million Catholic members would boycott all Hollywood theaters if screen sexuality weren't controlled, a new movie czar, Joseph Breen, proposed a new production code, which was finally adopted in 1934. The code determined the morality of many American movies for the next 30 years. No movie could get the Seal of Approval, as it was called—meaning it couldn't get distributed—if "it lowered the moral standards of those who would see it."

Incidentally, this is an interesting subject in connection with sexvids. The effect of film censorship changing the conditioning or morality of a society is carefully analyzed by Mollie Haskell in her excellent book, *From Reverence to Rape*, in which she studies the way women have been portrayed in film since the early 1900s. Haskell shows clearly that, prior to the 1930 moving picture production code, treatment of women was much more honest and egalitarian, both sexually and otherwise, than it has been since. The anything-goes X rating of our current production code has unleashed, at least in adult films, a new breed of sexually aggressive women and a totally unrestrictive sexual morality. The widespread viewing of sexvids in the coming years raises the question of whether the extremely loose morals and manners depicted in films will affect monogamous marriage and the family or eventually create less restrictive marriage styles.

Realistic or not, the 1934 movie production code controlled all scenes between men and women in bedrooms—whether the scenes were sexual or not. Twin beds were the order of the day. Husbands and wives were never shown in bed together, and unmarried lovers never passed the threshold of a bedroom door. No sexual words were ever said and no swearing was permitted. Clark Gable telling Vivien Leigh, "I don't give a damn!" in *Gone with the Wind* (1939) was a breakthrough of sorts.

The first reversal of these and many other sexual edicts in the first production code occurred with the censorship of a religious movie that was only incidentally sexual. The hierarchy of the Catholic church was shocked by Roberto Rossellini's film, *The Miracle*. It told the sacrilegious story of a Catholic peasant woman (Anna Maganni) who believed that St. Joseph was the father of her child. As a result of the efforts by the Legion of Decency, the movie was censored out of New York theaters, but this was contested all the way to the Supreme Court by the producers and theater owners. In 1952, the Court declared that censorship of *The Miracle* violated the Fourteenth Amendment and interfered with the separation of church and state. A byproduct of this decision was that within the next decade many of the sexual "verbotens" of the production code were no longer enforced by the rating board. The Seal of Approval was given to *The Pawnbroker* (1965) and to *Who's Afraid of Virginia Woolf?* (1966). By 1968, various Supreme Court decisions had made nudity possible in movies, and even a brief description of copulation appeared in *I Am Curious (Yellow)* (1969).

Increasingly nervous and fearful of repercussions, Hollywood producers decided they had better police themselves. Thus, Jack Valenti was appointed the new censorship czar of the moving picture industry. A new rating system appeared very quickly: G (for General Audience), M (for Mature), R (for people over 18) and X (for people over 21). In 1971 M was changed to PG (Parental Guidance). During the past ten years, the morality of PG films has loosened considerably and in many cases is more permissive than in the early R movies. For a time it looked as if R-rated movies might move gingerly into the visual sex area staked out by X-rated films. But if you have watched R-rated movies over the past ten years you'll discover that although they may present frontal nudity and offer soft-core sex and what used to be considered obscene language, most producers are more cautious than ever about showing explicit sexmaking and any extended scenes containing frontal nudity. Theater chains such as General Cinema enforce their own form of censorship by refusing to distribute films that may aggravate suburban customers.

David Friedman gave me his reaction to what he calls the "pussyfoot" attitude of major film producers, which of course applies to many of the regular Hollywood-product distributors, too. "The independent film producers and distributors led the fight against prior censorship in the United States, resulting in the abandonment of many city and state censorship boards all over the country. During this time, the major film producers did nothing. The producers of X-rated films pioneered the home video business and were in the market two years before the majors took their first timid step."

This raises one of the big issues yet to be decided in the final battles of visual sex. Keeping in mind both the present and future, is a simple X rating for sexvids adequate? During the past decade, X-rated films have been subjected to a fairly effective environmental censorship based on zoning and the location of adult theaters. Adult films were confined to theaters in certain zones of downtown cities or in occasional drive-ins off the main traffic lanes. Until recently, only an occasional adult theater would be located near a prime shopping center. Yet even though at least three million people find their way to these theaters each week, they still are not located in areas that might offend middle-class Americans or that are usually seen by young children or teenagers. But remember, too, that the U.S. middle-class is a sneaky lot, as shown during Prohibition when millions of high-minded citizens, who would never go to a speakeasy or admit that they liked to drink, pulled down their curtains and made gin, wine and beer in their kitchens or cellars. The analogy to sexvids is obvious. Despite the women's movement against pornography, sexvids are rapidly becoming a giggly phenomenon and are being shown in thousands of suburban homes today. Women who wouldn't be caught dead in an adult theater, and who are outstanding members of various women's clubs, watch them with varying degrees of enthusiasm and disgust.

Eventually, explicit sex on tape must provide a whole new rating game, especially if the makers of sexvids want female approval. Anyone who has watched sexvids or adult films in theaters is well aware that "X-rated" covers the whole gamut of human sexuality, both normal and abnormal, with innovations being provided weekly by the producers.

And it should also be kept in mind that the range of human sexuality in the 650 films I have watched on tape (and the 2,000 or more in the Supplemental Listings that I haven't seen) exceed the imagination and even the reality of Kraft Ebbings's *Psychopathia Sexualis*. After ten years, patrons of adult theaters who have seen hundreds of porno films are either pretty jaded or totally desensitized to normal sexual experience on the screen. To compensate, many sexvids offer bondage or discipline sequences or entire tapes in which the participants get sexually aroused by tying each other up or whipping each other while they wear leather clothing. There are sexvids that offer enemas, golden showers and probably even Marquis de Sade's defecation and the eating thereof (although I haven't seen any that actually show coprophagia). Most adult film reviewers (sometimes it is difficult to call them critics) rate the films on their ability to produce a hard-on or, at the very least, some tingling in the male crotch. Continually seeking after novelty, producers and directors of even the best sexvids offer kinky sexual behavior that often borders on cruelty or sadism, or they link sex with violence against females. These sexvids degrade not only the participants, but human sexuality in general. But until we learn how to exalt human sexuality they will continue to be made.

Arthur Lennig concludes his essay on censorship with the following thought, some of which I have excerpted: "No one can prove that films with graphic sex or violence have a harmful effect on viewers, but there seems to be little doubt that films do have some effect on society and that all of us live with such effects. . . . The question of how society will function when all checks that a few thousand years of civilization have imposed have disappeared . . . has yet to be answered."

As I have tried to make apparent, my feeling is that the exploding at-home market for sexvids will eventually change the character of sex films that we will be watching on tape or disc in the coming years. But thousands of the sleazier films will coexist on tape and disc with the new product. A rating system that breaks down the contents of sexvids not only lets the new buyer beware of kinky areas of human sexuality that don't appeal to particular people, but it eventually could also create separate markets. Ultimately, it could pinpoint a new kind of censorship, which I believe will become pretty widespread, and drive totally deviant sex films underground or eliminate them altogether. Keep in mind, despite media publicity, that the so-called perverse market is a very small market, with limited profitability. Thus, the rating categories I am offering extend far beyond any such system now available. Also, please note that I have not included any male homosexual sexvids in the filmography. There are several hundred gay films on tape. If you would like a listing, you can get it from Lambda Video; the address is given on p. 56. Having watched a few of them, it is apparent to me that they, too, should have a more definitive rating system. What I rate deviational kinky (e.g., anal sex) is probably considered quite normal within the male homosexual community.

Playboy, Penthouse and a few non-sex-oriented video magazines review a few of the current sexvids and adult films, but the sexual variations within particular films on tape are usually only hinted at in their reviews. As I have mentioned, there is a group of magazines entirely devoted to adult films and sexvids. The best is *Adam Film World*, which runs short reviews of all films but does not indicate, in many cases, whether these are available on tape or who the key distributor is. In its reviews, the number of X's after a film title indicates its degree of erotic content. Three X's mean hard-core; two mean simulated sex; and one X means soft-core (i.e., the film has some nudity and erotic content). Stars after the X (one, two, three or four) indicate the overall erotic content. And O means not erotic by hard-core standards. Although it is not defined, by *Adam Film World's* standards, the word erotic as used by their reviewers is male-oriented. The reviews offer a synopsis in a few sentences of the story line along with some positive or negative reaction. Interestingly, reviews of most foreign films carry a one-X rating. Proudly or not, the United States leads the world in the production of truly hard-core films.

Screw's current rating system is an erect penis symbol. One erect penis means not recommended—you get the least for your money; two erect penises mean reliable—you get what you pay for; three mean recommended—you won't go wrong here; and four mean highly recommended—the best of its kind available.

Incidentally, the reviews that appear in *Screw*, like many of the reviews from the following magazines, are masterpieces of sexual put-down, reducing human beings and sexmaking to a moronic level. As a supplement to these reviews, *Screw* offers an additional rating system, which judges a film on a percentage basis covering the following areas: Sexually Explicit, Sexually Erotic and Technical. Here's an excerpt from *Screw's* review of *Summer School:* "Sandy tells about her cunty sorority . . . and one member, Mary, a cute little pussy whose chore is to service the school's gardeners. . . . Having fucked and sucked both men dry her initiation is secure. . . . Jack (another character) must sample the sweet taste of Ms. Smith's cunt . . . but before he can ram his cock into her snatch, he must learn how to eat pussy properly. Jack however . . . acts like he's sucking on cock as the horny teacher fills her mouth full of her burning juices. . . . Jamie (another sorority sister) tells Jack, 'This is fun, take it all please.' . . . She straddles his waist, riding his cock like a bitch in heat. . . . Another female tells Jack, 'Suck my toes, you prick. Smell my cunt. Tell me how much you want to suck this juicy cunt. Lick it . . . that's a good little doggie.'" *Screw's* reviews are obviously male raincoat-crowd-oriented, and they prove one thing: If you translate sick visual sex into words, it gets even sicker.

Video X—unlike *Screw*, which is a newspaper—is a full-color monthly magazine. It does not rate films, but it does review them in the same far-out manner. Here's a review of one of the *Swedish Erotica* films, which are available on both tape and 8-mm film. "Donna nibbles Alice's clit as Bill shoves his hot hammer up the barbaric blonde's soaking slit. Bill then has the girls cunt bump for a bit before shooting his sticky jism all over Alice's pussy while Donna laps it up and flicks her tongue at his churning balls."

Hustler's reviews are a little tamer, and *Hustler* reviews its films with a penis symbol in varying degrees of erection: Full, Three Quarters, Half, One Quarter and Totally Limp. *Porn Stars*, another new monthly devoted to only adult films, uses a stag symbol. Four stags represent top erotica, while one means not erotic at all. *Velvet* magazine, a little more sexually sophisticated in content than *Hustler*, uses a symbol of a woman lying on her back with her legs in the air. Legs wide open is the highest rating; legs somewhat closed—you have to work very hard to get it up; Legs completely closed—might remind you that there's life below your belly button, but you'd have more fun at the zoo.

During 1980 many of the reviews that appeared in *Velvet* were written by William Margold, an adult film actor and producer himself. The interesting thing about them is that Margold withholds no punches on the quality of many films. Here are some of his comments on two films, *Three Ripening Cherries* and *Champagne Orgy*: "*Velvet* readers can avoid two turds with one stone-cold review. . . . *Champagne Orgy* is even worse than awful. . . . Troy Benny, the director, may well have turned the cameras on and walked out of the room during this unarousing excuse for adult entertainment. What is supposed to be a cast party degenerates into an orgasmic-less series of grunting and grinding grapples during which many of the holes and poles spend more time looking into the camera than in each other. Cum shots are of course the main course, and Benny never misses the chance to show us a man's seed from every angle possible. If I were a spermatozoon in *Champagne Orgy*, I'd file for residuals." Margold's review of *Three Ripening Cherries* is in the same vein, in that the same director bombards the eyes with the same cum shots over and over again. (But Margold has appeared in at least one film that is even worse than these—see filmography.)

Cinema X, another monthly devoted to the field, tries to be very professional and rates films specifically on direction, acting, screenplay, editing, production, music, costumes and cinematography (E for excellent, G for good, F for fair, P for poor, L for lacking). The most detailed, buyer-beware reviews appear in a small magazine, *Source Video*, which has no illustrations and approaches the film content with amazing dignity. The editor, Matt Kovac, sells sexvids and is determined to do all he can to upgrade the product.

One thing is obvious. None of these reviews is directed at a female audience or at a more select male audience that may be more idealistic about sex and the kind of female they copulate with. So before I explain the rating system I have devised and applied to the Main Filmography in this book, I will tell you why I believe that this type of rating system (or a variation on it) is inevitable.

The first reason is that the emerging female audience and a (hopefully) reconditioned male audience will be much more intrigued if they know what they are buying. The second reason is more complex. In 1969, *Variety*, a show-business magazine that is against censorship, confessed: "Reasonable people of whatever political persuasion find hard-core appalling." I disagree with this. Billions of words have been written over the past few hundred years trying to define pornography and obscenity with no conclusions except that what is obscenity to me or you varies with our background, education and the age in which we live. There seems to be no common denominator, but I think there is. The reason that I continually propose a merger of sexuality and religion in my novels is that a viable and healthy society must never become so "sophisticated" that it forgets or denigrates the sheer wonder and beauty of the human body or the mystery, never to be fully penetrated, of its existence over a given number of years. Lifetime sexual attraction may vary in degrees, but a constant of the human condition is humans caring for each other. Sex for pleasure and procreation under happy circumstances is the sine qua non of our lives. Without this kind of environment other human rights don't have much meaning. Societies that continually degrade human sexuality—like those of the Middle Ages in which women were said to consort with the devil and were eaten by snakes and toads, or those of today in which women are simply cunts or pieces of ass and men are pricks getting their rocks off—are the societies that eventually terminate other human rights.

But don't get the idea that I'm on the side of born-again Christians. On the contrary, I'm probably a lone fighter in the most crucial battle of visual sex. I do not believe in censoring visual sex. Rather, I think all of us should try to redefine and carefully label what degrades human sexuality. Only then can we lay the foundations for new approaches to human sexuality and lift our life processes out of the slime and slop being continuously heaped upon us—not just by X-rated films but by much of our mass media and the advertising profession—which may claim to be horrified by sexvids but does not hesitate to objectify women and use them as a continual sex tease to sell their products or services. Perhaps, with new labeling, we can be rid of sex degradation and sex teases. Scorn, laughter and pity are more effective weapons than censorship.

Another approach is to diffuse much frustrated human sexuality through practical methods such as the legalization of prostitution (something the women's movement should think about) and the creation of "sexual release environments" in which men and women cut off from regular sexual channels can still enjoy a human privilege. Sexmaking subsidized by Medicare if necessary, for those who can't afford it, may not be as silly as it seems. Millions of healthy men and women who enjoy sex with each other must face reality: There are millions of other quite normal citizens who have no regular avenues for sexual pleasure.

Men and women come into this world needing to love and care for each other. When they are in their late teens, people look for a sexual release that is something more than a "fuck." Sexual kinkiness and sexual sadism are by-products of a society that uses sex as a tease—yet talks out of both sides of its mouth on the subject. Thus, a repressive society that denies these loving and caring needs creates sex hatred that runs the gamut from sexual violence to kinky sex—which are simply substitute ways of expressing self-hatred.

So, in judging sexvids, I am proposing that penile-vaginal sexmaking and oral sexmaking is normal sex with—or without—a marriage commitment. Sex without love and recreational sex, for good or bad, has always been a basic element of human life. (A very interesting book worth reading on this subject is called *Sex Without Love*, by Russell Vannoy, Prometheus Books, New York, 1980.) I believe that normal sex, as defined above, can be experienced privately between any healthy man or woman in approximately the same age range—and also between men and women separated by a fairly wide age differential, depending on the physical condition of the older partner. My feeling is that the quality of the orgasm originates in the mental rapport between the participants. Of course not everyone agrees with me. I also affirm that *watching* actors (on a screen or television tube) enjoying normal sex together or masturbating alone or in the company of another couple who are friends (when it isn't reduced to a gymnastic exercise or an orgy) can be a way of learning about normal sex—even though the viewers might prefer sexmaking with one other person at a time. Also, masturbation *is* normal sex—but as a substitute, not as a way of life. On this basis, the following N (Normal) ratings have been derived:

N = Normal and Includes Oral Sex

NL = Normal—Laughing and bawdy sex.

NR = Normal—Romantic or deeply caring sex.

NN = Normal—Noncommitted sex without love but with momentary caring.

NM = Normal—Masturbation or self-love.

D = Deviational*

DK = Deviational kinky variations in normal heterosexual sex, including not generally accepted anal sex, golden showers, group sex, etc.

DB = Deviational bondage and discipline as sex stimulants.

DS = Deviational sadistic, violent and victimized sex.

DC = Deviational sex with children under 16. There is no DC listing on any sexvid in the filmography, but many viewers will be convinced that some of the females acting in some films are under 16—which of course is the producers' intention.

BI = Bisexual—Sexmaking with a member of the same sex.

CC = Collector's Choice.

R means R-rated or "soft-core" (no explicit genital sex).

P/D means Producer/Director in that order. If only one name is given, the individual acted in both capacities.

F/A means Featured Actors and Actresses (as many as I've been able to determine from dealers' catalogues and other sources). If information is fragmentary it means that thus far no one has copied the essential information off the film credits. If *no* date is given, this means the film was produced sometime between 1970 and 1979. An exact date may be impossible to determine since many films were not copyrighted. If no distributor name is given it means that the tape is temporarily "out of print" but could be reissued.

While there are many video cassettes totally devoted to homosexual sex (male or female) available, the thrust of this book is heterosexual. Unless otherwise stated, the appearance of a **BI** rating refers to sexmaking between two women. One or two scenes of this type are a convention in sexvids, and the women are usually called lesbians. I think that bisexual is a better characterization, since in the majority of sexvid plots (and probably in actuality) most of the women actresses are not lesbians, and they are capable of moving from male to female sexmaking with no apparent reservations. Males with bisexual leanings rarely appear in heterosexual sexvid plots. The reason is obvious: It would make the "straight" male audience very uneasy.

The **DK** category could conceivably be revised in the future. Many kinky-sex enthusiasts believe that what they enjoy is normal. For many people, group sex, swinging or wearing clothes of the opposite sex is considered normal. Amazingly, in the 1980 *Cosmopolitan* sex survey to which 106,000 women responded, 15 percent regularly had anal sex. In a *Redbook* survey in 1975, 20 percent of the women engaged in anal sex; and a 1972 Play Foundation study found that among wives under 34, nearly 25 percent had occasionally tried anal sex. So perhaps in the future, anal sex might be considered normal. But for most people today it is still in the kinky area.

In my opinion, once heterosexual sexmaking becomes dependent on external stimuli beyond the clean human bodies of a particular man and woman for sexual arousal and completion of the sexual act, it ultimately tends to deny the other person. On the other hand, I have not given a **DK** rating when a sequence involves only three persons, two of whom are of the opposite sex. This is a fantasy of millions of men and women, and I have even proposed in one of my novels, *The Rebellion of Yale Marratt*, that a ménage à trois should be a legal form of marriage. My feeling in the **DB** (deviational bondage) category is unequivocal: It reflects a kind of sexual degradation. In my opinion, both the **DB** and **DS** categories will eventually be self-censored by the producers of mass-market sexvids. But

*With the exception of **DS** and **DK**, of which many examples are included in the filmography, all other ratings are nonjudgmental classifications. I'm sure that you'll learn these classifications quickly. Hopefully, they may encourage producers and distributors to offer more sex with laughter (**NL**) and sex with affection (**NR**) in future sexvids.

human responses in these areas continue to challenge all movie makers, who are well aware of the erotic qualities of aggressive sex, and of mixing sex and violence. For this reason I have included three horror films in the filmography (*I Spit on Your Grave*, *The Texas Chainsaw Massacre*, and *Halloween*) to show how filmmakers are using the **R** category to get away with material that would get them arrested if they simply added a penis or vagina to their films.

For the most part, if I have rated sexvids in any of the categories with a total **DK** or **DS** rating, let the buyer beware. It's sure to be a stomach turner; you'll find it difficult to laugh. On the other hand, in contrast to the **DS** category, the **DK** category by itself depends on your individual hang-ups. If the weird variations on sexmaking don't appeal to you, you may still find them so silly that you can laugh.

If you have read this far, you realize that from my standpoint an **NN**, **NR** or **NL** rating (or any combination of these) is a reasonably healthy sexvid, but nevertheless will probably contain some of the sexvid conventions discussed previously. Also note that when I have given a sexvid an **NR** rating, it doesn't mean that the entire sexvid is "romantic." Actually, the **NR** rating often indicates caring sexuality, even though the participants may not be in love. The word *romantic* has many overtones, and if you would like to explore them more fully, I highly recommend Nathaniel Branden's book, *The Psychology of Romantic Love* (J. P. Tarcher, Los Angeles, 1980).

I'm predicting that the adverse reaction of millions of women in the coming years will eliminate many of the old-style sex conventions that they disapprove of. Eventually (and perhaps to the shock of many feminists) noncommitted but romantic films (**NR**) with a predominantly romantic approach will dominate the adult film market. There are thousands of untapped stories, including extended "soap-opera" scenarios that can be developed to offer "caring-romantic" explicit sexmaking. It's a wide-open field for adult film screenwriters. As this new era of female-oriented sexvids develops, I'm sure that men (who are presumably more aroused by visual sex than women are) will not be disappointed or feel deprived by this type of sexvid. Men will simply discover that catering to female fantasies will not only create much more responsive sex partners for them, but they will be just as aroused by female sex fantasies as they are by the current male variety. And men will discover—if they haven't already—that most women really enjoy sexmaking, too—and with lots of snuggling, hugging and conversation before, during and afterwards.

There are several other caveats on these ratings. Almost all of the films have lesbian relationships; I have labeled them **BI**. Many women find these scenes disgusting. Also, many producers and directors are well aware of the erotic qualities inherent in violence or a **DS** category as mentioned above—and they know that these films are prone to attack by women's organizations and religious groups. How do they get around this? With laughter—but in a very weird way. You'll discover that many recent sexvids have scenes which, for a few minutes, seem to be very sadistic. They are, however, quickly followed by some silly situations that are supposed to relieve the tension and make you laugh. I haven't labeled any of these films **NL**, though many of them contain contrived humor as a staple.

A good example of this rather tricky approach is *Ms. Magnificent*. Richard Aldrich, who produced and directed it under the name Damon Christian, told me that he detests anal sex scenes, but his financial backers insisted on having one—so he gave it to them in spades. The title of *Ms. Magnificent* was changed from *Super Woman* because the producers of *Superman* threatened to sue. In one scene, an actress (not one of the featured stars) is forced to go down on her knees while a man fucks her anally. At the same time, he slaps her buttocks viciously, and as he thrusts into her from behind, he insists that she tell him how much she enjoys it. Just as the scene is getting very gritty, Super Woman arrives and tumbles the nasty man on his back. Amazingly, the woman who has been sodomized is laughing happily (giving the impression, anyway, that she's not too unhappy). She claps enthusiastically while Super Woman nearly twists his balls and penis off in a nerve-wracking—for a male—sequence. Presumably, the viewer, who may be female, gets her revenge and laughs. In another scene, Super Woman is overcome by a competitor from another planet named Cretia Borgia who has a magic amulet—a simulated penis about 14 inches long. Using it as a dildo, Cretia straps Super Woman to a chair and is about to disembowel her. While Super Woman is shrieking in pain (only about half the dildo is in her vagina)—presto! a young man and woman appear. Speaking with English accents, they ask if this is the supermarket. They are looking for cucumbers. Cretia, with the huge dildo strapped around her middle, promptly offers it to them, thus saving Super Woman's vagina and intestines from certain destruction.

In addition to the above ratings, I have given more than 100 of the sexvids in the Main Filmography a **CC** (Collector's Choice) rating. This is a tricky rating. One man's cup of tea is another man's poison. In his book *Reverse Angle* (Clarkson Potter, New York, 1982), John Simon covers 245 major Hollywood films produced in the same decade as the films I have reviewed in the Main Filmography. He recommends only 15 of them! The important thing to keep in mind is that a Collector's Choice rating is assigned within the adult genre itself. An adult film with a **CC** rating may not measure up to a four-star Hollywood production. But in many cases, from the standpoint of technical filmmaking and cinematography (and often even dialogue), they equal and often surpass many of the trashy made-for-TV films, soap operas and Hollywood films (which often have budgets ten times or more those of most adult films). Many of the producer/directors of adult films are just as capable as those making regular **R**-rated films. One thing is sure: Even though most bankers won't finance the adult filmmaker, these men and women will never get the opportunity to turn in the million-dollar box office failures that have plagued Hollywood in the past few years.

Finally, if you read the filmography from beginning to end you will discover I have not only given **CC** ratings to films that are **NR** or **NL** rated, but also to a few that are **DS** and **DK** rated. As I have noted, the conflict involved in films that contain rape scenes often forces the director into an emotional interplay that may be lacking in more compliant sexual involvements.

5

Making Your Own Sexvids

Inevitably, if watching sexvids becomes a stimulating part of your life, you'll probably decide that the least expensive way to enjoy them is to make your own. Blank videotapes cost less than $10.00 each, and in extended play are good for six hours of taping your own sexmaking! Cameras that plug into your VCR are already selling at discount houses for as low as $500. By the end of the decade videotape cameras will be as convenient and inexpensive as 8-mm cameras ever were—and you don't have to send your tape out for developing!

Before I describe some approaches to making your own tapes, I will tell you about Susan's Video Exchange, which offers you the opportunity to see how others are doing it—without committing yourself, if you prefer. If you send Susan's an original videotape of you and your companion making love, they will exchange it—at no cost—for a sixty- to ninety-minute tape containing up to four other couples' tapes (which they combined on one longer tape), *and* they will return your original tape to you. If you are just curious, however, Susan's will sell you their tapes for $55 each, and offer you a continuing service as a nonparticipating voyeur.

Thus, if you are interested in sex exchange with another couple, unlike swinger's magazines (which must rely on still snapshots that are often gross and do not reveal much about the people involved), Susan's Video Exchange provides a way you can learn just about everything you want to know about particular couples that are sexually adventurous. But perhaps even more important, Susan's Video Exchange provides a "safe," yet pleasantly dangerous and sexually provocative, exposure for thousands of young "experimenters."

In one current offering from Susan's Video Exchange there are four different couples, none of whom, before they sent their tapes to Susan's (or probably even now), are acquainted with each other. First we see Earl and Debra, a couple in their late twenties or early thirties. You quickly realize that in addition to Earl's sexual abilities, he is a perfectionist and is trying to make an attractive tape. You see Debra in their bathroom washing and combing her hair, preparing for sexmaking. As you will discover, this required more than one placement of the video camera, either on a tripod or hand-held. After the bathroom scene, Earl sets up the camera in a position near the bed so he can see most of Debra's body. The lighting is clear and sharp; there are no close-ups, but there are attractive shadows. From that point on, and for the next twenty minutes, you watch Earl and Debra enjoy each other orally, as well as through penile-vaginal sex in many different positions. Occasionally, Earl interrupts the action and zooms in on Debra's lovely body, but there are few facial close-ups. While they mostly avoid watching themselves on the monitor—something most home filmmakers have a hard time avoiding, and which is easy to detect and often amusing to watch—unfortunately, they scarcely converse at all. Maybe it was a first try.

On a longer tape, prepared entirely by one couple (Greg and Rena), Greg tells you that he rented the camera for the project. Despite his lack of camera experience he provides a very interesting opening. Rena, a very attractive woman in her thirties, is sitting languidly on her living room couch, fully dressed. As she runs her hands over her body, Greg, in a voice-over, tells you: "This is my wife, with whom I have lived for seven years. We've had an open relationship, and during this time we've gotten together with many different couples. As you can see, Rena has a very beautiful body (at this point Rena is slowly undressing), and sharing sex with other people in our lives has brought us very much closer together because we always share our total feelings and reactions." Throughout the entire taping Greg, who finally moves into camera range, not only makes love with Rena (she puts a cock collar on him, which he later removes). As they kiss and taste and merge bodies, they not only talk to each other, but to the unseen viewer as well.

For about $1000 to $1500 above the cost of your VCR, you can now be your own screenwriter, producer and director. Before you begin, if you're male you should immediately start practicing Tantric sexual control. If you don't learn how to control your ejaculation, your first sexvid may be over before you start to record. Assuming that in most cases men will take the initiative (presumably because they enjoy visual erotica more), you obviously will need a coopera-tive, laughing, fun-loving female partner. She must agree along with you to be both actress and cinematographer, and you can be sure that if she will help you direct your personal sexvid, she will also operate the camera.

So by now, you and your friend have pulled down the shades in whatever room you've turned into a temporary studio. Depending on the kind of video camera that you are using you may or may not need floodlights. Experiment with raising and lowering your floodlights and the different shadow effects they create on your bodies. If you have white walls or light wallpaper you'll probably get enough light for a color video camera by aiming just one floodlight at the ceiling. Make sure, in advance, or before you turn on your camera (which should be securely resting on a tripod to keep a steady focus) that it does not point directly at your floodlights. If you turn the lens directly into such a bright light you may burn out your vidicon tube, which ordinarily should have a life of several thousand hours—and you will have to buy a new one at a cost of about $200.

Before you turn on your camera, put a few records or tapes on your stereo for background music. Your video camera will have an excellent microphone built into it near its carrying handle. Home video making does not require a supple-mental microphone.

Now turn on your camera. Presumably (again I am assuming that you are male), you have learned how to operate the camera and have connected it to your VCR, which is already hooked up to your television. If you are using a camcorder you may not want to hook into your television, but while you can check back and reshoot with a camcorder it's more fun to watch the action in progress. On the other hand, a camcorder extends your shooting area and lets you move your sexvid production around the house or outdoors. But if you're hooked to your TV as monitor, you can explain to your co-moviemaker, who is probably protesting vehemently that she's sorry she ever agreed to such insanity, that your television tube is now a monitor, and later, when you push the play/record buttons on the VCR, it becomes a recorder.

Show her the release/pause button on the camera and how it controls the movement of the tape in your VCR when the play/record buttons are down, and how you can stop the tape (and the recording). Explain to her that at any time during your recording you can depress the pause button and stop the tape for about five minutes. This gives you time to change positions and angles and check them on the monitor to create a superior sexvid. She'll have to understand, too, how to use the zoom lens for close-ups.

Don't buy a video camera that doesn't have a zoom lens. Learning how to zoom in for a close-up takes about two minutes. Before you turn on the play/record button, you should experiment, monitoring yourselves in living color on your television screen. Let her get used to long shots and the fun of zooming in on your body (standing and sitting) and taking close-up shots of your penis, while she makes sure that your body is sufficiently lighted by monitoring the television. Assuming that she has been using the camera on a tripod, take it off and show her how easy it is to perch it on her shoulder.

Hopefully, she's stopped protesting by now and is enjoying the taping as much as you are—so snap on the play/record switches. You've already convinced her that in order to make a really interesting sexvid you can't shoot it just from one angle. You can set the camera up in a fixed position on the tripod, focused on her. Now with the camera running, sit down next to her and see the miracle. There you both are—watching yourself and each other on the tube. When you play your tape back and watch it together on your television you'll quickly discover that the fixed position will get boring to look at. Therefore, be sure to change the camera's position, or hand it back and forth to each other. If you're a video nut determined to produce a better sexvid than you ever could have bought from professionals, you may have to declare same time outs while she helpfully restores your erection.

This is where the laughing, talking (remember you are recording your voices, too), fun and romance come in. One warning, though: a wise male will have made love to his woman and brought her to at least one orgasm without coming himself. This will not only make her more mellow about your video insanity but hopefully will make her more amenable about stopping the action anywhere in process while you change personal and camera positions. Assure her that you really aren't trying to make a six-hour sexvid in one night and then show her the real fun. Play back your production thus far, and watch yourselves to determine what positions and shots (long, medium, or close-ups) you need to use to make your sexvid more explicit or romantic.

To avoid jumping up and down every few minutes, you may want to produce your sexvid with a hand-held camera. Since the camera won't be in a fixed tripod position, you both can't appear in your sexvid at once (unless you prop it up somewhere). But it will give you a chance to see your genitals as others see them.

No professional video or film producer ever made a movie film or videotape this way. They can rely on editing after the filming or taping of various scenes—you can't. But you are discovering, and I assure you that it can be done, how to make a continuous sexvid with no breaks between scenes, using many different camera angles, and how to create a finished product without any editing. You have to learn to do this because unlike half-inch reel-to-reel tape used by professionals, or three-quarter-inch cassette studio tape, you can't edit half-inch video cassette tapes, unless you wish to buy additional equipment costing up to $500 or more. But never mind, all creative arts have built-in limitations. If the bug hits you, you can learn not only how to produce off-the-cuff tapes of your own sexmaking, but later you can also work out simple shooting scripts that will let you create a home-made masterpiece!

If you are determined to tape the actual sexual thrusting that is so boring on most sexvids, you will require a very cooperative partner. You'll have to put your camera on a tripod, and it will take some experimenting with the camera angles and personal positioning (and some mutual patience) to get superior results. Since I hope you won't feel compelled to ejaculate outside her vagina, like the heroes of sexvid films, you can arrange the camera so that it is focused on *her* face when she climaxes. Later, when you play it back, you'll have the sounds and sighs—and the sheer beauty—of a woman's face (or your own) in the act of sexmaking and orgasm. And you'll discover that facial beauty and sexmaking includes both contortions and agony as your organisms strive for the final release—then ecstacy and warm laughter as you float placidly after consummation.

While I'm sure that you'll invent your own scenarios, here is a simple one. Start with a camera-held long shot of your environment. Your lady can be entering the room fully clothed or naked, and do what you rarely see done on most sexvids—talk! (But don't argue.) If your lady is dressed, she may slowly undress. She can leave something on for you to take off. Or you may prefer to put the camera on a tripod and undress her. Now it's her turn to use the camera. She can take a long shot of you undressing, whether she's holding the camera or not, and can pan it slowly over your erection. Now, after following you with the camera to your sofa or bed with a long shot, she joins you. Glancing surreptitiously at the tube, ensure that you are both on camera. My God, you are! Now she can kiss your penis, and you can kiss her breasts, her vulva. But remember, nobody else is out there holding the camera, following your movements. And remember something you may have learned from years of watching the tube: What makes the action interesting is close-ups interspersed with medium and occasional long shots.

Of course, if you have a video camera and are in a synergetic relationship or in a corporate marriage you may have other people available to help you make your sexvids. Or, if you are a swinger, you'll probably have little difficulty in finding many sex partners and recording your sexual activities.

Finally, singles who are cohabiting or pair-bonds may discover a new way of eroticizing each other by making their own personal sexvid—alone, with themselves as the hero or heroine.

It's very easy to do. Set your camera up on a tripod or prop it up on pillows. Put a tape in your recorder. Turn on your television. Now walk to and fro or lie down, always staying within the range of your camera. Lo and behold, there you are, with no help from anyone, on television! Snap on the play/record button and position yourself. Now snap up the camera-release button. You are now recording what you see—yourself. With a little ingenuity, and aided by background music on your stereo, you can strip, do erotic dances, caress yourself and intersperse the action with amazing shots of your genitals, buttocks or breasts. Now take the camera off the tripod and prop it so that it's pointing up at you. (Never aim your video camera directly down at the floor. At such a sharp angle, some particles may be released in the tube.) Now, when it is aiming up at you, snap the camera-release button on again. There you are in naked glory on your television screen! But you are taller and more graceful than you ever realized, and you are seeing views of yourself (and recording them) that you've never seen before. Now, if you really dared, you could create a half-hour tape of you turning yourself on. Smiling and gesturing at your absent lover, you can tell him or her how much you want them. You can show, with your hands on your body, how you wish it was his or her hands. Later, or the next day, with the lights turned low, you can tell your lover, "Honey, today I made something just for you!" Turn on your tape. You should have it ready and waiting to be rerun on your television. And now let your partner discover an erotic you that he/she never knew existed!

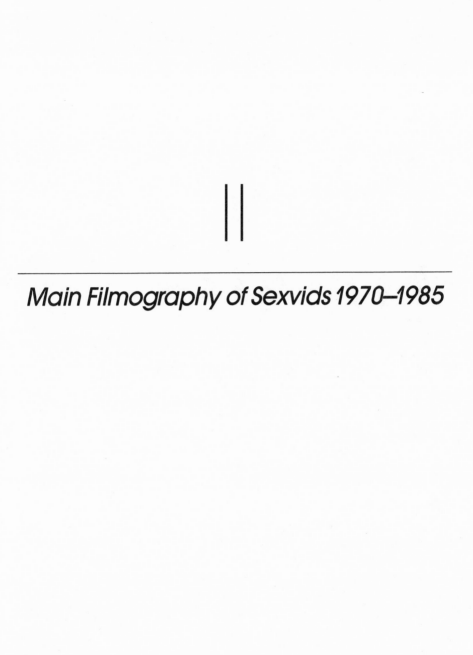

II

Main Filmography of Sexvids 1970–1985

All of the Best . . . and Some of the Worst Adult Films Produced Between 1970 and 1985

As this book developed, it became obvious to me that adult film/X-rated films/porno films (whatever you wish to call them), instead of disappearing forever after a short run at one of the nearly 800 adult theaters around the country, are now gaining a new kind of lasting power with the advent of videotapes and video discs. Somewhat like the transition from hardcover books to paperbacks (but in this case at much higher prices than in the theater), thousands of different sexvids will be available for many years to come.

Unlike more conventional films, in which clothing styles may date the film, fucking and nakedness never go out of style. Thus, as the transition from the film to tape proceeds, and in their new form, as sexvids, it occurred to me that someone should attempt to compile a complete catalogue of adult films that were originally created on film (and currently are sometimes made directly on tape), offering a guide, with some insights, to the millions of potential purchasers as to the best of the sexvids.

Deciding on the best sexvids—either those currently being shot directly on videotape or those produced from films between 1970 and 1985—wasn't easy. In addition to the Main Filmography that follows, in which I have rated and summarized over 1,300 films on videotape, there is a Supplemental Listing of more than 2,840 additional sexvids, which I have not seen. If you have never purchased a sexvid, or are considering expanding your sexvid library, my feeling is that most of these 1,300 sexvids will be around for a long time. If they are withdrawn by a particular dealer or distributor, or are no longer sold by a particular distributor, they are likely to become collectors' items. In future decades they will provide insights into the sexual world of the 1980s. Perhaps like the various forms of erotica that were prevalent in ancient societies, sexvids will become artifacts of this particular time and culture. If a new kind of sexual world, which I have alluded to in this book and proposed in my novels, ever comes close to reality, our grandchildren watching these films may not only find them funny, but in a different world of easy, loving, laughing, human sexuality, will probably find them, in many cases, totally incredible.

I have not put the running time on any of the movies unless they are less than

60 minutes. *Deep Throat* runs 62 minutes. So do most of the *Swedish Erotica* tapes, which were originally designed as "loops"—three or four sex "story" vignettes running 15 to 20 minutes each—and in many cases were available (and still are) as 8-mm films. Most of the films made in the late 1970s, and especially those made in 1980 and 1981, run anywhere from 72 to 90 minutes, with a few exceptions that run as long as 120 minutes. Keep in mind that 10 or 15 minutes one way or the other does not make a better film, and that soft-core versions of X-rated hard-core movies (the kind that often appear on cable and subscription television) have all the genital sex close-ups and erect penises eliminated, with a loss (depending on your point of view) of 10 to 15 minutes from the original. Unless otherwise indicated, all tapes except former stag films where noted are in color. Many of the tapes are available in a soft-core version and are already appearing on late-night subscription and cable television channels. Many women prefer these soft-core R versions, which provide a transition for them, and with which they can better cope and enjoy because the sex is much more subtly expressed.

It also should be noted, in both this Main Filmography and in the Supplemental Listing, that when I have listed featured actors and actresses I have not included them all—particularly the females. One of the conventions that many sexvids adhere to is to offer a cornucopia of female stars. Many simply make "guest appearances," and are only in one scene that has little or nothing to do with the plot (if there is one). For example in the film *A Girl's Best Friend*, in which Samantha Fox appears as the lady in red, she is on screen only about five minutes; the film is totally oriented around Juliet Anderson and Veronica Hart.

Also, if you can watch any videotapes on either a Sony 26-inch television screen or on the General Electric Wide Screen 4000, you will probably enjoy them more. The Sony offers a brilliance that is unobtainable at this writing in any U.S.-made television, and the General Electric is an absolutely amazing job of rear-projection television with a 50-inch screen that gives you the feeling that you really are at the movies. Of course, human genitals seen on a 50-inch screen in the close-ups are many times actual size!

Without the help of the distributors I have credited in the dedication, who lent me specific tapes that they control (in many cases they financed the original production costs), I never would have been able to put this unique sexvid filmography together. While I have become very friendly with many distributors, I have *not* let the friendship (as you will discover) influence the particular ratings that I have applied to some of their tapes. My feeling is that my ratings will not hurt the sale of any particular tape, particularly when these ratings carry a DS, DK or DB notation. Since I believe that the future of sexvids lies with those rated NN, NR and NL, like any critic I have my own preferences. (*Worse* is a totally subjective word.) Like it or not, there is a continual demand, for example, for Bondage and Discipline tapes, and many people are fascinated by the kinkier side of human sexuality. In an odd way, for those of us who shudder when we watch, they may provide a learning experience that can only be summed up: "There but for the grace of God go I."

You should also understand that some of the adult films produced in past years are not controlled exclusively by any one distributor. The original producers of a film, or those who now control the rights to some of the older films, have occasionally negotiated joint selling agreements with more than one distributor. Or the film owners, for one reason or another, may have discontinued an exclusive tape sale agreement with a particular distributor and assigned the sales rights to another.

In the following sexvid filmography, I have tried my best to key the tapes to the exclusive distributor who lent them to me, even though other distributors may offer the same tapes. Many of the original distributors/owners of these tapes will sell adult films directly to you by mail. The complete listing of their addresses precedes the filmography. If you order from any that don't sell by mail, they will pass your letter on to a preferred mail order dealer, or you can try to find a retail video store that handles adult films. Many stores do carry adult films, but in the smaller cities they may only have a limited stock. In some cases, they will be glad to order for you, using the information in this book, and may even be willing to reduce their mark-up. The dealer cost on most of the tapes is probably not more than $35 to $40. Practically all the distributor/owners listed in the following pages will be happy to send you their mail order catalogues if you send them a check for $5.

If you order by mail, your tapes will be sent via United Parcel Service, and they will be packaged in distinctive, trademarked packages that identify the distributor. If you prefer to order by mail, but not from the particular distributor listed, you will find many regular mail order dealers advertising in various video magazines—who in many cases discount adult films to as low as $60. Keep in mind, too, that many dealers advertising are not the original distributors. Companies such as VCX, Cal Vista, Quality, Video-X-Pix, Video Home Library, Essex and the Mitchell Brothers are the original owners of particular tapes, and you will also find their ads in the video magazines.

If you discover a particular film on tape that I have missed, either in the Main Filmography or the Supplemental Listing, I hope you will drop me a line in care of the publishers, giving me any information you may have on the film so we can incorporate it into a future edition. Thank you.

7

Adult Film Owner/Distributor Listing

*A.B. Video
2119 Osborne Street
Canoga Park, CA 91304

ABV West
2119 Osborne Street
Canoga Park, CA 91304

AD Video
1566 La Pradera Drive
Campell, CA 95008

*AVC—Adult Video Corp.
18121 Napa Street
Northridge, CA 91325

Action Video
Route 2
Box 10
Santa Fe, NM 87501

Active Home Video
9300 Pico Boulevard
Los Angeles, CA 90035

Allied Video
106 Berkert Street
Bethpage, NY 11714

American Broadcast Video
P. O. Box 17546
Denver, Colorado, 80217

*Ambassador Video
21540 Prairie Street
Unit C
Chatsworth, CA 91311

Anthony Spinelli Productions
22222 Sherman Way, Suite 100
Canoga Park, CA 91303

*Arrow Films
85 East Hoffman Avenue
Lyndenhurst, NY 11757

*Astronics Ltd.
90 Golden Gate Avenue
San Francisco, CA 94109
(Many Astronic tapes are now being offered by other distributors. See footnote.

*Atom Home Video
13360 Beach Avenue
Marina Del Rey, CA 90292–5622

*Baker Video
330 Bakersville Road
South Dartmouth, MA 02748

Banana Video
1399 Western Avenue
Gardena, CA 90247

Big Top Video (see H&S Sales)

*Bizarre Video Productions
150 Lafayette Street
New York, NY 10012

*Bizarre Tri-Star
5848 Naples Plaza, #204
Long Beach, CA 90803 (Name changed to California Star Productions.)

*Blue Video
3615 Carnegie Avenue
Cleveland, OH 44115
(Blue Video sold most of their line to other distributors. See footnote.)

Boccaccio 100
(Some Boccaccio films have appeared on tape. Those listed are still on 16-mm film and to my knowledge have not been transferred to tape.) Ray Felder who controls these films is located in Tempe, AZ 85283

Boss Video
4650 Bel Air Road
Baltimore, MD 21206

*Broadcast Quality
7800 Southwest 57th Avenue
Miami, FL 33143

Catalina Distributing
6611 Santa Monica Boulevard
Los Angeles CA 90038
(All-male video tapes—none of which are reviewed here.)

*CBS/Fox Video
23290 Commerce Drive
Farmington Hills, MI 48024

*CDI Home Video
(See Cinderella Distributors.)

*CPLC
1765 West Adams Boulevard
Los Angeles, CA 90014

*Caballero Control Corp.
Order from Video Mail Order Company, 21540 Blythe Street
Canoga Park, CA 91304.
(Caballero controls Swedish Erotica and several other labels and has taken over the distribution of all Cal Vista tapes.)

*Cal Vista Corp.
6649 Odessa Street
Van Nuys, CA 91406

*California Star Productions,
5848 Maples Plaza #204
Long Beach, CA 90803

*California Supreme
P. O. Box 38670
Hollywood, CA 90038

Catalina Video
6611 Santa Monica Blvd.
Los Angeles, CA 90038

Channel X Video
4774 Melrose Avenue
Hollywood, CA 90029

Choice Video
21624 Lassen Street
Chatsworth, CA 91311

Cinematrex Corporation
16121 Sherman Way
Van Nuys, CA 91406

*Cinderella Distributors
8021 Remmet Avenue
Canoga Park, CA 91304

Cinema Tech, Inc.
8745 Shirley Avenue
North Ridge, CA 91324

Classic Editions Video
4933 McConnell Avenue
Suite R
Los Angeles, CA 90066

Classic Productions
P. O. Box 952
Metaire, LA

Class X Video
Box C
Sandy Hook, CT 06482

Coast to Coast Video
85 East Hoffman Avenue
Lindenhurst, NY 11757

*Collector's Video
No longer active. Tapes available from Gourmet Video

*Command Video
1540 Broadway
New York, NY 10036

*Competitive Video
(CAL VISTA) 6649 Odessa Street
Van Nuys, CA 91406

*Creative Image
P. O. Box 38307
Hollywood, CA 90038

Creative Video Features
7618 Woodman Avenue
Unit 6
Panorama City, CA 91402

Creative Video Services
500 N. Ventu Park Road
Newbury Park, CA 91320

*Diverse Industries
7651 Haskell Avenue
Van Nuys, CA 91406

*Dreamland Home Video
20611 Plummer Street
Chatsworth, CA 91311

*Embassy Home Entertainment
1901 Avenue of the Stars
Los Angeles, CA 90067

*Eros (King of Video)
(No longer distributing X-rated films. See footnote.)

Erotic Video
(See Superior Video.)

*Essex Video
P. O. Box 1055
Northridge, CA 91324
(Listing in first edition as Select/Essex. Name changed in 1983.)

Excalibur Films
424 West Commonwealth
Fullerton, CA 92632

*F.I.V.—Video Voyeurs Club
P. O. Box 114
Murrysville, CA 15668

*Four-Play (4-PLAY) Inc.
3075 No. California St.
Burbank, CA 91504

*G.M. Video
3645 India Street
San Diego, CA 92103

*Golden Girls
P. O. Box 55254
Valencia, CA 91355

Gold Medallion Editions
Great American Soap Opera Co.
11140 Chandler Street, #1100
North Hollywood, CA 91601

*Gold Stripe Video
P. O. Box 180
Nesconset, NY 11767

*Gourmet Video
13162 Raymer St.
North Hollywood, CA 91605

H&S Sales
P. O. Box 126
College Point, NY 11356

*Harmony Vision
116 North Robertson Avenue
Los Angeles, CA 90048

*HIFCOA—Hollywood International Films
1044 South Hill Street
Los Angeles, CA 90015

High Class Productions
18720 Oxnard Street
Suite 103
Tarzana, CA 91365

Highbridge—Audubon Films
313 East 74th Street
New York, NY 10021

*Hollywood Video Productions
16787 Schoenborn Street
Sepulveda, CA 91343

*Home Entertainment Club of America
(Video Audio Electronics)
153 West 4th Street
Arcade Building
Williamsport, PA 17701

*I.V.P. (Innovation Video)
19410 Business Center Drive
Northridge, CA 91325

I.P.I. Video
2312 South Brentwood Boulevard
St. Louis, MO 63144

Independent Distributors
430 West 54th Street
New York, NY 10019

Intact Productions
Box 2218
Astoria Station
Long Island City, NY 11102

*International Home Video Club
(See Video Club.)

*Intropics Video, Inc.
7131 Owensmouth Avenue
Suite 104B
Canoga Park, CA 91303

*J.L.T. Films Inc.
480 Central Avenue
Northfield, IL 60093

*Janus Films & Video
7505 Foothill Boulevard
Tujunga, CA 91402
(Name changed to Liberty Films.)

Kenyon Video
(See Sound Video.)

Kemal Video Enterprises
630 Ninth Avenue
Suite 907
New York, NY 10036
Kemal Tapes now distributed by
Caballero

Key Video
3529 South Valley View Boulevard
Las Vegas, NV 89103

L.A. Video
24–12 South Thurman Avenue
Los Angeles, CA 90016

Lambda Video
P.O. Box 323
East Rockaway, NY 11518
(Male homosexual and lesbian tapes)

D. T. Lang
210 Fifth Avenue
New York, NY 10010

Lightning Video
P.O. Box 4384
Stamford, CT 06907

Lipstick Video
(See Video Tape Exchange)

Love Television
(See Superior Video.)

*MCA Home Video
70 Universal City Plaza
Universal City, CA 91068

Magnum Entertainment
9301 Wilshire Boulevard
Suite 602
Beverly Hills, CA 90212

*Mastervision
969 Park Avenue
New York, NY 10028

*Masterpiece Video
7901-B Canoga Avenue
Canoga Park, CA 91304

*Media Home Entertainment
5730 Buckingham Parkway
Culver City, CA 90230

*Russ Meyer
R. M. International Films, Inc.
P.O. Box 3748
Hollywod, CA 90078

*Mitchell Brothers
895 O'Farrell Street
San Francisco, CA 91409

Moonlight Entertainment
9811 Owensmouth Avenue, Unit C
Chatsworth, CA 91311

*Monterey Video
7920 Alabama Avenue
Canoga Park, CA 91304

Movies at Midnight
(See note under Blue Video.)

Morning Glory Productions
604 Main Street, #D
Susanville, CA 96130

MSI Video
5020 Sunnyside Avenue
Suite 112
P. O. Box 825
Beltsville, MD 20705

*Naturists
P.O. Box 132
Oshkosh, WI 54902

*New Wave Productions
P.O. Box 66425
Los Angeles, CA 90066

New World Video
1888 Century Park East
Los Angeles, CA 90067

*Now Showing Video
953 Harrison Street
San Francisco, CA 94107

*Orchids International
1460 F. Monterey Pass Road
Monterey Park, CA 91754

T. Page
Box 348
2008 Deerpark
Fullerton, CA 92631

*Paradise Visuals
9311 Eton Avenue
Chatsworth, CA 96311

Parliament Video
12011 N. Sherman Rd.
N. Hollywood, CA 91609

Penguin Productions
15015 Ventura Boulevard
Van Nuys, CA 91403

Platinum
4521A Van Nuys Boulevard
Suite 215
Sherman Oaks, CA 91403

Pleasure Series
P.O. Box 6500
Englewood, NJ 07631

Pleasure Productions
7131 Owensmouth Avenue
Suite 29A,
Canoga Park, CA 91303

Quality X Video Cassettes
(All Quality X tapes now handled by
Video-X-Pix. See listing.)

Ed Rich Productions
1950 South Ocean Drive
Hallandale, FL 33009

SKJ Productions
P. O. Box 16191
Philadelphia, PA 19114

*Select Essex Video
(See listing under Essex Video.)

*Select-A-Tape
(Most Select-A-Tapes being offered by
other distributors. See footnote.)

*Silhouette
(See T.G.A. Video Ltd.)

Sound Video Unltd.
(Electric Blue Tapes now distributed by
Caballero)

Spectrum Video Distributors
5303 Sunset Boulevard
Los Angeles, CA 90027

*Standard Video (Innovation)
16838½ Saticoy Street
Van Nuys, CA 91406

*Super Video Productions
(Super Sight & Sound)
28853 Orchard Lake Road
Farmington Hills, MI 48018

*Superior Video
495 Ellis Street
#2938
San Francisco, CA 94102

*Susan's Video
P.O. Box 759
Frederick, MD 21701

Swan Video
5608 Fort Hamilton Parkway
Brooklyn, NY 11219

T.G.A. Video Ltd.
8821 Shirley Avenue
Northridge, CA 91324

T.M.X.
355 West 52nd Street
New York, NY 10019

Tamarack Productions
7618 Woodman Avenue
Suite 12
Panorama City, CA 91402

Tao Productions
7046 Hollywood Boulevard
Suite 203
Hollywood, CA 90028

Target Video (See Essex.)

*Uschi
P.O. BOX 663
Walnut Creek, CA 91789

Valiant Int. Pictures
4774 Melrose Avenue
Hollywood, CA 90029

*VCA
(Video Company of America)
9333 Osso Avenue
Chatsworth, CA 01311

*VCX
13402 Wyandotte
North Hollywood, CA 91605

*VCR
(Video Cassette Recordings, Inc.)
8745 Shirley Avenue
Northridge, CA 91324

VPX
P.O. Box 300
Brooklyn, NY 11214

Ventura Video
6860 Canby Avenue
Suite 101
Reseda, CA 91335

*Vestron Video
1011 High Ridge Road
P.O. Box 4000
Stamford, CT 06907

*VidAmerica Productions
235 East 55th Street
New York, NY 10022
(Some VidAmerica tapes being handled
by Vestron Video.)

*Vidco
1207 Vose Street
North Hollywood, CA 91605

Videatrics
51 East 42nd Street
Suite 1803A
New York, NY 10017

Video City
3371 Mount Diable Boulevard
Lafayette, CA 94549

*Video Club
(International Home)
220 Shrewsbury Avenue
Red Bank, NJ 07701

*Video Exclusives
Box 1900
Gary, IN 46409

Video Express
(Also Video Factory)
664 North Michigan Avenue
Chicago, IL 60600

*Video Gems
731 North La Brea
Los Angeles, CA 90038

*Video Home Entertainment
7037 Laurel Canyon Boulevard
North Hollywood, CA 91605

*Video Select Entertainment
6649 Odessa Avenue
Van Nuys, CA 91406

Video Showtime
P.O. Box 16165
St. Louis, MO 63105

Video Station
345 Main Street
Huntington, NY 11743

Video 2000
P.O. Box 54
Elwyn, PA 19063

Video Tape Enterprises
P.O. Box 34037
Coral Gables, FL 33134

Video Tape Exchange
1440 North Crescent Heights
Los Angeles, CA 90046
(Male Homosexual Films)

Video Tech
P.O. Box M-827
Gary IN 46401

Video Vista
90 Golden Gate Avenue
San Francisco, CA 94102

*Video Home Library
75 Spring Street
New York, NY 10012

Video Warehouse
P.O. Box 12007
Merrillville, IN 46411

*Video-X-Pix
430 West 54th Street
New York, NY 10019

Vision Video Productions
P.O. Box 25669
Los Angeles, CA 90025

Vista Video
8055 Lankershim Boulevard
North Hollywood, CA 91605

*Visual Entertainment Productions
16134 Covello Street
Van Nuys, CA 91406

Vivid Video
15127 Califa
Van Nuys, CA 94111

*Western Visuals
15745 Stagg Street
Van Nuys, CA 91406

*Wet Video
9333 Oso Avenue
Suite #1
Chatsworth, CA 91311

*Wizard Video
5303 Sunset Boulevard
Los Angeles, CA 90027

*Wonderful World of Video
(Formerly Wonderful World Tapes, now
handled by other distributors. See footnote.)

*X-Tra Vision
6616 Eleanor Avenue
Hollywood, CA 90028

But please note that linking adult videotapes with a particular distributor in this volatile industry is a hazardous business. Since the first edition of this book was published in July 1984, the following distributors have either become inactive, gone out of business, or stopped handling adult films: Astronics, Blue Video, Eros (King of Video), Freeway, Highbridge, Kenyon, Lambda, Movies at Midnight, New Wave, P.V.X., Scorpio, Select-A-Tape, T.M.X., TVX, Unicom, VBM, VidAmerica, Wonderful World of Video, Xana Home Video. While there have been no changes made in these above distributors' names against reviews that appeared in the previous edition, if you are looking for a tape attributed to one of the above companies, you can be pretty sure that it is still being offered under one of the following labels: Caballero, VCX, Essex, VCA, Video-X-Pix, or Video Home Library.

You will also note that there are many new companies in the address listing, and many of these are independent producers who have decided for one reason or another to distribute their own tapes.

About five companies in the address listing refused to supply me with review tapes for fear of negative reviews or because they didn't want the production dates of their tapes listed. If you don't find a particular tape reviewed, the chances are good that you'll find it listed in "Supplemental Listing of Sexvids" at the end of the book. By comparing the list of individuals and distributors mentioned in the Acknowledgments with the address listing, you can determine the "cream of the crop" of producers and distributors, who went all out with me and supplied the additional 650 tapes that are reviewed in this revised and updated edition.

There are many mail-order sources for adult videotapes, and their prices occasionally run as low as $9.75 each, on an order of 10 or more. But most older tapes produced in the 1970s range in price from $19.95 to $39.95 (for one-hour tapes and older tapes) with brand-new tapes of current productions running about $69.95 tops, in most cases.

Video Shack at Broadway and 47th Street, New York, NY 10036 or Price Busters, P.O. Box 28130, Las Vegas, NV 89126 can supply most of the tapes reviewed or listed in the Supplemental Listing.

*Means that this company controls and/or distributes particular tapes attributed to them in this book.

8

Classics

ALICE IN WONDERLAND
CC NL NR NM
*1975 XTRA-VISION & MEDIA and VID
AMERICA soft-core version*

P/D—Bill Osco, Bud Townsend
F/A—Bradford Arndexter
F/A—Kristine de Bell

There's both a hard-core and soft-core version of this one. A laughing, musical version of Alice, it is one of the few explicit sex films in the past ten years in which sex is neatly interwoven into the story line. Kristine de Bell is a captivating actress (the only one, incidentally, who has made the transition from porno to regular films). For my money the hard-core version is superior to the soft-core. (Xtra-Vision offers the hard-core direct via mail order.) Basic scenes eliminated from the soft-core Media version are Kristine in a loving and nicely photographed first masturbation experience and Kristine enjoying oral sex with the Mad Hatter, plus a few other genital sex scenes. The difference in length is about ten minutes. Most women will enjoy either version. The hard-core version costs about $30 more than the soft-core one.

AMANDA BY NIGHT
CC NN DK NM NR
1980 CABALLERO CONTROL

P/D—Harold Lime, Robert McCallum
F/A—Richard Bolla, Jamie Gillis, Frank Hollawell
F/A—Veronica Hart, Samantha Fox, Lisa de Leeuw

Nominated Best Film for the 1981 Fifth Annual Erotic Film Awards. It should have received it. Amanda Heather (Veronica Hart) is a high-class Los Angeles hooker who works with a couple of other girls, Gwen (Samantha Fox) and Beth (Lisa de Leeuw). Friday (Jamie Gillis), Amanda's former pimp, offers her a $1,000 night job with a big shot who wants one girl to play the dominatrix. Amanda refuses the assignment, but Gwen and Beth take it, and Beth is murdered in a swimming pool fracas with Mr. Big. Gwen, who is on drugs, knows who the murderer is, but Friday, to get his way with Mr. Big, takes care of her—and is about to "waste" Amanda, too, but she is saved by Ambrose Hart (Richard Bolla), a lieutenant in the police department who wears a white hat. It's a story of the good guys and the bad guys, including one sergeant in the vice squad who uses the hookers for his own pleasure and is a thoroughly nasty guy, as is our anti-hero, Jamie Gillis. Bob McCallum (not his real name) proves in this one that a good director with a seamy underworld story of believable call girls and police can mix sex, murder and violence in a 1980s-style adult film that will keep your interest to the romantic ending, with good guy Lieutenant Ambrose falling in love with Amanda—and not using her. There's no lack of sex and good acting by all, especially Richard Bolla (with Ron Jeremy and Jamie Gillis) as the good guy against the bad ones. Veronica Hart proves she's an actress who could bridge the adult film gap into legitimate films. Worth owning.

AMERICAN SEX FANTASY
CC   NN   NL   DS (one scene with Jamie Gillis)
1976   INT. HOME VIDEO CLUB

P/D—Jim Holiday, Beau Buchanan
F/A—Toni Roam, Shelly Dynah Mite, Jennifer Jordan, Peony Jones, Susan Barrett

Except for Jamie Gillis (who plays his usually perverted character role) and Jennifer Jordan, you have never seen most of the women and guys who appear in this one. But the director has a real sense of humor, and some of the sequences are so silly that you can't help laughing. Also, many of them have original music and accompanying words which are quite singable. The first one sets the theme: "Did you ever want a little more out of life?" Four women who live respectably in suburbia work for Lenny, who runs a whorehouse where male patrons are offered the opportunity to live out any fantasy they can think of. One of the women, Shelly (Shelly Dynah Mite, who isn't a bad actress), is going to quit the business and marry Michael Hum. She finally manages to at the end of the picture (in a whorehouse after Michael Hum—to her shock —has taken on all her girlfriends and worn them out one by one). In the interim, various women service the clients. One of them is a very plump guy who pretends

he is the Shah of Oklahoma. Another client is actually pushing 70 and has dreams of making love to the little girl he took care of when she was only six. Shelly, dressed as a 15-year-old, convinces him that he is the first to have sex with her and he is her teacher. The result is so ecstatic that they tip over their leather chair and have a hard time extricating themselves. Another client wants to enjoy his dead lover, Claudia. He gets her laid out with silver dollars holding down her eyes and candles and organ music playing. But she revives and takes care of him. Barney brings in his son, who has grown up in Georgia and is a virgin, to get "his pop corked." Jennifer Jordan does the job very romantically and lovingly. All the clients can use credit cards—Master Charge, Visa or traveler's checks. One nasty scene with Jamie Gillis.

ANNA OBSESSED
CC   NN   NM   NR   BI   (but totally plot oriented)
1977   HOME ENTERTAINMENT

P/D—The Strangers, Martin & Martin
F/A—John Leslie
F/A—Constance Money, Annette Haven, Susan McBain

You'll watch this one from begining to end. Although you get a few moody clues as it goes along—a naked woman whose face you never see walking up a flight of stairs whom Maggie (Annette Haven) dreams about; a radio announcer telling about a Long Island rape/murder of several women; and Jamie Gillis's name on the credits (though as far as I can determine he's not in the flick)—you won't anticipate the shocking ending. The environment is surburbia. The story is about the marriage of David and Anna Carson (John Leslie and Constance Money), which is no longer working. Anna no longer climaxes with David. She masturbates and David knows it. David enjoys great sex with his secretary (Susan McBain). Anna meets Maggie, a photographer, and rediscovers her lost sexuality in Maggie's arms. "I love David," she tells her, "and I love you. If you could only help me reach him." Maggie invites them to dinner, and in an erotic threesome Anna has an orgasm (she has been fantasizing being raped while she makes love to David). But then the top blows off. I won't tell you how it ends, but you won't forget it. Put this on your list of top 25 sexvids. Worth owning. Most women will like it. It's one of the few that totally revolves around one male.

AUTOBIOGRAPHY OF A FLEA
CC NN NL
1976   MITCHELL

F/A—John Holmes, Paul Thomas
F/A—Jean Jennings, Annette Haven

Based on a seventeenth-century pornographic story, the infamous flea (in a voice-over) lives on a lovely young girl with occasional vacations on priests who lead her into a life of sin, biting them occasionally so that all is not pleasure. No collection of sexvids is complete without this one, which is among the few laughingly explicit films ever made with a continuously connected story line from beginning to end. Beautifully costumed, too.

A VERY SMALL CASE OF RAPE
CC NN NL BI
1981   TED ROTER PRODUCTIONS

P/D—Ted Roter
F/A—John Hollyfield, Steve Event
F/A—Gena Lee, Heather Gordon

Ted Roter is an interesting guy. He produces adult films also under the name Peter Balakoff. His films are more subtle and more fun than many adult films. He has also appeared in some of them (see listing on *The Psychiatrist* and *Prison Babies*). This one is the story of Lisa (Gena Lee) and David (Steve Event) who at the very beginning are happily married in a wedding chapel and leave for their honeymoon. Alas, Lisa has a headache on the wedding night, and you soon discover that she should never have married David. She wants romantic sex and lots of talk, and he wants a lusty partner who can

respond to his needs twice a day at the very least and enjoy sex as much as he does. Their next-door neighbor friends, Renee (Heather Gordon) and Doug (John Hollyfield), are in just the reverse position. Renee wants to do it every day, but Doug is too occupied with business problems; once a week would be enough for him. David finally grabs Lisa one morning before a very important feminist meeting she is planning to hold in their house and tells her that he has to make love. She refuses—in the morning after breakfast—ugh! He rips off her morning coat and forces her to screw while she screams and sobs that he's raping her. Being a women's libber, she tells what happens to her friends and they advise her to sue David for rape. (Roter was obviously having fun with a true story.) To bring everything to a happy ending, it seems that Renee is about to cut off Doug's prick with a carving knife unless he promises to use it as a husband should—and *he* sues *her* for rape! Everything comes to a happy conclusion when Lisa discovers that Doug is her kind of man. He loves to spout poetry when they make love, and David finds that Renee is a match for him anytime. "I never thought an extended family could be such fun!" Lisa announces as they switch spouses on a regular basis. Most women—sexually demanding or passive—will chuckle at this film. What's more, there are no come shots—and while there's plenty of sex and nakedness, the camera never lingers long on the genital action.

BABY FACE   **CC   NN   BI   DK   DS**
1977   ASTRO

P/D—Alex de Renzy
F/A—Otis Sistrunk
F/A—Cuddles Malone, Amber Hunt, Linda Wong

Best Film Direction, 1978 Erotic Film Award. The intriguing story line is about Dan (played by Otis Sistrunk, a former Superbowl star with the Oakland Raiders), who seduces a 15-year-old nymphet (or is seduced by her) and is caught an hour and a half later by Momma, who tries to castrate him for defiling her daughter. An alternate title could have been *The Training Camp*, the story of a male whorehouse whose clients are upper income, very sexually verbal and demanding women. To top it all, de Renzy gives a 15-minute sequence of a woman who exhausts ten guys. You've never seen anything like it!

BABYLON PINK
CC NL NM NN some DK
1979 QUALITY and TVX

P/D—Chuck Vincent, Henry Pachard
F/A—Bobby Astyr
F/A—Samantha Fox, Georgina Spelvin, Vanessa Del Rio

Best Film, 1979 Erotic Film Award. *Screw's* Best 10 for 1978, #3. A sexvid with an intriguing plot and a down-to-earth story. Much humor, silly fantasy and bawdy laughter. The best sequence in the film, which includes fantasy sex with Bobby Astyr's wife (played by Vanessa Del Rio), is a long one. Bobby Astyr, as a weak little salesman peddling his wares in the office of a cold-blooded female executive vice-president of a cosmetic company, Samantha Fox, imagines that she suddenly capitulates and obeys his every sexual command. When he comes back to reality, wiping his brow as he leaves her office, it's with her panties. Maybe it wasn't a fantasy? Most women will laugh at this one. Worth owning.

BEACH BLANKET BANGO-
CC NN NL NR
1975 EROS and FREEWAY

P/D—Richard Aldrich, Morris Deal
F/A—Ric Lutz
F/A—Renee Bond, Cindy Taylor

This one has a very bad title. Sex on the beach isn't the basic plot. If you were in college in the late 1960s, you'll enjoy the half-truth/half silliness of the story. Renee Bond is more fun than Annette Funicello ever was. She gets pregnant by one of the guys. She doesn't know which, but she loves them both. Then, while they are in Vietnam, she marries a man with money. A laughing, sexy sexvid that could be re-

filmed with a bigger budget, or Richard Aldrich could remake *The Harrad Experiment!*

BEHIND THE GREEN DOOR
CC DK DS
1975 MITCHELL

P/D—Mitchell Brothers
F/A—George McDonald, Johnny Keyes
F/A—Marilyn Chambers

A young woman is kidnapped and taken to a sex club to broaden her sexual horizons. She is subjected to every imaginable kind of sex. An ugly film, but one you won't forget. Worth owning on a historical basis because when it was made there was nothing equal to it photographically or story-wise—and Marilyn Chambers really looked like the girl in the choir.

BEL AMI **CC NN NR NL**
QUALITY

P/D—Bert Torn
F/A—Harry Reems, Bent Warburg, Bie Warburg
F/A—Christa Linder, Maria Lynn, Jacqueline Laurent, Lucienne Camille

I'm sure that if Guy de Maupassant could come back to life he'd enjoy this modern version of his story. George du Roi (Harry Reems) is a moralistic, naive writer and poet who is doing an article about the Erotic Museum and *Playhouse Magazine* in Stockholm, Sweden. Forestiere, a handsome grey-haired man who is editor of the magazine and curator of the museum, tries to corrupt George by offering him $3,000 for an erotic poem instead of the paltry sums George usually receives. He gives George a gift of a statue with a huge phallus, and before George knows what is happening to him he is on an erotic merry-go-round, seduced by at least ten different very lovely Swedish women, and one black African princess. All of the women are refreshingly unsubtle about their sexual needs (every man's dream?), and one after another George is enjoying their happy, unleashed female sexuality. The sex in this Swedish film not only has interesting backgrounds and settings indoors as well as outdoors, but it is humorous and caring at the same time in a sophisticated, continental style that escapes most U.S. films. The entire action revolves around George's seduction by various women. This was Harry Reems's last movie.

BENEATH THE VALLEY OF THE ULTRAVIXENS **CC NN DS NL BI**
1980   RM INTERNATIONAL FILMS

P/D—Russ Meyer
F/A—Ken Kerr, Pat Wright, Henry Rowland, Robert Pearson, Michael Finn, Don Scarborough, Abram Katcher, Deforest Cowan, Steve Tracy
F/A—Francesca "Kitten" Natividad, Anne Marie, Candy Samples, June Mack, Lola Langusta, Sharon Hill, Uschi Digard

If *Supervixens* was really *Apocalypse Now,* this one is *Our Town,* or *Middletown!* (See reviews of other Russ Meyer films on pages 63, 73, 74, 90, 93, 97, 101, 107, 139, 148, 152.) Stuart Lancaster is the commentator on the action in Smalltown. It's the story of Lamar Shedd (Ken Kerr) and his wife, Lavonia (Frances Natividad), who is a nymphomaniac. She also gets mad at him when he poops out and takes off on the town with Mr. Peterbilt (Pat Wright). Never mind. Lamar works for Junkyard Sal (June Mack), a black woman who teaches Lamar how to make love while Lavonia is taking on Rhett (Steve Tracy), who tells her that he's only 14. Lavonia is also taking care of Semper Fidelis (Michael Finn), who works for Frederico's of Wisconsin and sells sexy underwear and a bust developer that you can attach to your water faucet. Of course, Lavonia doesn't need it. Never mind. Lamar relaxes after a hard day in the junkyard at a strip joint called The Other Ball when Lola Langusta (she really is Lavonia moonlighting from her household duties) does a sexy striptease number. And on and on the story of Smalltown goes, with Lamar taking on the big-busted evangelist of Radio Dio, and Lavonia in a dentist's office making out not with the dentist but with his assistant, Uschi Digard. All the women get socked on the jaw, and the guys knock down doors. Asa Lavender (the den-

tist/psychologist) uses a chainsaw to burst through one to get at Lamar Shedd who has been enjoying his wife, Lavonia, who also is having sex with Uschi Digard. But you know who wins out at last—the ladies with the large breasts. If you think this is the end of the Vixens, it isn't. *Jaws of Vixen* will be released soon!

BEYOND THE VALLEY OF THE DOLLS **CC DK DS BI**
1970   TWENTIETH CENTURY FOX

P/D—Russ Meyer
F/A—Dolly Reed, Cynthia Myers, Marcia McBroom, Edy Williams, Erica Gavin
F/A—John LaZar, Michael Blodgett, David Gorisa, Duncan Mcleod.

Roger Ebert, now a well-known film critic and potentially the future biographer of Russ Meyer, wrote the story and screenplay for this film, which cost $2 million to make (a substantial sum for the 1970s). Although he lost control of ownership, Russ thinks this is his best film. The first hour or so offers very fast, sophisticated cutting, exceeding anything you are likely to see in current films. It tells the late 1960s story of a female rock group composed of Kelly MacNamara (Dolly Reed), Carey Anderson (Cynthia Myers), and Petronella Danforth, (Marcia McBroom). It begins at senior graduation from college where the girls are featured singers and makes a fast cut to Los Angeles, where Kelly is about to inherit a large portion of her Aunt Susan's estate, which Aunt Susan believes, despite her lawyer, Porter Hall (Duncan McLeod), belongs to Kelly. This is a secondary plot. Although everyone gets mixed up eventually, the main story concerns the three girls' rise to fame against a very sleazy Hollywood background during which their college manager, Harris Allsworth (David Gorisa), gets thoroughly shafted by Ronnie Z-Man Barzell (John La-Zar), one of the top rock impresarios in Hollywood. Ronnie corrupts everyone he contacts, including the girls. He changes the name of the group from The Kelly Affair to The Carrie Nations. Pot smoking, drug taking and booze dominate their lives, and the nice girls and their managers all get seduced by various Hollywood "sickies," including a moving picture star whose name is Lance Rock (Michael Blodgett) and a porno film star, Ashley St. Ives (Edy Williams), who wants sex in such unusual places as her Rolls-Royce and on the beach. But the real Mr. Nasty is Ronnie the Z-Man, who manages to get to bed with Kelly even though Kelly is supposedly in love with Harris. Petronella Danforth in the meantime falls into bed with a famous black boxer, where she is caught red-handed by her boyfriend whom the boxer beats up. Lance beats up Harris. Time passes and at the height of their career Harris is reduced to being a gaffer on television shows where the girls are appearing. He falls from the top of the stage, stoned on drugs, after getting Casey pregnant. Casey has an abortion. Are you getting confused? Russ and Roger could exhume this plot and turn it into a never-ending soap opera. But not with the ending, which will thoroughly shock you. Seems that Ronnie Barzell is really a transsexual who, in his alter ego, becomes Superwoman. In bed with Lance as a gay, he suddenly reveals that he has breasts. By this time he has Lance tied hands and feet and threatens to castrate him. He finally slashes off his head (no kidding—with a sword) and then as a part of a Gotterdammerung party supervised by a guy dressed in a Nazi uniform, Ronnie pokes a revolver in Ashley's mouth and he pulls the trigger, blowing her head off. Before he is killed himself by Harris, he slashes off Casey's head. The picture ends with Russ Meyer in a voice-over providing a moral and why each character was the architect of his/her own fate. There's some nudity and lots of sex, but not explicit.

THE BITCH CC R NR
1979 VIDEO GEMS

P/D—Edward Simons, Gerry O'Hara
F/A—Michael Coby, Ian Hendry
F/A—Joan Collins, Sue Lloyd, Caroline Semour

Move over Sidney Sheldon and Harold Robbins, here is a more super-sophisticated sex film than any ever made from your novels. This is the story of Fontaine Kahled, divorced wife of a millionaire Greek, whose only remaining asset (al-

though she is used to the lifestyle of a multimillionairess), is The Hobo, a far-out disco in London that has seen more affluent days. With just a dash more explicit sex—a style I predict will dominate cable and subscription films in the near future—this film could be a model for adult filmmakers. Fontaine gets involved with Nico Cantaflora (Michael Coby), an adventurer who has stolen a supposedly very valuable diamond and is in trouble with the Mafia. Both Fontaine and Nico think the other has the monetary solution to their problems. The story has many plot twists, interesting English scenery (it was produced in Europe), and much choreographed sex without love. The group sex scene as it slowly develops in an indoor swimming pool at an English country estate is an aesthetically photographed, fun-to-watch, and how-to-do-it piece for X-rated filmmakers. Joan Collins (star of *Dynasty*) provides some pretty explicit sexmaking that you're unlikely to see on television.

BLONDE AMBITION CC NN NL
1981 QUALITY

P/D—John and Lem Amero
F/A—Eric Edwards, Jamie Gillis, Richard Bolla, Wade Parker
F/A—Suzy Mandell, Dory Devon, Molly Malone

If you want to buy only one adult film that I guarantee you'll watch more than once and show to friends—buy this one. Produced by the Amero Brothers, who have been making adult films both R and X since the early 1960s, the story, plot and dialogue are so hilarious and so well integrated that it verges on being the script for a Broadway musical—one that would be far more fun than *The Best Little Whorehouse in Texas*. All it needs is music by Stephen Sondheim. What's more, the original movie cast has Suzy Mandell. (If you are a "Benny Hill" watcher you've seen her as the dizzy blonde on his shows. Now she's Sugar Kane and much more naked.) Dory Devon as Candy Kane, Molly Malone as Aunt Sibyl and Eric Edwards as her nephew, Stefan, all are believable actors. They could be retained in a Broadway version. The story begins in Coyote Falls, Wyoming, where the Kane sisters offer their totally hammy musical act in the Tumbleweed Saloon. Stefan, a millionaire, sees the show with his butler/chauffeur (Richard Bolla). The Kane sisters' agent has offered them a job in New York, if they'll send him a hundred-dollar retainer. Stefan subsidizes them and flies them back to New York in one of his private jets during which Suzy appreciatively takes on the chauffeur in a very funny scene as Bolla describes what is happening to him in terms of gourmet cooking. In New York their agent has disappeared with the Kane sisters' money, and Suzy has managed to get her $1.50 Newark-made Egyptian brooch mixed up with Aunt Sibyl's million-dollar Buckingham brooch, which Stefan is bringing to London so Aunt Sibyl can auction it off for charity. In the meantime the Kane sisters, who are living in Stefan's apartment get a job to appear in a porno version of *Gone with the Wind*, being produced by Ben Dover (Jamie Gillis), head of Miracle Pictures, whose slogan is: "If it's a good picture, it's a miracle." In a scene directed by Ben, the Yankee soldiers arrive and the Southern girls, who wonder what they are ever going to do, obligingly raise their hoop skirts for them. Suzy Mandell is the star of the show. The Kane sisters, trying to recover Aunt Sibyl's brooch, appear as transvestites in a homosexual nightclub (a natural for a Broadway musical), and Suzy does a strip on ice skates for a nude pianist who is also wearing skates and finally joins her. The sex is explicit but controlled—your laughter won't be!

THE BLONDE GODDESS
CC NN NR NL BI DK
1982 VIDEO-X-PIX

P/D—Bobby Bouchard, Bill Eagle
F/A—Jonathan Ford, Ron Jeremy
F/A—Susanna Britton, Loni Sanders, Jacqueline Lorians, Tamara West

Howard Farber—the financial Big Daddy behind many adult films, president of Distribpix, owner of the World and Circus Theaters in New York City—admits that

he's in the business "strictly for the bucks," but he hates boring adult films. This one, financed by Farber, opened in the World Theater in April 1982 after much fanfare, with a reserved-seat first night audience, new female star Susanna Britton, and something that Farber didn't promote—a new male star, Jonathan Ford (as Elmo Smathers), a worthy in-the-sack competitor of John Leslie and Richard Pacheco. Most of the scenes in this sexvid involve Jonathan in amorous dalliances. As for *The Blonde Goddess*, it's a good title, and Susanna Britton is adequate. But the title doesn't give you a clue to the whacked-out story line. Seems that Elmo is a comic book artist who has created many famous Marvel Comics such as *Jungle Jane, Flying Aces*, and a *Star Wars* kind of comic called *Megazon*. Elmo's problem is that, like all good writers, he lives the lives of his characters in his imagination. So there he is, first as Louisiana Smith (an Indiana Jones, *Raiders of the Lost Ark* hero) rescuing his heroine, Jungle Jane, from an ancient Mexican goddess, Amorella (Susanna Britton), who presides over some ancient ruins. (Portions of this film were actually shot in Mexico and France.) Elmo saves Jungle Jane but falls in love with Amorella. Next, as a World War I flying ace, he shoots down the Black Baron and lands his triplane on a French country estate. Together with Ron Jeremy, who lands his biplane on the palatial grounds, they take care of two French contessas in some of the most athletic screwing you've ever seen on your screen. Next, in a black-and-white sequence as Jack Hammer (who talks like Humphrey Bogart), Elmo is in pursuit of the villains that have stolen a priceless Persian relic, the Abou Dabou Dildo; and finally as Tony Steele (a Clark Kent type of character), he's on the planet Activa where the Blonde Goddess is under attack by Megazon, a weirdo.

BODY MAGIC **CC NN DK BI NR** (a little)
1983 SELECT ESSEX

P/D—Mark Corby, Sven Conrad
F/A—Rick Ardonne, Joey Silvera, Bill Dee
F/A—Kathleen Kristal, Kelly Cole, Penny
  Arcade, Victoria Slick, Linda Templeton

Mark Corby and Sven Conrad, with this film and *Doing It* (see listing p. 80), are aiming at a new audience of sophisticated, upper-income couples, of which I believe there are at least five million. These are men and women (not the raincoat crowd) who enjoy adult films and want a super-glossy portrayal of life—*Playboy*-style with explicit sex. Mark Emery (Rich Ardonne) is a renowned still photographer teaching his craft to Laura (Kathleen Kristal). The film opens with 15 minutes of very erotic, high-style still picture shooting with very seductive ladies all packaged in with eye-catching cinematography and editing. The dialogue is a voice-over commenting on Mark and coolly appraising him. "Photography took all his energy but he loves it. It was the best electric train a boy could have, but now without love, and after many sexual encounters [not shown], Mark remembers when he worked for fun." But at this point in his career he was doing it for money. Among the explicit sex scenes that Mark is presumably shooting with a 35-mm camera, you watch a country music party and an "orgy" in a barn; and even further-out group sex at a fraternity party to which he has been invited—although Mark is long past his college days. Mark never participates in any of the sex scenes. He thinks he's falling in love with Laura, but she tells him that she would be "too inhibited." In the words of the commentator, "They talked, they became friends, they toasted life and each other—and for the first time in his life he was turned down." They finally come together in bed. While there is much explicit sex throughout the film, even in the final scene where Laura and Mark are making ecstatic love, the camera never focuses on their genitals.

BODY TALK **CC NN NR BI DK**
1983 VCX

P/D—Robert Holcomb, Pedie Sweet
F/A—Steven Tyler, Randy West
F/A—Angelique, Kay Parker

Along with *Foxtrot, Irresistible, Undercovers,* and *Roommates* (see listings) this film was nominated for Best Picture in the 1983, 7th Annual Erotic Film Awards. If I had been a judge, and *Roommates* had not been on the list, I would have picked it for Best Film. All of the actors and actresses would have been high on my list of Best. The film offers something else. While I wouldn't want to take bets, my guess is that both Angelique (who plays Cassie) and Kay Parker (who plays Laura) are past forty. Kay Parker's breasts are more languid than Angelique's, who has probably supported hers with foam. Angelique is a Joan Blondell look-a-like, if you can remember her in 1940 films. The story is about T.J. (Randy West) who is younger than Laura and his friend Mark (Steven Tyler) whom T.J., at Laura's request, introduces to Angelique. Mark is a promising sculptor but has been rejected by his father who wants him to make money in the business world as he has. Mark does not know that Angelique has been supported mostly by Jeremy (a 60-year-old lecher) for many years. Jeremy has never had sex with her and refuses to kiss her, but pays to watch through the eyes of a portrait hanging on her bedroom wall when she has sex with her johns. Mark falls in love with Cassie, and Cassie with him. She finally tells Jeremy, to his shock, that she's not going to live on his money or in his house anymore. She uses her savings to buy Mark a studio near Mill Valley, and then she discovers—she has been falling down—that she has bone cancer. In the meantime, Mark's father, not knowing she is dying, convinces her to break up the relationship with his son. He's now willing to subsidize Mark in his career. Not knowing why Cassie is rejecting him, Mark goes to a year-long seminar on sculpting in Italy, but he's still very much in love with her. Finally, Laura and T.J. tell his parents the truth, and Mark flies home from Italy to find Cassie in bed—she obviously will die. She's under nurses' care. They embrace, and the film is over. Believe it or not—a tear-jerker porno movie! Put this one in your top fifty listing! Women will like it, especially all the warm, caring separate sex scenes between Randy West and Kay Parker, and Angelique who is a big-boned woman (she must weigh about 140 pounds) and Stephen Tyler. As good or better acting, throughout, as you'll find on any soap opera.

BORN ERECT CC NN NL DK
CABALLERO

P/D—Jon Sanderson
F/A—Eric Braun, Peter Straus
F/A—Christine Roberts, Vicki West, Monika Metzger

Produced in West Germany, this one has good cinematography with funny, sophisticated dialogue, and a refreshing change in background ambiance. Leo (Eric Braun) is born with a perpetual erection. Twenty-eight years later he still has it. For Leo this is not funny. Leo tries his doctor, who tells him he really should leave well enough alone. Most men would love to trade places with him. His doctor tries to help him, by attaching him to a wet dream machine, but to no avail. In the meantime he's offered increasingly high monetary rewards to appear on television in a vitamin commercial. But he refuses. He even tries his cousin's machine shop with a grinder and various other tools, but refuses the electric saw. Finally, he takes the vitamin pill manufacturer's offer—eats a few pills during the commercial—and you guessed it, he loses his erection. Worth owning.

BORDELLO CC NN BI NL DK (but laughing, too)
1974   ARROW

P/D—Lee Hessel
F/A—James Morrison, Alan North
F/A—Lonny Federsen, Leni Kjelland, Ingerlise Gaarde, Sune Pilgaard, Connie Nielsen

Put this one in your small collection of absolutely delightful adult films which com-municate a joyous feeling of sexual laughter and caring sex. With a few exceptions (*Alice in Wonderland* and *Autobiography of a Flea*), American filmmakers have yet to produce the laughing sophistication of European films. This one is Danish. The time is the late 1800s—the telephone has been invented. Lonny is the daughter of a prosperous Danish farmer, who along with his wife, fall into their pigpen, suffocate in the mud, are trampled over by the pigs and die. Lonny goes to live with Aunt Hilda and Uncle Wolfgang, who immediately tries to crawl into bed with Lonny. Early one morning, she escapes in a hilarious nude chase through the countryside during which Uncle Wolfgang falls into a seat in the outhouse. Lonnie goes to Copenhagen to live in Aunt Anna's Charm School for Young Ladies, which is devoted to culture, learning and the beautiful life. It's really a bordello, but absolutely luxurious with everything in good taste. The founder, a male, drops dead during sex, and the Charm School is left to either a Mormon priest in America or Baron Raymond of Krakow, both of whom arrive to claim the premises and a diamond hidden therein. From this point on you spend about an hour with lovely Danish girls engaging in an amazing variety of sexual experiences. All this occurs to the accompaniment of music from Strauss, Wagner, Chopin and Borodin. The entire story is told in a unique voice-over style—voicing what the actors are thinking or doing. And Lonny, who loses her virginity to the Baron, marries him!

BOTH WAYS
CC NN NM NR DK BI (Male)
1975   INT. HOME VIDEO CLUB

P/D—Jerry Douglas
F/A—Gerald Grant, Dean Tait
F/A—Andrea True, Katherine Miles, Darby Lloyd Raines

If you are a woman and discover that your husband is in love with another man, what would you do? Here's one of the few adult films made thus far that has total character exploration, excellent acting, and a sensitive, well-told story. David Wyman is a young, wealthy Harvard Law graduate and corporate lawyer who lives in Westport, Connecticut, and is married to Janice. They have a son of about six who is very much a part of the story. David's meeting with Janice is told in intercut flashbacks, but somewhere along the line David recognizes that he is attracted to men, too. He meets Gary (Dean Tait), who is in his final year at Yale. "I've discovered there's a lot of people in the world. Why limit yourself to one half the population?" he tells him. Gerald Grant and Dean Tait, one dark, one blonde, are handsome, attractive males and they fall in love with each other. Janice realizes that David isn't always as sexually attentive to her as he has been. First she thinks it's just years of marriage, then she wonders if there is another woman. She asks David if he wants a divorce. But David is very clear in his mind. He tells Gary, after a lovemaking scene that is caring and believable: "I love Janice, I love you and I love my son. No more. No less." But Gary has his doubts. He's very much in love with David and tries to break off. Then he takes a job as a bartender at a private party to which David and Janice are invited. All the women are trying to seduce the bartender who finally tells one of their husbands, "Your wife is lovely and a nice person, but you don't have to worry. I'm as queer as a three-dollar bill." Their love affair slowly alerts Janice, and the Wymans' housekeeper. In a disastrous confrontation David tries to take Janice and Gary to a matinee together. Gary tells him, "I'd rather have half of you than 100 percent of anyone else that I can think of." But Gary wants to tell Janice, who has already guessed what is happening, the truth. David is shocked and clouts him with a beer mug Gary has given him. Gary falls dead on the floor. You can put this film in your top ten. It can stand muster with any regular Hollywood film. What's more, women will like it—even the orgy party. Buy it or rent it. You'll watch it more than once—even if you're totally male and heterosexual. For those who wish to read more in the area there's a fascinating book written long after this film was made by a couple who experienced what they claim is not such an exceptional problem as you might think. It's called *Barry and Alice* by Barry Kohn and Alice Matusow (Prentice-Hall, New Jersey, 1980). Hollywood's film, *Making Love*, is nowhere so frankly open.

BREAKER BEAUTIES CC NN NL BI
VIDEO-X HOME LIBRARY

P/D—Steven Barry
F/A—Richard Bolla, Bobby Astyr, Wade Nichols
F/A—Sharon Mitchell, Kitty Suckerman, Jean Dalton

A laughing sexvid with a consistent story line that interweaves most of the adult film conventions into an interesting plot. It is especially well acted by Richard Bolla and Bobby Astyr, who combine sexual antics with happy slapstick. Tom (Richard Bolla) drives a rig with his partner. At home with his wife (Sharon Mitchell), he's a dud in bed. But on the road behind the wheel he's known to all the CB ladies by his "handle"—Big Bear. The plot involves getting his wife to discover that Tom can be a Big Bear at home too if he gets rid of his "super slag drags," which she can do by talking truckese and CB to him. Much of the action takes place in an overnight truck stop run by Big Mamma, who provides a "rest stop" and bedrooms for the truckers as well as a country-western music floor show featuring Johnny Rash and Linda Rongtits, who actually sings sexy country-western songs. In the things-you've-never-seen-before department, there is a detailed sequence with Baruch as a trucker who actually swallows razor blades followed by a thread. In camera close-up he recovers them. Most women will giggle at this one.

BRIEF AFFAIR CC NN BI NR
1982 CABALLERO

P/D—Jo-Anne Lewis, Louie Lewis
F/A—Paul Thomas, Mike Horner, Joey Civera
F/A—Annette Haven, Brigitte Monet, Loni Sanders, Lisa de Leeuw, Sharon Mitchell, Nicole Noir

"Did you ever have a really terrific day—one when everything seems to be working out?" asks Annette Haven, playing the part of Sinclair West, a dancer who is studying modern dance at the Lewis Academy of Performing Arts (see comments under *Every Which Way She Can*, p. 87). She asks the question as she wakes up in the morning with her new lover Rudy (Paul Thomas). Unfortunately, Paul must go to New York and she may never see him again—but she loves him. He makes her late for school, but why worry? "I never made love in the morning before. It's more romantic than the pas de deux from *Sleeping Beauty.*" With that, the story continues, until the end, under the roof of the Academy, where you quickly find an escapee from a mental home (Joey Civera) who chews gum and has wandered into the women's locker room. Pam (Nicole Noir) hides him in her locker so she can continue her enjoyment of sucking his cock. As one of the students studying dramatics, Sharon Mitchell performs in front of a video camera being run by another student in one of the funniest scenes, "Seduction, the Essence," that she has ever done in an adult film. She explains as she seductively strips why she prefers certain words like tits rather than breasts or boobs, and why her genitals demand different words for different occasions like pussy, twat, cunt, etc. Lisa de Leeuw leads a mixed company of about 30 students, all dressed in leotards or gym clothing in a body stretching exercise, which everyone performs very seductively. Then Lisa is seduced by Brigitte Monet to improve her marks, and finally Annette reappears doing a modern dance to original music and proving that she has more than just sexual abilities. Rudy returns from New York—seems Sinclair didn't realize that he was a choreographer, and they return to her apartment for warm, romantic sex, dancing in her bed. Paul Thomas should receive an award as adult film's most romantic lover.

CAMILLE 2000 **CC NR This film should carry a commercial R rating.**
1973 HIGHBRIDGE ENTERTAINMENT

P/D—Radley Metzger
F/A—Danielle Gaubert

A modern, jet-set version of Alexandre Dumas's novel about a consumptive prostitute, mistress of the Duc de Mauriac. Marguerite and her lover, Armand, prove in this sexvid that Radley Metzger can (but hasn't yet as Henry Paris, his adult film a.k.a.) make the kind of explicit sex film that would entrance women *and* men. The sad story of Marguerite has the twists and turns of a soap opera, but it is exquisitely photographed, and the acting and dialogue are believable. If the sex scenes had been more sharply focused, instead of choreographed, Metzger would have produced the first classic porn film worth owning.

CAN I DO IT IF I NEED GLASSES? **Far-out R rating**
1976 MEDIA

P/D—Mike Callie, I. Robert Levy
F/A—Robert Pelz, Roger Behr, Ollie Prater, Moose Carlson, Jeff Doucette
F/A—Saba, Deborah Klose, Talie Chochrane, Ann Collier

A rapid-fire, sexual "Laugh-In," but you can be sure you will never see it on commercial television. It has nutty sequences like a naked woman in a hotel room puting out her husband's shoes to be shined. The door slams behind her. A drunk coming down the corridor tells her: "That-a-boy, shorty, give it everything you've got!" Or Little Red Riding Hood being encountered by the wolf, who tells her: "I'm going to eat you up." She responds, "Doesn't anyone fuck anymore?" Or, "Which one of you painted my horse's balls yellow?" a guy yells in an 1800s-style cowboy saloon. "I did. What about it?" a tough guy answers and shoves his pistol in his face. "Oh, that's nice. I just wanted to tell you that the first coat is dry." There are at least 50 more—all played fast and furiously for belly laughs. Verbally, you can't subtract the jokes from the often very funny scenes, which are played with great enthusiasm by the cast. They'll love this one in Sandusky, but it may not play so well with the more sophisticated jet set.

CAFE FLESH **CC NN NM BI DK**
1982   VCA

P/D—Rinse Dream, F. X. Pope
F/A—Andrew Nichols, Paul McGibonney, Joey Lennon, Neil Podericki, Robert Dennis, Kevin Jay
F/A—Pia Snow, Marie Sharp, Darcy Nichols

This one will give you the cold shudders. I don't see how it could ever have been popular on the adult film theater circuit, although in a frightening way it covers all the porno bases. Even if you don't buy it for sheer entertainment, see it—somehow! It should be on the top of any list of 25 best porno films. The time frame is five years after the first nuclear war. Ninety-nine percent of the population that has survived are able to exist, but they are mutants who no longer feel any sexual pleasure and are repelled by flesh-to-flesh contact with the other sex, or even the same sex. They are known as the Sex Negatives. One percent of the population who still feel sexual pleasure are compelled by law to entertain the Sex Negatives and try to stimulate them back to normal. These are the Sex Positives. Every night they put on elaborate shows in clubs like Cafe Flesh. Sadly, sex between the Sex Positives (watched by the Sex Negatives, who look as if they escaped from a charnel house—some have radiation burns or look like Auschwitz survivors) is totally depersonalized. Women called "Moms" run the clubs. The master of ceremonies of Cafe Flesh (superbly acted by Andrew Nichols) is even worse off than the Sex Negatives. He lost his "weskit" in World War III. Some of the sequences in the night club reenact the day of the nuclear holocaust. Sex is equated with mechanical things like the pumps on an oil fill, or a naked typist who insistently repeats "Do you want me to type a memo?" Amidst all the Sex Negatives there are Nick and Lana, who live together. They remember when sex was joyous and nice—but try as he may Nick is totally repulsed by contact with Lana. The film ends with the master cocksman in the country, a guy named Johnny Rico, arriving at Cafe Flesh. To the amazement of the patrons, Lana walks to the stage, feeling sexual attraction for the first time. The film ends with the blank look on Lana's face after she has been forcefully screwed doggy-style by Rico. It's impossible to describe the clever photography, the good acting and total feeling of the film. Rinse Dream (why does he use an a.k.a.?) also made *Nightdreams* (see listing, p. 110), which has a similar quality. Art film houses should try this one for the late, late crowd. You'll need a pick-me-up afterwards.

CAPTAIN LUST AND THE PIRATE WOMEN **CC NN NL BI DK (but silly)**
1979   INTERNATIONAL HOME VIDEO CLUB

P/D—Beau Buchanan
F/A—Jake Teague, Jamie Gillis, Wade Nichols
F/A—Sharon Mitchell, Veri Knotty, Ming Toy

Put this one in your top ten adult films. Can you mix sex with laughter? Sure! Can you mix totally erotic scenes into a far-out, hilarious story line? Yes! Can you produce a film with a lot of action, dramatic at times, but with the characters spoofing the drama? You bet! With this one Beau Buchanan opened the door for a thousand gothic-novel-style stories with eighteenth-century backgrounds. The plot involves Jack (Wade Nichols—as swashbuckling as Errol Flynn ever was and more handsome) and his sister Anne Forsythe, who have been cheated out of their inheritance—the Count of Monte Cristo's fortune of gold and jewels. Jack is the Count's missing son, but Captain Lust (Jake Teague) doesn't know it. Lust is on his way to Sacrifice Island where the treasure is buried, and aboard his brigantine is his Cuntessa, who services him on command. He locks her up with a padlock (no kidding—only Veri Knotty could perform this feat) to make sure that she's unavailable to his crew. Jack and Anne smuggle themselves aboard Lust's ship, and Lust, not knowing they are brother and sister, forces them to have sex together while he watches (a scene right out of a gothic). But Lust has an enemy—the pirate Captain Surecock (Jamie Gillis), who mans his ship, the *Jolly Roger,* with a crew of pirate women. Surecock is after the Count of Monte Cristo's treasure, too. Except for a few scenes on a tropical beach (where Jack saves a native girl, Poon (Mai Ling), from being sacrificed—only virgins are sacrificed by the natives and Jack remedies that), the entire action was shot in the Caribbean on an actual brigantine, the *Black Swan.* The pirates are properly costumed, and in one of the final scenes there is a 15-minute battle between Lust's crew and Surecock's pirates—many of them half naked—equal to many Hollywood productions. This is a sexvid that most couples will enjoy. It has a large cast of extras, and most of the sex scenes aboard the ship are accompanied by old bawdy songs and sea chanteys such as "Fire Down Below," "Blow the Man Down," "Bringin' in the Riggin'" and many others with funny, sexy lyrics, plus an original— "Oh, Captain Lust, He's Really Mean and Horny-o."

CARNAL GAMES **CC NN DK BI**
  BLUE VIDEO

P/D—Bob Gripe, Ralph Lander
F/A—John Leslie, Jake Teague
F/A—C. J. Laing, Sharon Mitchell

The opening sequence of this one will keep you intrigued for the first ten minutes. Despite a lot of kinkiness that follows, the story line hangs together pretty well. Thom, a middle-aged, wealthy man marries Kate because she looks exactly like his sister who died in an automobile accident. He enjoyed watching her make love to her various suitors because later she made love to him. "I was the only love she really wanted," he'd say. Jake Teague and C. J. Laing do some of the better acting you've seen in adult films. Teague looks like an old-time matinee idol. C. J. Laing occasionally looks as if she could be Barbra Streisand's sister. Women may like some of this sexvid if they close their eyes to an extended orgy scene.

CARNAL HAVEN **CC NN BI DK** (depending on your point of view) **NR** (a little)
1976   HIFCOA

P/D—Troy Benny, Sharon Thorpe
F/A—Jon L. Dupre, Miguel Jones, Joey Civera
F/A—Sharon Thorpe, Leslie Bovee, Annette Haven, Pat Lee.

A sex education porno film? Sure enough —and unlike the *Love Tapes* (see listing, p. 101), which are more clinical, this one has many top stars, including John Leslie when he was known as John L. Dupre. A voice-over takes you on a tour of the marital lives of four couples who have been married for varying lengths of time. None of them are having any fun in bed. Sample dialogue: "It's not the same. Why do you drink so much? You're turning into an alcoholic. Our daughter is grown up— there's no need for us to be married any longer." Or: "You're spending too much money. I don't like the way your breath smells. You smoke too much. Your hairspray stinks." Or: "You're too fast. Why are you always in such a hurry? The truth is, I don't really enjoy it anymore." Then a voice-over tells you that "complete sexual relief" is essential to your health, and your psychological and emotional well being. Solution? Go to Doctors Klein and Wasserman's Sex Clinic where real doctors teach old married couples, in groups, how to revitalize their sex lives. You learn the Inca Knot, the Gypsy Grip and the Figure 8. Everyone learns by doing and watching and trying. And Sharon even offers private discussions and enjoyment of female homosexuality with Annette and Leslie.

CATHERINE & CO **CC R NL NR**
  VIDAMERICA

P/D—Leo Fuchs, Michel Boisrond
F/A—Jean Claude Brially, Jean Pierre Aumont, Vittori Caprioli
F/A—Jane Birkin

A French-made movie with Jane Birkin as Catherine—a young, lower-class English girl who comes to Paris to attend L'Ecole Cordon Bleu and learn to be a chef. Unable to eviscerate a chicken with her hands, she sleeps untouched, at first, with kindly Frenchmen who feed her, but then ends up in bed with François, who makes romantic love with her. Unfortunately, François is engaged to be married to a wealthy French girl, and Catherine decides not to sleep with just her friends anymore. Learning about business from one of her friends who is a wealthy broker, she incorporates herself and her friends, who now include a wealthy artist who teaches her snobbery, a rich Italian with six daughters and the elevator boy in her apartment. Together with the stockbroker, all become her stockholders—*not* clients. Each is entitled to Catherine's services one day a week. Finally, although François wants to marry her on the condition that she be monogamous—and even though she has bought her stockholders out—she can't do it. "I love you," she tells him, after he is married, "and you can have Sundays." Jane Birkin is delightful, sexually provocative and naive at the same time. She will delight most men and most women under 40. Whether you buy this one or join the Vid America Rental Club and borrow it, it's worth watching.

CENTERFOLD CC R
VIDAMERICA

P/D—Chet Harmon
F/A—Bob Cannarela
F/A—Martha Thomsen, Kathleen Sands

A fascinating documentary-style tape of two former *Playboy* centerfold playmates posing for Bob Cannarela. Unlike *Playboy* (which uses 8 × 10 negatives) Cannarela uses a fast-shooting 35-mm camera. The tape is worth owning for several reasons. The tape was not produced by *Playboy*, but whether the editors of *Playboy* realize it or not this kind of tape sounds the death knell for the *Playboy*-style static four-color female images in men's magazines (see the V.I.P. and Kenyon entries) and presages the future for video-style magazines in which the women are moving, talking and much more complete persons than naked ladies with staples through their navels. Within the next ten years, sexy video magazines on discs or tapes will eliminate the men's magazines, which depend on female nudity for their sales. A second reason for owning this tape is that many women will enjoy watching the facial and body transformation of two pretty women into glamorous sex objects. From a feminist standpoint a beautiful sex object is not a total woman, but the question emerges whether clothing and make-up as sex enticements and attractions are not a valid part of the joyous sexual game between men and women. Another question that older women will quickly raise is why men, old or young, never grow up and want to look at young naked women. Finally, if you are female and have the shape, the potential interaction (sexual) between your male friend or spouse, leading you as the willing "sex object" in a photography session, is intriguing. You'll run this one at more than one mixed gathering to answer these questions.

CHARLI CC NN NR NL BI
1981 VCX

P/D—Godfrey Daniels
F/A—Eric Edwards, Randy West
F/A—Jesie St. James, Annette Haven, Arcadia Lake

If there's a new wave of adult films aimed at the at-home female market, this one is not only a pacesetter but it also opens up approaches to a huge female audience (and male as a by-product). It uses a soap opera technique, presenting aspects of most women's lives that they can identify with, as they can with Jesie St. James, who does a good acting job. Men may have a more difficult time since why Jack (Eric Edwards), who has been married to Charli (Jesie St. James), for six years would have to fantasize about other women when he makes love to her is hard to understand. But Charli is having her marital problems, too. "Remember how his touch was electric," she asks herself, "and it made you forget everything but just the two of us? Remember, Charli?" Now it's no longer that way. Jack is working too hard. At night, in bed, lying naked beside him, Charli asks: "Don't you want to look at Johnny Carson?" Jack doesn't and when they finally make love he's too fast. During the hour and a half you live Charli's and Jack's lives as they fantasize sex with others, and as various friends of the same sex give them advice, Charli even buys the porno tape *Insatiable* for Jack as a birthday present. Godfrey Daniels has not only told an interesting story—it ends happily, of course—but the dialogue, editing and cinematography and even a bisexual scene with Annette Haven as Angie, Charli's friend, are tasteful and believable. If you've never seen an adult film before, buy this or rent it. You may change your mind about the potential future of explicit sex on film, especially when it is so nicely story-integrated.

CHERRY, HARRY & RAQUEL
CC NN BI
1979 RM INTERNATIONAL FILMS

P/D—Russ Meyer
F/A—Uschi Digard, Larissa Ely, Linda Ashton
F/A—Robert Aiken, Charles Napier, Bert Santos, Franklin Bolger

David Friedman thinks that Russ Meyer likes breasts so much that they should make him chairman of the board of the Carnation Milk Company. In this one, Uschi Digard acts as she does in many others as the off-screen commentator to the action, which brings back Harry Sledge of *Super Vixen* fame (see listing p. 139). This time he's Harry Johnson and almost—but not quite—so bad a guy. He's still the sheriff of a dusty Arizona town, but in this one he doesn't slap any ladies around. In fact he's quite romantic. Seems that Franklin (Franklin Bolger), a rich old guy who gets what he wants, is smuggling marijuana (in cahoots with Harry) from Mexico. Apache, an Indian representing the Indian losers of the past, is determined to get his piece of the money action. Before he goes to the hospital for a checkup, Franklin sleeps with Raquel (Larissa Ely). Dissatisfied with her work, he gives her to Harry to get rid of her. Harry takes her home, and then Russ gives you several sequences of quite erotic sexmaking, including an extended scene during which Raquel runs naked out into the desert and buries all of herself in the sand except her

head and Harry slowly uncovers her. Harry's assistant, Enrique, has a wife, Cherry (Linda Ashton), who is a nurse at the hospital where Franklin has checked in. Harry is taking care of her, in addition to Raquel. But then Franklin informs Harry he wants some of Cherry, too. Harry just shrugs and shares the wealth, and Cherry restores Franklin's manhood in a very funny bedroom scene in the hospital. In the meantime, Apache is shooting everyone connected with Bolger. First he finishes off Enrique (Bert Santos), Cherry's husband, when Enrique, who knows Cherry is unfaithful to him, is driving with some of the loot and figuring how to get his revenge on Harry and Cherry. Apache's murder of Enrique is violent and gory. He mows him down with Harry's jeep. Apache also gets to Franklin in his hospital bed. You don't see this one happen on screen, but when Cherry tries to arouse him sexually he is covered with blood and sleeps on—forever. It all ends with a mad shoot-out between Harry and Apache while Cherry and Raquel, who have discovered each other, aren't unhappy that they are sharing Harry. Instead they are in bed with each other enjoying life while their man is getting wiped out. Meyer's films have excellent color transference to tape, and he makes use of a camera technique that many Hollywood directors overlook: very brief shots intercut with the action show what the character is thinking. In the case of Meyer's characters, it's sex, of course, with big-breasted women.

CHINA GIRL
CC NN NR (occasionally) DK BI
1974 SELECT ESSEX

P/D—Sumner Brown/Palo Uccello
F/A—James Young, Tom Douglas, Barry Fry
F/A—Annette Haven, Pamela Yen

Way back in 1974, Sumner Brown produced an adult film that has the style of a 1980s film. For the first 15 minutes there is no genital sex. You meet the villains, who are about to steal the new engram formula, which will change basic memory retention in the human brain and is of great importance to the United States. But an unnamed country, whose representative is Howard Smythe, is willing to pay huge sums of cash or diamonds for the secret. Bob Dragon (James Young), a sinister Chinese importer who ties his enemies in cloth sacks and dumps them off wharfs, tells Smythe through his emissary, Madame Wu (Pamela Yen) that he can get the formula. It is partially known by each of the creators, Dr. Olinsky and Dr. Teresa Hardgrave (Annette Haven). In the meantime, U.S. agent David Chase (Tom Douglas) is trying to save the formula for the United States. The story falls apart a little on the mad premise that the creators of the formula will reveal their secret not by torture but through an excess of pleasure. "Torture based on pleasure is just as effective as torture based on pain. Exceed the limit, and your subject is broken," says Dr. Chan. Of course Dr. Olinsky is quickly driven to the wall by four women working on him all at once for hours on end. But not Teresa Hardgrave, who is not only a top scientist, an Olympic skier, and a champion backgammon player, but a sexpot to boot. She exhausts every male Madame Wu can toss up against her and finally Madame Wu, too! Dr. Chan gets very upset. He's about to go back to tried and true torture methods when David gets free from his handcuffs and finishes off Dr. Chan. This film was made before Annette Haven had her teeth capped, but she's still very pretty.

CINDERELLA CC NN NL in a corny sort of way
1977   VIDAMERICA

P/D—Charles Band, Michael Pataki
F/A—Sy Richardson, Kirk Scott
F/A—Cheryl Smith, Yana Nirvana, Marilyn Corwin

A soft-core musical with no crotch shots but plenty of naked sex. Watch this one with a group of two or more couples and with a few glasses of wine (or scotch). Primed with alcohol is the only way to get into *Cinderella*. (No pun—that's what it's all about!) In the process, the Prince's Lord Chamberlain cuts off his finger (literally, no kidding) as he watches two maids strip. Her fairy godfather endows her with a "snapper betwixt her thighs" and the Prince, who has never climaxed, searches blindfolded in bed with numerous commoners on the night of the ball to discover one who can cure him. She, of course, is our darling Cindy.

CHORUS CALL CC NN BI NR
1979   TVX

P/D—Davis Freeman, Antonio Shepherd
F/A—Richard Bolla, Bob Hollander, Joe Nassivera, Bobby Astyr
F/A—Kay Parker, Darby Lloyd Raines, Beth Anne

Add this one to your collection of better sexvids. Integrated with a story line that revolves around Mona Randall (Kay Parker), a Broadway superstar who can hire and fire members of the cast of shows she appears in, Mona fires Cheryl, an ingenue who is competition for Elena (Beth Anna). While the story gets forgotten and the sex-making takes precedence, the various scenes of lovemaking (note the word) between Richard Bolla and Darby Lloyd Raines, between Kay Parker and Bobby Hollander, and between Joe Nassivera (now Joey Civera) and Susan London are all lovingly photographed, and in these one-to-one scenes there is a caring ambiance, which you don't often see in adult films. Even a threesome with Civera, Parker and Anna looks like athletic fun. There's a very funny production number sung by three women: "I'm an A-cup, I'm a B-cup, I'm a C-cup—Six Tits in a Row." Much of the film's action takes place in a Broadway theater. Words and music to this one and "Chorus Call" and "My Love" by Antonio Shepherd. Most women will enjoy the way he directed this one.

COMMON LAW CABIN CC NM BI
1967   RM INTERNATIONAL FILMS

P/D—Eve and Russ Meyer, Russ Meyer
F/A—Jack Moran, Franklin Bolger, John Furlong, Ken Swofford, Andrew Hagara
F/A—Alaina Capri, Babbette Bardot, Adele Rein

Note the date and the rating. Russ hadn't perfected his sex-and-violence bit in this one as much as later films, but even though you may catch it on subscription television, it's pretty far out. Imagine a remote tourist place way up the Colorado River on a lake called Adobe, where a middle-aged guy, Dewey Hoople (Jack Moran), runs a game-hunting lodge that can accommodate a few people at a time for a day or weekend. Populate the lodge with his second, much younger wife (Frenchy) Babette Bardot, and his daughter by his first marriage, Coral (Adele Rein), both of whom measure 42–24–36. Add to this melange Cracker (Franklin Bolger), a guy in his sixties, who rounds up tourists for them, and let him convince Sheila Ross (Alaina Capri), who is married to Dr. Martin Ross (John Furlong), who has heart trouble, that they should move out of their fancy resort downriver and have a day of adventure at Hoople's place. Add to this a red-headed former cop, Barney Rickard (Ken Swofford), who has stolen a fortune and is hiding out from the Missouri police (you don't know this until you're halfway through). While Barney is nearly smothering in all the big breasts on the place, a Russ Meyer dynamic situation is building. Before it's over, the doctor, watching his wife trying to seduce Barney, dies of a heart attack, Cracker is shot dead by Barney, and Barney and Sheila end up dead, too, but not until all of them, including Hoople's daughter and wife, get smacked on the jaw and on the ass more than once.

COUNT THE WAYS **CC   NN   NR**
1976   TVX

P/D—Anne Perry
F/A—Jason Welles, Jack Beardsley
F/A—Yvonne Green, Charla Miss

This precedent-setting sexvid has a strong story line. It was nominated for the Best Picture Award in 1976, at the First Erotic Film Festival, and should have received it. It is about a professor who falls in love with a student although he's engaged to marry the dean's daughter. It has excellent dialogue, extended, very believable warm, caring sexmaking scenes, an original musical score, excellent background photography and environmental ambi-

ance. One-to-one sex in all sequences with no group sex or bisexuality. Highly recommended. Perry has produced an adult film in advance of the inevitable future direction of these films. Women will like it. Worth owning.

CRY FOR CINDY **CC   NN   some DK (anal)   potentially NR**
1975   ARROW and TVX

P/D—Henry Locke, Wendy Locke
F/A—Fred Tames
F/A—Amber Hunt, Marianne Fisher

The flashback story of a call girl who puts her boyfriend through school, but becomes entranced with the easy money of her profession. When she tries to escape from her pimp, she commits suicide. Crying for Cindy, you can reflect in flashbacks on her life. Many women may identify with this sexvid. Amber Hunt does one of the better acting jobs.

CRY UNCLE **NN   NL   Commercially could be rated R**
1974   VCX

P/D—David J. Disick, John C. Alvidsen
F/A—Allan Garfield
F/A—Madeline Le Roux

John Alvidsen, who directed this film, made the transition to "straight" films and in 1981 released *The Formula* with George C. Scott. While the dialogue is occasionally dated, and all the girls wear mini skirts (when they're not naked), this one is a small classic proving that sex and laughter and sheer silliness can be intermixed. Allan Garfield, as Jake Masters, private eye, is trying to solve a murder so complicated that you soon lose the plot, but it doesn't matter because Jake has sex with all the female suspects, including one, to his amazement, who has been murdered. With a very big belly, a bald head and bewildered expression, Jake Masters is a film hero who should have appeared in more films. John Alvidsen missed a sequel bonanza. This film could be shown on subscription television.

THE DANCERS · CC NN NL NR
1982   VCX

P/D—Anthony Spinelli
F/A—John Leslie, Richard Pacheco, Randy West, Joey Civera
F/A—Georgina Spelvin, Vanessa Del Rio, Kay Parker, Mai Lin

Put this one near the top of your list of the best 25 sexvids. It won the Best Screenplay award for Michael Ellis (who also wrote *Nothing to Hide*), and Georgina Spelvin won Best Actress at the Sixth Annual Erotic Film Festival. It wasn't nominated for Best Picture because the emphasis is on *male* stars and *male* strippers. But the film is entirely heterosexual, very well acted and really funny. It stars Jackie (John Leslie) and his Dreams: Randy West, who plays the part of Sebastian, a male stripper who is very much in love with himself and his new sexy, curly hairdo; Richard Pacheco who plays the part of Jonathan, a male stripper who really wants to be a Shakespearean actor; and Joey–Mr. Bad (Joey Civera), who is a professional football star reduced to stripping after a head injury. All four of them travel from town to town, staying a few days as the feature attraction in local clubs that offer male strippers for Ladies Only nights. The stripping is very cleverly intercut into developing the story, during which Jackie gets involved with the nightclub owner (Kay Parker) and makes very romantic love to her, and Sebastian gets involved with a waitress in a local hash-joint, Frances (Vanessa Del Rio). Joey is bedding down with the town nymph, who plays in bed with any and all comers while her husband is working, and Jonathan ends up in the sack with Katherine (Georgina Spelvin), an "old maid" to whom he confides his acting ambitions and teaches lines from Shakespeare. As the nights pass, Jackie, dressed in a white tie and tails, features one stripper—thus giving each of them a chance to reveal themselves to a totally lascivious cheering female audience. The tape is worth buying or renting to get at-home female reaction to the whole concept of male strippers and to find whether women enjoy watching men being seductive and using their bodies as a sex tease, as well

as to see which one of the strippers they prefer. Each of them does it differently and totally in character with the parts they are playing. Randy West, with a superb body, is very egotistical, Richard Pacheco is the boy-next-door female fantasy as he scatters rosebuds from his jockstrap, and Joey Civera is a bad-ass, wearing only chaps and brandishing a whip when he appears. In all cases the females clamber up to the stage to stick money in their favorite jockstraps, get a quick feel and get kissed by the stripper. A few even try to go down on the strippers. But Spinelli never lets the strip acts get out of hand, and they are typical of what hundreds of thousands of women have journeyed in groups to watch at local clubs. In my novel *The Byrdwhistle Option* (Prometheus Press, Buffalo, New York, 1982), I have played with the idea and described an afternoon session at The Big Bamboo and Jumping Banana—a similar club). The story ends just as you would expect. After Sebastian has practically convinced Frances that he can get her a singing part in a Hollywood movie, and Jonathan promises Katherine that he will think over her proposition to move in with her—she has enough money so that he never has to work again—Jackie and his Dreams beat it out of town together, convinced by Jackie that they really have it made. "We've got the best job in the world . . . they say. We set women on fire . . . We're artists . . . When the lights go down we submerge ourselves into the souls of every woman in the joint."

DEBBIE DOES DALLAS
CC NN NL NM
1978   VCX

F/A—Jim Clark
F/A—Bambi Woods, Misty Winter

A laughing sexvid that fulfills at least one male fantasy—joining the girls in the high school shower. Nicely photographed with women who really seem like the teenagers that you will remember making love to in the back seat of your automobile, if you're male. Or, if you're female, you may identify with them. This one was a best seller in 1980—second only to *Deep Throat.*

DEEP THROAT CC NN NL some DK
1972 ARROW

P/D—Gerard Damiano
F/A—Harry Reems
F/A—Linda Lovelace

The story of a woman who can't reach an orgasm until she discovers that her clitoris is in her throat. More people have seen this film in adult theaters (often in a censored version) than any other adult film. It's a sexvid worth owning since it establishes many of the conventions that have dominated adult films for the past seven years, and of course it's far superior to most of the films that preceded it. Arrow offers it together with *The Devil and Miss Jones* on one tape. Worth owning.

DEFIANCE CC DS DK BI
1975 VCX

P/D—Jason Russell, Armand Weston
F/A—Fred Lincoln
F/A—Jean Jennings, Day Jason

This is a sexually more frightening film (and much more explicit one) than *Straw Dogs,* or *The Snake Pit* or even *Behind the Green Door.* Caught sniffing dope by her religious mother, Kathy is first sent to the psychiatric ward of a hospital where she is raped by the inmates and an attendant in a most brutally believable rape scene. "Rescued" by a doctor who is a follower of the Marquis de Sade, she is tortured until horrifyingly, in the *Journey of O* tradition, she begins to enjoy her pain, debasement and degradation. Worth owning to test your own reactions. Should the Marquis' writings be censored or do we dare to expose the insanity of his theories by openly showing tapes or movies like this? And whatever happened to Jean Jennings, who is a good actress?

DEVIATIONS CC NN NL DK BI
1983 SELECT ESSEX

P/D—J.D. Blackthorn, Domingo Lingo

F/A—Mike Horner, Don Hart
F/A—Shanna McCullogh, Adrienne Bellaire, Robin Everett, Connie Lindstrom, Lile Marlene.

The first four ladies in this one, listed above, who play the parts of Ellen, Ginger, Goldie and Connie—anyone of whom a normal guy would immediately fall in love with; the sharp clear filming; and a plot that sadly went astray is the reason for the CC rating. The story is about a female rock group called The Four Foxes who are so fresh, innocent and bland that they can't get any night club gigs, and are having a hard time paying the rent for their apartment. For the first half of the film they are all believable young women, who have sexual limitations they will not exceed. Goldie manages to get rid of the old guy—he's forty—who's trying to evict them for unpaid rent by sucking him, and riding his face while he jerks off, but she avoids actual screwing. The others ask her how she managed to do it. "Wasn't it degrading?" Then, Ginger gets caught up by a guy, Ziggie Rockstein, who tells her that he's an agent who can put them all on the map. "You need a gimmick." But his gimmick is to get Ginger, who finally agrees, into the sack—but only if he will come up with some good ideas for them. Alas, afterwards, he's too exhausted to think. Ellen and Connie answer an advertisement to pose for a photographer, (a Woody Allen style guy), no undressing. But for the $100 they need to pay the rent, he finally convinces them to capitulate, and both of them take him on. Then, the group decide that the only way they can survive is to forget their morals. Even though they are really nice girls they'll change their name to the *Deviations.* From this point the potential for character development gives way to one orgy after another (Ellen even makes love to a boa constrictor) and culminates in their getting a job in a Gold Coast night club inhabited by sophisticated clientele "who would murder them, if their sexy presentation is all an act, and they're really just goody two-shoes." For the last fifteen minutes, the foursome sing their new obscene songs "We're the Deviations; Go Down on Me, I Love It So When You Go Down on Me; and

I Don't Want a Cannibal, I Want an Animal." Meanwhile the entire audience in the club is gradually stripping and eating and sucking everything in sight including Ginger, Goldie and Connie who decide this is the price of success. Only Ellen walks out in disgust. But her boyfriend, a tax accountant, who doesn't make much money thinks it may be the only way. Obviously, the ending caters to the porn theater audience, but it could have been much more subtle and a better film if all the girls had stayed in character.

THE DEVIL AND MISS JONES
CC NN some DK
1972 VCX

P/D—**Gerard Damiano**
F/A—**Harry Reems**
F/A—**Georgina Spelvin**

The story of Justine Jones, a virgin spinster who, horrified by her sexual compulsions, commits suicide in one of the most dramatic scenes on sexvids. Before entering hell, she is granted a reprieve to experience the totally lustful life that she has missed. This film established Georgina Spelvin as one of the few real actresses appearing in adult films, and Damiano rose head and shoulders above his *Deep Throat.* No collection of sexvids is complete without this tape, which epitomizes Gerard Damiano's continuing Catholic conscience.

DEVIL AND MISS JONES II **CC NN NL**
1983 VCA

P/D—**Howard Beach, Henri Pachard**
F/A—**Jack Wrangler, R. Bolla, Michael Bruce, Bobby Astyr, Joey Civera**
F/A—**Georgina Spelvin, Jacqueline Lorians, Joanna Storm, Anna Ventura, Samantha Fox**

To appreciate this film you should first watch *The Devil and Miss Jones* (see listing) which is a somber film and more melodramatic. Among other things you'll discover that although Georgina Spelvin is ten years older, she's even prettier and sexier, and Henri Pachard has a wild sense of humor which Damiano does not. The dialogue between Lucifer (Jack Wrangler) and the Devil's Advocate (R. Bolla) is so super-sophisticated-silly that I'm sure that much of it will pass over the heads of most past fifty and many young porno-film addicts. Everyone you can remember is in hell, including Cyrano de Bergerac, who gives good nose, and Captain Ahab, who is an expert with his wooden leg. When Justine Jones (Georgina Spelvin) arrives, Cyrano (who the Devil's Advocate admits really doesn't belong in hell) is about to bring Justine to a climax when the orgasm alert alarm goes off. You can screw all you want to, but long ago the Devil's Advocate made a rule which is strictly enforced. No orgasms! After all, this is hell. (Pachard lifted this idea from an idea proposed by Ingmar Bergman.) But Lucifer is weary of hell, and he hasn't had any fun for a long time. So he listens to Justine and promises her anything she wants, if she pays no attention to the Devil's Advocate and brings him to a climax. Seems he hasn't come in centuries. Justine gives old Lucy the best orgasm he can ever remember. He shoots fire all over her! And of course he doesn't want to let her go back to earth. He finally relents, but she can't go back in her old body. So Justine first becomes Roxanne (Jacqueline Lorians), the highest-priced call girl in New York, and soon she's giving Arnold Arnold (Bobby Astyr) the opportunity to realize his greatest fantasy. He wants to screw a woman dressed as the devil—complete with a simulated devil's head on his cock. Next Roxanne is taking on an Arab sheik. "Don't shriek, sheik!" she tells him when he comes. All the while down in hell Lucifer and the Devil's Advocate are watching as Justine satisfies her lusty nature. They even hope that Roxanne checks his oil! But Lucifer is sorry he ever let her go. (Under the rules she can't ever come back.) Because he's so jealous Lucifer decides that in the future he'll personally make the selection of any female body that Justine inhabits. Soon she's inside an Army WAC (Joanna Storm) who flagrantly showers with the enlisted men, and seduces the Captain. Then she's a former Tupperware representative (Anna Ventura) who is now selling sex toys to men. Hoping to calm her down, Lucifer decides to put her inside Sister Angela, a nun (Samantha Fox) but is advised by St. Peter in a phone call to heaven that "he'd better not fool around with our people." In despair Lucifer abdicates the throne and arrives in Roxanne's bedroom. Beautiful as Jacqueline is, Henri Pachard made one mistake. He should have turned her back into Georgina. The interchange between Jack Wrangler and Richard Bolla is great fun, all of the acting is good, and the dialogue is so slaphappy that you can't help laughing, but the raincoat crowd probably won't like it.

A DIRTY WESTERN   **CC   NR   DS**
1975   ARROW and VCX

P/D—Michael Dassin, David Fleetwood
F/A—Richard O'Neal, Geoffrey Parker, Dick Payne
F/A—Barbara Bourbon, Verne Rossi, Simone

This is the most believable sexvid, with perhaps the best acting and cinematography you've seen in any of them. It is also the most frightening. The time frame is the 1890s. After seven years in prison, three convicts have escaped. Jim, a rancher near the prison, is leaving for a cattle drive, and his wife, Sarah, is planning the wedding of one of her three daughters. A tender love scene sets the prelude for the horror to come. After Jim has left, the three convicts arrive. They rape Sarah several times, once in front of her daughters, and then they hang her by her arms, naked, in front of her farm house. Then they kidnap the three daughters for hostages and fun and games. A very brutal rape scene occurs when Luke, the oldest convict, rapes the youngest daughter. The posse and Sarah finally track them down and Sarah discharges her shotgun into the oldest convict's face. This film raises an inevitable question: Why do violence, murder and rape make more sexually exciting films than stories dealing with normal emotions?

DIVERSIONS   **CC   NN   NL   BI   DS   DK**
1979?   HOME ENTERTAINMENT

P/D—Valerie Ford, Derek Ford
F/A—Timothy Blackstone, Gilly Sykes
F/A—Heather Deely, Jacqui Rigby

Put this one on the top shelf of your collection of classic sexvids. Produced in London, it begins in a London railway station with a handcuffed woman being escorted to Eastern Women's Prison by a male and female guard. During the journey by rail, Heather Deely, a very attractive British actress, takes you into her memories and fantasies (you are never sure which) as the English countryside rolls by. As she mentions during the film, "It's a good thing you can't see what other people are thinking. It's like having a telly in your head." Move over Nancy Friday. In the next hour you see Heather (in fact or daydream) being seduced in a barn by her lover, who recites a Shakespearean paean to apples ("They have lovely buttocks, and a navel"). You see her being raped in World War II when she, a Red Cross nurse, is captured by Germans. As she recalls it, her current lover is on top of her, and she reaches under the couch and stabs him to death with a long-bladed knife. Then she's in Soho driving a Jag and picking up another guy. Back on the same couch, he turns out to have the teeth of a vampire, and when she tries to stab him the knife won't penetrate his skin. Then she's being raped by army officers, two males and one female, of an unknown army. Then her fantasies turn humorous, and she decides to try whipping and bondage only to discover that her first client thinks he's renting her flat and not her, and finally she dreams of buying a nineteenth-century camera, which she takes home. It comes to life with the long-dead photographer taking sexy nineteenth-century-style pictures of her. If you want to start a controversy, show this one in mixed company—women will watch it both horrified and amused—and ask the women how their fantasies compare with Heather's.

DIVINE OBSESSION
CC NN NM NL (occasionally) NR DK DS
1979 TVX

P/D—David Wynn, Louis Su
F/A—Tony Dexter, Alan Marlo, Levi Richards, Eric Edwards
F/A—Julia Franklin, Terri Hall, Bree Anthony, April Summer

Here's a sexvid that will keep you interested from the beginning to the end. You quickly know that Julia (Julia Franklin, who is appearing with two other women, Patti (Terri Hall) and Peaches (Bree Anthony), in a sex show), is going to murder somebody. Before she appears on stage she has the gun behind the curtain. In flashbacks intercut with the continuing strip and sex show, watched by a small audience of lascivious-looking men, you follow Julia's memories from her life in a small town in Ohio, where she wasn't much of a student but appeared in all the high school plays. She was in love with Ted, who taught her math when she wasn't exciting him upstairs in her room in her parent's house. After high school in Ohio, Julia goes to New York and quickly finds that the way to the top is giving *more* than she gets. Reciting Shakespeare (Juliet, from *Romeo and Juliet*) while she undresses for a porno filmmaker, she's still saying Juliet's lines (very well) as she has sex with Eric Edwards, who is casting a porno movie. Then to her surprise she makes a porno film, *Sunset of Passion,* which makes her a national celebrity. In a funny television interview with a William Buckley look-and-talk-alike named William F. Buckley, pseudo-Buckley tells the country that this particular porno film is great art. But despite her fame, Julia is arrested by the FBI, and before she's free of obscenity convictions all she has left are two fur coats and $26,000. But she has met Peter, a student at the university who lives with James—and soon she's head over heels in love with Peter. But her friends warn her. Peter is not all he seems to be, and James is really the guy who loves her. Soon Julia discovers that Peter is engaged to another woman —and he's never been very faithful. So Julia gets tangled up with a Mafia-like guy who tries to move in on her. Worse, Ted, the boy back home whom she thought was so nice, is visiting New York. He no longer is a nice guy and rapes her in a hotel room. Who is Julia going to murder? In the final scene she points the gun at various men in the audience and then suddenly puts it in her own mouth and pulls the trigger. "You never hit bottom," she has said. "There is no bottom. You just keep falling." Julia Franklin, a redhead, is a good actress. Everything bad happens to her—but many women will sympathize.

DOING IT CC NN DK NR
1983 SELECT ESSEX

P/D—Mark Corby, Sven Conrad
F/A—Eric Edwards, Mike Horner, Billy Dee, Jon Martin
F/A—Drea, Lily Marlene, Babie Bendum

It's interesting to compare this film with *Body Magic* (see p. 66). It's in the same super-sophisticated genre. Filmed almost entirely outdoors, it revolves almost entirely around Eric Edwards and Drea (I never did find out their screen names) who are financially secure and live near San Francisco in a beautiful home with an outdoor swimming pool and separate jacuzzi that will make your mouth water. For the first 15 minutes you meet them—together with their friends and servants—during an afternoon and evening. An anything-goes orgy ensues, which includes underwater sex, two guys making it with one gal on the edge of the pool, etc. Then the day comes to an abrupt end, and you hear Eric and Drea in their living room talking about how nice it was—and how extra special their friends are. But Drea notices that Eric is "getting one of those I-want-something-else looks in his eyes again." Bang, you see a masked man on a motorcycle chasing Drea over the manicured grounds. When she collapses and you think she's about to be raped by a knife-carrying maniac, it turns out to be Eric, laughing. "What the hell do you want?" she demands. "Kicks," he replies, and immediately they are off on a camping trip on his motorcycle, taking a mad tour on two-lane roads north of San

Francisco. Through the wine country, they highball it—stopping at Old Faithful to take a mud bath. They end up in an amusement park riding the roller coaster, wandering in turning tunnels, and circling in swaying sky rides. Next they meet two gals and a guy protesting a hydroelectric plant under construction that will deplete the hot mineral waters in which they are swimming. They end up spraying bottles of champagne over each other, swimming in a sylvan lake naked and switching partners in a temporary sexual nirvana. Then Eric and Drea high-tail it to a Howard Johnsons. Starving, they eat and are served in fast motion. Camping out later Drea remarks: "It certainly looked like you were enjoying yourself with that little blonde today," and Eric replies: "Well, you were having a good time, too." With no jealousy or recriminations, she grins at him and tells him, "Your trouser mouse is playing peek-a-boo again." And they make love under the stars. Running out of gas, they end up in a commune run by a guru named Jacob, who naturally has a few female acolytes, and soon they all are communing with each other and sex-making to Indian ragas. Finally, after saving them from a guy and gal who chase them with guns on posted property—via fellatio, of course—Drea announces, "I don't want to do this anymore. I want to go home to my jacuzzi and hot-oil massages and champagne." And presto, the next morning, at peace with himself again, Eric remarks: "After all our traveling around and all the people we've met, I've discovered something. I've got everything I need right here"—which he quickly proves witth Drea's enthusiastic help.

DOWNSTAIRS UPSTAIRS
CC NN NL BI
1980 SELECT/ESSEX X-TRA VISION

P/D—Bob Augustus, Lisa Barr
F/A—F.J. Reynolds, Bobby Reed, Dan Quick
F/A—Kay Parker, Seka, Lisa DeLeeuw

Mommy, daddy, sister and brother Bun live upstairs in a nutty, you-can't take-it-with-you Hollywood ambiance. The Buns not only enjoy their guests sexually around an outdoor swimming pool, but when Olive, a hillbilly maid arrives to live downstairs, she joins the fun and games and one by one services all the members of the family. While there's no resemblance to the famous PBS series, all in the cast in this one seem to thoroughly enjoy themselves.

DRACULA EXOTICA
CC DS DK BI NL (occasionally)
1981 TVX

P/D—Ken Schwartz, Warren Evans
F/A—Jamie Gillis, Mark Dexter, Eric Edwards Bobby Astyr
F/A—Samantha Fox, Vanessa Del Rio

Ken Schwartz (who also did *Fiona on Fire*, see p. 90) proves again with this one that he can tell a story that will keep you interested. In his second appearance as Dracula (see *Dracula Sucks*, see p. 207), Jamie Gillis has perfected the role which seems to come naturally to him. In the story of a twentieth-century Dracula (the time is approximately 1990), the Count, who was born in Transylvania, arrives in New York City aboard a freighter. Since he lived behind the Iron Curtain, the FBI suspects that he's a Russian agent. Samantha Fox, who looks like Surka, a woman he defiled in 1490 (you see all this in the first sequence, which is elaborately costumed and takes place in the Count's castle) and who now works for the FBI, tries to discover the truth. While you'll lose the plot, you'll keep watching to the end. Dracula takes over Vanessa on the freighter (she has just finished taking care of the entire merchant marine crew), and although stabbed in the heart by a sailor, the Count manages to screw her and drink her blood. After turning her into a vampire and enjoying her so much, he tries to hire her as a secretary ("Can you type?" Answer: "Yes, 50 words a minute.") One guy discovers Vanessa dead in a coffin. Enjoying necrophilia, he brings her to life and she bites him. Before it is over everyone has nasty fangs. Feminists should encourage their male lovers to buy this one, and thereby find out, should they laugh as they watch it, where they are coming from.

DUTCH TREAT **CC NN NL DK**
1974 VIDEO X HOME LIBRARY

▓▓▓

P/D—Navred Reef
F/A—Roger Caine, Zebedy Colt
F/A—Carrah Major-Minor, Lucy Duvall, Christy Kluiver

I watched this one after I watched *Playgirls in Munich*. I have no idea which one was made first but Roger Caine and Zebedy Colt portray the further adventures of the same characters, Chuck and Barney, this time in Amsterdam. Which one is the funnier is difficult to decide, and whether there is a third episode in another country I haven't as yet discovered. Continuing to read *Sex in Europe*, a paperback, this time they spend their last few dollars and fly to Amsterdam with a Dutch phrase book and lots of chutzpah to guide them in their sexual encounters. In the red-light district, Chuck finds a prostitute and fails to ask her price. He is delicately relieved of 10 guilders for "kissing my breasts"; 10 guilders for kissing you-know-where; 25 for sucking; 25 for you-know-what; 25 for the room; and 25 for coming a second time. Later Chuck and Barney end up in an Amsterdam sex club. After watching the show, Chuck decides they should become American porno film producers. As a result of their advertising, at least 12 women offer their services and are interviewed in crazy but erotic sex sequences. Poor Barney ends up in a sauna, with *his* Dutch Treat turning into a rubber doll, and two lesbians completely ignoring him. "I can't even plug the dykes in Holland," he complains. Our heroes are finally arrested by the Dutch police and shipped home air freight in two separate boxes. If you got hooked on *Playgirls in Munich*, you'll want to see this one.

EASY **CC NN NM NR & BI**
1978 CAL VISTA

▓▓▓

F/A—Sam Norvell, Anthony Spinelli
F/A—Jack Wright, John Wilson
F/A—Jesie St. James, Georgina Spelvin, Desiree Cousteau

Nominated for the Best Film of 1979 at the Fourth Annual Erotic Film Festival. Kate Harrison, a schoolteacher, has lost her husband to another woman teacher at Clifton High. She's "easy"—not always because she wants to be, but because she can't resist her own sexual compulsions. From a student who forces her to have oral sex, to his friend who rapes her (but in the process she acquiesces), to a blind piano tuner who tells her that he's the best stud in town, to a fat man who accosts her in a bar (played by Anthony Spinelli) with whom she refuses to go to bed, to an author, Victor (Jack Wright), who seduces her but already has a girlfriend (Georgina Spelvin) and who beats her and rapes her, to her final love, Matt, whom she adores, but who forlornly tells her that he's married, poor Kate wants to be wanted—not just for her body—but she can't find the right man. Jesie St. James has a very expressive face. What makes this film more interesting than most is that Spinelli concentrates on her face. Whether she is climaxing or not, both the contractions on her face and her joy makes you believe that she is.

THE ELEVATOR **CC NN K NR DK**
(two couples)
1974 BOCCACCIO 100

▓▓▓

P/D—Not given
F/A—Not given

Have you ever been in an elevator alone with a member of the other sex and wondered what would happen if it got stuck between floors? That's what happens in this one—and it's on a Friday afternoon. To keep things going for an hour you have to know who is who. Peter is married to Joyce, who once was a lot of fun in the sack but now gets very moody and thinks that Peter is fooling around. Jane is secretary to Howard, a lawyer whose offices are in the same building as Peter's. Howard may be fooling around with his lady clients, but he lives with Jane and tells her he loves her and wants to marry her. You see in flashbacks both of these couples enjoying each other's bodies and one in which Peter and Joyce play switchies with another couple. But now Peter and Jane are in the elevator, and Peter kisses Jane, who is frightened. "Sorry, I didn't mean to do that," he tells her. "Yes you did," she replies. And of course, they are soon happily screwing on the elevator floor. When the elevator finally starts to move they scramble into their clothes but no one is waiting on the ground floor. They kiss each other good-bye fondly. "Tell your boyfriend he's got one hell of a girl," Peter tells her. "Joyce should love you," Jane sighs back at him.

EMMANUELLE, THE QUEEN OF SADOS
CC HARD R DS
1982 VIDAMERICA

P/D—Evangelos Founistakis, Ilias Milonakos
F/A—Harris Stevens, Vagelis Vatran, Gordon Mitchell, Pantelis Agelopu
F/A—Laura Gemser, Gabrielle Tinti, Livia Russo, Nadia Nero

I am writing this review just as Jerry Falwell has launched a mail order campaign to support new legislation to censor cable television, and as Sidney Niekerk, retiring president of the Adult Film Association of America and president of Cal Vista, warns members of the AFAA not to sell hardcore films to pay television. He is sure that hard-core on pay television will inevitably bring repressive legislation, which brings up the question of the difference between Hard R and an XXX rating. It's not very much, as you will discover if you watch this film, which incidentally is the best I have seen of the Emmanuelle series with Laura Gemser. It seems that Emmanuelle has married a very sadistic man, who, with the help of his secretary and a business associate, regularly tortures her, ties her up and beats her prior to screwing her. In the opening scene you have quick memory flashbacks of this while Emmanuelle is in bed with her lover, whom you will later discover is known as "the killer with the red rose." In addition to screwing with him, she is paying him to kill her husband—which he does a few scenes later by blowing up his private plane. The remainder of the plot revolves around the fact that the killer is blackmailing Emmanuelle who has indirectly inherited all the guy's money (he was very wealthy) and now has custody of his 15-year-old daughter. In addition to much female nudity and sexmaking, without any male genitals showing of course, Lydia enters the story as a 15-year-old virgin. There are no credits on the film to determine who she is, but the girl (based on her breast development and facial features) is certainly under the U.S. standards of 18 years old. She is very pretty, and her first love affair with a 17-year-old boy is very well handled. Then the assassin, who is blackmailing Emmanuelle, rapes Lydia in a terrifying scene and leaves her lying naked on the beach in a pool of water. The film concludes with Emmanuelle making a date with the killer and firing a revolver at him point blank. Shot in Greece and Cyprus, the film is much more professional than most adult films. The rape scene is not gratuitous. It's the focus of the plot, but it raises the question of who, in a society that has censored the publication of a book such as *Show Me*, with underage youngsters pictured fondling each other, this film will fare on television, for which it was designed.

EMILENNE   CC   NR   BI   This one actually has an R rating.
1978 VIDAMERICA

P/D—Andre Genoves, Pierre Braunberger, Guy Casparil
F/A—Pierre Oudrey
F/A—Betty Mars, Natalie Guerin

A fascinating story of a ménage à trois. Claude falls in love with Nicolle. To have more time with him, Nicolle seduces his wife, Emilenne, who has repressed her bisexual leanings in her marriage. Claude seems to have the best of two possible worlds. There are some amusing scenes where they all play sexually together, but then Nicolle tries to dispossess Emilenne and become the sole woman in Claude's life. She gets pregnant but Emilenne loves the child more than she does. This is a very erotic film with no hard-core sex, but much female nudity.

EMMANUELLE R BI DK DS
1974 COLUMBIA FROM INTERNATIONAL HOME VIDEO CLUB

xxxxxxxxxxxxxxxxxxxxxxxxxxxxxxxxxxxxxxxxxxxxxxxxxxxxxx

P/D—Just Jaeckin
F/A—Alain Cuny, Daniel Sarky
F/A—Sylvia Kristal, Marika Greene, Jeanne Colletin, Christine Boisson

There are two Emmanuelles. Sylvia Kristal was the first one, Laura Gemser the second. Sylvia is much more naive than Laura and perhaps is closer to the Emmanuelle of Emmanuelle Arsan's presumed autobiographical writings of the same title published by Grove Press. Nearly ten years ago, *Emmanuelle* was released in major cinema theaters throughout the United States to audiences who stood in line to see human sexuality depicted so openly. It's still not a film you are likely to see on commercial television. The entire action takes place in Bangkok, Thailand, where Emmanuelle's husband, Jean, is a diplomat who has been transferred to the French embassy. It's a boring life for the wives but Jean tells her: "You may play tennis, golf, explore the canals and you can make love." Not necessarily to Jean. Unlike most husbands with such a beautiful wife, Jean believes that Emmanuelle needs to experience new depths of eroticism. Emmanuelle timidly tries by masturbating together with a neighboring wife's daughter. Then she falls in love with Bee, who is blond and very beautiful. When Emmanuelle returns after hopelessly pursuing Bee (during which time Jean has sadistically screwed a wealthy bisexual friend of theirs), Jean suggests that Emmanuelle can get her revenge on Bee with another lover. "I'll help you find him," he says. The lover who will teach her all there is to know about sex is Mario, a septuagenarian. With Mario's guidance, and while smoking hashish, Emmanuelle becomes the sexual prize of the winner of a vicious Thai boxing match while Mario watches. Then she is raped by two Orientals, and shares Mario with a male lover. It's a pretty decadent philosophy, and it totally disengages sex from one's brains. You would never believe that a woman as lovely as Emmanuelle, who really enjoys normal sex, would need any instruction in the kinky stuff. If you've never been to Bangkok, there's some nice background scenery of the canals and upper-class living. If you want to know more about Sylvia Kristal, *Playboy* offered an interview with her on their video *Playboy Magazine of the Month* in 1982.

EMMANUELLE IN AMERICA Hard R CC DK BI
1978 VIDAMERICA

xxxxxxxxxxxxxxxxxxxxxxxxxxxxxxxxxxxxxxxxxxxxxxxxxxxxxx

P/D—Joe D'Amato
F/A—Roger Browne, Lars Boch, Paeoli Senatore
F/A—Laura Gemser, Gabrielle Tanti

Laura Gemser succeeded Sylvia Kristal in the Emmanuelle role. She's dark-skinned, perhaps Italian, but looks and acts like a very cool Thai woman. This film should serve as a model for explicit adult filmmakers—if it had a few actual genital close-ups it might bridge the gap. Of course, then it could never be shown on cable or subscription television but it would certainly be more palatable to the female audience because it has a story line and Emmanuelle is a very sophisticated woman. She's a photographer who takes pictures for skin magazines as well as doing investigative reporting. She wears a camera on her wrist bracelet, and will stop at nothing to gain her objectives or expose the villainy of those she's probing. The first guy is Eric van Deeren, who has an estate on Long Island in which he keeps a private harem of a dozen beautiful women who will cater to every whim of his guests. Those chosen live in such luxury they sob pitifully if Eric rejects them. As a novitiate, Emmanuelle joins the group, and eventually proves with her trusty camera that Eric's wealth comes from drug dealing. You discover that she has exposed him only after she suddenly ends up in Venice with a friend of Eric's, the Duke, who has invited her to one of his parties on the Grand Canal. Her boyfriend, Bill, wants to marry Emmanuelle and save her from the decadent world she's messing around in, but Emmanuelle doesn't believe in marriage, especially when she discovers that the Duke is not only selling forgeries of famous paintings but enjoys his wife best in a threesome in which Emmanuelle willingly participates. At the Duke's party, the pièce de résistance is a huge cake which contains a solid gold peanut. Whoever gets the peanut in his/her cut of the cake gets a special prize. An old senator finally announces that he has the peanut. His prize is a naked young woman inside the cake who is covered with whipped cream. When he starts to gobble her, everyone else takes the hint and soon they all shed their beautiful tuxes and gowns and are happily eating each other. Next, Emmanuelle is back in the United States investigating a stud service on Long Island. The guys wear only towels which the prospective female purchaser can pull back before buying. Emmanuelle takes care of the owner of the place, a woman, by stripping her and making love to her. There's more! But the fascinating thing is that in scene after scene, Joe D'Amato has given you everything you ever saw in an X-rated film—plus a dollop of decadence that may turn you off.

ENDLESS LUST **CC NN NM DK BI**
1983

P/D—Erica Fox
F/A—John Hollyfield, Ron Jeremy, William Margold, Larry Moore
F/A—Gena Lee, Hilary Summers, Georgina Spelvin

Peter Balakoff, a.k.a. Ted Roter, did not direct this one but his name is listed as screenwriter and his style is evident throughout the film (see listings for *The Psychiatrist, A Very Small Case of Rape* and *Prison Babies*, pp. 211, 61, and 122). Also, although through some oversight Gena Lee's name does not appear on the packaging (she often appears in Roter films), she is the star of this one. Georgina Spelvin appears only momentarily in one bisexual scene. The reason for the CC rating is largely because of Gena and the clever way the film is put together. The many, many sexual scenes are intercut into ongoing interviews, first between re-

porters and television cameramen who are questioning Senator Jack Doucette (John Hollyfield) and his wife Erica (Gena Lee) about the wild sex scandal that he's involved in—and has just erupted in the nation's capital. Doucette denies everything, but the brief intercuts tell a different story. Although Erica agrees to stand by him and tells the reporters that she still loves him, after he is found guilty she immediately poses nude for *Scum* magazine and appears on national television ("The Larry Moore Show") where once again, over the next half hour, wild Washington sex orgies are depicted and intercut with Larry's interview. But Erica never describes the events verbally. The approach keeps you interested and the interview with Larry Moore has a semblance of reality. When Moore asks Erica about internal security she smiles archly. "Oh, I wear a diaphragm." But of course, he's referring to senators who may be passing top secrets to women who could be foreign agents. Erica describes daisy chain parties, and a President's nephew who services various senators' wives— once even in the Rose Garden while the President was being interviewed. Some of the orgy scenes run interminably—one to the accompaniment of Ravel's *Bolero*. The film ends up with Larry Moore pursuing Erica to her home for an afternoon of dalliances during which she continues to expose the seamy side of Washington. She tells him that if her darling "Jackie-poo" has told her the truth "the country is being run by lust-filled sex maniacs." But she loves dear old Jackie-poo because he has launched her on a new career. At the beginning of the film Gena warns you that any resemblance to actual events and real people is purely coincidental, but she concludes, "If you believe *that*, you'll believe anything." If you have read your newspapers in the past few years, some of this story may not sound far from reality. At least it provided the groundwork for a porno film more interesting than most.

THE EROTIC ADVENTURES OF CANDY
CC NN NL
1978 WONDERFUL WORLD OF VIDEO

P/D—Gail Palmer
F/A—John C. Holmes, Turk Lyon, Paul Thomas
F/A—Carol Connors, Georgina Spelvin

This film preceded *Candy Goes to Hollywood*. There is very definitely a female touch in this sexvid. Laughingly "based on Voltaire's *Candide*," it is funnier than the sequel. Among others, there is a sequence of Candy making love with her Spanish boyfriend (who can't speak English) interrupted by her father, who catches them both in bed. The father has a heart attack as the boy leaps out of Candy's arms. It has a real Chaucerian touch that escapes most film producers. Worth owning.

EROTIC MEMOIRS OF A MALE CHAUVINIST PIG
CC NN NM NL DK
1973 QUALITY

P/D—John Butterworth
F/A—Paul Taylor
F/A—Georgina Spelvin, Tina Russell, Amy Hunter

"I seem to be one of those people whose destiny it is to be married." So begins Barney (Paul Taylor) the hero(?) of this one. "I use the word destiny even though I don't enjoy being married," he says. "I'm not comfortable married, but it's like smoking. Presently, I'm in the middle of my fourth attempt to quit marriage. Already I'm involved with Alice (Georgina Spelvin) but I have no intention of marrying her." Thus begins the story of Barney, who records his screwed up love-life on a tape recorder even as he is living it. There are three women in his life: Alice, who tells him in detail how he should make love to her. And then there's Susan, played by Tina Russell, a woman with whom Barney has never had a serious conversation. Susan doesn't want to be touched—but she does her exercises naked while Barney watches and she really enjoys masturbating just as long as he only watches her and masturbates, too. And there's Chris-

tine, a former hooker. Christine loves him so much that she takes an overdose of sleeping pills. Barney finds her in his bed with a note pinned to her: "Dear Shit: Why not use me one more time?" Saving her life, he finally makes her his fifth wife.

ERUPTION **CC NN BI DK**
1976 CAL VISTA

P/D—Stanley Kurlan
F/A—John Holmes, Eric Evol, Gene Clayton
F/A—Leslie Bovee, Susan Hart

If you're old or watch late, late shows, you've probably seen the first version of this one played by Barbara Stanwyck and Fred MacMurray in James Cain's *Double Indemnity*. The plot is to collect a million-dollar life insurance policy on the husband's life so that the lover and the wife can share it—and each other. This one has John C. as the bad guy and Leslie Bovee as the wife. John strangles the husband (he's hiding in the back seat of the Cadillac) and they put his body in the trunk. Leslie is lovingly delighted to be rid of the old man. What makes this one more interesting than most is a consistent story line that only occasionally gets off track, good photography (it was shot in Hawaii) and, in one sequence, close-up studies of Leslie and John that may interest many women as well as men.

EXPECTATIONS **CC NL NN almost NR and beautifully photographed BI**
TVX and SELECT/ESSEX

P/D—J. F. Cohan, Arvid Beller
F/A—Jack Wright, Joey Civera
F/A—Suzanne Wright, Delania Ruffino, Desiree West

If women are ever going to like sexvids, they'll approve of most of this one. It has a thin story line about women who change apartments and lovers and enjoy exquisitely photographed sensual and erotic sexmaking with each other's lovers. This sexvid could easily cross the line between sex education films and porn. It offers a feeling tone that is absent from many clinically produced sex education films and occasionally you can even emote with the actors and actresses!

EVERY WHICH WAY SHE CAN
CC NN BI NL (occasionally)
1981 CABALLERO

P/D—Jo-Anne Lewis, Louie Lewis
F/A—Mike Horner, Herschel Savage, Paul Thomas, Joey Civera
F/A—Loni Sanders, Serena, Lisa de Leeuw, Sharon Mitchell, Dorothy Le May, Lysa Thatcher, Nicole Noir

Every which way you can ever imagine, your every-which-way-and-loose fantasies take place at Lewises Corral. (Note the name. The Lewises are a husband and wife team with a new formula for adult films—locate them in one particular environment and proceed from there—see *Brief Affair* listing, p. 68, where the location is the Lewis Academy of Performing Arts.) Lewis Corral is a nightclub where Clit Westwood (Loni Sanders) becomes the female Clint Eastwood and describes the action in a voice-over: "What I do for a living is not important. I do what I have to do to get by. . . . You know what I mean." The action of the night at Lewis Corral gets going with Lysa Thatcher and Nicole Noir as wrestling ladies—performing in the hay in an extended female scene where the ladies occasionally get more involved in each other's crotch than wrestling, and are cheered on by the crowd, which yells, "You're supposed to be beating her, not eating her." Loni as Clit watches Paul Thomas being sucked off in the cloak room by Serena and wishes she were her: "A bird in the bush is better than a hand any time." Sharon Mitchell takes one customer to his car, which fortunately has a sun roof. They are interrupted by a motorcycle gang of three guys including Paul Thomas and Joey Civera, who are about to rape Sharon. But Loni appears without her panties and Sharon and she suck them into submission, after which they pour gasoline on their jeans and burn them. In the meantime, Serena is doing a strip act inside the club while Lisa de Leeuw is brashly finishing a guy on the floor in the sawdust—followed by an invasion of the motorcycle gang with baseball bats. After they are quickly subdued by Mike Horner (a Clark Gable lookalike), Mike and Loni end up in bed in a long romantic sexmaking sequence. Most women under 40 won't object to this one, and may even laugh a little.

EXPOSED
CC NN NM NR BI NL DK (but plot-oriented)
1979 SELECT/ESSEX

P/D—Wesley Emerson, Jeffrey Fairbanks, Anthony Spinelli
F/A—John Leslie, John Seeman
F/A—Shirley Woods, Kitty Shane, Sharon Caine

Willie (John Leslie) and Annie (Sharon Caine) celebrate their first anniversary in a very romantic sexmaking scene in their living room. "You're the most wonderful lover I ever had," Annie tells him. "Did it come naturally or did someone teach you how? You must have been a porno star." And, of course, Willie was and though he's now running a photographic studio, he succumbs to a job offer from Max (who in real life is neither George Spelvin nor Anthony Spinelli, porno film director, but is presumably Sam Weston), who offers him $1,500 a day for five days to star in his new flick, *Cheerleaders in Bondage*. Simultaneously, when Willie is mowing his lawn, his next-door neighbor recognizes him and threatens to tell his wife unless Willie services her too. Pretty soon Willie is so exhausted from his work that he's not functioning in his marital bed. This is a laughing sexvid that will keep you interested to the finale when Annie turns the tables on Willie and takes a job in the film he's acting in. Most women will like this one—and obviously, if John Leslie was their next-door neighbor, would recognize him, too. This one proves that Leslie is one of the few porno stars who can give a genuinely funny performance, and the film itself generally laughs at porno movies.

EXPOSE ME LOVELY
CC NN NR (occasionally) BI DK
1976 QUALITY

P/D—Armand Weston
F/A—Ras Kean, Bobby Astyr
F/A—Jennifer Welles, Jody Maxwell, Cary Lacy,
   Iminu, Annie Sprinkles, Eve Adams

Frosty Knight (Ras Kean, who is a very handsome guy—what happened to him?) is a very nice private detective (not Mike Hammer style) and a lover of women. Karen Spencer (Cary Lacy), a very wealthy woman, tells him that her brother is missing and her father is trying to find him before he dies. They have quarreled but she doesn't tell Frosty the reason why. Of course, Frosty and Karen make love, and as Frosty pursues the clues leading him to Karen's brother he not only gets involved in a carefully developed deepening mystery and several murders, but he enjoys sexmaking first with Cary, a young woman who has a studio in a former synagogue and is later murdered, as well as with Vicky (Iminu), a sexy black lady who has a shaved head and performs an erotic dance in an apartment where he is following up a clue. Iminu dances with a white woman and the contrasting tones of their flesh as they dance and embrace are handled with great camera art. Frosty's search for Keith Spencer even leads him to Shelly, his ex-wife, played by Jennifer Welles, where he finally finds the answer to Keith's disappearance—seems even Karen didn't know the truth. *Variety* reviewed this one "as a monumental achievement on the hardcore circuit."

EXTREME CLOSE-UP
CC NN NR BI DK
1980 CABALLERO

P/D—Aaron Lin, Charles de Santo
F/A—John C. Holmes, Jamie Gillis
F/A—Gloria Leonard, Delania Raffino, Denise
   and Diane Deneuve

Laura (Delania Raffino), a very attractive woman, is married to George (Jamie Gillis), who appears only once in this film in a very romantic, delicately photographed sexmaking sequence, which most women will enjoy watching. "I'm going to miss you," he tells her, and as she dozes she has a recurring dream of being raped near a huge estate. "If going to see Marguerite Heller (Gloria Leonard) is doing this to you," he tells her as she wakes screaming, "don't go—you don't have to." But Laura is writing a book about Marguerite, who is a famous photographer, and has invited her for the weekend to a lush country place that looks vaguely similar to the site of Laura's dream. During the next few days Laura is plunged into a sophisticated environment of erotic sexmaking and capitulates in romantic sequences on beaches and in bedrooms to Jonathan (John C. Holmes), who falls in love with her—even though he is Marguerite's lover and the perpetual house guest of an older woman. Eventually, Laura resists Jonathan's prayer that she'll run away with him, and the film concludes with her returning to George more than a little sexually and mentally confused. Over and above the story line, good editing, cinematography that has a European ambiance and sophistication lacking in many American adult films, the photography manages to make depersonalized sex (even in an extended orgy scene) not too sleazy or boring. Most women will enjoy this super-sophisticated symphony of sex.

F CC NN BI NL NR (one scene)
1979 COLLECTORS VIDEO

P/D—David Frazer, Svetlana
F/A—John Leslie
F/A—Annette Haven, Seka, Chris Anderson,
   Beckie Bitter, Kandi Barbour, Mary
   Darling, Geraldine Gold, Kassy, Rhonda
   Jo Petty, Laura Smith, Piper Smith, Ingrid
   Jenning, Andrea Paroucci

The reason I've listed the entire female cast on this one is that it should make you wonder. How you can produce a film with 13 women and one guy? Svetlana did it, and has thereby given John Leslie a legend equal to John Bunyan. John, as Cannonball, is a taxi driver. His wife is so dumb she can't even warm up a TV dinner. In his cab on his CB, he reaches a female who calls herself Dream Girl. Later, when his cab breaks down in a deserted area, he knocks on the door of a home that looks like a castle. And quickly the fantasy begins. His first encounter in the house is in a room filled with dolls, all attractive, all dressed in doll costumes. When he lifts a doll's dress he can't believe his eyes. "I never saw a doll with pubic hair." After taking care of the dolls, he wanders into a dream 1920s whorehouse. (It seems that somewhere in the house, Dream Girl, Annette Haven, is supervising his dreams and making them reality.) The brothel is occupied by Seka, Rhonda Jo Petty and Chris Anderson, who work him over very thoroughly. Next, he's at the door of a cave similiar to Ali Baba's and he finds a Golden Girl. (She's painted gold.) He finally meets another guy, David, who tells him they must be lost in a wet dream factory. Finally, John finds Annette, who gives him one last shtup before she sends him home to his wife.

FAMOUS SMOKERS Volumes I & II
each 80 minutes running time
CC NN NL
WONDERFUL WORLD OF VIDEO

Volume I includes several of the most famous stag films ever made, such as Candy Barr in *Smart Aleck*, as well as *The Payoff, Bachelor's Dream, Good Year, Sexcapade in Comic Land, The Priest* and *Fatso*. In Series II there is *The Nun, The Dentist, The Marrieds, Artist Models* and Marilyn Monroe (?) in *Appleknockers*. These two sexvids are a laughing antidote to balance any sexvid library. All accompanied by dubbed-in popular songs of the 1940s and 1950s.

FANTASEX CC NN NL DK NR
1976 COMMAND

P/D—Bud Green, Cecil Howard, Robert Norman
F/A—Jeffrey Hurst, Michael Jefferies
F/A—Terri Hall, Jennifer Jordan, Juliet Graham, Lindee Mitchell

Add this one to your shelf of sexvid classics. The title is misleading. Maybe it should have been titled *Bernie's Complaint*, since Bernie Lipshitz (Jeffrey Hurst) is a mommy's boy and strictly accountable to her after a day's work editing porno books at the Babcock Publishing Company. Mr. Crotchmeier, the owner, is a nasty character with a secretary named La Verne, who services Crotchmeier in his office. Poor Bernie and another employee, Jane (Terri Hall), a proofreader, are exposed to so much porno that they live in a fantasy land and thus compensate for their total inadequacies as sexual persons. In a funny scene, Jane reads aloud from a porno book while Crotchmeier in an inner office has La Verne on top of his desk and unknowingly acts out her words. Then Bernie is playing poker with a bunch of tough guys who are listening to a ball game at the same time—but after a day at the office Bernie can't concentrate. He becomes a character in a porno book—*Big Bart*, a Mississippi riverboat gambler enjoying the belle of New Orleans in bed. Later, at home, Mommy Lipshitz, who gets out of her wheelchair when Bernie isn't looking, is whining and complaining while poor Bernie is in the bathroom with a fantasy woman from one of the books he has read. Then, angry at Mommy, he suddenly becomes a Richard Widmark character and wheels her to the top of the stairs and gloatingly pushes her down. Next he's Buzz—a Hell's Angel, but on a bicycle instead of a motorcycle, bumping into a woman crossing the street. (He dreams that she jumps on the handlebars and he pedals off with her for some joyous sex.) Then, back at the office listening to La Verne excoriate him for not getting enough work done, he becomes a ruthless killer with a knife who strips and forces her into fellatio. Then he's a ringmaster at the circus and Crotchmeier is a clown obeying his orders. And later he daydreams about Jane, who has a mother to take care of too and her fantasies are interplayed with his as she (a famous pianist) is playing the "Hungarian Rhapsody." Finally, he has a fantasy that he has married Jane. In a canopied wedding bed they are making ecstatic romantic love, and she's telling him, "You're safe in my arms now. I'm your wife. Rest your tired head on my breast." The tape ends in reality. He tries to ask Jane for a date, stammers, can't make it and goes home to take care of Mommy. Jeffrey Hurst did an excellent acting job in this one and could have become a competitor for John Leslie.

FASTER PUSSYCAT, KILL! KILL! CC DS
1977   RM INTERNATIONAL FILMS

P/D—Russ Meyer
F/A—Dennis Busch, Stuart Lancaster, Hay Barlow
F/A—Tura Santara, Haji, Lori Williams, Linda Bernard

Russ Meyer isn't very faithful to his heroines (except for Haji and Uschi Digard, who appear in many films. Each one has a new big-breasted female who can subdue any man. In this one Varla (Tura Santara) is the tough leader of two other dead-end kids. Rosie (Haji) and Billie (Lori Williams) challenge Tommy (Hay Barlow) to a race around an improvised track in the desert in a Porsche, Triumph and an MG. Tommy has a girlfriend, Linda, who watches the action in dismay, which ends with Tommy losing the race and being literally beaten to death by Varla, who is a karate expert and breaks his back. Tying up Linda, the three of them race across the desert in one of the cars. They have discovered that a crippled old man (Stuart Lancaster) is living with his sons Kirk and the Vegetable (Dennis Busch), a big, retarded guy. The old man presumably has a large stash of cash, and Varla and the girls are determined to get it. Before they find where it is hidden (in the old guy's wheelchair), he tries to rape Linda, who by this time the girls have drugged. She's trying to escape all of them. First Varla wipes out the old man, then the Vegetable is stabbed by Rosie, but he pulls the knife out of his back and plunges it into her heart. Then Varla chases him around the yard with her Porsche until she has him up against a wall where she crushes him to death. When she tackles Kirk, she nearly kills him too, but Linda bounces a rock off her and eventually Varla is left bleeding in the desert to feed the vultures. For some reason this one was shot in black-and-white. While it is as violent as most Meyer flicks, there's not very much nudity.

FINDERS KEEPERS . . . LOVERS WEEPERS CC NM
1978   RM INTERNATIONAL FILMS

P/D—Russ Meyer
F/A—Paul Lockwood, Joey Duprez
F/A—Anne Chapman, Lavelle Roby, Jan Sinclair

Sometimes Russ Meyer gets a little mellow and produces a film in which the women are still big-breasted but are not so macho. This film has Russ Meyer's usual dollop of violence but only the men get hurt. This is the story of Paul (Paul Lockwood), who runs an expensive roadside night club. Paul is married to Kelly (Anne Chapman), but he's not performing very well in bed with her, and she knows why—he's sleeping with Claire (Lavelle Roby), who runs a high-class whorehouse. After Claire has worked Paul over she turns him over to Christina (Jan Sinclair). After a joyous turn in the sack with her "naked baby" she sends him home to Kelly. In the meantime there's a couple of bad guys who are planning to rob the club's safe, and Kelly convinces Paul that if he isn't going to "stop buzzing the brillo with every mother and daughter in town" that he should at least let her become an entertainer in his nightclub. It all ends in a violent scene in which Feeny and Cal, who are trying to open the club safe with a blowtorch, finally get Paul tied up and Claire as well. They stretch Kelly over a pool table and hump her but before they are through Paul gets loose. Even though they have a blowtorch (can't figure out why Russ didn't let them use it), he finishes them both off. He and Kelly live happily ever after.

FIONA ON FIRE CC NN NM BI DB DS with an NR ending
1978   TVX

P/D—Kenneth Schwartz
F/A—Jamie Gillis, Sam Dean

F/A—Amber Hunt, Gloria Leonard, Marlene
Willoughby

Kenneth Schwartz has proved with this
sexvid that it is possible to tell a dramatic,
totally involved mystery story with good dialogue. He uses the *Laura* plot theme and
interweaves every aspect of human sexuality from incest to S&M and a vividly
frightening rape scene on a New York
subway. You won't know the answer to
who "murdered" Fiona until the last
scenes, but in between you will see some
excellent film editing and good photography as well as top acting by Sam Dean,
who plays a black detective, and Amber
Hunt and Jamie Gillis, who do as good an
acting job as appears in many television
and Hollywood films. Worth owning.

FLESH GORDON   CC   Hard R or
X   NL (in a silly ass way)
1978   MEDIA

P/D—Howard Ziehm, William Osco, Michael
Benveniste
F/A—Jason Williams, John Hoyt, Joseph
Hudgins, William Hunt
F/A—Suzanne Fields, Candy Samples

At the Fourteenth Adult Film Convention
David Friedman ran a raffle with the winner being the one who could answer the
most of 20 or more questions about the
industry. Two questions were: What was
the biggest-budgeted X-rated film made
in the U.S.? And: Was *Flesh Gordon* originally shot with explicit sex? The answer to
the last is yes (it's not in any version available on tape) and to the first, *Flesh Gordon* beat out *Sodom and Gomorrah*,
costing over a million dollars to make.
You'll see why if you watch it. Since it precedes *Star Wars*, you'll wonder if George
Lukas didn't swipe some of the planetary
scenery. It seems that Emperor Wang The
Perverted (William Hunt), also known as
The Protuberance and His Ass Holiness, is
shooting sex rays at earth from the planet
Porno. During the bombardment everyone gets so horny that they have sex with
anyone in sight. On his way back from Ti-
bet in a Ford Tri-Motor plane (Ford actually made airplanes in the 1930s) in which

Flesh Gordon (Jason Williams) is flying
home to investigate the sex ray problem,
Flesh is sitting next to Dale Ardor (Suzanne
Fields). Then the plane is hit by the sex
rays. Even the pilot can't resist—he's
humping a stewardess as the plane goes
down. Flesh jumps out with Dale in his
arms in a parachute and they screw on
the way down. Landing near an eerie-
looking house, they are accosted by Flexi
Jackoff, who has built a spaceship
shaped like an erect putz. Of course, they
must take off immediately to save the
world from Wang. On the Planet Porno
they encounter penisauruses who spring
from the earth and try to penetrate Dale,
and they are captured by Wang's troops,
known as Dildoes. Wang covets Dale and
wants to make her his new queen. His former queen, L'Amour, is awarded to Flesh
after he survives an encounter with six female harpies who are determined to castrate him. Armed with the queen's pasties,
which have a magic power greater than
anything on Porno—including the Emperor's jewels—he places them in his
consort's vagina for safekeeping. Together, they try to destroy Wang and return the throne to Prince Precious (a gay),
who promises peace(?) on earth and
Porno when he's returned to power. It all
ends in a sequence that makes King Kong
look tame as Flesh Gordon shoots down a
monster—the God of Porno—who is bigger than King Kong, and doesn't hesitate
to strip Dale, whom he brandishes in his
clutches from the top of the castle. Dale
and Flexi finally shoot a death ray up his
ass and save the screaming Dale from a
fate worse than death, and Prince Precious pats Flesh's ass happily and tells him
he can't wait for him to come back to
Porno.

FOR RICHER FOR POORER
CC   NN   NR   BI
1979   VCX

P/D—Gerard Damiano
F/A—Richard Bolla, Bobby Astyr
F/A—Georgina Spelvin

This sexvid proves that Damiano, six years
after *Deep Throat*, is still one of the most
creative directors/producers in the adult

film industry. It is the story of a conservative, middle-class, middle-aged woman whose husband has left her for a younger woman. In fantasy he is still dominating her life and she is the kind of erotic female she has never dared to be. It's a classic that should be in every sexvid library. Most women will relate to Georgina in this one. Don't give up on sexvids until you've tried it.

FOR THE LOVE OF PLEASURE
CC NN NL NR (almost) DK BI
1979 SELECT ESSEX

P/D—Ed Brown
F/A—Jamie Gillis
F/A—Suzanne Nero, Veri Knotty, Serena

Simon Black, a down-and-out bum, steals a car, breaks into an apartment and is about to get away with the loot when a woman turns on the light, points a pistol at him and demands that he strip. Her husband arrives home. Simon gets dressed but he's still in her bedroom. What can she do? She shoots him dead. Next scene. Simon is in heaven—he thinks—and an angel in the form of Annette Haven, called Shiva, teaches him how to make love to a woman in what is perhaps the best porno sex-education sequence you've ever seen. But Simon is condemned to satisfy his lust for women and food. In the process he eats a ten-pound roast beef, holding it in his hands, enjoys a virgin and discovers that he's in a nonstop sex marathon culminating in an orgy in which five women wear him to a frazzle. "I used to love food and sex," he pleads with Shiva, "but I'm exhausted. I can't take it anymore. Get me out of heaven." To which she replies, laughing diabolically, "What makes you think this is heaven?" Beautifully filmed with bell-clear lighting, you can't help smiling occasionally at this one, especially when Jamie Gillis goes berserk in one scene and does a mad nude dance.

FOXY LADY **CC NN BI DS**
1978 CAL VISTA

P/D—Jake Matthew
F/A—John Leslie Seth Wagner, Paul Crandall

F/A—Valerie Driskell, Sandy Pinney

Clifford (John Leslie) is a gambler who is always broke but has expensive hobbies such as hang gliding. Ginger (Valerie Driskell), his wife, loves him but is angry at his spendthrift ways. But Clifford is a charmer. After a mild depression, drinking at a bar, he is picked up by one woman and happily takes on her roommate. Next day he's even better in front of the fireplace with his wife. Exhausted after their lovemaking, Valerie goes to make him a sandwich in the kitchen of their ranch house and she is kidnapped by two guys who have previously spotted Clifford and think he is rich. They are holding Valerie for $10,000 and of course rape her. When Clifford gets the ransom note, a girlfriend who suddenly appears suggests his only solution is to rob a bank—which he does. In the meantime, Ginger is not only being enjoyed by the two kidnappers but by their girlfriends as well, with the most detailed close-ups you've ever seen. Poor Ginger—she escapes the kidnappers but because she's on an island she can't get away. She is captured by a black man who promises to help her but only after she has sexually relieved him. Eventually, Clifford discovers that his girlfriend has been working with the kidnappers, but he saves his wife. You'll watch this one from beginning to end. The sexvid proves one thing: If there is sufficient conflict—this time rape and kidnapping—it's possible to hold a movie picture storyline together.

FRANKENSTEIN **CC NL (?) DK DS**
1973 VIDEO GEMS

P/D—Carlo Ponti, Paul Morrissey, Andy Warhol
F/A—Joe D'Allessandro, Udo Kier, Arno Juerging
F/A—Monique Van Vooren

If you want to take an hour-and-a-half trip into macabre, blood-spurting madness, then buy or rent this tape. Guaranteed: If you survive watching it without getting sick to your stomach (or laughing your head off at the total insanity of it)—you have never seen anything like it! Imagine, if you can, Baron Frankenstein (Udo Kier) married to his sister, Catherine (Monique Van Vooren). They have two children and they live in the Baron's castle, where he is working with Otto, his assistant, on a creature that is both male and female. They will populate the world with a whole new race of monsters who will be at the Baron's beck and call. To accomplish this he needs the head of a man who strongly craves women to attach to his new male body. With monstrous clippers he severs the head of Stasha (Joe D'Allessandro), thinking that the local farmhand is a likely candidate. But, alas, he does not know Stasha doesn't enjoy women and wants to be a monk. In the meantime, Stasha's friend, who does enjoy women, is hired by Catherine to service her in bed because the Baron no longer sleeps with her. Scene after bloody scene ensues, including the Baron having an orgasm on the bloody carcass of his female creation, and telling Otto: "If you want to know death, you have to fuck life in the gall bladder." The film is gruesome but transpires in a svelte European environment, so you don't know whether to laugh or cry. Interestingly, although this film is X-rated, there is never any genital exposure (even in the Baron's laboratory).

GOOD MORNING AND GOODBYE
CC NM
1977 RM INTERNATIONAL FILMS

P/D—Russ Meyer
F/A—Don Johnson, Stuart Lancaster, Tom Howland, Toby Adler, Patrick Wright
F/A—Alaina Capri, Haji, Karen Ciral, Sylvia Tedemar, Carol Peters

Unlike most adult filmmakers, Russ Meyers has an affinity for older men—especially when they are hooked up with young women. Perhaps he's reflecting on his own life. He was married to Eve, the co-producer of many films. It was a love marriage that ended with Eve's tragic death in a terrible airplane crash in Tenerife in 1978 in which hundreds of lives were lost. In this film, Burt Boland (Stuart Lancaster, who appears in many Meyer films and is in his late fifties) is married to Angel (Alaina Capri). Burt can't make it in bed with Al-

aina, and she's not very happy about it. Alaina is a tramp, and although Burt is very wealthy she's sleeping with everybody in the desert town. "My needs are very big, Burt. I'm not ashamed to admit it. I'm a biological freak." Alaina is not a good stepmother for Lana (Karen Ciral), Burt's daughter. The fact is that Lana hates her because she can take her boyfriend Ray (Don Johnson) away from her right before her eyes. And Alaina is also screwing the pants off the guy who owns the local sand and gravel company, Stone (Pat Wright), who is calmly screwing Herby's (Tom Howland) wife, Lottie (Megan Timothy). When Herby catches him in bed with Lottie, Stone beats him to a pulp. In the meantime Burt is consorting in the forest with a sorceress (Haji). Russ Meyer loves to introduce big-breasted women frolicking in woods who have nothing to do with reality and I'm sure he'd agree his pictures don't either. Anyway, the sorceress is restoring Burt's manhood until finally he's better than any 19 year old. Both he and Herbie nearly get tossed in Stone's stone crusher and buried in a gravel pit, but Herby kills Stone, and Burt, badly beaten but still mobile, comes home and finds Angel in bed. He teaches her a thing or two that he learned from the sorceress. From now on she'll only get under him under his roof and in his bed. No ladies are beat up in this one—so you might catch it on late-night cable or subscription television.

HAPPY DAYS **CC NN NL NR**
1976 INTERNATIONAL HOME VIDEO

P/D—Beulah Brown, Beau Buchanan
F/A—Joe O'Brien, Sonny Landham
F/A—Cindy West, Arlan Blue, Georgina Spelvin

Most women, especially if they are in their late 20s or 30s, will laugh and identify with this film. It has totally explicit sex but with *no* come shots, and *no* bisexual sequences. It belongs in any list of the top ten. It's Wayne and Debbie's twentieth-anniversary party and they've invited a group of their friends. After a few drinks they start to tell each other about their first sexual experiences or what sex was like 20 years ago. First, there's the two-couple date on a cold winter night. They are sharing a bottle. Before the guys take the girls home they try to make out in the car. In a family garage with the door closed (the engine turned off), the car radio playing 1950s songs and commercials continuously through the action, the guy in the back seat is making out fine with his gal, but the guy in the front seat is frustrated. "Gary! Stop it please! I'm not that kind of girl! I'm engaged to Tom. What'll he think? Gary, you're messing me all up. If I let you touch the tops of my breasts, is that as far as you'll go? Gary—put my panties back on. You think this is a big joke, don't you? Gary, why are you doing this? This is the first time ever. You're taking advantage of me." In the meantime, the guy in the back seat has his woman naked, and is tapping Gary on the shoulder asking if he has a "safe." The scene ends hilariously when the gal in the front seat gets her heel caught in the horn—and they can't stop it blowing. Every scene that follows is something that could have happened to you or your friends. One woman tells about her first job in a French restaurant where she fell in love with the handsome French cook who couldn't speak English. When she goes to his apartment, she uses his French dictionary and finally manages to write in French a note for him, "Je suis un virgin"—after which he is very, very gentle with her. Then there's a guy who when he was 19 bought a book, *How to Hypnotize Anyone.* After practicing on his rabbit, he tries the maid. She plays along and obeys him when he tells her, "Now, it's a pony. Climb on and take a ride." And then there's the guy who brings a kind of wild girl in high school home to his cellar while his parents are out and tries to make her on a mattress in the basement, only to hear his Grandma suddenly arriving in the midst of things. Then there's the gal who gets enamored with a leader of a rock band, who amazingly is very loving with her. Finally, there's Debbie, who married her stepbrother after she seduced him, and at this late date Wayne, her husband, reveals that her mother (Georgina Spelvin) gave him lessons in how to make a woman happy. Buy it or rent it—even if

you are not as old as I am, it will make you nostalgic.

HARD SOAP CC NN NL one almost DS scene with humorous overtones
FREEWAY

P/D—**Richard Aldrich, Bob Chinn**
F/A—**John C. Holmes**
F/A—**Candida Royalle, Laurien Dominique**

A silly, laughing satire of soap operas, complete with organ music to enhance the melodrama about poor Dr. Johnny who can't get it up with his horny wife. Most women will laugh at this sexvid, and in many scenes may identify with Candida and Laurien, who are not only physically beautiful but are also good comediennes. They should play suburban housewives more often.

THE HARRAD EXPERIMENT CC R (Nudity but no explicit sex)
1973 WIZARD

P/D—**Dennis Stevens**
F/A—**Don Johnson, James Whitmore**
F/A—**Laurie Walters, Victoria Thompson**

When I first saw *The Harrad Experiment* on screen in a Boston theater (I had not been consulted on the screenplay), I was shocked—not by the story that finally appeared in the film, although strange bits and pieces that never appeared in the novel were added, but rather by what was omitted. The movie left off sexually, at least, about halfway through the book and never dealt with the group marriage of Insix, the three young couples around whom the story of Harrad evolves. I realize now that in 1973 when the movie was made (or in 1967 when the novel was first published) that the ideas expressed in the book were, and still are, shocking to a very large percentage of Americans. The movie has never appeared on commercial television, not because of the frontal nudity (edited versions of the film exist) but because the *idea* of Harrad goes far beyond the kind of cohabitation that now exists on many college campuses: that young men and young women would live together with at least four different roommates over a two-year or four-year period without marriage but with complete physical and mental intimacy. Unlike Harrad, today's cohabitation is really a kind of trial marriage, and there is no guided Human Values course for the participants. If some daring adult filmmaker would like to make a film called *Harrad II*, I think it would reach a wide audience. In any event, at the moment, according to *Video Retailer*, this version of *The Harrad Experiment* is a college and university "cult film." It is nicely romantic and manages because of James Whitmore's good acting to convey many of the Harrad ideas.

HARRAD SUMMER **Rated PG (No explicit sex and minor frontal nudity)**
1974   WIZARD

P/D—Dennis Stevens
F/A—Bill Dana
F/A—Laurie Walters, Victoria Thompson

This sequel, which was deliberately made with PG ratings because of inability to get full theater distribution of *The Harrad Experiment* in the suburbs, bombed and was quickly withdrawn. Actually, it is a fun movie and still has the two key females, Victoria Thompson playing Beth and Laurie Walters as the perfect Sheila. The guys are not the same as in the original movie, and the story that is told does not appear in the novel. But it is a natural offshoot from the novel since the Harrad students did have summer vacations (in the novel only Stanley's was detailed). Bill Dana as Harry's father provides all the fun and reflects parental shock to the Harrad idea. The summer vacation is seen through the eyes of three very different kinds of parents and their reaction to Harrad. Sam Grove in this version is also wealthy but he's a far cry from the Sam Grove in the original novel. Dennis Stevens has a screenplay (written by me) called *The Harrad Game,* which I think is funnier than *Animal House,* but thus far no financing to make a "hard R" movie has developed.

HER NAME WAS LISA
CC   NN   NM   BI   DB   DK   DS
1979   VCA

P/D—Robert Michaels, Richard Mahler
F/A—Bobby Astyr
F/A—Samantha Fox, Vanessa Del Rio

The scary story of Lisa's (Samantha Fox) short, sleazy, squalid life begins with her nude body in a cellophane bag in the morgue. It's told in flashbacks from the funeral home where she is laid out in a coffin and is being visited by her friends Paul and Stephan. Lisa works in a massage parlor along with her friend, played by Vanessa Del Rio. Paul offers her a job posing as a model for lurid photos, which will appear in magazines published by his client, Stephan. Stephan, a crude, lascivious guy, takes Lisa away from Paul and sets her up in an apartment equipped with all the paraphernalia of bondage and discipline. During the next hour Samantha proves that she is a good actress in a film which was made long before *Babylon Pink.* As a tough, cold-hearted woman who really doesn't like men, she plays a dominatrix, handcuffing Stephan to his bed. In retaliation, he invites a couple of his friends over and they rape her, after which Stephan completes the job. Finally, Lisa, who is constantly ingesting bennies and Quaaludes, gets hooked on heroin and totally disintegrates. The seamy story is well told—but it's depressing. *Screw* listed it number two in the top flicks of 1979.

HIGH SCHOOL MEMORIES
CC   NN   NL   NR (almost)
1981   VCX

P/D—Anthony Spinelli
F/A—Jamie Gillis, John Leslie, Richard Pacheco
F/A—Annette Haven, Chris Hopkins, Dorothy Le May

This one opened in March 1981 in California at a Pussycat Theater with all the glamour of a Hollywood première. The elite of the adult film industry arrived with the engraved invitations. Told via flashbacks, it is presumably the fifth reunion of

certain people at Wahoo High School—
not the students. A former teacher, Janet
Templeton (Annette Haven), and Coach
Silenus (Jamie Gillis) were fired five years
before because of certain improprieties
on the night of the big game. Now in a
flashback, while they are sitting in a bar,
they recall the bus trip of the football
team and the cheerleaders on their way
to a nearby city where the big game will
be played. The bus ride turns into an orgy.
Coach Silenus is particularly aggravated
with Nunzio (John Leslie), one of the players who is being thoroughly worked over
by Dorothy Le May. But the plot isn't important and you never see the big game,
which gets lost in the sex shuffle. There are
six separate sexmaking sequences: one
involving Richard Pacheco, two involving
John Leslie, two featuring Jamie Gillis, and
one with Annette and the 17-year-old star
quarterback of the team. And *mirabile
dictu*—all of them are one-to-one encounters with an amazing amount of loving, caring foreplay. There is no group sex
in the flick and no bisexuality, and Jamie
Gillis who, as Coach Silenus five years before, was a typical nasty Gillis-bastard, is
now a reformed, gentle, lovable man.
When he makes love with Chris Hopkins
and Annette (if you've watched him in
hundreds of other flicks) you won't believe
your eyes. He's as gentle as a lamb. Even
Annette is amazed and early on asks him
if he has had a prefrontal lobotomy. Obviously Spinelli was aiming this film at home
audiences and he has succeeded. If you
are a woman, you'd enjoy all the males as
lovers, and if you're male, vice versa. In either case, you'll end up humming the
haunting theme song "Pages in a Book"
that accompanies all the lovemaking.

HOLISTIC MASSAGE CC R
BROADCAST QUALITY

P/D—Rachael Harris, Beverly Hinton

Watching this film, I wondered if video
can give the old human potential movement an entirely new direction. Watching
nude couples massage each other in the
privacy of your own home and learning
how to do it is not only less scary than tak-

ing your clothes off with total strangers,
but with the right couples watching it can
not only lead to emulation, but going a
step beyond to lovemaking, which this
tape does not provide. *But,* keep in mind
in the two long and detailed sequences
—one with a naked woman massaging a
naked man, and the other with a naked
man massaging a naked woman—you
are told what is happening and how to
do it in a voice-over. Even though they
stay away from each other's genital
areas, the holistic touching and integra-
tion of the masseuse and the person
being massaged is a loving experience.
With this tape you can really learn the lay-
ing on of hands, breathing with your partner in perfect rhythm and how to make a
person feel taller than he or she really is.
Essentially you learn how the doer and re-
ceiver interact, which is the basis of all
sexmaking. Worth owning.

HOT LEGS CC NN NR
1980 WONDERFUL WORLD OF VIDEO

P/A—Gail Palmer, Bob Chinn
F/A—Paul Thomas
**F/A—Jesie St. James, Laurien Dominique,
Sharon Cain**

The only concession to the raincoat
crowd in this sexvid is the male fantasy of
women in black silk stockings and garter
belts. Hot legs is the name of the nylons
which are presumably being promoted
by a multimillion-dollar advertising campaign. Beyond the silly plot, Bob Chinn
and Gail Palmer have produced a totally
female-oriented sexvid with one romantic
sexmaking sequence after another. A film
that should turn many women on—and
hopefully their lovers. If you have never
purchased a sexvid before, this is a good
one.

V—THE HOT ONE CC NN NM DK
1978 CAL VISTA

P/D—Robert McCallum
F/A—John Leslie, Paul Thomas
**F/A—Annette Haven, Laurien Dominique, Kay
Parker**

Screw listed this film as number four of the Best 10 of 1978. V—or Valerie (Annette Haven, who does an excellent acting job in this one)—is married to Paul (John Leslie) but they aren't making it together sexually. It's difficult to tell why except that as a child her mother caught Valerie showing herself to the boys and called her a whore. Now Valerie is slipping out of bed at night and cruising in sleazy areas of San Francisco and offering herself to guys in a porno theater and to a sailor for $5. Then she discovers a high-class whorehouse and becomes an 11:00 A.M. to 3:00 P.M. hooker who takes on freaks, such as a drunk who passes out on her, a school superintendent who wants to be spanked and a guy who can only do it with blue lights with a woman he calls "Mother." McCallum ends the movie with the conclusion that Valerie will never reform. And he also raises the age-old male question that goes back to Lilith and Eve: Is woman the seductress?

HOT RACKETS CC NN NM NL BI
1979 CAL VISTA

P/D—Sam Norvell, Robert McCallum
F/A—Jon Martin, Mike Fairmont, Turk Lyon
F/A—Candida Royalle, Laurien Dominique,
    Desiree Clearbranch, Chris Cassidy

A happy-go-lucky sexvid that proves that other guys besides the two Johns and a Jamie can provide a welcome change in male actors. In this one, Jon Martin is Herb Adler, a wealthy tennis addict, who isn't making it with his not-too-sexy wife, Liz (Candida Royalle). Liz soon finds that the tennis club where Herb spends all his time has a female masseuse, Laurien Dominique, and playmates like Mike Fairmont, who help relieve her of her sexual hangups. At this club they play tennis in the nude, which certainly makes it more interesting for non-professionals, at least, and they join each other in the steam room and jacuzzis and on the massage table. There's a long scene with Desiree Cousteau (formerly Clearbranch) enjoying both Martin and Fairmont and playing her Pretty Peaches role, and a funny scene in a greenhouse with Turk Lyon and Chris Cassidy, who play the role of chauffeur and maid. Surprisingly, even the group sex scene in this one, which takes place outdoors around a swimming pool, seems like healthy exercise.

THE IMMORAL MR. TEAS CC R
1959 RM INTERNATIONAL FILMS

P/D—Russ Meyer
F/A—Bill Teas
F/A—Ann Peters, Marilyn Westly, Dawn Denelle,
    Michele Roberts

According to Turan and Zito (*Sinema*), the "nudie cutie" was born in 1959, the year Russ Meyer, a one-time army combat man and cheesecake photographer, raised $24,000 and made *The Immoral Mr. Teas*, "the most notorious and erotic film released in the United States until Grove Press put *I Am Curious Yellow* on the market in 1968." The film made Russ Meyer a millionaire. Nearly thirty years later, even though there is no explicit sex and the ladies you see naked reveal only "T and A," you will probably never see this film on commercial television, but it will obviously be a staple on late shows on cable and subscription TV. It is typical "nudie" fare—and actually funnier than many of the current cable offerings. Cleverly produced (French style?), the film star is Mr. Teas, a bachelor and deliveryman for a dental supply house who lives on Cantlay Street somewhere in Los Angeles. Although his actions and thoughts are accompanied by sexy accordion music and there is a voice-over commiserating with him and the state of the world, neither Mr. Teas's voice nor the voices of any of the actors are ever heard. Quite simply, Mr. Teas needs a woman. But he never gets to touch female flesh. His life is filled with daydreams of women undressing. He can't keep his eyes off women—even clothed—and as he watches their deep cleavages or their asses in motion, he sees them—and so does the viewer—delectably naked. As the picture progresses, his ability to see women naked improves. Finally, using this gimmick in the year 1959, Russ Meyer treated male audiences to more female nudity than had ever appeared in any U.S. motion picture. Single-handedly, Russ had, in his words, "filled a vacuum" and created a new industry that has produced many thousands of films that make *The Immoral Mr. Teas* a little dated—one step ahead of *September Morn*. But it's still a collector's item. An interesting sequel could be made using the same format and letting the *Son of Mr. Teas* go all the way with his fantasies, but hopefully as "genteely" as his daddy.

IN LOVE CC NN NR
1983 VCA

P/D—Chuck Vincent
F/A—Jerry Butler, Michael Knight, Michael Bruce
F/A—Kelly Nichols, Tish Ambrose, Johanna Storm, Samantha Fox, Veronica Hart

With this film Chuck Vincent has set the pace for all Hollywood filmmakers, who I predict in the next few years will test the general "hard R" or X market and offer lovemaking which reveals an erect penis and a happily receptive vulva. Since Playboy collaborated in the $750,000 financing—making this film one of the most expensive adult films ever made—it will no doubt appear on the Playboy Channel in a soft core version. But this is one adult film that, male or female, you will enjoy uncut. So rent or buy the video tape. If you are a film aficionado, you will also enjoy another first: Frederick Fell Publishers, Inc., 386 Park Avenue South, New York, NY 10016, is offering a complete illustrated screenplay of the film for $8.95. You may enjoy following it the first time you watch the tape and you will surely watch it more than once. The editing is slick, and fast, and in some sections without the actual screenplay in front of you you may not get all the nuances of what is happening. This is the story of Andy Whitman (Jerry Butler), who works for his wife's father's fast-food franchise, Jiffy Hamburgers. Andy is traveling around the country peddling the franchises. Ron Sullivan and Bob Sumner, both producers of their own adult films, play the parts of two fast-buck dealers with great gusto to whom Andy makes his first sale. The time is 1962, and it begins

in Key Largo in a beachfront bar. Jill Travis (Kelly Nichols) walks out of the bar after drinking too much and is nearly raped by two kids. Andy rescues her. Although he is married to Melinda (Veronica Hart), the boss's daughter, he is overwhelmed by Jill, and she can't resist him either. Their lovemaking in different environments not only shows time passing but is photographed with loving warmth in one sequence after another and they even tell each other about their first sexual experience. Andy is so much in love with Jill that he tells her that he is going back to New York and ask Melinda for a divorce. Jill, who has the same deep attraction (obsession) for him, refuses to let him ruin his marriage. For the next twenty years, the film pursues separate events in both of their lives. They have other lovers but they never forget each other. In many scenes when they are making love, Jill's or Andy's actual lover is replaced in clever cinematic transpositions by the one they never can forget. Andy's marriage to Melinda finally collapses at a New Year's Eve party. He is seduced by Elaine (Samantha Fox) in a bedroom of the penthouse at the stroke of midnight. Melinda, who is now pregnant, is desperately searching for him and is aware of what he has been doing. As a result his father-in-law fires him as Vice President of Jiffy Hamburgers. A few years later, broke, and living in a seamy part of town, Andy offers a hooker ten dollars for love—all he gets is a disinterested ten minutes during which the hooker reads *Cosmopolitan* and ignores him when he can't get it up. In the meantime—it's now the late 1960s and early 1970s—Jill has given up supporting a bearded country folk singer who can't sing and is secretly screwing her best friend. Jill joins a hippie commune in California; Roland, the leader of the group, takes her on an acid trip which is frighteningly realistic. She is blamed for the death of a male friend who is also on LSD and goes to prison, where she writes the story of her love for Andy, and it becomes a best seller. In the meantime, Andy has started his own restaurant chain and is now a millionaire. In the last scene they find each other, and you know they are going to live happily ever after. The plot is right out of Judith

Krantz, or Sidney Sheldon, or your favorite soap opera, but the dialogue, the character development and the very realistic sex scenes integrate the sex drives of Jill and Andy. The camera lingers on their faces while they are making love much more than on their genitals, and their conversation reveals the kind of people they really are. For the first time in an adult film, Chuck Vincent creates a real empathy between the viewer, male or female, and the actors—especially Jerry Butler and Kelly Nichols, who can act as well as or better than many of their "legitimate" Hollywood peers. Hopefully this film is not one of a kind but reflects the long-awaited "new wave" of adult films.

INSATIABLE
CC NN NM BI NR (occasionally)
1980 EROS

P/D—**Godfrey Daniels**
F/A—**John Leslie, Mike Ranger, David Morris, John Holmes, Richard Pacheco**
F/A—**Marilyn Chambers, Jesie St. James, Serena, Joan Turner**

Insatiable has probably been the largest-selling adult film on video cassettes during the past two years. At the Consumer Electronic Show in Las Vegas for two years (and at the Summer Show in Chicago), long lines of men wait to get Marilyn's autograph on a full-color picture of herself, mostly naked, at the Eros, King of Video, booth. Fair warning! While I have given it a CC rating my feeling is that most women won't identify with Marilyn. Read the title of the film again. Marilyn is *insatiable*. All she wants to do is have sex. If most women feel the same way, they won't admit it to anyone. Also, Marilyn is a happy masochist. See the *Never a Tender Moment* listing (p. 299). There is no plot to this film, but there is much wealthy ambiance and background cinematography in London and on an English estate to which Marilyn (as Sandra Chase, a famous model who was wealthy even before she was a model) flies to England with her friend and agent Flo (Jesie St. James). There they are met by Aunt Victoria and

Sandra, who is seeking a more private way of life away from the madding crowd, and tells Flo that all she really wants in life is a man who can keep up with her sexual appetite. Driving her Ferrari, she picks up a guy who ran out of gas, and she not only shows him how to siphon it out of her tank by sucking a rubber hose, but although she's never seen him before, before she's finished she fellates him. Finally, when Roger Renee (John Leslie) arrives—he's going to make a film with Sandra—you're sure that he'll be Sandra's soulmate—but surprise! He's in love with Flo and while he's making very romantic love to her on the veranda of the beautiful English country estate, Sandra (Marilyn) is masturbating upstairs in the bedroom fantasizing about John C.

ITALIAN STALLION
CC NN BI DK DS
1970 WONDERFUL WORLD OF VIDEO

P/D—**Morton Lewis; editing Gail Palmer**
F/A—**Sylvester Stallone, Nicholas Warren, Frank Micelli**
F/A—**Henrietta Holm, Jodi Van Prang, Barbara Strom**

Any woman who has empathized with Rocky (Sylvester Stallone) in his various movies and would like to see how he acts as a lover will enjoy this movie. While you see Stud (as Stallone is called in this sexvid) naked, and you see him making love with Kitty (Henrietta Holm) as well as with a beautiful black woman and several other white women—you never see him erect. Otherwise, as Gail Palmer, who introduces this version tells you, if you are not accustomed to watching naked people making love, you better leave the theater. Gail puts the date of this film as 1970, and tells the story that for his performance Sylvester got $200. What she doesn't tell you is that this version has a copyright date of 1978. It would be interesting to see the original version, what she edited out—and how she got her hands on the film. The characterization of Stud is similar to Rocky. He is a loving guy who is frustrated by life and as Stud by his own driving sexuality. Even though Kitty takes very good care of him and she's happy when he drops the soap in a shower so that "I can get closer to my favorite part of his body." Nevertheless, when Stud is flashed in the park by a naked woman wearing a fur coat, he can't get her out of his mind. In desperation, he smashes a window and cuts his hand so that it is bleeding. The film ends with a long, very erotic nude dance done by a black woman at a small party where three couples are smoking joints. Everyone is eventually having sex with everyone else but for some reason the extended scene is happily naive and interesting to watch. Stallone presumably tried to stop this film from being shown. My feeling is that most women who like his style would be happy to see him follow through and be an all-around naked lover in his Rocky movies. Maybe he'll do it in *Rocky IV!*

LAST TANGO IN PARIS **NR DK**
VIDAMERICA

P/D—Bernard Bertolucci
F/A—Marlon Brando, Jean Pierre Leaud
F/A—Maria Schneider

Still rated X, and not likely to be shown on commercial television or many subscription services without cuts, *Last Tango* is a breakthrough movie that's worth owning on tape to study Bertolucci's film technique, which plunges you into the middle of things and lets you slowly discover the characters and events as the action develops. And you will be intrigued by the dialogue, which is often gripping, gruesome and shocking. Excellently acted by Brando and Schneider, the sex scenes, including the famous one where Brando butters Schneider's ass to humiliate her with anal sex, and even the four-letter words are mild by current standards. But they were standing-in-line shocking less than a decade ago when this film was released. I predict this will happen to many of the adult films reviewed here. The story line of a 45-year-old American who is married to a Frenchwoman, Rose, who had a lover and committed suicide a few minutes before the film begins, and who seeks surcease from his sorrow and confusion with a 20-year-old woman whom he

dominates, is just as unbelievable as many current adult films, but the acting and dialogue will make you forget that a young woman "without a name" would come back for more with an older guy who doesn't want her to know his name either.

LEGEND OF LADY BLUE
CC NN NR some DK
Bi in which the lead actress does not participate
1979 TVX

P/D—John Brown, A. Fabrizzi
F/A—John Leslie
F/A—Maureen Spring, Gloria Leonard

Best Film 1979, Third Annual Erotic Film Awards. Best Screen Play, Best Costumes, Best Film Editing. *Screw* dissented because of the romantic elements, which did not produce the appropriate arousal. Even in the conventional orgy scene, which takes place in a barracks in Vietnam, the erotic elements are well handled and very interesting. All women (and hopefully many men) will empathize with the scenes of young love between Chris and Casey, and many years later his love for her, which is strong enough to rescue her from a hooker's palace. Maureen Spring is a simpatico female—not beautiful, but human. Most men and women will identify with her.

LICKERISH QUARTET **CC NN NR**
1972 HIGHBRIDGE ENTERTAINMENT and VIDAMERICA

P/D—Radley Metzger a.k.a. Henri Paris
F/A—Frank Wolf, Paolo Turco
F/A—Erika Remberg

This one has a commercial R rating. It's a four-character drama. You'll understand this sexvid better if you look up lickerish in Webster's. A little-used word today it encapsulates human sexuality somewhere between lust and lechery. It begins very erotically in an Italian chateau where a wealthy, lickerish family threesome are watching porno films. Later they believe they identify one of the female actors, who is now riding a motorcycle in a local carnival daredevil show. She goes back to the chateau with them, completes the quartet, and has very erotic sex separately with the father, mother and son during which they all search for their identity as human beings. A great film—worth owning.

LITTLE ORPHAN DUSTY   **CC   DS   NR**
(a little)
1976   TVX

P/D—Jaacov Jaacovi, Bob Chinn
F/A—John Holmes, Turk Lyon
F/A—Rhonda Jo Petty

Best Actress, 1977 Erotic Film Award, *Screw's* Best 10 for 1977 (#10). If you are male and wish to test your sexual arousal to rape scenes, this sexvid provides you with three separate sequences—one with a motorcycle gang that takes on Rhonda Jo Petty. They later try again with her and two other women. The weird NR rating is a counterpoint to the rape scenes: John Holmes tells Rhonda Jo that he loves her and wants to marry her even though she's pregnant by the rapists.

LORNA   **CC   DS**
1959   F.M. INTERNATIONAL FILMS

P/D—Eve Meyer, Russ Meyer
F/A—Hal Hopper, Mark Bradley, James Rucker, Doc Scott, Franklin Bolger, James Griffith
F/A—Lorna Maitland, Althea Currier

After his very successful *The Immoral Mr. Teas,* Russ Meyer produced a few films, such as *Eve and the Handyman* and *Erotica,* which weren't on target. Then, in *Lorna,* which is almost a PG-rated film by today's standards, he made his first blend of sex and violence. Incidentally, Russ would prefer that all his films carry an X rating, but the world has caught up with him. Quite a few of them in the 1980s would not. On the other hand, because other of Russ's X-rated films probably came into focus when he shot *Lorna,* this film should not be missed. It was shot in black-and-white. There is relatively little nudity in the film. The story is about Lorna, who has been married to Jim for a year, living with him in a back-river shack where he works in a salt mine along with a couple of unsavory characters who are constantly impugning Lorna's morality and suggesting to Jim that she's screwing all day long with unknown lovers—which, in fact she is. There is one at least, a guy who has just escaped from prison. He discovers Lorna bathing in the river and quickly proves to her what she has been missing sexually with Jim for the past year. Russ described the movie as a "primitive work of art in which black is black and white is white and there is no shading or distortion." To point up his moral, an evangelist preacher pops into the action several times and predicts the terrible ending. In almost all of his later films there is a big-breasted woman explaining the events or laughing at the silliness of the performers. Interestingly, Russ ran an advertisement in *Variety* for a big-breasted woman to play the part of Lorna. Lorna Maitland was one of 134 women who tried out for the part! Whatever happened to her?

THE LOVE TAPES   **CC   NN   DK**
(depending on your own
conditionings)
1980   BLUE VIDEO

A Robert Lynn Production
F/A—C. More Ashley, Ron Hudd
F/A—Merle Michaels, Denise Sloan, Marlene Willoughby

They are in two volumes—two two-hour tapes which are only sold together. Current retail price is approximately $150. They are also available as eight separate half-hour tapes. I can't imagine buying them this way. They cover Foreplay, Positions, Masturbation, Oralism, Analism, Dominant Female, Threesome and Swinging. Nicely photographed, with background music and a sexy female voice-over with a British accent. With the sound turned down she will light up your bedroom while you do it yourself—instead of watching.

LOVE YOU **CC NN NR BI DK**
1980 CABALLERO

P/D—John Derek
F/A—Wade Nichols, Rob Everett
F/A—Annette Haven, Leslie Bovee

John Derek, husband of the famous Bo, proves with this film that a small cast, good dialogue, and superb cinematography can create a totally erotic film. Buy it or rent it. You're not likely ever to see it on cable TV. Annette, as Charlie, is married to Steve (Wade Nichols). Leslie Bovee, as Lynn, is married to Mark (Rob Everett). They are all nice people, but Lynn is more sexually amorphous than Charlie or Steve. Along with Steve, Lynn has promoted a weekend where a helicopter will land them on an otherwise inaccessible island off California's coast. The object of the weekend is to act out Steve and Lynn's fantasies of spouse exchange. Charlie is very frightened by the idea but is pushed into a situation where Mark will make love to her while Lynn and Steve are also caressing her. Charlie is so responsive that before the evening is over Steve is very jealous of his wife, and although he instigated the weekend, he is shocked, particularly when the next morning Charlie tells him she loves him and he tells her that he loves her, too. The following night, after deciding that they are probably all insane, and after a warm, funny discussion of their insanity on the beach, they return the favor and this time Mark makes love to Lynn with Steve and Charlie cooperating. Gradually, as they accept their insanity, they end up discussing whether the ladies can tell who their male partner is. Blindfolded, they discover that they can't. While I have given this a DK rating for group sex, the total ambiance of the film is loving and caring, and Annette climaxing with the camera on her face is beautifully done.

MARILYN AND THE SENATOR
CC NN NL BI DK (but laughing)
1979 HIFCOA

P/D—Carlos Tobalina
F/A—William Margold
F/A—Nina Fause, Diana St. Clair

U.S. Senator John Wolfe (William Margold, who occasionally looks enough like one of the Kennedys to be related to the family) is married to Mildred (Diane St. Clair). Although his wife is practically a nymphomaniac in bed, he also has Nancy (Sharon Thorpe), a Washington D.C. hooker, on the side. Marilyn Susan Right (Nina Fause, one of the few really blonde porno stars) wants the senator to be the father of her child. The senator is happy to oblige. In the meantime, while his assistant, Queep, is videotaping him in the Watergate Hotel where he has his rendezvous, Nancy tries to fluff him up for Marilyn. With a Washington D.C. background, much silly but funny dialogue, appropriate military and patriotic musical backgrounds and sharp cinematography, this is a tape worth owning or renting. Most women will laugh at the cool sophistication of the senator's three women who all give him quite a workout. Eventually they find out why he goes limp with Marilyn (really he does, the camera proves it over and over again): he's turned off by the idea of having a child. And of course it ends up with all three women confronting him with the horrible truth. They're all pregnant, *by him*—and you're sure that from now on they have more in common with each other than with the Senator.

MEMORIES WITHIN MISS AGGIE
CC NN NR NM
1974 ARROW and HOME LIBRARY and VIDEO-X and SELECT/ESSEX

P/D—Gerard Damiano
F/A—Eric Edwards, Harry Reems
F/A—Deborah Ashira, Kim Pope, Darby Lloyd
    Raines

If you've never seen this one, you've missed a sexvid classic, and in my opinion, Damiano's best film. You'll enjoy comparing it to Ingmar Bergman's films or Edith Wharton's famous novel *Ethan Fromme,* which it parallels in a bleak way. Superb acting, casting, dialogue and cinematography. The time of the story is probably the 1930s. The place is probably New England or a midwestern town. You meet Miss Aggie telling Richard, a strange man who lives with her in an isolated farmhouse, that when she was young she had spark-ling eyes—like a princess. "I was real blonde, and had scarcely ever seen a man then." Richard, whose face you don't see until the end, tells her she was never blonde. Aggie's memories are really her daydreams. In them she's not a lonely, homely spinster, but a sex-driven, beau-tiful woman (portrayed by other ac-tresses). Gradually you discover how Rich-ard came into Aggie's life. And finally, in a horrifying scene, you learn that she kept him prisoner by stabbing him in the eyes the night she almost, but didn't dare, sur-render to him—not because he was chasing her but because he was leaving her for good in the morning. Aggie's memories are revealed in explicit sexual detail in romantic sequences and in a masturbation scene that will bring tears to your eyes. This is a woman's film that you're not likely to see in adult theaters. Buy it!

MIDNIGHT BLUE CC DK some NL
1980 VIDEO-X-PIX

P/D—Al Goldstein

These are scenes from Al Goldstein's tele-vision show, *Midnight Blue* (cable TV), which they didn't dare run on cable. It in-cludes a long section with the woman who set a new world's record—not yet re-ported in Guinness—by bringing 83 guys to orgasm in one night at Plato's Retreat. A gymnastic married couple will also aston-ish you with their sexual positions. There is a Santa Claus episode and a short story with Samantha Fox and Bobby Astyr (who have cohabited for years anyway) in a funny sequence, "I Gave at the Office." A Christmas present for those who have everything!

MEMPHIS CATHOUSE BLUES
CC NN BI NR NL (occasionally)
1982 CABALLERO

P/D—Elliot Lewis, Louie Lewis
F/A—Michael Morrison, Mike Horner, Jon Martin, Herschel Savage, Joey Civera
F/A—Annette Haven, Lisa de Leeuw, Rhonda Jo Petty, Dorothy Le May, Danielle and Kimberly

All of the ladies listed above live in a cat-house in Memphis that has been in bus-iness for more than a hundred years. Mavis (Annette Haven), who runs the place, says, "My mother was a hooker and my grandmother was the best piece of ass in the Civil War." Unfortunately, Rever-end Nobel Pickett is trying to rouse the town against the place and put it out of business. His problem is that Mavis has been sleeping with the local sheriff (Mike Horner) for six years and her girls are very nice to some of the best male citizens in town. The action is better than you will see in the movie *Best Little Whorehouse in Texas,* but many ladies will not be happy with the nonstop sex that Mavis provides her customers. Not only do they seduce the assistants of the minister, but the guys end up praying for the girls as they plunge into them and sing "Glory, Glory Hallelujah" when they come. Mavis teaches a new girl (Danielle) how to give the sheriff fellatio. The girl has been nearly raped by someone in the town (guess who), but she does love fellatio: "It tastes like a warmsicle instead of a popsicle." When it becomes apparent that a re-straining order is going to be issued against "The Feline Farm," the sheriff tells Mavis that he has always loved her and since she has slept only with him for the past six years, she should marry him. At the wedding everything turns out okay as Danielle recognizes Reverend Pritchett—he was the guy who almost raped her, of course—and Mavis and the sheriff live happily ever after with the lucrative busi-ness still operating.

MIDNIGHT HEAT
CC NN NM BI DK
1983 VCA

P/D—Robert Michaels, Richard Mahler
F/A—Jamie Gillis, Howard Feline
F/A—Cheri Champagne, Sharon Mitchell, Susan Nero, Joey Carson, Tish Ambrose

For the first 20 minutes of this film, you be-come totally involved in trying to grasp the atmosphere and figure out what is happening. Much of the outside world that Jamie Gillis watches from his apartment and a seedy hotel in the Bowery is filmed in watercolor-style, slow motion. You wonder who this man is, who tells a character: "I am Lazarus, come back from the dead," and mentions in passing T. S. Eliot's "Hollow Men." All you know about the character—he is nameless—is that he must be a low-level hit man. In the very beginning, he walks into a business office and shoots a man, who evidently knows him, with a .45 caliber revolver. Immediately afterwards, he goes to a woman's apartment and while he is coolly fucking her, the door opens. You know he is going to be caught. But unexpectedly the guy, who you know must be out to get him for the murder, walks into the room. Just after Jamie climaxes, the man grabs him, kisses him on the lips, and tells him coldly, "I'll be seeing you in the streets." Jamie, who has a wife (Sharon Mitchell), is constantly staring out of windows. "What's so interesting out there?" she demands. And then she tells him, "Honey, I'm leaving you. You are a cold, remote man. You never let anyone get close to you." After hiring two women from an escort service, he insists they perform for him in his run-down hotel room while he watches. Later, watching the street traffic below, Jamie tells one of them to stay for the night. Some very fascinating dialogue occurs between them. After examining his revolver, she asks him, "Do you ever think about the people you kill?" He tells her that he does and that he's caught up in his own fantasy of "living on the edge." She tells him that she wants affection more than sex, "someone who really likes her." Later he tells her that "only a person in constant terror of annihilation can experience life the way it should be experienced." He asks her, "Would you kill me if I asked you to?" When she declines he asks her, "If I paid you?" Then while he's screwing her doggy-style, he asks her, "Someone sent you here, didn't they?" She nods affirmatively into the camera and he strangles her with his belt. You never see her face while he rides her and tightens the belt. Alone with her body as the film ends, he's once again staring out the window. Jamie Gillis proves with this one that he's a fine actor and can portray a tormented man. He should get the AFAA

award for Best Actor in 1983, but it's unlikely because this film will give the raincoat crowd the cold shudders. It's worth watching as a tour de force by a producer and director who dare to try something new.

THE MISS NUDE AMERICA CONTEST AND THE MR. NUDE AMERICA CONTEST CC (Nudity—no explicit sex)
1975 WIZARD

P/D—James Blake
F/A—Dick Drost, owner of Naked City; Cheryl, his mistress; his mother, Edith; his father; judges (one of whom was Harry Reems); hundreds of contestants; and thousands of visitors

The entire 78 minutes of this one were filmed at Naked City (Roselawn, Indiana). Unlike *Nudes-a-Poppin* (see listing p. 112), which concentrates on another event, The Nude Miss Galaxy Contest, this film is a composite shot over a period of one year—including winter at Naked City. While the beauty contest (1975) concludes the tape, it is very well edited and is a fascinating story of Dick Drost's life. He appears constantly through the film in an electric wheelchair. At about six years old he had muscular dystrophy. "I went to grammar school and partway through high school," he says. Then, it was impossible for him to walk. He never went to parties. But finally, as a young man, he convinced his parents that he'd like to visit a nearby nudist camp, "which was pretty run down." The family saved and skimped and finally bought it and it became the famous Naked City, located right in the middle of the Bible Belt. Today, it has 300 acres, an Olympic-sized swimming pool, a heart-shaped lake and several million-dollar buildings designed for playing together naked. Mother Edith is interviewed and tells how they really don't make a lot of money. Cash flow is negligible in the winter. You see the family, including Cheryl, Dick's mistress, eating alone on a cold winter night. Cheryl is bisexual but she loves Dick and he satisfies her in bed and that, according to her, is something because although she was brought up Catholic and was supposed to be a nun, she's really a nymphomaniac. Cheryl bathes Dick and helps him in and out of bed, but Dick admits that his contracts with employees (and presumably female contestants in the nude contest) state that they will be available to him sexually if he so desires. Drost admits that he'd like to be president, or preferably a king or emperor, but he'll be happy if he lives to franchise Naked City. There are interesting scenes between Drost and Hare Krishnas, during which Drost tells them he'll be happy to buy and read their literature if they'll read his. They tell him he's "agitating the male mind." With his father, who is drinking too much, Dick admits that although they are financially successful, he is not really happy at Naked City—or with his father. Harry Reems appears as one of the judges, and Dick keeps trying to contact Hugh Hefner, who he claims does not like him largely because they are so much alike. A very interesting exploration into a man who is definitely a survivor— even though as Harry Reems says, is "egomaniacal," and not at all sure of where he is going.

MISS SEPTEMBER (WHATEVER HAPPENED TO HER?)
CC   NM   NR   DK
1973   HOME ENTERTAINMENT

P/D—**Jerry Deney**
F/A—**Nick Harley, Ultra Max, Eric Edwards, Marc Stevens, Jason Russell**
F/A—**Tina Russell, Helen Madigan, Kathy May**

Tina Russell died on May 18, 1981. She was 30 years old. Eroded by cancer, she weighed only 75 pounds. Had she lived and continued in the business she probably would have been one of the top stars for many years to come. Tina wrote two books, one on the male and female sex organs, and another titled, *Porno Stars,* published by Pinnacle, which evoked much of her philosophy. She was married to Jason Russell for many years in a sexually open marriage. "My husband Jason and I often shared our love with another female or male or couple. But it was always a spontaneous interaction with close friends, and not a planned party. . . . I am an insecure person and cannot trust many people fully enough to abandon myself to them. As a result I have always preferred a one-to-one relationship," she wrote. Although Tina made more than 100 films, she refused to do S&M sex, sex with children or animals, or anal sex. "I have spent much of my life searching for the transcendental orgasm . . . but it has been a search for quality through selectivity . . . not quantity. . . . A transcendental orgasm is totally and completely letting go. You are completely with yourself, your orgasm and your partner." With that background you can add this tape to the top 25 adult films produced in the past ten years. The search for Barbie Handleton, a sensitive, very loving, highly sexual college graduate who poses for a nude photo in *Town House* magazine, is instigated by a wealthy man who falls in love with her picture. As played by Tina, you have the feeling in her scenes with Eric Edwards, Marc Stevens, a Latin lover, and even a bisexual scene with Helen Madigan, that Tina is not only a good actress but is very much being herself. The story is intriguingly told. Harris Keyes (Nick Harley) is employed by a Mr. Forbes to locate Barbie. Wherever she may be, and whatever she may have done, Forbes doesn't care. He wants her. The price to find her and bring her to Forbes is $50,000—and for Barbie, wealth and a wedding ring. As Harris conducts the search and interviews her various lovers he discovers that despite himself, he too is falling in love with her. The kind of person she may be is revealed in stories that various males and one female tell about her. In the process, although the director didn't relate Tina's actual life, you'll have a feeling that Barbie/Tina are very much one and the same kind of person. Both men and women viewers will like her. The story ends with an orgy scene—but interestingly, the four couples involved never play switchies or get in daisy chains, but have sex with only one other person in the group environment. Obviously, later filmmakers have played one-upmanship and gone all out in later endeavors along this line. The story ends with a "beginning" as Harris drives off into the night with Barbie after telling Forbes, "Don't call me, anymore. I'll call you." And *mirabile dictu*—you never see Harris and Barbie in the sack.

THE MISTRESS   **CC   NN   NR**
1983   CAL VISTA

P/D—**Jack Remy**
F/A—**Eric Edwards, Randy West, Richard Pacheco**
F/A—**Kelly Nichols, Anne Turner, Susan Key, Brooke West**

Karen Richards (Kelly Nichols) works for Lampert Associates, a high-powered New York company whose chief, Carl Reese (Eric Edwards), is married, with children, but enjoys lunchtime and occasional weeknights in the sack with Karen. Karen is also involved with Paul Summers (Randy West), who is wealthy and married to Ellen. She previously traveled a lot (leaving time for other ladies in Paul's life), and has now accepted a job with Lampert Associates, which means that Paul is going to have less time for Karen. Both guys are first-class egotists who give Karen the impression that she's the best thing in their lives, but they keep an eye on the clock when they are with her to make sure they get home to their wives on time. Carl is the worst. He not only goes to bed with Karen but sets her to secure accounts for him by being sexually available to some of his key male clients. Poor Karen—all her friends tell her to stop being a patsy for married men, but she is a loving person, the kind who might have a not too demanding lifetime affair with some married guy, if he had only been reasonably fair with her. The film spends most of its time following Karen to bed with either Carl or Randy. Karen occasionally reflects on her own insanity. "All I really wanted was for Carl to want me," or "There wasn't anything I wouldn't do for Paul." While Karen's motivations could have been better developed, this film is far superior to most adult films. There is no bi-sexuality. The "come" scenes are few and not prolonged. And the lovemaking is erotic and quite believable—almost as if there were no cam-

eras watching. Kelly Nichols is plumper than she was in *In Love* (see listing) and proves that she's an actress that many women can empathize with. And there may be women like Karen in the world—who are unwilling "to make the commitment" that a single guy would ask. Bring it home to your wife or lady friend and get her reaction.

MONDO TOPLESS   **CC   R**
1976   RM INTERNATIONAL FILMS

P/D—**Russ Meyer**
F/A—**Babette Bardot, Sin Lenee, Donna X, Pat Barringer, Darla Paris, Darlene Grey, Veronique Gabriel, Denise Duval, Anudavita, Heidi Richte, Gigi La Touche, Yvette La Grand, Lorna Maitland**

When I was a young man in college one subject that often came up in bull sessions was whether one was a "tits man" or an "ass man." This was long before Hugh Hefner finally, in the 1950s, convinced the world that U.S. males were breast-oriented. In protest I wrote a novel, *That Girl From Boston*, in which the female heroine, who is always wearing skin-tight jeans, has the most beautiful behind a male ever set eyes on. Russ Meyer makes his preference for breasts—big ones—apparent in this one-hour tape. He is your voice-over tour guide, and he takes you on his "big boobie" expedition from San Francisco to Paris, Copenhagen, and Germany to see the breasts of all the ladies listed above in motion. The lovely ladies give you many little "tit-bits" about their lives: "I can't find a bathing suit to fit me." "I guess I'm an exhibitionist—I enjoy being looked at and appreciated." "I don't wear a brassiere but I try to project a childlike innocence." And one lady tells you she requires a size 38 DD bra. Women with "cup cakes" won't like this film. And guys who are into bottomless females will be disappointed since Russ's interest is in topless naked ladies.

MS. DON JUAN   **CC   R   BI**
1975   WIZARD

P/D—**Roger Vadim**

F/A—Brigitte Bardot, Michelle Sand, Jane Birkin
F/A—Robert Hossein, Robert Walker, Jr.

Joan (Brigitte Bardot) believes she is a female reincarnation of the famous Don Juan, who died over four centuries ago after a lifetime of seducing and betraying women. The reason I have included this R-rated film (you can probably catch it on cable or subscription TV and Brigitte only appears naked a couple of times) is that the subject matter is very close to many X-rated films which star actresses like Seka, Juliet Anderson and many others who portray the dominating seductive females in adult films. The big difference is that Bardot does it with dialogue and facial expression rather than T and A—although, of course, these are basically her offerings to the men who fall under her spell. "Seducing is easier," she informs a female friend. "Conquering is more difficult." Her first conquest is the young priest to whom she is asking absolution for her crimes (not really—he's her cousin and she's hell-bent to seduce him) and to whom she recounts some of her conquests. They include Pierre Gossard (Robert Hossein), a very macho man who is married. She finally entraps him and leads to his destruction, which begins when he is photographed naked at a masked ball she has arranged. The pictures of him, a famous lawyer, are published in the scandal sheets and ruin his career and marriage. Next she takes on Louis, who is married for the third time to a very beautiful, much younger woman, Claire (Jane Birkin). Louis is vastly wealthy and extremely macho. He tells her, "Some day I'll devour you. I love French cooking." But she masticates him by arranging for him to catch her in bed making love with his wife. Then when he proposes a threesome, she coolly rejects him, although he wants her more than his wife. He beats her face with his hands. She's bleeding but she does not capitulate. Finally, while Pierre, now a drunk, is still shadowing her (she refuses to speak to him), she takes a young guitarist (played by Robert Walker, Jr.) in a nightclub. After a night with her, realizing the hopelessness of his love, he cuts his wrists with a broken wine glass and bleeds to death. It all ends unhappily with Joan seducing the priest and then being burned to death by Pierre. At the last minute she shoves him out the window and saves his life. In an inferno of lighted gasoline she's burned to a crisp and he's buried in the sand by bulldozers.

MUDHONEY CC NR DS
1976 RM INTERNATIONAL FILMS

P/D—Russ Meyer
F/A—Hal Hopper, John Furlong, Stu Lancaster, Frank Bolger, Nick Wolcuff, Sam Hanna, Mickey Foxx
F/A—Antoinette Christiani, Rena Horton, Lee Ballard, Lorna Maitland

The time frame on this one is about 1943. Prohibition is still in effect. Maggy Marie (Princess Livingston) is a toothless lady who looks like a living incarnation of Mammie Yokum. She has two daughters: Eula (Rena Horton), who is deaf and dumb with big breasts, and Clarabelle (Lorna Maitland), who takes care of the local yokels from Spooner, Missouri, for 25¢ and $1—while Mommy Maggy Marie sells them moonshine. Her best customer is Sidney Brenshaw (Hal Hopper, who looks like Leroy Brown of later years, and who is undoubtedly the meanest man in town). Sidney is married to Hannah (Antoinette Christiani) but he doesn't just make love to her—he comes home drunk and rapes her. Meanwhile, a handsome guy named Calif McKinney (John Furlong) has just gotten out of jail after five years for manslaughter. He didn't mean to kill the guy—and now he won't fight anybody including Sidney, who beats him up regularly and knows that Calif is in love with Hannah. But they are very moral people. Although Uncle Luke, who owns the farm that supports both Hannah and Sidney, encourages Calif to take over (Luke knows he's going to die of a heart attack) they both realize that Hannah is married. She must be faithful to Sidney. Sidney makes friends with Brother Hanson, an illiterate preacher, screws Eula (everyone takes a crack of Eula, who is beautiful, loving and speechless!) and enrages the town against the goings-on at the Wade farm, where Sidney tells everyone that Calif is horny for his wife. Uncle Luke, who has left all his money to Calif so that he can take care of Hannah, dies of a heart attack. Only Russ Meyer could figure out a graveyard scene like this one. Luke is stretched out in an open casket. Sidney arrives drunk at the burial site and Calif and he have a vicious fistfight during which they all tumble into the open grave —including Uncle Luke, who is thrown out of his coffin. Later, Sidney burns down the farm, rapes Brother Hanson's sister and drowns her in the pond, after which Brother Hanson decides that they don't need the law to hang the bastard. But wait! Hannah doesn't want Sidney hanged without a trial, and Calif tries to hold off the mob. Sidney finally ends up dangling from a rope, and the film ends with the moral, "One man's evil becomes the curse of all." This film finally gave Russ Meyer the basic direction for all his later films, a mixture of sex and violence with virtue finally triumphing but only after the blood is dripping out of your TV set.

MYSTIQUE **CC NN BI DS DK**
1979 INTERNATIONAL HOME VIDEO CLUB

P/D—**Robert Norman**
F/A—**Jake Teague, Randy West, Ron Jeremy**
F/A—**Georgina Spelvin, Samantha Fox, Helen Madigan**

Alma (Georgina Spelvin), who has a not-quite-terminal, unidentified disease, is told by her doctor (Jake Teague) that she must quit her job as a successful magazine photographer and lead a less stressful life. Alma has a home in Connecticut on the ocean but she has no friends or family and is an intellectual who has given herself to men very often. But she dreams about her doctor, and then she sees a mysterious woman in red, Cosima (Samantha Fox), on the beach in front of her house. Alma tells her that it is a private beach but finally invites her in for tea. Big mistake! Cosima does not enjoy the classical music, Mahler's songs, and a concerto for voice and orchestra that fills the rooms of a very attractive home. Cosima quickly seduces Alma, and Alma falls desperately in love with her. When Alma asks

Cosima if she loves her too, Cosima refuses to answer. Soom Alma is completely dominated by Cosima, and her male friends are not only sleeping with her under Alma's nose, but catch Alma in her circular tub and rape her viciously—and later, once again in her living room while some of them are smashing up her classical phonograph records. "You've gone too far. You've defiled my home," Alma tells Cosima. "Get out of my house." But Cosima knows she's in command. Alma can't bear to have her leave. When Alma asks her: "What are you doing to me? I love you." Cosima's answer is: "I'm teaching you how to live. You haven't learned to celebrate life!" Robert Norman had a good story but screwed it up with a celebration of life that seems to totally depend on sex. Presumably, Alma's doctor is a symbol for a kind of God. Worse is the concept that Alma "created" Cosima. "I needed you because I had missed so much of life," she says. Most women would settle for Alma's life before Cosima—frigid or not.

NAKED CAME THE STRANGER
CC NL NR NM BI
1975 QUALITY and TVX

P/D—**Henri Paris**
F/A—**Levi Richards, Alan Marlow**
F/A—**Darby Lloyd Raines, Mary Stuart, Helen Madigan**

Gilly and Billy run a radio talk show together. "We get you to work, we get you home, we even may teach you to roam," is their slogan. Billy is already roaming with their script girl, Phyllis. He has "the three-year, five-month married itch." Gilly knows what's going on, and tries to get her revenge with some of their male friends, whom she meets at a costume party. In her first attempt she can't even get the guy up. In a second try a few days later, she offers another friend a chance to tie her and whip her but discovers that he prefers to be whipped. On a Fifth Avenue bus (actually photographed in Manhattan traffic) she is more successful, giving another friend the fellatio of his life, but her most successful encounter is so good she becomes a silent movie star (in a very erotic extended satire on old sexy silent flicks). But Billy still roams—until Gilly solves the problem by seducing Phyllis so thoroughly that Phyllis decides to leave, not because she's in love with Billy but because she is with Gilly. Radley Metzger should put his real name on this one instead of Henri Paris, his a.k.a. The film, even in the explicit sex scenes, has Metzger's class and a European ambiance. What's more, he proves a porno star can act. This is probably the best film Darby Lloyd Raines has made. It all ends up happily in bed with Gilly proving she's equal, if not better, than Phyllis—anytime. Most women will enjoy this one. Worth owning.

NEON NIGHTS **CC NN NM BI DK**
1981 COMMAND

P/D—**Cecil Howard**
F/A—**Jamie Gillis, Eric Edwards, Jake Teague**
F/A—**Lysa Thatcher, Kandi Barbour, Arcadia Lake**

In her bedroom, Sandy's mother is screwing with her boyfriend, Robert Prince (Jamie Gillis—you have to watch the whole tape to figure out who he is)—because you realize what you see on screen may be a figment of Sandy's (Lysa Thatcher) imagination, you finally end up not knowing whether everything you've watched is really Sandy's imagination. In any event, you follow Sandy's fantasy from her detailed camera close-up in the bathroom with washing instructions provided by Robert, to her getting caught by her mother, to telephoning a friend Bonnie (Kandi Barbour) and asking her to take her to New York (Bonnie is too busy servicing her tennis instructor) to a tour de force scene where she is picked up by Harlan, a magician (Jake Teague), driving a van. She is brought to a motel where he hypnotizes her and floats her off the bed while he has sex with Sweet Marie (Jody Maxwell), his girlfriend, and she imagines it's happening to her. In New York Sandy's point of view is lost for about 20 minutes while you get acquainted with Rhonda (Arcadia Lake) and her stud (Eric Edwards) in preparation for Sandy's final arrival in

New York, where Rhonda has been waiting for her—she's a casting agent—and Sandy is just whom Mr. Prince has been waiting for for his new show. Then, lo and behold, you're back where you started with Sandy waking up in her own bed, but only after having seduced Mr. Prince in her imagination on her own terms. Cecil Howard offers enough nonstop, artistic hard-core, cinematography to guide filmmakers for a long time to come. Ladies past 35 may not like this one, but the storytelling technique does keep you interested.

NIGHT ON THE TOWN **CC R**
1982 KENYON VIDEO

P/D—**Simon Nuctern**
F/A—**Don Carroll, Chrysis, Alan Nichols, Casey Wayne, Jack Weaver**
F/A—**Marilyn Chambers**

This unique one-hour tape concentrates entirely on the New York night club, Cage aux Folles, and interweaves the acts put on by the various male performers with dressing room discussions of what kind of people they really are. In addition, a you-are-there sensation is provided by a live audience, which includes Tiny Tim sitting at a table with Annie Sprinkles, and a magic act in which Veronica Hart (her name is not on the credits) emerges from a box in which the magician has inserted swords—minus the evening gown she was wearing. Marilyn Chambers appears twice, totally dressed, and proving with two songs "Shame on Me" and "Morning, Noon and Nighttime, Too" that she can sing sexy songs very effectively. But the really fascinating part of this tape is the guys, who come in three varieties: gays, guys who enjoy playing the female role but who are not transvestites, and one transsexual (she/he has silicone breasts). In the words of one of the performers, they are offering "glamour drag." Their acts include low-down female comediennes, Mae West–style interpretations, sexy French bistro-type singing, and one who starts out his act in an evening gown and wig with a song, "What Is a Man," eventually stripping down to his jockstrap. Other than Marilyn Chambers, who appears only twice, the only other female entertainers appear as female tigers in an act where their trainer is a bald-headed black man whom they all snarl at very effectively. With a drink, and good companions, you'll think you have spent an hour in the audience at the Cage aux Folles.

NIGHTDREAMS **CC NN DK BI**
1981 WONDERFUL WORLD OF VIDEO

P/D—Rinse Dream, F. X. Pope
F/A—Kevin Jay, Fast Steppin Freddie, Ken Starbuck
F/A—Dorothy Le May, Loni Sanders, Jennifer West

Most men deprived of sex will probably have wet dreams. What about women who don't reach orgasms? With this question as a basis, many women may watch this sexvid quite fascinated—but will probably refuse to answer whether their dreams approximate Mrs. Van Houten's (Dorothy Le May). The sequences presumably take place in a psychiatric hospital where the patient is being watched by two doctors through a one-way mirror. One is a female. Dorothy knows she's being watched. "You think I'm a suburban housewife with two kids, a bagful of credit cards and a husband who can't get it up," she screams at them. "But that isn't me," she says—and she proves it as you watch her night dreams (nightmares?) First, she is in a nursery at night. Jack-in-the-boxes jump out with erections, clowns with pointed chins penetrate her while she has fellatio with horrible-looking toys that come to life. Next she is in a park. Late at night, two female witches in cowboy hats are watching her beside a fire they have lighted. A song, *Ring of Fire*, with erotic lyrics, is being sung as background music while the witches play with her. Then, she is in a tent with four Arab males. In the background, what sounds like an Arab prayer is being chanted. She is lying on an oriental rug naked, and finally the Arabs, who are passing a hookah, attack her. Next she's sitting naked on a dead man's lap. She unbuttons his clothing, taps his chest and it sounds hollow. He suddenly screams like a demon and when she unbuttons his trousers a fully formed fetus emerges. Then she's in a bathroom late at night, caressing herself. A fully dressed man wearing a hat attacks her and they dance together as she finally capitulates —ballet style. Then she's in her kitchen preparing breakfast and the black man on a Cream of Wheat Box comes to life. Then she is in hell—strewn with corpses, burning fires, skulls and a demon. Finally, she's walking into a lovely bedroom naked. She's wearing only a veil. A handsome man, naked too, is waiting for her and she enjoys a warm, caring sexual encounter. The cinematography is fascinatingly erotic and scary. Sometimes the explicit sex is a metaphor for lust incarnate. And Dorothy Le May does a good job as a sex-starved woman.

NOT A LOVE STORY **CC X**

P/D—Bonnie Sheer Klein
F/A—Linda Lee Tracy, Susan Griffin, Marge Atwood, Kate Millet, Kathleen Barry, Robin Morgan

This film, produced by the National Film Board of Canada, proves one thing. The pornography that incenses the people against porn is more interesting than the diatribes against it. Presumably, Linda Lee Tracy, who was a stripper, is converted after being shown the truth about her trade by Bonnie Klein, the director and tour guide. She realizes for the first time why feminists such as Susan Griffin, Kate Millet and Robin Morgan are fighting pornography and trying to censor it. Both the audience and Susan are taken on a trip through the porn emporiums of Forty-second Street, where they see Suze Randall, a porn photographer in action. They also see clips from porno movies (*The Private Afternoons of Pamela Mann*) and watch a total environment of sleaze and degradation where males indulge their repressed sexual fantasies. The reason I have given it a CC rating is that while the tape provides no answers, if you show it in mixed groups it will immediately create a pro and con discussion.

NOTHING TO HIDE **CC NN NL NR**
1982 CAL VISTA

P/D—**Benardo Spinelli, Anthony Spinelli**
F/A—**John Leslie, Richard Pacheco**
F/A—**Chelsea Manchester, Erica Boyer, Misty Hagen, Holly McCall, Raven Turner**

Much more than *Talk Dirty to Me* (see listing, p. 142), which features John Leslie and Richard Pacheco in a relationship similar to John Steinbeck's Lenny and George, this film (which won the 1982 Sixth Annual Erotic Film Award for Best Picture along with *Roommates*), points the direction that adult films will take for the next five years or more. The story line is similar to *Talk Dirty to Me*—in fact it could be called a sequel. Lenny (Richard Pacheco) is a "backward" guy when it comes to women, and he watches in amazement his best friend and pal, Jack, who scarcely has to look at a woman but she is panting to have him. The story of Jack's conquests begins on this tape with Lenny warning Jack, who is in Elizabeth's (Elizabeth Randolph) bedroom that her husband (Richard Dove) just arrived downstairs. Momentarily, Jack is ready to run for his life—the scene is right out of Chaucer—but he turns back and finishes bringing himself to a climax before he jumps out the window and takes off in a high-powered car pursued by the cuckolded husband. Next Jack is talking seriously to a woman who is sunbathing on the beach, and who admires his philosophy of life. Soon another woman is ready to jump in the sack with Jack but he tells her: "If you're going to have sex with me, you gotta have sex with Lenny, too." She shrugs, "Why not? I never made love with a retard." But then Lenny meets Karen (Chelsea Manchester), who clumsily falls into him—she's wearing roller skates. Lenny has found his soulmate. From this point on the interaction between Karen and Lenny is handled very romantically, as the two innocents slowly discover each other and finally make love for the first time. When Lenny tells Jack that he's going to marry Karen, Jack doesn't believe his ears. In Jack's world you never confine yourself to one woman. An old friend, a heavy-built, bearded guy who runs a food stand on the beach (played by Anthony Spinelli, who should star in one of his own films), tells Jack that he's upset with Lenny, who is sure that he can make it on his own. He tells Jack that his problem is that Lenny is the child he never had, and that "children leave home every day." The film concludes with Jack being best man at Lenny's wedding. All of the explicit sex in this one is enacted from the female point of view—including a funny scene with Jack and Patti (Holly McCall, who, as she grows older, has developed a lushly erotic female body). Most women under 50 will like this one.

NUDE MISS FLORIDA **CC (No sex . . . just normal girl-next-door types competing unashamedly for prizes)**
1980 BROADCAST QUALITY

This hour-and-a-half tape is the proceedings of the Annual Nude Beauty Contest held at the Seminole Health Club, Davie, Florida. Contestants are sponsored by firemen and local garages. Available at $49.50, it is worth owning to show your friends the joy of being naked and the possibilities of nude beauty contests. While it is not yet published, I have written a *New Feminine Sexual Manifesto*, which offers a number of very different approaches in which feminists who really enjoy themselves as women could defuse the antagonism and sexual frustration that occurs between men and women most of their lives, beginning with the adversary relationship that occurs in early childhood when young boys and girls live virtually segregated lives because of parental fears they may discover each other as sexual creatures. One proposal in this manifesto would be nude beauty contests sponsored by organizations of all kinds and held on the Fourth of July and other holidays. Qualifications for physical beauty would be weighted in such a way to deemphasize so-called perfect female and male shapes. Thus it would be possible for women with pretty faces (or homely faces) but with or without other provocative sexual features to win. When Dave Clark, of Broadcast Quality, sent me this tape for inclusion in this filmography he insisted, "It wouldn't turn on an ant." But I think he's wrong. Viewed both subjectively and objectively, the human body is a lovely sexual turn-on equal or superior to any other esthetic experience. Many adult filmmakers fail to realize this, and many films never show a woman or man walking or playing together naturally naked. While the idea of such contests embracing *all* age groups and including males may seem Utopian, they could be structured as a joyous experience which would include erotic dancing by both males and females as a laughing part of their accomplishments. And perhaps in another century, when we learn to wonder at our sexuality instead of denying it, such contests could include erotic, provocative preliminaries to sexmaking offered by male and female dancers within pre-defined limits of two to three minutes. With this premise and this tape, you can surely start an interesting discussion.

NUDES-A-POPPIN **No explicit sex**
1979, 1980, 1981 SUPERSOUND & SIGHT

There are *three,* two-hour tapes of the Annual Erotic Beauty Contests held at the Ponderosa Sun Club, Roselawn, Indiana, each year. The tapes sell at $69.95 each, but purchased as a threesome are available at lower rates. The 1980 and 1981 tapes were shot directly with video cameras and are much sharper. The proceedings include the beauty contest in which the participants (as many as 50 or more women from various dance and go-go clubs in Indiana and other midwestern states) compete for cash prizes, cups and the honor of being Miss Nude Galaxy of the particular year. In addition, they dance very erotic dances for the largely male audience, which overflows the outdoor grounds each summer. Many of the women are totally uninhibited and as they dance—in full detail (to the video camera at least) to most of the men standing in the front row. A feature of the 1981 tapes is an extended sequence of two naked women mud wrestling in thick mud with a naked male referee. There are many other mud wrestling tapes available. See the classified ads in various video magazines. Mud wrestling or Jell-O wrestling with women in abbreviated bathing suits is a feature attraction in many major cities. I have a feeling that watching women soil their bodies while they slither together helplessly in the mud is simply a modern-day manifestation of the early Christian teachings that women are basically evil, and Eve's descendants are seducers of men. Watching them degrade themselves in mud is equivalent to the woodcut engravings and paintings of female sexuality in the Middle Ages when the only way artists could portray human sexuality was by portraying not the vice itself but the *punishment* of vice. Thus a common appearance in art of the time was toads eating female vulvas and female breasts, accompanied by snakes enjoying the feast. Consider, too, the many drawings of women copulating with goats and other animals (see reproductions of paintings by Hieronymous Bosch). Supersound & Sight also offers a complete mud wrestling tape. The film is interesting, especially to start a discussion that I'm sure will separate most women's views from those of their male companions.

NUDES-A-POPPIN' JULY, AUGUST 1982
CC R
1983 SUPER VIDEO

P/D—Carl Friedlander, David Galloway

These two videotapes, each running close to two hours, are a great improvement over the videotapes made in previous years at the famous Ponderosa Sun Club (located in Roselawn, Indiana). The nude beauty contests, the erotic dancers, the strippers, the go-go dancers are all staged more interestingly—with good related music and comments from the master of ceremonies, Gene Burton (who looks and sounds like Ronald Reagan's younger brother would—if Reagan had a younger brother!). The cameramen, shooting directly on videotape, have improved their techniques a hundred-fold.

Using interesting camera angles, they move in and out of the on-stage action, capturing expressions on the ladies' faces as well as offering revealing close-ups of their bodies.

Both tapes offer nude body painting contests featuring both male and female contestants, and some of the results (especially in the August tape) are side-splitting and spectacular. The August tape also offers nude disco dancing with guys and gals, which is amusing to watch. The Ponderosa may be onto something—nude rock could add a lot of fun to out-door summer events!

Most of the contestants are professionals—in all sizes and shapes—who dance in midwest night clubs. Unlike the old-time strippers, these ladies suntan in bikinis and quite a few of them have breasts and be-hinds that look like white beacon lights waving on a dark shore. Here and there some housewife nudists join in the fun, and despite their weight, compete against the slimmer ladies.

These are fun tapes that you can put on your television as ice breakers for a party, and will undoubtedly get a mixed company interacting—verbally at least—as fast as alcohol.

Super Video Productions also has separate tapes of mud wrestling events at the Ponderosa.

OCTOBER SILK **CC NN NL BI that's unique**
1980   TVX and COMMAND

P/D—Cecil Howard, Ron Sullivan a.k.a. Henri Pachard
F/A—Bobby Astyr, Rob Everett
F/A—Candida Royalle, Christie Ford, Samantha Fox, Gloria Leonard

This one has at least half the beautiful women starring in adult films in it. In addition to the above, Lisa de Leeuw, Arcadia Lake, Merle Michaels, and Tara Smith also appear. Scene after scene not only keeps you smiling with its good dialogue, but despite the typical vignette approach, it is well integrated. The title doesn't tell you much but in most scenes the women are

in total sexual charge. Most women will enjoy the sexual silliness of this one, which is as good as *Babylon Pink* (see p. 62) or better.

ODYSSEY **CC NN BI DK several NR sequences**
1977   WONDERFUL WORLD OF VIDEO

P/D—Gerard Damiano
F/A—Gil Perkins, Wade Nichols, Richard Bolla
F/A—Susan McBain, C. J. Laing, Vanessa Del Rio

"In the beginning we are born. In the end we die. The middle is called life." Thus begins the most erotic and one of the best films that Damiano has made. The beginning is the story of Charles and Diana, who have been married for a few years and no longer turn each other on. After a highly stylized orgy scene at Madame Zenovia's, Charles and Diana remove their masks and you watch them in the most erotic sexmaking scene you've ever seen on your screen. The middle comprises three women who reveal their sexual frustration to their psychiatrist. And you will cry at the end for Susan McBain as Nicole, a lovely, skinny New York model who, after being put down by a porno flick producer and a photographer for a bizarre magazine, returns to her apartment, fantasizes herself with a romantic, caring lover and shoots herself. Excellent cinematography and good dialogue. Worth owning. Women will identify with this one.

OH! CALCUTTA **CC R NL NR (in the ballet scenes)**
1971   VIDAMERICA

P/D—Kenneth Tynan, Jacques Levy
F/A—Mark Dempsey, George Welbe, Mitchell McGuire, Bill Macy
F/A—Patricia Hawkins, Nancy Tribush, Raina Barrett, Samantha Harper, Margo Sappington

A complete, two-hour version of the famous nude musical that played on Broadway for twelve years—and is still playing. I'm not sure when this version was recorded, but it has most of the original cast appearing in miniskirts and a Spiro Agnew joke gives a clue. Obviously, some of the skits are changed in the current version, but this one is worth owning. There is no explicit visual sex but plenty of explicit vocal sex and much nudity. It begins with the audience arriving in the theater while the actors backstage are getting ready. Many of the skits will remind you of old-time burlesque. There's Jack and Jill measuring each other's genitals; there's sexy "Letters to the Editor" sung by the cast. There's a cohabiting couple with the boyfriend disgusted by the take-charge way his girlfriend makes love—he tries to loosen her up; a married couple whose sex life has cooled inviting a couple of old wife-swappers (now swingers) to their home; a Victorian gentleman who tries to seduce his lady and gets caught in his own trap; a Masters and Johnson sex scene with the two subjects hooked up to electric equipment as they make love; a naked ballet scene in the country which couldn't have appeared in the stage version; a lovely, erotic, classic modern dance scene featuring George Welbe and Samantha Harper, called "Clarence and Mildred," with a song-over story to accompany the nude dance which is worth the price of the tape. It raises the question: Why can't nudity be incorporated into much more of modern dance and ballet? Rent this one or buy it from VidAmerica. It will shock some, delight others.

OLD, BORROWED, STAG
CC   NN   NL   BI (with fairies, too!)   DK
1975   QUALITY

P/D—Al Di Lauro

Here is an hour and a half of your (or someone's) great grandfathers and great grandmothers having sex. Unlike the *Famous Smoker's Series* (see listing on p. 89 which has more or less complete segments from famous stag films), this film was created by editing scenes from at least a dozen stag films, plus animated stag cartoons and intercutting them with actual scenes from newsreels and films which go back to the early 1900s. Silent, of course,

and in black-and-white, it has piano and orchestral accompaniment from the music of the times and amusing sexual conversation inputs (you have to read them) which resurrect old words and phrases—such as stink-finger, back scuttle, step-ins, a stiff prick knows no conscience, and fairies—as well as several pretty complete segments from *The Farmer's Daughter*. She urinates in the jug of water she is carrying to the hired man in order to seduce him (a trick hundreds of centuries old). The Modern Magician, who can strip a lady with a wave of his hand, pulls a rabbit out of her "box" (another passe word) and makes his wand disappear inside of her. Also there are cuts from Mexican films (Mexico was a source of many stag films), especially the one featuring a dog. Most of this sexvid is joyously naive compared with modern-day adult films. I don't know about you, but I find it intriguing that all of the people on this tape have disappeared from the earth (of course by now they may have been reincarnated). It proves one thing: Close to a hundred years ago men (if not women) were just as amazed at their sexual drives as we are. If you wish to know more about stag films, read *Dirty Movies (1915–1970), an Illustrated History of the Stag Film*, with a complete filmogaphy of stag films by Al Di Lauro and Gerald Rubin (Chelsea House, New York, 1976).

ONCE UPON A TIME
CC   NN   BI   NL   NR
1975   INTERNATIONAL HOME VIDEO CLUB

P/D—Annette Haven
F/A—David Blair, Paul Thomas, Carl Regal
F/A—Amber Hunt, Abigail Clayton, Annette Haven, Tina Orchid

Annette Haven proves in this film (probably one of the first she ever appeared in) that if you have a good idea you can make an interesting erotic film on a very small budget. This one, which was shot entirely outdoors, uses the time machine premise, and Annette as an anthropologist is able to study the sexual behavior of Cro-Magnon man and other early men and women who appeared on earth several million years ago. It's all tongue-in-cheek, but the sexmaking is caring and believable and there are no caveman antics such as might appear in a 1980s film. In fact, some of the sequences with drumbeat background, or with Debussy's "Afternoon of a Faun," during which Annette, presumably as an anthropologist, is making love to Paul Thomas in a long, caring sequence, make you believe momentarily that these are happily primitive people. Annette proclaims at the ending that the film was made to change American sexual attitudes, and she makes a concession to the raincoat crowd with printed intercuts to some of the action such as: "Man who screws on grass has piece on earth," or "Don't talk with your mouth full," or "Watch the tool, fool." This is a happy sexvid which most women will enjoy and perhaps even learn a little about playful sexmaking. Without realizing it, some eight years later Annette was on the fringes of a subject that actually intrigues anthropologists. In her book, *The Evolution of the Sex Contract* (William Morrow, New York, 1981), Dr. Helen Fisher explores the sex life of early man, and shows how vestiges of it still linger in our own sex lives. Using the theories evolved by Fisher, some producer should give Annette Haven a second chance at making this movie with a strong story line. It could make a really fascinating adult film.

ONE PAGE OF LOVE
CC NN BI NR
1983

P/D—Ted Roter
F/A—Anthon Richard, Tovia Israel
F/A—Gena Lee, Nancy Hoffman

Gena Lee doesn't appear in many films, but Ted Roter and she must like each other. In Roter films, she emerges as a very good actress. Gena has an open, naive, almost sorrowful facial beauty that entrances many male viewers. In this one there are no come shots. The explicit sex shots are not labored, and the character development is intriguing. Rick (Anthon Richard) is a writer—he cooks up "True Confessions" stories to make a living. Leaving his girlfriend, Mona, he wanders around bars at night to make contact with people and soon meets Suzanne (Nancy Hoffman), who takes him home to a loving encounter in bed. To his surprise they are watched by a very attractive woman whom Suzanne introduces to him as her sister, Manon. Rick is intrigued with Manon, but he soon discoveres that Suzanne pimps for her and that Manon is mentally backward and plays with dolls. Rick falls in love with Manon. He's sure she can be cured. Suzanne insists she'll always be like that. Rick is surprised to gradually discover that Manon is almost totally amoral. She likes to play sexually with men. She masturbates when it pleases her and she can become very highstrung and nasty when she's frustrated. Rick wants to marry her—but first takes her to a psychiatrist, Dr. Gesheit (Ted Roter), who gradually discovers the real problem. When Manon was very young, her father seduced her and then killed himself. Her refusal to grow up is the result of this traumatic experience. Rick is sure that he can help Manon and prepares for the wedding. He even agrees to take Suzanne on their honeymoon because she is Manon's only other friend—and they have made love together as a threesome. But then, on her wedding day, Manon goes into a tantrum. Rick is very considerate. Back to Dr. Gesheit they go. After waiting in the outer office for an inordinately long time—Gesheit has assured Rick that Manon can be cured—Rick opens the door and sees Manon fellating the doctor. The film ends with Rick walking disconsolately down the street. The raincoat crowd may turn thumbs down on this one, but most women will find it quite fascinating—and sympathize with Anthon Richard, who is a good actor, too.

THE OPENING OF MISTY BEETHOVEN
CC NN NL BI DK
1975   QUALITY and TVX

P/D—L. Sultana, Radley Metzger a.k.a. Henri Paris
F/A—Jamie Gillis, Ras King, Jacqueline Beudant, Terri Hall, Gloria Leonard, Mary Stuart

This film won the first Erotic Film Festival Award in 1977. If it were made today it would probably win again. Among other things, it has Constance Money, who appeared in only two other films, *Mary, Mary,* and *Anna Obsessed.* She also had a bit part in *Confessions of a Peanut Butter Freak.* Metzger has retold the *Pygmalion* story of Professor Higgins and Eliza Doolittle with a sexual twist. Seymour Love (Jamie Gillis) runs the House of Love in New York City, and also has written numerous books on human sexuality. In Pigalle in Paris, he discovers an American woman in a brothel—Dolores Beethoven, who calls herself Misty (Constance Money). Misty is not a very sexy whore. She's in it for the money. Here is the perfect Galatea for Seymour. He convinces her that he can make her a top society hooker. Taking her back to New York, he gives her a long course of instruction but never has sex with her himself. When she's ready they fly back to Rome.

The ultimate goal is to pawn Misty off on Larry Layman, who runs *Golden Rod* magazine and make her his choice of *Golden Rod* Girl of the Year. In the process Misty rebels. "I can't fool people. I'm not a phony," she says. So Seymour, who is a tough cookie and is determined to achieve his goal, hooks her up with an earplug into which he can transcribe a tape recording to guide her on what she should do in servicing a count, one of Rome's top society males. Misty succeeds, becomes the talk of the town and Seymour nearly loses her to Layman. But it all ends in a long sequence of romantic sexmaking. There is much highly sophisticated humor, such as transatlantic flights where you can fly First Class with Sex or First Class Non-Sex, etc. The story could have been sharpened tremendously if the love interest between Misty and Seymour had been more carefully developed. But most women will like Constance Money.

OVERNIGHT SENSATIONS
CC   NN   NL   BI   silly DK and DB
1976   ARROW

P/D—Robert Benjamin
F/A—John Leslie, Tahoe Jonathan, Joey Civera
F/A—Sharon Thorpe, Annette Haven, Victoria Starr

As Max the director, John Leslie (who is listed in the credits as John Leslie Dupre) tells you that this is a documentary film of porno stars making porno films. The story line is that Max falls in love with Susie (Sharon Thorpe) and when she wants to act in one of his films he's shocked. Throughout the film there is a strong feminist line which the actresses evoke: that "they can do any damned thing men do—better." And Max is finally put in his place by Susie and Starr, who collar him like a dog and make him prance around to act in his own films. Although porno films are obviously not made this way, the film gives a refreshingly naive approach by having the actors talk directly to the viewer, and also watch each other in the act of sexmaking. After the conventional orgy scene they all appear naked on camera, *Oh! Calcutta* style, and comment on the fact that they really do like each other. Most women who think men should be put down occasionally will like this one.

PAUL, LISA and CAROLINE
CC   NN   BI
1976   SELECT/ESSEX

P/D—Peter and Belinda Balakoff
F/A—Tovia Borodyn, William Margold
F/A—Gena Lee, Diane Miller

Paul (Tovia Borodyn) is a producer of television commercials in his late forties. A heavy-set, attractive man, he marries Caroline (Gena Lee), who is in her twenties. But he's sexually involved with Lisa, who asks him: "Why did you marry her? You should have adopted her." Paul quickly establishes with Caroline, to her shock, that he's not monogamous. Slowly, he convinces her to try group sex with Lisa, and from there he moves her into an unconsummated spouse swap with friends of theirs, then to a swinger's ad for which they both pose nude, which leads them to a private swing club, a human potential group—and back to a wild party in their own milieu of upper-income friends. In the process, Caroline and Lisa are becoming involved with each other and Caroline is suddenly discovering that Paul is jealous of her even though, as she points out: "I'm only doing what I thought you wanted me to do." She suggests they stop all this nonsense and be monogamous. But Paul persists, even though he often is not getting it up with some of his conquests. At this point you have been watching, with good acting and good dialogue, a slice-of-life story of extramarital sex and sex teasing among the upper-income group. Since Caroline and Lisa really care for each other I was hoping (as the author of the novel *The Rebellion of Yale Marratt,* which proposes the legalization of bigamy) that the movie would conclude with a happy ménage à trois. Unfortunately, Paul becomes so jealous of Caroline and Lisa that conventional sexual morality takes precedence, and returning from a trip and finding them in bed, he shoots and kills them both. While this film was made in the middle 1970s, if the director could get hold of the original and re-edit it a bit, and if it was taped properly, it would be one of the best sex-vids made, with actors and actresses you have never seen before, but would like to see again. Trivia note: Peter Balakoff and Tovia Borodyn are both aliases for Ted Roter.

PEACHES & CREAM **CC NN NR BI**
1982   SELECT/ESSEX

P/D—Mark Corby, Robert T. McCallum
F/A—Dale Meador, Paul Thomas, Jerry Heath, Aaron Stuart
F/A—Abigail Reed, Chelsea McClane, Annette Haven

This is an adult film with class. Annette Haven as Sunny, a girl brought up on a farm by a drunken, lecherous stepfather (Dale Meador), plays in all the sex scenes, even a bisexual one with Chelsea McClane. They are all romantic and caring and believable. Whether she's on a blanket with Jerry Heath making love beside a pick-up truck, or in bed with Paul Thomas, she reflects the character she is playing (herself?), a loving person who "has the habit of adopting people" and making them, through her love and honesty, better people than they were. The story line is

developed in a way to keep you interested trying to figure the sudden transition from her farm background to a svelte, super-sophisticated San Francisco environment where she has escaped her stepfather. As an added attraction, two female black dancers, entirely naked, entertain at a party where Annette/Sunny appears in her transformation. Gradually you realize that Sunny, four years after her farm days, has been working for a very smooth, white male pimp who has rescued her from being a waitress in a hash house. The memories of her boyfriend on the farm are never far from Sunny's mind, and on the advice of her therapist, whose marriage she has straightened out (she's very nice sexually to him, too), she returns after many years and finds that her boyfriend now owns the home in which she was born. Her stepfather is dead, and her boyfriend has married a plain Jane and has a baby. You can't go home again—but, without any sexual overtones, they are very caring with each other. Finally Sunny even reforms her pimp, and walks away while he looks at her wonderingly! Most women will identify with Annette. The only question this film raises is why does Chelsea Manchester, Tigr, Chelsea McClane (all one and the same woman who has a naive schoolgirl quality) use so many different names? As Chelsea Manchester she nearly won Best Actress in the Sixth Annual Erotic Film Festival. The same applies to Jerry Heath, whom adult film aficionados will recognize as Jon Martin.

THE PINK LADIES
CC NN NM NL BI DK DB (but funny)
1980   VCA

P/D—Robert Michaels
F/A—Richard Bolla, James March, Jesie Adams
F/A—Samantha Fox, Kandi Barbour, Robin Byrd, Marianne Willoughby, Vanessa Del Rio

Can anyone produce an adult film with almost continuous sex and almost no story line but so outrageous and far out that most men and women who watch it can't help laughing—or even occasionally identifying with the characters? Robert Michaels has in this one. What story there is is hooked to four suburban housewives who play racketball together and have fairly dull marital lives. Many of the fantasies are fantasies many male and female viewers have probably experienced. They include a naked young man watching four women playing racketball together. They are playing naked. When they see him they make love to him from head to toe. This scene is followed by showers and a conversation in the ladies room in which they are all sitting on the toilet and talking to each other. This is followed by one woman in bed with her husband imagining herself as a sword swallower while Ron Jeremy actually *does* swallow his own penis. Another scene follows with a woman imagining herself in a whorehouse where the girls are waiting for the clients and a pretty black girl is masturbating as she plays the piano. This is followed by a husband sitting on a toilet reading bondage magazines and imagining his wife tying him up. In another scene, all the ladies in the gym ride exercycles and enjoy the feeling of the saddles on their vulvas while pink and blue men using the gym equipment eventually take over and enjoy them (Tom Ungerer, robot fashion). Then Vanessa Del Rio appears as a femme fatale. At the commuter railroad station she seduces each one of the husbands, but plays different roles. Totally insane, this one needs several couples watching it together plus a couple of drinks.

PLAYBOY VIDEO, Volume One CC R
1983 CBS-FOX VIDEO

P/D—Hugh Hefner

During the past two years, Playboy has given up its Playboy Clubs for the most part, sold off its London casino and book publishing company and is concentrating on the magazine, which is very profitable, and video. The Playboy Channel, which is available on pay cable television,

now has over a million viewers. If you have cable and it isn't shown in your city, local censorship may prevent it. Where I live, the managers of the cable system refuse to offer it. Playboy began a video interpretation of the magazine on January 29, 1982. Thanks to a friend who has a satellite in Grand Rapids, Michigan, I watched the first six monthly offerings, which he recorded for me. Obviously, Playboy is competing with itself at the moment by offering tapes. It raises the question of whether those who can watch the monthly Playboy Video Magazine on pay television will record the magazine each month, and whether this will cut into the sale of video cassettes. Perhaps Playboy can successfully ride both horses—especially if the Playboy Channel is hemmed in by local censorship. The other problem is with the video magazine format itself. Once you've watched it and shown it to a few friends, will you ever want to watch it again? Certain sequences such as the intercut jokes and the Playboy memories which appear on this tape don't bear repetition. But there is another answer, and I suspect that Playboy may already be planning in that direction. If this kind of tape could be sold for under $20—sustained perhaps by some advertising—there's obviously a huge market that will make Hugh Hefner wealthier than he already is. Volume One gives you a fast-cut flashback on Playboy Bunnies and Playboy nostalgia for the past 25 years. Then Lonnie Chinn, Playmate for January 1983, appears and reveals more of herself mentally and physically than she or the photographers could ever do on the printed page. Next there is a laughing excerpt from the girlie show at the Crazy Horse Saloon in Paris which makes you wish you had cash to afford to see it in person. That's followed by a frank discussion of how she feels about sexmaking by Barbara Carrera, who appeared in a remake of the Mickey Spillane film, *I, The Jury* (1982), in a naked bedding-down scene with Mike Hammer. From there you are cut to the Fourth Annual Playboy Jazz Festival with performances by various stars. Followed by a Ribald Classic called *The Crafty Lover* by La Fontaine, which is filmed attractively in soft focus with no explicit sex but plenty of sexmaking. The Playboy Interview follows, and this one is with John Derek, who is 55 and has been married three times to women much younger than himself, including Ursula Andress and Linda Evans of *Dynasty* fame. He discusses love, sex and his current marriage to Bo Derek, nee Mary Kathleen Collins, 25. The tapes conclude with Sharon Tweed receiving the 1982 Playmate of the Year Award from Hugh Hefner ($100,000 plus a Porsche)—and in Sharon's case, Hugh's undying(?) love. They've lived together for two years. Future tapes will probably offer the Playboy Forum and Playboy Advisor. Their only competition at the moment—despite other entries in the video magazine field—is *Electric Blue* (see listings p. 280).

THE PLAYGIRL **CC NN NM NL NR**
1982 CABALLERO

P/D—Roberta Findlay
F/A—Ashley Moore, R. Bolla, Bobby Astyr
F/A—Veronica Hart, Samantha Fox, Tiffany Clark, Sharon Cain, Merle Michaels, Candida Royalle

Put this one in the top 25 of the most controversial sexvids you have ever watched! It's fascinating for more than one reason. First and foremost, it was made by a woman who is probably not a feminist, but is likely well aware that she is expressing, via the story, a new approach to feminism by reversing the male/female sexual roles. Second, *every* actor and actress in this film—especially Veronica Hart, Samantha Fox and Richard Bolla—does a superb acting job. Third, Roberta Findlay has put the whole thing together with a sense of laughter—so that although the story line is unbelievable, you get carried away with it. Laura (Veronica Hart) is married to Carl Bond (Ashley Moore, who is aging handsomely). They are in an open marriage that tops any open marriages you ever heard about. Carl, a millionaire publisher, provides the money and Laura adopts artists, musicians and novelists and

not only helps push them to the top of their profession, but is the best in-the-sack companion they ever had—up to a point! When they achieve success she wearies of them and kisses them goodbye. Since they all fall in love with her they can't believe what is happening to them. Only men weary of women—not vice versa! Carl is very easygoing. He knows all about Laura's conquests, but she reassures him that he is the one and only. Nick Ray (Bobby Astyr), who plays a leader of a rock group, can't believe it when Laura tells him good-bye after very happy sexmaking during which they are both wearing stereo headphones and he teases her with her microphone. Nor can Danny, a painter whose first showing she has subsidized. But love finally catches up with her in the form of David Fuller (Richard Bolla), a frustrated novelist who works for Carl writing blurbs for the new books Carl will publish. Laura is so charmed with Richard's novel you are left with the feeling that she may divorce Carl, settle down and be monogamous. Since in real life Veronica has sent out wedding invitations and at the Sixth Annual Erotic Film Awards told me, "I'm quitting the business—do you think I'm crazy?" (all with a twinkle in her eye), the story has a ring of truth. If Veronica continues making pornos her husband will certainly have to be as cool as Carl is in this movie. And that's where this film is neatly controversial. It should spark a great deal of marital discussion in living rooms and bedrooms all over the country. Watching Veronica with her amusing dialogue and her good acting raises the question—especially since this film was made by a woman—could most women, if they dared to, actually be this sexually provocative? Or is Roberta simply reinforcing a male daydream? Most men who watch it would have been happy to be introduced to sex so lovingly as is a young virgin boy in one scene with Veronica and Tiffany; or receive the detailed sexual instruction Veronica supplies as she teaches Richard how to really make love to a woman (Merle Michaels) while she watches. Many women may give their men answers to the above questions that will surprise them.

PLEASE, PLEASE ME CC NN NR BI
1976 ARROW

P/D—Paul Lyon, Jay Niney
F/A—Paul Thomas
F/A—Erica Strauss, Sharon Thorpe, Bonnie Holiday

A true-to-life domestic marital drama. After six years of marriage, Mary fantasizes her sex life with Jack, who with her at least is a missionary-position lover and has no imagination. A friend tells him to introduce his wife to sex aids such as vibrators and dildoes, and when he does she tells him in shock: "Look at this crap! This isn't what I mean by no imagination. This does it. I'm through with you!" Mary tells him she needs a job. He tells her that she's on one of her stupid ego trips. Separated, Mary tries sex with an old college friend in a caring bisexual scene, and with a former black lover who proves that he can be romantic. In the meantime, Jack goes to a psychiatrist (she's very Germanic, fat and blowsy) and discovers that "the emotional fulfillment from sex comes from fantasy." Not with her obviously—so Jack imagines screwing with her receptionist. It all ends happily. Mary returns to Jack, no worse for wear for her extramarital fling and decides that he may be the best after all. Many women will like the occasional reality of some of the sex scenes and the dialogue, and Erica Strauss is very pretty.

PORTRAIT CC NN NM DK BI NL
1974 ARROW and SELECT/ESSEX

P/D—Gerard Damiano
F/A—Jamie Gillis
F/A—Jody Maxwell

Imagine a sexvid that runs for about 15 minutes with no explicit sex. But don't worry, Damiano quickly makes up for it in a unique flick that plays with a woman's schizophrenic fantasies, which she describes to her psychiatrist. Linda (Jody Maxwell, who does a nice acting job) tells him about her obscene phone calls—to which she masturbates while listening to some stranger tell her that she is lonely and needs him. On her next visit, Linda is wearing pigtails and sucking a Coke bottle very suggestively which quickly turns into unidentified penises. In another visit she describes to him a two-couple party where the boyfriends get the two girls drunk so they can go to bed with each other's girls (wives perhaps—you're not sure). Finally the psychiatrist gets so intrigued when Linda arrives in her first manifestation as a hooker that he tells her that his own relationship with his wife is not that good, but he could cure her in bed. To which she disdainfully responds: "Okay, I have Thursdays free. It'll cost you a hundred dollars a pop." The long, two-couple sequence of group sex in this one in which all four of the participants are pretty bombed with booze is done in silent film–style, in color and is often amusing.

PLEASURE SHOPPE
CC NN NM NL with an extended DK group sex scene
1979 CABALLERO

P/D—Alan Vydra
F/A—Jean de Villroy
F/A—Candy Dallas, Susan Rosebush, Felicia

This one might become a sex education sexvid for male senior citizens. Male chauvinists will also be proud of Jean de Villroy, who is in his seventies but is totally virile. In the back room of a bookstore owned by Mr. Hoffman and his three sons, if you're female and know the password ("I'm looking for a magazine and I'm lonely"), you can get properly serviced by Daddy or two of the older boys who fill in for their father when he's pooped. The young ladies really adore Daddy even when he can no longer get it up. The only plot revolves around Alex, the youngest son, who is a virgin but eventually proves his manhood in a pre-arranged seduction scene.

PORNOGRAPHY IN NEW YORK
CC NN DK BI
1972 ADULT VIDEO

P/D—Milton Vickers, Betsy Moss
F/A—None

Although it was made twelve years ago and adult films on videotape were unheard of, and live sex shows and massage parlors didn't have the "class" they now do, this sexvid (introduced by the district attoney of New York's Nassau County, who tells the listener he must prosecute pornography since it is in violation of the law) is still pretty much where it's at—a look at the seamy side of the human sexual coin. A girl and a guy selling flowers in Times Square tell how they made porno films for the money: "Why not? We sleep together, anyway." Lesbians and homosexuals describe their sexual motivations in very natural, unrehearsed dialogue (and of course all of them show the intimate sexual action involved in their relationships). An owner of an adult book and sex aid store displays his merchandise and shows artificial vaginas, dildoes, vaginal jellies, etc. A woman who makes plastic molds from the erected penises of males shows how she does it and why. Girls available for body painting are seen in action and describe (in voice-over, as do all the participants) how much they enjoy their work. You visit The Pleasure Chest, which sells appurtenances such as chains, whips, handcuffs, clamps etc. enjoyed by the S/M trade, and a prostitute tells the problems and rewards (financial) of her trade. A believable, true-to-life documentary that you will never see on commercial television.

PRACTICE MAKES PERFECT
CC NN BI
1978   QUALITY

P/D—Sam Norvell, Torgny Wickman
F/A—Charles Canyon, Eric Edwards, Knud Jorgeson
F/A—Madelain La Foret, Darby Lloyd Raines, Kim Pope, Anita Chris, Anne Magie

This film won the 1979 Erotic Film Festival Award for the Best Foreign Film. Why Eric Edwards, Darby Lloyd Raines and Kim Pope, the only American actors to appear in the film, went to Sweden to make it is probably a good story in itself. What makes the film different is that it all takes place on a very large Swedish farm, run by Squire Richard (Charles Canyon), a mighty cocksman who insists that his agreeable female staff should pull down their panties and take care of him at a moment's notice. Come to live with him is Cousin George (Eric Edwards) who is very shy with women. Richard points out the boars in the piggery and the rams among the sheep. "It's exactly the same with man. A man must never forget his animal power," he says. But Cousin George can't get it up when Richard arranges with his cook to introduce him to the pleasures of the bed. Cousin George is saved by Esther (Darby Lloyd Raines), a schoolteacher who has managed to reject Richard. Esther has a secret to overcome: her own shyness. She pretends she's a prostitute. In the meantime, Richard's housekeeper is shocked at the general lasciviousness around the farm and is planning to blow this Sodom and Gomorrah off the map. Fortunately, just as she's about to light the fuse on a pile of dynamite, a guy takes her hair down and makes love to her in the barn and she's quickly converted into a believer. This is a nicely bucolic sexvid which proves that interesting environments make the sex more palatable.

PRETTY PEACHES   **CC NN NL one DS scene**
1978   ASTRO

P/A—Alex de Renzy
F/A—John Leslie
F/A—Desiree Cousteau, Juliet Anderson

Best Actress, 1979—Third Annual Erotic Film Festival Award. Pretty Peaches is a female Candide . . . everyone's victim, but she is so happy-go-lucky that her misfortunes never affect her. After her jeep collides with a tree, she's flipped onto the ground. Unconscious, she is revived by a penis, of course. After that her memory is suddenly lost and to recover it she gets the most detailed enema you've ever seen. Women may not identify with Desiree Cousteau (or Carol Connors who plays a similar type as Candy), but she's so naive that most men will want to play Big Daddy with her. Juliet Anderson, who was born in

Helsinki, Finland, makes her screen debut in this one as the maid of Pretty Peaches's father. Worth owning.

PRISONER OF PARADISE
CC NN NR BI and some not very believable DS
1980   WONDERFUL WORLD OF VIDEO

P/D—Gail Palmer, Bob Chinn
F/A—John C. Holmes
F/A—Seka, Sue Caroll

The time is World War II, December 7, 1941, Pearl Harbor Day. You may not believe your eyes or ears but John C. tells an Oriental woman he loves her and will return in 60 days to marry her. Then, in the attack, she is killed. He goes to sea and his ship is torpedoed. John is washed ashore on a tropical island. Women will enjoy watching John bathe naked beneath a waterfall, and climb trees to get coconuts. The photography (shot in Hawaii) is excellent and romantic. But now you really have to suspend disbelief. A Nazi colonel ("Hogan's Heroes" style) is running a POW camp—with three women (one Japanese). They've captured two American nurses and are torturing them. John C. is captured. But John wipes out the bad guys and gals and lives happily ever after with the nurses, who even get pregnant.

PRISON BABIES **CC NN NR DK BI**
1976

P/D—Ted Roter
F/A—Patrick Wright, Peter Balakoff a.k.a. Ted Roter
F/A—Kristi Fletcher, Sally Petersen, Maria Karina, Karen Cooknell, Hilary Scott

Ted Roter must be a frustrated psychiatrist. In this film, and in *The Psychiatrist* and *Paul, Lisa and Caroline* and *One Page of Love* (see listings pp. 211, 116 and 115), he plays the part of a psychiatrist. To my knowledge he's the only producer/director who appears in explicit sex scenes, which has some point because he couldn't hire a middle-aged actor who would appeal to women more than he does himself. In addition, most of the actors who appear in his films, while competent, rarely appear in other films, and like this one, most of his films are too sparing of detailed genital sex to appeal to the raincoat crowd. Presumably a true story, this one revolves around Kathy (Kristi Fletcher—a believable and fairly plump teenager), whose father has left home and whose mother has a new lover. Kathy runs away and gets involved with a lesbian who makes porno movies and treats her royally on her yacht. They make love in some caring bisexual scenes. When Kathy is making her first porno movie, the set is raided by the police. Kathy ends up in the Redland State Home for Girls, which is inhabited by some pretty tough young ladies. The female warden insists all the girls are criminals, but one of her assistants, who is also in love with prison doctor (Ted Roter), believes in the girls and gets him on their side. While she and the doctor are making love, Kathy is brutally beaten by some of the girls, but the film ends with Kathy realizing that the doctor is on her side. The doctor's only sexual relationship in the film is with an assistant warden. She has an evil lesbian counterpart who forces the girls to service her. Scenes between the doctor and the assistant are romantic, and the bisexual scenes with Kathy and a roommate who protects her from the really bad girls are unusually caring. Because of the environment of the story there is quite a bit of lesbian sex, but Ted Roter has produced a "thinking" style adult film which is closer to life than most.

PRIVATE AFTERNOONS OF PAMELA MANN **CC NN BI DS (one extended rape scene)**
1974   TVX

P/D—Radley Metzger a.k.a. Henri Paris
F/A—Marc Stevens
F/A—Barbara Bourbon, Georgina Spelvin

At least cinematographically, Metzger has tried to make the sex scenes in this film artistic. But the story of Pamela, who can't get enough sex, and her husband, who aids and abets her, escapes Metzger in silly dialogue. There is a very erotic bisexual scene between Georgina and Barbara Bourbon. In the heterosexual scenes Barbara can out-"deep-throat" Linda Lovelace. Metzger sets the pace for the outer limits of choreographing sex-making on film. Nothing like it had been seen before 1974, but today it is well copied.

PUNISHMENT OF ANNE
CC DK DB DS BI
1979   HIGHBRIDGE ENTERTAINMENT

P/D—Radley Metzger
F/A—Carl Parker
F/A—Mary Mendum, Marilyn Roberts

You won't ever forget this sexvid. Despite the rating, it's like no sadism/masochism film you've ever seen. If depiction of sexual pain and horror can become a classic, Radley Metzger has done it with this one. Exquisitely photographed in Paris, it's the story of Anne, a beautiful masochist who "belongs" to Claire. In the course of a very erotic buildup you watch Anne (through the eyes of Jean, a male friend), who is excited by submission. First she is punctured by a rose thorn which Claire presses against her upper thigh. After whippings, Anne is nearly drowned in a bathtub and then hung in a chamber of horrors where she is tortured. Worth owning for its total shock value.

PURELY PHYSICAL
CC NN NM BI NR
1982   SELECT/ESSEX

P/D—Billy Thornberg
F/A—Joey Civera, Michael Morrison, Sidney Fellows, Albert Johnson
F/A—Laura Lazare, Juliet Anderson, Jade Wong, Lysa Thatcher

Here's a unique, believable background for an adult film that allows some interesting character development and will keep you interested through the last scene. Kathy Harrington (Laura Lazare, who ranks with Annette Haven and Arcadia Lake as a beautiful lady) takes a job as night clerk in a local motel and decides to keep a journal (she's studying writing at a local university) about her experiences. Of course, she never does know what goes on behind the various closed doors but she's got a good imagination and eventually gets romantically involved with one guy who is a traveling salesman and passes through the town twice a month. Although the rooms are all the same, he prefers Room 22. A young high school guy checks in with his "wife," Jade Wong (who looks like a Chinese Brooke Shields). She's been around but she's very loving and romantic with him on this, his first time with any woman. Juliet Anderson as Claudia Sinclair is a frustrated female executive without a man. She tries to pick up Kathy for a night in the sack, but Kathy rejects her. After which, alone in her room, a very lonely woman, she sadly makes love to herself. It's the best scene Juliet Anderson has ever played. Charley, a plump guy with a woman he's picked up in a local bar, checks in. For the first time in his life he's found a woman with whom he can communicate. She presumably enjoys "movie trivia," on which she's also an expert—or tries to convince him she is. But he can't get it up. After that, disgusted with him when he passes out, she lifts his billfold, and it's obvious she doesn't give a damn about movie trivia. Joey Civera arrives dead tired. Two women hookers sent by his friend Barney burst into his room. Since he isn't interested in sex, they enjoy each other while he watches and holds one in his arms and the other laps her to a climax. Finally Kathy's traveling salesman checks in again and asks for a 6 A.M. wake-up call. She gives it to him in person the next morning, and he decides that he needs her to become his permanent wake-up partner.

REFLECTIONS **CC NN NM DK**
1974   VCX

P/D—William Dancer, Michael Zen
F/A—Paul Thomas, Dave Penny, John Leslie
F/A—Annette Haven, Kathy Thomas, Bonnie Holiday

Good acting (especially by Annette Haven), good dialogue and a strong story line would put this one in the top 50 sexvids. Beautiful Cousin Joan has come to visit for the summer. In a drive-in, she refuses to fool around with her cousin Bob, although his sister Connie is in the backseat (she's also a virgin) going at it. Bob is determined to get to bed with Joannie (even Daddy has fantasies about her when he's making love to Mother) but Joan resists him. He's so hard-up that his sister Connie masturbates him, and it seems when they were all kids, and Joan came for the summer, they all played doctor together. Bob offers Joan a sleeping concoction (the parents have gone on vacation) and in a lightly erotic sequence makes love to her while she lies out cold on the bed like a corpse. You have to suspend disbelief to accept this until later when Joannie (Scarlett O'Hara–style) proves she never drank it. The conventional orgy ending in this one gets a bit yucky but Joannie gets her revenge on both Bob and Connie and it comes as a neat surprise.

REPRODUCTION OF LIFE   CC
1981   MASTERVISION

P/D—Numerous
F/A—Commentators—no actors

If you read many or all of these reviews of adult films, you will be well aware that, in my opinion, while they shouldn't be censored out of existence, too many of these films are simply concerned with the mechanics of sexual arousal and the individuals involved do not care about each other. They seem to have no awareness of the infinite wonder and amazement of the human body and human sexuality. Somewhere in the next century I predict the answer will be found in religions that exalt human sexuality and in teaching young people from childhood the beauty, wonder and joy of humans surrendering to each other in the act of love. Underlying every embrace of a man and woman is the potential for the creation of another life. The potential doesn't have to be realized, but the awareness of it is basic to the human psyche. Such awareness illuminates and fulfills sexmaking beyond sensual gratification. Most men and women don't receive this kind of sex education. This tape is a coming event that casts its shadow before. Eventually we will

have many more that provide an at-home sex education which parents and their children can share together. And hopefully, young people will grow up in a new kind of video world where they can watch their own peers: child actors, obviously—despite the Supreme Court—but interacting with boys and girls in their own age groups, and in films where wonder, caring, joy and love are the motivating elements. *Reproduction of Life* is composed of three separate films. The first, *Birth of a Kitten*, is a 12-minute segment that most parents and children have never witnessed intimately unless they were fortunate enough to have a female cat. There is no voice-over, but the camera watches the mother cat's face and the actual birth of all her kittens. Young children, six years to old age, will identify with the mother cat—a loving female—as she welcomes her four kittens to life. The next segment, *Human Reproduction*, uses no live people, but works with animated drawings and voice-overs, male and female, describing human sexuality and reproduction. It should be seen by every girl or boy before they enter their teens. The combination of vocal teaching with moving drawings to explain human sexuality, impregnation and birth and the roles that the male and female play in the process is far superior to the printed word or still pictures. The chances are good that most of the readers of this book will learn aspects (or be reminded) of mysteries that he or she has forgotten. The final segment is for older children in their later teens. Titled *Prenatal Development*, it raises the question of malnutrition and unpleasant maternal environments on the unborn fetus. It suggests that prenatal environments may be the most influential encounters of a human being's life. After you've seen this film you'll watch your favorite porno stars in action with an increased sense of wonder.

RENDEZVOUS WITH ANNE
CC   NN   BI   NR   NL   one short DK scene
1975   BLUE VIDEO

P/D—Lowell Pickett
F/A—Lou Mann, Mark McDonough, Stephen Wilcox
F/A—Lisa Troy, Keri Carpenter, Cazander Zim

Anne Stewart is being paged in the San Francisco airport. Four Anne Stewarts arrive at the information desk. The call for one, a grandmother, is the one being paged. The other three, all young women, introduce themselves to each other, and the next hour and half you get acquainted with all of them. The first Anne is a virgin who just graduated from high school. Refreshingly naive, she learns about sex and loving from an artist she meets in a park in San Francisco. Joyously, she takes her clothes off to pose for him and they end up in a warm, loving sex scene in his bed. The second Anne meets a guy who is disillusioned with women and in a hotel room they talk and timidly embrace in a friendly encounter during which he discovers that he's not as impotent as his former girlfriend insisted he was. The third Anne (married back home) is visiting her sister. She has recently discovered her husband "in flagrante delicto" with his secretary, which is why she left home. But she meets a guy who is very warm and caring and even though he takes her to a group sex party where she watches the action quite horrified, she learns a lot. Lowell Pickett, who produced nudie, breast-and-behind sex exploitation films in the 1970s produced and directed this one. It is a small classic of the genre. All of the one-to-one sex scenes are friendly, conversational and caring—even the one bisexual scene between two of the Annes is amusingly talkative as they tell each other about their sexual encounters. Women will like it—the female dialogue is believable and the women are prettily average.

RESURRECTION OF EVE
CC NN NR and DK (but believable and totally plot-oriented)
1973   MITCHELL

P/D—Jon Fontana, Artie Mitchell
F/A—Johnny Keyes
F/A—Marilyn Chambers, Kani Jones

This sexvid (better than *Behind the Green Door,* see page 62) proves that an intelligent story line can be blended into a sexually erotic movie. Cinematically equal to any Hollywood product, it has a story that keeps the viewer intrigued by the clever interweaving of Eve's life from a child of 13 to her later life with a very jealous disc jockey who believes she's sleeping with a black fighter (Johnny Keyes). She isn't. After an auto accident Eve becomes Marilyn Chambers and marries the disc jockey who gradually talks her into "swinging" and then gets jealous of her when she finally enjoys it. Most women will like this one. It has many romantic sequences, and excellent acting. Why didn't the Mitchell brothers do it again?

ROOMMATES   **CC   NN   NR   DK (but totally plot-oriented)**
1982   VIDEO-X-PIX

P/D—Chuck Vincent
F/A—Jamie Gillis, Jerry Butler, Bobby Astyr, Jack Wrangler
F/A—Samantha Fox, Veronica Hart, Kelly Nichols

If you think that porno film stars can't act; if you think adult filmmakers can't tell a story; if you think that sexmaking between a man and woman can't be fascinating to watch, then buy this sexvid. As of 1983 it is one of the ten best adult films ever made, and it may well be number one. Chuck Vincent calls it a "cross-over" film, meaning among other things that it can be shown in the theaters of major exhibitors as well as adult theaters. Chuck may be gambling on the major exhibitors, and he may not please the raincoat crowd, but he has a million-dollar bonanza in the home video cassette market. (*Roommates* will probably be edited for cable or subscription television, which will be sad because the sexmaking is beautifully honest.) It's the story of Billie (Samantha Fox), a former high-priced call girl who is trying to get out of the business and start a new life. She has a job in a studio making television commercials (which are cleverly worked into the plot), but Billie is indebted to a former pimp, Marv Lester (Bobby Astyr). To cover the cost of her expensive apartment (since she's not making enough money on her new job), she advertises for roommates. She gets Joan (Veronica Hart), an aspiring actress who has just arrived in New York from her hometown in Ohio where she has been involved with a married man who is using her for sexual variety. Even though she's in love with him and believes he loves her, he has no intention of marrying her. The third roommate is Sherry (Kelly Nichols), who also has just arrived in the city. Sherry is hoping to reach the top of her profession. Chuck has interwoven the sex lives of these three women with the story of their triumphs and failures. Joan finally finds real love with Eddie (Jerry Butler), a guy who thinks he is gay, but succumbs to her country-girl freshness in a charmingly romantic and explicit sex scene. Sherry gets involved with several different guys, especially a pervert, scarily acted by Jamie Gillis, who tells her he loves her but basically hates women. After watching her being raped in the studio, he masturbates over her shuddering, naked body and later he beats her viciously. Billie, who almost escapes her past, falls in love with Jim (Jack Wrangler) and she makes love with him in a really fun-loving sex sequence. But later, to her shock, he discovers her with four "johns" who she's servicing against her will because if she doesn't, her pimp, Marv, will see that she loses her new job. Beyond the interesting story, Chuck has created one explicit sex breakthrough scene after another. The scenes are romantic and laughing or when they are definitely sexist, the viewer has no doubt about it because of the natural and superb acting of Veronica Hart and Samantha Fox, as well as Kelly Nichols, all of whom respond to sexmaking the way any normal woman would. Chuck has created many beautiful precedents, cinematographically as well as psychologically, in a film which will be a sexmaking guide to R-rated and X-rated filmmakers for a long time to come. I'm sure that all women—even those against pornography—will endorse Chuck's comment: "I'm not interested in making sex films anymore. Many people I have talked with have been turned off by watching them. The sophistication of the American public is very acute. The sex industry has to take this into account. I'm trying to put a little class in the product." He most certainly has!

S.O.S. (Screw on Screen)
CC NN NL DK BI (male, too!)
1975 QUALITY

P/D—David Buckley/Jim Buckley
F/A—Spider Webb
F/A—Honeysuckle Divine, Jody Maxwell

If you have never seen a copy of Al Goldstein's *Screw*, here's a chance to watch it live. Even though the film was made nearly ten years ago and Jim Buckley has long since left *Screw* to Goldstein (where is Buckley now?) and Al is a much skinnier version of his former fat self, the visual recreation of the famous tabloid newspaper isn't much different than if it were made today from a current issue. This is a tape that offers a number of sequences in "the things-you've-never-seen-before department." Skipping through the calmer sequences, hosted both by Buckley and Goldstein, Al tells you how he started *Screw* in 1968 and how he has been fighting "sexual hypocrisy" and people "who are afraid to know what makes us tick" ever since. You are then shown a long segment from a famous stag film in which a very homely woman, wearing glasses, who was known in stag circles as "Wheathead" has sex with everyone in sight. Al explains his Peter Meter rating system of adult films. (He puts down Damiano's *Portraits* but extols a film called *Rainbow*, now called *Wet Rainbow*—see listing on page 153.) It's so good he would take his then wife to see it. But the pièce de résistance of the film is three segments—first with Spider Webb, who considers himself the best and foremost tattoo artist in the business. In 1975 he was still tattooing "hikers, priests, nuns, dancers, actors, street people" (according to Spider it's an ego trip for the tattooist and the tattooees), despite the fact that New York City made tattooing illegal in 1969. This is followed by about 10 minutes with Honeysuckle Divine, billed by *Screw* as the Dirtiest Broad in the World. Seems Honeysuckle read about *Le Petomain* (the guy in the early 1900s who became famous because he could blow a tune of farts out of his anus; Honeysuckle perfected the skill). Even nuttier than Honey is Jody Maxwell, billed as "the singing cocksucker from Missouri" (Jody is pretty enough), and in an extended sequence demonstrates on one guy how a woman should really give oral sex without using a "cheating hand." Not too much *Deep Throat*. Jody can vibrate with her mouth and can sing songs while she's blowing a guy—she actually does, singing "Old MacDonald Had a Farm." Way back in 1969 I was on a television talk show with Al Goldstein and Father Morton Hill (the founder of Morality in Media). I tackled Al, claiming he was degrading human sexuality, and Father Hill because he was censoring any manifestation of it. My theory? We should exalt human sexmaking. Alas, in the 1980s we're a long way from my approach—and, thankfully, Father Hill's. Either way you shouldn't stop laughing at what sex-driven sillies we mortals be.

SADIE **CC NN NR**
1980 EROS

P/D—**Larry Price, Bob Chinn**
F/A—**Jerome Deeds, Gary Dana, Joseph Darling, John Hires, Larry Price**
F/A—**Chris Cassidy, Deborah Sullivan, Diahana Holt**

When this film was reviewed by the men's magazines, it was almost a unanimous thumbs down because it didn't raise peters up. While the drama can certainly be faulted as a little amateurish, it certainly deserves a CC rating as a daring attempt to introduce explicit sex into the framework of the famous *Rain* story by Somerset Maugham, which in 1922 became the very famous stage play, *Sadie Thompson*. Chinn and Price had updated the story to the Vietnam war and substituted a rightwing moralistic senator for the righteous minister in the original story. Also added: a local Rajah and a Colonel, both of whom have their fingers in the drug trade, which Senator Chester Daniel is investigating. As a by-product, he is trying to wipe up sin, corruption and sex in the war zones. Sex is exemplified in the person of Sadie Johnson (Chris Cassidy), who has been kicked out of a house of prostitution in Danang and has come to Borneo on the *Island Queen*—the same boat as the senator, his wife, Bessie (Deborah Sullivan), and his adopted daughter Honore (Diahana Holt), together with several soldiers. One Sergeant Jocko, and another called Bear, are soon shacking up with Sadie and Honore. Interwoven with the drug plot is the conversion of Sadie whom Senator Daniels is convinced must not only repent her sinful ways but serve time in jail in San Diego. He is committed to taking her there on the next boat. Most of the action takes place in the lobby of Doc's Hotel with occasional switches to the bedroom action. John Hires as Doc and Chris Cassidy do nice acting jobs, but Chinn and Price lose their way in the side plots, and should have concentrated on the temptation and seduction of the senator, who finally hangs himself after he discovers he can't stop touching Sadie's breast *under* her nightgown. Sadie as a good person in love with Jocko—and a loving woman beneath the hooker charade—is developed. For the most part the sex scenes are believable and interesting. Most women will find this one inoffensive, will like Chris Cassidy, and would tell Price and Chinn to try again with another literary gem. The advantage of working with a well-known story is that it gives the directors a framework to stay in, and a chance to see if they really can develop character and sex at the same time.

A SCENT OF HEATHER
CC NN NR NM BI
1981 VIDEO-X-PIX

P/D—**Bill Eagle, Phillip Drexler**
F/A—**Paul Thomas, R. Bolla, Neil Peters, Felix Krull**
F/A—**Veronica Hart, Vanessa Del Rio, Lisa Be, Christie Ford, Jessica Teal, Tracy Adams**

Put this one in your list of the top 25 sexvids. It's a gothic romance in an English castle, complete with subdued lighting and believable costuming, even down to the ladies' underwear. There are only one or two anachronisms, such as the ladies wearing heels too high, an electric bedroom light and a modern telephone. The acting of Paul Thomas, R. Bolla and Veronica Hart is exceptional, and the dialogue is a laughing, happily corny 1980s version of Victorian conversation. Heather (Veronica Hart) has been brought up in a convent. She is pledged to marry Frederick (Paul Thomas). If she's not married by the end of the year, she will lose her grandpa's inheritance and the castle. Prior to the wedding night Aunt Phyliss (Lisa Be) tells Heather about her own frustrated romance (shown in a flashback). Although she is now an old maid, she knows more about sex than Heather. "Do you know what that place between your legs is for?" she asks her. "Of course," Heather replies, "To go to the toilet." On their wedding night, Frederick is fascinated with his virgin wife. When he shows her his penis, she's delighted. "It's so soft and cute." But a few minutes later she can't believe her eyes. "It's so big—you're not going to try to stick this into me?" "After you taste it," Frederick tells her. But, alas, a few minutes later, just as he's about to make his bride a woman, Uncle Roy knocks frantically on the door. There's a terrible family secret he has just discovered. Frederick and Heather are really brother and sister. The wedding night can't be consummated. How all this came about is revealed in a flashback which is silly but believable. What to do? Frederick is a moral man—as much as he loves Heather he can't have sex with her. Heather doesn't really care. She wants him, brother or not, but Frederick insists, although they will stay married, they must take a vow of chastity. Poor Veronica—all she has left are her fingers. Freddie has the maid and cook (Christie Ford, Vanessa Del Rio), but alas they're not enough, he really wants his sister. Feeling sorry for Heather ("The poor girl is as frustrated as I am"), he arranges with Tom (R. Bolla), his chauffeur, to take care of her. He even has a peephole where he can watch them. When he is driving Heather on a shopping trip, Tom lets the old family Rolls break down near a farmhouse. Soon he's in a hayloft with Heather and she is discovering the joys of copulation. "He didn't even come inside me because I might have a baby,"she says. But poor Fred has left the castle. Later, still totally enamored with his sister, he finally returns. They must have one night together, Frederick tells Heather, to consummate their love—after which they will commit suicide. With the poison beside them on a night table Frederick is about to penetrate his wife and then once again dear old Uncle Roy knocks frantically on the bedroom door. It's all a mistake (explained in detail that will set your mind reeling): Frederick and Heather are not really brother and sister. Alas, to his chagrin, Frederick suddenly is impotent. "You thought you were going to have sex with your sister," Heather tells him, "but now that I'm your wife, you don't desire me." It's true, but all is not lost. Heather telephones a neighboring castle where Tom (who left after his one-night stand) is now employed. To his delight Tom now has two jobs: drive the Rolls and sleep with Heather.

SECOND COMING OF EVA
CC NN NM BI DK NL (silly ass)
1975 CAL VISTA

P/D—A. M. Rahs, Mac Ahlberg
F/A—Peter Berg, Jack Frank, Jim Styf, Kim Frank
F/A—Teresa Svenson, Bridget Maier, Agda Daal, Suzy Anderson

Produced either in Sweden or Denmark (there's nothing on the credits to help determine which), this sexvid has very attractive women whom you've never seen before, and an almost indefinable happy-go-lucky, slapstick sophistication that escapes American filmmakers. It's not really the story of Eva, although her sister sends her to Count Beau Gillinstake's live-in school for young women. Rather it's the story of Gillinstake's inheritance of his wealthy Uncle's country manor estate somewhere in Sweden. In the dubbed-in dialogue a lawyer arrives, presumably from the United States, to check up on the count and make sure that he's living a life of impeccable moral standards. Of course, he isn't. The count has hired a faculty of young men to teach the young ladies, "who are so horny they have to be put away by their parents" and provide the environment for "moral growth." Opening day of the school—after the parents and guardians have left—turns into a champagne party orgy in which the Baron, who is in his forties, joyfully participates. Eva, who is a virgin, quickly gets initiated into sex by a female roommate but she doesn't really climax until she falls in love with a handsome male instructor and then she wails so ecstatically that she sounds like a siren going off. I would guess in the original version that the moralistic young lawyer who arrives is *not* American but is supposed to be a Swedish inspector of schools. In a funny extended scene, after he is seduced, and then "raped" by five young ladies in the library, he proceeds to exhaust each and every one of them in turn, and finally takes on Eva's sister, who has arrived to take Eva home because she's discovered her blissfully having sex with her instructor.

SECRET DREAMS OF MONA Q
CC NN NL NR NM BI DK
ARROW and ADULT VIDEO

P/D—Charles Kaufman
F/A—Wade Nichols, Tom Baker, Richard Rimmer
F/A—Monique Cardin, Ushi Inger, Inga Bjorg

Add this one to your list of totally sophisticated sexvid classics that are worth owning, and which most women will enjoy. It's impossible to describe except that you gradually realize the sexual fantasies you are watching are either Mona's or her husband's (Bob). They range from laughing, romantic to silly and kinky, all one after another. The first section is for music lovers as Mona as herself (and as several other women) makes extended love to the background music of a concerto and a symphony. Bob scarcely hears her say: "We've been married five years and we can't even fake a decent conversation.

Talk to me!" He's dreaming of being a big executive with naked women secretaries, and later in bed can't get it up unless he is looking at *Playboy* bunnies as he makes love to his wife. As for Mona, Do women really have such crazy fantasies? This is a sexvid which will start conversation between young couples. It's Monique Cardin's first film—and there's only a couple of others. Two big questions: Whatever happened to Wade Nichols? He's a charming male actor. And note the name Richard Rimmer. He's no relation—but he is a handsome black lover, one of Mona's wash-day dream men!

SECRETS CC R NR
1978 VIDEO GEMS

P/D—John Hanson, Phillip Saville
F/A—Per Oscarsson, Robert Powell
F/A—Jacqueline Bisset, Shirley Hopkins, Tasrka King

With luck you might see this one on pay television—if not, it's a tape worth owning. It is not X-rated. Jacqueline Bisset as Jennifer Wood, a woman in her late twenties with a ten-year-old daughter, is married to Alan (Robert Powell). In this film she is the first major Hollywood star to appear naked in a believable sexmaking sequence that will captivate most females and offers a verbal exchange between her and a first-time (but probably not last) lover that should be watched and listened to carefully by adult filmmakers. After passionate lovemaking with Raul, who is older than she and who has been attracted to her because she resembles his wife who died of cancer, Jennifer sighs, looks at him lovingly and comes back from her complete surrender with one word: "Hello." And he grins and responds to her with a hello. Their gentle, after-lovemaking conversation covers even their children and her husband. It is warmly caring and romantic because it reveals two people sincerely trying to reach out to each other. Simultaneously, her husband, Alan, is having a brief affair with another nice woman who has been aptitude testing him for a job with a computer company, and their daughter Judy has been testing her budding sexuality on a young man who is a gardener and sends her home with an azalea plant. Each relationship has an aura of caring lacking in most adult films. Moreover, the afternoon of "adventuring" and Jennifer's needs in her own words: "Sometimes I just need to be irresponsible . . . to be taken care of," and Raul telling her: "It's good to get away from normal life and explore other avenues to discover oneself"; and Alan's feelings, "I love Jennifer but it's really difficult to live with someone a lot of the time." . . . All are evocations of "What is love?" The refusal of the producers of this one to interject guilt into the "secrets" makes this a film that really points the way to the future of adult films. *Secrets* has much in common with my novel, *Thursday My Love* (written before *Secrets*). I offer it to an adult filmmaker of the future with a challenge to film the sex scenes, as written, graphically with full touching and display and caring—*plus* conversation.

SEDUCTION OF LYNN CARTER
CC NN NM BI DK
1975 ADULT VIDEO

P/D—Wes Brown
F/A—Jamie Gillis, Tony Rousso, Peter Gibbs
F/A—Andrea True, Sharon Thorpe

Most women will watch this one from beginning to end. It has excellent, believable dialogue, and the scenes are erotically photographed. As in many of the best adult films the story focuses on one woman, Lynn Carter (Andrea True, who no longer makes adult films). Lynn has been married 15 years and has a 13-year-old boy. In bed with her husband, who is about to leave on a two-week business trip, they make love and he asks her if she's ever been curious as to what it might be like to be with another man. She tells him she's never been interested but wonders what his reaction would be if it did happen. He tells her he would understand and not be violent. The next day, after he's gone, she meets Sean (Jamie Gillis), who is waiting to see the doctor she is visiting to get a hair removed from her eye. Jamie convinces her to have lunch with

him and woos her so convincingly that she goes to his apartment. Andrea does an excellent acting job as a hausfrau who is both terrified and entranced by the very cruel and nasty Gillis: "You make me feel like a whore," she tells him. But he excites her, and controls her sexually against her will. By the time her husband returns she's addicted, and Jamie has continued her sexual degradation. Bewildered, she tells her husband and he is totally shocked. He demands a minute-by-minute explanation of what it was like with this other guy. There is no attempt to resolve the marital infidelity. The film concludes with Lynn still a prey to her new addiction.

THE SEDUCERS **CC R DS**
1976 VIDEO GEMS

P/D—Larry Spiegel, Peter Traynor
F/A—Seymour Cassell, Michael Kalamanson
F/A—Sondra Locke, Coleen Camp, Beth Brickell

Originally titled *Death Games*, this one is a frightening blend of horror and sex which has come to be the main ingredient of many films in the 1980s. It reverses the sadistic role which is usually in the male domain and gives it to Jackson (Sondra Locke, of later fame in *Every Which Way But Loose*) and Donna (Coleen Camp), two young women who suddenly appear rain-soaked and forlorn at the front door of George Manning's (Seymour Cassell) palatial home, north of San Francisco. George, a wealthy businessman, is married to Karen, who has gone to San Diego where their son is being operated on for appendicitis. Pretending that they are lost, Jackson and Donna ask if they can telephone friends to pick them up, but there are no friends, and while they are waiting, they are coolly examining George's home. To his surprise, he suddenly finds them naked in the bathroom in a huge tub bathing happily together and they immediately convince him to join them. By the next morning they own him. Almost convinced that they are the "jailbait" they claim they are, as they help themselves to everything in sight and generally create mayhem, he finally scares them sufficiently to leave—if he'll drive them to the bus terminal in San Francisco. But when he returns that night they are back waiting for him. They knock him out, tie him to a brass bedstead and later drag him bumping all the way downstairs. They tell him he is their surrogate father (a unique theme song floats through the picture— "Who's the Best Friend I Ever Had . . . My Old Dad." Before it's over they murder a delivery man by knocking him out and shoving his head in a small aquarium, and they leave George either dead or a babbling idiot—you're not sure which. You'll make this one your Halloween special. Very scary acting by all concerned.

SENSATIONAL JANINE CC NN NL
1979   AVC and CABALLERO

P/D—Hans Billian
F/A—Male actors not identified
F/A—Patricia Rhomberg, Linda Rogers, Irene Silver

Many European-made adult films approach sexmaking in a more realistic and joyous way than most American-made films. As Janine, telling about her introduction to sex in London in 1910 in her mother's boardinghouse, Patricia Rhomberg, with a lovely face and body combines innocence, sauciness and just plain sexual enthusiasm together with down-to-earth conversation during sexmaking that is warmly funny. From her mother's boarders to her priest and stepfather, Janine never gets enough—though her men do. Most women will like this one. A small classic that evokes an era. Worth owning.

THE SEVEN SEDUCTIONS CC NN NR
1980   EROS

P/D—Aaron Lin, Charles de Santos, Christie McDonald
F/A—Richard Pacheco
F/A—Annette Haven, Georgina Spelvin, Kay Parker, Carol Doda

All through this film, especially in the basic premise that quality with one woman is better than quantities of female flesh, you can detect a female director's and scriptwriter's presence. Not only that, but by concentrating on one male, Richard Pacheco, the story permits, through the medium of Madame Lau (Annette Haven), the exploration of male versus female sexual drive. Seems that Christopher Hamilton, a wealthy British playboy, has come to Hong Kong in his own flying boat to experience, with the help of Madame Lau, a sorceress of sorts, the outer limits of human sexuality. To prepare him for the experience, Madame Lau gives him a long exquisite oil massage with loving attention to his penis, and he in turn caresses her body as she slowly rides him to nirvana. There is no climax, and she explains that this is his introduction to tantric sex. At his request she then provides a *Playboy* centerfold girl whom he has always admired, but the lady makes love to him totally silently and then, since she is an illusion created by Madame Lau, she disappears. "The world as you know it has never existed," Madame Lau tells him. "You speak in riddles," he responds. "You are your own riddle," she smiles, "seeking only to experience perfection." At his request, she provides as many women as Marilyn Chambers had men in *Behind The Green Door* (five) to service him, "his cock in one mouth, his balls in another." But this doesn't make him happy because he thinks they are all pretending and not really enjoying him as a person. When she offers him five more ladies, at the moment of his climax they turn into plastic mannequins grinning mindlessly at him. Then he admits that the first time he really experienced love was with Lucy, his first girl. Obligingly and charmingly, Madame Lau becomes Lucy and in a very nice first love scene he makes caring love with her on her family's sofa—and he's *actually* wearing a condom. When he finishes and shows it to her, he tells her wryly: "All our children are in here." Then he tells Madame Lau that once an older woman, Mrs. Barrington (Georgina Spelvin), was very nice to him and taught him about sex, and presto, you are on top of a penthouse apartment in a warmly amusing scene watching Georgina and Richard converse and make love in the bright sunlight. Every older lady in the audience would like to have Richard for a lover! Finally he admits to Madame Lau that the love of his life was/is Veronica (Kay Parker), the woman he deserted. Madame Lau suddenly becomes Veronica. On a blanket beside a lake he makes love to Veronica in a sexmaking sequence that all women should approve of, and he concludes, "More is not enough . . ." Veronica, who really loves him, is better than the faceless women of his fantasies. Add this one to your collection of superior adult films, with good acting throughout.

SEX MANIAC'S GUIDE TO THE U.S.A.
CC   Hard R
1982   KENYON VIDEO

P/D—Romano Vandertes
F/A—Many not identified

Moral Majoritarians will shudder at this tape because it covers many of the sexual "insanities" they fulminate against. It begins in a car wash in Los Angeles where practically naked ladies entertain male patrons with views of their female goodies as they slop soap and water over the cars. Application for employment in this car wash from women weary of working nine to five in offices average 100 a week. Next you get a tour of Plato's Retreat in New York City, which is a sexual social club with 40,000 regular members who enjoy copulating on the premises in the "mat room," or dancing naked on the dance floor, or swimming together in the pools, or relaxing naked in hot tubs or enjoying the complimentary buffet while they cuddle together in screening rooms and watch adult films. It's swingers' paradise, where the guy or woman you come with is not likely to be the only one you screw with on a particular evening. This segment is followed by a quick view of topless boxing between Vanessa Del Rio and Veronica Hart. Then you are taken on a tour of a company on Seventh Avenue which specializes in making leather clothing—plus the whips and chains and gadgets for those who enjoy bondage and discipline. This is followed by a funny sequence with male strippers performing for an all-

female (mostly in their 40s) audience. The ladies shove money into the performers' jockstraps for a quick feel and clap enthusiastically at the erotic stripping. Then there's Captain Sticky, a 400-pound guy whose career is to fight the never ending battle against the enemies of sexual pleasure. This is followed by a tour of Frederick's of Hollywood, that specializes in seductive clothing for sexy ladies, such as crotchless underwear, bottomless girdles, rubber hip pads and inflatable bras that you blow up yourself, etc. Then you are taken on a tour of Studio 54 in New York City, a sexy disco which features an Orgasmatron, a gadget which ejaculates whipped cream on the ladies, and offers a jello jacuzzi for those who wish to escape the cares of the world in 100 gallons of yellow jello. Then there's a new franchise for B and D enthusiasts called Rent-a-Dungeon where you and your mate of the evening can torture each other to your heart's content. That is followed by a sky diver's wedding ceremony where the bride and groom jump naked and are married on the way down. Plus a course offered to American housewives on the art of self-defense and How to Seduce a Man. Followed by cowboys, 1980 style, who fly their airplanes into bordellos in Nevada, complete with airstrips where they can enjoy a little extramarital sex. If you aren't worn out yet, there are segments on prostitution coast-to-coast via massage parlors, an All-Bare Miss America Pageant and a segment of a Black Mass with a naked girl being worked over by a devil in the Church of Satan in Lynn, Massachusetts. Obviously, there are no born-again Christians among the far-out sexual enthusiasts on this tape!

SEXUAL PLEASURE EDUCATION SERIES
PLEASURE SERIES

P/D—Ted McIvenna, Laird Sutton
Consultants—Wardell Pomeroy, Erwin Haeberle
Actors—Many, but not professional and identified by first name only

Originally the Sexual Pleasure Education Series was offered by the Institute for Advanced Human Sexuality and The National Sex Forum (both founded by Ted McIlvenna with headquarters in San Francisco) as the Creative Sex Series. Working with Wonderful World of Video, four one-hour tapes were produced, but distribution through regular video outlets was not up to expectations. Now the series' new name is The Pleasure Series (a Penthouse organization). At least 16 tapes are planned to be released through 1983. If you have the original Creative Sex Series which have been discontinued (or can purchase them), Volume I now appears on both Volume I and Volume III of the Sexual Pleasure Series. Volume II of the Creative Sex Series, *Sexual Vacations* and *Creative Sex Settings,* has been eliminated. Also Volume IV of the original series, *Creative Oral Sex* and *Creative Sex Fantasies,* has not yet reappeared in the *Sexual Pleasure Series. The Creative Use of Sex Aids* is now a separate tape. Two additional tapes, *Gay Men* and *Gay Women,* have been added, making five tapes available as of October 1981.

SEXUAL PLEASURE EDUCATION SERIES, VOLUME I **CC   NN   NR**
$49.95   PLEASURE SERIES

("For couples who want a better sex life")

The entire series is intercut with erotic pictures from the institute's collection and is guided by Loretta Haroian, a psychologist, offering personal and voice-over interpretation. On this tape you can watch a variety of your next-door neighbors talking about and making love, including an extended sequence of a couple in their 40s sexmaking in their bedroom in a tender, romantic and caring way. Also, there's a joyous, loving, laughing sequence with Ed (Ed Brecher, who has written many books on sex) making love with Sally. In case you've given up sex because you're too old, be advised that Ed is in his 70s and Sally in her late 60s which makes this tape something to see. There's also a sequence with a young couple making love in new environments—in this case in the woods by a lake. I'm sure that before the proposed 16 tapes are completed, Ted McIlvenna will explore the fun of sexmaking in even more imaginative

places—such as on top of the World Trade Center overlooking New York City!

SEXUAL PLEASURE EDUCATION SERIES VOLUME II **NN   DK**
$39.95   PLEASURE SERIES

Sex Aids

This tape explores a wide variety of sex aids and shows attractive people using vibrators, dildos, anal vibrators, cock rings and sexy female underwear as a turn on. Sex aids as an aspect of sexmaking turn me off. On the other hand, there is no question that sex aids in solitary masturbation are helpful for non-orgasmic women to discover how to achieve orgasm, and for men to enhance a lonely sex life. Ted wants to create a new aura for sex aids as a part of normal sexual behavior and suggests the word "Erotons" for sex toys with the emphasis on play rather than aids. But loving talk is really the nicest sex aid, and as Wardell Pomeroy points out: "Talk is a four-letter word, too." But you have to have something to talk about, which is a subject for future tapes. Whether using sex aids is a bit kinky is up to you.

SEXUAL PLEASURE EDUCATION SERIES VOLUME III & VOLUME V **CC   DK**
$49.94 each   Male Pleasuring Volume III, Gay Women Volume V   PLEASURE SERIES

This filmography does not list several hundred sexvids which are available for gay men or gay women (note: I do consider the lesbian sex that is an integral part of many adult films not as gay but rather as bisexual since the women make love with men as well as other women). However, these two tapes provide an opportunity for heterosexuals to overcome their repugnance for same-sex lovemaking (not easy for many males) and learn that playful, caring sex can be a natural component of relationships between men who prefer men as lovers and women who prefer women as lovers. If you have never watched homosexuals in the act of love and heard them discussing their feelings for each other this tape is an interesting learning experience. The reason I have labelled it DK is that for homosexuals as well as heterosexuals I think group sex is in the kinky category. Unfortunately this tape has little one-to-one homosexual sex-making.

SEXUAL PLEASURE EDUCATION SERIES, VOLUME IV **NN NR**
$39.95 PLEASURE SERIES

Sex Approaches

On this tape, Loretta Haroian points out four key attitudes males should have in their relationships with females. A woman wants to know you have chosen her as a total person; she wants your undivided attention in essentially what is an act of courtship; she wants to feel that you are sensitive to her needs and desires; and she wants endorsement and validation of herself as a person *after* sex. The tape then proceeds to show you the interpersonal sexual exploration of three separate couples. One unmarried couple engage in laughing discussion over a bottle of champagne whether they will go to the ballet or to bed. Bed wins and romantic caring sex ensues. A couple meet in a laundromat. He's washing his tennis balls. She proposes they spend the time waiting for their laundry in a hot tub which is in a building a few doors away. Another couple explore how they feel about sex by looking at sex books and erotic art in a bookstore. Later they enjoy each other so much that she forgets her sunburn.

SEXUAL PROBLEMS, PRIMARY CARE OF **R**
VIDEO CLINIC   AMERICAN MEDICAL ASSN

Diagnostic and Therapeutic Guidelines

I'm not sure whether the AMA will rent this tape to laymen. It was designed for doctors. It sells for $300 and the AMA rents it for 15 days to nonmembers for $45. There is no explicit sex but there is an ongoing dialogue between Harold I. Lief, M.D., professor of psychiatry of the University of Pennsylvania, and Domeena C. Renshaw, M.D., professor of psychiatry of Loyola University, covering basic problems of human sexuality from the patient's and doctor's points of view. As the moderators point out, "Doctors, no matter what their specialty, are the community front-line sex therapists." Harold Lief for many years has been advocating and pushing for many more courses in human sexuality, particularly sexual problems, which future doctors have to deal with in their own lives as well their patients' lives. While some doctors may not find this tape very sophisticated, my feeling is that it is a forerunner of the kind of sexual learning tapes that eventually will appear (not yet in 1983) on the market. Drs. Lief and Renshaw, and others, discuss many aspects of interpersonal sexuality between themselves and with patients, beginning with a young woman who wonders, "Am I normal?" Seems that there is a change in her marital sex life—she takes too long to "get ready" and John is inside her and ejaculates before she comes. It goes on to patients with diabetes, heart trouble, impotence, etc. The conversation between Lief and Renshaw is a good learning experience for millions of married couples—and, in fact, could make it easier for doctors to elicit answers from patients who, prior to seeing it, might be too embarrassed to talk. The discussion and sexual arousal which Dr. Renshaw calls DAVOS—Desire/Arousal/Vasocongestion/Orgasm/Satisfaction—and factors inhibiting good sexual enjoyment, such as anxiety, anger, alcohol, aging, drugs, depression, deliberate control and dissociation would be educational for millions of young and old couples. Tell your doctor to buy it and rent it to you!

SEX USA **CC NN DK BI**
1972 ARROW

P/D—Gerard Damiano
F/A—Various unidentified porno stars

Like Matt Cimber's *Man and Woman*, which made him a million dollars in the early 70s but so far as I know is not on tape because it is by today's standards so unsophisticated, this film poses as a sex documentary and uses the device of a half-dozen sober citizens (lawyers, writers, homemakers) discussing pornography and censorship pro and con. In between, a group of presumably ordinary young people discuss their own sexuality in what looks like a college environment. Actually they are porno stars. This is an interesting tape because it tries to offer visual sexual portrayals in the framework of serious discussion of how to enjoy human sexuality. Thus, in its time it would avoid censorship. But Damiano, who obviously put it together as a much younger man and offers an extended discussion himself about sex, has to earn a buck and appease the raincoat crowd, who want it explicit and kinky. The voice-overs, male and female, particularly an unknown English woman (who is also featured behind the camera in *The Love Tapes* offer interesting how to commentary and occasionally there's dated comments like an off-camera female who tells you that she "digs oral sex and particularly 69"—or guys who tell you they learned from lesbians who knew how better than most men. If coming events cast their shadows before, perhaps some day a sexvid of this type could be very natural and deal with human realities much better.

SEX WORLD **CC   NN   some BI**
1978   SELECT/ESSEX

P/D—William Thornberg, Anthony Spinelli
F/A—John Leslie
F/A—Leslie Bovee, Sharon Thorpe, Annette Haven

Best music score, Erotic Film Awards 1979. *Screw's* Best 10 number one. A weekend at a sexual health center that caters to (supposedly) innermost male and female fantasies. Excellent cinematography. Some good acting and an excellent montage of interracial sexmaking.

SKINFLICKS **CC   NN   NM   DK   DS**
1978   ADULT VIDEO and VIDEO-X HOME LIBRARY

P/D—Gerard Damiano
F/A—Jamie Gillis, Anthony Hudson, Joseph Scott
F/A—Beth Anna, Colleen Davis, Sharon Mitchell

Damiano not only directed this film but appears in it as Al, a nasty character who owns a strip joint and finances adult movies. In this behind-the-scenes story of porno films, the director is ten days behind on a movie that was supposed to be produced in three weeks. "An epic he wants," Damiano as Al comments on Tony Hudson, who plays the part of the director. The plot revolves around an inside look at making of porno films, and one of the stars, Colleen Davis, who falls in love with Tony Hudson. Tony reflects Damiano's true feelings. "Ten thousand years of civilization," he tells Colleen, "Where has it led us?" Damiano proves it with Jamie Gillis who is in the advertising business but has seen all of Colleen's films and believes she wants some "dirty" sex as much as he does. In a terrifying rape scene (Jamie captures her after she tells him that off-camera she wants a relationship and not just sex), Jamie ties her up. He puts Colleen through total sexual degradation while she whimpers, at his command, that she loves every minute of it. As in many of Damiano's films, there is an uneasy truce between his own Catholic morality and the reality of the adult film industry which he subtly makes apparent. Someday when the adult film classics are available on tape or discs for about $20, collectors will want to own all the Damiano films. Note for the curious: Jill Monro, who was male and had a sex change operation (see *Screw*, July 13, 1981), appears in this film and also *Double Your Pleasure* and *Centerfold Fever.*

SKINNY DIPPING **R**
THE NATURISTS

P/D—Edin and Ethel Velez

This is a joyous, one-hour tape of the naturist (not nudist) "clothes optional" lifestyle which is slowly becoming a way of life for millions of Americans who have created and enjoy "free" beaches in various parts of the United States and the world. Even more than the nude beauty contest tapes that I have put in this filmography, this tape celebrates the joy and wonder of the human body, young and old, fat and skinny—and even pregnant women and nursing mothers—people of all ages enjoying the freedom of their naked bodies in the sun, the air, the ocean and mountain streams. If you have read any of my novels you will know why I have included this kind of tape in this book. Lee Baxandall, who heads up The Naturists (a worldwide organization, P.O. Box 132, Oshkosh, WI 54902), calls the tape "A unicorn—the only one in its genre which is between pornography and puritanism, and beholden to neither and crippled by neither." My hope is that before the turn of the century you will be able to watch this kind of film—and natural nudity—on both commercial and cable television. When this happens, while they will still make adult films showing a man and woman sexmaking together, the films will exalt human copulation and not degrade it as many of the current films do. In his letter to me Lee was hesitant about having this tape included . . . and among other things he asked: "Why don't you turn over a chapter to a woman to evaluate the difference between porn and eroticism?" Unfortunately, many women are no better equipped mentally to do this than men. I'm sure of one thing—a nicely shaped naked female body, young or old, is an erotic experience for most men, and I hope the same is true for women. This tape covers the free beaches at Riis Park, twenty minutes from Times Square; the beaches in Guadelupe, "the most clothes-free resort in the Western Hemisphere"; a mountain resort called Smitty's in upper New York State; and the famous Blacks Beach near San Diego. The Velezes interview people from all walks of life who tell you how much fun it is to shed your clothes. You learn the problems caused by some shocked local lawmakers who are always trying to legislate other people's morality. If you never have taken your clothes off—out in God's sunlight, and played naked together with your friends, or even if you have, you'll enjoy this tape. You can order it from the above address for $69.95—and (even without ordering the tape) you can join the Skinny Dippers and become a naturist for an annual membership of $15 a year which includes a subscription to *Clothes Optional Newsletter*.

SMALL TOWN GIRLS
CC NN BI DK DS DM
1979 VCX

P/D—**William Dancer, Tony Janovich**
F/A—**Harry Freeman, John Seeman, Dave Morris, Aaron Stuart, Michael Morrison**
F/A—**Serena, Valerie Darlyn, Dorothy Le May, Blair Harris, Shirley Wood, Jesse Adams**

This title is a complete misnomer. These are not small town naive little girls from the country but super-sophisticated ladies competing in a $50,000 contest run by *Play-Around* magazine for the best article a woman can write about her fantasies. Four women have qualified. Cindy (Dorothy Le May) has rape and bondage fantasies. Barbarella (Valerie Darlyn) wants to be a voyeur and be watched screwing. Anne (Blair Harris) wants to make love to a big beautiful man on a beautiful yacht. In addition to writing about their fantasies, the finalists are given five thousand dollars by the magazine owner, and they must actually live out their fantasy. Unknown to them, the owner of the magazine has enlisted four men to aid and abet them. This, of course, is one way of saying, especially about the sadistic and/or masochistic scenes, that it was all in fun, that it really never happened. But you won't think so when you see Cindy suspended by a maniac rapist on a what he calls his "ferris wheel," two planks crossed in an X on an axle which he can spin around and to which he ties her and strips her. Then he rapes her while she protests. Barbarella pretends that she's a fortune teller at an amusement park, and before she is through she gets her voyeur wishes. Anne is the only one who has any nice sex. She finds a yacht, rents it and the Captain, and off they go—sailing, screwing, and falling in love. Danielle (Serena), the fourth contestant, wants to screw an unknown man in the back seat of a Rolls Royce while the chauffeur watches. She also wants the man to obey her completely. The hired chauffeur spots a guy in a tux who quickly discovers that Danielle is quite freaky. She gives him a vibrator and tells him to shove it in her ass. "I want you to hurt me with it!" she tells him. He does. She screams in pleasure, and finally opens the car door and throws him out on the sidewalk. The CC rating may be dubious, but you'll keep watching, because you can't believe your eyes! Oh yes, *all* the ladies win the contest because the editor is so impressed with their deeds and fantasies.

SODOM AND GOMORRAH
CC NL NN DS DK
1977   MITCHELL

P/D—Mitchell Brothers
F/A—Sean Brancato, John Keyes
F/A—Gina Fornelli, Jacqueline Brody

Supposedly the most expensive explicit sex film made (until *Caligula*), this sexvid has a story line (Hollywood Biblical), though it gets muddy at times because it is relived through the future. This sexvid is worth owning, historically, because it reveals the potential for retelling hundreds of Biblical stories with more explicit sexuality.

SOMETIME SWEET SUSAN   **CC NR**
(with a totally believable sequence)
VCA

P/D—Craig Baumgarten, Fred Donaldson
F/A—Harry Reems, Neil Flanagan
F/A—Shawn Harris, Sara Nicholson

Best Picture Award, Adult Film Association. If you need proof that an adult film can be made which incorporates explicit, caring sexmaking, good acting, good editing, excellent dialogue, and an interesting story, buy this one. Most women will really like it. This is the last film that Harry Reems made and the only one in which Shawn Harris appears. Both prove they are good actors. It is the story of a girl (with a schizoid personality) who is picked up by the police. Is she sweet Susan or aggressive Sara? In the process of finding out, you will watch some really warm, loving, joyous sexmaking between Harry and Sara and between Harry and Shawn. You can also preview this one in an edited version which runs on some adult subscription television stations.

SOUNDS OF LOVE   **CC NN NM BI**
1981   CABALLERO

P/D—Alan Vydra
F/A—Gerald Koehn, Don Hart
F/A—Annette Haven, Jesie St. James, Loni Sanders, Misty Blue

If you'd like to hear Annette Haven and several other ladies reach a climax in Dolby stereo, and you have the equipment to play it on your VCR set-up, this one deserves a collector's choice. Also, the only male star, Don Hart, takes care of all of the females listed above, in addition to three others. The plot? It's a gimmick to hold your attention to the continuous, happy belly-bumping. Seems that Annette's husband, Richard, a musician, never takes care of her properly in bed, but with a $3 million sound studio, he's determined to capture the sound of human orgasm—"the highest level intensity of human sound," according to him. Then he, or anyone else, can replay the sound. This may seem silly, but had Alan Vydra known how far commercial digital synthesizers would develop he might have written the screenplay differently and better. The fact is that synthesizers can now be programmed to mimic *any* human sound and play it back, and electronic music has entered a whole new creative phase. Donna Summers made a "climaxing" record a few years ago which was a big seller. Why not an "Orgasm Concerto For Synthesizer and Orchestra"? Since Vydra didn't have this perspective, the story concerns Richard, who hires Don Hart to tap telephones and generally bug the premises of nice young ladies so that he can record their climaxes. This becomes the raison d'etre of one sex scene after another. There is one in which Annette and Jesie St. James make very romantic bisexual love together after Jesie has been rejected by Annette's husband. Finally, when Richard discovers that Annette is having the ultimate in noisy climaxes (which she is enjoying with Don Hart just to show him what he is missing) and Richard's recording the whole business, he suddenly gets jealous and does just what he promised to do in the beginning. He blows the house, the studio and everybody to kingdom come!

SPECTACULAR EVENING IN PARIS R
1978 VIDAMERICA

P/D—Harlan Kleinman
F/A—Yves Mourossi
F/A—Lauren Hutton

Lauren and Yves are your tour guides to the nightclubs of Paris. It's better than the tour you'd get as a "paid extra" on one of those one-week in Paris tours. It includes a general tour of Paris in the early evening—then one after the other, a feature sextion of the shows at Moulin Rouge, New Moon, Empire Theatre, Lido, Michou, L'Espace Cardin, Madame Arthur, Casino de Paris. Other than the transvestites at Michou and the transsexuals at Madame Arthur's, the show scenes are no different than you would see in Las Vegas. The nudity is all confined to female T and A. The reason that I've included this tape here is that while writing this book I have tested many varieties of sexvids on different age groups. It's interesting that most ladies past 50 find this one pleasantly titillating. In the 1980s the boundaries of sexuality for most Americans still stop at the waist, especially for the males, which older ladies still can't enjoy watching.

STORY OF JOANNA
CC NN DK DS BI
1975 ADULT VIDEO

P/D—Gerard Damiano
F/A—Jamie Gillis, Zebedy Colt, Stephen Lark
F/A—Terri Hall, Juliet Graham

Damiano didn't make this one for the raincoat crowd. A supersophisticated, moody, decadent film with an intellectual dialogue that interweaves a theme of love, death, sex and lust, it will keep you morbidly watching to the shocking end. Joanna (Terri Hall) is discovered in a Continental restaurant by Jason (Jamie Gillis), a moody, malevolent European libertine who takes her to his ancestral castle "to perform a task that I am unable to perform myself." Joanna is entranced and falls in love with him, but Jason tells her, "If you're expecting me to love you in return you're wasting my time ... You'll never understand anything until you know who you

are." From an exquisitely photographed nude ballet scene, to a lonely night in bed where she is masturbated in her dream by detached male hands, to a romantic love scene not with Jason but his manservant (played by Zebedy Colt, who also performs the only homosexual scene that I've ever seen in a film for heterosexuals), to being whipped, chained and defiled by Jason, Joanna never stops loving him. Eventually you discover Jason is dying of cancer(?) and wants to "die by the hand of someone who loves me." And he finally does! Terri Hall has a very evocative face, and she does a fine acting job. A few years ago a description for this blending of masochism and sadism would have been called "porno chic." It's worth owning.

STRANGERS CC NN NR DK
1972 SELECT/ESSEX

P/D—Larry Price
F/A—Michael Simon, Quentin James, Adam Richards
F/A—Michelle Simon, Lisa Marie

This is the only film that I have seen that deals straight-out with swinging—which is surprising because 10 years later, swinging (according to Bob McGinley, president of North American Swing Club Association) is alive and well with quite a few million people involved nationally. And numerous magazines such as Odyssey and Select cater to their search for sexual delight with spouses other than the ones they married. In this sexvid, Paul, who owns a recording studio, is married to Andrea (they have a child). They are both bored with the in-bed aspects of their marriage but they love each other. They try all the marriage manual approaches—pretending that they are someone else, even spending a night in a hotel making believe they are adulterers named Thelma and Harry. Paul makes believe he is a rapist invading their bedroom, but Andrea giggles. Then they buy a swinger's magazine and after discussing the meaning of all the code words, like B/D, Greek, French, European, watersports (bondage and discipline, anal sex, oral sex, spanking, and peeing on each other, in case you don't know), they respond to 15 advertisements and pick out a couple named Tom and Marie, who own a 32-foot motor yacht and are about their age. On the first meeting they quickly make it, on the boat together with each other's spouse. But Andrea wants to keep looking. Their second attempt is with a horny pot bellied-man and his wife who want to take pictures of them copulating. Andrea has a pre-agreed-upon dizzy spell and they escape. The final attempt is the Venus Swing Club, which runs swing parties at various members' homes on weekends. They leave flabbergasted after the first evening, just before one of the members, a woman, tries to cut her wrist in the bathroom. Swingers, of course, won't agree that what they call "social sex" is anything like it is portrayed here—but the film is pretty honest. The dialogue between Paul and Andrea, who must be a husband-and-wife team, is quite realistic. This is a good tape for couples to watch and discover where they are at vis-à-vis mate swapping.

SUMMER SCHOOL
CC   NN   NL   some BI attractively done in a shower
1979   VCX

P/D—Godfrey Daniels
F/A—Gary Linden, Don Fernando
F/A—Laurien Dominique, Lisa Loring, Lynn Thatcher

Queensbrook College Summer School is where everyone would like to further his/her education. Laurien Dominique is the coed every guy would like to take to bed. Most women will approve of her as she and her friends dominate the male professors and show them how to really make love to a woman.

SUPERVIXENS   **CC   NN   DS   NL**
1975   RM INTERNATIONAL FILMS

P/D—A. James Ryan, Russ Meyer
F/A—Charles Napier, Charles Pitts, Henry Rowland, Big Jack Provan
F/A—Shari Eubank, Ushi Digard, Christy Hartsburg, Haji, Ann Marie, Sharan Kelly

Robert Ebert, the famous film critic, who is a very close friend of Russ Meyer and worked with him on *Beyond the Valley of the Dolls,* may one day write a biography on what makes Meyer tick. Russ has left him an extra $15,000 in his will if he does a definitive job. In the meantime, to gain some insight into the tragicomic insanity of Russ Meyer films, I have tried to give some passing insights in the various reviews. I have given them all CC ratings because in the 1980s Meyer has very definitely become adored by cult movie film buffs. This one is the first sequel to *The Vixens.* Unlike *The Vixens, The Immoral Mr. Teas, Lorna* and *Mudhoney* (see listings), which you may see in their entirety on cable or subscription, you will never see *Supervixens* or many of the others uncut. In their originals they are X-rated *and then some.* Not because they actually show penetration, but because of the language—it's wild. The coupling of sex and violence is so damned horrifying you don't know whether to scream or chuckle. Meyer is quite pragmatic about it. He told Al Goldstein in a *Screw* interview in 1977, "I think violence is entertaining . . . it also works for me in the number of asses that cover seats in the theatre." So, *Supervixens* introduces you to Clint (Charles Napier, I think), who works in a filling station run by Martin Bormann (Henry Rowland)—yes, you read the name right. Bormann speaks German and remembers Hitler well! Poor Clint is married to Angel (or is shacking up with her). Angel is not only a sex maniac but she's totally jealous of Clint. Convinced that he's screwing around during the day, she tries to beat him up when he gets home to their bungalow. Failing that, she axes his pick-up truck, smashing it to pieces, but not before he has beat her up so much that a neighbor calls the police. One of the cops, Harry Sledge, is very attracted to her. After Angel has spent a few days in the hospital he arrives at the bungalow when Clint isn't there. Angel quickly seduces him into bed. But Harry (who looks like a young, beefy Marlon Brando) can't get it up. Angel excoriates him in no uncertain terms, and before you know it Harry is beating her up. She temporarily escapes into the bathroom. The violence and sex (she's teasing the hell out of him behind the bathroom door, which she has locked) keep mounting and finally culminate in the wildest, most sadistic scene you've ever seen on your tube (not exceeding *I Spit on Your Grave* . . . see listing, page 233). Harry jams kitchen knives through the door to get at her, and that failing, finally batters the door down and flattens Angel beneath it. The knives in the door stab her. She is still barely conscious. He puts her in the tub (which she has drawn to take a bath), puts her head under water, and drowns her. Then he burns down the house. And that's only the beginning—Clint, afraid he will be accused of murdering his wife, hitchhikes out of town and has three more encounters with big-breasted women who seduce him and he comes out the loser. Months later, he arrives at a filling station in the desert being run by Supervixen—Who is she? Angel reincarnated! Soon Harry arrives to fill up his car, and the ending is even more violent than anything you've seen thus far, with Harry trying to kill both of them by throwing lighted sticks of dynamite at them, finally blowing himself up. All of this transpires while you are watching some of the loveliest and biggest breasts you've ever seen.

SUSAN'S VIDEO EXCHANGE
CC   NN   NM   NR
SUSAN'S VIDEO

P/D—You and your companion
F/A—Same

You can buy amateur productions directly from Susan of average couples (some swingers) who have made their own sexmaking tapes. Prices are $55 for an hour or longer tape. After watching these tapes, you'll be intrigued enough to make your own. My guess is that one day the Japanese will introduce an auto-focusing timer that will attach to your video camera and over a period of an hour can be programmed to zoom and pan or make close-ups and wide-range shots. It obviously will be a big seller. Also, like me after watching thousands of couples copulating, you may wonder if someday sexmaking might be incorporated

into Olympic gymnastic competitions. Seriously—young couples in good physical condition could portray many ancient tantric positions and with background music make copulation as graceful and aesthetic as any of the gynmastic events now offered.

SWEET SAVAGE   **CC   NN   NR**
1979   TVX

P/D—Anne Perry
F/A—Aldo Ray
F/A—Beth Anna, Carol Connors

Best Actor, First Erotic Film Festival Award. Aldo Ray is the first regular Hollywood actor to appear in a porno film, but he doesn't copulate. *Screw* lists this film in its Worst 10 Awards because it isn't sexy enough. But this happy Western about an Indian girl returning to the reservation after living in the East has some very romantic, but explicitly sexual scenes. Most women will like this one, and it points to a future where women will dare to produce sexvids for women and in the process show men what sex and loving is all about. This sexvid shows the unrealized potential for sexy Westerns.

SWEPT AWAY   **CC   R**
1975   COLUMBIA

P/D—Lina Wertmuller
F/A—Giancarlo Giannini
F/A—Mariangela Melato

Many porno film producers are trying to bridge the gap between the art movie houses and the X-rated theaters, but the kind of film that plays to a sexually unsophisticated adult theater audience is usually not the cup of tea of the art houses. In my opinion the at-home video market will solve the problem and cater to an untapped audience with explicit sex in films which evolves directly out of the story line. While *Swept Away* is not sexually explicit, an extended sequence during which a lower-class Italian seaman retaliates against his capitalistic female employer is one of the most sexually erotic and controversial ever filmed. Not only does it symbolize the continuous war between the haves and have-nots, but to feminists it angrily raises the question of male domination and the male-female power struggle, as the two protagonists are temporarily forced to revert to a primitive existence where the female is dependent on the male for the food she eats, and must eventually capitulate to him sexually in order to survive. The overt and subtle power-play between male dominance and female submission, with the female the ultimate winner, make this a sexvid classic. Worth owning. It's a guide for future adult filmmakers to an inexhaustible subject.

SUGAR COOKIES
CC BI DS DK NR (almost in a lesbian way)
1975 VIDAMERICA

P/D—Lloyd Kaufman, Theodore Gersuny
F/A—George Shannon
F/A—Mary Woronov, Lynn Lowry, Monique Van Vooren

This is a fascinatingly-frightening sexvid that walks a thin line between adult X-rated films and art films. You'll probably never see it played in an adult theater. There's plenty of naked sexmaking but no hard-core closeups. You'll probably never see it on subscription television either because it's more "R" than most "R" movies. So buy it or rent it from VidAmerica because it will keep you entranced to the bitter end. It also features one of my favorite actresses, Lynn Lowry, who has a wide-eyed, naive face. She's never appeared in hard-core flicks but is also in Radley Metzger's *Score*. The story is about a very wealthy, handsome, decadent heel, Max Fabel, who convinces sexy movie star Alta Lee, who loves him, to play a weird kind of Russian roulette. He gives her the choice of killing him (she's naked) or putting a revolver in her mouth and pulling the trigger—which *he* does. His girlfriend, Camilla, covers for him and convinces the police it's suicide. Then Camilla gets her revenge by discovering another woman who looks just like Alta, named Julie (Lynn

Lowry plays both parts). Camilla is bisexual but prefers women. The film now moves into a long, beautifully developed lesbian relationship, which suddenly turns sadistic. Later, Camilla restages the scary opening and this time Max is killed, and she leaves Julie holding the bag. Why they titled this one *Sugar Cookies* is anyone's guess, but it mixes sex and murder and good acting in a way you won't see in your surburban movie theater.

TABOO **CC NN DK BI NR (occasionally)**
1980 VCX

P/D—Kirdy Stevens
F/A—Mike Ranger
F/A—Kay Parker, Dorothy Le May, Juliet Anderson

A standard story line in adult films is the married couple who are no longer making it sexually (usually it's the wife's fault and thus the films cater to the frustrated male audience). In this one Chris tells his wife, Barbara Scott (Kay Parker), "Every time, you act as if you're doing me a favor." "You know I don't like to do it with the lights on," she tells him. Before this sorry conversation is over, hubby packs his bag to join his teeny bopper secretary. What makes this one different is the problem of who gets their 19-year-old son, Paul (Mike Ranger)! He can go to Daddy, if he wants to, but Paul chooses Mommy—and you soon discover why. Even though he has Ellen (Dorothy Le May) and her girlfriend to service him, he is always watching his mother, especially when she's naked or taking a shower. In an extended scene without any musical background he watches her in her bedroom, and he sees her admire herself naked in the mirror as she slowly dresses. What makes all of this believable is Kay Parker, who does a good acting job and looks as if she might well be in her late 30s and might possibly have a son like Mike Ranger, who really looks not more than 19 or 20. Her girlfriend Gina (Juliet Anderson) gets Mommy a date with a guy who takes her to a suburban home filled with swingers—six couples in a daisy chain on the living room floor and all the bedrooms filled. Barbara is thoroughly shocked and does not participate, but back home at last, she can't sleep. She hears Paul groaning in his bedroom and finds him lying naked in his bed, dreaming. Unable to resist, she kisses his penis and soon has it in her mouth. The next day she is shocked by her behavior, leaves him a note and tells him they can talk about it tonight. She has got a new job and is employed by a former lover. But Paul isn't shocked by Mommy. "It happened and I want it to happen again," he tells her. The tape ends with Barbara in bed with Jerry, her new lover, but no resolution to the incest which she has enjoyed. This one is interesting to watch and may fascinate a lot of women. But the real story of mother-son incest has yet to be told in adult films.

TAKE OFF
CC   NN   NL   NR (occasionally)   DK
1978   QUALITY

P/D—**Armand Weston**
F/A—**Wade Nichols, Eric Edwards**
F/A—**Leslie Bovee, Georgina Spelvin, Annette Haven**

Seems Daren Blue (Wade Nichols), a multimillionaire, former gangster was born about 1900. But now (the time is the late 1970s), instead of being an old man, he looks as young as he did in the 1920s when the miracle happened. Henrietta (Georgina Spelvin), a wealthy older woman, fell in love with him. As Daren tells the story to Linda (Leslie Bovee), a guest at one of his parties, the screen shifts to black-and-white and you see Henrietta taking Daren on a picnic in a chauffeur-driven Rolls. In 1920s-style ambiance which includes silk stockings and a wind-up phonograph, they make love. Unknown to Daren they are being filmed by Max, Henrietta's chauffeur (shades of *Sunset Boulevard* with Gloria Swanson!). Later when Henrietta shows the film, projected by Max, to Daren, Daren wishes that he would never grow old. Instead the man in the film would grow old in his place (cf. Oscar Wilde's *The Picture of Dorian Gray*).

Mirabile dictu—that's what happens. Actually this intriguing gimmick is not so far from reverse reality as it might seem. If you become a sexvid aficionado, you'll soon discover that ladies like Renee Bond, Tina Russell and Andrea True, all of whom made adult films more than ten years ago and no longer do, will always remain (on the film at least) very beautiful young ladies. Using the never-aging theory gives Armand Weston the opportunity to cover, in nicely integrated, hammily told stories, three decades of Daren's life. They include Wade Nichols amusingly imitating Humphrey Bogart as he recounts his life with John Dillinger and Virginia Slims (a vamp played by Annette Haven), and in a thoroughly mixed up story line he metamorphoses into a Marlon Brando-like character. Most women will grin at this one and enjoy Wade Nichols, who is handsome, and all of the female actresses. Weston proves that if adult filmmakers would orient their story around one or two persons—in this case Wade Nichols—the viewer can stay tuned even through the explicit sex scenes, if only to see what happens.

TALK DIRTY TO ME   **CC   NN   NL**
1980   CABALLERO

P/D—**Jerry Ross, Anthony Spinelli**
F/A—**Richard Pacheco, John Leslie**
F/A—**Juliet Anderson, Jesie St. James**

The *Screw* accolade, "the Best porno film ever made," is an amazing turnabout for *Screw* since this sexvid has no kinky sex, no bisexuality and more than one funny sequence, including two women comparing pubic hair and brushing and primping it to please their lovers. This is the story of Jack, who claims that within three days he can have any woman panting to jump in the sack with him, and his friend Lennie, who is so shy he doesn't dare ask. Jack as John Leslie services four adoring women, one of whom is Jesie St. James, who overhears him talking dirty to some other female. It's not a good title since the dirty talk is normal sex talk. Most women would enjoy John Leslie as a bed friend. This film not only won the Fifth Annual Erotica Film Award as the Best Picture of the Year (1981), but John Leslie was also chosen Best Actor.

TANGERINE CC NN some NL with the ladies in command
1978 VCX SELECT/ESSEX

P/D—Mark Corby, Robert McCallum
F/A—Ken Scudder, Howie Greene, Milt Ingersoll
F/A—Cece Malone, Holly McCall, Laurie Blue

This sexvid, brightly photographed, has a consistent, if silly story line. McCallum provides three women (Tangerine's daughters) who aren't 15 or 16 but occasionally look like nymphettes (especially Holly Mc-Call, who will remind you of Judy Garland) to cater to male fantasies about their teenage lovers. This sexvid also may be one of the first to dispense with one-to-one female bisexuality and offer instead three or four women sexmaking with one man and themselves at the same time thus giving the male viewer the best of both worlds. Women under 40 may enjoy this one.

TALK DIRTY TO ME II
CC NN NM NL NR
1983 CABALLERO

P/D—Jerry Ross, Tim McDonald
F/A—John Leslie, Paul Wright
F/A—Bridgette Monet, Blair Harris, Nicole Black, Analis Person, Louise Jackson

John Leslie was nominated for, and received, the Best Actor award at the 1983 Erotic Film Festival for this film. Unlike most sequels, this one is equal to or better than the original film simply because of John Leslie. He has a knack of combining sexmaking (he'd call it fucking) with a sense of laughter ("It can't be for real that I'm screwing with this lovely woman") with a feeling that he really likes each and every woman he screws. As in the original, Leslie is the superstud whom no woman ever refuses. But in this one the part of Lennie (played by Paul Wright instead of Richard

Pacheco) is not developed. Jack (John Leslie) is the hero—and the original theme of big brother to a retarded character (inspired by Steinbeck's *Of Mice and Men*) is played down. The story revolves around a Dr. Anne (whose real name is Esther Huckaby) played by Bridgette Monet. Though she has no medical degree, Dr. Anne, a cool, collected, sophisticated woman, handles all kinds of sexual and interpersonal questions directly on television from a live audience. Disgusted with her dishonesty, Jack (Leslie) tells a customer at the bar where he is bartender, "I'd like to tell her to suck my dick." "If you feel that way about it, why don't you tell her yourself?" is the response. But when Leslie finally gets in the television show audience, he asks Dr. Anne, "What's more fun than fucking?" Instantly, the Dr. Anne Show, which has been running downhill and is about to be terminated, breaks all the ratings, and the sponsors want Jack as a regular guest. How Dr. Anne locates him (or he locates her by arriving at her home to inspect the plumbing and instead plumbs the maid) is the story line. It ends up in bed with an extended romantic sex scene during which Dr. Anne becomes convinced that Jack is right. Appearing on her last show in a sleek red, low-cut pant suit, she tells her audience, "Nothing is more important than fucking, right?" Bridgette Monet has improved her speaking voice in this one, and is slowly becoming a better actress. The film proves that with a good screen play, an adult film can be sexy and fun to watch, too.

TEENY BUNS
CC NN CI occasional NR
1978 WONDERFUL WORLD OF VIDEO

P/D—Godfrey Daniels
F/A—John Simon, Tyler Reynolds, Jerry Barr
F/A—Judy Harris, Phyllis Wolf, Donna Ruberman

Quite frequently the sexmaking in this sexvid is much more caring and believable than you will see in most adult flicks. An extended sequence between John Simon and Judy Harris (who has a most appealing face to go with what seems like a teenage body) is erotically photo-graphed and Judy responds much the way you'd expect a teenager to respond. After Judy gets $100 for a taxi ride home, her friends quickly discover they can get paid "a whole lot of money for doing what they enjoy doing anyway." Younger women may like this one.

TELL THEM JOHNNY WADD IS HERE
CC   NN   almost NR
1976   FREEWAY

P/D—Richard Aldrich, Bob Chinn
F/A—John Holmes, Tyler Moore
F/A—Annette Haven, Felicia Sanna, Veronica Taylor

Holmes as Johnny Wadd is, as usual, the perfect lover. In one scene after another, Johnny makes love to women the way most women would enjoy. This is a fe-male-oriented sexvid. The story line about narcotics smuggling from Mexico is harm-less. Handsome Richard Aldrich, like Alfred Hitchcock, always appears in his films. In this one he gets shot and killed by the baddies.

THE TEXAS CHAINSAW MASSACRE
CC   R   DS
1974   WIZARD

P/D—Tobe Hooper
F/A—Gunnar Hansen, Allen Danziger, Paul Partain, William Vail
F/A—Marilyn Burn, Tori McMinn

There is no nudity or explicit sex in this tape, but you should watch it and com-pare it with explicit sex films and then de-cide if you were a censor which one you would want your children to watch. Keep in mind that this is a cult film and is shown in college university towns around the United States with no protest from censors that an X-rated film would immediately evoke. It's the story of Sally Hardesty, her brother Franklin (a cripple), her boyfriend Gary, and their best friends, Pam and Kirk. Driving a van, they have just come from a cemetery where a vandal has been dig-ging up bodies and cutting off their heads, arms and legs. Sally's Granddaddy

Hardesty is buried in the cemetery and parts of him are gone. Driving home in the van, they pick up a hitchhiker who is obvi-ously quite demented. He and Franklin (who is older) discuss how cattle were killed in the local slaughterhouse. (They were stunned on the head and then their throats were slit—but now it's done with an air gun instead of a hammer.) The hitchhiker slits his own palm with a knife, cuts up Franklin with a straight razor, and they throw him out of the van. Soon they are passing the farm where old Grand-daddy used to live. Sally remembers visit-ing there. They stop and try to buy more gasoline at an isolated gasoline station. The owner crazily ogles them and tells them to stay away from her Grand-daddy's place—it's abandoned and fall-ing down. The tension is very carefully built. After exploring the deserted house, Pam and Kirk wander off to another nearby farmhouse which likewise seems deserted except for a noisy gasoline gen-erator. Inside lives the maniac Leather Face. First he captures Kirk and then Pam, and while you don't see the decapitation, you know he has sawed off their heads with his chainsaw. Sally goes looking for Pam and Kirk, pushing Franklin through the scrubby land in a wheelchair. Leather Face finds them and decapitates Franklin. For the next half-hour you watch Sally being pursued through the woods by the maniac, brandishing the chainsaw, cut-ting his way through a dark forest after her—she stumbling, screaming and torn. Finally getting back to a filling station and thinking she's been saved by the owner, she discovers he is the brother of Leather Face and the hitchhiker, who are there with their exhumed Granddaddy. Beaten and bleeding, Sally is carried back to the farmhouse where during a horrendous night she promises to do anything they ask her if they'll let her go. She escapes once again—with all three of them pur-suing in the early morning to the highway. She finally escapes with the driver of the pick-up, but has obviously gone totally mad herself. The interesting thing to ask yourself about this film is whether it could have been produced with a maniac chasing a guy instead of a woman? Whether there is explicit sex or not—this story obviously combines sex and violence.

THAT'S PORNO CC NN BI DK
1979   CAL VISTA

P/D—Adele Robins
F/A—See below

This is a good tape if you want to get acquainted with many of the major male and female stars in the business. Most (but not all) are identified by name by the hosts, Jesie St. James and John Seeman, who also have a little sex between these cuts from many unidentified full-length films or loops. The following all appear on this tape, performing every kind of oral, genital, anal and bisexual sex play that you can think of. The male stars appearing are: Jon Martin, John Seeman, John Leslie, Jamie Gillis, Tyler Horn, Joey Civera, Eric Edwards, Marc Stevens, Ric Lutz, Mike Ranger, John Holmes and Johnny Keys. The female stars are Georgina Spelvin, Serena (as a redhead), Abigail Clayton, Tina Louise, Desiree Cousteau, Annette Haven, Jean Jennings, Desiree West, Terri Hall, Suzanne McBain, Lindy Dorn, Karen Devin, Juliet Anderson, Constance Money, Vanessa Del Rio and Jesie St. James. You'll need a stop motion on your VCR to catch some of the faces, should you wish to remember them.

THIS FILM IS ALL ABOUT . . .
CC NN DK BI
1972   ARROW

P/D—Gerard Damiano
F/A—Various "real" people

Damiano obviously enjoys making documentaries. His problem is that he had to produce a film acceptable to the raincoat crowd. This one escapes that trap for the most part, except for an extended cut from XXX-rated 16-mm. pornies, which dominated the Times Square area during the early 1970s. Except for the 16-mm. ten minutes or so, and a cut from *SEX USA* of about five minutes, this is original material that is currently and historically very interesting. Damiano interviews theater man-

gers, strippers, bookstore owners and model studios devoted to photographing women or painting them with poster paints. There is an extended interview with Mary Phillips, who is an active feminist (with NOW); a discussion with a leader of the Gay Alliance during a parade in New York City; an interview with Alex, who says he has appeared in over 200 porno films and is rarely turned on by women; a long interview with Al Goldstein and Jim Buckley, who at the time was part owner of *Screw* with Goldstein; plus a live sex theater sequence and the making of a "peep show" film—the kind of film popular before the advent of explicit sex loops.

THOROUGHLY AMOROUS AMY
CC NN NL DK BI
1978   VCX

P/D—Aaron Linn, Catharine Montgomery, Charles de Santos
F/A—Peter Johnson, Paul Thomas, Nick Jones, Rocco Haper
F/A—Tracy O'Neil, Christine Heller, Candida Royalle

Amy (Tracy O'Neill) is jogging through the parks and streets of San Francisco. Before she gets back to her home, eight guys enamoured by her swinging behind are jogging after her. Amy is so amorous that she could take them all on, but she only manages three. One guy lies flat on his stomach in a net hammock with his penis protuding. He's taken care of by Amy who lies underneath. The two others join her in her waterbed. In process she gets a phone call from her husband, who tells her he will be home from a trip tonight. She tells him to tiptoe in and not to wake her because she's going to be so tired from all the housecleaning she's done. But worry not, when hubby arrives home she takes care of him and again in the morning too. She's making breakfast in curlers and a robe. He gooses her, the scrambled eggs land on the floor and Amy is soon slithering on top of them with her husband happily on top of her. Before the day is over Amy soothes her clitoris with her electric toothbrush, answers the doorbell for a black cop who is checking out a neighbor's house next door for va-grants; answers the doorbell for a vacuum cleaner salesman and a cosmetics lady, and happily screws with all of them. Then her next door neighbor arrives without his wife. She has hidden the others in various closets while she takes care of new arriv-als. Then the story of the insatiable Amy suddenly falls apart. The guy's wife and sis-ter arrive and the husband (Paul Thomas) who Amy has just serviced gives her sister (Candida Royalle) amyl nitrate to sniff and screws her while his wife and Amy watch. It all ends up in group sex with Amy's husband joining the fray. But some of it is happily silly.

THE TIFFANY MINX
CC NN NM BI DK DS
1981 SELECT-A-TAPE

P/D—Robert Walters
F/A—Richard Bolla, Carter Stevens, Jeffrey Hurst
F/A—Crystal Sync, Jennifer Jordan, Marlene Willoughby, Samantha Fox, Candida Royalle, Merle Michaels

I can't figure out why this film wasn't put up for the 1981 Erotic Film Awards. The adver-tising on the film and tape is misleading. The stars of this film are Richard Bolla, Jeffrey Hurst (who is a contender for a top leading man), Marlene Willoughby, Crystal Sync and Jennifer Jordan. All of them do an excellent acting job. Did ac-tor Carter Stevens (who has produced many, many adult films) have a hand in directing? It has a strong story line without sacrificing most of the adult film conven-tions, but handling them in a totally differ-ent way. Wealthy Jessica Grover (Crystal Sync) is married to Paul (Jeffrey Hurst), who is managing her properties together with Anne (Marlene Willoughby), Paul's secre-tary. Right off you know that Paul is a bad guy. "I can't leave Jessica," he tells Anne. "I'm living off her money." Telling Jessica that he must work late, he's happily in bed with Anne. "Don't worry about Jessica," he tells Anne. "I'm not." Their sexmaking is in-tercut with Jessica going to bed alone in her big house and a prowler, Ben (Carter Stevens), whom you've seen previously

with Samantha Fox. Ben holds a knife to Jessica's throat and rapes her, and during the act she takes a pair of scissors off her night table and plunges them into his back. Did Paul hire Ben to kill her? You're not sure—and the story takes off in a new direction. Jessica, shocked at having killed a man, goes for the summer to their beach home on Long Island where Matt (Richard Bolla), a proclaimed stud to wealthy women, has just arrived. Matt has moved in with Pinky (Jennifer Jordan), who is in the real estate business and has a place on the beach not far from Jess-ica's. Matt is determined to seduce Jess-ica. Pinky doesn't like what's happening. Paul is obviously trying to drive Jessica mad with guilt about murdering Ben. After screwing Pinky in a motor boat on Long Island Sound and telling her that he will cut her in on money he plans to pry out of Jessica, Matt strangles Pinky and tosses her body into the ocean. The story goes right down to the final scene, which will surprise you, but even better, most of the sex sequences, especially Bolla with Jennifer Jordan and earlier with Merle Michaels and Candida Royalle, have an interesting, believable spontaneity. Most women will like this film and will relate to Crystal Sync, who is a convincing de-ceived wife.

THREE A.M. **CC NN NM BI NR**
1975 CAL VISTA

P/D—Robert McCallum
F/A—Charles Hooper, Rob Rose
F/A—Georgina Spelvin, Clair Dia, Rhonda Gellard, Sharon Thorpe, Judith Hamilton

Don't pay any attention to the title (it's a poor one), nor to the illustration on the package. Robert McCallum has made one of the few adult films for mature audi-ences. It's erotically photographed, the di-alogue is good, the story is believable and the acting, especially Georgina Spel-vin's and Charles Hooper's (who will re-mind you of Tony Perkins), is excellent. Most women will like this one. The hetero-sexual sex scenes are loving and caring—even an incestual one between brother and sister, and it has the most erotic bisexual scene you have ever watched, with Georgina and Judith Hamilton in a shower. It's the story of Kate (Georgina), who is Elaine's sister and has lived with them for many years helping bring up their children, Stacy and Ronnie. Elaine believes that her husband has been faithful to her but doesn't know that he has been sleeping with her sister, Kate, who tries to get him to leave Elaine and marry her. In a very believable scene in a marina, Kate strikes Mark with a bottle and he falls overboard and drowns. Later Elaine re-enacts her guilt and finally drowns herself. Amazingly, in the sex scenes McCallum uses the camera to watch the females' hands and faces in the act of love. Worth owning.

TOUCH ME **CC NN NR BI**
1971   SELECT/ESSEX

P/D—Larry Price, Sam Weston
F/A—Buck Flower, Ric Lutz
F/A—Tiffany Stewart, Renee Bond

This may have been Renee Bond's first porno flick. She and Ric Lutz are the only actors you will ever see again in later films. Amazingly, the director has used his right name. Sam Weston is much more famous now in porno filmmaking and is one of the hottest directors—Anthony Spinelli is one of his aliases. This one is better than many of his later films. If you have ever been to an encounter group weekend, which were so popular in the mid 1970s, then you will immediately recognize the dialogue and the participants. This one involves a marathon group which includes a husband and wife, three single women, and three single guys, all with different hang-ups—mostly sexual. They are frigid, too aggressive with their friends, or too involved in religiously induced sexual fear. Dr. Lloyd Davis, played by Tom Stevens, is determined during the next 24 hours to teach them all how to enjoy pleasure simply—his approach is "sensory awareness." And as usual in groups of this kind someone who is further out than the rest gets things started: "Doctor, how can I feel anything with all these clothes on? Can I take some of them off?" Dr. Lloyd responds to

the group, "You can remove all of your clothing if you wish, or as much as you wish." Soon half the group is naked, and some are still dressed. After the first 12 hours the aggressive ones are challenging each other and copulating. They act out rape fantasies in front of the group, and the viewer is exposed to explicit sex in a totally different context than most adult films. This film is no *Bob and Carol and Ted and Alice*, which quit before anything happened, and it doesn't stray too far from the actuality of this kind of "therapy," which is still offered today by various groups in the human potential movement. Adult filmmakers should review this film. After ten years it is still more fascinating than many of their offerings. Good for couples and their friends to watch together.

A TOUCH OF SEX
CC NN DK BI ND
1975   ARROW

P/D—Lon Stephens, George O'Connor
F/A—Harry Wilcox, Seymour Clinton
F/A—Penelope Dixon, Candy Horn, Darleen Saunders

Mark Markson (Harry Wilcox) is a middle-aged songwriter who writes romantic, 1950s-style June/spoon songs which no one buys in the rock era. His friend Bif pays his way to California and tells him that he will promote him into fame. Unfortunately as soon as he lands in L.A. Mark has a dybbuk around his neck in the form of two very horny couples who meet him at the airport and screw in the car all the way to Bif's house. Mark's problem is that only *he* can see these disturbers of his sexual peace, and they pop up everywhere—in recording studios, in a private airplane, in a restaurant where he is taking new-found love Mary Jane. Mark is so shocked he tumbles a waiter into a woman diner whose cheese soufflé drops into her dress—which her male friend promptly eats off her. Worse, they follow Mark on a boat in which he's practicing to become a musical deep sea diver. Finally, he takes Mary Jane on a picnic, and to his shock she, the only other person who can see these sex crazies, is seduced by them.

Mark is finally seduced out of his virginity as he sings one of his songs in a night club. Wilcox is a good actor and occasionally this one is quite amusing. It raises the question of why someone hasn't produced an adult version of *A Midsummer Night's Dream.*

UP CC DK DS NL BI
1979 RM INTERNATIONAL FILM

P/D—**Russ Meyer**
F/A—**Edward Schaff, Robert McClaine, Monte Bane, Larry Dean, Bob Scott**
F/A—**Janet Wood, Raven La Croix, Frances Natividad**

Only Russ Meyer can create a sadistic sexual satire that finally leaves you nothing to do but laugh . . . nervously. Censors could raise the question of the education of the viewer. If you are sophisticated enough to laugh, you know that Russ is taking you for an insane buggy ride. But are all the people who see his films that sophisticated? The story on this one is so complicated that for the first half-hour you may think the plot will never unravel. On top of that it has Frances Natividad acting as a Greek Chorus, plus a couple of other big-busted women commenting on what fools we mortals be, in between the action. Their breasts and words will leave your tongue hanging out! Margo Winchester (Raven La Croix) is the big-chested heroine. She's jogging along a country road when local Sheriff Homer Johnson (Monte Bane), driving a Mercedes cruiser, tries to pick her up. She refuses him but a few minutes later a guy named Leonard Box (Larry Dean) corners her and she gets into his pick-up truck. Box immediately goes ape over her. But never try to rape a Russ Meyer heroine! This one is a karate expert, and though Box knocks her out and manages to rape her, she comes to and lifts him up. In the middle of a mountain stream she tosses him down so hard that she breaks his back. She's quickly arrested by Homer, who is more interested in getting into her pants than putting the lovely woman in jail. Besides, she's helped the world get rid of a piece of scum. Soon Margo is curling Homer's

toes—literally, and he gets her a job at Alice's Restaurant, where she draws such an appreciative clientele that Alice (Janet Wood) and Paul (Robert McClaine) have to expand the place. They open a new place called Alice II and Margo becomes the feature attraction. But now Alice ain't too happy with her husband, who is messing around with Margo, too. In a counterpoint plot, Paul is whipping and buggering an Adolf Hitler lookalike who pays to have it done. The grand finale of all this lust takes a half hour. It will leave your eyes popping! A local woodchopper, Rafe (Bob Scott), who weighs about 250 pounds and is six feet tall, spies Margo doing her act at Alice's. He picks her off the bar and while she's struggling and screaming, tears off her clothes and rapes her across one of the tables while the male crowd cheers him on. Paul tries to save her, but Rafe clouts him silly. Homer arrives and sees his woman being molested. He plunges one of Rafe's axes into Rafe's back. Do you think that stops Rafe? No way. He pulls the axe out of his back and whops it into Homer's chest. Blood is spurting out of Rafe like a geyser, but Rafe picks up both Margo and Alice and trudges off into the night with them. He's followed by Homer, who is erupting with blood but now has a chainsaw. When he catches Rafe, he damn near saws him in half. Think the sexvid is over? No way! Alice is determined to kill Margo for seducing her husband, and almost does before she admits that her real name is Eva Braun, and she was Hitler's mistress. You'll have to watch it twice to figure it all out. But you'll never forget it.

UP 'N COMING CC NN BI DK
1983 CREATIVE IMAGE

P/D—**Godfrey Daniels**
F/A—**Herschel Savage, Richard Pacheco, John C. Holmes**
F/A—**Marilyn Chambers, Lisa de Leeuw, Codi Nicole, Loni Saunders**

Miracle Films, who made this one, has a slogan: "If it's a good film . . . it's a miracle." This one isn't a miracle, but it's a good film. The story is about Cassie Harland (Marilyn

Chambers), who is a country-Western singer on her way up, and Althea Anderson (Lisa de Leeuw), top singer in the country who is on her way down and overdosing on pills and booze. Told by Johnny King (Herschel Savage), a big country-Western promoter: "You sell sex the way Colonel Sanders sells chicken. Are you as good as you sound?" Cassie responds, "I'm better" and proves it. In her rise to the top Cassie has to challenge Althea. She tosses a drink in her face and tells her she's a drunk. After which Althea assigns her goon squads to get her. Cassie takes refuge in a laundromat where the guy is using Ivory Snow and dreaming about her. Marilyn was once the Ivory Snow girl. Cassie finally makes it and gets her own bus and caravan. To get to the top she has sex with two guys at the same time, as well as taking on Codi Nicole. Richard Pacheco as a disc jockey doesn't think she's a very good singer but tells her she's got great sex charisma. He has a fantasy of interviewing "a beautiful woman like you naked." She coolly unzips him and totally deep-throats him, after which, leaving him panting, she tells him: "When I get to the top I'll be back to finish you off." This tape is worth seeing to keep up to date on Marilyn, who I would guess is now forty. All her ribs can be counted, her pussy hair is heart shaped, but she's more interesting now than when she was younger. Lisa de Leeuw should win a best supporting actress for her role as Althea. No Hollywood professional could have played the part better. Godfrey Daniels gives you some nice cinematography and takes you to Catalina on a shopping trip with Marilyn.

But the film would have been much better if he'd eliminated John C. Holmes, who only appears for a few minutes as a famous country-Western singer. Holmes doesn't sing. His name is Charles Strayhorn. For some reason, you never see Holmes's face, but he's as skinny as Marilyn, and she can accommodate all of his fantastic strayhorn in her mouth. Obviously Daniels was catering to the box office with Holmes. It's Holmes's first film after finally being released from prison on drug charges. The film concludes with an unnecessary orgy scene—or maybe it was necessary. Marilyn is a pretty freaky lady—see the various listings on her films.

URBAN COWGIRLS
CC NN BI DK NR (but only with Georgina)
1981 CABALLERO

P/D—Cliff Stern, Laura Stevens, Tsansudi
F/A—John Leslie, Eric Edwards
F/A—Hilary Summers, Victoria Hart, Georgina Spelvin

This one tied with *Talk Dirty to Me* for the Best Picture, Fifth Annual Erotic Film Festival 1981, and also gave Georgina Spelvin the Best Actress in a supporting role and Tsansudi the Best Director award. Beyond a couple of scenes at Rock-a-Bye Billy's Dance Hall (owned by John Leslie) to establish the title, the real background is presumably upper-class women, divorced, widowed or not, making it with their husbands, who slip away to the nightclub dance hall for fun and games with whomever they encounter. They're dressed as cowgirls, of course. Amanda (Victoria Hart) is a slutty, wealthy widow who picks up guys for romantic evenings before her fireplace in an expensive home overlooking Los Angeles. Marianne (Hilary Summers) is in love with Billy and he with her, but their encounters are all in their imaginations (very romantic) until they discover each other. But the story of Kate (Amanda's sister), played by Georgina Spelvin, is a little sexvid classic that makes this one worth owning if you're a Spelvin fan. Kate is married for a long time to Paul (Aaron Stuart). Sexmaking is perfunctory, as you see in a funny early morning bed scene. Next Kate is trying to seduce Paul with a gourmet dinner which includes oysters. She's dressed as a French maid with her ass sticking out, but Paul falls asleep. So poor Kate decides to slip away and take her sister's advice and live it up at Rock-a-Bye Billy's Dance Hall. Fortunately, Paul hears her make the date with Amanda on the telephone, and on the brink of disaster saves her, brings her home and they make passionate love for the first time in years. It's interesting that after ten years, directors, story writers, and producers of adult films are still, as this film reveals, ambivalent about their audience. Half the time they cater to the male raincoat crowd and the other half they try to be romantic.

VIOLATION OF CLAUDIA CC NN BI
1977 QUALITY

P/D—Billy Bagg
F/A—Jamie Gillis, Don Peterson, Waldo Short
F/A—Sharon Mitchell, Crystal Sync, Long Jean Silver

When Claudia (Sharon Mitchell) awakens in her sumptuous bed in a sumptuous home after dreaming a sexy dream, she turns sleepily to her husband for some morning sex. "I'm sorry, dear, I have a busy day," he tells her. Jason (Don Peterson) is glad that she's going to take a tennis lesson at the club. He's obviously preoccupied. Claudia's tennis instructor, Kip (Jamie Gillis), offers her a job working for him in a call girl service in a fancy apartment, complete with two-way mirrors. Kip invades the massage room, where Claudia is having an after-tennis massage. She's quite horrified. "Go away, please. I'm a married woman. How did you get in here?" she asks. Kip doesn't answer but he soon gets into her, and she goes to work for him. Why not? That night Jason, at dinner, is doing some office calculations. He asks her what she did today and she answers, "I had a very interesting fuck." Jason doesn't hear her then or when he tells her that he's going on a trip and she says she hopes his plane crashes. The only reason I've given this one a CC rating is because of the senator. Played by Waldo Short, who is bald, not over 5'5", and rather plump, he's Claudia's client. (She's now working afternoons for Kip.) The senator arrives with a black bag filled with whipped cream, a bottle of cherries, a paint brush and chocolate and butterscotch sauce. Telling Claudia to undress and lie on a table where he has spread a tablecloth, he follows suit and soon is wearing only an apron and a chef's hat. Then chuckling happily, he decorates her like a birthday cake, and finally offers her choice of chocolate or

butterscotch. Poor Claudia decides that marriage—even to Jason—isn't so bad. She rushes home. Jason isn't expecting her and she finds Jason in bed—no, *not with the maid*—but with Kip! Seems Jason prefers men to women and arranged the whole deal with Kip. Poor Claudia!

VISIONS CC NR BI DK
1977 QUALITY

P/D—Chuck Vincent a.k.a. Felix Miguel Arroyo
F/A—Wade Nichols, Peter Andrews, David Christopher
F/A—Susan McBain, Victoria Corsaut, Betty Brook

Larry (Wade Nichols), a composer, is working late when this film opens. As he walks down the corridor getting ready to leave, a strange woman suddenly appears and beckons to him. She vanishes. Then he's accosted by a couple of thugs who are about to rob him. One, standing behind him, slugs him with a crowbar and he drops to the floor, bleeding profusely. During the rest of this film there is *no dialogue whatsoever*, and you gradually realize as the ambulance arrives and medics pound Larry's chest that he is in cardiac arrest, hovering between life and death. Unconscious, his mind floats into a world of detached sexual bodies caressing him, and then he's with a woman (Susan McBain) who is caressing him and almost mothering him in a very tender, caring sexmaking sequence. From there he is plunged into a circus-like orgy with painted women in swings, clowns, men wearing hard hats, and then, against a white background, three naked women discover him and are caressing him while three naked men watch. Then a fish net is thrown over his head. Two women strap him to a table and one plunges a knife into his breast, and once again he's being made love to by a woman, caringly, who gets out of bed and bids him goodbye with tears in her eyes. The camera returns to the medics, who have given up. Larry is dead. Chuck Vincent may not have realized it when he was making this one and filling in the action with very appropriate background music that this erotic sexual ballet would be a forerunner and point the way to *Roommates* (see filmography, p. 125). Buy or rent this one. Most women will like it. Vincent told me he shot this one in two days, which goes to show if you have a good basic idea, carefully worked out, a quickie can be better than a million-dollar epic.

VISIONS OF CLAIR
CC NN NR BI DK
1977 WONDERFUL WORLD OF VIDEO

P/D—Zachary Youngblood, Thomas Erp
F/A—John Rolling, Jay Gamble
F/A—Annette Haven, Bonnie Holiday, Susan Bates

My interest in watching over 650 adult films during a period of three years was maintained by discovering, within the conventions (and hence limitations) of the genre, a number of classics of adult filmmaking. This is one. Ron (John Rolling), an artist, tells Clair (Annette Haven) that he can't capture her naked beauty on canvas. "It's not real," he tells her. "I can't even imagine having sex with your body." Clair, who does seem quite ethereal, proves to him in an extended caring sex sequence that she is attainable. Four years later, Clair is living with Ron, who is slowly deteriorating, and his wife Daphne (Bonnie Holiday). They have another artist friend, Rohane (Susan Bates), and both she and Daphne have come under Clair's spell. Who is Clair? Is she a lesbian? Is she a mirage? "My visions of Clair," she tells herself before a mirror, "are whatever I want them to be." Did she invent Ron—and Rohane? Maybe they don't even exist? In one of her visions the viewers experience an other-worldly, mystical orgy in an extended sequence in which Clair is the central figure of beautifully choreographed sex. In another, while she is in bed with Daphne, she is watched by Rohane, who does a dagger dance piercing her skin until blood flows—or does it? Is it all figurative, symbolical? Immediately thereafter her skin is untouched. The bisexual scene is preceded by an erotic dance during which the camera watches Annette and Bonnie to-

gether for many minutes. Most women will be fascinated with Clair.

VISTA VALLEY P.T.A.
CC NN NM DK BI
1980 QUALITY

P/D—Benardo Spinelli, Anthony Spinelli
F/A—Jamie Gillis, John Leslie, Aaron Stuart, Dewey Alexander
F/A—Jesie St. James, Juliet Anderson, Kay Parker, Dorothy Le May, Shirley Woods

Miss Martin (Jesie St. James) is the new English teacher at Vista Valley High School, where two former female teachers already have been raped, and a male teacher has been mugged and beaten. But it's not New York City, it's Southern California. And it's not *Blackboard Jungle*—rather it's a kind of Peyton Place. First, there's Daddy Davis (John Leslie), who has a son, Greg Davis (Dewey Alexander). Right off Greg is out parking with Sharon's (Juliet Anderson) daughter, Sandra (Dorothy Le May). Eventually Daddy Davis calls on Sharon, whose husband has divorced her—Daddy's wife has disappeared too, and Daddy is telling Sharon that he "can always tell when a lady's husband is gone and she needs a little." Sharon sure does, but in the process they are interrupted by her daughter Sandra, who tells her, "Mommy, you are a slut after all." Then Sandra takes Daddy into the bedroom, even though he's just climaxed with Mommy. At first Mommy is shocked, but she joins them in bed and Daddy happily tells her, "I'd better tell Greg—we could have a good family-thing going here." Next in Vista Valley there is Kay Parker and Aaron Stuart, who have been married 16 years. There are Walter and Mildred, also with a daughter who defies discipline. And Mildred is rejecting Walter in bed because he attacks her about once a week for sex and then climaxes before she does. She falls asleep beside him and masturbates while he's snoring. Then there's Jamie Gillis, a religious zealot who likewise has no spouse but goes to whorehouses where he masturbates while he watches a whore masturbate. The trouble with Jamie is that he's in love with his daughter, played by Shirley Woods, and in a very effective and believable scene, he introduces her to the joys of sex. Tying this altogether is Jesie St. James, who tries to make all these middle-class kids study but is finally tricked by Greg Davis and is raped while standing against the wall in an unoccupied house before all the hung-up fathers arrive. Miss Martin will have to leave Vista Valley, they tell her, because she was going to expel Greg and because she believes that their children can be disciplined (they obviously can't). But not before they all take a poke at Miss Martin. Is she angry with them? Well, not quite. When it's all over she leaves town with Greg Davis. In bare outline it's pretty silly, but Spinelli manages to put it all together with some interesting and fairly believable sexual encounters, and as usual he appears to put his blessing on things. He's the fat, plump, likable guy who appears with John Leslie in a bar scene. Many women will identify with Kay Parker in this one, and Shirley Woods, too. John Leslie is his usual slap-happy self.

VIXEN CC NN BI (no explicit genital interaction)
1968   RM INTERNATIONAL FILMS

P/D—Russ Meyer
F/A—Garth Pillsbury, Harrison Page, Jon Evans, Vincent Wallace, Robert Aiken, Michael Donovan O'Donnell
F/A—Erica Gavin, Jackie Illman

Russ Meyer's first film, The Immoral Mr. Teas, was censored in one city after another when it was released in 1959. Today you can probably catch it uncut on cable or subscription television. After Mr. Teas, Russ made Lorna, which revealed more T and A. Then Russ made The Vixen for $72,000. (It has probably grossed over $10 million, and from the standpoint of earnings is the most successful picture ever made.) Today, Russ, who has been called King of the Nudies and the Barnum of Boobs, is an active, aggressive multimillionaire who could retire if he wished but probably still gets, in his own words, "a hard-on" when he shoots a successful scene with one of his big-busted, wildly aggressive female stars. Russ thinks his best film is Beyond the Valley of the Dolls. It's the only one that RM Films does not control and Russ only owns 10% of it. (The tape is controlled by Magnetic Video.) Other than that film and a bomb, Seven Minutes, based on the Irving Wallace novel, RM International (Russs's company) distributes all his films on tape, and they are packaged under the general heading Bosomania. Meyer's makes no bones (pun intended) about it, he's "obsessed with female breasts." In an interview in Home Video (May 1981), he told Diana Loevy, "They do a lot for me. They titillate me, they turn me on, they excite me, they rejuvenate me." On the other hand, Russ, who shows plenty of female frontal nudity and some male, never shows one penetrating the other in his films. "It leaves nothing to the imagination," he says. Russ combines sex and violence and a fast-moving story, along with good cinematography and great editing that will carry you along to the finale—with your mouth hanging open. The Vixen is the story of Tom Palmer, a Canadian bush pilot, who takes parties fishing and hunting in the North woods in his four-passenger Cessna airplane. He's married to Vixen (Erica Gavin), who loves him and makes love with him at the drop of a hat, but Vixen is amoral. "I'm just a plain and simple chick," she tells David Payne, who has arrived for a fishing weekend with his wife. "When I'm attracted, I respond." So does Payne's wife, Janice! Before the weekend is over the four of them have spent more time sexmaking with each other's spouse than they have fishing. Strangely, although you are sure that Tom knows his wife is no angel, no one gets angry. You even have a feeling that the Paynes will return for another weekend of frolicking in bed, in the leaves and in the lake with the Palmers. Meyer scatters the seed of his story line when you first encounter Niles, who is a handsome black man and is a friend of Vixen's brother. Vixen teases Niles, but makes it apparent that she'd never let him touch her. Niles redeems himself by saving her life and Tom's and refusing finally to hijack Tom's Cessna and fly it to Cuba, where black people are presumably respected. The last 20 minutes of this film have no sex, but instead Niles's rejection of communism for good old America.

WANDA WHIPS WALL STREET
CC NN DK NL NR
1982   VID-X-PIX

P/D—John Christian, Sven Nuvo, Larry Revene
F/A—Jamie Gillis, J. T. Ambrose, Ron Jeremy, Ron Hudd, Kurt Mann
F/A—Veronica Hart, Samantha Fox, Sharon Mitchell, Lisa Be, Chantel Duclos

If you can accept the absolutely unbelievable premise on this one—that an attractive young woman, Wanda Brandt (Veronica Hart), can take over a top Wall Street investment firm with her sexual ability—then the film turns out to be one of the better 1982 sexvids. Actually, with some of the true-life sexual involvements that quite frequently break loose from political and business sources, the story of Wanda and her secretary, Janet (Lisa Be), literally sleeping their way into stockholder control of Tyler Securities, for a few hours at least, may only seem incredible. (Actually in 1982 a small firm, Drysdale Government Securities Inc., nearly created a Wall Street economic collapse involving billions of dollars in government bonds.) What makes the story work is an underlying sense of laughter and very good acting by Veronica Hart. A few scenes that make this one different from many others include Wanda conning a young broker into a broom closet on the ground floor of the New York Stock Exchange, getting him totally undressed and convincing him to close his eyes in anticipation of the oral delights she is promising him. While he is dreaming of such joy, she is dressing in his suit and hat. She leaves him bare-assed in the closet and uses his identification card to get on the floor of the stock exchange. Or there's a scene on a yacht in the Hudson with everyone merrily screwing while in the background the phallic towers of Manhattan are stolidly watching. And then for a complete switch, Jamie Gillis, as Lou

Perrini, hired to investigate Wanda's slippery deals (pun intended), proves that he can be a very romantic male lead. He makes love with Wanda on a blanket on the shore of her summer home against a woodland background. To top it off, there are no bisexual scenes!

WET RAINBOW **CC NN NM NR BI**
1974   ARROW

P/D—Roger Wald, Duddy Kane
F/A—Harry Reems
F/A—Georgina Spelvin, Valerie Marrow, Mary Stuart

If you don't believe that adult film stars can be good actors and actresses, or that directors and producers can handle stories that come to grips with human problems, then buy this one or rent it. It's early Georgina, and she's quite pretty, and Harry Reems proves that he's one of the few good male actors who have made porno films. I'd guess that with the raincoat crowd this film was a box-office flop. But it proves that intimate little stories about marital problems, interwoven with explicit sex, are the perfect subjects for adult films on home video. It's the story of Valerie (Georgina Spelvin), a Greenwich Village artist who is married to Jonathan (Harry Reems), who teaches photography, and their involvement with Rainbow, a pupil in Harry's class who gives him a nude photo of herself. Rainbow is not a designing female. . . just a forthright loving one. But first Valerie is jealous of her, then is attracted to her and wonders if she's a dyke. Confused and jealous, Valerie imagines Jonathan screwing Rainbow as well as herself making love to her, which she finally does. Then she is totally shocked at her lesbian tendencies. All monogamous women will applaud the ending when, after the loving, Valerie ends up in Jonathan's arms and Rainbow is left out. Among other things is the most believable anal sex sequence (between Valerie and Jonathan) that you've seen in any adult film. Women will like it. Worth owning.

WICKERMAN **CC**
1973 MEDIA

P/D—Peter Snell, Robin Hardy, Anthony Shaffer
F/A—Edward Woodward, Christopher Lee
F/A—Diane Cilento, Britt Ekland

This one is not strictly a sexvid. The entire movie, which was produced in Scotland, takes place on Summerisle, an imaginary island off the coast of Scotland which has renounced Christianity and reverted to pagan religions and sex worship. The time is now. A very religious Scottish detective comes to the island to locate a missing girl, and what happens to him will totally astound you. All the paganism in this movie is authentic. Britt Ekland does a nude dance out of sight of the detective, which is more erotic than anything you've seen in adult films. Media is making a mistake in promoting this as a horror film, and although the subtle attack on Christianity will horrify some people, that is probably the reason that the film does not appear in the suburbs or on cable or subscription television. It is obviously the reason that the original film wasn't released for six years after it was made. This tape is worth owning. It is beautifully photographed and well acted. You'll watch it more than once, and if the star, Edward Woodward, charms you, you can see him again in *Breaker Morant,* an Australian movie that reveals that immorality in war is far more scary than sexual immorality.

YOUNG BUTTERFLIES
CC   NN   NR   some NL and Bl
1974(?)   BLUE VIDEO

P/D—Joseph W. Sarno
F/A—Harry Reems, Eric Edwards
F/A—Maria Forsa, Zoe

Many women will identify with this film as they are both attracted to and repulsed by Frank (played by Harry Reems, who stopped making porno films about a year later). Frank makes love nicely to many women but is faithful to none of them. Denise, a German farm girl, is bored with the narrow-minded village she lives in and flees to Munich, where Frank takes her over for a while before telling her to get out of his life. There is much romantic lovemaking, but it is occasionally intercut with too-long scenes of hard core close-ups. This is one of the few adult films where sexual jealousy is the motivator of the action. It has interesting European backgrounds, and Maria Forsa is a naturally appealing woman. As one of the butterflies in Frank's life, she personifies the sexual symbolism that has always been associated with butterflies.

The Education of a Virgin

BABY CAKES **CC NN NR (for a few minutes) BI DS**
1979 SELECT/ESSEX

P/D—**Bob Chinn**
F/A—**Randy West**
F/A—**Rhonda Jo Petty, Jamie Leigh, Victoria Slick, Misty**

How they figure out titles for some of these films is a mystery. Cakes, I suppose, are buns—or behinds. Two of the babies are friends of Suzie (Jamie Leigh) and they put their cakes on 10-speed bikes because Suzie (Jamie Leigh), who is not a sexpot like they are, wants to race her bike in the Grand Prix bike race which is going to be held in Los Angeles. Unfortunately, they all live in San Francisco. Not having much money, the only way they can get there is to pedal down on the Pacific Coast Highway—about 500 miles—and do it in a week. It's a nice premise for adventure, and it happens that first night when they stop at a motel. Rhonda (Rhonda Jo Petty) and Denise (Victoria Slick) immediately find two guys to shack up with. They're not shy. Rhonda tells the guys within minutes: "I'm Rhonda, this is Denise. Let's go in your room and have some fun." In the meantime, Charlie (Randy West) appears, and virginal-looking Suzie is just the woman he's been looking for all his life. But Suzie is not the jump-in-the-sack type. "Can't we just sit and look at the ocean for awhile," she asks, and Charlie, entranced, does. Next day back on their bikes they are being pursued by two evil-looking guys in a camper. The second night they stop on a fire-lit beach where Charlie, driving ahead, has set up tents. Suzie still won't capitulate, but Rhonda sets her up—bisexually—for Charlie, who soon appears and makes a woman out of Suzie. Next morning Rhonda and Denise are kidnapped by the two villains who were following them—and miles away in the camper, naked, her hands tied, she sneers at the guy: "You're just a fucking punk! I ain't movin' an inch. You ain't gettin' nothing out of me." Even though she has an orgasm, she still is trying to punch him silly before she and Denise (who is talking with her captor) are rescued.

BABY LOVE AND BEAU
CC NN BI NL NR
TVX

P/D—**Daemian Lee**
F/A—**Pete Templar, Rod Jacobi**
F/A—**Jennifer Holmes, Dewey Alexander, Chris Cassidy**

You may never see most of the people who appear in this one ever again, but they do a good naturalistic acting job—especially plump-faced Jennifer Holmes as Baby Love, and Pete Templar as a sailor. Baby Love seduces her sister's boy friend, Justin—hoping that he will take her on a clothes-buying expedition to Paris. But Justin leaves without her, even though, still wearing her roller skates, she has given him her "all." Sister Susan soothes her that night in bed by kissing away her sexual frustrations. But the next morning Baby Love meets Beau Harris, a sailor with three days' leave and two months' pay which he quickly loses to two hookers who, after screwing his pants off, offer to play bondage with him. When he's properly tied they beat it with all his money. Broke, he goes to a stag film with a dollar he has found. It's run in black-and-white and must be fifty years old. But wait—next day Baby Love, roller skating with a watermelon, crashes into him, and for the next half hour you can watch their romantic joyous *lovemaking*, including an extended scene on a deserted San Francisco beach as they frolic in the waves and make love on the beach. The sex in this one is caring, the dialogue natural, the people very normal and average. All coupled with some laughter. What's more, Baby Love is a *natural* blonde. For some reason few natural blondes ever appear in pornos. Worth owning.

BELLA
CC NN NM NR (occasional) BI
1974 ARROW

P/D—Christopher Duncan, Alexander Kubelka
F/A—Eric Edwards, Dana Stone, Jake Teague
F/A—Tracy Adams, Arcadia Lake

In an upper-income environment of stately brick homes, Bella (Tracy Adams) comes home from school, calls for her mother and finally discovers her next door in the basement garage owned by Tom, their neighbor. They are passionately making love. A few scenes later Tracy is driving to the airport to meet Daddy, who is very wealthy, but after making love to mother is always leaving on business trips. You may not believe what now happens but you have never seen anything like it in adult films. Tracy visits Tom (why Tom is living alone in this big house is not explained) and tells him, "I know all about you and mother. I know a lot of things kids don't know. Teach me how to make love." Of course, Tom does. How can he resist? Very quickly you discover that he should have. Bella doesn't want to share Tom with her mother, and she not only threatens and almost does tell Daddy, but she telephones Tom and says, "That whore of a mother of mine is on the way over to your house. If you touch her I'll kill you." And she almost does, until she and Mommy call a truce, and Mommy has a better idea: "We'll share him, honey." All of this is told to an original composition performed by the Rome Symphony Orchestra, and is photographed by Carter Stevens. Tracy Adams really looks about 16, and since Daddy (Jake Teague) never does find out what is going on between his wife and daughter, many women may find it a reasonable solution.

BLUE ECSTASY IN NEW YORK
NN DK DS BI
1980 TVX

P/D—Kemal Horulo
F/A—Jamie Gillis, Eric Edwards, Richard Bolla, Bobby Astyr
F/A—Leslie Bovee, Samantha Fox, Candida Royalle

Jamie, Samantha and Bobby better be careful. It's hard to tell in this one whether in reality they are as sleazy as the characters they are presumably portraying. Chillis-Gillis, as David, is a dealer in cocaine, and he's usually snorting it directly off Samantha's, Leslie's or Candida's breasts. He screws the ladies with his usual detached, ass-slapping precision. While Bobby Astyr watches, he works over Samantha (who is looking a little the worse for wear) from stem to stern. Then he proceeds to viciously abuse Leslie. Believe it or not there's a plot, of sorts, that ties all this stuff together. Seems that Veronica (Leslie Bovee) is a very prudish young lady who hates sex and thinks men only want her for her body. But her alter ego, or doppelganger, with whom she lives, and who materializes and talks to Leslie, is a very uninhibited young woman. If Horulo had stayed with this story instead of trying to merge Veronica's personalities utilizing the aggression of Jamie Gillis, it could have been much more dramatic. You'll probably watch it to the end but will feel as if you need a bath afterwards.

THE BUDDING OF BRIE CC NN
a little DK
1979 TVX

P/D—David Friedman, Henri Pachard
F/A—Eric Edwards, Richard Bolla
F/A—Hilary Summers, Jennifer Jordan

The story of Brie Livingston, working her way up—with lovely sexual aplomb—from waitress to a Hollywood star. The story line continues through this sexvid and is cleverly told by skilled photography and editing which interweaves the sexual elements and will leave women viewers crying for and empathizing with Brie. This is a film that in a soft-core version could appear on late-night TV. Directed by Henri Pachard, a.k.a. Ron Sullivan, who directed *Babylon Pink.*

CONFESSIONS OF A TEENAGE PEANUT BUTTER FREAK CC NN NL BI one DK sequence with a black and white guy with a willing white female
1974 EROS and FREEWAY

P/D—Jack and Alf Albumin, Gerald Graystone
F/A—Rex Roman, John C. Holmes
F/A—Jennifer Mason, Sharon Taylor

Poor Billy—our teenage peanut-butter-loving hero finds it hard to relate to girls. Aunt Opel introduces him to oral sex. Billy's teenage cousins handcuff him and rape him. But Priscilla, to whom he confesses the pains of growing up, loves him. Some of the quite normal, pimply faced women in this one, along with Billy, don't look much over 18. A much younger John Holmes appears in one scene. It all ends

happily, and believe it or not, after one quite nice romantic sex scene, Billy marries Priscilla!

DADDY'S LITTLE GIRLS
CC NN BI NL
1983 CABALLERO

P/D—J. Angel Martine, John Christopher
F/A—Dan Stephens, Ashley Moore
F/A—Brooke Bennett, Anne Ventura, Sharon Kane, Chelsea Manchester

Daddy is a hillbilly. His girls Roxy (Brooke Bennett), Suzanne (Sharon Kane) and Jacky (Chelsea Manchester) know that the sheriff is about to foreclose the mortgage on the old homestead, so they offer their neighbors an invitation to a mud wrestling match in their backyard—wearing bathing suits, no less. A city slicker arrives and tells the sheriff how they can promote a much bigger event by matching Roxy against a professional Tony Cimoli (Anne Ventura). The backyard version didn't raise enough money, so Roxy, the most likely challenger, agrees to take on Tony. Subplots are about Suzanne, with her boyfriend who wants to marry her but is broke, and Jacky, who screws the city slicker to get to Hollywood. Brooke Bennett, who is a plump young lady—my bet is she weighs about 140 pounds, and is big breasted—provides all the interest in this film. On the tile bathroom floor, she leaves Dan Stevens breathless in a very erotic and believable sexmaking scene. Later she does it again on the trunk of an automobile—both giving and receiving with great enthusiasm. But the tour de force is the wrestling match between her and Anne Ventura. Both are buxom women. The match which lasts at least ten minutes is not sexually revealing, but both Brooke and Anne really work at it—egged on by the cheers of the local hicks.

DESIRES WITHIN YOUNG GIRLS
CC   NN   BI occasional NL and NR and a laughing spoof of DB
1977   CABALLERO CONTROL, VIDAMERICA (soft-core version)

P/D—Harold Lime, Ramsey Carson
F/A—John Leslie, John Seeman
F/A—Georgina Spelvin, Clair Dia, Annette Haven

Best Film, Best Actress and Best Screenplay, 1978 Erotic Film Festival. Imagine Georgina Spelvin, whose second husband has died (screwing in the saddle), trying to find rich husbands for two teenage daughters (Annette Haven and Clair Dia). "Ball rich and marry rich," she tells them. This amusing and occasionally romantic sexvid runs for two hours. Several scenes with Clair Dia and Annette Haven reflect warm, loving sexmaking. The story line is fairly consistent, and women will applaud the ending because at 40, Georgina gets the millionaire her daughters rejected.

FELICIA   **CC   NN   NR   NM   BI**
1976   QUALITY

P/D—Max Pecas, Roger Michel
F/A—Toche
F/A—Rebecca Brooke, Beatrice Harn

If you are in your mid-30s and have been married for ten years, would you like to have a very attractive 18-year-old nymphomaniac virgin—a young woman feeling all the compulsions of her as-yet-unleashed sexuality—visit with you for a three-week vacation? Highly affluent Paul and Gabrielle (Gabby) live in Deauville (this film was made in France), and they meet their friend's daughter at the airport. Paul is very much in love with Gabby, but he's quickly aware that Felicia is spying on them making love and listening at their bedroom door. Gabby pays little attention to Felicia, but she slowly becomes aware of her as she takes photographs of her for a record album cover that she is doing, photos supposed to symbolize purity and innocence. Before she knows it,

Gabby is "seduced" by Felicia, who exudes a combination of sexual innocence and newly discovered sexual power. After teasing Gabby into making love to her (the bisexual scenes are caring and believable), she goes to work on Paul. While Gabby is away in the city, Felicia walks (naked) into his study. He doesn't capitulate for quite a long time. But Felicia implies to Gabby that Paul already has had sex with her and Gabby believes her and not him. Finally only a saint could resist. Paul takes her in anger and then tells her: "I'm sorry. Did I hurt you?" Everything about this film has a class and style and a confrontation with sexual reality that isn't in the American idiom. Scene after scene is beautifully acted—extended lovemaking between Paul and Gabby underwater in their swimming pool by moonlight, near a fireplace; Gabby at Paul's request caressing herself to a climax in front of a mirror while he watches, and a very naturalistic scene with Felicia and a boy her age—she experiencing oral sex for the first time, coolly watching him ejaculate and then telling him, "I didn't feel anything," are beautifully acted. This is a sexvid that most men and women can share together. The English dubbing isn't too bad, but it would be nice if there was an original French version.

FLIGHT SENSATIONS   **NN   BI   DK**
1983   VCA

P/D—Packaged by Adele Robins
F/A—Phil Tobias, Turk Lyon, Herschel Savage, Johnny Keyes, Don Hart, Mike Ranger, Eric Edwards, John Holmes, Jamie Gillis
F/A—Seka, Desiree Cousteau, Josephine Farmer, Desiree West, Pat Manning, Leilani, Connie Peters

When you see so many names in the cast—beware! It's probably not an original film, but a package of loops or scenes from other films that you may have seen before. This one is tied together with Herschel Savage and a gal, who I can't identify, acting as a Flight Lieutenant and Stewardess. Driving toward the San Fernando Valley, they recall various tidbits which include a very young Desiree Cousteau, doing it with a much younger Seka and Paul Thomas. Then there's Jamie Gillis, and John Holmes inundating Seka with their gyzym, followed by Desiree West giving a guy a sexual massage while she explains what she's doing. Then there's a guy stained red and chained both by his arms and prick while two dominatrixes work him over. They finally forget all about him while they enjoy each other. It concludes with a four-way-split scene of four different actions all going on at the same time, and is finally wrapped up with a scene from a porno film, *Little French Maids*, with Johnny Keyes, and John Holmes and Don Hart taking on Connie Peters. The boys in the fraternity house may love this one, but most women won't.

FOREPLAY **NN NM BI**
1982 VCA

P/D—**Mike Davis, Vinnie Rossi**
F/A—**Paul Thomas, Starbuck, Ron Jeremy, Julian Michel**
F/A—**K. C. Valentine, Cara Lott**

Chloe (K. C. Valentine) gets a job in a hotel boardinghouse. A virgin, she is too shy to have ever made love. Her only confidante is a suit of armor (she calls him Arthur) ensconced in the front hall. Among the boarders is Greg Herpis (Ron Jeremy) *"Not* herpes—*Herpis,"* he says. Presumably he's an intern at a local hospital who uses his room in the boardinghouse to practice on female patients. "Dr. Herpis at your servis" takes his girlfriend's temperature by lapping her all over. Chloe decides that the only way she can get a sex education is to install two-way mirrors in the various rooms so she can watch the action. To hear the sound as well, she installs an intercom. How all this is managed is left to your imagination. But as Chloe watches two female roommates in bed and a guy who thinks he's a musical conductor conducting a sexsymphony, you discover the truth. The place is not a boardinghouse at all, it's a place where people can act out their fantasies—whatever they may be. Chloe's fantasy is to have the knight in armor screw her—and sure enough, Chloe gets her wish in the form of Paul Thomas, who

emerges from the creaking contraption. As Chloe says, "Imagination is a wonderful thing." You can imagine a better story than this one, I'm sure.

THE GOOD GIRLS OF GODIVA HIGH
NN DK BI
1979 VCX

P/D—**Bill Eagle, Jim Clark**
F/A—**Richard Bolla, Bob Presley, Ron Jeremy**
F/A—**Kitsy Storme, Danielle and Daphne, Susan de Angelis, Merle Michaels**

The young women who attend Godiva School for Girls (it's not a high school) all sleep in the same barracks-style room, wear white knee socks, saddle shoes and pigtails, and are all virgins. Except for Merle Michaels, you've never seen most of them before. Occasionally some of them actually do look like teenagers, and that of course is the raison d'etre for this flick—to cater to the middle-aged male Lolita daydream of enjoying a nubile, loving body. What story there is involves Charlie (Richard Bolla), the middle-aged hero with whom his peers may empathize, the school handyman. He teaches the girls the joys of sex, including anal intercourse in an extended scene. There's also a horny Miss Lena, who won't let the girls have a disco graduation party, and an extended sequence in which Daphne and Danielle satisfy your curiosity about sharing your bed with twins. (They wear the guy to a frazzle.)

JAILBAIT **CC NN BI one silly DB scene**
1976 WONDERFUL WORLD OF VIDEO

P/D—**Carter Stevens**
F/A—**Wade Nichols**
F/A—**Tina Lynn**

What makes this sexvid different from most is the amount of dialogue—even in the middle of sex—and plot line that finally gets off the ground when it concentrates on a presumably 16-year-old high-school baby sitter who services her classmates while she chews bubble gum, and incites them to masturbate while she watches. Plus there is a female who can tie her labia in a knot and stretch it out far enough to push piano keys with it! Tina Lynn was probably in her 20s when this film was made, but she gives a good performance as a cold-blooded teenager, and the conversation between her and Wade Nichols is often believable.

JOY NN BI DK DS
1975 QUALITY

P/D—Derek Davidson, Harley Mansfield
F/A—Jake Teague, Richard Bolla
F/A—Sharon Mitchell, Melinda Marlowe

Joy (Sharon Mitchell) is on her summer vacation from high school. A virgin, she refuses to have sex with her boyfriend on the basketball team, but when she goes home, her mother is out shopping, and two burly guys knock on the door. When she lets them in, they strip and rape her. At first she screams, then suddenly she is climaxing, and enjoying it. When they leave, she screams at them, "I want more . . . more!" Suddenly turned into a woman who demands sexual satisfaction, she hurries to her boyfriend's house, finds him in the shower and fellates him. Within days, New York City is plagued by a new phenomenon: a female rapist! And she isn't afraid of being mugged herself. No siree. She works the lonely streets at night and attacks Richard Bolla, who hasn't climaxed with his wife in years. In a back alley, she strips him and reduces him to a happy blob. Next she seduces a guy in a subway train. They are the only ones in the car, but she forgets her panties with the monogram Joy on them—and the police are after her. Before she is through, she has turned on half the women in New York City. Crime ceases as female after female grab guys on the streets and in elevators and rape them. She finally gets brutally raped herself by a black cop who handcuffs her to a stairwell while he does the job, and she ends up in jail where she convinces Jake Teague (as Lieutenant Handcock) to untie her from a stretcher. After that, she sucks his pistol (no kidding). That ain't all, folks! Forced to leave the city and still needing more, she takes on all the guys in the men's room at the airport. Don't bring this one home to your wife

and girlfriend unless you want to start an argument. Can a man be raped?

LITTLE DARLINGS
CC NN NL NM BI
1981 VISUAL ENTERTAINMENT

P/D—Jim Clark
F/A—Richard Bolla, Jake Teague, Jerry Butler
F/A—Lysa Thatcher, Juliet Jay, Suzannah Ash, Lorelei Palmer

The CC rating on this one is not for the tape as a whole but for a couple of scenes which defy the U.S. Supreme Court rulings against child pornography. Keep in mind that there are no females in this one who are under 18. They may all be past 20 for all I know. But two of them, facially and in the they talk and act, really make you think they are not much older than 16. The story is about a camping trip for the Eager Beavers (six young ladies dressed in plaid miniskirts, knee-length hose, saddle shoes and hair ribbons). Their leader is Buddy Bargain (Jake Teague, who must be close to 50), wearing a Boy Scout leader outfit. The van he picks them up in from their suburban homes breaks down before they reach the campsite. But fortunately there is an old, New England-style hotel up the road run by Miss Buckworthy and her manager, Arnold Roberts (Richard Bolla). There are plenty of rooms for the girls. With that setting, Richard Bolla literally screws himself to death (in fantasy, of course—but the fantasies are explicitly shown). Before one of the young ladies loses her virginity with Buddy Bargain, you listen to the slightly older girls discussing men. Soon the girl asking the questions is asking still more from Buddy Bargain, who invites her into his room and tells her some answers. The conversation that ensues as he teaches her how to fellate and screw is quite believable, and Juliet Jay, who plays the part of the innocent being screwed by granddaddy (who is partially bald and never takes his glasses off), really only looks about 15 or 16. Lysa Thatcher, in a bisexual scene during which she teaches another girl how to masturbate, doesn't look over 17, either. Which of course was why this flick was made.

LITTLE GIRLS LOST **CC NN NR**
1983 VCA

P/D—Pierre Balakoff, Ted Roter
F/A—John Leslie, Eric Edwards, John Hollyfield, Ron Jeremy, William Margold
F/A—Tigr, Veronica Hart, Gena Lee, Jennifer West

If you check other listings of Ted Roter's films, you will discover that he and Pierre Balakoff are the same person. Ted usually makes adult films with good story lines and some character development. This one is no exception and may be his best. The story is about three aspiring actresses Cathy (Tigr a.k.a. Chelsea Manchester), Alicia (Veronica Hart), and Stephanie (Gena Lee who invariably appears in Roter films) and one aspiring actor Paul (John Leslie). They all meet in Hollywood at an acting class being given by Aaron (Eric Edwards) and Cathy quickly moves into the same apartment with Alicia and Stephanie. Cathy is the idealistic one (Tigr plays the same naive role she did in *Nothing to Hide*). She won't compromise herself, and she refuses coldly to suck and fuck her way to the top. Stephanie is more pragmatic. The minute nasty directors or producers tell her she's a great actress and is going places, but she has to play ball (balls and cock), she knows what they mean and quickly complies. Alicia, from Toledo, Ohio, is not quite so idealistic. She falls in love with Aaron, hoping, of course, that he will advance her career, but to her shock she catches him in the sack with two other starlets. Paul is a sad case; he can't seem to break through and get a good part because "he's too handsome," and he refuses to play games with a big name fag director. Cathy falls in love with Paul, but Paul is convinced that she's screwing with Aaron to get a coveted part. She isn't, but Stephanie tells him that Cathy is as ambitious as she is: "In this racket there's no room for love." Paul is easily seduced—and is caught by Cathy in flagrante delictu with Stephanie. Cathy forgives him, though, at least until she sees him at a party in a loving encounter with the gay director.

In the meantime Stephanie is going downhill rapidly in a degrading relationship with Jeff (John Hollyfield), a big director who has promised her a part. It all comes to a head when Cathy, who hasn't screwed with anyone but Paul, gets an offer for a big part in a top Hollywood production. In the interesting finale, she's about to sign a contract with the top man, who is Ted Roter himself. Then to her shock, after she signs the contract, he tells her, "In this instance if you really want the part, you have to accept the fact that I want you as a woman." Cathy undresses reluctantly and tells him angrily, "If you want my body, you can take it, but you'll never have the part of me I value most." Astonished, Ted tells her to put her clothes back on. He thanks her for the amazing performance and tells her, "You better leave before I call your bluff." All of the acting in this one is professional. Presumably, this is Veronica Hart's last X-rated film. In the film her last lines are: "I'm going home. I guess I'm not cut out for this kind of life." Actually, Veronica quit to have a baby. She sent me a birth announcement. Christopher Michael was born April 2, 1983, at 10:02 A.M. at Mt. Sinai Hospital. He weighed 8 lbs. 11 ½ oz. I'm trying to persuade her to write a book about the industry and herself.

LITTLE GIRLS BLUE **NN DK**
1978 VCX

P/D—William Dancer, Joanna Wilson
F/A—Paul Thomas, Ken Cotton
F/A—Tamara Morgan, Elaine Wells, Casey Winters

A few of the girls/women in this one actually look and act like 16-year-olds most of the time—except one female, Marium (Lola Dunmore), who looks as if she has been "done" too much. The girls in Townsend School for Girls, a boarding school, spend their time seducing male teachers to improve their marks. A thin story line involves the coach, who loves one girl and gets seduced by Casey Winters. Because he does it in the dark with her, he doesn't know she is very pretty until later. Many sequences of sexmaking are educational if you watch them in frame-by-frame slow motion. But who is director Joanna Wilson?

LITTLE GIRLS BLUE II NN NR (a little)
1983   VCX

P/D—Joanna Williams, William Dancer
F/A—Eric Edwards, Carl Lincoln, Keven James, Bill Buck, Jack Blake
F/A—Barbara Klouds, Sharron McIntyrye, Chris Petersen, Shirley Duke

The sequel is a better picture than the original because it adds a touch of romance. This time the girls from Townsend School for Girls are having an eight-week vacation from school at Camp Townsend. The featured girls are different actresses from those who appeared in the first picture, but they have the same story names. This time Marium is a very pretty girl. It's not easy to call them women because facially, at least, with wide-eyed expressions, saddle shoes, pigtails, etc., for the most part they really look like young teenagers between 15 and 17. Which of course accounts for the popularity among older males of the earlier film and this one, too. Buffy teases the physical education instructor (Eric Edwards) and lures him into bed, where he teaches her fellatio and is very gentle with her. Marium falls in love with a foreign student who is counseling at the camp. She helps him learn English and he makes tender love with her. The other two girls are not so selective but manage to take on a guy who comes to repair the camp motorcycle. Amazingly there's no bisexuality. Most women won't object to this film—and it may remind some of their youth.

LITTLE ME AND MARLA STRANGELOVE NN BI some silly DK and DB
1979   ARROW, VCX, SELECT/ESSEX

P/D—Helen Terries, Kirdy Stevens
F/A—Ric Lutz, Rob Rose
F/A—Dianne Dale, Nancy Hoffman, Christine Carr

If you have teenage daughters, they may be spending their afternoons after school the way these kids are. Marla is the sexpot. Her friend Debbie is almost a virgin: "Whenever I've done it I was sort of raped." The girls watch Daddy's porno movies in the playroom and compare Johnny Wadd's size with their own boyfriends' size, they fantasize bondage and discipline (a filmmaker's trick of offering reality by presumedly making it unreality) and they invite two boys back to Debbie's parents' house when the parents are out. Debbie fights one guy off but lets him play with her, and Marla goes all the way. It all ends when they are caught by Debbie's mother and father. Very pretty young women who look like teenagers and guys you've never seen either—plus a dialogue that will often remind you of your high school days.

PORTRAIT OF A SEDUCTION CC NN BI
1976   TVX SELECT/ESSEX

P/D—Anthony Spinelli
F/A—Robert Cole, Jeffrey Stern
F/A—Vicki Lyon, Monique Cardin, Rita Stone

Nominated for the Best Screenplay, Erotic Film Festival 1977, it's the story of a woman who marries an older man with a teenage son who goes all out to seduce her and succeeds. Superior film storytelling with fast jump cutting and voice-over to explain flashbacks and give them credence. At times, the story line gets lost as Spinelli tries to cover all the sex film conventions, but the acting is occasionally pretty good, and the sexvid gives some idea of the potential when a daring producer concentrates on one or two women in a film and develops characters.

REVOLVING TEENS NN BI DK
1974   VIDEOSHOWTIME

P/D—Not given
F/A—Harry Reems, Eric Edwards
F/A—Helen Madigan, Tina Russell

Mrs. Potts is the headmistress of a girls' school where somehow or other there are male students. Courses include learning badminton, manual training and gymnastics—you know the kind. Harry Reems is the manual training teacher who is seduced by Mrs. Potts when he tells her he's going to quit. Eric Edwards is the gym teacher. He tumbles with the girls (there are only two), and one of them gets stuck with her ass in the air as she is somersaulting. Never mind, Edwards untangles her. The title is appropriate—they may not be teens, but everyone who appears manages to revolve with everyone else. This is early Harry Reems for Reems collectors.

SEDUCTION OF AMY
CC NN BI DK and DS but plot-related with an NR ending
1975 WONDERFUL WORLD OF VIDEO

P/D—Dale Martin
F/A—Brian Davidson, Terrence Vitez
F/A—Tiffany Smith, Gwen Fore

This weird sexvid pits Gideon, who owns a French chateau which may be inhabited by reincarnated friends of the Marquis de Sade, against Amy, a virgin who has been nearly raped and viciously attacked in a nearby forest. The soft-lighted erotic photography creates confusion that will keep you interested. Gideon tells Amy he is condemned to make the women he loves suffer. This is quickly proved with women in chains in the wine cellar. Nevertheless, in an extended romantic scene of tumbling, naked sexmaking on sand dunes, Amy succumbs to him. In total concept and surprise gothic ending this sexvid is almost a classic.

SORORITY SWEETHEARTS
CC NN BI NR
1983 CABALLERO

P/D—Ted Gorley, Paul Vatelli
F/A—Don Hart, Herschel Savage, David Smith
F/A—Bridgette Monet, Lisa de Leeuw, Linda Shaw

Cindy (Bridgette Monet) is the only woman in the sorority who is still a virgin. She dreams of a white knight (shown) while her sorority sisters Sugar (Linda Shaw) and Bobby Jo (Gretchen Sweet) are happily screwing away with their more prosaic boyfriends. Lisa de Leeuw, as Jean the sorority housemother, also has a boyfriend in town. The sorority sisters decide that they've got to get Cindy laid. They create a very nice candlelight din-

ner and invite "three studs." Everyone dresses formally for the dinner and a very handsome guy, Mark (David Smith), in a very sensuous scene slowly undresses Cindy. Halfway through ignoring his pointed "Do you like to suck cock?" (Of course, she does), Cindy asks him, "Do you want to go up to my room?" Some very romantic sexmaking follows, with some comic relief as one of her roommates watches with her boyfriend through a keyhole. The reason for the CC rating is that practically all of the sex scenes are caring sex, and even an old toughie like Lisa de Leeuw concludes the flick in a loving merger with her boyfriend. For the record someone must be oiling Bridgitte's squeaky voice—a few more films and she may prove a challenge to Annette Haven and Veronica Hart.

A SUMMER IN TROPEZ **CC R**
1981 THORN EMI Available from I.P.I.

P/D—David Hamilton
F/A—Not identified except by first names

Here's a film that's the other side of the coin from *Sizzle* (see listing), which depicts, woman as the seductress. In this one seven very young women (between 14 and 18, I would guess) are living in a way never explained, in a very expensive country estate in St. Tropez near the Mediterranean. All of them are reflections of the eternal woman, the virgin, the innocent. They are photographed by Hamilton in his well known still-photographic style which makes them all seem like a young man's dreamy fantasy. This is what girls and first love is all about. There is no conversation in the film, only the young women's laughter as they wander on the beach, ride horseback, swim naked, wake up in the morning, play with each other tenderly and appreciate each other's bodies in a way that verges on lesbianism but is quickly dispelled when one of the young lady's rapture and first love with a young man is explored. He is identified as Renaud, who is a caretaker on the estate. Most of the movement is like a still-life in motion—ethereal, transcendental, dreamy, other-worldly. The one scene where heterosexual love is evoked will remind you of your own first love and leave you wondering why the mutual awe that floats young lovers on a cloud can't last a lifetime. But one warning—while the Debussy-like musical score and photography meld together, an hour of watching may be just too sweet for most people. Interestingly, the film is copyrighted by J.V.C. (Japanese Victor Corp.), who must have underwritten the production costs.

SUMMER OF LAURA NN NM BI
1975 VCX

P/D—Y. B. Wellington, David Davidson
F/A—David Hunter, Eric Edwards, Wade Nichols
F/A—Marsha Moon, Helen Madigan, Kim Pope

Remember *The Summer of '42?* This is a sexual offshoot of the same story. Two teenage boys spy on Laura making love with her husband, who is leaving for the army. They read sex books and masturbate and fantasize getting laid, and then take their girlfriends to a skin flick, *It Happened in Hollywood,* and they get laid on the theater floor. Finally one of them, Richie, goes to Laura's house, finds the telegram that tells her that her husband has been killed in action. Richard immediately makes it with Laura. Both Laura and her husband never stop verbalizing sex while they make love, and Laura evidently likes it because she tells Richie to talk to her while he's doing it. The big problem with making sex films about teenagers is that the actors must be over 18 and everyone in this one is over 25. But the director tries hard.

THREE RIPENING CHERRIES
NN BI DK
1979 HIFCOA

P/D—Troy Benny
F/A—Misty, Dorothy Le May, Mary Ryan
F/A—David Morris, Aaron Stuart

Three presumably teenage girls arrive home from school and Mommy is waiting to talk with them about sex. Seems that Mommy, who was a girl in the late 1950s, was first penetrated by a lascivious older

schoolteacher, but after a few escapades married Daddy and never has had sex with anyone else. Troy Benny treats you to a few minutes of Mommy and Daddy making very romantic love—and then pulls out all the stops. Our teenagers not only enjoy each other sexually, but they have group sex fantasies which are quickly brought to life on the screen. After 40 minutes you can't tell their fantasies from realities. Finally the girls come back to "reality" and try to seduce their schoolteachers. One ends up with the high school coach, who takes her to a motel, but he's so exhausted from his athletic endeavours no matter what she does, he can't get it up. William Margold's review of this one in *Velvet* was, "Troy Benny turned the camera on and left the room." On the other hand, with the sound turned off it provides an extended sex dance as background for other pursuits.

VALERIE NN BI
1975 VISUAL ENTERTAINMENT

P/D—Steve Brown
F/A—Not given
F/A—Katrina Rexford

Valerie is supposed to be 15. An orphan and a virgin, she is adopted first by Mr. and Mrs. Fettucini, who already have adopted Maggie. She is 18 and screwing Mr. Fettucini after Mrs. has gone to bed. Maggie teaches Valerie about boys and indoctrinates her with a dildo. Later Valerie still hasn't made it with one of her boyfriends (he ejaculates before he can get inside her). Mrs. Fettucini catches Maggie and Valerie playing with the dildo and sends Valerie back to the orphanage, where she is quickly adopted by Mrs. Kelly. At Mrs. Kelly's daughter's birthday party Valerie is finally screwed by a clown entertainer. Then she's adopted by a young Mrs. Oldfinger, whose husband, Rodney, is 76. She is waiting for him to die so she can inherit his money. Rodney confides in Valerie that he has no money left. Sitting in his wheelchair he convinces her to take off her clothing piece by piece so that he can see what he's long forgotten—how delightful a young female body is. Standing naked before him, the old guy dies happily of a heart attack, and poor Valerie is once again back at the orphanage. Mrs. Fettucini repents and re-adopts her, but poor Valerie—this time she's caught fellating Mr. Fettucini (at his request) by Mrs. Fettucini. Katrina Rexford doesn't look 15, but she has a beautiful 20-year-old body.

VANESSA **NN DK (R-rated)**
1977 VIDAMERICA

P/D—Eric Tomer, Hubert Frank
F/A—Anthony Diffring, Gunther Clemens
F/A—Olivia Pascal

Vanessa (Olivia Pascal) is a virgin. She has been brought up in a convent in Paris, but she and her friends know all about sex from reading art books like *Eros in Pompeii.* Her Uncle Richard, her only relative, has just died and left her his estate. Arriving in Hong Kong, where he lived, she discovers that she is the owner of a chain of luxury brothels and an extensive farm. Her stepbrother believes he has a claim to the estate, but her uncle's will can't be broken. Vanessa is taken over by a young, sexy woman whose uncle is her guardian and whose lover is Major Cooper, a wealthy pervert who lives in a sexual never-never land. He introduces Vanessa to a female bondage trap which she can't resist and inserts her wrists and ankles. While she is helpless, he strips her and flagellates her before she is finally rescued by Prince Bander, a taxi driver and yogi. He demonstrates that he can copulate with women at a distance, and proves it by engaging Vanessa in mental sexual intercourse of which she is fully

aware. Her stepbrother tries to seduce her, and her friend tells her that "everyone here is sex crazy. It must be the climate." Vanessa eventually returns to Paris, still a virgin, to grow up so she can enjoy her new luxuries. This is a super-sophisticated, beautifully photographed and edited sex film with much nudity that often upstages *Emmanuelle* in lasciviousness. Even though it's rated R, it's one that you're not likely to see on subscription TV.

YOUNG & INNOCENT **NN DK BI**
1981 VCX

P/D—Beau Janson, J. Angel Martine
F/A—Ron Hudd, Ron Jeremy
F/A—Tiffany Clarke, Brooke Bennet, Tamara West, Debbie Lee Jones

This one is supposedly the story of a week at a summer camp. Camp Duck is run by Mr. and Mrs. Wasserman (Ron Jeremy and his wife). The "girls" arrive by bus and are told: "Your parents should have kept you home and let you watch TV all summer." The "girls," unfortunately, are not young—they're all over 25—and they most certainly aren't innocent. A better title would have been *Bored and Knowledgeable.* Typical conversation, between the ladies, who are trying to seduce every male in sight goes like this: "You mean you've never been hosed? Don't worry here; at Camp Duck you'll get hosed." One girl jerks a guy off and tells him brightly: "Now, I'm ready." He frowns and tells her: "Sorry, I'm not." Tiffany Clark tells her cabinmates: "Look, I didn't douche. If you taste me, you can taste the come." And on and on, until it all ends up in one cabin in a writhing, groaning, group grope.

10

Comedies

.

BLONDES HAVE MORE FUN
NN NL BI
1975 SELECT/ESSEX

P/D—John Seeman
F/A—Joan Seeman, John Leslie
F/A—Seka, Dorothy Le May, Jesie St. James

This one should be retitled *The Ultimate Aphrodisiac PQM2*. Professor Brains invents it and Herb (Jack Wright) sells it in Magical Health Market Stores at $10 a bottle. It will not only grow hair on bald heads, but it turns old ladies into nymphomaniacs; it stops the birds singing in a drunk's head (John Leslie) and gives him a perpetual erection, during which time he wears out all the ladies in a whorehouse, including Seka. It turns Jesie St. James into an indefatigable lover, and saves Dorothy Le May's boyfriend, Jack, from premature ejaculation, which is such a problem for him that he ejaculates in his pants if a woman looks at him sexily. The humor is burlesque-baggy-pants-comedian style, but occasionally you can't help laughing. Some producer/director should re-explore this idea with a story that gives a male actor what every man wants—continuous virility and the problems it causes him and his consorts, some of which are raised in *Born Erect* (see listing, p. 67).

BUBBLEGUM **CC NN BI NL** (sophisticated)
1983 VCA

P/D—Damon Christian
F/A—Eric Edwards, Mark Goldberg, Stu Greenfeld
F/A—Honey Wilder, Tina Ross, Candy Cummings, Blair Harris

Richard Aldrich (Damon Christian) is a very handsome young guy who has an overriding sense of humor which infiltrates his many films. A few years ago he started drilling in this oilfield—a satire on soap operas (see listing *Hard Soap*). In 1982 he formed his own production company called The Great American Soap Opera Company. The potential is endless. Whether there will be a Bubblegum sequel—or this one continues for many episodes—Aldrich is off to a good start. Very wealthy John (Eric Edwards), reading the *Wall Street Journal* at breakfast, ignores his wife, Carla (Honey Wilder), as he has for years. She wants to talk with him about their daughter, Paula, who is coming home from college this weekend. Paula is having an affair with Sammy (Mark Goldberg), whom Carla disapproves of. But John's too busy to listen. When he's gone to work the upstairs maid takes care of

Carla, and she the maid, in an extended bi-sexual scene. But it's soon apparent that Carla has had a lover, Sid (Stu Greenfeld), for many years, and although Stu doesn't know it, he's Paula's father. The problem is that Sid is Stu's son. Suspecting his wife after all these years, John has hired a private detective, who learns the truth from the maid and tells John. In the meantime Paula arrives home with her college friend, Bubblegum, who is majoring in economics. Soon Sammy arrives, and he and Paul are really having good sex in the garden of the mansion. But they are seen by Paula's horrified mother, Carla. In the meantime Daddy John (who is thinking about Paula in a flashback) remembers her in her bedroom softly calling "Daddy, Daddy," to him in a seductive voice. John gets so excited that he's playing with himself. But he's saved from masturbation by Bubblegum, who has been taking a very *soapy* shower. At this point the story gets lost a little as Aldrich intercuts a too-long sex scene with the maid and the detective, who has just arrived at the mansion with Daddy and Bubblegum, who are humping away upstairs. Anyway, the next morning at breakfast, Daddy John confronts his wife and daughter with the truth. Paula runs upstairs, horrified, and she takes a very *soapy* bath, during which Sammy arrives and gets in the tub with her. He tells her that it's all right, he's not her brother. His mother told him that she was having an affair with another man when Sid was born. But Paula suddenly wonders if the other man was her father, Daddy John. Probably. But the hell with it. They squiggle down happily in the soapy tub and make love.

CANDY GOES TO HOLLYWOOD
CC NN NL BI plus one DK Mazola party orgy
1978 WONDERFUL WORLD OF VIDEO

P/D—Gail Palmer
F/A—John Leslie, Howie Gordon
F/A—Carol Connors, Wendy Williams

From a male point of view, there are some very funny scenes in this sexvid, including satires called the Dong Show with Chick Bareass, Jack Farson of the Last

Night Show, and Samuel Goldlicker of Mammoth Movies. Candy, beautifully played by Carol Connors, is a dumb blonde that many gentlemen prefer. She gives men a protective feeling—but women won't enjoy seeing Candy hypnotized by John Leslie and told that she is sucking a vanilla ice cream cone, which she happily agrees is very delicious.

CENTERSPREAD GIRLS
CC NL NR BI
1982 CABALLERO CONTROL

P/D—Harold Lime, Robert McCallum
F/A—Richard Bolla, Eric Edwards, Michael Morrison, Frank Hollowell, Paul Thomas, Jon Martin
F/A—Annette Haven, Veronica Hart, Jesie St. James, Desiree Cousteau, Georgina Spelvin. Lisa de Leeuw, Tara Aire, Jacqueline Brooks, Lilli Rogers

Can you put six top female porno stars in a film, an equal number of male actors, and give everyone time to act in an integrated story line as well as copulate? It ain't easy! But Lime and McCallum have done it in this one and at the same time offered a smattering of romance as well as quite a bit of laughter. All the characters in their story have names, but to eliminate confusion, it's easier to use their screen names. Georgina Spelvin is the owner of a men's magazine called *Panther*. A group of "respectable" male citizens, which include Eric Edwards, a former porn star who has gone straight; Frank Hollowell as a senator who has never satisfied his wife, Jesie St. James; Michael Morrison as a businessman with kinky tastes in sex; and Paul Thomas as an evangelist preacher with sex on his mind, convince Richard Bolla, a judge, to spearhead a Moral Majority group which will put Georgina's magazine out of business. Georgina enlists the aid of women who have formerly posed as centerspread girls for the magazine to co-opt and corrupt these "good" citizens. Veronica Hart plays the part of a woman who has become a lawyer; Desiree Cousteau is now a famous television talk show interviewer; Lisa de Leeuw is a painter and sculptress, and Annette Haven is a rising "legitimate" film star. Each of them and several others mentioned above are assigned the task of bringing a particular guy to his knees literally and figuratively. The best sequences are with Annette Haven and Eric Edwards (whose name in the story is Lindon Loveless). Seems that after years of sex with beautiful women, Lindon can no longer get it up. He is totally amazed at Annette, who is patient with him. Later Annette soliloquizes as to whether she could ever really make a porno film and do what she did with Eric: "I don't think I could do what I did with someone watching." Veronica plays it all for romance and affection with Richard Bolla, with whom she'd like to start a law practice. Desiree Cousteau plays her most natural part since *Pretty Peaches* with Paul Thomas when she convinces him to videotape an interview and then leaves the camera on when she seduces him into bed. The denouement is silly, and of course the plot is too—but it all hangs together. Most women will laugh. If it's one of the first tapes you buy or rent, it will introduce you to quite a few of the top stars, whom you will see again and again.

CHAMPAGNE FOR BREAKFAST
CC NN NL BI DK
1979 SELECT/ESSEX

P/D—Chris Warfield
F/A—John Leslie, Ken Scudder
F/A—Leslie Bovee, Bonnie Holliday, Kandi Barbour

Champagne (Leslie Bovee) is the vice-president of Britton Cosmetics. She's been "tremendously successful at success," but she uses men and doesn't surrender to them, mentally at least. Through an employment agency she hires a "fag" to chauffeur her Rolls Royce and be her bodyguard. Harry (John Leslie) has just finished a hitch in the Navy and pretends he's gay. Mostly this is a laughing sexvid with John Leslie getting "the stonies" when two women try to seduce him. He thinks they're perverted, but he's great with one woman at a time, and he even performs admirably with a female attendant in the

back seat of the Rolls in a three-minute car wash. In the meantime, Champagne is paying for studs to service her, getting rejected in high-class bars, screwing with a hard hat who turns her upside down with her legs around his neck, seeking fulfillment with three guys at once or a young stud in a motel who has only 15 minutes to do the job, and even offering Harry a gay lover to take care of him. Finally dressed as a sailor, she finds true love with Harry. John Leslie and Leslie Bovee are good comedians. By concentrating most of the silly story line on Bovee she becomes a more interesting woman.

CHOPSTIX   **NN**   some silly DK and BI
1979 TVX

P/D—William Dancer
F/A—Samantha Morgan, Serena, Barbara Harold

Don't let the title on this one mislead you. It's not Oriental. Chopstix is a catering service whose mission is to pay off the mortgage on a huge estate so that our heroine, and not the bad villain lawyer, will inherit it. It should be funnier than it is.

DAISY MAE   **NN**   **BI**
WONDERFUL WORLD OF VIDEO

P/D—Vincent Rossi
F/A—Holly Joy, Heather Gordon

Mostly filmed outdoors, the natural scenery in this supposed spoof of L'il Abner (it's Pussypatch instead of Dogpatch) is better than the boring story line. If you can tolerate an hour of continuous fucking and sucking with dialogue like: "Lick it, pappy", or "Eat them balls" while macho hillbilly men whack their women's behinds and screw, then you'll like this one. Two songs: "The Bullshit Blues" and "Billy C" have slapstick lyrics.

EROTIC ANIMATION FESTIVAL **CC NL**
1980 VCA

P/D—Chuck Vincent
F/A—Jeffery Hurst, Jeff Peters
F/A—Lorell Brownell, Kathy Hickman

This is a one-hour tape of short films created by one of the best and most imaginative filmmakers in the adult film business, Chuck Vincent. You'll laugh a lot at this tape and show it many times to your friends. The first two sections are with puppets or anything that's handy to feed Chuck's vivid imagination. Number one, titled *No Strings Attached*, offers tiny mannequins with vaginas and penises. Two of them are in bed in the morning screwing in their dollhouse. Then after being watched by an Indian head (without a body) through their bedroom window, Daddy goes to work and the Indian head is joined by a creature from outer space. In short order the prickless Indian and the creature from outer space are in the bedroom, and lo and behold the extraterrestrial has two pricks, both of them green. Happily waving them he penetrates the ecstatic lady front and back side. The second story is titled *Le Toy Shoppe*. You, as the bodiless devil, with your eyes rolling and no prick, can't believe what is happening in a store that looks like Child's World or Toys R Us. There's an adult toy section where all the sex aids, including inflatable dolls, dildos, and toy soldiers shaped like phalluses come to life. Then the inflatable dolls and flying pricks happily discover each other, after which the whole place gets so hot it blows up. The next one, *The Appointment*, has live characters and is hilariously funny. I'm sure it has won an International Film Award. Two middle-aged people are having an extramarital affair. They meet in a deserted amusement park. They are always looking behind in fear that someone (their spouses?) might be checking on them. Furtively, they soon repair to a rooming house, where they rendezvous once a week. Unknown to them, the room is bugged by a weirdo with a tape recorder, and an arthritic landlady listens through the floor with her ear cupped to a tumbler. For the next ten minutes, wildly passionate after a week's separation, they scramble out of their clothes and make love while a radio gives appropriate cooking recipes. It's all shot with high speed photography, which emphasizes their lust and fear of discovery. You'll laugh yourself silly—as you will at the final episode, called *Wild Honey*, which opens with a guy underneath his car trying to fix it. His wife, unseen, is yelling at him to do something useful—like chop some wood for the fireplace. Winter is coming. Soon, the guy (Jeffery Hurst) is out in the woods busting his ass chopping. He hears noises in the woods but ignores them. Then he's suddenly accosted by a young woman with a shotgun. Dressed in abbreviated blue jeans, she forces him to strip. "Oh," she marvels, "is your little pee-pee scared?" She fires the gun but it doesn't go off. For the next few minutes he angrily chases her through the woods. He finally catches her in a meadow, and they make passionate love. If you haven't guessed who the woman is, I'm not going to tell you.

FIRST NUDIE MUSICAL **Rated R**
1977 NILES

P/D—Mark Haggard, Bruce Kimmel
F/A—Stephen Nathan
F/A—Cindy Williams

Other than a nude chorus line at the conclusion, this sexvid is Grade B Hollywood and wouldn't qualify as a sex exploitation film either. But it is harmless soft-core entertainment, typical of many produced by Medea Entertainment, which you can watch on subscription and cable TV.

FOXHOLES **NN BI NL**
1983 SELECT/ESSEX

P/D—Bob Augustus
F/A—Randy West, Jeff Baird, Phil Tobis
F/A—Lisa de Leeuw, Linda Joy, Vanessa Del Rio, R. J. Reynolds, Pat Manning, Drea, Juliet Anderson

Combine a "M*A*S*H" environment and a *Private Benjamin* plot and put the whole business back in a basic training camp during World War II. Congress has just endorsed the Women's Auxiliary Corps, which brings in 12 women—a platoon—who must prove they can do anything men can do in the Army *and better.* You now have the basic plot. The Colonel and Major Storm (Phil Tobis) are determined to get rid of the women, but Sergeant Riker (Randy West) leads the Pink Army (the ladies) to victory. They totally seduce the Blue Army (the guys), who are out-maneuvered by bobbing breasts, tantalizing bottoms and a group of ladies who would rather make love than war. The camp's Dr. Honey Bottoms (Judith Anderson) offers a different kind of combat practice in sick bay. Interesting to compare this film with *Puss 'n Boots,* which is the same subject. Bob Augustus must have had a much bigger budget than Chuck Vincent because with tanks and artillery he creates a more believable `unbelievable` Army. Most women under 40 will laugh at this one.

FRINGE BENEFITS NN NL (in a kindergarten way)
1975   INTERNATIONAL HOME VIDEO CLUB

P/D—Pendulous Productions
F/A—Eric Edwards, Kenneth Angle
F/A—Michelle Magazine, Georgina Spelvin, Angel Street

You can judge the intellectual caliber of this one, an early 1970s effort, by the fact that the director and producer's names are not given and by the names of the characters. Dr. Tessy Tightwat (a much younger Georgina Spelvin) is a virgin who is head of the Tightwat Institute for Sexual Research. Employees refer to it as Hard-on Heaven. Harry Flatout (Eric Edwards) arrives for treatment for his impotence. He's been working for Mr. Cockpole (president of the Spurt Over Oil Corporation), but now Flatout tells Tessy, "I need to be fixed up and I mean up." Seems he instituted a sex-hour as a fringe benefit for Spurt Over employees. Cockpole is having an affair with his secretary, Elaine Ziplove. Flatout wants Cockpole's office for his own rest and recreation periods, and he especially wants to initiate two new employees, Marianne Lubglob and Kathy Thunderfart. On and on it goes with Flatout's

impotence finally being resolved by Dr. Cherry Popper's new invention, an Electro Testicular Cock Erector, which together with his assistant, Miss Motor Mouth, give Harry a permanent hard-on and make him the new hero and vice president of Spurt Over Oil.

HEAVENLY DESIRE CC NN DK with a group sex ending but much NL
1979   CAL VISTA VISUAL ENTERTAINMENT

P/D—Jaacov Jaacovi
F/A—Johnny Keyes, Jamie Gillis
F/A—Serena, Seka

A laughing sexvid which raises the possibilities of doing the whole Thorne Smith series with Myrna Loy and William Powell as adult films. It begins in the old West, when Ralph the Kid, a near-sighted killer, and his girlfriends are shot down at high noon. They return to today, rising from their graves to a sorority that now exists on the site of the old bordello. Serena and Seka are ghostly housemothers holding the fraternity brothers' putzes when their girlfriends won't and encouraging all the young people to enjoy themselves sexually. There is a unique bi scene with both Serena and Seka convincing a young woman they are her boyfriend. Also Johnny and Serena are featured in a nice black and white sequence.

HERE IT IS—BURLESQUE CC NL R
1979   VESTRON VIDEO

P/D—Michael Brandman, Marty Callner
F/A—Morey Amsterdam, Pinky Lee, Patrick Bagwell
F/A—Ann Corio, Tami Roche, Silki St. James, April Maitland

If you've never seen burlesque, or if you have and forgotten its whizbang slapstick humor, which was a training ground for the older television comedians, then don't miss this tape. If anything, it proves it needs a sequel because the nature of the burlesque acts are perfectly adaptable to small-screen viewing and ideal for projection-size television. It's a sexy sexvid, but sexy silly in a way that most mixed audiences in the 1980s and even young teenagers will enjoy. The nudity is all T and A, and the most famous burlesque skits include "Here Comes the Judge" (Morey Amsterdam); the girls in the chorus who walk with a bouncy, ass-bumping walk and play end-man to the baggy pant jokes; the male vocalist who looks like a fruitcake; the xylophone player (Pinky Lee) and of course the female strippers who take it off with bumps and grinds ever-so-slowly and teasingly. One has mammoth knockers and can twirl tassels attached to her breasts and rump. One that you never saw in places like the Old Howard in Scollay Square years ago when I played hooky from high school is a male stripper like Patrick Bagwell who does a strip act equal to, if not more erotic than any of the female strippers. When I was a teenager, Ann Corio came onstage wearing a big picture hat. She was dressed like the girl in the Sunday School choir, the one you loved but didn't dare speak to. Sadly, in this one, although Ann was only 50ish when it was made and was still quite pretty, she does not strip. In memory of the genteel way that Ann Corio took it all off, when I was a young man I combined her with another stripper, Sally Keith (she shook tassels in the Crawford House in Boston), and created a character I called Princess Tassel in my novel *That Girl From Boston*. Princess Tassel lives on an island in Boston Harbor and is married to Mad-Man Starch (a retired wrestler.) They have a daughter named Willa, who has graduated from Radcliffe. It's a funny, nostalgic story of a past era waiting for some adult film producer to bring it to life in a fast-moving, laughing sex film.

HIGH SCHOOL FANTASIES
CC   NN   NL
FREEWAY

P/D—Richard Aldrich, Morris Deal
F/A—Larry Barnhouse
F/A—Renee Bond, Nicole Riddell

A laughing sexvid. If you were in high school in the past 20 years you'll remember poor Freddy, the bumbling ass who could never make it with girls. All his friends are happily screwing, but not Freddy—until he finally invents a concoc-

tion that sexes women better than Spanish fly is supposed to. His first conquest is his high school English teacher, who drinks it in Coke. Richard Aldrich insists the idea of this sexvid, if not the action, is autobiographical. William Margold, who acts in, produces and reviews adult films, believes that *High School Fantasies* is "the best sex film ever made. I adore that film because it has caught all the humor of sex."

HOT AND SAUCY PIZZA GIRLS THEY DELIVER   **CC   NN   NL   BI occasional DK (anal) and a cranking dildo**
WONDERFUL WORLD OF VIDEO

P/D—Richard Aldrich, Bob Chinn
F/A—John C. Holmes
F/A—Desiree Cousteau, Candida Royalle, Laurien Dominique

The absolute silliness of this sexvid counteracts the deviational stuff. It's the best film Desiree Cousteau has made since *Pretty Peaches* and establishes her as one of the few comic actresses who make porno films. The pizza girls deliver sex and pizza to order. The villain is Night Chicken, employed by the Fried Chicken Syndicate to stop their lucrative pizza delivery service. Worth owning.

HOT DALLAS NIGHTS
CC   NN   NM   BI   DK   NL
1982   VCX

P/D—Tony Kendrick
F/A—Slim Grady, Turk Lyon
F/A—Hilary Summers, Raven Turner, R. J. Reynolds, Tara Flynn, Greer Shapiro

Offering a parody on TV's "Dallas," a sick-sex soap opera for the masses, isn't easy, but Tony Kendrick and the various actors in this one have succeeded in topping the ucky sex relationships in J.R.'s family with even uckier ones, and occasionally there is funny dialogue. Rock Brewing is the name of the old man. His wife Millie is played superbly by Greer Shapiro. R.J., the oldest son, has taken over the fertilizer empire and won't let Daddy come to work any more. R.J. wants to take over the Johnson Fertilizer Company. "There ain't enough shit in this town for the both of us," he tells his father, but to make more he has to mortgage the old homestead. Pat, the wife of R.J.'s incompetent brother Robbie, agrees to forge Robbie's name on the mortgage, but only after R.J. agrees to eat her pussy. R.J. is not too enthusiastic, but he's not making it with his wife, Mary Ellen, who is a drunk. Mary Ellen and Robbie have something in common—they detest R.J. So Robbie takes care of Mary Ellen so she won't have to masturbate any longer. In the meantime Lindy, the granddaughter, is trying to seduce Duke, the hired hand. But every time Duke gets close to climaxing someone breaks in before he comes—so poor Duke is out in the barnyard chasing chickens. In his words, "screwing beats jacking off." In the meantime it turns out that Pat is a masochist. She enjoys being tied up—using R.J.'s whips and chains, of course. And R.J. is busy consulting by telephone with J.R., who is arranging to have the Johnson Fertilizer factory burned down so R.J. can take over. But R.J. doesn't realize that Johnson is Mother Millie's brother. When she finds out what he has done she kicks him off the ranch along with Robbie—and Duke takes over. He's already gone to work for Millie's brother. "I'm full of shit," he tells her. "We ought to merge and get all this shit in one place." You can't help laughing, but whether it gets your shit together is something else.

HOUSE OF LOVE NN BI NL DK (in a silly Gallic way)
1978 BLUE VIDEO

P/D—Robert Lynn
F/A—Jacques Marboeuf, Pierret Raymond, Jean de Villroy
F/A—Collette Marevil, Denise Fevreier

This one was made in France. The actors listed on the credits of the tape are different from those given above. With the exception of the immediately recognizable Jean de Villroy (whose name is not on the box), I can't identify for sure any of the others. But even with the English dubbing, the dialogue manages to convey some of the silly Gallic humor of the original. Count Drisac (the 70-year-old Jean de Villroy) and his wife have a sexually backward son who is at least 25. He has a fiancée, chosen for him by his parents, but Humbert doesn't know much about the birds and bees. When his fiancée stares at him sexily, he faints. A doctor is called and he tells the count and countess that Humbert, the viscount, needs a few weeks in his clinic. Before the film is over, the count arrives too for a week of sexual refurbishing, and soon he is followed by the countess, who needs some oil in her sexual gears. The count hasn't screwed her for ten years, but you'd never guess it to see him in action with the nurses. Mademoiselle Betty, one of the nurses, takes care of Humbert, teaching him the facts of life. Meanwhile, the doctor is receiving a couple of country peasants, patients who pay him in home-grown vegetables. They tell him they are getting married tomorrow, but they are both virgins. The guy's problem is that he doesn't really know what sex is. Telling them to undress and lie on his sofa, the doctor eats his lunch, and verbally tells the guy what to do. It's all so silly that you can't help laughing occasionally—especially if you've had a couple of drinks.

IF YOU DON'T STOP IT YOU'LL GO BLIND
1980 MEDIA

P/D—Tom Parker, Mike Calle, Keith Braselle
F/A—George Spenser, Pat Wright, Garth Pillsbury, Herb Graham, Richard Stuart, Alan Sinclair and many others
F/A—Jane Kellem, Deborah Close, Ina Gould, Thelma Pelish, Ushi Digard and many others

This is a zany sequel to *Can I Still Do It If I Wear Glasses* (see listing). The format is a dirty "Laugh-In." You can be sure that you'll never see this one on commercial TV. It raises an interesting question. Whether you find it hilarious, medium funny or purerle depends on your level of sexual sophistication. My theory is that only about 10 percent of Americans are really sexually sophisticated and will abhor this tape. On the other hand, while it certainly won't appeal to the Moral Majority, it will tickle middle-class suburbanites and Rotary Clubs everywhere who enjoy a dirty joke.

Samples from among the hundreds which are dramatized: A young woman in a restaurant ordering everything on the menu, to the shock of her consort, who asks her, "Do you eat this well at home?" Answer: "At home no one wants to fuck me after dinner." Or a guy to a woman who he thinks he's screwing for the first time: "Do you know what this is? Do you think it's a wee wee? It's really a prick!" Response: "I've seen lots of pricks but this is definitely a wee wee." Or a woman assuring a guy, "There's no teeth down there," and tells him to take a look. "Do you see any teeth, stupid?" Response: "Are you kidding? With gums like that?" Or "I'd like to get into your pants," a guy tells a woman. Response: "Sorry, but—one asshole in my pants is enough." There's an hour and 20 minutes of this—fast and furious, concluding with the World Sex Awards (given Academy Award-Style) to a big theater audience for various achievements, such as Best Dramatic Performance in a Bedroom Situation; Longest Sustained Erection; Busiest Beaver; Most Orgasm with the Least Effort; Most Promising Nymphomaniac, etc. All followed by a big stage production with singing and dancing girls and Keith Braselle singing, "Don't Fuck Around with Love."

INTENSIVE CARE **NN BI DK NL**
(baggy-pants-burlesque style)
1974   BLUE VIDEO

P/D—**Jack B. Nuss, David Sear**
F/A—**Harry Reems, Don Allen, Bobby Astyr**
F/A—**Mary Stuart, Lyla Piccolo**

Dr. Scrotum (Harry Reems) speaks with an Italian Jewish accent. His first patient has a problem. His penis has shrunk from 12 inches to 7 inches. To help get it back to normal, Nurse Nookie takes it in her mouth but it gets stuck and she can't get it out. After various colored liquids are fed to him from test tubes and a string tied around his penis, Harry makes a sandwich out of the patient and Nurse Nookie. The next patient (Bobby Astyr) got his *schmeckel* caught in a grinder that was making chopped liver at the delicatessen. It's carefully put in a splint and bandaged. Meanwhile, looking for the cafeteria with-

out his glasses, our good doctor ends up in the hospital morgue conveniently equipped with a naked female corpse lying in a coffin. Harry humps her and she immediately returns to life as a kind of vampire. Finally there's Miss Piccolo, who has a problem. She was lonesome for her husband and so she played his recorder —you guessed where—and now it's stuck and whistles when she walks. The whole thing begins to look a little greasy . . . but if you're tipsy yourself when you watch it you may laugh occasionally.

IT HAPPENED IN HOLLYWOOD
CC NN DK BI NL
1972   WONDERFUL WORLD OF VIDEO

P/D—**Jim Buckley, Peter Locke**
F/A—**Harry Reems, Marc Stevens, Jamie Gillis**
F/A—**Melissa Hall and many other one-timers**

Sponsored by Al Goldstein and Jim Buckley, who at the time were the co-owners of *Screw*, a tabloid-style sex newspaper that has been in continous publication since 1968, this one has all the insanity of *Screw* on tape. It begins with Felicity Split's birthday present, given to her by Harry Reems—a bidet. When she sits on it a male face appears and the tongue laps her. Seems Felicity (a brunette Goldie Hawn look-a-like—*Variety* called this a porno version of "Laugh-In") is giving up her office job to work her way up to porn star. En route, she tells a new boyfriend that her pussy is so hot that she could boil an egg in it—and presto, a hard-boiled egg pops out. The guy she is talking to on the phone comes so hard it sprays out of her telephone. Then on stage you watch the Flying Fucks. Sure enough, after leaping through the air the woman lands squarely on her partner's erect penis— after which she rides a bike equipped with dildos; and Al himself (much fatter than he is now) appears as a High Priest. Add the Academy Award of Fuck Films (given by Jim Buckley, who has long since gone straight) and the big scene with Samson and Delilah where everyone is having sex to the music of "Hava-na-gila," and you have some of the silliness of this tape. The CC rating may be dubious but this film is a contemporary of *Deep Throat*

174 _____

and it has a baggy-pants burlesque style that probably can't be duplicated in the 1980s.

JACK AND JILL CC NN NL some BI and laughing DK
1979 QUALITY

P/D—Chuck Vincent, Mark Ubell
F/A—Jack Wrangler
F/A—Samantha Fox, Vanessa Del Rio

For this sexvid, Samantha Fox received the Best Actress award at the Fourth Annual Erotic Film Festival, 1980. *Screw's* Best 10 of 1979, number seven, it is one of the first sexvids to combine a great deal of dialogue with the sex action. Much of the dialogue is funny. Samantha makes a believable housewife. An interesting variation has two couples getting acquainted by playing strip poker and doing what the drawer of the high card prefers (in alternate deals) while they all watch . . . ending of course, in group sex. Younger women will enjoy it—especially the Romeo and Juliet scene.

JOINT VENTURE CC NN DK NL
1978 ADULT VIDEO

P/D—Not given
F/A—Gerard Damiano, Bobby Astyr
F/A—Vanessa Del Rio, Sharon Mitchell

This one should carry the title *The Wonderful World of Spurts*, which is what it is all about. Four women compete in a weekly event which Gerard Damiano and Bobby Astyr as co-anchors report to you live from Madison Square Hotel. Four women contestants (whose faces you see—you rarely see any male's face in the sex scenes) take on four males in various events called the "orals," the "anals," the "straddles," the "hand job" and a final orgy scene called the "freestyles." The other scenes give you all the adult film goodies, not one at a time but *four at a time*. Giving this one an NL rating is really a way of saying that it's so damned silly that you'll laugh in spite of yourself or burn it in horror.

JUDGMENT DAY CC NN NL NR (a little)
1978 CAL VISTA

P/D—Bella Maria, Jon Cutaia
F/A—P. J. Whigham, John Leslie, Turk Lyon, John Seeman
F/A—Angel Face, Moira Benson, Josie Farmer

Before you even know who they are, you are watching John Leslie and Moira Benson in an extended sexmaking scene. Afterwards, she asks John (they use other story names), "Do you still feel the same way you did last time?" To which he answers, "I do." He leaves the bed, turns on all the gas jets in the kitchen and goes back to Moira for one final orgasm before they meet their maker. Next scene you watch them and four other guys laboriously climbing a hill and St. Peter (P. J. Whigham, who is very amusing), wearing wings and a halo, is waiting for them. He reviews the guys' cases first. Seems one was exercising in his back yard. After screwing his maid near his pool, he suspended himself upside down on his exercise bar while she fellated him. He fell on his head and died. "Don't you get snotty with me," Saint Peter tells him, "or I'll send you to hell." And after listening to his case, he finally does. Then St. Peter reviews the case of a garage mechanic who went to fix a lady's car and ended up screwing her. He smothered to death when she sat on his face. St. Peter sends "this stupid twit" to hell, also. Next there's John Seeman, a vacuum cleaner salesman who demonstrates to a newly wed bride a new use for a vacuum cleaner. Her husband catches them in flagrante delicto. Thinking he's going to be shot (the husband only has a fake cigarette lighter), John jumps off the balcony to his death. He too is consigned to hell. One guy named Elgin Twitty (his screen name) is saved by St. Peter and taken to Paradise. He died of a heart attack because two women came into his home and were going to rob him. Since he had no money they made him strip and killed him with sexual kindness. John and Moira are also saved by St. Peter, who reverses their death. They really love each other but can't marry because John's wife won't give him a divorce. St. Peter fixes that and John's wife dies so that he can marry Moira and live happily ever after. It's so silly that most women will laugh, too.

KATE AND THE INDIANS
NN DK BI NL (but only if you've had a couple of drinks)
1979 SELECT/ESSEX XTRA-VISION

P/D—Bob Augustus, Allen Swift
F/A—Jack Shute, Mike Ranger
F/A—Kay Parker, Betti Good, Kandi Barbour

It takes about ten minutes before this one gets to the Indians and total insanity. But finally, to the accompaniment of the "Nutcracker Suite," Professor Von Martin and his student, Kate, are out in the desert with Indians, who are watching them eating watermelon and blowing bubble gum. Then Kate and the professor are lost in the desert, running around naked, while the Indians, including a midget, an uncircumcised Jewish Indian chief, and his two sons are fornicating among the cactus with the Indian girls and Kate. Lighting was no problem since it was mostly shot outdoors, and unlike most adult films is in constant motion. Plenty of low-class barroom style humor.

KINKY TRICKS
CC NN NL BI DK NR (momentarily)
1978 VISUAL ENTERTAINMENT

P/D—Bob W. Davis
F/A—Danny Flynn, Polo, Bill Lewis
F/A—Sharon Lucas, Cindy Lake, Fran Cooper, Diane Wilde, Lana Terry

This is a better sexvid than its title. The cassette box reveals the actresses' real names (or maybe the credits do?). Anyway, you'll recognize immediately Candida Royalle, around whom most of the story revolves, and Tiffany Clarke, who are *not* listed in the credits. Seems that Candy (Candida Royalle), who has lived with Elliott (Danny Flynn) nearly a year before, has ended up in the clinker for prostitution. She's been released because she's told the authorities she has a nice home where she can live. The home is Elliott's but, when she arrives, he's so broke he has

to sell it. Besides, he's in love with Allison. Good-hearted Candy really loves Elliott although he ignores her. She wants to help him. So she calls up all her friends. During the day the house, unknown to Elliott, becomes a kind of sex commune with Candy's various girlfriends meeting the needs of various boyfriends while Candy collects money from them to help pay the mortgage. In the things-you-can't-believe-you're-watching department, Tiffany has sex while a parrot rests on her shoulder and they keep time to jungle music. In another part of the garden, Candy plays Eve with a green apple. Upstairs a guy is being totally babied with a woman mothering him. In another part of the house a guy lying face down in a net hammock has a woman lying underneath him, and on a sofa a guy dressed in black silk stockings and a garter belt is bringing a woman to a climax with his toes. And in another bedroom two women discuss whether one of them can contain a penis as big as J. C. Holmes's. When Elliott finds out what is happening in his house, Candy tells him she did it all for him and they end up in bed. Ordinarily, this melange could have been very seamy, but it is done with a such slap-happy silliness that you can't help laughing.

KISS AND TELL (KOCK FM 169)
NN NM DK
CABALLERO

P/D—Suze Randall
F/A—Mike Ranger, Mike Eyeke, Tim Dennis
F/A—Suze Randall, Loni Sanders, Tippi Rocks

Imagine a radio station called KOCK 169 with a disc jockey named Dirty Dan who can say anything that comes into his head over the air, and who has no problems with the Federal Communication Commission. It probably would break all Nielsen ratings. Dirty Dan (Mike Eyeke) is a skinny blond guy who walks around in a long marcelled hairdo, a T-shirt and nothing else. In between advertising products like Auto Suc ("Attach it to your cigarette lighter, guys, and get a blow job while you drive"), he sings songs to his listeners: "Kock-A-Doodle Doo, Any Cock Will Do."

Or he tells them to dial H-A-R-D S-E-X and tell other listeners "how Cupid came into your life." He answers the phone, "Hi Bubby, You're live on the KOCK." The idea of this one and the conversation from Dirty Dan is better than the sex, which is continuous switching between the action in the station and in the listeners' homes. When one of his panting female listeners visits him, Dirty Dan and the guy in the control booth take her on. Then they make a sandwich out of her in one of the most detailed, close-up, double-insertions you have ever watched. Don't buy this one for your wife or girlfriend.

LET MY PUPPETS COME   CC   NL
(especially if you've been smoking pot or are a little bombed)
1983   CABALLERO

P/D—Gerard Damiano
F/A—Littel Louie, Al Goldstein
F/A—Penny Nichols, Lynette Sheldon

Like Beethoven with his Ninth Symphony deciding that he had reached the end of orchestral development, Damiano has finally given up on people and produced a sexy muppet movie. He doesn't have Mr. Frog, or Miss Porky, but he has rubber pricks and talking cunts. The cast of characters leads off with names like Clark Gobble, Anthony Quim, Clitoris Leachman, Robert Vasellino, Connie Lingus, Peter Rection and many more. The Board of Directors of the Big League Bocci Company are in trouble. They owe Mr. Big (who finally turns out to be a live midget) a lot of money, and the only way to bail the company out is to make a porno flick. The dialogue abounds with stuff like a female puppet telling her dog, "You're a dog." Answer: "Yeah, but I'm a cocker." After which he proves it. Pinocchio appears with Geppetto and is re-created as a transvestite who sings operatic music à la Nelson Eddy and Jeanette MacDonald. "When I'm calling you-ooohoo. . . . Excuse me. When I'm balling you." There are also arias about Quim and Cock. Then there are X-rated commercials: "New Sweet Fish Feminine Hygiene Spray; Climex watches —take a beating and still keep ticking; Lusterene—I hate the taste, but I'm so oral

I use it forty times a day." And finally when the puppets run out of gas, there's a few live ladies. One of them actually tries to screw a puppet but he only wants her bras and panties. The CC rating is not ecstatic, but obviously someone had to attempt to do it, and Damiano hasn't spared any effort.

LIPPS AND MCCAIN
CC   NN   NL   NR
1980   SELECT ESSEX

P/D—Richard Aldrich, Bob Chinn
F/A—Ric Lutz, Paul Thomas
F/A—Amber Hunt, Pat Rhea, Vickey Lindsay

This is a laughing sexvid. Lipps and McCain are two cowboy brothers who really like women. Most of the sex scenes are warm, friendly and caring. Most women will enjoy this one, which has much dialogue interspersed with the sex.

LITTLE ORPHAN SAMMY
CC   NN   NL   BI
1975   BLUE VIDEO

P/D—Michael Roberts, Arlo Schiffin
F/A—Jamie Gillis, Rocky Millstone, Lin Flanagan
F/A—Jennifer Welles, C. J. Laing, Andrea True, Kim Pope

This film was made long before *Annie* became a Broadway musical or movie. It's a satirical antidote for both of them. Crazy dialogue and good acting from just about everyone in the film add up to one of few funny pornos. Rocky Millstone (whoever he is—I've never seen him in any other film) plays Little Orphan Sammy. Lin Flanagan, a happy-looking Irishman with a potbelly, plays Daddy Sawbucks. Little Sammy, whose hair is dyed red, speaks in a tiny boy's voice. He believes "It is very nice and American to help all your friends." And he does—happily servicing horny nurses, a female doctor and the matron in charge of the orphange where Sammy lives. Sammy misses his Daddy Sawbucks and neither knows where the other has disappeared to. Daddy, a zillionaire, has never stopped searching for Little Sammy. Never mind. Hata Mari (Jennifer Welles wearing a black wig and speaking with a weird accent) has located Sammy in the orphanage and plans to use him as hostage to milk Daddy Sawbucks. She also has smoke dreams of screwing with her chauffeur, Jamie Gillis, as a happy moron who can only react to his first name, Dar. Hata Mari's nefarious scheme is to adopt Sammy and use him as the foil to ply Daddy Sawbucks' secret out of him. Sawbucks has the whole Arab world trembling because he knows how to convert garbage into oil. On top of that, he has cornered the market on garbage. He doesn't trust anyone, including Hata Mari, who telephones him at his office in a dump. But Hata knows Daddy's real secret. The only way Daddy can get it up is when he is actually wallowing in money. Soon she has Daddy Sawbucks almost naked—down to his baggy shorts. In the middle of the confusion, a service man from Ma Bell arrives. He's trying to lay a telephone cable but only manages to lay C. J. Laing, one of Hata's girls. It all ends with everyone happily screwing to the accompaniment of the "Star Spangled Banner" and "Stars and Stripes Forever" with money pasted to everyone's behinds, while Daddy and Little Sammy remind the viewer, "The American way is the best way" . . . and "The family that plays together stays together." Most women will chuckle along with their guys at the insanity of it all. In the 1980s the only one in the cast still making adult films is Jamie Gillis. But this one proves that silliness and sex can be happily combined.

MASH'D NN DK NM
1979   CABALLERO CONTROL

P/D—Emton Smith
F/A—Mike Jefferson, J. J. Jones
F/A—Andrea True, Annie Sprinkles

A sexier version of "M*A*S*H*" than will ever appear on commercial television. Although it has a copyright date of 1979, it probably was made a few years earlier. Backgrounds are reasonably realistic. Nurses screw in the jungle with MD's, doctors operate in tents while being fellated by the nurses, nurses crawl into bed with patients, two of them have a naked mudfight while the entire camp cheers and Hotpuss and Telescope (counterparts of the TV version) copulate in the shower while the camp watches them. Contrived humor—lower middle class, barroom style.

MEATBALL CC NN DK NL (but pretty puerile and contrived)
1974   ARROW

P/D—Gerard Damiano
F/A—Harry Reems
F/A—Singe Low, Linda Sanderson

Dr. Schmock (Harry Reems) sprinkles his new chemical compound, Preparation X, on hamburger he's cooking in his lab and it grows so big it pops out of the pan. When he eats it, it affects his putz, which begins to pounce around in his pants. Nurse Helen Bed (Singe Low) tries to bring it down but it goes up every hour on the hour; even Bertha, a masseuse, who is called in to help is exhausted. The only solution the two women can offer is to wring it out or amputate it, but Schmock has a better idea. He reverses the Preparation X formula and when he drinks it he becomes gay. Harry Reems's extended parody will aggravate homosexuals and delight macho males, as will the theory that the reason women aren't excited by the stuff when it is put in hamburgers is that women prefer meatballs. Harry Reems's silly facial expressions and his telescope that sees the present all at once and combines human sex with shots of dolphins with their mouths open, roller coasters, swimming fish, turtles, bumper cars, all accompanied by well matched background music for sexmaking may keep you amused.

MISBEHAVIN' CC NN NL (in a silly ass way)
1978   QUALITY

P/D—Bob Sumner, Chuck Vincent
F/A—Leslie Bovee, Gloria Leonard, Molly Malone
F/A—Jack Wrangler, Kurt Mann, Dick Gallan, Eric Edwards

There's an Angel (Kurt Mann) and a Devil (Dick Gallan) in this one—but they'll remind you of Abbott and Costello. They make a bet that given the choice of love or money in a marriage, one or the other will win out. The only one who can prove whether they are right is Rita Lawrence (Leslie Bovee), who has been married 14 times and obviously has settled for lots of money. So the Angel and the Devil attend a party Rita is running at her country estate to watch as Gloria (Gloria Leonard) tries to line up Rita's next husband, a wealthy old man, Mr. Cornwall. While Rita is conning him she is also being followed by one of her former husbands, Carlos, who threatens to commit suicide if she doesn't return to him. Rita takes on the hired hand in the barn, a headwaiter in a restaurant (while Mr. Cornball is waiting at the table) and then meets a rich young man played by Eric Edwards, whom she momentarily falls in love with. You'll have to decide whether love or money wins out. It's a totally silly sexvid with continuous one-liners. The actors even talk directly to the audience, pre-Elizabethan style, telling them what they are thinking.

NAUGHTY NETWORK
NN   NM   DK   BL   NL (on the sick throw-up side)
1981   CABALLERO

P/D—Linus Gator
F/A—Mike Ranger, Ray Cooper, Chris Parker
F/A—Delia Cosner, Tina Jordan, Lauren Hart, Sandy Browne, Nicole Noir, Stephanie Taylor

WHAC-TV, the number one X-rated network in United States, has offered such programs as "The Little Whorehouse on the Prairie," and "The Mating Game," but now they are previewing their new season for Blackie, Mr. Blackman, the president of the network (who is black). He wants to knock out all competitors, particularly straight programs like "General Hospital," which will be up against his "Genital Hospital." This sequence has Mike Ranger as the patient, getting his anal temperature taken by a nurse who masturbates him while she's doing it. Eventually he takes her vaginal temperature.

Then, there's "Trash" (to compete with "M*A*S*H*") which features a dominatrix as an enlisting officer who, in Little Rock, Arkansas, is recruiting more manly fighting men than any other enlisting location in the U.S. She tests out their manliness by whipping and domination and their ability to screw by way of a cooperating private (female) who is willingly chained to a swing with her ass in the air. Then, there's "Wild Crazy Kingdom" which features Spider and the Fly—a bisexual sequence in which the spider first eats the fly and then they eat each other. "As the World Burns" follows, but Blackman rejects it because it's too romantic—there are no "tunnel shots." Finally, if you haven't tossed your cookies yet, there's "Young and Horny," which begins with some high school kids sculpting phalluses by the seashore and talking about their sex lives. You learn about how one of the young ladies invited in a door-to-door salesman.

NEVER SO DEEP   **NN   BI   DK**
1982   VCX

P/D—Gerard Damiano
F/A—Mike Ranger, Paul Thomas
F/A—Loni Sanders, Brooke West, Victoria Slick, Tara Aire, Marie Tortuga

Many years ago Damiano complained in an interview that the biggest problem in making adult films is that porno actors can't act. Maybe so in the early days, but there are plenty of good actors and actresses around today. Nevertheless, Damiano picks one for this film, Loni Sanders, who really can't act. She gives you the feeling she's about to say "gee whiz" or "oh, wow" to every confrontation. Never mind, she has a beautiful body and in this one plays Ginger Trueheart, a private eye, who has a chauffeur, Sam Strong (Mike Ranger). Mike services her regularly and when she's not available takes on suspects or ladies who will lead them to their quarry. Their quarry in this case is, believe it or not, a woman with a butterfly on her ass. The great publisher Hugh Heffer (Paul Thomas) has fallen in love with her but has lost her. He never really knew what she looked like. But, "She's the best cocksucker I ever met . . . Sex has never been a problem for me," he explains to Ginger as women walk around the Heffer mansion half undressed. "But every time I think of this girl I get a hard-on." For a $5,000 retainer, and a $20,000 payout, Ginger takes on the job of finding the lady. There's one funny scene where Loni tries to interview a live model in a peepshow and must keep inserting quarters to make the screen go up. If you have never seen the San Francisco Gold Coast and its strip and sex clubs, Damiano takes you on a cinematic tour. Ginger interviews one lady who is sucking a guy off and she obligingly shares his cock with Ginger while she speculates where the lady with butterfly may be. Ginger finally finds her, and in a silly non sequitur Ginger does an X-rated television commercial only to discover that the script girl is the lady (Marie Tortuga) she is searching for. Hugh Heffer gets his deep throat from an expert, and Sam and Ginger go on to their next exploits. Please, Gerard, don't make a sequel!

NURSES OF THE 407TH
CC   NN   NL   NM   BI   NR (a little)
1983   CREATIVE IMAGE

P/D—Julian Ornyski, Tony Kendrick
F/A—Paul Thomas, Jon Martin, Joey Civera,
    Lynx Cannon, Herschel Savage
F/A—Jesie St. James, Kristin, Tigr, Laura Wren,
    Bonnie Jean

Along with *Insatiable*, and *Up'n Coming* (see listings), this is one of the first porno films to appear on a laser disc. Whether the disc version is soft core, I don't know, but this is a better film than *Mash'd* (see listing) although it closely parallels the famous television series. Jesie St. James is Captain Janet "Hot Hips" O'Reilly. Paul Thomas is Jack "Jaybird" Anderson and Lynx Canon is Colonel Arthur James. Canon is a dud, but the rest of them, including Corporal Specs (Joey Civera) and Herschel Savage, a major who arrives in the hospital unit with a broken toe gets his arm broken screwing a nurse, and finally ends blown up by a land mine on which the unit has been camping, all combine to offer some silly scenes and a good approximation of a sexy X-rated

*M*A*S*H episode*. Jaybird tells his friend John (Jon Martin) in front of Hot Hips that he'd like to enjoy her body as the All American Girl Sandwich—with her in between himself and Jon. Of course, he's totally rejected by Hot Hips who is in love with a guy back home, and in the meantime has her vibrator kit, and a friendly nurse to take care of her. After many mishaps and much copulating, during which Corporal Specs gets a birthday cake and two naked nurses, Jaybird finally traps a pretty willing Hot Hips. But after telling him that she really loves him, and making romantic love with him, she says: "When you get something special you really want to share it," and much to John's delight (He's been watching them, of course), she invites him to share the fun and she becomes a willing filling in the sandwich.

PLAYGIRLS OF MUNICH
CC   NN   NL   DK (but always laugh oriented)
1973   VIDEO X HOME LIBRARY

P/D—Navred Reef
F/A—Roger Caine, Zebedy Colt
F/A—Gretchen Kolber, Karen Hapsburg, Sylvia
    Renard

Two telephone repairmen with $14 between them, compelled by the lure of a paperback they are reading titled *Sex In Europe*, stow away on a plane and end up in Munich during the 1972 Olympic Games. You'll chuckle at this silly slapstick sexvid from beginning to end. It offers two crazy characters, a stud named Chuck (Roger Caine) and his worried, clucky pal, Barney (Zebedy Colt), who is forever getting in trouble in his search for sex. He never quite makes out while Chuck screws himself silly. Photographed in Munich, it not only has appropriate German background music to enhance the sequences but the 12 women that they get in and out of scrapes with actually speak German, and the comedy is enhanced by occasional subtitles translating the words our heroes don't understand. Zebedy is an excellent comedian, and sexmaking with a 200-pound fraulein, watching a mistress with her lover (closeup) or being seduced in a German whorehouse, he'll keep you grinning. The German women are much more sophisticated about sex than any American actresses, and Gay Talese would trade Sandstone for the German ski lodge in which they all end up in a laughing group sex sequence in an indoor swimming pool. Worth owning—as well as its sequel (see *Dutch Treat*, p. 82).

PLAYTHINGS **NN NM DK BI NL** (occasionally if you're bombed)
1982 VCA

P/D—Zachary Youngblood, Robert Pudenda
F/A—Jerry Bilt, Michael Morrison
F/A—Starr Wood, Simona Wing, Sharon Caine, Lysa Thatcher, Liza Adams

The only way to enjoy this one is with another couple sharing a pitcher of martinis or whatever may be your alcoholic pleasure. It's so bad it often becomes funny. Somewhere in the sci-fi future there's a guy named Dork from a planet called Neon who arrives on earth, which is being run by humanoids. One of them is using her vibrator and she's screwing up Dork's intergalactic reception. Dork, played by Jerry Bilt (note also the director's name Pudenda) is a sappy-looking guy who wears an "erotic belt" which makes it possible for the wearer to simulate sexual intercourse, or get blown without a partner. Dork doesn't understand the language of earth, so a sexy lady from Marin County, California, teaches him a new non-sequitur language which gets one rid of one's sexual inhibtions. Example: "What interesting balls you have! I want to fuck you. What kind of car do you drive?" or "What's that belt you're wearing on your chest? I think I love you." There's a theme song called "Me First," and the females have found a new use for Perrier bottles— you know where. On and on it goes while you wonder what kind of imbeciles would make such a flick and why anyone would be caught naked in it.

PUSS 'N BOOTS **NN NM BI DK**
1983 VIDEO-X-PIX

P/D—Chuck Vincent

F/A—Kelly Nichols, J. T. Ambrose, Sharon Kane, Cheri Champagne
F/A—Ron Hudd, David James, George Payne, Michael Knight

Released after *Roommates* (see listing, p. 125), this one, written and directed by Chuck Vincent, is a real letdown. I suspect that Chuck may have had to replenish his pocketbook by catering to a certain kind of male audience (still the biggest-paying customers) who don't care whether the plot is subtle or there is any characterization just so long as there's lots of nitty gritty sex. Most of the sex in this one is pretty gritty. Kelly Nichols plays Puss Malone. Like *Foxholes* (see listing), the movie trades on the Goldie Hawn–*Private Benjamin* theme, except you never know why Puss is in the Army. Right from the beginning all Puss wants to do is get out. What story there is takes place supposedly in a WAC Army barracks, or in a local barroom where Puss pays a local stud $70 to fuck her so she can get pregnant and thus discharged. Later she tries various other maneuvers, such as a Section Eight. After discovering her stud has a vasectomy she ends a tavern brawl, subduing everyone in sight with karate chops. Bobbi (J. T. Ambrose), as a private first class, commands two male privates, who are on guard duty, to drop their pants. After she sucks both of them erect, she backs her ass up to them and orders them to see what they can do. Following her commands they eat pussy. "Now try my asshole!" she tells them. They are evidently mute since they say nothing. "No wet 'em and insert them," she tells them. "Now soldiers, you may come when you are ready." Nora (Cheri Champagne) seduces April (Tara Aire) in the showers and when she's caught accuses April of being a dyke. April thereby gets what Puss wants—a discharge from the Army. Later, while Cheri is using a dildo in the toilets, she excites herself by looking at sexy pictures in *High Society* magazine. (Do women look at pictures when they masturbate? I doubt it.) To avenge April, Puss and Bobbi cajole the evil Nora into putting on rubber leotards. They tie her up and shove a dildo into her while she screams, "Don't stop! I love cock." Even in the five minutes of a romantic scene, Puss never removes her garter belt and stockings, thus letting Chuck Vincent offer all the adult film conventions packaged in one film. While the female soldiers are presumably in charge in this one, don't expect *your* woman to respond enthusiastically.

ROLLERBABIES **CC NN DK**
occasionally NL in "a silly ass way"
1979   WONDERFUL WORLD OF VIDEO

P/D—Carter Stevens
F/A—Robert Random, David Williams
F/A—Yolanda Salvas, Susan McBain, Terri Hall

It's the twenty-first century. Sex is outlawed because of the population explosion. People eat sex-suppressant pills. Cool Whip comes by the bucket and is pistachio flavored. "Fuck and Suck" is a national TV show. Yolanda Salvas, a black, baldheaded woman, sucks lollipops and anything else in sight. Irving Rochsov has created a female android who can say, "I gotta make pee-pee," and who to his dismay gets pregnant. Susan McBain has starred in *Deep Thought*—and in the things-you've-never-see-before area can give a guy a hard-on and a climax without touching him. To top it all, the Rollerbabies can have sex on roller skates. Watch this one with your neighbors and a few drinks. You can't help laughing at the total insanity of it.

SEX ROULETTE **CC NN NL DK BI**
1978   CABALLERO

P/D—Alan Vydra
F/A—Jean de Villroy, Robert Le Ray
F/A—Vanessa Melville, Anita Berenson

Combine Balthazar, a black midget dressed like a priest who stands on phone books to screw, and makes porno movies for his boss, Jean Villroy, a very wealthy, past-70 playboy (see *Pleasure Shoppe*—Jean looks like a U.S. senator should look). Add Jean, his niece who loves roulette but hates sex, add a Riviera–Monte Carlo ambiance, recombine with Jean de Villroy, who can't always get it up but his midget friend can, and you have a European-made film which handles kinky sex

with humor and sophistication that somehow make it more palatable than American films. This one is crazy enough that you can't help laughing. Worth owning.

SOCIETY AFFAIR **NN BI DK**
1982   CABALLERO

P/D—Harold Lime, Robert McCallum
F/A—Harry Reems, R. Bolla, Jack Newtown, Frank Holowell
F/A—Veronica Hart, Kelly Nichols, Tiffany Clark, Tara Aire, Lauri Smith

In 1972, two years after he appeared in *Deep Throat*, for which he was paid the sum of $100, Harry Reems was arrested by the FBI in New York and charged with a national conspiracy to transport obscene materials in interstate commerce. He was convicted in 1976, but an appeals court reversed the conviction, and then the prosecutor, Larry Parrish, tried to put the cost of the $4-million trial on the defendants. Harry received the support of thousands of people and many top Hollywood actors. But he quit the business and has not appeared in any porno flicks for the past six years. Harry is a professionally trained actor and has appeared in many legitimate plays, and with the National Shakespeare Company (see also note under listing for *Demented*). All of this raises the question: Why did he return to the porno scene—and why in particular did he make this film? One thing: he's so busy screwing, he has little time for acting. But then the story doesn't demand much from anyone except the joys of copulation. Seems that Rick, as played by Harry, is a small-time crook who has never really made a big killing. His former partner, Alexis (Veronica Hart), has moved on to bigger game—rich families like the Austins, whose son is about to marry Lillian (Kelly Nichols). Alexis discovers that their son, Howard Austin, is an exact lookalike for Rick, and she conceives the idea of Rick marrying Lillian instead of Howard, and then she and Rick can abscond with the wedding presents. To accomplish this, Howard is fed a mickey which keeps him comatose (believe it or not) in his bedroom closet for three days. Rick arrives to play the part of Howard, and before the wedding actually occurs he (as Howard) interrupts his stepmother making out with the maid, who wears only a garter belt and an apron; he screws his sister in the bowling alley of the estate, takes on three girl caddies in an afternoon bachelor party planned by his father at the golf club, and on the wedding day screws the bride while she's waving out the window at the guests who are arriving for the lawn party on the estate after the wedding. Prior to the actual wedding he discovers his bride and father are conspiring to cheat him out of his mother's inheritance and that Lillian loves Daddy more than she does him. Just as the minister is about to pronounce them man and wife, Rick denounces the whole family—shoves the wedding cake in the bride's face and absconds with Veronica and the wedding gifts. Howard enthusiastically approves and has recovered from his knockout drops and rewards Alexis and Rick with a check for $ 1 million dollars for saving his inheritance. Unfortunately, the way the story is told—presumably for laughs—the characters are, in Harry's words, "such a bunch of dummies" that you can't identify with anyone. Except perhaps Harry and Veronica, when at last they wrap up the picture and themselves in bed together very romantically. The same story could have been told much more effectively if Harry only played the part of Howard and was saved from his unscrupulous father and bride by Veronica—at the same time eliminating about half the other women panting after Harry's cock. Some American filmmaker should take a second look at Harry's best pictures—*Bel Ami* and *Young Butterflies*, both of which were made in Europe.

SUMMER CAMP R
1980 MEDIA

P/D—Mark Borde, Chuck Vincent
F/A—Jake Barnes, Michael Abrams, John Mclaughlin, Matt Michaels, Ray Holland
F/A—Colleen O'Neill, Alexis Schreiner

If you have subscription television which offers after-hour sex movies, you'll get your fill of these "nudies" which only provide plenty of frontal female nudity (and rear view). Presumably the people who make them have more money to spend than the adult filmmakers, and you'll note that this one was directed by Chuck Vincent, whose adult films always appear in softcore or "cool" versions. This one is about Camp Malibu, which has seen better days and is about to go bankrupt. The owner's solution to restore the camp is to invite the campers, who were only six or seven when their parents sent them, back for a reunion (and work) weekend—ten years later. So now all the little angels have returned and are thinking about making out with each other. In the women's dorms the horny girls run around topless and are spied on through a skylight, taking showers, by the equally horny males. One guy, Horse (Ray Holland), is a John Belushi type and is always unzipping his pants to show himself. Some of the girls seduce the camp cook, the medic and happily screw with anyone in sight. Then the whole thing turns into a kind of *Animal House* when the girls fill the guys' beds with shaving cream, dead fish and short sheet their beds. The guys raid the girls' dormitory, steal their underwear and try to hump them. And there's a football game between the guys and gals where the gals always end up willingly on the bottom. Dirty words abound—and "Fuck you" is written in shaving cream on the walls. You may laugh occasionally—but not if bucolic sex turns you off or dirty jokes bore you.

TITILLATION **CC NN NL NR (almost)**
1982 SELECT ESSEX

P/A—Damon Christain
F/A—Eric Edwards, Randy West, Ray Simpson, Mike Zempter, Mike Horner
F/A—Kitten Natividad, Heaven St. John, Gina Gianetti, Sandra Miller

Russ Meyer should love this film. Not only has Richard Aldrich (a.k.a. Damon Christain) rescued Kitten Natividad, one of Russ Meyer's famous big-titted ladies, from oblivion, but he has upstaged Meyer with a hilarious story about jugs, titties, mounds, lungs, busts, nobs, boobies, knockery, yaboos, chichis and bazooms that will keep you (both male and female) intrigued but chuckling and laughing a lot right through to the end. Seems there's a very rich old man, Felix Fitswilly (nicely played by Ray Simpson), who after collecting just about everything in the world, now in his old age is collecting big tits—a pair in particular that will fit a brass bra he has had molded. The owner of such mammaries will not only inherit his entire fortune but get anything in the world she may want while he's alive. In addition, the person who locates the lucky lady will get a $50,000 reward. His secretary, Brenda (Heaven St. John, who has breasts you could suffocate in), still does not have big enough boobies to fit Fitswilly's special bra. She wants more than the reward. She wants the crazy old bastard's fortune. So she hires Spado Zappo (Eric Edwards) and Pigeon Johnson (Randy West) to locate a particular woman named Candy (Kitten Natividad) who, from pictures they have, must have the qualifying mounds. From this point on the plot proceeds with cross- and double-cross. It's a little hard to swallow, but Aldrich makes it all palatable with silly Sam Spade-style voice-over dialogue and Eric Edwards's very good acting. Zappo is so broke the cockroaches have moved into his bed. He uses his last bullets shooting at them. He tells the listener, "I looked into her cold blue eyes and they were green. They didn't fit either. She looked like sex, but I hadn't changed my underwear." When he tells Brenda that he's a private dick, she replies, "You mean your dick is private?" But she quickly tumbles into the sack with him "because a hard man is good to find." In addition to the crazy dialogue, the sex scenes in this one are really different. Mike Horner makes love to a Cheryl Carter in an extended erotic way that almost any woman will identify with. Later Horner (called Rooster in the film), who is shacking up with Heaven St. John, gets involved with another woman, Sandra Miller (they are trying to locate Candy), in a threesome that I might have ordinarily given a DK rating, but this one is actually amusing as they finally exhaust each other and fall happily to sleep in each other's arms. A sex scene with Randy West and Cheryl

Carter runs for quite a few minutes with no soundtrack or phony moaning and groaning. Interestingly, though all the women are very sexy, none of them are very young, and none would win a beauty contest. Aldrich could develop a good thing with more stories featuring his private dicks.

X-RATED CARTOONS DS DK
VCX

Here's some of your favorite fairy tales, plus Bugs Bunny and Porky Pig retold with the cartoonist's sexual imagination running wild and occasionally beserk. Filled with Walt Disney-style violence—you can watch Hansel disemboweling the wicked witch with his penis while Gretel grins approvingly, or the Seven Dwarfs crawling into Snow White's vagina, or the evil witch in Sleeping Beauty being blown up with a firecracker in the dildo she's using, and many others. In truth you've never seen anything like it. Most women will detest this one.

THE YOUNGER THE BETTER
CC NN NM BI
1983 CREATIVE IMAGE

P/D—Michelle Kreimn
F/A—Ray Hardon, Bill Thorpe, Jerry Davis
F/A—Jennifer West, April Davis, Gaylene Marie,
    June Flowers

This one gets a CC rating because the dialogue, the acting and the plot are so corny that you can't help laughing. The story is about poor Vanessa (Jennifer West). She's a hooker, married—her husband Nino (Ray Hardon) was her former high school math teacher. Now he's her business agent. She does the work in the sack, and he cooks the meals and cleans house. The only problem is that Vanessa is 34 years old. She notices that she's not making as much money as she used too. Her customers want younger women. Sobbing, she brings the problem to Nino. He immediately comes up with an idea of how they can get rich and Vanessa won't have to work at all—split the profits fifty-fifty with three younger ladies in their teens whom they will hire. Vanessa will teach them all she knows. Soon they have three women all under 20 (they really only look about 19) living with them and taking on clients for $200 a night. But the hero of the film is Ray Hardon. You've never seen him before. He's a nice guy and he really loves his wife, Vanessa. She blows him while he's making dinner, and he happily, with her help, teaches one of the young ladies how to suck cock. "Blow it, kiss it, lap it like a lollipop, and bite it gently like a hot dog." All the young ladies are very nice with their customers. One of them takes on two motorcycle cops at the same time, and they also enjoy watching Nino make love to Vanessa which he does to the accompaniment of lots of "Darlings" and "I love yous." Vanessa concludes the tape by telling her protégées: "If I never teach you anything else, always remember how special true love is, and never stop searching for it." Amen!

YOUNG, WILD AND WONDERFUL
NN   DK   NL (in a silly ass way)
1980   VCX

P/D—Jim Clary
F/A—Richard Bolla, Eric Edwards, Jake Teague
F/A—Arcadia Lake, Merle Michaels, Hilary Summers, Kandi Barbour

Professor Peterson and his assistant take their Mount Virginia Art School class to the Museum of Natural History by bus on a field trip to help them in their courses in art and archaeology. The museum director provides an introductory slide show during which the professor gets seduced and loses his underwear to one of the coeds. Various students imagine themselves as Goya's Maja Nude, Modigliani's famous nudes, or Paul Gaugin's Tahitian ladies. In the process Merle Michaels fellates a dozen "Romans" in her fantasy and has sex doggie style. Later, trying to act like an innocent teen-ager, she services the curator. Everyone looks as if they are ready for their fifteenth high school reunion instead of just about to graduate.

Jerry Butler and Jessyca Wylde, with feeling.
Courtesy of AVC Adult Video.

Seka. Blonde, loud, and brassy.
From *Blonde Heat,* courtesy of VCA Pictures.

Ginger Lynn. Just like ginger…hot and sweet. Courtesy of Caballero.

Kay Parker. She's not getting older, she's getting better. Courtesy of Caballero Home Video.

Taija Rae. You know what she wants.
Courtesy of Caballero.

Vanessa Del Rio. Puerto Rican man-
cruncher first class. Courtesy of
Richard Milner, *Swank* magazine.

Marilyn Chambers and Richard Pacheco.
The Ivory Soap girl meets the boy next door.
Courtesy of Richard Pacheco.

Tara Aire. She'll never go hungry again.
Courtesy of Leisure Time Booking.

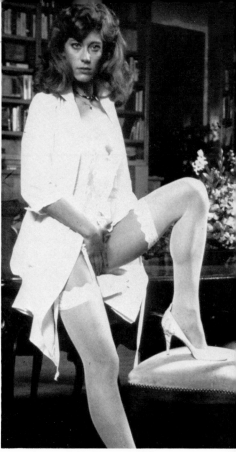

Joanna Storm. There's a storm blowin' in tonight. Courtesy of GM Video.

Tamara Longley. Deep voice, warm heart. Courtesy of Caballero.

John Holmes and Ginger Lynn. Johnny Wadd meets Miss America...on a steamer trunk. Courtesy of Wirth Mentioning P.R.

Kandi Barbour. Cool and hard to handle. Courtesy of Scotty Cox, Liberty Films.

Rhonda Jo Petty. Too sexy for her own good. Courtsey of Scotty Cox, Liberty Films.

Kelly Nichols. Small town girl being bad in the big city. Courtesy of Chuck Vincent Productions.

Annette Haven. Sweet face, perfect body, fiery dream girl. Courtesy of Morgan Communications.

John Leslie. But it's also a cigar. Courtesy of Caballero.

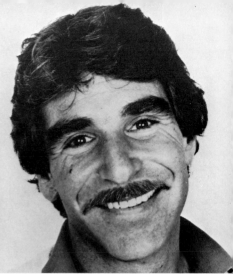

Harry Reems. Nice smile. Courtesy of Caballero Home Video.

Paul Thomas (with Lisa de Leeuw). Sleek and seductive. Courtesy of Richard Milner, *Swank* magazine.

Richard Pacheco. The guy you'd bring home to Mom and Dad. Great photo collection, too. Courtesy of Richard Pacheco.

Amber Lynn. Everybody in the pool! Courtesy of Caballero.

Joey Civera. Rough but loving.
Courtesy of Richard Milner, *Swank*
magazine.

Samantha Fox and Jack Wrangler. In the clinch in
Jack 'n Jill. Courtesy of Chuck Vincent Productions.

Ron Jeremy and Merle Michaels getting to know each other in *Fascination.* Courtesy of Chuck Vincent Productions.

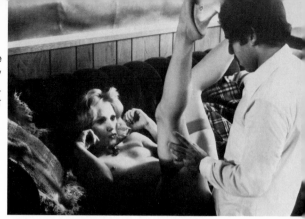

Surprise! A scene from *Sizzle.* Samantha Fox and Jamie Gillis. Courtesy of Chuck Vincent Productions.

Annie Sprinkles goes in for a little pocket pool. Courtesy of Richard Milner, *Swank* magazine.

Candida Royalle, the author, John Leslie. Courtesy of Adult Film Association.

11

Historical

BLUE MAGIC **CC NN BI DK**
1981   QUALITY

P/D—Par Sjostedt
**F/A—Jack Wrangler, Ron Hudd, George Payne,
   Josh Andrews**
**F/A—Candida Royalle, Samantha Fox,
   Veronica Hart, Merle Michaels**

Candida Royalle, who is married to the producer of this one and presumably wrote the original screenplay, must have been brought up on Grimm's fairy tales. It has some of the elements of the gothic novels which appeal to millions of women, and it has excellent costuming and background music both from eighteenth century composers and Scott Joplin-style piano music in some sex scenes. Filmed in New York on someone's estate, it is supposed to be Woodhurst Castle. It actually does look like a small one. Natalie Woodhurst (Candida Royalle) is the owner. No one knows much about her except that she may have lived several centuries. As it turns out, her longevity is obviously related to continuously satisfying her sexual needs. She meets Mr. Gettys (Jack Wrangler), a detective who crashes her private weekend party to which she has invited three couples (played by Samantha Fox and George Payne, Veronica Hart and Ron Hudd, and Pattie Love and Josh Andrews). After she has made a voodoo doll of him to seduce him she says, "You shall be overcome with lust and provide the pleasure I need to sustain immortality." While the turn-of-the-century ambiance is very well done (and breaks a new path for adult film stories), the story deteriorates when Natalie transforms Maria from a gentle kitten type into a steely dominatrix during which Ron Hudd and George Payne (because they are under Natalie's spell, too), at her command service her in every way imaginable. This extended scene is intercut with a bisexual scene between Veronica and Samantha in crinolines and corsets which is equally unbelievable. But women will enjoy the costuming. I've given it a CC rating because it raises a question that many husbands and boyfriends may want to ask their women: Do women ever fantasize slave-adoration and submission from men, as obviously some men do about women?

COMING WEST **NN NR DK (caring
group sex)**
early 1970s   BOCCACCIO 100

P/D—J. S. Scott
F/A—Unknown (credits not legible)

Three women driving in an open convertible to Fort Laramie flash themselves back to the old West, where one was a hooker and they've been abandoned by a stagecoach driver. There follows a long romantic sexmaking sequence with much mouth kissing, foreplay and concentration on the woman's face as she experiences sexual ecstasy. It finally concludes in a "normal" come shot with the woman on top. This is followed by a long Adam and Eve sequence of lovemaking in a forest beside a rushing brook. The women, wearing nineteenth century costumes (including voluminous cotton undergarments), are attractive, and even a final group sex sequence is quite caring (see note under *Fanny Hill*).

CONNIE AND FLOYD   **NN**   **BI**
COMPETITIVE VIDEO

P/D—Paul Clark, Gene Knowland
F/A—Serge Bonghart
F/A—Genevieve Bouvier

Floyd Baker (Serge Bonhart), wanted in 20 states, picks up Connie (Genevieve Bouvier) in his 1925 Buick sedan and although she's never met him before, she obligingly blows his horn. Afterwards, she tells him, "I hope you don't mind. I swallowed it." They rob a bank, have a picnic, take snapshots of each other. Floyd takes her to a hideout in the woods where he makes love to her still wearing his gun and holster. Pretty soon his pal arrives with three other molls. Connie is angry and will only screw with Floyd—but Floyd is less discriminating. Before the day is over, the sheriff arrives and forces one of the molls to suck his "doohickey" but eventually shoots Floyd's pal and the three women. Connie and Floyd escape but make the mistake of taking time out to screw in the grass. The sheriff catches up with them and shoots them both (see note under *April Love*, p. 273). Even though they can't act, everyone concerned seemed to have fun making this one, which has 1920s background music.

COUNTRY COMFORT
CC   NN   NR   BI   NL
1981   SELECT ESSEX

P/D—Bob Augustus
F/A—Randy West, Tommy La Roc
F/A—Georgina Spelvin, Rhonda Jo Petty, Drea, Ginger

Put this one in your top ten sexvids for couple viewing. Good acting, good dialogue, good costuming and believable characters are combined in a post-Civil War time frame. Martha (Georgina Spelvin) is running a Southern farm with her two daughters. Clare (Drea) is the oldest but is rather shy and bashful, and Farina (Ginger) is the fresh, wise-guy younger sister who is constantly spying on everybody—especially her sister-in-law Beth (Rhonda Jo Petty), who is making out in the barn with Marsh (Tommy La Roc), the hired man. Beth is in love with Marsh even though she's married to Martha's son. Tom Savage (Randy West), a soldier returning from the war, arrives in this menage and tells Georgina that her husband and son were killed on the battlefield. Mother Martha is sad, but she's very attracted to Tom. Tom's character is indicated by his words to Marsh: "There's two things you don't do with women—fall in love or marry them." In the meantime, Farina seduces Tom in the barn and he gently makes a woman out of her, and later he introduces shy Clare to the joys of sex. Finally, Tom, who is really a nice guy, "can't keep his hands off Martha" either. For a long time Martha rejects him. "I gotta have something else, Tom," she tells him. "Security, for one thing." And Beth is having her problems. She's afraid to tell Martha she's in love with Marsh and they want to get married. Martha finally capitulates to Tom in a romantic evening of sexmaking, but the next day at breakfast before Tom arrives, Farina tells Mama that Tom has enjoyed her and Clare too. Angrily, Mama returns with Tom, "the prize bull"—a pistol held to his head. But Tom resolves her fears by telling her he loves her best and wants to marry her. Martha looks at him happily, but tells him from now on he must leave her daughters alone. Then Clare suddenly announces: "Gee, I'm hungry. I feel like some pickles and strawberries." They all look at each other in consternation and say "Oh, no!" Tune in next week!

(New) EROTIC ADVENTURES OF CASANOVA **NN BI**
1979 HIFCOA

P/D—**Michael Merlino, John C. Holmes**
F/A—**John Holmes, Peter Johns**
F/A—**Susan Silver, plus many others impossible to identify**

Can you imagine John C. (for Casanova, of course) Holmes wearing a white peruke, an embroidered blue silk coat, linen blouse and knee breeches? Sniffing not snuff but cocaine, he is an eighteenth-century swordsman literally and figuratively, who looks better than Errol Flynn ever did in his prime swashbuckling days. And, as always, John is a considerate lover. Just when you are hoping that the period piece will continue—it does go on for about 15 minutes with nice costuming and believable acting—suddenly you are back in Southern California. John is consulting a psychiatrist, telling her about his dreams and a box he purchased in an antique store which has some letters written by Casanova and a bottle of ancient cologne which makes anyone who smells it immediately horny. John has used it at his partner's home (they are wealthy and have sold oil leases on their land), and in the process seduced or were seduced by his partner's wife (not intentionally) as well as his two daughters and the maid, Rose. His partner is so angry with him that he demands John give him the new sexual thrill Rose has taught him (anal sex). You don't see it happen on screen, but John admits to his psychiatrist that he did it to Paul to save his life . . . after which the psychiatrist smells the cologne and succumbs to John, too. This one raises a question. How did John C., who is the director, convince so many attractive young women to appear in this film? You've never seen any of them since.

FANNY HILL **CC NN NR**
1968-1970? BOCCACCIO 100

P/D
F/A
F/A—**Caramel Monterray**

Although this obviously was a low-budget film, the producer tries valiantly to give it seventeenth-century costuming and ambiance. Fanny's voice-over commentary on the action (which covers the first part of John Cleland's famous novel) tells you what she is experiencing emotionally and sexually in a naive way that is highly amusing. Because it concentrates on one woman, for the most part, many women will find this tape more interesting than later films, and the sexmaking is more natural. While I have listed this film under Boccaccio 100, the company does not sell tapes directly at this moment and is looking for a distributor. I'm sure that eventually many of the 100 or more 16-mm films and master tapes of older films produced in the early 1970s that Boccaccio 100 has access to will be available through one of the regular distributors listed in this filmography.

EDUCATION OF A BARONESS
DK DS BI NL of the sick kind
1979 CABALLERO

P/D—**Sacka Nudamko**
F/A—**John Gatto, Robert Albar**
F/A—**Aude Le Coeur, Brigitte La Have, Susan de Lojr**

The setting is Europe, 1930. Baron DuPont is driving with his chauffeur in his Rolls Royce to see Melania who whips him. Charlotte, the baroness, meanwhile is masturbating in her ornate bathroom while Alice, her maid, is being accosted in the kitchen by a gangster on the lam, and Alice's brother, who is a blind accordion player. With Alice's help, Mr. Finch takes over the house and forces Charlotte to switch roles with Alice. He shows Alice the only way to treat the rich is to "give it to them up the ass," which he does literally. He also warms his cold kidney dinner, which the baroness, half-naked, is forced to serve him. Blind John chases her around the salon. But believe it or not, it all ends happily because the baroness adores her rapists.

IN THE SPRING NN NL
Early 1970s BOCCACCIO 100

Three men in the nineteenth century, wearing appropriate costumes, tell each other how they got seduced into marriage in the spring, of course, when they were in the throes of passion. The first, a music and opera lover, falls madly in love with Louise, who sings his favorite aria from *Carmen*. He wrestles her out of her clothes, promising to marry her. Alas, after marriage he discovers she only knows this one aria. She sings it endlessly and scolds him incessantly. The second man finds Suzanne "marvellous in the culinary department," but after he is seduced by her seven gourmet meals, he beds her and marries her, and she never cooks anything different. The third foregoes singing and cooking for great sex—and finds a little minx who is so inventive in bed that she is an artist, "a veritable gem." In the things-you've-never-seen-before department, sitting in a wicker basket suspended over her bed Jacqueline twirls on top of him, and makes love to him in a black iron tub. Alas, her passion is a cover-up for her idiocy. She hasn't a brain in her head. After marrying her, he's ready for the missionary position and conversation (see note under *Fanny Hill,* p. 187).

IRRESISTIBLE NN NR DK BI
1983 SELECT ESSEX

P/D—Sandra Winters, Edwin Brown
F/A—Richard Pacheo, Misha Garr
F/A—Samantha Fox, Gayle Sterling, Starr
   Wood, Dorothy Le May

Walter Brooks (Richard Pacheo as a Walter Mitty-type) runs a travel agency and is married to Arlene (Samantha Fox), but for some reason never made clear, he is sexually frustrated and daydreams about women all the time. Driving on the way to work, he fantasizes a loving encounter with a hitchhiker he sees (Dorothy Le May). In his fantasy, she invites him into her apartment and adores him with her body and mouth from top to bottom. "Alas," he sighs. "Nothing like that ever really happens to me. Girls don't like me." Never

mind. The screenwriter has a gimmick. A man named Miracle Meyer (Misha Garr, who is in his 60s) drops into his office. Seems he's a travel agent too and has a marvelous machine which will transport you back in time. The price of a trip is only ten bucks. On his way home from work, Walter decides to take a trip, and presto, he's in Egypt and Cleopatra (Starr Wood) is delighted with this man from the future who lives in Marin County, California. But she finally orders him tossed to the crocodiles because he tries to warn her about Julius Caesar and she doesn't believe him. Next trip, he's in Venice and in the sack with Juliet (Gayle Sterling—the time machine doesn't give a damn whether the characters are historical or fictional). He seduces Juliet, but Romeo catches them in flagrante delicto. To Meyer's horror, Walter reports that he has transported Juliet back to San Francisco and she's living in a run-down motel. She has turned from virgin to nymphomaniac. After an orgy scene in the motel, Walter goes to bed with his wife, Arlene, but he's still dreaming about unattainable women—this time Mata Hari. In a schmaltzy conclusion, he decides the woman he really wants is Arlene—on their wedding night many years before. Meyer obliges him and he and Samantha Fox finally make love. Pacheo is a better actor than this silly material warrants. In the end Meyer is dancing with a woman his own age (presumably Arlene's mother provided by Walter) but you never see them naked. In Hollywood adult or R-rated films—no matter who is producing—sex stops after producing 40. I offer my novel *The Byrdwhistle Option* as a fun movie to some daring producer. The main character, Heyman Hyman Youman, is 62, very handsome and a believer in daily sexmaking as the key to longevity.

THE JOURNEY OF O NN some DK
1976 TVX

P/D—C. F. Kennedy
F/A—Vanessa Jorson, Marilyn Berg, Georgina
   Spelvin

This is not as masochistic as the novel *The Story of O,* on which it is loosely based. For some reason the extended oral sex is boring. Ophelia is cured of her frigidity and goes home to her husband after a sojourn with some male libertines.

LOLLIPOP PALACE **NN DB BI**
1973? ARROW & SELECT ESSEX

P/D—**Kirdy Stevens**
F/A—**John Holmes, Ric Lutz**
F/A—**Frenchie Dior, Bunny Savage, Laura Bacalle**

For one hour you'll think that you're in a 1930 San Francisco whorehouse with believable backgrounds and low-price nookie. It's run by a madam called Frenchie who imitates Mae West. The customers of Lollipop Palace are sailors (one of them is given a good whipping by one of the ladies during which he gets a better erection) and hayseeds, including two Greeks who just arrived in this country (one can't speak English, the other must watch and interpret—thus two for the price of one). When the ladies aren't screwing men, they're reading sexy books or making love with each other. There's no plot. One for the books: A hayseed complains after he pays, "She chewed me so much it still hurts." Frenchie blithely replies, "Next time we'll file down her teeth." As for John Holmes in this one—I couldn't find him without looking twice and you probably won't either.

A MAN WITH A MAID (The Naughty Victorians) **CC NN NL BI DK DS**
1983 VCA

P/D—**John Butterworth, Robert S. Kinger**
F/A—**Beerbohm Tree, Raymond Court-Thomas**
F/A—**Susan Sloane, Angel Barrett, Jennifer Jordan, Heather Austin**

There is no way I could avoid giving this one a DS rating with the system I have established. But, notice also the NL rating. Despite the DS rating and an uproar from some women who may see it, I'd put this film in a list of the top 25. The story is presumably based on one of those Victorian novels written by libertine men for men only. Cleverly set to the music of Sir Arthur Sullivan, the story begins on April 12, 1878, the day *H.M.S. Pinafore* opened in London. Alice (Susan Sloane) is arriving in London for a quick visit to the townhouse of her fiancé, Jack. She's not accompanied, as proper ladies should be, by her maid, Molly. Terrified of thunderstorms, she lets Jack (Beerbohm Tree) lead her downstairs to a padded, soundproofed room. To her surprise and maidenly distress, Jack tells her he has had enough of her teasing. She quickly discovers that the room (in what was a madhouse) is equipped with bondage bracelets, stockades and mirrors that drop from the ceiling. "It is designed for your violation, my dear," he tells her in a very courtly way, "the surrender of you to me of your maidenhead." Cuffed and hanging, wailing, "Have pity on me, Jack!" she is ignored by him as he slowly relieves her of her eighteenth century corsets and lace. He gloats over her lovely body, "equal to a magnificent Botticelli." He gives her the choice of submitting freely or being taken against her will. "I will not submit, I defy you," she says stoutly, and presto, finds herself strapped from the ankles and wrists, with a harness supporting her middle, while the arrogant villain laps her to a climax. After that he lowers her onto a lovely bed where instead of taking her maidenhead, he takes her anally. Despite her shock it's apparent that she's getting excited. Two weeks later she returns and she tells the viewer, "There must have been an element of lust in my blood which Jack wakened, not created." This time she has brought her cockney maid, Molly, with her, and with Alice's help she quickly gets the hanging treatment. But Jack finds her "quim" has been used before, and Jack tells Alice he only wants virgins. He turns Molly over to Alice. In the last segment of the film, Molly brings Lady Margaret and her daughter Cicely. Both of them are very haughty and aware of their importance, but now both Molly and Alice assist in the conquest of the mother and daughter. There isn't any question that Jack actually rapes four women. But it's really a funny spoof on eighteenth century pornographic novels. You can't help but laugh at the silly, but very proper English dialogue. The ladies finally plot together to give Jack his comeuppance. With their help, one of his students with a huge penis takes Jack's maidenhead—you know where! I presume this is an English-produced film. Whoever is responsible should produce an "Upstairs Downstairs" based on the original PBS presentation.

PINK CHAMPAGNE **CC NN DK NL** (occasionally)
1980   CAL VISTA

P/D—Mark Corby, Sven Conrad
F/A—Jon Steele, Rick Fonte, Jeff Parker, Ron Jeremy
F/A—Lisa de Leeuw, Lorell Winston, Aimee Leigh, Lauri Pearl, Tiffany Clark

The time on this one is the late 1920s or early 1930s in Hollywood. All the actresses are fellating men to get ahead (no pun intended), and none more so than April (Lisa de Leeuw), who lives with the famous Zagfield in a Beverly Hills mansion. Zagfield, played by Jon Steele, looks a lot like Franchot Tone, if you can remember that far back. In this flick he's sexually far out, and enjoys watching April fellate his chauffeur in the back seat of his Rolls Royce. April believes that a star is only the product of those who make her one, including all the boys in publicity whom she services happily. In the meantime, down at the studio Zagfield is getting fellated by various women who want to be the star of his new musical. He takes April to a new bordello called Starlight, where there are studs as well as whores. They all pretend (for their clients) that they are actually the stars of Hollywood—Mae West, Marlene Dietrich, Charlie Chaplin, Douglas Fairbanks, etc. Thus you can have the illusion that you are screwing with your favorite movie star. But the reason for the CC rating is the ending, during which Zagfield is running a house party which turns into an orgy, but during which he at last finds the woman of his dreams, Shirley Dimple (Loreli Winston). He pursues her to a bedroom in the tower of his estate while they make romantic love (she's supposed to be a virgin). Tschaikowsky's Sixth Symphony is intercut with scenes from the party downstairs, which is jumpin' and humpin' to jazz music. It all ends up in a Busby Berkley-style musical number where the women, otherwise glamorously costumed, only have bare behinds and breasts.

THE SPIRIT OF SEVENTY SEX (1776)
CC NN NL BI DK
1976   VCX

P/D—Ms Ricki Krelmn
F/A—John Holmes, Tyler Reynolds, Jeff Lyle, John Toland, Ebenezer K. Bartholomu
F/A—Annette Haven, Ann Carraday

This one might also have been titled sexual episodes from colonial history. Among other things it is probably the only porno film shot in Boston, Massachusetts, with much local New England scenery. The time is now. But somehow Ebeneezer, who is wearing a tricorn hat and has arthritis and a voice that would get him a job with Pepperidge Farm, relates the sex life of various historical figures. There's Colonel George Washington who tells Martha (Annette Haven) that he has a twitch that must be itched. A very young Annette Haven helps him soothe it under a cherry tree. There's Paul Revere on his way to warn his countrymen about the arriving British, but he's stopped by a fetching behind. "I know good buns when I see them —even when they're under wraps." There's Ben Franklin playing with his kite and electricity in the fields, and a young lady arrives who is having problems with her "crumpet." Franklin with electricity—a vibrator and his tongue—helps her assuage her crumpet fire. There's John Alden, who hasn't met Priscilla yet but who is into Indian broads. And there's John Smith (John Holmes) in a short episode who tells Pochahontas, "Boy, you've got great tits!" There's The Minutemen (you know how they got their name), and finally once again there's Martha Washington who is having identity problems and thinks she's Betsy Ross, but George doesn't care, it's just like having another woman. This is for the most part a happily silly sex tape with some good dialogue. Ebeneezer Bartholomu (whoever he is) ends the tape in an ancient cemetery examining the headstones of his "damned depraved relatives."

A THOUSAND AND ONE (1,001) EROTIC NIGHTS **NN BI NR (last scene)**
1982   SELECT/ESSEX

P/D—Sandra Winters, Stephen Lucas
F/A—John Leslie, Jon Martin, David Morris
F/A—Annette Haven, Lisa de Leeuw, Mai Lin

In case you don't know, the *Arabian Nights*, and *Supplemental Nights*, in a full, unexpurgated edition (with about 400 pages to a book) was translated by Richard Burton. The unexpurgated version comprises 17 volumes. In this version, Annette Haven cons the sultan (John Leslie) into sparing her life (the sultan doesn't trust women and has them executed, after one night of screwing) by telling him 1,001 stories. Thus at least three years should have passed but no one changes costumes much, and in one scene when the sultan is supposedly tracking down his adulterous wife (Lisa de Leeuw) across China, actually he's riding a horse along the Pacific Coast. If Sandra Winters and Stephen Lucas had actually skimmed through the unexpurgated *Arabian Nights*, they could have found sexier stories than appear in this flick. But alas they take off on their own and Annette (who is a very pretty Scheherazade) tells John a three-part story of the genii and the fisherman, who gets three wishes, all of which involve screwing first with a wealthy woman and then her daughters, and finally one which she doesn't tell him until the next day. Besides Jon Martin as the lucky fisherman, there's a prince on a golden horse who can ride backwards and forwards in time. David Morris, as the prince, screws a Japanese girl and his life is ended by a samurai, but he reappears in the nineteenth century screwing a madam in Paris whose lover appears and shoots him dead. In between there's a long sequence during which Annette shows the bemused sultan how three women can enjoy each other sexually. As in the original, Scheherezade wins the sultan's love.

UPRISING AT BOX CANYON **NN DS**
BOCCACCIO 100

In the hundreds of sexvids that I have watched only this one, *A Dirty Western* and *Sweet Savage* use an old West background. There's a gold mine of subjects that could be explored combining westerns with adult films. This is a story of the good guys, who are panning for gold when a horse-drawn wagon passes their encampment with four "trollops" dressed in eighteenth century clothing. They are on their way to Box Canyon to service the miners. The bad guys, on horseback, see the wagon and decide to have some of this stuff for themselves. They tie up the women, hang one by her arms from the limb of a tree and although she's kicking and screaming, they force her to fellate them and then rape her while the others watch. Soon they take on the other three women, who are pretty tough cookies. Our "ladies" are eventually rescued by the good guy miners and after they hang the bad guys from a tree limb, they all have loving and sweet sex together.

THE VELVET EDGE **NN BI DS (mildly) DK NR (one scene)**
SELECT ESSEX

P/D—John Hannah, Eddy De Witt
F/A—Turk Lyon, Max Savage
F/A—Jennifer West, Debbie Sands

The title refers to a crossover beyond normal sex into kinkier varieties. Sergei has organized an orgy of friends, or if you prefer, a group sex party, during which one woman is hooked up to a thrusting vibrator and another experiences anal sex against her will. Sergei tells the story of his grandfather in the 1920s and what amounts to two Bonnies and two Clydes who discover each other in a holdup and merge forces. In the process, though they are temporarily enjoying an idyllic love life in the backwoods, one of them irritates a Mexican, who shoots up the guys and beats and rapes the females. There's lots of antique autos in this one and much of the same old slurping.

12

Travelogues

ALL AMERICAN GIRLS **NN BI**
1983 CABALLERO

P/D—**Bob Bouchard, Craig Ashweed**
F/A—**Stephen Douglas, Ken Star**
F/A—**Cassie Blake, Jacqueline Lorians, Jillian Nichols, Joanna Storm, K. C. Valentine**

Here's a sexy variation of Chaucer's *Canterbury Tales*. Six sorority sisters are invited to London by Miss Caroline—one of the sisters who has married into the British aristocracy. The reason for their visit is to tell her at a dinner party "the nastiest and dirtiest thing that has happened to them since graduation." The attempt, throughout the film, is to give it a continental, super-sophisticated atmosphere. For this purpose there are background shots of London, Paris, Las Vegas, and Hong Kong, where the various ladies' stories take place. The stories include one sister who spends a summer in Paris and meets two Frenchmen—though they speak no English and she no French, they have a lovely time in a hayloft outside Paris. Another sister goes to Las Vegas where she meets a really sophisticated lady who breaks the bank playing blackjack and crap but gets trimmed at roulette. Having no money left and no credit, she bets herself and the sorority sisters—and of course loses. After which they take on the croupiers quite willingly. Another sister and her friend, bored with a violin soloist that her mother has invited for an evening soiree, flashes his assistant by lifting her skirts. He forgets to turn the musical pages and is soon on the staircase with them while the impresario continues playing for her mother's guest and no one knows that three of them are screwing to a violin accompaniment. Another story takes place in Hong Kong where one sister visits "a meditation garden" and services a brute of a guy that she's never seen before. The pièce de résistance is the sister who seduces her college professor at Fisherman's Wharf, first blowing him under the table. Then he finishes by screwing her, to the delight of the other diners, on top. The best you can say about this mess is that you've never seen most of the guys or ladies before.

AMOUR **CC NN NR DK BI**
1980 BLUE VIDEO

P/D—**Robert Lynn, Jorg Heliser**
F/A—**Georges Blue, Rolf Medus, Siegmar Deubner**
F/A—**Fritzi Ross, Gaby Hiller, Martine Gerrault**

Adult foreign films—at least those that make it to the United States—often have more interesting story lines and some character development, which elude the

American product. You'll watch this one to the shocking ending. Fritzi (evidently using her screen name) is on a summer vacation. Hitchhiking around Europe, she has evidently had a bad evening's experience with some guy who picked her up and with whom she spent the night in a motel. The next day she is picked up by Leo, who is driving somewhere below Barcelona, Spain (although it often looks like Torremolinos and the Costa del Sol). Leo has a rented villa for the summer and he takes Fritzi there where a romantic sex-making interlude ensues. But a week later when they are eating out, a group of two guys and three women sitting at another table intrude on their happy world. One of them, Walter, who has been discoursing loudly on sex and fucking, invites them to join them at their table. They meet Gabby and the other women and a poet, Victor, who philosophizes on love in a gentle way that totally contrasts with Walter's crudeness. Victor insists that "only through sex is it possible to know the mind, body and soul of a particular person. The tragedy is men and women's failure to understand this simple truth." Gabby doesn't care about souls or minds. She tells Fritzi, "Do you mind if I borrow your boyfriend's cock and balls?" Soon they are all back at the villa, and during the next few days Leo becomes totally entranced with Gabby and forgets Fritzi. Fritzi is pursued by Walter, a rough and tumble character who is tattooed, even on his prick. He tells her, "Fucking is what's life is all about." Fucking, by his standards, has nothing to do with love. Drawn to his craziness and jealous over Leo, Fritzi responds to him. At the bullfight, an extended sequence which is nicely photographed, sex is supposedly stimulated by death in the ring, à la Hemingway. Fritzi sits on Walter's prick and they both climax as the bull is slaughtered. The next day Walter rents a motorboat and screws her while the boat is traveling at high speed in a wide arc. But during all this it is apparent that Fritzi really loves Leo and she's shocked that he has let their love deteriorate. "You fucked around first," she tells him. "I wanted you to really love me but you didn't." She leaves for Barcelona with Walter, who can't understand why she's wrecking their summer com-

mune by fleeing. They soon discover that Leo is in pursuit. The film climaxes in a wild fist fight between Leo and Walter after which Walter shoots Leo and kills him. He tosses Fritzi's barrack bags out the window of his car and yells goodbye to her. The movie ends where it began, with Fritzi thumbing a ride to complete her vacation.

BANGKOK CONNECTION NN BI
mild DK and NL on the silly side
1979   CABALLERO

P/D—Alan Payet
F/A—Not identified
F/A—Linda Jade, Marlene Gillis, Jennifer Sax

While the few Oriental women in this sexvid are probably not Thai and the exterior shots were probably taken from some travel film, our hero, Aloysius Dunbar, is an amusing Candide-style cluck. In search of sexual El Dorado he manages to get his cock banged (in Bangkok?) and is unable to avoid at least a dozen women who want to and do "fucky-wucky" with him in the course of this 120-minute tape. This is a European-made film (probably German) and has sexual silliness about it that many American filmmakers are unable to capture.

BLUE PERFUME NN BI DK DB
1979   HOME ENTERTAINMENT

P/D—Charles Vienna
F/A—Peter Halcombe, Howard Nelson
F/A—Margo Neal, Rena Brown, Dawn Starr

There's a lot of talk about Formula 69 (Blue Perfume) in this one. It presumably turns on both men and women and is about to be launched in an advertising campaign on British telly by Dawn Starr, a Soho stripper with the slogan "Ooh, I'll take everything off but my Formula 69." But after the wife of the perfume factory manager gets strangled, he spends the next day in bed (not very contritely) in a sunken tub screwing Dawn Starr. It finally moves to an English country estate where the bad guys, who are attempting to steal the formula, are attending a Roman orgy. Finally, John, the manager of the factory, devises a truth or torture game during which a woman is stretched on a medieval rack and confesses that she is an accomplice to the murder. With their clothes off, the British are genitally no different than their American cousins, but this British-made film with a London-Soho ambiance is a change from New York and Los Angeles and the faces are not so familiar as the American porno stars.

BODY LOVE CC NN BI DK
1983 CABALLERO

P/D—John Nichols, Larry Brown
F/A—Jack Gatteav, Gene Sorlin, Tony Morena
F/A—Lolita da Nova, Glenda Farrel, Gilda Jacobs, Roberta Jones, Carmen Royale

This is a surrealist sex film with excellent cinematography and the sophistication of a European production, which it may be. Note the people listed above—all beautiful people—but you've never seen them before. The far out Emmanuelle Arsan type story is about a Baron (Gene Sorlin) in an unidentified country who owns a castle-château. He has a daughter, Martine (Lolita da Nova) and a new wife, Glenda (Glenda Farrel). The Baron's premise for living is: "I am especially fascinated by the unique experience, the one that hasn't been tried before." You'll have a moment of suspense at the beginning when Glenda leaves in her Mercedes and arrives at another château which seems empty. She walks the room, and looking in a mirror gasps as she discovers a man watching her. Then two other men grab her and seem to be about to rape her, but suddenly she is begging them to do it to her. A few scenes later she returns home naked. The Baron is playing a grand piano and asks her if she enjoyed it. She tells him, accompanied by detailed flashbacks, how much, and concludes: "I hope you don't mind, darling." In the meantime Martine is on the roof of the château with one of her father's girlfriends who is about her age, and soon they are engaging in a highly passionate bisexual encounter, after which Martine tells her "I don't want you to have sex with girls or any men. Your body is meant for me."

Seems also that Martine has her own sexual slave on the grounds of the château. Nana, a Uruguayan lady, lives in a trailer, and does anything that Martine commands her. This includes lapping a very extended sensuous blow job during which he says: "I never experienced anything like this in my life." The film concludes with Martine arriving in one of the rooms of the château in a leotard where some twenty people in various stages of undress are waiting and seem to be in a hypnotic trance. Even if you have been in a group therapy session, you've never seen anything like this. In a totally sensuous prelude to an eye popping sex orgy Martine brings them back to reality with her fingers flying near their faces and bodies but not touching them. Then after some fifteen tape minutes of the wildest sex you've ever watched, the participants including Martine are all happily sleeping on the floor. Martine, once again dressed in leotards, tip-toes out of the room and closes the door. That's all. You'll probably watch it a few times to listen to the sexual philosophy which abounds in sophisticated dialogue.

BON APPETIT NN NR (one extended scene) BI (momentary)
1979 QUALITY

P/D—Robert Sumner, Chuck Vincent
F/A—Randy West, Kelly Nichols, Gloria Leonard

Chuck Vincent must have needed a European vacation, so he took Randy West, Kelly Nichols and a cameraman on a tour (I'm kidding—as the credits reveal many, many people were involved). The story moves from San Francisco to New York, to Paris, to Munich, to Las Vegas, to Fire Island, to Rome, to Hollywood, to Washington, D.C. (quickly showing the Washington monument as the ultimate phallic symbol) to Amsterdam, back to Paris and Rome. All this jetset sex background requires you to believe that wealthy society lady Alexis Summit (Gloria Leonard) would bet Faith (Kelly Nichols) a waitress, a quarter of a million dollars that she can't seduce the world's ten best lovers (predetermined by Alexis) and do it within a 50-day time span in all parts of the world.

Scott Desmond (Randy West) must go along to surreptitiously record each conquest on film. On top of that you've got to believe that after he's watched Faith screwing her way to glory in one scene after another, he falls in love and wants to marry her. Well, Kelly, who is pretty and really looks like a small-town girl being bad in the big city, makes the hour tolerable, and Chuck Vincent, who is on record for saying he's bored with come shots and bisexual scenes, offers only a few in this one. Daddy can bring this one home to Mommy but she may decide that she wants to take a world tour, too!

EMMANUELLE AROUND THE WORLD
NN BI DK DS
1977 WIZARD

P/D—Jerry Gross, Joe D'Amato
F/A—Juan Rassimo, Don Powell, George Eastman
F/A—Laura Gesmer, Brigitte Petroni

You may see this one on cable or subscription television with some scenes deleted. But Joe D'Amato continues to walk the razor's edge between X and R ratings. Italian-made, on what must have been a fairly large budget, *Emmanuelle* begins in San Francisco, where our heroine is in the back of a moving van screwing with David Morris (a regular porno star) who appears only in this scene—and he's not copulating either. Before she leaves San Francisco for New York, Emmanuelle loses her clothes in a short scene where she's stripped by an elderly man when she enters the wrong hotel room. After that she's in New York City—then on to India where her editor has sent her to investigate a sex cult run by an Indian guru who is offering his devotees a weird mixture of tantric sexual meditation (extended sexual intercourse) and a section where women are trained in the martial arts of the Kama-Sutra. (If such daydreams were really offered in India the country would be truly overrun.) Never mind Emmanuelle screws up tantric sex by sitting on a naked male devotee and immediately bringing him to a climax—after which she takes on the guru himself, who ejaculates prematurely. Then on to Rome, where she's hot to un-

cover a white slavery racket run by Mafia types who kidnap foreign women and sell them into white slavery on the Ivory Coast. Emmanuelle nearly takes the trip herself but is saved so that she can go on to Hong Kong in search of another aspect of the subjection of women, and from there to Macao where she captures a guy named Chang who tries "to reduce his women to utter degradation." And then to Iran to alert a local emir (obviously before Khomeini's time) that his palace is being used for orgies to corrupt foreign ministers, and finally back to New York, where a sleazy senator picks up Kristine de Bell (of *Alice in Wonderland* fame and who in 1977 hadn't yet made it into conventional movies). Poor Kristine does a very erotic nude dance on a nighttime wharf overlooking the Hudson River—and in the process a tough bunch of guys take over and viciously rape her. But as in all these Emmanuelle flicks, which have a European kind of decadent sophistication, much is left to your imagination.

EMMANUELLE IN BANGKOK **R**
VIDAMERICA

P/D—Joe D'Amato
F/A—Ivan Rashmov
F/A—Laura Gesmer

Not only do you get a cook's tour of Bangkok in this sexvid covering palaces, bazaars, canals, cockfights, Siamese boxing and dancing and elephant safaris, but halfway through her continuous adventures, Emmanuelle (played in this one by Laura Gesmer, an Italian actress with an Oriental look) ends up in Casablanca, where you get plenty of Moroccan ambiance. This Italian made film with dubbed-in voices has no plot. Emmanuelle is in Bangkok as a photographer/ reporter to interview the king (she never makes it). But while she's there, she makes love with Roberto, an archaeologist, a Siamese houseboy, Ji, a female Thai masseuse who gives soapy, nude body-to-body massages, Jimmy, an American tourist, and the prince, a cousin of the king who enunciates the philosophy that permeates the original novels. Emmanuelle is amoral, an earth mother who "knows how to suspend herself in a tunnel where time (even the act of sex) has no meaning"— except for the moment, or as pleasure becomes pain, she may experience the "grand ecstasy," "le petit mort." All of which is quickly proved on the tube when Emmanuelle is captured by five men affiliated with the prince who strip her and rape her and with whom she becomes erotically involved. You never see a penis in this film, but sexmaking in bed and out with male and female occur one after the other. Emmanuelle loves women as well as men. In a way they may not be willing to admit, many women will identify with Emmanuelle but realize in real life their male consorts would not permit them to be so polymorphous.

EMMANUELLE, THE JOYS OF A WOMAN
NN BI DK
1976   PARAMOUNT

P/D—Yves Rousset, Rouard, Francis Giacobetti
F/A—Umberto Orsini, Frederic La Gache, Henry Czarniak
F/A—Sylvia Kristal, Catherine Rivet, Marion Womble

None of the *Emmanuelle* films were made by producing members of the Adult Film Association, and it's interesting to note that such respectable Hollywood companies as Columbia and Paramount control the two Sylvia Kristal *Emmanuelle* films, which in my opinion are essentially sleazier than many so-called adult films. This is sad because there is no more beautiful actress than Sylvia Kristal, but making her the purveyor of Emmanuelle Arsan's almost ugly sexual philosophy just doesn't ring true. You can't believe it. This second Kristal-Emmanuelle episode begins with her on her way from Bangkok to join her husband, Jean (not the same actor in the original *Emmanuelle)*, who is temporarily reassigned to Hong Kong. En route in a steamer she (for no plot-motivated reason) is assigned to a woman's dormitory slung with hammocks. She refuses to sleep with the ship's radio operator but obligingly brings a fellow woman passenger who was raped by three Filipino women when she was a child to a

climax in her hammock. Arriving in Hong Kong she finds Jean—but spouts the same philosophy. He's being shaved by a Chinese woman. Eventually Emmanuelle gets to bed with Jean but not before she flashes her eyes at Christopher, a temporarily grounded drug dealer who is bunking in the household. The next day they visit a Chinese shop which specializes in erotic foods and curios, and soon she is having her pubic hair woven with needles (no kidding) by an old man who specializes in erotic acupuncture. It works and gives Emmanuelle some highly erotic dreams which are duly recorded by the camera. Next she and Jean and a young woman, Anne Marie, whom Emmanuelle is intent on seducing, are all in a private bathhouse. They are massaged by naked Chinese ladies who perform the massage by rubbing their whole bodies sensuously against their clients. A few days later Emmanuelle is at a Hong Kong Polo match. Spying a guy in the male locker room who is tattooed from head to foot, she can't resist him and is quickly lapping his tattoos while he reciprocates. Questioned by Christopher as to what Jean thinks of a wife who needs an old man to use acupuncture to make her come, Jean responds: "I prefer that Emmanuelle lives as she likes. We are both free . . . There's no danger in playing around—the danger is falling in love . . . I don't love Laura [a woman he's involved with who is married]. I love Emmanuelle." Well, each to his own, as they say. While I personally don't believe in lifetime monogamy, I have to admit that being married to a nymphomaniac who will hop into bed with guys whose first name she doesn't even know is a bit scary. What makes this film honest is its super-super sophistication, conveying the belief that if you are rich it's all part of the game. The same story wouldn't be believed if Sylvia/Emmanuelle were a young matron in Sandusky, Ohio! But if you like fairy tale glamour and exotic settings . . . there's still one more Emmanuelle film. It was released in 1982 and titled *Goodbye Emmanuelle* (maybe prophetically). This time Sylvia/Emmanuelle is married to an architect and the action takes place in the Seychelles.

HAPPY HOLIDAY **NN   NM   BI   DK**
1978   CABALLERO

P/D—Alan Vydra, Jon Sanderson
F/A—Karl Blake, Stephen Roberts
F/A—Olinka Johnsson, Nina Lund, Karen Karlsson

Screw's Best 10 of 1978, number seven. A male voice-over holiday tour guide opens this one with a tour of London and offers comments on the action throughout the tape. Claudia, who lives with her boyfriend in London, is on her way to Hamburg to visit her daddy and stepmother. "Just because they enjoy each other doesn't mean that they can't enjoy other people too," she says. Which sums up this European-made film. Daddy collects pornography. Stepmommy runs a stud service. Claudia's lovely virgin sister masturbates most erotically for ten minutes. Often sickly—ucky, it has a European master-male ambiance that American women will detest.

INTRODUCTIONS **CC   NN much BI**
1978   WONDERFUL WORLD OF VIDEO

P/D—Georges Fleury
F/A—Jacques Insermini
F/A—Chantal Naura, Emmanuelle Pareze, Tenzer Twins

You think that you've seen them all? Not until you've watched Jacques Insermini play the part of a wealthy French businessman. (The film was made in France.) In his late 50s he's balding, heavy built with a full belly, but muscular and in his own words, "I'm built like a bull." His wife solicits young women to join them in threesomes at their summer place. Back in the city (Paris) he takes care of twins and several other women. Things you have never seen before but are coming to if you live long enough—an older man ejaculating. Of course, Jacques's women are all 20 to 30 years younger than he is. He should be matched with Georgina Spelvin!

I, A WOMAN-II **NN   DK (R-rated)**
1968   VIDAMERICA

P/D—Peer Guldbransen, Mac Ahlberg
F/A—Lars Lunoe, Hjordis Pettersen
F/A—Gio Petre, Kate Mundt

If you saw *I, A Woman,* the first film, also produced in Sweden in the mid-1960s, you'll remember that Siv (Gio Petre), the nurse, has more than one sexual encounter in the film. When it was finally cleared through U.S. Customs, there were long lines in downtown theaters to see it. Now, in the sequel, Siv is married to Hans Henrich Holm (Lars Lunoe) a cold-blooded Swede who collects antiques and spends all his money on art objects which he considers superior to their human creators. He has weird sexual control over his wife and only enjoys sex when he has degraded her. He takes nude photos of Siv, shows them to one of his customers, Mr. Swensen, and invites Swensen for the evening to partake of Siv. She agrees but only if she can use the money to pay their common creditors, such as the butcher, wine seller etc., whom Hans coolly ignores as inferior people who should be happy to subsidize him. The sex sequences, particularly with Hans watching Siv and Mr. Swensen, are highly sensual and erotic, although the story line is hard to swallow. Siv goes back to work as a nurse to pay their bills, and it turns out that Hans was a former high-ranking Nazi officer. The sexual buildup and the camera study of sexmaking is a bigger turn-on than many X-rated adult films.

THE JOY OF FOOLING AROUND **CC   NR   NN   BI**
1979   CAL VISTA

P/D—Jean Claude Ramon, Pierre du Bois
F/A—Kevin Raymond, Sal Pontini
F/A—Monique Du Prez, Erica Swanson, Valerie Ashley

Best Foreign Film of 1979, Erotic Film Award. This is a love story that takes place on a Greek island. Pierre Constantine (Kevin Raymond) is a wealthy shipbuilder who finds his wife in bed with her lover. Shocked, he wanders to the marina where his yacht is moored, takes the tender and drives it hellbent into the bay where it explodes. Simultaneously, Carlo, a handsome devil but a thief (he's stealing ancient Greek icons from the churches on the island), tries to smuggle them out on a schooner. Surprised by the captain of the ship, he murders him. In the meantime, Constantine, thrown into the water and stunned by the explosion, drifts ashore, where he is rescued by the daughter of a fisherman who has a shack on a deserted beach on one side of the island. Constantine has amnesia, but Flora, who owns the hotel on the island has a reputation for sheltering down-and-outs, and she's angry with Carlo, her lover. Only Marina (Monique Du Prez) believes that Peter Constantine is innocent. The story begins when Monique rescues Peter and only as it evolves do the details come together very gradually as both Marina and Flora fall in love with Peter. Good acting, splendid photography with a Greek island ambiance and warm caring sexmaking will keep you intrigued. Most women will identify with both of the female actresses as well as the sexmaking scenes. The day may come when European-made films like this one will be more popular with American women than most of the American products. The sex is just as explicit but the genital aspects are not so prolonged, and the men, even when they are scoundrels, seem to like women.

THE JOY OF LETTING GO
CC NN NM BI
1976 SELECT/ESSEX

P/D—Summer Brown, John Gregory
F/A—Leslie Hughes, James Kral, Frank Dudley
F/A—Dominique St. Pierre, Pamela Strass, Susie Sun Lee

This one has a European ambiance to it cinematographically, and you've never seen any of the actors or actresses before (or since?). But it demands that you accept the premise that Michelle Martine (Dominique St. Pierre), is married to a very wealthy man, perhaps 20 years older than she. He is very moralistic and when he is traveling around the world leaves her in care of a bodyguard, Herbie. She is so sexually frustrated she gets involved with a pimp named Dancer and his girl-

friend, Annette, and takes a job, for a lark, as a paid prostitute—after which she takes on a compatriot Frenchman; a husband and wife who advertise for a third; gratuitously helps a guy in a porno theater masturbate, as well as helping a young gas attendant achieve nirvana in the men's room. Over and above the unbelievable story, during which her bodyguard is held captive by two females who wear him to a frazzle, is Dominique St. Pierre. In the words of Summer Brown, a female adult film producer, "When she walked in my office, I thought she was in the wrong place. I interview beautiful women every week but none with such elegance coupled with a shy vulnerability." It's Dominique's almost suppressed laughter and pixie grin that holds this one together and proves that certain women can make you believe anything. Most women will like her.

JUNGLE BLUE **NN BI DK**
1978 HIFCOA

P/D—Troy Benny
F/A—Bigg John, Jose Ferraro
F/A—Nina Fausse, Iris Medina, Susan Fuentes

Did you ever see a woman sucking off a gorilla? Amidst continuous intercutting of the animals, vegetables and minerals in Peru and Colombia (where this one was actually filmed), you see this romance progressing. A dastardly Sylvia (Nina Fausse) arrives in Peru with Hank and locates her friend Jane who tells her about E-go (that's the way it's pronounced—the actor's screen name is Bigg John), who is a second Adam that God put on earth in Peru. But E-go acts more like Tarzan to match Jane, who is looking for her daddy, a scientist. E-go tells her he was his friend but now alas, he is dead. But Sylvia and Hank have other plans—they want to steal the jewelry from the Peruvian tribe of headhunters and head shrinkers. They plan to poison everybody with poison candy. In the meantime, while Nina Fausse is no Bo Derek she soon has E-go's diapers off. In one day E-go manages to explore both Sylvia and Jane and find true love with Jane. Hank and Sylvia poison the Cashibo tribe and shoot holes in

E-go's chest. Sylvia is bitten by a rattler. Hank shoots her and is escaping with the loot when E-go mows him down with a blowgun and a poison dart. This one becomes goofily giggly if you're reinforced with a couple of drinks.

LAURA'S DESIRES NN NM BI with a DK finale
1979 CABALLERO

P/D—Heiner Stegelmann, Heoko Hagemann
F/A—Unidentified
F/A—Sigrun Theil, Iris Stern, Stephanie Ross

This is a German made film which offers a bisexual, heterosexual, ménage-à-trois mélange. The plot gives you nothing you haven't seen before except many attractive male and female European faces and background scenes of Munich. Laura is trying to decide which of her seven lovers of the past week she really loves. They include men as well as women, black and white. In the things-you-may-have-wondered-about department— How to become a member of the Mile High Club? Screwing in an airplane at 5,280 feet or higher, Laura and her friends and the pilot show you how!

MADE IN FRANCE (THE CAT) NN BI NL (French style)
1974 INTERNATIONAL HOME VIDEO CLUB

P/D—Not given
F/A—Jacques Marbouef, Robert Lercy, Andre Gray
F/A—Claudia Zante, Denise Fevier

This is a quickie made in France. Originally it was titled *La Chatte*—in translation "The Pussy," with a double entendre, of course. One night when Clair Fontange (Claudia Zante) is making love with her husband (Jacques Marbouef, a.k.a. Jean de Villroy) who is much older than she is, they are continuously interrupted by her cat, who wants to go out or come in. Finallly, he grabs it, sticks it in a wicker basket and puts it in the cellar without telling her. Grieved at the loss of her pussy, Clair first offers a monetary reward with no results, and then posts a notice in the village. She offers one unforgettable night to anyone

who returns her cat. Soon she is inundated with cats but alas not her missing pussy. And all the ladies in the village are very angry with her because one by one their husbands are enjoying Clair's favors. To save the day, her husband, who doesn't dare tell her that he kidnapped her pussy, finds a way to get it back to her. There's a lot of Gallic humor and much Gallic sex and bodies that you've never seen before, and French style, older men having much younger bed companions than most of their American peers.

MONTENEGRO CC R BI NL
1981 THORN-EMI

P/D—Dusan Makavejev
F/A—Erland Josephsen, Per Oscarsson
F/A—Susan Anspach

Unlike many adult films, this Swedish-made film can probably be rented in any video store. If you catch it on cable TV one very erotic dance sequence will be eliminated—an attractive stripper is chased around the dance floor by a mechanical penis. She finally sits on it. Marilyn Jordan (Susan Anspach) is a bored American housewife who plays a somewhat similar role as Liv Ullmann in *Scenes from a Marriage*. According to Martin: "I have no problems. My wife has problems. She has disappeared." Vacillating between staying home in Stockholm with her two precocious children or leaving with Martin for a business trip to Brazil, she finally follows him in a taxi to the airport, where she is delayed by customs and misses the plane. He, too, misses the plane and goes home. But she is picked up by some Yugoslavians who are all living communally in a happy madhouse bar and restaurant called Zanzi Bar. One of them, Montenegro, falls in love with her, and she finally decides to give up her sexual repressions and make love. She is toasted by other males in Yugoslavian (translated in subtitle): "I swear to the sky of blue/ How nice it would be fucking you/ Please take your pick of my emballage/ So I can park it in your garage." In the meantime Martin, whom she has telephoned and informed that she may not be coming home at all, is having his own happy little sex party in his home. When Marilyn does return she serves the whole family, including her psychiatrist, poisoned fruit. It's all in fun, of course, although a footnote at the end of the film insists it's a true story.

THE NIBBLERS **CC NN BI DK**
1979 TVX

P/D—John Thomas
F/A—John More
F/A—Christine

There's a slaphappy sophistication to some foreign-made sex films—a lack of a sense of shame, perhaps, or no feeling that sex is evil or naughty. Satisfying one's sexual needs is a natural daily event—and in French films (this is one), it is assumed that a wife will have a lover and a husband a mistress. George is married to Eva, who is very prudish in bed. She suspects that he has a mistress because he hasn't been to bed with her for three weeks. Instead of a divorce, George asks her if she will do what he asks her to. He wants to help her get "released." He takes her to a sex shop, buys her sexy underwear, picks up a prostitute in the park who fellates him and shows his wife how to do it. Then he introduces Eva to his mistress, Samantha, who doesn't know Eva is his wife. In order to keep George happy, Samantha has supplied other friendly women from time to time and thinks Eva is one. Samantha makes love to Eva who is a bit shocked—but even more so when Samantha suggests she try another man besides George. By this time Samantha has discovered that Eva is George's wife, and she's not too happy with George. Eva tells Samantha, "I'm not going to do it—I'm not going to cheat on my husband." But of course, she does. And when George finds out, he doesn't mind because Eva's becoming so much better in the sack. The film concludes "I got my husband back by sharing his adventures. I love you, George." "I love you, too, Eva." Maybe it happens in France—but not in America—yet!

PUSSY TALK **CC NN NM BI**
1975 TVX

P/D—Francis Le Roy, Danille Bellus
F/A—Nils Hortz
F/A—Penelope Lamour

This is a French-made film which originally was titled *Une Sex Qui Parle*. It is dubbed in English. I have the feeling that the French version has a less strident voice emerging from the heroine's vulva and more subtle sex talk. The lovely female can't control her talking pussy, which not only tells her husband about her sex life before and during marriage, but also contradicts her and tells her husband, "She really hates you!" Theoretically this sexvid should have an NL rating, but it's not very funny. But it has better photography and is more subtle than most American sexvids.

UNDERCOVERS **CC NN NL BI DK**
1983 CABALLERO

P/D—Virginia Anne Perry-Rhine
F/A—Lawrence Rothchild, Bobby Astyr, John Fielgud
F/A—Samantha Fox, Sharon Mitchell, Becky Savage

This one was one of five films nominated for Best Picture, at the 1983 7th Annual Erotic Film Awards. Virginia Anne Perry-Rhine is the wife of Joseph Rhine, a well-known California lawyer and advisor to the Adult Film Association. I have great hopes for Virginia Anne. She made two films, *Sweet Savage* and *Count the Ways*, that I've given an unqualified CC rating. (See listings.) On this one the rating is dubious, but the acting of Lawrence Rothchild and Samantha Fox save the totally insane plot. Virginia Anne and Joe must have lugged their cameras all over Europe because it was shot on location in London, Venice, Istanbul, Nice and Karulla, Greece, which makes it more interesting to watch. The story is about Lachma (Becky Savage) who has had an atomic device implanted in her vagina by an organization called Enema (run by Sharon Mitchell). Anyone who screws Lachma immediately becomes a babbling idiot. Her targets are the diplomats of the world. Harry the Creep (Bobby Astyr), who employs Dilly (Samantha Fox), wants to get the device to sell it to the highest bidder.

So does Q (John Fielgud—yeah, that his screen name) who is head of the British Secret Service. Q rescues Commander James (Lawrence Rothchild) from a Turkish prison and gives him a decoder which, if placed near a woman's pussy, emits sounds that will identify the woman. Commander J's job is to find Lachma (no one knows what she looks like), extricate the device, and save the world from Enema. Anne Perry-Rhine must have been smoking pot when she thought this one up. Supposedly a spoof on James Bond and 007 films, Rothchild saves the picture with good acting as a total bumbling idiot. Interestingly, he never appears naked in any of the sex scenes except as a patsy. The plot is so complicated that it was obviously difficult to keep all the various actions going—let alone even partially believable. Samantha Fox and Bobby Astyr disappear halfway through. But silly stories haven't stopped *Octopussy* from making millions of dollars. The sex is explicit and with Lachma and her gang often grimy. But shame on you, Virginia Anne—the "come shots" are never ending. Virginia Anne should return to romantic films—or develop Lawrence Rothchild (who is in his late forties) as a comic sex star. The scene where he convinces Lachma to let him reclaim the atomic gadget with a vacuum cleaner would have been even funnier if the script had been written so that Lachma falls in love with him, and tries to save him by not letting him fuck her, which he doesn't, anyway, even after he's removed the horrible gadget from her pussy.

WHITE HEAT **NN   BI   DK**
1982   CABALLERO

P/D—Burt Rose, Michel Le Blanc
F/A—Gabriello Pontello, Danny Berger
F/A—Olinka, Lisa Shine, Myka, Sarah Claudia

If you want a change of scenery—human as well as environmental, this film (French-made, probably) was shot in the Alps with a ski lodge background. Voices are dubbed but the ins and out are not that much different. The story, such as it is, begins with a handsome young man, Michel (Gabriello Pontello), waiting for a woman

in a restaurant. He's never met her before but he's taking her for a weekend (based on another woman friend's belief that Jackie is just the person he needs). When she arrives, Jackie (Olinka—a Marilyn Monroe lookalike) drives with him to the lodge. He spills champagne on her, which is an excuse for undressing her. Then he pours the whole bottle over her and laps it off. He soon discovers that despite her half-hearted acceptance, she's really looking for a marriage partner—and she hopes this encounter with him is the prelude to marriage. She soon discovers Michel is not about to confine himself to one woman. When the other couples arrive for the weekend with a pretty sexy black maid, they all swing into action. Jackie, horrified, drinks too much. She starts to strip and then, disgusted with herself, runs to her bedroom. Luckily, Mr. Right finds her and makes love with her. After several pleasant episodes she leaves with him, obviously to live happily ever after. Unfortunately, Snow White, as Michel calls her, is not really developed as a virginal character so you can't believe in her rescue by the nice prince. But there are some nice copulating and skiing scenes in the snow.

YOUNG WIDOWS **NN   BI   DK**
1981   CABALLERO

P/D—Bert Wolff
F/A—Richard Allan, Charles Schreiner
F/A—Jenny Feelings, Barbara Stephens, Diane Dubois

Only a Frenchman could have thought up this plot. Filmed in Paris, it's the story of Phillipe, a horny young man who reads the obituary columns in *Figaro*. He's searching for situations where the bereaved widow is younger than her departed husband, who has died suddenly. Phillipe usually arrives immediately after the funeral and tells the grieving wife (though not all of them are unhappy) that he was a friend of her husband—one that she obviously didn't know about. Soon he has his arms around her and is consoling her as he removes the widow's weeds. They are always black with black stockings and panties to match, of course.

Phillipe tells a male friend of his that his profession in life is to make women happy. He certainly is very good at it. Many women watching Phillipe might decide it's a sex education film to show men how they should make love to a woman. In the things-you've-never-seen-before department, Phillipe discovers one widow who is bisexual. Soon they are joined by her maid. Phillipe straps a dildo on his behind so that when he moves his ass, taking care of the woman in front of him, he is also servicing the lady behind him. His male roommate conceives a variation on the theme. He puts an obituary in *Figaro* saying that his wife has passed away suddenly—the theory being that women will come to him, and he won't have to get into situations like Phillipe, who arrives at one home where the corpse is still in the living room. The theory works and Phillipe has to stay home to help take care of the female avalanche which arrives to soothe the grieving widower. Unfortunately, the tape loses a CC rating because the women are much too eager to slide out of their drawers. Using the same plot and concentrating on one wealthy widow would make a more believable and character-revealing story.

13

Supernatural

AUNT PEG'S FULFILLMENT **NN BI DK**
1982 CAL VISTA

P/D—Arthur Cutter, Wes Brown
F/A—John Leslie, Jonny Keyes, Richard
Pacheco, John C. Holmes, Aaron Stuart
F/A—Juliet Anderson, Suzy Reynolds, Sharon
Malberg

This is one of several sequels to Aunt Peg Norton (Juliet Anderson), a ball-breaking movie producer. In this one she takes on five different guys and three women. Juliet Anderson gives the impression in practically all of her films that she can "fuck them all but six and use those for pall bearers." She's the kind of woman who would incite a man to whack her bottom and see if she could be subdued a little. That would probably be suicidal. There is no plot in this one—just Aunt Peg subduing all of the men listed above. But a few scenes stand out—one with Pacheco and Suzy Reynolds has the usual Pacheco caring sexmaking style, and a few scenes in which Johnny Keyes (of *Behind the Green Door* fame) takes on on separate occasions, Juliet and her niece (Sharon Maiberg) are an interesting contrast in black and white screwing and well photographed. Its interesting to keep in mind that less than 25 years ago, Ralph Ginzburg published a still series showing black and white sex in his magazine *Eros.* These pictures were probably responsible, as much as anything else in the magazine, for his long prison sentence. We've come a long way, baby!

BABY ROSEMARY **NN DK BI**
1975 SELECT ESSEX

P/D—Bill Steele, Howard Perkins
F/A—John Leslie, Ken Cotton
F/A—Sharon Thorpe, Leslie Bovee

Rosemary's Baby this is not. But *Baby Rosemary* (played by Sharon Thorpe) has such an involved plot that you'll keep watching in spite of yourself. In the process you will hear Rosemary tell John (John Leslie) that she is going away to teach at some college and not to take liberties with her—"Sex is always so degrading." John meets a hooker, Eunice (Leslie Bovee), and Rosemary goes to visit her stepfather who brought her up after her mother died. He now lives in a derelict hotel where Rosemary is raped. Two years pass. John is now a cop in San Francisco, and Rosemary is a teacher in a religious cult whose novitiates recite a sexual incantation: "Father Night, Father Spirit. Penetrator of the Eternal Woman, let thy molten liquid flow through our beings." Rosemary's father is dead, and the action moves to a funeral home. Rosemary becomes less frigid in the funeral home where the undertaker screws two women at a time—on their backs with a pillow in between them. All of Rosemary's friends arrive in the mortuary to pay their respects to Rosemary's father, who is lying dead in his casket but whispers in a voice-over, "I'm alive, don't bury me." Whether they finally do or not, he should certainly have been revived by the orgy in front of the casket and daisy chain with five female penitents.

THE BLONDE   NN   DK   BI
1980   VCX

P/D—Eliot and Harry Lewis
F/A—David Morris (many others but no credits given)
F/A—Annette Haven, Mai Lin, Dahje Taan, Brooke West

A nonstop fuckathon with many beautiful nymphomaniacs and satyrs being sexually fulfilled (with no guilt feelings) in the sophisticated setting of an upper-income Beverly Hills home. It's owned by a former Hollywood sex queen, Valerie Vincent (Annette Haven), who has been dead ten years. Whether she was murdered or committed suicide is never answered. Whether the film reflects some aspects of current reality or is totally futuristic, one thing you can say about it is that the participants work each other over and watch others being worked over with an amazing twenty-first-century aplomb which includes talking with others during sex. Will this ever happen? All I can tell you is that after you've watched a few hundred sex films the aesthetics of sex will intrigue you more than the act. As for the story in this one, it's about Angela, who has just arrived in Hollywood to make a movie based on Valerie Vincent's life. The ghost of Valerie appears in her bedroom and watches herself in her new incarnation having sex with her maid. Then the ghost of Valerie's former love appears, and he has sex with Valerie. After that, the film ends so suddenly you think perhaps because this is a low-budget job (probably produced for not more than $25,000) that the Lewis Brothers ran out of film.

BLUE VOODOO   CC   NN   BI   DK
1983   GOLD STRIPE

P/D—Armand Weston, Dianna Chambers, Romeo Davis
F/A—Wade Nichols, Jamie Gillis, R. Bolla, Joey Civera
F/A—Serena, Samantha Fox, Camille Sands, Jeanine Dalton, Vanessa Del Rio, Sharon Mitchell

Most of the action of this tape takes place in a night club which features Serena, Samantha, and Sharon as strippers and Vanessa and Camille as behind-the-scenes witches who are expert in the art of magic and Haitian voodoo. Camille, as the Black Widow, wears a spider ring which comes to hypnotic glowing life and allows the beholder to participate in his/her fantasies. The plot—what there is of it—involves a nasty character Jason (Wade Nichols) who has convinced Serena to raise ten thousand dollars as a kind of dowry, if he's going to marry her. At his request, when he has her money in hand, she fellates him (not too happily) after which he tells her that he would never marry a whore like her. Vanessa promises Serena revenge (but as the price she must—shades of Rumplestilskin!—surrender her baby, by Jason, to Vanessa when it is born). After that the story disappears for nearly an hour, before you see the horrifying conclusion. In between times, you watch Vanessa in an extended bisexual scene with Jeanine Dalton which is lovingly photographed. Samantha another stripper in the club appears in a happily silly scene with Jamie Gillis. As a baby in a crib she's wearing only a diaper. Trying to get to "Daddy" she breaks the crib, she sucks her bottle and squirts milk all over herself. Jamie screws her while the background music is playing "Love to Love You Baby." The Black Widow offers Joey Civera, and R. Bolla a chance to relive a Roman orgy. After which, conferring with Vanessa, the Black Widow tells Samantha it's time to take revenge on Jason. In the dressing room, while Samantha squats over a sink, Jason helps her wash her vulva, and he laps her to a climax while she supports herself against the ceiling. In the meantime the Black Widow is on stage strip-ping. As Jason works toward a climax with Samantha on top of him, he is suddenly clutching his chest. On stage, the naked Black Widow has produced a sharp dag-ger. Pressing the point into her breast, she is bleeding profusely as she dances. In-tercut into her death dance, Jason is screwing Samantha and he's suddenly bleeding in the same spots that she has cut herself. Horrified and bloody they con-tinue to screw, and then the Black Widow plunges the dagger into her stomach and Jason dies a victim of voodoo. The reason I've given this tape a CC rating is that while the sex is totally explicit and quite extended, it is not so boring as most adult films. Varied cinematography with many interesting superimposed close-ups of faces and genitals shown simultane-ously, and fading in and out of the more comprehensive shots, make it interesting to watch. The musical background also enhances the action.

DESCENDANTS OF GRACE
NN DK DB BI
1974 BLUE VIDEO

F/A—Richard Bolla, Bobby Astyr
F/A—Erica Havens, Deborah Penson, Paula Morton

According to movie critic Jack Kroll, "Stu-pid movies can destroy your brain cells." Home video has solved the problem by giving viewers fast forward and an envi-ronment where they can complain aloud. Keep in mind that there are at least 1,000 adult(?) films on cassettes which are not listed in this filmography, but inevitably I have seen some of the worst, and this is one. The descendants of Grace are ghosts, Grace's grandfather, grand-mother and mother, who inhabit the old mansion. During his life, old Granddaddy, played by an overweight Richard Bolla, "never got enough," but he's still trying. This one has extended sequences of his penis plunging into oozing vaginas. The hero-ine, Grace, ultimately sticks a long knife in her heart so that she can copulate with Granddaddy through infinity.

THE DEVIL INSIDE HER
CC NN NM DK DS
1978? BLUE VIDEO

P/D—Leon De Leon
F/A—Rod Dumont, Zebedy Colt
F/A—Terri Hall, Jodi Maxwell

This is one of the few adult films that utilizes the medieval Christian belief that human sexuality is essentially evil. The setting is En-gland, 1826. Two daughters, Hope and Faith, of a fanatically religious farmer (played by Zebedy Colt, who wrote the screenplay) are in love with Joseph, a hired hand. The father rejects Joseph for Faith, and Hope, shocked that Joseph is paying no attention to her, invokes the devil. "I'll give my soul to possess the one I love." Instantly, she inherits a grotesque devil with an enormous penis and balls that he can almost twist around it. Believ-able cinematography and good acting are combined with devils, witches, and mothers, fathers and sisters who are pos-sessed, momentarily, by the devil to per-form horrible acts on each other. Satanic background music, performed as a kind of Gregorian chant, will keep you in-volved in this one from beginning to end. In the long history of eros denied there are many, many comparable stories wait-ing to find their way into scary, explicit films, which are hypnotic in spite of their unbelievability.

DELICIOUS **CC NN BI DK**
1981 VIDEO-X-PIX

P/D—Bill Eage, Phillip Drexler
F/A—Richard Bolla, Ron Jeremy, Aaron Stuart, Arthur West
F/A—Veronica Hart, Candida Royalle, Desiree Cousteau, Nicole Scent

Divina (Veronica Hart) is a woman many males, married or not, would like to have around. She's a sorceress, who, with a flick of her wrist, can show herself to you, *and only you*, naked and ready for action. In-visible and soundless to others when she wishes, she offers her goodies to most men and occasionally to ladies. Lady Caroline (Candida Royalle), who lives in what is supposed to be an English country estate with Harold Dixon (Aaron Stuart), her wealthy husband, doesn't really enjoy him in bed. Usually she only lets him suck her tits, and she doesn't want his penis in her vagina. This, of course, drives Harold to his only other source of pussy—the household maids. When Caroline catches him in flagrante delicto with Katty (Desiree Cousteau), she fires her and won't hire a replacement, Divina, until Harold promises to keep hands off her. Of course, now Harold's problems are over since in a jiffy Divina can bounce naked in bed on top of him—even while Caroline is in the room, totally unaware of what is happening. But Maurice (Richard Bolla), the butler, Ron Jeremy, a household servant and Caroline's brother can't make out with Divina. So they plot to destroy her, or at least get her fired. Divina foils them by seducing Caroline just as Caroline is about to tell her she must leave. Not only does Divina seduce Caroline, but she turns her into a horny lady who finally, after all these years, enjoys her husband, too. The story falls apart totally when the three male rejects convince Divina that they need her help in the boiler room. To their shock she gives them all huge erections which she quickly sucks. Brother James is so enamored of Divina that he wants to crawl inside her and live there forever—a wish she quickly grants him. The CC rating is a little shaky but Candida and Veronica give the males detailed views of their vulvas when they make love and Nicole Scent, with her husky voice, pixie face and boy's body, is a potential new star. Not for ladies past 40.

DEVIL'S ECSTASY
CC NN DK DS BI and occasionally NR
1974 XTRAVISION

P/D—Robert Keith, Brandon Carter
F/A—John McNight, David Lamont
F/A—Deborah Whitney, Tara Barr, Debbie Garland

This mixes sex with witchcraft and Satanism. You'll watch it from beginning to end. Our heroine has weird origins. Her father and mother are dead, and when she returns to her birthplace, her aunt, who really is a witch, seduces her and sacrifices her to Satan. But her twin sister, Elaine, takes her place. Pretty soon her boyfriends, who come to find out what has happened to her, are wiped out, too. Interesting cinematography, and sexmaking is photographed from new angles and is frequently caring and interesting to watch.

DEVIL'S PLAYGROUND
NN NM DK DB BI
1974 VCX

P/D—R. Owen Teegee, Rik Taziner
F/A—Paul Tonas
F/A—Kelly Guthrie, Desire, Bonnie Holiday

A sleazy-looking Lucifer, up from hell, seduces nymphettes (several of them don't look much older than 15) while they chew bubble gum and grimace unhappily. That's the story line of this quickie, which is strictly a combat-zone theater production. It will make most viewers sad that women of any age could get in such sorry straits that they would let themselves be used for a few dollars.

DIRTY LOOKS **CC NN DK BI**
1982 VCA

P/D—Chuck Vincent
F/A—Jack Wrangler, Jeffrey Hurst, Roger Caine, Frank Adams, Ron Jeremy, Bobby Astyr
F/A—Samantha Fox, Christi Ford, Merle Michaels, Vanessa Del Rio, Leslie Bovee, Kelly Nichols, Annie Sprinkle, C. J. Laing, Beth Anne

Most sexvids created by patching together cuts from other films aren't worth much. This one, reviewing some of the best moments of Chuck Vincent's adult films, is not only a fast introduction to the many stars listed above, but it proves Chuck is one of the top two or three producer/directors in the business. With the exception of the film *Bang, Bang*, which I have not seen, all the other films mentioned below are listed and reviewed in this book. Al Goldstein (publisher of *Screw*), in his thinned-down, new image, and Gloria Leonard (publisher of *High So-*

ciety) tie the various segments of this tape together with some zany conversation. The best cuts are from *Jack & Jill,* where Jack Wrangler and Samantha Fox play macho husband and domineering wife in an opening sequence where the viewer at first doesn't know that they are married. This is followed by a funny scene in which Ron Jeremy tries to impress Christi Ford with an exquisite dinner he has prepared, only to discover that food doesn't interest her—she prefers to suck cock. This one is from *Fascination.* Ron Jeremy also appears in a scene from *Sizzle* in which a kidnapped Merle Michaels proves harder to handle than the kid in O. Henry's "The Ransom of Red Chief." Other cuts include erotic sexmaking with Samantha Fox and Frank Adams from the film *Bad Penny,* and from the same film, a scene in the elevator control box on top of a high-rise building in which Samantha seduces a repair man (Roger Caine). He is oblivious that his greasy hands are leaving a trail all over her white gown and body. There's the very funny Romeo and Juliet balcony scene from *Jack & Jill,* played by Roger Caine and Vanessa del Rio. A scene from *Games Women Play* where Leslie Bovee and Jack Wrangler have an early-morning quickie in a stairwell in a building off Times Square is included, and there are also cuts from *Dirty Lilly, Visions, Le Toy Shoppe* and *Roommates.* And there's a silly one with Jeffrey Hurst and C. J. Laing making detailed verbal love as they talk to each other naked on the telephone, describing every gesture they are making. Only after climaxing do they discover they aren't talking to their respective spouses.

DRACULA SUCKS or DRACULA'S BRIDE
DS DK
1979 MEDIA

P/D—Darryl Marshak, Phillip Marshak
F/A—Jamie Gillis, John Holmes, John Leslie
F/A—Annette Haven, Serena

There are soft-core and hard-core versions of this one. Media has the soft-core, which eliminates penetration shots, but not a closeup of John Holmes's penis bitten by a female vampire, or the count "eating" his bride. The hard-core *Dracula's*

Bride provides some sexual relief from the stilted dialogue, but not the close-ups of the count biting female breasts with blood spurting out of the mouths of vampires dripping with blood. Jamie Gillis obviously enjoys himself as the red-eyed Dracula, and this one finally proves what all Dracula movies insinuate—that blood and semen are part of the count's repertoire.

DRACULA (Blood for) **NL DK**
1974 VIDEO GEMS

P/D—Andy Warhol, Paul Morrissey
F/A—Joe D'Allessandro, Udo Kier
F/A—Victoria Desica, Maxine McKenzie

Andy Warhol must have made this film at the same time he made *Frankenstein.* Both films have the same key actors. In this one, Udo Kier plays the count. His secretary, a fearsome character himself, tells him, "You must have the blood of a virgin or you'll be dead in two weeks." So the count, a Romanian, carrying his coffin on top of a 1930 Ford, is driven to Italy, where Catholic girls remain virgins until they are married. They settle in with the Fiore family, who own a run-down country estate and are nearly broke because Poppa goes to the casino and loses all his money as fast as he gets it. Mother Fiore is determined to marry off one of her four daughters, who are now forced to work in the fields to sustain the house, to the count. But she doesn't know that two of them have been screwing with the gardener (Joe D'Allesandro) and are not virgins. The count soons discovers the truth. When he takes on Sofiria, humping her as he bites her neck and sucks her blood, he is suddenly sick to his stomach and vomits her blood in the bathtub for a yucky couple of minutes. When he tries to seduce Rubina in the bathroom, she suddenly realizes she can't see his reflection in the mirror, but the poor count is foiled again and can't digest her blood. The gardener suddenly realizes the count is a vampire. He breaks Pearlia's (the 14-year-old daughter's) hymen as he screws her (to save her)—and Dracula emerges from behind the curtain and laps up the blood that has dripped from Pearlia's vagina.

The homeliest daughter *is a virgin*, and the count finally gets what he came for. But the gardener chases him around the estate and hacks off his arms and legs in a blood-spurting mess. The gardener finally kills him and Esmeralda. You may feel as if you should wipe the blood off your television tube when you finish.

FRIDAY THE 13TH, PARTS 1, 2, and 3
R DS
1980-1982 PARAMOUNT

P/D—Steve Miner
F/A—There is no continuity of actors or actresses in the three films since most of them are murdered.

None of these three films was made by an adult filmmaker. There is no explicit sex in any of them—but there is sex *and* violence. The only reason I have included a few of the horror genre in this book is that they reflect the kind of perverted morality that condones censorship of adult sex-making on television and in films but refuses to censor films where hacking and chopping up females (and some males) constitutes the entire action of the film. In Sweden, no visual portrayal of consenting adult sexmaking is censored, but violence is. The British are trying to devise a code to label video cassettes of this type (among others are *I Spit on Your Grave* (see listing, p. 233), *SS Experiment Camp, Driller-Killer*). Each successive part of the *Friday* trio churns the sexy slice-and-dice machine a bit further. Part II continues the story of Jason Vorhees, who has turned Camp Crystal Lake into a massacre ground for teenagers. Presumably, as a young boy he drowned when the camp counsellors were so busy making love they were unaware his canoe had turned over. In Part I, his mother seeks vengeance for him and chops up at least four young men and drives a young woman crazy (she finally hacks off the mother's head). The second film takes place five years later. The campgrounds are deserted and kept off limits by the local police. It is now known as Camp Blood. But a half-mile away on the same lake, a group of young camp counselors, equally divided between male and female, have come together for training in summer camp work. One young lady swims naked in the lake, unaware that she's being observed by a prowler. All the women are sexually provocative, and most of them are easily enticed into the sack. It slowly becomes apparent that Jason never really drowned. He has turned into a psychopath who lives in the forest and wreaks vengeance on anyone crossing his path. Before the film is over, he splits a police officer's head open with a claw hammer, strangles a wandering bum, hangs one of the campers by his feet and slits his throat, stabs two of the counselors who are in bed together screwing—with a spear that goes through both of them—stabs two other ladies to death, and even after one woman saws his arm off with a chainsaw, recovers sufficiently to finish off all but two of the counselors. Part III was filmed in 3D. In the summer of 1982, long lines of mostly young people waited happily to see detached eyeballs and decapitated heads soar into the audience at them. Jason is dead. Long live Jason!

HEAT WAVE **NN DK BI**
1973 COMMAND

P/D—Midas Gettrich, Umberto Corelone, a.k.a. Cecil Howard
F/A—Dante, David Morris, Robert Brown
F/A—Susan McBain, Georgina Leonard

The devil, who calls himself your libido, the itch in your brain that gets you in the crotch, is your tour guide in this one. What do five unrelated couples do in a heat wave? You guessed it. The devil helps all of them break through their repressions. This one is totally male-oriented. It ends with a total orgy lasting about 15 minutes.

JEZEBEL **NM DK BI**
1979 CAL VISTA

P/D—Sam Norvell, Charles Adamson
F/A—Neil Oakley, Henry Woods
F/A—Ladye McCormick, Brenda Hale

Strange faces but familiar genitals doing nothing you haven't seen before in a series of loops—some reviewers call them vignettes. This one is tied together with a transmigration fantasy. Presumably, Jezebel, a housewife who is experiencing marital frustration with her husband, wakes up masturbating because her sex life is nonexistent. With the devil's help and a gypsy's 1,000-year-old liquor ($20 a sip), she becomes a woman who takes on four guys at once. But never mind, she has a female friend who lives in the house next door, and a male friend who wears a mask and provides stud service for lonely housewives. After she's enjoyed so much sexual fun, like the lady in *The Devil and Miss Jones,* she wants to keep going, but the devil owns her and he disintegrates her.

THE KINKY LADIES OF BOURBON STREET
CC NM BI DK
1978 QUALITY

P/D—**Frances Le Roi, Henri Outrandy**
F/A—**Dawn Cummings, Helga Trixi, Madja Mons, Veronique Monod**
F/A—**Brenda Reed, Jacque Conti, Carmelo Petix**

If you buy or rent this film you'll have to run it twice or more to figure out what is really happening. And that's the reason I gave it a CC rating. You keep watching and can't figure out whether you are in the past or present—and some of it is pretty gross. It begins in a churchyard cemetery. The film is French made and obviously must have had another title because it has nothing to do with New Orleans's Bourbon Street. A mysterious woman is walking toward some simple crosses which you soon discover have photographs of three women on them—Charlene, Penelope and Alice. Their voices emanating from the grave greet Maude. Within the next 15 minutes you discover they have all committed suicide—Charlene by inhaling gas; Alice by drowning and Penelope (I think it's Penelope), a singer who performs a song in French that translates to "Drowning in Your Eyes," by putting a stick of dynamite in her vagina and lighting it! You witness all their deaths. But I'm not sure whether Penelope dies before or after she has walked out of the cemetery naked one morning and greets four guys collecting trash with a cold

stare, after which she unzips their pants and fellates all four of them, astonished but willing. And Maude is ready to kill herself: "Dying is something too important to do just any old way. I want to die in the best way possible—by being fucked to death." She listens to the admonitions of her friends from the grave. "You mustn't die, Maude. You're our only connection with life." The film ends with what must be her last visit to the grave. She's an old woman, but her consort somehow or other hasn't aged. There's probably something I missed but if you take to watching *all* the porno films ever made for a living, you'll never have time to retrace your steps!

LURE OF THE TRIANGLE **CC NN**
1979 VISUAL ENTERTAINMENT

P/D—**Robert Angrove, Phillip Ronald**
F/A—**Mike Cone, Scott Daniels**
F/A—**Patricia Rivers, Victoria Lee**

Here's a sexvid with a totally different background. The lure is the Bermuda Triangle, and of course not incidentally, the female delta. The entire film was shot off the coast of Florida. Jack owns a palatial home on the inland waterway and a fifty-foot cruiser called *The Proud Peter.* He has a girlfriend, J.P., who is not adventurous. Another couple, Harry and Linda, are living in the house with them on vacation and are happily screwing their time away. But Jack has an uneasy belief that he lived before in the lost city of Atlantis, and the city still may actually exist somewhere in the Bermuda Triangle. So he persuades the others to leave with him on an exploration trip. Running around the yacht happily naked, they are soon scuba diving and making love underwater with their original partners. There are no swappings or bisexual scenes in this flick. In the things-you've-never-seen-before department, you watch them in a long underwater ballet wearing their diving tanks, occasionally taking the oxygen inhalers out of their mouths so they can enjoy oral sex, and actually copulating in the briny deep among the tropical fishes. When they return to their ship the compass is suddenly spinning, the clocks and the radio have stopped, and they are evidently near the fabled spot of the lost city. But the girls get nervous so the guys take them back to shore, put them aboard a hydroplane bound for home and immediately take off back to the spot, where lo and behold, two naked ladies from Atlantis, mermaids without tails, emerge from the sea and take them over. Obviously the producer couldn't afford to technically deal with the subject in a Hollywood spectacular, but male or female, you'll enjoy the underwater sexmaking.

MARY, MARY **CC NN BI with some female-oriented NL**
1975 SELECT/ESSEX TVX

P/D—Bernard Morris
F/A—John Leslie, Jeremy Smith
F/A—Constance Money, Sharon Thorpe

Who is Bernard Morris? This one storywise and cinematographically is head and shoulders above most sexvids. Commencing with an exquisitely photographed underwater sexmaking ballet scene, the participants emerge with the female demanding: "You did it again! Why did you come so soon?" Presto, Old Nick appears and offers the solution for a permanent hard-on in trade for the man's soul. Never mind that the basic plot gets lost, somehow or other the film hangs together from beginning to end with strong environmental ambiance, and silly lines. Amazingly, at the end, the devil comes to collect.

NOCTURNA **This one carries an R rating, and can be seen occasionally on television.**
1979 MEDIA

F/A—John Carradine
F/A—Yvonne de Carlo

Don't expect to see Yvonne de Carlo naked in this one. She's gotten old and plump, and John Carradine as Count Dracula has false teeth which click when he bites. Nocturna is their daughter. The plot is that she has fallen in love with a young man and wants to go straight, settle down and have kids and stop being a vampire. "You have no right to love," her father tells her. "You can only procreate your own kind." There is no explicit sex but a lot of female nudity, plus a rock group sequence that is sexier than the dance John Travolta did in *Saturday Night Fever*.

PANDORA'S MIRROR **NN BI DS DK**
1981 CABALLERO CONTROL

P/D—Warren Evans
F/A—Jamie Gillis, Frederic Foster, Ron Hudd
F/A—Veronica Hart, Kandi Barbour, Merle Michaels, Marlene Willoughby

Pandora's Mirror has a plot device which would have been much more effective if Warren Evans had used it to carry Pandora back into her past lives, thus concentrating the film on one actress. But Evans uses it as an adult film convention to hang together at least five unrelated glimpses of the sexual lives of people who have performed before the mirror. Thus it is possible to keep male viewers from being bored (presumably) by just one set of female equipment, even though the five other mouths and vaginas in this one don't perform much differently from each other. Whenever the story gets back to Pandora (Veronica Hart), it is interesting and told with a lot of creepy atmosphere. The owner of the antique shop warns Pandora the mirror is dangerous ("It has a soul of its own") but she gets so attached to it she never does date her boyfriend, Peter (Jamie Gillis). He gets rid of his aggressions by having anal sex with her girlfriend. In the meantime the bulk of the film reveals a seventeenth-century beauty being raped by soldiers in Colonial uniforms; a 1920s actress (Marlene Willoughby) whose scandalous behavior with young boys and women is the talk of Hollywood; an audition on a Broadway stage in which a young actress masturbates at the director's command; a scene in a club devoted to orgies during which Merle Michaels ingests several men at once and finally, as Veronica is performing the same feat in front of the mirror, lo and behold, she disappears into it to stay there forever for the edification of future owners. Alas—it all adds up to nothing you haven't watched before, *except* Veronica.

THE PSYCHIATRIST   **CC   NN   BI   DK**
1978   SELECT/ESSEX

P/D—Peter Balakoff, Belinda Balakoff
F/A—Tovia Borodyn, Richard Parnes, Van Star
F/A—Gena Lee, Diane Miller, Natcha

I can't figure out why Tovia Borodyn, a Belgian and just as fascinating as Charles Boyer ever was, didn't go into straight films. He would have been a matinee idol. In this one he plays Dr. Maurice Rondeau, a psychiatrist who runs a clinic where he treats patients with various hang-ups, including satanic possession. While he tells his classes at the university that possession by the devil is ridiculous, it slowly develops that everyone who ever enters his clinic is soon in the devil's control, and the doctor himself, who's exceedingly smooth with his patients (most of them are women), is running a cult that would make Jim Jones roll over in his grave. A new nurse, Jean Lowell (Gena Lee), who has read all the doctor's books, arrives to do research and takes a job at the clinic. Soon she is obediently fellating Dr. Rondeau, and although she tries to get him arrested, the police believe she is the crazy one. Inside the clinic, there are nightly meetings with the devil and the patients, dressed in cowls, arrive to accept their "punishment." Jean is thoroughly hypnotized and although patients have committed suicide, the doctor continues in business and Jean finally becomes his new wife. Good acting and filmmaking reflect a woman's touch. Gena Lee has big brown eyes a person could drown in. And in case you're interested, Borodyn, Peter Balakoff and Ted Roter are one person and is still busily producing, but not acting in, adult films.

RING OF DESIRE   **NN   BI**
1982   SELECT/ESSEX

P/D—Peter Balakoff
F/A—Paul Thomas, Ron Jeremy, Chris Parker, William Margold
F/A—Gena Lee, Georgina Spelvin, Jennifer West, Hilary Summers, Monica Faberge

One thing many adult movies have in common is a fairy tale origin. High-income people (kings, princes and princesses) drive Rolls, Jags and Mercedes and discover magic potions or amulets (frogs into princes, beans in beanstalks) that make them nicer or worse than they were. In this one the amulet is a ring which makes whoever owns it totally seductive. Chris Parker, as a lawyer, buys it from a young woman (the witch or good fairy). Wearing it, his secretary immediately undresses for him. In appreciation he gives her the ring. She loses it to Paul Thomas, a magazine photographer who immediately seduces two women. The last one, Jennifer West, wears it home and Georgina Spelvin (looking a little the worse for wear) enjoys sex with her lesbian roommate. After Georgina has taken care of Jennifer, she seduces a young couple and then gives the ring to a director, William Margold, who picks up a prostitute. She can't resist him but later steals the ring. Before you finish, John Hollyfield, Hilary Summers, Ron Jeremy and Monica Faberge (a real redhead) seduce or are seduced by the owner of the ring. Occasional laughter and good dialogue, plus a Goldie Hawn-style portrayal by Hilary Summers and Ron Jeremy as a good guy, redeem this one. The ring, of course, comes home to roost on Chris Parker's night table, put there by his wife's masseur, Ron Jeremy, who screws her once a week.

SENSUAL ENCOUNTERS OF EVERY KIND

DK   DS   BI
1978   SELECT/ESSEX TVX

P/D—Harold Lime, Ramsey Carson
F/A—John Leslie, Turk Lyon, Chris Cassidy
F/A—Serena, Leslie Bovee, Dorothy LeMay

There's a special talisman, you have to believe, a jewel hung on a chain which makes the wearer sexually irresistible, but only works once for each owner. This is a sexvid convention which makes it possible to tie together various unrelated episodes. The first wearer is Leslie Bovee, who gets raped by three gardeners. At first she fights them off furiously, but afterwards she hires them to work four days a week instead of two. Next is Georgina Spelvin, who is a French teacher and inadvertently seduces two students, a male and female, who rape-seduce her. This is followed by Serena, who gets screwed on a bidet and in a bathtub with vibrators and dildos by a man who is presumably a senator running for reelection. If you haven't quit yet there's John Leslie, a coach in some kind of girl's school. He and the women use the gymnasium and steam room for sex. There are no sensual encounters you haven't seen before.

SEXCALIBUR NN BI DK
1983 SELECT/ESSEX

P/D—Dadas Christi, Dinin Dicimino
F/A—Ken Starbuck, William Margold, Jeff Conrad
F/A—Maria Tortuga, Jennifer West, Drea, Lee Carol

Don't buy this one for the story—it's pretty confusing. Nevertheless, the director manages to package all the adult film conventions on one tape—this time in 3D! I watched it on a forty-five-inch General Electric rear projection screen and had a devil of a time following the tuning instructions to get a light blue screen overall. (Rear projection screens offer a limited viewing angle.) But ladies' legs were right there protruding from the tube. You must wear red and blue paper glasses provided with the tape. With a little juggling of your tube, you may even have to duck the come shots! Third dimension effects depend on the original camera placement and the type of shots that are filmed. Sometimes you experience the third dimension internally within the tube, which is not as effective as when you get the illusion of the character, or his or her anatomy, emerging from the tube. The cameraman on this one needs more practice. Some day holography will replace the stereoptic effect, and when that happens the action will really move out of the tube and offer unlimited potential for adult film producers. As for the story—it seems that our heroine (Maria Tortuga), who lives in the present, discovers in her dreams that in a previous

century she was a sorceress. A mask which she has purchased in a local secondhand store transports all who behold it with uncontrollable lust. The action moves back and forth between the present and her dreams in another era. She is rescued by a knight in armor who is about as graceful as the Tin Man in *The Wizard of Oz.*

SEXORCIST DEVIL DK DS
1974 ARROW

P/D—Hans Leek, Sven Hellstrom
F/A—Kelly Guthrie, Wayne William
F/A—Eva Galaunt, Lilly Lamarr

Somewhere in the marsh lives Volta, a sex-mad devil who runs a Satan-worshipping cult. You only see Volta in action after he leaves the swamp to avenge himself on Ernest Von Kleinschmidt, a demonologist, and Janice Lagney, a free-lance photographer and writer. They uncover secret parchments telling about his evil practices. Volta seduces Janice's roommate. Once Diane, a prostitute, is in his power, he tells her to stab a 240-pound client who is taking a shower to get ready for sex with her. She obliges Volta. Then she kills Janice and finally Dr. Kleinschmidt, who tries to use the cross and various exorcisms to send Volta back to the evil place he belongs. Kleinschmidt fails and Janice spits his blood all over him before he tumbles in her swimming pool and drowns. If the devil hasn't immobilized you halfway through, the best thing to do with this one is to try and forget how you wasted your money. It's not scary, only amateurish.

THROUGH THE LOOKING GLASS CC NM BI DK
1976 QUALITY

P/D—Jonas Middleton
F/A—Jamie Gillis, Douglas Wood, Mike Jefferson
F/A—Catherine Burgess, Laura Nicholson, Maria Taylor, Terri Hall

This is a sexvid classic that mixes a Daphne du Maurier or Stephen King kind of story into a terrifying gothic drama, a story vein that for some reason or other adult filmmakers have overlooked. Whoever Jonas Middleton is, he knows how to build effect on top of effect and make you believe his heroine, Catherine Burgess (played by Catherine Burgess, whom I haven't discovered in any other adult film), is truly possessed by a satanic demon. He lives on the other side of an old mirror in the attic of her ancestral home—and he resembles her father. The entire film concentrates on Catherine, who really looks as if she were born to the aristocracy. She lives with her husband, Richard (Douglas Wood), in her family home. They have one daughter, Jennifer (Laura Nicholson), who realizes her mother has a strange compulsion to visit the attic and brush her hair (naked) with a silver brush that her Grandaddy (Jamie Gillis)—now dead—gave to her mother. Catherine keeps asking her husband to help her, but Richard thinks she's neurotic, and he doesn't know that every time she looks in the mirror, a demon who resembles her father beckons to her to come through the looking glass and live with him forever on the other side. "Where will you take me?" she asks. "Where you will be adored," he responds. "It's not real," she protests. "What is real?" he counters. "Your world out there?" Finally unable to resist—even though she's booked an airline flight (against her husband's wishes) to leave the house, Catherine follows Jamie into the mirror. And then you are literally immersed in a weird, totally insane sexual hell. Middleton gives you a 15-minute cinematographic tour of madness that must have been inspired by Hieronymus Bosch's paintings. It will literally scare the hell out of you—or make you want to throw up—and Jamie as Catherine's daddy is at his worst. A demon, laughing insanely, tells Catherine: "There are no mornings here, no nights. You'll never grow old, Catherine." But after a few minutes of floundering in his sea of despair, Catherine looks pretty haggard, and so will you if you dare to watch it to the end.

TRASHI **NN NM DK BI**
1980 CABALLERO

P/D—Jo Anne Lewis, Louis Lewis
F/A—David Morris, Joey Civera, Michael Morrison
F/A—Lisa de Leeuw, Loni Sanders, Dorothy Le May, Sharon Mitchell, Carol Doda, Serena

Dr. Schtup (Michael Morrison), a latter-day Dr. Frankenstein, has created a whole houseful of female robots out of the best parts. "Every woman has some good parts," he says. His latest creation is Trashi (Lisa de Leeuw), who, when she leaves the birthing couch, does what every good woman should do. Fellate her creator—what else? Bic Boner (David Morris) is asked by Inspector Crotch (Joey Civera) to investigate the evil goings-on at Schtup's house. Before they get to the bottom of things (pun intended), all three of them end up on the birthing couch themselves, tied down and in their robots' control. All of the actresses listed above are among the robots. The only problem is that the difference between female robots and real-life porno stars is difficult to discern. Never mind, Lisa de Leeuw finally becomes a real woman. "I feel, I really feel," she tells David Morris, who kisses her tenderly at the end.

14

Star Vehicles

ALL ABOUT ANNETTE **NN NM BI**
1982   SELECT ESSEX

P/D—**Sondra Winters, Stephen Lucas**
F/A—**Jamie Gillis, Joey Civera**
F/A—**Annette Haven, Mai Lin, Tres Dover**

Nothing Much About Annette would have been a better title for this one—which is sad because a film that *really* explored Annette Haven's thinking in the areas of female sexuality would be fascinating. The only direct discussion that occurs with Annette takes about three minutes, during which she tells Al Goldstein, "I cook, I sew, I clean, I knit baby booties . . . the only difference between me and lots of women is that I think sex is okay, and I'm not afraid to say so . . . The whole point of my being in the industry is to help change American attitudes and establish that sex is a good thing. I still conduct myself as a lady." But if you really want to know more about what makes Annette Haven tick, watch the sexvid *Once Upon a Time* (see listing, p. 114), which Annette created and directed herself. Other than that, a long cut from *For the Love of Pleasure* (see listing, p. 92), which Annette tells Goldstein is her favorite movie "because I play God," and a few cuts from *China Girl,* there is nothing about Annette on this tape. Two things make it interesting, however—a long masturbation scene performed by a

woman at a supposed casting director's request. Her name is Judy. As the camera cuts between her face and her fingers working on her clitoris and vulva, she forgets the camera and slowly brings herself to orgasm. In another *nothing*-about-Annette sequence, two women discuss their bisexual feelings and how making love together differs from sexmaking with a man. None of the "all about" or "inside" tapes listed in this filmography tell the viewer much about the actresses or actors involved.

ALL ABOUT GLORIA LEONARD **NN BI**
one silly DK with Gloria sucking three cocks at the same time and a double insertion with Jamie and Marc
1979   VIDEO-X-PIX

P/D—**Howard Howard, Gloria Leonard**
F/A—**Marc Stevens, Jamie Gillis**
F/A—**Gloria Leonard, Ming Toy**

A film about a woman by a woman. Many women will be quite fascinated with this sexvid, especially scenes where Gloria verbalizes in a long dialogue how she feels while she is screwing, and as she experiments with a vibrator connected with a wiggly reproduction of a male head. The final scene with Gloria in bed with two men is, according to a recent survey of Cosmo girls by *Cosmopolitan* magazine, a common experience for about 25 percent of them. Like this one or not, Gloria is a pragmatic woman.

AUNT PEG **NN NM BI**
1980 CAL VISTA

P/D—Arthur Cutter, Wes Brown
F/A—John Holmes, Jamie Gillis, Mike Ranger, Michael Morrison
F/A—Juliet Anderson, Seka, Serena, Shirley Woods

This is the first of several Aunt Peg movies (see Supplemental Listing). If Juliet Anderson keeps it up as Aunt Peg, she will probably become as famous as John C. Holmes as Johnny Wadd. She's a matinee idol for the raincoat crowd (but most women will detest her). Miss Peggy Norton, or Aunt Peg (Juliet Anderson) is a producer/director of porno films. But off-camera she is better than any of her actresses. John Holmes only appears momentarily, and although he is appearing in a film Aunt Peg is making, she never gets her hands on him. Never mind, she makes up for it, not only with Franco (Jamie Gillis), who has come from Italy to star in her pictures, but also with her niece (Shirley Woods), who has arrived from the Midwest. She eats her in the back of her Rolls Royce, and eventually she and Seka work over Franco and, still not satisfied, taste and lap each other. Despite the continuous all-day sex, Aunt Peg can't help herself. She masturbates when she showers at night.

BAD PENNY **NN NL and NR but only occasionally**
1978 QUALITY

P/D—Howard Paul, Mark Ubell
F/A—Don Peterson, Kurt Mann, Roger Caine
F/A—Samantha Fox, Molly Malone

Screw's Best Ten for 1978, number three. The entire story revolves around one female, which is unusual for adult films. Penny Hickey is trying to find the answer to a riddle and in the process has to screw at least five men in order to inherit her uncle's fortune. Good New York City photog-

raphy. This is a silly story with even sillier background music from Strauss.

BARBIE'S FANTASIES **NN NM BI DK**
1974 VIDEO-X HOME LIBRARY

P/D—Claude Goddard
F/A—Jamie Gillis, Jeffrey Hurst
F/A—Jennifer Hurst, Sue Kelly, Jenny Lane

Jenny Lane is the star of this one, and if you're interested, Jeffrey and Jennifer Hurst were (are?) married. Jeffrey is a hammy actor, but Jenny Lane comes through as she did in *Couples* as a believable teenager. On the other hand, what makes this a bit different from the run of the mill includes a sequence with a black female (Sue Kelly, who has a beautiful face and body) and a white male, Jeffrey, who is yuck. There is a weird sequence with a guy who is tattooing his penis while two women watch (he's also tattooed all over and the girls wear identifying "butterfly" tattoos) and a unique scene with Jenny Lane seducing her young brother. You never see his face, but his voice and hairless body, except for a few pubic hairs, put him at about age 14. Jenny is very warm and sisterly with him as she teaches him the joys of sex. It's a scene that might well enhance a good story line between an older female and a young boy with or without incest.

BEYOND FULFILLMENT **NN BI**
1971–1973 SELECT/ESSEX

P/D—Billy Thornberg
F/A—John C. Holmes and several others
F/A—Claudine Grayson, Barbara Barton

If an hour and half of John C. Holmes fulfilling himself isn't enough (see *Fulfillment*, p. 221), here's a follow-up with John in a couple of loops and several other guys doing the job—with one of them concentrating on anal sex. The loops in this sequel are tied together by Claudine Grayson, who tries to convince you that women are more knowledgeable about sex than men. She's about as reliable in her philosophy as Shere Hite. A totally boring sexvid—literally and figuratively!

BEYOND DE SADE **CC NN BI DK**
1979   MITCHELL

P/D—Mitchell Brothers
F/A—Marilyn Chambers, Tanya Robertson,
Carol Christy

On the premise, evidently, that the viewer could only take so much of Marilyn Chambers's delight in pain, this is a continuation of Marilyn's masochistic behavior begun in *Never a Tender Moment.* This one takes place in the famous Mitchell Brothers' Kopenhagen Lounge in San Francisco. Men wearing masks seated around the perimeter have phallic-looking flashlights with which they can caress the performers and see and explore their genitals better. Marilyn begins her act with a sensuous disco dance in which her labial ring is clearly revealed. Then she's joined by two women (one black), and for the next 15 minutes they thoroughly enjoy each other's vulvas and breasts. According to Marilyn, "If you don't do bizarre things and enjoy doing them, that will screw you up. So, 24 hours a day, I think of all kinds of ways to have sex." On this hour tape there's a second unannounced feature which runs for about 25 minutes called *Family Affair.* It's much tamer. Daddy, Mommy and Daughter can't ever seem to spend an evening together because unbeknownst to each other, they are with their respective lovers. The CC rating is not because I'm a supporter of Leopold von Sacher-Masoch but rather because this is the only real-life demonstration of masochism I have ever seen. It's mind-boggling!

BLONDE IN BLACK SILK
NN DK DS BI
1979   QUALITY

P/D—Bill Eagle, Phillip Drexler
F/A—Eric Edwards, David Bellow, Jake Teague,
Ron Jeremy
F/A—Serena, Merle Michaels, Arcadia, Erica
Mathews

By the time you've finished this one, you'll be as well acquainted with Serena's genitals as you are with her pretty face. It begins with her as a contessa who made millions copying high-style fashions in a Seventh Avenue dress shop. She's in bed with her lover, Jerome. It ends with a rape scene, ensuring that Serena will go down in adult film history as the most-raped woman. This one has a twist, however. There's a scary ten or 15 minutes during which Serena is chased through the bombed-out Bronx by three guys on a motorcycle. She's stretched across it. You've never watched a more frightening rape. But it ain't for real! Turns out that the contessa, who has a high sex-drive, paid the guys to do it. The story is about Heather (Merle Michaels, who once told me she was studying journalism at night school.) She's a reporter for *Metropolitan* magazine, and her assignment is to write a biography of the contessa. The contessa obligingly gives her background details. It includes stories about her assistant, Carol, who can fellate a buyer (Jake Teague) in the nine and a half minutes it takes the helicopter to fly from Kennedy Airport to downtown Manhattan. Another assistant's Mercedes isn't functioning. She brings it to a garage while an attendant, Bobby Astyr, is pumping gas. She invites his boss to screw her and balances herself spread-eagled on the car lift. Then she happily satisfies both of them. Finally, there's Eric Edwards. He's in charge of the band at the Magdelene School for Girls. He punishes one girl (a baton twirler) for making it with Serena in the school camper on Fifth Avenue (while a parade is passing) and beats her bare fanny with his hand.

BLONDE FIRE **NN BI mild DK**
1979   EROS & FREEWAY

P/D—Zaven Avedis, Bob Chinn
F/A—John Holmes
F/A—Seka, Jesie St. James

Blonde Fire is a diamond which Johnny Wadd has come to Capetown, South Africa, to purchase for a client for a million dollars. Seventy-five minutes later, after making love to four women Johnny Waddstyle—which means that he gives as much as he gets, even to one who tries to kill him but whom he handcuffs to the bedposts—Johnny recovers the diamond from where another woman has hidden it. You guessed it—in her vagina.

BOTTOMS UP CC NN NM BI DK
1974   EROS

P/D—Gerard Damiano
F/A—Douglas Stone, Marc Stevens, Eric
   Edwards
F/A—Tina Russell, Karen Clark

The reason that I've given this one a CC rating is that it really is a collector's tape but not for those who can't wonder a little. It begins with a bum panhandling in Central Park. "Please, I'm hungry," he tells Damiano, who appears momentarily as a park-walker and rejects him coldly. Then the bum spies Tina Russell sitting on a park bench. She shares her sandwich with them. You begin to think that an interesting sexvid with a story is about to develop. And that brings on your wondering. Why did Damiano ever make it? Tina Russell died in May 1981 of cancer. She was 31. The entire film after the opening places the camera in one or two positions and focuses on Tina screwing, sucking and getting screwed by more or less faceless people. Although the actors listed above are in the film, you'll never recognize them. Finally, as if Damiano were psychic, he predicts Tina's death. In the film Tina gets into bondage and discipline as the continuous, plotless screwing and sucking continues. Finally after she nearly strangles a guy with the rope of her whip, a woman puts it around Tina's neck. Though you don't see her die, her ring falls off, and the woman with whom she's been involved in a foursome picks it up, and smiling, puts it on her own finger. The end.

CALIFORNIA GIRLS NN DK BI
1980 FANTASY VIDEO BY CABALLERO

P/D—Not given
F/A—John C. Holmes
F/A—Rhonda Jo Petty

Rhonda Jo and her pretty girlfriend, who is not identified in this one, are presumably disco roller skating queens and they both can skate pretty well on California sidewalks. But you never see them in the big disco contest which is the theme of this tape and in which they fellate their way to victory. Rhonda and her friend are competing against John C., who, when he is roller skating, unfortunately looks as if he might fall on his ass or tip forward and break the famous jamoke. If you buy or rent this one, it is because you are a Holmes aficionado. Rhonda Jo tries, but she can't take *all* of the magnificent instrument, though she works at it for at least 20 minutes. Rhonda Jo and her friend also enjoy sexmaking with each other in her bathtub. If you've never seen a woman masturbate using the tub water faucet with her legs over her head, now's your chance. Produced on a shoestring budget, it is better than most of the low-priced sexvids.

CELEBRITY CENTERFOLDS
CC NN BI NM DK
1983 VISUAL ENTERTAINMENT

P/D—Bobby Hollander
F/A—Merrick Flint, Tom Byron, Steve Douglas
F/A—Cody Nichole, Laurie Smith, Laureen Wild,
   Pepper Hinds, Ricky Lane

When I put this tape on, I thought for a moment I had seen it before. It took me an hour of searching among these reviews to discover that I was both right and wrong. *Paper Dolls* (see listing, p. 255) has a similar approach. This is a better tape and I have given it a CC rating because I'm sure that most people who watch adult films wonder about the women and guys who make them and what makes them tick. Hollander asks them all many questions, such as, "How do you feel when you are showing all you have? When did you first have sex? Do you like anal sex? Do you enjoy giving head or blow jobs? How do you deal with the multiplicity of your sex life?" Of course he quickly slides over answers. But for the most part, unlike the men's sex magazines in which the women porno stars give ecstatic responses to similar questions, these women seem unusually forthright and honest. Laureen Wild started at 19. She laughs when Hollander says that he's heard she has a "tight pussy." She hopes so—and hopes to keep it tight for life. Both she and

Cody Nicole (see *Sex Boat* listing, p. 258) tell him the first thing they look at when they see a man in a bathing suit is his "buns, or ass—not his crotch." They enjoy male posteriors. "People think porno stars are brainless," Hollander tells Cody, who is a six-footer and very pretty. "They have no class." Cody convinces him he's wrong. "Don't get in the business unless you have your head together," she tells him. "But for the most part, sex is fun, especially when you do it with someone you like." The fascinating overall impression from this tape is that these women may be prototypes of the twenty-first century women who are totally at ease with themselves as naked ladies or ladies enjoying sex whether it be as work or as a romantic, more intimate part of their private lives. Women who have a male outlook about their sexual needs—"I can still love you and have sex with another man whom I don't love"— will require basic adjustment in their moral standards for many men. In addition to the women listed above, Hollander also interviews Merrick Flint, who has a body Charles Atlas would envy. All the interviewers put on laughing demonstrations of sexmaking for the edification of the viewer. Surprisingly, Merrick Flint, known as the Iron Man, has a normal-sized penis which evidently has not kept pace with his other body-building routines.

CHINA CAT   NN   BI   DK (with Johnny doing an anal)
1978   FREEWAY

P/D—Richard Aldrich, Bob Chinn
F/A—John C. Holmes, John Seemen
F/A—Monti Stevens, Ellen Welles, Jennifer Richards

Johnny Wadd gets involved with Charley's Devils (Angels to you) in this one. He has the Jade Pussycat, leftover from another film, and they want it. In the process Johnny is, as usual, a delicate, considerate lover even when one of them orders steak tartare and tells him she loves raw meat. A Chinese girl tries to stab him, and another "devil" gives him knockout drops. It all ends happily and harmlessly.

CONFESSIONS OF LINDA LOVELACE
DK   BI
1974   ARROW

P/D—Unknown
F/A—Harry Reems
F/A—Linda Lovelace

Linda Lovelace is only in this film through a rehash of most of the footage of *Deep Throat* and a loop she made. It's all tied to together with a long sequence from another film called the *Love Witch* by an actress who looks like Linda but isn't (she appears in a veil as she comes from a cemetery and in purdah when she becomes a chaperone to an Arab sheik's daughter). She applies for a job during which she recounts, as you see it on film, what has happened in her life and what is happening to the sheik's daughters as she guides them into womanhood. Arrow should withdraw this tape. It's a con job to cash in on Linda Lovelace, and they have many much better tapes. This one will scare away future buyers.

DEAR PAM: NN   NL (in a silly way)
BI   DK
1976   INTERNATIONAL HOME VIDEO CLUB

P/D—Harold Hindgrind
F/A—John C. Holmes, Tony Perez, Eric Edwards
F/A—C. J. Laing, Jennifer Jordan, Crystal Sync

Harry Phallis (Eric Edwards) writes a letter to Pam Slanders (Crystal Sync), who runs a very moral advice to the lovelorn column for a New York newspaper. In the letter he tells Crystal all about his love life, which includes seducing Gladys Migraine (C. J. Laing), a virgin, to the accompaniment of background music, which repeats, "Harry, fuck me" over and over again. A few weeks later, Gladys informs Harry that he's the father of their baby. Her boyfriend, Norman, couldn't have done it because he had a vasectomy. In the meantime, one night when he comes home Harry finds his stepdaughter sleeping in his bed and murmuring "Bobby, oh Bobby, fuck me." So that she doesn't wake up and feel disappointed (she's crawling in her sleep all over Harry, anyway), Harry obliges. Conflict is provided by Jennifer Jordan,

Tony Perez and John C. Holmes, who, as Citizens for Decency and Morality, are investigating writers of such letters to Dear Pam. The most amazing thing about this sexvid are the penises of Gillis and Perez. (Perez's is equal in length and girth to Johnny's.) All of the women are aghast at the size of them: "My God—this is awful; it will never fit." "You can't fuck me with that thing. You must be kidding." Nevertheless, C. J. Laing manages to deep-throat all of Holmes's wad.

DEEP INSIDE ANNIE SPRINKLES
CC BI DK
1982   VIDEO-X-PIX

P/D—Howard Howard, Annie Sprinkles
F/A—Jake Teague, Ron Jeremy, Ron Hud,
Roger Ram
F/A—Annie Sprinkles, Judy Bilodeau, Lisa Be,
Heather Young, Sassy

All through this tape, which runs an hour and 27 minutes, Annie Sprinkles talks to the guys—not women. But women may want to watch it and be horrified. She tells you her real name is Ellen. She's a Leo. She shows you pictures of herself when she was three, five and 16 with her hymen still intact: "I was afraid it was going to hurt," she says. Then 17, "When my cherry finally got popped." After showing you snapshots of her Mom and Dad, who know what she does for a living, and proving that she's a typical American girl, Annie asks, "Would you like to see what I can do with two hunky men, right now?" She blows them one after the other with total deep throat, and then she discusses her tits. She likes big tits and hopes you do. In fact, she likes them so much that pretty soon she's sucking Sassy's tits, and Sassy is sucking hers. After they rub their cunts together for a while, Ron Jeremy arrives and she brings Ron to a climax—between her tits, of course. Then Annie tells you "I really like a man's ass, and I love to have my ass played with too." But best of all from Annie's point of view is peeing on her guy. In a 20-minute segment, Annie not only reaches a climax but pee-pees on the guy who is eating her vulva. This is followed by a 20-minute-long slumber party which Annie arranges for her girlfriends—

Heather, Bobby, Diane, Judy, Lisa Be and Sasha—which with Annie makes seven. Before you have finished watching this segment, you'll know the different ladies' vulvas better than their faces. Then Annie grins and tells you, "Hi lover. I want to be alone with you—just you and me. I'd like to spread my legs for you . . . You know what I'm thinking about? I'm thinking about you licking my pussy." After which, since you're not there to help her, she takes care of herself with a vibrator. But Annie tells you not to be disappointed. If you see her movies playing anywhere, be sure and go inside. She loves to watch her own films, and who knows? She might just arrive and sit down beside you. Suiting the action to words, she goes inside a theater and takes care of an old gentleman (Jake Teague) who can't believe the lady on the screen has come to life. After an hour and a half, you'll know Annie's body better than you do your own, but you still won't know what really makes her tick.

DESIRES FOR MEN
NN NM DK BI DS
1981   MITCHELL BROTHERS

P/D—Mitchell Brothers/Carol Connors
F/A—Herschel Savage, Lew Mann
F/A—Carol Connors, Long Jeanne Silver,
Nicole Black, Eric Boyer, Jesse Adams

If you are expecting to find the Carol Connors who appeared in the *Candy* series—the naive, trusting, blue-eyed clinging vine—forget it! Carol presumably directed this one herself, and it is strictly for the hard-on male trade who in their entire lifetime are not likely to meet such a sex-hungry bitch as Gena (Carol Connors). She's continuously fishing in guys' pants, extracting their gelungs and saying, "That's it, you hot, stiff prick. You like that, don't you?" Of course the engorged organs don't talk back. They just explode. What plot there is centers around Carol's mother getting very alarmed over the gossip about her daughter's sexual proclivities and trying to get her married. Gena doesn't care whom she seduces; she even fellates her best friend's husband just after he's returned from his honeymoon while his wife is passed out in a chair from drinking too much champagne. But the pièce de résistance, if you can call it that, is a ten-minute detailed close-up of Long Jeanne Silver stumping Carol for ten minutes or more with what remains of her leg. It's pretty throw-uppy to watch. There's also a scene in the Mitchell Brothers' famous Kopenhagen Lounge (which is constantly being closed down and reopened) where nude entertainers sit in the laps of the audience, put on a live sex show while mixed audiences watch and, in this sexvid, get turned on, of course. If you want to see more of Long Jeanne Silver—there's a sexvid devoted wholly to her—see the Supplemental Listing.

DR. LOVE AND HIS HOUSE OF PERVERSIONS **NN BI DK**
1978 VCA

P/D—Robert Michaels
F/A—Bobby Astyr, Mark Anthony, Levi Richards, Rick Iverson, Alan Adrian
F/A—Mary Stuart, Samantha Fox, Margo Barnett, Susie Gold

Dr. Franken Schlong, a.k.a. Dr. Love (Bobby Astyr), in addition to treating nonorgasmic female patients, is creating a monster in his laboratory with the help of a female assistant. The monster, which looks quite plastic, has a huge schlong, of course, and finally ejaculates in a continuous nonstop stream, after which the lab blows up. In between, the female assistant prepares one female patient for the good doctor with a rubber-gloved vaginal massage (shown in amazing full-screen detail) which ends in an ecstatic orgasm. Later, Dr. Love examines another patient (Mary Stuart) whose vagina is too small. He enlarges it with a vibrating dildo after lubricating her with his tongue, and then without asking enlarges her anus, too— much to her surprise and happiness. He also demonstrates how to achieve orgasm with his patients in his outer office in a four-way participation. When the monster blows up, the picture ends with the wording, "To be continued." You'll probably hope not.

EXHAUSTED **CC NN**
1982 CABALLERO

P/D—Julia St. Vincent, Bob Chinn
F/A—John C. Holmes
F/A—Seka, and a dozen other female stars who have appeared with Holmes in movies directed by Bob Chinn, and produced by Damon Christian

If you want to get acquainted with John C. Holmes's magnificent, uncircumcised, 13½ inch penis and the faces of practically every female porn star who has appeared with him since he became Johnny Wadd, then this is a *must* film to buy or rent. What's more, most women will probably like it because Holmes reveals himself as essentially a nice guy in the various discussions which are cleverly intercut. By his own admission he has had sex with over 14,000 women! That includes various orgies, five or six women who usually appear in the various 2,500 porno films he has made, plus freebies of his own choosing. Divide this by ten minutes per female (which is pretty quick) and you come up with over 2,000 hours. Since John C. must be approaching 40, that really only works back to about 200 ten-hour days. Is it work? No way! John C. is asked by an interviewer, "If you had to do it all over again, would you do it?" Answer: "I wouldn't change a stroke." It must have been play. Some things you may not know about John C. are revealed. He had made 1,000 porno films before he was discovered by Bob Chinn and Damon Christian, a.k.a. Richard Aldrich, who literally recreated him and made him an Errol Flynn-style detective named Johnny Wadd. In various films reviewed in this filmography, I have noted John C.'s appearances as BC (before Chinn) and AC (after Chinn). So—what is Holmes really like? This film was made before his arrest as accessory to a shocking murder in the Laurel Canyon area of Los Angeles, and there is no reference on the tape to the fact that John has/had an expensive cocaine habit that kept him broke. In the area of sex and how he treats women in his personal life, he admits that he is three persons: "Myself—the guy who goes to the bathroom and sits on the throne and is the real me. . . . The fantasy me, which is a figment of *your*, the viewer's imagination, and the particular character that I am playing." So when he is with women, even his off-screen relationships are usually not too long-lasting because "women have expectations of being with the guy they see in the film—They don't accept me for who I really am. I'm just a human being." According to Seka, who on this tape has long blonde hair and looks prettier than she ever has, sex with John C. is the best she had ever had in her life. "He knows how to give head, and he's very gentle," she says.

FASCINATION NN BI NL NR (in one sexmaking scene)
1980   QUALITY

P/D—Chuck Vincent, Larry Revene
F/A—Ron Jeremy, Eric Edwards
F/A—Candida Royalle, Veronica Hart, Merle Michaels

In films, Ron Jeremy is usually the bad guy and has a minor role. Probably not over five foot six, he has a magnificent penis which in other films he often quite easily puts in his mouth. In this one he doesn't have to. As Ernie Gordon, a guy who has always lived at home and been driven crazy by Mom, he can't seem to make out with women. Discovering a book called *How To Become a Successful Seducer*, chapter by chapter he puts the advice into practice. The first requirement is to have his own bachelor's pad and cut the umbilical cord. Momma is very shocked when he tells her he's moving out, but he breaks one of the book's rules: "Don't give a key to your apartment to your mother." Ernie has no choice. "Leaving home after all I have done for you," Mommy sobs. But Mom doesn't stop Ernie from following the rest of the rules. "No seductions until your pad is ready. It should have a respectable look on the surface." Poor Ernie—most of his seductions get screwed up without him getting screwed. First, woman's husband arrives just before Ernie climaxes, and he forces Ernie to watch him really service his wife. Then Ernie invites Merle Michaels, who never stops talking. He prepares an elaborate dinner for his next conquest and, course by course, she rejects his offerings. She finally confesses, to his shock, that he shouldn't have bothered. She enjoys sex more than food. Finally, his father filches Mom's key to the apartment and brings his girlfriend there (unknown to Ernie). At the same time, his sister, Victoria (Candida Royalle), arrives with her boyfriend and soon Ernie comes home with two macho women he has picked up in a singles bar. With everyone playing hide and seek in the apartment, the hookers really work over Ernie. Chuck Vincent (who, like many adult film producers, makes an appearance in his films) can be seen in this one. He's sitting in a porno theater beside Ernie, smoking a cigar. This is a film that will appeal to many a middle-class bachelor who may empathize with Ernie and his cornucopia of women, and many women will think Ron Jeremy, as Ernie, is kind of cute.

FULFILLMENT NN NL
1972–1973   SELECT/ESSEX

P/D—Billy Thornberg
F/A—John C. Holmes, Edward Roehm
F/A—Sharon Yorke, Barbara Barton, Claudine Grayson

If you are a Johnny Wadd (John C. Holmes) aficionado, you should own this one. (He claims he's made 3,000 films and screwed 14,000 women.) It's a collection of loops that Holmes made before Richard Aldrich and Bob Chinn recreated him as a Clint Eastwood-style detective, in the famous Johnny Wadd series. Here, his hair is marcelled, brown and wavy, but his redoubtable penis is something to see. How one woman manages to deep throat him, and another tiny slip of a woman manages to contain him reveals the potential of some mouths and vaginas. The loops are tied together by Edward Roehm, a heavy-built man wearing a top hat who tells you in a Dutch accent that Johnny Wadd is a legend in his own time, and with his 13½ inch penis is the Paul Bunyan of the bedroom. All through the film, Johnny is very gentle with the women: "Tell me if I'm giving you too much. Don't let me hurt you." The NL rating is a test of your ability to laugh whether you're male and envious—or female and scared to death.

INSIDE DESIREE COUSTEAU   much BI   some DK
1979   VCX

P/D—Leon Gucci
F/A—John Holmes
F/A—Desiree Cousteau, Serena, Susan Nero

This sexvid is literally inside Desiree. She doesn't act the *Pretty Peaches* part and spends more time with Serena and other women than with Johnny Holmes. But she is still the melting woman of most male fantasies. It ends with the typical group sex scene.

INSIDE GEORGINA SPELVIN
NN   BI   NM some NL
1974   WONDERFUL WORLD OF VIDEO

P/D—John Christopher
F/A—Marc Stevens, Jeffrey Hurst
F/A—Georgina Spelvin, Darby Lloyd Raines, Linda Terry

There's more of Darby and Linda Terry in this one than Georgina, but the few scenes in which she appears as Gloria Box reveal a laughing woman and a silly one who may be closer to reality than the dramatic actress. Some amusing scenes include a younger Marc Stevens trying to prove with the help of two ladies (a joint effort) tha he really has 11 inches erect. Linda Terry takes an extended piss for guys who have never seen a woman urinate and masturbates in the tub with running water. Harmless . . . but no plot!

INSIDE JENNIFER WELLES   NN   BI one DK mass suck off
1977   VIDEO-X

P/D—Howard Howard, Jennifer Welles
F/A—Ken Anders, Richard Bolla
F/A—Jennifer Welles

If you like Jennifer Welles, you may enjoy this plotless sexvid of a woman screwing herself and every male in sight from stem to stern, or you may run it fast forward because you'll get bored with the 22 men in this film.

INSIDE MARILYN CHAMBERS
CC   NN   BI   DK
1976   MITCHELL BROTHERS HOME ENTERTAINMENT

P/D—Mitchell Brothers
F/A—Johnny Keyes, George McDonald
F/A—Marilyn Chambers

While you still won't really know what goes on in Marilyn Briggs's (Chambers's) mind after you have watched this one, it's by far the most interesting of the "inside" porno star films. Not only Marilyn, but Johnny Keyes and George McDonald discuss the making of *Behind the Green Door* and *The Resurrection of Eve*, and they give you some insight into their feelings and emotions in making porn films. Marilyn enjoys acting out her rape fantasies, and Keyes tells how he had five "nuts" (climaxes) with Marilyn during one scene, but nevertheless managed to keep thrusting inside her. George McDonald reveals that after having sex with Marilyn for several hours and not climaxing, or being able to, with the crew watching he asked her in the shower to relieve him—which she did by hand because she was too sore to continue vaginally. There are many behind-the-scenes of porno movie making. Some scenes are included which were edited from the final version of the two films for one reason or another. But if you really want to see inside Marilyn Chambers, rent or buy *Never a Tender Moment* (see listing).

INSIDE SEKA   NN   NM   BI   DK
1980   VIDEO-X-PIX

P/D—Howard Howard, Ken and Seka
F/A—Ken and others
F/A—Seka, Merle Michaels

Complete with a theme song, this one stars Ken, Seka's husband, plus about 20 other people you've never seen before in an adult film. Ken obviously hasn't a jealous bone in his body. Seka loves them all: the long, the short, and the tall, and one, two, three at a time. She also, in her own words, has a "juicy pussy" for Merle Michaels. An extended sequence with Merle and Seka and one with Seka masturbating (ten minutes or more each) are really a sex education for males. This is a male–oriented sexvid, replete with strip scenes, garter belts and black silk stockings. An extended sequence inside Plato's Retreat completes the tape with a non-stop group sex scene. The film ends with Seka's statement, "Ken and I have been married six years and have never been separated during this time. All the scenes in this picture are true and accurate representations of my actual experiences." You'll know a great deal about Seka's body when you finish but what goes on in her mind is still a mystery. Worth owning because after this can only be the deluge! If you want more of Seka, see the tape *Rocking with Seka.*

INTIMATE REALITIES #1
NN NM DK BI
1983 VCA

P/D—Richard Wright
F/A—Ron Jeremy, Kevin James, Steve
   Saunders, Ken Starbuck, Tom Byron, Mark
   Richards
F/A—Serena, Cara Lott, Shawna Evans, Ricki
   Lane, Gina La Rosta, Dominique, Lori
   Smith, Candice Ray

Serena, dressed in a white circus ringmaster costume, is your host to this sex circus which purports to give you "a unique inside view of the sex lives of adult film actors." It doesn't! But there's Ron Jeremy screwing Gina La Rosta—presumably her first time on film—with some very athletic sexmaking. Then there's Shawna Evans as a sexual submissive, being strapped to what is evidently known in the trade as a "sexual inversion cot." Dressed in tight black satin, Dominique whips and teases her while she's upside down and laps her from head to foot. But Shawna enjoys it and murmurs ecstatically. "Don't stop." Soon two guys arrive and they try a foursome. In between Serena plays with herself and then Ken Starbuck screws Candice Ray on top of a nice looking private bar in someone's Beverly Hills mansion. They are followed by Ricki Lane and Mark Richards who places Ricki in a plastic seat which is supposedly a "black monster." Actually it's a special

screwing chair that tips the female pelvis invitingly upward and spread. Larry Flynt advertised them for many years in *Hustler.* If you want further details try my novel *The Byrdwhistle Option* (Buffalo, New York: Prometheus Books, 1982) in which I satirized them as a mail order item. Finally in this one there's Cara Lott and Kevin James watching themselves on five television monitors as they screw and suck, and Serena wraps it up in bed with Lori Smith because: "I really like ladies a lot." Let's hope they do better with Intimate Realities #2.

THE LIBERATION OF HONEYDOLL JONES **CC NN BI NL NR**
1978 VCX

P/D—Aaron Linn, Katherine Montgomery,
   Charles de Santos
F/A—Not given on the credits
F/A—Virginia Winter, Tracy O'Neil, Candida
   Royalle

Some women may not think this one should have an NR rating. You have to accept Honeydoll's morals (or lack of them), but she is romantic—even when Bobby Jarvis' Daddy catches and rapes her. "I wanted to push him off, but it felt good. It was so dirty—me and Bobby's Daddy, but it was so nice," she says. Or when she takes off with two travelling salesmen and stays with them in a nearby motel taking them both on in bed. Seems Honeydoll (Virginia Winter) has a Mamma, a Daddy and two very horny sisters—Big Sister, and the younger Laureen. Honeydoll is in love with Bobby Jarvis, their neighbor, whose Daddy owns a run-down Southwestern squatter farm that's as disreputable looking as her own. Daddy Jarvis and the Joneses have been feuding for years, and while Honeydoll dreams of doing it with Bobby, her sister beats her to it. Laureen (Tracy O'Neil) also enjoys a little sexmaking with Big Sister. But Big Sister's husband, the "Cadillac Man" (he buys and sells old Cadillacs and isn't very faithful either), takes on Daddy Jarvis' daughter (Candida Royalle), who very obligingly screws with him on top of a Cadillac. Daddy Jarvis catches them and whips her bare behind, but in the process she unzips his pants and asks, "Am I doin' it right, Pa?"

Answer: "Sweetest daughter a man ever had." What makes this one worth seeing is that it was actually shot on a farm and hence is pleasant change from typical New York City or Los Angeles backgrounds. The cinematography is very naturalistic, as is the sexmaking, and Honeydoll finally gets her man—Bobby forgives her—and lives happily ever after. At least until, as she explains at the end, she meets Frank and Jerry.

THE LIFE AND TIMES OF XAVIERA HOLLANDER NN NL BI DK
1974   QUALITY

P/D—Larry G. Spangler
F/A—Rick Cassidy, John Holmes, Ric Lutz
F/A—Samantha McClearn, Karen Stacy, Paula Stone

Xaviera acts in this one both as a voice-over and (fully dressed) guest star in the story of her life which is acted by Samantha McClearn, a nicely buxom lady of about 130 pounds. As her Xaviera alter ego, Samantha has her first sexual encounter in the back seat of a limousine with a wealthy guy from whom she has hitchhiked a ride afer a day at Hollywood High School. "After that I screwed everybody," Xaviera tells the listener, "the entire football, baseball and basketball teams. I knew that after this introduction that sex was something I wanted to practice over and over like an athlete. Practice makes perfect." Xaviera not only loves men but enjoys women, too, and feels no guilt with her female lovers. A long sequence takes place in what presumably was one of Xaviera's brothels (she considers herself the world's foremost madam) and her girls play scrimmage football wearing only tops—no bottoms. Xaviera (named after the famous Catholic brothers) also enjoys John C. Holmes (you wouldn't recognize him except for his famous member), plays sexual games with three guys dressed like the Three Musketeers, and gets screwed on top of a pool table. At the end she gets married and thanks the preacher with fellatio.

MAI LIN VS SERENA   DK   Total BI
1982   HIFCOA

P/D—Troy Benny
F/A—Carlos Tobalina, Ray Guerra, Jon Martin
F/A—Mai Lin, Serena, Jesse Adams, Retama
Haag, Jade Wong, Anne Fisher, Melanie Smith, Martine DuBois

If you're male and bring this one home to your wife or girlfriend, you may end a long friendship. The plot? Carlos Tobalina offers $25,000 to either Mai Lin or Serena, whoever can prove herself "the hottest" or sexiest. Presto, our ladies are in a restaurant and Mai Lin tells Serena, "See that guy over there? I'm going to fuck him." Soon everyone in the restaurant is happily screwing. Next scene is practically a repeat in a bar where Mai Lin and Serena are having a "happy hour" with some girlfriends, and soon everyone is stretched out lapping each other. They are joined by the bartender and a few males who wander in. But the pièce de résistance is the conclusion. Mai Lin and Serena have an ordinary bathtub painted pink. They are in some kind of hotel with several dozen males waiting to join them in their room. When the guys arrive, both ladies get in the tub facing east and west, and as the guys flow into the room (some of them are wearing masks—probably because they don't want to be ever identified), Mai Lin and Serena jerk and suck them off until they literally are enjoying a shower. Although Carlos decides that they both win the bet and each will get $25,000, my guess is that they probably didn't get any more than $500 apiece, and the whole thing was shot on a long weekend.

MARILYN CHAMBERS'S FANTASIES #1 CC NN BI DK
1983   CREATIVE IMAGE

P/D—Not given
F/A—Not given
F/A—Marilyn Chambers, Annette Haven

The only reason this has a CC rating is for Marilyn Chambers's aficionados and those who may wish to speculate on what makes Marilyn tick sexually. Unfortunately, only about half the tape has Marilyn on it. The rest are fantasies that she presumably has about screwing in olden days, but are actually two long cuts from *The Spirit of Seventy Sex* (see listing) and really screws up (pun intended) this tape. The section in which Marilyn appears first is an old one with John C. Holmes, who arrives in her gymnasium where she has been exercising (wearing a bathing suit) and doing gymnastics that would confound Jane Fonda. Holmes punches a bag naked and soon his doughty weapon is inside Marilyn's vagina. The second bit is an eye-popping, unbelievable fifteen minute bisexual sequence on the floor of a single-lane bowling alley where you will become better acquainted with Marilyn's labia, vagina and rosebud than you are with her face. In the process she attempts to insert a duck pin into her tunnel, and the tape concludes with a bowling ball coming down the alley aimed straight at her crotch.

MARLENE'S WORLD **N N BI DK**
1977   BLUE VIDEO

P/D—Mister Mustard
F/A—Jim Crane
F/A—Marlene Willoughby, Samantha Fox, Merle Michaels

Despite the title, this is not an "inside" or "all about" Marlene Willoughby... which is just as well. It's really about Dolly (Merle Michaels), who is married to Elton (Jim Crane), and because he's complaining about the bills and the high cost of living, decides to get a job. En route she encounters Marlene (Marlene Willoughby), a hooker. Marlene convinces Dolly to try her first trick. Dolly is so naive that when she gets him in the hotel room she tries to kiss him until he directs her to where her mouth should be. Proudly bringing her first earnings to Elton, who is supposed to become a doctor (he really doesn't look as if he has graduated from the sixth grade), she doesn't know that the next day he has spent her hard-earned money on a black hooker. In keeping with the O. Henry-style plot, finally Marlene works out a *triple* for Dolly, which includes Samantha Fox, who has also been paid for fun in the sack by Elton with Dolly's money. Naturally Dolly is

surprised when she finds that the john is her hubby, Elton. Pretty ho-hum.

MS. MAGNIFICENT **NN BI DK and one DS anal scene**
1979   SELECT ESSEX

P/D—Richard Aldrich, Joe Sherman
F/A—John Seeman, Robert McCallum
F/A—Desiree Cousteau, Jesie St. James

Superwoman is the only dirty word that is bleeped out of this sexvid. Richard Aldrich, a.k.a. Damon Christian, was forced to change the name to *Ms. Magnificent* by the owners of *Superman*. If the story had concentrated on Superwoman and saving females from nasty bastards as she does with one guy, yanking and twisting his penis so hard that all male viewers will shiver, more women might like this one.

PLATO'S—THE MOVIE **NN much DK some BI**
1980   SELECT ESSEX

P/D—Richard Aldrich, Joe Sherman
F/A—William Margold
F/A—Seka, Lisa de Leeuw

A totally plotless sexvid, unless you can accept that Seka (her real name is Dorothy Hundley Patton) is a reporter investigating what is happening at Plato's Retreat West before it closed down. Richard Aldrich lost his sense of humor in this one. But Seka gives a good acting performance, presumably enjoying anal sex among other things.

PLEASURE CRUISE **NM NL BI**
Early 1970s   BLUE VIDEO

P/D—Don Lang
F/A—Harry Reems
F/A—Andrea True, Sandy King

Captain Nemo (Harry Reems, whom you first see with his penis in a sneaker as he watches his wife, Andrea True, undress) owns an ancient motor yacht. He takes three couples aboard for a weekend cruise in what looks like Long Island Sound. Andrea True, who has an English accent, admits she was born in London.

Reems obviously enjoyed himself making this film. He is totally zany—seducing and being seduced by the female guests. In between, as what story there is progresses, Andrea pants at the male viewer with close-ups of her, and invites the watcher to jump out of his seat and relieve her "hots" for him. There's lots of natural kissing, foreplay and genital closeups with no come shots in this flick, which runs for about 60 minutes.

ROCKIN' WITH SEKA **NN BI DK**
1980 CABALLERO

P/D—Billy Thornberg, Ziggy Zigowitz
F/A—John Holmes, Jamie Gillis
F/A—Seka, Patricia Lee, Judy Carr

Seka's an airline stewardess in this one, and, as Sweet Alice, tells about her recent sex life. A plotless, nonstop, garter belt, black stocking, sucking and fucking (GBSF) epic. Most women will detest Seka. She's so clinically sexually aggressive that in real life she'd probably scare many men into permanent impotence. Things you've never seen before: Roberto—an electric penis designed so that the female user can control the stroke speed and length. It competes with John and Jamie. Seka sucks lollipops, but like Ronald Reagan's jelly beans, too much of either will turn your stomach.

SERENA, AN ADULT FAIRY TALE
NN BI DK
1979 WONDERFUL WORLD OF VIDEO

P/D—Vinnie Rossi, Fred Lincoln
F/A—Jamie Gillis, Paul Thomas
F/A—Serena, China Leigh

The story line, if you pay attention, is about a modern Cinderella left to a mean old madam and her daughters. Serena, as Cindy, has all her orifices thoroughly explored. For economy's sake, the midnight ball is held downstairs in the madam's house, but Cindy's fairy godmother gives her permission to attend and tells her that she "may fuck and suck to her heart's content until midnight." You've seen everything before (except Serena) in detail.

SOFT PLACES **NN NM BI DK**
1977 TVX

P/D—William Dancer, Wray Hamilton
F/A—Phil Tobias, Paul Thomas
F/A—Annette Haven

Adult filmmakers who are trapped by all the must-be-included conventions of adult films have a difficult time incorporating them into one believable plot. Even if you suspend disbelief, you won't believe this one. Monique's (Annette Haven) husband, Michael, dies in an accident. You never see him, but he leaves a will on audio tape which his lawyer, Marshall (Paul Thomas), tells Monique is unbreakable. Seems that Monique was frigid, and their sex life a mess. Now, beyond the grave, Michael is going to get her. If she wants to inherit his millions she must do five things. 1. Learn to love herself—ergo, masturbate. 2. Exhibit herself to a strange male and suck his cock. 3. Give herself to another woman. 4. Show her power as a woman by teasing men and forcing them to rape her. 5. Finally love a man as much as he loved her—so much so that the guy can urinate on her face and she'll still adore him. Marshall is adamant. Monique must carry out the terms of the will if she wishes to inherit the money. So she does. By the time she gets to condition number four, Marshall changes his mind and decides that Michael's will can be broken. In the final scene Monique is in bed with Marshall, enjoying normal sex, but suddenly she tips an urn over on the sheets. It's filled with Michael's ashes and she happily rubs them on Marshall's back, thus proving that she was better than Michael ever realized. Male Annette Haven aficionados may like this one—the entire sexual action with a few minor exceptions is concentrated on her. But many guys will wonder why she does it, and how after all these years she still manages to stay so pretty.

SULKA'S WEDDING **CC DK BI NL**
(Note there is no other N-rating. There's nothing normal about the sex in this one.)
1983 CABALLERO

P/D—Kim Cristy, Mike Stryker
F/A—Craig Roberts, Ron Jeremy
F/A—Sulka, Sharon Mitchell, Tigr, Jamie Ling, Jennifer Thomas, Mindy Williams

A few years ago, Sulka, who was a transsexual with full breasts and a penis, made several tapes, including *Dream Lovers* and *The Transformation of Sulka* (see listings, pp. 263 and 228). Evidently she had an operation to remove her penis and now she has a vagina. So someone got the mad idea to make a film about Sulka's wedding day. You see her calling friends and inviting them to the wedding and a garden party reception afterwards. In the meantime, while Sulka is playing with herself, remembrances of when she had a penis (also while masturbating) are intercut into the conversation. Ron Jeremy arrives and she sucks him off. He's screwing her doggy-style when the doorbell rings. Sulka tells him coolly he'll have to take care of himself. He immediately does, by putting his cock in his mouth. "Fuck it—I'm just as good as she is," he says. To add to the insanity, throughout the film the radio is turned on to AM and FM radio stations KOCK and CUNT, respectively. The commercials offer kits to do your own home surgery and remove unwanted testicles; derma drugs to hide the pimples on your ass; mobile abortion clinics; a new country band called Saddle Sores, and a rock song called "Spread Your Legs, Baby." If this isn't enough, every time a beautiful new woman appears on your tube (with the exception of Sharon Mitchell and Tigr, a.k.a. Chelsea Manchester, you slowly discover they have pricks between their legs which neither Tigr or Sharon hesitate to suck off. Tigr takes on two men orally while suspended from the ceiling at her own request. Finally the wedding occurs between Craig Roberts (known in the film as Paul) and Sulka, after which there is an extended wedding party orgy. Why the CC rating, you may ask? Simply because you've never seen anything so balmy in your life, but you'd better be half-mulled when you watch it, or you'll throw up. And yes, you'll see Sulka's new vagina in close-up detail.

TEENAGE DEVIATE   NN   DK   BI
1976   VIDEO-X-PIX

P/D—Leo de Leon, Ralph Ell
F/A—John Jean
F/A—Annie Sprinkle, Ms. Dunkle, Nikki Hilton

This is one of the most realistic, believable hard-core sexvids you can buy. An excellent story device has Annie Sprinkle talking to her psychiatrist and telling him about her overprotective mother, whom she leaves to live in New York City with her cousin, Audrey, a hooker. Annie Sprinkle does a superb acting job. The dialogue is believable and natural. Annie's problem ("I always end up in situations where I like the guy but he doesn't turn out the way I thought he would be") gives her instant identification with millions of women. Worth owning. Proves that concentrating on one female is more erotic than skipping through a film story with a half-dozen.

TRAMP (THIS LADY IS A)
CC   NN   NL   BI   DK
1980   CAL VISTA

P/D—Chuck Vincent
F/A—Richard Bolla, Ron Jeremy, Kurt Mann, George Payne, Bobby Astyr
F/A—Samantha Fox, Gloria Leonard, Merle Michaels

Buy or rent this one to watch nicely plump Samantha Fox play all her various roles in one film. She won the Best Actress award in 1980 at the Erotic Film Festival for the second year in a row (in 1979 for *Babylon Pink*). As Dana Sue in this one, she's being divorced by her multimillionaire husband (Richard Bolla) after a quick marriage arranged by her friend Vera (Gloria Leonard). Richard has discovered she isn't one of the prestigious Boston Hancocks she proclaimed herself to be, and she wasn't really brought up on Beacon Street in the Back Bay—she is nothing but a tramp. Dana Sue doesn't think so, even though at 16 years old she sucked lollipops and her best boy friend's cock. She shows her stepfather how she did it with Frank in the back seat of his car. "I'm a very bad girl," she tells him just before her mother catches her in flagrante delicto. "But isn't it fun!" Then, kicked out of her poor white trash home by Mommy, she hitchhikes to New York, blows the driver in appreciation, and is soon watching a live sex show hosted by Ron Jeremy with Veri Knotty as a dominatrix. Veri Knotty concludes her act of beating a woman into submission by doing her specialty—tying her labia in a knot. Dana Sue is properly appreciative of her talent. Her companion at the theater, Vera, hires Dana Sue to appear in a porno movie where she can play the female hussy and beat up Bobby Astyr. (In real life Bobby and Samantha sleep together.) Finally, on her Jamaican honeymoon, Richard, her new husband, is running in and out of the bedroom catering to her various demands. Meanwhile, she has the bellboy stashed in the bathroom and happily blows him while she tells Richard to be gentle with her, she's a virgin. Back home in Richard's palatial mansion, she jumps in bed with the butler and maids, and finally, "a prisoner to Richard's warped moral values," she's sequestered in her bedroom. But she's not alone. She's got a guy in bed with her whom you never have seen before. Richard catches her as the guy leaves. You still don't see his face. Next day in court where the divorce settlement is being determined, the judge finally appears. She smiles happily at him. But not until he faces the court do you know who he is. Her last lover, of course!

TRANSFORMATION OF SULKA R
1981   BIZARRE

This half-hour tape has no explicit sex. It begins with Sulka explaining in a voice-over as she walks along a beach the difference between homosexuals, drag queens, transvestites and transsexuals. Sulka is a transsexual. You see her dancing almost naked with very large, artificial-looking breasts—but obviously the shoulders and legs of a female. Unfortunately, except for a number of still shots, you never see her with a penis. Evidently the movie was made after Sulka was operated on and provided with a vagina.

15

Cops and Robbers

A GIRL'S BEST FRIEND **NN DK BI**
1981 QUALITY

※※

P/D—Robert Sumner, Henri Pachard
F/A—Ron Jeremy, Richard Bolla, Bobby Astyr
F/A—Juliet Anderson, Veronica Hart, Samantha
**   Fox, Jody Maxwell, Merle Michaels**

Mrs. Lautrec (Juliet Anderson) and her son, Paul (believe it or not, Ron Jeremy), are jewel thieves. While Mom entrances people like the count (Richard Bolla) in the sack, Son ransacks the mansion, looking for the Fairchild diamond to complete a set of two they have already acquired. Before the diamond moves to New York (sold by the count to Irving Greenfield, a very wealthy importer), son Ron ends up in the sack with Lady Colgate and her daughter, played by Merle Michaels, who shares Paul. Back in New York, still after the elusive diamond, they meet Irving Greenfield (Bobby Astyr) at a New York disco. Son Ron filches his billfold after being masturbated at the bar by the Lady in Red (Samantha Fox, who never appears again). Mom returns Irving's billfold telling him he must have dropped it in the disco club. Irving invites Mom to a dinner at his house. Turns out Irving is related to Henry VIII . . . and while Son, as chauffeur, is screwing Charlotte, the maid in the kitchen, Irving is literally eating Mom as she lies stretched out on the dining room table. Mom discovers that the Fairchild diamond is in Irving's safe, but so does Charlotte, who finds the combination and writes it on her breast. While the guests at a masquerade party are enjoying each other, Charlotte steals the diamond. Disgusted, Mom and Son join the orgy party, and so as not to look conspicuous, Mom tells son to make love to her. "Mom, you couldn't," he says. "Son," she replies "You wouldn't?" But of course they do and become great lovers and live happily ever after with Charlotte, whom they catch trying to steal their diamonds. Juliet Anderson plays her cool, aloof, almost masculine self. Her semi-detached, totally assured approach to sex in reality might emasculate most men. This film may appeal to a highly sophisticated upper-income New York or San Francisco audience, but it won't play well in Sandusky.

ABDUCTION OF LORELEI
CC NN DS BI (lots of)
1978 BLUE VIDEO

※※

P/D—Richard Rank
F/A—John Galt, Charles Neal
F/A—Serena, Jenny Gillian, Monique Perrij

For better or worse, the first 25 minutes of this sexvid has the most believable kidnapping-rape scene you've ever seen. It will frighten most women, but perverse or not it probably reaches primitive areas of most male brains and will sexually arouse them. It's worth owning for a male-female discussion on this point. It begins deceptively with Serena, playing the part of Lorelei, an obviously rich young woman who is shopping through high-class stores, looking at expensive jewelry and clothing and finally buying lipstick. Driving later in her Lincoln Continental, she uses the car telephone to call her father and discovers he is leaving on a short business trip. You are now aware that she is being followed. When she stops again near a shopping center, a van and another car pull up beside her. Two men jump out, grab her, toss her in the van and one of them viciously rapes her for ten or 15 minutes in the van while the other guy drives. Later, as the captive not only of the two guys, but a woman, Lorelei is tied and abused. Then, the turnabout occurs. The woman, Jenny, unties her. The de rigeur bisexual scene occurs and the plot slowly runs down. Instead of maintaining the shock and trauma of her rape or trying to escape, Lorelei is suddenly enjoying her female captor sexually. Before the flick is over, one of the guys shoots and kills the other guy when he tries to rape Lorelei. But eventually Lorelei seduces the guy who raped her and murders him so that she can live happily ever after with Jenny, the female kidnapper. Good acting for the most part. This one raises the question: If you portray any kind of violence in the arts, including sexual violence, shouldn't the material reflect some moral judgment against the violence? This one really doesn't.

ALLEY CAT NN BI DK DS
1983 ALLEY CATS PRODUCTION

P/D—Bosley M. Crawford
F/A—Sal Vitelli, Ron Jeremy, Buddy Hatton, David Christopher
F/A—Alexis X, Stephanie Sunshine, Lindy Jackov, Laurie Jackov

Among other things Bosley Crawford is the editor of *Adult Cinema Magazine*. He produced this film on a low budget in New York City with unknowns except for Ron Jeremy who should have begged off. But parts of the film and especially the dialogue are so sickly squalid and seamy that they may have a ring of truth. It most certainly is like no other porno film. The time frame is the future when nude female boxing has become a national spectator sport. Alley Cat (Alexis X) is determined to become champion of the world without compromising herself in the locker room where between and after fights her sisters are screwing managers so that they can get matches. Alley Cat is determined to get to the top. Two female boxers pin Alley Cat down while Ron Jeremy ramming into her proves what she's been missing. The locker-room scenes of cruel sex and dialogue are interspersed with quite a few scenes of naked ladies slugging it out with each other in the ring. Alexis X comes through as a sad but believable tough lady. You can buy this tape direct from Alley Cat Productions, Box 1363, RCU New York, NY 10185. In all probability your video dealer won't have it. Alley Cat Productions will also send you details of a film that *you* can star in called *My First Porno* which includes beautiful ladies playing with and talking to the snapshot of yourself that you send them.

AMERICAN PIE NN BI
1980 SELECT/ESSEX

P/D—Damon Christian, Jeffrey Fairbanks
F'A—Eric Edwards
F/A—Lysa Thatcher, Arcadia Lake, Kitty Shane

The first adult film to be produced with Dolby sound. This one is presumably a tongue-in-cheek "Ransom of Red Chief" plot. While the wealthy Daddy Chandler is screwing the French maid and his wife is upstairs in bed with her boyfriend, two seedy characters kidnap their debutante daughters. Along with a waitress they've picked up to help them collect a $20,000 ransom, they hide out in a mountain lodge. But Daddy thinks his sophisticated daughters are playing a joke on him. "You can have them," he says. So what do they all do together? You guessed it! Potentially a plot with many conflicts. Alas, it got sidetracked. But just to prove you can't trust the critics, *Adam Film World* rated this film number ten in their 1982 annual listing of the top ten adult films. As will be apparent if you read all of these reviews, I personally like Richard Aldrich, a.k.a. Damon Christian, but know he can do and has done better.

ANYTIME, ANYPLACE **CC NN NL**
1982 VCX

P/D—**Helen Terrie, Kirdy Stevens**
F/A—**Mike Ranger, Jesse Atlanta, William Margold**
F/A—**Seka, Nicole Noir, Tara Flynn, Lee Carol**

Some day, some adult film producer is going to do with Seka what Blake Edwards did with Julie Andrews—reverse the image. Kirdy Stevens comes closer to the idea in this one than any other director. This time, Seka is given a chance to act (she can) not as a dominating woman but as a fluffier, more vulnerable one. As Lynne, she's played off between two ex-cons, Skinner (Mike Ranger) and Chickie (Jesse Atlanta). After some very nice sexmaking which opens the film, Lynn asks Skinner, "Why do I have to fuck Chickie all the time? I love you. I just want to ball you." But Chickie is Skinner's former cell mate. "What's mine is his," he tells Lynne, and a few minutes later, when Skinner picks Chickie up in a van, he tells Lynne to get in back and take care of poor Chickie, which she does reluctantly. When she finishes, Chickie looks at her adoringly and tells her, "I wish you loved me as much as you do Skinner." With this underlying relationship, the trio embark on a series of burglaries because this is the easiest way to make a living. Since they are mainly after jewelry, Skinner contends, "We're doing people a favor. They'll collect more from the insurance company than we steal." From this point on, Helen Terrie, who wrote the screenplay, tells a Chaucerian story that involves all three of them. First, in one wealthy home (where to their later dismay Seka steals only perfume, animal stuffies and soap), the female owner arrives home with her lover, trapping them in the next room. To top it off, while she (Nicole Noir) is blissfully screwing, unaware that she's being watched, her husband arrives home and her lover has to join the thieves. In sequence after sequence they are bumbling crooks who can't even pawn the stuff they make off with. Thinking they are stealing computers from an electronics company while Lynne tries to seduce the guard, they later discover they have stolen boxes of dildos. When Seka goes off on her own, she ends up in someone's wealthy mansion in the midst of an orgy which is interestingly choreographed. One of the women loses her huge diamond which Lynne quickly appropriates and leaves. Amazingly, there are no bisexual scenes, but one sequence that could have been eliminated at the very end is with Lee Carol, whose breasts look as if they were pasted on her. Ultimately, after Lynne leaves Skinner in disgust that she has to service his friend, Skinner, of course, realizes that he can't live without her.

COVER GIRL (CHERYL HANSON)
NN BI
1981 SELECT ESSEX

P/D—**Alex de Renzy**
F/A—**John Leslie, David Morris, Joey Civera**
F/A—**Cheryl Hanson and other unidentified "cover girls"**

Alex de Renzy, who created *Pretty Peaches* (see p. 121) lost his touch on this one. A top model agent, known in the trade as a total bastard, is murdered just as Cheryl arrives for an interview. Thinking she is having sex with the agent, whose name is Max Fowler, she doesn't know he's dead until she tries to take a shower after her session. Who was the murderer? Then, who should fall out of the shower but the real Max? Who did Cheryl actually sleep with? Believe it or not, she didn't see his face, but she remembers a tattoo on his thigh. For the rest of the film, Joey Civera as the detective tries to find the guy with the word Lulu tattooed on his leg. Cheryl Hanson has a pretty face but can't act. Beyond one scene where you watch a tattoo artist inscribe a tattoo on a lady's ass, there's nothing in this one you haven't seen before.

DOUBLE EXPOSURE OF HOLLY
NN DK with some nearly DS sex
1977 TVX

P/D—Ronan O'Casey
FA/—Jamie Gillis, Bobby Astyr, Don Petersen
F/A—Catherine Earnshaw, Annie Sprinkle, Terri Hall

Sex, drugs and murder are mixed with such involved editing and jump cutting that you'll quickly lose the blackmail plot. The story line revolves around the videotaping of Holly's sexual activities by a gangster employed by her lover who plans to blackmail her new boyfriend and expose her to her husband. A line from the sexvid: "Holly uses people like toilet paper. She wipes her ass with people." So does this sexvid.

EXPENSIVE TASTES **CC DS DK BI**
1978 VCX

P/D—William Dancer, Jennifer Ray
F/A—Joseph Nassi, John Leslie, Ken Scudder
F/A—Fannie Essex, Elaine Wells, Phaery Burd

A sick, scary story about a man who looks for young virgins, dates them and entices them to his apartment, where his three friends (one a woman), all wearing ski masks, burst in and rape his victims (and him, as a cover). The rape sequence is done twice with thoroughly nauseating detail and pretty good acting. If nothing else, this sexvid provides a test tape for psychologists investigating male sex arousal by rape and for any male who wishes to test his own subconscious feelings.

FAST CARS/FAST WOMEN
CC NN BI NM DK
1979 SELECT ESSEX

P/D—David Tear/Scott McHaley
F/A—Ken Gibson, Al Chiurrizzi, Ron Jeremy
F/A—Kay Parker, Carolyn Jackson, Lisa Lane

The CC rating for this one is because it tells a coherent story, intermixed with much sex, that is equal to any you'll see in your average television serial. Molly Davis (Kay Parker) is a very cool and wealthy woman who owns racing cars. A guy named Orson McNight (Al Chiurrizzi) manufactures McKnight Tires and has tampered with one of her cars in a previous race and the driver, a woman, was killed. Now Molly has hired a new driver, Christy Hollis (Lisa Lane), a champion driver who will race in the All American 500 (race track unidentified). Christy is a good driver, but when she uses sex to obtain her objectives, like fixing a speeding ticket or trying to get a new guy hired as a pit boss, she's the one who gets screwed—figuratively as well as literally. Ron Jeremy as Dutch and Al Chiurrizzi as Orson look as if they stepped out of a Godfather movie. But their dirty work is foiled by one of the good guys.

HUMAN EXPERIMENTS **CC R**
1980 VIDAMERICA

P/D—Sumner and Edwin Brown, Gregory Goodell
F/A—Geoffrey Lewis, Aldo Ray
F/A—Linda Haynes, Ellen Travolta, Mercedes Shirley

Although this film is not a so-called adult film because there is only brief nudity and no explicit sex, I have included it because like many porno films, it depends on a common plot—the subjection of women. Rachel Foster (beautifully played by Linda Haynes) receives a life term in a woman's prison after being found guilty of a triple murder which was actually perpetrated by the deranged son of a family she didn't even know. Once in prison, she falls into the hands of an insane psychiatrist whose mission in life is to bring recalcitrant female inmates into total subservience so that they become docile and good citizens in the prison. The horror, violence and implied sex between the doctor and his female patients in the prison could never make an even faintly believable story if the prisoners were male instead of female. As it stands, even though Rachel finally murders the doctor, it plays to male power fantasies. While the chase through the subterranean chambers of the prison and capture are unbelievable, it's a good film to challenge males and ask them to reveal their own power fantasies over the female.

I SPIT ON YOUR GRAVE **CC   DS (Hard R)**
1979   WIZARD

P/D—**Joseph Zbeda, Meir Zarchi**
F/A—**Camille Keaton**
F/A—**Eron Tabor, Richard Pace, Anthony Nichols**

This film was not produced as a porno or adult film. Because it shows no erect penises or vaginal-penile penetration, it can and has been shown in drive-ins and regular theaters. In some city areas it is considered a cult film. Some may think it was produced by Women Against (not only) Pornography but against men. With that prelude, let me tell you that this is the most stomach-turning mixture of sex and violence you ever have watched and exceeds the DS categories of all but a few of the adult films in this filmography. But it's worth owning or renting to test your own reactions. It's the story of Jennifer (Camille Keaton), a very pretty young woman who is driving to a summer cottage she has rented somewhere in the country beyond New York City. Alone, she is going to spend the summer writing a novel. Three young men at a gasoline station see her arrive, and one, a guy who is married and has two kids, gives her directions to get to the cottage on a lonely country road beside a river. When she orders groceries by telephone from a local store, Michael, a slighty retarded delivery boy in his middle 20s, delivers them to her on a bicycle. She is friendly, tips him, and he tells the guys back at the station how nice she is. They ask him if he'd like to screw her and promise they will work it out. A day later they are on the river in a boat equipped with a high-powered outboard. They wave at Jennifer, circle the cottage on the river and she waves back. Next day Jennifer, wearing only a bikini, is sunning as she lies in a rowboat that belongs to the cottage.

The guys rip by in their speedboat, pick up the boat's painter and tow a screaming Jennifer up the river into a wooded glen where they strip her and first try to force Michael on her. After that, they rape her viciously and leave with her bathing suit and rowboat. Naked and sobbing, she tries to find her way back to her cottage. Again they are waiting for her in the woods a half-mile up the river. Stretching her naked on a rock, they rape her again. It's not over yet—when she gets back to the cottage there they are. This time, Michael manages to rape her as do the rest of them on the living room floor. You have now watched Jennifer naked, bloody and covered with mud, get gang raped for nearly a half-hour. She's unable to call the police—they've torn out her telephone. She is presumably dead. Their leader, Stanley, the married guy, thinks Michael has stabbed her to death (at his command) so she won't talk. Instead he has wiped her blood on the knife and brought it back. Two weeks pass and Stanley wonders why the cottage hasn't attracted any attention—it should be stinking by now with rotted flesh. When the story returns to Jennifer, you can't immediately understand why she hasn't got in her car and hightailed it back to the city. Instead she calls the store to have Michael deliver some more groceries. When he arrives, she is wearing only a nightgown and though this time he really plans to kill her, she seduces him out near the river by a tree. When he's on top of her, climaxing, she slips a noose around his neck that she's prepared in advance. In a wink of an eye, Michael is strangling and dying as she swings his body over the river. Stanley is next. He gets his in her bathtub where she has seduced him, pretending that she loved his rape. Getting in the tub with him, pretending she is about to massage him, she picks a knife from under the bathmat, castrates him and bolts him in the bathroom to die. One of the other guys ends up with an axe between his shoulder blades, and the last tries to save himself as she nearly drowns him in the river. Many women who watch it will shout, "Hurray for Jenny!"

INTIMATE ILLUSIONS NN DK BI
1980 SELECT ESSEX

P/D—Paul Levis, Jerry Smith
F/A—John Leslie, Sylvia Rodgers
F/A—Constance Penny, Phaedra Grant

For a couple of minutes, you may think this one has a plot. There's a holdup in a grocery store, a wild car chase, equal to any in a regular Hollywood scenario. Then the cop (John Leslie) goes to bed with a hooker he takes on the chase, and the burglar (Jerry Smith), called The West Side Rapist, is raped by John Leslie's wife, played by Phaedra Grant. For the next hour, it is all nicely photographed and everyone enjoys everyone else's body from head to toe, including two women in an interestingly choreographed bisexual dance. Finally, after all the actors who appeared in the opening scenes have disappeared, you are treated to a half-hour scene in a disco with music provided by the Filthy Four, who are blown by helpful females as they play, and a *Saturday Night Fever*-style tour de force performed by six couples whose nude consorts obligingly suck away at their male partners during the dance.

JADE PUSSYCAT NN NM BI one DS
sequence
1977 FREEWAY

P/D—Richard Aldrich, Bob Chinn
F/A—John C. Holmes, Steve Balint
F/A—Georgina Spelvin, Linda Wong

The Jade Pussycat, stolen from a museum in Tokyo, is worth a half-million dollars. The bad guys (including Linda Wong) steal it from the guy who stole it and murder him. The original thief's sister employs Johnny Wadd to find out what happened to him. Before he solves the case, Johnny gently services (and is serviced) by four women, including Georgina. In a humorous sequence, Linda and Georgina explore each other's genitals and anuses; a woman is raped and doesn't enjoy it, and Johnny ends up owning the pussycat. Next installment is titled *China Cat!*

LIQUID LIPS NN NM BI one DS
sequence
1976 EROS

P/D—Richard Aldrich, Bob Chinn
F/A—John C. Holmes
F/A—Monique Starr

Johnny rides again—this time employed by the FBI to decoy heroin smugglers from Mexico who are dumping the stuff in San Francisco. In the process, Johnny watches a stripper on the Gold Coast do an extended and very erotic dance, and a government investigator captured by the hoods is sex-teased by a moll who gives him an overdose of heroin and literally sucks him to death. As usual, Johnny shows his identification to four women who are all orally and vaginally delighted by the length and girth of it. Richard Aldrich does not appear in this one since as Sam Kelly he was murdered in the previous installment, *Tell Them Johnny Wadd Is Here.*

LITTLE ORPHAN DUSTY PART II
NN BI DK
1982 CABALLERO

P/D—Jaacov Jacovi
F/A—Rob Everett, Eric Edwards, Danny Lazare
F/A—Rhonda Jo Petty, Angel Cash, Tress

Someone is trying to kill Little Orphan Dusty (Rhonda Jo Petty), and after you watch this one, you may wish he had succeeded. Jacovi offers a story line, but he's so intent on pleasing the raincoat crowd (and working on a low budget), that after about ten minutes you lose interest. Someone is following her in a Rolls Royce through San Francisco, taking pot shots at her. She is soothed by Dr. Goldman (Rob Everett?), who is about the plumpest guy you've ever seen in an adult film. He soon is replaced by John Perry (Eric Edwards—the only one in the film who can act). John figures that the solution lies in Dusty's parentage. After a visit to the orphanage he discovers she is the daughter of Annie

Harris (Angel Cash), an aging but wealthy former Hollywood screen star. As the plot thickens, it develops that Anne's young lover, Rick (Kevin Gibson), is trying to murder Dusty so she'll have no claim to her mother's fortune. Of course, Dusty had no idea who her mother was until our hero finds out. In the meantime, at the orphanage, Dusty remembers where she hid the dildos years ago when she was there, and in a grimy-slimy close-up three-way masturbation scene, she shows the new occupants of her old room in the orphanage how to take care of themselves. The Legion of Honor Award goes to Kevin Gibson for being able to get an erection with Angel Cash, who has long, white, Santa Claus-like whiskers hanging down to her shoulders and speaks in a simpering, eyeball-rolling manner that would unnerve even a John Bunyan. Rhonda has shaved pubes and can't act, either.

MORE   **NN   NM   BI   DK   DS**
1973   BLUE VIDEO

P/D—**Leo de Leon, Ralph Ell**
F/A—**Harry Reems, Bobby Astyr, Harry Valentine**
F/A—**Sue Rowan, Gloria Haddit, Delaine Young**

This one is so repulsive and nasty that it should receive one of the top ten saprogenic awards for adult films. (Look up saprogenic in your dictionary!) On that basis, you still may want to watch it. Despite Harry Reems who tries to laugh his way through, it's pretty slimy. Marie and Louise are living with a black guy who gets bumped off while they are in bed making it together. Steve Cochrane (Harry Reems), the detective, gets the case. Two of Sam Slack's (the guy who had him wiped out) boys, are described by Marie, who has serviced them both, as "a little one with big cock (Bobby Astyr) and a big one with a little cock." They tell Sam that "Jim's quim" is putting the finger on him. So Sam ties her to the bed and is getting ready to put cement shoes on her when our hero bursts in and saves her. He's uncovered the whereabouts of Sam by screwing the plumpest woman you've even seen in pornos—she eats bananas while she's humping.

ORIENTAL TREATMENT   **NN   DK**
1978   ARROW

P/D—**John Evans, Harold Lee**
F/A—**Rob Rose, Lanny Roth, David Lane**
F/A—**Kuoto Gee, Marsha Judd, Lucy McMillan**

The story of Sgt. Pecker, a very homely but well-built policewoman who is on the narcotic squad and screws drug informers to get information on cocaine pushers. A police chief screws her as well as another policewoman, whose sister is on drugs and screws in a floury bed (no kidding!) with the guy who is blending the stuff. Another guy is secretly taking movies of Sgt. Pecker in her stakeout where she is screwing the police chief. Finally, if you've lasted this long, Suki Yu (Kyoto Gee) appears, sniffs coke through the de rigeur $100 bill, and at last provides the Oriental Treatment with her mouth and lovely vertical vaginal opening. If you've wondered what it might be like to bed a Chinese woman, this one will give you a ten minute preview.

PUNK ROCK   **NN   NM   DK   BI   DS**
1979   INTERNATIONAL HOME VIDEO

P/D—**Carter Stevens**
F/A—**Wade Nichols, Richard Bolla, Bobby Astyr**
F/A—**Jean Sander, Susaye London**

While Carter Stevens never denies his viewers any grisly aspect of human sexuality, he does try to tell a story that goes from A to Z. Stevens believes that *Pleasure Palace*, which has 60 minutes of dialogue, is one of his best pictures. This one runs a close second in dialogue. A seamy story of city low life without the sex, it isn't too much different from those you can watch on weekly television cops-and-robber serials. James Dillinger is a detective who has been kicked off the police force because he's too independent. But as a private detective, he has just rescued the daughter of a wealthy Connecticut businessman from the drugs and squalor of New York City. In appreciation, Jennifer, who really isn't very virginal, sleeps with him. But the group he has rescued her from are indignant. They murder Jim's friend Travis—Jim finds him dead on his toilet. The murder was committed to get Jim out of his apartment so they could kidnap Jennifer and bring her home to her own people. Not her Daddy, of course. As Jim tries to track Jennifer down, he spends the evening listening to punk rock in a club where groupies and dancing girls are blowing both horns and guys. Finally, he finds her where she is being worked over, rather willingly, by a couple of seedy-looking guys. In a concluding five-minute dialogue, he resolves all angles of the story just like an old time Republic B movie. But he has missed a crucial clue. Richard Bolla (who never takes his clothes off in this one), even though he is head of the police detectives, is really the guy who killed Jim's friend, Travis. Bolla shoots Nichols dead—and that's that, folks!

THE SEDUCTRESS NN DK BI
1982 SELECT ESSEX

P/D—Damon Christian, Bob Chinn
F/A—Richard Laidlaw, Lazzlo Landani, Billy Dee, Damon Christian
F/A—Lee Carroll, Lisa de Leeuw, Kathy Marcourt, Yvette Cole.

The time is September 26, 1978. The place is Las Vegas. George Anderson is married to Cindy (Lisa de Leeuw). A politician, he is in a position to work with hotel builders to circumvent the building codes, particularly relating to fire law standards (sprinklers in rooms, etc.). John McCord (Billie Dee) is married to Rosie (Kathy Marcourt). There's also David Hamilton, who is a big-shot in local politics, and Renee (Lee Carroll), a high-priced whore. Finally, there's Richard Aldrich (Damon Christian—the producer of the film). He's a photographer who uses Renee as the lure to get the big shots in a motel room equipped with a two-way mirror. Thus he can photograph them making it with Renee and ruin their careers, if they don't ignore building codes, by blackmail. All of this could have been the basis for a strong story about political corruption ending in the tragic MGM and Hilton Hotel fires in Las Vegas. Christian finishes off the picture with actual stock shots of both hotels burning—but unfortunately the story got lost in the various bedrooms. The longest foursome scene on record has Lisa de Leeuw and Yvette Cole in the motel with two guys, one of whom (Billie Dee) goes home to his wife. After confessing that he has been trapped (photographed through the two-way mirror) screwing with two different women—and it was blissful—he takes on his wife, Kathy Marcourt (who looks a little like Desiree Cousteau). The conversation between Billy Dee as John and Kathy Marcourt as Rosie is one for the book. By this time Kathy is happily lapping him. "Why did you cheat on me?" she demands. "I do it so well you don't need anyone else." After which Kathy proves it. Renee, who is the fall girl, ends up dumped in a ash barrel, dead after an overdose of junk. And you finally realize after an endless screwathon that Damon Christian is the villain in more ways than one. With a tight, fast screenplay and more erotic sex scenes, he could have made an intersting whodunnit.

SEX MUSEUM NN NM DK
1976 VIDEO SHOWTIME

P/D—Alec Beon
F/A—Ted Kesey, Jo Ambriz, Ed Stark
F/A—Annabelle, Mona Jenks

A totally amateurish slimy-grimy about Professor Mucklestein, who creates living sculptures out of people he's fed mickies or bopped on the head. He coats one of them, Tricia, the girlfriend of Dick Sticker, in plaster. But he screws her before he seals her. To find Tricia, Sticker hires Pussy Valentine, a private eye who wears a garter belt, a jacket that hangs just above her bare ass and a felt hat. Pussy does daily workouts before she goes on the job—masturbating. When she breaks into the studio, she asks, "What kind of asshole would do this?" You'll ask the same question about the tape.

WATERPOWER **CC DK DS BI**
1975 VIDEO-X HOME LIBRARY

P/D—Gerard Damiano
F/A—Jamie Gillis, John Buco, Eric Edwards
F/A—C. J. Laing, Marlene Willoughby, Gloria Leonard

If Jamie Gillis had gone into straight films he would probably have been as popular as Charles Bronson or Clint Eastwood. He'll scare you to death in this one, in which he portrays a sex pervert—an enema bandit who accosts women in their apartments, ties them up and before he rapes them gives them an enema (supposedly based on a true incident). Thinking about his first victim, an airline stewardess whom he has watched screwing through a telescope in his apartment, he says: "She's dirty. Just a toilet. If I cleaned her out she would be clean again. She'd thank me. She'd be glad I cleaned her out." Damiano gives this sexvid a long, scary buildup with Jamie discovering that he is orgasmic when he watches an enema being given to a woman in a sex palace called Garden of Eden, which specializes in B&D, S&M, infantilism, cross dressing, French and Greek cultures and high colonic irrigations. Suspected by a policewoman, C. J. Laing, in the final sequence, he captures her and tortures her in a long frightening sequence. The agony of the enemas is written on his victims' faces. Whatever your shock feelings may be, you'll watch this from beginning to end, and you'll have to admit that both the acting and cinematography are great. Worth owning—if only to initiate discussions on whether a film like this should ever be made.

16

Family Sagas

ALL THE WAY **NN NR BI**
1980 COMPETITIVE VIDEO

P/D—Jack Hoffman, Chuck Williams
F/A—John Reese
F/A—Georgina Spelvin, Cindy Bell, Nicki Ronson

Delores (Georgina Spelvin) is married to a writer, Everett (John Reese), who is evidently writing a novel that's too true to his own life. He's having an affair with Kitty (Nicki Ronson), but then you discover that some of Delores's uneasiness is because she's in love with Russell, a handsome black man who takes very good care of her sexually. Everett discovers Delores in the barn in the hay with Russell and is about to shoot him when a woman who has run out of gas knocks on his shoulder and asks his help. He takes her to a gas station, and to pay for the gas she takes on Everett and the station owner (also in the hay). But Everett really loves Delores, and when she leaves him a note that she's running away with Russell, he follows her to a bar where's she waiting (Russell never shows up) and persuades her to come home, that he loves her no matter what. Georgina fans will want to own this tape. She does a nice acting job, and the interracial sexmaking with Georgina and her lover is nicely done. In fact, it's the only sexvid I have seen where love is presum-ably a factor between the black and white characters (see note under *April Love*, p. 273). And unlike many sexvids, it has a country town and farm atmosphere.

ANYONE BUT MY HUSBAND
CC NN NM DS BI NL occasionally
1977 VCA

P/D—Robert Norman
F/A—Tony "El Goncho" Perez, Eric Edwards
F/A—C. J. Laing, Bree Anthony, Jennifer Jordan

Sam, a history teacher, has been married to Nora (C. J. Laing) for six years. Nora is only 22, but Sam likes "young stuff." The film opens with Sam in bed with one of his high school students. In the meantime, he's neglecting Nora and he returns from his matinees completely pooped and flops in bed to sleep. Nora's only recourse is to masturbate, which she does very erotically. Her psychiatrist tells her she must have an affair—presumably to make Sam jealous. Guided by her girl-friend, she ends up in an art gallery owned by a super-sophisticated artist who is going to recreate *her* as a work of art. He promptly does by tying her to pulleys in his studio. Hanging her by her arms, he strips and whips her—after which they have ecstatic sex in an extended sequence. "I was terrified," she tells her friend the next day, "but actually it really was a little exciting . . . but I prefer to go to bed, not to the morgue." Next she tries a poet—but he's so flowery he forgets what he's doing. "Aren't there any men left in the world who want a good lay?" she asks the viewers. There sure are! "El Goncho" means "the hook," a fortune teller tells her, and presto, there he is— Tony Perez. Finally, Nora's husband, Sam, mends his ways and comes home. But it's Nora's turn. Now she's too tired to do it. Like Barbra Streisand, C. J. is a Jewish girl with a homely face that is often pretty. She's a better actress than most. The CC rating is for her and El Goncho, whom I've never seen since.

CONFESSIONS OF A WOMAN
NN DK BI
1978   SELECT ESSEX

P/D—Anthony Spinelli, Leonard Burke
F/A—John Leslie, Ron Rodgers, Eric Marin, Joey Civera
F/A—Cindy Johnson, Karen Cusick, Barbara Lovelynn

Gary (John Leslie) plays a schnook who is so preoccupied with his work that he fails to service his wife properly. He leaves her hanging without a climax in bed even though she has taken very good care of him. So, Carol (Cindy Johnson) gets dressed and follows a guy on a motorbike in her Honda, and he teaches her how to give better head by sucking on his finger. That night, while Gary is extolling her virtues as a model wife and telling her female friends how he and Carol love each more now than they did six years ago when they got married, Carol is upstairs in the bathroom, fellating his boss. Then in a sicky scene, she's discovering a woman whose husband wants to be dominated. Finally she's playing a hooker to act out a fantasy she's always had. For $200, a fat guy works her over in a hotel room, after which she tells him that she has to leave and get dinner for her husband.

COUPLES **NN BI NL DK**
1976   VIDEO-X HOME LIBRARY

P/D—Rod Whipple, Claude Goddard
F/A—Jamie Gillis, Jeffrey Hurst, Rodney Farrell
F/A—Cindy Price, Gwen Fisher, Mary Stewart, Lisa Love

The credits on this one give the actresses names as Angel Barrett, Cindy Lane and Gloria Haddit. Evidently, they all "had it" because I've never seen their faces in other adult flicks. Which is too bad because the two wives, Alice and Faith, are interesting to listen to—especially when they test each other out for a bisexual scene (because their marriages to Bob and Dave are so dull and sexually unsatisfying). Bob and Dave (Jamie Gillis and Jeffrey Hurst), are on their own trip, and as they drive to work, they too discuss their dull marriages, and an encounter they each had with teenage girls (told in flashbacks with girls who really seem like teenagers). Bob and Dave contact Charley to line up women for them after office hours, and Alice and Faith decide to become call girls, as arranged by their former friend Rita. Charley and Rita are in business together, and you guessed it—after an expensive trip with Rita, Bob and Dave don't find extracurricular sex so good, nor do Alice and Faith after a session with Charley. Charley arranges a date for Bob and Dave with two new girls, who are of course their wives. After the great switch, marriage and a new sexual partner, neither finds the other's wife dull. Most women will get a chuckle or two at the conversations in this one.

DO YOU WANNA BE LOVED?
CC BI DK
1975   ARROW

P/D—Larry Yost, B. A. Smith
F/A—Paul Tanner (actually Paul Thomas), Joey Nassivera (now Civera), Tyler Horne, Lou Behr
F/A—Renee Bond, Anita Sand, Nancy Paige

Melanie (Renee Bond) is married to Jim (Paul Thomas), who, on his way up the executive ladder, is putting business before pleasure. Slightly beserk, she follows a guy into a men's room (she's dressed in men's clothes) and sexually assaults him. Fortunately, she can't remember what she does after the act. To remind Jim of the pleasures of life, they go for a weekend to Pleasant Valley Lodge where everyone is engaged in a very spermy weekend, including Joey Civera, who with both Renee and Anita (she's the redhead—Renee has the beautiful, petulant face) is worn to a frazzle. It finally reaches a crescendo at the big Saturday costume party orgy where the featured entertainer shows her oral ability with volunteers in the audience. When Jim tells Melanie that "Love should be private. It shouldn't be in front of a whole bunch of people," she agrees, and it almost becomes romantic. But not quite. Jim falls asleep—so what can Melanie do except join the orgy going on downstairs in the lodge? Renee Bond quit the business long ago and is now a more prosaic working wife, but she was very pretty when this one was made.

EUROPEAN LOVERS NN DK NL (silly)
1978   BOCCACCIO 100

P/D—Vidal Bernstein, Robert Grayson
F/A—Richard Mars
F/A—Josephine Cox

I don't know whether this is a French- or English-made film—the dubbing is pretty good. Elizabeth, who is in love with Harry, a professor at the university, invites her niece and girlfriend, Dory and Susan, to spend the weekend with her. Dory brings her boyfriend, Charles, and Susan brings Jimmie. Poor Elizabeth isn't getting much sex from Harry. That night when she discovers that the girls are not asleep in their room, Elizabeth gets a little frantic and goes on the town. She finds a bar where she picks up two guys who work her over very thoroughly. Back at the house in the morning, Susan wakes up with Jimmy. But she becomes very passionate with Charlie when he and Jimmy switch roommates. Next day the girls, who have Harry for a professor, tell the boys that they are going to the zoo, but after viewing the monkeys playing with each other they call Harry and give him a thoroughly

happy afternoon. Back home the boys have convinced Elizabeth to play strip chess—anyone who loses a piece must take off a piece of clothing. Everything works out happily when Harry decides to marry Elizabeth. And you just know it's going to be one big happy family.

EUROTICA (EL GRECO) NN BI DK
1983   GOLD STRIPE

P/D—Danielle Peters
F/A—Not given

This half hour tape is one in a series, under the over-all title Eurotica, which were shot directly on videotape. If you have a video camera, this one may give you some ideas on how to produce your own short story on video tape. It's the story of a young Jewish girl, obsessively in love. Her lover (presumably a Greek but he looks more Norwegian) beats her and he's very cruel to her, but she can't give him up. Her sister, who is worried about her (she's run away from her life as a Jewish princess), arrives and tries to persuade her to come home. Then the Greek arrives. He tells her sister to undress, after which he screws her rather brutally, slapping her buttocks incessantly and kneading them roughly while she moans but not too unhappily. The older sister watches and joins the action. Most ladies in the audience will not like this one. Other tapes in the Eurotica series, which I have not seen, and I presume are developed to sell at low prices are: Office Dictator, Eye to Eye, Dressed to Finesse, The Baby Sitter, and Party Line.

FOOTBALL WIDOW CC NN NL some DK
1979   SCORPIO

P/D—David Summers
F/A—William Margold, Chuck Starr
F/A—Seka, Janice James

A half-hour, shot directly-to-videotape sexvid aimed at a male-female home audience. (It sells for about half the price of adult film sexvids.) Promo: "Pick up Football Widow today and score a touchdown in your bedroom." This is a laughing story about a young woman whose husband prefers pro football on TV to her enticements. She rips the cord off the set and when her husband leaves, offers herself to the TV repairman among others. After a group sex party she reunites with hubby and all is well. This and many other Scorpio tapes point the way to a new type sexvid that will appeal to many women and offer sex education to boot.

GAMES WOMEN PLAY
NN DK BI NR (one scene)
1980 TVX

P/D—**Chuck Vincent**
F/A—**Frank Adams, Jack Wrangler, Roger Caine**
F/A—**Leslie Bovee, Merle Michaels, Kelly Nichols, Samantha Fox, Veronica Hart**

Although the males in their lives might wish it, most women have never played these kinds of games. It's spring in New York City. Frank (Frank Adams), who is married to Sarah (Merle Michaels), takes some quick sex with Leslie Bovee in a hallway off Times Square. George, who works at the same advertising agency as Frank, has an extended lunch with Alice Walker (Veronica Hart) and a very romantic dessert in her bed afterwards, although he's married to Milly (Samantha Fox, whom you never see naked). Alice has already been through two husbands since graduation. Frank is jealous of George and takes it out on Sarah. After beating her up a little, he screws her and tells her how much he needs her. Sarah, who is bisexual, confesses her screwed-up marriage to Margo, who is also bisexual and is married to Mark—and obligingly offers her body to all his poker partners. Chuck Vincent must have been watching soap operas because that's not all. There's Roger Caine, who is married to Leslie. She spends mornings in the hall with Frank but also plays occult sex games with her husband while Bobby, their six-year-old son, is at the grandparents. At the end, Milly announces that George is taking her on a honeymoon to celebrate her pregnancy, and Alice is at the celebration party, which miraculously doesn't turn into an orgy. But like me you'll wonder about the massage oil, candlelight, and raga music

sexmaking between Leslie and Roger. How come all that oil doesn't gag her?

HALF THE ACTION **NN NM BI DK**
1980 TVX

P/D—**B. Ron Eliot**
F/A—**Mike Ranger, Ron Jeremy**
F/A—**Becky Bitter, Donna Jones, Terri Galko**

Half the action is money. The other half is sex. Mike Ranger plays Marvin Lee (you can reverse the first and last name, of course). He has been playing house with Michelle (Becky Bitter, taking an appropriate name) and after several years has kicked her out. Michelle angrily returns to their condo, cuts the oil painting over the fireplace in half, measures out their cocaine and grass in equal portions and then finds Marvin upstairs with two women in bed. She takes one of Marvin's women, too—and Marvin's 50-foot ketch. Immediately, she and one of Marvin's women turn it into a seagoing whorehouse. The price for a tour of the islands is $1,000 and includes all the sex you can eat or otherwise enjoy. Michelle's lawyer advises Marvin that "if a woman moves in with you half your ass is hers—and if you're gonna play, you gotta pay!" Marvin eventually gets his boat back and runs it more efficiently than Michelle—sexwise at least. Much of this film was shot on the ketch, but I couldn't figure out where—sometimes it looks like the coast of California, sometimes like the British Virgin Gorda. The scenery is more interesting than the sex.

LIKE MOTHER LIKE DAUGHTER
NN NM DK BI
1979 VCX

P/D—**Eugene Paul, Ernest Danna**
F/A—**Ralph Carl, David Fine**
F/A—**Kelia Kane, Lesia Harris**

Momma and her second husband are into group sex and swinging, and her daughter and girlfriend join them or watch their parties. Daddy Bruce hasn't seen his daughter since she was three and is now returning from Japan to get custody of her. He divorced Mommy years ago because she was a sex maniac. Daddy is puritanical, but Tricia and her girlfriend save the day. They pick Daddy up in his rental car, and Daddy, who doesn't recognize his daugher, tells her he likes young girls. Tricia proves that Mommy and daughter are just alike. Daddy goes back to Japan where the women are nicer. For better, but mostly worse, this sexvid offers actors and actresses you've never seen before and can't believe either.

LOVE SECRETS NN BI
1976   VISUAL ENTERTAINMENT

P/D—Gerold Greystone, Sudray Martin
F/A—John Seeman, David Blair, Frank Michaels
F/A—Tracy O'Neill, Ann Sylmar, Candida Royalle

Alan Wineman (John Seeman) and Lil (Tracy O'Neill) have been married a long time. They have never been sexually honest with each other. "If she really knew about me, she'd divorce me in a minute," Alan thinks as he fantasizes about making it with his neighbor, his secretary and other women he believes are sexier than Lil. "My husband would kill me if he really knew what I wanted," Lil thinks as she fantasizes really wild sex with her girlfriends, boyfriends and other guys. After a hard day's work (living out his fantasies) Alan comes home and after supper adjourns to the bathroom, where he plays with himself. Disgusted that he's so sexy, he wanders into the bedroom, where you have already been watching Lil caressing herself very erotically in front of her mirror. Shocked at being caught, she sobs, "Oh, Alan, I'm so sorry. I don't know what to say." Then, for the first time, they confess to each other. She'd like to make love beside the swimming pool or in the back seat of their car; he in the woods. "Let's promise from now on we'll do the things we really want to do with each other," says Lil. There's a moral in this one that may intrigue many guys and gals.

PORTRAITS OF PLEASURE NN NM BI DK
1974   BLUE VIDEO

P/D—Bo Koup
F/A—Jon Black, Juan Pedos, Four Huck, Bud Wipp
F/A—Susan McBain, Sharon Mitchell, Candy Split

This is a raincoat-crowd, greasy-sleazy sexvid. But instead of giving the male viewers the feeling that man is in control, many guys may watch this one and decide to give up women forever. Anyone married to Candy Split—the first woman to appear on your tube—would want to run for the woods. She wakes up in bed, reaches for her husband and immediately says, "Come on, I want some action," as he groans, "Not again." "Come on, what good are you?" she yells at him. Of course, he's not a very nice character either. "God-damn you—a telephone pole wouldn't satisfy you," he says. Next scene: Rod is meeting Susan McBain, who admits that up to now she only enjoyed women but is willing to take a whirl in bed with him. When her roommate, Sharon Mitchell, hears about it, she tells her, "Women are fools. Men are no good. Sure, you like that man inside you once in a while. But you can't have a relationship with a man like we can." To convince her, Sharon tells her and Candy (who it seems is a friend of theirs, too) to each pick up a guy. Together they'll prove that men are fools. Candy gets a kid who doens't look over 16, and she teaches him cunnilingus. Susan gets a black guy who doesn't need any lessons, and Sharon, to Candy's surprise, arrives with her husband, Rod. Sharon tells her; "I'm going to teach him a lesson." When it's all over, Rod is flattened out cold.

SEDUCTION NN DK BI
1974   VIDEO-X-PIX

P/D—Ralph Ell
F/A—Jamie Gillis, Ray Paul
F/A—Andrea True, Annie Sprinkles

Lois's (Andrea True's) friends are frustrated suburban housewives whose husbands are always going away on business trips and "come too soon." Lois gets more attention from her dog than her husband

Max. So while their husbands are away, they all go to a swing party where there are plenty of males belonging to other women to be seduced by and to seduce. Lois falls in love with Derek (Jamie Gillis), who is a heel. After he screws her (at least he can last longer than Max), he tries to get rid of her. At this point Lois goes out of character and tries to seduce Derek over the phone in lustful conversations that no self-respecting female would ever have with a man, even if she adored him. Max finally comes home and still comes too fast. Potentially a believable story about sex and marriage, this one falls short on characterization and leaves the field wide open.

SCORE **CC NN BI**
1975   HIGHBRIDGE ENTERTAINMENT

P/D—Ava Leighton, Radley Metzger
F/A—Carl Parker, Calvin Culver, Gerald Grant
F/A—Claire Wiever, Lynn Lowry

Good acting, excellent dialogue and editing. Elvira and Jack, who have been married a few years, are swingers. Either of them would jump into bed with a porcupine if it suited their sexual fantasies. Along with Betsey and Eddie, they are somewhere in Europe in the town of Leisure. The score is a toss-up. Can Elvira and Jack seduce Betsey and Eddie, heterosexually or bisexually? It really doesn't matter. Betsey and Eddie are the innocents—a version of Martha and George's guests in *Who's Afraid of Virginia Woolf?* The bisexual seduction scenes are cleverly intercut. After a bisexual night with Elvira and Jack, monogamous innocence is replaced by, "It doesn't matter who you love just so long as you love." Excellent erotic filmmaking by a master of the art.

SUNNY **NN DK BI**
1980   VCX

P/D—Robert Lynn, Warren Evans
F/A—Jeremy Wyatt
F/A—Candida Royalle, Marlene Willoughby

Marlene Willoughby as Eva (Mark's mother) is trying to regain control of the multimillion dollar estate that his father (her husband) left to Mark. Through an agency she hires Sunny (Candida Royalle) to seduce Mark. Sunny decides she doesn't have to share the proceeds with Eva, but finds out too late that Mark knows from the beginning that both Eva and Sunny are out to get him. In the process Mark is fellated by his mother and screws her and Marlene, who, next to Candida, is the hammiest actress you've ever watched in a sexvid. A very attractive 60-year-old woman, the countess something-or-other appears in this one, but the director muffed it. Instead of having Mark go to bed with her, the Countess reenacts her youthful sex life by commanding Sunny to do it for her with Mark while she watches. Pretty silly.

SWEET YOUNG SINS **NN DK BI**
1973   VIDEO SHOWTIME

P/D—Jack Film Productions
F/A—Not given—no one you've ever seen before

Here's one day in the life of a suburban nuclear family: Mommy and Daddy with two children in their late teens; Rita and Rich. At breakfast, baldheaded Daddy demands to know where Rita is. She didn't come home last night. Seems she stayed out with Tom. Rich is in a hurry to leave for football practice. No sooner does Daddy leave than a young black delivery boy arrives and Mamma delightedly caresses him. Soon she is fellating him, and within minutes she's stretched out on the dining room table happily being shafted by her new chocolate-colored friend. Mommy gets rid of him just in time. Rita arrives home with Diane, carrying schoolbooks, and soon she and Diane are in her room exploring each other's bodies. Mom discovers them and Rita demands, "Can't I have any privacy in this house?" Not with Mom around—she joins the action. That afternoon when Rich arrives home, pooped after football practice, Rita and Diane search him out in his bedroom and revive him orally. Daddy finally arrives home, has a cocktail with Mommy and is trying to get into her pants on the sofa when Rich pops into the living room naked to watch the proceedings. Doesn't bother Daddy or Mommy a bit. As Rich joins the fun, Daddy laughs and says, "The family who lays together stays together." Rich responds appreciatively as he works over Mommy, "You taught me all I know."

TABOO II **CC NN BI DK**
1983   VISUAL ENTERTAINMENT

P/D—**Kirdy Stevens**
F/A—**Eric Edwards, Kevin James, Ron Jeremy**
F/A—**Dorothy Le May, Kay Parker, Juliet Anderson, Honey Wilder, Cara Lott, Bambi**

On the premise that you have seen *Taboo* (see listing, p. 141), the story begins with Barbara Scott (Kay Parker), whose son, Paul, is now living with his father. Gina (Juliet Anderson) is her lesbian friend who adores cock, too. But this is only a gimmick to develop the story of another family where Mommy (Honey Wilder) and Daddy (Eric Edwards) end up in the sack with Junior (Kevin James) and their daughter, Sherry (Dorothy Le May). I've given it a CC rating because the dialogue is often more believable than most adult films, and the response to incest is more believable. Also Kevin James and Dorothy Le May (when the camera is not too close to her face) actually act quite convincingly as teenagers. Kevin is a cocksman. His tail is constantly wagging the dog. He discovers Kay Parker likes young men and is quickly in the sack with her. But he really likes his sister better. Driving to school, he can't keep his hands off her, and in their very affluent home (Daddy is wealthy), he is always popping into her bedroom unannounced. He finally convinces his girlfriend, Mary Lou (Bambi), whom he is screwing, to persuade Sherry that a threesome would be fun. Thereafter Sherry is hooked on Junior. In the meantime Daddy is having an affair with his secretary, and Mommy is not getting any attention in bed. When Daddy does perform, he doesn't listen even when she pleads, "Don't come yet, I'm not ready." Junior is aware that all is not right in the parental bedroom, and his hands linger on Mommy. But he doesn't go into action until Mommy catches him in bed with Sherry, and Mommy is totally horrified. Daddy is away on a business trip, but she

tries to reach him with the awful truth that their children are enjoying each other in bed. Fortunately Junior catches her in time. He confesses how bad he is and that it's not Sherry's fault, but his. What's a mother to do? She soothes Junior a little too much and before she knows it she's in bed with him—guilty but enjoying it. When Daddy calls to find out what happened, she tells him everything is all right and after he hangs up, she stares into the tube. "I fucked my son," she sobs. The film should have ended there, but, of course, Daddy and his daughter have to do it too—of all places in bed with Mommy wearing a nightshade and sleeping on the other side. Mommy doesn't wake up, but after daughter has sneaked back to her bedroom, Daddy (remarkable man that he is) makes tender love to Mommy and it's obvious that they have no further need for Junior and Sherry. Kirdy Stevens tosses in a gratuitous orgy scene near the end, complete with Juliet Anderson organizing a daisy chain. It adds nothing to the film.

TEENAGE HOUSEWIFE
NN NL DK BI
1976   BLUE VIDEO

P/D—**Not given**
F/A—**Bobby Astyr, Bill Coney, Hugh Westy**
F/A—**Susan McBain, Sharon Mitchell, Nancy Hoffman, Mary Beth**

Susan (Susan McBain) is not a teenage housewife. She's in her 20s. The film begins with a monologue as she walks through a garden. "I thought when I was marrying him, I was marrying a mature, worldly man. It's true that Bob is older than I am, but does he have to be so conventional? He's turned out to be such a bore. Why does he have to be this way?" Believe it or not, her staid husband, who only wants to have sex in bed—and not on the kitchen table or standing on his head, like his wife—is Bobby Astyr. When she tells him she wants anal sex, he's horrified at the thought. Susan soon discovers that a neighbor in the same apartment building, Jack (Hugh Westy), has the same weird ideas about sexmaking as she does, and of course, his wife, Jennifer (Sharon

Mitchell), is just like Bob—very staid, a woman who likes the missionary position. All of this has the potential for an interesting story—one that is even conceivable about a very sexy woman who exceeds her husband's sexual needs and conditioning. For a moment or two you think it may happen. There's some funny dialogue between Susan and Bob and Bob and Jennifer—but you can quickly guess how it will end in adult film land. Bob and Jennifer think they are missing something, Susan seduces Jack in her canvas exerciser, which stretches her legs for explicit viewing, after which she invites the whole apartment building to an orgy. What choice do Jennifer and Bob have but to join the fun? Susan McBain, who I don't think makes porno flicks anymore, has a very appealing face—and body.

THAT'S MY DAUGHTER **NN   DK   BI**
1983   VCX

P/D—Charles de Santos
F/A—Eric Edwards, John Leslie
F/A—Lisa de Leeuw, Karen Sweet, Sharon
  Mitchell, Arcadia Lake, Mona

Wealthy Harry Joseph (played by an unidentified man in his 50s) hasn't seen his daughter Wendy (Karen Sweet) in many years, and she doesn't remember him at all. She's been brought up by her stepfather, Max Stempo (John Leslie). As the film begins Harry is screwing one of his many girlfriends (Lisa de Leeuw) and at the same time watching a porno film on a 45-inch screen in his ski lodge. He recognizes his daughter (He has pictures of her—but she none of him) and yells: "That's my daughter!" He immediately hires Angela (Sharon Mitchell) who, with her boyfriend John, runs a private detective agency to find Wendy. The ensuing story is the search for Wendy who has now become Stephanie. She's a rather slimy person who screws with everyone in sight, and even pays a black stud to service her. Max is in love with her, but up to this point has not screwed her. When he does he asks her the impossible—to be faithful to him. In the meantime, Angela has traced Stephanie to a high-priced whorehouse, only to discover that she is now wearing a

wig, and is on her way to screw with Harry. Before they can stop the incest, Harry has discovered that Stephanie is really his daughter—but what the hell, he enjoys her anyway. As for Stephanie, she doesn't give a damn—just so long as she gets paid. I have a feeling that this film was made about 1979 because Eric Edwards looks much younger, and John Leslie looks embarrassed about the whole thing. But VCX is offering it as a 1983 release. Other than some different scenic backgrounds ski lodge, and screwing on a schooner, and a sequence where an unnamed actor in a night club is trying to penetrate a naked young lady with a dildo mounted on the turret of a remote-controlled toy tank (he does) it's nothing you haven't seen before.

TOUCH ME IN THE MORNING
CC   NN   BI   NR
1982   CABALLERO

P/D—Elliot Lewis, Louie Lewis
F/A—Paul Thomas, Michael Morrison, Mike
  Horner
F/A—Veronica Hart, Lysa Thatcher, Lisa de
  Leeuw, Sharon Mitchell, Nicole Noir,
  Becky Savage

Skyler Barnes (Paul Thomas) and his wife, Jenny (Veronica Hart), are in bed when this one opens. The entire story is an alteration of their various sexual fantasies. Seems that Skyler is so busy earning a living and drinking too much on an expense account that he can't get it up with his wife. Worse, when she accuses him of not being interested anymore, he shoves her down on the living room rug, but he really can't get an erection, and she laughs at him hysterically. From that point on, while they lie in bed through the night not touching each other, they each have dreams. Jenny's include making it with her hairdresser (Michael Morrison) and his female assistant in a threesome; then she thinks of seducing the guy next door (Mike Horner), who is younger than she is, and enviously watches him screwing his girlfriend in the garage. Before her marriage to Skyler (he never pushed her for sex, even then) she remembers making it with her girlfriend Sharon Mitchell. Skyler's fantasies include meeting a girl on a park bench (Lysa Thatcher) who invites him back to her office, plays with her pussy with a banana he offers her from his lunch and then lies back on her desk where she makes romantic love to him. He also remembers smoking pot with Sharon while she fucks her boyfriend on the bed and he laughs himself to sleep; and finally he enjoys Ravel's "Bolero" to a screwing sequence with Lisa de Leeuw. And now it's morning. Jenny sobs in his arms and he tells her he's sorry about last night (when he couldn't get it up) but, "I love you." After that he calls his office and tells them he won't be in that day. Then Skyler leads Jenny to the living room couch and shows her that he's a great lover after all. The CC rating is really for the sex scenes, which are mostly gentle with soft-focus and vaseline-covered lenses.

ULTIMATE PLEASURES **NN BI DK**
1977 HIFCOA

P/D—Merino Fortes, Bruce Van Buren
F/A—Peter DuBois
F/A—Nina Fausse, Iris Medina

After some weird footage that shows various people copulating against a San Francisco daily life background, the credits finally appear and a young man named Jim is trying to convince his pretty wife, Rose, that he's horny and needs to have sex. He hasn't been inside her since last Sunday. "I'll fuck you tomorrow morning," she tells him. "But right now I've got a headache and need to sleep." Then she lies on the bed naked, legs open, with a view of her vulva that he can't keep his eyes off as he lies on the couch in the living room. When he tries after she emerges from the bathroom, she announces that she has her period. (It's interesting that in no sexvid that I know of does a guy enjoy a woman during her period.) After this auspicious beginning, when you hope that you might learn more about this couple—she works in an office, he drives a taxi—somehow they end up in a sex clinic. Again you have hopes as she tells the female doctor the truth: she never has climaxed and is not good in bed and

that's why her first husband probably divorced her. After that, it's all downhill as Jim and Rose live out their fantasies which offer nothing you haven't seen before, except a sequence of a naked woman (not Rose) kneeling in a tub. Six (count them) guys pass by and she fellates them one by one. Among all this is a diatribe against cigarette smoking and ecological destruction. John Holmes is not in this flick, but Annette Haven appears in one of the group sex scenes.

UNNATURAL FAMILY **NN DK (almost DS)**
1975 VIDEO SHOWTIME

P/D—Not given
F/A—None you've ever seen before

The family (a mixture of Irish and Italian), lives on the Lower East Side. Penny, one of the daughters, is getting married to Tony (I think that's his name), but except for one lengthy scene where they try each other out before the wedding, most of the action centers on other members of the family. There's Daddy doing the dishes with Mommy. Lifting her skirt while she's up to her elbows in the dishpan, he decides she still has a nice ass. Cooperatively, she anoints his penis with soapy dishwater made so from a convenient container of Dove. And there's Vinnie, a Mafia type who returns to his own apartment and proves who's boss by grabbing his wife, Janey, by the hair and yelling at her, "Tell me you want it." Sobbing, she finally tells him what he wants to hear. Later another relative, John, who's taking care of the ring and flowers, remembers he doesn't have a date for the wedding. After searching through his datebook and being rejected by former flames, he calls Janey, who tells him to come over for dinner—she'll think of someone. He's having a candlelight dinner with Janey when Vinnie, drunk and jealous, arrives. Vinnie forces John, at knife point, to undress. He strips Janey, and while he shoves his "vengeance" in her, she is forced to fellate John. Why does she put up with Vinnie? Later she tells Penny, "I was working for Vinnie's daddy in a sweatshop where he was boss." Daddy's price for the job was occasional servicing by Janey. When she got pregnant, Daddy forced Vinnie to marry her. Listening to all this, Penny wonders if she should cancel the wedding. Most of the dialogue and acting in this one is believable, as are the sex sequences. A kind of porno Paddy Chayefsky-style slice-of-life drama.

WICKED SENSATIONS
NN   NM   DK   NR (sort of—at the end)
CABALLERO

P/D—Jerry Ross, Ron Chrones
F/A—John Leslie, Paul Thomas
F/A—Annette Haven, Mai Lin, Diana Holt

Pierson (John Leslie), a famous novelist, isn't making it with his wife, Heather (Annette Haven), who, believe it or not, goes to bed with curlers on and wearing glasses and wonders why he doesn't make love to her. Since Annette's body is in good shape, most men won't understand why either. But Pierson is continuously peering in on his friend George's sexmaking. George (Paul Thomas) lives across the street and leaves his lights on. Ultimately, Pierson tells Heather he can't stand her any longer; he's going skiing with George. Actually he's met Candy (Diana Holt), and he's benumbed by her face (and ass, of course, though he hasn't seen it bare). He knows that Candy is going for the weekend to Kirkwood in the California mountains, so he and George arrive in a van. George immediately takes on a woman he picks up (Chris Cassidy), and while he is screwing her to a fare-thee-well in the women's room (other women walk by, watch, shrug and leave), Pierson is in a wild session with Candy. (Diana Holt is very pretty.) But alas, when they finish, she tells Pierson that she's not a one-man woman. "I love my old man Robert," she tells him, "and we have an open marriage and even try threesomes." Pierson is shocked. He would never share his wife or woman with another male. He rushes home to Heather and they live happily ever after—following some fervid sex.

WOMAN IN LOVE   **NN   BI   DK   NR (occasionally)**
1980   TVX

P/D—Kemal Horolu
F/A—Richard Bolla, Ron Jeremy, Paul Thomas
F/A—Laurien Dominique, Vanessa Del Rio, Veronica Hart

Christine (Laurien Dominique) is married to Alex (Richard Bolla), who is so involved in his business that Christine tells him that he has "shacked up with a slide rule" instead of her. He's so tired in bed that all he can do is roll over and go to sleep. Christine meets wealthy Giorgio in a dress boutique run by Simone (Vanessa Del Rio), and he invites her to one of his famous sexual free-for-alls in his penthouse apartment, where she is properly shocked but quite entranced with Erie (Ron Jeremy, who in most flicks is a real bad guy—among other things he can suck his own cock). Eric is romantic with her, but Christine is married and Eric has a model, Veronica Hart, who will literally stand on her head to satisfy him. After a brief affair with Eric, which is aborted when she discovers his relationship with the model, Christine has a tender love affair with Giorgio. She's so much in love with him that she leaves Alex a note telling him that she's running away with Giorgio, but Giorgio takes off for Europe by himself and leaves her a rose in remembrance. Poor Christine—sobbing, she stumbles home to her husband, who forgives her. If Horolu had concentrated 100 percent on Laurien, who is a very natural actress and expert at playing suburban housewives (she appears in only a few films), he would have made an adult film that many women who have been married ten years or more might identify with. Unfortunately, he screws things up with ten minutes of totally unrelated bondage and discipline and transvestite junk that you would do well to erase for a second watching.

17

Role Playing

AIRLINE COCKPIT **NN** **BI** **DK (group sex)**
1973   BOCCACCIO 100

P/D—Not given
F/A—Not given

The women in this one are supposedly airline stewardesses. The cockpit is between their legs. The women are uniformly nice looking. First there is a pretty woman, Connie, with one guy in bed, and then another guy comes in with his woman and they go in the bedroom and can't wait to get their clothes off. In the meantime, a pretty woman is listening to the action, fantasizing she's in the middle of things (when she isn't) and reading Xaviera Hollander's book, *The Happy Hooker*. There's an interesting sequence when the guys want to switch and one of the girls indignantly refuses. This one looks like a 16-mm film that the participants probably did for a few bucks and lots of laughs.

BABE **NN** **NM** **BI** **DK**
1982   ARROW

P/D—John Christopher
F/A—Roderic Pierce, Ron Jeremy, George Payne
F/A—Samantha Fox, Tiffany Clark, Bobbi Jackson

Babe (Bobbi Jackson) is a top New York model who practically keeps Samantha Fox's model agency in business. She has plenty of men but basically detests them. She wants her freedom. Then her dear old grandpa, whom she loved, dies and leaves her 20 million bucks, BUT not until she's married, and that must occur within 30 days or the old boy's estate goes to charity. Inheriting money and enacting the provisions of some crazy's last will and testament seems to be a favorite of adult filmmakers. In this one, a further gimmick is that Samantha knows that if Babe marries the wrong man, and at the same time has so much money, she'll quit the agency and Samantha will be out of business. What to do? Samantha enters the venture capital business, offering Babe's inheritance to a series of clucks if they agree to marry her. They are obviously men that Babe will never climb into bed with. Then, whoopee! Samantha finds just the right guy—an impoverished actor, Chad Collins (Roderic Pierce), who has daydreams of mounting nude versions of Shakespeare and other Elizabethan and Greek dramatists in Broadway productions that will cost millions of dollars and use up all of Babe's inheritance. Thus she'll have to continue to work for Samantha. During the reception, Babe goes to bed with another guy and the groom is blown in the bathroom by his old girlfriend. Samantha's plan is working! Then Chad's play opens and instead of being a ten-million-dollar flop, *Variety* calls it the best *Oedipus* of the century. Instead of being poor, Babe is going to be twice as rich. But never mind, it's always blackest before the dawn. Chad agrees with Babe that they both need their careers, and Babe comes back to work. Ain't that nice? As for the sex, you've seen it all before, except one scene where young guys who work for Samantha and whom she's servicing tell her, "You're pretty good for an old lady!" Tempis fugit, even for porno stars!

BALL GAME   **NN   BI   DK   NL**
1980   CABALLERO

P/D—Anne Perry
F/A—Laurence Rothschild
F/A—Candida Royalle, Lisa de Leeuw

The baseball game between the inmates of the Women's County Jail (the Beavers) and the male guards (the Dicks) doesn't get played until this sexvid is more than halfway through. To wear them out, the night before the game the women capture the guards and one by one suck and fuck them to blobs. Is Anne Perry not so subtly trying to prove that when it comes to sex men are very much the weaker sex? In this one Anne has pragmatically proved to the male reviewers who put her down for the romanticism of her films *Sweet Savage* and *Count the Ways* that she can produce a male fantasy film equal to any male production. But most women watching it will shrug or say ugh.

BARBARA BROADCAST   **NN   BI   DK**
and DS in one extended bondage scene
1977   QUALITY & TVX

P/D—
F/A—Jamie Gillis, Bobby Astyr
F/A—C. J. Laing, Annette Haven, Constance Money

Among other things in this sexvid, C. J. Laing urinates in a dish and is screwed by a human dishwasher. This is a plotless flick gravitating around a posh New York restaurant where the female waitresses lie on the table and offer themselves as hor d'oeuvres, and the male waiters offer sperm salad dressing squirted on the lettuce. If the waitresses drop anything, they must give the headwaiter a blow job. Unfortunately, it's not very funny—only sad.

BLAZING ZIPPERS
NN   NM   NL   NR   BI
1974   SELECT/ESSEX

P/D—Boots McCoy
F/A—Big John Henderson, Gerry John, John Seaman
F/A—Melissa Jennings, Anne Beatty

Melissa (Melissa Jennings, who is nicely homely, wears no makeup and has a country look) keeps having sexual dreams in which she is screwing a cowboy or being raped by two of them. So, Melissa goes to her girlfriend's shrink, Dr. Grooveright. He tries to convince her that he's a cowboy at heart, but not succeeding, tells her that she needs a Western vacation where she can really do it with a cowboy. Way out West, Melissa gets a job as bartender in a male pub known as Toots. And soon she's enjoying Toots as well as a black cowboy on the joint's pool table after hours. But the rodeo is coming, and soon Melissa is involved with Jimmy-Bob. Toots is screwing Hank Wilson (Big John Henderson) so much he can scarcely rope a steer. In the meantime, in a nice outdoor country scene, Melissa and Jimmy-Bob make love romantically, and you just know they are going to get married and live happily ever after. Most women will probably feel some empathy with Melissa Jennings, who is such a nicely average American female—physically at least!

CB MAMAS   **NN   BI   NM**
1976   MITCHELL

P/D—Mitchell Brothers
F/A—Joey Civera, David Morris
F/A—Leslie Bovee, Sally Foremost, Pat Lee

The second her businessman husband leaves their suburban house for work, Leslie Bovee shoves all the kitchen debris in a plastic bag, takes the curlers out of her hair, changes into a seductive dress and answers the door to her neighbors— all ladies of the same age. She turns on the CB and announces "Breaker, breaker. Beaver Country to Animal Kingdom. There's a fire in the oven." After that you never see a CB again. The guys who arrive are evidently truckers, but you don't see their trucks—only their cocks. When hubby comes home from work, Leslie tells him, "You smell like a distillery—enjoying yourself while I've been cleaning the fucking house all day."

CANDY STRIPERS NN DK BI
1978 ARROW

P/D—Bob Chinn
F/A—Paul Thomas
F/A—Amber Hunt, Nancy Hoffman, Sharon Thorpe

Screw's Best Film of 1978. A censored version eliminates one scene of fist fucking, which brought this sexvid to trial after a Los Angeles police raid in 1980. When you stop to think about it, where's the best place to make an adult film? In a hospital, where there are plenty of beds. In the event you don't know what candy stripers are, they are high school kids (female) who volunteer to deliver flowers, magazines and candy to the patients, saving money for hospitals and thus learning hospital routine. This crew of the three females listed above go a step further and wash the male patients' pricks, collect urine samples, blow the doctors in linen closets, suck off male patients, eat the nurses and get in bed with male and female patients at the drop of a hat. A nonstop fucking and sucking flick. The redeeming feature of this sexvid is the background music, which includes original songs, "Yankee Doodle gets it up and it's a dandy. Yankee Doodle keep it up and with the girls be handy . . . and Poogie Woogie, baby . . . all night long . . . Poogie Woogie baby, love can't be wrong." Maybe poogie-woogieing will enter the vernacular.

COED FEVER NN DK BI
CABALLERO CONTROL

P/D—Harold Lime, Robert MacCallun
F/A—Jamie Gillis, John Leslie
F/A—Serena, Annette Haven, Brooke West, Vanessa Del Rio, Samantha Fox, Juliet Anderson

The guys in Upper U Omega Fraternity are low class. The girls in Alpha Epsilon Zeta sorority are about to be featured in a national magazine, Newsmonth, owned by the father of one of the sisters, but only if they date the less horny Phi Upsilon Delta brothers. The story line is not only pretty silly, but worse, the actors and actresses look as if they should be working for their doctorates rather than their undergraduate degrees, or just working. On the other hand, most of the top porno stars, male and female, make at least one genital appearance in this one, and no one can deny that they are about the right age to portray the nice-looking neighbors you meet in your apartment building, in suburbia or in church. There are the usual "don't come-inside-me" sequences, as well as a sorority initiation party with vibrators and paddling of coeds, bare behinds and forced fellatio for one sister as punishment. Many of the coeds wear garter belts, of course. In the things-you've-never-tried-before department, one coed supports herself on a hand bar suspended from the ceiling of the fraternity house while she rides her male friend. A weightless fuck, or the old male dream of the girl in the basket with a hole in it. Women will find this one pretty ucky.

COSMOPOLITAN GIRLS NN NM DK
1981 VCA

P/D—Not given
F/A—Matt West, Ron Jeremy, Rick Iverson, Ron Hudd
F/A—Tamar Lynne, Miranda Stevens, Lisa Bee, Marilyn Gee

While none of the three women depicted in this one are shown reading Cosmopolitan magazine, who knows? They may have been included in one of the surveys of the sex lives of Cosmopolitan readers that the magazine regularly makes. The film opens on a weekday morning in Manhattan with three separate single women awakening in their beds. As you watch them wander around their kitchens naked, take showers or look down at the city from their high-rises, you hope the story of one day in their lives will be better than it turns out. One of the ladies is a dentist, and when she isn't fantasizing herself in the chair and the male patient servicing her, she is undressing the next male patient and climbing on top of him in the chair. The next lady, Lisa Bee, whom you'll recognize by a mole above her left breast, is a receptionist. Her employer, Ron Jeremy, who is busy screwing his clients (you never know how he makes a living), makes it apparent if she wants to keep her job, she's next. The third lady models underwear in the hope of landing a job—but all she manages is to land on the floor under a hefty buyer. At night they all return to their separate apartments and, as the camera cuts from one to the other, with vibrators, dildos and their own fingers, they prove they can take care of themselves better than any of the men they have been involved with.

CREME RINSE CC NN NL BI DK
1976 VIDEO SHOWTIME

P/D—F. Lee Ballher, Dick Cocks
F/A—John Holmes, Peter Packer, Caesar
    Balstic
F/A—Renee Bond, Ginger Peachy, Linda Licks,
    Angie Cinsalo

Despite the fact that the producer of this one has hidden behind an obvious pseudonym, it's better than many sexvids. Obviously inspired by the 1975 movie *Shampoo* it raises a question as to why more porno filmmakers haven't explored the possibility of a hairdresser's salon. This is the only one I know of. Tony and Bob own the place, and do all the work on their customers. Neither is John C. Holmes, but they are nice-looking guys. Tony bets Bob his half ownership that he can score with more of their lady customers than he can. Bob accepts the bet, and Renee Bond,

who is their appointment manager, takes care of Bob. In very natural dialogue, they discuss sex, the hairdressing business and the bet. Tony arranges a party, to which he invites their customers, married or not. All attend, and soon a happy orgy ensues. It is interrupted momentarily by John C. Holmes looking for his wife, who is being happily scored by Tony or Bob. The bet ends in a tie.

FANTASY GIRLS NN BI DK
1976 ASTRO

P/D—Alex de Renzy

As usual, Alex tells a consistently integrated story. This one gives no credits to the actors and actresses except the wording, "Thanks to my friends, the players who made this film possible." It has only a few people of either sex that you've seen before or since. The flick is the story of a massage parlor and the lives of the women off and on the job. One extended bisexual scene could be used as a training film for men on how to arouse a woman. The film subtly accentuates male dependence on women (the masseuses who are serving them). One poor guy offers $500 to climax *inside* a woman.

FANTASY WORLD NN occasional DK
1979 WONDERFUL WORLD OF VIDEO

P/D—Gail Palmer, Eliott Lewis, Bob Chinn
F/A—Jon Martin, James Price, Paul Thomas
F/A—Jesie St. James, Laurien Dominique,
    Sharon Cain

Three sailors have been to sea for six months. Together with three female telephone operators from Dayton, Ohio, they get all their sexual fantasies fulfilled, including two girls sleeping with one guy. Two romantic love scenes follow (this is a Gail Palmer sexvid), one with a lover singing romantically at a white piano in a white suit in a white bedroom, and one with a Japanese girl giving a sailor an extended sexmaking ceremony. Whether Gail is actually director or not, this sexvid shows a woman's touch.

FRAT HOUSE **NN presumably NL but not much**
1979   VCX

xxxxxxxxxxxxxxxxxxxxxxxxxxxxxxxxxxxxxxxxxxxxxxxxxxxxxx

P/D—Rod Richards, Sven Conrad
F/A—Randy Allen
F/A—Aimee Leigh, Lisa de Leeuw

At Faulk U. (university), both in the sororities and fraternities such as I Phelta Thi (ugh), sex is a way of life. The humor in this one is slapstick and often puerile. Brothers cut the pockets out of their pants and entice women to look for a quarter so they can make a phone call. And there are statements like "How can I say I love you when you're sitting on my face?" Or there's an advertisement for Brim lubrication with novocaine so that the purchasor can enjoy "your chocolate speedway. Rub on Brim and you can fill it to the rim." An X-rated *Animal House* it isn't.

FRENCH FINISHING SCHOOL **NN NM BI DK DS**
CABALLERO

xxxxxxxxxxxxxxxxxxxxxxxxxxxxxxxxxxxxxxxxxxxxxxxxxxxxxx

P/D—Richard Tantolini, Lois Chapman
F'A—Claude Irrison
F/A—Brooke West, Cathy Grenier, Desiree Cousteau

A Reeltime Pleasure Film, this one was produced in Europe by Beate Ushe, a German millionaire from her chain of European sex shops. Of course, she makes films too. Beate has announced that her films will appeal to women, but she doesn't make it with this one. The entire plot revolves around Brooke West as Samantha, one of the girls in the upper-income school who spies on a male teacher, Eric (Claude Irrison). She tries to blackmail him with photographs she takes of him seducing another student, Kathy. (If this is Desiree Cousteau, I didn't recognize her and neither will you.) Eric turns the tables on Samantha by screwing her on the hood of his car while three other guys jerk off over her, and then whisking her to a medieval mansion where she is stretched out on a long table and worked over by a black midget, a huge breasted woman and a guy in a leather mask wearing a cock ring. Never mind.

Kathy, who loves the professor, too, is upset that Samantha has stolen him away. So she murders Samantha with a pistol. No kidding! Brooke West is a lovely woman, but you may weep that she's so cool about it all.

GARAGE GIRLS **NN BI DK NL NR (last scene)**
1981   CAL VISTA

xxxxxxxxxxxxxxxxxxxxxxxxxxxxxxxxxxxxxxxxxxxxxxxxxxxxxx

P/D—Bernardo Spinelli, Robert Neeallum
F/A—John Leslie, John Seeman, Jon Martin
F/A—Lisa de Leuuw, Dorothy Le May, Chris Cassidy, Brooke West (the Garage Girls), Georgina Spelvin, Susanne Nero, Dewey Alexander

The humor in this one, which is almost continuous, is not the kind that will inspire female laughter. Rather, it is male barroom or fraternity humor. Thus in 1982 not all adult filmmakers agreed with Chuck Vincent (see *Roommates* listing, p. 125). The Garage Girls have nothing special to distinguish them. They have just finished a mechanic's school course and opened a garage, which among other things provides towing service (described by one male actor when he has his toe in one of the ladies' vaginas as toe-ing service). They all wear coveralls that let their breasts overflow beyond the straps, and of course they wear nothing underneath. Two of them, Dorothy Le May and Chris Cassidy, take on a whole poolroom full of guys, but Lisa is faithful throughout the film to Aloysius Duke (John Leslie), the patrolman on the beat who passes by their garage. He showers with Lisa in a long, wet sexmaking scene, and, wearing a gorilla suit, chases the bad guy who has been trying to blow up the garage or put it out of business with stink bombs. Seems he and his buddies are mechanics who resent women's libbers horning in on the business. There's also a happily silly Bonnie and Clyde chase scene through the city with the hold-up guy and gal ending up in the garage. They are quickly subdued by one of the girls with a karate maneuver. And Georgina calls for aid when her camper, with some not-so-young Youth Corps campers, breaks down and her charges spend the afternoon fornicating. Men between 18 and 40 may laugh their heads off, but most women won't.

GINA, THE FOXY LADY **NN   DK   BI**
COMPETITIVE VIDEO

P/D—Jason DuPrez, Franz Beckman
F/A—B. J. Boggs, Jack Roven, Desiree
    Cousteau, Dorothy Le May

Buck (Jack Roven?) is a good-looking Mexican who tries to make a living gambling. Whether he's playing poker with black and white pimps who have plenty of dough (openers are $50 with $5,000 pots) or shooting crap or pool, he's a loser. Gina (Sandra Stevens?), a sad-looking woman with a pixie face and boyish haircut (the kind of woman who brings out a protective instinct in some men), has no choice but to go whoring to pay Buck's debts. To compound his callousness, he screws her girlfriend Nancy (she encourages him because he's depressed) in a very unusual outdoor screwing sequence with the Golden Gate Bridge in the background. Buck owes Prince, a black pimp, several grand, and Gina is the pawn. She tells Prince it doesn't matter; he can do anything with her he likes. But Prince likes her and warns against Buck. Sure enough, he gets deeper in debt, and Gina is screwing two or more at a time, but she only wants Buck. This one has a believable underdog story line reflecting a sad slice of life in lower-class America. The story ends with Gina, who most certainly is not a foxy lady, running sobbing to Prince for protection and Buck getting gunned down by one of his creditors.

THE HANDYMAN AND THE STEPDAUGHTER **NN**
ASTRO

P/D—Richard Bennett
F/A—Jessie Adams
F/A—Kathryn Glen, Leslie Lane

It looks as if this one might have been shot directly on videotape. Two very aggressive but young and fairly attractive females play doctor with the boy next door (in this case the gardener), and they offer him $25 to service them. As for the stepdaughter, the plot(?) is that Mommy won't have sex with Daddy anymore because he got too fat. The stepdaughter doesn't mind, and when she arrives, Mommy catches her with Daddy and decides to join the fun. Pretty ucky.

HEALTH SPA **CC   NN   NM   BI**
SELECT/ESSEX AND TVX

P/D—Clair Dia
F/A—John Seeman, Robert Girard
F/A—Abigail Clayton, Kay Parker

If you've ever thought about the possibilities of a fully equipped gymnasium as a place for sexmaking, this sexvid covers all bases, including belt massage vibration during oral sex or intercourse, or coming while riding an exercycle or a roller massage, or screwing, eating and sucking in the swimming pool. The premise of this female-directed film is that sexercise is the way to keep healthy, and maybe it is! It even has a story line about a hung-up, sexually repressed woman doing an exposé on a health club. Most women will enjoy this one, and Abigail Clayton's acting, which occasionally is surprisingly good.

LE STRIPTEASE **R**
1983   GOLD STRIPE

P/D—Danielle Peters, Felix Daniels

Gold Stripe offers 14 half-hour tapes in this series, each one confined to a separate stripper. Unless they keep the price low, I would bet they may have to combine two or three strippers on one tape. I've seen two of the tapes—one a classic featuring Sharon Mitchell who begins wearing a flowery print dress and long stockings. She is nicely watched by the camera against a pale blue background and she moves from an almost virginal strip to a hot seductive finale. The other one is Electra Blue in Leather who strips to a rock song called the "God Damn pushing man/ I've smoked a lot of grass/ Popped a lot of pills/ But I've never had nothing my spirit could kill." This lady is a whorish-style stripper.

LET'S TALK SEX NN NM BI DK
1983 CABALLERO

P/D—Ted Gorley, Paul Vatelli
F/A—Bridgette Monet, Linda Shaw, Patricia Manning, Becky Savage, Tina Ross, Kitten Natividad
F/A—David Cannon, Kevin James, Don Hart, Herschel Savage

In case you haven't heard it—phone sex where you can call up a number and listen to a woman try to turn you on verbally, with the time charged to your Master Card or Visa (or aural sex as it is called) was the big gimmick of 1983. *High Society* magazine offered a no-charge variation. If you called their special number the New York Telephone company shared the profits with the magazine. In March 1983 calls from the State of Virginia's government agencies to hear *High Society's* 57-second sex message exceeded 2,000 calls. So that's the plot of this one. For good measure the ladies at Dial Fantasy whom you telephone for some steamy sex talk turn the caller on so much that you can actually see his fantasy come to life right on your tube. Thus one guy enjoys his fantasy of breaking into a nurse's apartment (Bridgette Monet), waiting for her to come home, forcing her to undress, making her fellate him and then having sex with her which she enjoys as much as he does. A young man wants to make it with his stepmother while Daddy is away. The ladies at Dial Fantasy obliging make it happen for him over the telephone but you see it really happening on your screen. Another guy wants to make it with two women. Two women at Dial Fantasy get so turned on helping him live out his fantasy that lo and behold you are suddenly watching four women making it—in different locations—with two of the fantasy ladies eventually asking the poor guy to join the fun. Finally, one of the ladies (Becky Savage) becomes so hooked on a guy that keeps paying for her aural sex turn-on that she meets him in person, which is probably the daydream of any guy who ever made a phone sex call in the first place. Don't bring this one home to your favorite lady. It's only for horny guys!

LOVE AIRLINES NN BI DK
1978 WONDERFUL WORLD

P/D—Andy Binner, John Fowler
F/A—John Leslie, Bill Anderson, Jean de Villroy
F/A—Georgina Spelvin, Doris Tyler, Brigitte Graham

Georgina is president of Sex Airlines—also known as Love Airlines. John Leslie arrives in her office to apply for a job as steward. The airline already offers stewardesses who service the male passengers, plus continuous porno movies and female pilots who put the plane on automatic pilot and service each other. In her office, Georgina tells John about one particular flight. She evidently has omniscient vision, since some of the action takes place off the plane and she wasn't actually on board. Nevertheless, in first class on this flight are a novelist, an Arab, two cowboys who are practical jokers, an actress who is now a big star (but her boyfriend isn't) and Jean de Villroy (see *Sex Roulette*, p. 181). He actually is 70 years old and plays his usual role—the rich man who can keep it up practically forever, but can't ejaculate! In an off-the-plane sequence, woman after woman tries to make him come but collapses from exhaustion. Finally at 30,000 feet, he tries a ploy recommended to him by his doctors. He disinfects three stewardesses' mouths and they do the job, after which everyone on the plane joins in a celebration orgy. Finally we're back to Georgina and John, and she asks him, "Do you think you're equipped to be a steward?" And he proves that he is—on top of her mahogany desk.

METER MAIDS NN DK
1968-1970 SILHOUETTE VIDEO

P/D—Bob Kirk
F/A—Frank Ryan, John Rand, Rick Smith
F/A—Linda Baile, Toni Scott, Ann Brady

Three meter maids arrive at a barroom after a hard day's work. Three guys arrive, and the owner closes the bar. Pretty soon all six are happily having sex. When the girls arrive home late in the evening, their respective husbands are waiting and each girl takes care of her "old man," too. But one husband is suspicious. He catches his wife in a lie and calls the other two to meet with him and their spouses at two o'clock in the morning to get to the bottom of things. They all do—each other's spouses's bottoms! What makes some of these very early adult movies more interesting is their relative naivete and the homeliness of both the males and females. The men also pay much more attention to the women, and there is often more natural sexmaking than in later films which often accentuate kinkiness (see note under *Fanny Hill*, p. 187).

N.Y. BABES **NN DK BI**
1979 HOME ENTERTAINMENT, ARROW

P/D—Neil Grant, Bobby Hollander, Kurt and Andrew Barat
F/A—Bobby Astyr, John Leslie, Jamie Gillis
F/A—Gloria Leonard, Serena, Vanessa Del Rio

Imagine a pro softball team of porno stars who (for about ten minutes) play softball—the N.Y. Babes against the San Francisco Dolls. The players have clothes on, but some locker room sex is intercut. In addition to the gals listed above, the N.Y. Babes have Helen Madigan, Candida Royalle, Marlene Willoughby and Rikki O'Neal on their team. The story quickly deteriorates to a house party at the home of the owner of American Softball League to celebrate the victory, during which O'Calley (Jamie Gillis), owner of the team, is literally shafted in the ladies room by Gloria and Marlene, who are after a better contract for the team. Bobby Hollander, publisher of *Cinema X* magazine, put this one together. Its real claim to fame is a most erotic striptease, performed by Serena at the disco party after the game. Many of the porno stars have perfected a style of striptease dancing that would make old-time burlesque stars turn over in the grave in embarrassment. It's surprising that some

adult filmmaker hasn't combined erotic dancing into a full story line.

OLYMPIC FEVER **NN BI DS (one scene) Occasionally NL**
1979 ARROW

P/D—Phillip Marshak
F/A—Paul Thomas, Ron Jeremy, William Margold
F/A—Seka, Serena, Kristin

This one was made before the United States declined to enter the 1980 Olympics, but it doesn't detract from the silliness of the plot. The Russians are trying to eliminate Kristin from the 200-meter freestyle swim event because their spies have determined that no one can beat her—she even exceeds the male records. What is her secret? Protein injections by mouth. How does she get them? You guessed it! In between, the story has a more intriguing background than most since it was shot in the winter in the mountains where the swim training camp is located. A feature of this one is William Margold, who produces, acts in and reviews, with acerbity adult films for many magazines. In the things-you've-never-seen-before department, the coach (Margold) screws one of the team in the snow. Kristin, the Olympic contender, is captured by the Russians and beaten, but she wins with a final injection of protein from the coach. Theme song: "I didn't know, but I've been told an Eskimo's pussy is mighty cold."

PAPER DOLLS **NM BI**
1982 GOURMET

P/D—Not given
F/A—A male interviewer
F/A—Linda Shaw, Cara Lott, Tina Marie, Shana, Chrissy Beauchamp

Paper dolls are young ladies who appear in skin magazines that you'll find in adult bookstores, like *Exposed, Velvet, Cheri, Beaver, Chic, Hustler, High Society, Porn Stars,* etc. This is a good fraternity house tape for sex-starved brothers who in all probability have a collection of these magazines and wish their own girlfriends were so eager to show their "split beavers" to them. First you meet Shan, who is 20, and shows her shaved vagina to a middle-aged male interviewer. She has absolutely no compunctions about showing her genitals in front of a camera. She lost her virginity at 17. She still masturbates and gives a demonstration on how she does it. She can come three times in an hour. She's never tried anal sex and never will. Next there's Tina Marie. She's 18, five feet 11, and a 39D with a 28-inch waist. She lost her virginity at 15½. She loves fellatio, and she likes to masturbate. If you'll send her a SASE care of Gourmet, she'll send you a picture of herself "with her boobs out." Next is Linda Shaw. "Sucking cock is my favorite position," she tells the interviewer. He tells her that her labia is folded over and looks like a little butterfly. "Can you make it wink?" She can! Linda also loves to make it with women and she and Tina Marie give you an extended session. Alas, no one asks them the questions most psychologists would like to ask, beginning with, "What are you really like—and what are you saying because it's an easy way to earn a buck?"

PLATINUM PARADISE NN BI DK
some silly NL
1980 COMMAND

P/D—Cecil Howard
F/A—Bobby Astyr, Eric Edwards
F/A—Kandi Barbour, Samantha Fox, Vanessa Del Rio

You wake up to morning in the Big Apple. Ballet teachers, ballerinas, hookers, gigolos and women's clothing buyers are all blending work and play. The ballet instructor cuts a crotch hole in the ballerinas' leotards; the gigolo brings his client to climax five times but refuses to try it in her nose; a dress model takes on the two buyers at the same time; the gigolo takes a hooker to bed thinking she's a paying client and a wife telephones her husband and asks if he can guess what she is doing right now. You guessed! This one has a good theme song and an interesting cinematographic New York City ambiance.

PLEASE, MR. POSTMAN NN BI DK
1980 VCA

P/D—Elliot Lewis, Louie Lewis
F/A—Jessie Adams, Richard Pacheco, Paul Thomas, Michael Morrison
F/A—Chelsea McLane, Loni Sanders, Nicole Noir, Holly McCall

In what seems to be a Coldwater Canyon post office, Jessie Adams and Loni Sanders sort the mail and deliver it. Before going on their routes, they also service each other among the packages and mail. En route, they deliver various letters and bundles to people which are all sexually related. Chelsea McClane (a.k.a. Chelsea Manchester and Tigr) gets a package supposedly containing her home movies, but when she runs them for her girlfriend it turns out they are homemade porno flicks delivered to her by mistake. Never mind, they turn her girlfriend on, and soon they are rubbing tits and lapping each other's vulvas. Next Loni delivers to Richard Pacheco a package which turns out to be the underwear of a famous actress he's in love with. Never mind, Loni looks just like her, and soon she's modeling the underwear for Richard in a typical Pacheco scene. After he screws her and she's asleep, he kisses her ass and gently covers her with a blanket. Next two women get a package filled with sex aids sent to them by three guys in their apartment building—and soon all five are in bed together. Michael Morrison gets a swinger magazine and calls several women. He gets a dominatrix and a more loving one, and they enjoy his penis while he tries all of their orifices. Next Paul Thomas is in bed while his wife, Holly McCall, is opening her package in the bathroom. She slowly blows it up and it turns out to be a male rubber doll with a big schlong which gets stuck in her vagina. Yelling for help, Paul reluctantly leaves his television set, extricates her and provides a real man. Outside of Pacheco and Holly, who are more interesting to watch than most porno stars, this one gets a C minus.

PROBALL CHEERLEADERS
NN NL NM BI DK (anal)
1979 ADULT VIDEO

P/D—**Jack Mathews**
F/A—**Johnny Keyes, Turk Lyon, Ric Lutz**
F/A—**Jennifer West, Debbie Evans, Candida Royalle, Lisa de Leeuw, Suzanne Nero**

Nominated for Best Film at the Fourth Annual Erotic Film Festival. Women who are a little overweight will identify with the ladies in this one. My guess is that Candida must weigh about 140; Lisa about 135 (she's really a redhead), Debbie about 145 and Suzanne 135. They are cheerleaders for a team called the Cactus, which is owned by Mr. Prissy Pringle. He, along with Aunt Frieda (Jennifer West), coach of the Prickettes, believes sex will give you cancer and the team should have no orgasms during the season. Too Long (Johnny Keyes) is betting against the team and trying to get the Prickettes to seduce the new player, a guy named Potts (Turk Lyon). All of this is combined into much silliness with a locker and shower scene that is funnier than *Debbie Does Dallas*. It also includes Candida giving head to a dildo strapped onto Aunt Frieda, who is afraid of men but has an orgasm anyway; a long, funny conversational sex scene between Johnny Keyes and Candida; cheerleaders reviving injured players you know how and an extended scene of sexmaking in the rain and mud, all tied together because "it's against the rules for a Prickette to grab a member of the team by his member."

RHINESTONE COWGIRLS   **NN BI DK**
SELECT/ESSEX

P/D—**Damon Christian**
F/A—**Richard Ardo, Richard Barnes**
F/A—**Tiara O'Malley, Yvette Cole, Rhonda Jo Petty**

During the first ten minutes, you'll have big hopes for this film. To the accompaniment of an original country western song, "Glory Bound" (which should become a Grand Old Opry favorite) you see Roger (Richard Ardo, a likeable newcomer to adult films) hitching a ride on a country road. He's picked up by a farmer, and sitting in the rear of the truck, his feet in manure, he reads a letter from his wife, who has divorced him after their last terrible night together. In a very attractively photographed sexmaking scene with much emphasis on the lady's hands and face, you watch them making love until they are interrupted by two plainclothesmen who handcuff Roger and lead him away from his distraught wife. Seems that Roger is an embezzler. After this somewhat unbelievable scene, the story line gets Roger involved with Marcie (Tiara O'Malley), a real tough lady who owns a country western bar in Cactus Corner where Roger is hiding out. Marcie learns of Roger's past (by digging in his pockets after she's screwed him to a fare-thee-well). A dominating sexomaniac, she controls not only Cactus Corner but her waitresses, whom she refuses to let Roger date. Just when she seems to have the upper hand, Roger and Carol (Yvette Cole), a waitress, tie her up and force her to smoke angel dust. They high-tail it out of Cactus Corner to get Roger's cache of stolen money and live happily ever after. Rhonda Jo Petty appears with two other women in a threesome to restore the bar singer's manhood, which has been erased by his encounter with Marcie. Buy this one for the music.

SAN FERNANDO VALLEY GIRLS
NN BI DK
1983 CABALLERO

P/D—**Jo-Anne Lewis, Louis Lewis**
F/A—**Jamie Gillis, Eric Edwards, Paul Thomas, David Morris, Joey Civera**
F/A—**Juliet Anderson, Sharon Mitchell, Janey Robbins, Shelly Ray, Chelsea Manchester**

In case you haven't heard, young ladies who live in the San Fernando Valley a few miles from Los Angeles presumably speak a different language from most American girls, and use words like "bitchen" and "switchen." They call hats which they don't wear "Joannies." They "bag their legs in panty hose," go in for "bikini waxing"— shaving their pussies so the hair won't show at the beach, and they give good head called "durs." On top of that they are very vocal about their sexual enjoyments. To understand the language in this one you should buy *The Valley Girl Dictionary* (a Bantam paperback). Or watch it twice. You may wonder if the valley girls are simply a media-created event to inspire teenagers throughout the country. Unfortunately, the ladies in this one aren't teenagers. Juliet Anderson's name is on the billing but I never did find her, and Sharon Mitchell, Chelsea Manchester look a little the worse for wear and tear. There's no plot—a competition of some kind ensues where different ladies try to prove who is the most representative of the "Vals." One gal tells Eric Edwards, "I love to be able to suck your dick and have it between my tits at the same time." Another tells about her boyfriend, "When he comes it could fill one of my mother's Tupperware bowls." Jamie Gillis screws one lady while the other one sits on her face and gets serviced by her. Jamie finally tells both of them "Gag on this for a while." And David Morris does a transvestite act, and Paul Thomas, as the valley hairdresser, does a lot more than bikini waxing. The only thing surprising about this one is that, with the exception of John Leslie and Richard Pacheco, it features so many top male stars.

SATIN SUITE **NN BI DK**
1980   QUALITY

P/D—**John Eagle, Phillip Drexler, Jr.**
F/A—**Eric Edwards, Richard Bolla, Jake Teague, Roger Caine**
F/A—**Samantha Fox, Arcadia Small, Lemmon Young, Christie Ford**

Falcon Eddy (Samantha Fox), also known as the Dragon Lady, is the editor of *Eighteen* magazine, one of many published by "a sprawling empire" called Rothwell Industries. "Using her body as a tool, a total weapon," she is trying to take over the entire corporation. In the process, her models must enjoy sex with her. Her top assistant negotiates deals for her in the company limousine (a Rolls Royce, of course) and takes clients to "lunch" (eating each other) as the chauffeur drives the car through a car wash. To achieve her goal, Falcon Eddy videotapes her sex episodes with married clients young and old and then threatens to give the tapes to their wives. She rehires a fired alcoholic accountant (Richard Bolla), and he agrees to help her milk the company. Add to this her corruption of an IRS agent (Eric Edwards). She gets him blown on the Staten Island Ferry by a presumably underage girl and then tapes him screwing her in his apartment. You have most of the scenes in this one. Ladies will not like it. If Samantha Fox doesn't stop playing nasty roles, she'll begin to look like Jamie Gillis.

SEX BOAT **NN DK BI NL but only occasionally**
1980   VCX

P/D—**David Marsh, Svetlana**
F/A—**Randy West, Dana Dennis**
F/A—**Silva Miser, Kelly Nichols, Roxanne Potts, Linda Reeves, Jeanette James, Kandi Barbour, Pene Le Paz**

If you can imagine it, two men dressed as women sneak aboard a cruise ship which caters only to young married women whose husbands want to get rid of them by sending them on a six-week cruise. For good measure, the captain and crew are also women. This is one way of getting 18 women (count them) in one place with two guys who are happy to service them all. A nonstop fuck and suck flick. After seeing thirty-six female breasts and eighteen female behinds and vulvas within an hour and a half, you won't even be able to recall one of the female faces you've seen or for that matter their genitals either. One of them, Randy West, manages to screw five different women one after another. (He finishes off by kissing each of them tenderly before he climaxes.) The directors have the ship invaded by pirates who chase the girls all over the boat and "rape" them in scenes that turn into happy compliance.

SWINGIN' STEWARDESSES
CC NN NL
1972   ARROW, VCX, CABALLERO

P/D—Erwin Dietrich, Michael Thomas
F/A—Bernard Wilcensky, Detlev Hayes
F/A—Eveline Trager, Ingrid Steeger

There are four of them on a transatlantic flight to Zurich. The first one agrees to go to bed with a sophisticated gray-haired man who looks like a jet-setter but is actually a salesman for cuckoo clocks. He takes separate rooms in the hotel but falls asleep before she finishes her shower. The second gal jumps into the Trevi Fountain, takes off her dripping clothes in the hotel because the manager is complaining and walks naked to her room, where she beds the copilot, whom she finally marries. The third takes on a muscle man, Svend, in Copenhagen, and Olaf takes her to a private showing of Danish sex films. The fourth meets a Russian in Munich who takes her to his commune. A joyous, fun-filled sexvid with much female nudity and much copulation but no explicit genitals showing. Most women will enjoy this one.

TAXI GIRLS **NN DK DS BI**
1979   SELECT/ESSEX

P/D—Jaacov Jaacovi
F/A—Mike Ranger, Ric Lutz, John Holmes
F/A—Nancy Suitor, Serena, Nancy Hoffman

The police pick up all the hookers on Hollywood Boulevard and stick eight of them in one cell together. Within moments, they have snagged a cop and given him the business, but one of them has figured a better way to do it. If they owned taxis, they could get all the male customers they want without walking the streets and provide both transportation and copulation. The premise in this one is that six women cannot only service one man better than one or two, but they can make him do things he wouldn't ordinarily do—like give them a loan to start their taxi business, or sell them taxis cheap, etc. In the things-you've-never-seen-before department, one customer who hasn't the money to pay the driver is given an inflatable doll which he obligingly fucks in the back seat.

TROPIC OF DESIRE **NN NM BI DK**
1978   WONDERFUL WORLD OF VIDEO

P/D—Eliot Lewis, Gail Palmer, Bob Chinn
F/A—Jon Martin, Ken Scudder
F/A—Georgina Spelvin, Jesie St. James, Kitty Shane

The time is 1945. World War II is almost over. The fleet is in Honolulu with a lot of sailors looking for Rita, the nicest girl in the Pink Flamingo, the famous bordello (also known as Frances's Place—see *From Here to Eternity*). Rita has gone, but there are plenty of girls left with Georgina (as Frances) in charge. The only thing that holds this one together is the 1940 musical background and the Hawaiian ambiance. There is nothing to indicate a female producer behind the scenes.

WEEKEND COWGIRLS **NN BI DK**
1983   CREATIVE IMAGE

P/D—Cindy Lou Sutters
F/A—George Beaumont
F/A—Debbie True Love, Angela O'Day, Kelly Matthews, Starr Johnson

Whoever Cindy Lou Sutters may be, together with Hans Andersen, she has videotaped at least three of these hit-and-run 60-minute movies (most of the big ones last up to 90 minutes), *Plato's Retreat West* and *Teenage Dessert* (see listings for two others). This one involves Debby Truelove, a voyeur, who travels around on a motor bike and spies on her girlfriends making love. When she finally performs she tells you that she wants a guy who can do it three or four times in a row. One of her girlfriends likes to make it with truck drivers and she services at least ten a day. There's nothing you haven't seen before except the next to last scene with a real homey, plump, bald-headed guy, in his 40s, making it with a lady in a middle-class backyard swimming pool, which is the kind of pool that is protected from next door neighbors by cement blocks. There must be at least a million other identical pools in Southern California.

WHAT'S BEHIND THE GROUPIES?
NN DK
1975 VIDEO SHOWTIME

P/D—P. Lumger
F/A—Not decipherable on the credits

Mickey Saint thinks he's potentially as big a rock star as Mick Jagger. To get to the top, he hires two gals as groupies to convince his agent and a record producer that he's the tops. First the gals prove their talents on him. Next day, they are separately working over two older guys and telling them that Mickey Saint "is the best thing I ever heard. I'd do anything if you'll give him a chance." Individually they do. One never takes her glasses off while she is being penetrated from stem to stern; the other keeps talking about Mickey while she sucks away. They finally succeed. Can Mickey sing? Hell no—he plays a harmonica (presumably with a group). But never mind, the groupies love him. He screws one while the band plays on and an *unseen* audience applauds strenuously. This film raises a question. With all the potential for rock star-oriented movies, why hasn't any adult filmmaker made a good one? Maybe the porno stars can't sing but they could dub in the voice. I nominate Richard Pacheco for the male lead.

18

Fetishes

ANGEL BUNS **NN   DK**
1981   QUALITY

P/D—Robert Sumner, David Mackenzie
F/A—Richard Bolla
F/A—Veronica Hart, Tiffany Clark, Lisa Beth,
   Diana Flores

If you are male and bring this one home to your wife or girlfriend, the chances are she won't like it as much as you might. Not unless anal sex is her bag. In the Thorne Smith style, there's an angel named Angel Buns (Veronica Hart, wearing a blond wig to make her look ethereal). Angel Buns has a mission on earth to help men like Sidney Purtzer. Poor Sidney owns a women's shoe store. He can't help it, he's constantly staring at women's vulvas as he helps them try on shoes. Alas, he never manages to get his hands on one, or his penis in one. While Angel can't commingle with humans or she'll lose her angelic privileges, she can copulate with other angels. She introduces Sidney to Angel Dick, whose specialty is anal intercourse. "There's something about an asshole that never fails to turn me on," he tells Sidney, and he teaches him how by carefully buggering Angel Buns. Angel Buns offers Sidney all the sexual delights he has missed, including sex with a teenager and two women at once. She also guides him on how to really enjoy being blown. It all ends up with Angel Buns losing her wings because she falls in love with Sidney, which is against the heavenly rules. Note —this one has no bisexual scenes, which is unusual. But maybe it should have been called *Anal Buns!*

BLACK SILK STOCKINGS
NN   NM   BI   NL (one scene)
1975   SELECT/ESSEX

P/D—Billy Thornberg
F/A—John Holmes, Joey Civera, John Leslie
F/A—Annette Haven, Patricia Lee, Linda Wong,
   Monica Welles

Like *Sheer Panties* (see listing), the link between a number of loops in this one is black silk stockings. Both tapes begin with a male panegyric to the sexual attraction of silk stockings or panties that could be used as advertising copy by Frederick's of Hollywood. Looping from A to Z, John Holmes first enjoys himself with Patricia Lee, a beautiful black lady, and then with Annette Haven in a luxurious mountain lodge. In a funny sequence as a professor, he teaches women the nature of the male penis and uses his own, from soft to hard, as a unique example. In between, Joey Civera screws Monica Welles in a sequence during which she never stops telling him, "Oh, honey, I love it. Your cock is so nice. Oh, fuck me," etc., etc., for ten minutes. The wrap-up loop is Linda Wong, Annette Haven and John Leslie all lapping and tasting each other.

BLOOMER GIRLS NN BI DK
1974   VIDEO SHOWTIME

P/D—Not given
F/A—Not given

A maker of women's panties invites his male customers to a showing at his summer place. They bring along a girlfriend, and he has two models. The two women model various Frederick's-style panties while their girlfriend gets exasperated at their interest in the models. A fight ensues, but the girls finally apologize to each other, and all six of them end up happily screwing and playing switchees. Save your money.

CHINA LUST NN DK BI
SELECT/ESSEX, VCX

P/D—Summer Brown
F/A—Linda Wong, Desiree West

On Grant Street in San Francisco, a couple pays $100 for a jade carving of an erect penis. They take it home and, of course, try it. In the meantime, some other people are looking for it because whoever owns the jade penis achieves new orgasmic heights. Two guys steal it and try it on their girlfriends, and one of them sticks the carving in a guy's anus while he's screwing her. The only redeeming features of this one are the two Chinese women (Desiree and Linda).

CONSENTING ADULTS
CC NN DK BI
1982   VIDEO-X-PIX

P/D—Gerard Damiano
F/A—Mark Stevens, Joey Civera, Ron Jeremy, Ron Hudd
F/A—Annie Sprinkles, Veronica Vera, Sharon Mitchell and many others

I've given this one a CC rating not because it's a top adult film, but rather to alert those who may be fascinated with kinky sexual behavior. The film poses as a documentary in some sections. Damiano enjoys doing this (see other Damiano listings). He begins with a ten-minute segment photographed at Dick Drost's Ponderosa Sun Club in Roselawn, Indiana. It's a male and female nude beauty contest in which the females reveal more of themselves than in other tapes which feature an hour or more at Ponderosa (see various listings). From there, it cuts to an inane sequence with Mark Stevens adoring his cock and telling you about the joys of masturbation, or ladies like Veronica Vera sucking his cock. In riposte, Annie Sprinkles tells you how "good it feels going in and out," and Veronica tells about her fantasy of being raped in a dark alley by a loving rapist. Then you have ten minutes with Jim, who is The Master Piercer of Labias in Southern California. You watch him prepare an ecstatic lady and finally pierce her labia in close-up detail, after which he puts on her labia ring. Marilyn Chambers wears one. It gently tickles while a woman walks and presumably keeps her ready for action. The comment is made that if Jim pierces the lady's labia, two rings can be joined by a tiny lock and her lover can be given the key to assure her chastity. Next you listen to Veronica Vera read from a pornographic novel she's in the process of writing while she enacts out her version of the "joys of sex." She tries to give the impression that young women are as lustful as the most lustful men. "For me, sex is not the most important thing—it is the only thing. I love to fuck. I love to come." But Vera never sounds very romantic. This is followed by a long interview with Damiano in which he discusses cock sucking—the good and the mechanical—while Sharon Mitchell demonstrates the best technique on Ron Jeremy. Damiano finally admits he enjoys being sucked twice as much as he does lapping ladies' pussies. After that you are introduced to a new indoor sport—female wrestling. Viewers spend the evening in an apartment, where a mattress, covered with vinyl, is dragged into the living room. Then two women, greased with Mazola, slip back and forth over each other and are eventually joined by the males. The tape concludes with an evening at the Casino Royale where, in between the porno movies, two young ladies blow male volunteers from the audience. Obviously there are a lot of "consenting adults" you may never want to know, or prefer to confine to Krafft-Ebbing.

DEEP STROKE **NN   DK   BI**
COMPETITIVE VIDEO

P/D—Robert Speller, Peter Evans
F/A—Buck Ellen
F/A—Yvonne Elders, Gina Nadeau

Ellen's husband, Bart, a bearded, hairy guy tells you at the beginning that she has become a nymphomaniac and he doesn't know whether she should be committed. But as it turns out, it's all his fault. He's convinced her to go to a swap party and although Ellen tells him, "I'm not changing my mind. I want to go home," eventually she discovers a guy with whom she enjoys it more than Bart. And Bart has finally made it with Rhonda Fisher, his neighbor and friend's wife. This is the standard story about swingers and the wife who gets to enjoy it more than her husband. Unfortunately, the potentially interesting story gets lost in the continuous sex sequences. If nothing else, surprise your friends and turn on this one, or one like it, at your next cocktail party—but leave the sound off. It's guaranteed to generate amusing conversation—or total shock! (see note under *April Love*, p. 273).

DIRTY BOOK SHOPPE **NN   BI   DK**
1974   BOCCACCIO 100

P/D—Not given
F/A—Sonny Diner, Kebb Lieser, Rich Allson
F/A—Judy Cinders, Beth Laws, Sara Melo

Three girls on vacation in the big city wander into a dirty book store and read each other stuff from the books they examine. Some of what they read is visualized on screen. Soon they are examining the sex gadgets, and one finds a package of condoms. "What do you do with these?" she asks the owner. "Blow them up," he tells her, and she does, into a huge balloon which finally breaks. Then the girls are rubbing dildos against their dresses, after which they undress and take on the owner of the store, who gets some help from a customer who wanders in. After they are all satisfied—one guy is collapsed on the floor—they put on their clothes and promise each other they will always take a vacation where there are dirty book stores.

DISCO LADY **NN**
1978   EROS & FREEWAY

P/D—Richard Aldrich, Bob Chinn
F/A—Mike Ranger, Ric Lutz
F/A—Rhonda Jo Petty, Robin Savage

Note the rating. There's no bisexuality in this sexvid. It's New Year's Eve at a disco club called The Disco Lady, where women blow men in the ladies' room or the men's room. Take your pick. Most of the women have shaved vaginas. But what really makes this one different is Producer Richard Aldrich's appearance. Richard tells his film wife (after he has told her that he has been extramaritally involved) that if she goes out tonight, he'll kill her—and he tries to in the nightclub in a delayed action sequence that is dramatically very effective.

DREAM LOVERS **CC   DK**
1980   CABALLERO

P/D—Kim Christy
F/A—Craig Roberts
F/A—Sulka, Loni Sanders, Frances Lopez,
Naughty Nikko, Magnificent Margo

Hold onto your hat! You've never seen anything like this sexvid. It features Sulka, a transsexual, before her sex change operation. Lying naked in bed with beautiful silicon breasts (filled?), a lovely, hairless (except for pubic hair) female body and a heavily made up, but definitely feminine face, Sulka reaches between her legs and you watch her playing with her erect penis and full breasts. The sequences that follow gravitate around Sulka's apartment and a Finochio-style San Francisco night-club where transvestites and transsexuals gather. A few of Sulka's friends have normal penises and vaginas, but they don't seem to be perturbed by Sulka's prick, which she tucks between her legs when she puts on pantyhose. In a mindbending sequence, a man called Jack picks up Sulka, who takes him to her apartment where another transsexual is enjoying his girlfriend. Sulka gives Jack a "fix" which turns him green (literally!) and there is a clever sequence of color negative photography as Sulka and Jack enjoy each other's pricks. To top off the things you've never seen before, Sulka and another transsexual enjoy each other's pricks while they are connected anally with a dildo. Essentially, some of the tape is homosexual, but heterosexual males will probably find it more palatable because the transsexuals look like women from the top down. It's probably not cricket to rate this one DK. Transsexuals can't help their genetic conditionings. I have given it a CC (collector's choice) rating because it certainly gives perspective on the range of human sexuality. For more in the same vein see listings under *She/Male Encounters*, (p. 269) and *The Transformation of Sulka* (p. 228).

EROTIC CLOTHING AND MARITAL AIDS **NN NM BI**
1982 VPX

P/D—Sal
F/A—Unknown

Sal says this is one of his most popular tapes. Obviously designed for the male audience, it features two women, one white and lean, one black and zaftig, modeling Frederick's style underwear to a background of Scheherazade music. The names for the garments are Enticer, Expose, Mistress, Conquerer, Arouser. A guy also appears modeling see-through jock straps and behind embracers called Players, Snugglers and the Trap. In the second section, marital aids are demonstrated, including double dongs (a lengthy dildo to connect two vaginas), squirmy vibrators (a dildo that allows the user to turn it like an egg beater), peter squirters (dildos that ejaculate), electra shaft (a vibrating dildo), silver egg (battery powered to vibrate when inserted in a vagina) and ben-wa balls, which jiggle together when a woman inserts them in her vagina. In addition, there are cock rings, gadgets to suck a male cock, inflatable vaginas, orgy oils of all kinds, and finally sex games which are pictured and not demonstrated. VPX provides a catalogue from which you can order most of the products.

GARTERS AND LACE **NN BI DK**
1975 SELECT/ESSEX

P/D—Billy Thornberg
F/A—John Holmes
F/A—Leslie Bovee, Patricia Lee, Barbara Barton, Aubrey Turner

This one offers four sex loops made in the early 1970s. It's tied together by a woman named Aubrey Turner who models lace and see-through bras and panties and in a sprightly, teasing voice, tries to seduce the hard-on audience. Collectors of early John C. Holmes, when his hair was marcelled in waves, may find it amusing. John C. was just as big. Three of the loops have him servicing a young lady in her swimming pool. She's a brunette who strips in her bedroom and goes ga-ga at the sight of his tool. In a later loop, he takes on Leslie Bovee and refers to himself as Johnny Wadd. The first loop has Patricia Lee, a Chinese lady, and an unidentified male.

HOT TEENAGE ASSETS **NN BI DK**
1978 WONDERFUL WORLD OF VIDEO

P/D—Zachary Youngblood, Damian Lee
F/A—Zeos Saavadi, Curt Crotchkiss
F/A—Chris Cassidy, Kathy Malwin

Accentuate the word *assets* on this one. It's not really about teenagers. The actors are all in their 20s. Kathy has a boyfriend, Jed, who puts a finger in her anus while he's screwing her. Margo makes love to Kathy and sticks a vibrator in her anus and Kathy has her first climax. But that's not all, folks! Eventually Kathy meets Dr. Goode, who runs sensitivity training fuck groups.

With his help, everyone lives anally ever after.

I LIKE TO WATCH **NN NM BI DK**
1983   CABALLERO

P/D—Paul G. Vatelli
F/A—Don Hart, Kevin James, Herschel Savage, David Smith
F/A—Bridgitte Monet, Lisa de Leeuw, Patricia Manning, Little Oral Annie, Linda Shaw

It continuously amazes me that month after month there's a market for men's magazines and porno films that are essentially no different from last month's version. This tape joins the "You've-see-one-you've-seen-them-all" category. To try to be different it offers the premise that watching is as much fun as doing it. Most of the action takes place in the home of Leticia (Patricia Manning) who is presumably a designer of women's lingerie. Her maid watches the plumber, who has come to fix the furnace, plumbing Kim, one of her assistants, who tells the plumber to come to the attic where at her request he sodomizes her (shown in great detail) and then sans washing she fellates him. Laura, her niece (Bridgitte Monet), whose boyfriend Michael (Don Hart) hasn't ever asked her to make love watches Leticia screwing with tears in her eyes at what she's missing. Later she steals Linda's (Lisa de Leeuw) panties and nearly has an orgasm rubbing them on her face and pussy, but is saved in the nick of time by a phone call from Linda who invites her over so that Linda's boyfriend, Montag (David Smith) can watch them making it—after which he enters the room and takes on Laura while Linda watches. In the meantime Michael is finally accosted by two young ladies who take him on in Leticia's living room while they are watched by mannequins. This is presumably one of Bridgitte Monet's first pictures. She has a classically beautiful body, a lovely face but her voice is nasally squeaky, and she's a terrible actress. (Note—see Talk Dirty to Me II in which she is the female lead. In this one her vocal chords are under better control.) Don't bring this one home to momma!

LESBIAN ORGY **BI**
1980   WIDE WORLD OF VIDEO

F/A—Victoria, Ruth Jones, Sharon Asnes

Seven young ladies, and one with a butterfly on her ass, spend the afternoon naked in an attractive living room doing everything possible that naked ladies could do to each other, including finger fucking, occasional fist fucking and playing with dildos. This is a direct videotape probably made with a home camera. Eighty-seven minutes of sex with no live penises!

THE LITTLE BLUE BOX **NN BI DK**
1978   BLUE VIDEO

P/D—Arlo Schiffin
F/A—John Leslie, Jamie Gillis, Alan Clements
F/A—Jennifer Welles, Leslie Bovee, Gloria Leonard, Sharon Mitchell, Ming Toy

Figuring out a gimmick that will tie together an hour and a half of continuous sexmaking ain't easy. This one offers the Little Blue Box, a gadget sold by Ms. Azure (Jennifer Welles) to a writer, John Michaels. He is married to Jen (also Jennifer Welles, wearing a black wig), who is not so much fun in bed as she used to be because she's become a feminist. So John fantasizes screwing with Leslie (Leslie Bovee), a friend of theirs who in real life he has never made a pass at. Of course, his fantasies are vividly portrayed on screen. But on the premise of the old advertising slogan "Twice as much for a nickel, too," when Ms. Azure arrives with the Blue Box, it magically turns on the television. The owner of the Little Blue Box can watch screwing on TV while he is doing it! So John and Jennifer (oops, Ms. Azure) screw on the couch while wifey, Jen, is out working, and at the same time they watch porno stories about a girl being picked up for shoplifting a dress (she gets undressed by the store detective). Ming Toy, as an ingenue, tries to convince a porno movie producer that she can perform (she does, with Jamie Gillis). The pièce de résistance of The Little Blue Box is Channel 69. When you punch this button it brings to life your own fantasies on your own TV. Of course,

John pushes it and presto, he vanishes into the tube with four lovely ladies, all listed above, who adore him from eyebrows to toenails as well as each other. When Jen comes home and finds her old man on the tube enjoying "four cunts," what choice does she have? She pushes the button, too, and joins the group. Jennifer Welles can act, and she has a lush, big-breasted body, but the ladies in the house probably won't jump for joy at the sight of her and Leslie.

MAKE MINE MILK NN NM BI DK
SILHOUETTE

P/D—Not given
F/A—Not given

Like *Milk Maid* (see listing, p. 266), this one has the same unidentified lactating woman who describes her sexual enjoyment in a voice-over as it is happening to her. It may have been shot the same weekend that *Make Mine Milk* was shot with a big hangover in San Francisco. Milky's girlfriend, Myra, brings a guy home to their apartment. It quickly goes away as he gets his cock sucked. Finally another guy arrives and Myra sits on his prick and nurses on Milky's tits as Milky rides her guy facing forward. The sex continues the next day unabated as Ken and Barbara arrive, and Ken happily sucks Milky's tits while she and Barbara suck his cock.

MARASCHINO CHERRY NN DK BI
1978 QUALITY

P/D—Morton Berman, Radley Metzger (a.k.a. Henri Paris)
F/A—Wade Nichols, Waldo Short, Eric Edwards
F/A—Constance Money, Gloria Leonard, Annette Haven, Jenny Baxter, Susan McBain, C. J. Laing, Leslie Bovee

Maraschino Cherry (Gloria Leonard) runs a high-class cathouse in New York City. All the above actresses work for her and are experts at cock sucking, of which there is an inordinate amount in this sexvid—well over two dozen mouth-induced ejaculations with only a quarter as much pussy eating! M.C. also offers her clients all the pleasures of bondage and discipline in her Dungeon of Secret and Holy Delights. Her male clients include a guy who ejaculates whenever he sneezes, a guy who asks the woman servicing him if he can get VD from the toilet seat, several unidentified guys, and Wade Nichols, who is sleeping with M.C., and a guy who tells her he has a problem communicating with women. When Maraschino asks him his profession, he tells her, "I'm a gynecologist." She solves his problem by turning him into a toreador, and he learns how to dominate women. In the things-you've-never-seen-before department (and may never want to), Annette Haven stretches out naked on a grand piano and sucks off one guy while Gloria and another guy eat her. Radley Metzger must have made this one on a lost weekend. It's a far cry from *Score, Punishment of Anne* and *Camille 2000*, but it does have a big touch of masochism which intrigues Metzger.

THE MILKMAID NN NM BI DK
SILHOUETTE

P/D—Not given
F/A—Not given

This film was probably shot on a Saturday or Sunday afternoon for under $1,000. But it has one thing going for it that many men may like. Everything our heroine Milky does is described by her in a voice-over. She's lactating but her breasts aren't very full of milk, and she really enjoys sucking and being sucked. Her encounters include the lady next door, who drops in for a taste of milk. After that, they lap each other's vulvas. Later they are joined by a guy and a gal and finally by another guy. If you are a male who is intrigued by screwing with a full-breasted mother, unfortunately this lady evidently served dinner to her child before the film was shot. While I have pointed out several films that show lactating mothers joyfully squirting their milk into receptive male mouths, I have not been able to locate any of the famous Angel Cash's full-length films on tape. There's *A Hard Worker, A Girl Named Angel* and another *Milky Mama*, but they are all on 8-mm film. *Milky Mama* features Angel in all her lactating glory.

MORE THAN SISTERS   NN   DK tries for NR but doesn't make it
1979   BLUE VIDEO

P/D—Robert Lyon, Russ Carlson
F/A—Jamie Gillis, Eric Edwards, Russ Carlson
F/A—Leslie Murray, Coleen Anderson, Marlene Willoughby

If you see Russ Carlson's name on a sex-vid, you can be sure the plot will be immensely complicated. This one has many New York scenes attractively inter-cut into the story, and like Carlson's *Slaves of Pleasure* proves that despite occasion-ally insipid acting, it's possible to make adult films that are erotically appealing—but not when the director gets hung up and tries to give the raincoat crowd its money's worth, as this one does. The story is about Siamese twins separated at birth with no body scars remaining and no knowledge of each other's existence. Alice is happily married, and Eva is in an in-sane asylum in Quebec. Now, at this late date (they are both in their late 20s), Eva communicates telepathically to Alice the sexual trauma she experiences as she's raped and buggered by doctors in the in-sane asylum. Jamie Gillis, a psychiatrist, with the help of a detective gets to the *bottom* of the problem (not with Alice but one of his female colleagues). Everything you've ever seen before in an adult film is in this one, plus a few additional kinky scenes as Eva is "restrained" sexually by the doctors in the asylum. The plot didn't require that the twins be Siamese and needed no insane asylum—simply sisters who are totally different kinds of women communicating with each other tele-pathically. This kind of story construction—playing off the immorality of one against the morality of the other—could have created a really interesting sexvid. This one, unfortunately, isn't.

NANCI BLUE NN NM DK BI
1979   SELECT/ESSEX

P/D—Kenneth Berger
F/A—Ron Jeremy, Mike Ranger
F/A—Kandi Barbour, Tawny Pearl

Ron Jeremy is a detective. His daughter, Nanci Blue, wants to follow in his footsteps, but he doesn't encourage her. Daddy is working on a case of women who dis-appear and get screwed but can't re-member what happened to them. In the meantime, Nanci is in love with Rod (Mike Ranger), who wants to marry her, but she can't climax with him. The fact is, she has never climaxed, not even with good old Dad, whom she seduces to find out the secrets of the case he is working on. The bad guys (one is a woman, played by Lisa de Leeuw) capture Nanci. With their zap-per, which makes one forget what hap-pens, they zap her into a climax and teach her the secrets of "sustained or-gasm." And so she marries Ron and they live happily ever after. Concludes with an orgiastic wrap-up that takes five minutes and altogether is pretty yucky.

ON WHITE SATIN NN NM BI DK
1980   VCX

P/D—Harry Lewis, Eliot Lewis
F/A—Spender Travis, Joel Caine, Paul Thomas
F/A—Seka, Lisa de Leeuw, Lisa Thatcher

A guy and a girl in a fraternity house are watching porno flicks. The guy pushes the girl (Lisa Thatcher) to sleep with him. "I'm a satin woman, not acetate," she tells him. "I don't want to do it on this smelly couch. Can't I just jack you off, instead?" An hour later she gets the white satin sheet spread over the couch, but not until Lisa de Leeuw as a new bride (who talks and acts like an old-time hooker) has made it on the white satin sheet in a honeymoon motel, and Paul Thomas as linen service man has picked up the sheet and res-cued Seka and her girlfriend whose car has broken down. He spreads the sheet in the back of his pick-up truck and takes on both of them and finally gives the sheet to Seka in appreciation. A little the worse for wear, she dons it and wears it to a toga party which of course is a Roman orgy. This one couldn't have been budgeted for more than $25,000 but will probably gross a million in adult theaters and will sell over 5,000 tapes, as a minimum. Thus it is profitable for all concerned except the actors and actresses who are paid five or six hundred bucks for a few days' work—with no residuals.

ORIENTAL HAWAII NN BI DK
1982 HIFCOA

P/D—Troy Benny
F/A—John Leslie, Jerry Heath, Jon Martin
F/A—Mai Lin, Jade Wong, Jesie St. James, Rhonda Jo Petty, Danielle

Mildred and Bob Walker (Jesie St. James and John Leslie) have four kids (Rhonda Jo Petty, Danielle, Jerry Heath and Jon Martin). They live in Hawaii in a home that certainly must be worth a quarter of a million dollars, but Dad is out of work and Mom is serving the family spaghetti for the umpteenth time. So they decide to rent two rooms to students at the University of Hawaii. Immediately Mai Lin and Jade Wong respond to their advertising and jump in the sack with Rhonda Jo and Danielle. They play games with Rhonda's "toys"—a collection of dildos which they happily stick into each other's vaginas and anuses for at least ten minutes before the new roomers invade the brothers' rooms, where they quickly are bouncing on engorged rods. Mai Lin gives Daddy John Leslie some special pills to change his attitude toward Mommy Jesie. It seems that despite his poverty Daddy John has been paying a hooker $100 a week for an afternoon of more enthusiastic fucking than provided by his wife. Daddy takes the pills and in his dreams he's humpin' and pumpin' away not only on Mommy, but with his daughters and the two new roomers. When he wakes up his dreams come true, and Mommy Jesie enjoys her sons as well as him. This is a man's daydream tape about complacent women whose sole object in life is to service them. Chief cook at HIFCOA is Maria Tobalina, a very pretty woman who is married to Carlos.

RANDY, THE ELECTRIC LADY NN some DK and DS and one scene that is almost NR
1979 ASTRO

P/D—Phillip Schumann
F/A—Roger Frazer, Cyrus Jones
F/A—Desiree Cousteau, Monica Sands, Lisa Rush

Poor Desiree—strapped to a fucking machine by a Nazi type, she is experiencing orgasmic problems. But worry not, her body is manufacturing Orgasmine when she does climax. Injected into the bloodstream in the form of a serum made from Desiree's blood, it produces permanent erections and nymphomaniac women. Ann Perry, who did not produce this film but is distributing it, thinks, "It will appeal to women." It does have one scene that is almost romantic. The screenplay was written by Terry Southern of *Candy* fame.

ROBIN'S NEST NN DK BI
BLUE VIDEO

P/D—Vic Burton
F/A—Eric Edwards
F/A—Samantha Fox, Arcadia Lake, Crystal Day

This one begins with the bridegroom carrying the bride over the threshold. Six months later they are swearing bitterly at each other, and the bride, Robin, leaves the nest (or takes her nest with her, depending on how you look at it) and moves in with a woman friend. After that it's all downhill. This is a sexvid for men who enjoy watching women make love. Scene after scene is offered of female twosomes, threesomes and foursomes. Eventually the newlyweds find each other at an orgy.

SENSUAL FIRE NN NM BI DK
1979 HIFCOA

FA—Troy Benny
F/A—Jamie Gillis
F/A—Serena, Dorothy Le May, Jesie St. James

"Thank you for being such a gentleman," Serena tells Jamie in bed. "Were you this nice with your first wife?" Jamie is so nice in this one that you can't believe it's Jamie. He is so nice he agrees to have Serena's daughter, Tina (played by Dorothy Le May), live with them in the spare room. At a distance Dorothy does look like a teenager. Jamie can't help himself. He's always spying on her through a hole in his bookcase that looks into the spare room. And it gets so that he's thinking about Tina so much he can't climax with Serena. His psychiatrist tells him he has an obsession for young stuff, supplied by Jesie St. James (who is evidently not young enough). Then Father Carlos (Carlos Tobalina), a priest, suggests that he must have been in love with a girl in high school who looked like Tina but with whom he never made it. Solution: find a Tina lookalike. But even that doesn't work, so he invites Serena and Tina/Dorothy to a costume party/orgy. Unknown to them, he arrives as Zorro or Don Juan, take your pick. He seduces Dorothy while Serena is busy elsewhere. Finally his lust has gone and no one is the wiser, or sorrier. But then in bed the next night, Serena asks him to do her a favor. "Make love to Tina like you make love to me so she can know what a real lover is like." Pretty hokey but there are lots of marital "I love you's."

SHE-MALE ENCOUNTERS Collection 1
DK
CONNOISSEUR SERIES CABALLERO

P/D—Not given
F/A—Carnal Candy, Magnificent Margo, Sulka

The flick opens with Margo, a black transsexual, talking girl-talk with Candy and then cuts to Candy beside her swimming pool. Later, when she's taking a bath, you finally see it—her penis!—as she washes her full breasts and plays with herself. A seamstress who is invited to fit Candy to new lingerie doesn't seem surprised, and she happily sucks Candy off. Candy returns the favor. Watching what looks like a woman literally fucking a woman is a little mind-boggling. But this is only the first episode. Next, you see big-breasted Sulka lying near her swimming pool being watched by a guy. Eventually when she takes off her panties because they bind her penis he doesn't seem too surprised and happily sucks her off and fucks her anally. After that, Margo, who is bigger and tougher than the others, seduces a delivery boy (he's at least 25). It all ends with Sulka and Margo picking up a male hitchhiker and taking him back to their apartment so you can watch three busy cocks with no real home for their excite-

ment. Most women will probably detest these tapes, or laugh (hopefully sadly) at men who want to be women and are cursed with a prick. And heterosexual males will wonder if they have been conned into watching a gay flick.

SHE-MALE ENCOUNTERS Collection II
DK DS
1980 CABALLERO

P/D—Not given
F/A—Carnal Candy, Sultry Sylvia, Luscious Lynn, Tantalizing Tony

If you were left gasping to see more transsexuals after viewing Collection I, here's a sequel. It begins with pretty Sultry Sylvia enticing a poolman on her patio to fuck her. The big blond guy moves in, kisses her mouth, gets to her very pretty breasts and when he finally wiggles her swimsuit down over her balls and penis, he doesn't seem too surprised. He even obeys her instructions: "Suck me off, you motherfucker!" Next episode is Tantalizing Tony with her maid, Carnal Candy. He spanks Candy's ass until it is bright red, and then, speaking in guttural German intermixed with English, he commands Candy to suck his high heel followed by his cock while he masturbates Candy. If you're still watching, the next episode shows Luscious Lynn in her bedroom being spied on by a male prowler who finally breaks in, robs her and "rapes" her. How? By blowing her, of course. The final episode is back to Tony, who plays with herself and talks in German. Finally donning a dominatrix outfit (leather and latex), she repairs to the basement where she has a male slave in a leather mask suspended by chains from the rafters. In a mixture of German and English, she informs him "I'm going to rip the cock off your body," and while he yells she nearly does. Aren't you glad you're normal?

TEEN ANGEL **NN DK NR (almost)**
COMPETITIVE VIDEO

P/D—John St. Pierre, Dave Miller
F/A—Frank Ford
F/A—Melba Teague, Sharon Demsted

This one begins with Jim and Sharon's wedding day. After the marriage and a tour through San Francisco, the Baumans arrive at Jim's home, which Sharon has never seen. It's a two-story house in the older part of the city. Sharon is reluctant to visit the bedroom. She's a virgin! But you'd never guess it two minutes later when she's demonstrating remarkable oral proficiency with Jim's cock. A few days pass, and Sharon is out shopping. A teen-aged newspaper girl rings the doorbell and convinces Jim to subscribe to home delivery. A week later, when she arrives to collect she has to go to the toilet. And there she is sitting on the hopper, thinking of Jim and masturbating while he's in the living room doing the same thinking of her. Next scene they are in bed. Sharon comes home from her sister's unexpectedly, and finds them. She doesn't scream, but calls a taxi. But she does go berserk because in the next scene, Jim's friend, a black guy who is being serviced by two women (one black, one white), tells Jim that he must help him rob a bank. Jim needs the money for Sharon's psychiatric care. Final scene—a shot of Alcatraz where our heroes are spending a few years because they goofed up the robbery. You keep thinking this one might have been a good, tight story, but it doesn't make it.

TREASURE BOX **NN DK BI**
1981

P/D—Robert Lynn, Jerome Robinson
F/A—John Leslie, Eric Edwards, Gary
   Goodman, Cecil Johnson
F/A—Nancy Hoffman, Chris Cassidy, Mimi
   Morgan

If you like an involved plot and you are into anal sex, you may give this one your own private collector's choice rating. Practically all of the women lie on their backs with their legs around their head, thus exposing their anuses for easy penetration by the various males. As you will see, this has something to do with the plot. The plot concerns Richardson Miles (John Leslie), top porno king of America, who has just died. You see him in his coffin. But his brother, Rumpleton Miles (John Leslie), who looks just like him, has survived as has his daughter, Heidi Ho (Nancy Hoffman), and an adopted black nephew, Brindle (Cecil Johnson), who has a white girlfriend P.L. (Chris Cassidy). Richardson's will is not on paper—it's written symbolically into a special porno film he has made which gives the clues to where he has hidden most of his estate, a huge sum of cash, so that it won't be taxed by the IRS. The relatives mentioned above and their friends, Inspector Cleausneau (Gary Goodman) and Dr. Alvin Topsy (Eric Edwards), plus the Internal Revenue men all try to unravel the clues which include four gamblers searching a naked lady's vagina, a red-haired woman and a brunette swimming naked together in a private swimming pool, two couples screwing together in a living room while they are served drinks by a butler, and the pièce de résistance, a guy stripping the redhead. The various groups who are after the money divide up, and one of them, led by Richardson Miles, reenacts the various elements in the porno film to see if they can decipher the various clues—hence the triple doses of anal sex. The plot has some of the overtones of the famous Stanley Kramer chase movie, *It's a Mad, Mad, Mad, Mad World*, but none of the happy laughter.

19

Vignettes

AFTERNOON DELIGHTS
1980   CABALLERO

P/D—Cliff Carter, Warren Evans
F/A—Eric Edwards, Larry O'Brien, Bobby Astyr
F/A—Merle Michaels, Veronica Hart, Vanessa Del Rio, Samantha Fox

Essentially five loops, this one is held together by lots of Ravel "Bolero" background music and five guys who instead of playing their usual Tuesday night game of poker write down the sex lives of their former wives and read them to each other. If you accept this hokey glue, you can watch the five flashbacks showing how their upper-income wives were spending the afternoon while their husbands were earning the bread. First is Merle Michaels, who seduces two guys in hard hats who are grinding up the asphalt with a phallic jack hammer. Next is Veronica Hart at the dentist where Bobby Astyr's female assistant gives Veronica nitrous oxide for a cavity and then they both work her over. Vanessa Del Rio spends her afternoons in porno theaters servicing the whole frustrated male audience. Samantha Fox is a dominatrix, a master-race female who likes to subdue males, and finally Serena, with a boyish brunette haircut that shows this flick was made early in her career. If you are interested in how a woman can handle two men at the same time, the cameraman gives you a long, explicit close-up of the action.

AMERICAN DESIRE
CC NN NM DK BI
1981   CABALLERO

P/D—Lasse Brown
F/A—Richard Bolla, Allan Clement, Jake Teague, George Payne
F/A—Veronica Hart, Lysa Thatcher, Mai Lin

Bob (Richard Bolla) and Sheila (Veronica Hart) live in a fabulous beach house overlooking the Connecticut shoreline. They aren't married, but they've been together so long that Bob is no longer very spontaneous in the sack. Looking at his penis under the covers, Sheila murmurs, "He doesn't seem to be in the mood." Bob continues to look at television. "Poor thing, I think he's broken ... Seems to be a case of sexual fadeout ... I feel like an old married woman ... it's gone, we don't have it anymore." Bob's solution is that they should have a holiday with new lovers. Sheila goes home to Daddy (Jake Teague) and is shocked to discover him screwing with a young Chinese woman (Mai Lin). She meets George (Alan Clement), a young writer, and for a moment thinks he's the kind of man (monogamous) she really wants, but then she catches him in bed with Daddy's mistress, and to her shock Daddy doesn't mind sharing his Chinese wealth. In the meantime, Bob (Robert is Bolla's real first name) tries an escort service and ends up with a dominatrix who wants to whip him. Then he picks up a hitchhiker (Lysa Thatcher) and discovers that she's a masochist—she wants to be whipped, "but softly." Obligingly, in an old farmhouse filled with antiques and a convenient hayloft, she kisses Bob's shoes, and he masturbates her while she adores his cock. Up to this point, Veronica as Sheila is a very believable actress and the New England settings are a nice change from the usual West Coast backgrounds. But then Sheila visits an empty house that used to belong to her grandfather. The guy who owns it appears. Without further ado, and while she protests violently at first but finally capitulates with increasing moaning cooperation, he strips her, masturbates her with a black-fingered glove and fucks her on the floor. The promotion on the box in which this cassette comes states, "The metamorphosis of a woman from housewife to sex goddess." Believe it or not, after this rape session, Sheila/Veronica floats happily downstairs in her garter belt and encounters a guy wearing a hard hat who is wandering through the empty rooms picking up her clothes, which her former seducer had scattered all over the place. Without further ado, Sheila opens up his trousers and sucks his prick. "I can't believe this is happening," he moans in delight, and neither will you. The reason for the CC rating is Veronica and R. Bolla's acting and the cinematography, which rises above a story line that could have been made much more believable. In case you are interested, Sheila and Bob are reunited and live happily ever afterwards.

THE ART OF LOVE   **This could almost be rated R**
EDUCATIONAL TECHNOLOGY SERVICES

P/D—An unidentified man who acts in it along with his wife

Have you ever wondered how the plump guy and his slightly overweight wife who live next door make love? This is an hour-long, homemade sexvid—the kind thousands of couples are making right now and I predict hundreds of thousands will be making them with their own video cameras. One reason for buying might be to satisfy your voyeuristic needs or as a warning how not to make your own sexvid. The main problem is that the guy in the flick set the camera up alongside the bed and rarely changed the camera position. At the end of the tape, he sings a hymn of praise to her in an original song called "My Love for You." His wife probably objected to the whole idea. She lies passively on the bed for quite a while while he massages her through some Frederick's-style underwear. You never see her totally naked and when she is performing fellatio the wide-angled lens makes it seem pretty far away and diminutive. A female voice-over tells you that if you make love and don't talk, you're not communicating. But other than the voice-over you rarely hear the couple talking. Perhaps the best reason for buying this one would be to prove to a recalcitrant female that she could do better.

APARTMENT GIRLS   **NN BI DS**
1980   COMPETITIVE VIDEO

P/D—Alex Demento, Bernard Laszlo
F/A—Larry Thomas
F/A—Linda Talley

You'll never know in this one whether the girls are wives or come with the apartment rent. You meet them one by one in bed in the morning as the alarm goes off at seven A.M. One female goes to the bathroom and returns to fellate her man. Another tells the guy, "It's so early, can't you wait? Don't you have to go the bathroom?" He tells her, "I'll go later." The tape cuts back and forth between apartments until finally they all meet in one apartment and play switchees. In the things-you've-never-seen-before department—a bagel is used as a cock ring. It all ends with one of the guys suggesting they all get dressed and go see an X-rated movie (see note under *April Love*, p. 273).

ANGIE, UNDERCOVER COP   NN   DK
(but only occasionally)
1979   BLUE VIDEO

P/D—Navred Reef
F/A—Roger Caine, Eric Edwards, Bobby Astyr
F/A—Samantha Fox, Vanessa Del Rio

A local minister spying at his neighbors complains to Sergeant Blowjack (yeah, he's bald) that everyone is screwing in plain sight. Angie and Kowalaski are assigned to the case. About all you can say about this one is that everyone in suburbia is having sex—outdoors in their backyards, next to their swimming pools, in the middle of washing the family automobile. As Kowalaski tells Angie, "I've seen more coming today than in my whole life." He isn't kidding—and you will, too! If you own a video camera, and have a private backyard, with a few loving friends, you could make your own version of this one.

APRIL LOVE   NN   BI
1980   COMPETITIVE VIDEO

P/D—Tom Rogers
F/A—Tom Lawn
F/A—Jennifer Sands

This one begins with Henry in bed making love to a woman. Suddenly, there's a knock on the door. Turns out they aren't married. Next scene, Henry is on a couch with his ankles bandaged. Henry and "Henry, Jr." evidently jumped out the window and Henry broke his ankles. Two of his girlfriends arrive to take care of Henry, Jr. and one of them is a redhead with a mean-looking pimple on her ass. But if you've wondered what a redheaded female looks like naked, this one will give you the answer.

NOTE; Competitive Video is Cal Vista's response to sexvids like *Swedish Erotica, Limited Edition, Peep Shows* and *The Diamond Collection* offered by competitors. Like them, Competitive tapes sell for about half the price of regular tapes ($49.50 or less) and run for an hour or a little longer. Unlike them, in some cases, which makes Competitive more interesting, they offer one story line, for an hour, instead of three short unrelated vignettes. Except for one *(All the Way* with Georgina Spelvin), you've never seen the actresses or actors or heard of the directors before in the fourteen Competitive tapes listed in this filmography. But in some cases, as I will note, the stories are well told and equal to the bigger-budgeted productions. Often the sexmaking is more natural and you believe the people are really having climaxes. Also the actors are often quite homely, bony and have acne. They will occasionally remind you of stag films from the 1930s and 1940s. But if you wonder what your next-door neighbors look like when they are making love, Competitive will satisfy your Peeping Tom instincts. The sex is usually pretty normal, plus the conventional lesbian scenes, of course.

AUNT PEG GOES HOLLYWOOD
NN   DK   BI
1983   CABALLERO

P/D—Paul G. Vatelli
F/A—Judith Anderson, Rhonda Jo Petty, Lisa de Leeuw, Little Oral Annie, Lorna Mills, Tara Hudd
F/A—Ron Jeremy, Jeff Conrad, Kevin Jaye

Aunt Peg (Judith Anderson)—her name doesn't appear on the box, just Aunt Peg —is casting for a new porno movie. She's even looking for a new director. Within the first few seconds of the tape Tara Hudd is opening her labia for Kevin Jaye, and telling him "I can't wait to taste you." Six steamy copulations later, which include all the people listed above, except the producer who should hide his face in shame, Jeff Conrad finally locates Aunt Peg in Mexico. As a potential new director he has to prove that he can do it as well as tell others how to. This leads to a fifteen-minute three-way deal with Judith Anderson, Little Oral Annie and Hunter. Believe it or not, rather than upchucking there's a way to laugh with this tape—particularly at this threesome. Run it in slow motion! You'll not only get well acquainted with Judith's vulva, but you'll guess from expressions on her face that her ecstasy is a little put-on.

BABY DOLL **NN BI DK**
VIDEO X HOME LIB

P/D—R. Zeller
F/A—Stephen Long, David Book
F/A—Candy Mason, Bonnie Lane

A plotless, ucky-fucky, nonstop sperm-shooter with people you've never seen before or will again. Presumably taking place in surburbia, it involves a teenage girl (Candy Mason, who is probably Mexican and looks about 19) and a lady who sells cosmetics (Avon-style) but prefers kissing and fellatio. Candy's "uncle," whom she calls Daddy, has white hair and a graying beard that mixes interestingly with Candy's black pubic hair—but other than that it's nothing you haven't seen before.

BAD GIRLS **NN NM BI DK**
1981 COLLECTORS VIDEO

P/D—David Frazer, Svetlana
F/A—John Leslie, Ron Jeremy, Richard Pacheco
F/A—Pia Snow, Jasimine du Bai, Victoria Knoll, Leonara Bruce

Four models who are also photographers take their vacation together in a Winnebago camper, which they drive into the San Bernardino Mountains (I think—the location is not identified). These are all women you haven't seen much of in adult films. The outdoor setting, the magnificent scenery and four young and horny ladies around a campfire discussing their sexual needs (they have just picked up a 16-year-old Boy Scout in the camper and teased him, but that was all) could have been an amusing premise to build on. Even a bisexual scene around a campfire where two of the women, after they have been swimming in the lake by moonlight, discuss making love to their own sex and finally try it is well done. They haven't ever done it before, and afterward they ask each other, "No guilt feelings?" Answer: "No, but I don't want to make it a habit." Even an encounter with John Leslie, who is chopping wood, gives you a feeling that this might have been an interesting film. But, alas, it quickly falls apart with most of the film being devoted to Habrina's Dungeon—a den of sadomasochism presumably hidden in the forest near where they have camped for the night. It's run by the Judge, who tells one of his monks, "We are crusaders in a world of forgotten values. We are truly male chauvinist pigs, and I for one am proud of it." If you are male and bring this one home to your wife or girlfriend, and if you laugh or look as if you are interested from this point on, you can count on it—she'll tell you that *you* are a male chauvinist pig, too!

BALLING FOR DOLLARS **NN NM BI**
1980 ASTRO

No actors or actresses are identified on this tape, except John C. Holmes, who appears in a threesome.

Mostly this one is a series of loops with the women, who presumably work for a collection agency. Instead of collecting for their company, they collect some sex for themselves. It begins with a woman masturbating in a shower sequence that is far more interesting than anything Brian de Palma offered in *Dressed to Kill*. It then proceeds to a woman picking a guy up in a van and offering to service him and two women taking on a guy in a garage who was working on his car. He relaxes and works on them, or are they playing on him? Women won't like this one—but the actresses are in control of the male actors.

BEAUTY AND THE BEAST **CC HARD R**
1982 KENYON VIDEO

P/D—Not given
F/A—Dick Richards, M.D.
F/Z—Seka. Others not identified

Despite the rating, you're not likely to see this one on subscription television. A doctor with an English accent emcees this tour through what is subtitled "a sex freak circus." En route, you meet Sulka (after her operation on January 18, 1982). But there are some "before" shots (for other tapes of Sulka in action see listings). Then you meet Moby Dick, a guy with a white whale that hangs to his knees, then a dwarf who stands on a chair to have sex (no genitals showing). Then you watch a guy having extended sex with a life-size inflatable doll. Dr. Richards explains this is a reasonable "partner substitute" when no partner is available. Next a female dressed as a male is gradually stripped by a transsexual male guy dressed as a woman. Then, you meet the Boston Batswanger, who has a complete set of male and female genitalia. And you meet guys who have their macho images restored with complete body tattoos, ladies with large labias, and transsexuals who perform in nightclubs and act more feminine than most women. Finally, intercut with these scenes Seka takes on 17½-inch Long Dong Silver.

BEAUTY PAGEANT NN NM DK BI
1981 ADULT VIDEO

P/A—J. D. Middleton, Stephen Phillips
F/A—Ken Roxoff, Bud Weiser
F/A—Nancy Suiter, Rita Starling, Bobbi Boobes, Mary Mufkin, Nancy Nukee

What plot there is in this one concerns the Sleepwell Waterbed and a decision to hold a Miss Sleepwell Contest to stop the declining sales of waterbeds. But after that you only see one waterbed for a few seconds in action—the rest of the film was probably shot on a Saturday afternoon in the California home of the producer or one of his friends for under $5,000. It includes the ten young ladies who compete in the contest, pose naked around the luxurious swimming pool and service and are serviced by the judges on floors and couches and near the pool in continuous fucky-sucky sequences. With the exception of Nancy Suiter, they are all people you've never seen before and the dialogue degenerates to inanity.

CALIFORNIA GIGOLO
NN NM BI and DB
1979 WONDERFUL WORLD OF VIDEO

P/D—Eliot Lewis, Bob Chinn
F/A—John C. Holmes, Don Fernando
F/A—Veri Knotty, Kitty Shane, Vanessa Tibbs

This one starts intriguingly in Palm Springs with Johnny Holmes following a woman into the tram entrance for a trip up the mountains and telling her: "I can really show you some fine loving." But then it strays back to Beverly Hills and nonstop sex. Nothing much to distinguish it except Veri Knotty's ability to tie her labia lips together in a knot when she is masturbating. Harmless, with one good thing: a nice Hollywood-Beverly Hills-Malibu ambiance in the cinematography.

CANDY STORE NN DK some silly
DS whipping scene
ASTRO

The only identified actor or actress on this one is Candy Samples. Who's she? In the sexvid, she's madame of the "Candy Store," her own house with five or six girls to serve the clients. If the client isn't satisfied, Candy will finish him off. This is a low-budget quickie which required only a living room and a bedroom to make, and a total budget probably under $10,000. Some of the girls actually talk with their customers in what is occasionally natural conversation. In addition there is one gratuitous whipping scene, one virgin sold to Candy and promptly deflowered, and one extended group sex scene with all the girls and one client which all takes place in the same bedroom.

CARNAL HIGHWAYS NN BI DK
HIFCOA

P/D—C. H. Howard
F/A—John Seeman, Fernando Fortes
F/A—Marlene Monroe, Seka, Maria Renee

Two horny, but not brainy guys drive a trailer and rig from Los Angeles to San Francisco, and during the trip are serviced by six women, including Seka, who you think might wrap things up with usual sexual proficiency, but next thing you know they are in a sex education class with six more women. Sexvid buffs might want this one for early Seeman and Fortes appearances. Both of them have worked behind and before the lenses of innumerable pornos. Nothing you haven't seen before.

CENTERFOLD FEVER **NN BI DK**
1982 VID-X-PIX

P/D—**Richard Milner**
F/A—**Richard Bolla, Ron Jeremy, Marc Stevens**
F/A—**Tiffany Clark, Kandi Barbour, Samantha Fox, Lisa Be, Veri Knotty, Annie Sprinkles**

Richard Milner, who is the author of a fascinating book and ostensibly a very straight guy, has produced with this one, a totally whacked-out sexvid for sexually frustrated males. If you show it to your wife or girlfriend you may create another member of W.A.P. (Woman Against Pornography). On the other hand, I deliberated whether to give it a CC rating—I finally didn't. Beyond the silly plot which involves Mr. Scuzzi, editor of *Skin* magazine (Richard Bolla), whose secretary is always fellating him under his desk (he's looking for the perfect Centerfold Girl), some of the sequences belong in the things-you-can't-believe department. First is Kandi Barbour interviewing Marc Stevens, who appeared in many porno films in the 1970s. She's trying to determine whether his famous 10½-inch penis has shrunk in his old age. Marc admits that he's pushing 40, but it hasn't. Marc admits that he has had sex with at least 3,000 women—and that doesn't include when he was "stud cocking" (providing the erect penis in films when the actor whose face is on camera can't get it up). Marc also does an erotic strip dance later in the film with Jill Munro that is interesting to watch and really belongs in some other film. But the throw-uppy stuff is all the women listed above watching Marc and Jill and having lesbian sex. One of them asks the other five, "Wouldn't it be nice if we could find a man?" And of course, they do—Richard Bolla. In the meantime, Annie Sprinkles is fellating three guys at once while her husband(?), Leo, is muffdiving with Tiffany Clark and then, after doing an unbelievable bosom dance, she offers to teach American women about oral sex. At least in this one Annie doesn't sprinkle on anyone.

CHINA DE SADE **DS DK BI**
1979 VCX, SELECT/ESSEX

P/D—**Aaron Linn, Charles de Santos**
F/A—**Ari Adler, Dale Meador**
F/A—**Linda Wong, Tracy O'Neil**

Apocalypse Now, Part II might have been the title of this sexvid. Colonel Krieg, after going native in Vietnam, escapes the looney bin where he has been incarcerated and opens up office in a tenement house in San Francisco. There he, and all the playmates he can find (à la Marquis de Sade) discover and promote the joys of pain to enhance pleasure.

COMING HOME BABY **NN**
1975 VISUAL ENTERTAINMENT

P/D—**Harvid Accett**
F/A—**Jon Gregory, Steve Blander**
F/A—**Diane Steele**

Trevor (Jon Gregory) arrives home after 18 months at sea in the merchant marine. He calls Vicky, his fiancée, but she doesn't answer the phone because she's too busy having sex with a new boyfriend. Trevor hitchhikes home and is soon picked up by a guy and a gal in a van. Eskimo fashion, the guy shares the woman in the back of the van with Trevor. Next he's picked up by a gal in a cabriolet with a sunroof. She pulls off the highway, opens the roof so that Trevor can stand up in the car and she fellates him. Then she leans out the window while he takes her doggie style. Back to the highway, she tells him, "Have a good day," and he answers, "Thank you, ma'am." It's getting late, but during all this time Vicky is still with her boyfriend. Trevor, passing through a big city, gets slugged on the head. A kindly girl leads him to her apartment, where she immediately opens his pants. Trevor gets home finally, but he never stops coming!

A COMING OF ANGELS
NN DK with continuous DS overtones and a 3-way BI between the ladies
1979 VCA

P/D—Joel Scott
F/A—Jamie Gillis, John Leslie, Eric Edwards
F/A—Annette Haven, Abigail Clayton, Leslie Bovee

Best Actor and Best Supporting Actress Awards, 1978 Erotic Film Festival. It begins with a five-minute intriguing introduction of a guy and a gal playing in the snow, but quickly deteriorates into a plot that seems to revolve around a guy who reaches his orgasms not as a participator but as a voyeur. Several amusing scenes of men brought to a high pitch and then left gasping while women chuckle. Pretty settings in a mountain ski lodge.

DAUGHTERS OF EMMANUELLE
NN BI NM DK
1983 VCX

P/D—Joshua River, Michael B. Webb
F/A—Ron Jeremy, Kevin Gibson, Star Buck, Doug Rossi
F/A—Rhonda Jo Petty, Jeannette James, Jennifer Russell, Stephanie Taylor

Don't buy or rent this one expecting to see some connection with Emmanuelle films (see listings). There is none, except that presumably her daughters are more sexually inhibited than Mama. There are two stories. The first is about Barbara (Rhonda Jo Petty), who is engaged to Paul (Ron Jeremy) but is embarrassed to be seen naked by him. He hurts her when he screws her. He finagles her a job with a men's magazine photographer, and quicker than you can say Jack Robinson Rhonda becomes a sex maniac wearing out Ron Jeremy—if you can believe that! It's not easy to believe that Rhonda Jo is so virginal, especially when she reveals her partially shaved vulva. Obviously most modest ladies don't depilate their nether parts. The second story is about Kay (Jeannette James) and Howard (Kevin Gibson). Howard can't get an erection unless he watches his wife masturbate, or unless he watches porno movies. Kay reluctantly obliges him but decides to investigate the Institute for Better Sex Relations to discover what's wrong with her. Unknown to her Howard is attending the same Institute. His instructor is a lady, of course. Hers is a guy. Eventually, the coun-

sellors, who don't know Howard and Kay are married, arrange for them to go to bed with each other—wearing masks. Believe it or not Howard wears a lion's mask, and they don't know it's each other until they have been sucking and bumping away for fifteen minutes. The makers of this film should try De Maupassant short stories. They're more believable!

DEEP ROOTS **CC NN NL and NR and DK occasionally**
1980 XTRA/VISION

P/D—J. J. Camer, Lisa Barr
F/A—Jesse Chacan
F/A—Liz Renay, Anita Sauds, Mary Swan

Jesse Chacan, as Billy the Indian (he really looks like one), leaves the reservation to discover the real world. His girlfriend tells him that he has roots and will return, which is the only reason for the title. In Los Angeles, Jesse meets a woman who offers to pose for him (he's an artist), and they poster paint each other's body in a nice erotic sequence. Billy enjoys the fleshpots of Los Angeles. Somehow or other this sexvid hangs together and amuses, perhaps because two of the women, Anita Saunds and Liz Renay, are quite plump and natural, middle-class appealing females. (Anita Sauds has freckles on her chest and belly.) Anita has her red pubic hair cut, trimmed and blow dried by her male hairdresser who then obligingly services her in the chair. Liz and Anita do a burlesque striptease together and the film concludes with a too-long orgy costume party which is occasionally funny and occasionally kinky. At the end Billy goes back to the reservation—and his roots.

DEEP RUB **NN BI DK**
1980 VCX

P/D—Leon Gucci
F/A—Paul Thomas, John C. Holmes
F/A—Desiree Cousteau, Serena

A male-oriented quickie designed for the raincoat crowd. Even though it comes complete with a theme song, ladies in charge won't like this one. Desiree learns how to be a masseuse from Paul Thomas, and eventually after servicing three guys on a sailing sloop, pretending she's an Oriental woman, massaging Annette Haven you know where and bringing a guy to a climax in four minutes, she earns her MDR (Master of the Deep Rub) degree and is awarded a phallic statue. Desiree gets no chance to play her *Pretty Peaches* role in this one, and you'll wonder if since that flick she's had silicone treatments.

DIRTY LILLY **CC NN BI KD ending occasional NL**
1979 VIDEO-X-PIX

P/D—Mark Ubell
F/A—Eric Edwards
F/A—Beth Anna, Sharon Mitchell

The title on this one is misleading. Beth Anna informs the viewer immediately that she bathes twice a day. As Dirty Lilly, she plays the part of a happy moron in pigtails (wearing knee socks and a little girl dress) in a delightfully hammy way. Silly scenes include her naive appearance on a porno movie set, and with a muscle man who ties her up and then has sex with another woman. Unfortunately, the ending is sick-sick with Beth Anna taking on five Satanists. Beth Anna, along with Desiree Cousteau and Carol Connors, is a kind of sexually pragmatic, in-control female, despite her seeming innocence.

ECSTASY GIRLS **NN and one mostly laughing DB and DS sequence**
1979 CABALLERO CONTROL

P/D—Harold Lime, Robert McCallum
F/A—Jamie Gillis, John Leslie, Paul Thorpe
F/A—Nancy Suiter, Desiree Cousteau,
    Georgina Spelvin, Serena, Leslie Bovee

This film was nominated for Best Picture at the 1979 Erotic Film Award and is *Screw's* Best 10 of 1979, number two. If you are willing to suspend disbelief the story line, once it gets going, hangs together for two hours and is interestingly photographed. It's about photographing five women in the act of sex and proving to their prudish

father they are immoral so he will disinherit them. Things you've never seen before include Desiree climaxing while standing on her head, Nancy Suiter enjoying whipping and bondage, and Serena and Jamie sexmaking in an almost NR sequence.

800 FANTASY LANE
CC NN BI DK DS
1979 CAL VISTA

P/D—Monique Du Bois, Svetlana, Robert
    McCallum
F/A—Jamie Gillis, Bud Weiss
F/A—Serena, Desiree Cousteau, Chris
    Anderson, Candy Summer, Lisa de Leeuw,
    Aimee Leigh

VD, or Victor Durgis (Jamie Gillis) and his friend, John (Buddy Weiss) own a filling station. Reading an advertisement of Hollywood Star Realty ("manned" by a dozen women who specialize in million-dollar properties for oil millionaires), they transform themselves into big-time operators of Durgis Oil and arrive for a tour of some very palatial Los Angeles estates, with a half-dozen or more luscious realtors as their guides. After this promising beginning, the co-director, Svetlana, went fantasy mad and offers some of the funkiest sex scenes you've ever watched, including an S/M chamber with five women in a sunken tub. A pot-induced fantasy involves a circus animal trainer in a cage with various striped and spotted naked ladies snarling and biting as he strokes them with his whip. When she made this one, Svetlana was catering to the kind of male fantasies that most women won't appreciate. Pretty far out . . . and wins awards in the things-you've-never-seen-before department.

EIGHT TO FOUR (8 TO 4) **NN BI DK**
1981 CABALLERO

P/D—Eliot Lewis, Louie Lewis
F/A—Hubert Savage, Paul Thomas
F/A—Annette Haven, Veronica Hart, Lois
    Sanders, Lisa de Leeuw, Juliet Anderson

The interesting (and sad) thing about this film is that if you pinpoint 1970 as the breakthrough year for explicit sex films, 11 years later it still incorporates all the old adult film conventions: seven women having sex in one film, practically all of them wearing garter belts; at least a dozen come shots; two extended lesbian scenes, and extended fellatio by women who can't live without it. Obviously, creative breakthroughs by producers and directors who can integrate sex and story for more mature audiences than the raincoat crowd are hard to come by. There is a story of sorts patterned after the *Nine to Five* movie. Annette Haven as Lisa plays the Jane Fonda role, and she eventually "gets" Mr. Jarvis, the office manager, who is a prick literally and figuratively, as well as Miss Patrick (Juliet Anderson), one of the top officials of the company, Osborne Insurance Agency. She hires men based on their G.Q.—genital qualifications— and then in her plush office provides some of the most acrobatic sexmaking you've ever watched on your tube. And the other women, Lisa de Leeuw, Veronica Hart and Lois Sanders (who xeroxes a guy's penis in the copy room) are all beautiful—and sexperts who can lead a man quickly for their own satisfaction. Worth seeing if you're a male, mostly to wonder if you could cope with these aggressive women, who literally emasculate male egos. This one appears on late-night subscription television, but in an edited version with no genitals showing.

EROTIC LOVEMAKING (L'Amour) R
STAR VIDEO

P/D—Jean Luis Mongur
F/A—Many young French people

Here's an hour of beautiful young, naked French women being caressed and kissed from head to foot gently and passionately by handsome French men. Off-screen, a lady with a French accent describes the joys and how-to's of arousing a woman and the many ramifications of sexmaking. Romantic action is interspersed with Charlie, a boorish character who is in such a hurry to get into his girlfriend he hasn't time to take his pants off. There are no hard-core scenes. Amazingly, however, the couples engage in every kind of loving sexuality, including oral sex without showing their genitals. This is the kind of tape which obviously will be typical of the kind of sex play you will see continuously on the new Playboy Television Cable Network. It should appeal to the Playboy audience, who prefer their sex glamorized. In fact, the lady commentator puts much emphasis on baths before and after. This may be the first of a forthcoming flood of new how-to-do-it and-win-the-fair-young-maiden's-gratitude tapes. But unless the participants actually become persons who reveal what is taking place in their brains, they never will be very erotic.

ELECTRIC BLUE 001 **Nudity but no close-ups of genital sex. Further out than most subscription or cable TV**
1980 KENYON VIDEO

P/D—Adam Cole

Electric Blue is the first with a video sex magazine that is now published quarterly and ultimately will probably force the Playboy Channel (on Escapade, cable TV which they own) to get much sexier than they are now. Ultimately, the Playboy Channel and particularly *Electric Blue* may eliminate *Playboy, Penthouse* and *Hustler.* How can still photographs compete with hundreds of naked ladies talking to you and shaking their breasts and behinds at you? Electric Blue 001 was originally numbered 002—but evidently, as Kenyon got organized and kept publishing, 001 eliminated 002. One elimination from the original version which Kenyon should rectify is to put back an extended nude erotic disco dance by Marilyn Chambers, who is the hostess of this hour program. In between the segments she reveals that she's wearing a ring on her labia: "It's a turn-on when I walk." Various sequences on this tape, which moves fast, are an erotic bisexual massage, nude disco dancing, and interviews with Moby Dick and Long Dong Silver. As a counterpoint to the sex, the tape offers death in a film of the famous 1976 Indianapolis 500 Auto Race during which two drivers and a spectator were killed in a crash. This is followed by clips from several Russ Meyer films showing his big bosomed heroines in action, and a story about brothels for the elderly and retired in upper Manhattan in which women in their 50s, 60s and 70s earn an extra five or ten dollars by servicing older men who actually prefer them to younger women. Each tape concludes with a Nude Wives Special which presumably are tapes of young women taken by their husbands to qualify in *Electric Blue's* continuing $500 prize for those selected. Unlike the nude wives portrayed in *Hustler* and other men's magazines, these ladies tell you why their husbands enjoy their bodies and what their particular sexual preferences are.

ELECTRIC BLUE 003 **X-rated (no genital sex)**
1981 KENYON VIDEO

P/D—Adam Cole

The second *Electric Blue* commences with an erotic dance by three women who a poor black guy in prison has summoned up in his imagination. Danced to a tune called "Galaxy" ("I'm the ruler of the galaxy"), it looks as it might have been featured at Richard's Revue Bar, the famous nightclub in London's Soho. Next, Fanny, a former model who has become a photographer for *Club* magazine, takes sexy pictures of herself, presumably with cables attached to her cameras. But no photographer will ever believe it. As a counterpoint to sex, you get some surfing scenes from *White Waves*, a film made by Rod Sumptner, followed by the stag movie Marilyn Monroe presumably made in 1956 (all she does is undress and play with her breasts). *Playboy* (see listing) insists it really isn't Marilyn. Next, on to a female roller derby where the participants practice mayhem with each other and try to rip off each other's clothes. A discussion of Americans' eating habits and a potential cure of junk food addiction follows. Then there are a number of excerpts from porno films, including *Sunny, Coed Fever,* and *Ecstasy Girls,* and finally another session with Long Dong Silver having sex. When he comes on top of her he presumably gets inside her—but it's doubtful. If he

did he'd come out of her mouth! Britt Ekland hosts this one (in a night gown) and you can see her naked for a moment in an old movie with Tony Curtis—but you can see more of her in *Wickerman.* I'll take a bet that eventually *Electric Blue* will expand these tapes to an hour and a half and sell them for under $25. How? By selling advertising on them. Really a natural.

ELECTRIC BLUE 004
KENYON VIDEO

P/D—Tony Power, Roger Cook

Seka is the hostess. Her claim to fame in this one is that she takes on Long Dong Silver in a skit in which she plays a southern maiden, and Long Dong is a returning confederate soldier. Other episodes on this tape include an inside view of Mustang, a Nevada brothel where the ladies tell you the toughest work of the night is how to tell the guy that she's going to wash him. Then you are watching scenes from a Jayne Mansfield film made before she was decapitated in an automobile accident. Jayne soaps herself naked in a bathtub, and sings, "Lulu, I'm in Love." Then there's an interview with the hermaphrodite, the Boston Batsman. There's an interview with two women who enjoy luxury living but couldn't afford the apartment of their dreams singly. Together they can— and enjoy each other in bed to boot! Then there's Amanda Lear, a rock swinger who swirls a lighted phallic baton as she sings, racing speedboats and an Electric Blue Swing Party in what looks like Plato's Retreat. It concludes with the feature of the month, Nude Wives Special. *Playboy* is now offering similar but not quite so censorable or sexy material on the Playboy Channel, Escapade.

ELECTRIC BLUE 005 **Hard R and BI**
1982 KENYON VIDEO

P/D—Adam Cole

Desiree Cousteau is the hostess of this one. Before it's over she manages to get cunnilingus from several different women plus the cameraman and John Holmes—

though you never see their penises. There is much simulated sex, and it is obvious that *Electric Blue* will be much more popular on subscription television than much of the soft R stuff that now appears. In this one, you spend a day in Spain with Amanda who meets a ladies' underwear salesman. She caresses herself with his clothing line—you never see him—but she tells you that he did get his hands in her knickers (she's English). This one offers you some fascinating sky-gliding shots and a tour of an Oriental peepshow that's turning people on in New York City's Chinatown. If you pay your entrance fee you can watch through a grill just about every kind of live sexuality you ever dreamed about, and you can participate if you wish to pay a bit more. Once again the Boston Batswanger, appears. She/He wasn't aware that she/he was different until he/she was about 12 years old. Then there's an extended bisexual sequence, followed by a scary report called San Francisco Splash-Down. Seems that more than 100 people have committed suicide by jumping off the Golden Gate Bridge and falling at 80 miles an hour into the bay. Then there's a Sex Maniacs' Guide to the U.S.A., which covers topless car washes; nude male disco dancing; S/M factories where you can enjoy(?) pain; naked parachute jumping; topless boxing; erotic bakeries; et cetera. Midpoint on the tape is a 3-D bisexual scene. You have to put on the red and blue cardboard glasses to get the third dimensional effect. It's not bad, but it can be improved. One day, holography will solve the problem.

ELECTRIC BLUE 006 R
1982 KENYON VIDEO

P/D—Adam Cole
F/A—Vanessa Del Rio, Terri Hall, Bridget Bardot, Suze Randall, Sulka and others

The difference between *Electric Blue* as a video magazine and *Playboy* is something like the difference between *Hustler* magazine and *Playboy*. Whether Playboy Video (see listing) decides to compete with less glamorized and more "down to earth" vulva close-ups and erotic sexual behavior on the part of their females remains to be seen. In 006, Vanessa Del Rio is the hostess. Dressed in a Lupe Velez costume and accompanied by a mariachi band, she eats a banana lasciviously, telling you, "I eat the whole banana." Later, she gives you a close-up look of her labia, which she tastes approvingly with her fingers. Terri Hall appears in a Venice Beach, California, sequence in which you get a quick tour of the beach and the crazies (who are calmer than they were in the 1960s) as they roller skate by, beach muscle men practicing their exercises and young women rolling their pelvises in tight jeans. In an apartment overlooking the beach, Terri lies on her bed, strips and masturbates erotically to a climax, making the male viewer wish he were present to supply the missing ingredient. A brief interview with Sulka brings you up to date (see *Sulka's Wedding*, p. 226) with the fact that she had her penis and balls removed (not so coarsely stated) January 19, 1982 and is now a woman. Other sequences cover a woman playing with herself in a chauffeur-driven Cadillac as she's driven through Hollywood, a cut from *Electric Blue's* tape, *Nude Jello Wrestling;* a cut from a censored version of *Alice in Wonderland* (see listing, p. 59), an interview with Suze Randall, who changed from a career of modeling to become a photographer of nude ladies. Suze admits she prefers anal sex to sex the regular way since she doesn't climax readily. The tape is topped off with cuts from a Bridget Bardot film with another lady going through sexual motions without a male partner and a survey of a Los Angeles establishment where you can rent a dungeon, complete with chains, racks and leather gadgets to satisfy your masochistic or sadistic compulsions.

ELECTRIC LIGHT VOYAGE NR
1979 MEDIA

P/D—Stephen Cole, Astralvision, Inc.
This is a light show.

A one-hour light show tape that is totally erotic. You can watch it with the sound track turned on, or better still, choose your own music on your stereo and then undress and turn down the lights. Stephen Halperin's music, such as "Zodiac Suite," works beautifully. It's great for sexmaking. Before 1990, many homes will have whole walls in the living room playing Astral vision just the way you play music. I hope some producers of adult films will see the possibility of computer animation using the human form to totally eroticize sexmaking in some upcoming production.

11 (ELEVEN) **NN DK BI NR at the end**
1981 VCX

P/D—Elliott and Harry Lewis
F/A—Jon Martin, Jesse Adams
F/A—Brooke West, Dhaije Taan, Susan Nero

Here's *"10"* carried to its illogical conclusion. Our hero tells his psychiatrist he dreams about a girl, though he hasn't found her, who is "eleven" on a scale of one to ten. If nothing else, the sequences with various women on his way to finding "eleven" prove one thing. The average female is very much in control of the male who is always in need of sexual relief. This one won't add anything new to your fantasy life—except a sequence where two people make love in a coffin, proving perhaps that an orgasm really is "une petite morte." When our hero finally finds his woman, they make love not to Ravel's "Bolero" but to Tschaikowsky's "1812 Overture"—with our hero's cannon going off, of course!

EROTIC AMATEUR VIDEO Volume 6
BI
1982 VPX

P/D—Sal
F/A—Unknown

"Sal," the chief cook and bottle washer of VPX, is an entrepreneur in the adult film industry with a new concept that even he hasn't taken, as yet, to its inevitable conclusion: couples *paying* Sal to videotape them while making love. Sal's theory is that porn tape aficionados are weary of watching film after film with Seka or Serena or Samantha, so he films amateurs.

He probably doesn't have to pay them very much because he provides a very nicely furnished bedroom and tells them to go ahead and make love—there will be no cameraman in sight or anyone else to inhibit them. Reason? Sal has designed the room so that it can be "watched" through two-way mirrors. Several camera eyes watch the lovers from different angles, allowing close-ups and long shots. His tapes are shot direct on videotape and the color is very sharp. In different volumes, all of which sell for $39.95 and run for an hour, Sal offers a single woman masturbating, a couple enjoying sex and group sex in various combinations. Volume 6 is bisexual—or perhaps even straight lesbian. The two women really seem to like each other. If you don't like lesbian sex, you'll get bored.

EROTICISE **R**
1983 VESTRON VIDEO

P/D—Ed Hansen
F/A—Kitten Natividad, Gigi Anthony, Kit Fargo, Rita Gardner, Ashley St. John, Summer Tenaya

Inevitably someone would realize that men as well as women were buying the *Aerobicize* and the *Jane Fonda's Workout Tapes.* Their lady friends may be exercising, but most of the guys probably open a can of beer while they enjoy watching the women. You can't see Jane Fonda in her birthday suit, but you can see Kitten Natividad (she of the huge mammaries) and five other lovely ladies. They are happily exercising on a porch overlooking what seems to be the San Fernando Valley. In the beginning, they are dressed in workout suits but then a breast slips out here, and a behind there. About halfway through they're completely naked. Throughout the tape, in the close-ups, the ladies grin suggestively at you, and moisten their lips sexily with their tongues. The only thing better than watching this tape would be exercising naked with the opposite sex. Why not? If we had a sane society—coed sports, sans clothing would be a way of life.

EVERY INCH A LADY
NN BI DK NL (in a mind-boggling way)
1975 QUALITY

P/D—John and Lem Amero
F/A—Harry Reems, Marc Stevens, Jamie Gillis
F/A—Darby Lloyd Raines, Andrea True, Kim Pops

Before Crystal La Verne (Darby Lloyd Raines) finds Cino (Harry Reems) sleeping in the hallway of her apartment, she was a struggling hooker in Greenwich Village. Taking Harry into her rooms, he's quickly in bed with her, but just before she climaxes, he tells her that it's going to cost her twenty bucks. Soon they are in business together offering "Escort Services, Massage, Models"—but they quickly discover they can make more money offering perversions. A few years later they are the prosperous owners of Deviation, Inc.—and presumably very much in love with each other. But watch out. Suddenly you discover that Crystal's secretary (Andrea True) has been sleeping with Cino, and Crystal (after receiving a diamond from Cino and buying him a house—before they are to finally get married), unknown to them, catches them in bed and overhears a plot to kill her and thus inherit the business. She turns the tables on them and the gas from the stove and blows them up. But, of course, this plot is only a weak glue to hold together the sex sequences. There's several weird ones in the things-you've-never-seen-before department. There's Marc Stevens, who can't get it up unless a woman says dirty words to him, so Kim Pope reads to him extensively from a dirty book. And the pièce de résistance is Dr. Infinity, who can fellate himself, and as an employee of Deviation, Inc. does so in an extended sequence.

EXOTIC FRENCH FANTASIES
NN NM BI DK
ADULT VIDEO

P/D—John Herbert Glick, Michael McDermott
F/A—John Holmes
F/A—Linda Lovelace, Andrea True

Why this one required both a director and a producer is a mystery. A combination of foreign film loops, it was put together with much patching and cutting of sex sequences from European films, with a weak attempt to tie the mulligan stew together by adding a presumed writer and secretary who in voice-overs and occasional intercuts try to convince you that you are watching stories being written by the author. Most of the sex sequences are pretty yucky. As for Linda Lovelace—her appearance in a "shaved clam" episode is grimy. Whether it's Johnny Wadd she's fellating as advertised on the box in which this tape comes is a matter of conjecture. You can live without it.

EXTREMES **NN NM NL DK**
1981 CABALLERO

P/D—Alan Vydra
F/A—Eric Edwards, Joey Civera, John Leslie
F/A—Serena, Jesie St. James, Susan Nero

The producer of this film is a 62-year-old West German grandmother, Beate Uhse, who is determined to crack the U.S. market for adult films through her American subsidiary, Reeltime Pleasure Unlimited. Beate, who owns, among other things, 400 adult theaters in Europe, runs a mini-conglomerate doing about $150 million annual sales. In all the films she produces, she rules out bestiality and sadomasochistic sex and insists that none of her films degrades women. You have to watch this sexvid (which was shot in San Francisco) at least twice to know what is going on. If you have your TV connected to your stereo you can hear it in stereo, which makes it a first. A series of vignettes, the story includes an auto that can fly and takes John Leslie and Joey Civera from San Francisco to Hamburg. In between, you see a guy and his woman covered with feathers, and the woman asking "Do you want me to lay an egg again?" Response: "I wonder why I ever married you." Cut to a totally mad S&M palace in Hamburg where the women wear leather masks. You never see their faces. Next, there's a long sequence in a waterbed. There's such a fast-changing panorama and weird cutting that whether you applaud or not, you'll watch it to the end. Despite its European sophistication and interesting cinematography, Beate missed the beat on this one. Most American women will not cheer it!

EXPLORING YOUNG GIRLS
DK BI NM
1975 ADULT VIDEO

P/D—Chris Smegna, David Stitt
F/A—Rick Chamberlain, Wade Nichols
F/A—Vanessa Del Rio, Harriet Hart, Erica Havens, Sharon Mitchell

A yuckie-quickie during which four porno stars tell a psychologist about their early sex lives and why they are making X-rated movies. (A subject which if it were done legitimately would make a good film.) Vanessa's first experience is at a Halloween party. Another woman loses her virginity in a summer camp called Camp FaBago, where she screwed with the counselor while the kids watched. Another had sex continuously for eight hours in a group sex orgy, and another is turned on by ugly men. Essentially this is a film about nasty adults playing doctor with each other. No one in the film, despite pigtails, white socks and saddle shoes, is under 25.

FANTASY NN BI DK
1978 VCX

P/D—Gerard Damiano
F/A—Paul Thomas, David Morris
F/A—Georgina Spelvin, Nicolle O'Neal, Kyoto Sunn

Nominated for the Erotic Film Award in 1979. Bowing to the pressure to produce films with at least five women experiencing sex—all within an hour—Damiano has produced another film of vignettes. The unrelated fantasies mostly of women include double fellatio, double insertions and lesbian encounters. While everyone gets what they want, no one seems much happier afterward. The film concludes with the whole cast waving happily at the viewer with the Golden Gate Bridge in the background.

FEMALE ATHLETES NN BI and DK ending with conventional orgy sequence
1977 VIDEO-X-PIX

P/D—Leon Gucci
F/A—Paul Thomas, John Holmes
F/A—Annette Haven, Desiree Cousteau, Serena

In this one you can see John Holmes before he became Johnny Wadd and Desiree Cousteau before she became Pretty Peaches. All are very young and beautiful. The title is a misnomer. Annette Haven saves *Sports Life* magazine from bankruptcy by orienting the magazine to coed sports. The plot gets lost in transit, but there are some silly scenes with women kung fu experts defeating their male opponents and then reviving them, you know how. Things you've never seen before—oral sex in a swimming pool, including underwater come shots. Despite the feminist plot, except for sexmaking on a sailing yacht with Annette and Paul Thomas, women won't like this one.

FIREWORKS NN NM BI DK NL (If you believe in insatiable women)
1981 CABALLERO

P/D—Alan Vydra
F/A—Ted Harlow and many others
F/A—Caroline Grace, Nadine Russell, Joan Berry

You've never seen most of the women before (they are all beautiful) or the guys. The story is tied together by "firemen" who are on 24-hour duty and supply live male bodies to put out vaginal "fires" and "burning bushes." In addition, there is a 15-minute Mazola party with at least a dozen naked guys and gals squirming and there is copulating all over each other, creating a fleshy sex ballet which might be called *Garden of Delights* after Hieronymous Bosch. You can watch one woman (Nadine Russell) on her knees sucking four males (whom she has requested from the firehouse) while she determines which one of them will have the pleasure of entering her vagina. She wears them all out, after which reinforcements are sent in and ten more guys arrive (one weighs at least 400 pounds) and she takes them all on, too. In the final scene, a busload of ten women arrive at the "firehouse" and the ladies married or not pick out guys who service them when their boyfriends or husbands aren't available. Unless your lady enjoys dominant women, or is one, despite the unusual cinematography, she won't like this sexvid.

THE FILTHY RICH   NN   NL (for the dialogue) DK
CABALLERO

P/D—Michael Zen
F/A—Jack Wrangler, Hubert Savage, Randy West
F/A—Samantha Fox, Lisa de Leeuw, Jesie St. James, Vanessa Del Rio

It seems that Tiffany Tremaine (Samantha Fox) has never had an orgasm with her wealthy husband, Trent. In the first scenes on satin sheets, she is trying desperately, but downstairs in the mansion, her maid, Frieda (Jesie St. James), and Jarvis (Hubert Savage), the butler, are wearing out the cotton sheets. She and Trent listen on the mansion intercom and order breakfast. Then Tiffany decides to switch roles with the butler and maid, and she agrees to go to Loadstone, run by Werner Garhard, head of "pornographic est." Its motto is: "Assholes Share Your Space." As the wealthy Tremaines Jarvis and Frieda pretend *they* are filthy rich. Chili Caliente (Vanessa Del Rio) arrives. She is the new cook, hired by Tiffany before she left. Chili wears a mini-miniskirt and no panties when she serves as the new maid. Chili also "mixes Ex-Lax with Spanish Fly—so I can come when I go." Magnolia Thunderpussy, representative of Slave-On Sex Aids, arrives at the door while Frieda (stimulated by the Spanish Fly Chili has put in the Mexican beans) is servicing the pool boy (Randy West). Thunderpussy (Lisa de Leeuw) is her magnificently big-breasted, abrasive self. And up at Loadstone, Tiffany, in her crash course of sharing space with other assholes, is being screwed in front of a cheering audience by Trent. It all ends in an orgy where the participants are eating watermelons, bananas, and finally dine on Tiffany who now has become a tigress

in the sack and elsewhere. She crawls on top of the banquet table. A lovely voice-over at the beginning and conclusion (whose a.k.a., I happen to know, is Sweet Mouth) comments on the action. Sweet Mouth has a sweet voice and is probably as much fun in bed as any of the stars in this one. But she hasn't appeared in an adult film yet!

FLIPCHICKS   NN   NM   BI   DK
1975   VIDEO SHOWTIME

P/D—Butterfly Films
F/A—Marc Stevens
F/A—Darby Lloyd Raines, Georgina Spelvin

Darby and her roommate wake in bed to a telephone call from Mr. Schwartz, who tells them to pay the rent on their apartment or move out by noontime. Her roommate staggers sleepily into the bathroom while the camera watches her, and then climbs into the bathtub to masturbate with the water running and her legs stretched against the shower wall. In the kitchen, Darby greets their apartment neighbor, who has just lost his job. The only solution to their monetary problems is to make a porno movie—*Deep Throat* has grossed $2½ million. If they are going to be sword swallowers, they might as well do it for money. Auditioning prospects for their movie, who should arrive but Marc Stevens who undresses and kneels in front of Darby on her desk: "Can you get it up?" she asks. "All by myself? Let's make it a joint effort. Two hands are better than one." He then tells her in detail how to get him up. She's soon joined by her roommate who helps her measure the growing phenomenon. Then Gloria Box (Georgina Spelvin) arrives. Darby and she audition each other for an extended period, after which Mr. Schwartz bursts in and tells them to move out. But Georgina teaches him how to enjoy a "41." It's better than 69—a female delight—she fellates him and Marc at the same time. Next Marc suggests an 8-59, which you soon discover is a sandwich with Georgina, Marc and Mr. Schwartz. Schwartz decides that making porno movies is better than being a landlord.

FOXTROT NN NM DK BI
1982 COMMAND

P/D—Cecil Howard
F/A—Jake Teague, Richard Bolla, Ron Jeremy,
Bobby Astyr
F/A—Marlene Willoughy, Veronica Hart,
Vanessa Del Rio, Tiffany Clark, Sharon
Mitchell, Merle Michaels, Samantha Fox,
Sandra Hillman

My suggestion for the preliminary judges of the Seventh Annual Erotic Film Festival, which was held in July 1983, was that they face market realities of porno films and have two awards for Best Picture. One would be for films aimed at the female and couples audience which have a definite story line tending toward the romantic, some characterization, and no come shots or bisexual scenes. The other would be the best picture for horny males and the raincoat crowd. On this basis, *Foxtrot* would be a strong contender for the horny-male award. While all of the characters, who are encountered on the day before and through New Year's Eve, have screen names, it's impossible to remember them. The tape commences with Jake Teague, playing the part of a rich old millionaire, immediately enticing the family maid into bed with him when she serves breakfast. Within seconds it has cut to Richard Bolla watching Marlene Willoughby through binoculars. She's masturbating in her room across the street. His wife, played by Veronica Hart, is making a date on the telephone and complaining about his voyeurism. But Marlene, who knows that he is watching, is more intriguing. Then you are cut to Vanessa Del Rio, who is savoring her boyfriend's genitals. He returns the favor. Next Merle Michaels is making it with Sharon Mitchell and her sailor home from the sea. Ron Jeremy arrives in the apartment and discovers them. Minutes later, they are lying naked on their backs on top of each other. He doesn't last long, and to his sorrow, when he ejaculates they calmly continue to make love to each other. Bolla is now making it with Marlene, and Ron has discovered Veronica disconsolately wandering the streets. She joins him in his room and tells him, "Don't talk. I don't want

to know your name. It's weird, isn't it, fucking a complete stranger? It's a goddamned *foxtrot*. I want you to do terrible things to me." Finally it's New Year's Eve and Jake Teague is still running around, naked, although hundreds of guests are arriving at his mansion, and a New Year's Eve party is in full swing with an orchestra and a caterer. The caterer, who it turns out is Vanessa, falls into Teague's arms and he screws her in the laundry on top of the washing machine—turning it on so that it will vibrate her. But he finally climaxes—believe it or not, between her feet. Before you are finished with this one you will know the various actors and actresses' genitals as well as their faces. Including Sandra Hillman as a very homely Jewish woman who plays a babysitter to Samantha Fox's (unseen) yowling kid while Samantha is bouncing on the penis of the trombone player in the orchestra. It all ends up with scenes from Times Square on New Year's Eve. Run the tape on your television about an hour and half before midnight on New Year's Eve, and turn the sound off—it could provide silly background for certain kinds of New Year's Eve Parties.

THE FUR TRAP CC NN DK BI
1973 ADULT VIDEO

P/D—Not given
F/A—Bill Berry, Richard Bolla, Marc Baramy
F/A—Colleen Anderson, Marlene Willoughby,
Kelly Mint

Begins with Ted and his wife Sheila (Colleen Anderson) arguing about anal sex. He wants to try it—she is horrified. Ted works for an advertising agency, but his campaigns aren't paying off for his clients' products, Purr Detergent and Ardor "for specific odors where you need them." Sheila tells him it's gotten to the point that "your business problems are affecting our sex life. I'm going to get a job." Despite Ted's objections, she does. In the loft of a furrier she learns how to cut furs and sew them. In the things-you've-never-seen-before department are both heterosexual and bisexual sex in a pile of furs. What makes this one more interesting than most is Colleen Anderson, who acts the unsophisticated housewife role very well. She finally takes a one-night job, and with a female friend arrives in a cake at a stag party which is being run for a fellow at the office where Ted works. This provides the final orgy scene—with Sheila shocking Ted and then inviting him to anal sex, after which she assures him: "Oh, Ted, you're the only person I ever wanted. We can make it together."

THE GIRLS OF MR. X **NN BI**
1978 CABALLERO

P/D—A. G. Schmidt
F/A—Hans Engles
F/A—Angelique Brown, Dominique Frazer

Mr. X's several ladies, whom he treats lavishly and like a "chevalier sans raproche," are always disappearing on him and enjoying quickies in unlikely places like ladies' rooms, in the woods or on beaches, in boutiques, ballet classes and with riding instructors in stables. Plotless, but with several long scenes of interracial sexmaking with both black male and female lovers which are nicely photographed. The European ambiance—this one was made in Germany—makes it more interesting than most sexvids with nonstop sex.

GIRL SERVICE **DK BI**
1980 COMPETITIVE VIDEO

P/D—E. Tense
F/A—Caro Keff
F/A—Rod Tuiet

When the male actor's name sounds like "Rod to eat" and the director is E. Tense, you can't expect too much. My ratings don't mean much either because no one, including the director who may be one of the actors in this one, takes the action or the "plot" very seriously. Mr. Carson pays $1,500 to kidnappers for women whom he resells for $2,500 to his clients. The women, trussed up, arrive in the trunk of a chauffeur-driven Cadillac in a busy thoroughfare—and although they are obviously bound no one seems to pay any attention to them. Nor do the women protest too much. In fact, they are very cooperative with their new owners (see note under *April Love*, p. 273).

GRAND PRIX **NN DK BI**
COMPETITIVE VIDEO

P/D—Sam Norvell
F/A—John Durgess
F/A—Monique DuBois, Jacqueline Marrows, Sally Roberts

Maggie is going to marry Burn (his real name is Jim) within the week, but she wants him to give up racing. "But racing is my whole life," he tells her. "I want you to be your whole life," she tells him. He goes to a stag party with Bob and they both examine Bob's girl until she complains. Then Maggie and her friend share a dildo which Burn discovers later in the friend's room and identifies Maggie's smell on one end. Then Maggie goes to a bridal shower in a motel room next to the racetrack, but no one shows up except her friend. They listen to a guy trying to make it with a girl in the next room. First thing you know he knocks on their door. He needs some Vaseline to breach the ramparts. But before he gets back to his room, they take care of him, each jumping on and off of him and Maggie hogging the key position as she explains to her friend, "I'm getting married tomorrow." Then, sure enough, she's in bed with Burn/Jim and he's given up racing cars. One problem: you never did see him or his friend in a racing car (see note under *April Love*, p. 273).

HER LAST FLING **CC NN BI DK**
1977 HIFCOA

P/D—Bruce Van Buren
F/A—Roger Dickson
F/A—Sandy Feldman, Sue Yu

What would you do if you were in your late 20s and doctors told you you were dying and had at the most three or four weeks to live? Sandy (Sandy Feldman) tries gambling at Las Vegas, buys a Cadillac with the relatively small money she has saved and tries group sex. The sexual anonymity of group sex as a kind of death surrender could have been developed into a fascinating theme. "The only way to get to know people is at an orgy," Sandy muses. Sandy tells no one that she is dying (including a potential lover). And here is another undeveloped theme. As a male (or female) how would you feel about having sex with someone who will be dead in a week? The group sex at various parties is almost continuous in this one but is surprisingly caringly photographed and engaged in by the participants, most of whom you've never seen before. One of the silliest scenes you ever watched is three guys, naked, sitting on a sofa in a room that looks like a suite in the Golden Nugget in Las Vegas (fake nineteenth century). All three of them play with themselves while they watch four lovely ladies making it with each other. The producer got cowardly at the end. It seems the doctor made a mistake—Sandy is not dying. Sandy Feldman is quite attractive. What ever became of her?

HIGHLIGHTS **NN DK BI**
1975-1979   INTERNATIONAL HOME VIDEO

P/D—Many
F/A—Many

If you want to make a fast survey of a few of the adult films reviewed in this filmography, this one-hour tape (according to the Home Video Club, the most popular in their line) offers short scenes from *Captain Lust, Deep Throat, Happy Days, Punk Rock, Mystique, American Sex Fantasy, The Love Couch, Wet Rainbow, Fringe Benefits, Sexual Witchcraft, Devil in Miss Jones, Dear Pam, Pleasure Palace* and *Slip-up*. Too much of the best parts can be too much a "good thing," especially for women. If you wish to order the complete tapes, International Home has them all available (see preface to this section). Incidentally, TVX, VCX, Cal Vista, Select/Essex and many others offer preview tapes from sexvids which appear in their catalogue, but you can never figure out the story line from these short excerpts.

HIGH RISE **CC NN NM BI DK**
1972   QUALITY

PD—Danny Stone
F/A—Harry Reems, Jamie Gillis, Marc Stevens
F/A—Tamie Trevor

"If only my husband could show me affection," Tamie tells her psychiatrist. "We don't fuck anymore." "You need a fast course in sexual stimulation," he tells her. Discovering that she's looking for a new apartment in a high-rise (a double entendre, of course), he suggests that she expand her sexual horizons with some of the residents. Behind the first door she knocks on she finds Harry Reems, a mother-fixated railroad-buff playing with his electric trains, but Tamie soon proves that she has more delights to offer than transformers and railroad engines. Mother hears them playing and knocks down the door just as Harry is coming. She chases Tamie down the hall but loses her when Tamie knocks on another apartment door and is let in by two lesbians who are enjoying each other and include her in the revelry. This sequence is totally choreographed, using mirrors. In the words of Turin and Zito (*Sinema*, Praeger Inc., New York, 1974), "It is one of the most elegant love scenes to appear in hard-core films." (Note the date of the film.) Next Tamie opens a door on Jamie Gillis and happily faints in his arms, after which he undresses her and they make ardent love even though his wife is waiting in the next room. Finally, Tamie opens the door on a far-out sex party, the likes of which you've never seen in any adult film. It includes a tassel-twisting stripper, a huge-breasted Egyptian belly dancer, a nude guy punching a punching bag, another stripper masturbating in a coffin and innumerable twosomes and threesomes. But underlying all the vignettes is a sophisticated sense of humor, culminating in the revelation that the psychiatrist is actually Tamie's husband to whom, after a session of sexmaking, she suggests (now she's the psychiatrist) that he too could benefit from a day in the same high-rise.

HONEYPIE **NN NM BI DB DK**
1974   QUALITY

P/D—Not given
F/A—Al Goldstein, Bobby Astyr
F/A—Victoria Sloane, Jennifer Welles

There's no particular honeypie in this one. The sex sequences are tied together by the gimmick of visualizing letters written to *Metro (Screw)*, a newspaper run by Al Goldsmith (Al Goldstein). His editorial assistants are Bobby Astyr (who when this was made probably hadn't met Samantha Fox) and Victoria Sloan, whose claim to fame is that she wears a vibrator in her vagina and plays with herself in a taxi on her way to work. Al Goldstein appears in his former plump-plump incarnation. He's the totally vulgar editor—in one scene he's being fellated in his office by a secretary but in reality his pants are zipped up. The scenes include Jennifer Welles seducing a boy who is supposed to be 14 (he doesn't look much over 18). Plus, there's a bisexual scene with Serena (possibly her first film) and a silly scene with two guys making out with an older guy's wife and escaping through the back door when he returns. BUT don't stop! If you have ever wondered about bondage and discipline, then buy or rent this tape. It has one of the most sickly believable scenes you've ever watched.

HOT CIRCUIT   **NN   BI   NL**
(occasionally)
1971   ARROW

P/D—**Paul Wyatt, Paul Glicker, Richard Lerner**
F/A—**Jack Dusquesne, Elmo Hassel**
F/A—**Sally Paradise, Kit Fox, Simone Fallique, Pris Teen**

The first lap in the Hot Circuit is a 42nd Street strip joint. In a cinema verité style, you are taken backstage where a con man traveling salesman is trying to seduce the strippers. He finally succeeds with one of them, but the lights go on in the alcove he's taken her to and the audience in the club can see him. Next there's the salesman who tries to install an air conditioner and is seduced by two babysitters who steal his pants and tie him to a jungle gym in the backyard. In other, equally silly episodes there is a woodcutter, an adventuress, a nymph, a porno film producer who interviews various potential actresses and another salesman whom a woman invites home and who prefers to eat her pastries than to eat her. Historically, this sexvid has a silly naivete about it that will remind you of the better stag

films. It's one of the first that went beyond the exploitation films of the 1960s and provided explicit sex with all the standard adult film conventions.

HOT COOKIES   **NN   NM   BI   silly DK**
1978   WONDERFUL WORLD OF VIDEO

F/A—**Abigail Clayton, Serena**

A series of vignettes. One is about a Beverly Hills socialite who wants to screw a stranger in her chauffeur-driven Cadillac and does. Another is an artist who wants to paint a masterpiece which can only be experienced erotically by him and his subject. Another an extended Victorian picnic with two women who make love to each other while their lone boyfriend is sleeping. They pour wine into each other's vaginas. The sequences are held together by Serena and her father, who come from outer space. It doesn't add up to much.

HOT LINE   **NN   BI   DK**
1980   CABALLERO CONTROL

P/D—**Harold Lime, Anthony Spinelli**
F/A—**Jon Leslie, Eric Stein, Jon Martin**
F/A—**Jesie St. James, Pat Manning, Nicole Noir, Phaedra Grant**

Spinelli and Lime flipped their lids on this one. Seems that Jesie (Jesie St. James) is having a mid-life crisis. It's her thirty-fifth birthday. For the next hour and a half, you watch her drinking gin, popping pills and imagining the lives of her friends and enemies. The gimmick between the various vignettes is Jesie's telephone—a hot line. First there's Justin, the stupid bartender at Victoria's Place. Victoria (Pat Manning) has fired Jesie because she's in love with another cocktail waitress, but Justin goes to her rescue. He catches Victoria making love with another woman and puts a collar around her neck, pours a glass of gin down her throat and forces both of them to sodomize him. "You love it! Don't you?" he yells at Victoria as he nearly chokes her to death, and of course, she and her girlfriend do love it! But the film was obviously made for the totally whacked-out denouement, during which Jesie, wearing a black wig, seduces her father, both as herself and her sister Kathy (Nicole Noir). And believe it or not, her father is John Leslie, who (for revenge) she refuses (after a wild orgasm herself) to bring to a climax and forces him to masturbate on her chest! Seems that Daddy loved her sister better than he did Jesie. But it's all a day-dream—because at the end everyone is waiting in her apartment (including Daddy), to celebrate the birthday she's sure they've forgotten. You'll only wish Lime and Spinelli could dream better dreams than those they dreamed for Jesie.

HOT LUNCH NN DK BI
SELECT/ESSEX

P/D—William Thornberg, Harold Perkins
F/A—Jerry Heath
F/A—Desiree Cousteau, Christine de Shaffer, Brigit Olsen

If all women were as aggressive as the four female stars in this one, much of the male population would be wearing cock pieces. But not Andrew Moran (Jerry Heath, a.k.a. Jon Martin), around whom the entire film revolves. Andrew arrives from the country with a wife in the big city and takes a job first as a dishwasher then as an encyclopedia salesman. Finally, be-cause "he gets anything he wants with his dick"—a female comment—he be-comes an account executive for a book wholesaler. The only thing different about this one is that it concentrates on the vir-ility of one male. As far as the title goes—it's a metaphor, obviously. The only Hot Lunch in the picture is a seamy restaurant run by Juliet Anderson and is memorable in the things-you've-never-seen-before department when she masturbates with another woman behind the counter using a rolling pin, spoons and various other res-taurant hardware.

HOUSE OF A THOUSAND DELIGHTS
HARD R
TED ROTER PRODUCTIONS

P/D—Ted Roter
F/A—About 30 guys and gals you've never seen before

I think this is an early Ted Roter production (see other listings—*Prison Babies, The Psy-chiatrists, A Small Case of Rape*, pp. 122, 211, 61). In fact, it may extend back to the days when Dave Friedman was making "tits and ass films." In any event, because there is no explicit sex you may see it on cable. If you last through an hour and a half of it you still won't know what the hell it's all about, unless you stay to the bitter end. It ends where it begins with the alarm clock buzzing. The whole thing is a sex dream of a klutzy young guy. The house of a thousand delights is dream peregrina-tions from one silliness to another. A bishop is blown while his priests sing "Joy to the world, our lord has come." A sur-geon is about to operate on a naked young lady who suddenly smiles at him. He immediately drops his surgical gown and jumps on her. A courtroom judge in-sists "justice must be served with kisses"—from head to foot. In ancient Egypt, a fe-male painted as a snake takes a bite out of Cleo's tit. And there's a half-hour Ro-man orgy where various female "cap-tives" dance for Caesar, and everyone belly bumps together without revealing any penises erect or otherwise. It oc-curred to me while watching this one that if you have a dozen cooperative friends and access to St. Vincent de Paul's old clothing sales, you could costume a film like this yourself and shoot it with your own video camera—providing you had a fenced-in backyard!

IN SARAH'S EYES NN BI DK
1976   VIDEO X HOME LIBRARY

P/D—Carter Stevens
F/A—Eric Edwards, Tony Richards, Marc Stevens
F/A—Lorraine Alraune, Anna Livia Plurabella, Lynn Harris

The gimmick that holds this one together is the sexual fantasies of a klutzy, Jewish virgin, which are better—even after she is married—than reality. The fantasies come on her as she is talking to her psychiatrist or while she is eating dinner with her future husband and their friends, or while they're are playing Monopoly, and even during her wedding reception, during which she imagines an orgy in which she is the center attraction. On her wedding night after some perfunctory sex with her new husband, she asks: "Is this all there is to love and lust?" Never mind, while he is sleeping she re-creates him into a virile lover who beats her and screws her at the same time from stem to stern. Among her fantasies is a sharply-focused extended sexmaking scene with a black telephone repairman. While there's nothing new in the sex scenes, this sexvid may induce conversational input between lovers and young marrieds.

INDECENT EXPOSURE
NN NL NR DK BI
1982   CABALLERO CONTROL
::

P/D—Harold Lime, Robert McCallum
F/A—Richard Bolla, Eric Edwards
F/A—Veronica Hart, Jesie St. James, Georgina Spelvin, Arcadia Lake, Nicole Noir, Chelsea

Richard Bolla split the Sixth Annual Erotica Awards as Best Supporting Actor for this one with Richard Pacheco. If McCallum hadn't been diverted by sexvid conventions—attempting to offer too many delectable women showing their genitals in one film—he might have created a top film. All of the acting is good, The conflict is between Tony Rossini (Richard Bolla), a con man fashion photographer who wants to screw all his models, and his girlfriend, Lialeh (Veronica Hart), who arranges his appointments but wants him to be more selective. Rossini's friend Teddy Purlis (Eric Edwards) comes along on a photographing trip in a van. He's with June (Jesie St. James), who is afraid of her sexuality and although she works for Rossini, has never screwed with him—all this has unrealized potential. But little comes through and it's almost impossible for the actors to develop these parts. Too often McCall ignores Louis Malle's (director of *Atlantic City* and *Pretty Baby)* dictum: "The photographing of naked bodies making love takes you out of the film. It does not put you in it." Thus the conflict between the principals is sustained as Ted first makes out with Kama, the owner of a natural foods store, who is posing for Rossini. Kama shows Ted how to enjoy sexual meditation and sexual eating by tickling him with a celery stalk. After that he grabs a bunch of grapes and squeezes them over her body and gives her her grape massage while she's climaxing. Then, the guys move on to photograph a ballet class while the ballerinas, unbeknownst to their teacher, drop their leotards and wiggle their asses. In these sequences, and several others either Rossini or Purlis is happily screwing with various models. In disgust, Lialeh and June turn to each other, but after an interesting bisexual scene discuss their need for men rather than women. Finally, their last client, Ariel DeVayne (Georgina Spelvin), a very wealthy woman and her butler, Harmon, resolve the problem. They mate Ted with Lialeh in a romantic sequence—and Georgina takes care of Bolla. In a funny sequence she seduces him into her bed and manages to snap ropes around his wrists. After tieing him up, she sits on his face and tells him she's going to give him a new course she's been experimenting with, "Cunnilingus 101," and he better not make her angry or she'll turn him over to her butler for more unsavory things. But it isn't going to be easy. "I haven't come in a very long time," she tells him. While he's tied hands and feet to the bed, she uses the squeeze technique every time he's ready to come until he's a pitiful mess—after which she blindfolds him. While she's talking to him, Jesie St. James as June appears. She is suddenly sexually released and proves to blindfolded Bolla how good she really is. After a romantic scene between Eric Edwards and Veronica Hart, they are all reconciled and drive off into the night to live happily ever after.

INSIDE HOLLYWOOD . . . THE ANNE DIXON STORY   **CC   NN   BI**
1980   ARROW
::

P/D—Leo Dancer, Renee Deneuve
F/A—Mike Ranger, William Margold
F/A—Seka, Pat Manning, Becky Savage

Originally this was a separate half-hour tape shot live with video camera by Scorpio. Scorpio also offered other half-hour videotapes, such as *Football Widow* and *A Love Story*. These have been recombined on one-hour tapes by Arrow, which offers them under the general title *French Erotica*, some of which combine three short stories and others which have just one story running for an hour. I have given this and the following (all on Volume 3) a CC rating for several odd reasons. First, they are the kind of stories that several couples with a video camera could easily script and shoot themselves. Second, in many cases, the dialogue is more interesting than many sexvids probably because dialogue and not a wandering camera tells most of the story, and finally because *The John Barfield Story* offers something you've never seen before in a porno flick!—death in the saddle! The plot of *The Anne Dixon Story* is old hat. Seka is a rising actress who is taught the secret of success by Hedda Hooper (Pat Manning), which includes servicing Hedda and every male in sight to get to the top. Errol Flint (Mike Ranger) is the bad guy actor who all women want to star with in a film, and Charley Read (William Margold, a Kennedy lookalike) portrays, quite easily, another slimy Hollywood character.

INSIDE HOLLYWOOD . . . THE JOHN BARFIELD STORY **CC   NN   BI**
1980   ARROW

P/D—As above
F/A—Ron Jeremy, Vic Falcon
F/A—Becky Savage, Laura Wench

Lita Layworth (Becky Savage), a rising actress, tells her cocky agent Wilson (Ron Jeremy), "You're cock's too short, your stroke is too short, your timing is lousy, and you talk too much." But she falls in love with John Barfield (Vic Falcon), one of the top Hollywood stars, and he with her. Unlike most Hollywood people it isn't bodies or sex alone: "They could get into each other's heads." But Lita doesn't realize that John is a sick man. Does he have T.B. or heart trouble? Never mind, he makes happy love to Lita, and she's ecstatic.

Then, he climbs on top, and at the moment of his orgasm collapses on top of her. Thinking he's only exhausted, she is shocked to find him dead. (This plot was used in *Private Benjamin*, but it wasn't half so realistic as Becky Savage's scream and trauma as she extricates herself from his lifeless body.) The famous poet William Carlos Williams wrote a play on this theme involving a married man with his mistress in a hotel room which would make a much better movie. Having known Williams when he was alive, I'm sure that he'd be grinning down from heaven if some adult film producer would tackle it. This sexvid falls apart at the end with Lita overcoming her guilt at John's death by experiencing sex with a female for the first time, after John's death.

JELLO WRESTLING CIRCUS (NUDE)
CC   HARD R (no explicit sexmaking)
1982   KENYON VIDEO

P/D—Adam Cole, Veronica Mellon, "Jelly Baby"
F/A—Many female wrestlers

You can put this tape on the top of your list of things you have never seen before. Unlike mud wrestling, Jello wrestling (at least as shown on this tape) is a new, intimate kind of structured burlesque feature that can be offered in any nightclub with a stage or space enough so that the audience can stand around and watch the wrestlers. Instead of sitting in the orchestra of a burlesque house as your granddaddies (or an occasional grandmommy) did and watching the queens undress to sexy music, in the 1980s you stand close to what is simply a backyard wading or swimming pool. It's made of plastic and filled with Jello. The female wrestlers, mostly in costume, appear and kiss the guys, who pay a few dollars for the privilege and cheer for their favorite. Kissing the contestants also includes feeling their half-bare behinds. After the preliminaries, the ladies, dressed in swimsuits and leotards, flop into the Jello on their knees and slowly pull off each other's clothing. At the same time they are trying (not very hard) to pin their opponent. Soon the ladies are totally naked. In the best two falls out of three, the guys watching a few feet away get what they came for—totally revealing exposures of flesh while the ladies (I presume they are well paid for 15 minutes' work) slip around and clutch each other's bodies in the Jello. This tape has three separate matches between different women and finally ends up with them pulling a guy in the audience (who was paid for the privilege) into the pool. All of them slide around naked and are quickly joined by some other guys and gals from the audience. Any normal guy watching Jello wrestling most certainly will be sexually aroused. There seems to be no problem in Jello wrestling contests to control macho males. They simply watch and cheer for their favorite. I predict that before Jello wrestling has run its course, it will become a middle-class suburban, backyard summer phenomenon. It's a faster way than hot tubs for young people to get acquainted! The tape concludes with a Nude Wives Special. These are homemade videotapes which guys shoot of their gals. They are competing for prizes for the best amateur videotapes.

LADIES NIGHT **CC NN BI DK**
1980   VCA

P/D—Elliot Lewis, Harry Lewis
F/A—Paul Thomas, Richard Bern, Herschel Savage, Billy Doe
F/A—Annette Haven, Lisa de Leeuw, Chelsea McClane, Nicole Noir

If your wife goes out with the girls while you stay at home watching Monday night football on the tube, she may be having more fun than you are. Betty (Annette Haven) is watching a porno flick on one TV. Her husband, Bud, is sitting in a hot tub watching football on another. "If you don't want to do anything else but watch football—fuck you!" she says. She calls her girlfriends, Angie (Nicole Noir) and Irene (Lisa de Leeuw). They all have the same problem, but they have a solution. They meet at The Diplomat, a male strip joint. In addition to the strippers, it is filled with anonymous males who enjoy being sucked off by sexually frustrated wives. Irene finds one guy who can't wait to explore her lush body and soon they join

another couple stretched out on a pool table. (There are at least a dozen porno flicks that use a pool table as the place for a female to rest her ass and open her legs. Maybe it's because pool tables and pool balls carry sexual overtones, or maybe because pool tables are the right height for a male standing entry, or maybe because at least the felt is not so rough on a female behind.) Annette watches the strippers with Nicole. (They are not very good—nor is Paul Thomas, the master of ceremonies who doesn't strip.) But Paul is in top form when he finally seduces Annette in a very caring sex scene. Nicole's new friend leads her to his convertible parked in the alley and asks her for the usual female attention to his penis. He can't believe it when she tells him, "I don't like to do that." But after much convincing, she gives in and enjoys it. Among the things you've never heard before, Paul Thomas actually sings, musical-comedy style, to Annette Haven. The CC rating may be dubious but the sex scenes are better than most, with Chelsea McClane (a.k.a. Tigr, Chelsea Manchester) offering acrobatic sex like you've never seen in a hot tub with the husbands who stayed home to watch football.

LAS VEGAS LADY **NN NM DK**
1981   VCX

P/D—Bob Chinn
F/A—Mike Ranger, Sean Sullivan, Gary Everhart
F/A—Drea, Donna Joy, Billy Dee, Candy More

When Helen (Drea) can't get a man—usually she can—she masturbates, which is the way this one begins. In a hotel room in Las Vegas, Helen uses the telephone while the camera gives you a tour of the older city, not the strip, and presumably sets the atmosphere. But after a close-up of a slot machine paying off, our heroine departs Las Vegas with a cowboy, John (Mike Ranger), who may not know the time of day but knows he enjoys Helen's mouth—until they arrive in San Francisco, where he tries Helen's roommate in a pad Helen maintains with her winnings. But Helen doesn't mind—she lets John enjoy Kathy (Donna Joy) and goes to her room and plays with herself. A story of sorts emerges when it turns out that John is not as dumb as he seems but is in cahoots with Bob (a guitar player who looks like Kris Kristofferson) to steal Helen's money. But Kathy beats them to it—and Helen, thinking it's John who has taken it, calls in a hit man who shoots John (no kidding) and John dies. Ho-hum!

LEATHER PERSUASION **DK**
1980 BIZARRE

P/D—Bradford Edwards, C. B. Remington
F/A—David Greer, Brian Allen, Davis Freeman
F/A—Susannah Deyer, Sharon Taylor, Paula Park

There's one thing about tapes with the Bizarre trademark. They offer the entire armory of bondage and discipline equipment (which by the way they sell by mail through their subsidiary company, Centurion). But if you are looking for real sadism and masochism, nothing that I have seen which they offer approaches some of the tapes in this filmography labeled DS. This one is the story of Tamila and her hunchback manservant, Toto, who live in a great house in the woods with a dungeon. They capture three young schoolteachers who are out bicycling in the country, drug them, strip them, tie them up and untie them, dress them in leather, then put them in handcuffs and then undress them and put them in racks. They don't whip them because they are planning—after they've taught them submission—to sell them to a South American millionaire white-slaver. The girls are rescued by the police, who are really friends of Tamila. There's no sex in this one—lots of naked women. Tied up and gagged—and at the end you know you've been had. Especially if you recognize Captain Deal, one of the cops, who is not Davis Freeman but David Friedman—past president of the Adult Film Association and who will go down in history for sexploitation films with much T and A but no sexmaking.

LIGHTS CAMERA ORGY **NN BI**
1979 LOVE TV

P/D—None given

F/A—Mike Ranger
F/A—Meggan Morris

A potpourri of sex loops combined with interviews with the kind of people who appear in "quickies" and make them. One sequence showing the making of a quickie with the cameraman and director telling the actor and actresses what they expect them to do could have been made much more interestingly. Another presumably depicts sexual meditation, or tantric sex, but despite the raga background music, it ain't!

LIMITED EDITION. Volume One (Late 1970's) **NN DK**
ADULT VIDEO

P/D—Unknown
F/A—Many—both male and female

There is a total of 12 volumes in this series. Each tape runs about an hour with four stories in 12- to 15-minute sections. Volume One features Georgina Spelvin, Annette Haven and two unknown females as well as Bobby Astyr, Eric Edwards, Richard Bolla and several unidentified male actors. Volume One is average-guy and his wife or girlfriend-oriented. Georgina is cooking dinner naked, and her husband decides that he would rather eat her than food. Annette Haven is watching football with her husband and finally seduces him from the game to more enjoyable flesh games. Eric Edwards complains to a call girl that she lacks enthusiasm, and he doesn't know whether she's worth her price—after which she proves she is! Bobby Astyr and Richard Bolla are worked over by one woman who does a good job on both of them. The amusing thing about this and I presume the succeeding volumes is the amount of continuous conversation between males and females as they explain to each other how to do "it" to them, and what turns them on the best. Thus the series becomes a kind of sex education—particularly for males. In other volumes you can see Jamie Gillis, Helen Madigan, Jennifer West, Blanca Luz, Candida Royalle, Susan Nero, Aubrey Nichols, Maria Torres, Meggen Morris, Turk Lyon, John Seeman and many unidentified men and women.

LIPS **NN BI DK**
1981 CABALLERO

▓▓

P/D—Paul G. Vatelli
**F/A—Paul Thomas, Herschel Savage, Ron
    Jeremy, Billy Dee, John Ogden**
**F/A—Lisa de Leeuw, Vanessa Del Rio, Heidi,
    Brooke West, Tigr Minette, Kath Harcourt**

John Matlock (Paul Thomas) runs a sex therapy clinic somewhere in the hills of Southern California. In this film you come for the weekend or a week and go away cured of your sexual inhibitions and the sexual stress that may have caused them. Herschel Savage and his wife, Kathy Harcourt (they have screen names but you won't remember them), aren't enjoying each other in bed anymore. Neither are Vanessa Del Rio and her screen husband, Billy Dee. But the good doctor knows the problem in every marriage revolves around the male. He tells Vanessa that she needs to experience anal sex. Not the least perturbed, they strip and when Billy Dee goes to work on Vanessa, she moans. The doctor joins his patients and soon Vanessa is the filling in a sandwich between them. Ron Jeremy is having problems with his wife, too. She refuses him completely in bed—always is having a headache. But when she arrives, Tigr Minette (a.k.a. Chelsea Manchester), who works in the kitchen and has never had straight sex, shows Jeremy's wife the joys of gay sex. Watching them through binoculars, Ron opens his pants, and is so horny that he has no choice—he sucks himself (no kidding—Ron can do it) and takes pictures of his lonesome cock until another lady comes along and relieves him of his agony. Although Tigr connects herself up with Ron's wife with a two-way dildo, when Ron joins the party and slips his cock into Tigr, she's instantly transformed into a heterosexual. In the meantime in another room, Lisa de Leeuw, assistant to Paul Thomas is teaching females how to really suck cock, including the "butterfly flick" in between "deep throats." A really interesting film could be made with a Sandstone or Elysium background (Elysium is an active nudist and interpersonal relationship center in Topanaga), but this isn't the film. If you watch it slightly bombed, you may chuckle at the silliness of it all.

LOVE DREAMS **NN NM BI NR**
(final scene)
1981 CABALLERO

▓▓

P/D—Alan Vydra
F/A—John Leslie
F/A—Abigail Heath, Susan Nero, Morgan Jones

According to the box promotion on this tape, Julia Perrier, a very pretty French girl who was only 18 when it was made, was paid $500,000 to appear in this film. Since the going rate for top stars is about $1,000 a shooting day (no pun intended) I doubt it. At that price I'm sure some top Hollywood stars would be tempted. In any event, the hook in this one to tie the sequences together is that Julia (she uses that name in the picture) has come to America to learn English and will accept the job of a maid in a nice home. Her employment agency gets her a job with an old guy with 100 cats who wants to smell her panties—so she leaves in a hurry. Next she's out in Mill Valley in a very swanky home with a father and mother and two daughters. Before she leaves, she catches Mommy in bed with her lover and inadvertently saves her life when Daddy returns. In the hall, Daddy insists she fellate him and makes so much noise Mommy hears him in time. Julia entices Mommy's lover (when Mommy is out) into bed with her and one of the daughters. Her next job is with a wealthy man who has an old Grandpa (the mother's father) living with them. One funny-sad scene is Daddy in bed with this Mommy. She tries to entice him to make love with her but he has to fantasize with girlie magazines to get it up. All he wants to do is get it over with, but she wants to prolong it, pun intended. Next job is with Mr. Franklin (John Leslie), who lives alone. Presumably he's 44. Who could resist Julia? Mr. Franklin doesn't, and lo and behold enjoys her so much they get married. This is a Reeltime Pleasure Production under the general direction of Beate Uhse, a German woman who insists she is making female-oriented adult films. Not yet, Beate!

LOVE GODDESSES NN DK
1981 VCA

P/A—Adele Robbins
F/A—John C. Holmes, Jamie Gillis, Mike Ranger, William Margold
F/A—Seka, Juliet Anderson, Crissi Stevens

An inexpensive way to create a "new" sexvid is to tack together cuts from older films with 10- to 15- minute loops which were originally sold on 8-mm film. The famous Swedish Erotica series of numerous tapes (see listing) makes no pretense and offers one-hour tapes of unrelated vignettes or short stories. This one provides a seamy linkage in the form of Venus and her consorts on some planet in outer space. Intercut with their rather slimy slithering Venus is trying to decide which is the best earthly love goddess. It's between Seka (Sweet Alice) and Juliet Anderson (Aunt Peg). One of the vignettes with Seka, John C. Holmes and Jamie Gillis provides the only unique sequence in this tape. Something you rarely see in sexvids is two top male porno stars sharing one woman. In this 15-minute segment Seka sucks one and is fucked by the other, and then reversing, and then finally each of them takes her on separately. "Put it in really deep," Holmes tells Jamie. "She loves it deep." Then on the edge of the couch, her head on the floor, J. C. Holmes plunges all 13 inches into her. Seka's competitor for the title of Love Goddess is Juliet Anderson, who is more acrobatic than Seka and moans and cries more. Both ladies are obviously on a protein diet of semen. Venus awards both of them the title, after which she and several other women finish off William Margold and another slimy-looking character.

LOVE STORY NN some DK but with an erotic NR ending
1979 SCORPIO

P/D—David Summer
F/A—William Margold, Chuck Starr
F/A—Seka, Janice James

This is a half-hour videotape never shown in adult theaters about Carol who thinks she's frigid, but doesn't blame her husband. Even in bed, Carol/Seka can't get

him up. So she goes to a psychiatrist who, together with a gynecologist, prove she's quite normal, and then she finds a man who is sick of one-night stands and really wants to know the woman he goes to bed with. William Margold, who appears in this one and several other Scorpio tapes, is a fairly reliable film critic who appears in *Velvet* magazine.

LOVE WITCH NN DK NL (but only occasionally)
1973 ARROW

P/D—Unknown
F/A—Marc Brock, Robert Sargent, Harry Reems
F/A—Ann Marshall, Linda del Toro, Cathy Parker, Ami Nitrate

This one begins and concludes with a mock porno trial in Tennessee in which Harry Reems is both the judge and the arresting officer, and the prosecuting attorney for a porno film producer looks suspiciously like Al Goldstein did many years ago. The film which is before the court is called *The Love Witch*, the name of a yawl with a crew of lovely women aboard. What happens on deck (the film was shot in Miami) is more interesting than the unbelievable studio shots below deck, which show bedrooms you wouldn't find on an ocean liner. As the film progresses, Harry Reems, in one of his manifestations, none of which are naked, makes off-camera comments on the actors, such as, "that guy has pimples on his ass," etc. The only thing unusual about the film is the extended underwater sex, which is nicely photographed but doesn't show how they breathe down there. In the conclusion, Harry Reems as defense lawyer for the film, sings cantor-style about the joys and rewards of watching porno films.

MADNESS Hard R (no explicit sex)
VIDEO TAPE ENTERPRISES

P/D—Famous Specialties Productions
F/A—Not given

This one follows the format of such video magazines as *Electric Blue* but has no hostess, or anything in particular, tying together the various sequences. It runs close to two hours and gives you a view of many things you've never seen before. First, there's a guy stretched out naked in a very exotic setting that looks like a witch's lair, complete with skull and cross-bones. The witch is a pretty lady who quickly disrobes, pours massage oil on the guy and herself and then for the next ten minutes gives him a "slick sleeve screwing" without any genitals showing. Next, two young women, one in a leotard, one in a tight-fitting bikini wearing boxing gloves, spar with each other for ten minutes or so with no holds barred. Their breasts are continuously falling out of their suits. All of this was shot in someone's living room. Soon they are joined by two other skimpily dressed young women and the boxing turns to wrestling and pillow fighting. It's all very good-natured. There are no winners but the girls get more exercise than they would doing Aerobicises. (Incidentally a tape of the same name put out by Paramount is very popular and considered soft-core pornography because many guys like to watch girls exercising in leotards and dream their own dreams!) The boxing wrestling section lasts close to a half-hour. Accompanied by soft rock, if nothing else it reveals a happy way to keep in shape. Next is the famous cut from a Marilyn Monroe film in which she flipped around naked showing her breasts and behind but no genitals. *(Play-boy* has supposedly traced the film to a Monroe lookalike.) Then you have a half-hour cut from the National T-Shirt Contest, which seems to have been held in a radio station (KMMT) and is crowded with a mixed audience of young people watching the typical girls next door model T-shirts and eventually strip them off and dance very sexily—topless. This is followed by a segment where the contestants shed their jeans and dance around in nothing but abbreviated panties. What makes it all quite fascinating is the girls are not actresses, but typical American females. This is followed by two ladies on the stage of what looks like a burlesque house. They are wearing bathing suits. Covering themselves with massage oil, they try to wrestle each other out of their suits. This is followed by a sequel where they try again, this time in a wading pool filled with mud.

Then there's a nude fire dance, followed by a very sexy male and female strip dance done ballet style. Then there's a session with Sulka, who is a transsexual. The tape switches gears with a long section on marital aids—everything from a Squirmy Rooter with a handle that a lady can turn when she inserts it to ben wa balls, orgy oil and motion lotion. A black woman and a white woman demonstrate how to use many of the items. It finally concludes with a 15-minute tour of the Reeperbahn—the famous street in Hamburg, Germany, devoted to every kind of sex you ever dreamed of.

MANDY'S EXECUTIVE SWEET
NN   NM   BI   DK
1982   ADULT VIDEO

P/D—Clark Matthews, Jack Genero
F/A—Lee Carol, Susan Nero, Gypsy Lee
F/A—Ron Jeremy, Ray Wells, Broderick Sterling

This one proves that in the 1980s, there is still a large male audience out there who don't care about plot or characterization but just want continuous sucky-fucky sequences. If you can give it to them by shooting an 80-minute film on a weekend, why not? The story(?) is about Mandy (Lee Carroll, whose breasts remain erect no matter what position she's lying or standing in) can't get a job because times are so tough. In the executive suite, she cleans toilets and sucks the bosses. Eventually after trying the copying machine to copy her breasts, she finds a discarded interoffice document that proves one of her bosses is up to some dirty work at the crossroads. Before she confronts him with her knowledge, she services the big boss, Ron Jeremy, in the parking lot in the back seat of his car, during which he never stops talking. A few days later at a board meeting of the company, Ron and other directors, including the villain who has been stealing the company money, discuss "deposits" and "withdrawals." Mandy, who is cleaning up the director's room, quickly discovers she's the bank. Stretched out on the director's table, she obligingly fellates them, after which she takes command of the company, promising to rat on all of them for one reason or another if they don't elect her president. Ladies won't like this one.

THE MASTER AND MS. JOHNSON
NN BI DK
1981 SELECT-A-TAPE

P/D—Sterny Herpowitz, Peter Balakoff
F/A—Larry Moore, Randy Lane, John Hollyfield, Bill Margold
F/A—Jennifer West, Monique Faberge, Dawn Perry, R. J. Reynolds

The Center for the Advanced Study of Research in Remedial Sex Therapy is run by the Master, Ludwig Van Strudel Wasser who flips off fast Yiddish one-liners to his patients and his associate Ms. Johnson. He supplies surrogate lovers, Halevah and Peaches, and also a guy for women like Iris who is married to Woody who can't get it up with her. Among Ludwig's other patients are Blind Billy who lost his eyesight when the car he was driving hit a truck carrying sulphuric acid, but Billy isn't really blind only traumatized. There are also jealous lesbians, and transsexuals, a guy dressed as a woman, and a woman dressed as a guy who beats his ugly wife when she doesn't make proper love to him, and a flasher who masquerades as a private detective. Ludwig and Ms. Johnson cheerfully help all the patients to relieve their sexual frustrations. Finally the patients are invited to a primal training buffet, and the film concludes with a fifteen-minute yucky-fucky orgy. If you run it in fast forward, you may think you are visiting the snake pit in a mental asylum. For what it may be worth, at the very ending the real Ludwig returns to the Institute, and it seems that the Ludwig you were watching is only his assistant who was offering his own version of remedial sex therapy. Ted Roter a.k.a. Pierre Balakoff appears somewhere in this one, but I couldn't find him. Maybe he edited himself out at the last minute—embarrassed to be caught in a sickie-quickie which doesn't compare with his better films.

MIDNIGHT BLUE II **NN DK BI**
1982 VIDEO-X-PIX

P/D—Richard Jaccom, Al Goldstein

F/A—Al Goldstein
F/A—Annie Sprinkles, Veronica Hart

Al Goldstein, with his *Midnight Blue* series, is offering the kinkiest video magazine around. (He's planning to issue it quarterly and *Midnight Blue III* is coming up.) It's further out than *Electric Blue* or *Shades of Blue* (see listings), but this one, except for a couple of sequences, has too many cuts from porno movies such as *The Satisfiers of Alpha Blue* (see listing), in which Lysa Thatcher fellates three guys. (According to an interview with Damiano made in 1980, this was the most erotic scene he has ever shot.) There are cuts from *Deep Throat, Delicious* and *Amanda by Night,* all of which fill up a good half-hour of the tape. The interview with Damiano doesn't tell you much. And when Al visits Veronica Hart at home, she's washing the floor and later ironing a shirt—believe it or not. This is a typical *People* magazine-type approach which doesn't tell you much about Veronica. The best thing about the tape is a seduction scene put on by the Aubrey Cross Players (who are they?), in which an aspiring actress is seduced and slowly, partially willingly and partially fighting it, has sex with a guy she never has met before. Finally, if you want to see what actually occurs in the peep shows on Forty-Second Street in New York City, where guys stand in little booths and put in a quarter for a five-minute live view of naked ladies who spread their legs or bend over, Al Goldstein has choreographed it on this tape into a daffy-silly-sorry 15-minute sequence that is too close to actuality for comfort. It's a sexually hung-up world!

MISS BARE FANNY CONTEST **R no explicit sex scenes**
1982 VISTA VIDEO AVAILABLE FROM I.P.I.

P/D—Dale Zunz

A day at one of the many naked beauty contests held at Dick Drost's Ponderosa Sun Club in Roselawn, Indiana, during the summer. The 50 or more ladies are mostly strippers from clubs in the Midwest. They happily reveal it all to the males, who crowd around the walkways and point cameras at them. While the ladies often pose spread-eagled or bend over with their behinds in the air for the poor guys who have never seen such sights, the video cameraman in this one is more cautious. He obviously does not want an X-rated tape. Many dance sequences are filmed in slow motion. Some ladies have tattoos on their behinds, some pimples, and there is a prize for body painting. But the emphasis is not particularly on bare fannies. In medieval times in Europe, a part of many harvest festivals was a contest to determine the most alluring female bottoms, but in those days the ladies weren't naked. They simply lifted their skirts. Most women will be quickly bored by this tape, or will get angry if they think their male is making mental comparisons or is simply bemused with his fantasies of so much unembarrassed female flesh.

NEVER A TENDER MOMENT
CC BI DK DS
1979   MITCHELL BROTHERS

P/D—Mitchell Brothers
F/A—Marilyn Chambers, Tanya Robertson,
Carol Christy

You can believe the title on this one! I've given it a CC rating because you have never seen anything like it—and may never want to! The DS rating is for a later segment called *Hot Nazis*. The first half-hour of the film concentrates entirely on Marilyn Chambers whom you see doing an erotic dance with camera close-ups of her famous labial ring. (She must have had her labia pierced because essentially it's a large earring.) Then two women —one black—in dominatrix costumes appear and they tie her with ankle cuffs and beat and abuse her. If the above is not enough there are two unadvertised specials on this 52-minute tape. The second one is called *Southern Belles* and shows a number of women, some black, wearing crinolines and big hats, all masturbating with huge dildos and some with two-way jobs. The real shocker is the second feature, which runs for about 20 minutes and is called *Hot Nazis*. First you see two naked women behind a wire containment lustily servicing each other to

the accompaniment of German music with translated English words. Then the guards arrive, both male and female, find a Star of David, and for ten minutes or so rape and beat the woman prisoners brutally. You won't find many women who will cheer this sexvid, but they will gasp at the Marilyn Chambers segment. It offers an interesting subject for discussion about pain and pleasure in sex.

NEW LOOK #1   **R**
1981   BLAY RCV

P/D—Claude Gorsky, Catherine Pourbeau,
Sygama
F/A—Many

Like *Electric Blue, Shades of Blue* and *Playboy Video Magazine,* this is something new in the world, a video cassette magazine which will be issued quarterly and maybe more often. Video cassette magazines walk a thin line between the kind of documentary material you can watch any night on television or on cable TV. The trick is to offer something you may never see on commercial television, and that, at the moment, is the sexual and erotic. Two of the interviews on this tape, one with the director Bob Rafelson, who directed *Five Easy Pieces* and *The Postman Always Rings Twice* with Jessica Lange, and another with Francis Ford Coppola, are a little more in-depth than the average commercial television material but nothing unusual. The rest of this tape you're not likely to ever see on commercial television or late-night subscription television. There is no explicit sex but a segment titled "The Well Undressed Woman" features a new Paris beauty salon which cuts, trims, dyes in one, two or three colors, lovely ladies' pubic hair. A blue, white and red French flag job goes for $40. Then there's a section called "Tamara" with a lovely woman who delights in showing her body to people and for whom dancing naked is another way of making love. In "The Lady's a Gas" you meet a pretty young woman dressed in blue jean shorts cut so high you can see the curve of her ass whenever she bends over—which is often. A candid camera watches her while she services customers in a filling station and asks them suggestively if they need a lube job or how their bushings are. When she checks a customer's oil, she says, "This is a hand job." Another feature is "The Girls of Bangkok"— a trip up one of the canals in a boat with an outboard motor watching pretty Thai girls bathing naked or waiting for customers. Finally, there's an interview with Courresgia and Nuria, a photographer with a very beautiful black model expressing the sexual joy of life. My suggestion for future issues is to concentrate on two or three subjects—or even one in depth. For example, sexual life and loving in Thailand—or any foreign country—could be expanded and contrasted with America. An entire film could be devoted to sex-gone-wild in Bangkok—with hundreds of clubs and thousands of Thai girls providing every imaginable kind of sex for the tourist trade from Europe and Japan—and America!

NIGHTLIFE **NN BI**
1983 CABALLERO

P/D—Jo-Ann Lewis, Louis Lewis
F/A—Don Hart, Herschel Savage, Joey Civerea, Michael Morrison David Smith
F/A—Bridgitte Monet, Loni Sanders, Dorothy Le May, Ginger, Gayle Sterling

This one begins hopefully with a guy in bed with his woman—David (David Smith) and Joanne (Bridgitte Monet) He tells her, "I love you, Joanne. I want to marry you." She doesn't answer. "I made a pretty heavy statement," he says, "but you're ignoring it." She replies: "If we were two normal people we'd be out buying furniture." After that you've got to be smoking pot to believe any of it. Seems she's a hooker, and although David is a millionaire, she enjoys her profession so much, ploughing around the grimy streets of the Gold Coast in San Francisco, and working in a brothel, that she can't give it up for marriage. On top of that, Bridgitte's high nasal voice not only detracts from her beautiful face and body but makes you wonder why David wants to listen to her for a lifetime. The sexual action approaches the outer limits with Dorothy Le May and Loni Sanders curing a psychiatrist, Joey Civera,

as they both work him over. In the things-you've-never-seen-before there's Crazy Harry (Don Hart) who likes to eat his lady upside down hanging from a trapeze which is installed in the whorehouse. Ultimately she blows him upside down, too, as they swing to and fro, while in another room Honey Wilder and Michael Morrison are screwing in bed. Honey Wilder has a new-style crotch shaved between the legs and up her perineum to look like she's still in her puberty but with the hair below her belly still intact. In *Bubblegum* (see listing) she let it grow back. This uggie concludes with David begging Joanne, "If you can't marry me, at least be as nice to me as you are to your other johns." And she is.

ONE WAY AT A TIME
NN NM BI DK
1979 CABALLERO

P/D—Alan and Laurie Colberg/Alan Colberg
F/A—John C. Holmes, Don Fernado, Rocky Raccoon, John Hardon
F/A—Aubrey Nichols, Michele Moore, Lisa Loring

The credits on the box on this one claim that the female stars are Diane Darlington, Sharen Caine, Lisa Loring and Mimi Morgan. But the female credits on tape are as listed above. In all probability none of them are actual names, which is typical for hit-and-run productions. You've never seen any of the women before, and John C. Holmes appears only in the initial sequence making very nice love to Mom (Aubrey Nichols), who has two daughters Julia (Michele Moore) and Barbara (Lisa Loring). Her daughters catch her having sex with John. Feeling guilty, she buys them mopeds so they can have their own adventures. The only thing that makes this tape faintly interesting is that the women are such hammy actors (but beautiful). If you had a video camera you could shoot a more believable story yourself. The gal who plays Julia is the tiniest (about 5' 2"), most perfectly shaped woman that you have ever seen in a porno flick. She looks like a doll when she's in bed with a six-footer. Mom is pretty and she's working so hard (you know how) that her boss (not John C.) promotes her to vice-president at double the salary, and of course she shows her appreciation properly.

THE OTHER SIDE OF JULIE
NN NM BI DK
CAL VISTA, VCX

P/D—Charles Gifford, Anthony Riverton
F/A—John Leslie, Richard Logan, Joey Maseria
F/A—Suzannah French, Gloria Roberts, Jackie O'Neil, Paula Donnelly

Mike Robbins (John Leslie) runs Stag Enterprises along with Scotty (Richard Logan, who in the first sequence is killed in a spectacular car crash) and Frank (Joey Maseria). Among other things, Stag employs a stable of women who service San Francisco males and pay Stag a percentage of the take. During the day, Mike drives a white Corniche Rolls convertible, but in the evening he arrives home to a middle-class suburban wife driving an Oldsmobile. Worn out from his sexual encounters, he's unable to service Julie (Susannah French), who takes care of herself in the bathroom (while he's recovering). She even succumbs to her Cousin Kim, who is unmarried and has just arrived. In the meantime, Aunt Isabel (Jackie O'Neill), who is looking for her daughter, Kim, is picked up by Mike (who has never met her). His unfailing line is "Do you believe in reincarnation? I never met you, but I'm sure I knew you in another life." Eventually, he's trapped by Aunt Isabel (because he stole her jewelry and she doesn't believe his story that he needs the money for an operation on his poor sick mother). She wears him to a frazzle and Julie discovers what he's been up to. Then Julie takes over Stag Enterprises and runs it herself. This one really should have been titled *The Other Side of Mike*. John Leslie plays the role with his usual charming impudence and indefatigable penis. And Jackie O'Neill, disgusted with Leslie's "wet noodle," has a cool, cute, sexy charm which is different.

OUTLAW LADIES **NN BI DK**
1981 QUALITY

P/D—Eldon Byrd, Henri Pachard
F/A—John Leslie, Richard Bolla, Bobby Astyr, Joey Civera
F/A—Marlene Willoughby, Jody Maxwell, Juliet Anderson, Samantha Fox, Veronica Hart, Merle Michaels, Candida Royalle

Not even Henri Pachard, who won the 1980 Erotic Film Award for *Babylon Pink* (see listing), can make a top adult film with so many characters. If you want to see what Pachard looks like, he appears in a scene as a photographer with Marlene Willoughby. Marlene is a fashion model (all the actresses and actors have different names in the story, but the story names don't really matter). In addition to Marlene, the outlaw ladies are Juliet Anderson, who is married to Bobby Astyr, and Jody Maxwell, who is married to Richard Bolla. Juliet and Jody are very unhappy with their hard–working husbands. One is a lawyer and one is an investment banker, and they are always arriving home late. So Julie and Jody hire a stud. Juliet adores him, fellates him, tells him not to be nervous and then asks Jody, who is watching, to insert a dildo with a pointed tip in her anus while the guy is still in her vagina. She has a delicious climax, especially when Jody turns it on and it vibrates. Then there's Samantha. She's married too, and John Leslie is painting her picture, but at night she and Jody pick up sordid-looking characters like Joey Civera in bars. When he tries to wash before servicing both of them, Samantha tells him not to. In the meantime Bobby Astyr is being fellated by Marlene. Richard Bolla, after being turned down by his law partner, Veronica Hart, goes to Merle Michaels' apartment. She's been married to Harold but now is divorced. And Veronica, who knows John, invites him up to her office (after telling her husband, Harry, that she's working late on a murder case). When John arrives, she tells him her secret need. She even has the cold cream waiting, and John gives you a good view of himself entering Veronica's anus. Merle Michaels (as Felicia) is the only believable one in the film, and Bolla tells Veronica the next day they have to fire her. Merle doesn't care. She may have lost her job but John Leslie has just called her for a date.

PEEP SHOWS #7 and ALL LESBIAN
NN BI DK
1980 WONDERFUL WORLD

P/D—Unknown
F/A—See below

Called "your private video arcade," there are at this writing 12 one-hour Peep Show tapes, each composed of as many as seven loops with minimal or no story. The people involved are in different sexual situations of anywhere from eight to twelve minutes each. This is the kind of film loop you would watch in the back rooms of adult stores by putting in quarters—and up to a buck to see all of one loop. The *All Lesbian* tape includes Jesie St. James with Lisa Sue Corey, Carol Connors with Delania Ruffino, Georgina Spelvin with Dorothy Le May, Chris Cassidy with Amber Hunt, Nancy Hoffman with Sharon Thorpe, The Victorian Lesbinas and Serena with China Leigh. If nothing else, you get acquainted with the faces and genitals of many actresses who appear in other films where they enjoy men as well as women. *Peep Show #7* is the only other of this series I have watched (or want to). Each episode title on the box pretty much tells you what to expect: *It's All Pink Inside* (white guy with a black girl); *Vanessa Has Her Mouth Full; I Can't Sleep When You Sit on My Face; Montana Does Her Thing; 69 with a Kicker* and *The Nasty Voyeur's Delight.* Actors and actresses in this one include Annette Haven, Chris Cassidy, John C. Holmes, Seka, Jean Jennings, Wade Nichols, Vanessa Del Rio, Candida Royalle, Christine de Shaffer, Rik Lutz and Nikki Anderson. All the loops are original and not cuts from longer films.

PEOPLE **NN DK**
1978 Quality

P/D—Gerard Damiano
F/A—Jamie Gillis, Richard Bolla, Eric Edwards, Bobby Astyr
F/A—Serena, Samantha Fox, Paula Pretense, Kasey Rodgers, Sue Swan, Kelly Green

Damiano-style, with an underlying moral tone of sin and retribution in a few of them, this sexvid comprises six unrelated stories. Part One, *The Game,* is the story of sex games that a husband, Jamie Gillis, and a wife, Serena, play. You think when you see him painting a downstairs wall in an affluent home that he is a hired painter. Upstairs while he's working she's taking a bath and arousing herself in the bathtub. Then Jamie opens the bathroom door and tells her he's leaving. But instead, they end up screwing. He is very rough with her (she's not unhappy) and commands her: "Up and down—nice and easy." Part Two is titled *Goodbye,* and if you are a woman watching this you'll wonder if Damiano forgot vaginas. The lady is losing her husband, but she fellates him in one valiant attempt to make sure he comes back to her someday. Part Three is called *Once Upon A Time,* and if you think Blake Edwards was original with Ravel's "Bolero" in *"10,"* you'll discover that Damiano beat him by four or more years. Only in this one, three women in costume —is it a Victorian ball?—fellate two guys. The process takes all of ten minutes while the Bolero drones on. Part Four is titled *The Exhibition.* A dominatrix in leather clothing is whipping a woman who kisses her from head to foot, and a guy in a cage arrives, is released and two women service him. Then there's Part Five in which Damiano appears with Samantha Fox playing the part of his daughter. She's in love with a man, but Daddy tells her, "I know that you're all grown up but you are still my little girl." Daddy obviously wants to go to bed with her—but Damiano-style, resists his compulsions. Finally there's Bobby Astyr in a hotel room waiting for *The Hooker,* who plays innocent with him but really is a lady who knows the time of day. Whatever point Damiano was trying to make about people and human sexuality gets lost in the shuffle.

THE PERFECT GIFT **NN DK bucolic NL**
1979 LOVE TV

F/A—David Morris
F/A—Bonnie Holiday, Judy Carr

The Perfect Gifts are of course your sex fantasies. In the first episode of this one (shot directly on tape with very average-looking people), the guy who can't satisfy his girlfriend gives her at least six bodyless penises which she enthusiastically fellates. The second gift is Deepstroke. A husband services his wife in an extended, but conversationally interesting sequence that covers all aspects of normal sexmaking. The final episode is what every guy wants for his birthday—his own real live doll—this one given to him by his wife. A little yucky but half the price of regular tapes, and amateurish enough to give you the feeling you could have made it yourself.

A PLACE BEYOND SHAME   **NN   NT   BI**
1979   VISUAL ENTERTAINMENT

P/D—Fred Lincoln, Roger Caine
F/A—Seka, Lori Blue, Veri Knotty, Lisa Adams
F/A—Don Fernando, Paul Thomas, Jon Martin

Here's brown-eyed Seka with a clean, classic, chiseled face, snow-white hair on her head, a shapely body and very black pubic hair. In this one she's a computer programmer who is presumably frigid. But never mind, her shrink can help her "get in touch with her thoughts." Under hypnosis, Seka sees herself being screwed on a motorcycle (she loves the bike more than the guy) and you watch her getting married and fellating her bridegroom before he gets out of his tux. All her recollections are played by other women, a technique that Damiano used in *Memories of Miss Agee*. It can get confusing, but offers the male viewer the opportunity to see the breasts, behinds and genitals of more than one lovely woman—but alas, not what goes on in their heads. Of course, that may not be very interesting anyway. Seka is not so brassy in this one. Younger women shouldn't be threatened by her. If you see her in real life she's nothing to write home about, but on screen she's a cosmetician's dream girl. And on her knees, or with her legs in the air, she does provide male viewers with close-up views that would embarrass their more sedate girlfriends.

PLATO's RETREAT WEST
NN   NM   BI   DK
1983   CREATIVE IMAGE

P/D—Cindy Lou Sutters
F/A—Mike Ranger, Randy Radisue, Gene Miller
F/A—Sandy Sunshine, Millie Moon, Desire Elms, Too Tall Teresa, Big Tits Malloy

Don't confuse this one with the glossier *Plato's West* produced by Damon Christian (see listing). It's the same place, I guess, but no longer quite so sophisticated. This one has a cinema verité effect which tells you that Mike Ranger is the manager of the Plato's swing club and he takes you on a tour which concentrates on a locker room and the big stage area where most of the action takes place. If you enjoy watching group sex and lots of sucking, blowing, screwing and eating with little care of who is doing what to whom, this may be your cup of tea. There is also much nude roller skating on the stage which also finally ends in a roller-skate orgy. Sutter has produced two others in this 60-minute genre (see listings on *Weekend Cowgirls* and *Teenage Dessert*).

PLAYBOY VIDEO Volume II   **R**
1983   CBS-FOX VIDEO

P/D—Hugh Hefner and many others

I think Playboy Video magazine has a great profit-making future, but not at the present prices for the tapes, and/or discs. For the most part these tapes will survive only as one- or two-time viewing at the most. An amusing way to pass 81 minutes, but not at 80¢ a minute. All Playboy has to do is extend the tape length to about two hours and sell advertising (as sexy as possible) and then offer the tapes for about $15. I predict this way they would have a monthly sale of at least a half-million tapes. Volume Two moves faster than Volume One and begins with the Great Playmate Hunt in which 4,000 women were interviewed and Candy Loving (presumably that is her real name) was chosen to represent Playboy's 25th Anniversary Celebration. As she is photographed naked, a photographer tells her, "Make yourself appear very warm, very lush, very loving—but use no facial muscles." If you want to read a sexier, funnier sequence on the same subject try *The Harrad Experiment* when *CoolBoy* photographers glamorize. Beth Hillyer and her Harrad roommates offer helpful comments. Next there is an interview with Sylvia Kristal, the original Emmanuelle lady, who reveals that she feels happier in the company of women than of men. There's A Ribald Classic based on Boccaccio's The Mercenary Mistress who is tricked by a lover who pays for her services with money borrowed from her fat old husband. The copulation scenes are softly vaselined. Then, there's the Great Playmate Playoff which takes place on the grounds of the Playboy Mansion, and during which Playmates dressed in bikinis compete in games with each other designed by male chauvinists who want to see the "best" a female has to offer. Feminists will abhor this sequence, and won't believe that their peers would happily become such exhibitionists for a buck. There's a very sexy cut from a Duran Duran, produced by E.M.I., Music-on-Television-style tape, and it features a song called "Girls on Film." This is followed by a discussion that you've heard before on the various uses of the word fuck as noun, verb, and adjective. And then there's Dudley Moore being interviewed and revealing that he's only five feet two and has a club foot but now lives happily with nearly six-footer, Susan Anton. Dudley gives you his favorite poem. "Oh, little Flo/ I love you so/ Especially in your nightie/ When the moonlight flows—across your tits/ Oh, Jesus Christ, Almighty!" The tape winds up with a tour of the Young Rubber factory, and an extended interview with Playboy Playmate Lynda Wiesmeier who works for a dermatologist and likes to take long showers—especially with loving friends. (You watch her showering, but with no friends.) Lynda also loves to eat (salads and shrimp) better than anything else— with one exception, of course, making love.

PLEASURE MASTERS NN BI DK
1975 ASTRO

P/D—Alex de Renzy
The only actors listed are Kiko and Lil

Two unconnected stories. The first is about a guy with a Japanese housegirl who watches him entertain his girlfriend, take a shower and bidet-washes afterwards. Then the Japanese girl takes over and the girlfriend (now sucking lollipops and with unaccountably shaved pube) becomes the housemaid. The second story is much more interesting. In San Francisco in 1890, a coach drawn by horses is lost in the fog. The occupants (all male) end up in a brothel and have a wonderful time. They discover the next morning that it burned down many years ago and all the occupants were killed in the fire. The nice costuming and period ambiance should have been used in a longer and better film.

PLEASURES OF A WOMAN
NN NM BI
1983 CABALLERO

P/D—Cindy Scott, Jethro Bunel, Skip Mason
F/A—Bill Weston, Herschel Savage, Edward Elite, Dick Bogart
F/A—Adrienne Plushette, Jill Flaxon, Julie Duree, Vanilla Joy, Gigi Rigoletto

This one was made strictly for the horny guy in a raincoat. Presumably it tells the stories, in their own words, of seven voluptuous suburban women, upper-income ladies, and their sex fantasies. I'm sure that if you show it to your favorite woman (which might be a valid experiment) she will tell you it's a piece of crap. The first lady is presented in the tired old adult film plot of the woman whose hubby is glued to the television set watching football, hockey, basketball, and depriving her of good screwing. Whether it's a fantasy or reality, is hard to tell, but she frankly invites the guy next door who's washing his car to enjoy a screaming moaning session on the living room couch. All the while her husband is in the den watching sports. This episode concludes with the husband discovering them, and instead of being upset, he watches and jerks off. The next lady speaks to you in dialogue from what Al Goldstein would call a "male stroke book." She enjoys taking care of herself. "I love it when my fingers feel the wetness between my legs." She is intercut with a female traveling saleswoman who is in a taxi on the way to the airport. She confides to you that she hasn't time for real love affairs or male friends, because she's so busy. But never mind her best friends are here in her vibrator kit. Then lovingly introduces you to them, one by one. She has given them her favorite male actor names Robert Redford, Richard Pryor and John Travolta. Next there is Sally who is a secretary. She's taking dictation from her boss about something called "Semen Proposals" and pretends to faint. For ten minutes or so while she's unconscious he undresses her and screws her on his desk. Then there's the lady who is introduced to sex by her mother's cleaning lady, and another woman tells about how she serviced a guy who is 80 years old. Unfortunately this one is not shown. She only tells you how wrinkled he was, "But his cock shows no sign of wear." It finally concludes with the fantasy that you've seen before of a lady being screwed by three different guys, all anonymous, and wearing weird masks, while they copulate to the accompaniment of a piano concerto.

REVELATIONS NN NM BI DK
Early 1970s   BOCCACCIO 100

P/D—Richard Wilton
F/A—Harold Black, Ken B.
F/A—Joan J., Sarah L., Mary Jackson

Two attractive women, one in an office, one in a beauty parlor, discuss their sex lives with an unseen sexologist and seem, from a male standpoint, to reveal their sexual emotions, encounters and fantasies in believable dialogue which is intercut with actual sexmaking and a continuing voice-over. It's interesting to compare female reality with this dialogue, and women, particularly younger females, may enjoy contradicting the sexuality of these women as they express it—obviously for a male audience. The big question is whether most women would answer a male so bluntly without resenting the invasion of their sexual privacy (see note under *Fanny Hill,* p. 187).

SALLY'S PALACE OF DELIGHT
NN DK NR (final scene)
COMPETITIVE VIDEO

P/D—Roger Harts

F/A—Dick Pole
F/A—Shell, Britt Reed

Plump, heavy breasted, and thick eyebrowed (you never see her naked), Sally runs a stud service for neighborhood women. Zack, one of her studs, is black and he's much in demand. After one sequence, Zack disappears—presumably to give in-house service to another of Sally's clients—a 60-year-old woman. "All you have to do, Zack, is sit in front of her naked with your animal pointing at the ceiling," Sally tells him. "What else can a 60-year-old woman do but look?" Unfortunately, you never see this sequence. Another stud takes care of a very pretty, flat-chested young lady who is into sadomasochism. She ties him up, after which they reverse roles and he nearly strangles her with his "animal." Then you hear Sally talking to a male client on the phone (while she's filing her fingernails) and helping him to masturbate, verbally. The sexvid concludes with an amusing scene with James, another stud, whose assignment is to convert a woman who "digs chicks." "Men are disgusting," she tells him, but she's fascinated when he slowly strips in front of her. James converts her to men in a surprisingly romantic, well-photographed, long lovemaking sequence with Tschaikowsky's Fifth for background music.

SUPERCHARGER NN BI DS NR
COMPETITIVE VIDEO

P/D—Anthony Pirelli
F/A—Howard Worth
F/A—Suzanne Charmlaine, Patti Buckner

Whoever the director, cinematographer and editor were on this one, they are not only quite skilled, but story aside (there isn't one), they obviously enjoyed creating different camera angles, montages and new perspectives on sexmaking and female nudity. It begins with supercharged racing cars roaring around the racetrack. After views of the people at the track, the camera finally concentrates on one couple. The woman wishes they were somewhere else so they could make love. Her boyfriend wishes he was racing, but he didn't qualify. Goodbye story, but surprisingly they make love very romantically on a blanket behind his car. After that, without goodbyes, you are watching a lovely woman taking a bubblebath in a suburban house. Her doorbell rings; a big guy is impatient to get in. She answers it wrapped in a towel. It's a guy she knows, but despite his invitation she doesn't want sex. He threatens to knock her out unless she cooperates, then rapes her. She escapes, and runs naked through the streets to her girlfriend's house. Trying to soothe her, the two friends end up caressing her, and in a few minutes they are all having sex together when the husband (boyfriend?) arrives home. They happily shower together, and then the couple you met at the racetrack arrive. Champagne is broken out, they literally bathe themselves in it, after which they have a happy, silly orgy, four women and two guys, with multiple images and montages, and with the cameraman having as much fun as the participants.

SAN FRANCISCO EROTICA VOLUME I
NN BI
ASTRO

No producer, actors or actresses provided

A poor competitor of *Swedish Erotica*, this tape contains three sex loops, *Lawn Party, Tiffany for Breakfast,* and *After Dinner*. The first quickly ends up in the living room in a 15-minute fuck and suck sequence of three women and two guys. The breakfast sequence—presumably with a husband and wife—moves rapidly to the couch in the living room where there is, surprisingly, some conversation with the sex. *After Dinner* is an evening with two couples playing doctor. Playing it slow motion or fast forward on your VCR will produce the only humor on this one.

SATISFIERS OF ALPHA BLUE
CC NN BI DK
1981 ADULT VIDEO

P/D—Gerard Damiano
F/A—Richard Bolla, Herschel Savage, George Payne

F/A—Lysa Thatcher, Sharon Mitchell, Annie Sprinkles

I've given this one a CC rating because it certainly belongs in the top ten films women will detest. Hence, perhaps they should watch it to see a master of the genre giving the raincoat crowd what they really want in spades! The time is the twenty-first century—there are no more wars, no more poverty—and the only thing left in this "almost perfect" world is continuous fucking and sucking provided by the satisfiers, who are both female and male. They work(?) for sex resorts like Alpha Blue. Both Algon (Richard Bolla) and Griffin (Herschel Savage) have "unlimited use cards" at Alpha Blue and Griffin can't get enough. He comes at least three times a day. "What about love?" Algon, who is nostalgic and would like to return to the past, asks him. "There's pussy," Griffin replies. "It's not enough." "You're right—there's never enough pussy." The satisfiers' specialities are coded into a computer. Griffin orders three ladies at a time. Soon three of them are happily fellating him. One of the hostesses (Sharon Mitchell) is also a teacher in the sex arts, and in one scene she gives detailed instructions (visually carried out) on oral sex. One of the most flagrant satisfiers in Alpha Blue is 805 (Lysa Thatcher), and Algon falls in love with her. He even manages to find a chicken and wine (no longer generally available in the twenty-first century), and they have a sensuous dinner eating it together. But 805 thinks he's ridiculous when he talks about love. "You can have me anytime. I'm the best fuck in Cubicle 7," she says. "But that's not love!" "I don't need love, don't talk about love," she says. But it all ends happily, as Algon finally convinces her that from now on she wants him, and him alone. She actually has an orgasm and moans, "I love you." Maybe you can attribute all this discussion of love versus plain sex to Damiano's Catholic conscience. But Damiano's eye is on the box office buck and not heaven. The cinematography is unusual, with many close-ups that reveal the actors' and actresses' blue veins on their behinds and breasts and penises.

SEKA FANTASIES **NN BI DK**
1981 CABALLERO

P/D—Ted Snyder, Bobby Hollander
F/A—Randy West
F/A—Sara, Chris Cassidy, Connie Peterson

George is breaking up with Marge (Connie Peterson), and Seka, who is running a new business, Outcall Fantasies, knows how to cure her disgust with her ex-husband. She provides three guys to take care of Marge. Within moments they arrive and find Marge in her outdoor sauna, naked of course, and ready for action. Seka has brought along another woman and they and one of the guys adjourn to the upstairs living room—the place is built on the side of a hill. Seka strips to much enthusiastic comment from the guys. Later she supervises a double insertion for Marge, and the viewer gets a detailed camera examination. "It's just what you wanted, isn't it baby?" she tells/asks Marge, who moans, "Oh yeah, oh yeah!" Seka discovers Randy West, one of her employees, being worked over in bed by Chris Cassidy and she attacks her angrily. Randy is supposed to save his strength for another client, but she forgives and provides Chris' fantasy—two men to fellate at once. In the meantime, three horny women call for one guy to be sent over and when he arrives they have a contest. Don't bring this one home to Mama.

SENSATIONS **NN DB DK DS BI**
1975 CABALLERO CONTROL

P/D—Lasse Braun, Alberto Ferro
F/A—Brigitte Maier

This sexvid was the big adult movie of the Cannes Film Festival in 1975. It is the story of Margaret, a sexually inhibited American woman and her meeting with super-sexually-sophisticated Europeans. The sensations include a man with a metal hook for a hand, women who ride horses, breasts shoved into vulvas, women chained to wheels and much, much more—with no plot.

SEVEN INTO SNOWY **NN NR some DK and one NR scene**
1977 TVX

P/D—David Friedman, Anthony Sheperd
F/A—Paul Thomas
F/A—Abigail Clayton, Kay Parker

Best Music Award—Second Erotic Film Festival. This sexvid is memorable for a long, romantic scene on a deserted California beach that would grace any film, and a lover who actually tells the woman, "I love you." Unfortunately, the Snow White plot deteriorates pretty quickly.

SHADES OF BLUE I **NN NM BI**
1982 ASTRA VIDEO NOVACOM PRODUCT

P/D—David Butler, Michael Krueger
F/A—Drea

Porno star Drea hosts this new video magazine, which will appear quarterly. "I don't need a towel," she tells the viewer as she says hello beside a swimming pool. "I'd rather be naked." It offers not only Drea stroking herself between the various segments, but a gal washing her Mark IV with a hose. Wearing abbreviated Levi's, her breasts clearly revealed through her wet blouse, she finally finishes and with the hose between her legs (you probably never thought of that before) uses it to happily masturbate. Next there is a rock group segment with naked gals and guys happily rubbing together, followed by a gal in a gym utilizing various equipment to reveal her body. Next is a woman in a barn currying her horse. She finally strips and rides him naked (in a saddle) through the countryside. Of course, young women and horses are very popular sexual symbols. Then—in the things-every-young-woman-will-want-to-try, a young lady is sucking a popsicle. She tests it on her breasts, likes the sensation, and is soon caressing her body with the melting ice, but not before she manages to give herself a deep vaginal freeze. One segment covers Dick Drost's famous nudist camp at Roselawn, Indiana, and there's a short interview with Dick, who is a total paraplegic (but never lacks sex). For a complete documentary on Dick Drost, see listing, p. 104, *Nude Miss America Contest*.

There's also an interview with Wendy du Near, who won the Nude Entertainer of the Year Award (see listing, for Nudes-a-Popping, p. 112), and who reveals her entire body when she dances. "I pretend I'm making love when I dance," she says. Then there's some more bisexuality. And finally a nude guy appears and takes care of Drea before she says goodbye.

SHARON DK BI
1971 HOME ENTERTAINMENT
SELECT/ESSEX

P/D—Navred Reef
F/A—Zebedy Colt, David Christopher, Jamie Gillis
F/A—Jean Jennings, Sharon Saunders, Susan McBain

A nonstop gang-banger that will make you feel as if you should take a bath after a few minutes. My copy of the tape on a 60-minute reel (with a large plastic insert) runs out of tape—or maybe there was nothing left to say. Presumably photographed in Atlanta, Georgia, the premise is that Southerners, male and female, are a pretty horny lot even if they live in an Atlanta suburb and mostly are still in high school. It all begins with Zebedy Colt (as Daddy) taking a shower with his daughter, Suzanne, and telling her later on the couch in the living room (while she's laughing and chuckling at the size of Daddy's erection), "You sure don't take after your mamma. All she puts in her mouth is cornbread. I'm gonna break you in right. Whoever marries you is gonna get a good one." And when he comes, "That's the way, baby. That's the stuff that made you, and now it's back in your mouth." If that doesn't curdle your stomach—stay tuned.

SHEER PANTIES NN BI DK
1979 SELECT/ESSEX

P/D—Billy Thornberg
F/A—John Holmes
F/A—Annette Haven, Linda Wong, Sharon Westover, Susan Strong, Barbara Lester, Stella

Emceed by a huge-breasted woman named Stella who provides comments between the sequences, this one is a series of loops. Wearing sheer panties which are quickly discarded, most of the women listed above take extended sucks on the famous Holmes' penis and manage to contain it in their vaginas. In between, Annette and Linda savor each other's clitoris, and a guy that the woman describes as "dorky-looking" gets stuck in an elevator with her. You may survive it better with your fast-forward button.

SHOPPE OF TEMPTATIONS
NN DK BI
1978 ARROW

P/D—J. Arthur Sportjacket, Jerry Ross
F/A—John Leslie, Mike Ranger, David Blair
F/A—Nikki Masters, Andrea Lange, Ruby Sapphire

If you walk into this gift and curio shop, and the little incense maker is bubbling (dry ice?), you may have an irresistible impulse to copulate. The pretty owner, Luray, asks no questions. She isn't even startled by guys with "their dicks in their hands." She just spreads her legs. Pretty soon there are more fucking, naked people (or is it naked people fucking?) than there are souvenirs in the shop. Even the haughty Baroness Von Furburg (Ruby Sapphire a.k.a. Juliet Anderson) can't resist and shares the Baron with Luray. An ickie-lickie with an orgy ending that can be amusing, and become a communal sex ballet but only if you are a little blotto and run your VCR in fast forward.

SIZZLE CC R
1982 JLT FILMS Available from I.D.I.

P/D—Paul Hertzberg, Chris Tyner
F/A—Kitten Natividad, who strips and acts as hostess to other strippers who are identified by first names only

Feminists who get upset with their peers who take an opposite tack and enjoy flaunting their sexual differences should study this tape. Millions of guys will happily accept that a woman's brains may be equal to their own, but the ladies have something else too—lovely bodies which were designed by whomever God may be to stimulate the male and keep the world procreating. Can men do the same for women? You bet—but not until a great many women are unafraid to admit that they enjoy a naked male. In the meantime, any lady, career woman or housewife can learn how to do it from this tape, which is much more erotic than watching women mud wrestling. The various strippers include ladies who laughingly accept zipper help from some of the male audience on the circular stage. Each of them offers some of the most unusual and sexy dancing you ever watched —including a flamenco strip, a woman who performs as a robot stripper and is absolutely unique (she could play Olympia in the *Tales of Hoffman*) and Kitten Natividad herself. Her huge mammaries don't interfere a bit as she waves *all* of herself in a laughing sexual invitation.

SIZZLE **NN NL DK**
1979   QUALITY

P/D—Mark Ubell
F/A—Roger Caine, George Payne
F/A—Samantha Fox, Merle Michaels, Veri Knotty

An amusing sexvid offering five unrelated short stories. A pretty gangster moll's gang of hoods—six or more—service her on command in every orifice: An O. Henry "Ransom of Red Chief" take-off follows, with the Red Chief an insatiable, sassy hillbilly girl who nearly screws her kidnappers to death. Next is a conventional bedroom scene of a woman and her lover enjoying themselves before the husband arrives home, and then there's a family soap opera where the sisters get mixed up in bed with the wrong husbands. Finally, Samantha Fox drowns herself but returns wearing a fishnet to continue her amours.

SKIN ON SKIN **NN**
1981   CAL VISTA

P/D—Bernardo Spinelli, Anthony Spinelli
F/A—John Leslie, Richard Pacheco, Jon Martin, Aaron Stuart
F/A—Eva Hausman, Pat Manning, Juliet Anderson, Erica Boyer

Presumably, all depicted in this sexvid are average, normal people—just like you and me. There's Juliet Anderson, who is married to Joel Caine. He's busy with his bar and serving customers like Anthony Spinelli (the producer who plays the part of a harassed husband—Spinelli always appears in his movies. He's bearded and plump and smokes cigars). He hasn't time to service his wife properly, so Juliet calls the TV repairman, who is delighted to soothe her itchiness. Then, there's Jon Martin, who is demanding extra special service for his flight to China, and Mai Lin arrives to provide it in bed before the flight. This is followed by a sequence with Richard Pacheco, who has a date with Pat Manning's daughter—but instead in her fantasy he bounces Mommy on the sofa. And there's a guy reading a beauty care ad and sure enough his doorbell rings and the Avon Lady, after opening her cosmetics case, quickly strips and bounces on him. This is followed by Aaron Stuart in bed beside his wife dreaming that he is getting an obscene phone call from a husky-voiced lady who tells him to "Meet me in front of your house in ten minutes." He does and adds some spice to his boring marital sex life. Finally John Leslie is interviewing Eva Hausman, a model from Germany, and looking at her portfolio, but in his imagination he is happily screwing her on the couch. She in turn is enjoying the same fantasy. Note the ratings on this one—no bisexuality, no group sex. If Spinelli had enlarged his own part as the father of Richard Pacheco (Spinelli could be a top-drawer character actor), the sexvid might have been really funny.

SKINTIGHT **NN NM BI DK DS**
1981   CABALLERO

P/D—Mike Weldon, Ed de Priest
F/A—Paul Thomas, Randy West, Aaron Stuart
F/A—Annette Haven, Lisa de Leeuw, Mai Lin, Lee Carroll, Maria Tortuga

Poor Samantha Denver (Annette Haven). She's a surrogate, a therapist working at Dr. Chambers' (Paul Thomas) Sex Clinic. She tells her roommate, "I have sex all day. The last thing I want to do is go out on a date with a guy." But it's all right with a woman, and soon you are watching Annette's lovely mole on her left buttock as she enjoys her. She also handles a male premature ejaculator, showing him how his wife can use the "squeeze technique" to keep her husband erect. Other therapists in the clinic are teaching an impotent male how to get an erection by becoming a master of women. "Suck my cock, you bitch," are the key words. In her weekend hideaway, Samantha treats Randy West, who pleads with her not to excite him too much. But her real problem is obscene phone calls, which she continuously gets. It won't take you long to figure out who initiates them. It's Dr. Chambers himself. The poor guy has sadistic fantasies in the form of Lisa de Leeuw (who is a figment of his imagination). He arrives at Samantha's home to try them out on her (but Samantha has left the clinic—she's working on her masters, and is going to marry Randy West). So Dr. Chambers takes out his frustration on her roommate, Marie (Marie Tortuga), and rapes her in a violent conclusion.

STAR VIRGIN **NN some silly DS and DK and occasional NL**
1979 VCX

P/D—**Nisan Eventoff, Linus Gator**
F/A—**Mike Ranger, Johnny Harden**
F/A—**Kari Black, Tracy Walton, Jeanette Harlow**

This is not a science fiction sexvid. What makes it more interesting is that you never know what the next sequence will bring. It begins with an afternoon at Monroe High School in 1950 "where sex began," and proceeds to a night in Transylvania (with a black-and-white, silent technique that has unexplored possibilities) where our heroine is raped by both Dracula and a man in a Richard Nixon mask. Next, there's Starstruck, a football hero who is KO'ed in the big game and brought back to life by two cheerleaders sliding on his face and nether parts. And there's a woman who can blow out a lighted torch with air she has sucked into her vagina. She later dances with a boa constrictor.

THE STIMULATORS **NN BI DK**
1983 VCA

P/D—**Not given**
F/A—**Ron Jeremy, Dave Ruby**
F/A—**Cheri Champagne, Maria Sentyr, Niko Vendette, Silver Starr**

In the mid 1980s there's still obviously a continuous demand for plotless "quickies." Else why would they be made? This one tries to convince you that Cheri Champagne is a porno movie producer and Ron Jeremy her assistant. All the action occurs on about five different sets, mostly inside one house. It begins with Cheri forcing Ron to strip and watch a porno movie with her while she tries to determine if the actors will arouse him. If they do, she can hire them for her next production. You thus watch Ron and Cheri screwing while they are watching other couples on a screen screwing, and presumably, if you're lucky you are watching with some nice lady making love, too. I would guess this film was shot entirely on a weekend by a cameraman who was producer (the producer/director is not identified in the credits). Assume an actor's budget of about $500 each for ten persons and you have $5,000. Add another $10,000 for the producer and lighting man and materials and you've spent $15,000. If you can sell the product to a distributor for a $10 per-cassette royalty, all the distributor has to do is sell 1,500 cassettes and you, as producer, have done very well for a weekend's work. Then there's the possibility of adult film theater distribution with even larger revenues. So what's stopping you? All you need is a private home and backyard and a half-dozen cooperative friends. If you don't have a video camera, you can rent one, but make sure you pull the curtains in case the neighbors may be watching!

SUZE'S CENTERFOLDS **NN DK BI**
1980 CABALLERO

In the style of *Swedish Erotica*, these are two one-hour tapes with four loops on each, running about 15 minutes. Collection One offers two young women using a dildo together in excruciating detail; a parlor maid dusting the furniture and wearing only an apron and a bra while the master of the house watches and plays with himself before taking her on; a plumber who arrives to unplug a sink, and plugs the owner instead, and a six-foot blonde who dances so erotically for her boyfriend that the mirror in her apartment becomes steamed. More of the same in Collection Two. These loops are standard fare in the adult peep show parlors, where it costs about a dollar in quarters to watch a 15-minute segment.

SWEDISH EROTICA VOLUMES 27 & 28
NN BI DK
1978-1981 CABALLERO

F/A—See below
F/A—See below

Probably the best known of all adult films, *Swedish Erotica* comprises more than 52 one-hour tapes. They have been available in the past on 8-mm film and continue to be a big seller in this form. The tape versions are all produced within the past few years and most of the famous porno stars, past and present, appear on them. Each tape has three episodes and the entire series amounts to about 150 short sex stories. Most of the story lines are concerned with upper- and middle-class people, and the stories are easier to sustain, amidst much genital sex, than the longer hour or more films. They also resolve the problem of showing five or six women on one film to satisfy the male viewer. The six stories on these tapes cover Seka waking up in the morning with her horny husband and taking a bath to get ready for sex with him; Seka looking at sex magazines in another story and getting very horny; Lisa Woods running for city council and ringing doorbells to solicit signatures; Shannon looking for a job at a disco and Desiree Cousteau as a nurse giving oral therapy. Designed for young men and males who dream about sex-obsessed women who can't get enough, *Swedish Erotica* episodes are well photographed. But most women will be convinced that the actresses must have acquired their libido on some other planet. If you send $5 to Caballero (see address on page 55) they will send you a catalogue which describes all of the various *Swedish Erotica* tapes in some detail, and also their many other sexvids. *Swedish Erotica* one-hour tapes sell for $49.95, and Caballero will make a special price to any aficionado who wants to own the entire series.

SWEET DREAMS SUZAN
NN BI DK DS
1980 EROS

P/D—Jon de La Carde, Leon Valenti
F/A—Aaron Stuart, Mick South, Jon Martin
F/A—Rhonda Jo Petty, Bonita, Dorothy Le May

A continuous problem for adult film producers and directors, if they try to offer a film that encompasses all the adult film conventions, is to make the story approach as unique as possible. It ain't easy! This one uses the dreams of one woman, Suzan (Rhonda Jo Petty), to embrace a number of unrelated situations which she describes to her psychiatrist. Suzan does this in a voice-over to a visualization of her dreams. It seems that Suzan's dreams are more sexually oriented than she is in real life. In her first dream, she is at a party near a swimming pool in a private home. All the guests are wearing masks. A stripper is the center of attention and eventually the male guests go down on her. And then she is watching herself in her dream fellating her own brother. Suzan verbalizes through three more dreams, which include a long segment with her school nurse, her sister-in-law and her mother's housekeeper, and then her piano teacher, who seduces a girl selling Girl Scout cookies. Finally in a scary, extended rape scene she dreams about being tied up by three guys who rape her orally, vaginally and anally. Interestingly, in this, her final dream, she does not comment on her rape in the voice-over that accompanies all the other dreams. The rape scene will frighten most women, especially when Suzan cooperates. The tape could be the basis of a controversial evening with couples—the women being asked if the voice-over dialogue reflects any feminine feelings or is simply male contrived.

SWEETCAKES **NN NM BI DK**
1976 QUALITY

P/D—Hans Johnson
F/A—Jennifer Welles, Linda Wong, Serena, Brooke and Taylor Young
F/A—Ras Kean

The gimmick that is supposed to hold this unrelated series of loops together is an interview between Jennifer Welles and Ras Kean, who is supposed to be the world's foremost erotic photographer of women. Instead of still photographs, he recalls various moments of sex that he filmed. Thus you are treated to a scene where Serena and her maid, Sun Flower, welcome Johnny back from the war with the North, and both of them happily work him over in the barn. A barn was obviously less expensive to photograph than the bedroom of a southern mansion. Then a high school girl tells her boyfriend how she masturbates and invites him home after school (Mommy and Daddy are working) to show him how. This is followed by Linda Wong offering to do anything a handsome guy wants for an evening for $100. What he wants is to tie her up so that all her orifices are available to him and so that she can't resist. He does. Some ten minutes later, untied, they are in bed together laughing. Seems that they are really married and a psychiatrist told them to try this game to improve their marriage. Finally Jennifer and Ras get it on—and the tape is over. This is a sweetcake you can pass up.

THE TALE OF TIFFANY LUST **NN BI DK**
1981 TVX

P/D—Henry Paris/Gerald Kikoine
F/A—George Payne, Ron Jeremy
F/A—Arlene Manhattan, Misty, Desiree Cousteau, Samantha Fox, Veronica Hart, Vanessa Del Rio, Merle Michaels

Henry Paris, a.k.a. Radley Metzger (under which name he has made some memorable films, such as *Camille 2000, Punish-*

ment of Ann and *Score*) slipped his gears on this one. I guess Tiffany is Arlene Manhattan. She slips in and out of the story as she takes a day off from fidelity and leaves a note for her husband: "I'm not going to say 'hello punkin' to you any more when you come home . . . I'm going out without panties for this first day of my life . . . I want to feel free. I can't say when I'll be home." Intercut into this action is Vanessa Del Rio, hostess of a radio talk show called "The Florence Nightingale Show." She talks to people over the air and interviews people from the audience, viz, Merle Michaels, who tells her, "I've got to give some head, right away. Else I'll overeat." To which Vanessa responds, "Oh yes, the Modified Scarsdale Diet." Throughout the film, Vanessa acquiesces happily to audience requests for sex. In between glimpses of Vanessa, Tiffany goes in search of freedom. First she goes to bed with Veronica Hart, whom she never met before. Then, taking Vanessa's advice (somehow she ends up in the audience for the talk show), she goes to a strange bar and fellates the first male who tries to make her. Escaping from the bar, Arlene goes to the Sincerity Health Club where Veronica Hart's lover has followed her. She screws with him in an extended scene under a shower—after which she decides that she better get home before her husband finds the note she left. This is a sexvid for the hard-on audience. Women will not like it. Most guys may think that small-breasted Arlene has a prettier face than Veronica, but after all, what do faces matter?

TARA **NN BI DK**
1980 INTERVID

P/D—Leon Gucci
F/A—Jamie Gillis, Zebedy Colt, Bobby Astyr
F/A—Seka, Veronica Hart, Samantha Fox

Tara (Seka) is a photographer's model for Harold (Jamie Gillis). Her daddy (Zebedy Colt), an old renegade, is having an affair with Angie (Veronica Hart). Angie is also screwing her heart out with Harold, which makes Tara very jealous. Joyce (Samantha Fox), who is servicing two guys, tells her not to worry, it'll all come out in the wash.

As a photographer, Jamie is his usual crass self, telling Seka to bend over and spread her cheeks so he can get a better view of her—at the same time two other models are fellating him while he clicks away at Seka. Veronica and Seka make it together in an extended bisexual scene, and Veronica, who evidently paid her dues in this one, screws everyone in sight to a fare-thee-well. One funny scene: Bobby Astyr (who always appears in films with Samantha, with whom he lives in real life) takes on Seka, and after laughing his head off, he finally falls asleep on top of her. The film concludes with this word to the wise from Zebedy Colt: "This is 1980. We're all grown-up people. So, if *it*—whatever *it* is—feels good, do it!" Most women will say yuck to this one.

A TASTE OF SUGAR NN BI DK
1976 ARROW

P/D—Kirdy Stevens, Helen Terrie
F/A—Joey Civera, John Seeman, Mike Strong
F/A—Serena, Ellen Wales, Marlene Cipher

If you are a swinging hostess and have to run a wedding reception you may try Louise's (Serena's) approach. Order a wedding cake to be eaten *off* the naked bride's body by the guests. Before the bride and bridegroom arrive, Louise and Larry, who are running the party, play oral and genital switchies with Teach and Coach, who are married and arrive first. By the time the rest of the guests arrive, you are watching a non-stop fuckie-suckie, finally involving six couples. There's a song in this one, "We Could Love Forever," which Kinsey was the first to deny. Assuming that male orgiasts last longer than the Kinsey statistics—or about fifteen minutes—what do they talk about when the males can't get it up anymore, no matter what the females do or offer?

TEACHERS AND CREAM NN BI DK
BOCCACCIO 100

P/D—Not given
F/A—Georgina Spelvin, Helen Madigan

Boccaccio 100 is packaging some of the older porno films originally shot on 16-mm film—two to a tape (so I understand) at a price of around $39.95. (See other reviews of some Boccaccio 100 tapes and the Supplemental Listing for others.) These films were probably produced between 1965 and 1975 and represent a transition to sound from the stag films of the 1930s and 1940s. This one has a tiny story line about Mr. Boynton, who teaches English at PBS 114. To supplement his income he has made porno films with Rock Stone, a guy who shoots on weekends—most of his scenes are on the living room couch or in the bedroom. Mr. Boynton's moonlighting has been discovered and he has been fired. In disgrace, he's about to jump from the Brooklyn Bridge when two of his students dissuade him. He takes them home and shows them some scenes from his films, and they can't wait—and don't—to become porno actors. Very unsophisticated by 1984 standards but plenty of sex.

TEENAGE DESSERT NN BI DK
1983 CREATIVE IMAGE

P/D—Cindy Lou Sutters
F/A—Mike Ranger and others
F/A—Sandy Sunshine, Desire Elms, Big Tits Malloy, Too Tall Frieda

One of three 60-minute jobs (see *Plato's Retreat West* and *Weekend Cow Girls*) which was probably shot directly on videotape. It offers faces and genitals and roller skating at Venice Beach, California as you've never seen before, but not much else. The ladies are all long past their teens. There's Giuseppe—when he's not making pizzas, he's turning women into desserts covering their pussies with sliced bananas, cool whip, and cherries and eating it off—something you've watched in more than one porno. The film concludes with a dinner party where four couples all formally dressed quickly forget the food on the table and dine off each other for about 15 minutes.

TEENAGE MADAM DK DB DS BI
1979 VCX

P/D—R. Owen Teegee, Rik Taziner
F/A—John Holmes, Mark MacGregor, Paul Thomas
F/A—Desiree West, Bonnie Holliday, Kathy Marsa

Dr. Gonad, a psychologist, visits Madam Rose's brothel to interview the girls and find out why they got into the profession. There are no teenagers in this one, nor anyone who looks like one. These are loops tacked together and include an early John Holmes. A first grade retarded child could have mede a better film, and certainly could have thought of something more exciting than a truck driver who dresses in women's clothes and sobs to one of the girls, "Please don't spank me, Mommy, I'll be good!" The only reason to own this one is for historical interest, and sheer amazement that anyone (including Bob Rimmer) could watch it.

TEENAGE PLAYMATES NN DK BI
LOVE TV

No director's, actors' or actresses' names are given.

A direct-to-tape quickie with Gail, who occasionally looks like a teenager. There is no plot, just a lot of "goes intas" and oral sex, all climaxed by a head-eating contest during which the viewer is asked to pick the winner from among ten loopy-loops of different women—one after another and with penises attached to no particular bodies.

TEENAGE FANTASIES PART II NN BI
1974 ARROW

P/D—Various directors of separate sequences
F/A—John Holmes in most sequences
F/A—Renee Bond, Victorie Winter, Suki Yu

"Hi, my name is Renee Bond. My favorite fantasy is oral sex. I like being in control. I like the taste." So says Renee as she works over a detached penis in the beginning and between the sequences in this composite. Detached penis? Well, obviously not—but you never see the rest of the male body to which it belongs. Renee talks to the guy in the audience who may be holding his own, and she tries to give him the feeling that the one on the screen is really his. Among the other fantasies in what really are separate loops, Renee is a fairy princess and the horny toad turns into John Holmes, who can't stop saying, "Oh yeah . . . Oh yeah!" as she fellates him. Next is a mile-high fantasy which finally takes place on the ground on a private plane . . . in the cockpit, of course. Renee's friend, Suki Yu (a Japanese girl), proves that her a.k.a. is well chosen.

TELEFANTASY NN DK BI
1979 ARROW

P/D—Vittorio Gasso, Bob Chinn
F/A—John Leslie, Mike Ranger, David Blair
F/A—Mimi Morgan, Desiree Cousteau, Christine de Shaeffe

In the beginning, you have hopes this one might develop as a sex satire on television news programming. It has John Leslie as a believable anchorman who asks women, "Do you think of sucking me off when I'm on TV?" And there's a female news director who wants to get sex into the programming and improve the ratings of KCIZ-TV. Unfortunately, it quickly goes downhill when the action moves out of the studio and into massage parlors, where the news team is presumably obtaining interviews. If you last to the end, you'll see a few unique scenes, like a detailed examination of Desiree Cousteau's vagina being lapped and Desiree lapping in turn. Run slow motion, the tape may teach you some things about oral sex given or received that you never knew before. Included is this conversation with John Leslie in a massage parlor with a woman he has just watched servicing another client: "I don't like sloppy seconds," he says, and she replies, "That's silly. Don't think of it that way. I'm all warmed up. You don't have to do anything to get me ready."

TEENAGE STEPMOTHER NN BI DK
VIDEO-X HOME LIBRARY

P/D—Benson Hurst, Claude Goddard
F/A—Jamie Gillis, Marc Stevens
F/A—Darby Lloyd Rains, Lynn Stevens

Before your VCR has even warmed up, the nonstop screwing and sucking in this one commences with the marriage of Jamie to Darby Lloyd Raines, who is supposed to be a teenager, but ain't. Darby has a sickness. She must have sex every hour on the hour and makes no never minds who the male or female is. Jamie has two teenage daughters to bring his new wife home to—and before Judge Crawford (Marc Stevens, known as Mr. 10½) performs the vows, Darby is masturbating him and screwing doggie-style with Jamie. When they get home, you discover that Jamie's daughters look older than Darby—if that's possible. There's a way to make this a fascinating sexvid which you can run as a background for sedate parties. Find a couple of good ballet records. Put them on your stereo. Turn on the videotape. Put your VCR in fast forward. Turn off the TV sound, and you will have a unique, modern Group Sex (indoor and outdoor) Copulating Ballet. You may even decide to assign it an NL rating!

TIGRESSES **NN DK BI**
1979   VIDEO-X-PIX

F/A—Eric Edwards, Ron Hudd, Dick Rimmer
F/A—Samantha Fox, Vanessa Del Rio, Rikki O'Neal

This one is comprised of four short stories with a common theme—women in command of men. One gal beats her men friends at swimming and handball, takes them both on in bed and tells them how to satisfy her. Another picks up sailors and serves them smoked salmon that looks like a vaginal opening. Two sisters take on a black man in an extended interracial sequence, and Vanessa pretends she can only speak Spanish to get her way with men. Big question: Who in this movie is Dick Rimmer? I can't identify him. He's no relative I know of—and of course the name may be a sexual pun.

TINSELTOWN **CC NN NM BI DK**
1980   VCA

P/A—Carter Stevens
F/A—Eric Edwards, William Margold, Randy West, Mike Ranger
F/A—Danielle Ray, Loni Henderson, Ashley Brooke

This one tells the familiar Hollywood story from casting couch to fame as an actress, but with several twists that make it interesting—at least for a sexvid. First, Carter Stevens tells three stories. One is about Mary Jo Harman (Danielle Ray), who comes from Oklahoma to be an actress; another is about Pat Norman (Loni Henderson), who is a senior at UCLA and also wants to be an actress; and the third is about a $500-a-day hooker (Ashley Brooke) who prefers hooking to acting. But because she has such charisma, she convinces Jerry Kaminski, (Eric Edwards) that, even though she can't act, she can be a great star just being natural. William Margold plays the part of the fast-talking agent who takes over Mary Jo's career, which ends in a back alley making porno loops, and Loni Henderson falls in love with a sadist, whose contribution to her career is as a star in higher-class porno flicks. What keeps the tape interesting is fast editing, and the fact that in reality none of the women are very good actresses but perform well for Carter Stevens. In the things-you-can't-believe department, each woman relaxes before going to a big Hollywood party by masturbating: one in her bathtub with the water running on her vulva, the other with her own hand and fingers, the third with her usual vibrator.

THE TRAVAILS OF JUNE **NN DK BI**
1974   VIDEO SHOWTIME

P/D—Not given
F/A—John Leslie
F/A—Sharon Mitchell

It will take you a few minutes to recognize John Leslie in this ucky-fucky. He's wearing glasses and a moustache and is not the featured player. Neither is Sharon Mitchell. The woman who plays June is not identified, nor is her savior(?) Dan Crockett, a reporter for the *Washington Post* who is uncovering a story about high Washington officials who are provided with kidnapped girls who must do their sexual bidding. Sounds as if it might be sadistic, but it isn't because everyone enjoys everyone else—even June who has been fed some juice that makes her very sexy. Never mind, Dan doesn't care what she's done. He gets the gang arrested and the story, if you can call it that, ends with him hugging her and telling her, "I'm thinking serious thoughts about you." Nothing to bring home to your lady.

TROUBLE DOWN BELOW **NN DK BI**
FANTASY VIDEO BY CABALLERO

P/D—Mansfill Warwick
F/A—No male actors' names given
F/A—Connie Petersen, Maria Tortuga

A plotless, low-budget, one-hour sexvid designed to sell at lower prices than most. Actors and actresses you've never seen before stare at the camera too much and never stop screwing or sucking each other, all to the incessant beat of rock music. After some initial dialogue, Connie's psychiatrist tells her she is an anal woman, and he advises her that she is married to an anal retentive man. Eventually her psychiatrist takes care of her anus and vagina. But after the interview, conversation ceases. Some of the women are attractive, and the guys splay their labias with their fingers in extended close-ups, offering sights you've never seen before. Most of the group sex action takes place in a suburban middle income home that by today's inflated standards would sell in California for over $200,000. I'll bet their neighbors didn't know what was going on.

THE UNTAMED **NN DK BI**
ASTRO

P/D—Harold Lime, Ramsey Carson
F/A—Jeffrey Stern
F/A—Jill Jackson, Kay Parker

A plotless crotch opera. If you think sucking penises or playing "goes into" for more than an hour is amusing, you may enjoy it. If you watch this one in mixed company, it's sure to engender enough "ughs" from the women to create conversation and laughter.

VIDEO KIXS MAGAZINE, VOL. 4
NN DK
1983 ROLD STRIPE

P/D—Danielle Peters, Felix Daniels
F/A—Vanessa Del Rio, hostess

I haven't seen the first three volumes of this video tape magazine. This one isn't quite so professional as *Electric Blue* and *Playboy* (see listings) but Gold Stripe, in this and other tapes, seems to be emphasizing female eroticism rather than genital sex. And along with its other fashion tapes, *Body Beautiful, Frederick's of Hollywood, Shape Up,* and *Beauty Bible* (which I have not seen) is obviously going after the female at-home audience. As with other tapes in the magazine format, this one has various sections. *Adult Cinema Hot Spots* reveals an unidentified lady in a 1940s style black and white stag film. She plays with her very full breasts and thoroughly massages herself. This is followed by a modern young woman who also is enjoying herself but with no genital close-ups. An extended sequence offers a woman called *Black Velvet* who is presumably famous in Europe. She does an extended strip during which she perspires heavily and offers a running comment on her feelings in a voice over: Example: "The whole room comes alive with the erotic aroma of my wet pussy." The tape concludes with a busty woman who fantasizes herself as a stripper. Intercut into her fantasy you discover that she's actually a secretary to a guy who is trying to seduce her. She ends collaring him with a leash and making him happily obey her commands.

THE VIDEOSEX REVOLUTION **NN NR**
1983 SUSAN'S VIDEO

P/D—Amateurs
F/A—Gals and guys next door

You can buy this hour long compilation of 40 different couples screwing at home in their living rooms, bedrooms and kitchens from Susan's Video for $39.95 (see listing Susan's Video). The tape is a much longer composite from actual homemade tapes provided to Susan's either in exchange for tapes of an other couple, or because the couples involved are swingers and are using this method to contact others who'd like to exchange spouses with them. Each excerpt runs about a minute and a half and is sufficient to give a pretty good view of each couple's copulatory abilities (the ladies are very noisy climaxers) and an appreciation of their bodies. The tape is coded with the first names of the people involved and the state in which they live. If you want to see a particular entire tape—as received by Susan—you can order specific ones by the number assigned, and thus get better acquainted. Most of the couples do not talk much in these excerpts and full screen close-up of their faces is rare, but if you want to see how young America, behind closed doors, makes love, you'll be amazed that so many people are not self conscious about exposing themselves. This tape is interesting and revolutionary! And in some cases imaginative.

WEEKEND FANTASY **NN DK DS BI**
1980 VCX

P/D—**Elton Marc, Joe Luchine**
F/A—**William Margold, David Morris**
F/A—**Jennifer West, Kathy Konners, Tawny Pearl, Christine de Schaeffer**

"Are you ready to jerk off, men? Do you have your pants down, men? I've got a hot story to tell you. Ushers, close the door." So says Jennifer West, who throughout this tape talks directly to her unseen audience of horny men—presumably masturbating. The story, if you can call it that, involves four guys who have a week-end cabin, and a hostess who directs traffic and offers the men masochistic (the word is not used in the film) women. The worst one of all this is of William Margold, who portrays about the nastiest person (including Jamie Gillis) you ever watched on the screen. In one scene, he dumps a lady in a muddy barnyard and beats her a bit more before she fellates him. Margold is a porno film reviewer for *Velvet*, who presumably excoriates films like this. A really ugly film. In addition to the ratings above, I give it a 7-S rating. Sleazy, slimy, seamy, slutty, sadistic, sicky, spermy—you'll add some more after you've watched it.

WET DREAMS **NN NM BI**
1980 WONDERFUL WORLD OF VIDEO

P/D—**Robert Foxx**
F/A—**Clyde Clone, Peter New**
F/A—**Suzy Spazz, Diana Strawberry, Bo Bridgett**

The only reason for buying or renting this tape would be to discover that you probably can make a better one with your own camera in your own living room. It was shot directly onto videotape, and poor Suzy has the most unreal foamed-filled breasts you've ever seen. But in things-you've-never-seen-before close-ups, she can vibrate her labia and vaginal muscles before and after she masturbates. Obviously, in the vernacular, she can milk a penis. Another woman in an extended masturbation scene cools her vulva and anus with ice cubes. And a guy wearing a female mask—probably the embarrassed director—finally takes her on after she's done a better job on herself.

20

The Update

Six hundred fifty new reviews of current and older films. These films are classified by the same system used in the rest of the filmography. Please note the addition of one new category, "Documentaries."

The manuscript of the first edition of *The X-Rated Videotape Guide* went to the publisher in December 1983 and was published in July 1984. It contained 650 reviews of adult films and a "Supplemental Listing" of an additional 1,700 that I had not watched.

During the last six months of 1983 and through 1984, adult films were being released at the rate of 75 or more a month. This second edition of the guide reviews another 650 films, which makes a total of 1,300 or more reviews. The supplemental listing of films that I haven't reviewed continues to grow and now numbers 2,840 tapes.

But the truth is that many new releases are no better (or worse) than the thousands of sexvids produced during the last 15 years. Most buyers or renters have no way of telling whether a particular tape has a good story line or is just a patched-together collection of loops or a nonstop fuckathon shot directly on video over a long weekend.

One thing is obvious. If you enjoy watching adult films regularly or even infrequently and want to see the best within the genre (or see films that reflect your own fantasies), you need this guide. There is no other X-rated videotape guide on the market where one viewer, like myself, has actually watched all the films reviewed and in many cases has cross-referenced these in terms of actors and directors, or recognized that in the mid-1970s many films produced were better dramatically and storywise than many of the current productions and achieved this with no lack of explicit sex.

Nor does any other guide recognize that many early porno films, produced between 1970 and 1980, are actively being promoted, sold, and rented with no indication of when they were made. Nor does any other guide, or the distributors themselves, reveal many of the retired actors, and particularly the actresses, who were just as pretty as the current crop.

But there is one unique adult-film guide that I think every filmmaker, producer, director, and writer, and you, if you are a sexvid aficionado, should own. It's published in two huge volumes by Scarecrow Press, 52 Liberty Street, Metuchen, New Jersey 08840. Written by James Limbacher, it's titled *Sexuality in World*

Cinema. In 1,511 pages, the author has pinned down 13,000 sexual films produced in every country of the world and organized them into 26 categories such as "Step to the Rear" (anal sex), "Once Too Often" (bigamy and polygamy), and "World's Oldest Profession" (prostitution). In many cases he gives the dates of the films and the directors' (but not the actors') names, plus a one-sentence summary. But there are no detailed reviews such as you will find here.

As in the previous edition, I make no claim to have watched all the best adult films. But after exploring this area for the past four years (in between writing novels in a totally different vein) I'll stick my neck out and tell you that in the current "Supplemental Listing," which is very comprehensive, I doubt if there are another 200 films that I would give a "Collector's Choice" rating. Many of these were probably filmed in the 1970s, prior to the current flood.

Many readers of the first edition have discovered that reading these reviews, whether they see the films or not, constitutes a kind of happy-go-lucky sex education. I've been pleased with the many letters sent me in care of the publisher. Some of these have been from sociologists and educators who realize that watching adult films has become a way of life for hundreds of thousands of Americans. How this may affect marital and interpersonal relationships in the coming years is a subject that I'm sure you'll find discussed in books and articles by sociologists, psychologists, and family counselors.

If you buy or rent adult films and have seen the original packages (in some states, this is unlikely since video dealers keep sexvids under the counter, don't sell them, and rent them in plain vinyl boxes), you are aware that during the past few years sexvid packages have become minor graphic-art masterpieces. Designed by experts to encourage your purchase, they are printed on glossy stock in four colors and often are embossed. The description of the contents is glowingly written to make you feel that here at last is the most erotic tape you've ever seen.

Whether I receive a tape in an unprinted vinyl box as a review, or screening, copy or it arrives in the retail-store package, I ignore the blurb sheets and box copy. I never read a review of a tape until after I have watched it. Thus I am like an explorer searching for a sexual El Dorado: a film that offers upbeat sex, a fairly good story line, and some character development, and isn't afraid to break away from the adult-film conventions.

My criterion for a CC (Collector's Choice) rating, whether I personally like the story line or not, is a tape where the sex is caring and takes place between people who seem to realize (even remotely) that we are all vulnerable human beings. And my feeling is that there is no human being more vulnerable than a woman kneeling doggie fashion or lying with legs spread to receive the "gift" of the male. Thus when you find an NR or NL rating, in this respect the tape is above average or has one or more scenes that reflect human sexual caring. If on the other hand I have given a film a CC rating with DS and DK elements, I have made a point to tell you why. If you find an NN, BI, or DK rating, in my opinion it's an inferior film, but I have tried to give you enough of an idea of the contents so that you can make your own decision.

When I was discussing this second edition with my editor, he wondered if I should confine the book only to sexvids with CC ratings. But in reality there are thousands of viewers (maybe millions) who would not agree with these ratings and who actually prefer out-and-out "fuck films" featuring totally uninhibited young women whose speciality is turning on the male viewer.

My CC ratings are aimed at the married-couples market, either one couple or a group of couples who are friends, and/or a single guy dating a single woman. Within this group there may be some couples who go in for group sex, or kinky sex, but most of the women (and probably many of the men) prefer one-to-one relationships, with one man or woman at a time.

Surprisingly, in real life many of the adult-film stars are totally monogamous. As I was writing this I received a second birth announcement from Veronica Hart, who is no longer making adult films. She now has two children, and the picture she sent along of the boys and her husband reveals a very contented mama. Richard Pacheco's wife (they also have kids) told me that so far as she's concerned, Richard's job is only slightly different from any actor's work. He not only kisses a woman, but she can suck his penis and he can put it inside her. But from Richard's standpoint, and hers, this genital relationship does not mean sexual involvement with the person after working hours. The Pacheco's are not, as I have suggested in many of my novels, interested in expanding their monogamous life with another couple.

Like me, my CC audience will enjoy recent films produced and directed by Candida Royalle under the overall grouping *Femme*, or a videotape like *Turning on with Kelly Nichols*, or Anthony Spinelli's *Reel People* (see various reviews). But I'm well aware that a huge audience of males would simply shrug. No matter what your preferences may be, I urge you to experiment with the tapes that I have not extolled and to make your own judgment.

In the process, you can decide which part of the sexvid market you identify with. I break it down as follows:

1. Average married couples, or unmarried cohabiting couples. Many of these couples live in suburbia and are not as sexually sophisticated as urban married couples. Hundreds of thousands of them have not watched many adult films but are intrigued by them. Most of the women in this group detest bisexuality (BI) and are not happy with "cum shots." Most of them can't believe that any woman would want jism shot in her mouth or on her face.

2. There is a large, sophisticated urban audience with women who just chuckle at the above or any deviational sex. Most of these viewers will give many Henri Pachard films a higher rating than I have because Pachard/Ron Sullivan, who produces and directs in New York City, has a flair for this kind of film.

3. Then there are male singles, who can be further subdivided into fraternity-brother males who daydream about women like Traci Lords, Joanna Storm, Desiree Lane, and Ginger Lynn, who are about their own age and seem to enjoy sex more than most of the fellows' girlfriends. Their older counterparts are single or married, beer-bellied, barroom, Veterans of Foreign Wars types who like these ladies, too, but aren't particularly happy when they portray marital bliss or play romantic parts. They are the older generation, whose motto was: "If you fuck and run away, you'll live to fuck another day." Hot, horny, slapstick sex without too much story line appeals to them as well as to many of the fraternity types. The hard core of this group read the sleazier men's magazines, including *Gallery, High Society, Velvet,* and several devoted entirely to X-rated movies.

4. Then there is a highly specialized market that seems to be growing, with many voyeurs from other groups who can't believe what they are seeing. These are the people who have sadomasochistic feelings and evidently enjoy tapes that I have labeled DB (deviational bondage and discipline). Twenty-six tapes of this type were eliminated from the first edition by the editor, and I have received numerous letters asking about them. In this edition I have convinced the editor to include these tapes, and I have added a few more.

You should understand that DB and DS are two separate categories that often seem to overlap, but BD, for the participants, is somewhat different. S&M behavior involves the belief that sexual pleasure is enhanced by light pain; it has a willing victim, who can be either male or female but usually in sexvids is female. Whether this be a psychological component of female behavior I leave to psychiatrists. But quite a few people are evidently turned on by sexual punishment, which includes spanking. There are several hundred of these films in the "Supplemental Listing," and most of them come from California Star Productions and Bizarre.

If you are interested in this kind of deviational sexual behavior, I recommend that you read some of the literature. See the note under the review of *Curiosity Excited the Cat,* and try some of these books: *Sadism & Masochism,* by Albert Eulenberg, Bell Publishers, New York, NY, 1984; *S/M, The Last Taboo,* by Gerald and Caroline Breene, Ballantine Books, New York, NY, 1974; *S/M, Studies in Sadomasochism,* by Thomas Weinberg and G. W Levi Kamel, Prometheus Books, Buffalo, NY, 1984.

Within this category there are male viewers of all kinds (whether they will admit it or not) who are aroused by rape scenes in films, which I have labelled DS. As I have mentioned elsewhere, rape and capture of the female is probably built into the male genes. Like it or not, the conflict engendered often makes for a more interesting film. That is why PG-13 films and many television dramas play on the fringe of rape by putting the female in jeopardy. When I have given a tape a DS rating, it may not involve the whole film, but it usually means that a woman is the unwilling victim of a male's sexual drive.

I don't think that sadistic behavior should be totally censored on film. We have to come to terms with the fact that the kind of mentalities that produced the Holocaust still exist in the world. The Hitlers and Stalins and their followers didn't get that way by watching adult films. But in reviews of films with DS ratings, I have often asked the question, Should this filming of sexual violence be permitted? Should we actually see a bloody murder or rape, or should it take place offscreen? Whatever the answer, obviously the filmmaker should not condone it.

Finally there are the gay and lesbian films, each with their specialized audience. I have reviewed a few "all-girl" tapes, but I keep wondering why men who enjoy these are so shocked by the "all-guy" tapes. Both categories bore me.

In a different vein, you will note that there is a new address listing in this edition, with many new names of producers who have formed their own distributing companies. Why are there so many new companies? Why are there so many new adult films? Will boredom set in? Will the market become glutted? The answers are all related to the so-called VCR revolution, which is not only changing American movie- and television-viewing habits, but is also reaching a very big market for adult films that didn't exist before. Millions of people are discovering that they can be sexual voyeurs in the privacy of their own homes, and they are fascinated to compare their own private bedroom activities with others' and learn how other people do "it."

If you read the historical background of the adult-film industry on pages 10–24, you'll discover that future shock has occurred at an unbelievable rate. In 1983 there were about 850 adult theaters in the United States. Now there are fewer than 250, and most of these are having a hard time surviving. The guardians of your morality and mine have continued with an unrelenting campaign to close down adult theaters and now are aiming their guns at video stores that sell and rent X-rated tapes. Amusingly, their success in closing theaters has been largely due to a diminishing audience. Stopping the sale or rental of adult video cassettes will prove much more difficult. The audience who used to go to adult theaters would prefer to watch X-rated films in their homes, bars, fraternities, and social clubs, and the demand for videotapes is growing.

When the first edition of this book was published, about 11 million VCRs had been sold. By the middle of 1984 there were 20 million VCRs in American homes. Predictions are that by 1990 there will be 42 million. While the adult-film share of the total video market seems to have shrunk to 17 percent, the total market for prerecorded video cassettes is now close to $1 billion annually. In

1984, over $100 million of adult tapes were sold at wholesale, with retail prices exceeding $300 million. Leaders in the industry expect a 25-to-30-percent increase in adult video cassette sales in 1985, with the increase continuing at this rate until 1990. Keep in mind that much of the present sale is direct to video stores who rent many more sexvids than they sell. Well aware of this, the big distributors have cut their prices on tapes from films produced in the 1970s to a retail range of $14.95 to $39.95, and even current releases seldom exceed $69.95.

If they can sell enough tapes, adult-film producers are no longer dependent on the theaters for their profits, but now the big worry is that so many people have jumped on the money-making carousel that a kind of Gresham's law will prevail, and the sex quickies, shot directly on video on a long weekend, will drive out the better-made films shot on 35-mm film and transferred to videotape.

Many of the old-line producers, like Cecil Howard, Dave Arthur, Richard Aldrich, and Anthony Spinelli, to mention a few, who insisted that you can't make a quality film directly on three-quarter-inch videotape, have already made one or two direct-video films. There isn't any question that, unless it's in the hands of experts, lighting for video is flat and the editing possibilities, compared with those of film, limited. But the real problem is that many producers believe that there is an unlimited market of horny males, young and old, who don't give a damn about character development or story line but only want to see the latest uninhibited female bodies and life-size genital and oral-genital close-ups. They may be right, since *Playboy* and *Penthouse* survive with essentially the same naked ladies with different names from issue to issue.

But my feeling is that whether the sexvid is shot on video or film is not so important as whether the producer/director is willing to spend a little more money to get a good screenplay with some realistic dialogue and is willing to tackle interpersonal relationships in the framework of human sexuality, or sexual fantasies, and is aware of the potential of the small screen for this kind of intimate storytelling.

One of the leaders of the adult-film industry (he probably wouldn't give a damn if I mentioned his name) wrote me:

> At the 1985 Consumer Electronic Show there were at least 10 new companies. I've never seen any group of crapshooters so anxious to kill the goose that lays the golden egg. Not content to release the 100 or so feature films that are being ground out annually, they have to augment this staggering profusion with made-for-video quickies. Ours is the only racket where a five-day shooting schedule is a major item, and a TV quickie has a production time about as long as it takes five Portuguese fishermen to gang bang a broad on a New Bedford pool table.
>
> These TV quickies cost about $15,000 to grind out. Figure a $15.00 net profit to manufacture; cassette and wrap, $5.00; transfer, $3.00. Sales commission, $3.00; and you can wholesale at $27. All the producer has to do is sell 2,500 cassettes to break even.

Based on the $100-million estimate for adult video cassettes sold in 1984, a rough guess would mean that 5 million individual cassettes were produced, a figure I think is too low. But assume that 1 million of them were sold direct to the consumer by mail order or through video stores and that the other 4 million were rented by video stores. If each sexvid is rented only five times, this means that in 1984 20 million or more viewers watched an adult film, or if you assume that the same people rented more than one tape, the figure for individual viewers still may be larger since usually more than one person watches a rented tape.

Adult film statistics for 1985 claim 55 million adult film viewers. More than voted for the President.

Obviously, the future of the industry, and whether enough money is made to permit bigger film and videotape budgets, depends on sales of 5,000 to 10,000 or more cassettes of individual films. From this standpoint adult-film producers are better off than most publishers of books, which require a sale of at least that many copies of a book for them to show a profit. Adult-film distributors have a big backlog of very good sexvids made in the 1970s that can be sold at under $20 and still show a profit. Unlike regular Hollywood films, they will never grow old, since the subject matter and human nudity haven't changed, and there is a growing group of "collectors" (I would number them in the hundreds of thousands) who want to build their own sexvid libraries.

Unfortunately, adult-film producers are their own worst enemies. Many of the new producers are at war with the Adult Film Association of America, which for the past 10 years has not only fought the legal problems of the industry but has tried to upgrade the films being produced and has created a star system that attracts the viewer to watch his or her favorite actors and actresses.

One of the big gripes has been that the AFAA Erotic Film Awards are unduly influenced by selection committees composed of personnel of the major distributors. The adult films nominated for best picture at the Erotic Film Awards on July 11, 1985, were *All the Way In; Body Girls; Dixie Ray, Hollywood Star; Every Woman Has a Fantasy; Firestorm; Great Sexpectations; Jack & Jill 2; L'Amour; Let's Get Physical; Stiff Competition; Talk Dirty to Me, Part III; Trinity Brown, Up, Up and Away;* and *Viva Vanessa.*

If you check the reviews in this edition, you'll discover that I have given "Collector's Choice" ratings to about half these films. But what ever happened to the following films that were produced in 1984 and not nominated? *Reel People, Hot Pursuit, Public Affairs, Bodies in Heat, Matinee Idol, Aphrodesia's Diary, Inflamed, Nasty,* and *Femmes: Christine's Secret,* which I think were equal to or better than those nominated.

Protesting against the choices, a new group was formed, the X-Rated Critics Organization (XRCO), who chose *Great Sexpectations, Every Woman Has a Fantasy, Firestorm,* and *Go for It* as their nominations for best picture. But prior to their announcement of the winner, William Margold (who with his wife, Drea, a former porn star, writes and produces many films), made the statement about adult films that blew the mind of the industry. "The bottom line," he wrote, "is that we deal in meat. Our XRCO awards show is going to reflect this."

Margold's remark sent cold shudders through the industry. About the same time, *Newsweek,* in its March 8, 1985, issue, was alerting America in a cover story titled "The War Against Pornography" and *Mademoiselle* magazine was summing up in its April 1985 issue the Andrea Dworkin–Catherine Mackinnon attempt to make pornography a civil-rights issue in a cover story titled "Is One Woman's Sexuality Another Woman's Pornography?"

Margold's implication, believed by many who never stated it so bluntly, that the adult-film business deals with human genitals as so much meat, was not the kind of publicity needed, especially in the current moral climate.

But unfazed, Margold wrote an unpublished letter to *Newsweek:*

> Your piece spanked voyeuristic sensibilities for daring to be titillated by damsels in designed distress. With lots of pseudointellectual babble, all the Mackinnons and Dworkins of the world finally do is drown in their own self-pity, becoming little more than a gaggle of emasculators who have pounded their dentata vaginas into censoring sheers. As one who has perpetrated cinematic violence on the fairer sex in such X-rated attractions as *Hot Skin, Weekend Fantasy,* and *Lust Inferno,* I can honestly say that I bore

the brunt of bruises (even in places you wouldn't have any idea of looking) in order to keep my female costar fit enough to lay-for-pay another day.

Chuck Vincent tried to stop the waving of a red flag in front of the bull with a letter to the members of the AFAA:

As members, we have always stood firmly on the side of improving the quality of adult films. We believe that viewers want good production values and emotionally as well as sexually satisfying stories. We don't treat performers as pieces of meat because we recognize their humanity and artistic goals. The formation of an awards group dedicated to applauding dehumanization and debasement is a giant step backwards for the entire industry. Margold strips away the artistic merit of our work and is an open invitation to the Jerry Falwells and foaming-at-the-mouth feminists to march right in and shut us down.

During all this there was some doubt whether the AFAA would finally hold the Ninth Annual Erotic Film Awards at the Sheraton at Universal City. They finally took place, but the industry has yet to learn the tenet of revolution, "United we stand, divided we fall."

There isn't space here to cover the details of the sexual civil-rights issue that Dworkin and Mackinnon managed to develop in the form of an ordinance for the city of Minneapolis and which has since been passed into law by Indianapolis and Los Angeles. Thus far rejected as unconstitutional, the proposal, which is given in full in the issue of *Mademoiselle* mentioned above, is still very alive. Dworkin and Mackinnon's statement of policy that introduces the antipornography law reads as follows: "Pornography is sex discrimination, posing a substantial threat to health, safety, peace, welfare and equality of citizens in the community." The model law then states that pornography promotes violence against women, keeps women subordinate, inhibits access to equal employment, education, and opportunity, and in essence describes pornography as a meat market. Fortunately, in late February 1986 the Supreme Court, without listening to argument rejected the Indianapolis law as unconstitutional under the 1st Amendment.

So, to change the metaphor, it really comes down to what is one man's or woman's meat is another's poison. Hopefully, if you read these reviews (many people tell me they make great bathroom reading) you may discover that watching sexvids can become an amusing change of pace from regular films. In the process, you will become an explorer yourself. It's not all wasteland. I'm sure you'll find a few adult films that appeal to you, and I'll wager that in the long run you'll prefer films that express (however remotely) sexual wonder and the amazement of all of us as sexual creatures.

And unlike Hollywood stars, sexvid actors and actresses are really a kind of repertory company who appear over and over again in different films and occasionally get a film and story built around them that reveals that they can act as well as copulate. When that happens you'll discover that you are suddenly more interested in them as human beings. And you may wonder why practically all the top male porno stars (John Leslie, Jamie Gillis, R. Bolla, Paul Thomas, Richard Pacheco, Harry Reems, Herschel Savage) are Jewish and why only two women, Annie Sprinkles and Joan Robbins, that I know of, are Jewish. Perhaps one answer is that Jewish men really enjoy women as persons as well as sexual creatures and have not been brought up with Christian guilt about human sexuality.

And I'm sure of one thing: If you watch many sexvids you'll gradually discover that there are certain men and women you enjoy and prefer as physically and emotionally naked people. Thus you will take one step toward fulfilling the philosopher's rule for greater understanding: Know thyself!

Classics

ADULT 45, VOLUME 1
CC NN BI
1985 DREAMLAND VIDEO

P/D—Jerry Ross
F/A—See Below

Here's a 60-minute AMV (adult movie video) produced in MTV style. While MTV walks a sexual razor's edge, AMV goes all the way. Most of the sequences are cuts from various Jerry Ross films and are identified at the end. With MTV-style cutting and editing, and with sex scenes played against provocative, original rock music, the sexmaking takes on a totally different, ballet-style dimension. The songs, with vocals, like "Dirty Talk," "Sparks," "Bad Bad Girl," "I Can't Give It Up," "Lolita," and "Wave Length," are as good as any current Top-40 stuff. The fast-moving scenes offer Annette Haven and Herschel Savage, Kimberly Carson and John Leslie, Ginger Lynn and Tom Byron, Susan Hart, Bunny Bleu and Jamie Gillis, and Diane Holt with John Leslie.

ADVENTURE IN SAN FENLEU
CC NN BI
1985 CABALLERO

P/D—Jose Benzaref
F/A—Sophie Garnier
F/A—Richard Alba

The CC rating is for the story that might have been. But this European-made film is too confusingly told and may have been cut to 60 minutes for American consumption. It takes place in a resort hotel on the Costa del Sol, a favorite location for Jose Benzaref (see review of *The Whore's Port*). Two married couples on vacation meet in the dining room, and it's quickly apparent that one wife, Maria, is not very sexually active with her husband, Don. The other wife, Sophie, is sure that her husband, Pierre, is having an affair. He is! He's screwing a hotel maid. Seems that some of Don's business activities are close to the hotel, and soon Maria is propositioning Pierre to come to their room. Later, Don gives Sophie her first extramarital adventure. Don is finally subsidizing Pierre to remain on vacation (Pierre, who is short of cash, promises to pay him back in Paris). But then, after some discussion, instead of carrying on separate affairs (the guys don't know their wives have already switched), they adjourn to one hotel room where the wives, giggling and a little embarrassed, watch each other suck the other spouse's cock.

ADVENTURES OF RICK QUICK, PRIVATE DICK
CC NN NM NL NR BI DK
1984 CABALLERO

P/D—Herbert von Eggenburg, Kristin Leavenworth
F/A—Bunny Bleu, Helga Sven, Beverly Bliss, Topaz
F/A—R. Bolla, Steve Powers, Rick Cassidy

At last R. Bolla has been given a starring role, and he proves that he is a great comic actor. As Gary Kendall, he's a starving writer who still manages to live high off the hog in a home in Los Angeles on a canal where he can go rowing for exercise. Waving at her from his boat he meets Julie (Beverly Bliss), an artist who has just moved to California from Minnesota so that she can really experience life. Gary gives her the impression that he's a novelist, but actually he's so hard up he's doing porno scripts for a female producer, R.V. (Helga Sven), whose name is Regina Vagina. On a deadline to produce a script, he invents the character Rick Quick and is so entranced with him that he actually becomes Rick and shares all his fictional screwing adventures while at the same time he's happily seducing Julie and taking care of Suzie (Bunny Bleu), his answering-service gal. Julie, who is painting and sculpting, wants to model his prick on a nude male statue she has partially completed. He finally convinces her that she must hold it to keep it erect. She falls in love with him but arrives one morning to find him in the sack with Suzie. At the same time she learns that his so-called novel is nothing but a "filthy porno script."

As his alter ego, Rick Quick, poor Gary is so busy screwing his heroines and keeping out of trouble with gangsters that he doesn't know whether he's coming (pun intended) or going. This is a clever screenplay with amusing dialogue, and Bolla and his ladies are fun to watch.

AFAA (Adult Film Association)

EIGHTH ANNUAL AWARD SHOW
CC NN BI
1984 ESSEX

P/D—Jack Genero
F/A—See below

You may not want to own this tape, but if you're interested in adult films and adult-film makers you'll want to rent it. It runs more than an hour and a half, and is pretty much the complete show (price: $85 a person) that was put on at the famous Coconut Grove on Wilshire Boulevard in Los Angeles on March 14, 1984. The Erotic Film Awards, complete with statuettes of a nude lady holding a spear, are patterned after the Oscars. David Friedman was the genial master of ceremonies, and other behind-the-scenes people you will see are: Ron Sullivan (Henri Pachard), director of many adult films; Sidney Neikerk, president of Cal-Vista, one of the major distributors; and Jimmy Johnson, president of the Pussycat chain of adult theaters. The show consists of Las Vegas–style topless dancers (not porno stars), a stand-up comedian, and the showing of film clips from the five films nominated in each category. Before you are finished, you will know the faces (and genitals, if you can distinguish them) of 50 or more porno actors. *The Devil in Miss Jones, Part II* won best-picture and best-director awards for Henri Pachard; the best-actress award went to Kelly Nichols for *In Love;* best actor, Paul Thomas for *Virginia;* best supporting actress, Kay Parker for *Sweet Young Foxes;* best supporting actor, Ron Jeremy for *Suzie Superstar;* best-screenplay, Rick Marx and Chuck Vincent for *In Love;* best-cinematography, Rahn Vicker for *Virginia;* best original

song, "If I Love You Tonight," from *Suzie Superstar;* best erotic scene, *Virginia.* Check the Index for reviews of the various winners.

ALEXANDRA
CC NN BI (unwilling)
1983 VCA

P/D—E. Clayton, Daniel Walker, Dave Friedman, Robert Freeman
F/A—Eve Sternberg, Lauren Wilde, Joanna Storm, Ashley Summer
F/A—Eric Edwards, Red Wilson, R. Bolla, Michael Gaunt, Steve Douglas

Alexandra, who is on her way to Rome, knows all about Diane (Joanna Storm), who made a porno movie before she became an airline hostess and landed wealthy Cliff Ballard (Steve Douglas). She also knows that Jennifer (Lauren Wilde), married multimillionaire Foster Holloway (R. Bolla), owner of a huge chain of stereo stores, is screwing around with a younger guy—even though Foster has legally parted with half his estate to convince Jennifer to marry him. And she knows that Patricia (Ashley Summer), who is married to an impoverished writer, Martin (Eric Edwards), has capitulated to her weirdo boss, Jason Starrett (Michael Gaunt), and thus has become a vice-president in the ad agency he controls. Early on, you see Alexandra in a rear view, fully dressed, in a flashback that does not reveal her face and you learn that she has also been to bed with all the guys mentioned above. But now, as Jennifer and Diane are going shopping prior to a party at Jason's to which they have all been invited, Alexandra calls them on Foster's limousine telephone and coolly tells the ladies that tonight at the party all their little extramarital and premarital secrets will be revealed. All the acting in this one is good, the dialogue is amusing, and Ashley Summer (a.k.a. Rachel Ashley) is especially effective as a woman who is not happy with her double life and tries to avoid sleeping with her husband after an afternoon with her boss. Rachel/Ashley also appears in *Every Woman Has a Fantasy.* As for Alexandra, you never do see her face, and to all the ladies' relief, she gets caught in the trap she sets.

ALL-AMERICAN GIRLS IN HEAT, PART II
CC NN NR BI
1984   CABALLERO

P/D—Bob Bouchard, Bill Eagle
F/A—Shauna Grant, Shelley Rey, Laurie Smith, Rose Linda Kimball, Karen Summer, Misty Regan
F/A—Blake Palmer, Tom Byron, Ron Jeremy, Ken Starbuck, Paul Thomas

These are not the same *All-American Girls* who appeared in the first film (see review), and this time they tell their stories of the "juiciest, sexiest thing that has happened to [them] in the past year." There are six of them aboard a multimillion-dollar yacht, and the best story wins the prize, Tom Byron. Byron has the face and body of a naive teenager, and the ladies can't wait to get their hands and mouths on him. As for the stories, two of the girls tell about their bus trip through Texas on the way to Los Angeles and how they took on the driver, Ron Jeremy, and two horny guys at a gas stop. Then one gal wearing a wedding gown tells how she was picked up by a Smokey-and-the-Bandit type who was being chased by Sheriff Buford Butterworth. Eventually he was rescued from the law by a friend in an army tank who demolished the sheriff's car, but not until his new-found girlfriend was happily screwed, too. The CC rating is for the Shauna Grant episodes, which are appropriately romantic, and for the scenery (supposedly the film was shot in Tahiti, Bora-Bora, and Hawaii), especially the breathtaking sequence shot on a deserted beach with the surf providing a perfect accompaniment to the sexmaking. Shauna (as Laura) appears in a romantic sequence in a hayloft at her aunt's home in Dublin, where she is vacationing, and Paul Thomas is her poetic Irish lover. The film concludes with another lush scene as her real lover, Fred (Blake Palmer), the guy she wants to marry, lands in a helicopter on a lonely beach with tropical forest, cliffs, and a waterfall background and they make de-

licious love together. Most women will enjoy these parts.

AMATEUR PRODUCTIONS, VOLUMES 2, 3, 4, AND 5
CC NN BI DK
1984   BAKER VIDEO

Like Susan's Video (see reviews) Baker Video advertises in various video magazines and offers tapes of average Americans who can't resist videotaping their sexmaking. If you are interested, Baker will probably arrange to buy your tapes or will sell you tapes from their collection. Apparently, making private sex tapes is becoming a favorite pastime of many Americans. There are many more tapes in the Baker collection (see their entry in the address listings). Volumes 3 and 4 are one 60-minute tape that includes a husband and his wife (my guess). She's sucking her husband's cock while he wears tinted glasses. The camera is in a fixed focus, as is true of most homemade sex videos. Camera placement and changing position, of course, make the results more interesting (see the chapter on making your own sexvids). The second segment in this first 70-minute series has a changing focus, with close-ups, and you quickly realize that a third party is operating the camera. It turns out that it's another couple, and in an amusing sequence one husband gets in bed with two women, one of whom sucks his cock while the other watches, laughing, but won't put her mouth on it. Nevertheless, she gives it an occasional shake. Then the cameraman takes his place on the bed, and the proper lady sucks her husband's cock while the other laughs and helps her along by tickling his balls. Volume 5, which is a 60-minute tape, offers something you are never likely to see on commercial sexvids. First, you watch three ladies, each weighing somewhere between 160 and 180 pounds, playing together on a living-room floor while a male records them happily kissing and lapping each other. This one should have been titled "Weight Watchers," because the guys who finally appear are as plump as the horny ladies.

Another sexvid on Volume 5 is amusing because it likewise involves a couple of pudgies. A buxom wife, wearing a garter belt, invites a passing guy in for coffee. He asks her where her husband is, and she tells him, "He's gone to work, but I know how to take care of what you got in your pants." "Nice looking pussy," he comments when she spreads her fat thighs for him on the breakfast table. You soon realize that they are really husband and wife and obviously made this little story for a laugh. For other Baker tapes, see reviews of *Secret Dreams* and *Night Times*.

AMERICAN BABYLON
CC NN NM BI
1984   VCA

P/D—**Richard Mahler**
F/A—**Tish Ambrose, Taija Rae, Chelsea Blake, Lonnie Lee, Bobby Astyr, Michael Gaunt**

When you're beginning to think that porn-film producers have no imagination, try a Richard Mahler film (see reviews of *Corruption* and *Midnight Heat*). Mahler gives everyday reality a surrealist touch, which will keep you watching and wondering what is happening and what is going to happen next. What's more, he proves that the key to a good adult film is a small cast of good actors. Tom and Mary (Michael Gaunt and Chelsea Blake) live somewhere in Connecticut, next door to Robert and Joan (Bobby Astyr and Tish Ambrose). Neither husband is paying much attention to his wife. Mary does aerobics and leaves milk and a sandwich for Tom when he comes home from work, and a note that tells him, strangely, "I'll see you after a time." Robert, who is totally devoted to his hobby of collecting and watching porno movies, invites Tom over to watch one with him. He ignores Joan, who stands behind the projector for a moment watching in disgust and tentatively exploring her own neglected crotch. She tries to divert him, but he pushes her away. "I wish you wouldn't do that. . . . Evaporate," he tells her. When Tom arrives, he show a film in which Taija Rae, wearing a flame protector, has sex doggie style with a guy likewise masked and

carrying a huge lighted blowtorch in one hand. To Robert, who watches his films dressed in an army camouflage suit, there is a "joy in watching which requires no formal commitment. I've turned it into a way of life, Tom," he tells him. "It's my salvation. I watch, oh God, how I watch." Back home in bed after some perfunctory sex, Tom and Mary are awakened by a phone call. Tom takes it and is shocked to find it is Joan telling him to meet her tomorrow at a local restaurant. Mary doesn't know who the caller is, and from that point on in spite of himself Tom is involved with Joan. Tish Ambrose now proves that she's a top actress. (See also *Corporate Assets*.) With a mole over her left breast and a soft, pitiful, but erotic expression on her big face, a little overweight, she is the perfect neglected wife. Unknown to Mary, who one day, frustrated herself, takes a rifle and shoots out the TV, Tom is involved with both Joan and Robert, who continues to show him porn movies and philosophize about menopausal males in bondage—which finally becomes a reprise for this fascinating sexvid. To top it off, Bobby Astyr never has sex with anyone!

THE ANALYST
CC NN BI DK
1975   IVP (formerly CVX)

P/D—**Gerald Graystone**
F/A—**Candida Royalle, Angela Tufts, Jocelyn Martin**
F/A—**Tyler Reynolds, Paul Scharff**

Anita (Candida Royalle) is married to Preston (Tyler Reynolds), who always wants to fuck but scarcely listens when she complains that he "should be more gentle." And she most certainly doesn't want anal sex with him. Anita talks to her best girl-friend, who doesn't understand because she enjoys cock in all three orifices. She sends Anita to a male analyst, who has a female assistant. Before it's over the analyst makes Anita an "analist," and they enjoy some group sex that even includes the husband, who is now a happy patient. Ten years later, directors like the Dark brothers and Hal Freeman are producing one anal-sex film after another. All of them assume that women enjoy "being caught from behind." (And, of course gays presumably enjoy it.) But in the heterosexual films, the guys never expose their own ass to ladies or dildoes if they can help it. Why are women expected to enjoy it so much? One well known porno actor, who's writing his autobiography, wrote me that he was seriously considering giving up making sexvids because he was afraid of contracting AIDS. But AIDS or not, anal sex, if you believe adult film makers, is what their audiences want to see. (See notes under *Pleasure Bed.*)

ANGEL ABOVE, DEVIL BELOW
CC   NN   NM   NL   DS
1975   CAL VISTA

P/D—Not given
F/A—Brittanny Lane, Mindy Brandt, Starlyn Simone
F/A—Robert Bedford, Lamar Gilbert

Probably produced before *The Devil in Miss Jones* and *Pussy Talk* (see reviews), this is an adult-film classic that you shouldn't miss. It's very funny and cleverly photographed, and you've never seen any of the actors or actresses before or since. Randy and her mother live in a New England–style home somewhere in suburbia. Mama, who is only in her late 30s, is happy to screw with the handyman who does carpentry work for her. Randy hears them screwing while she's in bed reading an ancient book about devil worship. She moans in Latin, calling up the devil, and sure enough, he arrives, a horrible-looking creature who caresses her naked body, after which he disappears inside her cunt. It's the devil's new home, and what's more, he talks through her pussy, using vile language. He growls through Randy's labia at George, her mother's boyfriend: "Randy wants you!" George can't resist, but to Randy's shock, when George practically rapes her, the devil bites his prick, and she shoves him head over heels down the stairs. A doctor is called, and when he examines Randy's pussy, the devil moans, "Eat me, you son of a bitch." He nearly dies in the process.

Finally a guy arrives who falls in love with Randy, and it's a war between him and the devil in her pussy. The nice guy finally fucks the devil to death, and he and Randy live happily ever after. All this is interspersed with some very funny sequences, including one in which Mama screws a local politician and smokes his cigar while he takes her doggie style, and another one when Randy's pussy is gagged with adhesives to shut the devil's mouth.

ANGELA, THE FIREWORKS WOMAN
CC   NN   NM   BI   DS   DK
1975   VCA

P/D—Carmen Rodriguez, Abe Snake
F/A—Sara Nicholson, Helen Madigan, Erica Eaton
F/A—Eric Edwards, Ellis Deigh, Lefty Cooper

Put this one in your top-50 list. Just when I'm about to cry uncle and say I'll never watch another yucky-sucky again, I discover one like this that restores my faith. Surprisingly, many good sexvids were made in the 1970s, when there seemed to be a greater interest in developing an integrated story line and in exploring believable sexual problems. This one was shot somewhere near Mystic, Connecticut, with excellent cinematography. It's the story of Angela (Sara Nicholson) and her brother Peter (Eric Edwards) growing up together in a picturesque New England town. They are totally in love with each other until Peter decides that they are being very immoral. He finally leaves her to become a Catholic priest. Years later, he returns to the town as an ordained priest at the local cathedral. Angela has never loved anyone else, and she still can't understand why he rejects her. He convinces her to seek work with a wealthy woman parishioner. But he doesn't know that the woman has a sadistic lover who decides to brutally train Angela in what he thinks is the art of being a woman. Escaping from them, Angela runs to her sailboat. Far offshore she anchors. There is no food. After drinking the whiskey aboard she falls overboard and is rescued by a couple who get her involved in a threesome. Later, inadvertently attracting the attention of two local fishermen, she is brutally raped in an ice house by one of them. You may not accept the way Angela finally convinces Peter, on the Fourth of July, that he should abandon the priesthood and live with her, but you'll watch this one again. It's the only adult film I have seen that dares to tackle sex and religion.

ANGEL ON FIRE
CC NN NM BI
1979 ESSEX

P/D—Roberta Findley
F/A—Darby Lloyd Raines, Jennifer Jordan, Judy Craven
F/A—Jamie Gillis, Mark Stevens, Eric Edwards

You can bring this one home to your wife or girlfriend and she'll cheer Roberta Findley, who wrote the story as well as directed it. It begins in bed. After some detached screwing by an undignified guy and his girlfriend, she asks him, "Why can't we get married? I love you." He tells her to forget this marriage crap. Crying, she tells him, "You have to marry me. I'm pregnant." "You stupid cunt!" he yells at her. "You've been lying to me. You stopped taking the pill." He slugs her and tells her to get out of his house and that she can raise the bastard herself. A few minutes later, still pissed off, he's crossing the street and is struck by a van. Dead, he arrives in heaven, where Angel #9 tells him he must do penance. He must either go back to earth as a woman and have his heart broken by some male or go to hell. "You must be kidding. I'd rather be dead than be a woman," he replies. But he has no choice. Back on earth he's Stephanie (Darby Lloyd Raines). Roberta Findley gets her vengeance on males by making Steve very much aware that now he's in a woman's body. Steve as Stephanie loves his breasts and pussy and is totally charmed with his new body. So is Jeff (Jamie Gillis) when Stephanie takes a job with him as a model. First, Jeff makes beautiful, romantic love with her as they listen to the "Aranuez Concerto." But pretty soon he

tells her that he doesn't want to be tied down, and when she's too persistent he tells her that she's a stupid bitch. "You can suck my cock occasionally, but stay out of my life." The film ends in a neat reprise of the beginning, with Stephanie telling Jeff she's pregnant and Jeff beating her. "I can't take it any longer," Stephanie moans. "The pain of being a woman is too severe." Up in heaven, Steve is forgiven. He's done his penance. Angel #9 rewards him on a fleecy cloud. If you wonder where Eric Edwards was during all this, he was Angel #10, enjoying himself with other angels.

THE ANIMAL IN ME
CC NN BI NR
1985 STANDARD VIDEO

P/D—Helen Terrie, Kirdy Stevens
F/A—Colleen Brennan, Karen Summer, Gina Valentino, Heather Wayne
F/A—Greg Ruffner, Jerry Butler, Tom Byron, Peter North, Eugene Scott

In this one, Pepper (Karen Summer), a young nurse, is the daughter of Maggie (Colleen Brennan), who writes romantic fiction for women that is published by her divorced husband, a wealthy publisher. Mama Maggie is a sexpot who has a very crude lover, Travis (Greg Ruffner). But Pepper detests Travis and is constantly avoiding him. Mama Maggie agrees with her ex-husband that she could do better than Travis. "But he appeals to the animal in me." Maggie can't help herself. She has the hots for any willing young man, including Dr. Jerry Morgan (Jerry Butler), who is having a very romantic affair with Pepper. But she has made it apparent to him that she's a one-to-one person who doesn't screw around. Alas, after coming home from a dinner date with her father, Pepper thinks she hears Mama in the bedroom with Travis. But Travis appears and tells her the truth: Maggie has seduced Pepper's lover, Dr. Morgan. Grimly, Pepper decides to hell with the monogamous life and takes on Travis. It would be interesting to know the age difference between Karen Summer and Colleen Brennan. Sometimes Karen looks about 20 and

Colleen about 38, making the mother-daughter relationship believable, but sometimes Karen, in close-ups, looks like an old hooker.

APHRODESIA'S DIARY
CC NN NR BI
1984 CABALLERO

P/D—Serge Lincoln, Gerald Kikoine
F/A—Arlene Manhattan, Joanna Storm,
 Lisa Cintrice, Marianne Flower
F/A—Kevin James, Ron Jeremy

Arlene Manhattan, a beautiful natural blonde, is either French or has mastered a French accent. In the film, her name is Adrienne, not Aphrodesia. The title must have been added later as more euphonic. Adrienne tells her story, which begins on a farm in France, where she learned "at a very young age that [she] could excite men." She leaves Alan, her first lover, to go to Paris to earn a living, and she is quickly picked up by a French porn producer who will pay her $500 for a day's work. She doesn't actually perform, and her face, as she watches others, reveals her disapproval. She's paid with an airplane ticket to New York, where, the director assures her, she can make a good living. Walking the streets of New York, she encounters a happy-go-lucky con man named Jeff (Kevin James), who is trying to raise money with a fast-playing card shuffle called "monte." She wins, but he has something else in mind for her. Supposedly, he is a playwright who needs some big financing. He takes her to his loft, where Adrienne takes a shower and carefully douches before making love to him. Adrienne falls in love with him and agrees to try to help him raise the necessary money to launch his play. He makes beautiful, romantic love to her, but it slowly develops that he has another girlfriend, Susie, and that he is obviously using Adrienne. When she returns after one assignment, he has disappeared. Sad, she goes home to Paris, where Alan finds her. She eventually becomes very wealthy by writing and publishing romantic, sensuous stories and is happily married to Alan. Women will empathize with Arlene, who has a very expressive face. The acting and dialogue are good, with the exception of an extended bi scene with Vanessa Del Rio, which is totally out of character for Adrienne/Arlene/Aphrodesia.

APHRODITE
CC NN BI DK
1982 VESTRON

P/D—Adolphe Viezzi, Jean Aroy, Robert Guest
F/A—Valerie Kaprisky, Catherine Jourdan,
 Capucine, Delia Boccard
F/A—Horst Bucholz, Yves Massard, Paolo Baroni

There are many films with an R rating or no rating, like this one, that never make the big theater circuit. Called "art films," they aren't designed for the teenage market and they often dare to play on the edge of explicit sex, with well-known actors stripping down to essentials (see review of *Your Ticket Is No Longer Valid*). You'll enjoy this film more if you're familiar with Pierre Louy's famous short novel *Aphrodite*. It's the story of Chrysis and Demetrios and their tempestuous love. Harry (Horst Bucholz), a wealthy armament maker, proposes to a group that he has invited on an Aegean cruise on his yacht that they reenact the novel using an entire Greek island to celebrate the reincarnation of Aphrodite, who the ancients believed returned twice in each century. The year is 1914. The period clothing gives way to Greek costumes and a splendid orgy. Valerie Kaprisky, who played opposite Richard Gere in the American film *Breathless*, plays the part of Chrysis. I doubt if this version could ever get an R rating, but it is superior X.

AROUND THE WORLD WITH JOHNNY WADD
CC NN
1975 VCX

P/D—Donald U. Cunard and six others
F/A—John C. Holmes. Ladies not identified

The CC rating is because, as Johnny says: "I'm one of the wonders of the world. I have the biggest cock in the world, and

I've been using it since I was seven years old. It's been inside 10,000 women at least, and none of them have been dissatisfied." Thus begins an odyssey that takes him from his home in San Francisco to Las Vegas, New York, London, Paris, and Rome. You get fleeting glimpses of these cities and detailed close-ups of the 10 women he encounters, who discuss the miracle of his cock in hushed tones, when they aren't actually bubbling over it. "My cock is a responsibility," he tells the viewer. "I must use it. Fortunately, I can fuck four or five hours a day, but I'm still looking for that special woman who can make my cock disappear in her mouth, cunt, and ass." J.C. doesn't find her on this trip, but his continuous voice-over discussion of his schlong and the admiration of the women who enjoy it may give less-endowed guys an inferiority complex.

THE ARRANGEMENT
CC NN NM BI DK
1984   CAL VISTA

P/D—Steven Anderson, Sid Holland
F/A—Marilyn Jess, Ann Hoover, Jean Baker, Chris Kennedy
F/A—Jean Pierre, Randy Damon

You can ignore the credits, which I'm sure do not list the true names of the French stars who appear in this film. It was made in France and has pretty good dubbing. The hero is an architect named Paul Pasquier. Paul has a very sophisticated teenage daughter and a maid whom it looks as if Paul is going to marry. But Lisa, the daughter, vows that she'll never let her daddy marry that woman. She contrives an elaborate scenario in which Daddy is seduced either by her or her look-alike girlfriend at an orgy that she arranges at her boyfriend's family's mansion (they're away on holiday). The film finally ends with Paul not knowing whether he's screwed his daughter or her look-alike friend. For diversion, in the "things-you've-never-seen-before" department, Christine, the maid, masturbates with a vacuum-cleaner hose. Later she sucks up Paul's prick in it in a laughing scene on the bedroom floor.

BABYLON BLUE
CC NN NL NR DK
1983   VIDEO-X-PIX

P/D—Michel De Jou, Jackson St. Louis
F/A—Bridgette Monet, Tish Ambrose, Sharon Kane, Jacqueline Lorians, Joanna Storm
F/A—Joey Silvera, David Cannon, Michael Gaunt, Alex Adrian

Martin (Joey Silvera) has just been released from a six-month prison term for being a high-class gigolo. Missie (Sharon Kane), an expensive call girl with her own stable of ladies, is waiting to pick him up in her limousine. She has started a new business, a house of pleasure in an apartment on the Upper East Side of New York where she offers the opportunity to satisfy any fantasy. Prices can run up to $1,000 for a trick. But Martin isn't too happy with the business and especially with crazy married women like Mrs. Baker (Jacqueline Lorians), who wants to be fucked while her ass is suspended in the air. Missie also has hired Cheryl (Bridgette Monet) and Jack (David Cannon) to work in her establishment, along with several other ladies, including Joanna Storm. Martin continues to tell Missie that he's fed up with the racket, and to her horror Cheryl and Jack (who presumably turn tricks also, but you never see them in action except with each other) have fallen in love. (In real life they are Mr. and Mrs. Cannon). "Let's call it quits together," Martin tells Missie. "What will we do?" "Make love like normal people," Martin replies as they finally walk arm in arm out of the park. Joey Silvera and Sharon Kane are a good comedy team who can maintain a verbal fight to the finish but then make up quite naturally.

BANG, BANG, YOU'VE GOT IT!
CC NM NL BI DK
1975   QUALITY/VIDEO-X-PIX

P/D—Chuck Vincent
F/A—C. J. Laing, Misty Grey, Jennifer Jordan, Marlene Willoughby, Annie Sprinkles
F/A—Jeffrey Hurst, Jaime Blume, David Savage, Wade Nichols, John Christopher

Remember "Laugh In" on TV? Here's an explicit-sex version created by Chuck Vincent that you shouldn't miss. The sex comedies change so fast and there are so many that I can give you only an inkling of them. It begins with C. J. Laing being telephoned by Jeffrey Hurst, who tells her that he's so horny that he's playing with himself. And so is she, she tells him, because she misses him so much. Soon they are telling each other over the phone how nice their genitals feel to each other. C. J. finally reaches a climax and sighs, "That really was nice, Freddie." But that isn't his name. He's got the wrong number. Next Jennifer Jordan, à la Julia Child, is preparing a dish called "the Bulgarian blow job," during which a nude guy is prepared for eating. This is followed by a fast cut to a woman smoking Vagina Slims (which she demonstrates). Next is a medical-advice segment, during which a doctor answers sexual questions: "Is it harmful to masturbate with my electric toothbrush?" "Okay, but not in the bathtub!" Then Jeffrey Hurst reads from Mother Goose such stories as "Goldilocks and the Three Dykes" and "Little Red Riding Hood," with C. J. Laing playing the girl and Wade Nichols the wolf. There's a classic soap-opera segment with a woman arriving at her psychiatrist's office and going into very funny detail of how she became frigid. The psychiatrist is screwing her, but she pays no attention to him. There's a show "What the Fuck Do You Do?" (remember "What's My Line?"), in which a panel guesses Annie Sprinkles's line. This only skims the surface of this mad sexual slalom, which will keep you laughing—either happily or in shock.

BARE ELEGANCE
CC NN NM DK
1984 MASTERPIECE

P/D—Jerome Bronson, John Stagliano
A/F—Crystal Breeze, Elaine Sutherland, Karen Summer, Dorothy Onan, Rikki Blake
F/A—R. Bolla, Billy Dee, Francois Papillon

I've given this one a CC rating for perversity. You can underline the DK rating and then some. It begins with Jana (Crystal Breeze), who wants to be an actress, picking up a couple of guys, telling them her name is Chastity and screwing them on a San Francisco hilltop without even asking them their names. Then it cuts to the affluent home of Ellis Howard (R. Bolla), who was a film producer but quit because none of his films "expressed his soul." The guys invite Chastity to meet Ellis, who tells Jana, "I hear that you're quite a slut.... Your ass, dear lady, is all that is needed to meet my approval." (Ellis inspects all his ingenues doggie style with their behinds in the air). Jana wants to be alone with Ellis and convince him that she can act and that with her he can once again make a great movie. But Ellis avoids her. Seems that, among other things, he's a masochist who has regular appointments with a dominatrix who makes him crawl around on his hands and knees. To get rid of Jana, Ellis sends her to Francois, an acting teacher who tells her, "Bend over and drop your drawers." Then he connects her and three other aspiring actresses with dildos. "Acting begins here," he smugly assures them. Eventually it turns out that Jana has something in common with Ellis. She has pain-and-pleasure dreams from which she wakes up screaming. Encountering him, finally, at an extended poolside orgy at his house, she finally woos him away to his bedroom and they make joyous love and presumably will become "normal" people once again.

BATTLE OF THE STARS
CC NN BI DK
1985 NOW SHOWING

P/D—Lawrence T. Cole
F/A—Traci Lords, Christy Canyon, Mal Lin, Nina Hartley
F/A—Peter North, Billy Dee, Mike Horner, Steve Drake

Battle isn't quite the right word for this tape. In sharp, clear color, it's a 90-minute contest to determine whether Traci or Christy is the best sex companion. After watching, the viewer (presumably male) can vote for the winner by sending his choice to *Adult Video News, Cheri,* or *Spectator,* whose addresses are given. There's no enmity between Traci and Christy. Neither has any doubts as to her sexual superiority. Cole provides continuous facial, genital, anal, and breast close-ups, as well as very erotic dialogue. Traci likes to tease men, and Christy likes to play with them and watch them get horny. Traci likes guys to come all over her and rub her while she's getting fucked, to pull a guy's hair, and to dig her fingers into his ass. Christy loves to lap them. Essentially, this could be a sex-education film for women. But the average woman will probably hate it and not want to enter into competition with such uninhibited ladies. Unlike *Playboy* or *Penthouse* mannequins, Traci and Christy are real, live dream competition who know all the tricks. If any man can watch this one without getting a tingle in his dingle, he's too old to dream anymore!

BATTLE OF THE STARS, ROUND 2: EAST VS. WEST
CC   NN   NM   BI   DK
1985   NOW SHOWING

P/D—Lawrence T. Cole
F/A—Kristara Barrington, Heather Wayne, Nina Hartley, Gaye Sterling
F/A—Tom Byron, Jesse Adams, Don Fernandez, Jonathan Younger

Using the same sexy, talky, fucky format with many facial and genital close-ups, Cole now gives you two more ladies, Kristara (a.k.a. China Lee) and Heather. An additional feature of this one is Tom Byron, who discusses the sexual attributes of both women and tells you intimate things about them. Unlike Traci and Christy, who are better actresses, these girls don't provide imitations of various male actors, like Jamie Gillis and John Holmes, making love to them, or of Ginger Lynn climaxing. But in one sequence Heather comes through quite believably when she giggles and refuses to do some of the things that Cole, off camera, asks her to do. Obviously, Cole has only scratched the surface of this kind of tape. He should make one for the ladies.

BEHIND THE SCENES OF AN ADULT MOVIE
CC   NN   NL
1981   CAL VISTA

P/D—Sam Norvell, Joe Sherman
F/A—Samantha Fox, Veronica Hart, Danielle, Jesie St. James, Georgina Spelvin, and others
F/A—Ron Jeremy, Herschel Savage, John Leslie, Joey Civera, and many others

About 50 percent of this one consists of cuts from other Cal-Vista movies interspersed with some interesting conversation with Veronica Hart, Samantha Fox, Ron Jeremy, and a few other people who go into detail about how they got into the adult-film business; their reaction to their work; its effect on their sexual relationships offscreen (enhanced and improved for some of them because now they are no longer acting); female reaction to bisexuality (positive between Samantha and Veronica); the problems of the male getting a hard-on while being watched by the film crew; and female reaction to men with big cocks. Veronica, who is married and had her second child in 1985, tells Ron that she wouldn't want him for a boyfriend. He's too big. But Samantha can't make it with men with little weenies. As for the actual making of an adult movie, most of the time is spent showing scenes from *Expose Me Now* (see review) and what actually occurred when this film was being made.

BETWEEN LOVERS
CC   NN   NR   NL
1983   CABALLERO

P/D—Marga Aulbach, Henri Pachard
F/A—Jesie St. James, Georgina Spelvin, Mai Lin
F/A—John Leslie, Joey Silvera

Henri Pachard produces better films when he works with a woman (see review of *Public Affairs*). You can be sure of it—most women will be delighted with this one! Bradley (John Leslie), a wealthy lawyer, is married to Maggie (Jesie St. James), who is gaining some success in a new business, Maggie's Fashions. She has an office in San Francisco, where she lives, and one in Santa Monica, to which she commutes quite frequently. Returning from a trip to Santa Monica, she's shocked to find Brad in their bed with Mai Lin. He tries to grin his way out of it and assures her that it won't happen again, but she angrily dumps the drink he hands her over his head and goes back to Santa Monica, where, very lonely, she meets Dexter (Joey Silvera) in the Lone Star Bar. Although she has not left Bradley permanently, she hasn't forgiven him, and she keeps seeing Dexter. She tells Carol (Georgina Spelvin), her partner in her fashion business, that she loves them both. Carol tells her, "It's illegal for a woman to have two husbands at the same time." But Maggie figures she can work it out, and she agrees to marry Dexter. Now she has a husband in each city, and it works for a while. But unknown to her, Brad, trying to find out what is going on, flies down to Santa Monica when he's supposed to have gone to Seattle, and soon he meets Dexter in the same bar. Neither know that they love the same woman, and there's a very funny scene where they are both talking to her on the telephone from Dexter's apartment and only she knows that they have met. The ending will surprise you. The guys never share Maggie together, as would happen in most adult movies. Instead, Brad promises to be a model of virtue and Maggie agrees that her revenge, marrying Dexter, was overreacting.

BETWEEN THE CHEEKS
**CC   NN   DK   NL (but only if you are
anally oriented)**
1985   ESSEX

P/D—**Walter Dark, Gregory Dark**
F/A—**Ginger Lynn, Treanna, Gina Valentino, Lori
Smith, Sheri St. Clair, Summer Rose**
F/A—**Jack Baker, Steve Powers, Mark Wallice,
Tom Byron**

I've given this one a CC rating only because it's a classic in anal-sex video, which was the big seller on cassettes in 1985. If you're not into anal sex, you'd better skip it. All the ladies listed above are penetrated anally (in detailed close-ups) by the cocks of the guys (and in many cases two or three preparatory fingers), and a few of the guys enjoy rimming.

The connection between the sequences involves a group of morons who are being taught the joys of anal sex by a black dude. You watch re-creations of their own experiences. The ladies listed above don't seem to object to where the guy's cocks have been, and they lap them enthusiastically between insertions.

THE BITE
CC   NN   NM   BI   DK
1980   ESSEX

P/D—**Jerry Denby**
F/A—**Jennifer Jordan and other, unidentified
ladies**
F/A—**Hardy Harrison, Eric Edwards, Alan Marlo,
Sonny Landham**

Remember the movie *The Sting* with Robert Redford and Paul Newman? Here's one about a sex con man. There's the Toledo Kid, a.k.a. Reggie Kinkaid (Eric Edwards), who sells shares of stock in a non-existent company to Francis E. Dobbs (Hardy Harrison), an upright Toledo, Ohio, banker with a drive for larceny and a fast buck. Then there's Johnny Memphis (Alan Marlo), who arrives in town with Sweet Kate (Jennifer Jordan), whose father was known as the Flim-Flam Man. Now you have the con team, with Jennifer/Sweet Kate supplying practically all the sex in this lighthearted sexvid. The time is the 1930s, and the ambiance is maintained throughout, down to 1930s automobiles and ladies who wear garter belts. In their second scam they create a temporary whorehouse in Toledo. It is filled with rented ornate furnishings, and all the ladies are in the proper 1930s costumes. Nice acting by all, especially Jennifer Jordan.

BLACK ANGELS
CC   NN   NM   BI
1985   VCA

P/D—**James Ranier, David Christopher**
F/A—**Candy Staton, Streeta Taylor, Tash Voux,
Delilah Devie, Edwina Thorne**
F/A—**Ron Jeremy, George Payne, David
Christopher, Johnny Nineteen, Dave Ruby**

The CC rating on this one is not for the story but for the ladies, three black gals and two white, all of whom are totally expert in the art of seductive copulation and fellatio. Tash Voux is a pretty, white, Jewish (my guess) girl who offers her boss, George Payne (he's married, but they've stopped for a quickie on the way home) the most awe-inspiring sexy, leg-splaying, ass-splaying, erection-special strip dance you've ever seen. It would get her top billing in any stripper's contest. After this, she offers her vulva in an acrobatic backstand pose that is a wonderment to behold. Not to be outdone in the nonstop sex, Ron Jeremy (the hero) services two of the black ladies (one is a six-footer) and reveals for white guys, who have never seen black female genitals, every nook and cranny of her nether region. There's also a big, 250-pound black guy (Johnny Nineteen), who has a prick with what looks like a diameter of two inches. His willing white companion can scarcely get it in her open mouth. As for the story about Lennie (who runs a commune near New York City for aspiring actors (mostly actresses), it's just a hook on which to hang the banging.

BLACK ON WHITE
CC NN BI
1975 IVP (formerly CVX)

P/D—Sandra Day
F/A—Cinnamon, Ella Ryme, Lonnie Love
F/A—Charles Breen, Bobby Bang

Jewish Ralph is married to Jewish Martha. They live in all-white suburbia. Black Lil is married to black Sonny. They move in next door. Neither Ralph, who is sure that blacks will destroy the value of their property, nor Sonny (who responds to Ralph's "What is it like to be on welfare?" with "What's it like to be Jewish?") looks as if he could be a good neighbor. But Martha likes Lil and wonders what it would be like to go to bed with a black man. Attuned to each other, they are soon in bed together. But then Sonny walks in and wants to know what the fuck is going on. Nothing that he's adverse to, really! He joins them, and soon Martha has her question answered. The women ar-

range an evening together, and although there's no sex, the guys soon find out that they really like each other. A few days later Ralph sees Lil at a bus stop and gives her a ride home. While he's diddling, she coolly verbalizes what he's thinking: "Let's go fuck." After that they all become such good friends that they happily exchange spouses and become one big, happy family. (See notes under *Pleasure Bed*.)

BLACK THROAT
CC NN NL (maybe) DK
1985 VCA

P/D—Gregory Dark, Walter Dark
F/A—Traci Lords, Erica Boyer, Christy Canyon, Purple Passion, Lady Stephanie
F/A—Jack Baker, Kevin James, Mark Wallice, Peter North, Craig Roberts

For the most part, the Dark brothers don't make tapes for the couples market. Show this one to most women and they won't laugh. But there's another market of guys in fraternities and horny old men in their lodges who will probably watch this in total awe, and may even chuckle at the total insanity of it. Its fast, nonstop cuts from one suck and fuck to another will remind you of MTV, and it comes with its own rock music, with the chorus, "You're gonna see black heads sucking on white heads and white heads sucking on black heads." Not only that, you'll watch very sharp close-ups during the nonstop sex, and wild camera angles and backgrounds. I've given it a CC rating because the whole tape falls into the things-you've-never-seen-done-like-this department. Or you might prefer a 7S rating: "sheer scuzz with sick, sleazy, slick, sophisticated sex." So what's the plot? There isn't any. But it begins with a guy talking to a rubber rat, Mr. Bob, who philosophizes with him and is his confidante. After a wild session with Debbie (Traci Lords), who gives him a workout that would exhaust two guys, he's invited by Roscoe (Jack Baker) to discover Madame Mambo's House of Divine Inspiration Through Fellatio, and soon you are watching oil-slick penetration of both black and white female orifices, with lots of full-screen shots, and Erica Boyer, whose screen name is Double Penetration Slut, proves her ability as she's buggered and screwed simultaneously. There's another workout with Traci Lords that goes on for 10 minutes, and you'll wonder how her vagina survived it. Feminists will watch this one in horror.

BLONDE VELVET
CC NN BI NL DS (plot related)
1976 QUALITY/VIDEO-X-PIX

P/D—Dexter Eagle
F/A—Jennifer Welles, Suzanne McBain, Sharon Mitchell, Alexandria
F/A—R. Bolla, Bobby Astyr, Jake Teague, Roger Caine, David Innis

This is a happily slapstick spy story, with the tongue-in-cheek sex style (pun intended) of many 1970s adult films. The impossible-to-repeat story involves Mark Slade (R. Bolla), who works for the United Nations, and Eva Kovacs (Jennifer Welles), who hates men because "they think with their cocks and fuck all over the world." She's intent on exposing quite a few of them, who are members of the United Nations Security Council. She has video-taped them all screwing her or other women, thus making them security risks. The price for her silence is $5 million put into a Swiss bank. There are some extended sex sequences in a posh indoor swimming pool in New York City and one in which you really believe that Dexter Eagle got inside the U.N. building and filmed a very young Bolla screwing Suzanne McBain in one of the conference rooms. There's also a flashback, in black and white, of Eva trying to escape a Hungarian soldier during the revolution and being raped by him. It's a wild mélange that includes Bobby Astyr as Dr. Weird Love, who is ready to amputate any enemy pricks. It's amusing.

BLUE HEAT
CC NN BI NL DK
1975 IVP (formerly CVX)

P/D—Young Lee
F/A—Anne Hall, Jessie Chandler, Christine Kelly, Chris Cassidy, Dorothy LeMay
F/A—Jim Thornton, Norman Mince, David Blair

This is a down-to-earth film about the making of porno movies in the 1970s, when they were shot on 16-mm film. This one is set in Cleveland, of all places. Somewhere in the background is "the family," who "are calling the shots" on the film and waiting for the final version. One of the producers is staying in a Howard Johnson's motel, where he is serviced by an outcall lady. Chris Cassidy and Dorothy LeMay appeared in many movies in the following five years, but today only Jesie St. James (listed as Jessie Chandler) is still making sexvids. Jessie, in this one, is a runner delivering a 16-mm dubbing tape to a film editor who is trying to add sound to the completed film. He needs sexy sounds to match the action. Jessie finds that she can provide sexier groaning if she is actually doing it while she sighs and moans into a mike. (See notes under *Pleasure Bed.*)

BLUE ICE
CC NN BI DK DS (plot related)
1985 CABALLERO

P/D—Joe Repaso, Phil Marshak
F/A—Jacqueline Lorians, Shanna McCullough, Danielle
F/A—Herschel Savage, Jamie Gillis, Paul Thomas, Ron Jeremy

This one has so many plot twists that it will keep you bewildered right up to the surprise ending. As Ted Singer, Herschel Savage is the star, and once again he plays the loving, tough-guy/good-guy role that should endear him to many female viewers. In this one, as a private detective, he shares his apartment with Dottie (Shanna McCullough), a hooker who's always bringing home the wrong kind of men. Ted has to protect her against guys like Ron Jeremy, and deep down he really loves her. Promised $100,000 by the Big Man (Jamie Gillis, of course), who has an expensive lady friend, Messina (Jacqueline Lorians), if he can locate an ancient book,

The Bogen Gelder, Ted soon discovers that the American Nazi party is also searching for the book. Supposedly, when it is opened, it will give the owner amazing revelations direct from God that will allow the Nazis to conquer the world. Before Ted locates the book, which is encrusted with jewels and sealed in gold, he falls in love with Messina and has to rescue her and his drunken friend Johnny (Paul Thomas), who has the book, from the enemy. He finally delivers the book to the Big Man. When they unlock it, they are shocked to discover what's inside.

BLUE JEANS
CC NN BI NL NR DK
1983 VIDEO-X-PIX

P/D—Angel Martine, John Christopher
F/A—Brooke Bennett, Sandy Gazelle, Sharon Kane
F/A—David Messa, Jerry Butler, Ron Jeremy, Michael Bruce

Debbie (Brooke Bennett) is married to clothes designer Gene Howard (David Messa). They live in a slightly above-average home in the suburbs of New York City. They make very romantic love together, and Debbie, it develops, has helped Gene design a new line of jeans that are sure to be popular and will save Gene's company from bankruptcy. All is well until Debbie calls at the office unexpectedly and catches Ellie (Sharon Kane) blowing a somewhat reluctant Gene. After many years, Debbie has just "run into" a former boyfriend, Tony (Jerry Butler), who tells her that she should have married him and that he always loved her more than Gene did. Debbie refuses his invitation to his hotel room, telling him, "You must realize that I'm married now." But the next day, after she catches Gene with his pants down, she's in the sack with Tony. In the meantime, she's hired Rick (Ron Jeremy), their former grocery delivery boy, as a house boy, gardener, and cook. Her sister Cindy (Sharon Mitchell) is arriving to visit for a while. Despite the marital confusion and Debbie's anger at Gene, the new line of jeans has taken off (no pun), and an important French buyer is about to ar-

rive from Paris to place a big order. He's invited to the Howards' home for dinner. Ron Jeremy is making a ragout, into which Cindy dumps some marijuana, and soon they're both slurping booze and screwing in the kitchen. Rick eventually passes out, naked, on the floor. Debbie can't believe her eyes when she sees the mess. Gene and the French buyer are in the living room, and Cindy has "fixed" their drinks, too. Tony telephones Debbie and tells her that he's coming to save her. He finally does, and they "elope" while a funny orgy is occurring in the living room.

BODIES IN HEAT
CC NN NM
1984 CABALLERO

P/D—Paul Vatelli
F/A—Annette Haven, Lisa de Leeuw, Star Weatherly, Billy Dee, Janey Robbins
F/A—Herschel Savage, Eric Edwards

Harry Reed (Herschel Savage) is a tough detective who doesn't hesitate to knock off a prostitute before he lets her go, or to screw around with the female dispatcher (Janey Robbins). He also has an assistant, Storm Trace (Lisa de Leeuw), who wears tight blue jeans—despite her 150 pounds. Storm wants to go to bed with him, but he tells her, "I don't believe in dipping my pen in the office inkwell," which she doesn't find very amusing. Neither is she very happy when he is called to investigate a robbery at the home of wealthy Moira De Salvo (Annette Haven), who claims that burglars have stolen a $10,000 antique watch. Harry inspects the bedroom with an evil eye on Moira. But nothing happens until Moira telephones and tells him that she thinks her very jealous husband, Lawrence (Eric Edwards), is planning to murder her. Soon she convinces Harry, who can't resist her and makes very passionate love to her in her Oriental-rugged living room (a sequence you won't fast forward), that if he really loves her he should help her kill Lawrence. What's more, they will be rich when Lawrence has gone to his Maker. If you remember, Barbara Stanwyck and Fred MacMurray, the story now becomes a variation on

Double Indemnity. Harry gives Moira a poison that he assures her will give Lawrence a heart attack, and since he will be the investigating officer she will never be found out. Later, in a neat double twist, Moira gives Harry the poison and you think he is about to trick her into drinking it herself. It seems that Moira and Storm are friends and have conspired to rid the world of Harry. Although it's not clear, Lawrence evidently survives. The facial resemblance between Annette and Jane Seymour, a more legitimate Hollywood actress, is astonishing. As for Vatelli, he proves again that, with a good story line, he can produce a film that you will enjoy.

BOILING POINT
CC NN BI DK
1984 ESSEX

P/D—Jack Sloane, Paul Levis
F/A—Sylvia Rodgers, Phaedra Grant, Constance Penny, Paula Brown, Desiree Cousteau (momentarily)
F/A—John Leslie, Jon Martin, John Seeman

Halfway through this one the director must have forgotten the story he was telling. The last half has no connection to the first, but offers one of the most effective bisexual sequences I've ever seen, followed by a surrealistic orgy. The story begins with a prostitute, Angel (Sylvia Rodgers), servicing a client (John Seeman) by telephone, after which she goes to a local market. Before she can buy any groceries she's involved in a holdup by Jon Martin (the West Side Rapist), who flees in a wild car chase when he's accosted by a plainclothesman, Tosy (John Leslie). Martin ends up hiding out in Tosy's bedroom, proving that he's not really a rapist, since Tosy's wife can't wait to jump in the sack, and later the bathtub, with him. At the same time, Tosy, who has reluctantly let the fugitive get away, goes to bed with Angel. But when Tosy arrives home, Martin is still there with Tosy's wife. Martin escapes through the back door, steals Tosy's car, picks up a young lady on her way to go baby-sitting, and that's that! You never see any of them again. But the baby-sitter ends up in bed with the woman she's

come to sit for, and their sexmaking is cleverly intercut with a carousel and painted horses moving up and down, after which you are suddenly at a disco orgy where the guys and gals are dancing together either half naked or stark naked. A few gals are blowing the musicians while they play, and then in a long sequence, seven naked guys are dancing with and being blown by seven naked ladies as they move in rhythm to the music in a neatly stylized orgy.

BORDELLO, HOUSE OF THE RISING SUN
CC NN NR NL
1985 ESSEX

P/D—Chuck Vincent
F/A—Norris O'Neal, Amber Lynn, Tish Ambrose, Taija Rae, Marita Ekberg
F/A—Jerry Butler, Scott Baker, Buck Adams, Stephen Lockwood

Chuck Vincent has done it again (see reviews of *Roommates* and *In Love*). Breaking many of the adult-film conventions, he has come up with a story about the happy days in a New Orleans whorehouse when the customers were treated like gentlemen and the madam and the ladies really cared about their patrons. As a matter of fact, whether he realizes it or not, Chuck is making an undercurrent social statement in this film against the "meat market" view of sex which dominates some producers' thinking. With the exception of Taija Rae, who plays a bitchy belle, all the women are loving people who enjoy what they are doing. The plot is simple. The House of the Rising Sun is 49-percent owned by Gloria, who is now a lovely old madam. On her death bed, she leaves her ownership to Cas Wilcox (Norris O'Neal), whose unknown partner is Transworld, a conglomerate. Their hatchet man arrives and complains that the place is not contributing its share of the corporation's profits. To Cas's horror, Transworld's solution is to modernize the place—install water-sports rooms, bondage rooms, and Marquis de Sade facilities, all of which can be paid for on one's credit cards. Soon the place is a sleazy joint catering to weirdos. But never mind, the president of Transworld arrives and understands what a warm, comforting place a bordello should be. In between, there's some nice sexmaking provided by Tish Ambrose with a young-looking Bobby Spector, and Marita Ekberg, a first-timer, with a customer who falls in love with her. Taija Rae provides some acrobatic sex. But Norris O'Neal (a Mary Astor look-alike) never undresses or goes to bed with Jerry Butler. I have a feeling Chuck is experimenting by incorporating "legitimate" actors and actresses into the porno scene without the necessity of them fucking and sucking.

BURLEXXX
CC NN NL BI DK
1984 VCX

P/D—Vince Benedetti
F/A—Gloria Leonard, Joanna Storm, Carol
    Cross, Samantha Fox, Annette Heinz,
    Sharon Kane, Honey Wilder, Renee
    Summers
F/A—Ron Jeremy, R. Bolla, Jerry Butler, Bobby
    Astyr, George Payne

If you've ever wondered what old-time burlesque, carried to the extremes of the sexual world of the 1980s, would be like—here's your chance to see. Just as in the days of yore, most of the action on this one takes place on the stage of the Paradise Theater, with a big live audience watching the action. Ron Jeremy is the master of ceremonies and also takes part in various skits as well as tossing off at least a hundred jokes and one-liners. But the jokes are only a small portion of the silliness and are followed by many different skits and, of course, stripping, which is offered supererotically by Joanna Storm, Annette Heinz, and Samantha Fox. One skit incudes Bobby Astyr arriving at the Best Little Whorehouse, run by Gloria Leonard. He's Willie Lohman, or Rohman, selling Bibles or maybe Dribbles. He's followed by Dixie Doo, a stripper, who challenges the audience with all kinds of funny sexual repartee and who, after taking a bubble bath in a huge champagne glass, sucks a conical lollipop that she sensuously inserts into her vagina and then gives to a guy in the audience. There's a typical burlesque skit in a schoolroom, with a female dunce played by Renee Summer and the bad boy by Jerry Butler. They soon have the teacher stretched out on her desk. There's also Ron Jeremy in the pokey being sent a rubber doll by Sharon Kane so that he can have something, after so many years, to put his dick in. There's a male stripper, in a baseball uniform, playing with his ball and a bat that finally ejaculates. There's a boxing match between half-naked ladies that finally turns into a wrestling match. And there's a totally silly skit in which Ron Jeremy and Bobby Astyr are challengers in a cock-boxing match. Their female trainers keep them hard enough between rounds to swing their dicks at each other. The AFFA should put Vince Bendetti and Richard Miler (a very brilliant guy who composed the music and has written several books including *Black English*) in charge of running the next Erotic Film Festival with porno actors instead of the boring outside talent which they hire who are as sexy as dried turnips. It could be done without the explicit sex which this one offers and if videotaped as they did the 7th Erotic Film Festival (see reviews) it would be a best seller.

CALIGULA
CC NN BI DK DS
980 PENTHOUSE PRODUCTS

P/D—Bob Guccione, Franco Rosselini, Tinto
    Brass
F/A—Teresa Ann Savoy, Helen Mirren
F/A—Malcolm MacDowell, Peter O'Toole, John
    Gielgud, Guido Mannari

The above are only some of the many actors and actresses in this film, which cost over $15 million to make, thus qualifying it as the most expensive porno film ever. Actually, when the film was first released as an X-rated flick, at high box-office prices, it was soon apparent, after many bad reviews, that it wouldn't recover costs in the theaters. To get wider distribution, an R-rated version was turned out, eliminating six and a half minutes of explicit sex in various sections of the film.

Fortunately, the full-length, X-rated version is now available on tape. I have given this two-and-a-half-hour movie a "Collector's Choice" rating because, campy or not, overacted or not, "a relentless series of decapitations and disembowelings" or not, "sick chutzpah" or not, it can't compare with the life of Caligula as described by Suetonius in his *Lives of the Twelve Caesars,* which was written only a few years after Caligula died. Before you rent or buy this tape, read Suetonius. The book is in paperback in bookstores or in your library. You'll discover how cheap life was in the year A.D. 48, and if you want a more up-to-date sequel, try *Salon Kitty* (see review), which was also directed by Tinto Brass and which covers aspects of wartime Nazi Germany.

CAMPUS GIRLS
CC NN NM
1973   QUALITY/VIDEO-X-PIX

P/D—Richard D'Antonini
F/A—Diana Baker, Judy Gillis, Carol Dempsey
F/A—Mick Allman, Joey Gerardo, Buddy Boone, William Constantine

While their names are listed in the credits as Diana Baker and Mick Allman, they're better-known screen names are Mark Stevens (now retired from adult films) and Tina Russell (now dead from cancer). The CC rating is for Tina and Mark, who have just graduated from college and are reminiscing over their college days. There was Marlene, Mark tells Tina, who had the reputation of giving the best head on campus. This shocks Tina a little, but Mark is more shocked when she tells him about Barbara, who actually slipped away from campus and made a porno movie. Then Tina tells him about Mary Anne, who got her honors degree by servicing all the professors. All these little stories are reenacted, but the interesting part of this sexvid is Mark and Tina's dialogue, during which Tina casually plays with Mark's uncircumcised prick; he goes out for sandwiches before they finally make very nice love together.

CERTAIN FURY
CC R DS
1984   NEW WORLD VIDEO

P/D—Gilbert Adler, Stephen Gyllenhaal
F/A—Tatum O'Neal, Irene Cara
F/A—Nicholas Campbell, Moses Gunn, George Murdock, Peter Fonda

You can probably catch this one on late-night cable TV, or you can easily rent it. There's some nudity and no close-up genital sex, but it would be censored in Sweden. You can add it to your collection of the most violent movies that you've ever seen. It begins early in the morning in a courtroom where a number of young women are being brought on drug, larceny, and prostitution charges. Among them are a tough-looking redhead, Scarlet (Tatum O'Neal), and a light-skinned black girl, Tracy (Irene Cara). They are both in their early 20s and up to this moment have never seen each other before. Then, as a doped-up blonde girl is being charged, she slits the court officer's throat with a knife and her girlfriend in the courtroom opens fire with a submachine gun. Within minutes, a dozen people are slaughtered. Scarlet and Tracy, running in a wild panic to escape both the killers and the police, head for the streets of San Francisco and soon are deep in the sewer system, fighting rats and sewage and nearly being caught by a policeman pursuing them. But he drowns in the muck when he lights a cigarette and the sewer gas around him explodes. Still running, they end up with Snipper (Nicholas Campbell), one of Scarlett's ex-boyfriends, who tries to rape Tracy in the shower in his apartment and tells her, "For a nigger, you're stupider than you look." Never mind, she beats him to a pulp with a baseball bat, and then Scarlet and she are separated for a while as Scarlet plunges lower and lower into the depths of an Oriental drug hideout, where they finally come together once again, still dodging the police. It all ends with Scarlet slain by the cops.

A CHANGE OF PARTNERS
CC NN NR BI DK
1982 CABALLERO

P/D—Francis LeRoi
F/A—Joan Keller, Catherine Rover, Barbara Collins
F/A—Guy Royer, Jack Gatt, Emile Bren

Martine and Bob live in Paris. You don't know that they have just gotten married until after Bob has "play" raped Martine in the elevator, at her request. When the elevator door finally opens, their friends shower them with confetti. Total lovebugs, they are off on their honeymoon to the French seacoast (probably Biarritz), where most of this film was shot. Martine's school friend, Joelle, has invited them to a villa where she lives with her husband and her peripatetic sister Angie. Immediately, you discover that Joelle and Eric are not happily married. A very funny-sad arrival scene ensues where the newlyweds go to bed early and the disillusioned husband and wife listen to their happy moans by the hour. It quickly develops that Joelle owns the villa with her sister Angie, who is a very devious and sexy lady. Her friends are a group of local Hell's Angels. Before the honeymoon weekend is over, Angie has seduced Eric, who isn't getting any loving from his wife, Joelle, and then she goes to work on Bob, who resists her because he is very much in love with his new bride, Martine. Finally Bob can't help himself and capitulates. Angie also convinces Joelle to try sex with her friends, and Joelle is completely degraded by guys who screw her and never take off their helmets. Then Angie gets Martine so bombed that she ends up being fucked by local fishermen. Finally Angie departs, happily bare-ass, on a motorcycle. After one night of spouse exchange, the two couples return to their original mates with no recriminations. Most women will like this one and would be delighted to spend a week, or a month, making love in this romantic villa and seacoast environment.

CHICKIE
CC NN BI NL
1975 FANTASY/CABALLERO

P/D—Bill Mizner, Charles Dodgson
F/A—Blaise Pascal, Emmeline Parkhurst
F/A—William Booth, Cotton Mather, I. M. Zoroaster, Thomas Paine, Jamie Gillis (who is not listed, unless one of the above a.k.a.s is him)

Chickie Tetrazzini is a good-natured gal who works in a massage parlor. She also has a job as a policewoman. She can't save any money because she's so generous with everyone—she's always making donations to orphanages and charities. Even though they don't turn her on, she obligingly screws with a 250-pound guy and one who wears his sunglasses and socks. Her female police sergeant is a woman-firster and has the message that power belongs to women tattooed on her chest. But Chickie doesn't pay much attention to her. Even hard-as-nails detective Jamie Gillis falls in love with Chickie, and he has a fight with another guy who claims she belongs to him. "If she's your woman, why was she sucking my cock for the last three nights?" he demands. But then Chickie wins the New York lottery and suddenly is so overwhelmed with people wanting a piece of the loot, and her, that she just disappears. (See notes under *Christy.*)

CHINA SILK
CC NN BI DK
1984 MASTERPIECE

P/D—Jerome Bronson, Steve Scott
F/A—Kristara Barrington, Ginger Lynn, Cara Lott, Colleen Brennan, Gina Carrera, Debbie Green
F/A—Harry Reems, Herschel Savage, Eric Edwards, Ken Starbuck

Here's a modern dope-and-smuggling story told with expert editing, and cutting and good acting, plus it's carefully interwoven with explicit plot-related sex that will keep you interested from beginning to end. It begins 15 years ago in Cambodia, where American soldier Harry Parker (Harry Reems) has been wounded and is saved from certain death by a peasant girl, Lily Chang (Kristara Barrington). Now Parker is a tough police captain in San Francisco investigating dope smuggling, and he has just discovered that Lily, now an American citizen, is the head of the operation. To his shock, Mike Shaw (Paul Thomas), an undercover detective working for him, is murdered. Shaw's corpse, even though he's never taken dope, shows a severely punctured arm. The coroner forestalls investigation by insisting that Shaw OD'd. Mike's widow, Nancy (Colleen Brennan), asks Harry to help bring the criminals to justice. It's her husband's last wish that he be cremated. Before it's over, with a neat plot twist, Parker, with Nancy's help, double-crosses his own cops and the FBI (Eric Edwards), who are also investigating the case. He and Nancy take off with a million-dollar stash of heroin in a Chinese vase that is similar to the one that contains her husband's ashes. But only after both she and Parker have wept together at the crematory.

CHINA SISTERS
CC NN BI DK
1979 ESSEX

P/D—Anthony Spinelli
F/A—Vicki Lyons, Tina Wong, Lisa Grant
F/A—Jack Wrangler, Jack Wright, Robby Robinson, John Leslie

If you watch *Portrait of a Seduction* (see review) before you watch this one, you'll see that Vicki Lyons was quite a good actress. It would be fascinating to know what has become of her. In this film, she plays the part of a Chinese-American, Gloria Chinn. Now living in San Franciso, Gloria is 32 and teaches English at Glenwood High School. Worried that her sister Barbara (Tina Wong) is experiencing only rough, groping sex from her peers, Gloria shows her how a woman should be loved by a man. Later, unable to help herself, Gloria brings a 17-year-old high-school student home to discuss literature and makes love to him. In the meantime, her sister has fallen in love with Billy (Jack Wrangler), a gay man—which Wrangler acknowledges that he really is in his book *The Jack Wrangler Story* (see review of *Jack & Jill II*). Lying naked with Barbara, Billy moans, "You're so beautiful. What's the matter with me?" Gloria knows, and

she sticks a dildo in his anus while he's trying to get into Barbara. It works. Later, Barbara thinks that she has found true love with another young man who is very shy. But he can't make it with Barbara either. His father (played by John Leslie) tries to prove to Barbara that it's just because of Gary's youth and shows her how Gary will improve with age. But Gloria never finds a man of her own.

CHRISTINE'S SECRET
CC NN NM NR
1984 VCA

P/D—Per Sjostedt, Candida Royalle, R. Lauren Neimi
F/A—Carol Cross, Chelsea Blake, Taija Rae, Marita Ekberg
F/A—Jake West, George Payne, Joey Silvera, Anthony Casino

In her third *Femme* film, Candida, with Per Sjostedt, tries to tell a complete little story, but following the style of the previous films, it still is a vignette. Christine (Carol Cross), a single woman, comes back for a summer vacation to a country home being run as an inn by Marilyn (Chelsea Blake) and Phil (George Payne). Also staying at the inn are newlyweds on their honeymoon, and in the background Marilyn's daughter Heather (Taija Rae) is happily making love with Joey Silvera as Tommy, a hired hand from another farm. That leaves Jake, the caretaker of the inn, to take care of Marilyn. All the sexmaking is warm, loving, and caring. There is no conflict and little dialogue, but it has a sensuous summertime environment and various sequences (such as Christine swinging in an old-fashioned tree swing and being fantasized naked by Jake, who makes love to her as she glides into him; or Tommy and Heather making love outdoors behind the barn) with which most guys and gals will quickly identify. Candida's next move must be to try to tell a real story with some characterization. To do it she has to focus the story on just a few characters and offer a little conflict. When this happens she should be able to reach a huge home market of single and married lovers.

CHRISTY
CC NN BI NL
1975   FANTASY/CABALLERO

P/D—Steve Harris
F/A—Andrea True, Cindy West, Anne Christian
F/A—Harry Reems, Mark Stevens, Eric Edwards, Peter Smith

The CC rating is not only for all the old-timers in one film but also for the unglamorous, but believable, second-floor Greenwich Village apartment environment. Mark Stevens and Andrea are sloppy people who live by their wits and have a 15-year-old daughter, Christy, who pretends she's older. Christy gets a job as a stripper in a nearby pub. Her boyfriend, John (Eric Edwards), doesn't want her to work there, gets in a fight with a black guy who tries to paw her, and ends up in the clink. Christy, in the meantime, cons a wealthy guy into making love with her in the family apartment, where they are discovered by Mom and Dad. Dad threatens to call the cops because Christy is a minor, unless the guy coughs up some dough. Frightened, the poor guy writes them a check for $2,500, and when he's gone they all end up laughing their heads off at their good fortune. In the meantime, Mama isn't getting enough sex with Daddy, so she tries Harry Reems, the Fuller Bra man. She also goes to bed with her daughter because it's a loving thing to do. So does Daddy.

Note: This is one of the many Fantasy/Caballero tapes that sell for under $30 and for the most part were made between 1972 and 1978. Since they have no copyright dates in the credits, I have compromised with the year 1975 in most cases. They run for 60 minutes and are attractively boxed. But there is little or no information on the box as to who the actors and actresses are or what the story is. They were all shot on film, and even if it was 16-mm, the color is usually pretty good. Many of the male actors are still performing, but most of the females have disappeared. Most of these early films reflect a more naive and experimental quality than you'll find in current films. A few that I have given CC ratings do deal with aspects of real life.

CLASSICAL ROMANCE
CC NN NR
1984   MASTERPIECE

P/D—Jerome Bronson, Richard Mailer
F/A—Jacqueline Lorians, Desiree Lane, Renee Summer, Lisa Lake
F/A—Paul Thomas, Herschel Savage

Eric (Paul Thomas) is a talented classical pianist who dissipates his energies "chasing cunt," smoking pot, and playing syrupy music in bars and nightclubs. He lives with Monica (Desiree Lane), who can't understand why he is still studying "Chopin." Monica can sing, and together they could make a fortune in the right clubs. She's already paved the way to the top by screwing with the owner of a big chain of clubs. Laura (Jacqueline Lorians) is married to Charles, a wealthy businessman who hates music and screws around plenty with other women. When Laura meets Eric at a resort restaurant, it's love at first sight. But she leaves before he wakes up, and he doesn't even know her name. With a little help from his, and her, friends, he finds her. But soon Charles is aware that Laura is having an affair. He punishes Laura by making her come to bed with a whore whom he has invited into their bedroom. But Eric arrives and tells Laura, while Charles is standing threateningly beside her, to run away with him. She must make a choice.

For a minute you wonder what it will be. But Laura finally rushes to the car where Eric is waiting and gives up her life of wealth for a pianist who finally (à la *Flashdance*) is going to get his great opportunity to prove himself on the concert stage. Richard Mailer is a director who tries to tell a good story. In this one he proves that, given a chance, porno actresses like Jacqueline Lorians can act. Compare this one with her throw-uppy role in *Making It Big* (see review).

COME FLY WITH US
CC NN NR (a little)
1974   QUALITY/VIDEO-X-PIX

P/D—Oscar Tripe
F/A—Pamela Field, Daniela DiOrici, Veronica Mellin, Susan Foxworth

F/A—Kevin Andre, Eric Edwards, Oscar Tripe, Dorian Patch, Jamie Gillis

Three stewardesses land in New York in the middle of summer. A limousine is waiting to take them to Lake Placid for a weekend of relaxation, mostly with guys that they've never seen before. En route, two of them relate their experiences with other lovers. Margaret has met Jay, an equestrian. After a day of horseback riding she makes love with him in the stable. Another stewardess, Lisa, tells about meeting Alan (Eric Edwards) in Central Park, where he was playing chess against himself, and soon had invited herself back to his apartment on 70th Street. But sadly, neither Margaret nor Lisa really liked the guys enough (they were too nicey-nice) to continue with them. Same with Elena, who met a nutty guy, David (Jamie Gillis), who snatched a dress she was trying to buy in a boutique and promised to pay for it if she would go back to his apartment and model it for him. When she did, he invited her to a fancy-dress ball and soon appeared in a 19th-century British uniform. With the hi-fi playing Strauss waltzes, he unbuttoned his trousers and gave her the gift between his legs. By this time the limousine has arrived at Lake Placid, where finally Elena (a woman you've never seen before in adult films) meets a guy who obviously will become her one and only.

A COMING OF ANGELS: THE SEQUEL
CC NN BI
1985 CABALLERO

P/D—Not given
F/A—Ginger Lynn, Colleen Brennan, Annette Haven, Kelly Nichols, Jill Ferrar
F/A—Paul Thomas, Eric Edwards, Jamie Gillis, Herschel Savage

It's interesting to compare this one with the original, which was made in 1977 (not 1979) and on which I have now changed my mind. The first one deserves a CC rating, also, and although the original's plot is hard to swallow as is the sequel's, the first is probably a better adult film. The only female carry-over is Annette Ha-ven, nearly 10 years older but just as pretty. Leslie Bovee, Amber Hunt, and Abigail Clayton no longer make adult films and are replaced by Ginger Lynn and Kelly Nichols as the angels. Eric Edwards and Jamie Gillis play different roles. In the first one, as Mark, Jamie's a sadist who either totally hypnotizes women or chains them up in the cellar of his New England home with the help of Robert (John Leslie), who screws them while Mark watches. Although he degrades some of his captives, they still want Mark sexually, but he will not, or can't, satisfy them. Eventually, with the help of Andy (Eric Edwards), they are both put out of business. Note that the first film claims to be based on a novel of the same title. In all probability, "Charlie's Angels" did not exist when the first one was made. In the sequel, Jamie is a U.S. senator married to a lush, Colleen Brennan, who drinks because of him but finds love in the arms of his campaign manager, Eric Edwards. Herschel Savage has kidnapped Jamie's daughter, Jill Ferrar, and is holding her for a substantial ransom. But the truth, which the angels—now controlled by Charlie (Paul Thomas)—know is that she loves Herschel and this is a way for mommy and daughter to revenge themselves on their callous husband and father. Annette is the most interesting angel in both tapes.

COMING TOGETHER
CC NN BI DK
1985 CABALLERO

P/D—Paul G. Vatelli
F/A—Kimberly Carson, Colleen Brennan
F/A—Herschel Savage, Greg Ruffner

Tracy (Colleen Brennan) is married to Mark (Herschel Savage), but she's worried that their sex life is not as zoomy as it once was. Mark assures her that he never thinks about his former girlfriend, Jackie. But this weekend he's going duck hunting with a male friend. Anyway, Roxy (Kimberly Carson), Tracy's college roommate whom she hasn't seen for many years, is arriving for the weekend, and they can have a good time remembering their youth. Faithful to Mark, Tracy pleads a headache and won't go out on the town with Roxy, who brings a guy she has picked up back to the house and plays with him in the Jacuzzi and in bed. The next day, sure that Mark is cheating on her because his duck-hunting friend has telephoned and isn't with Mark, Tracy goes to a swinger's party with Roxy and manages for most of the evening to stay aloof from the action. But she finally capitulates and then the next morning is disgusted. But she can't put up with Mark's deception either and finally leaves with Roxy for better things. The CC rating is largely for Colleen Brennan, who proves that she's a good actress in this kind of part and can actually weep a few tears.

THE CONNECTION
CC NN NL
1983 ORCHIDS INTERNATIONAL

Presumably the Japanese censor *Playboy* and *Penthouse* magazines and airbrush out pubic hair, and presumably American pornos are not for sale in Japan. But the demand for sex on film is not easy to censor. I can't believe that these films were made for export only. The people at Orchids International, who let me preview these tapes, plan to add subtitles and English dubbing. I prefer subtitles. I watched all five films in this guide in Japanese and sexmaking in any language isn't too difficult to follow. This one begins with a shot of a woman ejecting three tennis balls from her vagina, and another woman ejecting three eggs. One of the eggs immediately hatches, and the lively chick takes a peck or two out of a guy's penis. Soon a group of Japanese young people are off in a van for a holiday. The bus stops by a seashore. One sad guy measures his penis with a tape measure and slaps it indignantly because it's so small. Two ladies busily wash their vulvas with a scrub brush. In the bus, a guy tries to play a guitar using his prick as a pick, and another guy tries to extend his, using a vacuum cleaner. After this silliness they all arrive at a mountain lodge, and they settle down to extended screwing. In one scene a Japanese girl finds her boyfriend sleeping on the floor and works him over

very thoroughly, speaking to him in broken English. In another scene, a guy arrives with a tape recorder playing Japanese rock and is soon dancing on a dining room table. Joined by his woman, they strip each other and make love. No plot obviously, but full of the unexpected.

CORPORATE ASSETS
CC NN BI NR DK
1985 ESSEX

P/D—Ed Leonard, Thomas Payne
F/A—Tish Ambrose, Rachel Ashley, Amber Lynn, Sheri St. Clair, Tamara Longley
F/A—Eric Edwards, R. Bolla, Herschel Savage, Nick Random, Harry Reems, Jamie Gillis, Francois Papillon

This one is so superior to many adult films that you may keep thinking it could have been better, especially if the character J. W. Sieverson, a multimillionaire capitalist who entertains top Washington officials in his mansion, had been better developed. As it is, all you know about J.W. is that he's very rich, has a private secretary, Jill (Tish Ambrose), and has three call girls (Rachel Ashley, Amber Lynn, and Sheri St. Clair) on the payroll to service his honored guests and do certain dirty work for him by getting rid of older executives like Bill Saunders (Harry Reems), who has heart trouble. Two of the girls arrive in Bill's office and literally fuck him to death and later have an argument over "an old man's prick." But the plot centers around Jill, who has been J.W.'s secretary for 12 years and whom he thinks he owns. Then he discovers that Jill has been writing love letters to Winston (Eric Edwards), who is in a mental institution. After seeing his best friend (her brother) killed in Vietnam, and after raping a Vietnamese woman whom he may have murdered, Winston had a breakdown. Jill has never met Winston, but they have fallen in love by mail. When Winston finally arrives in Los Angeles, their love grows even stronger with the sight of each other. But they are being tailed by Louis Sorrento (Herschel Savage), J.W.'s tough bodyguard and executioner. Jill is dragged out of Winston's arms, and J.W.

arranges that Winston will see Jill giving J. W. head. Winston flees in disgust. J.W. tells Jill that if she tries to leave him it will be the end of Winston. But Winston forgives Jill, and it all ends in a wild shoot-out at the mansion, with J.W. as the only survivor— until he is stabbed by one of his call girls, whom he's turned into an imbecile. If all the unrelated sex had been eliminated and the time devoted to a real tug of war between J.W.—not as a totally nasty man but a man who discovers belatedly his need for a loving woman—and Jill and Winston, this would have been a better film. But genitals, not minds, still dominate sexvid producers' thoughts.

CORRUPTION
CC NN NM BI DK
1984 VCA

P/D—Steve Crown, Richard Mahler
F/A—Kelly Nichols, Tiffany Clark, Tanya Lawson, Tish Ambrose, Vanessa Del Rio, Alexis X, Nicole Bernard
F/A—Jamie Gillis, Michael Gaunt, Bobby Astyr

The CC on this one is not for the story. The producer or director would probably tell you that it's about the interplay of good and evil. The people in this story are all pretty scummy characters, and you'll have a hard time figuring Jamie's involvement with most of them except his half brother, Bobby Astyr, who is ex-officio devil in charge of a decrepit bar with underground rooms where Jamie can play voyeur and watch the modern purgatory of noncommitted sex through peepholes. In addition to two women enjoying each other in a shower, he sees a guy playing "bad little doggie" to a woman brandishing a whip (the guy, to his shock, looks just like him), and he sees a dead woman on a bier. With organ music playing, a clown wearing a top hat strips her and pulls her over to the edge of the bier and screws her wildly, with no sign of life from her until the very end, when her eyes pop open. Soon after, Bobby Astyr tells Jamie, "They've got your sister, Felicia. They don't trust you to come up with the dough." Never mind, Bobby takes care of whoever "they" are by shooting one of them

in bed while he's servicing Felicia. Why the CC rating? For the moody photography, for Nicole Bernard as a stripper, and for the musical background, which includes selections from Bach and *Boris Gudunov.*

CRIMES OF PASSION
CC R
985 NEW WORLD VIDEO

P/D—Barry Sandler, Ken Russell
F/A—Kathleen Turner, Annie Potts
F/A—Anthony Perkins, John Laughlin, Bruce Dawson

In the 1980s, for the most part, sexual words and discussion are uncensored in R movies. Inevitably, sex will also become a little more explicit, as it does in this fascinating film directed by Ken Russell (*Altered States, Women in Love, Tommy,* and *The Devils*). This one features Kathleen Turner (*Body Heat, Romancing the Stone*) and Anthony Perkins, who typed himself as a looney years ago in *Psycho.* This is the story of an unfulfilled woman, Joanna (Kathleen Turner), who in her straight life is a dress designer totally devoted to her job. Joanna has no male friends, but her alto ego, China Blue, which Kathleen plays with a sexual aplomb that most porno actresses would envy, is a nymphomaniac. As China Blue, her price is $50 for the night, and she will screw with just about anybody, including a scary evangelist, Peter Shayne (Anthony Perkins), who haunts the seamy sidewalks where she offers herself. Peter tells her that he will save her because, in essence, she and he are one. He carries a bag, which she discovers contains rubber dolls, penis pumps to aid ejaculation, and vibrators. In the meantime, Joanna's boss, thinking that she is giving design secrets to a competitor, has hired Bobby Grady to investigate her. Bobby is married to Amy. They have two kids, but Amy has never liked sex and doesn't like to talk about it or hear a sexy story. Inevitably, as Bobby encounters China Blue, the roughest, toughest, sexiest whore that you've ever seen in any adult film, he is totally enamored. It all ends where it began, in an encounter group with Bobby explaining, after China/Joanna is nearly murdered by Peter, that he's left his wife and moved in with China.

DAMES
CC NN BI DK
1985 ESSEX

P/D—Crystal Bleu
F/A—Karen Summer, Sharon Mitchell, Aurora, Gina Carrera, Sheri St. Clair, Tish Ambrose
F/A—John Leslie, Paul Thomas, Eric Edwards, Herschel Savage, Buck Adams

Here's a big-budget adult film that goes all out to capture the changing atmosphere of a formerly high-class saloon/speakeasy, which in later years has become Lovie's, a plastic-table-top bar where the bartender arranges sessions with call girls. It begins in the present with Eric Edwards, as a plainclothes detective, raiding the place and getting ready to arrest the bartender and a 75-year-old piano player, Harry (Paul Thomas), for pandering. Harry is questioned by a television reporter, Lucy (Aurora) and in a series of flashbacks tells Lucy the story of the place, beginning in 1928, when it was Vera's (Sharon Mitchell's) place and Vera served booze and sang for wealthy gangsters who arrived dressed in tuxedos. Harry remembers the night that Johnny Domenico (John Leslie) tried to make Vera and she told him coldly, "I don't like your style." No woman ever did this to Johnny, and that night a couple of hoods almost raped Vera (they were Johnny's guys) before Johnny saved her from them. But later, after she had gratefully screwed with him, Vera learned about the setup and knocked Johnny out. Then Harry remembers the place in 1944, when it was the Star Lounge. Sailors and soldiers filled the joint, and Madge (Gina Carrera) ran the bar and gave herself to a paraplegic (Herschel Savage) whose woman got drunk and took on a gang of guys in the men's room. In 1954, Harry admitted that he fell in love with a hooker, Dolores (Karen Summer), and you see how he saved her from the police and how they made romantic love on top of the baby grand piano. Finally,

Harry remembers the night in 1975 that Charlotte, a big-time model, arrived and danced with a pretty blonde woman (Tish Ambrose), after which, discovering that they were both lesbians, they ate each other and played with each other at one of the tables. Before Eric puts the padlock on the place, Lucy gives Harry a respite and takes Eric out in the back room, where they enjoy some contemporary copulation.

DANISH PASTRIES
CC NN NL BI DK
1972 QUALITY/VIDEO-X-PIX

P/D—Robert Sumner, Finn Karlsson
F/A—Lone Helmer, Sigrid Rasmussen, many others
F/A—Ole Soltupt, Bent Warburg, Benny Hansen

Adult-film makers should study early films like this one, which has a boisterous, Chaucerian sexual humor that they can't seem to capture in the 1980s. It was made in Denmark, with very good English dubbing added later. The time is the 19th century. Seems that a young Mr. Armand is supposed to inspect a girls' school in a small Danish town as soon as possible and arrive with something to suppress the young women's horniness. Something that has not occurred in many centuries is about to happen: The planet of Venus will be in conjunction with the town, and everyone will go sex mad. Actually, it's already happening. The 20 or more schoolgirls, who wear blue monk-style robes and nothing under them, are driving the mistress in charge batty. With no men available, they are kissing and hugging each other, and when the old lady in charge puts them in a dungeon to repent, they escape and go directly to the town brothel. But the madam doesn't want them. She has too many women already and not enough paying customers. Meanwhile, a young chemist has just discovered a foolproof aphrodisiac and is on his way to town and to the girls' school to try it out. Somehow Mr. Armand's sexual suppressant and the chemist's aphrodisiac get switched in the brothel, which they both mistake for the girls' school. The chemist drinks the suppressant, and the women play with his flaccid cock in disgust. But he soon gets his formula back and not only puts it in the drinking water at the girls' school but also tosses it in the town reservoir, after which the entire town goes on a sexual binge. You can't help laughing at the silliness of it. The beautiful Danish young ladies are nice to look at, and your wife or girlfriend will like the guys.

DARK DREAMS
CC NN BI
1974? VCA

P/D—Candida Ference, Roger Guermantes
F/A—Tina Russell, Darby Lloyd Raines, Kitty Eat, June Dulu
F/A—Harry Reems

The date on this one is my guess. VCA rediscovered it in 1985. In the previous edition of this guide, this film had simply a no-information listing. It's one of the best films made in the 1970s and should be way up there on a top listing. It's a sexy, scary, supernatural sexvid. Surprisingly, VCA lists the featured male actor as Tony Lee, when it is actually Harry Reems, who couldn't have been more than 25 when the film was made. Honors also should go to the cameraman, Werner Hlinka. The story takes place on the wedding day of Jack (Harry Reems) and Jill (Tina Russell). Driving through the New York countryside in a new Edsel with "Happily Married" signs and cans tied to their car, Jack stops to get rid of them and then tries to make love to Jill, who is a little prudish. Then a few minutes later he has a flat tire, with no air in the spare. Nervously, they knock on the door of a Victorian mansion to see if they may use the phone. Jill wonders, "What if an evil old lady answers the door?" And, sure enough, one does (Darby Lloyd Raines, marvelously disguised). The rest of this unique film is an extended sexual nightmare, during which both Jack and Jill live in a fantasy world that may reveal their true sexuality. As the old lady, actually a witch, is making a tea that drugs Jill, she turns into a beautiful woman and leads Jack upstairs to bed. A man in a black hood with the mark of the devil on his forehead picks up Jill and strips her, and she is made love to by a mysterious woman, after which the devil dresses her again in a 19th-century gown and she is held spread-eagled while Jack makes love to her. In between there is a very erotic topless belly dancer, and the old witch keeps telling Jack that he shouldn't limit himself to his wife. "Give her to us and we will give you many succulent women." All of this daydream, which ends where it began, with Jack and Jill knocking on the front door of the mansion, is accompanied by erotic music and lighting and superb camerawork.

THE DEBAUCHERS
CC NN DK
1972 QUALITY/VIDEO-X-PIX

P/D—Jacques Robeau
F/A—Tina Russell, Susan Cono, Nessa Trudu, Darla Bartun, Angela Schenk
F/A—Jason Russell, others

It's important to note the date of this film. It features the late Tina Russell as May and her husband, Jason, as Jack. When the film was made there were very few adult theaters. Video cassettes showing humans copulating, with or without a story line, didn't exist. From this perspective, the film is more interesting than many current films. May, who lives with Jack, must get a job because Jack is out of work, and if he had a few bucks he would like to buy a motor bike on which they could take off and enjoy life. May goes for an interview to appear in an "experimental film" that is being made by a very wealthy guy, Tom Waters, in a Gothic mansion, complete with a scary-looking butler, a maid, and a psychiatrist. Despite his wealth, Tom is a sleazy character who farts and burps at dinner. His doctor admits to May that Jack is a weirdo. But his money, which he tosses around at the drop of a hat, in $100 bills, is good. So May, though she's scared to death, stays and soon discovers, to her horror, that he wants her to undress and play with herself while he films her. Tom has the house guarded and won't let her leave. Within the day, May telephones Jack to come save her. But when Jack arrives Tom convinces him, with lots of bucks, to talk May into screwing with him while Tom records the event. May is shocked and filled with hatred for Jack. She confides her problem to the 50-year-old doctor, who is sympathetic and who May makes love with (a sexmaking sequence between young and old that you rarely see in sexvids), but the doctor tells her that he can't save her. Tom has too much on him. Anyway, Tom wants to shoot only one more scene with her and Jack. Supposedly they will be fully clothed, but May knows that she must defend herself. Sure enough, although Jack is dressed and so is she, Tom has in mind a "snuff scene." Jack is going to drown May in the swimming pool. He almost succeeds, but May, trusting no one, has strapped a knife on her thigh. As she is about to drown, she plunges the knife into Jack. Tom only laughs: He's got his snuff scene, and it doesn't matter which one is dead.

DEBBIE DOES 'EM ALL
CC NN BI
1984   CAL VISTA

P/D—Sam Norvell, Bob Vosse
F/A—Shanna McCullough, Angel, Lana Emerson, Lili Marlene
F/A—Jamie Gillis, Lynx Cannon, Rod Grant, Elmo Lavino, Nick Niter

Don't confuse this Debbie (who is Angel) with Debbie (Bambi Woods) who "does Dallas" (see review). If brunette women are your preference, Angel is certainly the prettiest woman making porno movies, and with her naive, virginal look it's hard to believe that she's as sexually insatiable as she appears on film. In fact, you may wonder why she ever decided to make sexvids. Anyway, in this one she sleeps with Fred (Lynx Cannon), who wants to marry her, but she has finally gotten a job as an airline stewardess, and although she loves Fred, she's often unavailable as she lays over (pun intended) in various cities. Her college friend Pamela (Shanna McCullough) is also a stewardess, and in various cities, such as Miami, Dallas, and Chicago, she has gangster friends, like Anton (Jamie Gillis), with whom Debbie, after just meeting him in a Miami bar, is

soon happily copulating. Knowing that she's flying to Chicago early the next morning, Anton gives her a present he'd like her to deliver to a friend of his who will meet her at an elevated stop. Luckily, she sees the guy being arrested before she gives him the package, which contains several million dollars' worth of cocaine. Pamela takes it off her hands and sells it for 20 grand to another gangster and then like a good friend tells Debbie she only got $4,000 and gives Debbie half. In between all this there are believable scenes aboard an airline with the usual screwing in the toilet and the pilot getting blown by one of the stewardesses. The story could have been told much more dramatically, but never mind—it has Angel, who finally gets reunited with Fred at a masquerade orgy.

DESIRE
CC NN NR N (a little)
1985   VCX

P/D—Vinnie Rossi
F/A—Kay Parker, Tamara Longley, Misty Dawn, Mai Lin, Ruby Smart
F/A—Randy West, Ron Jeremy, Herschel Savage, William Margold

Lilli (Tamara Longley, she of the deep voice) leaves her lover, Toby (Herschel Savage) because of desire. Now many years older, Toby is still bewildered at losing the only person he ever loved. (For some unexplained reason, Toby as an old man is played by William Margold instead of Savage. Maybe Savage was busy on other projects.) Still mourning his loss, wealthy old Toby hires Kay Parker, a psychologist, to find out what desire is. Her first volunteer subject is Mai Lin, who defines desire as wanting two men at once when you have only one. Next comes Ron Jeremy, a stand-up comic (Jeremy really is), who under Kay's questioning finally admits—despite all the women he has screwed—that he doesn't enjoy sex anymore. He's in love with a mannequin. In a funny sequence, Jeremy makes very erotic love to his almost-real dummy, who comes to life briefly. But he doesn't know what desire is, either. Her next subject, Randy West, proves to Kay what desire is so far as she's concerned. He's a handsome former football pro, and she wants him! Finally, Kay tells you, "Desire is an attempt to add tangible feelings to an intangible entity." Wow! After that bit of philosophy, Tamara reappears to old Toby in a dream and tells him that the reason she left him is that he desired money more than her. So don't say you never learn anything by watching adult films.

DIXIE RAY, HOLLYWOOD STAR
CC NN BI
1983   CABALLERO

P/D—**Billy Thornberg, Anthony Spinelli**
F/A—**Juliet Anderson, Lisa de Leeuw, Veronica Hart, Kelly Nichols, Samantha Fox**
F/A—**John Leslie, Cameron Mitchell**

This is the best cops-and-bad-guys adult film that I have seen so far. Why it wasn't nominated for the 1984 Erotic Film Awards beats me. Nick Popodupolis (John Leslie) not only is the only "screwing male" in the film—but he ultimately beds all the luscious ladies mentioned above. Dixie Ray (Lisa de Leeuw) was, back in the '30s, a top Hollywood star. Now, in February 1943, she is a has-been, and she hires Nick to recover pictures of her that were presumably taken by her husband, Charles Barkeley, with her skirt flying in the air and revealing her pussy; the photos could endanger her film comeback (remember, this is 1943). Strangely, she has the negatives, which she gives to Nick for safekeeping, and soon Nick is being bashed on the head and kicked in the balls by sundry characters who want them. Dixie's daughter, Leslie (Kelly Nichols), Veronica Hart, and Samantha Fox are all involved. Before it's over, you've guessed that Dixie Ray has purposely set up Nick and has murdered her husband, but, in a philosophical conclusion, you realize she will get away with it by telling the jury she did it because her husband seduced her daughter. Good acting by all, especially Lisa de Leeuw.

DON'S PARTY
R NN NL
1976   VIDAMERICA

P/D—**Bruce Beresford**
F/A—**Jeannie Dryman, Veronica Lang, Cindy Raymond, Kit Taylor**
F/A—**John Hargreaves, Harold Hopkins, Pat Bishop, Graham Kennedy**

Here's an R movie that, with luck, you might catch on cable TV—if not, rent it or buy it. Don (John Hargreaves), a professor in Sydney, Australia, who is in his early 30s, has been married to Kath for quite a few years, and they have one child. At this point in their marriage they don't see eye to eye on much, especially Don's enthusiasm for other, more sexy women. On election night, Don invites five couples to watch the returns in his home. Kath (Jeannie Dryman), who is a delightful actress, is not too enthusiastic about the odd assortment of couples, most of whom are Don's friends, but they quickly arrive and start consuming the cases of beer and liquor and the food that Don has bought and Kath prepared. Before the evening is over there are continuous, hilarious sexual regroupings and much straying with other people's spouses. The election returns are quickly forgotten while Kath gets increasingly incensed at Don and his guests, who end up invading the swimming pool of a next-door neighbor (who is out of town). It comes very close at the end to an orgy and a spouse switch, and it proves that, with a relatively small budget, adult-film makers, if they weren't so intent on filling half of 80 or 90 minutes with genital close-ups, could offer plenty of sex plus a slice of life that more viewers could identify with. You'll see plenty of female nudity and humping in this one, but no explicit sex.

DREAMS OF MISTY
CC NN NM BI
1985   VCX

P/D—**Bill William, John C. Holmes, Max Strand**
F/A—**Misty Dawn, Shalimar, Tantala, Pat Manning, Shaun Michelle**
F/A—**Nick Random, Scott Irish**

When Dr. Banks (Misty Dawn), a sex therapist, arrives in her office, she finds Sherry (Shalimar) masturbating on her desk. Then, in a surrealist flashback, you see a terrible dream that Sherry has been having of being accosted in a wheelchair by a naked man. He is about to rape her, but she rises from the chair and kicks him in the balls, and then she sees Dr. Banks at the end of a long hall, naked and doing ballet exercises. She joins her, and they make love, and once again the naked man, whom you now recognize as John Holmes, appears. But this time, holding him in an arm lock, she practically strangles him, after which she and the doctor enjoy big John's schlong. All this is a prelude to the story of how Dr. Banks became a doctor and what her childhood was like, which she now tells Sherry. You see her 10 years earlier (with her small breasts, Misty Dawn really looks like a teenager). She's showering, and she hears her mother and father making love in the next room. In the ensuing days it becomes apparent that Daddy has a lover, his secretary, and Mom is bisexual and enjoys one of her club friends in the privacy of her home. Both Mom and Dad arrive home with their extracurricular mates. They are unaware of each other or daughter, who has come home from school early because she is not feeling well. Playing with herself in bed, she's having fantasies of screwing with the naked men whom she is looking at in *Playgirl* magazine. But then she becomes aware of the activity in the rest of the house. Finding Daddy with his mistress and Mommy romping with another lady is enough to make anyone a little batty. Instead she became a doctor, and is happy to tell Sherry that her father and mother didn't get divorced but decided to put up with each other's peccadilloes. Misty Dawn, Pat Manning, and Nick Random do a good acting job, and Random is perfectly cast as the upper-income horny father.

DRILLER
CC NN BI NL DK
1985 VCA

P/D—Timothy Green Beckly, Joyce James
F/A—Taija Rae
F/A—Mr. J., Dick Howard.

If you're so old that you've never seen Michael Jackson's best-selling rock video *Thriller,* you may not appreciate this one, which is billed as a "poon-porn parody." It begins with Mr. J., a guy who looks like Jackson and sings in the same falsetto voice while he's cheered by every sexy female in sight. Dan (Dick Howard) takes Louisa (Taija Rae), his girlfriend, who is in her early teens, home after the Mr. J. "Driller" concert. Dan wants some quick sex on the living-room couch, even though her parents are upstairs in bed. Finally rid of Dan, Louisa goes to bed and turns on a late-show horror movie on TV. After watching werewolves and vampires, she's soon immersed in her own nightmare—an even scarier story. Horrible male and female creatures invade her bedroom, as does Mr. Driller, singing a catchy rock song. What follows includes monsters with fluorescent pricks, Driller turning into a horrible creature with an 18-inch prick that twirls and dances into Louisa's vagina, screwing in a graveyard, and a zombie orgy to end orgies, plus much more, all cleverly photographed and choreographed and with rock music that blends it all together. The producer of this one is also the producer of *Cafe Flesh* (see review), which became a cult porno movie.

EASY ALICE
CC NN BI DA
1976 VCA

P/D—Not Given
F/A—Linda Wong, Annette Haven, Candida Royalle, Leslie Bovee
F/A—Joey Silvera, Paul Scarff, John Leslie

Who Easy Alice is is a mystery that I never solved. The film was made earlier than 1976, because none of the actors or actresses listed above is given his or her usual screen name in the credits. Nevertheless, the story of one day in the life of Joey Silvera has a slice-of-life reality that captures one's interest. It opens with a director trying to shoot a porno quickie and discovering that the female actress absolutely refuses to act with the male because he's too rough with her. The assistant director puts in a call for Joey, who is living with Linda Wong and is happily screwing her. But despite Linda's grim response ("You're not going to make another porno?"), Joey can't refuse the $150 for a one-day shoot. Joey is so nice to the female that after the shoot (pun intended) she applauds him. But then Joey and the bad guy (Paul Scarif) go out together. Early in the morning they walk into a laundromat, where the only occupant, Candida Royalle, is trying to do her laundry. By this time Joey is bombed enough to help Paul tease her a little, but he's horrified when Paul jumps her and in a scary scene rapes her on the floor. Joey is no hero. He runs, leaving Paul and the helpless Candida, who can't escape Paul, who can't believe that she didn't enjoy herself. By the time Joey arrives home, early the next morning, Linda has spent most of the evening with Annette and her boyfriend in the threesome "paying Joey off." But even though Joey won't promise her that he'll stop taking porno jobs, she still loves him, and he goes to bed with her. *Pal Joey* would be a better title for this one.

EAT AT THE BLUE FOX
CC   NN   NL
1984   VCA

P/D—Damon Christian
F/A—Ron Jeremy, Herschel Savage, Harold Greene, Gerald Greystone
F/A—Pamela Mann, Kitten Natividad, Desiree Lane

In 1964 when the first novel I had written, *The Rebellion of Yale Marratt,* was being promoted for a movie (still not made) and I was traveling up and down the coast of California promoting "bigamy as a solution for the divorce rate," I ended up in Tijuana, Mexico, with my wife and my brother and his wife where we discovered the famous Blue Fox. That night we all saw sexual sights we had never dreamed of—including a packed house of American males who not only ate food at the Blue Fox, but all the pussy in sight. The next morning—Sunday—the obliging Mexican ladies all attended Mass, and I'm sure God blessed them for being good wives and earning a little extra money from the crazy Americanos. Richard Aldrich a.k.a. Damon Christian has tackled this story in a largely cleaned-up version of the Blue Fox, and, with a chuckle, has incorporated overtones of Humphrey Bogart and Casablanca. It seems that Rick Simpson owns the Blue Fox now, but it has fallen on hard times. A super highway is being built to bypass Tijuana (and although Aldrich doesn't mention it, today you can get wilder shows in Los Angeles and San Francisco). To top it off, the Mexican police and their obnoxious fat Mexican Chief of Police have closed the joint and arrested the strippers who also entertain the customers in the backroom. (This is factual, but Richard Aldrich's backrooms look like the Ritz Carleton compared to the former Blue Fox stalls.) The story line is lighthearted. Ron Jeremy is the star of this production. (He's a cross between Jamie Gillis, as a bad buy and himself as a comedian.) His adversary is the Mexican Police Chief. In a very funny twist, the Chief of Police discovers that the super highway won't actually open for two years because someone has blown up the connecting bridge, so because the tourists are once more pouring into Tijuana, he insists on keeping the Blue Fox open. What's more, he takes over the kitchen and serves a dinner of Mexican specialties to a packed house. They no sooner eat it than they all get "Montezuma's curse," and have to stand in line to get to the men's room. The smell is so bad some are even wearing gas masks. In this madcap melange, Richard Aldrich manages to give you all the explicit sex you might expect, but he always underlines it with a sense of humor. Erotic film Oscars to him and Ron Jeremy and all the ladies.

EROTIC ADVENTURES OF LOLITA
CC NN NM BI DK
1982 VIDEO-X-PIX

P/D—Leon Gucci
F/A—Tammy, Chelsea Manchester (a.k.a. Tigr), Copper Penny, Terri Stevens
F/A—Ron Jeremy, Henry Margolis, Ralph Harper,Ron Hamilton, Steve Parks, Doug Hamilton

Leon Gucci proved in this early sexvid that he can make a good film—given a reasonably good story and good actors. The Lolita title must have been added afterward, because the key characters, Tammy (who really looks like a 15-year-old without makeup) and Tigr (with a perpetual worried-teenager look) use their own names. They live in farm country, and Tigr, who has seen her mother and father copulating for the first time, talks it over with her horse, wondering what they were doing and why. This question leads her to explore her own crotch, and soon she is caught masturbating by the hired man, who helps her out. Her friend Tammy (Lolita) still doesn't know what it's all about, but Tigr fills her in and then makes love to Tammy. Tammy soon demonstrates that she's learning fast by tongue-kissing Daddy, on her birthday, to Mommy's shock. When Mommy and Daddy are at work, a salesman selling vibrators and sex toys arrives and soon is showing them to Tammy, who discovers, with him, the delights of screwing. Later, she quickly attacks an insurance agent. Before it ends, Tammy, made up like a whore, is trying to get $100 for her services and Tigr is having an affair with her own mother.

EROTIC AEROBICS
CC NN NL BI DK
1985 VCA

P/D—Adele Robbins
F/A—Sharon Mitchell, Rene Summer, Kristara Barrington
F/A—Scott Irish, Paul Thomas, Randy West, William Margold

You can detect a woman's touch in this one. Adele uses an aerobic dance group with about 20 adult-film stars. (You'll recognize many of them who do not appear in the interwoven stories.) They're dressed in workout clothes, dancing and exercising to the commands of a female instructor, and they provide the integrating element for a group of funny little memories that are crossing the minds of some of the dancers. You see Randy West dragging a half-naked, reluctant Kristara Barrington through the woods into an old western town and tossing her into a metal cage, through which she blows him. Then when he enters the cage and tries to screw her she escapes and runs naked down the street. The next diversion is with Paul Thomas, dining at home, on a perfectly set table with a woman, in an unfinished house that is composed only of studs. He recites Shakespeare, including: "What a piece of work is man, how noble in reason," while his tuxedo-dressed butler unzips himself for the lady's lips and then ejaculates in her salad. That's followed by another female capture sequence which is seductively lighted and during which a guy makes love to a woman's floating pussy. Next Renee Summer, tits out, in an old-fashioned western-style saloon, seduces a guy while he's singing "Ghost Riders in the Sky" to a guitar accompaniment. It all ends back with the dancers, who are still fully clothed, removing their workout suits and having a happy orgy. You may want to join in the between-scenes aerobic dancing, but you'll be a little disappointed that, while they finally copulate naked, they never exercise without their clothes.

EROTIC PLEASURES
CC NN BI NL
1984 CABALLERO

P/D—Frances LeRoi
F/A—Marilyn Gulle, Chris Martin, Rene Douglas, Dolores Manta

Three lovely French ladies live in a typical French apartment house that has a cast-iron elevator surrounded by a staircase. Martine is married to a guy who never stops complaining that she doesn't know how to cook or keep house. All she wants to do is make love, but he is too busy trying to make a living so they can live in the style to which she is accustomed. Joelle is a schoolgirl who lives with a balding father who is appalled by her friends and would be even more shocked if he knew that all his daughter wants to do is lose her virginity. Arlene is a rich girl who pays her gigolos and would dearly like to find a man who loves her for herself. The three women know each other only as people who live in the apartment building. A few days in their lives are interwoven against a wonderful Parisian background. Martine decides to cheat on her husband with a former boyfriend who is still a bachelor and lives in an environment of unwashed dishes, unmade beds, and clothes strewn everywhere. He makes very nice love to her, and there's even some extended romantic afterplay, but he thinks she's pretty bitchy when she refuses to do the dishes or clean his apartment. Next, her girlfriend proposes a threesome with her husband, but in the process the husband calls up the guys next door to come to the party. Indignant, she walks out, telling her girlfriend, "I'm not screwing everyone in Paris." She finally decides to be nice to her husband, but he arrives home and tells her that he's fed up with her and she'll be hearing from his lawyer in the morning. In the meantime, Joelle bumps into a guy near the Arc de Triomphe who brings her back to his apartment, presumably to relieve her of her virginity. But he can't get an erection unless she whips him and tells him, "You're my slave." Shocked, she is sure that this isn't the way it is usually done, but she whips him harder than she anticipated, after which she stalks out. Her girlfriend tells her that she has a brother who will be happy to make love to her, but before the brother arrives she seduces Joelle and tells her that she's sorry but she has no brother. Finally, her professor comes home and does the job very tenderly— and there is even blood on the sheet afterward. But alas, he leaves her a note saying, "Adieu." After being screwed doggie fashion by a gigolo who drinks coffee, smokes cigarettes, and ogles himself in the mirror while she is leaning across the dining-room table, Arlene pays him and tells him to get the hell out of her life. The next day as she is hailing a taxi she

encounters a very handsome, rich-looking young man and tries to get the same cab. They share it, and before long, as they pass the Seine and the Eiffel Tower, Arlene has hiked up her skirt and is happily bouncing on her new friend's lap. At last she thinks she has found a man who loves her not just for her money. But alas, she has to pay for the cab because he forgot his wallet. Her next encounter is with a most poetic man, who brings her back to his hotel room. While he skillfully makes love to her, he recites romantic poetry. Afterward, floating on a cloud, she watches him dress. He tells her he is going to bring back champagne to celebrate, but she soon discovers that he has left her with his hotel bill. Most of the sexmaking in this one is either quite romantic or just plain funny, and the film has a laughing French comme-çi-comme-ça sophistication that escapes most American films.

EROTIC RADIO WSSX
CC NN BI NL
1984 VCA

P/D—Robert Beachwater, Bob Augustus
F/A—Renee Summer, Tanya Lawson, Desiree Lane, Bunny Bleu, Kay Parker
F/A—Herschel Savage, Ron Jeremy, Brian Curtis, Scott Irish, Mark Harris, William Margold

All the young married couples in this San Fernando Valley town set their clock radios to WSSX and wake up to Peter Rabbit (Herschel Savage), an all-night disc jockey who sounds more sexy than their husbands ever do, especially in the morning, when the camera flits between the bedrooms of Renee Summer, Desiree Lane, and Tanya Lawson, who are left in bed unsatisfied by their husbands. When the men are gone, the ladies telephone Peter and some of them give him their address or a meeting place because he's not adverse to a little sexual adventure. And they have long sexual conversations on the phone with him, in which one of the husbands (Ron Jeremy) recognizes his wife (Renee Summer). In the meantime, Peter has been fired for screwing a female interviewee, Clarissa Redbone (Kay Parker) from the California Institute of

Sexocology, because their sighs and groans were broadcast over the air. But he is saved by a woman who manufactures and sells cosmetics door to door, who wants to advertise on WSSX because she knows that Peter is reaching her customers, literally and figuratively. The dialogue in this one is often quite funny, and acting honors go to Herschel Savage, who sounds just like a late-night disc jockey, and Renee Summer as the sexually frustrated housewife. Many years ago, in San Francisco, a guy who called himself Count Marco had a program not quite so far out sexually but almost. Living in a French provincial double bed, eating breakfast, the Count accepted phone calls around nine o'clock every morning from ladies who jammed the phone lines and made it possible for him to drive to work in a Rolls Royce.

EVERY WOMAN HAS A FANTASY
CC NN NM BI NL
1984 VCA

P/D—**Sandra Winters, Edward Brown**
F/A—**Rachel Ashley, Shantell Day, Lisa George, Erica Boyer, Martina Nation**
F/A—**John Leslie, Robert Byrne, Blake Palmer**

Ben (John Leslie) is married to Terry (Rachel Ashley). She meets with a group of her friends once a week and, as Ben discovers while he's in bed with Terry, in addition to exchanging recipes, they tell each other their fantasies. These fantasies are brought to life on the screen and include being tied, naked, to a dining-room chair while your husband takes pictures of you, or inviting the handsome young delivery boy in the house and watching each other as you both masturbate (a most detailed scene, as you watch the lady's finger playing with her engorged clitoris and shivering vulva as she climaxes), or a female news commentator who is reading the news but is really thinking about undressing in front of the TV cameras so that all can behold her (also playing with herself). Ben gets so wrapped up in these fantasies as his wife retells them, while they are making love in a very believable marital bedroom encounter, that he fantasizes the

ladies' fantasies (and ends up screwing all the ladies listed above). He finally convinces his wife to bring a tape recorder to the next meeting. But that proves insufficient. He wants to see the ladies' faces as they tell their fantasies, so he hides in a closet. But the tour de force is when Terry insists that if he is so interested, he can do what Dustin Hoffman did in *Tootsie*, become a woman, and she will take him to the next meeting as her husband's cousin. John Leslie as a woman is much prettier than Hoffman, and funnier. Rachel Ashley is a good actress, and she really looks like a plump, big-breasted, big-ass wife from suburbia who could attract any man. She does in a scene with Robert Byrne in a hotel room (her fantasy come true?), which is exceptionally well done. Whether they agree or not, most women will like this film. Incidentally, lest you think the idea of women exchanging their sexual fantasies is far out, remember that truth is stranger than fiction. In the San Francisco area, there is the Kensington Ladies Erotica Society, a group of upper-class, middle-aged ladies that meets once a month in Berkeley, California, to read aloud erotica they have written themselves. Some of the selections were published in 1985 by Ten Speed Press, and the $8.95 paperback has sold surprisingly well.

EXPERIMENTS IN BLUE
CC NN BI NL DK
1981 CABALLERO

P/D—**Frances LeRoi**
F/A—**Christine Craig, Michelle Thomas**
F/A—**John Vincent, Patrick Dally**

This one is advertised as one of the 10 best films on the European circuit in 1981. Made in Paris, it has an underlying sense of laughter that escapes most American producers. It also offers many interesting Parisian exterior and interior scenes that will make you want to take off for Paris. The first 10 minutes cover the first four wedding anniversaries of William and Joelle Le Brandt and Joelle's increasing awareness that with William business comes first; he's always rushing off to some meeting or going on a selling trip to London. But he does bring home a pretty maid to help Joelle with the housework—and surprisingly never touches her. After reading a book that her brother has written about sexual freedom, Joelle decides that it's time for her to experiment. Soon she is blowing a surprised but willing chauffeur while he stands near his limousine in busy Paris traffic. Then she tries the maid, and a few days later a session with the husband of a friend, during which the wife prepares her ass and vagina by rubbing them with sliced cucumbers while her husband paws the carpet barefoot like a bull in heat, waiting to take her doggie style. Although William is sleeping with a hooker in London, he's really in love with Joelle and can't stop thinking about her. He'd fly home immediately, but he's grounded in London by a transport strike. Joelle, in the meantime, in a hilarious scene, is so sexually deprived that she parks her Volkswagen at a busy intersection not far from the Arc de Triomphe, puts down the car roof, slips down her panties, and masturbates behind the wheel, to the surprise and amusement of male tourists passing by. By the time William arrives home, Joelle has been to a group-sex party sponsored by her brother, but tired as she is, she's happy to see William again and is still loving.

EXPOSE ME NOW
CC NN NM BI NL
1982   CAL VISTA

P/D—Sam Norvell, Roy McBride, Joe Sherman
F/A—Danielle, Lynx Cannon
F/A—Herschel Savage, Ron Jeremy, Richard Pacheco, Paul Thomas

Abel (Ron Jeremy) is a bad ass, and Shane (Herschel Savage), his brother, is a simple guy who loves everybody. Their wealthy uncle dies and leaves his entire estate, including a mansion, to Shane on the condition that, like him, between 6:00 and 9:00 (69, of course) every evening he devote his time to doing good deeds. To Abel he leaves "jack shit." Exasperated, Abel tries to sell their uncle's mansion out from under Shane while Shane, wearing his boy-scout uniform, is wandering around

the town helping old ladies across the street and letting a girl scout practice tying knots on him so that she can qualify for a merit badge. "Girl scouts have strange activities these days," he sighs, as she ties him up, opens his zipper, and blows him. In the meantime, Abel has hired Sondra (Danielle) and a couple of other ladies to show the mansion to potential buyers, who included Paul Thomas as a British millionaire and Richard Pacheco as the gardener of a Mexican millionaire, as well as a lady executive who enjoys women and cucumbers. Naturally, the ladies also show their own genital properties to the prospective clients. One of them, to Abel's disgust, mixes up the Mexican millionaire with the millionaire's gardener. After a very satisfying session on the couch with Richard, she asks if he's ready to buy the house, but he sadly tells her, "I can't even afford toilet paper. I steal it at the filling station." Finally, Abel gives up and decides that he's destined for marriage with Sondra. In the meantime, Shane has gotten married. They are finally happily reconciled with each other and with each other's wife. There's a lot of silly laughter in this one that will keep you amused.

FANTASY FULFILLED
CC NN NR
1975   FANTASY/CABALLERO

P/D—N. Conts
F/A—Mary Love, Tracy Npeit, Alisa Troy
F/A—Henry Gite, John Pais, Tim Ward

If you've ever thought about spouse swapping, once called wife swapping (which differs from swinging because it occurs among a small group of friends), then you'll find this one amusing. It has realistic dialogue and a group of very average-looking men and women, one of whom, Peggy, is old enough to have saggy breasts. John and Peggy awake to a morning sex encounter, a shower, and the arrival of their niece Louise from Boston. A party is planned for the next evening, and Chris and Irene, Freda and Bob, and another couple are invited. Louise goes out for the evening with a boyfriend, and the three couples are soon discussing marriage and sexual boredom and the advantage of having sex with a different person after many years of marriage. Soon they decide to give it a whirl and are nervously undressing and guiltily making love in different rooms. They have scarcely returned to the living room to say good night when the niece returns and is amazed that they could do such a thing. Next day, she makes love romantically with her boyfriend, and you're sure that *she's* not going to fool around when she's married. (See notes under *Christy.*)

FAREWELL, SCARLET
CC   NN   BI (subdued)   NL (happily corny)   DK
1979   COMMAND VIDEO

P/D—Cecil Howard
F/A—Terri Hall, Jennifer Jordan, Kim Pope, Dulce Mann, Darby Lloyd Raines, Kati Maria
F/A—J. P. Parradine, Eric Edwards, Roger Caine, Doug Wood, Al Levitsky, Barry Christian

Don't miss this early Cecil Howard film. Howard told me that it wasn't up to the standards of his later films, but it has a vintage 1970s feel (when directors and producers were competing against each other rather than going for the fast buck), and it mixes sex with laughter and sheer silliness in a way that makes it fun to watch. Scarlet (Terri Hall) is a lady whom all her friends loathe for one reason or another. But they wouldn't miss the parties she runs in her mansion. One of her group-sex orgies is in progress, and tonight all the participants must strip naked and put on blindfolds. Men and women can find each other only by playing touchies. When you're finally screwing you don't know with whom. In the midst of things, some guy who must have been peeking, gets Scarlet and shoves a dildo down her throat. She gags and dies. No one hears her scream or knows who did it. Enter Dexter Sleuth (J. P. Parradine), a not-too-bright private detective, who is hired by Olga Rich, Scarlet's maiden aunt, to find who done it. Sleuth investigates one person after another and with each is sure that he's got the real murderer. Scarlet's life and sexual relationships with Con-

nie Columnist, Beatrice and Anthony Broker, Celeste Star, and Senator Graft are revealed in flashbacks, and in every case she has screwed up their lives. A very funny sequence shows her being directed by Sam Smut, a porno-film producer, whom she refuses to listen to. She gets so horny for the leading man that the crew has to pry them apart. Throughout the cinematography is erotic and interesting. The story drags a little at the end as Sleuth brings all the people together in the familiar "one-of-you-in-this-room-did-it" ending. Who did it? The butler, of course.

FELICITY
CC   R   NN   NR   BI
1976

P/D—Russell Hurley, John Lamond
F/A—Gloria Annen
F/A—Christopher Milne

You may catch this one on the Playboy Channel or Select TV. There's plenty of sex and nudity but no hard-ons. Using the Fanny Hill technique of a young woman telling the story of her early sex life, Felicity (Gloria Annen) reveals herself in a voice-over while you watch her actions. (At least in the first half. In the second half her motivations are pretty confused.) The story begins in England, where she is a schoolgirl. Finishing school, Felicity is invited for the summer to Hong Kong to stay in the home of a wealthy friend of her father. From this point on, the film, which is British made, creates an erotic background of a cosmopolitan Chinese city and will remind you a little of *Emmanuelle* (see review), as Felicity watches her friend and her husband make love, tries sex with a Eurasian woman who is guiding her around the city, loses her virginity to a wealthy playboy on the hood of his car, sleeps with a Chinese stranger on a sampan, and is finally saved by a young Englishman, Myles (Christopher Milne), from being raped as she cruises the city alone. Once she finds Myles, a long love affair ensues (including screwing with him on top of a bus), but then Myles is transferred up the coast, and Felicity has sex standing up in a sleazy bar as she works her way north in search of him. She finally finds him on a deserted beach with a broken arm, and the romance continues for a while, at least. You'll enjoy the tour of Hong Kong, and it proves that with a bigger budget, an interesting, almost-X-rated film can be made.

THE FELINES (The Cats)
CC NN BI
1975 VCX

P/D—Stanley Miels, Daniel Daert
F/A—Janine Renaud, Pauline Larrieu, Nathalie Ziegler
F/A—Jacques Insermini, Georges Gurrett

Here's one of the best French-made adult films with the lushest backgrounds you've ever seen. It belongs in any top-50 list. Maude (Janine Renaud, who also appears in *Marianne Bouqet*; see review) is married to Oliver (Jacques Insermini) a 50-year-old, balding, beefy, but very wealthy Frenchman. Oliver has a mistress, Clare (Pauline Larrieu), and although he makes very nice love to Maud when Clare isn't available, he isn't about to give up Clare, and Maud is likely to get her face slapped if she indicates that Clare is wrecking their marriage. Then one night while Oliver is away, Maud meets Florence (Nathalie Ziegler) at the home of a friend. She knows that Oliver is a patsy for strange pussy, and she thinks that if she brings Florence home, maybe he'll forget Clare. With Florence under her own roof, Maud thinks she can control Oliver better. Thus begins the seduction of Oliver, at which Florence (who doesn't look over 17) is an expert. In the meantime, Florence is also wooing Maud and thus making her future in this wealthy world doubly secure. Oliver has a cold parting with Clare, and the film ends with Oliver subduing a wild stallion, but you know that his mind is on Florence, who now has him in her power, too.

FEMALE INPERSONATORS OF THE YEAR PAGEANT
CC PG
1984 NEW WORLD VIDEO

P/D—Howard Schwartz, John Moriarty
Hosts: Ruth Fuzzy, Lyle Wagner
F/A—see below

A PG tape in an X-rated guide? There's a reason, and even though there's no overt sex in this one, you're not likely to see it on network television, largely because it raises the question of whether the 30 contestants for best female impersonator of the year are transvestites or gay or a little of both. One thing you can be sure of, they are not transsexuals. In various cuts, after watching some of the most beautiful women you've ever seen, you see them stripped to the waist. Unlike transsexuals, they have no breasts (see review of *Trisexual Encounters*). Shot on video at the Shamrock Hilton Hotel in Houston, the hour-and-a-half show begins with all 30 guys, beautifully made up in wigs and evening gowns, parading across the stage. If you met any of them on the street you'd turn and look twice. Is she a Hollywood actress, or a wealthy guy's playmate? Twenty of the contestants are eliminated by the judges, and the remaining 10 ladies (guys?) model both evening gowns and casual dresses. In the close-ups, their gestures and walks are not those of men. They are women! Even more so later, when they imitate Tina Turner, Ann-Margret, Shirley Bassie, Barbra Streisand, Marilyn Monroe, and Liza Minelli. The guy who calls himself Naomi Sims won the contest, with a standing ovation as Liza Minelli. Women will watch this tape utterly fascinated, and guys will wonder what motivates a man to impersonate a woman. Incidentally, if you wonder about the expression *in drag*, it presumably was coined by Shakespeare, meaning "dressed as girls," which of course was a way of life on the 17th-century stage.

FEMME
CC NR BI
1984 VCA

P/D—Candida Royalle, R. Lauren Niemi
F/A—Tish Ambrose, Sharon Caine, Rhonda Jo Petty, Carol Cross
F/A—Michael Knight, Klaus Multia, George Payne, Jerry Butler, David Israel-Sander

I told Candida (a picture of her with me is in the first edition) that she could make a movie of my novel *The Rebellion of Yale*

Marratt anytime, providing she played Cynthia and Jerry Butler played Yale. After watching this tape (the first of several called *Femme* and following the same plan) I'm doubly convinced that Candida (who has appeared in many adult films, some of them pretty awful) has proved that a woman can make a more erotic and loving film than any man. In six unrelated sequences (except for sensitivity and proof that female porno stars are real women) Candida and her husband, Per Sjostrom, have created a film that Women Against Pornography will have a difficult time labeling pornographic. Although it is totally explicit, there are no cum shots. The first vignette is titled "Rock Erotica" and in it Tish Ambrose and Michael Knight, dressed as punk rockers, screw to the accompaniment of a loud, unseen rock group. In the next sequence, "TV Idol," alone in bed fully dressed, Sharon Kane is watching a soap opera on TV. A man (Klaus Multia) appears, slowly undresses, and to the background music of romantic piano, undresses her. Without talking, they make love slowly and exquisitely, almost Tantric style. This is probably the most loving sex scene you've ever watched in an adult movie, and it is obviously a woman's dream of the way she likes to be loved. Next comes "Gallery"—which is really fun to watch, as first a guy and a gal are paying more attention to each other in an art gallery than to the paintings they have come to see. Soon another guy appears, and although none of them speaks to each other the guys are fantasizing making love to her and she to them. Carol Cross as the woman is delightful, and the two guys, Michael Knight and George Payne, would appeal to most women. This is followed by "Photo Session," in which Jerry Butler is snapping pictures of Rhonda Jo Petty and ends up making love to her after she oils him up, literally and figuratively. Two more episodes, "Sales Pitch," which offers a short bisexual sequence as the Avon–style lady sells cosmetics to her customer, and "Dressing Room," with Carol Cross and David Israel-Sander in another totally romantic sequence, conclude the tape. Except for the rock-music sections, all the others are accompanied by original Steve Halperin–style mood music. You'll want to own this one.

FINISHING SCHOOL
CC NN BI DK
1976 VCX

P/D—Lloyd Richards
F/A—Cinda Grazier, Margaret Silverman
F/A—Joey Silvera, Harry Wills

David Peters (listed in the credits as Neil Long) teaches political science at a university (not a finishing school) that looks, from exterior shots, like Berkeley. In his coed class, he can't keep his eyes off the young women. One of them, Laura (Linda Grazier), fantasizes that she sees him naked with an erection. When her friends invite her to a sex party, she shrugs at a guy who looks about 18. "You're too young. I need a man." Actually, Laura doesn't look much over 18, and is a plump 130-pounder. She looks like a girl you'd meet in church. Peters can't get his mind off her, either, but as his fellow teacher, a handsome black guy, tells him, there's plenty of other stuff on campus. Eventually, Laura, who is flunking Peter's course, is invited to Peter's office to discuss the problem, and soon she's got her wish. He makes the approach, and she happily screws with him. Afterward, he shrugs, puts on his pants, and tells her, "You wanted a good fuck. You got it. Now get back to class and do some work for a change."

FIRESTORM
CC NN NR BI DK
1984 COMMAND

P/D—Cecil Howard
F/A—Victoria Jackson, Joanna Storm, Kay Parker, Sharon Kane, Rikki Harte, Sharon Mitchell
F/A—Eric Edwards, John Leslie, Michael Bruce, George Payne, Kurt Mann

Put this tape in your top 10 for couple viewing. Nineteen eighty-four opened the floodgates on adult films shot directly on videotape. Many of them are low-budget quickies that do nothing to upgrade the image of adult films. But Cecil Howard, who shoots only on film, has gone all out technically and financially to prove that adult films (even with some of the conventions retained) can be interestingly plotted, with good character development. This story takes place in a wealthy "Dynasty"-style environment ruled by Magda Balcourt (Kay Parker) and her husband (John Leslie), whose attractive daughter Claire (Joanna Storm) is suffering psychological blindness caused by discovering her mother fucking Claire's first real boyfriend immediately after her birthday party. Magda has invited novelist Ken Cushing (Eric Edwards) to live in her palatial home and write the story of her life. You gradually discover that Cushing is basically a nice guy who has known quite a few women. You see him in happy action with Sharon Mitchell and Lisa (Victoria Jackson). Up until a few years ago he was living more or less monogamously with Lisa, but then he returned one day to their apartment and found her screwing in a foursome. His memory of this is like no group sex you have ever seen before— rather, it is a kind you might experience in a dream and not quite recall the next morning. As the story develops on several levels it is apparent that Magda's real reason for wanting Cushing to live in her house while he writes the story of her life is to seduce him and get her revenge on her husband for playing around with other women, particularly Barbara (Rikki Harte), a warmly sensuous blonde who you may be certain will appear in other films. But to the shock of both Magda and his friend Lisa (whom Cushing has rediscovered as a stripper in a bar) Ken falls in love with Claire. After making love with her in a very caring way (she can't see him and they are caught in the act by Magda), Claire runs away with Ken. But once again Magda ruins Claire's love life. She seduces Ken, and Claire hears them fucking. The shock restores her eyesight and ends the romance. Amazingly, Howard, with the help of a good screenwriter (Anne Randall), tells this complicated, almost incredible story so that you get involved with it

and believe it. He succeeds through excellent cinematography (ranging from sharp, clear lighting to chiaroscuro effects that suit the mood of the story), fast editing, good acting, and never staying too long on the genital aspects of sex. In the first edition I reviewed Cecil Howard's *Scoundrels, Platinum Paradise, Foxtrot, October Silk, Neon Nights, Fantasex, Babylon Pink, Heatwave,* and *Jailbait.* In this edition you'll find reviews of Howard's earlier films, *The Final Sin, Farewell, Scarlet, Lecher, Georgia Peach, Babylon Gold, Heavy Load, Handful of Diamonds,* and *Spitfire.* Cecil autographed the tape he gave me of *Firestorm*: "For Bob, X.T.C. Forever." It's a philosophy that permeates most of his films.

FLASH
CC   NN   DK   BI
1981   CABALLERO

P/D—Jack Genero
F/A—Hillary Summer, Raven Turner, Jane Lindsay, Connie Peters
F/A—Tommy La Roc, Don Bruce, Lloyd Allen, Lance de White

Who says that adult films are plotless? There's so much plot in this one that at times you'll think that Jack Genero got confused in the editing—but a second viewing will show you that he picked up all the marbles. It begins with Jessica Collins (Hillary Summer), a photographer for *Flash* magazine, being driven to the airport in a limousine to meet her girlfriend. Sucking a dildo in the backseat, she sees a suspicious-looking guy outside a bank reading *Flash* and tells the chauffeur to stop while she takes pictures. Spreadeagled in the backseat, the chauffeur helps her take pictures of the guy and another guy and woman emerging from the bank—and he services Jessica at the same time. Cut to a woman, Maxine (Raven Turner), having her hair washed and being completely made up by a hairdresser. They are making love but are being watched by one of the guys from the bank, who has seen Jessica taking the pictures. Switch to the bank robbers counting a bagful of stolen money and

Denise Rockland (Jane Lindsay), who is sobbing and watching in horror a fuck film of herself that she made years before when she was broke—but now will be exposed, if she doesn't cooperate, to defeat her father who is running for governor. Denise asks herself, "How did I ever get into such a mess?" And so you might, too. But you won't be able to quit now. Cut to Maxine and her boyfriend spraying each other with vegetable oil and then enjoying a slippery fuck. Cut to Jessica's boyfriend finding her in a tub, spanking her and playing S&M games with her, which Jessica adores. Cut to two guys taking Jessica to see her boss, the owner of *Flash* magazine, who you now discover is one of the bank robbers. Seems the magazine isn't doing too well. Then somehow, because her boss's flunkies thought that Maxine, her girlfriend, and not Jessica is the one who took the pictures of them, Maxine is taken to a farmhouse in the desert by her boss, and a few cuts later Jessica herself is kidnapped by one of the crooks, who forces her to blow him while he is flying them in a small plane to the hideout. But worry not, Jessica takes over (seems she can fly a plane, too) and rescues Maxine from her villainous boss in an eye-popping finale as she buzzes the farmhouse and kills the bastard. Jack Genero has made 50 or more adult films and knows filmmaking inside and out. He has also written an excellent how-to book (not yet published) on how to make adult films which goes into full financial detail as well as the technical and emotional problems of dealing with the actors and actresses, and he obviously enjoys making movies that are full of action sexual and otherwise!

FRENCH LETTERS
CC NN BI NR
1985 CABALLERO

P/D—**Robin Goodhill, Joe White**
F/A—**Shanna McCullough, Valerie La Veau, Lili Marlene**
F/A—**Paul Thomas, Billy Dee, Mike Horner, Gene Hardman, Francois Papillon**

The title is misleading. This is not a French-made film. The letters are simply the di-

ary of a young woman, Melissa (Shanna McCullough), who has recorded the main sexual events of her life, which we watch in retrospect. As a high-school student she and her girlfriend seduce their biology teacher (Mike Horner) at a summer camp. In college she falls in love with Chuck (Billy Dee), and they get married. Then after several not-too-happy years, she discovers a videotape that he has made of himself with another woman (Lili Marlene). Melissa's so shocked by his infidelity that she divorces him. But never mind. Her girlfriend, to whom she tells her problems, consoles her, and soon she meets Henri (Francois Papillon) a handsome Frenchman with whom she shares a hot tub on her patio, and she enjoys romantic love with him. But she's still drifting and then she gets a phone call from David (Paul Thomas), who asks her to meet him in an Italian restaurant owned by a friend of his. It's closed on Mondays, and they have the place to themselves. Even before they order dinner, she's stretched out on a red tablecloth in the restaurant with her legs open to receive him. The story ends where it began, with Melissa reading her diary and now happily married to David—and proves it once again in a romantic in-bed conclusion. Most women will like this one, and guys will be intrigued by the pretty, girl-next-door quality that Shanna McCullough exudes.

FROM HOLLY WITH LOVE
CC NN NM NR
1976 CABALLERO

P/D—**Robert Norman?**
F/A—**Marlene Willoughby, Joanna Miquel, Patti Sebring, Crystal Sync**
F/A—**R. Bolla, Tony Perez, Jeffrey Hurst**

The question mark after Norman's name is because the director is not listed in the credits; nor for that matter is the date of the film. But if you watch *Women Tormented* (see review), you'll note that the same beach house on Fire Island was used for both films, and the expert film technique is the same. What's more, you won't believe that R. Bolla was so handsome and Marlene Willoughby so pretty

10 years ago. The believable story concerns Holly (Joanna Miquel, a Puerto Rican actress who if she still made films would give Vanessa Del Rio some competition). She tells the story of her life in a flashback to a john, who wonders why such a pretty girl ever took up hooking. Seems that her mother and father died and she went to live with her older sister Trish (Patti Sebring) and her husband, Lou (R. Bolla). Lou couldn't keep his eyes off her. You can't blame him, since she was a virgin cock teaser who walked around the house naked. Despite his protests that Trish was not bringing her up right, Lou leaves her alone until the very end. Lou and Trish own a summer home on Fire Island, and Holly is quickly involved with the guys and gals on the beach and Lou grows more and more unhappy. Trish is always so sexually cautious with him in bed because Holly might hear them. Hal (Tony Perez, he of the big hook) falls in love with Holly. Trish picks up the local bartender when Lou goes to town on legal business with Marlene. Lou returns, but Trish rejects him and he rapes Holly. Holly totally rejects Hal (because he loves her) and screws in front of him with his nasty friend on a speedboat. In case you believe everything Holly has told you, you have to watch the ending of this well-made film to find the truth.

FROM RUSSIA WITH LUST
CC NR NL BI (laughing)
1984 VCA

P/D—George Kay
F/A—Cara Lott, Cody Nicole, Jesse Adamovich
F/A—Randy West, Igor Pregun, Bill Stewart

Put this one on your top sexvid list. Although the film obviously was not made in Russia, from the very beginning the director, with shots of Paul Stevenson (Randy West) arriving at the Moscow airport and being met by a female Russian guide, Natasha (Cara Lott), convinces you that you are in Moscow. Cara Lott, who does a superb acting job, speaks English as if she learned it in Russia. Randy is immediately on the make for Cara, who realizes that she is being followed by the KGB—in

this case, one female and one male. She can't go to his hotel, but she invites him to her family's cottage outside Moscow, and you are treated to a believable outdoor, bucolic, loving, sexmaking sequence where they both play naked in the barnyard, Cara being pulled in a wagon by a naked Randy, who doubles as her horse, and a naked Cara being bounced around in a wheelbarrow amid the horses and goats, with believable Russian background music that should make this an award-winning joyous, explicit sex scene. Cara then takes Randy to a steam bath, where a happy, hefty Russian, Igor (most of the characters actually speak Russian), has just made enthusiastic love to his assistant Olga. During the days that Cara is his guide, they drink enormous quantities of Stolly vodka and she takes him to her friend's birthday party, which ends in switching of partners and much happy singing in Russian and boisterous screwing that Americans might well assume reflects a Russian joy of sex. Randy is finally arrested by the KGB woman for distributing American pornographic magazines (he gives them to the guys at the birthday party) and degrading Russian women with group sex. But the KGBer can't resist him either, and the film ends with Randy at the airport being separately wept over by his two Russian girlfriends. It ends with a "to be continued." It should be. In a slap happy way it's believable as *Moscow on the Hudson* and proves that adult filmmakers with a little imagination can make a film that will keep you interested.

GEORGIA PEACH
CC NN BI DS (plot oriented)
1981 COMMAND

P/D—Michael Bernard, Cecil Howard
F/A—Jean Dalton, Hope Stockton, Michelle Damon
F/A—Jeffrey Hurst, Zebedy Colt (and a guy, who looks suspiciously like Cecil Howard, to whom the story is told)

This one has a copyright date of 1981, but I'm pretty sure that it was made in the mid-1970s. Although Command Video is pushing it in a fancy box, Cecil Howard was reluctant to send it to me because it's one of his earlier films and not up to his current standards. (See reviews of *Firestorm* and *Spitfire*.) Current producers should make one so good! The cinematography offers many of Howard's special film effects, especially a dramatic scene with Michu, the name Steve (Jeffrey Hurst) has given to the Georgia Peach, "the most beautiful woman I have seen in my life." In this scene, Jean Dalton (who has long since disappeared from adult films) describes her rape by three men to the professor's daughter Priscilla (Hope Stockton). In a clever, scary sequence, you watch anonymous hands, faces, and cocks work over her. The story, told by Steve, is about this southern gal who he believes was white-slaved from a southern village before she ended up in the professor's house as the professor's mistress. Steve sees her first through the window of the professor's (Zebedy Colt) study, fellating him as he reads ancient history to her. Jean Dalton has a very unusual, childish face. Hope Stockton is pretty, and Jeffrey Hurst, if he had stayed in adult films, would be a top star—along with Zebedy Colt, a great actor, who has also vanished.

GIRLS ON FIRE
CC NN BI NL
1984 VCX

P/D—Bill Amerson, J. Remy
F/A—Angel, Shanna McCullough, Kim Carson, Roxanne Potts, Vicki Vickers, Shaun Michelle, Ginger Lynn
F/A—Jamie Gillis, R. Bolla, Harry Reems, John Holmes, Bobby Bullock

Funny adult films are rare, and this one, which has a *Guys and Dolls* feel to it, has some good laughs. It could have been even funnier if the story had been tightened a little and the editing were better. Acting awards go to the guy and gal who play Tony Cardozo and his wife, Cherry, but I couldn't identify them from the credits. Anyway, Tony, a Mafia gangster, knows that his wife, Cherry, is cheating on him, and vice versa. She tells insurance investigators Danny (Jamie Gillis) and Greg (Bobby Bullock) in a squeaky New York City doll accent, "He's shacked up somewhere with a lousy broad, but I don't care. He's a lousy lay anyway." But Danny and Greg aren't. Checking Tony's house to find evidence of an insurance fraud he's attempting, they are soon both in her bed enjoying Cherry in the sack. Then Tony comes home unexpectedly. He points his pistol at Danny's head and pulls the trigger, but he has forgotten to load the gun! Danny and Greg, wearing only towels, rush for the door in a hurry and are pursued by Tony's hoods, one of whom is Rocco (John Holmes). You already know that a few doors away Launcelot, (R. Bolla), a gay lingerie designer, is rehearsing a fashion show and is warning his ladies not to mess around with men until the show is over. But, unknown to him, Danny, wearing a lady's bathrobe and shower cap, and Greg are already hiding out in the place, and Rocco, wearing women's clothes, has invaded the premises looking for them. Encountering Ginger Lynn, one of Launcelot's models, Rocco loses his gun out of his bodice. Ginger grabs it and tells him not to get any funny ideas or "I'll blow your balls right off." And she nearly does with her mouth and vagina as poor Rocco begs for mercy. Here and there it becomes corny instead of funny, largely because the chase isn't dangerously realistic enough, and the ending is contrived.

GLITTER
CC NN NR
1983 CABALLERO

P/D—Roberta Findlay
F/A—Shauna Grant, Kelly Nichols, Rhonda Jo Petty, Marlene Willoughby, Tiffany Clark, Joanna Storm
F/A—Jerry Butler, Michael Knight, Ashley Moore, Robert Walters

David Preston (Jerry Butler) is a shy guy who has been teaching at the university. His father decides to retire and turns over to his son a supersophisticated, multimillion-door-billing ad agency, called Glitter, that he founded. Guiding him will be vice-president and next-in-command Ms. Abby Benson, (Marlene Willoughby) a fast-talking middle-aged bitch who has fucked her way to the top of the ladder. She tells David's father, whom you never see, "Farley, you old bastard, I'm going to eat your kid alive," and she tells David, "Go into your dad's office and read magazines—play with yourself—let others do the dirty work." Which for her is servicing one male client who refuses to leave his wife and children and marry her. In the meantime you have already discovered that poor meek David is completely dominated by his girlfriend Paula (Joanna Storm). David's only friend, Brad (Michael Knight), is just the opposite from David. When Brad tells a woman to lie down and open her legs or to suck his cock, she can't wait to comply. Brad tries to make David more sophisticated but to no avail. David must choose between two models, Amy (Shauna Grant) and Marcy (Kelly Nichols), to pose for a client's product. Amy of course is a female duplicate of David. Marcy, like Brad, has done it all. If you read the review of *Shauna Grant, Superstar.* You may think Amy's conversation is right out of Shauna/ Colleen's own life: "I need to be sure. I want a commitment." She tells David that she comes from a small town in Michigan. "All I ever wanted is a house, kids, and a man who loves me." In an amusing sequence, David (who can't believe that Amy would ever love him) visualizes himself as a Rudolph Valentino—a sheik who has captured poor Amy and strips her and makes her do his will. Later, with his new-found assertiveness (because he's really in love), David takes command of the ad agency. Shauna and Jerry are ideally cast as young romantic lovers. Roberta Findlay went all out to capture the-girl-you-met-in-church innocence that was a part of Colleen Applegate's charm.

GO FOR IT
CC NN BI NR NL DK
1975 VCA

P/D—F. J. Lincoln
F/A—Tiffany Clark, Gabrielle, Teresa Orlowski, Shannon, Becky Savage, Jennifer West, Victoria Jackson

F/A—Joey Silvera, Michael Morrison, Nick Niter, Jon Martin

Totally oriented around Josh Holloway (Joey Silvera), who works in an ad agency for a bitchy woman, this one was partially shot with a European background and gives Joey and the various women a chance to act quite believably. On vacation, Josh tells himself, "No more women—no more working for women." But he is no sooner ensconced in a beautiful, estate-like hotel than he runs into Eva (Gabrielle), a charming natural-blonde German woman who can't speak English very well but is totally in love with him. "I am proud to have a woman like her," he tells his associates when he brings her back to California. "Some men bring back cars and paintings from Europe. I brought back Eva." Alas, he's so busy working to support his lush California home that he arrives home every night totally exhausted and can't take care of Eva properly, and she has nothing to do all day except wait for her Josh. "Am I so bad?" she asks him. "Why do you leave me alone?" Alas, he hasn't taught her that most American men have to work for a living. Poor Eva goes to a local bar and finds she's capable of enjoying two men at once. Good-bye, Josh! So Josh goes back to Europe determined to live without women, but he's soon involved with Caroline (Tiffany Clark), who is so horny that he has to take care of her in the airplane toilet on the way home. Back home, his female boss expects him "to deliver" and give an important female client anything she wants. When he refuses, she tells him, "You're not a businessman, you're a piece of shit." Then to his shock, he catches Caroline screwing with his best friend. Once again he goes back to Europe and finally ends up with Michelle. Silvera proves in this one that he can act the part of a believable average guy whose eyes are bigger than his prick.

THE GRAFENBERG SPOT
CC NN DK
1985   MITCHELL BROTHERS

P/D—Artie and Jim Mitchell
F/A—Ginger Lynn, Annette Haven, Traci Lords, Amber Lynn, Lili Marlene, Nina Hartley
F/A—Harry Reems, John C. Holmes, Rick Savage, Thor Southern

The big sex book of 1982 was *The G Spot* by Alice Ladas and Beverly Whipple. If you want to know about the supposedly true G spot, you had better read the book. But in case you haven't, this one is a semi-serious spoof on a spot in every woman's vagina halfway up to her cervix. If properly stimulated, it will cause her to ejaculate and have big, big orgasms exceeding any regular climax. Seems that Leslie (Ginger Lynn), who has finally found the man of her dreams, Michael (Harry Reems), has a serious problem. She adores him and he her, but when she climaxes she ejaculates. (You watch this "believe-it-or-not" phenomenon with your own eyes.) This is very shocking to Michael, who finally decides he needs "normal" women. Poor Leslie. She goes to Dr. Elaine Reynolds (Annette Haven) and explains her "problem" and discovers that the male who induces it should be delighted. Eventually, Elaine reveals that she, too, can produce a stream at the moment of climax. By now the stream is becoming practically a bath. Elaine also functions as a sexual surrogate in special cases like this, so she agrees to take on Michael and lets him discover with a finger probe into her vagina the fascinating truth. In the meantime, Leslie tries a few other men, including John C. Holmes, of course, and Michael tries a few other women who haven't discovered the G spot. But they are finally reunited, and the story ends with Leslie and Michael enjoying a happy, wave-splashing climax as her G spot engulfs them.

GREAT SEXPECTATIONS
CC NN BI DK
1984   VCA

P/D—David Stone, Henri Pachard
F/A—Kelly Nichols, Honey Wilder, Joanna Storm, Chelsea Blake, Tanya Lawson

F/A—Eric Edwards, John Leslie, R. Bolla

The CC rating is for one scene and for the picture that Henri Pachard could have made but didn't because he got lost en route. This is the story of Harry Crocker (Eric Edwards), a porno-film director, and Lewis Charger (R. Bolla), a producer of regular films who is about to make his first adult film. Casting takes a bit of time—especially deciding what to do about a mother who wants her daughter to be a porn star and doesn't care if the daughter has to do an anal scene. Lewis's wife, Honey Wilder, also tests all the stud stars for him. But the real plot is that Harry has fallen in love with a female porn star, Marilyn Camp (Kelly Nichols), and he can't bear to direct her in a scene with the Big Drill (John Leslie). Harry finally ends up confessing to Marilyn that he loves her, but Marilyn doesn't believe him and in an extended scene nastily puts him and sex in general down. There's some good acting in this section, and had Pachard built his entire story around a director slowly becoming enamored with a porn actress who in real life is disillusioned with men, he might have developed some characters and had a far more interesting story.

A GUIDE TO MAKING LOVE
CC NN NR
1973   VESTRON

Hosted by Bryle Britton, Rona Lee Cohen

Give this tape to your favorite high school graduate to make up for the visual sex education lacking in most secondary schools. It's less commercial than *The Love Tapes* (see listing) and more romantic than the *Sexual Pleasure Series* (see listing). Guided by the voice-over of one of the hosts, each section is followed by a discussion with the participants. They are photographed in soft focus sexmaking which is finally totally explicit. The sections included touching; sex exercizes (to keep you in shape for a lifetime of loving); romance; sexual arousal (including sex toys and useful vegetables such as carrots and cucumbers); stripping as an erotic art—both male and female; signs of arousal; kinds of kissing; fantasies to share or not to share; masturbation together; intercourse, with a variety of positions illustrated on a revolving bed; and orgasm as a combination of pain, pleasure and ecstasy. All of the performers are beautiful people and porno aficionados will be sure that one woman called Dana—presumably married to Dave—is Bridgette Monet or a very good look-a-like.

HEAVENLY NURSE
CC NN BI
1984 CABALLERO

P/D—Gerald Kikoine
F/A—Julie Burgundy, Christy Love, Kim Vogue
F/A—Charles Darnel

Angel Hart (Julie Burgundy, I presume, although there is no character listing on this French-made film) is a practical nurse who specializes in taking care of wealthy older men. The film might have been titled *Death in the Saddle*, with Angel, who is paid by impatient relatives to help their loved ones' quick departure so they can split the loot. Handsome Charles Lambert (who lives in a huge country estate) has a wife who is so sexually frustrated that she appears in local taverns wearing a leather coat and nothing else and blows wine-drinking patrons at their tables. One son is married to a bitch who shows her tits to Charles and tries to seduce him, but Charles is equal to her and all his relatives. Before the film is over, Angel has screwed with both sons and made love to both the wife and the daughter in a very cold-blooded way. Every time that she's alone with Charles, nursing him back to health, she straddles him and gives him a mind-bending workout that you are sure is the last one he'll ever have. But wait—just as his relatives are gathered to hear, they hope, of his demise, Charles appears with Angel. Thanks to her, he tells them, he's fully recovered! He's leaving the scurvy lot of them and is going to marry Angel. On their honeymoon, he's enthusiastically telling her that this is the smartest thing he's ever done. "I love you, Angel. You saved my life." She nods sympathetically as she prepares a hypodermic injection that will make her his sole heir. Nicely acted, this one has sex, good acting, and a story that will keep you intrigued.

HOME FOR UNWED MOTHERS
CC BI NM
1985 AMBASSADOR

P/D—Not given
F/A—Marcie Carter, Linnea Stevens, Shannon O'Rourke, Keli Stuart, Polly DuBois, Laura Leche, Jean Clarke

No guys appear on this 60-minute tape, and it would be fascinating to know how the director/producer managed to find so many pregnant or recently pregnant women. The box blurb, appealing to horny men, reads: "A Bizarre Orgy of Lactating Lesbians and the Secret Desires of Pregnant Girls." I've given it a CC rating because it's a film that young men who have never seen a mother with milk-filled breasts, or a naked woman in her last months of pregnancy, can watch to learn in advance what their wives (or girlfriends) may one day look like in real life. And hopefully as they watch it (not for sexual arousal—it isn't very sexy) they will experience some of the wonder and mystery of the female body. The first section is titled "Milky Mamas" and offers two ladies who are lactating. They are young and pretty, and while they have regained their shape, their breasts are very full of milk. One lady works on hers for a long time, milking it herself, and she finally uses a breast pump. This is followed by a surprising sequence in which one young lady nurses for 10 minutes or more on the other's full tits. The second section reveals Polly DuBois, Shannon O'Rourke, and Keli Stuart, who are all in their last few months. These ladies are shown separately, and all of them, despite their advanced pregnancies, are still so hot, presumably, that they keep moaning for the cocks of the guys who got them that way, and in the meantime they are using their fingers and a vibrator.

HONEYMOON HAVEN
CC NN NL DK
1977 QUALITY/VIDEO-X-PIX

P/D—Carter Stevens
F/A—Karen St. Joy, Lisa Marks, Carol Kay, Marlene Willoughby
F/A—Richard Bolla, Wade Nichols, Al Levitsky, Bobby Astyr

Here again is a happy-go-lucky porno tape with an "innocence" about it that eludes the more pragmatic 1980 sex-film makers. Honeymoon Haven Motel is located in Intercourse, Pennsylvania. R. Bolla is the room clerk and owner. Morris (Wade Nichols) arrives with his bride, Susan (Karen St. Joy), and before he has his suitcase open to toast them with a bottle of champagne, she has locked herself in the bathroom and is not sure that she wants to do "it." No amount of cajoling will make her come out, so Morris goes down to the lobby and is soon being regaled by Bolla with stories of other bridal nights going back to 1949, when a newly married guy arrives with his wife and then left in a hurry because he got a telegram that his first wife is still alive. The best man soothes her and saves the day, and night. Bolla next tells a story about a guy who is called back to his business on his wedding night and when he returns finds his bride in bed with a stranger, whom he knocks out cold. This totally impresses his ecstatic bride. Another wedding night that Bolla describes ends up in a threesome. Two young *just* married couples also arrive and discover there is only one room available, with one bed. Bobby Astyr is one of the guys, and the discussion of who is going to sleep where and with whom is amusing. Morris finally returns to his room, and his wife is still in the bathroom, but she comes out in a hurry when he tells her not to worry, he's going to drive her home to her mother.

HOT ACTION
CC NN NM BI NL DK
1982 CABALLERO

P/D—Gerard Kikoine
F/A—Amanda Laver, Bonnie Sailor, Brigitte Bordeaux, Dominique Buzot
F/A—Guy Lorant, Jack Gateaux

If you'd like to know what goes on filming a porno in France, this one is a behind-the-scenes look with a real sense of humor. Patricia Gordon (Amanda Laver) is a freelance writer and decides to write an article on the making of a porno film. Soon she's a daily voyeur at the filmings. She discovers that today more than half the films made in France and West Germany are pornos, and the director of this one has produced a hundred of them in three years. During the entire length of this film you have a feeling that you are watching the actual making of a sexvid, and the director's and actors' and actresses' comments on what they are doing are amusing. In addition, Patricia interviews the stars and technicians and discovers among many other things that "jackoffs and freight trains" are guys who are kept around to provide erect pricks but no faces. Finally, at the end, Patricia gets so interested she decides to appear in "just one."

HOT-BLOODED
CC NN BI NL (sort of)
1985 CABALLERO

P/D—Godfrey Daniels
F/A—Kay Parker, Angel, Karen Summer, Cara Lott, Colleen Brennan
F/A—Herschel Savage, R. Bola, Harry Reems, Ron Jeremy

The only reason for the CC rating is that there is no DK action. But what begins as a potentially good story, with Linda (Kay Parker), mother to Melissa (Angel), sleeping with her boyfriend, Chris (R. Bolla) in a bedroom next to Melissa's, and the mother-daughter conflict that develops the next morning when Linda insists that her daughter wear less sexy clothes, quickly degenerates. Later, when Chris tries to make Melissa understand her mother's point of view, Melissa counters by asking him to help her with her college homework. She quickly seduces him while Mama is downstairs doing the dishes. When Linda finds them in the sack, she tells her daughter that she's not sharing her man with any woman. For all she cares Melissa can go live with that sex maniac Uncle Phil (Herschel Savage), who owns a chain of video stores that specialize in adult tapes and offer adult sex toys. Soon Uncle Phil is being serviced by Melissa's friends (Karen Summer and Cara Lott), and he offers them all jobs in his video store for the summer, with a split-the-profit deal if they increase sales.

HOT SEX IN BANGKOK
CC NL
1984 MEDIA

P/D—Erwin C. Dietrich, Michael Thomas
F/A—Many beautiful Thai women not identified
F/A—Michael Jacot, Claude Martin

At the end of World War II, after spending a year in India and China, I was a roving Finance Officer and had the good fortune to get to Bangkok a few weeks after the Japanese surrendered. The smiling Thai women, dressed in black skirts with white blouses, were the most beautiful in the Orient, and you could take your pick (overnight for about $5) for an evening of happy sex and Thai dancing with pretty teenagers who had never been told that sex and making love wasn't the best thing in the world. If you're male and watch this film, you'll want to organize your own bowling team and spend a week in Bangkok, as the eight guys in this film did. The entire film was shot in the city, on the canals and in the nightclubs, and the guys pay $20 a night for the very pragmatic Thai ladies, who hope to marry them and be brought to New York as brides. One guy does fall in love and promises to return. After you've watched the various gals (all of whom are meticulously clean and are constantly showering—or washing their male companions), you'll agree with one of them who tells her American friend, "I very sexy girl. I going to show you the time of your life, good-lookin'." Or another who stands on one guy's chest barefoot and tells him, "Don't worry, I've been doing it my way for ten years and never had an unsatisfied customer." You'll wonder if she started screwing when she was six.

HOT TOUCH
CC NN BI
1984 VCX

P/D—Bill Williams, Jeffrey Kumquat

F/A—Mindy Rae, Fawn Parris, Renee Tyffany, Beverly Glen, Tanya Harris
F/A—Don Hodges, Nick Random

This one proves that even a bottom-budget film can be made that keeps you watching. The CC rating is for the people (you've never seen most of them before), who look like your next-door neighbors. Balding Jim (Nick Random) is in bed Sunday morning and his wife, Marsha (Renee Tyffany), who is dressed in a nightgown and wearing curlers and a blue skin-tightening face mask, arrives to make love to him. In the process she finally removes her curlers and the mask, but she wonders if he is happy. He assures her that she's the best little lay around. But she probes him and wants to know his fantasies. When he pictures himself as a young stud screwing with a few different young girls, she's not too happy, but of course, she understands that these are only fantasies. Jim feels so contented with Marsha that he tells his lover, the wife of a next-door neighbor, that from now on he's going to be faithful. But she suggests an evening of bridge, during which they may decide to play some other, more interesting games. Leaving a baby-sitter, who is soon in their sack with her boyfriend, the two couples stop playing bridge, and the wives initiate things by undressing each other. The switchies initiated by the ladies are soon followed by a happy spouse exchange. If you'd like to read a more subdued version of a two couple relationship, try my novel *Proposition 31*.

HOW DO YOU LIKE IT?
CC NN BI NM NL
1985 CABALLERO

P/D—Marga Aulbach
F/A—Sharon Mitchell, Helga Sven, Aurora, Pamela Jennings, Robin Carnes
F/A—Jamie Gillis, John Leslie, Tom Byron, Herschel Savage

Marga Aulbach aims her films at women, most of whom will enjoy this one and will identify with Sharon Mitchell, who proves that she's one of the top sexvid actresses. As Midge, she has been married to psychologist Alex (Jamie Gillis) for 10 years. She's a very loving wife and would be happy to go back to work so that they can buy a new house and a second car. But Alex doesn't want her to be a working wife, and lately, although he's still very loving (Jamie Gillis plays a nice guy in this one), he's often preoccupied, and occasionally he's just too tired after working late at night on group-therapy sessions, which he presumably offers his clients, that he can't take care of his wife. The truth is that he's supplementing his income by offering a call-girl service and occasionally, although it's strictly business, he has to teach some of the surburban wives he's employing how to earn their money with the tricks he provides.

None of his friends, nor Midge, knows that he's a pimp, not even Dr. Herb Morrison (John Leslie), whose dental office is next door to Alex's in a downtown office complex. Herb is a bachelor who has a difficult time keeping his female patients from fingering his crotch while he explores their dental cavities and ignores their other offerings. For many years Herb has wanted to seduce Midge, but Alex is his best friend. Then, one night, he happens to look out his widow, and sure enough, next door he sees Alex in bed with another woman. He immediately calls on Midge and bets his Mustang against an evening in the sack with her that Alex is having an affair. After she sees Alex in action with her own eyes she still can't believe it, but she keeps drinking Herb's vodka and finally decides, "What the hell? If Alex can play around so can I."

ILLUSIONS OF ECSTASY
CC NN BI DK
1985   NOW SHOWING

P/D—Lawrence T. Cole
F/A—Ginger Lynn, Lili Marlene, Sheri St. Clair
F/A—Jamie Gillis, Billy Dee, Mike Horner, Jonathon Younger, Jon Martin

Merlyn the magician (Jamie Gillis, who is perfectly cast), with his assistant, Melanie (Ginger Lynn), offers hypnomagic in a nightclub act that transports selected people from the audience into the realm of their sexual fantasies. Lili Marlene ends up on a sex trip in the arms of a black man on a faraway island. But the audience boos Merlyn because only the girls know what is happening to them. The mental effort of performing this kind of magic is totally exhausting for Merlyn, and Melanie wants him to quit the business and transport them to a magically romantic place, but Merlyn can't give up, and he continues the next night with Billy Dee, whom he transforms into an Arab sheik with a harem while other volunteers go back in time to ancient Rome or to another planet. Finally, to please the audience, he gives them what they all want—a fantasy orgy, which turns into reality and is raided by the police. Melanie finally convinces Merlyn to retire and become a romantic lover. Typically, Cole moves the story along with a voice-over theme song.

ILSA, SHE WOLF OF THE SS
CC DS
1976   VIDEATRICS

P/D—Herman Traeger, Don Edmonds
F/A—Dyanne Thorne, C. D. LaFleur, Nicole Ridell, Sandy Richman
F/A—Gregory Knoph, Tony Mumolo, Jo Jo Deuvile

Put this one at the very top of any list of horrifying sexvids. It's the most sadistic film I've ever watched. There is no normal sex. (For the record, this and the other Ilsa films were not made by any member of the AFAA.) Interestingly, many video-rental stores don't classify the Ilsa films as porno. You never see an erect male or a female spread shot. But there's plenty of humping, nasty nudity, and blood-covered males and females. The excuse for this grimy story is given at the beginning: "The film that you are about to see is based on documented facts"—with some story action thrown in, of course, to make it entertaining. Most of the action takes place on a set that will remind you of the long-running TV series "Hogan's Heroes." The story is about Ilsa (Dyanne Thorne), the Nazi commandant of Medical Camp #9, which has both male and female prisoners. The females, some Jewish, are sterilized and then sent out in the field for the enjoyment of the German troops. The men are Jews and prisoners of war. Some of them who please Ilsa are invited to spend the night with her, after which she has them strapped in her "operating room" and told: "Once a prisoner has slept with me, he'll never sleep with another woman." After which, with the help of female attendants, she castrates them. If possible, the women get even more sadistic treatment. You watch all of them being inspected, naked, by women guards and doctors. They are strapped to racks, put in stocks, and tortured to see how much pain they can bear. Those who disobey Ilsa are flogged to death and hung upside down, naked and bloody, in front of the command post. All the women are sterilized by Ilsa, with what amounts to a vibrating hot iron. A visiting Nazi general eats a merry dinner while a naked, gagged woman, with a rope around her neck, is standing barefoot on a huge cake of ice. When it melts, she is hanged by the neck. Later, at his request, Ilsa pisses on the general: It's the only way he can get an erection. Only one American soldier, Wolfe (Gregory Knoph), is among the prisoners. But he's able to control Ilsa because, mirabile dictu, he can fuck and fuck her, all night long, and not ejaculate—something he has learned to do from childhood. Of course, Ilsa can't live without him. Eventually, with his help, the prisoners fight their way out of the camp in a bloody massacre of most of the Germans. A German officer is sent to kill Ilsa, whom Wolfe has strapped naked to the bed with her silk stocking. But evidently she doesn't die, because there's a sequel, which I'm sure you can locate in most video stores—if you can watch more of the same. All of which raises the question of censorship. In the July 29, 1985 issue of *Screw* there's an interesting essay by Marco Vassi (a well-known porn writer) who proposes: 1. that depiction of rape and child violation be made illegal; 2. that erotic art, which he carefully defines, have no legal restriction; 3. that all pornography as distinguished from erotic art be restricted to porn centers and mail order; 4. that property and facilities for these centers be made available by local governments; 5. that depictions of meta sexual activity in which the participants are willingly involved not be outlawed (that includes Bondage and Discipline). Vassi's concept of "meta sex" is

people touching one another intimately. Pornography is the depiction of meta sex. Sex itself is the method of perpetuating the species. If you read this essay, you'll come to the conclusion that one of the top pornographers would outlaw the Ilsa films—truthful or not.

INFLAMED
CC NN BI DK
1984   NOW SHOWING

P/D—Lawrence T. Cole
F/A—Misty, Debbie Greene, Renee Tiffany, Blair Harris
F/A—Dan T. Mann, Jon Martin, Lynx Cannon, Don Fernando

Put this one on your top list of really erotic sexvids. The theory is that porno films are really fantasy films, but in most cases they never tackle pure fantasy within the story line. Throughout this one Lawrence Cole has merged outstanding erotic phallic photography with a voice-over contest between God (light) and the devil (fire and brimstone) for the soul of Misty, whom the devil calls Satania. "Long ago," the voice-over tells you at the beginning, "there was no good or evil. Only the sun ... but amidst the flames, there was a rebellious flame...." In a mysterious opening, Misty, on a black horse, is led by a cloaked figure to the edge of hell, where amid flames and satanic music, she is made love to by an unseen devil, who penetrates her *with light* and brings her to a wild, writhing climax like none she has ever experienced with an earthly creature. "I will continue to give you what you need," the voice-over tells her, "but only if you obey me. You will incite and inflame men, to capture their souls for me. Take this chalice and in it capture the souls I need." Needless to say, men's souls are in their semen. (Interestingly, this is an ancient belief that extends far back into Chinese and Eastern literature, when men were taught by courtesans how to delay or even avoid ejaculation to ensure their longevity.) Following the devil's commands, Misty (who deserves an Erotic Film Award for her performance) collects the jism from a local tribal chief, who was impotent until she and another devil's helper teased him alive and made him a phallic giant. She also collects from two male strippers, with Satania encouraging them to take off their jockstraps, and several other kinky sources. Balancing Misty's admission in this morality play that "the drug of lust is pouring through my mind. I am lost. I am truly enslaved" (more than once she succumbs to ecstatic coupling with her unseen lover while flames shoot around them), is the voice of God, who says, "I will stop her and save her with love." But when Innocence arrives (a handsome blonde guy on a white horse), she captures even his semen and pours it into the fiery pit. Then she demands that the devil keep his promises to her. He must assume the shape of a man, which he does reluctantly. You never see him except as a shadowy figure. In a mind-bending climax afterward, Misty/Satania announces triumphantly that she has captured Satan's soul and taken his power. "I am now the Queen of both Good and Evil." Add this one to your list of adult-film classics.

IN THE PINK
CC   NN   NR   BI
1983   VIDEO-X-PIX

P/D—Sam Lake, Bill Eagle
F/A—Jacqueline Lorians, Gina Carnale, Joanna Storms, Lorri Smith
F/A—Scott Baker, Zebediah Colt, Joey Silvera

Put this one near the top of your "'Collector's Choice" sexvids. Unlike some American-made sexvids that try to capture a foreign background with stock shots, much of this one must have been shot in Paris, London, Venice, Vienna, and Luxor. The actors are actually in the crowds, buildings, and squares in various cities. Blake Covington (Scott Baker) is a very sophisticated art dealer who has recently married Mariange (Jacqueline Lorians). At the moment, he is in Venice with his assistant Heather (Joanna Storm), whom he's bedding in one of the hotels near the canals. Back in Paris with Heather, he introduces her to Mariange briefly. But a musician friend of his, Umberto (Zebediah Colt), playing the piano, is waiting for him in

another room in the mansion. Umberto tells Blake a sorrowful story about the woman he has just married, Angelina (Gina Carnale), who is much younger than he. He discovers on their wedding night that she's not the virgin she's supposed to be. She told Umberto that Blake seduced her before the wedding ceremony. Umberto is so shocked at this treachery that he pulls out a revolver, shoots Blake, and runs. But Blake is not dead. He tells Heather, who has witnessed the shooting, that his wife and the whole world must believe that he's really dead, and that he will not pursue his life under another name. The reason for the subterfuge finally becomes apparent: Blake is trying to buy the famous Hapsburg portraits from the Baroness of Hapsburg in Vienna. She refuses to sell them to Blake Covington, but might let them go to his estate. In the meantime, Mariange, now a widow, who was married only a few weeks to Blake, is guided by Heather on a whirlwind tour of Europe. She should forget Blake and enjoy her sexual self with new companions, including the baroness. Mariange is soon in a European sex tour enjoying men in various cities, including one of the Queen of England's guards (Joey Silvera), whose pants she unzips outside Buckingham Palace. In another fascinating scene she and Heather seemingly make love in one of the rooms of the Louvre. The ending provides a surprise twist that reunites Blake with his wife, who knew what was happening all the time, and leaves Umberto, who turns out to have been a hired actor, finding romance with Heather, who can't believe that Blake deceived her so completely to get the Hapsburg paintings.

INTIMATE ENTRY
CC   DS   BI
1977   HOME ENTERTAINMENT

P/D—John Klugerman, Helmut Richler
F/A—Laura Cannon, Ruby Runhouse
F/A—Tim Long, Helmut Richler

The screen credits give the title on this one as *Forced Entry*—but whatever its title you can put it in your book as the most frightening sexvid you will probably ever watch. A psychopathic, sex-crazed Vietnam veteran, wearing a cap with an American flag stitched on it, is running a filling station, where he obtains the addresses of young women by telling them that he accepts only credit cards. He stalks them through the streets of New York to their apartments with a gun and a trench knife in his belt. The veteran's madness is accentuated throughout the film by black-and-white flashbacks from actual Vietnam War footage—with wartime incidents that parallel his own need to continue to kill. He rapes and murders two women, forcing them to suck him off first, and he rapes one anally until she bleeds. No matter how compliant, abject, and sobbing they are, after he comes he hates them. He finally follows two female college students who are freaked out on drugs to their apartment. When they laugh hysterically at him and offer to do anything he wants them to do, he kills himself. A real horror film that blends sex and aggression and detailed graphic on-camera murder showing slit throats and trench knives stuck in breasts and stomachs.

INTRUSION
CC NR BI DS
1975 IVP (formerly CVX)

P/D—Barkley Heath, Arthur Nouveau
F/A—Kim Pope, Lynn Bishop
F/A—Michael Cattore, Levi Richards

This one begins ominously with a car driving toward Little Neck, New York. Before the car arrives at its destination, a young married couple are having breakfast in the kitchen of their suburban home. Kim Pope, the wife (a very pretty natural blonde who no longer makes sexvids), tells her husband that she's nervous in the house when he's away on sales trips, so her girlfriend, Gail, is coming to stay with her. Before he leaves they make very romantic love in the kitchen and on the living-room floor. A few minutes after he's gone, the car arrives and a man gets out and cuts the telephone wires. Although Kim has never seen him, he barges his way into the house, knocking her to the floor. "Be calm," he tells her as he forces her

upstairs to the bedroom. "Nothing is going to happen to you." But soon, after plundering the house of silver and jewelry, he forces her, at knife point, to undress. Sobbing, she tells him that he promised he wouldn't hurt her, but he gets increasingly rough and ties her, naked and open-legged, to the bed. Forcing oral sex on her, he's interrupted by the doorbell, and he soon has her girlfriend naked in the bedroom, after which he proceeds to rape them both. In the process, Gail's fingers find the knife he's been threatening them with, and she stabs him to death. This is a scary rape film in which the women do not capitulate willingly, and it takes place within a believable environment. (See notes under *Pleasure Bed.*)

I WANT TO BE BAD
CC NN NR NL
1984 CAL VISTA

P/D—Sam Norvell, Robert McCallum
F/A—Kay Parker, Stephanie Taylor, Jacqueline Lorians, Tara Aire
F/A—Paul Thomas, Jon Martin, Blake Palmer, Mark Wallice

The CC rating is for Kay Parker and a happily silly story of Kay as Jan Jenkins, married to Charlie (Jon Martin), who has played around ever since they were married. With reason, evidently, because Jan is not that much fun in bed. Charlie, after hearing his secretary complain, "I'm sick of your wham-bam, slang-bang scenarios," leaves on a trip to Seattle, where he is unwittingly fed an aphrodisiac by Trish (Tara Aire), the new wife of a millionaire customer, and soon Trish is munching a happily numb Charlie from head to foot. Back at the ranch, Fred Appleby (Paul Thomas), a friend of Charlie, arrives to ask Jan if he can use Charlie's VCR to view a new tape (Cal-Vista, of course), and Jan sneaks into Charlie's den to see what's going on. Shocked at the action and embarrassed (she never acted that way with Charlie), she's soon turned on by the tape, and she experiments with Fred, after which she admits for the first time in her life: "I'm a liberated woman. From now on, what's good for the goose is good for the gander. If Fred fools around, so can I." She soon does, with a young guy (Mark Wallice) who delivers drinking water. In the meantime, Charlie's secretary has quit and gone to work for Fred, and Fred advises Charlie that he should reexplore his relationship with his wife. Charlie tries, but Jan angrily pushes him into the swimming pool and furiously rejects him. He chases her into the bedroom and locks the bedroom door, and she fights him as he tries to make love to her. She soon capitulates but refuses his offer of a second-honeymoon cruise. "All I want is you to make consistent love to me," she tells him sweetly. Obviously, he will now, because she's more fun in the sack.

JACK & JILL 2
CC NN NR BI
1984   VCA

P/D—Chuck Vincent
F/A—Samantha Fox, Carol Cross, Crysta Cox, Taija Rae
F/A—Jack Wrangler, Jerry Butler

The CC rating on this one is dubious. It takes Chuck the first 20 minutes or so to get into the main story. With the exception of a romantic 15-minute interlude, the whole tenor of the film is too glossy and sexually sophisticated to be remotely believable or even funny—although audience laughter is certainly hoped for. Chuck financed this one by giving everyone except the actors a share of the profits and no pay during the production. Trading on the first film (see review), he offers Samantha Fox as Jill and Jack Wrangler as Jack—but the opening scenes of their daffy marriage don't work as well or as believably as in the first installment. When you finally get through the insanity of their apartment being invaded by the "Macho Marauder," who screws his victims as well as robs them and who ties up Jack (whom Jill doesn't ungag when she discovers him) and their attendance at an orgy on Varick Street in Greenwich Village, the story line finally surfaces. "No more orgies," Jill tells Jack. "Swinging is dead, too. I read it in *Time* magazine. It's time we concentrate on our own sexual relationship." But then they meet Rachel (Carol Cross) and Josh (Jerry Butler), and it's love at first sight *for each others' spouses.*

Jack and Jill discuss various strategies for how they will seduce Rachel and Josh into a spouse exchange, but they are too embarrassed to broach the subject. Never mind, Rachel and Josh take the initiative. What follows is a romantic intercutting of the new lovers achieving sexual gratification they never achieved with their marriage partners. In fact, they are so enamored that as a foursome they visit a lawyer and separate, prior to a divorce, to each others' apartments. Then Jack discovers that Rachel enjoys girls as well as boys, and Jill, to her horror, learns that Josh likes booze and looking at naked women in men's magazines as much, or better than, he enjoys her. In one scene, sitting on the footboard of the bed, he masturbates while she squirms erotically and is unfulfilled. The total exaggeration of their incompatability with new lovers is supposed to be funny, but it doesn't match the previous romanticism. Chuck was on the edge of telling a story that many couples might identify with, had he stayed closer to reality by proving that the grass is not always greener in the other guy's backyard. You'll enjoy watching Jack Wrangler (who makes few films) more if you read his mind-blowing autobiography published in 1984, *What's a Nice Boy Like You Doing?* You'll not only learn that Jack, the son a top Hollywood director, has had a long-lasting, complete sexual relationship with Margaret Whiting (who in the 1950s was a top singing star) but is a homosexual who has made 25 or more gay films, and was, and is, the "Macho Man" of the gay community in New York and Los Angeles.

JACKPOT
CC NN BI
1979   VCX

P/D—Not given
F/A—Lisa Marks is the only actor or actress identified

Too bad the director didn't put his name on this one and the credits don't list the actors and actresses, especially the guy who plays the part of Neil, Lisa's daddy. He plays a cold-blooded gambler very effectively. Lisa tells a young stud how she became the sole heiress of her daddy's millions. She tells the story while paying him $1,000 for every orgasm she has during the evening. Seems that Daddy has a yen for his friend Doug's wife. Lisa's mommy didn't really care because she has a big affair going with the maid. Doug is a gambler, too, and soon Neil is betting a kiss from Doug's wife in a game of three-card monte. Losing to Neil, they play pinball for a dollar a point and Doug wins a few thousand bucks. Mommy suggests that they all play poker, and soon Neil has wiped out Doug and the ladies have quit playing. Neil challenges Doug to bet his wife against a check for $500,000. If you enjoy gambling at poker, you'll watch this play with interest. Neil finally wins with four kings against Doug's four queens, and while Doug and his own wife watch, he screws Doug's wife to a fare-thee-well on the pool table. But you know that during the card game the maid is in cahoots with Mommy and has fed someone a poisoned drink. You soon discover that it's Neil, when he drops dead during his orgasm with Doug's wife. Doug is in ecstasy. He has the check for $500,000, which Neil never tore up. But he soon is gaspingly aware that the maid and Mommy have poisoned him, too. The fuzz soon catch up with these bad ladies, and that's how Lisa got all of Daddy's loot and can now afford to pay $1,000 a climax with a stud of her choice. She has at least six in the 90-minutes this one takes to run.

JOANNA STORM WORKS OUT
CC NM
1985 GM VIDEO

P/D—Not given
F/A—Joanna Storm

Note the rating. In addition to "Collector's Choice," there's NM (normal masturbation). There may be other films of this type, but I have never seen any short female masturbation sequences in regular sexvids that held my interest as much as this one. One reason is Joanna herself. She's the only person in this 70-minute film, and until the very end, when she smiles at the viewer and gives her phone number, she seems unconcerned about who is watching. You are the voyeur watching an intimate, believable session of a woman making love to herself. It's a film that should interest sex educators as well as the average guy and gal. For 70 minutes you watch Joanna massage herself with baby oil and see her play with her clit and occasionally softly slap her vulva in between inserting two or three fingers into her vagina. She's in no hurry to climax, and she's consciously prolonging the buildup. Using a soft rope that she ties tightly in a loop between her labia and into the crevice of her buttocks and across her shoulders, along with clamps on her nipples, she is aware that mild pain will contribute to her buildup. Still walking a razor's edge, she whips her ass gently with a leather thong and then uses the handle as a dildo. Soon she tries another dildo, and finally she climaxes. When she climaxes it is not, as males might expect, a wild, screaming climax, but rather a slow, body-shaking, almost grateful release. Later, still at a high pitch, she uses a banana and a cucumber. Joanna, who is a brown-eyed blonde (as I have mentioned in other reviews), is pretty, with a vulnerable facial expression, when she is being herself, that brings out the protective instinct in many males. Since most people are reluctant to reveal how they masturbate, this tape could prove a conversation opener.

KEN CHAN, THE LAUNDRY MAN
CC NN NM
ORCHIDS INTERNATIONAL

P/D—Ken Kishi
F/A—Hiromi Janaka, Mieko Mizutani, Ken Kitabayashi

Ken Chan is happy-go-lucky, very handsome Japanese laundry man who doesn't actually wash clothes, but drives a pick-up and delivery van. He knows all the ladies on his route and laughingly points out semen spots on their bed sheets. After meeting him on his rounds the camera cuts to one of his customers, a very pretty Japanese lady who is putting shaving cream on her pussy, after which she shaves it and masturbates in an extended sequence during which she finally finishes with a phallic shaped Japanese vibrator that squirms like a happy snake when the battery power is turned on. Ken Chan convinces her that the real thing is better, so the next day they are on their way to the seashore where they have brought a picnic lunch. The camera watches her in earnest and proves that, genitally, American and Oriental women are indistinguishable. After making love to her, Ken Chan takes her home and telephones another lady. Posing as a friend of hers he tells her to meet him at a motel. When she arrives she's horrified to find that it's Ken Chan. "I loved you once," she says in Japanese, "but I not like you now." Never mind, though at first she protests violently, she soon is happily screwing with him. What makes it more interesting than American pornos is the environment and the language. If they dub in English, forget it!

THE KIMONO
CC NN DK
1983   ORCHIDS INTERNATIONAL

The packaging on this Japanese made film extols the kimono: "When you see a kimono it's like seeing a beautiful fantasy like drawing a colored leaf in the fall sunset, a beautiful butterfly as it flies from flower to flower. . . ." The film begins with a young man in some kind of conflict with his father. He ends up in a geisha house where the woman who surrenders to him as he unfastens her kimono and makes love to her whimpers, looks frightened and gives the impression that she is a virgin. She finally sobs in joy and fear as they make love. Japanese women are very emotional (at least in porno films) and are constantly sighing or sobbing ecstatically. The sex scene in this one are intercut with scenes of a Japanese garden in back of the house. As the film progresses various other women, including an American or English woman, who never speaks

English, and other men appear. There is a tea ceremony intermixed with extended explicit screwing, and when one of the guys ejaculates in a woman's mouth she tastes and swallows it in a slow extended facial shot. The men give the women as much or more oral and digital pleasure as the women give the men. In several scenes, with things you've never seen before, a man brings a woman lying on her back with her legs over her head to an agonizing climax with what looks like a gnarled Japanese vegetable root. In another scene, the American lady presents her vagina in a similar pose while a guy does a flower arrangement in it with long stemmed flowers. The film concludes with one of the girls being raped on a garden path by someone she actually knows. Afterward, with his semen dripping down her legs, she wipes it philosophically with her finger, tastes it, and walks off.

KINKY BUSINESS
CC NN BI NL
1984   DREAMLAND VIDEO

P/D—Jerry Ross, Jonathan Ross, Eastman Price
F/A—Tanya Lawson, Ginger Lynn, Laurie Smith
F/A—Tom Byron, Jerry Butler

Remember the R-rated film *Risky Business?* This one follows the Hollywood story much more closely than *Frisky Business* (see review) or any other adult-film variation on this theme. It's funny and works because Tom Byron as Matt looks amazingly like a guy in his late teens. In this one, he has a brother Vince (Jerry Butler) who no longer lives in the family mansion but has his own apartment. When the family has to go out of town for a funeral, Matt is left in charge of the house. Vince moves back in and calls a beautiful hooker, Angel (Laurie Smith), to show Matt how to do it. Matt falls in love with her but can't afford her. She's a working girl! But she has an idea! Soon the mansion becomes a self-supporting whorehouse, and Matt, learning the facts of life, becomes a cigar-smoking, devil-may-care whore master. As in the original, the parents return, but unlike the original, the house and Daddy's car have not been wrecked, nor does the hero in the original inherit so much money from his uncle that he never has to work again and can now marry the hooker and settle down in connubial bliss.

LADIES IN LACE
CC NN BI DK
1985   MASTERPIECE VIDEO

P/D—Dan T. Andrews, Jack Remy
F/A—Traci Lords, Christy Canyon, Kimberly Carson, Heather Wayne, Sheri St. Claire, Roxanne Roland
F/A—Eric Edwards, Billy Dee, Tom Byron, Dan T. Mann, Michael Jefferies

Linda (Traci Lords) is married to Tom (Billy Dee), and she's very competent in the bedroom, where Tom gives her a workout that would keep the average woman happy for a couple of days—but not Linda. She's insatiable, and she likes it rough. In the same yuppie neighborhood, Karen (Heather Wayne) is having a similar problem with her husband, Scott (Dan T. Mann), who keeps reading the morning newspaper when she tells him that she's having an affair with the postman. But not far away are Gregg (Eric Edwards) and Sandy (Kimberly Carson). They're swingers, and they still have a good time with each other, too. Sandy runs Great Expectations house parties for women only where she sells them sexy underwear, snaky vibrators, and massage oil in various flavors (chocolate, vanilla, and strawberry). When Linda tells Tom that she's invited to one of Sandy's parties, he immediately gets suspicious that there will be more than women present. There would have been, but Sandy tells Gregg it's for women only. Tom convinces his friend Scott to watch the party through Gregg's living-room windows. Scott is afraid they'll get caught, but he finally agrees. After some amusing scenes, suddenly it really does become a swinger's party, with the guys invading the house and everyone switching spouses and Linda/Traci finally making it with Tom Byron.

LADIES OF THE '80s
CC NN NM NR BI DK
1985   PARADISE VISUALS

P/D—Jim Wilson, Mark Richards
F/A—Jacqueline Lorians, Tamara Longley, Lana Burner, Sheri St. Clair, Clair Wright
F/A—Steve Drake, Dan T. Mann, Jesie Adams

Guys who bring this one home to their wives or ladyfriends may be in for a shock. This is a woman's sexvid. Right from the beginning five women tell Dr. Kay (Kay Parker), who listens off camera at first, whats wrong with men, their sex lives, and/or their marriages. The gals all have story names, but you'll remember their screen names better. Jacqueline Lorians tells Kay, "I'm disgusted with men who treat me like an inferior being." Sheri St. Clair says her kids "are little monsters, and everybody in my life, including my husband, wants a piece of me, but not the real me." Lana Burner, who has been married five years, is not sexually satisfied: "When he's done, we're done. I can count the times on one hand that I've been satisfied." Clair Wright tells Kay, "Everyone tells me that I should be independent. I was raised to be a good wife. But I feel so inadequate, and all my husband is interested in me for is someone to poke his thing into." Tamara Longley has a boyfriend who "is incredibly hung up and has no imagination when it comes to making love." So they've all come to Kay's Retreat (in which she offers Esalen-style group therapy and even a masseur, Dan T. Mann, who follows old-style Esalen credos and after a loving massage has loving sex with the lady—if she wishes. Lana gets a dream lover, Steve Drake, who makes love to her in a very romantic, soft-lighted sequence accompanied by dreamy music. Sheri and Jacqueline discover the joys of a woman loving a woman as they experiment with each other and a running faucet in the bath tub. There is much dialogue with Kay (who never appears in any sex scenes) about interpersonal problems and what each of them really wants out of life. Kay tells Tamara that she really thinks Tamara wants her man to be strong and take care of her. At the final session, Kay tells them "Life is a banquet." They can now enjoy the sexual experience of eating their "last supper" with their fingers, and for dessert they can eat each other, which they do—and prove, perhaps, that they don't really need men anyway.

LADY DYNAMITE
CC NN BI NR DK
1983 HIFCOA

P/D—Troy Benny
F/A—Colleen Brennan, Lili Marlene
F/A—Male actors not identified

Colleen, who in this film has been married 14 years, goes to her doctor (Carlos Tobalina, a.k.a. Troy Benny) for her annual medical checkup and discovers to her horror that she has a mild case of gonorrhea. The doctor gives her an injection and assures her that she will be free of symptoms soon. But Colleen is horrified. She's never been with another man during her entire marriage! When she gets home she tells her husband that he's an asshole and it's all over with them. Angrily, she decides that now she'll go to bed with every man who ever wanted her, and she soon finds them, plus a few female friends who enjoy each other as much as men. The reasons for the CC rating are Colleen Brennan and the caring sexmaking, for the most part, in which she gets involved. Colleen is a very attractive redhead, and Troy/Carlos proves that he can make loving sexvids, too, when he has the right actress.

LADY ON THE BUS
CC NN NL
1985 VESTRON

P/D—Neville D'Alemelda
F/A—Sonia Braga
F/A—Nuuno Lieal Maia, Paulo Cesar Periero, Jorge Doria

Sonia Braga, a Brazilian actress, is famous in the United States for *Donna Flor and Her Two Husbands*, which is a film you shouldn't miss. This one was made in 1978 in Brazil and is even more fascinating, not just for the story, but because, like some other foreign-made films (see review of *Your Ticket Is No Longer Valid*), it goes beyond a regular R rating to the edge of X and proves that the potential of sexvids has not been tapped yet. Solange (Sonia Braga), who has known Carlos all her life, finally marries him. But poor Carlos discovers that, although she claims to love him, she hates sex and is totally frigid with him. His father tells him not to worry: "Your mother was a saint, too. It was lucky that you were born at all." After 20 days of marriage, Solange is still a virgin, until Carlos in desperation finally rips off her nightgown and does it. But alas, he sets no fire burning in Solange. She goes to a psychiatrist, who doesn't help her much either. But soon she's taking a bus through the streets of Rio and picking up total strangers. What follows is scene after scene of some very erotic sexmaking, on a deserted beach, under a waterfall, in a cemetery, and on an empty bus after the driver has happily told the passengers that they must get off. Several of the guys Solange fucks fall in love with her, but afterward she calmly tells them, "I don't like you. I don't ever want to see you again." Her husband finds out what she's been doing and is about to kill either himself or her, but she tells her psychiatrist, "I want to hate myself but I can't." The film ends with Solange headed for another bus ride. You'll want to watch it again to see if you can find the missing link.

LADY ON THE COUCH
CC NN BI DK
1978 QUALITY/VIDEO-X-PIX

P/D—Oscar Tripe
F/A—Darby Lloyd Raines, Andrea True, LaNique Lope, Mary Stewart
F/A—Eric Edwards, Mark Stevens, Don Allen

Henry Trotter (Eric Edwards) has been married to Maggi (Andrea True) for 12 years. They have two kids, and she's been a perfect wife. Well, almost. Lately, neither he nor Maggie has been too good in bed with the other. Then Maggie is hit by an automobile. Rushed to the hospital, she is finally released, but now she has moments when she becomes a very lewd, highly sexed woman called Laura. Henry tries to cope with her, but then one night he's playing poker with the boys and to break up the evening one of them shows a porno movie, *The Lady on the Couch*. To their shock, Henry's wife is the star of it.

How this came about is explored in a psychiatric session with Dr. Paul Miller, who is told about the problem by Henry. Using sodium pentothal, Miller finally gets Laura first to reveal that she's led two lives for the past few years and has been involved with a black pimp, Big John. She also has made porno films for him and become well known as an exceptional porno star. As Maggie, she's totally unaware of her Laura life and her sexual proclivities. But Henry is shocked when occasionally she slips into her Laura role and becomes a wild sexpot. Of course, you watch Laura pursue all her extracurricular sexual activities as she describes them to the doctor. Her dual life is finally uncovered by Mark Stevens as a private detective. When Maggie finally admits to her Laura existence, she's cured, and a greatly relieved Henry takes her home, presumably to a happy hausfrau existence.

L'AMOUR
CC NN NR BI
1985 CABALLERO

P/D—Marga Aulbach
F/A—Angel, Kay Parker, Ginger Lynn
F/A—Harry Reems, Jamie Gillis, Tom Byron

This film was nominated as one of the best 1984 adult films at the Ninth Annual Erotic Film Awards held by the AFAA. In my opinion, it should have won best picture. It's very much a woman's film, and Marga Aulbach has proved (see review of *Wild Dallas Honey*) that little stories about real people, with good dialogue, can make adult films fun to watch. In this one, Vince (Harry Reems), who was married for 15 years to Ellen (Kay Parker) and had a son, Marc (Tom Byron), is now married to Gloria (Angel), who is younger than Ellen and pretty expensive to maintain. Vince has taken her on a European tour and bought her a brand-new house, but you discover, right from the beginning, in a phone conversation with Jerry (Jamie Gillis), a lawyer who was a friend of his and Ellen's, that he hasn't made his alimony payments to Ellen for quite a few months. Ellen has lost her job, and she's broke. Jamie tells Vince that he'd better

straighten out and pay up, but at the same time he advises Ellen it doesn't look too hopeful. Since she knows that Vince has a brand-new home with extra bedrooms, she tells Marc that they're both going to move in with Daddy and his new wife. After that the fun begins. Ellen arrives to find Vince in bed with Gloria. The expression on Ellen/Kay's face is a delicious blend of surprise and disgust. But it finally all works out happily, with some great scenes between old buddies Jamie and Harry, who have been making porno films for 15 years, and a happy-go-lucky secondary plot with Tom Byron, who is almost young enough to be Harry's son in reality!

LET'S PLAY DOCTOR
CC NN BI DK DS (plot related)
1977 CABALLERO

P/D—Not Given
F/A—No female or faces you've seen before, and none are identified.

Don't be misled by the box title on this one or by the list of actors, who are given on the box as Miss Temperature Rising, Jock Erectus, Sweet Sheets, and Betty Bed Pan. The box was obviously designed to sell to the beer-room crowd. Bur amazingly, it's actually a sex-education film (with a small plot added) that many women will find quite interesting. Obviously a takeoff on Masters and Johnson, their book, *Human Sexuality,* and their sex clinic, which once offered sexual surrogates, it's the story of Dr. Leon Flanders, who runs the Flanders Sex Research Project with his female assistant, Dr. Allcock, who falls in love with him. Most of the story is told in a voice-over by a woman with a cultured English accent, who explains the discoveries that Flanders is making with his female surrogates, his sex machine, and its mechanical phallus that allows the patient to control her excitement and orgasms and take pictures inside her vagina. It also deals with male impotence, and a surrogate shows how to help a man achieve an erection or control premature ejaculation. In the process, as you watch the volunteers along with the two doctors, you learn a little about them, including a surrogate who, against the rules, is actually married, and a volunteer who was born without a vagina. Presumably, this occurs in some female births, but a new vagina can be formed. Interwoven with all this is the story of bad guys in a pseudo sex laboratory where the doctors get involved with the patients. One of them tries to destroy Flanders and Allcock's credibility and their laboratory. It's an interesting film because it's so unexpected, and the good doctors, Flanders and Allcock, maintain strictly businesslike behavior with their patients.

LETTERS OF LOVE
CC NN NR
1985 CABALLERO

P/D—Ted Gorley, Paul G. Vatelli
F/A—Bridgitte Monet, Cindee Summers, Ginger Lynn, Kelly Howe, Debbie Northup, Pam Nimmo
F/A—David Cannon, Tom Byron, Greg Ruffner, Greg Rome, Herschel Savage

The CC is for the fact that there's no BI and no DK, which is a minor achievement in adult films and shows that someone is catering to the loving-couples market. In this one, Bridgitte (who is prettier and has improved her voice since her marriage to David Cannon) applies for the job of Candy, who handles the letters-to-the-editor column of a publication whose editor, Mr. Taylor, is none other than David himself. The tape then becomes a series of episodes dramatizing the letters that Candy receives and answers. The first is from Tom Byron, who finds the phone number of a call girl in a sexy magazine and calls her up—presto, she arrives at his parents' home ready to service him. This is the same plot that was used in the Hollywood film *Risky Business* and in several other adult films (see *Kinky Business* and *Frisky Business*), but Tom and Cindee Summers play it out better than any of these other films, with Alicia (Cindee Summers) as the hooker. The next letter is from a young man, Greg Ruffner, who has secret sex with his mother while Daddy's away. Trouble is that Greg looks older

than you'd expect his papa to look, but never mind, the sex with Mommy is happy. The next letter is from a young girl whose boyfriend took her to his parents' summer camp when they weren't there and after playing some nice unbuttoning games, they made happy love. The fourth letter is from Herschel Savage, who had a brief affair with his best friend's wife while the friend was away. Then there's a letter from Ginger Lynn, who hasn't climaxed in her life, but soon does when her boyfriend agrees to spank her, something she has always wanted. Finally, Bridgitte/Candy gets a letter from her boss, Mr. Taylor/David who tells her that the first time he saw her it was love at first sight. Soon they're happily making love in a mansion that any editor would envy. Since she and David were married a few years ago they presumably have sex on camera only with each other. When you watch them you'll have to admit they really don't need anyone else.

LINGERIE
CC NN BI
1984 CINDERELLA DISTRIBUTORS

P/D—Jerome Bronso
F/A—Jennifer West, Renee Summer, Lindy Shaw, Lisa Lake, Tina Marie
F/A—John Holmes, Herschel Savage, Eric Edwards, Blake Palmer, Ron Jeremy, Tom Byron

Monica (Jennifer West) is a lingerie designer who owns a factory producing lacy underwear, bras, and nightgowns that she designs herself. Stan (Herschel Savage) wants to marry her, but, although Monica's business is in serious financial trouble and a nasty, very wealthy competitor is stealing her designs and has bugged her house, she doesn't want to quit. It's her baby, and she knows that at the upcoming trade show, she'll take all the orders away from him. The plot revolves around which one of her employees is stealing her designs and giving them to the rat Charles Van Horn. Surprisingly, there actually is a factory sewing room, and Michael Adams (Eric Edwards) who manages the place, may be the bad guy because he's constantly trying to seduce one of the employees and thinks he's a better designer than Monica. Or Monica's assistant may be in league with Van Horn. Clever fast cutting keeps the various sex sequences and incidents, which are related to the main story, interesting. Ron Jeremy as a lingerie photographer finding a hick farmer (John Homes) and using Holmes's brass bed to photograph a model (Lisa Lake), whom he shares with Holmes, provides some silly laughter.

LIQUID ASSETS
CC   NN   NL   DK
1982   CABALLERO

P/D—Robert Walters
F/A—Sanja Sorrello, Samantha Fox, Veronica Hart, Tiffany Clark, Sharon Kane
F/A—Ron Jeremy, Bobby Astyr, Randy Grant, Richard Bolla

Depending on your degree of sexual sophistication, you may find that there are very few really funny sexvids. Laughter punctures hard-ons. Some people may find the laughter in this one a little sick, but the dialogue and plot are so happily goofy that you should give it a try. The stars are Bobby Astyr (Mr. Cashbox) and Ron Jeremy (Lawyer Fillpotts of Fillpotts and Slime). Poor Fillpotts. At the moment, he's so broke he doesn't have a secretary, only a rubber doll, which he screws in graphic detail, talking to her all the time. Cashbox enjoys some of the most acrobatic sex you've ever watched, with his girlfriend Samantha Fox. She blows him while he's standing on his head. But he is in deep trouble with the IRS, and Fillpotts and tax-loophole expert Rufus Quim (R. Bolla) figure that the only way to keep him out of jail is to go broke financing a Broadway play called *Piece and War*. To make it a sure thing, they should hire Tootsie LaMarr, Quim's sister (played hilariously as a loud, vulgar bitch by Veronica Hart) to star in the production. Tootsie insists on an audition—she tells them the producer always screws the star before she gets the job. But when she opens Cashbox's pants and sees his prick, she disdainfully calls it a vunce (*bedbug* in Yiddish). Then there's Suzy (Sanja Sorrello), who thinks she's the star about to be born. The box plug says that this one will appeal to lovers of Mel Brooks, and for once they were right. And if you've ever complained that in most pornos the lovers never talk, in this one they never *stop* talking.

LITTLE GIRLS OF THE STREETS
CC   NN
1985   L.A. VIDEO

P/D—L. M. Burton, Drea
F/A—Gina Valentino, Laura Lee, Shone Tee, Jane Nichols, Christy Canyon
F/A—Tommy Winchester, K. Starbuck, Jerry Paris, Dino Alexander, Scott Irish, Blake Palmer, Mark Jennings

Except for Tommy Winchester, who plays the black pimp Roscoe, all the guys listed above are tricks or johns that Roscoe's ladies take on in two different hotel rooms. This, of course, provides wall-to-wall screwing. The reason for the CC rating is that the film has a slice-of-life feel to it. The ladies ply their trade on Sunset and Hollywood boulevards. They are very careful not to be entrapped by cops and won't take money until the john undresses. Prices are never less than $40 for 15 or 20 minutes, and the ladies wash the guys' pricks and balls and inspect them carefully. Conversation is amusing. One of the ladies nonchalantly chews gum while her trick pumps away; one takes on a cop, who tells her, "I gotta make this quick. Just a blow job will do." Come morning they hand their earnings over to Roscoe, who expects them to average 11 or 12 tricks a night. Fifty tricks performed by four ladies gives him $2,000, which he has to split with them, but he can't today because he owes it to some shady character. After paying the guy off, Roscoe sighs, "Forty fucking dollars left. I can make more by being a TV repairman."

LITTLE GIRLS TALKING DIRTY
CC   NN   BI   NL (for silly sex talk)
1985   VCA

P/D—L. M. Burton, Drea
F/A—Misty Regan, Kristara Barrington, Sheri St. Clair, Kristie Deveraux
F/A—Tom Byron, Mark Wallice, Slim Green, Jesse Adams

The CC rating for this one is for one reason only. Due to the nature of the story, the ladies listed above never stop talking while they are fucking, and, surprisingly, the dialogue could stand alone (pun intended) as a phone conversation—without the visual portrayal. Of course, it doesn't and the ladies are forewarned by the woman (Kristie Deveraux) who runs the place, called "Finger Talking," that they must empathize with the guys who telephone the service—so much that they can practically see them. Tom Byron tells his female answer lady that he's sick and wants to have his temperature taken, you know where. Another guy remembers his school teacher and wants to have him fuck her. Another guy calls on a car phone speeding down the freeway. In all cases, the ladies talk the guys into happy euphoria.

LITTLE SHOWOFFS
CC   NN   NR   BI
1980   VCA

P/D—Zachary Strong
F/A—Cindy Carne, Renee Lovins, Lili Marlene, Montra Stark, Liza Windsor, Betsy Boudoir, Patti Perrier
F/A—Paul Whitecook, Mark Monroe, Peter Sheppard, David Habib, Hank Heathcliff, Steve Mileston, Roger Halycon

There are six fascinating little stories on this long tape, intercut in black and white with an interviewer who gives the various people (with whom he is talking quite frankly, in believable dialogue, about their sexual preferences and fantasies) a chance to act them out. You haven't seen any of the people listed above in other adult films, which along with excellent cinematography, and in each story a nice atmospheric build-up, contributes to the interest. The first story is the "Music Mas-

ter," with two women stripping before a Svengali-type rock musician in a strange fantasy nightclub and ultimately making love that includes him. "Pick Up" is about a woman who wants to be picked up by a motorcyclist, a stranger, whom she takes to her home where her bald husband, a concert pianist, is playing Chopin. They only have time to screw standing up, and when her husband finishes practicing the motorcyclist must leave. "Little Egypt" takes you back to the days of the pharaohs, where a brother and sister enjoy the fantasy of a really erotic sexual encounter. "Communion" takes place in a convent, where a young virgin dreams of a young lover, a total stranger, who climbs in her window to make love to her while in the distance the monks are singing Gregorian chants and outside the door a monk and nun are listening in shock. If you are familiar with Carl Orff's *Carmina Burana*, you'll wonder why some adult film maker hasn't made a sizzling mixture of religion and sex out of it. Two other episodes, "Museum Piece" and "Teacher's Pet," offer a lesson in fertility worship and a believable high-school teacher who introduces her special student to an afternoon of warm, loving sex. Most women will enjoy this one.

LORELEI
CC   NN   NM   BI
1985   L.A. VIDEO

P/D—L. M. Burton, Jack Remy
F/A—Kay Parker, Sondra Stillman, Rikki Blake, Debra Lynn, Danica Wood, Terri Morgan
F/A—Billy Dee, Dan T. Mann, R. Bolla

The CC rating is not for the story, which is a perennial with adult-film producers, about a famous dress designer whose latest creations are being stolen by some nefarious character or other. It's for the good shot-on-video color, and for Kay Parker, who once again proves, with Dan T. Mann (right at the beginning), that an older woman is just as much fun (or more) than a younger one. In this story, as Lorelei, after some rapturous sexmaking with Greg (Dan T. Mann), Kay gives him a job with her Lorelei Fashions. But, in the meantime, a gay character, Lance LeFleur (R.

Bolla), has hired Dirk (Billy Dee) to pose as a male model whom Lorelei is trying to hire and to steal her forthcoming high-fashion clothes designs. Dirk and Greg quickly get mixed up with all Lorelei's female models, and finally Dirk manages to steal the designs, but Lorelei follows him to Lance's house and proves that she's a master of men as well as of fashions by taking them both on and making Lance, temporarily, an enthusiastic heterosexual.

THE LOVE BUS
CC NN BI NL DK
1976   QUALITY/VIDEO-X-PIX

P/D—Oscar Tripe
F/A—Penny Ashcroft, Jennifer Jordan, Danilee D'Orlcl, Sharon Boxworth, Rhonda Blake
F/A—Jamie Gillis, Mark Stevens, Sonny Landham, Kevin Andre

On weekends, the bus takes people to the famous Gross Hotel in the "Borscht Belt" about 50 miles north of New York City. The bus has a special hostess who begins the get-acquainted process as soon as the bus leaves the Port Authority building. Not sex, but musical chairs. Unknown to the hostess and the bus driver, farmer Amos Johnson and his very pregnant wife own a huge old farmhouse hotel that is falling apart and has no guests. To divert the passengers from the Gross Hotel and keep them there would provide the kind of income needed for the Johnsons to survive and fix up the place, so Amos has a wonderful idea: Why not set up a roadblock on the main highway? When the bus driver sees it he's so surprised that he swerves into the woods and crashes only a few hundred yards from the farmhouse. Soon a few of the passengers are happily screwing with each other, but others are so discombobulated that they don't know where they are. Mark Stevens, as a bird-watcher who didn't make this trip to meet women, is soon screwing with Jennifer Jordan, who has been consulting with Dr. Psycoff (Jamie Gillis), a psychiatrist who has sex with his patients to help them over their hang-ups. While the situation's potential is not realized, there are some funny sequences.

LOVE-IN ARRANGEMENT
CC NN NL DK
1980   VIDEO-X-PIX

P/D—Mitch Delray, Charles Larkin
F/A—Merle Michaels, Arcadia Lake, Carol Cat, Vanessa Del Rio, Kandi Barbour
F/A—Rick Iversen, Eric Edwards, Ron Jeremy, Dave Ruby, Bobby Astyr

Remember the palimony trials of the early 1980s? Lenny, played by Rick Iversen, who is a good actor who only appears occasionally in porno films, plays the part of a stand-up comedian who has become very wealthy. Dolly, played by Merle Michaels, proves that when Merle had a chance she was a good actress. (By contrast compare her in *Silky*—see review.) Lennie and Dolly have been living together, and a voice-over before the palimony trial, in which Dolly is suing Lenny for a million bucks, half his wealth, announces: "What are the legal and financial ties that bind a man and woman who live and love outside the confines of marriage?" Lennie is first to appear on the witness stand. He tells his story in flashbacks, during which Lennie tries to convince the jury that he never really encouraged Dolly. He slept with her once and then she moved in, lock, stock, and barrel. Sadly, he soon discovered that she would screw anybody, including Ron (Eric Edwards), a movie producer, and then claim that she was doing it to advance Lennie's career. He also describes an orgy in which the guys arrive dressed as cats and the women as pussies. Dolly tells an entirely different story of their relationship, but under questioning by Lennie's lawyer admits that she never cooked a dinner, mopped a floor, or did the washing, which leads the lawyers into trying to determine, hilariously, what a good wife should do in a marriage. Finally, when Lennie's lawyer begins shouting at Dolly, Lenny gets angry with him. Seems he's still in love with Dolly, and they decide to get married.

LOVE LETTERS
CC R
1983 VESTRON

P/D—Amy Jones
F/A—Jamie Lee Curtis, Bonnie Bartlett
F/A—James Keach, Matt Clark, Bud Cort

This one probably will be shown on regular cable. Don't miss it. I've snuck it in here to prove my contention that a smart adult-film maker, recognizing the potential of the home market, could tell many stories like this one and still stay within the sexvid genre by making the sex a little more explicit. It's the story of Anna Winters (Jamie Lee Curtis, daughter of Tony Curtis), who is unmarried, in her 20s, and is proving that she's a comer as music director and disc jockey at a public TV station. She meets a man in his 40s, Oliver Andrews (James Keach), who is a successful designer, and she is immediately attracted to him, and he to her. From the beginning, he tells her that he's married. He loves his wife but not in the same way as he loves Anna. Anna's girlfriend warns her, "You have to remember that this guy sleeps with someone else every night." But Anna can't let go. As a counterpoint to her own love, her mother has just died and she discovers a packet of totally loving letters written to her by a man that Anna never knew existed. But her mother did tell her that she married her father (who is still living and is a nebbish) not for love, but because she was pregnant. What makes this film so engrossing is Jamie's acting. She involves you in her dilemma, from which there is no solution except that someone gets hurt. As for Amy Jones, who wrote the best story of this kind I have ever watched—if she reads this, I'll send her a copy of my novel *Thursday, My Love*, a story of adultery with a happy ending that would make a good R or X film.

LOVE, LUST & ECSTASY
CC R
1983 MEDIA

P/D—Evangelos Fournistakis, Ilia Milanako
F/A—Ajita Wilson, Mirille Damien
F/A—Missimo Saudurny, Starto Zasimis, George Minter

Shot almost entirely on the island of Corfu, this one will make you wish that you had rich relatives to visit there—especially one who looks like Sara (a beauty in her 30s with coffee-colored skin), who is married to Ari Velis, a Greek shipping tycoon. Ari, who is in his 50s, is recovering in a Swiss sanatorium from temporary paralysis. But Sara isn't lonely for him. She is having her portrait painted by Alex, and they are happily screwing together in the magnificent pool and on various lovely deserted beaches on the Mediterranean. Ari's secretary, Teresa, knows what is going on—but she doesn't tell Ari, who telephones every day from Switzerland and can never find his wife. The fact is that Teresa believes that she and Alex are really meant for each other and that Ari will have to give her up when he returns. In the meantime, Ari has hired an unscrupulous detective to check up on Sara, and he soon has a collection of photos of her and Alex screwing, which he has taken with a telephoto lens. He offers to sell them to Sara for 500,000 drachmas, but when Sara arrives with the payoff, he demands her body, too. Angry, she drives home, finds a gun and is going to murder him, but Teresa tries to dissuade her. The gun goes off accidentally and kills Sara—leaving Teresa with just what she wanted, Alex, who is returning from Athens. But alas, although Alex is finally convinced that he can't keep Sara, the police discover her body in the trunk of Teresa's car. Breaking the Ten Commandments obviously doesn't pay off! The interesting thing about this one is the island of Corfu and the continuous sexmaking and nudity with nary a male genital ever seen—quiet or erect!

LUSCIOUS
CC NN BI NR
1982 VIDEO-X-PIX

P/D—Chuck Vincent, Bill Slobodian
F/A—Samantha Fox, Lisa de Leeuw, Champagne, Vanessa Del Rio, Sharon Mitchell
F/A—Michael Knight, Kevin Gibson, Joey Silvera

Meeting after work at a local bar in Utica, New York, with a howling blizzard outside and temperatures 30 below zero, Samantha Fox, Lisa de Leeuw, and Champagne take the advice of the bartender, played by Chuck Vincent, and decide to get away from it all in Puerto Rico. They soon arrive at the Casa Luscious, a hotel managed by Vanessa Del Rio, whose boyfriend is Joey Silvera, a captain in the navy. The girls soon spot various guys, including one who is a stock-market genius (Michael Knight) who has daydreams of being a foreign agent. In his dreams he encounters Sharon Mitchell and a big-busted lady who tells him, "We gonna suck you and drain every last drop of oil out of your cock," which they do near a swimming pool. But reality in Puerto Rico proves better when he encounters Lisa de Leeuw. She and Champagne have been invited to go to a nearby island for the day by a navy ensign, Kevin Gibson (a.k.a. Kevin James), and soon they are a group of six picnicking on the island and making very romantic, one-to-one love under a waterfall and on the beach. Before they get back to Puerto Rico they are trapped in a cave in a thunderstorm, and back at the casa, Joey and Vanessa are worrying about them—but not too much as they make love. Most of the sexual encounters are loving and romantic, and the Puerto Rican scenery, with surf pounding on beaches, thunderstorms, sunsets, and dawns as background for the sex-making, make this a sexvid that most women will enjoy.

LUST AT FIRST BITE
CC NN DS DK BI
1979   VCA

P/D—Dale Alexander, Philip Morris
F/A—Annette Haven, Seka, Serena, Kay Parker, Nancy Hoffman
F/A—Jamie Gillis, John Holmes, John Leslie, Paul Thomas, William Margold

I reviewed this tape originally as a Media tape, *Dracula Sucks*, with a hard-core version, *Dracula's Bride* (see reviews), and I didn't give it a CC rating. In this complete VCA version, it comes together as a well-acted Dracula story featuring an array of adult-film actors that you're not likely to see again in one film—although all of them are big stars in the middle 1980s. The story line is that Count Dracula (Jamie Gillis) has moved from Transylvania to somewhere in southern California and taken up residence near what seems to be a castle complete with enormous fieldstone crenellations. It is now the Seward Sanitarium, run by Doctor Seward (John Leslie) and his assistant Kay Parker—and one male attendant (William Margold), who squeezes an apple to juice when he fucks and insists that all the patients are nuts. They become nuttier as Count Dracula fucks the females and sucks blood from their breasts, vulvas, and necks. Of course, once bitten, they bite the males. Before it's over, Serena is in a coffin being serviced by the Count, Seka is bitten by J. C. Holmes, who has been bitten by Annette Haven, who right from the beginning has been the count's first love. Despite the gore, the cinematography, the music, and the acting make this a better-than-average sexvid.

LUST IN THE DUST
R NL
1984   NEW WORLD VIDEO

P/D—Alan Glaser, Tab Hunter
F/A—Divine, Lainie Kazan, Gina Gallego
F/A—Tab Hunter, Geoffrey Lewis, Henry Silva, Cesar Romero

There's very little nudity in this one, but the theme is all sex and the search for buried gold. Shot in New Mexico, it's the kind of film that adult-film producers could easily make—the only difference being the addition of a few explicit sex scenes. What makes this one totally insane and funny is Divine, a sexy, 300-pound guy/girl with huge breasts (you never see them naked), big fat lips, mascara eyes, false eyelashes, and a falsetto voice. She plays the part of Rosie Valez, who has come to Chili Verde, along with Abel Wood (Tab Hunter; remember him?), a tough, gun-fighting hombre, and Hardcase Williams (Geoffrey Lewis, Clint Eastwood's sidekick in *Every Which Way But Loose*), a tough preacher/killer who loses all his battles with Divine. Then there's Grandma Big Ass, a 70-year-old woman who loves Abel, and Maguerita (Lainie Kazan, who is a real woman but looks enough like Divine to be her sister). Marguerita owns the local tavern, which is patronized by a gang of tough-looking characters, all aware that there's gold buried near Chili Verde that no one ever has found. Put all this action in a *Blazing Saddles* type of sheer wackiness, and add to it the fact that the map that shows where the gold is hidden was tattooed (one half each) on the two sister's asses (Divine and Marguerita) who were separated at birth, and you can't help watching this madcap western to its final delirious, crack-brained shoot-out.

MALES IN MOTION
CC   R
1985   AMBASSADOR VIDEO

P/D—Not given
F/A—See below

There's no audience, no sex, no erections, only male nudity in this 60-minute tape, but it has proved so popular with the ladies (and maybe the gay population) that Ambassador has released a sequel, *Males in Motion: Brief Moments.* It proves one thing: Women enjoy watching men "take it off" as much as guys enjoy women bumping and grinding their way down to basics. The eight guys who appear on this one are modern Greek gods. First there's Marcus the Cowboy, peeling down to denim briefs, which he erotically rolls over his behind and concludes his strip with his prick bouncing up and down while he rotates his ass suggestively. He's followed by Steve the Spaceman, who removes a Star Wars costume. Then comes Mike, dressed in a Madison Avenue gray suit, under which is a Superman costume; he soon displays a magnificent 10-inch bouncing schlong that John Holmes would envy. Next is Jeff the Cop, whose cock will arrest most women! He's followed by a good-looking, effeminate guy in tennis shorts, who smilingly offers his own racket and balls. There's also the Playboy, but the piece de resistance is Patrick the Explorer, who appears dressed as a raider of the Lost Ark. First he does a fire- and sword-swallowing act, during which he's half naked. Then he pulls a four-foot-long, live, spitting snake out of his pants and lets it roam over his torso as he finally dances naked with it contrasting its movements with his own dangling prick.

MARILYN CHAMBERS PRIVATE FANTASIES #3
CC   NN   BI   DK   DBD
1984   CABALLERO

P/D—Peter Moss, Ned Morehead, Kate Jillian
F/A—Gaylee Marie, Tantala
F/A—Nick Random, Rick Cassidy, John Colt, Dolph Stouber, Ron Jeremy

The CC rating on this one is only to be consistent with the other *Marilyn* tapes and is for those who wish to continue their exploration of every curve and crevice of Marilyn's body. But unlike *Never a Tender Moment* (see review), this one offers only one example of Marilyn's sexual joys. In a section called "The Newspaper Ad," Tantala, whose ad she answers, soon has her naked, chained and spread-eagled in her chamber of horrors, and she forces Marilyn to count as she whips her, and she tells her as she drops hot wax from a candle on Marilyn's nipples and labia, "Tell me how much you love it, my little animal." Marilyn does, and finally they make passionate love. In another sequence, Marilyn fantasizes herself as an old-maid secretary who seduces her boss; in another, when her boyfriend stands her up for a basketball game, she makes love to a male mannequin who comes to life; and finally, she visits her gynecologist (Ron Jeremy), who does his proctoscopic examinations with his prick, of course. Interestingly, with the exception of Jeremy, none of the guys listed above is a porn regular.

MARLENE BOUQUET
CC   NN   BI   NR   DK
1979   VCX

P/D—Louis Duchesne, Michael Lemoine
F/A—Janine Reynaud, Claudia Coste, Virginia Vignon
F/A—Michael Lemoine, Francois Canyon, Jimmy Hollosy

Most women will enjoy this fascinating story of a wealthy Parisian, Michel (who, I presume, is the same guy who directed this film and is a handsome Tyrone Power type). He stares at his ladies so intently that you wonder if he has a glass eye. I'd put this one on the top 50 of sensually erotic films, and it's one that you can watch more than once. Michel is married to Marianne (Claudia Coste, a most beautiful woman), but he is a man who can't resist women, and he controls them easily because he loves them so much. So Marianne puts up with his infidelities and even is well aware of some of the women, like Frances (Janine Reynaud, also a very beautiful woman), who wants him "for her own." Marianne tells Michel that he refuses to play by the rules of the game and that they will never grow old together. Michel reponds that she's bourgeoise, and when she refuses him in bed after she knows that he's been with Frances, he persists until he practically rapes her. But Michel can't resist beautiful women. At a dinner party, he picks up Edith, brings her home, and tries to work out a threesome, which Marianne resists. Marianne has a good friend, Phillipe, who really loves her and tells her that she's crazy to put up with Michel, but Marianne still wants him. Then Michel picks up an Englishwoman, a tourist from the lower classes, and he practically has to rape her before she acquiesces. When she does, she loves him, too, as do all the others. But he leaves her in bed, and this time he's disgusted with himself. You know that he's finally decided to return to Marianne for good. But it's too late. She's left him a note that she's going to marry Phillipe. It's all told with nice acting and very sensuous sexmaking.

MASCARA
CC NN NL BI DK
1983 CABALLERO

P/—Henri Pachard
F/A—Lisa de Leeuw, Lee Carroll, Tiffany Clark, Mistress Canice
F/A—George Payne, Ron Jeremy, R. Bolla, Bobby Astyr

Henri Pachard, a.k.a. Ron Sullivan, gives you a feeling in this one that women like Harriet (Lisa de Leeuw) and Lucy (Lee Carroll) may actually exist in New York City. By concentrating most of the action on them he not only proves that porno stars can act, but he also develops character and keeps your interest. In fact Lisa de Leeuw, who has been making adult films for nearly ten years, is one of the best actresses in the business. Lee Carroll also redeems herself in this one as Lucy, a high-priced call girl. Harriet is a secretary to R. Bolla, whose wife evidently isn't much fun in bed. Lucy arrives several times a week and takes care of him in his office. Harriet tries not to listen. During one session she gets a phone call from her mother in Cleveland. Mamma is trying to find out when Harriet is going to find a man and get married. But Harriet, who admits that she's usually "on a high energy sex kick" is double dating with a girl friend. The guys take them back to their apartment and after an evening where Harriet is very accommodating with her guy and her girl friend timidly gets a Jacuzzi screwzie with Ron Jeremy, Harriet's guy tells her the next morning, "I'll call you. Lock the door when you leave." As she leaves, Harriet shakes her head and sighs, "But you don't know my phone number." So lonely Harriet takes up with Lucy who is a very pragmatic lady about the men and women she services too. One lady is a female masochist. There's Jim and Bob, who Harriet takes on both at the same time and can't keep their names straight, and there's a transvestite (Bobby Astyr of all things) married to a dominatrix in a yucky scene which Pachard should have condensed. Finally, the film concludes, as it began, with Harriet taking the subway to work or home. Obviously, as Lucy comes frantically chasing after, Harriet is deciding that it's better to be lonely than to be a hooker.

MATINEE IDOL
CC NN NL NR
1984 VCA

P/D—David Friedman, Henri Pachard
F/A—Jesie St. James, Angel, Kay Parker, Colleen Brennan
F/A—John Leslie, Herschel Savage, David Friedman, Elmer Fox

Without Dave Friedman (chairman of the Adult Film Association), who wrote the screenplay for this film and produced it, this guide would never have been written. While Dave produced many "tits-and-ass" films in the 1950s and '60s and has underwritten some current films, this is the first one in which he appears as practically himself. Well, not quite! His screen name is Bernie Kuntz, and his partner in International Pictures is Harvey Cox (Elmer Fox). Cox and Kuntz have a new film underway, featuring Linda Hand (Jesie St. James) and Lance Hardy (John Leslie). Linda and Lance have made many pictures together, but it's a love/hate relationship that, right from the beginning, gets pretty hateful because Linda, during a filming, instead of sucking Lance's cock takes a big bite out of it and calls him "an arrogant asshole." They both refuse to go on with the shooting. Kuntz agrees with Linda's estimate of Lance but decides to replace them both. He and Cox audition various seductive ladies and come up with Daisy Cheney (Angel). Angel is very pretty, and this is really her first picture. In the meantime, Linda finds Bud (Herschel Savage), the guy who cleans her swimming pool, to replace Lance. In a mad sequence that only Dave Friedman could write, Linda and her friend Ginger (Colleen Brennan) make a plaster mold of Bud's cock to show to Kuntz. They keep him excited until it hardens by fucking his toes. It all ends up romantically, but to Kantz's and Cox's shock, Daisy and Bud mate up and Linda and Lance are reconciled. They all go to Reno and get married, and they telephone Kuntz and Cox and tell them that from now on they're not going to make any pornos. Dave provides a great laugh at the end, which I won't spoil for you. During the picture, Dave ducks a sexual encounter with Jesie St. James by telling her that he's been married for 28 years, but even that's not the truth in this fun-filled film: Dave has been married to the same woman for 35 years! Interestingly, Dave sets the pace for the industry with only one cum shot and no bisexual sequences.

MIDNIGHT DESIRES
CC NN BI DK
1977   QUALITY/VIDEO-X-PIX

P/D—**Amanda Barton**
F/A—**Karen Regis, C. J. Laing, Linda Lovemore, Vanessa Del Rio**
F/A—**Eric Edwards, Jamie Gillis, Ray Jeffries**

John (Eric Edwards), a high-income stock broker, and his wife, Amy (Karen Regis), are invited to play bridge at the 50-room estate of one of the wealthiest men in New York, Martin Van Nostrand (Jamie Gillis), who is married to Elaine (C. J. Laing). Martin can see to it that John will move up the ladder to vice-president in his investment firm, so they must be on their best behavior. They no sooner arrive at the palatial home than the butler delivers a newspaper to Martin with big headlines that Hitler has invaded Poland, and Martin begins to weep at the thought of his relatives who will be exterminated. John and Amy are bewildered, since the time is 1977 or thereabouts, but Elaine suggests, to cheer Martin up, that instead of playing bridge they tell each other their most obsessive sexual fantasy. She begins and describes herself as a naked prisoner in a windowless, doorless room from which she is finally delivered to hooded men with naked cocks in cock rings. With her head in stocks, she is whipped and fucked and humiliated. When she finishes, Martin analyzes her fantasy. She was not really humiliated—the people in her fantasy were obeying *her* orders. John reluctantly tells his fantasy with a prostitute and his girlfriend where he ends up making love to his girlfriend while the prostitute screws him with a dildo. "This was a cover-up for your homosexual tendencies," Martin advises him. Martin's fantasy involves his youthful desire to be heavyweight champion of the world, a goal he is unable to achieve in his fantasy because of gangsters who want him to throw the fight. So he fucks the godfather's girlfriend, Vanessa Del Rio. John tells Martin that his fantasy proves that he's really a "motherfucker" because his mother prevented him from being a boxer. Amy's fantasy goes back to the 18th century and involves being accosted by three highwaymen, with whom she ends up in a tavern getting happily screwed. They all agree that Amy is the most honest because her fantasy doesn't have any hidden meanings. She simply wanted to fuck. Whoever Amanda Barton was, she could tell an interesting cinematic story (see *That Lady from Rio*). The "cuckoo" feeling of the evening, which doesn't end in an orgy, is enhanced by the butler, who continues to arrive with newspapers covering major events of World War II as if they were current reality.

MIDNIGHT HUSTLE
CC NN BI DK
1985   VCA

P/D—Steve Brown
F/A—Juliette Orwell, Marilyn Zukor
F/A—Mike O'Dong, Jerry Putz, John Seeman, Jon Martin

Connie and Lisa (the two ladies listed above) and Harry and Phil (one of whom now has the screen name of Jon Martin) appear as high-school friends in this rerelease of a 1970s film. The guys try to make out with the girls at a drive-in movie, but the ladies are ostensibly prudish and won't even drink beer in the car for fear of getting caught by the police. But the guys do manage to play feelies. In the meantime, the girls, one of whom lives with a mother and her boyfriend, are really female Jekylls and Hydes. Rid of the guys, they take the subway from Oakland to downtown San Francisco seeking sexual adventures, which include a surrealistic photography-and-fucking session for one of them and a "poo-ectomy" for the other, performed by a doctor and nurse who put her in stirrups for a gynecological examination. In the meantime, their boyfriends, suspicious of them, have discovered that the girls didn't go to bed after the boys had brought them home, and they have followed them downtown, but have lost them. One guy pays $30 to get laid by a whore, who asks him if he's got a rubber. The guys finally confront their girlfriends, who promise to reform but soon are again pursuing their midnight hustles.

MISSING PIECES
CC NN BI DK
1985   INTROPICS VIDEO

P/D—Richard Mailer, John Seeman
F/A—Nina Hartley, Lili Marlene, Jill Ferrar, Carol Tatum
F/A—Mike Horner, Billy Dee, Jon Martin

This one gets a CC rating for the very sharp color (shot on video, I presume) and for Nina Hartley, who is a pretty good actress. As Lauri, she's married to a pro tennis player who is so busy keeping in shape and playing the game that he's a hop-on-fast-and-hop-off-fast kind of lover. Complaining to her friend Valerie, Lauri gets invited to a swinger's party with a half dozen couples in a San Francisco environment that looks very much like the real thing. Arriving alone, Lauri gets the immediate attention of several men but, in horror and shock at what she sees, she escapes, past a couple screwing avidly on the stairs, to an upstairs bedroom, where she calls Valerie in a panic. Valerie tells her to remember her marriage, and now the story proceeds in a long series of flashbacks that include a couple (Mike Horner and Carol Tatum) demonstrating sex toys. It all ends in a happy threesome, of course. Then Lauri is invited on a 35-foot motor cruiser to tour San Francisco Bay with a black friend of hers, and in gratitude, when the owner anchors the boat, they both take care of him. Finally Lauri, still at the swinger's party, after talking with Valerie, decides to join the fun. The next day when Jake (Billy Dee), her husband, tries to give her short shrift, she retaliates with a knockout seduction that no man could resist.

THE MORNING AFTER
CC NN BI DK
1977   QUALITY/VIDEO-X-PIX

P/D—Jean Jacques Robeau, Sidney Knight
F/A—Jean Parker, Cathy Neilman, Linda Shall, Lois Ester
F/A—Sammy Cole, Dandy Thomas, David Marcus

When you've watched several thousand porno films and you see one that was made in the United States with totally unfamiliar faces, you wonder who the people who acted in it and directed it were and why they never did it again. If you want an adult film with more story and dialogue than screwing, try this one. John Hickman (story names only are given here, because no one is identified in the credits) is a theatrical booking agent who travels a great deal and has let his younger sister, Gay, use his apartment. He returns to find her naked and stabbed to death in his bed. Did he do it? The police think he did. But you soon discover that Gay had moved out of their father's house because the old man beat her and their mother disappeared long ago. Their father hates their mother and his daughter, too. He tells John that Gay might not even be his own flesh and blood since both his wife and his daughter are damned whores. As you learn more about Gay, you have to agree that she isn't exactly the kind of girl you'd bring home to Mom and Dad. She wants to work in a club that is partially owned by her brother John and his partner Larry, but she can't do anything practical. But when she sees that the club offers live sex shows, she's very interested and would rather participate than be a stripper. But Larry falls in love with her, will let her be only a stripper, and warns her that he is the only person she can have sex with in the club. He soons finds that Gay isn't a one-man woman. Did he murder Gay? John thinks he did, and nearly kills him, but then John discovers the truth: The old man killed Gay when he discovered she was a stripper and after Gay taunted him: "You were always hot for my body, weren't you? So take it." Listening to her, knowing he wanted her, he stabbed her to death.

MY FIRST TIME
CC   NN   DBD   BI   DS (a little)
1979   ESSEX

P/D—Alan Schatz, Leonard Burke
F/A—Mimi Morgan, George Ilene, Sonya Spizer
F/A—Joey Civera, Jack Wright, David Blair

The title on this one is misleading. It's not Sue's (Mimi Morgan) first time in the sack with a guy. She's married to Joey (Joey Civera), a no-good guy who is too lazy to look for a job, so she has to support him. In between working for the phone company she decides to make a porno movie for the first time. The movie is being shot in a ritzy home, and she soon discovers that the owner, a young lawyer, is a swinger who rents the place out occasionally to porno-film producers. He's charmed with her and invites her to a swing party where the couples go to separate bedrooms. Sue brings Joey, and he's a little shocked to see her disappear with Jack (Jack Wright), the lawyer. Later, although Sue is a little shocked to be begged by a masochistic woman to whip her, she is really much attracted to the lawyer. He tells her to leave Joey and move in with him. Back home, she finds Joey screwing with the woman he met at the party, but when she tells him she's going to leave, he slaps her around and he and the women inject her with a sleeping drug. Never mind, she finally comes to, and when Joey sobs, "What am I going to do without you?" she replies, "I don't give a shit."

MY THERAPIST
CC   R   NL   NR
1984   MEDIA

P/D—Joseph Shaptel, Al Rossi
F/A—Marilyn Chambers, Judith Jordan, Kate Ward
F/A—David Winn, Buck Flower, Robbie Lee

Believe it or not, Marilyn Chambers in an R-rated movie proves that she is as good an actress as you'll see on most television dramas. What's more, this film has an interesting story line that makes you wonder why more adult-film producers haven't explored the area. Even Boston has a Sexual Health Center that offers sexual surrogates to help cure male shyness, premature ejaculation, impotence, and many other sexual problems. So this isn't fantasy, but a reality that is available in most large cities. As Kelly Carson, Marilyn is a sexual surrogate who enjoys her work and frequently gets involved in the emotional problems of her clients. One is Rip Rider, a famous country-and-western singer, who is 52 years old. Beautifully played by Buck Flower, Rip, who has been fucking since he was 12, is impotent. Among other things, Kelly saves him from murdering his girlfriend. But another client, impatient with her structured approach to regaining his sexual self-worth, comes close to raping her, and you realize that Marilyn is only about five-foot-three to this guy's six-foot-four (or more) height. During her non-working hours, Kelly has a boyfriend who falls in love with her, but he can't believe that she can love him and make a living the way she does. Tearfully, she tells him that she really likes her work and helping people. She can't quit. The tape ends with him sorrowfully saying good-bye on a beach. I think ultimately the video-cassette market for this kind of R-rated film, which won't play at suburban theaters, will effect a merger between X and R films.

NAKED AFTERNOON
CC NN BI NL NR
1976 CAL VISTA

P/D—Chelsea Lake, Alan Colberg
F/A—Abigail Clayton, Annette Haven, Sarah Mills, Clair Dia
F/A—John Leslie, Joey Civera, Turk Lyon, Mark McIntyre

"You are one wild chick, Thomasina," her boyfriend Sam tells her after they have had a happy session in the sack. "Let's get married." But Thomasina (Abigail Clayton) wants to pursue her career as an actress and doesn't think she's cut out to be a computer programmer's old lady. Unfortunately, at the moment, as a masseuse in a massage parlor who, for a fee, will satisfy orally as well as digitally, she is a long way from the silver screen. But then a handsome guy, whom she thoroughly satisfies, learns about her aspirations and gets her a part in a porno flick. Along with her, you now watch some realistic behind-the-scenes shooting of a porno film in which Thomasina jumps into bed with a guy she has never met and gets acquainted with him *after* they have fucked. But the director tells her the film won't be released for another eight months. The massage parlor is closed down by

the police, and Thomasina is out of work. Sam will still marry her, but she can't envision a dull, married life. Then, John Martin (John Leslie—in this early film he's still John Leslie Dupre), who is looking for a star for a legitimate film, sees her in the porno movie and, despite his assistant's (Annette Haven) dubious feelings, he finally locates her and gives her a screen test, and defying all reality, she becomes a legitimate actress. Leslie and Annette have only small parts. The story concentrates on Abigail Clayton, who has a kind of Diane Keaton facial vulnerability that is very appealing. I don't believe that she's now making adult films, but she was an interesting actress in this one.

NASTY GIRLS
CC NN DK
1983 VCX

P/D—Henri Pachard
F/A—Kelly Nichols, Joanna Storm, Tiffany Clark, Sharon Mitchell, Sharon Cain, Barbara Daniels
F/A—Dave Ruby, Ashley Moore, Alan Adrian, Michael Bruce, R. Bolla, F. J. Lincoln

The CC rating is for a clever slice-of-life idea that didn't quite get off the ground, but nevertheless Pachard does what few adult-film directors manage. He has created a number of different and interesting characters with whom the viewer can identify. Eve's Bar, owned by Pachard (who appears for a few seconds) is a typical pickup bar that exists in many cities. Regulars, like Kelly Nichols, Joanna Storm, and Tiffany Clark, gather there. They share an apartment, and hang out at the bar, looking to get laid by guys who can show them a good time in bed and out. Kelly acts the tough cookie, Tiffany the cool but willing lady, and Joanna, who can look at a guy and make him feel she needs a knight in armor, is naive. In addition, at the bar there's Barbara Daniels, who should receive some kind of award for playing a middle-aged alcoholic on the make. She ends up with a beefy married guy who comes to the bar for a night on the town. Another patron of the bar is R. Bolla, who has previously told his live-in girlfriend, Sharon Cain (she's a waitress in the bar), that he isn't going to see her anymore. He's been promoted, but only if he marries the boss's niece, Sharon Mitchell. Then he has the chutzpah to bring Sharon Mitchell to the bar while poor Sharon Cain serves them with tears in her eyes. Amid all this there's Fred Lincoln, himself a porno-film producer, holding forth all night at the bar with dirty stories and whatever comes into his head. The story goes nowhere, but the people make it interesting.

NASTY LADY
CC   NN   BI   NL   DK
1984   CAL VISTA

P/D—Sam Norvell, Bob Vosse
F/A—Tara Aire, Lynx Cannon, Rita Ricardo, Erica Boyer, Mai Lin
F/A—Jamie Gillis, Herschel Savage, Paul Thomas, Blair Harris

"I'm just a country lady," J.J. (Tara Aire) writes her high-school friend Katy (Lynx Cannon). "I'm coming to the city." Katy is head maid in a second-class hotel in San Francisco, where she has a sleep-in friend, Herschel Savage, and all the maids in the hotel are very accomodating with various hotel guests, like Paul Thomas. J.J. soon discovers that most of the guests in the hotel are very friendly and are happily screwing with each other in their rooms as well as in the elevator. Two hookers in the hotel, Mai Lin and Jade Wong, offer their combined services for $500. J.J. thinks that she wants to be a model, and soon she meets a young professional photographer who takes very nice pictures of her against San Francisco backgrounds. He finally photographs her nude, and she makes very erotic love with him. In the local nightclub, she encounters Jamie Gillis, who takes her doggie style while she's helping him run the stage lights. Her friend Katy is an aspiring singer in the club, but the stripper (Erica Boyer) steals the show by screwing on stage with a guy who inserts a candle in her vagina and lights it. The performance excites the customers into an orgy involving a dozen or more people, which is interesting because of the fast cutting and good cinematography. Finally, J.J. decides that she's not ready for the city and is soon on an Amtrak going home to the country. Tara Aire has a pretty face and a happy, believable acting style that is just as captivating as her lush body.

NASTY NURSES
CC   NN   NR
1983   CABALLERO

P/D—Paul Vatelli
F/A—Kay Parker, Janey Robbins, Misty Dawn, Patricia Manning, Becky Savage, Brooke West
F/A—Herschel Savage, John Holmes, Paul Thomas

The title is misleading. Starring Herschel Savage as Dr. Robert Matthews, Kay Parker as Joyce, his wife, and Grace Simpson (Janey Robbins) as a nurse, it opens with Matthews, who is enamored with Grace and sleeps with her in the hospital on nights he's on call. The story is as good as any afternoon soap opera—and provides believable hospital backgrounds, including an operation (Matthews is a surgeon) during which he loses his patient. The basic story involves Matthews, who, because his wife has found out about the affair, must make a decision between his wife and the nurse. He also has the problem of whether the hospital is going to be closed because of budget problems. Secondary plots include sexual hanky-panky in the hospital rooms—between a nurse who can't resist Paul Thomas and between a female doctor who can't resist a former high-school friend who is now a Hollywood star but arrives with a sprained ankle. John Holmes appears momentarily as a doctor who manages to spear most of the nurses. But Herschel gets acting honors as a believable doctor and as a man who returns to his wife and makes very romantic love with her. Interestingly, there is no bisexuality. Proves that Vatelli can make a good film when he decides to chuck the conventions.

NAUGHTY GIRLS
CC   NN   NR   BI
1983   SELECT/ESSEX

P/D—Sandra Winters, Ed Brown

F/A—Ron Jeremy, Richard Pacheco, Jamie Gillis, John Leslie, Randy West
F/A—Rachel Ashley, Honey Wilder, Hypatia Lee, Mona Page

The naughty girls and guys all live in a high rise apartment in Marina del Rey, a marina which is about twenty minutes from downtown Los Angeles. They all have names in this story—if you can call it that—but you won't remember them. Richard Pacheco is a computer genius and plays his usual girl-shy part. John Leslie is a repairman in the high rise. Jamie Gillis is a Professor of Sexology at a local university. Honey Wilder is the building social director, Hypatia Lee a former showgirl. Rachel Ashley wants to be a serious actress but learns the hard way, after being screwed on top of a pile of truck tires by Ron Jeremy, that you have to start at the bottom to get to the top. Never mind—she dumps a pail of paint on him in revenge, and Richard Pacheco falls in love with her at first sight. Randy West has a date with her, but he agrees to switch ladies with Richard and Randy ends up with Hypatia Lee. Meanwhile, Jamie Gillis is studying lesbian sex with a couple of students from the university. They follow his instructions while he takes notes. He's saved by Honey Wilder from a threesome as she faints (purposely) at his apartment door, after which he drags her in the bedroom and makes love to her. Regaining consciousness, she is more than a match for Jamie. Amusingly, that's all there is—except that everyone gets matched up, (John Leslie with Mona Page) and after extended romantic sequences of their "monogamous" lovemaking, it's obvious they will all get married and live happily ever after.

NEVER ENOUGH
CC NN NM NL DK
1983 SELECT/ESSEX

P/D—Gerard Kikoine
F/A—Lise de Leeuw, Maria Pfeffer, Danielle Guego
F/A—Christian Grovard, Marc Wyandl

While nothing on the packaging tells you, this is a foreign film made in Paris. The CC rating is only because the backgrounds are different, and you have a feeling that if the owners of the American version had simply let it appear in French, it might even be quite humorous. As it is, in addition to the dubbing, new credits have been provided which play on porno actors' names like John Lesly and Anita Haven. The plot is simple. A journalist is given the opportunity to save a sex tabloid that is about to go out of business with a continuing story of the sex life of romantic lady novelists. He has a live-in girl friend who quickly becomes suspicious of his activities—especially since the lady writers completely exhaust him and she can't arouse him. His first interview is with a lady who tapes her dreams—how this is possible isn't explained. But in the process you see her as a sex-starved lady telling her chef lover who has a carrot in his mouth which he plunges into her: "Deeper, deeper, I love your hard vegetable!" She's soon hovering over a cucumber! The next lady novelist still lives with her parents who have never let her grow up. In her thirties, she's making love to Walt Disney stuffed animals—especially Mickey Mouse. But she proves that she likes real men as well in a silly speeded-up film sequence. The last lady is Lisa de Leeuw, who must have been traveling through Paris at the time. Lisa likes it rough, tough and nasty. She enjoys it with a masked blackmailer in a subterranean garage, and is thoroughly gone over in a garbage dump by four brutal men. She enjoys it so much that she fellates all four of them. In between these sequences the journalist's lady friend blows him as he drives his Porsche through Paris, and eventually reclaims her lover.

NEW WAVE HOOKERS
CC NN BI DK NL (if you have a dark sense of humor)
1985 VCA

P/D—Walter Dark, Gregory Dark
F/A—Traci Lords, Ginger Lynn, Desiree Lane, Kimberly Carson, Kristara Barrington
F/A—Jamie Gillis, Jack Baker

Don't bring this one home to a female friend. The CC rating is for Women Against Pornography and the Moral Majority and for those who enjoy screwing that is disconnected to any brain reaction. Nevertheless, if you are sophisticated enough, you might laugh at the total insanity of it. The Dark brothers are chuckling all the way to the bank. Using the fast-cut techniques of Music Television—and sure enough, it often looks and sounds like MTV—this is supposed to be a hard-core version. It ain't for real, of course. It's a dream that Jamie Gillis and Jack Baker (a black dude who can talk fast and nasty) dream after they've watched a porno movie in their apartment. Their dream is about a new-wave hooker outcall service where all sucking, fucking, and masturbation (and even Ginger Lynn as the meat in a sandwich between two college guys) are accompanied by original rock music composed by a group called Plugz. It all ends up on a circular bed with four guys moving around the perimeter, stuffing themselves into 12 different female orifices. The X-Rated Critics organization picked this film for their Best Group Sex Scene Award.

NIGHT MAGIC
CC NN BI DK NL NR
1984   ESSEX

P/D—Adam Tarsiacus, Bob Loving
F/A—Lisa de Leeuw, Honey Wilder, Stephanie Taylor
F/A—Eric Edwards, Paul Thomas, Tom Byron

I have no idea who Michael Leonetti, the screenwriter for this one, is, but confining the action to the six people listed above allowed him to tell an amusing story with which many couples will identify. Eric is married to Honey, and he invites his friends Paul and Lisa, who are married, along with Tom and Stephanie (who are not married and are about 10 years younger), to spend the weekend at a camp in the Sierra Madre that his father won't be using. Quickly, you are with all three couples in Paul's Winnebago, which he is driving while complaining about the traffic on the freeways. The sexual banter between the older couples shocks Stephanie a little. It's a long and boring drive up

to the mountains, and soon, one after the other, they are fantasizing sexual encounters with each others' mates, which are more satisfying than sex with their own partners. Paul envisions a two-level conversation with Stephanie about horses and jockeys which leads to some happy screwing before the fireplace at the camp while their respective mates are still upstairs sleeping. Eric, who is taking a course in Shakespeare, imagines a delightful encounter with Lisa, during which they make love under a tree; she is Kate from the *Taming of the Shrew*, and they converse in Shakespearean language. In between these fantasies, they all come back to the reality of the Winnebago and continue to tease each other as Paul drives. Lisa dreams of a loving session with Honey, and the dialogue that precedes it and accompanies it is well done. Honey imagines playing a nighttime game of hide and seek. First she is discovered by Tom, and then Paul catches them screwing, and she tells him to make it a trio. Paul feels that he's not as good as Tom, who is much younger, and she must decide who is the best. When they are both snoring she finesses it by telling them they were both so good she can't decide. Tom, who loves to play softball, imagines a softball game with all three ladies, after which they shower together and play with his bat. When the six finally arrive at the cabin, they play a detective board game and they all fantasize an orgy at the same time. But then they finally to go bed with the mates they came with, and when the lights are out in their respective bedrooms, they happily wish each other good-night.

NIGHT PROWLERS
CC NN BI DK
1985   MASTERPIECE VIDEO

P/D—Howard Edwards, Will Kelly
F/A—Cara Lott, Heather Wayne, Susan Hart
F/A—Harry Reems, Herschel Savage, Steve Drake, Kevin James, Sasha Gabor

You'll find the plot of this one pretty hard to believe, but the acting is good and the bad guys, Nikki and April (Heather Wayne and Susan Hart), are any man's dream of a delightful, toothsome two-some. Two call girls have moved into an apartment in affluent Beverly Hills, where they are available to entertain guys like Mr. Hill (Herschel Savage) and his friends after the Saturday-afternoon television football games, while their wives have gone shopping. In addition to exhausting the guys, the gals case the joints where they are screwing. They come back after midnight and help themselves to the silver and art objects. When Mr. Hill is ripped off, he discovers that he's one of the many others in the area who have been burglarized. Sergeant Pete Welles (Harry Reems), who enjoys himself in bed with Sandy (Cara Lott), one of the police-women on the force, is constantly getting beat up by her boyfriend, another po-liceman, who tells him stay away from Sandy, whom he plans to marry. Who res-cues Pete after a good thrashing? You guessed it, our two classy hookers, April and Nikki, who at this point Pete doesn't know pick locks as well as cocks. Mr. Hill begs Welles not to tell his wife, but he finally gives Welles the gals' phone num-ber, which ends in SEXY (7399, if you check your phone). After that, Sergeant Welles catches the ladies in the act and sorrowfully sends his very friendly neigh-bors to the slammer.

NINE LIVES OF A WET PUSSYCAT
CC BI NN DS
1975   VCX

P/D—Navaron Films, Jimmy Boy L
F/A—Pauline La Monroe, Dominique Santo, Joy Silver
F/A—David Pirell, Shaker Lewis, Nicholas George

It would be interesting to know the back-ground on this sexvid, which has the aura of a foreign-made film. The credits state that it is based on a French novel, *Les femmes blanches*, and the cinematog-raphy is very well done. Gypsy, a woman in her late 30s, tells the story about her friend Pauline, who keeps her abreast of

her life via letters. Pauline is married to a very wealthy guy who is chauffeured around in a Rolls-Royce. His name is Da-vid, and Pauline tells you via Gypsy that David "can fuck and fuck and fuck and never lose his hard-on." David drives her wild, especially because he has other women. So Pauline takes on all comers and even seduces a guy in the rest room of a filling station while David waits in the car. A flashback tells you about her child-hood. Daughters of a very strict, Bible-reading Polish immigrant, she and her sister finally seduced Dad. Not long ago Pauline had an affair with a beautiful, coffee-colored princess from some Afri-can country who, in a digression, was raped by two black dudes. Pauline's on-going affair with the stable boy blends into her lesbian relationships. What makes the film intriguing is that even at the end, Gypsy, playing with tarot cards, is unable to untangle the threads of Pauline's pussy-cat life. As for the real pussycat, he's Gyp-sy's pet, but he doesn't contribute to the plot.

NOSTALGIA BLUE
CC NN
1983   VCX

P/D—Maurice Loctes, R. E. Perry
F/A—Sativa
F/A—Teddy Steele

Bobby (Teddy Steele) receives an old-fashioned trunk that belonged to his grand-father. He and his wife, Patty (Sativa), who are just about to make love, open it and find it full of women's clothes that were worn around the turn of the century and a huge reel of old 16-mm stag-party film. They're sure that Grandpa must have shown this prized possession to his male friends. Watching the film, which includes stag films as far back as the 1920s, Patty and Bobby talk joyously and humorously, in a voice-over, about what you and they are seeing. Along with the appropriate mu-sic of the time accompanying the vari-ous episodes, their conversation makes this a great addition to your collection.

(See also reviews of *Old, Borrowed, Stag* and *Famous Smokers.*) This one includes "Mr. Newlywed," during which a 1930s guy and gal prepare for their wedding night with a big application of Vaseline on her vagina; "Master Bator," in which the tax collector gets paid off in pussy; "The Novelist," who imagines such a sexy story that it can't be published; "The Dentist, Doctor Yankem," putting his patient under and then undressing her. Also included is a 1950s film where all the guys have crew cuts and the gals, after playing strip poker with their husbands, adjourn to separate rooms. But none of the girls really enjoys sucking their men, and they spit in handkerchiefs. One gal brings in her friend to do the job. Finally, there's a real oldie with a mustachioed guy screwing a 200-pound lady with a huge belly. Her friends can pick their dollar fees off the floor with their vaginas, and there's a guy who, after looking at dirty pictures, tastes a girl's panties; he's finally rescued by live women, who jerk him off into a cup and he drinks his own jism. As for Patty and Bob, while they talk a lot and finally go upstairs to make love, you never see them do it.

ONCE UPON A MADONNA
CC NN BI DK
1985 PARADISE VISUALS

P/D—Michael Phillips, Adam
F/A—Erica Boyer, Patti Petite, Little Oral Annie, Kathleen Kelly
F/A—John Leslie, Joey Silvera, Tom Byron, Ron Jeremy, Francois Papillon, Michael Phillips

If you haven't seen *Desperately Seeking Susan,* with Madonna, then you'll miss some of the fun of this parody, which uses the same plot. The CC rating is dubious, but the opening sequence with Erica Boyer as Susan (looking very much like Madonna) is one of the wildest "can't-get-enough" screwing scenes you have ever watched. Although you soon realize that they scarcely know each other, after five minutes, Susan happily imbibes Tom's (John Leslie's) jism, and you think that's that. Not at all! Tom still has an erection and sticks it in her ass, after which he sprays her with another spoonful and she has an

explosive climax. Moaning over "his poor tired cock," that's the last you see of Tom. Susan ties him up (in fun, he thinks) and then steals a diamond earring out of his jeans before she leaves. She's no sooner gone than a nasty-looking guy arrives and demands the jewelry, and when he can't find it, he strangles Tom. No Kidding! But never mind, there are other guys desperately seeking Susan and trying to reach her with personal ads in the local newspaper. These include Tom's friends Dick (Tom Byron) and Harry (Joey Silvera). As in the Hollywood version, there's a housewife, Rochelle (Patti Petite), who is married to a nerd, Garth (Ron Jeremy), and would prefer to be Susan's. Rochelle nearly gets strangled by Tom's killer, but she's rescued by Susan, whom the killer was really after. But now Rochelle has lost her memory. Fortunately, she hasn't forgotten how to suck and fuck. Before she recovers and the killer is caught, she and Susan take on all the guys that are desperately seeking Susan's various orifices.

ONE LAST SCORE
CC NN NM BI DK
1978 DIAMOND COLLECTION/C.D.I. HOME VIDEO

P/D—John Endler, Jerome Bryson, Robert Gold
F/A—Susan McBain, Heather Dougherty, Arlene Jamison
F/A—Gordon Wilson, Kenneth Brigg, Robert Rose, Robert Ness

Shot on Balboa Island, near San Diego, this one has a believable seamy, low-life environment and characters—Al Phangano (Gordon Wilson) and his first-choice whore Amy (Susan McBain)—who will keep you watching until the inevitable ending. Al lives on a motor yacht in a marina that is owned by some big shot you never see. Al is up to his neck in debt with bookies who have extended him credit on various horse races, football games, hockey games, etc., on which he has bet and lost. The money for betting comes from Al's ladies, whom he supplies with high-paying customers. Amy tells him, "Please, Al, I'm tired of hooking and watching you piss the money away on losing bets. Can't we stop and lead a normal life?" But Al can't stop. He has a tip on a horse from a friend who has screwed the jockey's black wife and has given him a sure thing on a 20-to-1 shot that has been set up to win a race in a few days. In exchange for the tip, one of Al's hookers agrees (in the things-you've-never-seen-before department) to give the black lady an enema while she's screwing with her white lover. In the meantime, Al has won a couple of bets and is now plunging all his earned and borrowed money on the one last score. Unfortunately, his bookie has been advised by Mr. Big to cut him off until he pays up past debts. Al keeps wiggling, finds a new bookie in Las Vegas, and gets caught by Amy "checking out" a new girl. Finally, as he's listening to the big race on his car radio, a nasty-looking guy who's been shadowing him during the entire picture arises from the backseat and strangles him . . . just as he hears that his 20-to-1 shot comes in first!

ORIENTAL BLUE
CC NN BI DK DS
1975   QUALITY/VIDEO-X-PIX

P/D—Lin Cho Chiang, Philip T. Drexler
F/A—Peonie, Bree Anthony, C. J. Laing, Kim Pope
F/A—Bobby Astyr, Jamie Gillis, Allan Marlo,
    Steven Lark

In the 1970s, it seems to me, they were making better porno films in New York City than in Los Angeles or San Francisco. This one gets a CC for the scary, sleazy New York City Chinatown background cinematography, which gives a feel for the city's underbelly where awful things like white slavery might actually be happening. Madame Blue (Peonie) is a tough lady who supplies women to Nick (Bobby Astyr). He provides women of all nationalities (the World Bordello Association) to whorehouses all over the world. Madame Blue keeps the women prisoners until they are finally overcome by her herbal aphrodisiacal "love juice" that she forces them to drink, after which they no longer want their freedom. All they want is cock. (See *That Lady from Rio* for a similar plot, but

it's not put together as effectively as this one). Madame Blue has a procurer, Brock (Jamie Gillis), who, for a fee, finds young women for her. A typical example is Angie (Bree Anthony), who has just arrived from Nebraska, been robbed of all her money, and is wandering the streets of New York City, sobbing and bewildered. While Brock hates Madame Blue and refuses to have sex with her, he likes the money she provides. Most women he brings to her end up imbibing her love juice and becoming insatiable lovers. But Brock is very attracted to Angie, and he refuses to turn her over to Madame Blue, which enrages her. It all ends dramatically, with Madame Blue and Nick kidnapping Angie from Brock and feeding her love juice, while Angie sobs for Brock to save her. He almost does—by agreeing to screw Madame Blue but then shooting her in the stomach before he finishes. But Madame Blue is too smart for him. Before she dies, she begs Brock to kiss her, and she finishes him off with a poisoned kiss. What happens to Angie is not shown, but obviously nasty Nick's dick takes care of her.

PARTY GAMES FOR ADULTS ONLY
R
1984   MCA

P/D—Carol Bromley, Kenneth More
F/A—Leslie Nurks, Cath O'Nell, Rhonda Shear
F/A—John Byner, Dustin Stevens, Blumen Young,
    Steve Tracy

This is a giggly-cutesy offering, the kind of games and conversation that people used to have in the 1940s and 1950s, with the guys hoping against hope that after the party they might get to bed with one of the more daring females. The games include blowing ping-pong balls across the room on your hands and knees with your behind in the air, a rope-tie in which a couple are hitched together and can extricate themselves only by a lot of rubbing and squirming against each other, a Tom Jones game of eating grapes while the women lasciviously suck carrots, eating food blindfolded and having to identify it (scatologically), the marshmallow-on-a-string game (to see who can chew the string to the marshmallow first) and risqué word games. Between games, you listen to the host, John Byner, recite limericks and imitate various Hollywood actors, and he intercuts "sexy" scenes showing a half-naked lady throwing horseshoes at a naked guy (rear view).

THE PASSIONS OF CAROL
CC NN NL BI NR
1975 QUALITY/VIDEO-X-PIX

P/D—**Amanda Barton**
F/A—**Merrie Holiday, Kim Pope, Rose Cranston, Daniela D'Orici**
F/A—**Jamie Gillis, Arturo Millhouse, Kevin Andre, Helmuth Richler, Mark Stevens**

If I were Video-X-Pix, I'd repackage this one in a snappy Christmas box and offer it as a stocking stuffer for the guy who has everything. Women will like it, too. It's Dickens's *Christmas Carol* retold in a sexier version. Instead of a crotchety old man, you have Carol Scrooge, who hates Christmas. She is the publisher of *Biva* magazine (the film was made about the same time that Bob Guccione tried to establish a magazine called *Viva*) and is a very nasty lady who rejects the magazine layouts provided by Bob Hatchett (Jamie Gillis). She keeps him working on Christmas Eve to meet the deadline on the next issue. Just as mean and nasty as the original Scrooge, she finally goes to bed on Christmas Eve and encounters her former partner Marley (Mark Stevens), who tells her she had better straighten out. "Being dead," he tells her, "is like an endless wet dream, and you wake up before you come." Soon Marley is exploring Carol Scrooge's vagina and she his cock to the tune of "Santa Claus Is Coming to Town." But the dream isn't over, and Carol proceeds through the Ghost of Christmas Past (at this point you even get a social message about a guy who died polluting the earth and how now in hell no one will accept his MasterCard or American Express card). With the Ghost of Christmas Future, Carol, after a tour of 42nd Street and Times Square, discovers, to her shock, that she has become a shabby street prostitute. She's rescued by

the Ghost of Christmas Present, a plump male, gay spirit, and they watch Bob Hatchett make very romantic love to his wife (Kim Pope) under the Christmas tree. Carol (whoever she is, she is a good actress) wakes up Christmas morning Scrooge style, and for the first time she loves everybody.

PERFECT FIT
CC NN NL BI NR DK
1985 DREAMLAND VIDEO

P/D—**Jerry Ross, Kurt Nielsen II**
F/A—**Traci Lords, Christy Canyon, Susan Hart, Gina Valentino, Laurie Smith, Kristara Barrington**
F/A—**Tom Byron, Mark Wallice, Francois Papillon, Peter North, Alan Royce**

Without Tom Byron, who plays the part of Ricky, a young guy who has been going with a gal for two years, they couldn't make a movie like this. He's a perfect match for Diane (Traci Lords), a young lady in her early 20s who thinks it's high time she was married. When he hesitates, Diane splits, but later at a poker party with his male friends (one of whom asks if he's still going with Diane and wants to take her on), Ricky has second thoughts and blurts out: "We're going to get married." "When?" "Next week!" Diane hears the good news via the grapevine, and her friends arrange a bachelorette party for her. At the same time, Ricky's friends are arranging one for him. They both use the services of Fast Eddie, who runs Porta Parties for various fees. He arranges both parties in the same hotel, with girls for one and guys for the other. But the hired performers are a long time showing up, and the guy who wants to go to bed with Diane nearly succeeds. Ricky saves the day, and he and Diane end up in the sack together. Traci Lords may be one of the gals some critics call "airheads," but in this one she's a believable girl-next-door. As for the bachelor- and bachelorette-party gimmick, it's used to better advantage here than in *Before I Say I Do* (see review).

PERSONAL SERVICES
CC   NN   NL
1975   CAL VISTA

P/D—Bella Bacalla, Michael Minghia
F/A—Claire and Connie Krumpert, Daphne Bliss
F/A—John C. Holmes, Peter Boll

The only familiar face in this one is a young John Holmes, who plays the part of sailor B. C. Buzzard. The happily silly story begins with a guy named Ronnie who has long sideburns and is balding. "I had gone three weeks without a piece of ass," he tells you, "and then I saw this advertisement in the personals. 'Queen of Sex will take on anyone and make them holler auntie. . . . I challenge any man to a duel of sex.'" Making an appointment, Ronnie soon discovers that there are conditions. The one who hollers auntie first loses, and the price for playing is $5 a minute. After three climaxes in some 75 minutes, Ronnie collapses and yells auntie when our heroine starts for his cock again. He pays up $375. Hardly able to walk, he goes to a local bar and finds B. C. Buzzard, who shows him his 14-inch cock. "It's a sad state of affairs," B. C. tells him. "I can get women to suck it all day, but no one will let me fuck with it." Needless to say, Ronnie arranges a return match with the Queen of Sex, and B. C./ Johnny, never taking off his knit cap, goes for two hours and 30 minutes and wears two ladies out. (While B. C. is "working," Ronnie discovers that the ladies are twins). When B. C. gets through, Ronnie gets his money back, and B. C. gets $650. One of the ladies moans, "We've lost a thousand dollars. At least I should have some fun." And she takes both of them on.

PET OF THE MONTH
CC   NN   NR
1978   VCX

P/D—H. J. Williams, Herbert Douglas
F/A—Michelle Roberts, Geri Daffron
F/A—Gary Roberts, Jackie Weaver

The title on this one is a misnomer. Michelle Roberts may have been the centerfold in some men's magazine, but in this one she plays a secretary on her way to Hawaii for a vacation. At the airport, a guy offers her a ride to a hotel and, finding that she has no place to stay, offers his home, which, lucky for her, overlooks a beautiful, deserted beach. From the moment she arrives, they begin making very romantic love against a beautiful cinematographic backdrop of Hawaiian sunsets and moonlight on the beach. Obviously wealthy, the guy is an expert at hanggliding, and the sexmaking is intercut with scenes of gliding over the Hawaiian coast in exquisite interludes that altogether comprise about 15 minutes of the film. Of course, the guy glides to a landing where our lady is lying naked and waiting for him. The film should have been titled *Hawaiian Honeymoon*, except that they never get married, and Michelle is soon back at her prosaic secretarial job. Most women will agree that this is the kind of loving that they can identify with.

PHYSICAL ATTRACTION
CC   NN   BI   DK   NR
1984   MASTERPIECE VIDEO

P/D—Jerome Bronson, Richard Mailer
F/A—Shanna McCullough, Pamela Mann, Bunny Bleu, Lisa Lake
F/A—David Cannon, Paul Thomas

Here's another strong adult story by Richard Mailer (see *Classical Romance*). This one begins with Bobbie Abbot (Shanna McCullough), a $100-a-night call girl, waking up with her john in a motel; he insists on one more shot. Reluctantly, Bobbi agrees. A few minutes later, she's out jogging. But you soon discover that she and her friend work full time for a nasty guy, Luther, who maintains an expensive home on their earnings and gets them johns every night. Bobbi is thoroughly bored with her work and wonders if this is all there is to life. But Luther sets her straight. "If it weren't for me you'd be back on Sunset selling your pussy for $5 a shot." Then Bobbi meets Ed (David Cannon), a runner who has injured his knee and is now coaching. He tests her speed and tells her that if she'll work at it she could compete in the upcoming women's time trials. Bobbi's big problem is that David doesn't know that's she's a whore. She finally has to tell him, but he still loves her. He even gets some of his buddies to beat up Luther in retaliation for his beating Bobbi. Bobbi has competition from another gal (Lisa Lake), who establishes a record in the things-you've-never-seen-before department by blowing Paul Thomas upside down for five minutes as she hangs from gymnasium bars. Amazingly, Bobbi finally prays to God. "Please, please," she begs. "This is my last chance for something good in my life." Of course, the Good Lord hears her. Shanna McCullough proves in this one that she can act as well as copulate.

PLAYING WITH FIRE
CC NN BI NR DK NL
1984   STANDARD VIDEO

P/D—Helen Terrie, Kirdy Stevens
**F/A—Brooke West, Cara Lott, Lindy Shaw,
      Cynthia Taylor, Karen Summer**
F/A—Randy West, Eric Edwards, Tom Byron, Ron Jeremy

Helen and Kirdy are the team that made *Taboos* and *Any Time, Any Place* (see reviews), and they prove that, with good dialogue and a fairly believable contemporary story, you can make adult films that have character identity and exist mentally as well as genitally. Catherine Marshall (Cynthia Taylor) is a working mother who is divorced and has two daughters. One is Virginia (Brooke West), who is about 20, and has an older lover, Frank (Eric Edwards). Frank loves Virginia but is attracted to Mommy, too. Her daughter April (Karen Summer) is a 17-year-old nymphomaniac who fills the house with her boyfriends while Mom is working. Danny (Randy West) is a supersalesman who likewise is divorced. He has a son, Les (Tom Byron). Danny keeps asking Mom for a date, but she keeps avoiding him. In the meantime, unknown to Danny, Les has been to bed with Catherine's daughter Virginia. Weeks later, in a romantic interlude, Danny finally gets invited into Mom's bed, after an amusing scene where she locks him out of her house and then undresses in front of a locked picture win-

dow while he watches. Never mind, she has finally hooked him. Danny marries her and moves into her house with his reluctant son, Les, who immediately is at war with April. Then Mommy discovers that Danny has slept with her daughter, and April can't wait to go to bed with her new father and his son. After some incestual exchange, it all ends happily, with Les and April sent to a military school and a girls' school, respectively, so they will keep out of each other's pants and April will let her new daddy's cock alone, except on holidays.

PLEASURE #1
CC NN NM NL BI NR DK
1985   L.A. VIDEO

P/D—Not given
F/A—Not given

This one proves that short stories, or vignettes, when they are carefully done, are more palatable than many longer sexvids. Each approximately 20-minute story was made in Europe with different backgrounds and actors, and they all have a Continental sense of laughter. The first story, "Paris d'Amour," begins early in the morning in an apartment near the Seine. A sleepy couple are making early-morning love, and another couple are arriving home. Before entering the apartment, they walk along the river and make love on the quay, overlooking Paris. Soon they enter the apartment and join the other couple in bed for a foursome. Next is "An Officer's Lady," which is set in Prussia around the turn of the century and is properly costumed. A policeman arrests a well-dressed young lady for urinating in the park and discovers that she's the wife of the captain of the local garrison. Before she is through with him she convinces him, sexually of course, that what she did was quite necessary. Then she makes love with a sergeant who arrives from the garrison. He's followed by a lieutenant. She hides the sergeant and another woman in her wardrobe closet when the lieutenant arrives. Finally the captain comes home, but he's half blind and can't see that the lieutenant is in his birthday suit.

Next is "Sex Show," which was actually shot in a small Paris nightclub. This one has an audience of about a hundred watching a ballerina dance to flute music (being played by a nude lady) around a nude male statue that slowly comes to life and soon begins a nude pas de deux. It all ends in a silly orgy done ballet style on the stage while the audience comments on the action. Finally there's "S.O.S. Save Our Sex," which is about two young ladies who have just missed a ferry going to a nearby island. Two guys offer them a trip over in a motor launch, and soon the ladies are suntanning, with the white one applying suntan oil to the black lady's anus—"the only place I get sunburned." After much happy screwing, during which one guy forgets to mind the helm of the boat, they pick up two additional ladies whose sailboat has overturned, and now the guys have two gals each.

THE PLEASURE HUNT
CC NN BI DK
1984   NOW SHOWING

P/D—Lawrence T. Cole
F/A—Ginger Lynn, Lili Marlene, Candi
F/A—Eric Edwards, Herschel Savage, Mike Horner, John Toland, Dan T. Mann

The CC rating is not so much for the far-fetched story, which is designed to keep you interested, but rather for, once again, Cole's clever use of several theme songs, with a female singer, to move the plot along—and also for Ginger, who occasionally proves in this one that she can act as well as screw with everything in sight. The plot is a doozy. Seems that Alex (Eric Edwards) is an old man who has Ginger, his child-bride lover. Presumably dying, he wants her to discover what love and sex are all about and makes it a condition of his will that she will follow his "pleasure map" and stop for instructions on all the places marked *X*. The first *X*, of course, is his lawyer's prick, and that is followed by one sequence after another of someone trying to prove that repulsive sex is the most exciting. Ginger experiences both filthy hillbillies, who cover her with chocolate sauce and screw her on

a dirty mattress, and acrobats who stand her on her head. She is constantly followed by a limping old man wearing mirrored glasses who is breathing so heavily that you just know he's going to get her, too. Sure enough, he does. And you've probably guessed already who it is. Alex/Eric, of course, and right from the beginning he really wasn't old. Rather he was testing her to see whether she preferred love to wealth, and now he knows the truth: She wants love and he wants her. In her best scene yet, Ginger concludes the film: "You're a cruel, mean son of a bitch," she tells him. "I could never forgive you for what you've done to me." And she doesn't!

PLEASURE HUNT II
CC NN BI DK
1985   NOW SHOWING

P/D—Lawrence T. Cole
F/A—Ginger Lynn, Mia Lynn, Susan Hart
F/A—Mike Horner, Steve Drake, Bill Dee, Tom Byron, Peter North, Don Fernando, Sasha Gabor, Mark Wallice, Buck Adams, Evan Taylor

Beginning with fast reprise cuts from the first film (see review) this sequel shows that Sharon (Ginger Lynn) still hasn't forgiven Alex for deceiving her. His lawyer (Mike Horner) now tells her that Alex was so depressed that he committed suicide. But he has left her a certified check for $1.5 million and a key to a secret map that will lead her to a great teacher who will take her on as one last student. The man (Sasha Gabor) lives on a mountaintop, and when Sharon/Ginger finds him, he tells her, "It's the age of the female. I have chosen you to become the most powerful woman in the world. . . . But there are agents in the world who want females to remain submissive." Thus begins Lawrence Cole's tribute to feminism *and* to Ginger Lynn. Using the pleasure-principle philososphy of Herbert Marcuse, carried to its logical extreme, Cole not only provides surrealistic sex scenes in which Ginger takes on practically all the guys listed above, but he provides lyrics and music written by himself and Shamus McGee to carry the story along.

PLEASURE PALACE
CC NN NL NR
1980 CAL VISTA

P/D—Carter Stevens
F/A—Serena and many unidentified ladies
F/A—Eric Edwards, R. Bolla, Jamie Gillis, Joey Silvera, Roger Caine, Bobby Astyr

Despite the copyright date my guess is that this one was made in the middle 1970s. It's not only Carter Stevens's best film (whatever happened to him?) but it's an unusual sexvid for a couple of reasons. There's no bi sex, and Eric Edwards, who's the hero, never screws with any woman on screen, and Bolla has sex only with Serena. Plus it has an interesting story and very good acting by Bolla, Serena, Edwards, and Jamie Gillis. Jimmy (Eric Edwards), who has been fired from the vice squad because he was too lenient on a pimp, teams up with a down-at-the-heels shyster, Mike (R. Bolla), and they spend $100,000 for a big, old-fashioned home in Connecticut that in reality is a massage/whorehouse that serves the local politicians. Mike is sure that there's something very fishy about the deal. The bordello, with Carol (Serena) in charge, is very profitable. Why was the original owner so eager to sell out? Mike and Jim soon discover that a New York gangster, Joe Buonofiglio (Jamie Gillis), also known as Joe Goodson, owns a $1-million home nearby and that their whorehouse is on his payoff list. It's so profitable that he's decided to take over the place. Goodson's gunmen are Roger Caine and Bobby Astyr, who mess up the ladies in the whorehouse when Jimmy and Mike don't pay off, and eventually they murder one of the ladies in the sauna. In the meantime, Mike has fallen in love with Carol (Serena), but he's shocked when she seems to be playing ball with Joe Buonofiglio. (He forces her to screw with him in a rough sex scene.) Jamie plays his best gangster part ever. Had he gone straight he would have made millions in this kind of role.

PLEASURES OF INNOCENCE
CC NN NM BI NL
1984 VCA

P/D—Bill Turner, Dick Thomas, Larry Revene
F/A—Robin Everett, Sharon Kane, Tish Ambrose, Tanya Lawson
F/A—John Leslie, R. Bolla, Eric Edwards, Alan Adrian, George Payne

In Des Moines, Iowa, Freddie (R. Bolla) and his assistant Dino (Eric Edwards) run a topless bar called The Cat's Meow. Out-of-town strippers get a lot more money per week than the local gals. Cindy (Tish Ambrose), a local stripper, convinces her friend Candi (Robin Everett) to take a bus to New York City with her, where Damion Farber (John Leslie), who runs a talent agency, will teach them (for $600) how to get jobs on the big-time strip circuit. Larry Revene's name on a film is a hallmark of excellence in cinematography, and this one captures the night-club mood and the environment of the rundown rooming house where the girls finally live when they arrive in New York. John Leslie is great as the sleazy agent who loves all his female clients. The story line, with clever editing, about two naive midwestern girls arriving in the big city hoping to become stars, is believable. Homely Robin Everett and pretty Tish Ambrose both prove that they can act. A clever subplot with Sharon Kane and Norman (Alan Adrian), a novelist who runs the rooming house, will keep you laughing.

PORTRAIT OF A SEDUCTION
CC NN BI
1976 ESSEX

P/D—Anthony Spinelli
F/A—Vickie Lyon, Monique Cardin, Rita Stone
F/A—Robert Cole, Jon Martin (listed as Jeffrey Stern)

If you're about to give up on 1980s adult films, explore around in the 1970s films and you may get renewed hope for the genre. This one has a dramatic, believable story and excellent acting. Only Jon Martin, who appears as a 1970s version of Tom Byron (a 17-year-old), is still making pornos. Vicki Lyon plays Kelly, a young woman who marries an older man, Jeff, who has a teenage son, Terry (Jon Martin). Vicki was an excellent actress and so was Robert Cole and young Martin. As Kelly, Vicki doesn't meet Terry until after she's married his father in London. But Terry, who is studying art in his last year of high school, is very talented. His girlfriend, Val (Monique Cardin, a woman as pretty as the 1980s Angel), poses for him and takes care of him in the sack. But Terry is a wise-ass kid who is occasionally quite brutal as a lover. When he sees Kelly it's obvious that he's going to seduce her, and he draws pictures of her blowing him, which he gives her. She valiantly tries to resist him but finally succumbs, and they always have the house to themselves while Jeff is at work. Feeling terribly guilty, she keeps trying to deny her physical need for Terry. You already know that Jeff, the father, is a moderate, once-a-week guy. After a wild passionate afternoon with Terry, Kelly refuses to have sex with Jeff. At first she tells him that she has a headache and that her period is due. But then, sobbing, she tells him the truth and begs him to forgive her. Although Kelly assures Jeff that she can end this insanity with his son, he's shocked and thoroughly embittered, and he calls her a slut and tells Terry to pack up and get the hell out of his house. Shrugging, Terry leaves, telling Kelly privately that she'll have more of a life with him and Val than with his father. If she has any sense, she'll meet him tomorrow afternoon, when he and Val are taking off. Will she? Won't she? Hopelessly rejected by Jeff, she decides to make it a threesome.

POSTGRADUATE COURSE IN SEXUAL LOVE
CC NN BI DK
1975   QUALITY/VIDEO-X-PIX

P/D—John Flanders, Harold Kovner
F/A—See below; also John Dugan and various
   students

Here's a sex-education film that you aren't likely to see in most colleges, let alone high schools. Aided by three couples (Bert Lewison and Bras Lewison; Darwin Burke and Randi Sablow; Danny Silman and Fran Carston), plus slides showing the visual history of sex, Professor Collins (John Dugan), who teaches a sex-education course at some fictitious California university, gives a lecture to his students on the dynamics of sexual love. The couples listed above illustrate foreplay, with a young man enjoying extended sexmaking as he arouses his lady and then, reversing positions, she plays with him. Another attractive couple illustrate that "position is everything in life." They enjoy making love as they merge, come apart, and remerge in 30 or more positions, all of which are romantically photographed. But the big surprise is when the professor discusses homosexuality and not only accepts this as a sexual variation but offers a film of two guys being affectionate and tender with each other and finally making love. "Isn't it ironic," he asks, "that this man could be jailed for loving his male friend, while another man will receive a medal for killing a fellow man?" The film ends with a 10-minute warning on the dangers of venereal disease and how to avoid syphilis and gonorrhea while still enjoying sex—even group sex, which is shown in one sequence in which you are told that it is a form of sexual release that the Greeks were familiar with thousands of years ago.

PRACTICE MAKES PERFECT
CC NN R NL
1983   MEDIA

P/D—Alois Brummer
F/A—Ulrike Butz, Logena Marks, Martha Meding
F/A—Victor Lange and many others not listed

You may see this one on cable. It was made in West Germany and proves two things: that Germans have a wild sense of sexual humor, and that they enjoy sexmaking night and day. It all takes place in a small town as a group of middle-aged men, gathered in a beer hall, tell stories about themselves and their neighbors. First, there's a woman who complains to a private investigator about her husband's infidelities and gets caught screwing with the detective on his desk as her ass hits the intercom buzzer. There's the pet-shop owner who arrives at the local brothel and has only a handful of change to pay for a lady. He starts out with a beautiful lady, who turns out the lights—and he ends up with the charwoman. Then there's the married guy trying to find a place to make love to his girlfriend in a sand bunker (the only place that they can find to be alone), but the sand truck arrives and fills it up just as they are about to climax. Or there's the wife of the pet-store owner screwing with her lover while loose parakeets, other exotic birds, a monkey, and a snake are all watching—and get involved in the action. She finally gets entrapped with her lover in an empty pet cage that was to be delivered to the pet store in a pickup truck, but the driver passes through a car wash first. There are many more, including three 60-year-old lechers being seduced by three young woman, who manage to stay out of their clutches. A good tape for a mixed group.

A PREY OF A CALL GIRL
CC   NN   DK   DS
1975   FANTASY/CABALLERO

P/D—Joe Davian
F/A—Valerie Dubois, Sue Denim, Susan Cheese, Sally LaBais
F/A—Richard Bolla, David Hatcher, Jack Lennan

This one begins with a flashy murder of a detective, Steve Stimpleton, on the waterfront, with someone shooting him from a moving car. The gangster, Mike, who had him rubbed out, is sure that one of his whores, who was Steve's girlfriend, has put the finger on him. The woman knows that she's in trouble and decides to leave town but phones her girlfriend, who's screwing with her own friend, Frank (a young Richard Bolla, weighing much more than he does now), who doesn't appreciate the interruption. But her friend tells her to come stay with her. It's too late. The gangster's thugs arrive and drag her screaming to Mike's pad, where Mike yells at her, "You're gonna tell me everything you told him." She insists that she told Steve nothing. For the next 10 minutes, in a very brutal scene, they strip her, put clamps on her nipples, which they yank, and whip her with leather thongs front and rear, after which they rape her. Finally, her girl-

friend, ignoring Frank's advice, alerts the cops, who arrive as Mike is throwing a big orgy replete with dominatrixes. The cops lead Mike off to the slammer, and our heroine is saved. There's one sex sequence in this one with a guy lapping a woman and vice versa, performed to the music of "Duelling Banjos," which is amusingly appropriate. (See notes under *Christy*.)

PRIVATE TEACHER
CC   NN   BI   NL   DK
1983   CABALLERO

P/D—Robert McCallum
F/A—Kay Parker, Stephanie Taylor, Joanna Storm, Janey Robbins
F/A—Tom Byron, Paul Thomas, Blair Harris, Mark Wallice

Many years ago, when I was running a business in Los Angeles, my brother lived high in the hills of San Pedro. He bought a high powered telescope with which you coud watch the ships in the harbor and look into the rooms of homes below you, if you were so inclined. This film probably doesn't deserve a CC rating, but the script offers much happily goofy dialogue and a neat survey of many aspects of Los Angeles. In the playoff between Jimmy (Tom Byron), who certainly doesn't look any older than 18, and his aunt Diane (Honey Wilder) and Kay Parker, who looks at least 10 years older, Byron is amusingly believable. Jimmy, to his aunt's dismay, stays holed up in his room whenever he's home from Valley Junior College. Unknown to her, he's glued to his telescope, watching the airline stewardesses across the street, who, whenever they are off duty, are busy offering themselves to all the men in sight and even giving some of them lessons in discipline. In despair, Aunt Diane hires Lillian Foxworth (Kay Parker), a private teacher, to find out what is bothering Jimmy and why he doesn't play sports or chase girls like a normal guy. Scene after scene is tongue in cheek. Aunt Diane is serviced by Eric Edwards, who she hears discussing the American sexual revolution on television. Before you know it, he climbs right out of the set and takes care of her. Jimmy really has his mind blown by an extended orgy (10 minutes of screen time) that he witnesses through his telescope. But his private teacher discovers the source of his withdrawal from society and soon convinces him that he must join the world and not live in his dreams, which he does by screwing with her—and Aunt Diane as well.

PROFESSIONAL JANINE
CC NN NL DK
1984   CABALLERO

P/D—Gunter Otto
F/A—Leila Visgo, Karen Gambriel
F/A—E. G. Marcus, Hans Klaus Beckhausen,
    George Daser

This is not a sequel to *Sensational Janine,* one of the most popular sexvids ever made (see review), nor does Patricia Rhomberg appear in it. It's presumably the life of Josephine Mutzenbacher, a 19th-century courtesan. Probably the title was changed because most people never heard of Josephine—and if you have a good thing going why not trade on it? In any event, this hour-and-40-minute costume film, with horses, carriages, bustles, and bloomers (made in Germany) evokes the Victorian atmosphere of the time, with much undressing and fumbling through mountains of clothing. In her rise to fame, Josephine marries a young, rotund butcher who warns her that he loves to fuck but is very jealous and will never share her with anyone. He soon catches her and her girlfriend taking care of a delivery boy and he kicks her out. A waiter tries to take over as her pimp, but she is rescued from him by a Hungarian soldier, who brings her home to the bucolic sex life of a family farm in Hungary. In the German beer halls, merry tradesmen eat tons of food while their helpful companions finger them or fellate them under the table. (In one wild scene they hoist an eager sausage maker over a 300-pound barlady, who lies complaisantly on a table, and they swing him back and forth inside her floating hairy custard.) Josephine now becomes the mistress of a soldier who is not adverse to sharing his

woman with his army buddies who have arrived for a recreational weekend at his farm. The evening festivities include a guy who plays an accordian while he services his lady, women who can pick up silver coins laid flat on the table by squatting over them, and women waving their naked bums at guys who are jerking off. You are then treated to a mind-boggling contest, the winner of which must ride a horse three miles in three hours, drink three bottles of vodka, and screw three ladies. The contestants swoop their ladies out of the crowd, onto their horses, and arrange the willing ladies so that they are facing the rider. You have a feeling watching this "sport" (the contestants are followed by the excited, cheering viewers in wagons) that it has its origins in actual country experience. So much nonstop sex would get boring in many films, but in this one the combination of a production that must have cost at least a half million dollars, a totally different environment, and the happy silliness of most of the encounters will keep you watching.

PUBLIC AFFAIRS
CC NN DK BI
1984   CABALLERO

P/D—Joyce Snyder, Henri Pachard
F/A—Annette Haven, Kelly Nichols, Cassandra
    Leigh, Annette Heinz, Chelsea Blake
F/A—Paul Thomas, Joey Silvera, R. Bolla,
    George Payne

This is one of the best dramatic adult films I have seen. It proves that you can work within the genre and still tell a good story with good acting. It's also the best film that Henri Pachard has made—and I suspect that the female guidance provided by Joyce Snyder is the reason. Produced and directed with real class, it tells the story of Nicholas Stern (Paul Thomas, who is perfectly cast and looks like a Kennedy offshoot), a New York congressman who is running for senator. Despite his public utterances and charm, he is not the believer in women's rights (or other things) that his adoring female followers think he is. Campaigning in a huge mobile home, driven by Tommy (Joey Silvera), one of his managers, Stern is constantly degrading Jodi (Annette Heinz), who meekly records his speeches and does secretarial work. When he needs release from the tensions of public appearances, he opens his trousers and tells her to blow him. "But don't get my suit dirty. I'll come in your mouth." Elvira Lawrence (Annette Haven), a TV newscaster, suspects that behind the facade Nick is a pretty gritty character, and she discovers that Tommy (who is really a nice guy who has been seduced by Nick) was a former pimp who had been arrested on prostitution charges before Nick got him out of the slammer. Worse than Tommy is Fritz von Holonval (R. Bolla, who in the film actually speaks German with subtitles), who is supplying millions of dollars to get Nick elected so they can make some fast real-estate deals. Actually, Fritz gets his money from multimillionaire heiress Mary Butterworth (Kelly Nichols), who long ago rejected Nick when he was a poor student at the University of Virginia Law School. All this is neatly woven together as Elvira keeps searching for the weak link in Nick's facade, and in a sadly realistic scene, tries to discuss it in bed with her coworker (George Payne), who has to leave before she climaxes to make the last train to Connecticut to be with his wife and kids. It all ends in front of Carnegie Hall on 57th Street in New York City. Why this film wasn't nominated for an Erotic Film Award is a mystery to me.

RAW TALENT
CC NN NL BI
1984 VCA

P/D—Joyce Snyder, Larry Revene
F/A—Lisa de Leeuw, Cassandra Leigh, Trish Ambrose, Chelsea Blake, Rhonda Jo Petty
F/A—Jerry Butler, Joey Silvera, Jose Duvall, Ron Jeremy

Before the credits appear on this one, you read the following warning: "This film contains subliminal suggestions that may result in a state of extreme sensual arousal. These messages are not visible to the average human eye. The producer accepts no responsibility for the viewer's sexual behavior that may result from these messages." Although the subliminal messages are there, and if you're alert you can pick them out, the real message is that a porno film can be made that will keep you interested from beginning to end. Again the reason is that the producer (a pretty female) has concentrated on just two people: Eddy (Jerry Butler), a hulk of a guy with a flaring temper who wants to be a legitimate actor, and Caroline King (Lisa de Leeuw), a zaftig, tough lady who when the film begins (the time is 1977) is making porno quickies and employing guys like Donny (Joey Silvera) for $100 a day. Donny and Eddy work as short-order cooks and countermen in a restaurant near Times Square. In a very realistic scene, Caroline directs Donny in a porno sequence, during which he can't get it up, gets his teeth caught in the actress's pubic hair (they shave her), and ejaculates inside her while Caroline is waiting for the cum shot. But Donny is not.as good at it as Eddy, who admits he doesn't like to act in pornos but needs the money so he can pursue his legitimate acting career. Time passes and Eddy becomes a nationally known soap-opera star. But then Caroline cashes in on him and publicizes some 25 porno films that he had made years before and which she is now selling in video cassettes. The producers fire him, and from riches he's back to rags. He locates Caroline, who has betrayed him, and screws her in the bathroom, forcing her head into a bidet and nearly choking her to death. She presses rape charges, but eventually she offers him a part in a new film (she's now making legitimate films) if he can play the part of a prizefighter. Her intent is really to get him beaten up, but little does she know that Eddy is an expert in the martial arts. You've already watched him, in the most realistic fight scenes you have ever seen in a sexvid, beat up three guys who try to mug him and practically wipe out Richie (Ron Jeremy) for screwing his girlfriend on the sly. The film ends with Eddy still down but not out. You can't help like Jerry Butler, who has a boyish face and the body of a heavyweight, and Lisa de Leeuw, who is beginning to weigh as much as the buxom ladies in Renoir paintings, is the nasty siren you can't help loving.

REEL PEOPLE
CC NN BI
1984   ARROW

P/D—Richard Farini, Anthony Spinelli
F/A—Juliet Anderson, Gail Sterling, Priscilla Shields
F/A—John Leslie, Richard Pacheco, Paul Thomas

Sam Weston (a.k.a. Anthony Spinelli), who introduces this film himself, has struck a home-video gold mine. The actors and actresses listed above are not the "reel people." They are simply foils to allow regular people to talk about their real selves, their sexual selves, their fantasies—and to realize their fantasies on camera. Unlike most adult films, *Reel People* lets the viewers become voyeurs to feelings and actions that in many cases (Spinelli hopes) parallel their own. To make this approach more interesting (and of course the sequences are not so spontaneous or unexpected to the Reel People as Spinelli tries to convey), Spinelli personally converses with the men and women who have agreed to appear. He talks in a voice-over with them, and they respond in their own voice-overs, as they are making love. In the process, the real people give their own reactions to what is happening to them, resulting in a nearly one-to-one ratio of dialogue and sexmaking. The participants in this one are Marie, who is 29 and a mother of three kids. She admits to being a total sexpot. When she's in a supermarket, she's turned on by looking at guys' crotches. Marie is delighted to get Richard Pacheco for a little fun in the sack, and as she makes love to him she gives you a running history of her sex life from high school on. Next Spinelli puts Jim, a 34-year-old electrician, together with Edwina, a 30-year-old schoolteacher who admits that she was once involved with a 15-year-old student. Next comes Chuck, who is 32 and realizes his fantasy of having two young women at once. Sabena, a bachelorette secretary, admits that she's a very sexual woman but can't believe her eyes when she sees Paul Thomas appear in her own fenced-in backyard. She hopes that the neighbors can't see them. One very pretty gal, Lucy, is offered John Leslie, but after much conversation she tells Spinelli that she never makes love when she's not in the mood and she refuses John, who is delighted because he so seldom finds a woman who doesn't want to fuck. Never mind, he gets Candy, who works in an insurance company and doesn't want steady relationships. Another Reel Person is Kay, who is bisexual and is rewarded with Juliet Anderson.

REEL PEOPLE II
CC NN BI
1985   ANTHONY SPINELLI PRODUCTIONS

P/D—Richard Farini, Anthony Spinelli
F/A—Kelly Nichols, Joanna Storm, Mariko, Candace
F/A—John Leslie, Randy West, Rocky Hane

Reel People II follows the same format as the first tape. Spinelli is improving the format, and this one has a few people who are "reeler" than the first one. Evidently, he had problems with the previous distributor and now is producing and distributing the series himself, with two more under way: *Reel People in Denmark* and *Reel People in Sweden*. This one introduces Mary, who is 21 and is never without a guy if she can help it. "I do it every night," Mary tells Spinelli, and she gets Rocky Hane, a porno star, to talk and fuck with. Then there's Candace, who can look at a champagne bottle and have sexual thoughts. Enjoying women as well as men, she wonders what an oriental woman would be like. She gets Mariko. One of my complaints about these tapes up to this point was that Spinelli's *Reel People* are all young and beautiful. But now he offers Frank, who is totally bald and weighs at least 275 pounds. Among other things, Frank is a B/D fetishist and a specialist in cock rings, which you'll be surprised to discover come in many sizes and shapes. Frank likes young women whose nipples get hard so he knows that they're not faking, and Spinelli provides one. Then comes Barry, a stockbroker, who is satisfied with his sex life but fantasizes having two gals at the same time. When Spinelli tells him that there are three young ladies waiting, Barry decides he's not ready right now! So Sean, a professional dancer, gets his wish—two women, a blonde and a brunette, Kelly Nichols and Joanne Storm, who take him to heaven. Finally, there's Mikey, a very sexy, attractive woman. She gets John Leslie, who ostensibly arrives on his day off to visit Spinelli and tells him that he really doesn't feel like working today. But Leslie changes his mind when he sees Mikey. These two tapes are great for couples and should engender some fascinating at-home conversation. But Spinelli still hasn't dared to deal with *all* the real people. The long and the short and the tall and the old and the fat and the skinny and the too pudgy guys and the too plump women and the homely people. Where are they? As you will discover when you watch these two tapes, Spinelli, who introduces them in person, and his wife Roxanne, who appears for a moment at the end of the second tape, are happy, plump well-fed people who are probably constantly dieting. So, play it again, Sam! You've got to love them all!

SALON KITTY
CC   R (hard, close to X)
1984   MEDIA

P/D—Tinto Brass
F/A—Ingrid Trulin, Teresa Ann Savoy,
   Rosemarie Lins, Sara Sperati, Maria
   Michaels, Stefa Sataflores
F/A—Helmut Berger, John Steiner, John Ireland,
   Bekim Fehimu

Note that Tinto Brass, who directed *Caligula* (see review), wrote the screenplay for this one, which also features Teresa Ann Savoy. Maybe he was trying to prove that Hitler and the Nazis had something in common with Caligula and his consorts. The film doesn't have any explicit X-rated scenes, but it has plenty of nudity and violence, with some really ugly sexual environments thrown in for good measure. Salon Kitty's is a brothel for upper-crust Nazi officers. The ladies who will serve the Nazi officers' sexual needs are lined up in a big auditorium, and at the command of the officer in charge, 20 or more of them strip naked and stand ready for

their first sexual inspection. Then they are shown some of the horrible misfits they must enjoy sexually, and this involves considerable sexual retraining by eager Nazi Brunhildes. It soon develops that the Gestapo wants to use the whorehouse as a listening post to identify officers who may betray the cause. A love story of sorts develops, and the lovers are finally freed by the conquering Americans.

SCANDALOUS SIMONE
CC   NN   NR
1985   ESSEX

P/D—Jillian and Nero St. James, Ted Roter
F/A—Kimberly Carson
F/A—Paul Thomas, John Hollyfield, Ron Jeremy

You've never watched a sexvid like this one. The plot is so interesting that it competes with the sex. Ted Roter, who appeares as Inspector L'oiseaux trying to solve a murder in a small town in the south of France, has surpassed his previous films, many of which have a CC rating. On top of that, although the entire atmosphere is French, I'd bet that the film was made in Los Angeles. It's the story of Marcel Duval (Paul Thomas), a wealthy banker who has fleeced most of the citizens in the town and has committed suicide. In the opening scenes, Marcel is laid out in a coffin, and the first one to come to pay his respects is an associate, Louis (John Hollyfield), who you quickly discover is not only as crooked as Marcel was but is having an affair with Marcel's wife, Simone (Kimberly Carson). He makes love to her in the living room, where the corpse is laid out, and their screwing is intercut with shots of the dead man. Then, to your horror, you see the corpse's eyes open, and he sits up in the coffin. "Come, come, cheri, you slut, aren't you glad that I'm alive?" he asks. Sure enough, Marcel has faked his death by taking curare, which put him in a cataleptic trance. Being "dead," he can't be prosecuted for swindling, but his partner can. Now Marcel conspires with his wife, who at the same time is conspiring with Louis, her lover. Someone is really going to die, but you don't know who Simone is going to waste, Louis or Marcel. Thanks to some excellent acting by Kimberly Carson, you never know whether it's her husband or her lover who is going to get a poisoned glass of wine and which one she will take off with. Ted Roter, who wrote the story, keeps you in suspense until the last moment, when he takes you to a beach in South America where Simone and her true love have fled.

SCHOOLGIRL BY DAY
CC NN NM BI DK
1985   L.A. VIDEO

P/D—L. M. Burton, Jack Remy
F/A—Summer Rose, Gail Force, Honey Wilder, Tantala Ray, Aurora
F/A—Steve Drake, Buck Adams, Francois Papillon, Nick Random

Here's a sexier version of *Angel*. Unfortunately, there's absolutely no motivation given for Tess (Summer Rose), whose mother is Catherine (Honey Wilder), to become a whore or to work for Madame Lila (Tantala Ray) afternoons and early evenings. It would have been simple to establish with some dialogue between Honey as the mother and Summer as the daughter, especially since Mommy is screwing around with younger men and Tess has obviously been raised in a single-parent household for some years. So the CC rating is for Summer Rose, who could probably be a good "legitimate" actress. She has an interesting face, and without makeup she looks like the all-American girl. With makeup, she's pretty whorish looking and not very erotic. Most of the action in this one takes place at Madame Lila's mansion, and the other reason for the CC rating is a sequence with Madame Lila and Vinnie (Nick Random) that shows an old whore taking care of a lecherous old man. Balding Nick Random and big, saggy-busted Tantala are perfectly cast!

SCOUNDRELS
CC NN NR BI DK
1983   COMMAND

P/D—Cecil Howard
F/A—Ron Jeremy, George Payne, Ron Hudd, R. Bolla, Sean Elliott, Dave Ambrose Chelsea
F/A—Lisa Bee, Manchester (Tigr) Copper Penny, Ann Turner, Sharon Mitchell, Tiffany Clarke, Tammy Lamb, Tess Myro, Marissa Constantine, Jay Tripper, Ariel Lee

Cecil Howard has always been an innovator in adult films—and this one which is a vignette on upper income suburbia, although it is wall to wall screwing, is interesting to watch. There are many surrealistic sex scenes—some shot with red and blue filters with unique camera angles. Simon (Ron Jeremy) is a wealthy psychiatrist. You meet him returning to his palatial home in Connecticut (Westport, possibly). His wife Linda (Lisa Bee) has spent the day presumably playing tennis but actually she's been in bed all day with his best friend Harper (George Payne) who also is a doctor. Simon suspects her, especially at the dinner table when she gets lies mixed up. Their daughter (Tigr) has presumably been studying for an exam but actually has spent the day in bed with two guys sharing their joints (pun intended). Nevertheless, although she has had wild sex with Harper, Linda also is very loving in bed with Simon. Seems that the first time Linda screwed with Simon, in medical school, Harper was watching and ever since she has wanted Harper too. But Linda is not above seducing Harper's nephew, which she does, and Simon isn't telling Linda all that goes on in his life. He not only fantasizes screwing the lady who sells him cigarettes, but he has something going with his secretary. So does Harper. And Simon takes afternoons off and goes to a "sports club" and beds call girls as young as his daughter. Meanwhile Tigr, in a fascinating scene decides to take a job as a hooker. A sailor pays her fifty bucks for the privilege, but after a very loving scene, asks for his money back. He wants to marry her and can't tolerate the idea of any other man ever touching her. All this nonsense, including psychiatric sessions in which Simon's patients, R. Bolla and Sharon Mitchell recount their sexual hangups are linked together by the "Laugh, Clown, Laugh" aria from *Pagliacci* and a still life of Simon, in whiteface clown's makeup, sitting between his wife and daughter. It finishes with Simon and his fantasy woman waiting to screw him in the back seat of his car. But it never happens, there's a head-on collision and they are killed. Maybe the film should have been titled *What's It All About, Simon?*

SECRET DREAMS
CC NN NM DK
1984 BAKER VIDEO

For more background on Baker Video see the review of *Amateur Productions.* This one (60-minutes long) is devoted entirely to one couple, a plump but pretty wife in her late 30s, Peggy, and her husband, whose name is not given. If you want to know what the couple next door look like making love and enjoying sex together, this one will give you a pretty good idea of what goes on behind closed windows and doors. It may even make you decide to record your own sexual activities, if only to see yourselves as others might see you—if you dared to let them watch. Peggy is a very erotic lady, and her husband talks to her continuously in a voice-over that he probably dubbed in later. He videos her in the shower, in bed, and before their fireplace. She plays with herself with vibrators and her fingers and in close-ups bumps her ass in a spread-eagled invitation to enjoy the delights between her legs. Her husband finally does, and she takes over the camera while he plays with himself almost to the point of climax. Then he manages to get in camera position with her, and they climax together. Later they play golden-shower games with each other. If you ever met them on the street, you'd be sure to recognize them. The husband also has not only figured out good camera angles for a fixed-focus camera but also experiments with interesting reverse-negative effects.

SECRET PASSIONS
CC NN NM BI NL NR
1982 CABALLERO

P/D—Joseph Rose, Burt Rose
F/A—Gretchen Meyer, Alma Katz, Heidi Maher, Lydia Loring
F/A—Claude Bach, Jean Luc Pitard, Felix Wurtman

It's sometime in the late 19th century in a small town in West Germany, where this film was made. Judge Gregor Van Klingenberg has just been made an honorary citizen because he has finally closed the town brothels. Everybody in the town, including his daughter Maria (but not his wife or the maid Frederike), thinks that he is a very virtuous man. Achim Ziedler comes to his home to interview him for a story in the local newspaper and sees him through the front window tinkering the maid's vulva with his riding crop and cruelly screwing her. Maria doesn't believe Achim when she sees him leaving the house and he tells her that her father is not as nice as he pretends. But Maria falls in love with Achim. In bed with his wife, the judge is very nasty to her, too. Then you learn more about Frederike in a flashback—and why she came to work for the hypocritical judge, and you also learn that she had three sisters (one of whom Maria's brother Hubert is screwing). Frederike also had a drunken father, who was screwing her sister. To bring the judge to terms, Frederike, Maria, and Achim conspire to expose the sex lives of the entire family, which include the judge's wife having an affair with the town doctor and brother Hubert being paid 1,000 marks by a young lady's grandmother to wean her from her dildo to a real prick. The costumes and silly, spoofy 19th-century dialogue and background music will make you laugh. If you enjoyed *Sensational Janine* and *Professional Janine* (see reviews), you'll like this one.

THE SENATOR'S DAUGHTER
CC NN BI NL DK
1979 CAL VISTA

P/D—Waldo Gest, Don Flowers
F/A—Leslie Bovee, Linda West, Gloria Throate
F/A—John Holmes, Peter Whigam, Bert Hupley

Remember "The Bionic Man" on television? This film was produced about the same time and still is a funny sexual spoof on the series. A senator's daughter (Leslie Bovee) has been kidnapped by Russian-sounding foreign agents. So have many other women in Washington. They are being brainwashed as spies to become "fully controlled seduction units." A major in charge of the Alpha Project to rescue them is working with a team of doctors to create a bionic man whom they can control and who will lead the government's agents to the harem where they are being held. The bionic man will be created out of a young man who is about to die anyway. In the meantime, John C. Holmes, playing a famous porno star, is driving home with an admiring female who can't keep her hands or mouth off his cock. He gets so excited that he crashes into a truck and she bites his prick off and gags to death. Nearly dead, Holmes agrees to have a bionic prick that will shoot one dart, bionic arms, and a laser eye. The operation to attach the cock is happily silly, and afterward, when Holmes finally recovers, he has a huge organ that ejaculates like a fire hose and has to be turned off electronically. Needless to say, Holmes finds the harem and saves all the women, but only after he has impaled quite a few of them on his bionic cock.

SEX-A-VISION
CC   NN   NL   BI
1985   DREAMLAND VIDEO

P/D—Jerry Ross, Ned Morehead
F/A—Gina Carrera, Tamara Longley, Melissa Melendez, Sheri St. Clair, Colleen Brennan
F/A—Herschel Savage, Joey Silvera

This is a very sexy, erotic tape with clear, sharp, copulating and cinematographic closeups, (CCC!) plus a funny story neatly acted by Joey Silvera as Darryl, a weak little nerd whose only friend is his dog Gus and whose only entertainment is watching a porno film in which Dick (Herschel Savage) is the lucky guy who gets all the luscious ladies. "Oh God, what I would give to be like that just once," Darryl groans. After you and Darryl watch Dick put his dick into a very lush lady's mouth and vagina and between her big breasts

(Melissa Melendez), Dick suddenly waves at Darryl and invites him into the tube. Thinking he's been dreaming or is drunk on one can of beer, Darryl groans: "I'd better switch to Kool-Aid." But he keeps watching, and after taking on Sheri St. Clair, Herschel /Dick shrugs and looks out of the tube at our hero and says, "This could be you, Darryl." He sticks his hand out of the tube and helps Darryl to climb in with him. Once in the tube, Darryl takes Dick's place and Dick goes in search of one of the female extras who has walked off the set of an ongoing porno film that Darryl is now playing in and joyfully getting laid "48 times!" Darryl arrives at his office the next morning and tells the secretary, Tamara Longley, a woman he has always dreamed of screwing, that he had a dream about her last night. "I had a dream about you, too," she tells him, "but I was angry with you. You were screwing everyone else but me!" This happily silly sexvid proves that with a little class, good dialogue, and lots of laughter, a superior adult film can be produced on a low budget.

SEX PLAY
CC   NN   NL
1984   ESSEX

P/D—Harold Lime, Robert McCallum
F/A—Kay Parker, Lori Smith, Lisa Lake, Danica Ray, Desiree Lane
F/A—Eric Edwards, R. Bolla, Herschel Savage, Paul Thomas, Richard Pacheco

Sue (Lori Smith) is secretary to Jeff Justice (Eric Edwards), a big Hollywood star known for his manliness. Her girlfriends, like thousands of others, have a Jeff Justice fan club and dream of going to bed with him—believing, for sure, that he would be more loving than their boyfriends. Unknown to Sue is that the unmarried Jeff, who has a beautiful home overlooking what seems to be Marina del Ray, has been impotent for a long time. But his agent (R. Bolla) knows, and the rumor has been spreading to such an extent that Jan Manly (Kay Parker), who works for the *American Enquirer,* is trying to find out the truth. Bolla hires a detective (Richard

Pacheco) to divert Jan, which he does in bed in a motel, and Jan falls in love with him. In the meantime, Sue's girlfriends are determined to get laid by Jeff. To his shock, they invade his home. One by one they try in amusing sequences to get him up and ready for action, but he remains limp. Finally, in disgust, they leave him, tied to his own bed. Sue, who has loved him ever since she was 12 years old and saw him in his first movie, unties him and restores his manhood.

SEXUAL CUSTOMS IN SCANDINAVIA
CC NN NM
1975   QUALITY/VIDEO-X-PIX

P/D—Eric Fosberg, Sid Knightsen
F/A—Ingrid Peterson, Angelica Bender, Judy Gringer
F/A—Alex Lindstrom, M.D., Sven Strobye, Jan Rinkberg, Nell Almebor

Made in Sweden, this is a sex-education film that is still pretty avant-garde by American standards even in the 1980s. It quickly establishes that the Scandinavians are against any laws that regulate sexual behavior between consenting adults. Ingrid Peterson, a psychologist presumably, who hosts this film, discusses the cases of several of her clients that she has handled, with an M.D. You soon discover that Scandinavian parents of an earlier generation have difficulty accepting their daughter's masturbation; and one young couple's marriage is in trouble because the husband feels inadequate and is not sure he'll have a sustained erection, so he ends up practically raping his unstimulated wife. Then there's a husband harassed by business problems who can't get an erection with his wife. Between Ingrid and Alex Lindstrom, all of these problems are examined in detail. They use live models and detailed analysis, with diagrams and charts of the male and female body, and they carefully discuss with their patients how to enjoy their own sexuality. The film concludes with a woman and a guy (who looks suspiciously like a young Jamie Gillis) showing how to overcome marital boredom with varied sexual techniques. What was Jamie doing in Sweden, where most

of this was made? Or was this section added as an afterthought? In any event, most couples will find it interesting and may learn some things they don't already know.

SEX WISH
CC NN NR DS DK
1976   CAL VISTA

P/D—Ralph Ell, Tim McCoy
F/A—C. J. Laing, Terri Hall, Candy Love, Dennea Benfante
F/A—Harry Reems, Zebedy Colt

Ken (Harry Reems) is living with Faye (C. J. Laing), and they are in love. The morning after Ken returns from a trip, and after a lovely evening of caring sex, he goes to work. A few minutes later Faye answers her door bell. She is greeted by a man wearing a stocking on his head. He rips off her clothes, ties her arm to a throat collar, gags her with an adhesive-tape bandage, and plays with her with a dildo while he jerks off. Then he whips her until her buttocks are bloody, after which, using a rapier concealed in a cane, he slits her throat. Zebedy Colt plays the insane, sadistic rapist. He sniffs amphetamines, wears lipstick and a cock ring, and acts like a retarded imbecile. Later, in a totally graphic scene, he forces a young black couple to have sex while he watches and comments in gibberish on the action and the woman's sobbing compliance. He tells the male to bite off her nipple, and when the man refuses he stabs and kills him, forces the woman to suck him off, beats her, cuts her throat, and then castrates her boyfriend. In one final, terrifying scene he handcuffs a woman to a fire escape and screws her before killing her. In between, as he terrifies the city, he is pursued by Ken, who is determined to kill him and finally does. Well acted, this film is worth owning if only to provide a controversial discussion as to how far filmmakers should go in providing details of a rape.

SEXY
CC NN NM DK
1984 ESSEX

P/D—Henri Dutranoy, Gilbert Kikoine
F/A—Dawn Cummings, Erica Madou, Katherine
Gambler
F/A—Guy Royer, Jacques Insermini, Jean
Deforets

This one was actually made in France in 1976 and titled *Delires Porn.* It wasn't picked up by Essex until now, but it proves that with a little character development the sex becomes much more interesting because it is related to an individual rather than to an automaton. Catherine (Dawn Cummings) is a young but dowdy secretary who wears glasses and teeth braces. She is the joke of everyone in her office, and she spurns potential friends in the apartment house where she lives. Totally alone, she sits at her typewriter and writes sexual fantasies in which she becomes either herself as a beautiful blonde or some other beautiful woman. In her dreamworld she transforms the street vegetable vendor, Jacques Insermini, into a tough hood who screws her with a cigar in his mouth. But one day, instead of dreaming, she notices a homely guy staring at her in a sidewalk cafe and accepts a drink of orange soda from him. Alas, back in his apartment, he's as shy as she is, and they both daydream what it would be like if they dared to make love with each other. There are some very clever scenes on this tape, including poor Catherine being discovered typing her fantasies by her boss, after which she runs out of the office in dismay and is accosted on the street by flashers and by one guy selling dirty pictures—all of which prove to be of her daydreams! It ends in despair as all her daydreams come to life at once in an orgy.

SHAUNA GRANT, SUPERSTAR
CC NN
1984 CABALLERO

P/D—Various, not listed
F/A—Shauna and unlisted male actors

On March 21, 1983, Colleen Applegate, age 20 (who a few years before had left her hometown in Minnesota and driven to Hollywood with her boyfriend), held a .22-caliber rifle to her head and pulled the trigger. It was 7:15 P.M. in Palm Springs, California, where she was living with her mother. At the Desert Hospital, she was put on life support systems, but she never regained consciousness. Two days later—Colleen, whose screen names were Callie Aimes and Shauna Grant—was dead. Prettier than Marilyn Monroe was at the same age, exuding an almost adolescent innocence, she never seemed on film or tape as sophisticated as most female adult-film stars. Why did Colleen commit suicide? Not only was she certain to become one of the top porno stars, but presumably she might have made the crossover into "legitimate" Hollywood films. Had Colleen killed herself four or five years ago, the media would have attributed her suicide to her revulsion and shock at her denial of her midwestern moral values. But surprisingly, in 1984 there was little or no mention of her death in the national press. Her story waits to be written. A daring adult-film producer and director could tell it straight or fictionalize it. She defied conventional sexual moralities, but so have hundreds of other adult-film stars—and they survived. What was happening in her mind? On this tape, Caballero, with a sympathetic female voice-over (who makes you aware that Colleen is dead but offers no explanation), gives you a survey of her career, from a loop that she did for Swedish Erotica called *Balling a Trucker* to sexmaking cuts from some of her films, including *Sex Games, Summer Camp Girls, Glitter,* and *Virginia* (her last film). All of the scenes reveal surprisingly caring sex, as do most of the films she appeared in. It was almost as if the producers and directors saw Colleen/Shauna/Callie as the first girl that they fell in love with. In the first edition of this guide I reviewed *The Young Like It Hot* and *Feels Like Silk,* in which she appeared as Callie Aimes. I also mentioned that she appeared in a loop (*Cindy's Bedtime Story*) "and is probably the most beautiful natural-blonde, virginal-looking woman in the business." When I wrote those reviews she was alive, and I suggested, even then, that the filmmakers should cast her in parts that let her be herself—and as herself she was a convincing actress. What was her real self? Of course, I don't know, but with this tape and the following (see various listings), which are all reviewed and which make a pretty complete filmography of Colleen, you can make up your own mind: *Celebrity Centerfolds #3, Personal Touch 1, Nice Girls Do, Maneaters, Flesh and Laces, Parts 1 and 2, Sex Games, Summer Camp Girls, All-American Girls in Heat II, Valley Vixen, Suzie Superstar, Private School Girls, Glitter, Virginia,* and *The Young Like It Hot.*

SHE'S A BOY TOY
CC NN BI NR
1985 DREAMLAND VIDEO

P/D—Jerry Ross, Ned Morehead
F/A—Amber Lynn, Gina Carrera, Sondra Stillman, Tamara Longley
F/A—Joey Silvera, Herschel Savage, Buck Adams, Gerald Greystone, Tyler Horn

The CC rating on this one is for Joey Silvera, who plays Tim, a starving legitimate screenwriter who has yet to sell a script, and Gina Carrera as Ronni, a nice girl who got herself involved with a married man, Derek (Tyler Horn), who fired her when his wife found out. Both Joey and Gina have warm, ingratiating screen personalities, and they make believable lovers. Poor Tim is in love with Sarah (Amber Lynn), whose daddy (Gerald Greystone) manufactures bathroom equipment and wants Tim to settle down and sell toilet seats if he expects to marry his daughter. If Tim hasn't sold a screenplay within the next week he has no other choice, Daddy tells him, or the marriage is off. Sarah sadly agrees with her father. Then Tim meets Ronni, who identifies with his problem and offers to help him sell a screenplay. But alas, rejections continue until she finds Sid (Herschel Savage), who produces porno movies. Tim can't believe his eyes when he sees one on a TV screen, but what can he do? Money is money, and without it he can't have Sarah. Of course, Daddy must never know that the screen-plays he is selling will feature Stormy Monday (Sondra Stillman), a big-name porno actress. When Sarah's brother Benjamin hears Stormy's name, he knows the truth. Before it's over, Benjamin is screwing with Stormy and providing better dialogue than Tim can write, and Sid fires Tim. But never mind, Ronni sells Tim's script to her former boss, and she and Tim get what they really want—each other!

SHOCKING
CC NN BI DK
1983 ESSEX

P/D—Frederic Lansac
F/A—Emmanuelle Pareze, Christine Chiriex, Karine Gambier
F/A—Jacques Insermini, Jean Guerin, Gilbert Servien

In the past few years filmmakers have given us the American TV movie *The Day After* and the British shocker *Threads* as warnings against nuclear warfare. In this one, the French give us an adult version. I've given it a CC rating only because it contains the longest orgy, about 80 minutes, that I have ever watched on a sexvid, and it reminded me of stories I heard when I arrived in Singapore at the end of World War II, when the British occupants of the Raffles Hotel knew that the Japanese would soon control the city. This one takes place at a dinner party in a wealthy estate owned by Jacques Insermini (a middle-aged actor, past 50, who appears in many French pornos). There are 10 guests. Outside you can hear gunfire and bombs going off. Intercut are pictures of the White House and the Kremlin, with a drunken southern President of the United States sipping bourbon and an equally crocked President of the Soviets gulping vodka. Both have red hot-line phones on their desks, but before the orgy is over, they have pushed the buttons and you see the nuclear blasts.

SISTER DEAREST
CC NN DK
1985 DREAMLAND VIDEO

P/D—Jerry Ross, Jonathan Ross

F/A—Traci Lords, Ginger Lynn, Sondra Stillman, Susan Hart, Sahara Breeze

F/A—Tom Byron, Harry Reems, Herschel Savage

On alumni Day at State University, Randy Jennings (Tom Byron with a moustache to make him look older) returns for his 10th reunion and discovers that, even today, the Gamma Nu fraternity brothers have a nude picture of his sister Vicki (Traci Lords), who was at the university, too, when he was a freshman. The snapshot lets him recall when he was a pledge at Gamma Nu. The captain of the house insisted that the virgin pledges accepted into Gamma Nu must get laid within two weeks. On the wall of the fraternity house is a chart of their progress toward sexual nirvana, including blow jobs, pussy eat, stink finger, dry hump, bare tits, and wet kisses. Two weeks later, Randy is the only virgin pledge left, which means that he may have to go in the Black Hole (the fraternity cellar) and take on two local hookers while the brothers watch. Randy is so shocked by almost having to do this, that he runs out of the fraternity party and is about to quit the frat. But Vicki, his sister, who, along with her friend (Ginger Lynn), has already screwed half the guys on campus, takes pity on Randy and arrives in his room to show him. Innocent-looking Tom Byron is the perfect college freshman, and Traci Lords, with her pouty coed expression, and baby-faced Ginger Lynn, plus the fraternity house parties, all combine to give this sexvid an authentic college feel.

sell. Georgina, as Bernice, and Tina, as Tracy, are sisters who were brought up by a Bible-reading mother and father. Tracy is always carrying a cross and praying for salvation to Jesus. She terrifies Bernice, who is very timid, by telling her that Bernice's best girlfriend is a consort of the devil. Bernice's friend responds that Tracy was known as "the walking chastity belt" in college. When the story opens they are sharing an apartment and Bernice is trying to resolve her fear of life by writing a story about her childhood. Bernice meets a young guitar-playing guy in New York City's Washington Square Park and has sex for the first time, but she's afraid to let Tracy know about it. In fact, she can't believe that the guy really wants her. Then one day her girlfriend and her boyfriend inveigle Bernice into a threesome. Tracy comes home, sees them, and is thoroughly shocked. She tells Bernice to get out of their apartment. Although Bernice is frightened, her friend tells her the only way to straighten Tracy out is to get her raped by some loving people, and Bernice must cooperate in setting up a little threesome game involving a helpful boyfriend. Tracy fights her rape at first, but soon she's enthusiastically enjoying both the guy and the gal as well as Bernice. To her sorrow, Bernice realizes that her sister has now become a nymphomaniac, and Bernice decides that it's her turn to seek salvation. She convinces her boyfriend that they can survive by playing hymns on the guitar while she passes the hat. Jamie Gillis and Mark Stevens appear only momentarily in roles not connected to the main story.

SLEEPYHEAD
CC NN NM BI NR DK
1973 VIDEO-X-PIX

P/D—Not given

F/A—Georgina Spelvin, Tina Russell, Darby Lloyd Raines

F/A—Jamie Gillis, Mark Stevens

Don't miss this one—and forget the title; it doesn't match the story. While the plot comes apart near the end in a too-extended orgy, it features Georgina Spelvin (who looks younger than she did in *The Devil in Miss Jones*) and the late Tina Rus-

SMOKER
CC NN NM BI DS DK
1984 VCA

P/D—Veronica Rocket

F/A—Sharon Mitchell, Joanna Storm, Diana Sloan, Troye Lane

F/A—John Leslie, David Christopher, Eric Edwards, Ron Jeremy

The CC rating on this one is only for those who enjoy weirdos, kinkiness, and a touch of sadism, all packaged together in such a way that you'll have a hard time figuring out what is going on. All the characters have screen names, but only Madame Suque (Sharon Mitchell) makes an impression. She runs a sex shop, complete with a B/D dungeon in the cellar. Ron Jeremy is her drooling assistant. Ron sells a vibrator to Troye Lane, and she uses it in the apartment she shares with her girlfriend, Diana Sloan, when they don't want to hassle with guys. Unfortunately, Madame Suque is out to destroy the world, and the last shipment of vibrators are really concealed bombs that can blow you to kingdom come. Troye tells Ron that she's perfectly satisfied with her purchase and will not exchange it for a less lethal one. In the meantime, John Leslie, representing the government as a self-proclaimed "faceless dick," is on the trail of Madame Suque. Troye and her roommate, Diana Sloan, are also being watched through a one-way mirror by David Christopher, the apartment janitor, who is married but has transvestite tendencies. He steals their clothes and the vibrator. Troye is captured first by Jeremy and Edwards, and finally she and Diana are brought to the dungeon, where they are gagged. Troye is suspended face down from the ceiling, naked. When she won't confess where the vibrator is, Jeremy and Edwards try to persuade her with their cocks. Masked, gagged, and hanging by her tiptoes, she is also pierced by a wiggly vibrator, which she seems to enjoy. In the meantime, before Madame Suque ends up strung up in the air by her captors, John Leslie provides a long, squalid fuck scene, screwing Joanna Storm on the kitchen table, on top of the stove, and on the floor, while her kooky husband (David Christopher) looks on, eating his dinner.

SNAKE EYES
CC NN NM BI
1985 COMMAND VIDEO

P/D—Cecil Howard
F/A—Laurie Smith, Rikki Harte, Brooke Fields, Joanna Storm, Cassandra Leigh, Sharon Mitchell, Blair Castle, Nicole Bernard
F/A—Jerry Butler, George Payne, Paul Thomas

In craps, snake eyes (a one on each die) is a loser. While Cecil Howard leaves the meaning for you to figure out, you'll soon discover that Tom (Jerry Butler) an advertising executive, isn't doing too well in his marital life. He has a long telephone conversation with his friend Jason (Paul Thomas), who may be double-dealing him, and he explains a weird dream that he's been having. He's imprisoned in a cage. Outside, a naked woman whom he can't reach is giving herself to another guy while he watches. The truth is that his second wife, Gloria (Laurie Smith), may still be in love with her former lover, Les (George Payne). But Tom is no innocent himself and has been having affairs with other women, particularly Rikki Harte, who asks him, "Do you like what you see?" "I like it," he answers. The conversation culminates in some very sensuous sexmaking, but afterward Tom's noncommital "I'll call you" indicates that he's a guy very much at sea and very jealous of his wife. He's also a little mixed up with his first wife, Lois, who is a very different woman from Gloria. Finally, Tom practically rapes Gloria on the dining-room table, but she responds, and maybe now she'll forget Les, but you can't be sure. Told on several levels, with the interesting cinematography that is Howard's trademark, the film is a slice of upper-income marital life that may bewilder you on first watching. But you'll watch it again and try to figure out the various nuances. Jerry Butler was picked a best screen actor in 1985 for this film by the X-Rated Critics Organization.

SNOW COUNTRY
CC NN NR BI
1983 ORCHIDS INTERNATIONAL

P/D—Shin Kuwahata
F/A—Yukiko Sasaki, Saburo Mori and others

I have given the five Japanese films listed in this guide CC ratings for several reasons. First, because they offer interesting insights into Japanese sex life. Second, because, while Japanese porno directors, like their American counterparts, may not be at the top of the commercial film industry, they do offer totally different sexual vignettes with much intercutting that provides fascinating background to whatever sex encounter may be in progress. Third, like European porno films, the varying Japanese backgrounds keep your interest, and for the most part the guys ejaculate inside the woman. This one takes place in a ski resort that looks somewhat like Aspen. Skiing enthusiasts will enjoy the many outdoor scenes including a complete stage show outdoors with Japanese ladies in kimonos and guys doing some kind of primitive drumming on a magnificent stage with a huge marble-looking edifice in the background. The story, as far as I can make out, without subtitles, that will appear on regular versions, is about a very pretty woman who arrives at the resort and realizes that her boyfriend who she was supposed to meet is in a hotel room screwing with someone else. As the story slowly unfolds, with plenty of explicit sex, our heroine is alone in a crowd, sadly watching the outdoor entertainment at the ski lift. Then she sees him with the other woman. She runs in dismay and is followed by another guy who picks her out of the snow. Soon they are making love, but alas, the next day in the hotel, when she's walking down the hall she hears sounds of lovemaking. Opening the door, she sees her new boyfriend making it with another guy. This homosexual scene which is offered in some detail may be cut a little in the version which is now available. But it's the key to the ending of the film. The poor woman, betrayed by two men, takes an overdose of a drug and walks out into the heavy snow. The last scene shows her sleeping in the snow where she will freeze to death while her new boyfriend is frantically looking for her. For Japanese audiences the label on the bottle is obviously self explanatory but so that American viewers will understand, the lettering "powerful drug" appears on the screen.

SOFT AS SILK, SWEET AS HONEY
CC NN NM BI
1985 ESSEX

P/D—Allan Shustak, Charles De Santos
F/A—Laurie Smith, Karen Summer, Asheya, Lili Marlene, Erica Idol

F/A—Jamie Gillis, Jon Martin, Blair Harris

Leslie (Laurie Smith) runs a small advertising agency and is so busy that she has no time for men, but she dreams of anonymous cocks—bouncing on them and being penetrated by them! This morning, she's having breakfast with Andrea. While Leslie and Andrea (Karen Summer) have breakfast, you are treated to some of the best dialogue and acting that you've ever watched in a sexvid. The flashbacks include their fantasizing writing a romance novel, and they talk about their own sex lives (Andrea is married to Michael, whom Leslie likes but considers a no-no). Leslie tells Andrea her fantasies of having two men at once and her reaction to a movie she saw in which Jamie Gillis takes on three women (one black) all at the same time. It concludes with Andrea and Leslie dallying in bed together, during which they are joined by Michael, but you see his face for only a second. *He's* the anonymous cock.

A SOLDIER'S DESIRE
CC NN DS (by Western standards)
1985 ORCHIDS INTERNATIONAL

P/D—Not given
F/A—Haru Yamaua, Natsuico Oxuda

Porno films are illegal in Japan and are presumably made undercover for export, but I'm sure that some are shown there surreptitiously. This one is a vignette about a Japanese soldier who is watching a young woman in the fields picking crops. She stops to pee, and he grabs her and forces her to come with him to a shack where he ties her up and asks if she's pregnant. She tells him that she's five months along, and her belly proves it, but she stops resisting him, and he makes love to her gently while she sobs a little. Untying her, he lights candles and drips the hot wax on her, presumably giving her quick pain and pleasure. She finally yells ouch and he stops and peels off the wax, and she invites him back to her house, where she gives him rice and beer. She tells him that her husband has been gone six months, and the soldier decides to stay the night, sleeping Japanese style, on the floor. As they make love, he has some more bondage-and-discipline fantasies, which he finally enacts with her. I have given many Orchid International films a CC rating, not because they are classics but because, porno or not, they reveal many fascinating sexual cultural variations. Most of the O.I. films in this book run 60 minutes. See reviews on the following: *The Connection* (renamed *Tampon Tango*), *The Kimono, Ken Chan, Love Melody, Snow Country, Forget Me Not, A Winter Story, Flying Sex Man, Tonight.* All films have English subtitles.

SPACE VIRGINS
CC NN NL
1984   CREATIVE VIDEO

P/D—Sol Starr, Phil Marshak
F/A—Kimberly Carson, Sharon Mitchell, Amber Lynn, Gina Carrera
F/A—Herschel Savage, Paul Thomas, Jerry Butler

Poor Jessie (Kimberly Carson) lives on a horse ranch with her three brothers, Kevin (Jerry Butler), Mac (Herschel Savage) and Tim (Paul Thomas). There are no other women for miles around, and she has to take care of their sexual needs. At night she goes out and wishes on a star that a beautiful blonde god from outerspace will rescue her. She loves her brothers, but she's overjoyed when the clouds get murky and churned up and three women, Sharon Mitchell, Amber Lynn, and Gina Carrera (they have interplanetary names), arrive from the planet Zona, where fucking had been outlawed. The only way they can perpetuate the species is to collect sperm from males on other planets. Soon they have drained the three brothers, who fall in love with them. The dialogue in this one is outrageous and will keep you laughing. It reflects the happy insanity of Bill Margold, who wrote the screenplay along with Mark Weiss. They also wrote the screenplay for *Passionate Lee* (see review). All the Earthlings' acting, especially Kimberly Carson as Jessie (you won't recognize her without her black wig), is convincingly hillbilly, and the ladies from outer space, two of whom speak computer-

style lingo and one of whom speaks only in musical chords, contribute to the fun.

THE SPERMINATOR
CC NN BI NR
1984   REDLIGHT/VIDEO-X-PIX

P/D—Howard A. Howard, Allen Stuart
F/A—Honey Wilder, Rachel Ashley, Crystal Breeze, Karen Summer
F/A—Jerry Butler, Joey Silvera, George Payne

If you're female, don't let the unfortunate title turn you off. This is a romantic sexvid with no kinky sex. Also the box copy is incorrect, proving that the people who promote these tapes often don't look at them carefully. Actually, Honey Wilder is the so-called sperminator, not Rachel Ashley. Brenda (Honey Wilder) runs an Esalen-like establishment called the Atwell Institute, to which people with sexual problems can go for a week or weekend and "achieve a new level of experience of themselves and others while they get in touch with their real sexual feelings." I don't know how Esalen at Big Sur, California functions now but in the 1970s when I was the drawing card for a few seminars there, this kind of pop-psychology approach included much friendly body touching and a kind of free love approach among the guests which became a sine-qua-non of most of the "human potential" programs, along with friendly hours spent naked together in the hot tubs. In this takeoff, there is an indoor tub (no hot springs à la Esalen). Honey and her "facilitators" concentrate on Heather (Rachel Ashley), a woman who has been turned off by her sexual experiences with male lovers. Another weekend guest is Jerry Butler, who makes a six-figure income and drives a Porsche but has never really "been in touch" with the many women he has bedded. And there's Joey Silvera, a wealthy bridge builder who doesn't spend enough time with his wife, Karen Summer. Brenda arranges a bisexual experience for Heather in the hot tub but later puts her in touch with Jerry, whom she has already shown how to let go when he makes love to her. George Payne, as a facilitator, shows Karen Summer how to relax when she makes love to her husband. After a weekend at the Atwell Institute, romance reblossoms for all the guests, and you may wish to make reservations yourself.

SPITFIRE
CC NN BI NL
1985 COMMAND VIDEO

P/D—Cecil Howard
F/A—Samantha Fox, Chelsea Manchester (a.k.a. Tigr), Annie Sprinkles, Gail Sterling, Sharon Mitchell, Susan Nero, Rikki Harte
F/A—R. Bolla, Eric Edwards, John Leslie, Joey Silvera, Michael Morrison, Jerry Butler

In an opening scene that will get your attention, John Leslie is talking to his wife from a Washington, D.C., hotel room, trying to reassure her that he's not screwing around, when Lacey (Samantha Fox) opens the door with a key (she's convinced the desk clerk that she is his wife), walks in, and makes it apparent that she intends to go to bed with him. He's never seen her before, but as the film progresses she tells the story of her marriage to Victor Kidd (R. Bolla), who is running for senator on a restore-chastity campaign. It becomes obvious that Victor is a devious man who has been transferring campaign funds to a secret bank account in Switzerland, with Lacey acting as a courier. Lacey's story comes to life as she tells it, and you discover that once she was a sex surrogate working for Dr. Vargo (Eric Edwards), who now has the problem of calming down their nymphomaniac daughter Catherine (Chelsea Manchester). Despite Daddy's political campaign to restore morality to America, Catherine is always in heat and will screw with anyone in sight. "Immorality is like a giant fungus spreading across the country," Victor tells his enraptured audiences, but he can't resist unzipping his secretary's (Annie Sprinkles) blouse and playing with her enormous tits. In addition to his daughter's and his wife's betrayal is that of his campaign manager, Eddie (Joey Silvera), who is screwing him up by going to bed with Sharon Mitchell, the female editor of a news magazine—nor can Eddie resist Victor's daughter. Victor finally allows the

TV cameras into his home to meet his family on network television. But, to his horror, his daughter strips herself and pleads to the unseen audience, "I'm so hot. Don't you want to reach out and fuck me?" Poor Victor drops dead, and then you discover that his wife has plans of her own. So does her daughter, who tries to poison her mother but drinks the wrong glass of champagne. This is a totally slaphappy film with ceiling to floor fucking, but it has Cecil Howard's usual classy style.

SPRINGTIME IN THE ROCKIES
CC NN BI NL
CDI VIDEO

P/D—Jim Reynolds
F/A—Lisa de Leeuw, Debbie Green, Pamela Jennings
F/A—Blake Palmer, Craig Roberts

Getting away from her boring nine-to-five secretarial job, Sandra (Lisa de Leeuw) goes backpacking in the Rockies, and to the accompaniment of a happy theme song falls down on a mountain trail. Flat on her back, she's soon being screwed by another backpacker, Derek (Blake Palmer) who has come equipped with Trojans in his first aid kit. The Young Rubber Company won't be pleased with Sandra's response—"Throw them away," she tells Derek, "they spoil all the fun." Meanwhile, somewhere else in the forest, two other young ladies are camping out, and one gets lost and is rescued by a ranger (Craig Roberts), who has previously supplied them with a CB radio to call him in case they need servicing beyond that which he has already provided. The CC rating is for the outdoor photography, which gives the various bouncing bodies a better flesh tone than most indoor shots, and for Lisa de Leeuw, who is a bouncy, laughing, zaftig female. The piece de resistance is a short ending that takes place 5000 years later. An extra terrestrial creature finds the discarded Trojan which he tries to slip on his tongue.

STAR OF THE ORIENT
CC NN BI DK
1980 IVP (formerly CVX)

P/D—John Evans, Harold Lee
F/A—Sarah Lorhman, Kyoto Gee, Marsha Judd, Lucy McMillan
F/A—Rob Rose, Joe Julians, David Lane, Lanny Roth

This one begins with a Madame Butterfly story. An American sailor tells his Japanese girlfriend, who loves him very much, the truth: He's going home and has a wife and kids in the States. During the first 10 minutes you get some nice acting by Kyoto Gee and you think this is going to be interesting, especially if she follows him to America. But you quickly discover that what you are watching is a film made by Arlynn Brandon. She's trying to sell it to a porno-film distributor, who agrees to buy it for $25,000 on the premise that she'll make him a hardcore one with B/D, water sports, and anal sex. She tells her mama, who is living in the Shalom Retirement Home, and despite the fact that mama is shocked at what she's doing, she goes ahead. The only time you see Kyoto again is as a female photographer. She's evidently a friend of Arlynn's who appeared in her film. Kyoto and a young American woman make love underwater in an Olympic-size swimming pool in an unusual and well-photographed bi-scene. As for Arlynn, she tries to make the porno film and even gets involved herself, but hastily accepts a job to do a documentary on Icelandic seals, with mama's approval. (see Notes under *Pleasure Bed*.)

THE STEWARDESSES
CC NN NM BI
1981 CABALLERO

P/D—Louis Sher, Alf Silliman, Jr.
F/A—Christian Hart, Janet Wass, Patricia Fein, Donna Stanley, Angelique Demoline
F/A—Michael Garrett and others

The CC rating on this one is not for the story, which tends to fall apart as it tries to explore the sex lives of too many stewardesses after they arrive in Los Angeles on a flight from Honolulu, or the involvement of one of them with a cold-blooded advertising executive, who makes a date with her on the plane. Rather, it's for a unique idea. Instead of making an X-rated movie softcore by removing the explicit sex, how about making an old R-rated movie that was probably made in the 1970s and didn't get off the ground into an X-rated movie by adding explicit sex? You are warned at the beginning that the sexually explicit scenes in this film were not played by the original cast. But you will have fun watching for the scenes where the actors and actresses finally get their pants and panties off and someone else takes over. In many cases they are cleverly intercut into the action—without showing faces, of course. Obviously, it's a wide-open field to "improve" some Hollywood films that never made it! But they need to find films with a more cohesive story line than this one, which concludes with the unbelievable story of a stewardess who is so shocked by her behavior with an ad executive, who has agreed to use her mouth in a lipstick campaign if she will blow him, that she jumps out the window of his high-rise apartment building.

STIFF COMPETITION
CC NN BI NL (insane style) DK
1985 CABALLERO

P/D—Paul Vatelli
F/A—Bridgitte Monet, Cindee Summers, Gina Carrera, Patti Wright
F/A—John Leslie, Kevin James, Herschel Savage, Dave Cannon, Ron Jeremy, Paul Thomas

Years ago, Philip Wylie wrote a book, *Night Unto Night*, about a future America gone sex mad. Here's an adult film that proves it's happening right now. Supposedly costing over $400,000 to make, it's partially a satire on America's mania for professional wrestling, boxing, or anything that can be turned into a sport. But beware of the CC rating. Most women will absolutely detest this degradation of the female. The subject is a world championship suck-off contest, the Super Bowl of Suck-Off, with a grand prize of $50,000 and women competing in a boxing-style ring to determine the winner—the lady who can blow an unknown man off faster than her competitors. The story comes replete with all the twists and turns and double-crosses of every boxing/wrestling film you've ever seen. Cynthia Silkthroat (Cindee Summers) is the retired world suck-off champion whose manager, Jake (John Leslie), decides to make a comeback to defeat newcomer Tammy the Tongue (Gina Carrera). Tammy is managed by Jeff (Kevin James). Another contestant, Patti (Patti Wright), is managed by Wayne (Herschel Savage), and the fourth is Linda Lonestar (Bridgette Monet), who is disqualified in the finals because she sucks off her manager, Bucky (Dave Cannon), to whom, incidently, she is married in real life. The Super Bowl is held in Las Vegas and is telecast nationwide. Paul Vatelli gives you the feeling that the arena is crowded with enthusiastic fans cheering their favorites in spectacular blow jobs to end all blow jobs. Tammy the Tongue is the winner!

SUCCULENT
CC NN NM BI DK
1983 VIDEO-X-PIX

P/D—Vince Benedetti
F/A—Kelly Nichols, Rhonda Jo Petty, Little Oral Annie, Tanya Lawson
F/A—R. Bolla, Ron Jeremy, George Payne, Jerry Butler, Jose Duval

The CC rating is for male chauvinists. Take a look and see why women hate pornography. After a telephone conversation with her boyfriend, or husband, you don't know which, during which he has telephone sex with her, telling her that he wants her to play with herself and pretend that he holds his cock in her hands, Jennifer (Kelly Nichols) goes to sleep and dreams that she is being sold to an Arab sheik for his harem. This is only the first part of the dream. It seems that some very nasty southern policemen arrest Jennifer for speeding as she's driving south for a vacation wearing a skirt that reveals her naked behind every time she bends over. Jennifer's dream allows her to be herself and other people, too. So you quickly discover that one of the arresting officers, a policewoman, wonders what's wrong with her husband. "Jim doesn't fuck me anymore," she complains, nor does her patrol partner, Officer Hynes. But he makes Jennifer spread her legs, and they both feel around in her ass and vagina to see if she's smuggling drugs. Finding drugs (not identified) in her car, they drag her into the police station, and the lady cop, whose husband doesn't fuck her, soon has Jennifer naked and makes love to her. R. Bolla, as the judge who finally puts her in the pokey, makes her blow him while Jerry, as a nasty police sergeant, screws her doggie style. Next day the male prison doctor takes Jennifer's temperature, in her anus, of course. Along with another woman they have arrested, she is soon forced to mouth wash his cock. Then Rhonda Jo Petty, as a policewoman, arrives for more fun. After some 90 minutes of continuous degradation, Jennifer discovers, in her dream, that the police are white-slaving their prisoners to the Arab sheik, Ron Jeremy. Jennifer finally wakes up and is happy that it is all a dream, but the point has been made, with a demeaning kind of female sexual surrender that will aggravate the hell out of most women. Maybe that's why Benedetti added the vignette *Box Balls* (see review), to give them their revenge!

SULKA'S DAUGHTER
CC NN BI DK
1984 CABALLERO

P/D—Kim Christy
F/A—Desiree Lane, Sulka, Lisa de Leeuw, Mistress Duscha, Colleen Brennan
F/A—Ron Jeremy, Eric Edwards, Craig Roberts, Herschel Savage

The CC rating is to be consistent (see review of *Sulka's Wedding*) and for the pure insanity of it. It begins in a hospital with Sulka giving birth to a baby and then cuts to a poor midwest farmhouse many years later where Eric Edwards, in overalls, and Lisa de Leeuw, middle-aged and pudgy, are telling their daughter Jenny (Desiree Lane), who is leaving them to go to the big city and make a living, that they aren't her real parents. Soon Desiree is working in a strip joint run by Herschel Savage and patronized by Ron and Sulka, who are producing a porno film but have lost their star performer and will go broke unless they find a new one. It's Desiree, of course. Ron is still married to Sulka and is screwing her, but only Sulka knows that Desiree is their daughter. She doesn't tell him until after daddy and daughter have happily bounced together on the living-room couch. But incest is the least of their worries. Ron finally asks Sulka something that has never occurred to him before, "How did you get pregnant?" She responds, "I forgot to take my pill."

SUMMER CAMP GIRLS
CC NN NL NR
1983 CABALLERO

P/D—Harold Lime, Robert McCallum
F/A—Shauna Grant, Joanna Storm, Kimberly Carson, Tara Aire, Janey Robbins
F/A—Herschel Savage, Paul Thomas, Frank Hollowell, Eric Edwards

Jennifer (Shauna Grant), whose Daddy is a Mafia type, is sent to Camp Quim, a summer camp for rich girls. Jennifer has led a very protected life, but like all the other young women at the camp, she wants a man. Unfortunately, Greg (Paul Thomas) who is assistant director, does his damnedest to avoid the women. J.B. (Herschel Savage) is the camp carpenter. His handyman and assistant is a gorilla called "the Animal." Marcie (Janey Robbins), the camp director, takes care of Greg in the gym, athletically screwing him on parallel bars and a horse, and blowing him as he lifts weights. But Greg tells her that the girls are getting out of hand and he can't handle them anymore. Jennifer and Veronica (Kimberly Carson) end up in a local bar, and Veronica gets the guys so excited that the girls are nearly raped, but Veronica tells Jennifer to run and she promises personally to take on the last two guys who don't drink themselves under the table. Interestingly, like other directors (see review of *Shauna Grant, Superstar*), McCallum spared Shauna any sleazy sex encounters, and

later, before she is almost raped by "the Animal," J.B. saves her and makes very romantic love with her. But her daddy finally arrives and catches them bare-ass in the barn and, gun in hand, tells J.B., "No one does that to my daughter and gets away with it." But J.B. responds: "I want to marry her, and I'm a Catholic." Daddy is so happy that he embraces him enthusiastically and accepts him into the Mafia family.

SUZIE SUPERSTAR
CC NN NR BI
1983 CAL VISTA

P/D—Sam Norvell, Robert McCallum
F/A—Shauna Grant, Laura Lazarre, Sharon Mitchell, Tara Aire, Stephanie Taylor
F/A—John Leslie, Joey Silvera, Jon Martin, Ron Jeremy, Ross Roberts

Here's a 90-minute adult film that belongs in any top listing and proves that with a good story, cinematography, and especially, good acting, that adult-film makers can make films as good as their legitimate Hollywood brethren. Suzie Mitchell (Shauna Grant, see reviews of her other films) is a rock star. Whether she actually sings the songs or her voice is dubbed, she's as effective, with a backup band, as Madonna. Unfortunately, both she and the band are in an air-tight contract with a lecherous character, Z. W. McKane (John Leslie), that prevents them from singing or playing with any other group for four years. To make matters worse, Suzie might be in love with Z.W., except he can't keep his hands off other women, and he screws her dispassionately. Angrily, she walks out on him and confesses her problem to Rick (Joey Silvera), a guitarist in the band who composes his own songs and sings one to her. But Z.W. is having her watched by Raoul (Ron Jeremy), his nasty bodyguard who fucks all the groupies in Z.W.'s limousine. Rick gets beaten up, and in the meantime Z.W. has made a deal for a one-night engagement at the estate of a multimillionaire Mafia godfather type, Lorenzo Loducca (Ross Roberts), whose daughter Priscilla is planning to have Suzie sing at her daddy's birthday party. The price arranged by Z.W. is $30,000 less than Suzie's regular price of $100,000 for an evening, but Priscilla happily rewards Z.W. for the difference. But daddy Lorenzo is shocked to discover, via Suzie, that his daughter is screwing with a no-account rock-band manager, and he would gladly cement-shoe him except that Suzie convinces him that he can hurt Z.W. more by forcing him to break his contract with her, which he gladly does. But Z.W. bounces back and soon has a new singer, Opal Kincaid (Sharon Mitchell), and Suzie has Rick, who really loves her. Men will fall in love with Shauna and Laura Lazarre (an Ali McGraw type), and the ladies will love John Leslie even when he's bad.

SWEDISH SORORITY GIRLS
CC NN BI DK
1978   CAL VISTA

P/D—J. Angel Martine, John Christopher
F/A—Colleen Anderson, Karen Havens, Paula Morton, Samantha Fox
F/A—Roger Caine, David Christopher, Joey Silvera

Pay no attention to the title. The ladies are not girls but mostly American women pretending to be Swedish, but because of the Swedish winter scenes and snow and skiing backgrounds, they'll make you believe it. Actually some of it may have been shot in Sweden. It begins in bed, with Ingrid (Karen Havens) making early-morning love to Sven (Joey Silvera, who has a fine Swedish accent), in what really looks like a Swedish bedroom, and telling him that her cousin Anne (Colleen Anderson) is arriving at the airport from America. They greet Anne happily, and Anne reveals to Ingrid that she hasn't had much to do with men in her life, or with women for that matter. Ingrid tells her that it's perfectly natural for women to enjoy each other and proves it to her. But later at a party, where they play strip poker (Anne wins every hand and everyone is naked except her), she meets Nils (Roger Caine), and her vacation is now full of happy loving and playing in the snow on a Swedish mountainside. Finally, Anne must return to America.

SWEET ALICE
CC NN BI NR
1983   VCX

P/D—Adele Robbins
F/A—Seka, Honey Wilder, Desiree Cousteau, Becky Savage, Drea
F/A—Kevin James, John Holmes, Mike Eyke, Bill Margold, Jamie Gillis

Billy Joe Williams (Kevin James) was married to Sweet Alice (Seka) more than a year ago. Now they live on his big ranch in New Mexico, with thousands of acres, horses and cattle, and no friends. All Billy Joe wanted was Sweet Alice, the only woman he has ever been to bed with. But Sweet Alice has run away to Los Angeles, and when the story begins, Billy Joe, after a year, is trying to find her and bring her home. He doesn't know that Sweet Alice has become famous as a porn star. But Billy finds a detective, Jamie (Honey Wilder). When he describes Sweet Alice, Jamie looks at him sympathetically. She's pretty sure that she knows what Sweet Alice is doing for a living! Discovering that money is no object with Billy Joe, Jamie agrees to find her. But first she decides to show Billy a videotape of one of Sweet Alice's films. Kevin James should have been awarded best actor of the year for the next scene, in which, tears pouring down his cheeks, he watches in horror as his wife and sweetheart sucks and fucks Jamie Gillis. But being a naive cowboy, he still thinks poor Alice has been led astray. If he actually can talk with her, he can save her and bring her back home. In the meantime, Jamie, who, like Billy, is a loner, is falling in love with him. Trying to dissuade him from reforming Sweet Alice, Jamie goes to bed with him. The contrasting romantic sex (some of the most caring and believable that you've ever watched in an adult film), with Seka/Sweet Alice being her typical dispassionate self and Jamie/Honey being the totally loving woman (she even takes Billy Joe on a picnic), makes this a love story that most women will enjoy. Hurray for Adele Robbins, Honey Wilder, and Kevin James, who prove in this one that even with a simple little love story an adult film can be interesting. As for the rest of the actors and actresses listed above, they are stereotyped to fit the plot.

SWEET CHEEKS
CC NN NM BI NL NR DK
1980   VCX

P/D—Adele Robbins
F/A—Becky Savage, Rhonda Jo Petty
F/A—John Holmes, Randy West, Mike Ranger

This one has a very poor title. It should have been called *Three Months to Live*, but that probably would have scared off the male-adult theater audience, to which it originally circulated. Put it on your top list of sexvids. Most women will like it. Adele Robbins knows how to create a female eroticism that escapes most male directors, and producing a story around one actress, in this case Becky Savage, who does a nice acting job, makes viewer empathy possible beyond sex. A wealthy woman, Regina, has been given three months to live with some incurable, unidentified disease. She tells Ken (John C. Holmes), "I love you, but I'm going to split. I have so much to do. I'm going to have a blast." And to herself she says, "Dear sun, don't run through the day. Come and stay with me. For now I know no yesterdays or tomorrows." Before her sun sets, she tries automobile racing, skydiving, motorcycle racing, and snowmobiling, all in daredevil sequences that are realistically intercut into the story. In between, there's lots of sex with different guys. She does it on a yacht with Mike Ranger and in a funny sequence on a mountaintop with Randy West, who is taking a bath outdoors in an old-fashioned bathtub, and after she turns him into a woman, temporarily, he laughingly puts a neck collar on her. She also makes love in a grease pit, slithering in grease with two pit mechanics to pay off a bet for losing a race. "I'm so busy running, I forget where I'm running to," she tells a female friend, but eventually she ends up back with Ken, who still loves her.

SWEETHEART
CC NN NM BI DS DK
1976   VIDEO-X-PIX

P/D—Roger Holt, Bo Koop
F/A—Jean Jennings, Susan McBain, Terri Hall
F/A—Wade Nichols, John Black, Philip Marlowe

Here's a group of old-timers who are no longer making adult films, in what you might call a happy rape story since the rapee protests at first but is soon enjoying the rape more than the rapists. This one comes complete with a gruesome story. Very wealthy Mabel Brooks (Susan McBain) married Foster (Wade Nichols) 15 years ago, and although Mabel can't wake up in the morning without happily grabbing Foster's cock, he's not so enthusiastic. You soon discover that he has been having a longtime affair with her cousin Carol (Terri Hall), who lives nearby. Mooning around the house naked and masturbating on her bed, Mabel is soon invaded by a black guy, Hank (John Black), and a woman, Lee (Jean Jennings), who have been casing suburban estates near New York City with the plan of robbing them. While Lee holds her, Hank rapes Mabel, who keeps telling them that she's not angry with them, that they can have all the money they want, but please don't hurt her. As they are collecting loot around the house, Mabel's lover, Jack, arrives and Mabel greets him on the front lawn of the secluded estate. She's afraid to tell him that she's a hostage to Hank and Lee. But she doesn't have to worry. Hank soon emerges from the house, and he and Lee tell Mabel and Jack to strip. They chain them to separate trees, and Lee happily blows a struggling Jack while Hank laps and rapes an unhappy Mabel. Meanwhile, Foster and Carol have been plotting to kill Mabel by giving her a heart attack since Mabel has heart trouble. But when they discover Mabel and her lover tied up, Foster has a better idea. He offers Hank $50,000 to kill them both and promises that he and Carol will cover for him. In the process, somehow or other Jack is being forced to screw Carol, and he suddenly yells and dies of a heart attack from so much exertion. Hank tells Mabel of her husband's offer, and he asks her to up it, but she gets her hands on the gun and shoots first Foster and then Carol, after which Lee and Hank cover for her by burying all the bodies (offscreen). In the final shot, she's become their willing servant in her mansion, which they have taken over. How's that for a plot? With continuous humping, of course!

SWEET PUNKIN, I LOVE YOU
CC NN NR NM BI DK
1975 VCA

P/D—Robert Michaels, Robert Norman
F/A—C. J. Laing, Jennifer Jordan, Crystal Sync, Marlene Willoughby
F/A—Tony Perez, John C. Holmes, Jeffrey Hurst, David Dixon, Eric Edwards

Punkin Peal (C. J. Laing—a Barbra Streisand look-alike who is no longer making adult films) is a hillbilly porno actress who has lost her job because she couldn't ingest the huge dork of John C. Holmes, who at the beginning of this flick is arguing with Tony Perez as to who has the biggest uncircumsised prick. But never mind, multimillionaire Jason Cream-Smith, who is 50 years older than Sweet Punkin, adores her and marries her, making her Mrs. Cream-Smith, to the shock of his upper-crust friends, who refuse to come to the wedding. Alas, finally in bed with Sweet Punkin, he hasn't got any further than tasting her sweet tits when he drops dead. Eric Edwards, his lawyer, is married to a bitch (Jennifer Jordan). He takes over and with the help of the butler (Jeffrey Hurst, who was one of the best comedy actors in adult films), decides to have an orgy for charity. This is a totally balmy, happy-go-lucky tape with silly dialogue that will make you laugh and a believe-it-or-not ending, during which C. J. Laing actually deep-throats Holmes and Perez, whom you haven't seen since the beginning of the film.

SWEET SURRENDER
CC NN DK
1980 IVP (formerly CVX)

P/D—Rudy Jason, Dirk Milford

F/A—Samantha Fox, Merle Michaels, Clea Carson, the Kurva Girls
F/A—Alan Levitt, Mark Valentin, David Morrison

Here's a CVX tape with a later date that runs 80 minutes. York Madison (Alan Levitt) has just completed a book about con men who use elaborate strategies to seduce young women. A female editor has read the manuscript and invites him in to discuss its potential sale. She asks him to elaborate on certain chapters, which he does, and he tells her the story of a guy who would borrow an office, pretending he was an M.D. setting up a practice to service stars like Robert Redford. He advertises for a female assistant, to whom he gives a thorough physical examination—including a vaginal exploratory with his prick—before hiring her. The next day, when the young lady (Merle Michaels) returns to go to work, he and the office are gone. One of the most ingenious guys, according to York, pretended he was a bodyguard to private parties run by groups like the Rolling Stones. He'd promise groupies that they could get into the action but they had to pay up pussy first. Poor Samantha Fox gets caught on that one. The tape ends with York servicing the female editor, after which she asks him if he has ever written about female con artists. He tells her that he doesn't know any. "You do now," she tells him as she gets dressed. "Thanks for the ride. You can take your manuscript and shove it!" (See notes under *Pleasure Bed*.)

SWEET TASTE OF HONEY
CC NN NM BI
1978 QUALITY/VIDEO-X-PIX

P/D—Not given
F/A—Bridette Lanning, Mary Anne Bardet
F/A—Art Stevens, Peter Bryce

By the time you read this, Video-X-Pix, which absorbed Quality in 1984, may have discovered that the Quality line offers some on the best adult films of the 1970s and may have repackaged them more flamboyantly and with more information on the boxes. But if you discover Quality tapes in their old packages, there's no information whatsoever on the boxes as to the nature of the film or who the actors are or who directed it. The 1970s were a scarier era, with long potential jail sentences a possibility for distributors, so they kept the packaging quite innocuous. In any event, if you're interested in adult films, you should explore Quality tapes (see the many reviews in this book) for some fascinating surprises, of which this film is one. I'd put it on my list of the top 50 adult films. The title is meaningless, and the tape gives no information on the director. The featured actress, Laura (Bridette Lanning), is a beautiful woman, and the story, told in cleverly conceived flashbacks, merges present and past neatly together. Laura has arrived at a small resort hotel. She's obviously quite wealthy, but her husband has left her, and once before she nearly committed suicide by slashing her wrist. Now she may be going to try again in the hotel, where she spent her honeymoon. The manager recognizes her and realizes that she's alone. Eventually, he practically rapes her in the woods near the hotel, after which she angrily whips him with a branch and tells him if he wants her body to fuck her properly. In the meantime, she can't keep her eyes off a newlywed, Peter, who is honeymooning in the hotel with his bride. Peter reminds her of her husband, and she finally seduces him in her hotel room when his wife goes for a hair appointment. Laura is carrying a revolver in her makeup case, which the manager, rummaging in her things, discovers and takes with him. But, like life, there is no perfect resolution. Laura leaves the hotel without seriously disturbing the newlywed's marriage, and the manager, whom she has never quite surrendered to and who must have known her before, tells her that he looks forward to her next visit at the hotel. You'll watch it fascinated by Bridette Lanning and wonder who she was.

SWEET YOUNG FOXES
CC NN NM NR BI
1984 VCX

P/D—Gail Palmer, Elliot Lewis, Bob Chinn

F/A—Hypatia Lee, Cindy Carver, Cara Lott, Kay Parker, Pat Manning
F/A—Eric Edwards, Ron Jeremy

Three beautiful young ladies have just completed their freshman year at Cal State and are looking forward to a summer of freedom. Laura (Hypatia Lee) needs a new boyfriend because the guy she once dated went to Harvard and is now summering in Europe with his parents. Laura and her mom, Julie (Kay Parker), aren't too happy with each other. In a very believable scene in which Julie tells her that she should stay home at night and stop drinking, smoking, and running around, Laura responds that Mom divorced Daddy so that she could run around, too. They enjoy a mother-daughter love-hate relationship. Maggie (Cara Lott), Laura's college friend, is so horny that all she thinks about is tumbling in bed with a guy, and she does, with Ron Jeremy after he's gotten her drunk. Their other friend, Kimberly (Cindy Carver), is a virgin. So while Julie is having a warm, loving evening with Raymond (Eric Edwards), who has been sleeping with her for two years and now wants to marry her because he's being transferred to St. Paul, the younger ladies all take off for a party being given by one of their college friends. During the evening, Kimberly, who has been shown how to apply makeup by Maggie to make her look sexier, loses her virginity. Laura finds a senior who never asked her for a date before because she was too young, and Maggie gets introduced to the joys of bisexuality by an older woman. Good dialogue, nice sharp color, and a slice-of-life story that's interesting to watch.

SYLVIA
CC NN BI DK DS
1976 VCX

P/D—Armand Peters
F/A—Joanna Bell, Penny Servant, Helen Madigan
F/A—Mark Stevens, Sonny Landham, Joe Fisher

Here's another entry for the top 50 sexvids. Again, it's one made more than 10 years ago. Remember the book and movie

Three Faces of Eve? This is the explicit-sex version, about a woman who has four personalities that dominate her actions at various times. As she assumes one, her other personalities are completely forgotten. As Sylvia D'Constant, she's a woman living alone in an upper-class suburban home. Sylvia is very religious. But when a vacuum-cleaner salesman (Mark Stevens) arrives and tries to demonstrate his machine, you suddenly see Sylvia's face light up lasciviously and she becomes Mona, an insatiably sexy woman whom men can't resist. Her glasses disappear, her tightly combed hair swings loose, and she wears poor Mark to a frazzle. Her cousin and a friend, who have come to stay with her for a week, arrive during this encounter and withdraw in a state of shock. But one of them, Sheila (Helen Madigan), is intrigued, especially when Sylvia puts sleeping pills in her straight cousin Toby's cocoa and Sylvia is transformed into Tony, a cigar-smoking lesbian with an entirely different hairdo. Sylvia also has another personality: Mary, who is in love with a guy who wants to marry her. But, as Mary, she's saving herself for the wedding night. When her poor fiancé finally convinces her that it's okay, since their wedding is only a few weeks away, and gets her into bed as Mary, she tries hard to continue, but suddenly she turns into Mona and shocks the pants (he isn't wearing) right off him. During all this, Toby, her cousin, keeps trying to redeem her. But little does she know that Mona is the product of Mona's mother, who repressed her sexuality when she was a kid. For her troubles, cousin Toby gets beaten and raped at an orgy from which she's trying to rescue Sylvia/ Mona, and her doctor nearly gets murdered by a couple of junkies that she's involved with. Even at the end, the doctor, who thinks that he's finally merged her personalities, discovers that the new lady is still a sexpot. You'll want to watch this one again.

TABOO AMERICAN STYLE, PART 1: THE RUTHLESS BEGINNING
CC NN NM
1985 VCA

P/D—James George, Henri Pachard
F/A—Raven, Gloria Leonard, Taija Rae
F/A—Paul Thomas, R. Bolla, Tom Byron, Frank Serrone, Adam Frank

Here's the first adult-film miniseries, a sexvid soap opera on four separate 80-minute tapes, a total of 5 hours and 20 minutes, which the producers have billed as a major Hollywood production: "Beyond 'Dynasty,' beyond 'Dallas'." The X-Rated Critics Organization picked it as the Most Erotic Film of 1985, and picked Gloria Leonard as the best adult film actress of 1985. The film also won best screenwriter and best director award for Rick Marx and Henri Pachard. On top of that, the series offers (following in the footsteps of *Taboo* 1, 2, 3, and 4; see reviews) the most popular adult-film sexual theme: incest! This one outdoes any you have ever seen, with a reasonably believable, well-acted story that will make Gloria Leonard the mother of the 1980s in future adult films covering two generations. The Sutherlands, who live in Connecticut or suburban New York, are millionaires who live in a completely remodeled turn-of-century, three-story home with quite a few acres of manicured grounds, which are tended by their handyman, Jack Chinzski (R. Bolla). Hardy Sutherland (Paul Thomas) is a Wall Street financial whiz, who, among other things, dabbles in legitimate motion-picture financing. His wife, Emily (Gloria Leonard), has the family well under control and manages to run all of their lives. But the truth is that she has been having a longtime affair with Jack. Their trysting place is the cellar of the mansion, among old garden furniture that Emily has set up so that they can make love in reasonable comfort once a week. But as far as Jack's kids—Lisa (Taija Rae) and Clete (Frank Serrone)—go, Emily tells her children, Nina (Raven) and Thomas (Tom Byron), that they must not associate with them. She feels they are lower-class social climbers. Nina, who is rebellious, pays no attention to Mommy and arranges for Lisa to spend the night with her brother, Thomas, in his bedroom, which is just down the hall from Mommy and Daddy's. On top of that she introduces Lisa to orgasm, although Lisa has screwed with several boys and Nina is a virgin. At the same time Nina smuggles Clete (Jack's son) into the house and balls him in her bedroom, finally losing her virginity. Mother Emily discovers what is going on and tells Jack that unless he can keep his kids home, their pleasant little dalliance in the cellar is about to come to an end. But Lisa hears her telling Jack (her father) and tells Nina, who already knows that Mommy is screwing her Daddy in the cellar, and not only arranges for Lisa to watch them but tells Daddy (at whom she's been casting lascivious glances) what is going on. Hardy catches his wife in *flagrante,* just as Tom is leaving for college (Brown University, no less) and announces to his crestfallen wife, "This family has been fractured, but it hasn't been destroyed. There will be no divorce, but what has happened will be a matter of complete secrecy." Realizing that her mother is in the pits, Nina confronts Daddy in the bathtub and begins her takeover as Daddy's "wife." You can't wait to see what happens next.

TABOO AMERICAN STYLE, PART 2: THE STORY CONTINUES
CC NN NM BI
1985 VCA

F/A—Same as Part 1

In Part 1, poor Emily has discovered that her husband may be willing to continue the marriage but their daughter has supplanted her and will soon convince Daddy to move Mother out of his bedroom and into the guest room. Emily tells her sad story to Dr. Berman (Henri Pachard, a.k.a. Ron Sullivan, who is also directing his best film), who puts her on tranquilizers so that she can stop crying and blaming herself for what has happened. He also calls Hardy and advises him that there are laws against father/daughter relationships. But Hardy is too far gone, and it's obvious that Nina is now learning how to control him. He paints her toenails while she tells him what she will and won't do, and she forces him to screw in Mommy's bedroom while Mommy watches them in shock. Emily tries to straighten her out by asking Clete to date Nina. Nina tells Lisa that she will,

but refuses Clete unless he'll take her in a threesome with his sister. Reluctantly Clete does, but Lisa goes into a state of shock because she has fucked her brother— even more so when Nina convinces her to massage Emily, who is now so far gone into never-never land that she doesn't know what is happening to her. But that's only the beginning. Discovering from Clete that Jack (his father) is out of work and desperate, Nina convinces Daddy Hardy to rehire him, and then, confronting Jack in the cellar, she dares him to jerk off in her hand, after which she wipes his jism on Mommy's face. Part 2 ends with Nina making a gift of Daddy to Lisa, who has taken a job in a massage parlor and is so hung up on what Nina has done to her that she's become a whore. But more problems are ahead. Tom is coming home from college for Christmas vacation, and he has no idea that his sister, Nina, is sleeping with Daddy. Stay tuned for Part 3.

TABOO AMERICAN STYLE, PART 3: NINA BECOMES AN ACTRESS
CC NN BI
1985 VCA

F/A—Same as Parts 1 and 2, plus Joey Silvera, Jake West, Carol Cross, Jeannie Silver, Sarah Bernard, Miss Tiger

Before Thomas comes home for vacation and weekend guests David, a legitimate film producer, and Deidre Weiss (Joey Silvera and Sarah Bernard) arrive, Daddy Hardy tries to make it clear to Nina that what they are doing isn't accepted in normal society: "You must never tell Tom that we've been sleeping together." What's more, Nina must move out of the master bedroom and let Mommy return to her proper bed until Thomas goes back to college and Daddy has arranged financing on a new picture with his friend David. Nina refuses at first but finally capitulates when she discovers that David is a movie producer. In the meantime, Thomas has been sleeping at college with art major Marilyn (Carol Cross), whom he brings home for the weekend, but he's afraid to tell his parents that they are having sex. Marilyn ends up in Nina's room.

But Nina has discovered from Tommy that poor Marilyn has never had an orgasm with him. Nina quickly rectifies that. She convinces Marilyn that she really is not a dyke but that women must learn from women, after which she puts a vibrator in Marilyn's anus, leaves it going, and brings Tommy out of his bedroom to finish the job properly. In the meantime, David arrives with his wife, Deidre, and after a boring evening with the Sutherlands, they are happily fucking in the guest room. Nina appears and makes it such a delightful threesome that David is sure that she has a great future as an actress. So much so that he fires the lead actress on a film that Daddy is financing and replaces her with Nina. In the meantime, Marilyn has gone back to college and Thomas discovers that his mother is not really menopausal but is a poor wretch whose only remaining love is for her baby, Tommy. She runs a bath for him, ignoring his remark, "For gosh sakes, I'm nineteen." Too old, obviously, for Mommy to wash his back and prick. But sobbing and getting in the tub with him, she tells Tom about Daddy and Nina. What's the poor guy to do with his mother fondling his erection? Of course, Nina comes home in time to peer into the bathroom. Which leaves you hanging breathlessly for the conclusion, Part 4.

TABOO AMERICAN STYLE, PART 4: THE EXCITING CONCLUSION
NN BI DK
1985 VCA

F/A—Same as Parts 1–3, plus Kelly Nichols, Sharon Kane, Jose Duval, and Stephen Lockwood

At the beginning of Part 4, Emily is once again consulting with Dr. Berman, who asks her if her husband is still sleeping with their daughter Nina. The answer is yes, but Emily is not concerned. She tells Dr. Berman that she too, has a young lover, and after some questioning, he's shocked to discover that it's her son, Thomas. Although Thomas is unable to resist his mother, and you watch them in some extended sex, he is obviously a little discon-

certed and is drinking heavily. Nina knows what is happening, but she's taken charge of the house and is spending her father's millions to launch her career as an actress. She's finished one picture with David Weiss, the producer, which was financed by her father, but Weiss has picked another and presumably better actress, Felicia Barrie (Kelly Nichols), for the lead in his next picture, much to Nina's exasperation. Nina discovers Felicia making love to Deidre (Weiss's wife), and of course she makes sure that Weiss witnesses the kinky business. He's so shocked that he gets rid of Felicia and gives Nina the starring role. In the meantime, Daddy Harding is hopelessly trying to control Nina before he goes bankrupt, and Nina is busy seducing Sid Holtzman (Jose Duval) into being her agent in an improbable scene where she provides Clete to fuck his wife while he watches (the only way he is turned on). She also seduces a critic, D.D. Dorfman, who has reviewed her as a "moronic, burlesque queen" of an actress. But never mind, C. B. Meyers, the biggest producer in Hollywood, thinks she has charisma equal to that of Jean Harlow and Marilyn Monroe, and soon he turns her into a million-dollar box-office star. Daddy Hardy, still living with Emily but missing Nina, dies of a heart attack, and Nina comes home for the funeral. In a reprise of Part 1, you hear her once again saying, "I'm going to get everything I want when I want it." And that's the clue that this miniseries has only begun. Other episodes are in the works. Surprisingly, in the process Raven, as Nina, has become a pretty good actress, and you'll probably want to see whom she takes over next.

TABOO III: THE FINAL CHAPTER
CC NN DK
1985 STANDARD VIDEO

P/D—Helen Terrie, Kirdy Stevens
F/A—Kay Parker, Honey Wilder, Lisa Lake, Pamela Mann, Colleen Brennan, Kimberly Wong
F/A—Jerry Butler, Blake Palmer, Ron Jeremy

Kirdy Stevens and Helen Terrie, who produce and distribute their own pictures under the Standard Video flag, are fascinated with incest and interfamily sexual relationships (see reviews of *Taboo I & II, Playing with Fire,* and *The Animal in Me*). This one is the continuing story of Barbara (Kay Parker), whose husband has left her, as has her older boy, Paul, who tells her at the beginning, via a phone call, that he can't handle his love for her anymore. Paul has left home, but Jimmy, Barbara's younger son, hasn't. He manages a rock group and has a girlfriend, Diane (Lisa Lake), who Mom doesn't feel is good enough for him. But Mom is trying very hard not to substitute Jimmy for Paul in her bed. She soon discovers that her friend Joyce (Honey Wilder) is actually screwing with her own son Bryan (Blake Palmer, who looks enough like Jerry Butler to be his brother). One day when she inadvertently walks in on them in bed, Joyce invites her to partake of the filial prick, which Bryan enthusiastically offers to his mother and to her friend. Eventually, mom ends up in bed with Jimmy, who is always watching her undress. In the meantime, poor Diane, who loves Jimmy, ends up at a wild orgy for record producers and agents to help promote Jimmy's rock group into national fame. The big problem you'll have with this one is why such attractive women as Kay and Honey must rely on their sons for sex. Honey Wilder tries to resolve this by proposing a toast to younger men, to which Kay enthusiastically drinks. Kay Parker, at this writing, has become director of publicity at Caballero, but she has announced that this does not preclude further acting in the right parts.

TABOO IV: THE YOUNGER GENERATION
CC NN NM
1985 STANDARD VIDEO

P/D—**Kirdy Stevens**
F/A—**Ginger Lynn, Karen Summer, Honey Wilder, Cindee Summers, Amy Rogers, Kay Parker**
F/A—**Jamie Gillis, John Leslie, Kevin James, Robin Cannes, Greg Ruffner, Joey Silvera**

In case you're confused, *Taboo I–IV* (four separate tapes), tied together by Barbara Scott (Kay Parker) and Joyce McBride (Honey Wilder) as mothers who are having sex with their sons and other relatives, has nothing to do with *Taboo American Style,* four separate tapes with a different producer and director. The only thing they have in common is that they are all pretty well acted and deal with the same subject, incest, which is a big seller in the 1980s. In this one, Dr. Jerome Lodge (Jamie Gillis) is a proper monogamist with two daughters who specializes in problems of incest and holds group-therapy sessions in his palatial California home. Honey Wilder is his patient, and so is Kay Parker, both of whom are trying to overcome their attachment to their sons. But they perform just a few of the sex scenes, and Kay's is a cut from the first *Taboo* film (see review). The main action concerns Jerome, who has a brother Billy (John Leslie) and whose wife, Alice, was in love with Billy before she married Jerome. It is now 18–20 years later, and the Lodges have two daughters. Naomi (Karen Summer) is a hot little lady who is expelled from boarding school because she sneaks a guy into her room. Her sister, Robin (Ginger Lynn), is prudish like Daddy, and when Jerome catches Billy screwing with Alice after all these years, he kicks Mommy out, and Naomi (who is probably Billy's daughter anyway) goes to live with them and Robin stays at home with Daddy. Ultimately, Daddy can't resist her and ends up in the bedroom (to her delight) and marries her *literally* (repeating marriage vows) as they finally make love together. In between, Naomi gets to bed with her daddy, Billy, and her dramatic coach, Danton (Joey Silvera). The sex is continuous, but amazingly, there is no bisexuality or kinkiness (DK).

TAKING OF CHRISTINA
CC NN DS
1975 VCX

P/D—**Jason Russell, Armand Weston**
F/A—**Bree Anthony, Terri Hall, C. J. Laing**
F/A—**Al Levitsky, Eric Edwards, Jack Thompson**

Put this one on your top-50 list. You'll be fascinated by the good acting, the fast editing, which heightens the dramatic effect, and the pre-story announcement that this film is based on an actual event that took place on October 1, 1974. Chris (Bree Anthony) is to be married within a week to Frank (Al Levitsky), but she's a good Catholic girl, and although Frank protests a little, she's saving herself for him on their wedding night. They see a movie together, and she's terrified by the violence. In another part of town, as Frank takes her home, a filling station is being held up by two guys, Larry (Jack Thompson), a psychotic killer who has spent much time in jail, and his easier-going buddy, Sonny (Eric Edwards), who tries to keep him under control. After stealing $400 from the old guy who runs the station, Larry stabs him to death. They then drive off and eventually hide out in a small deserted house. It's winter, and the ground is covered with snow. The following night, driving into town for groceries, Larry spots Chris waiting for Frank, who has promised to drive her home after work. Larry tries to pick up Chris, but she ignores him. He grabs her and, at knifepoint, shoves her into the car. Soon, back at the hideout, she's tied to the bed and is being raped by Larry while Sonny halfheartedly tries to stop him. In the meantime, Frank, who is a bit sex-starved and thinks Chris has deserted him, has gone to a strip club and is actually sitting next to Larry, who tries to start a fight with him over a bar girl who is trying to solicit Frank. Back at the hideout, while Frank goes to bed with the bar girl in a sad but loving encounter, Sonny is trying to persuade Chris, who is still tied naked to the bed, that she'd really have more fun going to Florida with them then getting married. She suddenly agrees and lets him have sex with her, and when Larry returns, she and Sonny are having a friendly conversation, during which she insists that her father has gone on a hunting trip. There's no one at home. If she's going to go with them she must have some clothes. They can have all the money that her father has hidden in the house. Larry is sure that she's lying and makes her fuck him and Sonny at the same time (they share everything) to prove that she belongs to them. By this time, you've guessed the bloody ending.

When she gets to her house, she manages to get inside ahead of them and blasts both of them into a bloody mess with her father's shotgun.

TALK DIRTY TO ME, PART III
CC NN NM BI
1984   DREAMLAND VIDEO

P/D—Jerry Ross, Ned Morehead
F/A—Traci Lords, Ginger Lynn, Amber Lynn
F/A—John Leslie, Jamie Gillis, Tom Byron

Jerry Ross likes to add new dimensions to Hollywood R-rated films (see reviews of *An Unnatural Act* and *Kinky Business*). This one is an X-rated *Splash*. The mermaid, who has no name, is Traci Lords. Traci has the male-fantasy dream body—a beautiful face with extra-big breasts and trim, boyish hips and behind. Seems that, unknown to Marty (Jamie Gillis), she's living in a pool at his son's (Tom Byron) girlfriend's house. The moment she leaves the pool her fins disappear and her legs come and go as she needs them. So the mermaid also visits the Ocean Park Naturist Club, which has a pool, and she learns phrases such as "Come in my face," "Put your cock inside me," "Eat my pussy," etcetera. Her best teacher is John Leslie who, as in previous *Talk Dirty* films (see reviews) is able to seduce ladies instantly. Of course, he can't believe that the mermaid is really a fish. A guy named Fast Eddie hears about the mermaid and offers John $1,000 to capture her. John takes the money, but he's in love with the mermaid and he certainly isn't going to let her be sold to Ocean World as a tourist attraction. It all ends up with John jumping in the pool with the mermaid and discovering how to breathe "down there"—literally and figuratively. There's a gratuitous secondary plot to tie this together in which Jamie Gillis and his wife conspire to ruin their son's love affair with Linda by having John Leslie screw her, with John thinking that Linda is the mermaid. She isn't! But it does nothing for the story.

TALK DIRTY TO ME ONE MORE TIME
CC NN BI NR
1985 ANTHONY SPINELLI PRODUCTIONS

P/D—Anthony Spinelli
F/A—Colleen Brennan, Niki Charm, Judy Jones
F/A—John Leslie, Harry Reems

Could you watch your wife make love with another guy? Could a wife make love with another guy with her husband watching? That in essence is the story line in this picture with John Leslie as Jack; Harry Reems as an obstetrician, Dr. Ted Roland; and Colleen Brennan as Ted's wife, Julie. The story of a wife not getting enough sex from her husband is a perennial in adult films. But what makes this one different is that Harry feels so badly about his inability to sustain an erection for very long with his younger wife that when he sees Jack in action in the park he asks Jack if he would take on his wife and give her the sexual satisfaction that he can't. He will watch them but not participate. If you can suspend disbelief then Spinelli, and I suspect his wife, Roxanne, who works with him on his films, gives you the most believable sexmaking, between Leslie and Colleen, that you've ever watched in a sexvid. There's lots of extended foreplay and silly conversation as you watch both of them getting more and more aroused and while the camera plays back and forth on Colleen's very expressive face and then glances occasionally at poor Ted/Harry watching her reach the kind of climax he hasn't been able to give her. Harry Reems's expression of agony (he doesn't undress or masturbate—usual adult-film procedures in this kind of scene) lets you know that he's a tormented man because he can't satisfy his wife. Later he watches her with another woman in a nicely understated scene, and then, mirabile dictu, when she comes to bed with him, he's got the erection he's been needing.

TEENAGE COWGIRLS
CC NN NL
1973 QUALITY/VIDEO-X-PIX

P/D—Hal Grunquist, Ted Denver

F/A—Amanda Blake, Sally Withers, Jane Wenstein
F/A—Long John Wadd, Wayne Johnson, Ted Armstrong

It's surprising how few adult films use an old-time western plot or background. This one is misnamed. It's a real shoot-em-up porno western with a continuous background of appropriate country-and-western songs. And although the camera rarely closes in on his face, you soon discover that this is a vintage John C. Holmes flick (he's listed as Long John Wadd), made when he was quite young and wasn't known as Johnny Wadd. In this one, he's Rio, a Robin Hood–type bank robber who services country ladies when their husbands are out cow punching. He's temporarily traveling with an Englishman, Duke Randy, who wears a bowler hat and speaks with an English accent. Arriving on horseback at various farmhouses and towns, they both take care of local wenches, but the Duke has a partiality to a pretty black woman he sees washing herself as she stands in a tin tub outside a squatter's shack. Both Rio and the Duke are being pursued by a bounty hunter who is after their scalps and the gold they have stolen from a bank. The film ends with a *High Noon*–style shootout in which John C. Holmes shoots the bad guy, who is using Duke's girl as a shield. John even looks like Gary Cooper when he twirls his gun. Shot almost entirely outdoors, it's no great shakes as a cowboy picture, but it's far more interesting than many current adult films.

TEENAGE FANTASIES
CC NN NR BI
1974 VCX

P/D—Not given
F/A—Renne Bond and many others not identified

When I was writing reviews for the first edition I couldn't get a copy of this tape. It's a classic of its time and better than *Teenage Fantasies II* (see review). It begins with a 500-word, or longer, introduction that was obviously included to justify its existence at a time when porno films led a precarious existence. "One of the major distinctions between man and the lower animals is man's capacity for imagery, for imagination—in a word, fantasy. Life itself may be based on a series of fantasy anticipations. . . ." After that prelude, you watch a very pretty lady, Renee Bond (now a Los Angeles housewife), sucking an anonymous cock with great enthusiasm and describing how much pleasure it gives her. Renee continues to appear between the four fantasies that comprise the film. These include a pretty young woman who would like to find a guy who would really fall in love with her but gets uptight when one tries to undress her. She finally capitulates to a guy in his late 50s who dreams of making love to a young girl once again, and he gets a young, happily compliant lady. A gal who dreams about her girlfriend making it with a guy gets her wish to join them, and so does a young guy, not over 18, who would like to be seduced by a girl and have her put "it" in her mouth.

TEENAGE SEX KITTEN
CC   NN   DS
1978   CABALLERO

P/D—S.B.
F/A—Renee Bond
F/A—John Holmes

I'd label this one a discovery. Renee Bond (whose name appears on the box) is listed in the credits as Lilly Lovetree, and there are equally silly names for the rest of the cast. Despite the box, John Holmes doesn't appear in the film. Whoever the director was, he was a skilled filmmaker. Renee Bond (long since retired from adult films) appears as Debbie, a young and sexy "teenager" who admits later in the story that she is really in her 20s. Her friend Shauna (who I think is played by Tina Russell) likes to make love but won't give herself to just anybody the way Debbie does. They want to go to Palm Springs for the weekend, a two-hour drive from Los Angeles. Neither they nor their boyfriends have enough money, but Debbie convinces Shauna to "exchange their assets" for a motel room. Shauna is not too happy about the idea, but their boyfriends don't

seem to object, so Debbie and Shauna end up in a sexual threesome with the manager of a motel. Up to this point, the sex has been lighthearted, silly, and laughing. Debbie, who is totally uninhibited, gets what she wants. Later, they go to a nightclub that features rock music. Soon Debbie is dancing with her dress in the air and is attracting some very unsavory characters. The owner of the club, a very genial black man, evicts her and tries to straighten her out. Sitting in his car outside the club, he gives her $20, telling her he wants nothing in exchange. But Debbie is so grateful she blows him, and while his head is hanging out the car window, the characters she incited in the bar slash his head open with a meat cleaver, after which they kidnap Debbie and take her to a shack out in the desert. Still unconscious, an ugly baldheaded character steals her bracelet, rapes her, and then leaves her with a retarded imbecile who keeps waiting for his turn. Conscious now, she fights him as he tries to force oral sex on her, and he grabs her by the throat and strangles her. He sobs pitifully when he realizes that she's dead. Searching for Debbie, the boys recognize her bracelet on the baldheaded guy, who has returned to Palm Springs for booze. The film ends with the boys murdering the retarded guy and tearing the balls off (literally!) the baldheaded guy—after which they bury Debbie and decide not to tell Shauna. Debbie is a runaway. It's a story that could appear on the front page of your newspaper, and it's a shocker, but it's skillfully told.

TEMPTATIONS
CC   NN   BI   NR   DK
1979   QUALITY/VIDEO-X-PIX

P/D—Dexter Eagle
F/A—Jennifer Welles, Gloria Leonard, Marlene Willoughby, Vanessa Del Rio
F/A—Jake Teague, John Leslie Dupre, Roger Cain

Note that this film goes back a few years, when John Leslie carried a French surname. As Raymond, he is confidential secretary and bodyguard to multimillionaire Mr. Hughes (Jake Teague), a man who has a beautiful wife, Rochelle (Jennifer

Welles), but unfortunately can no longer get an erection. Raymond arranges with various ladies so that poor Mr. Hughes can watch them screw with their boyfriends, but inevitably he gets caught spying and is beaten up by one guy. Marlene Willoughby, who runs an art gallery, is happy to have him pay to watch her and her female assistant, but Hughes isn't happy. He can't remember much of what happened. So Raymond has a great idea. With a TV camera, he records one session, which poor Hughes watches and falls asleep in. Later, when Hughes is watching it, his wife, Rochelle, finds him asleep with the tape running on his TV. The camera picks him out watching Vanessa Del Rio and others screwing with their boyfriends. Horrified that her husband is watching porno flicks of his own creation, she entices Raymond into bed, and soon they make a film together, which Rochelle calmly puts in place of the one that Mr. Hughes has. When he sees his wife making love, Hughes, for the first time, gets an erection, and later at a surprise-party orgy, Rochelle proves to him that Hughes is not impotent after all. If you have never seen Jennifer Welles in a film before (she was probably 40 when this one was made), you'll find it interesting to compare her good acting and voluptuous body with those of the current crop. Also, unfortunately, there's no male in the 1980s who can play old duffers the way balding Jack Teague did.

TEMPTATIONS
CC BI NL DK
1984   NOW SHOWING

P/D—Lawrence T. Cole
F/A—Desiree Lane, Gina Gianetti, Lili Marlene
F/A—Mike Horner, John Martin, Ron Jeremy, Herschel Savage, Don Fernando, Blair Harris, Nick Niter, Grant Lombard, Gary Hearn

The reason for the large cast of males is that Desiree Lane, as Laura Lee, is a marrying woman, and before she can settle down, she marries most of them. She just loves wedding nights. It's not easy to keep a story like this moving and continuously

funny, but Cole succeeds by matching the action to at least three very amusing country-and-western songs, as well as by the good acting of Desiree Lane. The first guy she marries, Jack (Mike Horner), can't believe it when she's gone, but the judge who married them sadly tells him that she's married another. Before it's over and she returns to Jack, she's married a woman with a husband, an elderly lecher who can't get it up, and then two guys at once.

THAT'S OUTRAGEOUS
CC NN BI
1983   CABALLERO

P/D—F. J. Lincoln
F/A—Franny Lomay, Natasha, Anna Ventura, Tiffany Clark, Sharon Kane
F/A—Jamie Gillis, Joey Silvera, Michael Bruce

You won't believe your eyes. Fred Lincoln has cast Jamie Gillis as a romantic lover in a film shot mostly in Paris that I'm sure wasn't brought in for under $300,000. Jamie has two identities. Living like Alec Guinness in a kind of *Captain's Paradise* in Paris, he has two apartments, one where he pretends to be a starving writer and is madly in love with Martine (Franny Lomay), a beautiful French woman. Actually, along with Rick (Joey Silvera), he's a top fashion photographer making plenty of money, with a Paris studio and a second apartment. Martine knows him as Paul—but somehow, unknown to her, he has met her sister, Michelle, who knows him as Phillip. Jamie is in love with her, too. The problem is that he wants them both, and if he could convince them to live with him in a ménage à trois, that would be heaven on earth. He tries to bring them together at a masquerade party, but when they discover that they have both been screwing him, they leave in shock and call him "a disgusting bastard." All the conversation between Martine and Michelle is in French with subtitles, and the background cinematography of Paris night and day contributes to the realism. You are left in doubt for quite a while as to what is going to happen to Jamie. But the French girls, after some soul-searching, decide that they can't live without him either, so they fly to New York, where he is now living, and elect to try a threesome.

A TIME TO LOVE
CC NN NR
1973   QUALITY/VIDEO-X-PIX

P/D—Harold Kovner, Jay Campbell
F/A—Tina Russell
F/A—Harry Reems, Howard Blakely

Although he's listed in the credits as Herbert Stryker (I think), the feature actor in this one is actually a very handsome and young Harry Reems, who is married to Kathy (Tina Russell), who is also not listed in the credits. But this is a unique sexvid that you have to see to believe. John (Harry Reems) and his college football buddy (Howard Blakely) come back to the university for their 10th reunion. John is now an ad executive, and Ned is a famous television commentator and a bachelor who has made love to women all over the world. In their reminiscing, they tell each other about their lives, and you discover that John, with one exception, has been totally faithful. He loves Kathy, and she loves him. The one exception occurred when Kathy was taking care of her sick mother and a nice young lady he met in a bar invited him back to her apartment for dinner. Later when he was making love to her, all he could see was Kathy's face and hear Kathy saying, "I love you, John." Embarrassed, he put on his pants and went home. John invites Ned to his home for the weekend, and you finally meet not only Kathy but their two children, a three-year-old boy and a four-year-old girl (something you rarely see in a sexvid), who give Daddy a tie for his birthday. Later, in bed, when they are making happy love, Kathy tells John she's worried about Ned, whom she also knew in college. She invites her unmarried cousin over to meet him, and finally Ned meets his one and only. In between Ned appears on television and gives a 1970s ecological and social message about the unholy alliance of business and advertising, the likes of which you have never heard before in any sexvid!

TOMATOES
CC NN NM BI NL
1968?   VCX

P/D—Joel Poete
F/A—Sheila Galore, Donna Rustle, Sara Nicholson and others
F/A—Tommy Toole and others

This film precedes *Deep Throat* by three or four years. I saw only one familiar face, Sara Nicholson, who appeared later in several other films. VCA released it on tape in 1985, and it is a collector's item for sexvid aficionados, reflecting, as it does, the happily silly touch of the earlier porno films. The various episodes are linked together by the story of a guy who is out of a job. Stanley Jones takes a job as a rent collector for a tough landlord, Mr. Watson, who promises him 25 percent of everything he collects from "those Hollywood nuts." Stanley assures him that he's a hard worker and a man above all temptations. His first collection is from a woman who squirts Cool Whip on his dick, and he soon forgets the rent. After knocking on one door after another, he encounters women making love to each other with dildos, but they're so happy to have a live prick that he's soon the object of their affections. One lady sprays the room with germicide and sucks a mint before she trades off her services for the rent, and he joins another in a coffin after interrupting a witches' black mass. In between rent calls, he reports back to Mr. Watson via telephone, growing weaker and weaker from his exertions and making no money as the day proceeds. Harry Reems appeared in a similar film that was made much later.

TOMBOY
CC NN NM NR NL BI
1983   VCX

P/D—William Dancer, Hans Christian
F/A—Melanie Scott, Kay Parker, Tina O'Ross, Alice Ward, Robin Wood
F/A—Doug Rossi, Tom Byron, Rudy Grand, Mark Wallice

The credits on this one, with the exception of Tom Byron, list different actors and actresses than does the box. Anyway, Melanie and Doug are a very attractive couple, and as a matter of fact, so is everyone else who appears in this happy-go-lucky story about high school seniors who play coed sports like football and volleyball together. One of them, Jan, is a virgin, and she knows she's as good as any guy in any sport. She can't believe that the the guys are all staring at her ass when she's centering the ball. One guy, Jeff (Tom Byron), is sure that, despite her claims to the contrary, she really is a virgin. He's constantly spying on her. To convince him that she's a woman as well as a tomboy, she lures Alex to her bedroom. Knowing that Jeff is listening under the window, she's determined to pretend that Alex is screwing her. Alex is a little bewildered by what is happening, but needless to say Jan is no longer a virgin. As a counterpoint to the kids, there's Mrs. Robinson (Kay Parker), whose husband has left her for another woman. Accidently, she encounters Ted (Mark Wallice) naked in his mother's home, and soon Ted is playing a delighted Dustin Hoffman, learning about sex roles and satisfying Kay's sexual needs in a romantic and loving sexual encounter.

TONIGHT
CC NN DS DK
1985 ORCHIDS INTERNATIONAL

P/D—Not given
F/A—Hanako Aomori, Keiko Hamada

Riding the subway into Tokyo, a young woman arrives with thousands of commuters from somewhere in the countryside. She finds a bar where she asks for Mr. Shimizu, but he's not there. A young wise-guy bartender offers her a cup of coffee and winking at his buddy puts a sleeping drug in it. The bar closes, and they carry her into the backroom and undress her. With her still unconscious, they rape her, and she finally wakes up protesting. In the meantime, another woman, who works in the bar, tells her not to cry over spilled milk. She can teach her how to perform as a combination sexy bar dancer and hooker. The guys in the bar watch as her new female friends shows her how, and they end up screwing the ladies to

exhaustion, after which our "country girl" picks up her clothes, puts them in her bag, and decides to go home.

TOO HOT TO HANDLE
CC NN BI (lots of)
1985 CAL VISTA

P/D—Sam Norvell, Bob Vosse
F/A—Angel, Kay Parker, Lili Marlene, Lynx Cannon, Donna Lindsay
F/A—Jamie Gillis, Blair Harris, Rod Grant, Don Fernando, Brandon Hall, John Toland (a.k.a. John Seeman)

If they had shot most of this one on the ski slopes of California and kept their eye on the basic plot, a male and female skier, Amanda (Angel) and Rick (Blair Harris), competing with other contestants to win a competition to ski in the Austrian Alps, they might have had a more interesting story. Instead, to get all the women and guys into action, there's another plot involving Michelle (Lili Marlene) and John (John Toland) to inveigle Amanda and Rick into endorsing their ski clothing—but only if they win the competition. Add to this Jamie Gillis, who appears as a ski instructor and gives Lynx Cannon lessons, after she has removed her dress in a non sequitur that has nothing to do with the story, and add a ski hospital supposedly next to the ski area, with Loretta (Kay Parker) as a nurse who nurses guys' cocks as well as their skiing injuries, and you have an incoherent mess. But with Loretta's help, Amanda patches her differences with Rick, who is prone to chase all the women in sight but suddenly recognizes true love. Rick and Amanda win the competition, which you never see—Michelle and John describe it to you as they watch a televison set. Ah, budget problems—and who said Angel could ski? But she can make love, and so can Kay Parker. They do it together and with guys watching them. It's the only reason for giving this one a CC rating.

TOO MUCH, TOO SOON
CC NN NR BI DK
1983 VCX

P/D—Michael Joseph, Vinnie Rossi

F/A—Becky Savage, Gina Gianetti, Drea, Misty Blue

F/A—Paul Thomas, Ron Jeremy, Bill Margold, Herschel Savage, Chuck Morrison, Tom Byron

Cindy (Becky Savage) is 18, just graduating from high school, and a virgin. Her girlfriend tells her that sucking a cock is just like lapping a strawberry ice cream cone. But Cindy wants to practice on the real thing. Julie arranges a date with Herschel Savage and Michael Morrison, who are "older guys," and Cindy is quickly initiated into the mysteries of sex. She enjoys men so much she can't stop. Then she meets Mark and falls so much in love that she can't even wash her hand for a day when he comes in it. But she's had "too much, too soon," and she can no longer concentrate on one guy, or on one cock. To his shock, Mark discovers her at a party blowing another guy. The romance is over and Cindy goes away to college. She's still in love with Mark, but on vacation she attends a swingers' party, complete with a magician who performs many tricks, including transforming the party into a happy orgy. Time passes, and now Cindy is living very luxuriously. She telephones Mark and asks him to visit her. When he does he asks for her forgiveness. But it's too late. Cindy is married to a pudgy guy twice her age who has a daughter. When he discovers that Mark was about to share his wife he kicks Cindy out. But Cindy doesn't give a damn—there's always another cock around the corner.

TOO NAUGHTY TO SAY NO
CC NN BI DK
1985   CABALLERO

P/D—Suze Randall, Victor Nye

F/A—Ginger Lynn, Cody Nicole, Lisa de Leeuw, Angel

F/A—Harry Reems, Jamie Gillis, Eric Edwards, Craig Roberts, Michael Morrison

It's a toss-up whether to give this one a DS rating. The sex action is not quite rape, but like *Succulent* (see review), it plays with a female dream of happy rape. The credits state that it is based on a character created by the Marquis de Sade, who

of course, is Justine. While Angel, who is the star, doesn't go through the same tribulations as Justine, she almost does. The film begins in a convent, where Angel and Ginger Lynn are innocent students—so innocent that Betty (Angel) presumably doesn't know what begat means when the Mother Superior (Lisa de Leeuw) reads to her from the Bible. But soon Angel, who is sitting out on the grass and picnicking with Betty (Ginger), falls asleep, and the rest of the tape is her dream. It includes watching Betty make love to a far-out character (Jamie Gillis, who has a roomful of sex objects) while she masturbates. Then Ginger takes her to a whorehouse of which Lisa de Leeuw is the madam, and Lisa auctions her off to some of her patrons, who include Colonel Vice, Senator Bribe (Eric Edwards), a bishop (Michael Morrison), and a Hollywood agent named Sidney Sweinstein. They are being worked over by ladies of the house, as Betty strips for them and they bid $10,000 for her services. Next she is accosted by a black guy on roller skates, who disappears, but when she tells two cops in a cruiser about it, they immediately strip her and screw her. After which she is chased by a mad flasher who tries to rape her, but she soon grabs his cock and sucks him off. Then she's dead—lying in a coffin and being taken by the devil himself (Harry Reems) who is wearing a tuxedo. She thinks she wakes up, but the dream continues as she is grabbed by a woman who undresses her in a car and makes love to her while two guys watch through the windows and jerk off. Poor Betty/Angel finally is awakened by her friend. With a smile, she tells her that she knows what begat means.

TOWER OF POWER
CC NN NR
1985   CAL VISTA

P/D—Sam Norvell, Robert McCallum

F/A—Annette Haven, Angel, Janey Robbins, Melanie Scott, Colleen Brennan

F/A—John Leslie, Harry Reems, R. Bolla, Herschel Savage

Move over "Dynasty," here's a 90-minute sex-packed story filled with the same kind of characters. But these characters don't have to make love offscreen. Note the rating. The actors in this one are so involved with each other that they don't have time for anything except heterosexual loving, which is almost an adult-film first. Fred Kingsley (R. Bolla), head of the multibillion-dollar Kingsley Industries, is married to Stella (Janey Robbins), but he lets his secretary, Annette Brady (Melanie Scott), pick out his wife's birthday presents. Annette also takes good care of him in the office, but Fred's not too active at home. Hugh Casey (John Leslie) is happily married to Linda (Angel). But Hugh thinks if Fred ever gets anything on him "he'll dump [him] in a minute," and Hugh never made him a vice-president. George Thompson (Harry Reems) is a vice-president of the company, but he's divorced and fiddling around with a call girl, Lilly (Colleen Brennan, who for some reason, is identified as Sharon Kelly) and he ignores Claudia (Annette Haven), who is a millionairess who owns 20 percent of the stock in Kingsley Industries. Claudia would marry Harry if he would settle down a little. In the meantime, she has a lover, Stella Kingsley's stepbrother Gabe (Herschel Savage). Linda Casey wants her husband to be vice-president, so she spends the afternoon with Fred Kingsley in a hotel room. But Kingsley has other problems. Someone in the organization has made it possible for a competitor to outbid them on a million-dollar job, and Fred is sure that the traitor is on the board of directors. Who's the traitor and why has she or he betrayed the company? Before the plot's resolved, everyone listed above has happily had sex with more than one other person listed above. You can be sure that there will soon be a sequel, with the baddie, who turns out to be Annette Haven, still playing a role similar to Joan Collins's "Dynasty" part—only Annette is prettier.

TRASHY LADY
CC NN BI NL DK
1985   MASTERPIECE VIDEO

P/D—Dan Andrews, Steve Scott
F/A—Ginger Lynn, Cheri Janvier, Amber Lynn, Cara Lott, Bunny Bleu

F/A—**Harry Reems, Herschel Savage, Tom Byron, Steve Drake, Francois Papillon, Mark Wallice**

The time is the 1930s, and the producer and director have gone all out to recreate the period clothing styles, automobiles, telephones, and speakeasy and bedroom atmosphere. Jesse (Cara Lott) is Dutch Seigel's (Harry Reems) moll. Fucking is her continuous verb/adjective, but she doesn't like to do it much. But Dutch likes his gum-chewing lady, and when she walks out on him he's disappointed with Kitty (Ginger Lynn), who he finds working as an innocent cigarette girl in his nightclub. Even though she's depressingly innocent, he knows that she has fucked Tony (Steve Drake), the manager to get the job. So Dutch takes Kitty over and hires Rita (Amber Lynn), who is Big Louie's (Herschel Savage's) doll, to train Ginger how to speak properly. Big Louie is in the slammer, but he hears about Dutch messing around with Rita and plans to wipe him out when he gets out, within the next week. He can't believe it when Dutch tells him that he hasn't laid a finger on Rita, omitting that Rita has laid her lips on him. In the meantime Rita has successfully transformed Kitty, who in an amusing scene practices adding fuck to every other word she says as she rehearses for Dutch in front of a mirror. It all ends happily, with the two big shots getting together at a convention in which everyone is frisked to make sure he isn't carrying any hardware.

TRINITY BROWN
CC NN NR BI
1984   CAL VISTA

P/D—Sam Norvell, Robert McCallum
F/A—Colleen Brennan, Tamara Longley, Melanie Scott, Kimberly Carson
F/A—John Leslie, Joey Silvera, Jamie Gillis

This one will keep you watching from beginning to end as you try to unravel who killed Tony Fortuna. His wife has been screwing around with Frankie Carbonne (Joey Silvera), a real tough hood, and Frankie is number-one suspect. But Trinity

Brown (Colleen Brennan), a freelance San Francisco detective who has been to bed with Frankie, is sure that he isn't the one. Zack (John Leslie), her detective partner, isn't so sure. Frankie has been identified by a gardener who is later shot before he can become a witness. In the meantime, there's Tony's wife, Angela (Tamara Longley), who in her whoring days, before she became a wealthy syndicate wife of Tony, has screwed with both Frankie and Zack. Our hero detectives gradually solve the crime by hopping in the sack (or on the floor or in a swimming pool) with the various suspects, with no strings attached and time out occasionally to prove that they really love each other best. Who killed Tony? A gal who tries to convince Zack that he's the father of her child, but you'll have to watch it twice to find out why. Colleen and John are a great team. The story is as good as you'll see on network TV. You can count on a sequel!

TRISEXUAL ENCOUNTERS #1 AND #2
CC   NN?   BI?   DK?
1985   L.A. VIDEO

P/D—L. M. Burton, Shannon
F/A—Angelique Ricard, Ava Hollywood, Dana
    Douglas, Pasha, Summer St. Cerly,
    Shalimar, Michael Marr, Sondra Stillman
F/A—Jamie Bleu, Rick Turner, Shaun Easton

Note the question marks after the various ratings. How can you define a man/woman (a "guy" with breasts and a cock) as normal? If two of them make love together, is it gay or bisexual? Anal intercourse may not be kinky for those half-and-half people. These two 60-minute tapes make comparisons with *Female Impersonators of the Year* (see review) inevitable. Unlike the impersonators, these people are really transsexuals, and Shannon, who introduces the various vignettes, reveals in words (you have no visual evidence) that, like Sulka (see reviews), she now has a vagina and no cock. But according to Shannon, 50 percent of the models used by the House of Dior and Pierre Cardin are transsexuals and are better-looking "women" than the real thing. So when

you watch these two tapes you can thank your lucky stars that you weren't caught in the middle. The tapes are divided into "little encounters" between the "trisexuals" listed above, with each other and with "normal" guys who get their cocks sucked and who suck the cocks of their companions as well as play with their tits. The trisexuals have body hair only around their genitals. Their penises are about average in length and circumference, and they ejaculate when stimulated. But dressed or undressed, down to their waist, they look and talk like women—and of course they delay the big surprise in sexual encounters down to the last minute.

TURN ON WITH KELLY NICHOLS
CC   NN   NM   NR
1984   CABALLERO

P/D—Harry Aaron, Ron Parchett, Elisa Howard
F/A—Kelly Nichols, Talja Rae, Brooke Field,
    Chelsea Blake
F/A—Klaus Multia

Here's a great wedding present for a bride. Amazingly, an adult-film star, together with whoever wrote the script and the cinematographer, has provided the best sexmaking instruction film that I have watched thus far. The film is shot in soft focus with ethereal background music and is intercut with segments showing erotic drawings from the past. From the beginning, Kelly Nichols makes it clear that the secret of good sex is the length of time that pleasure is extended. Throughout the hour-and-15-minute tape, Kelly gives you various suggestions, such as combining a woman's vaginal juice with a dash of perfume, for a natural aphrodisiac. She also suggests putting a drop of perfume on a light bulb to give a room a seductive fragrance. If an older woman has lost her lover, Kelly advises that she masturbate regularly. And so on. In addition, with much more loving advice, Kelly and all the various actresses listed above enjoy caring sex, and Kelly covers variety in sex—including where (in addition to bed) and when. She also covers music, ben-wa balls in a lady's vagina, and other devices. But she concludes that the best aphrodisiac is still romance. Most couples will want to own this one.

THE ULTIMATE KISS
CC NN NR
1984 AMBASSADOR

P/D—Jessie Mabry
F/A—Bonnie Stewart
F/A—Rick Cassidy

A 30-minute tape that would make a good wedding present. The bride may enjoy it even more than her husband. It offers a romantic sex education on the joys of foreplay, with the first section showing how a male should enjoy the woman's body and learn as he kisses her from head to foot that "her whole body is an erogenous zone." The loving action of the couple you watch on the screen is heightened by a warm, sexy female voice-over explaining how the woman is reacting and guiding the male. The second section of the tape reverses the love play, and the woman is talked to by a honey-tongued male voice-over. The dialogue, interestingly, in both cases includes anal kissing, but warns you, especially after rimming the lady, not to return to her genitals (no matter how clean she is and should be) before you wash away any potential bacteria. If this advice were followed in most adult films, they'd be a lot more soapier than the soap operas.

AN UNNATURAL ACT
CC NN NL DK BI
1984 DREAMLAND VIDEO

P/D—Jerry Ross, Tom C. Donald
F/A—Kimberly Carson, Desiree Lane, Bridgitte Monet
F/A—John Leslie, Eric Edwards, Ron Jeremy

If you've seen *Dona Flor and her Two Husbands*, a delightful Brazilian movie, then you know the plot of this one. This is a story John Leslie was destined to appear in, and it's a laughing, fun adult film that should amuse women as well as men. The story begins with four lovely naked angels. They're waiting in heaven for Michael Foley (John Leslie) to appear. He's an impoverished guitar player who only had two things going for him in life, a loving girlfriend, Teri (Desiree Lane), and a motorcycle. Going home after a nice evening with Teri, he is happily speeding through one of the Hollywood canyons when he is sideswiped by a Lincoln being driven by Blake (Eric Edwards), a producer of adult films, and his gay friend (a middle-aged actor whose name I don't know). Foley is dead. Blake and his friend don't report the accident, and the only person alive who misses him is Teri, who still has his guitar. Still mooning over him weeks later, Teri applies for a part in one of Blake's films, neither of them aware that they have Foley in common. Teri can't undress and appear naked before the cameraman, which she must do to get the part. Blake is intent on seducing her, but when he finally gets Teri in bed, Foley appears, completely naked, and watches them. Blake can't see Foley, but Teri can, and he harrasses her. "Don't do it, Teri," he tells her as Blake is trying to get her aroused. Teri tries to tell him to go away. Blake thinks she's talking to him. In shock, Teri faints. The rest of the film plays on the theme and is full of happy laughs. Foley appears in the ladies' locker room in a tennis club and takes on one of the ladies while she's making love to another. He hears Teri's roommate, Brenda (Kimberly Carson), tell Teri to stop moaning over Foley. "He had the sex appeal of a wet dishrag." Hearing her say that, Foley goes to bed with Brenda and gives her a sex dream she'll never forget. But Teri is afraid to make love with him. He's a ghost. He needs another body. Then, mirabile dictu, Blake, who is not really in love with Teri, drives his Lincoln off a cliff, and Foley is on hand to see the accident. At last he has what he needs, a new body—Blake's. In a funny closing scene, he makes Teri aware that even if he looks like Blake, he is really Foley. Two others who can see Foley when he reappears are Ron Jeremy and the gay friend, who provide some amusing interludes. Desiree Lane is a good actress, with an appealingly homely face, and Eric Edwards and John Leslie have long since proved they are as good as any of the young actors in regular films.

UP IN FLAMES
CC NN NL BI
1973 IVP (formerly CVX)

P/D—Not given
F/A—Kelly Mint; other female names not decipherable in credits
F/A—Frank Marks, Fred Lee, Bob Robbins, John Seeman

Put this one on your list of happily silly sexvids. Sex with laughter in adult films is not easy to come by, but following in the tracks of Cheech and Chong and their *Up in Smoke* film, this is the story of three very lazy, sloppy brothers who live in total squalor along with their cats. They smoke pot and manage to con everyone in sight in order to eat. The landlady, who isn't bad looking, tries to evict them, along with a gal upstairs who mixes pot with oregano and sells it to all comers. None of them pays the rent. The brothers decide that they must go to work, for a day at least. The older brother takes on the job of seducing the landlady. He tells her that the problem with the world is that there's too much distance between the owners of the world and the renters, but he doesn't quite solve their rent problem with her. He convinces a younger brother that even though he's never painted anything, except with a spray can, he can become a professional house painter, and soon the guy is painting rooms in the apartment and servicing a woman tenant. But when he's finished, she asks him to pay her. The other brother goes to work for Mr. Natural (John Seeman), who wears a fake beard and claims that his vitamin concoctions have kept him virile at the age of 82. Without the beard, he happily screws ladies who pass out cards telling where you can buy the stuff. Mr. Natural hires the third brother and pays him with beans that give off an aphrodisiacal aroma that women can't resist. No one earns any money, but they don't get evicted either. (See notes under *Pleasure Bed.*)

URBAN HEAT
CC NN NR
1985 VCA

P/D—Candida Royalle, R. Lauren Niemi
F/A—See below

I really think that *Ms.* or one of the women's magazines should review adult films, or at the very least interview Candida Royalle. There's a big market for her *Femme* series, but she probably won't be able to reach it easily through the conventional distribution channels. Like the previous *Femme* tape, this one continues a series of slice-of-life vignettes. The setting is a hot summer day in New York. There are six sections. "Friday Night at the Disco" features Sharon Kane, David Israel-Sandler, Marita Ekberg, and Klaus Multia. The atmosphere is highly sexual, and some of the dancers enjoy each other, all the way, in one-to-one sex. "Saturday Morning," with Taija Rae and Scott Baker, is sleepy early-morning sexmaking. "Elevator Seduction" offers a woman's fantasy of giving herself to a stranger in an elevator and features Chelsea Blake and K. Y. Lee. Then there's "Tar Beach," with Cassandra Leigh and David Scott oiling themselves with suntan lotion and then making it under a parachute on the beach. "TV Turn-On" and "Sunday Brunch," featuring Tish and David Ambrose and Carol Cross and Bernard Daniels, respectively, are in the same style of warm, caring sex with no cum shots. Candida has made her point with this and her first film, which are like watching sexual chamber music and will appeal to most couples. But now she must move on, using the same techniques to tell a complete story.

VIDEO GUIDE TO SEXUAL POSITIONS
CC NN NR BI
1985 AMBASSADOR

P/D—L. M. Burton, Drea
F/A—Gina Carrera, Sandy Fields, Cynthia Brown, Jessie Adams
F/A—Bobby Bullock, Dino Alexander

"Is your sexual life dull, listless, and boring? Are you yawning instead of yelping? Pep up your pooped-out play with new positions. Do it now and do it differently." Thus begins this tape, with a sexy female voice-over and erotic background music supplementing the action. The premise of this film is that "for most women having sex is easy but getting aroused is not, and kissing should be rediscovered as a part of extended foreplay." The sexmaking in all the sequences is romantic and includes extended female sexual arousal by a loving guy. The sexual positions and alternating fellatio and cunnilingus are tender and caring. It concludes with an extended viewing of a couple trying one position after another without coming apart for more than a second and a three-way sexual encounter with two guys and one woman, thus making this a tape that many females will enjoy.

VIRGIN & HER LOVER
CC NN BI NR DK
1980 VCA

P/D—Kemal Horolu
F/A—Leah Marion, Darby Lloyd Raines, Olinka Podany
F/A—Eric Edwards, Mark Stevens, Jonathan Jones

I have a feeling that this film was made a few years earlier than 1980. It has a 1970s-style psychological story line that keeps you interested throughout the film, plus exceptional sexmaking, cinematography, and good acting. The virgin is a mannequin! Her lover, Paul Gavin (Eric Edwards), keeps her in his bedroom dressed in a male masquerade costume that was worn at a party three years ago by the only woman he has ever let himself go with. She died in an auto accident. He tells this story to his psychiatrist, but unknown to the doctor, Paul has occasionally dated Julie (Leah Marion), the doctor's secretary, who has fallen in love with him. But she's very puzzled by his chivalrous behavior. Intercut between their almost first-love kind of romance, Paul goes home to his mannequin, who comes to life in his fantasies. She looks like the dead woman, and he makes love to her. Paul's troubles are compounded by his interest in lesbian behavior and as a director he has

produced a film called *Two Women* that features Darby Lloyd Raines in a believable bisexual scene. Julie, who has a very sensuous, soft-breasted body, is in love with Paul, so she furtively reads her boss's notes on the case, and soon she is impersonating the mannequin and Paul is cured. Horolu gives a sense of reality to most of his films that keeps you watching.

VIRGINIA
CC NN NL NR
1983 CABALLERO

P/D—John Seeman
F/A—Shauna Grant, Janey Robbins
F/A—Paul Thomas, Herschel Savage, Jamie Gillis

In one scene after another the cinematography is warm and romantic, the dialogue is better than average, and the cutting and editing are good. The film won six of the 1984 Erotic Film Awards, but the ending is for the birds. Virginia (Shauna Grant) is presumably the daughter of a photographer, Paul Thomas (who specializes in bird and animal photography, enjoys women, and his friends) lives in what amounts to an artist colony, which has a chimpanzee who enjoys hot tubbing with humans. What happened to his other wife (wives?), one of whom must be Virginia's mother, is not revealed, but when the story opens Paul has moved another woman into the house and is contentedly screwing her. He is unaware that Virginia is listening to their happy moaning. Virginia stays out of the sack with Jamie Gillis and in an amusing scene with Herschel Savage watches another couple screwing. While she kisses him avidly she doesn't surrender to him, because the truth is that she is in love with her daddy. Poking around in her father's dresser, she discovers that Daddy also has a collection of pictures of their friends screwing. Shocked, she decides that she can't go to a party with him in her new dress. She tells him, "I have to know whether I am living with a sick, degenerate man. Is my father a pervert?" He assures her that he is not but rather is paid by his friends to take the pictures, which harm no one. It is apparent that now, at last, Virginia is going to do what she has wanted to do for many years—go to bed with Daddy. The ensuing 15 minutes of loving sex are very romantic, even though Paul Thomas doesn't look old enough to be Shauna's father. You are ready to forgive them for their incestual joy, but you don't have to. Turns out Paul is a psychiatrist who's helping Virginia get over her hang-up on her real daddy.

VIRGIN SNOW
CC NN NL NR BI
1977   QUALITY/VIDEO-X-PIX

P/D—Dexter Eagle
F/A—Laura Hunt, Jean Jensen, Hope Stockton
F/A—Roger Caine, Trevor Mammik, Eric Edwards, Jeffrey Hurst, Richard Bolla

Virginia (I wish I could identify the actress in this one) tells the story. She's enrolled at college but is ready to give up her studies because so far her sex life has been a dud. She gets plenty of bed stuff, but she never has that magic feeling with a guy. She tells her problem to her best friend, Sally, who is living with Ben (Roger Caine). It's a cold winter day, and her professor, Victor Ashton (Eric Edwards), drops over. She tells him the story of their weekend up in the Adirondacks skiing with Sally and Ben and Marilyn, Sally's sister, who comes along and to Sally's shock is soon waylaying Ben and every other willing male in sight. These include R. Bolla, whom they have picked up in a van. He gets undressed before they arrive because he thinks that the ladies are going to screw him even before they check into the ski lodge. They don't, and Bolla breaks his leg skiing, getting Vanessa Del Rio as a nurse in the infirmary. In the meantime, Marilyn blows Ben as they ride the ski lift, and Sally catches Ben screwing Marilyn in the snow. But nothing phases Marilyn. That night in the lodge she sings a very pretty song titled "Virgin Snow," after which they adjourn to their room for a one-to-one group-sex party. Finally, after telling her story, Marilyn realizes that her professor is the guy who can put magic back into her sex life, and they prove it

together. The backgrounds in ski country are different, and the sex is cool 1970s style.

VIVA VANESSA
CC NN NL DK BI
1984   VCA

P/D—James George, Henri Pachard
F/A—Vanessa Del Rio, Renee Summer, Angelique Ricard
F/A—Eric Edwards, F. J. Lincoln, Jerry Butler, David Scott, George Payne, Henri Pachard, R. Bolla

If you're not a Vanessa Del Rio fan, you won't approve of this CC rating. Vanessa is the only well-known Puerto Rican female who has ever appered in porno films. There's no denying that Vanessa gives any film a kind of mad, devil-may-care flare, and just acting herself she's fun to watch. In this one, Henri Pachard (Ron Sullivan, who is also the director) is shooting a film about Vanessa's life. As the film progresses you watch Vanessa's introduction to the entertainment world by R. Bolla (as her agent). "This is strictly a formality. Take down your skirt, my dear. You are the merchandise," he tells her. While she gives him what amounts to a bored fuck (revealed by her facial expression) Bolla turns her over to Francois, who tells her he only wants her anally and ignores her plaintive "It hurts." Afterward, when he tells her to get out because he's not happy with her, she socks him on the nose. Then she meets Fred Lincoln (an actual porno-film maker who wears his long, white hair shoulder length). Watching her suck off a guy as a preliminary to getting a part, he yells, "A fuckin' star is born." In an eye-popping sequence (after Vanessa tells you that up to this time she has refused to perform with women), she appears with Angelique Ricard, a beautiful blonde with nice breasts—*and a big white prick*, which Vanessa obligingly sucks. She also takes on two guys in the men's room and shows them how she can lap her own nipples. In between these scenes, you see Henri Pachard desperately trying to set up other scenes. So you have it both ways, and you see how a porno film is made, with Vanessa in the middle of sex scenes telling Pachard, "This is boring. I've been on this fuck shoot for four days. It's weird. I'm ready to blow it"—or any guy in sight.

WET LADY
CC NN BI
1979   VCX

P/D—Walt J. Hoffman
F/A—Roxanne Neufeld, Ginger Hulsey, Adrian Michaels
F/A—Martin Noble, Manny Speigel, Gene Medlin

This one deals with the supernatural in a way that could have been scary, with overtones of the occult. It begins on a deserted New England beach. A woman suddenly arises out of the water. In a dripping-wet dress that looks like a shroud and with long, wet hair, she walks out of the surf and along the beach. Soon she's walking the streets of a country town, where she climbs in the window of a hatchback automobile that has been in a very bad accident but is still being driven. When the driver (a guy) arrives at his destination and opens the hatch, there she is, naked. She reaches up, unzips his pants, and blows him while, quite bewildered, he demands, "Who are you? What are you doing here?" Her only answer is a melancholy "I love men. I want to make love to you." Her further encounters are more prosaic. She can be seen by men but not by women, and her answer to all questions is: "I love men." She finally returns to the ocean and disappears. The unexpected style of the story keeps you watching, but could have been told to keep you on the edge of your chair—a reincarnation, perhaps, of a woman thrown overboard, or drowned by her lover.

WET T-SHIRT CONTEST
CC R
1984   GM VIDEO

P/D—Not given
F/A—Residents of Colorado and Arizona

Every August, somewhere along the Colorado River in Arizona, several thousand people congregate, most of them arriving by houseboat and motorboat at the small town of Fisher's Landing for the annual T-shirt contest. This two-hour tape records the events, which take place in temperatures of 115 degrees, with 25 or more female contestants who raise the male temperatures even higher as they compete for the first prize of about $450. As the day commences, the women put on T-shirts over their bikini bras, which they decorously remove under the T-shirt before they are doused with water. Once wet, of course, their breasts are revealed to the crowds of male and female onlookers, with endless cheers of approval. As the afternoon wears on and it gets hotter, the young ladies become a lot less shy and show their naked breasts. Tucking their bikinis high around their asses, a few daring ones even give you glimpses of their vulvas and pubic hair. The reason I've given this one a CC rating is that I doubt if many of the women are professional strip teasers or dancers. They prove that in America, in the 1980s, more and more women don't give a damn. If guys think they are sex objects, okay. When push comes to shove, they're in control and they know it. As for censoring this kind of silly sexuality (and even adult films) the moral majoritarians better forget it. Most young men and women spend a good portion of their waking hours thinking about sex or being sexy. On the other hand, most Europeans couldn't believe that any one would buy this tape or attend a Wet T-Shirt contest just to see ladies' breasts. All you have to do in most European countries is simply go to the nearest beach or the pool where many of the women, young and old, are happily bare chested and provocative, and the guys can watch them and enjoy their private fantasies.

WHITE FIRE
CC NN BI NR DK DS (story related)
1976   VCX

P/D—J. Thomas Simpson, Roger Colmont
F/A—Lisa Marks, Georgette Sanders
F/A—Bill Barry (but he looks like Herschel Savage)

Adult-film producers in the 1980s will have to go a long way to match the intensity of this film, much of which was presumably shot in Maine at a winter ski lodge. What's more, it's a film that most women will find quite fascinating. It's beautifully acted by Lisa Marks, a voluptuously built lady who plays the part of Vanessa Manchester, a magazine editor. It's a story of jealousy gone amok. In her younger days, Vanessa loved variety. She has never believed in marriage, but then she meets Tim at a swingers' party. Both of them have eyes only for each other. After that night, Tim tells her that he never wants another woman. Vanessa believes him, and though she moves in with him she still avoids marriage. Then, in an offscreen episode, she catches Tim *in flagrante* with her secretary. Wildly jealous, she drives alone to her cabin in Maine. She's so emotionally distraught that you begin to suspect that Tim is right, that it never happened. But now, living alone, snowbound, mixing drinks with sleeping pills, Vanessa begins to have wild sex dreams in which she fantasizes Tim making love to her and to other women, and then she thinks he's actually in the cabin with her. In a scene you won't believe, she makes love to him on a ladder, where she is finally dangling, holding his prick in her mouth as her only support, swirling in the air like a circus acrobat. Surrealistic oil paintings come to life and end up in a Hieronymous Bosch–style orgy that you'll watch through to the end because you never saw anything like it. In her imagination, Vanessa is raped by a guy who comes to dig her out of the snow, but then he suddenly doesn't exist. Tim finally arrives searching for her, and, trembling in his arms, without explanation, she vanishes into thin air.

way it really is. But a growing number of producers and directors (many of them women) are making films that reflect modern marital problems and at the same time reveal character. This one, with a real Texas background, will appeal to lovers everywhere. It's the story of Kelly (Honey Wilder) and Denver (Eric Edwards), a wealthy businessman, who were both in love with someone else before they got married and can't forget their former lovers. Kelly's first love was Duane (Randy West), a rodeo star, who has just been released from prison. For four years (crime unexplained) he has survived because of his memories of being in Kelly's arms. Thinking of him, after some perfunctory sex with Denver, who refuses to take her to Houston with him on a business trip, Kelly realizes that she should have married Duane. In the meantime, her sister Sandra (Sharon Mitchell) is married to the wrong guy, too. Butch beats her up regularly and doesn't screw with her enough. Kelly and Sandra decide to have some fun themselves and end up in a swinging roadside club, where they pick up a couple of guys and finally end up in a motel, where they are followed by Butch, who recognizes Kelly's Cadillac parked outside. This is a funny and very believable sequence, with Sharon and her guy (Paul Thomas) nearly getting caught in the sack, while at the same time, Kelly is still deciding whether to let the other guy into her pants. The story finally ends with Kelly and Denver parting and returning to their "true loves," but in between there's a rodeo sequence at a race track and some very fine acting by Honey Wilder who, with this one, joins the ranks of top female porno stars.

WILD DALLAS HONEY
CC NN NR BI (that's believable)
1983 CABALLERO

A WOMAN'S TORMENT
CC NN NR
1978 VCA

P/D—Michelle Aimes, Jeffrey Fairbanks
F/A—Honey Wilder, Sharon Mitchell, Tigr, Jasmine Dubois
F/A—Randy West, Eric Edwards, Paul Thomas

The premise of most adult films is that they are total fantasy—so to hell with life the

P/D—Robert Norman
F/A—Tara Chung, Jennifer Jordan, Marlene Willoughby
F/A—Jake Teague, Jeffrey Hurst

Here's a sexvid made by a skilled filmmaker who knows how to tell a realistic horror story with sex as an integral part. Whether Robert Norman made any films beside this one and *Mystique* (see review) I don't know, but don't miss this tape. It starts innocuously with a psychiatrist, Otis (Jake Teague) and his wife in bed and his wife complaining that he has climaxed before her. There's friction in their marriage, which soon becomes apparent when Otis and Estelle (Jennifer Jordan) are invited to a buffet dinner at Frances (the actress is unidentified) and Donald's (Jeffrey Hurst) home. Otis has been having an affair with Frances, and both their spouses are dimly aware of it. But Frances has bigger problems. Her retarded sister, Karen, is living with them and is temporarily alone at their summer home on what looks like Fire Island. Donald wants Karen to be put into a mental institution. She hasn't spoken for years. Intercut with the affair, which Frances is trying to cool down, you see Karen (Tara Chung) alone at the end of summer. Walking a lonely beach, carrying a suitcase full of clothes, she throws it in the ocean. The roiled sea reveals that there has been a big storm, and the power lines are down. A man from the power company has arrived to fix them. Karen, who you realize in flashbacks has been raped sometime in her past, wants a man but is afraid of sex, and she's carrying a long kitchen knife. She seduces the guy, who is very gentle and even talks a little, but when he tries to fuck her she plunges the knife into his back. This is the beginning of a horror story that ends with Karen murdering three other people, including Otis, who goes to the island at the request of Frances to find out why Karen doesn't answer the telephone. You'll watch this one, which has excellent acting, especially by Tara Chung, right through to the shocking end. If you compare it with *Mystique*, you'll find some of the same elements of sex and horror.

WORKING IT OUT
CC NN BI
1984 CABALLERO

P/D—Joe Williams, Phillip Gem

F/A—Joanna Storm, Erica Boyer, Janey Robbins, Danielle

F/A—Eric Edwards, Ron Jeremy, Herschel Savage, Mike Horner, Dave Cannon

The CC rating may be dubious, but with one unbelievable exception this one offers an integrated story line about a New York City hooker, Holly Hendrickson (Joanna Storm), who inherits a bankrupt health club from her Uncle Harry in San Francisco. The exception is typical of directors who shoot off the cuff and involves Holly in an airplane on her way to California to take over her inheritance. She rejects the advances of her seatmate, Ron Jeremy, who shrugs and immediately fantasizes screwing the hostesses on the plane. After a 10-minute diversion that has nothing to do with the plot, the director remembers and Holly arrives in San Francisco and discovers that Uncle Harry's health club needs a big infusion of money and labor to put it on its feet. Eric Edwards as Mr. Doherty, her uncle's lawyer, advises her to sell it or give it away. But Holly and her new friend, played by Erica Boyer, convince a contractor (Herschel Savage) to become a "joint" partner. The club quickly attracts male patrons, who enjoy a little servicing with the girls. The women customers have masseurs and studs, but the poor guys can't stand the strain. "We love getting paid for getting laid," they tell Holly, "but we're exhausted. Ten times a day is too much!" The club is about to go under, but then Holly and Erica offer "sexercising" for ladies only, to improve their performance in bed, and they soon have plenty of ladies performing their sexual aerobics.

WPINK TV
CC NN BI NL DK
1985 PARADISE VISUALS

P/D—Michael Philips, Miles Kidder
F/A—Christy Canyon, Tamara Longley, Ali Moore
F/A—John Holmes, Harry Reems, Ron Jeremy, Mark Wallice

Phil (Ron Jeremy) tells Cathy (Christy Canyon) that he has a great idea. People are bored with the same old killing and terror, news and situation comedies on TV. He tells her that they should take over the TV station where they work. After hours they can put on the kind of show that the public really wants to see. No sooner said than done, and as master and mistress of ceremonies Phil and Cathy show the viewers how to fuck and suck, they also prepare soap operas called *Secret Sperm, Lay of Our Lives,* and aerobic dancing with ladies "touching their toes and showing you where your penis goes." Trademark of the station is Phil's cock, which he can rotate clockwise or counterclockwise. Scorpio (Harry Reems), a goverment agent, is sent to shut down this sex madness, but he's soon seduced by Cathy, and the feature program *Beat the Cock* goes on as scheduled. Three blindfolded women compete to identify a famous cock by touch, taste, or insertion. John C. Holmes is the guest star, of course. The CC rating is for the silly, nonstop, sometimes pretty yucky, sperm-shooting insanity of it.

YOUNG GIRLS DO
CC NN BI DK
1985   ESSEX

P/D—**Bob Vosse**
F/A—**Shanna McCullough, Jacqueline Lorians, Erica Boyer**
F/A—**Paul Thomas, Herschel Savage, Billy Dee, Jon Martin**

This one has a slice-of-life feel to it—probably because it is supposed to be based on Erica Boyer's true-life experience. The opening sequence is at a high-school graduation slumber party, during which Mary Ann (Shanna McCullough) is revealed to be a virgin and ends up a little shocked when some of the girls begin tasting each others' pussy. You see her flying across country to a university in San Francisco, which in various outdoor shots looks like Berkeley. En route, after two bottles of champagne with Jon Martin, Mary Ann loses her virginity to him standing up in the toilet. A few days later, her psych professor assigns her and an-

other freshman, Erica, a joint paper (no pun). They must research "Sexual Experimentation and Its Worth." Accepting that unlikely assignment, Erica and Mary Ann have a common cause, but Erica, who is already doing erotic dancing in a Gold Coast club, leads the way. Erica's experiences, to write her thesis, include getting paid $500 to do an erotic S/M bisexual dance before a chained woman whom she releases from bondage (nicely photographed, with seductive vocal music). Then, dressed as a guy, complete with moustache, Erica pretends that she's a gay male—so she can have the homosexual experience. In a clever sequence, she blows a guy as a man and quickly turns and offers him her ass—as a male. Poor Mary Ann discovers that Paul Thomas, with whom she has fallen in love, enjoys guys as well as girls. Eventually, she experiences an orgy and is offered Herschel Savage on a platter at a surfer's party. Whether they wrote their psych paper is never revealed.

THE YOUNG STARLETS
CC NN NM BI DK
1976   QUALITY/VIDEO-X-PIX

P/D—**Harry Chow, Terrence Navilius**
F/A—**Maggie Pearson, Susan Deasy, Cynthia Crites, Carol Sands, Mary McMurphy, Barbara Cole**
F/A—**Dave Carson, Tom Hall, Mark Golden, Tony Vrenicar, Mike Epps, Jim Savage**

It's difficult to tell how much of this one is relatively true or totally fake. What gives it a feeling of reality is that, although none of the women above who appears in it (plus a few others), although they all claim to have made other porno films, is recognizable in any pornos I have seen. They are all very average, pretty-to-homely American girls who are presumably telling you how and why they made one or more porno films, and of course you are treated to cuts showing their sexual abilities. The reasons vary. A farm girl working in a restaurant couldn't believe that anyone would offer her $200 just to do what the animals do all the time. Other ladies tell about the advantages of making a porno flick over an eight-to-five job. One gal makes films only with her lover and finds it very exciting to be watched. Another grew up in a home where sex was casual, and she often saw her mother and stepfather making love. Made long before Anthony Spinelli's *Reel People* (see reviews), this one has some of the same flavor.

YOUR TICKET IS NO LONGER VALID
CC R
1978 VESTRON

P/D—Robert Lantos, Stephen Roth, George Kaczender
F/A—Jeanne Moreau, Jennifer Dale
F/A—Richard Harris, George Peppard

This unique film, which probably never "made it" at the box office, is one that you shouldn't miss if you want to see what I predict will create a merger between adult films and R films and will create a huge at-home audience who ultimately will give up trying to find films like this at their local cinemas. With a hair more explicit sex, it would have an X rating. As it is, Jason (Richard Harris), one of the world's top actors, is frequently naked and in bed with Jennifer Dale. Jason is a wealthy businessman who has just married Jennifer, who is in her late 20s. He quickly discovers that he not only has prostrate problems but is quite often impotent as well. His friendly enemy Jim Daisy (George Peppard) is in the same boat, but Jim is still making plenty of money while Jason's financial deals have also taken a turn for the worse. Jason tells Jim bluntly that they are both "pigs" and no damn good, but he really loves his young bride and literally sweats blood to perform with her in bed. He finally decides that he can't cope with his dual problems. He has a multi-million-dollar insurance policy, but his suicide would nullify it. The ending will shock you.

The Education of a Virgin

AWAKENING OF EMILY
NN NM BI
1976 DIAMOND COLLECTION/C.D.I. HOME VIDEO

P/D—Not given
F/A—Holly McCall, Stephanie Boyd
F/A—Herschel Savage, Michael Morrison

If you are an adult-film buff, you'll remember Holly McCall, who kept getting plumper and plumper and finally appeared in *Talk Dirty to Me II* (see review), where she won an award as supporting actress. In this one she's very young and plays a college English teacher who has invited Herschel Savage home to discuss his grades; soon she admits that she's practically a virgin. Later, she and Stephanie Boyd spend 15 minutes or so enjoying each other's genitals. Before you're finished, you will be well acquainted with Holly's labia, which in one film she tied together for fun.

BEAUTY
NN DK BI
1983 VCA

P/D—Warren Evans
F/A—Loni Sanders, Vanessa Del Rio, Laurien Dominique, Mai Lin
F/A—Jamie Gillis, Paul Thomas, Herschel Savage, Michael Morrison

Beauty Marr (Loni Sanders) has two older sisters, Faith and Hope, and a wealthy daddy, Benjamin, who has just returned from New York to his palatial home in San Francisco with some sad news. He has lost his entire fortune gambling with the notorious Martin Gross (Jamie Gillis), who among other things controls most of the pornography industry, owns several professional athletic teams, and is generally known as "the Animal." But Gross has seen a picture of Beauty, and he decides to be generous with Ben. "Send the kid to live with me for one year and you can keep your money and your business."

So, of course, in this version of the fairy tale, Beauty goes to live with the Beast. Surprisingly, while Gross is screwing everything else in sight, he leaves her alone, and eventually he asks her to marry him. You'll never believe that Jamie Gillis could be so nice, but it goes to show what a good woman like Loni with an innocent and virginal face can do to a man.

BLONDES LIKE IT HOT
NN NM BI DK NR (a little)
1984 ESSEX

P/D—Not given
F/A—Mary Monroe, Kathy Kay, Sadrina, Lisa Anderson
F/A—Jeff Moore, Paul French

Rosalie, a country girl, is taken by her mother to the big city (it looks like Nuremberg; the film was made in West Germany), where she will become an office nurse to Doctor Palmer, who is an M.D. with a weird assortment of patients and a secretary, Corinne, who loves him but is not jealous of him. Palmer is married to Bridgitte, who is well aware that her husband plays around but who wants to keep him because he's the best fuck she's ever had. Corinne recognizes Rosalie's possibilities and, presto, with new shoes and hairdo she's transformed. Now, in many scenes she really does look like Marilyn Monroe. Palmer is enthralled and invites Rosalie to a medical convention, which proves to be a quiet weekend at a chalet in the country. There is a very nice sexmaking scene outdoors with the pretty German countryside as a background. But Rosalie's boyfriend, George, has arrived serching for Rosalie, and soon he's in the sack with Bridgitte, who still wants to get "their studs" back to their original mates. She finally accomplishes it at a masquerade party. Before it turns into an orgy, George rescues Rosalie and takes her back home, where Mama catches them in bed and starts making wedding plans.

BROOKE GOES TO COLLEGE
NN BI
1984 VCA

P/D—James George, Robert Gouston
F/A—Brooke Fields, Cody Nicole, Lauri Smith, Jeanne Silvers, Sharon Kane, Carol Cross
F/A—Joey Silvera, Herschel Savage, Michael Knight, David Christopher, Michael Bruce

Brooke Shields was a student at Princeton in 1984—so here's a go-all-out story about Brooke Fields (a name obviously designed for its sound-alike quality). Brooke Fields is a famous movie star who has just made a film, *Paradise Blue* (cf. *Blue Lagoon*), and is now enrolled in State University, where *all* the girls detest her because she still is a virgin, and all the guys dream of screwing her. Brooke Fields looks enough like Brooke Shields so that you couldn't tell them apart on a dark night. She finally surrenders to the captain of the football team, who has screwed her in his dreams several times before. And, of course, all the other ladies at State University spend their study time in the sack.

CHERRY BUSTERS
NN BI DK
1985 VISTA VIDEO

P/D—Hector Castendenda, John Burroughs
F/A—Mindy Rae, Tracy Duzit, Melanie Scott, Fawn Paris, Sasha Gabor
F/A—Buck Adams, Billy Dee

The Cherry Busters, Buck Adams and Tracy Duzit, are swingers who rent their Hollywood home to Mindy Rae and Fawn Paris but first decide to have a going-away party and invite the future renters and their friends. There's no plot, but Melanie Scott, who sometimes plays a virgin (see *Tomboy*), takes on two guys at once and proves, along with all the other ladies, that there wasn't a cherry in the place to begin with.

CHERRYETTES FOR HIRE
NN BI DK DS
1984   FOUR-PLAY VIDEO

P/D—Loretta Sterling, Rock Hardson
F/A—Tiffany Clark, Serena, Maria Tortuga
F/A—Jamie Gillis, John Goodbar

Serena and Tiffany, "fresh from the country," arrive in Los Angeles and are employed by Harry (Jamie Gillis), a nasty guy who runs a strip joint and arranges rough sexual action (bondage and discipline) for his customers. He soon is screwing Serena to a sobbing fare-thee-well, and then he takes on Tiffany, stuffing her panties in her mouth and tying her arms behind her to get her ready for what's coming. Next they are "kidnapped" by a sadistic professor whose theory is that guilt and disgust make sex worthwhile. Naked, gagged, and drugged, they are chained to a wall, stretched out on examining tables, and poked in all their orifices by the professor and his female assistant. It's so corny that you'll have a hard time watching to the end, which finds Jamie in bed with both of them, telling them that it was all a put-on arranged for their benefit.

CORRUPT DESIRES
NN NM BI DK
1983   CABALLERO

P/D—Kim Christy
F/A—Rhonda Chantell, Ivory, Amy Alison, Colleen Brennan
F/A—Ron Jeremy, Johnny Davis, Marc Gold, Johnny Canada

"I can't make you happy in bed," Pamela (Ronda Chantell) tells Claude (Ron Jeremy). "You need to be corrupted and learn obedience," he tells her. It doesn't take Pamela long to be corrupted in this slimy-grimy tape. Under Claude's tutelage, she's soon so horny that she's masturbating and soliciting other guys to eat her while she sucks them and diddles their anuses. She seduces the delivery boy beside the swimming pool in a million-dollar home presumably owned by Claude. Finally, Claude finds her fellating Ivory, a beautiful blonde woman who has a *hard-on!* No kidding! Then Ivory and Pamela tie up Claude, and Ivory gives it to Claude, you know where. Pretty ucky!

EDUCATING MANDY
NN BI NR
1985   CDI HOME VIDEO

P/D—Jim Reynolds, Royce Shepard
F/A—Traci Lords, Christy Canyon, Gina Valentino, Heather Wayne
F/A—Harry Reems, Peter North, Ron Jeremy, Starbuck, Francois Papillon, Craig Roberts

Mandy's (Traci Lords) husband is cheating on her. So she confers with her bisexual girlfriends (played by Heather Wayne and Christy Canyon). In a series of flashbacks from her own life, Christy tries to prove that's the way of men, married or not. Mandy tries to get her revenge by screwing with the pool man. Heather tells her about a plumber who arrived while she was in the shower, but finally Mandy goes to see Jim (Peter North), a lawyer. Jim, it turns out, has wanted her all his life, and of course he will be faithful. Women may not like this film, but men will be entranced with the lush bodies of Traci and Christy.

EDUCATING WANDA
NN NM NL (corny) DK
1984   AMBASSADOR

P/D—Not given
F/A—Not given

Actually, one actress in this hillbilly drama, who has false eyelashes and wears makeup and overalls with nothing underneath, is identified as April Collins. She evidently is virgin Wanda. Her guardian, Uncle Cash, decides that Wanda really does need some sex schooling, and he gives it to her. The guys have pretty big bellies, and the women aren't 18 or very pretty, but it's all shot outdoors (presumably on a farm in the Ozarks), and the dialogue and action are so silly that you can't help smiling occasionally.

FEELS LIKE SILK
NN BI NL DK
1983   SELECT/ESSEX

P/D—William Hemmingway, Alan Everett

F/A—Callie Aimes, Rose Kimball, Jesie St. James, Diana Rogers, Sharon Mitchell
F/A—Jamie Gillis, William Margold, Dave Ruby

This one might deserve a CC rating for the believability of most of the sex encounters—all except one, which should be cut from the tape. This one has William Margold as a sex-crazed sadist who wears an army uniform and carries a riding crop. Sharon Mitchell and Diana Rogers are the stars. Sharon's a waitress, in a hash house where the chef screws the waitresses while Sharon does the cooking. Diana Rogers is a lady who has just arrived in San Francisco from Seattle, Washington, and is the virgin in the big bad city. After one night in a rundown hotel she tells her troubles to Sharon. Thus emerges the axis on which the story is to evolve. Sharon tells her that they can easily find a substantial home—she calls it a villa—close to downtown San Francisco where they will rent rooms to men who want a convenient place to take a woman. The rest of the story is devoted to the various arrivals and what they do in the various bedrooms which Sharon and Diana have wired with see-all closed circuit TV so that they can enjoy the fun.

FORBIDDEN DESIRE
NN BI DK
1984   NOW SHOWING

P/D—Lawrence T. Cole
F/A—Lili Marlene, Rita Cruz, Jesse Adams
F/A—John Toland, Ron Jeremy, John Younger

Why a woman who looks like Diane (Lili Marlene) would go to a bespectacled, homely professor of sexual enhancement and let him tell her how to do it and watch male surrogates show her how to get rid of her inhibitions is a mystery. Our professor (unidentified is the credits) puts her through a series of lessons that include stroking her own behind and anus, getting an oily massage from a guy and a gal who stroke her vagina as well, playing naked outdoors by herself, going to bed with a black stud who will do anything she wants, and screwing with two guys at once, after which she becomes a sexual sandwich.

HOT HONEY
NN BI DK
1977   QUALITY/VIDEO-X-PIX

P/D—Billy Bagg
F/A—Heather Young, Serena, Simone Sinclair, Robin Bird
F/A—Jamie Gillis, Jack Hammer, Bill Berry

Honey (Heather Young) has been going steady with Johnny (Jack Hammer) for four months, but she won't "put out" and she gets angry when he asks her for more than kissing. She finally walks out on him. She's been living with her brother Michael (Jamie Gillis), who has been in an automobile accident and can't walk. Returning home, she watches his nurse, Serena, pick him out of the wheelchair, put him in bed, and go to work on him. Seeing her watching, Serena calls for sisterly help, and soon Honey is learning what sex is all about. She returns to a surprised Johnny and shows him what she has learned.

KINKORAMA
NN BI DK NL
1975   FANTASY/CABALLERO

P/D—Not given
F/A—Not given

Mr. and Mrs. Smith have only recently been married, but they are having sexual problems and visit the famous Dr. Crenshaw (who looks a bit like Gloria Leonard). Seems that Mrs. Smith thinks it's disgusting when Mr. Smith wants to put his tongue in her mouth. How to straighten the lady out? Show her a sex film. I have a feeling, at this point, that the film was put together by combining scenes from a foreign-made film with the problems of Mrs. Smith. Along with her, you watch Elsa taking on the postman because her husband doesn't satisfy her; Lucy, a hired girl on a farm, being taught the facts of life by a repulsive old gap-toothed guy; and Hannah having sex with a priest. In the process, Mrs. Smith sees the light, especially when the doctor joins in and shows her how to suck her husband's cock.

MAKING IT BIG
NN BI
1984   CAL VISTA

P/D—**Vincent Davis**
F/A—**Jacqueline Lorians, Desiree Lane, Justine Love, Sharon Mitchell**
F/A—**Herschel Savage, Paul Thomas, Jerry Davis, Craig Roberts, Mark Wallice, Blake Palmer**

Cherry (Jacqueline Lorians) has won a scholarship to the Dumar School of Acting in San Francisco. She arrives from the country determined to make it big. If you expected that it would be a real school of acting, forget it. It's a school for learning how to fuck and suck properly, run by Dolly Dumar (Sharon Mitchell). Cherry is in competition with the only other student, Liz (Desiree Lane), for the honor of an audition by Herschel Savage, who is a big Hollywood producer.

MELANIE'S HOT LINE
NN BI DK DS
1972   COMPETITIVE VIDEO

P/D—**Gordon Ambers, Christopher Shaw**
F/A—**Angela, Margaret McCallum, Laurie Busch**
F/A—**Theodore Von Unkle**

The "hot line" refers to obscene phone calls that Melanie and her boyfriend make while Melanie's parents are away for the weekend. In the process they reach a woman screwing with a black guy who suggests to Melanie that it's more fun doing it than talking about it—so she tells Melanie's boyfriend, over the phone, how to proceed with Melanie, who presumably is a virgin. After that's over, she suggests on the phone that they all get together for a party, and they'll bring "The Whip," another black guy. Presto—you're watching "The Whip" in action with a masochistic white woman. Tying and chaining her to the cellar rafters, he whips her nearly unconscious, and then as she's hanging there, he masturbates her with a dildo, and proceeds to fuck her. Next scene they are all at Melanie's house and Melanie gets screwed and dildoed in a weekend vanilla-and-chocolate whip-cream fuck festival. Pretty seamy. But it

proves that you shouldn't make obscene phone calls—even in fun.

NAUGHTY NANETTE
NN BI DK
1984   VCA

P/D—**Leon Gucci**
F/A—**Desiree Lane, Karen Summer, Crystal Blue, Beverly Bliss, Jay Sterling**
F/A—**Francois Papillon, Jimmy Star, Nick Niter, Steve Powers, Doug Bennett**

In this one, Desiree Lane, who is presumably retiring from adult films, plays a 15-year-old nymphette. Wearing a little-girl blonde wig, she is first seen, with a swaying ass, walking through the streets to visit her daddy in his office. Daddy keeps her waiting while he screws his secretary (Karen Summers), who has just finished soothing Nanette's overheated vulva in the outer office. But Nanette is still not satiated, and she goes on to have sex with the grocery boy and six of Dad's clients.

RAW FOOTAGE
NN BI NL (occasionally)
1977   CABALLERO

P/D—**Walter D. Roberts**
F/A—**Marlene Willoughby, Lyn Manstone, Mary Ann Sweet**
F/A—**Wade Nichols, Larry Cox**

Here's an "oldie" that proves that some of the adult films made in the 1970s are more interesting (more dialogue, slower-paced stories, more naive, and less kinky) than many of those made in the 1980s. This one features Marlene Willoughby, who was even skinnier than she is now, as one of four high-school seniors whose horny guidance counselor, Wade Nichols, gets them jobs as apprentices in an ad agency as part of a high-school scholarship program. So there are two plots. In the secondary plot, the girls demoralize the ad agency, of course. But in the more interesting one, Wade Nichols is intent on seducing each one of the girls, some of whom are virgins. He does, but he gets it in the end.

Comedies

ALVIN PURPLE
R NL
1985 NEW WORLD VIDEO

P/D—Tom Burstall
F/A—Christine Amor, Valerie Blake, Diana Mann, Jacki Weaver, and many more
F/A—Graeme Blundell, George Whaley

The date on this one is the U.S. distribution date. The film was actually made in Australia in 1973 and proves, if nothing else, that the Aussies have a wonderful sexual sense of humor (see review of *Alvin Rides Again* and *Don's Party*.) Alvin Purple (Graeme Blundell), from the time he is 16, not only loves girls but can't think of anything except girls' breasts and pussies. They evidently feel the same way and can't wait to get their hands on his cock. The story covers Alvin's career from school to college, where a professor's wife, who is only 38, wants to mother him, to his appearance some years later at a party when he is unemployed but looking for the right job to suit his talents. Women are still popping up naked every time he turns around and are trying to bed him. Alvin becomes a bogus psychologist, and the women pour in. Adult-film producers should study this tape and learn how to produce a sex film with laughter.

ALVIN PURPLE RIDES AGAIN
R
1985 NEW WORLD VIDEO

P/D—Tom Burstall
F/A—Graeme Blundell, Alan Finney, George Whaley, Noel Ferrier
F/A—Jacki Weaver, Penny Hackforth Jones, Elli Maclure, Jill Forster, Abigail

The original Alvin Purple film (see above) was made in 1973, and I'd guess this sequel, which probably never got to the United States, was made a year or two later. Like the previous film, it begins with Benny Hill–style sex comedy and insanity. All women, young and old, can't wait to get Alvin into the sack. But then, unfortunately, sex takes a backseat.

BODACIOUS TA TAS
NN BI NL
CABALLERO

P/D—Paul Vatelli
F/A—Bridgette Monet, Patti Wright, Kitten Natividad, Pat Manning, Rosie Marie
F/A—Ron Jeremy, Dave Cannon, Greg Ruffner

Bodacious, in case you don't know, is a perfectly good English word meaning reckless or abandoned. Add *ta tas*, tits of course, and you have a useful way of classifying some mammaries. This is the weekend story of Jim, who is about to get married to Alice. His wealthy buddies, one of whom owns a Beverly Hills–style home and whose wife has gone away with Alice for the weekend, decide to take Jim on a last bash to a strip club where the above-named ladies perform. Before the evening is over, Ron Jeremy has arranged for a paid weekend with Bridgette, Patti, and Kitten, and you know after you've watched them at the strip club that they are going to be tops in the sack. Soon everyone is playing switches. The best thing about this one is the extended stripping. Bridgette and Patti are pretty good at it, but you ain't seen nothing until you've watched Kitten (one of Russ Meyer's favorites) shaking her tits and ass in the customers' faces. But in this one, Kitten, who says she likes to watch "girls get cornholed," never takes on any men.

BODY GIRLS
NN NL BI DK
1984 ESSEX

P/D—Bob Chinn
F/A—Hyapatia Lee, Robin Everett, Erica Boyer, Shanna McCullough, Desiree Lane, Tigr, Anne Thomas, Lona Emerson
F/A—Bud Lee, Francois, Eric Edwards

Jackie LaLay (Hyapatia Lee, who is wearing too much makeup in this one) owns a health club and gym specializing in female body development. She is assisted by her friend Jim Wilder (Bud Lee) and a handsome Frenchman, Arnold Feragano (Francois), who is an expert on the female body. The screenplay was written by Bud and Hyapatia could have made a very funny film, but the story of two guys (one very plump) who run a competing gym and want their gals to win the upcoming women's body-building contest got lost in the gymnasium, where all of the ladies listed above spend most of their time "developing the real muscle" of the gym's male patrons. In one amusing scene, the two male competitors are stripped by the girls and suspended from stirrups while Jackie sticks a dildo up the ass of one of them and another gal prepares an alum enema to shrink their assholes. The Laurel-and-Hardy aspect of this sequence could have been hilarious, especially if the fat guy had been shown completely naked, but except for one final scene, you never see the guys again. The film ends with Hyapatia (under the table) sucking the cocks of Francois, who is the judge (to make sure her girls win), and Eric Edwards, the TV commentator of the event. If your tape player runs in slow motion, try it on the long sequence with Bud Lee happily lapping Anne Thomas's vulva. He's an expert pussyeater. Bud and Hyapatia are married (like many porno stars).

CARNAL OLYMPICS
NN NM BI DK
1983 HIFCOA

P/D—**Troy Benny**
F/A—**Gayle Sterling, Susan Kay, Denise Damiano, Danielle Colleen, Rhonda Jo Petty**
F/A—**Herschel Savage, Hardy Cahuen, Bruce Murphy, Don Fernando, Tony Cassano, Paul Harmon**

Carlos Tobalina, a.k.a. Troy Benny, is a handsome, laughing man who appears in most of his films. He's never naked or copulating, but he makes up for it by giving those who enjoy it a fucking marathon. (He even has a film of the same title; see review.) In this one, a contest is being run by a men's magazine to find the hottest adult-film star. It ends in an unbelievable orgy, during which the ladies service 20 or more men and collect their semen in buckets. Carlos made this one when his wife wasn't watching.

DAISY CHAIN
NN NL BI DK
1985 STANDARD VIDEO

P/D—**Helen Terrie, Kirdy Stevens**
F/A—**Karen Summer, Tantala, Crystal Breeze, Cynthia Brooks, Lisa Lake, Colleen Brennan**
F/A—**Nick Random, Peter North, Kevin James, Francois Papilion**

Wealthy Phyllis Chandler (Colleen Brennan) wants to produce a porno movie starring Luke Lancer (Kevin James), largely because she wants to enjoy Luke's cock. The movie, titled *Daisy Chain*, will be produced by Bob Nigel (Nick Random), who thinks that Luke "has a cock for a brain." Sara Jane (Karen Summer) is the script girl and gofer who would rather be producing documentaries but isn't averse to fluffing a male actor's cock when necessary, or lapping various female pussies. The entire film is devoted to the making of the movie, and there are some funny scenes. You may think that you are watching behind-the-scenes the shooting of a porno film, but it is usually much more prosaic than this, and for the most part probably never ends up in an extended daisy-chain orgy, as this one does.

DALLAS SCHOOLGIRLS
NN BI NL (bucolic)
1981 VIDEO-X-PIX

P/D—**Seaman Louche, John Christopher**
F/A—**Tiffany Clark, Bobbi Jackson, Misty Middleton, Samantha Fox**
F/A—**Ron Jeremy, Eric Ryan, George Payne, Ron Hudd**

With the exception of Samantha Fox, the above young ladies get together at the home of one of them for summer vacation. They are immediately seen by Mr. Cobb, a fat, 40ish, balding handyman, who spies on them and provides the presumed comedy between six episodes that they relate to each other about their past sexual experiences as they play strip poker in one of the girl's bedrooms.

DEAR FANNY
NN BI NL (grade-school level) DK
1985 CAL VISTA

P/D—Sam Norvell, Robert McCallum
F/A—Janey Robbins, Gina Carrera, Mimi, Danielle, Pamela Jennings
F/A—Ron Jeremy, Billy Dee, R. Bolla, Nick Random

Here's another sexvid based on an advice-to-the-lovelorn column. Janey Robbins is "Dear Fanny," who answers a series of letters with the help of her assistant, Ron Jeremy, who helpfully stirs Fanny's morning coffee with his prick. A postman wearing a cock's head brings the morning mail and gets his cock serviced by another female assistant while Fanny deliberates over her letter problems, which of course are dramatized. At the end, Fanny reveals *her* fantasy. You guessed it ... in the fanny!

DEBBIE DOES DALLAS II
NN BI DK
1983 CABALLERO

P/D—Jim Clarke
F/A—R. Bolla, Ron Jeremy, Spike Adrian, Ron Hudd, Bobby Cohen
F/A—Bambi Woods, Lisa Cintrice, Ashley Welles, Daniella, Jeanne Silver, Lisa Bee, Bell Stevens

If Bambi Woods's plaintive face, skinny body and big breasts appeal to you, you may want to see Part II. Originally titled *The Best Little Whore in Texas* (but withdrawn for fear of legal problems), it offers a local Sheriff Little John (Ron Hudd) who keeps Aunt Sadie's Chicken Ranch in business. But the ranch isn't located in Texas, and it seems that poor Debbie is broke and has hitchhiked her way to some place in Northern California (it's snow covered) where Sadie, who really is her aunt, runs the whore house. Before she gets there she's picked up by the Sheriff who is sure that she's a hustler and probably selling drugs. He sticks her in the pokey (pun intended) and forces her to strip and searches her (you know where) looking for drugs. Having no choice, she works her way into

his good graces and he delivers her to Aunt Sadie, who tells her she can't stay. (Sadie thinks she's a good girl.) But Debbie is quickly introduced to carnal sin by several of the house ladies who take her to bed and convince her, somewhat reluctantly, that sex with women is just as much fun as with men. Unfortunately, *The Best Little Whorehouse* story never really gels.

DIRTY BLONDE
NN NM BI (lots of) DK
1984 VIDEO-X-PIX

P/D—Howard A. Howard, Eric Anderson
F/A—Danielle, Carol Cross, Cody Nicole, Honey Wilder, Renee Summers, Sharon Mitchell
F/A—Michael Knight, George Payne, Alan Adrian, Joey Silvera, David Scott

It was a toss-up whether to give this one a CC rating. It has a funny premise, the story of a guy who is such a red-hot lover that all the ladies want him, including his divorced wife, and his new fiancée. But he has disappeared. It also has Honey Wilder, one of the few sexy ladies (in her 40s, my guess) who is still making sexvids and is a pretty good actress. But the story gets lost here and there in the screwing and the bisexuality.

ECSTASY IN BLUE
NN BI NL DK
1978 QUALITY/VIDEO-X-PIX

P/D—Dexter Eagle
F/A—Annie Sprinkles, Terri Hall, C. J. Laing, Helen Madigan, Crystal Sync
F/A—Mark Stevens, Bobby Astyr, Jeffrey Hurst

Here's a 1970s film that hasn't much of a plot but has funny dialogue and good cinematography that will keep you amused. Manny (Mark Stevens, who is famous for his 10½-inch cock but is now retired from adult films), is the leader of his own cult of women who worship his cock. His assistant, Charley (Bobby Astyr), must find acolytes for him. He has little difficulty.

EXECUTIVE SECRETARY
NN BI NL DK
1975   FANTASY/CABALLERO

P/D—Not given
F/A—C. J. Laing, Cindy Reems, C. Gale Leonard
F/A—Big John, Bobby Astyr

This one features a very young Bobby Astyr, who runs a model agency. He's married and has a mistress (Gloria Leonard, I think; the credits identify her as C. Gale Leonard) who tells him that he better not cheat on her with his wife. He also has a secretary (C. J. Laing) whom he keeps imagining naked and who, although he doesn't know it, is planning to take over as both his mistress and his wife. This may be one of the first films that skinny C. J. Laing made. Bobby Astyr is a guy her own size, and they're both so bony that they look like a plucked chicken and a rooster when they fornicate. (See notes under *Christy.*)

FANTASEX ISLAND
NN BI DK
1984   NOW SHOWING

P/D—Lawrence T. Cole
F/A—Serena, Juliet Anderson, Holly McCall, Valerie Darling
F/A—John Leslie, Paul Thomas, Pu Pu

Here's an adult version of "Fantasy Island," complete with a midget and a guy named Dork who can offer males the chance to live out their fantasies. But I have a suspicion that, other than a tie-together provided by Dork and the midget Pu Pu, the rest of this film is a number of cleverly cut-in loops that were produced for other fantasy daydreams. They include a black cowboy who wants to experience a lady in a brothel, a Victorian card sharp who sells his sister to brothel owner Juliet Anderson, and John Leslie listening to one guy's story about screwing with a 13-year-old virgin. Leslie also appears in an unrelated loop with Holly McCall, who is listed in the credits as Holly Near. All through it, in the tie-together, Pu Pu complains that he's the only one who never gets laid. You keep thinking he will, but alas, he never does.

FANTASY FOLLIES II
NN NL DK BI
1983   VCA

P/D—Peter Eastwood, Drea
F/A—Serena, Tiffany Clark, Kay Parker, Becky Savage
F/A—Herschel Savage, Ron Jeremy, Eric Edwards, William Margold

This potpourri of silliness, conceived by Bill Margold, consists of stories told by Serena, who is in bed with a cold, to Becky Savage. The stories presumably reveal the lives of porno stars at home and on the set. They include birthday parties involving happy orgies, complete with birthday cakes and balloons and six or more couples eating each other while a bewildered puppy watches; woman who becomes the hors d'oeuvres; and naked ladies and guys wandering around a butcher's freezer labeled as hamburgers, pork chops, etc. Despite her cold, Serena and Becky end the follies by lapping each other from head to foot. The reason for the NL is a scene that has nothing to do with the rest of the tape and may well have occurred on a film set. Kay Parker suddenly gets the giggles as Eric Edwards is screwing her, and in take after take she continues to burst into inappropriate laughter so that finally everyone is laughing, too. Goes to show you that sex with laughter is one of the joys that most adult-film makers miss . . . including Bill Margold.

FANTASY LAND
NN BI DK
1985   L.A. VIDEO

P/D—Ned Morehead
F/A—Susan Hart, Brandy Alexander, Jay Sterling, Mindy Rae, Colleen Brennan, Sheri St. Clare, Nikki Dee
F/A—Harry Reems, Billy Dee, Robert Necki, Buck Adams

Another "Fantasy Island" takeoff. This one comes with Harry Reems as "Boss." Instead of a midget, he has Toto (Susan Hart), who talks with the proper accent. This one offers you five fantasies, which include Colleen Brennan, who is tired of being a wimp and wants to have a rough and tough cow-puncher lover, around the turn of the century. Next is a husband who is dominated by his wife but finally manages to take over. Two guys who would like to take on one chick at the same time also get their wish. Then there's a guy who would like to screw a big-breasted lady, and presto! he saves one from drowning in a nearby pool; he's soon drowning himself, between her tits and vagina. Two ladies lost in a forest are looking for cock, which suddenly appears in the form of a horny guy. The three of them are quickly zapped into a king-size bed. Finally, Boss/Harry gets his fantasy realized, too—a humping with Toto.

FLESH POND
NN NM DK BI
1983   HIFCOA

P/D—Troy Benny
F/A—Rita Ricardo, Shawn Mitchell, Candy Hart, Minx St. Clair, Raquel Martine, Drea
F/A—Helman and Carlos Tobalina, Reggie Gunn, Jack Mason, Tony Leigh

If you watch many sexvids, you'll discover that many directors have clearly definable styles and that you can practically identify "whodunit" even if his name is not given. This is true of Troy Benny, a.k.a. Carlos Tobalina, Kim Christy, Henri Pachard, and many others. Unlike Kim Christy, Troy Benny conveys an underlying sense of sexual silliness in his sexvids. But I'd take a guess that for the most part a film like this one will turn the average woman off. Uninterrupted sexual athletics are given temporary dramatic relief when two escaped convicts invade the flesh-pond party and "force" some sex on the participants at gunpoint. But most of the film, with no story, is nothing you haven't seen before—in spades. Some day Carlos Tobalina will find a happy-go-lucky story. Then he'll produce and direct a film which will not only be sexy but will keep you laughing. Hopefully, he will be the hero in it! In the meantime, as a change of pace, try *Anticipation, Lady Dynamite,* and *Casanova, Part II* (see reviews), which I have given

CC ratings and which prove that Troy/Carlos can produce romantic, sexy films, too!

A FORMAL FAUCETT
NN BI
1978   VCX

P/D—Vincenzo Rossi, Fred Lincoln
F/A—Norma Gene, Tina Austin, Lauri Blue
F/A—Ken Struder, Blair Davis, Rusty Rhodes

A take-off on "Charlie's Angels." The entire tape is devoted to Angel Faucett (Norma Gene) happily blowing and screwing various clients until she becomes the star of a TV detective series in which young ladies are exposed to dangers of all sorts.

HEAVEN'S TOUCH
NN BI DK
1983   CABALLERO

P/D—Warren Evans
F/A—Kelly Nichols, Joanna Storm, Sharon Kane, Gail Sterling
F/A—Michael Knight, Ron Jeremy

This one tries too hard for laughs and gives you a twist in the story that makes it totally ridiculous. Seems that Harry Artinger (Michael Knight), who is an upper-income executive, spends most of his time screwing every young woman in his office. Trying to satisfy them, he drops dead, but it seems that he has arrived in heaven before his time. With the help of an angel, he comes back to earth and takes over the body of Barry Armstrong, who owns the company he formerly worked for. He knows that he is Artinger, but no one else does. What happens to Barry isn't clear. But Barry's wife (Sharon Kane), and their butler, Finch (Ron Jeremy), have been wishing that Barry were dead. They have devised a sure means to accomplish it: A lady named Carlotta (Kelly Nichols) has lost quite a few husbands in the saddle, and she agrees, for a million bucks, to fuck Barry to death. Needless to say, she doesn't succeed. Finally, Barry's wife, who hasn't slept with him for three years, manages to do it, after which Henry/Barry returns to life as Bill Douglas and is obviously ready to start all over again.

HINDSIGHT
NN BI DK NL (guys may laugh but not gals)
1985 ISLAND HOME VIDEO

P/D—Richard Mailer
F/A—Heather Wayne, Stacey Donovan, Nicole West, Gina Valentino
F/A—Herschel Savage, R. Bolla, Craig Roberts, Greg Rome

Harry (R. Bolla) and R.J. (Herschel Savage) both consider themselves the world's best lover. Their girlfriends, Candy (Heather Wayne) and Carol (Stacey Donovan), who have screwed with both of them, agree that they are great but refuse to say which one is better. So they decide the only way to win the bet that escalates to $100,000 is by training a male who knows nothing about sex. Jeff (Craig Roberts) fills the bill. Before it's all over, Jeff, their enthusiastic pupil, decides that he, not either of them, is the world's greatest lover. Most women would give them all a Bronx cheer.

HOT NURSES
NN BI DK NL (bar-room style)
1977 CABALLERO

P/D—Anna Riva, Harold Hindgrind
F/A—Marlene Willoughby, Crystal Sync
F/A—John Holmes, Eric Edwards, Jeffrey Hurst, Zebedy Colt

If you enjoy burlesque-style explicit sex, you may like this one. It begins in an ambulance with a nurse keeping a guy alive by blowing him and the intern using a toilet plunger on his chest. When Doctor Mort (John C. Holmes) remarks, "Mrs. Schwartz needs an injection," you know what she gets. Marlene Willoughby is a fastidious nurse who puts on surgical gloves before she handles John's prick. And so on.

INDIANA JOAN IN THE BLACK HOLE OF MAMMOO
NN BI DK
1984 VCA

P/D—Not given
F/A—Barbie Dahl, Sara Bernard, Hazel Scott, Satin Summer
F/A—Melvin Ward, George Payne, Michel Le Boeuf

Joan (Barbie Dahl) is on some kind of expedition in the Polynesian islands. The ship explodes (all you ever see of it is the waves made by the prop). Next scene, Joan, her daddy, and Captain Jim are floating in a life raft and Joan, from lack of water, is hallucinating that she's sucking Captain Jim's cock. Quickly, after they float onto an island, Daddy is speared by a female cannibal and dies. Joan and Jim screw and soon they are captured. It turns out that Mama, who was on board the ship, too, has pulled Big Chief Mammoo's plug and he thinks that every thing is "unko dunko," which means that he enjoys white meat. Immediately, the pretty black native girls (Hazel Scott and Satin Summer) and the white survivors are happily integrated in an orgy.

LOVE IN STRANGE PLACES
NN BI NL (maybe, if you're whacked out, too) DK DS
1972 CABALLERO

P/D—Robert D. Walter
F/A—John Holmes, Jeffrey Hurst, Zebedy Colt, Eric Edwards
F/A—Janet Succatit, Cathy Bunmuddler, Marlene Willoughby

This is a totally whacked-out 1970s–style adult film featuring a young John Holmes as Doctor Hook, a surgeon, and Doctor Fraud, a psychiatrist, who are in charge of a hospital for the sexually insane. A new nurse, Nancy Blue, has just arrived and can't believe her eyes when she sees the various patients, who include a Cleopatra, a Napoleon and his Josephine, an Alexander Graham Bell, and assorted other sexual nuts, who receive psychodrama sex therapy, which ends up in a total orgy and one of the nurses being plied vaginally with a banana and anally with a carrot.

LUSTFULLY SEEKING SUSAN
NN BI DK
1985   TARGET VIDEO

P/D—**Jonathan Burroughs**
F/A—**Sondra Stillman, Summer Rose, Gabriella, Tiffany Duponte**
F/A—**Buck Adams, Billy Dee, D. T. Mann**

This is a very amateurish quickie, shot on video using the *Desperately Seeking Susan* theme (see review of *Once Upon a Madonna*). Susan in this one is Sondra Stillman, and the guy she robs after screwing him to a fare-thee-well is Billy Dee. The director gives you graphic close-ups of this long sequence, and when video is lighted this way you can count the pores on the actor's skin—not to mention the pimples on Sondra's behind. The woman who wishes to be Susan is Summer Rose, who is married to a guy who doesn't take care of her properly, but as soon as she's gone to become Susan, he does very well with two of his next-door neighbors. The whole, silly business is pretty hammily acted.

THE MATING SEASON
NN BI DK
1984   VCA

P/D—**Damon Aldrich**
F/A—**Julie Colt, Pamela Jennings, Renee Tiffany**
F/A—**Eric Edwards, Ric Lutze, Marc Goldberg**

Richard Aldrich, a.k.a. Damon Christian, had a good idea—make a really sexy version of *The Four Seasons*, which you'll remember was written by Alan Alda. Unfortunately, Aldrich spends so much time showing the actual screwing of the three couples involved, with so little character development, that the actors are indistinguishable one from the other and it's not funny.

MENAGE A TROIS
NN NL BI DK
1981   COMMAND

P/D—**Chuck Vincent, Ely Wooper**
F/A—**Jean Pierre Armand, Yvon Slave, Birdey Sylvie**

Presumably the theater version of this film is in 3-D, but the tape I have is in regular color with surprisingly few places where 3-D might have worked to make it sexier. And while Chuck Vincent is listed as producer, more likely he simply controls the rights to the American version of a French film. Unfortunately, instead of leaving it entirely in the original French (there isn't that much dialogue that you can't figure out), a W. C. Fields voice-over is added, reciting dirty limericks with responses from a Mae West–style voice, which adds nothing to the story. You can find grosser and funnier limericks in best-selling paperbacks, and if you are looking for a story, there isn't one. But I nearly gave it a CC rating for the three French girls, who live together and are very pretty and who love each other even more than do the guys who are watching them from an apartment across the street. The action presumably takes place on the day and night before Christmas. The guys arrive dressed as Santa Clauses, and in one case all three ladies work over his seemingly inexhaustible penis while he comments in ecstatic French. Another Santa Claus produces whip and leather garments, which the ladies' housekeeper (who is pretty plump) seems shocked by but quickly enjoys. It all ends up under the Christmas tree in an extended orgy, and since there are only two guys it requires double-ended dildos to take care of the lusty ladies. In the things-you-don't-usually-see department, one of the ladies, before performing her morning ablutions, enjoys a long and satisfying piss while the camera records every last drop.

ORIFICE PARTY
NN BI DK (cuckoo style)   DS (pretending)
1985   GOLD MEDALLION

P/D—**Damon Christian, Eric Edwards**
F/A—**Jessyca Wylde, Christy Canyon**
F/A—**Herschel Savage, Bobby Bullock, Steve Taylor, Nick Random**

Richard Aldrich, a.k.a. Damon Christian, is chief honcho of the Great American

Soap Opera Company, and evidently with this tape he has decided to distribute his own stuff. The big problem with the "story" is that you'll have a hard time telling the difference between what is "reality" and what is "fantasy" and whether the dialogue is funny or just sheer insanity. The action takes place in the offices of the Ajax Shipping Company, which in addition to handling regular freight also distributes porno movies. Jessyca Wylde has an English accent and a beautiful body that makes the tape less painful to watch.

PASSIONATE LEE
NN BI DK NL
1985   CREATIVE VIDEO

P/D—Sol Starr, Phil Marshak
F/A—Sharon Mitchell, Kimberly Carson, Bunny Bleu, Amber Lynn, Tiffany Renee
F/A—Jerry Butler, Ron Jeremy, Paul Thomas, Shone Tee, William Margold

"I'm getting out of this business. I'm going nuts," Lee Fontaine (Sharon Mitchell) tells her agent, Bill Margold (who along with Mark Weiss wrote the scenario for this one; see review of *Space Virgins*). "Have you any idea of how many cum shots I've had in my face in the past two days?" she continues. "Twelve! I used to like it, but I don't anymore!" Margold suggests a rest cure in the suburbs at his sister's house, where there is crabgrass and soap operas and everything that Lee misses about a normal life. Unfortunately, she's recognized by Eddy, who is the best friend of Margold's nephew. Complications ensue.

PIGGY'S
NN DK
1983   VCA

P/D—James George, Robert Houston
F/A—Lauri Smith, Blair Castle, Annette Heinz
F/A—Jerry Butler, Richard Knight, Paul George Payne

As in *Porky's*, if you saw those films, there's a bad guy, B. J. Westgate (Paul Thomas),

who owns a bar in Swamptown and is running for mayor. His competition is a rundown bar owned by Sylvia Morehead (Annette Heinz), who lives up to her screen name by blowing everyone in sight, including her son's friend, Jerry Butler. Jerry and George have just graduated from college and can't get a job, so they go to work in Ma's bar and soon find a formula that takes all the business away from B.J.'s. Live sex, of course.

R.S.V.P.
R NL
1983   PLATINUM PICTURES

P/D—Chuck Vincent, John Amero, Lew Amero
F/A—Lynda Weismeler, Veronica Hart, Kat Shea
F/A—Adam Mills, Harry Reems, Ray Culbert

The problem with this movie, which Playboy presumably helped finance, is that there are too many characters. I would estimate at least 30 are invited to Bill Edwards's (Adam Mills) luxurious home in Beverly Hills to audition, or just show their bodies, in the hopes that they might be cast in a new movie. The idea of building a story around a party, even this one, could be funny. If you want to watch it done by an expert, see *Don's Party*, an Australian film, which is also rated R and is much sexier and funnier.

ROMANCING THE BONE
NN BI NM
1984   VCA

P/D—Vince Benedetti
F/A—Barbie Dahl, Candace Daley, Hazel Scott, Satin Summer, Sharon Kane, Tasha Voux
F/A—George Payne, David Christopher, Frank Lance

You have to admit that adult-film producers have wild imaginations when it comes to renaming Hollywood films. The only resemblance between this one and the Michael Douglas film is George Payne, who is made up to resemble him a little. As Ron Sticker, a famous porno actor, he is reviewing his film of the above title for his fans. Sequences from the film first show him with what is called the "African duet"—Hazel Scott and Satin Summer. They live up to the film title by giving Ron an awe-inspiring mouth and vaginal wash while in between they take care of each other. Next Barbie Dahl, in what is supposed to be the Cave of the Rain, is overwhelmed by Ron's bone, and he explores her vulva in some close-up detail.

SEX IN THE COMICS
NN NL BI
1982   VCA

P/D—Huntington Shtup, Eric Von Letch
F/A—Bella Bush, Mona Bimbo, Clara Clit
F/A—Lance Hardon, Fenway Piles, Reggie Ball

You wouldn't expect live actors in a tape with this title, but as you can see above, the actors weren't about to identify themselves. Interestingly, I've never seen any of them before or since, but the men and women who made this tape, acting out various comic heros and heroines, obviously enjoyed themselves. The comic characters include Moon Mullins, Major Hoople, Dagwood, Dixie Duggan, Fritzie Ritz, and Dick Tracy. The guys wore comic masks, and the skits, which run one after another, are burlesque or "Laugh-In" style in format and occasionally will make you laugh.

SEXCAPADES
NN NL BI DK
1983   VCA

P/D—David Stone, Henry Pachard
F/A—Sharon Mitchell, Ashley Welles, Joanna Storm, Sharon Kane, Lee Carroll, Tiffany Clark
F/A—Eric Edwards, Michael Bruce, George Payne

Henri Pachard is evidently intrigued with the concept of the director, Harry Crocker (played by Eric Edwards in this film and also *Sexpectations*—see review), who

thinks of himself as a filmmaker and would prefer to be making regular films. In any event, he informs his wife, Miriam (Sharon Mitchell), who was shocked by his previous career, that like it or not he must make another porno film because they're broke and have been living too high off the hog in their town house on the Upper East Side of New York City. He's going to use the town house and a story line of a guy like himself who is trying to make it with the maid because his wife isn't that great in bed anymore. There are some funny behind-the-scenes shots of porno filmmaking as the crew, actors, and actresses invade the house. Poor Harry—Henri better forget him until he dares to tell a more believable story about a porno-film director.

SLIP UP
NN BI NL (Captain Billy Whizzbang style)
1974   CABALLERO

P/D—Robert Walters
F/A—Darby Lloyd Raines, Candida
F/A—Jamie Gillis, Mark Stevens, Eric Edwards

Here's another early porno made about the same time as *Deep Throat*, when many sexvids were totally slapstick and offered burlesque sequences with explicit sex. Most of these tapes are widely available and appeal to many male audiences. The story, such as it is, takes place at the Tighttwat Institute for Sexual Research, where Herman Killacunt (Jamie Gillis) has invented an electrotesticular cock erector. He tells Penelope Juiceslit, his nurse, that, given the right atmospheric conditions, he can give every male in the United States a permanent hard-on, and when they are seeking to relieve their agony he will take over the government. Before Herman is stopped in his dastardly scheme, Penelope has sex with Sam Suckatitty and Mr. Cherrypopper (Eric Edwards). Mark Stevens and Darby no longer make sexvids, but there are plenty of directors still turning out similar stuff.

STRIP FOR ACTION
NN (without erections being shown) NM BI NL (a little)
1982 MEDIA

P/D—Erwin Dietrich, Michael Thomas
F/A—Marianne Dupont, Christa Free
F/A—Michael Jacot, Mika Erras

Poor Elsie (Marianne Dupont)—she has beautiful legs, a classic pear-shaped ass, but only cupcakes for breasts. Be that as it may, Elsie is told by her ballet instructor that she better take up some other kind of dancing. So she goes to a male agent who specializes in hiring strippers for Amsterdam night clubs, where this film was probably made. Unfortunately, without big tits, she isn't going to be a star in this world either. What else can she do? She can try, unsuccessfully, to fuck her way to the top. The film concludes with a funny scene where Elsie goes into a sex shop patronized only by men, where she innocently plays with the vibrators and dildos while they watch in awe. For what it's worth—this is a soft-core film.

TEENAGE NURSES
NN NL (burlesque style) NR (one scene) DK
1975 QUALITY VIDEO

P/D—Oscar Tripe
F/A—Veronica Mellon, Sandy Morelli, Janet Champer, Nancy Wang
F/A—George Haucks, Fred Perna

Can you laugh at amputees in a Veterans Hospital in Bethesda, Maryland? After you watch this one you'll wonder if it was made just to show to war veterans, for laughs. Dr. Canute is assigned to change the entertainment program at the hospital, and soon he has the wildest collection of homely nurses you've ever seen, happily copulating with the doctors and amputees. Sick stuff.

WET, WILD AND WICKED
NN NM BI NL (occasionally)
1985 ESSEX

P/D—Thomas Paine
F/A—Colleen Brennan, Tracy Duzit, Becky Savage, Tantalia
F/A—Ron Jeremy, Harry Reems, Jerry Butler, John Johnson

Johnny Beamer (Ron Jeremy) has just graduated from college and is now a television engineer. His former roommate leaves him with an empty four-bed apartment, which he advertises in the university housing ads. Soon he has Colleen, Becky, and Tracy as roommates, and they immediately lay down the house rules: He can keep his hands off their asses. It's not easy for him because, in the meantime, the ladies are working their asses off entertaining their boyfriends all over the house. To get his revenge, unknown to them, he videotapes the action and sells it to a porno dealer. The tape includes Harry Reems enjoying two of them at once and an amusing kitchen fuck. Finally, the gals have pity on Beamer and take him on, but when they discover that he's been taping them, they throw him out of his own apartment. It ends with Beamer advertising for new roommates.

Historical

BEDTIME TALES
NN NM BI DK
1984 ESSEX

P/D—J. Essex, Daniel Morgan
F/A—Colleen Brennan, Honey Wilder, Karen Summer
F/A—John Leslie, Randy West, Paul Thomas

Five 15-minute, or less, loops presumably reflecting the sexual mores of the past 70 years. The Victorian era, the Jazz Age, the '30s, and the '50s pass. Finally, when you're happy it's coming to an end, it's 1985 and the participants, who are role-playing sex, can no longer distinguish reality from fantasy. You won't believe that people could spend their time making or acting in such yucky stuff.

CASANOVA II
CC NN NM NR BI
1982 HIFCOA

P/D—Troy Benny
F/A—Jesie St. James, Rhonda Jo Petty, Danielle, Shiela Parks, Anne Perry
F/A—John C. Holmes, Bjorn Beck, Carlos Tobalina, William Margold, Bill Kershner, Dorian Kupl

This is a better film than the *Erotic Adventures of Casanova* (see review), which also starred John C. It opens in Paris in 1751 with the arrival of Casanova (John C. Holmes), who gets involved in a duel during which he wounds a woman dressed as a man. She doesn't die from his sword but swoons over his schlong and gets pregnant with a son whom they name Don Juan. The same secret perfume that you couldn't smell in *Casanova's Erotic Adventures* (it's an aphrodisiac) is still available. Using it, Don Juan screws a good percentage of the young ladies of Europe. The costumes and acting are pretty good, and you will be surprised to hear Beethoven's *Eroica* as background music to one happy orgasm. Like the original, the film shifts to the 20th century, with the magic perfume coming to the aid of mankind in a surprise ending. You'll watch this one all the way through.

OPEN NIGHTLY
NN BI BL DK
1982 CABALLERO

P/D—Frances LeRoi
F/A—Julia Perrier, Sophie Dawson, Marilyn
F/A—Clyde Gerrard

The time is the early 1920s, in France. The locale is a brothel called Le Chat Rose, owned by a husband and wife who have a virgin daughter, Julie, who they hope will save the brothel from imminent financial ruin. There are some scenes in this film that will make you laugh, but only if you are a little bombed or feeling silly.

THE SEX ADVENTURES OF THE THREE MUSKETEERS
NL BI
1981 MEDIA

P/D—Erwin Dietrich, Michael Thomas
F/A—Inga Steeger, Nadia Pilair
F/A—Achim Hammer, Peter Graf, Jurg Gray, Thomas Larich

All four musketeers, Athos, Porthos, Aramis, and D'Artagnan, are in this film, but they don't do much except eat, drink, and belly bump indoors and outdoors with various barmaids, landlords' daughters, and a horny countess whose husband they quickly kill in a duel. Yvonne (Inga Steeger) is very pretty. There's nice costuming, some bawdy scenes, and backgrounds of West Germany, where the film was made, but if you're looking for a story, there isn't any—just endless soft-core humping—no erections and the camera never looks between the female legs.

WILD RIVER GIRLS
CC NN NM NR NL DK
1975 IVP (formerly CVX)

P/D—John Evans, Harold Lee
F/A—Lanny Roth, Rose Harmon, Lucy McMillan, Yvette Brando
F/A—Joe Julian, David Lane, Lee Donovan

Huck Finn and Tom Sawyer, in their late 20s, are walking the banks of the Mississippi River looking for a place to spend the night. In a barn, a pretty young lady undresses, lies in the hay, and plays with her breasts and clitoris very erotically. Unknown to her, she's being watched by the local sheriff. She's Becky, of course, and her girlfriends, seeing her being spied on, all "attack" the sheriff, who is soon in the barn playing in the hay with the three young fillies. Becky later finds Huck and Tom in the barn, and the next morning, in a romantic scene while they are all naked on Becky's bed, the guys talk lovingly to her and believe it or not, take turns combing her beautiful hair. The sheriff arrests Tom and Huck for disturbing the peace (pun intended) and makes them whitewash the barn. It ends with Mark Twain, with his arms around two of the ladies, saying, "The truth is, I always wanted to write a story like that." (See notes under *Pleasure Bed.*)

Travelogues

A FLYING SEX MAN
NN DK
1985   ORCHIDS INTERNATIONAL

P/D—Not given
F/A—Tsuyako Hime, Sachiko, Kijo

Watching Superman on TV, a Japanese boy is sure that he can fly, too. Soon he's swooping over downtown Tokyo and ends up in his girlfriend's bedroom. She's been sleeping in a net mattress and gets up to pee. (There is a great deal of female pissing in Japanese films.) The boyfriend watches her and then, although she protests a little, he ties her spread eagled to the hammock, after which he plays with her with a dildo, washes her vulva with Coca-Cola, rubs menthol-flavored lubrication on her labia, and finally, sliding under the hammock, gets a weightless fuck. She tells him that she lets him do all this to her only because she likes him, but now he must marry her. In shock, he climbs on the balcony and tries to fly but plops flat on his face in the grass. (She notes under *A Soldier's Desire*.)

FLYING SKIRTS
NN NM NI DK NL
1980   ESSEX

P/D—Michael Le Blanc
F/A—Mary Monroe, Kathy Kay, Sophie Zillers
F/A—Paul French, John Oury

Watching this one, I kept hoping that I could give it a CC rating. It has a potentially good plot and the fascinating background of a winter/summer resort in the French Alps, where it was shot. But the story, which takes place in the summer, falls apart about halfway through. Hugo takes his wife and daughter on holiday to a chalet in the Alps, but up the road he has sponsored his girlfriend in a room in an exclusive resort where he can get her for a little extramarital dalliance during his holiday. She brings Laura (Mary Monroe, a.k.a. Olinka) along with her to share the wealth. Unknown to Hugo, his wife has also made arrangements with a young man who is camping in a tent near the chalet so that he's available to her. Before it's over, all skirts, including their daughter's, are not only flying—they have disappeared. It ends with all of them copulating, for the third or fourth time, in the hay in a nearby barn. There's nice outdoor fucking on a mountainside and beside a mountain stream.

FORGET ME NOT
CC NN
1985   ORCHIDS INTERNATIONAL

P/D—Not given
F/A—Chikako Kawataba, Kitaro Baba

If you wonder what it might be like to spend an evening with a geisha girl, here's one version, which may be exaggerated or not. It begins with the lady washing herself in a flowing spring, dressing very carefully in a kimono, putting on makeup, and getting ready for the evening. She finally appears at a Japanese-style dinner where three young studs are waiting for her arrival. Struggling a little, she lets them undress her. They gently explore her body and tell each other to be nice to her as she blows them one by one and they enjoy her pussy. They all comment favorably on her sexual abilities and then they spread her out naked on a low dinner table and they sit around eating their rice and fish off her naked body, dipping portions in her vagina to flavor them. The evening finally ends with all the guys exhausted and snoring and the young lady getting dressed and leaving. (See notes under *A Soldier's Desire*.)

FRENCH SHAMPOO
NN BI DK
1978   QUALITY/VIDEO-X-PIX

P/D—Phillip T. Drexler, Jr.
F/A—Darby Lloyd Rains, Kim Pope, Helen Madigan, Annie Sprinkles
F/A—Bobby Astyr, Mark Stevens, Alan Marlo

As an Arab sheik, Waldo ben Said, who has an ugly daughter, Yolanda, who has warts on her nose and a few missing teeth, Bobby Astyr is the male star of this one. He has contacted a woman, Kim Pope, who runs a Fifth Avenue beauty salon and will give her $1 million if she can make his daughter marriageable. A male beautician, Mr. Marco (Mark Stevens), has a sure cure. His cock will make any woman beautiful, but his price is $2,000 and access to all the ladies in the salon, including the lesbian Francesca (Darby Lloyd Raines). When he's finished, Yolanda's warts drop off and she's so beautiful that even the sheik, sure that Allah will make him him pay for what he's doing, can't resist her.

FRENCH WIVES
NN BI
1970s VCA

P/D—Andre Carte Blanche
F/A—Andrea True, Tina Russell
F/A—Jamie Gillis, Mark Stevens

Although throughout this film you are given 15 minutes or more of French background shots and French narration, the film was really shot in New York City. How do I know? Because when Nicole (Tina Russell) arrives at what is presumably a French village, a train passes swiftly through. If you run the tape slowly you can read "Long Island Railroad." Never mind. It was an early attempt to create an adult film with something beside a bedroom.

HONG KONG HOOKERS
NN NM BI
1985 AMBASSADOR

P/D—Not given
F/A—Samantha Fong, Jean Quho, Loren Qui,
 Norma James
F/A—Bobby Astor, John Dalton

The Chinese ladies in this one are probably American born, but one of them speaks with a cute baby voice and sexy accent, has small breasts, probably weighs less than 100 pounds, and looks like a 15-year-old. Although not so tiny, the other Chinese ladies are equally attractive and never stop sexmaking with their guys and each other. The only non-Chinese woman

is a wealthy American bisexual who is taken care of by her Chinese maid. Bobby Astor in the credits is not Bobby Astyr.

HOT BODIES
NN BI DK
1984 CABALLERO

P/D—Michel Le Blanc
F/A—Olinka, Gabrielle Pontello, Kathy Menard,
 Aurore
F/A—Not given

Shot in Switzerland, this one gives you a nice tour of Zurich and the Alps, where Roland, a businessman, lives with his wife, Doris (Gabrielle Pontello). Unfortunately, Doris is not very sexy in bed (hard to believe), and as a result Roland is always on the prowl for new stuff. In an eye-popping scene, he picks up Olinka, a.k.a. Mary Monroe, on a passenger boat that traverses Lake Zurich, and to the amazement of other passengers, screws her while they all watch and a mate tries to collect their tickets. That's all you see of Olinka. But Roland has no compunctions and agrees that Doris should spend a weekend in the Italian Alps with her boss. When she's gone he immediately picks up two young female hitchhikers, invites them back to his apartment, and of course they're ready to move in. He finally gets rid of them after they invite a tough-looking guy to the apartment and he proceeds to wreck it. Never mind. Doris returns home and forgives him. After a weekend in bed with other guys, she's a newly released woman and ready to try anything, so they can live happily ever after.

HOT PURSUIT
CC NN NR BI DK
1984 VCA

P/D—Christopher Frederixis, Stanley Forest
F/A—Annette Haven, Jackie Jowes, Sandy
 Lane, Michelle Norris
F/A—Abel Caine, Sidney Derko, Sam Arthur,
 John Mann, Mark Raymond

Annette Haven has the only familiar face (and body) in this one, which was shot in

Amsterdam near Dam Square and has a total European sophistication. As you watch it, you'll be puzzled almost all the way through as to what is really happening. But it finally comes down to this: Annette (she has a screen name that doesn't matter) is a wealthy pop singer who is known for her naive, almost virginal songs, such as "I Don't Want to Be a Millionaire, I Just Want My Teddy Bear," which she actually sings wearing bobby sox and pigtails. Unfortunately, years ago when she was broke, she made a porno film, which has turned up in Amsterdam and if ever released will destroy her image. She is quite desperate and tells a detective appropriately named Dick (Abel Caine), "I don't care about the cost, I'm on the edge of self-destruction. Get that film." Dick's search leads him to a brothel, where you watch some weird action, including a black girl, wearing goggles, in a circular tub with two guys. She can hold her breath interminably and suck a guy to a climax underwater. You see his jism idly floating upward when she's finished. There's also a guy who is an S/M enthusiast, wearing old-time armor, with his balls exposed as he is being whipped. What ties this all together and keeps you watching is Annette, who is a great actress, and the intricate story, which begins with cuts from the porno film. But it is not apparent until the end, which includes a happy surprise for Annette that the director of the film, which is finally recovered, was so busy concentrating on her ass and genitals that he never revealed her face.

INGRID, WHORE OF HAMBURG
NN DK
1984 CABALLERO

P/D—Jose Benazeraff
F/A—Juan, Eric Dray
F/A—Olinka (a.k.a. Mary Monroe), Fabienne Parc, Helen Munoz

If you can figure out what is happening in the first 30 minutes of this one-hour tape, you're better than I am. Benazeraff makes a lot of European porno films, and while there often is little or no story, the loca-

tions and general ambiance make them reasonably interesting. And of course this one has Olinka as Ingrid, who can screw standing on her head.

A LITTLE SEX IN THE NIGHT
NN NM BI DK
1983 VCA

P/D—Michael Baudricourt
F/A—Francis Avril, Selina Starr, Alison Pink, Linda Vista
F/A—Rod Turner, Charles Long

A better title for this European-made film would be *Non-Stop Screwing Night and Day*. What story there is involves a genius named Peter who has a doctorate degree in just about everything you can imagine but has never had a woman. He arrives at his female cousin's palatial townhouse and develops a case of acute priapism. In the things-you-won't-believe department, the maid masturbates on the tile floor in the kitchen, rolling in spaghetti and crumbling it over herself to provide friction.

LOVE MELODY
NN NM
1983 ORCHIDS INTERNATIONAL

P/D—Ken Kishi
F/A—Asami Kobayahi, Kazuhiko Murata

Other than comparing American and Japanese sexmaking and Japanese facial expressions in the act of copulation, it has the style of an American-made quickie.

LOVE PLAY
NN BI DK
1977 CABALLERO

P/D—John Thomas
F/A—Emmanuelle Parezee, Martine Grimaud, Isabel, Evon Evler
F/A—Charles Schneider, Alain Saury, Pierre Danny

The DK rating for this one is not so much for the orgy but rather for the total kinkiness of this French-made film, on which Caballero has a release date of 1984. Call it supersophisticated French kinkiness. It concerns a guy named Etien La Crosse, who is married to Karen and of course is very wealthy. Karen is a dud in bed. So, unknown to Lena, who owns a boutique, he buys underwear and bras that Lena has tried on for him at his request thinking they are for another woman. But actually he collects them and hangs them on the wall of his in-town apartment. Of course, he ends up with both women.

MAKING A PORNO MOVIE
NN BI DK
1985 CABALLERO

P/D—Jose Benzaref
F/A—Michele Valentin, Odette Burel, Danielle Gueguad
F/A—Not given

Somewhere in a Mediterranean port town on the Costa del Sol, a porno-film producer is trying to make a new film. But he hasn't paid anyone for a previous film, and now he's trying to convince them, and a major investor and the investor's wife, to work for free. The producer/director shows the horrified investor how to make love to his wife, who suddenly becomes a willing actress. Soon everyone is engaged in an orgy, which the cameraman faithfully records and which becomes the new film. Unfortunately, when the producer tries to sell the iflm, the distributor tells him that the public doesn't want his "despicable movies" anymore. After watching this Benzaref bomb, neither will you. However, Benzaref is capable of better things (see *Whore's Port* and *Adventures in San Fenleu*, both filmed in the same general area).

MRS. WINTER'S LOVERS
NN BI NM DK
1985 CABALLERO

P/D—Jose Benzareff
F/A—Olinka (a.k.a. Mary Monroe), Gabrielle Pontello
F/A—Not given

Like *Yacht Orgy* (see review), this one is a 60-minute film shot in Spain, with wealthy, erotic, sexual backgrounds and two very beautiful ladies who both appear in other films made by Benzareff. Mrs. Winter is Olinka (a.k.a. Mary Monroe because she looks like Marilyn). The story is familiar. Mrs. Winter's husband has just died, and she will inherit his entire estate if she is chaste for five years. Unfortunately, Isabel, the stepdaughter, who is next in line, knows that her stepmother has a yen for the chauffeur, as do all the ladies who see him. It all ends with three ladies sharing the wealth and some nice sexmaking on the hood of a Bentley with the Mediterranean shimmering in the background.

PASSAGE TO ECSTASY
NN BI NL (here and there)
1985 CDI HOME VIDEO

P/D—Jim Reynolds, Bob Chinn
F/A—Stacy Donavan, Honey Wilder, Josephine Carrington, Buffy, Kristara Barrington
F/A—Harry Reems, Eric Edwards, Peter North, Herschel Savage

A "passage" with an Indian background sounds like a good concept for an adult film, but this one is no *Passage to India*. It presumably takes place in Bombay. The Indian ambiance is quickly established with a few shots of the city intercut into the beginning action. Living in the American colony, Julia (Josephine Carrington) invites her friends to a fourth wedding anniversary party on a Sunday afternoon. At the party, everyone screws everyone else.

REVOLUTION
NN BI DK
1985 CABALLERO

P/D—Jose Benzareff
F/A—Olinka, Gabrielle Pontello
F/A—Same males as in Yacht Orgy (see review)

Shot somewhere in Spain, the film is supposed to be set in a South American country, where El Presidente, following Marie Antoinette's dictum, is telling the *contras* to eat cake. In the meantime, he is screwing his heart out, especially with the ambassador's wife while the ambassador is provided with equally succulent delights. Outside, there is incessant shooting and sounds of battle, and finally either the *contras* or El Presidente's soldiers take over. It's hard to tell which, and the film ends abruptly. Maybe there was more in the original; this version was tailored to fit Caballero's *Once Upon a Time* series.

TAKE MY BODY
NN BI DK
1984   ESSEX

P/D—Michael Le Blanc
F/A—Mary Monroe, Olinka, Kathleen Menard, Laura Clair
F/A—John Oury, Gabrielle Pontello, Eric Dray

Essex missed the boat on this European-made film by not providing any identification of the beautiful people except Natasha (played by Mary Monroe, a Marilyn Monroe look-alike), in and around whom most of the sex action takes place. It begins mysteriously on a train headed for Paris when Natasha invites a handsome guy, Daniel (who, you later discover, is chief of some intelligence agency or other, and for whom she is working) into her compartment for some wild humping and bumping to the rhythm of the train wheels. A complicated espionage plot unravels. In one of the film's best scenes, Natasha and he screw on a circular bed that turns like a merry-go-round to enhance the dizziness of orgasm. (How can you live without one?) I can't quite give this one a CC rating, but before you're through you'll know Mary Monroe inside and out. Try running the circular-bed scene in fast-forward viewing for a laugh.

TEA FOR THREE
R
1983   MEDIA

P/D—Gerhard Janda
F/A—Iris Beerben, Mascha Gonska
F/A—Heinz Mareck, Eric Pohlman

Alfie, a medical student in Vienna, lives with Ina, who is helping to support him, but he's also occasionally relaxing from the stress of studies with Sonja. To his shock, they both get pregnant, and in nine months, on March 12 and 13, both give birth to handsome baby boys. The ladies are not very happy when they discover each other's existence, but they can't stop loving Alfie. Complications ensue.

A WINTER STORY
NN BI DK
1985   ORCHIDS INTERNATIONAL

P/D—Not given
F/A—Hiroko Fujido, Yasu Yamato

Two Japanese guys are dining with a young lady. One leaves, and the other tries to undress her. She protests a little, but soon they're making love on a sleeping mat. Next day she makes love to a woman. Then two guys join them and make it a foursome. The only winter aspect of this one is the two gals walking through a park in Tokyo. I have a feeling that this was an attempt to cater to American audiences with Japanese women. (See review of *A Soldier's Desire*.)

YACHT ORGY
NN BI DK
1985   CABALLERO

P/D—Jose Benazareff
F/A—Helena, Gabrielle Pontello
F/A—Richard Alstan, Lawrence Edwards

A 60-minute French-made film shot on board a 50-foot motor yacht off the coast of Spain. This one has no plot but beautiful close-ups of the sun-warmed bodies of three ladies and two guys who never stop screwing as they motor (with a non-participating captain) along the beautiful Costa Brava (or Costa del Sol). If you like these erotic backgrounds, try *Mrs. Winter's Lovers* and *Revolution* (see reviews).

Supernatural

DREAM LOVER
NN BI DK
1985   CDI HOME VIDEO

P/D—Jim Reynolds
F/A—Traci Lords, Susan Hart, Pamela Jennings,
    Sheri St. Clare. Dawn Adams, Stevie
    Taylor
F/A—Harry Reems, Tom Byron, Ken Starbuck,
    Francois Papillon

Haunted houses have been used in more than one adult film. This one has Harry Reems as Roger, married to Amy (Pamela Jennings). After a quickie in an old-fashioned bed in a mansion they are considering buying, Roger tells her he has to go to work and she can look the place over and decide. Amy discovers that the place is kind of weird. She sees people in a mirror copulating, and the stereo system suddenly comes to life. Outside, in a heated pool, she watches a guy making it with two women. But they all ignore her. Soon she enters a foggy room where the former owner is pumping away with some gal. He smiles at her and tells her that if she buys the house, he goes with it. When Roger returns and asks her decision, you know what it is!

THE ENCHANTRESS
NN BI DK
1984   4-PLAY VIDEO

P/D—Bruce Seven
F/A—Heather Wayne, Erica Boyer, Christy
    Canyon, Gina Carrera, Gina Valento
F/A—Mark Wallice, Tom Byron, Dan T. Mann,
    Peter North

Here's another fairy-tale sexvid with a magic gizmo. Catherine (Heather Wayne) owns it, and right from the beginning it conjures up two guys who busily lap her from top to bottom and fill her various orifices. She gives a crystal medallion to her friend Christy Canyon and it causes her to have her first orgasm. Christy loans the medallion to Erica, who immediately seduces her husband with a striptease. Erica loans the aphrodisiacal crystal to Gina but first sticks it in her vagina, with excellent results.

FEMME FATALE
NN DK BI
1985   VISTA VIDEO

P/D—Mike Stryker, Vanessa Cruz
F/A—Janey Robbins, Cody Nicole, Mai Lin
F/A—Paul Thomas, Blair Harris, Mark Wallice

Arriving to look over an empty old house that is for sale, Michelle (Janey Robbins) wanders through the rooms and nervously crawls up the stairs. She hears the sounds and voices of the former occupants and finds pictures of them in the attic. Not only can she hear them, but she actually believes that she can see them, and they include Paul Thomas chaining his wife, Cody Nicole, to the wall. She begs for his cock while he screws the maid, who is suspended from the ceiling. There's a bi scene with a fake sand dune ocean backdrop, and two masked guys arrive. The real-estate agent finally provides real dick for Janey's shaved and aching vulva.

FUTURE SEX
NN BI DK
1984   NOW SHOWING

P/D—Lawrence T. Cole
F/A—Amber Lynn, Gail Sterling, Jill Ferrari, Lynx
    Cannon, Lili Marlene
F/A—Paul Thomas, Mike Horner, Billy Dee,
    Herschel Savage, Dan T. Mann, Jonathan
    Younger

"Do not kiss, lust is bliss. . . . Love is against the law! Keep your passions raw! Betray those who love! Lust is loyalty to the State." If you watch this one and are entirely sober, you'll probably get nauseated. But Lawrence Cole obviously hoped that you'd laugh at the silliness. It ain't easy. Women are examined by androids, and females who are affected by love or kissing are eliminated or are cured on laser beds or in chrome bars where the Sextapo give them dildos to insert into each other or help them become lust sandwiches. A stop light, which is all you see of Older Brother (who is watching), flashes red when love is indicated and returns to green when it's pure lust.

THE HOUSE OF STRANGE DESIRES
CC NN BI DK
1985 NOW SHOWING

P/D—Lawrence T. Cole
F/A—Tamara Longley, Cindy Carver, Jill Ferrari, Gail Sterling, Maria Avelens, Justine, Monica Zon
F/A—Mike Horner, Steve Drake, John Seeman, Rick Savage, Don Fernando, Jesse Adams, Jonathon Younger, Grant Lombard

Jason (Mike Horner) and Terry (Tamara Longley) have just purchased a fascinating turn-of-the-century home somewhere in California (Cole is intrigued with this house and used it in *Nasty*, also; see review). The house is haunted by strange demons who, you discover much later, according to an occult specialist played by John Seeman, "live on the energy produced by sexual orgasms." But at first, Jason and Terry don't know this. Terry soon finds herself being screwed by unseen males. Jason thinks she's masturbating or fantasizing, but soon (he's an artist) he's being seduced by female demons who practically take control, not only of his penis but his fingers, and make him draw inexplicable sexual images. Neither Jason nor Terry can see each other's demons, but they compare notes and they hire Seeman, who can't dispell them either. It looks as if Jason and Terry are losing the war against the spirits and soon will be seduced into their world. Then the former owners of the house arrive and tell them they are sorry that they didn't tell them about the demons. They try to follow Seeman's solution: "If there is enough love in the house, the demons will withdraw." But after a wild sexual exchange, the guys suddenly disappear, leaving the gals. It's a losing battle, and Terry finally joins the demons. Never mind, she soon returns to Jason as a demon and tells him that now she'll never leave him. The story could

have been made much scarier, but Tamara is so pretty you wouldn't want anything really bad to happen to her.

I DREAM OF GINGER
NN BI DK
1985 VIVID VIDEO

P/D—Herschel Stevens, Scotty Fox
F/A—Ginger Lynn, Christy Canyon, Lori Smith, Lisa de Leeuw, Loni Sanders, Bunny Bleu
F/A—Paul Thomas, Greg Rome

After watching several Ginger Lynn films in a row (see reviews of *Ginger* and *Pleasure Hunt*), I was beginning to be afraid that I'd be dreaming of Ginger, too. In her *Vivid Video* appearances she presumably writes her own scenarios, which prove, if nothing else, that Ginger is still a child at heart and still likes the fairy stories of her childhood. This one is about a genie in a bottle that a medical-student friend of Michael's (Paul Thomas) gives to him, not knowing that a creature lives inside or that the creature is none other than Ginger, who can snap her fingers and make anything happen, such as dumping Michael in bed, naked and handcuffed so that she can have her way with him. She also interferes with his regular love life by tickling his girlfriend on the vulva with feathers when he's making love to her, and she's not adverse to screwing around with his friend Harold when Michael isn't there.

LOOKING FOR LOVE
NN BI DK
1985 VCX

P/D—Not given
F/A—Kimberly Carson, Jessie Adam, Mindy Rae, Pat Manning, Karen Summer
F/A—R. Bolla, Don Hodges, Patrick Long

Dr. B. Goodman (R. Bolla) is a sex therapist, but business is lousy. He needs a gimmick. Presto, a box arrives from a former colleague of his, Dr. Fritzer, along with a phone call telling him to be careful. The contents, an African aphrodisiac plant, are dangerous. It works, but not quite the way the doctor expected.

LUST IN SPACE
NN BI DK NL (but a little moronic)
1985   PARADISE VISUALS

P/D—Frank and Ernest Macintosh, Miles Kidder
F/A—Lana Burner, Ali Moore, Jessica Longe, Gina Carrera
F/A—Harry Reems, Rick Savage, Ron Jeremy, Tom Byron, Herschel Savage, Kevin James

Seems there's a planet Zitcom that's 46 light-years away. It's ruled by Vixanna (Jessica Longe), who has outlawed fucking for everyone except herself. Somehow, without benefit of flying saucers, Glinda Good (Ali Moore) arrives on a road near Los Angeles. Half naked, she speaks English well. Seeing Phil (Rick Savage) trying to get his broken-down truck started, she waves a magic hand over it. Presto, it starts, and he takes her to a motel, where she tells him the truth: She's an escapee from Zitcom. "I'm here to do as much fucking as possible before they catch me." A sequel is on the way. See if you can stay awake.

LUST IN THE FAST LANE
NN DK BI
1984   PARADISE VISUALS

P/D—Adam
F/A—Traci Lords, Ginger Lynn, Crystal Breeze, Sheri St. Claire
F/A—Tom Byron, Eric Edwards, Peter North, Mark Wallice

Jackie (Traci Lords) and Bill (Tom Byron) decide to get away for the weekend. They head toward Las Vegas on a back road and get a flat tire, but they have no spare. Seeking help at a lonely country house, they are greeted by Jake (Eric Edwards) and his wife, Louise (Ginger Lynn), who are in the midst of a swapsie party with some friends. Jackie and Bill are quickly involved in the fun and games, and while Bill makes some effort over the next 24 hours to leave, Jake tells him that he should relax and enjoy himself. Traci Lords and Ginger Lynn were the hot porno stars of 1984. They can't act, but they have beau-tiful bodies, and soon they are in the sack ecstatically moaning and screaming as they taste and finger each other's tits and vulva in an extended, nicely flesh-toned, shot-on-video sequence. If you can survive 80 minutes of detailed examination of vulvas and pricks and anuses all being thoroughly exercised, you won't be surprised at the ending. Jake suddenly turns into a ghoul (along with the rest of the party, who have sharp fangs showing), and he announces that they are vampires.

ON GOLDEN BLONDE
NN BI
1984   PARADISE VISUALS

P/D—Michael Phillips, Adam
F/A—Ginger Lynn, Chanel Lindsay, Christy Canyon, Janey Robbins
F/A—Jamie Gillis, Peter North, Tom Byron, Mark Wallice

Going to heaven prematurely is a plot gimmick of more than one sexvid. In this one, a lovely lady, Alice (Christy Canyon), after a wild early-morning session with her lover, goes out for her morning jog, has a pain in her chest, and drops dead. At the pearly gates, she meets the Heavenly Host, who tells her that her time wasn't really up yet. What to do? At the moment, all he can do is find her temporary bodies of women who are about to die anyway in the next few days. Alice objects, but soon she's being herself in other ladies' bodies and surprising their lovers, who scarcely recognize their new, lusty, sexy companions. It all ends happily.

THE OTHER SIDE OF LIANNA
NN NM BI DK NL (occasionally)
1984   L.A. VIDEO

P/D—L. M. Burton, Drea
F/A—Lisa de Leeuw, Tamara Longley, Cindee Summers
F/A—Steve Drake, Ron Jeremy, Dino Alexander, William Margold

Unlike many distributors, L.A. Video gives you a pretty good summary (not pornographic) and a cast of characters on the box. But if you're looking for somewhat subtle and motivated sex you won't like this one, which has a Grimm's fairy-tale story about one of the devil's helpers who has to pick up some new souls for the underworld. He arrives on Earth as Scratch (Ron Jeremy), a salesman for the Infernal Appliance Company, and finds Lianna (Cyndee Summers) in suburbia. She's a prudish housewife, but he gives her a music box that, when she listens to it, transforms her into a sexpot who shocks even her husband. It all ends up in Lianna's living room in an orgy.

RING OF PLEASURE
NN BI DK
1975   FANTASY/CABALLERO

P/D—Not given
F/A—Not given

"I want other men," our heroine tells a guy she's fellating in this 60-minute, over-blown loop. He gives her a ring and tells her that all she has to do is stroke it and she can have her heart's desires. Will it work? Of course. Everything works in fairy tales. First she gets a wealthy guy who can't wait to screw her. Then she and another gal take on a handsome guy who has been panting for them. Next she becomes a blonde and shares a guy with a gal. She evidently likes threesomes. It finally ends at a P.O.P.—pool orgy party— where she gets more men than she can accommodate. (See notes under *Christy*.)

RITES OF URANUS
NN BI DK
1975   IVP (formerly CVX)

P/D—Not given
F/A—Julie Hopkins, Janet Oawl, Vivian Parks, Lucy duLac
F/A—Frank Rowney, West Rogers, Jim Moore

During the late '60s and early '70s, there were many so-called families of the Charles Manson type. This is the story of one dominated by a guy called Uranus, whose acolytes wear robes and perform candlelight black masses, moaning their praise to the mighty cock of Uranus and inviting it "to enter my dark passage." Uranus speaks to newcomers through a horn and tells them they must give up their worldly possessions to become members of the Uranus family. One woman does, and after they take a lighted candle out of her ass, she fucks with Uranus, who seems to drop dead in the process. She tries to escape, but Uranus's high priestess puts her in a cell. The next day, to her surprise, there's Uranus, alive and assuring her he can never die and that she must be a good girl and do what she's told. This could have been a much scarier story. (See notes under *Pleasure Bed*.)

SEX DREAMS ON MAPLE STREET
NN BI DK
1985   ESSEX

P/D—Duck Dumont, Charles De Santos
F/A—Stacey Donovan, Janey Robbins, Ashley Grant, Lili Marlene
F/A—John Leslie, John Horner, Jon Martin, Don Fernando

This shot-on-video tape reflects Hollywood's new interest in ghosts. But in this one, even though both ghosts and humans bust their asses, you can't get very involved because it's all so unreal. Seems that the house on Maple Street, to which Rob (John Leslie) is invited to dinner, was a whorehouse in the 1930s. Madam Rose (Janey Robbins) and her girls still occupy the rooms, although they were killed in an automobile accident some 50 years ago. Stacey and John are visited by appropriate ghosts, two males and two females, and they have a merry old fucking time.

SEX RITUALS OF THE OCCULT
NN BI DK
1975   QUALITY/VIDEO-X-PIX

P/D—Not given
F/A—Not given

Introduced by a nice-looking guy, this one tries to give you the impression that you are watching bizarre, exotic, depraved sex rites from all over the world, including black masses, lesbian witches, and a dog as a sacred symbol. It's all kind of hokey. In its time it might have been considered far out, but now it's ony dull.

SEXTEEN
NN NM BI DS
1975 VCA

P/D—Lynn Metz
F/A—C. J. Laing, Bree Anthony
F/A—Jamie Gillis

Your hopes for this one quickly collapse. Jamie and C. J. Laing are happily screwing, with a wild storm pounding the shutters outside. They look up and the angel of death is watching them. Their time on Earth is up. They try to stall things by telling him far-out sex stories, which are so yucky you can't figure why he continues to listen. The first story is about a Lolita-style 16-year-old who is discovered dressing in Mama's clothes by her stepdaddy, who fucks her. Next a guy in Central Park is flashed by a young woman. He follows her to her apartment and screws her. Then there's a young woman who is about to marry a 65-year-old man (you never see him) but enjoys her black girlfriend first. But the story of two dykes with their maid, whom they chain up spread-eagled across the dining-room table and stick a riding crop in her vagina and a dildo in her anus, while she begs for mercy and the butler helps them, will turn most viewers off. Jamie and C.J. finally get rid of the angel of death by buggering him—no kidding!

SINDEROTICA
NN BI NL (hammy, low level) DK
1985 ESSEX

P/D—Alan Hitchcock, Leslie Marie, John Silver
F/A—Heather Wayne, Little Oral Annie, Patti Pettit, Lili Marlene, Catherine Drew, Mandi Randi
F/A—Mike Horner, Buddy Love, Chase, Ron Jeremy

Here's another version of the Cinderella story that is pretty yucky but may give you a few laughs if you enjoy sleazy humor. His Royal Highness (Mike Horner), King of Los Bubulous, lives in the city of Pussya guarded by his Royal Dicks and advisor (Ron Jeremy). His son, Prince Dick Charming (Chase), can get it up, but he has never ejaculated. Hence no children and no heirs to the throne. With his advisor's help, the king issues an edict that the woman who can make Prince Dick come will be the next princess. So Prince Charming takes off (pun intended) and finally arrives at the home of Sinderotica (Heather Wayne), her stepmother (Lili Marlene), and her two evil stepsisters (Little Oral Annie and Patti Petit). You can guess the rest.

STAR BABE
NN BI DK
1977 CABALLERO

P/D—Anne Perry
F/A—Tomi La Roux
F/A—Jason Welles

Anne Perry would probably like to forget she ever made this film, which arrived sometime after *Star Wars*. Star Babe, Milky Way, and Twinkletoes, all from other planets, are on a space mission aboard Starship Orgasm to save Earth from a nasty Darth Vader type in a white helmet, who is about to launch against Earth a missile filled with the semen of the weirdos who inhabit Phallus. It will impregnate all the ladies on Earth with weirdo babies who will then take over. Amazingly, the inhabitants of Phallus, who look as if they were going to a Halloween party, all have white pricks, which our heroines quickly subdue. If you're feeling silly, you might want to watch it and give it a "poor-doggie" award.

URGES IN YOUNG GIRLS
NN   NM   BI
1984   VCA

P/D—**Janus Ranier, David Christopher**
F/A—**Sharon Kane, Phaedra Grant, Tish Ambrose, Renee Summer, Sandy King**
F/A—**Joey Silvera, Eric Edwards, Dave Ruby**

There's a strange mirror in a boutique in New York City. When young women look into it they become very horny and are magically transported into the arms of one and even two lovers at a time. Eric Edwards takes care of these astral ladies in his apartment. Joey Silvera, who is in a hospital with "a pain in his dick," is cured by a lady from the boutique who arrives to soothe it in her mouth and vagina. This one was probably whipped out on a three-day weekend, and looks it.

THE WIZARD OF AAHS
NN   BI   DK
1985   ESSEX

P/D—**John Gold**
F/A—**Athena Star, Dee Vine, Rita Ricardo, Patti Petite**
F/A—**Ron Jeremy, Jon Martin, Steve Drake, Rick Savage, Mike Horner**

The time is 2069. Women rule the universe. Men are kept in a penal colony somewhere in outer space so that they can no longer start the wars that nearly ended civilization. All the women need them for is their sperm, which they receive from mechanical pricks. Passion and physical contact with males are prohibited. This idea may not be so farfetched, but the story is boring and the three homely, hammy ladies need to go back to their spaceship and learn how to act.

Star Vehicles

ALL NIGHT LONG
NN   BI   DK
1975   ESSEX

P/D—**Alan Colberg, Billy Thornberg**
F/A—**Sharon Thorpe, Rikki Gambino, Desiree West**
F/A—**John C. Holmes, Ric Lutze**

If you're a John C. Holmes enthusiast, you might want to watch this one, which was made some years before he became Johnny Wadd. Meant to be funny, it pits J.C. against Ric in a Golden Rod Contest, in which the winner will survive a series of varied sexual encounters and get back first to a Home and Hearts banquet where the prize will be given. After crashing around Los Angeles for six boring sucks and fucks, they both arrive back at the same time, exhausted, crawling through an orgy that stops long enough for both to be declared winners.

ALL THE WAY IN
NN   DK   BI
1984   VCA

P/D—**Gabriel Lobo, Robert Garcia, Bob Chinn**
F/A—**Candy Samples, Martina, Mai Lin, Shanna McCullough, Tanya Lawson**
F/A—**Eric Edwards, Ron Jeremy, David Morris, Francois, Pat Romano**

Candy Samples is the star of this one. She writes a "Miss Fantasy" column for *Ultra Flesh* magazine, which is run by Mr. Dicker (Eric Edwards) and Martina, a pretty woman who speaks in seductive slow motion, as if she were munching on cotton. Candy is not herself—she's fallen in love with a guy, but after a passionate, week-long affair he has left on urgent business and all she knows is his name—Pat. Now, back at work, Mr. Dicker announces that the magazine has been sold to a new buyer, P. J. Corona (Pat Romano) and they all may lose their jobs. You guess, of course, that P. J. is Candy's missing boyfriend, but you've got to sweat through 80 minutes of boring screwing before P. J. is reunited with Candy. He's bought the magazine because he loves Candy—and her column. All their jobs are safe, and everyone will live happily ever after. The only two reasons for watching this one are to see Candy bounce, lap, and play basketball with her size 48EE tits, also to speculate on why you never, in this or any other Candy Samples film, see her screwing without wearing a midriff-hugging corset. You may also wonder if Martina talks that way in real life.

AURORA'S SECRET DIARY
NN NM BI
1985   L.A. VIDEO

P/D—James Travis
F/A—Aurora, Rikki Blake, Summer Rose
F/A—Peter North, Rick Jackson, Peter Gunn

Aurora reads to herself from a diary that she kept before she was married and which she has never shown to her husband. As she reads and plays with herself, the episodes come to life. They include the day that she was washing her car and her boyfriend helped her and was finally washing her as he spread her legs on the hood of the car. Next, she is working at a recording studio where a "bad day" is relieved by some happy fucking. Next, a magazine editor is in the hospital where Aurora is a student nurse. He's being prepared to have a vasectomy. She shaves off all his pubic hair before she sits on his prick and then she discovers that she's in the wrong room. You rarely see a guy depilated in a sexvid. In other diary episodes, Aurora screws a guy in an empty building that, as a real-estate agent, she is trying to sell him, and she and an erotic stripper enjoy some womanly sex, after which they are joined by two guys.

BEVERLY HILLS EXPOSED
NN NM BI
1985   ESSEX

P/D—Mark Corby, Robert McCallum
F/A—Colleen Brennan, Tamara Longley, Mindy Rae, Tracy Duzit, Bunny Bleu, Jacqueline Roget
F/A—Harry Reems, Jerry Butler, Billy Dee

You can say one thing about Harry Reems. He's still flat-bellied, and he has his choice of the current crop of female sexvid stars. In this one, he's a wealthy businessman (doing exactly what, you never discover), and he's trying to swing a deal with a guy, Jeff Stimpson (Billy Dee), who arrives from Salt Lake City. Harry Town, as Reems is called in the film, has a daughter who has posed nude for some men's magazines, and a second wife, Colleen Bren-

nan, who uses a wiggly vibrator when she's not getting enough from Harry. What there is of a plot revolves around whether Stimpson can be seduced into the big deal that's being worked on by Harry. Of course he can, especially after he's enjoyed both of the sexy maids who flit about the mansion, and Harry's daughter. As for Harry, he enjoys them, too, as well as his secretary, Tamara Longley, who caresses him with her deep, warm voice and ties his prick in a happy knot with a velvet band as they drive to the office in a mile-long limousine.

BOLD OBSESSION
NN NM DK BI
1984   NOW SHOWING

P/D—Lawrence T. Cole
F/A—Linda Shaw, Sharon Mitchell, Rita Cruz
F/A—Jon Martin, Herschel Savage, Mike Horner

Linda Shaw, who has a beautiful, big-breasted body and I would guess weighs about 130 pounds, is the total star of this one. The other ladies appear only momentarily. The film also has the Lawrence Cole trademark, a theme song that advances the plot or becomes a voice-over telling what is going on in the heroine's head. Unfortunately, in this one not much. All she wants is to be watched doing whatever she's doing (mostly masturbating) by a man. Soon her stereo speakers come to life and a male voice assures her that he is watching but that she will never meet him. However, she must do what he wishes. First, she must meet a man who is waiting for her at the bottom of the staircase in her apartment. Sure enough, Jon Martin is waiting. Linda does an extended striptease for him, gradually revealing her crotch and behind. The staircase, of course, provides a new perspective on fucking, which makes it more interesting to watch. After that, Linda ends up jogging to a men's gym and finally gets her wish to be the main entree at her own party. Stretched out naked on a table, she is thoroughly eaten by two male and two female guests. The voice on the speakers comes to life again and gives her her final reward, "the taste of my cock." But it turns out that she is his fantasy (you never see him) and not vice versa.

BOLERO
R
1984   USA HOME VIDEO

P/D—Bo Derek, John Derek
F/A—Bo Derek, Andrea Occhipinti, Ana Obregon
F/A—George Kennedy and several unidentified males

When Derek's film was released in 1984, it bypassed the Motion Picture Board rating system, purposely, leaving the viewer with the impression that Bo appeared in some very explicit sex scenes. If she had, then Derek might have produced an X-rated adult film worthy of a "Collector's Choice" rating. But the problem is that the story of wealthy, spoiled Mrs. McGilvray (let's call her Bo), who has just graduated from an English girls' school (it's sometime in the 1920s) and is determined, with the help of her easygoing chauffer and friend, Cotton (George Kennedy), to get rid of her virginity with an Arab sheik (who resembles Rudolph Valentino) is pretty tough to swallow. After much silly buildup, Bo and a Spaniard make extended love in such low-key romantic lighting that you'll wonder why you waited. You can see more of Bo's body in the movie *10*. On the other hand, if you like erotic, exotic photography and a fairy tale about another, more romantic world, maybe you'll watch it for the "let's-pretend" kind of laughter that Derek hoped to generate.

CALL GIRL
NN BI DK
1984   CAL VISTA

P/D—Andrew Whyte
F/A—Marilyn L'Amour, Helen Shelly, Mary Anderson, Laura Forsman
F/A—Gabriel Pontello, Richard Hemingway

There's no doubt that in some camera angles and full-length shots, Olinka, a.k.a. Marilyn L'Amour, is a double for Marilyn Monroe. In this incoherent French-made film, she is presumably kidnapped by Caesar (Gabriel Pontello), a disbarred lawyer who does a little pimping. He touts her as a Marilyn Monroe look-alike, and the price for a night with her, even though she loves only him, is $25,000.

CANDY SAMPLES VIDEO REVIEW
BI NN
1984   FOUR-PLAY VIDEO

P/D—None
F/A—Candy Samples, Pattie Douglas
F/A—John C. Holmes and several unidentified guys

This is a 1970 collection of loops featuring Candy Samples, with a couple of sequences involving a young Holmes, whose prick Candy and Pattie cover with whipped cream, chopped nuts, and cherries, and then happily eat their way down. In case you don't know, Candy Samples is a lady with a 45DD cup size but otherwise is pretty skinny and sure likes to fuck. In other sequences, she enjoys herself with other guys in a Jacuzzi and in the sack with Pattie and no guys. For big-tit lovers.

CANDY'S BEDTIME STORY
NN
1983   DIVERSE-MAXIMUM

P/D—Jack Remy, Garvey Fox
F/A—Eric Edwards, Marc Wallice
F/A—Candy Samples, Callie Aimes, Mona Page

This is an hour tape which includes *The Peeper* as a separate half hour from the Candy Samples sequence. The tapes are also sold as half-hour jobs at a relatively low price. The Candy segment opens with Candy in bed with her husband. The story is about Candy and her meeting with a big Italian movie producer. This gives Candy an opportunity to take on two men in separate sequences and gives the viewer an extended introduction to her huge breasts. Candy also offers an extensive view of her genitals, but she never appears completely naked—depending on stretch garments, evidently to hold her stomach in. The second sequence, *The Peeper* features Eric Edwards making it with Mona Page, and then spying on Callie Aimes making it with Mark Wallice.

COMING HOLMES (HUNG LIKE A HORSE)
NN BI
1985   VIDCO

P/D—Tony Valentino
F/A—Susan Hart, Misty Regan, Ami Roberts, Cheri
F/A—John Holmes, Steve Powers, Tony Martin

This is a shot-on-video quickie for fans of John C. Holmes. It proves that even after a screen absence, his uncircumsised cock is none the worse for wear. In this one, John runs a bar/restaurant that employs topless dancers and strippers. He interviews four of them with his joint.

THE EROTIC WORLD OF ANGEL CASH
NN NM BI DK
1984   VIDEO-X-PIX

P/D—Howard A. Howard
F/A—Angel Cash, Juliet Anderson, Danielle, Bunny Hatton
F/A—Jim Sims, David Ambrose, Buddy Hatton, Felix Krull

"All I can think about is sex," Angel Cash tells you as she wanders half naked a-round her houseboat. It's on the New Jersey side of the Hudson River, overlooking New York. Angel's not kidding! There are 20 additional people in the credits who are not listed above, mostly more guys you've never seen before. Angel manages to copulate with or suck off most of them during the 80 or so minutes of this tape. Juliet Anderson, who is mistress of the ballet school that Angel attends, manages only two or three guys and gals, in a minor role. You soon discover that Angel can give milk when she squeezes her nipples. She also enjoys fist fucking. In the-things-you-can't-believe department, she encourages a lady friend to put her entire hand up, to her wrist, into Angel's vagina.

THE EROTIC WORLD OF LINDA WONG
NN NM BI
1985   VISTA VIDEO

P/D—Charles de Santos
F/A—Linda Wong, Vanessa Taylor, Cindy Carver, Morgan Ashley, Lili Marlene
F/A—Richard Pacheo, Mike Horner, Jon Martin, Blair Harris, Rocky Balboa

A series of vignettes in the life of a high-priced call girl of many talents. It begins with a tableau during which Linda tries to create some Oriental atmosphere by strolling back and forth in front of Mike Horner (a prince?), who is screwing Morgan Ashley while Linda offers some smoky comments. Next, she spends a good five minutes massaging Richard Pacheco's shoulder, which he claims is in pain. She finally turns him over and teaches him the joys of sex. Other sequences involve Lili Marlene servicing two brothers, evidently in Linda's establishment, and Linda taking on Billy Dee and Jon Martin, followed by a bi scene during which she laps up two women. With no story, the pseudo erotic atmosphere gets boring.

EVERY MAN'S FANTASY
NN BI
1985   INTROPICS VIDEO

P/D—Leon Gucci
F/A—Kristara Barrington, China Lee, Crystal Blue, Karen Summer, Nicole Blanc, Desiree Lane, Ebony Clark, Beverly Bliss, Lisa Lake, Joy Merchant
F/A—Francois Papillon

A real honest-to-God Frenchman, Francois Papillon has appeared in many minor roles in adult films, but I'd guess this is his first starring role. In fact, he's the only male in the film who copulates, and poor Francois is attacked by so many women that in the last frames, when Karen Summer, who plays two roles (Mrs. Smith and her sister), unzips his pants, the poor, shrunken thing has a bandage wrapped around it!

FLESH AND LACES, PARTS 1 AND 2
NN BI DK
1985 CABALLERO

P/D—Troy Benny (a.k.a. Carlos Tobalina)
F/A—Shauna Grant, Tamara Longley, Rose Lynn,
    Sparky
F/A—Jamie Gillis, Joey Silvera, William Margold,
    Carlos Tobalina

Carlos Tobalina is a warm, joyous kind of guy with a mad sense of humor and a conviction, evidently, that most guys who buy or rent adult films don't care much about romance but want wall-to-wall fucking. The gimmick that he hangs on this double bubble is that Jamie Gillis, in a hospital bed, is about to die. Jamie promises all of his huge estate to the heir, one of three sons and a daughter, who is getting the most out of his or her sex life. To determine the winner, he has all of their homes monitored with TV cameras. Lying in his hospital bed, he can switch from one fuck encounter to another. These involve a very long sequence of Shauna Grant arriving to take a job as a model with one of Jamie's sons and being screwed to a fare-thee-well, followed by Rose Lynn, as Jamie's daughter, taking on three guys at once. Then there's Joey Silvera, who does two female cops. All this and more, with Jamie taking on nurses who come in to check his temperature, goes on for 95 minutes. If that's not enough, there's Part 2, a separate cassette in which Jamie is still in bed—but Doctor Tobalina tells him that he's so improved that he's going to prescribe the best head in the hospital. "Who's that?" Jamie demands. "The head nurse," Tobalina grins at him. Jamie also gets help from Doctor Pecker (John Holmes, of course), and soon he and Jamie and three nurses are all in a hospital bed screwing. Before it's over Jamie is totally recovered. He tells his happy heirs, including his daughter, whom he has always wanted to screw and does, that they don't have to worry, they can all share and share alike. Both cassette packages feature Shauna Grant (see review of *Shauna Grant Superstar*), but Shauna appears only for a second or two on the second tape.

GINGER
NN NM BI DK
1984 VIVID VIDEO

P/D—Loni Sanders, Lisa de Leeuw, C. H.
    Stevens, Scotty Fox
F/A—Ginger Lynn, Tiffany Clark, Lisa de Leeuw,
    Loni Sanders
F/A—David Sanders, Greg Derek, Tom Byron

A new feature in the adult-film scene is the independents. Former producers and directors have decided that they can produce and market their own films on tape. With Vivid Video, Loni Sanders and Lisa de Leeuw have evidently decided that they, too, can get rich quicker by getting into the act from top to bottom. In addition, they have presumably signed up Ginger Lynn to act exclusively for Vivid Video (see review of *I Dream of Ginger*). A new one coming up is *Ginger on the Rocks*. With this, shot on videotape, they offer the story of a wealthy old man, Mr. Hobbs, who has told his grandson that unless he gets married and produces an heir, he won't get any money from Grandpa when he dies. Gramps himself interviews the potential wives for his grandson, Henderson, who is presumably in Europe. When he returns, Henderson is supposed to marry Ginger, who Grandpa picked out and has trained, during the course of the tape, how to seduce Henderson. In the process, she screws with every male in sight and even makes a luscious sandwich with two of them. But despite the training, when Henderson finally appears, he can't get it up with Ginger. At the last moment, you discover why: He's gay. Never mind; his lover is bisexual and promises to impregnate Ginger. Ginger Lynn has a beautiful body, but her babyish voice and often passive facial expressions may not appeal to many males.

HOLLY DOES HOLLYWOOD
NN BI DK
1985 VIDEO EXCLUSIVES

P/D—Mark Curtis, Ron Fellows
F/A—Christy Canyon, Cody Nicole, Pam
    Jennings, Traci Lords, Amber Lynn,
    Erica Boyer, Rikki Blake

F/A—Ron Jeremy, Mark Wallice, Craig Roberts, Blake Palmer, Tim Long, Rocky Rome

If you've been looking for a nonstop, merry-go-fuck-around, and you like big-breasted women like Christy Canyon who have a come-hither face and can suck three or more cocks at once, then this is the sum and substance of Holly (Christy Canyon) doing Hollywood. When she's not on camera, or if you grow weary of her, all the other ladies listed above appear at a P.O.P. (pool orgy party) where all the swimming is flesh to flesh. The film ends so abruptly that you won't have time to come up for air. Incidentally a good portion of Brian De Palma's movie *Body Double*, revolves about a woman named Holly, a porno star, who has made a movie with the same title as this one. While De Palma's film walks the razor's edge of pornography, this film and his are two different stories.

INSATIABLE II
BI   DK   SM
1984   CABALLERO

P/D—Godfrey Daniels II
F/A—Marilyn Chambers, Juliet Anderson, Valerie La Veaux, Shanna McCullough
F/A—Jamie Gillis, Paul Thomas, Craig Roberts, Billy Dee

The continuing story of Sondra Chase (Marilyn Chambers; see review of *Insatiable*) now involves Morgan Templeton (Juliet Anderson). Other than the interesting idea of costarring two 40-year-old porno stars, who are just as active as ever, the plot is the same old story of Sondra/Marilyn's insatiable need for cock, coupled with her masochistic need for punishment. In the things-you-can't-believe department, but which are obviously a Marilyn Chambers trademark, Jamie Gillis stretches her out on a massage table, puts a tourniquet around her neck, prods her with a pointed instrument, drips hot wax from a candle onto her nipples and labia, whips her with leather thongs, ties her hands in back of her, and screws her doggie style while he ass whips her. A more interesting story could have been told about what caused Marilyn's masochistic needs.

In the trivia department, Paul Thomas, who has a minor role, is identified in the credits as Phil Toubus. Maybe he couldn't believe what he was watching either.

INSIDE CANDY SAMPLES
NN   BI (lots)   NL (occasionally)
1985   L.A. VIDEO

P/D—L. M. Burton, Drea
F/A—Candy Samples, Cecily, Heather Wayne, Jessyca Wylde
F/A—Herschel Savage, Steve Drake

Candy Cox (Candy Samples, she of the 48EE bust) is a sex therapist who employs a female surrogate, Loretta (Heather Wayne), to provide sexual therapy for her clients. Loretta has a lesbian roommate (Cecily), and Dr. Cox also seems to enjoy women more than men. Loretta satisfies both of them and Vicki, the nymphomaniac wife of Rob (Herschel Savage), both of whom become patients on the recommendation of Vince (Steve Drake), who learns from Loretta (being instructed by Dr. Cox) the difference between "good sex" and "great sex." There's some funny conversation between poor Rob and his wife, Vicki (Jessyca Wylde), who can't leave poor Rob alone: "I can't get enough of you, Rob," she tells him as he lays totally exhausted in their bed, while she manages once more to shake him alive so that she can sit on him. But then she moans: "You came! I wasn't ready." "You've come twelve times already," Ron gasps. "But I like to fuck, Rob. I feel alive when I fuck." "Yeah, well I'm dead!" Loretta solves Vicki's problems and Dr. Cox presumably gets Rob on the right track, but you never see him screw with her.

INSIDE CHINA LEE
NN   BI   DK
1984   VCA

P/D—Leon Gucci
F/A—China Lee, Desiree Lane, Crystal Bleu, Karen Summer, Joy Merchant
F/A—Nick Niter, Dennis Keats, Jimmy Starr, Francois Papilion

Nonstop wall-to-wall sex with China Lee, shot in San Francisco. China Lee, a.k.a.

Kristara Barrington, is actually a Korean woman whom you'll recognize in future films because of her large aureolas and calculating face. In this one she has arrived from China because her uncle has died and left her a very profitable whorehouse. She quickly demonstrates that she's better than anyone who works for her. Gucci must have whipped this one out on a long weekend, but he feels no embarrassment about it. Evidently Kristara has a following of sex addicts who don't mind watching the same old stuff over and over again.

INSIDE LITTLE ORAL ANNIE
NN NM BI DK
1984   VIDEO-X-PIX

P/D—Howard Howard, Kenneth Morse
F/A—Little Oral Annie, Danielle, Taija Rae, Pam Weston, Carol Cross, Anne Cummings
F/A—Klaus Multia, Johnny Nineteen, George Payne, Marvin Hempstead, Michael Knight, Alan Adrian, Bobby Astyr

"I'm little Oral Annie," Annie tells you immediately. "I love sucking dick." Before the tape is over, some 83 minutes later, Annie is joined by her female friends listed above who can't live without a cock or dildo shoved in their vagina, mouth or anus. If you survive to the end, Annie cheers you up by telling *you*, the male viewer, "I'd love to have my lips around your cock." Even if Annie is an experienced sword swallower, you'd have a better time with a loving friend.

INSIDE MARILYN
NN BI DK
1985   CABALLERO

P/D—Silwa, Moll
F/A—Olinka Hardiman, Uschi Horn, Renate Putz, Swie Oberman
F/A—Peter Schuster, Siggi Buchner

Evelyn (Olinka Hardiman) is not too happy that she's always being mistaken for Marilyn Monroe (see review of *Call Girl* and other films with Olinka where the Marilyn image is not pushed). You'll have to admit when you watch this tape that in many of her facial shots and close-ups, and in her swaying behind and coy look, she really looks like Marilyn. To help the image, in this one, where she plays a model, she is photographed again and again in the famous Marilyn Monroe windblown-skirt shot with her skirt rising in the air to show her panties. Unfortunately, although she has a baby voice, in the American dubbing (Olinka probably can't speak English) her lips are often not well synchronized. Never mind. If you like Olinka, you'll be well acquainted with her face and genitals before you finish watching this one.

JOHN HOLMES AND THE ALL-STAR SEX QUEENS
CC NN BI NL
1985   AMBASSADOR

P/D—Not given
F/A—Serena, Uschi Digart, Candy Samples, Keli Stuart, Bobbi Hall, Valerie Clark
F/A—John Holmes, Johnny Keyes

This 90-minute collection of clips from John C. Holmes films has a CC rating, but only for Johnny's admirers. The cuts, which involve him sexually with all the women listed above, are interspersed with John's often humorous comments in a voice-over. With exception of Serena, all the women are 40DD-cup size, and in between there's a threesome with Uschi Digart and Candy Samples taking on Johnny Keyes (the black man of *Behind the Green Door* fame).

MARILYN CHAMBERS' PRIVATE FANTASIES #4
NN BI DK
1985   CABALLERO

P/D—Sonny Francis, Jack Remy, Peter Moss, Ned Morehead
F/A—Marilyn Chambers, Sheri St. Claire, Honey Wilder, Suzy Whitebond
F/A—Harry Reems, Herschel Savage, Billy Dee, Al Brown, Buck Adams

Here are four more episodes of Marilyn's presumably inexhaustible sexual fantasies.

MARILYN CHAMBERS' PRIVATE FANTASIES #5
NN BI DK DS
1985 CABALLERO

P/D—Sonny Francis, Jack Remy
F/A—Marilyn Chambers, Traci Lords, Tantala, Ami Rogers
F/A—Billy Dee, Steve Nadelman, Jerry Butler, Nick Random, Kevin Gibbons

In this group of Marilyn's fantasies, once again she reveals her pain and pleasure in two keyhole looks into what is presumably her private sex life.

MY SISTER SEKA
NN BI
1981 CABALLERO

P/D—Michelle Ames, Ron Barnet
F/A—Seka, Tina Ross, Sarah Sheldon, Vicki Steele
F/A—R. J. Reynold, John Leslie, Mark Slater, Dave Hartman

Six little episodes in Seka's life, during which she screws all the guys listed above in her living room, in her hot tub, in the office where she is secretary to a new young boss, with her girlfriend, and finally with some newlyweds, as Seka happily prepares the groom for the bride by showing him the joy of oral sex.

OLINKA, GRAND PRIESTESS OF LOVE
NN BI DK
1985 CABALLERO

P/D—Jose Benazeraf
F/A—Olinka (a.k.a. Mary Monroe) and others not identified

This one begins with a long bi sequence, after which Olinka, leaving a coastal town on the Costa Brava, is asked by another young woman if she can come with her. Why not? Olinka is going to meet some friends and get some sun. Soon they are in a Spanish villa enjoying the sun topless as well as some more bisexual lovemaking. Finally two guys arrive at the swimming pool and they switch from pussy to cock. Later, at a very sophisticated party, they soon shed their clothes and play pig-and-sow-pile.

PRINCESS SEKA
NN BI DK DS
1980 VCA

P/D—Leon Gucci
F/A—Seka, Serena, Veronica Hart, Samantha Fox
F/A—Eric Edwards, Bobby Astyr

Arriving in New York to seek a more challenging career, Seka moves in with her former boyfriend, Bert (Eric Edwards), who promises to find her something interesting to do. After several dead-end interviews and sex, she meets an old friend, Serena, who tells her how she was raped by two guys (you watch the action; Serena is a perennial rapee). Afterward, they gave her $100, and Seka suddenly realizes that this is the kind of challenging work she prefers, too. As for Bert, he ends up in the sack with both of them, of course, and to hell with marriage.

THE SEDUCTION OF SEKA
NN BI DK
1985 AMBASSADOR

P/D—Not given
F/A—Rhonda Jo Petty, Tina Verville
F/A—Mike Ranger, Steven Grant

This is a collection of Seka clips from previous films. Packaged in a four-color box, it may give the impression it is something new. It isn't. One clip goes back to Seka screwing with a couple of carpenters who she wants to fix her coffee table. In another she's watching bathers at Venice Beach through binoculars with her guy and soon she's screwing with him. Later they make a threesome with their babysitter, who they discover masturbating while she sits on a blowup of John Travolta's face. If you read all the reviews in this book, I'm sure that you can trace the original Seka films, plus another in which Seka enjoys a little bi sex with Rhonda Jo Petty.

SEX GAMES
NN NR (one sequence) DK BI
1983 CABALLERO

P/D—Paul G. Vatelli
F/A—Shauna Grant, Nicole Black, Becky
    Savage, Julie Parton, Cody Nicole
F/A—Kevin James, Ron Jeremy

Except for one scene with Ron Jeremy and Julie Parton, Kevin James is the only male in this film. He takes care of all the other women. As Peter (obvious pun), he loves his live-in friend, Nicole Black, but he also wants variety. He buys an Adam computer that has the power to tap into the secret files of a local computer-dating service. In the process he discovers the sexual fantasies of various ladies, commencing with Shauna Grant. Vatelli extends their sexmaking scene very romantically. The ensuing sex is caring and finishes with an eye-popping cum shot. She milks Peter's semen into a champagne glass, dilutes it with a little bubbly, and drinks it. This is the only sequence in which Shauna appears, and she is plumper than she was in later movies and is listed in the credits as Callie Aimes. After Shauna you'd think Peter might give up his search for better things, but the tape runs for 86 minutes, during which Peter resolves the fantasies of a variety of women that he locates via the computer. Worth seeing for Shauna's appearance as a believable, erotic sex companion.

STORMY
NN BI DK
1985 CAL VISTA

P/D—Sam Norvell, Joseph Bianiski
F/A—Linda Wong, Jacklin Morina, Valerie Perrier
F/A—John Holmes, Joey Civera, John Seeman

Strictly for John C. Holmes fans, this one portrays him as a San Francisco big-time operator with a string of call girls. John Seeman is his mousy treasurer, who finally is seduced by a couple of the ladies. Joey Civera is the pimp who searches for new ladies. Big John checks out every gal personally to see if she can handle a trick. In the process, he screws at least five women. In one scene, Jacklin Morina, a new-comer, becomes an oral, anal, and vaginal sandwich for him and Joey Civera. Linda Wong, Big John's hosekeeper (pun intended), is unable to ingest his big schlong either of two ways, but some of the other ladies do pretty well.

SWEET JULIE
NN
1975 FANTASY/CABALLERO

P/D—Not given
F/A—Many people appear, but no names are
    given except John C. Holmes

Here's a very young John C. Holmes, who runs some kind of call-girl service but immediately takes on a lithesome blonde who is taller than he is and very pretty, along with an equally tall and good-looking black woman. Cut to a van where women bring in one guy after another; without conversation, they join mouths and genitals, after which you return to Johnny and the blonde. This time he screws her alone while another gal raids his cash box. That's all folks. (See notes under *Christy.*)

A TASTE OF CANDY
NN NM BI
1985 L.A. VIDEO

P/D—L. M. Burton, Drea
F/A—Candy Samples, Stacey Donovan, Rikki
    Blake, Summer Rose
F/A—Paul Thomas, Herschel Savage

Mrs. Candy Tully's (Candy Samples) husband has gone to his Maker, and Candy, lying in bed alone, mourns him. But not for long. She puts an ad in the personals: "I need a 10-inch cock to slide between my 40EE tits." She gets many replies. If you want more of Candy Samples, see review of *Inside Candy Samples* and a new one coming up, *Rx for Passion*. But you'll probably never see Candy totally naked. Methinks her belly is a match for her tits.

THOSE YOUNG GIRLS
NN BI NM
1985 PARADISE VISUALS

P/D—Frank and Ernest Macintosh, Miles Kidder

F/A—Ginger Lane, Traci Lords
F/A—Harry Reems, John Holmes

After years of retirement, Harry Reems, now in his 40s, has returned to the porno scene. John Holmes also appears in this film. The story was written by Ginger Lynn and is supposed to be true. But John manages to get his super dork in only Ginger's orifices and doesn't, like Harry, manage to enjoy both Ginger and Traci. What story there is concerns the X-film world. The camerawork in this one is clear and sharp, with so many close-ups of our ladies' vulvas you'll feel that you are there.

UP DESIREE LANE
NN BI DK
1984   VCA

P/D—Leon Gucci
F/A—Desiree Lane, Nicole West
F/A—Nick Niter, Francois, Dennis Jones

Believe it or not (you shouldn't!), Desiree tells you that this is her autobiography. Incest at home leads to a porn career, and she goes looking to buy a yacht. Instead, she ends up on a schooner with a captain and crew who enjoy screwing in the rigging and in the fishnets. They should have made the whole film on board the schooner, which is an ideal place to shoot a sexvid, as proven by *Captain Lust and the Pirates* (see review).

WHAT GETS ME HOT
NN NM BI DK
1984   INTROPICS VIDEO

P/D—Richard Mailer
F/A—Traci Lords, Susan Hart, Bunny Bleu, Helga
F/A—Tom Byron, Mark Wallice, Sean Alexander

Guys who daydream about Traci's pouty lips, big breasts with large aureolas, and crinkly vulva, which she can't keep her fingers out of, may want to watch her first film appearance.

WITH LOVE, LONI
NN BI
1985   CABALLERO

P/D—Many
F/A—Loni Sanders, Lisa de Leeuw, Tigr
F/A—Paul Thomas, Richard Pacheco, Mike Horner

Host Jamie Gillis takes you on a reprise of many sex scenes from Loni Sanders's various films, including *Night Life, Trashi, Every Which Way She Can, Please, Mr. Postman, Brief Affair,* and *Eight to Four* (see various reviews). Loni is a pretty woman and guys enamored with her, or other sexvid stars, will find that Caballero's *With Love* series will help them remember her at night when they are dreaming. But women won't be impressed.

THE WOMAN WHO LOVED MEN
NN BI
1984   ESSEX

P/D—Adam Tarasiacus, Giovani Follini, Adam
F/A—Ginger Lynn, Karen Summer, Fawn Paris, Dorothy Onan
F/A—Eric Edwards, R. Bolla, Tom Byron, Blake Palmer, Shone Taylor

This one opens with the entire cast waking up in a wealthy Hollywood home where a dead woman is laid out. In a flashback told by her psychiatrist, Dr. Tom (Eric Edwards), you meet Linda Franklin (Ginger Lynn) who is a world-famous dancer but can no longer dance because she's in a depression over her incessant nymphomaniac desires for men. Linda's sexual encounters with all of the guys listed above take the rest of the film. And Doctor Tom, who, like some psychiatrists, believes that he can help his patients over their sexual difficulties, takes on Linda. Unfortunately, Linda is so impressed with his loving that she wants to marry him. He refuses, and she returns home, but she calls him, sobbing that he must come to her. He does, and believe it or not, as he's driving in the driveway, his brakes fail, and poor Linda, who is in the frontseat of a parked car blowing a friend, is killed. Did she choke to death on the guy's putz? You don't get the answer in Doctor Tom's sad wrapup!

Cops and Robbers

AFFAIRS OF JANICE
CC NN BI DK DS
1976   BLUE VIDEO

P/D—Leon de Leon, Zebedy Colt
F/A—C. J. Laing, Crystal Harris, Annie Sprinkles
F/A—Bobby Astyr, Ras Keen, Zebedy Colt

Zebedy Colt, the director, plays the villain, George King, an alcoholic artist. George's wife tells him that cobwebs grow between his legs. She has never been unfaithful to him with a man, but she loves Janice (C. J. Laing). The movie opens with George floating dead in a swimming pool. You'll stayed tuned to this one until its wildly sadistic end. Kirk (Ras Keen), who is also in love with Janice, is caught by George making love to her and George's wife. Tricking Kirk into posing as Prometheus (bound) for him, George strips Kirk, sprays him silver, chloroforms Janice, sprays her silver, brutally abuses her, and suspends her along with Kirk from the ceiling, both of them dead. He then calls the police, and his wife is accused of the murder. In between, irrelevantly, Bobby Astyr and Annie Sprinkles appear as guests of George and his wife, and Annie gets involved with Ras Keen (Kirk), who slaps her ass red while he screws her. But Annie gets her revenge. You may not like it, but you won't forget it.

ALLEY CAT
CC R PG13 or maybe R13
1983   VESTRON

P/D—Robert E. Waters, Victor Ordonez
F/A—Karen Mani
F/A—Robert Torti, Britt Helfer, Michael Wayne, Timothy Cutt

A neat mixture of sex and violence that probably kept it out of suburban theaters. Billie (Karen Mani), a pretty Eurasian woman who doesn't weigh more than 125 pounds, is a black-belt karate expert. Her grandma and grandpa are mugged by tough hoodlums led by Scarface (Michael Wayne), and grandma is stabbed. Searching for the gang, Billie finds them beating a young woman and about to rape her. You won't believe your eyes when you see Billie in action. She tosses big men on their backs and kicks them in the balls, and she can take on two or three guys at a time, even when they are swinging chains and bats at her. The girl she saves from rape is supposed to appear in court and identify the guys, but they frighten her and she drops the charges. Billie is so shocked by the minor fine that the judge imposes that she tells him off and is soon serving 30 days in a women's prison for contempt of court. Behind bars she has to fend off tough lesbians, but they don't dare mess with her. Her police boyfriend, Johnny (Robert Torti) wants to marry her, but she refuses. "I know your type," she tells him after they've made love. "Everytime you get laid, you want to get married." Billie finally tracks down the bad guys and, in a superwoman scene, kills all three of them.

BEAVERLY HILLS COP
NN NL BI
1985   TARGET/ESSEX

P/D—Giovanni Follini, Adama Taraisclus
F/A—Heather Wayne, Robin Cannes, Sahara, Sheri St. Clair, Kristara Barrington
F/A—Peter Pole, Peter North, Tony Martino

Don't confuse this with the *Beverly Hills Cop* that made Eddie Murphy a multimillionaire. Here you've got Ready Freddie Murphy (Peter Pole), who is just as good-looking as Eddie, but he won't get rich from this one. Freddie complains at the end, "Every one in this damned movie got some pussy, except for me. I gotta see the director." You can write it off for plot. In fact, all you can say about this tape is that all the guys and gals who made it seem to be having a good, chuckly weekend, even if they didn't get paid very much for their humping.

DEMENTED
R
1980   MEDIA

P/D—Michael Smith, Arthur Jeffreys

F/A—Sally Elyse, Deborah Alter, Katherine Clayton

F/A—Bruce Gilchrist, Bryan Charles, Chip Matthews

This one has the same plot as *I Spit on Your Grave*—a woman is raped by four guys and gets her revenge. But it is nowhere near so scary as the other movie, nor as believable. It's rated R, and while there is no explicit sex and the only nudity is a quick glimpse of the lady's breasts at the very beginning when she is being gang raped, the story trades on the sex-and-violence theme that is so popular in many horror movies. The plot concerns Linda Rogers, who is married to wealthy Matt Rogers, a surgeon who is having an affair with Carol and leaves his wife alone in their big house quite a few evenings a week. She has returned from a sanitarium, where she has finally recovered a little from the shock of her gang rape. But the boys in the neighborhood think she's fair game and invade her house wearing horrible Halloween masks. She kills them all, employing cleaver, piano wire, and shotgun. When her philandering husband returns home, she's waiting for him, too, with a meat cleaver. The only reason for buying or renting this one is that Bruce Gilchrist, the lady's husband, is really Harry Reems (whose real name is Herb Striecher). See *Society Affairs* for current information on Harry Reems, who has finally returned to making porno films. Harry proves in *Demented* that he is a far better actor than most of his porno parts reveal. It's intriguing that there is no mention of him as Harry Reems on the cassette box or advertising material that accompanies this tape, proving that crossing over to legitimate films, after making adult films, ain't easy.

EROTIC ADVENTURES OF PETER GALORE
NN NL (but corny) BI DK DS (but phoney)
1985 4-PLAY VIDEO

P/D—Not given
F/A—Dalana Bissonette, Shari Kay, Kitty Seeger, Cindee Summers, Barbara Bourbon
F/A—Rick Cassidy, Tony Lane, Bill Margold, Lee J. O'Donnell, Chick Wright, Hulk

Ian Fleming would turn over in his grave. Here's 007, James Bond, in the form of Peter Galore (Rick Cassidy), a secret agent who is trying to rescue a diplomat's daughter who was kidnapped by Harold Plum (Tony Lane) and is being held for ransom somewhere out in the desert (probably near Palm Springs). Plum is a dangerous fatso who can't get it up. Shot on videotape, most of the action takes place outdoors, and the whole thing is played for laughs by the actors, who obviously are enjoying themselves doing a corny spoof on James Bond movies.

EXPOSÉ
NM BI
1975 MEDIA

P/D—Brian Smedley Ashton, James Clark
F/A—Linda Hayden, Fiona Richardson, Patsy Smart
F/A—Ugo Kier

You may catch this one on cable. It could conceivably have an R rating. The reason that I'm including it in this guide is that this made-in-England film combines sex and an undercurrent of murder and violence in such a way that it will keep you following it to the bitter end. Basically, the story revolves around a very egotistic guy, Paul Martin (Ugo Kier), his girlfriend, Suzanne (Fiona Richardson), and a secretary, Linda (Linda Hayden), whom he hires to type his second novel at his remote country estate where he lives alone. He has made a half million dollars from his first novel (which, it develops, he didn't write), and you finally discover that Linda has taken the job of secretary to revenge her husband, the true author. Made on a low budget, this one proves that if adult-film makers would add explicit sex to a good story they might produce more interesting films. This one has the story, but implied sex, including rape, is not detailed.

GOOD GIRL BAD GUY
CC NN DK
1984   ESSEX

P/D—Ben, Pamela Ben
F/A—Colleen Brennan, Taija Rae, Sharon
     Mitchell, Carol Cross, Paula Meadows,
     Sandra King
F/A—Joey Silvera, Eric Monti, George Payne

This is a real "whodunit," with a good script
by Pamela Ben. Joey Silvera plays the
lead, Mike Costa, a Mickey Spillane–style
detective who takes on the investigation
of the murder of Velva (Colleen Brennan),
a legitimate actress who is appearing as
the leading lady in a new play by Arthur
Zoltan that will open soon on Broadway.
You see what leads up to the murder before Mike appears, but not the corpse.
Was Velva a slut or a saint? This is the
question that Mike has to answer as he
tries to find out who wanted to get rid of
her. The "ins and outs" and the complicated unraveling will keep you interested.
Joey Silvera plays a tough detective with
a heart of gold very convincingly, and
you'll never guess the "Laura-like" ending.

THE GOODBYE GIRLS
NN BI
*1977   DIAMOND COLLECTION/C.D.I.
HOME VIDEO*

P/D—The Sandwich Brothers
F/A—Hilary Summers, Candy Barbour, Tiffany
     Clark, Sue Carol
F/A—Kenneth Briggs, Ron Jeremy, Ryan Helm,
     Robert Rose

A 60-minute tape in which Al Goodbye,
who runs a bookie collection agency,
makes gamblers pay up their debts by
entrapping them with former hookers. With
the exception of a young Ron Jeremy,
who plays the part of a minister, I've never
seen any of the guys before.

HARD ACTION
NN BI DK
1975   FANTASY/CABALLERO

P/D—F. W. Hubert
F/A—Jo Feidsee, Mary Simon
F/A—Gene Giano

The above actors' names are on the box.
The credits list Paula Principe, Alva Harris, Doris Wiley, Paul Shelley, and Ralph
Stephens, which may allow some adult-
film historian a chance to trace them better. I've never seen any of them before. The
story could have been a scary one. A detective's wife reads that Harry Udo, whom
he put behind bars a few years ago, has
been paroled. She's frightened, and so
are their two teenage daughters, because
Harry has threatened to get his vengeance.
Enter Harry, who looks as if he's going to
rape the wife and then the daughters. But
he doesn't have to. They all want it. Still
wearing his hat, he fucks Mom, and she
happily accommodates him, although
she has just taken care of her husband
and was masturbating when Harry arrives.
He leaves her and kidnaps the daughters
in his car, and he takes them to a warehouse conveniently equipped with a bed.
The daughters also prove very accommodating. When furious Daddy arrives
with a distraught Mama, there's a wild
tussle, but soon they all agree it's more
fun to fuck than to fight. The whole thing
is so hammily acted that you can't help
laughing. (See notes under *Christy.*)

HOSTAGE GIRLS
NN NM BI DK
1984   VCA

P/D—James George, Jackson St. Louis
F/A—Danielle, Renee Summer, Brooke Fields,
     Taija Rae
F/A—Joey Silvera, Jerry Butler, George Payne,
     Klaus Multia

All the above young ladies share a suburban home, and right from the beginning you know they aren't getting enough
sex. One of them spends all her time in
the bathroom masturbating, and Brooke
Fields and Taija Rae, who do have boyfriends, know that the guys only want them
for a tumble in bed. But worry not, there is
a prison break and the escapees, Joey
Silvera, George Payne, and Klaus Multia,
running from the police, soon crash into
their home. The rest of the tape can be
summed up by Renee Summer's attitude.
She tells Joey Silvera, "Bet you fucked a
lot of assholes in prison. Bet that you re-

ally know how to do it." He quickly proves that he does, and soon the others take over the other ladies, with no protest, until one of their boyfriends, Jerry Butler, who has joined the party, escapes. Soon the police arrive.

LAS VEGAS GIRLS
NN NM NR BI
1983 HIFCOA

P/D—Troy Benny
F/A—Karen Hall, Liz Renay, Cynthia Morrow, Drea, Jesse Ronald
F/A—Brian Jensen, Raymond Andres, William Margold

A wealthy Texan hires a private detective to find his missing daughter, Lynn, whom he suspects may have skipped off to Las Vegas to become a hooker. (She has done this before.) The detective has a female assistant who is strictly business, and she and the detective investigate the fleshpots of Las Vegas without finding Lynn. Eventually they discover that Lynn has flown to Mexico, where she has married a wealthy rancher. Never mind, the detective's assistant finally relents and screws her boss's brains out.

LAST OF THE WILD
NN BI
1975 FANTASY/CABALLERO

P/D—Bill Berry, Joe Sekes
F/A—Ann Sapp, Pat Luis
F/A—John Banks, Rex Sayre

If you want an involved story line, here it is. Unfortunately, it would take a two-hour film, without the humping, to develop it properly. It begins with an escaped convict running madly through the deserted canyons of southern California. When he collapses in the brush, a young woman finds him, and he tells her his story of drugs, betrayal, and murder. (See notes under *Christy*.)

NIGHT OF LOVING DANGEROUSLY
NN BI
1984 PARADISE VISUALS

P/D—Michael Phillips, Adam

F/A—Traci Lords, Christy Canyon
F/A—Peter North, Stephen Drake, Jamie Gillis

Here's a sexvid with a complicated plot that doesn't come off because it is told rather than acted by the participants. It's supposed to be a murder story.

PLEASURE BED
NN BI DK
1975 IVP (formerly CVX)

P/D—Not given
F/A—Jane Clayton, Rose Simpson
F/A—Fred Huber, William Barnes, Joey Silvera

The guy tells the lady right from the beginning, "Enough of romance, let's fuck," and he admits that he's a prick in every sense of the word. "But that's what you really want," he tells her. She admits that she's married to a good man, but she can't wait to jump into bed with this animal. And he isn't kidding. He *is* a prick. While the "Bolero" is playing, a black male conspirator of his is snapping pictures of them copulating. Later, he threatens to show them to her husband unless she comes up with $5,000. She hires a detective (a very young Joey Silvera), who has a shootout with the bastard, kills him, and gets killed himself. *Note:* I have given all I.V.P./CVX titles a 1975 date. Most of them are attractively packaged and are labeled "Adult Film Classics." Most of them show no copyright date and were probably originally made on 16-mm film, within a year or two of this time. Unless otherwise noted, they run for 60 minutes. Many of them are so amateurish, with no effort to be otherwise, that they become funny to watch. Many have different names for present porno stars, and the producer or director doesn't let his name appear in the credits. Most of these early sexvids retail for as low as $19.95. But unless you are really an adult-film aficionado and enjoy seeing actors and actresses who are long gone from the sexvid scene, except for a few males who are still appearing, you probably won't find them as interesting as current films. I have given a few of them CC ratings because they rise above, in story and acting, many of those made in the same period and often are more naive than later films.

SCANDAL IN THE MANSION
NN BI DK
1984 CDI HOME VIDEO/CINDERELLA

P/D—Jim Reynolds
F/A—Desiree Ray, Lisa de Leeuw, Bunny Bleu,
   Helga, Heather Adams
F/A—John C. Holmes, Craig Roberts, Mark
   Wallice

A motion-picture tycoon is found dead in his bed by his French maid (Bunny Bleu), while a few rooms away in the mansion the housekeeper (Heather Adams) is screwing with the butler (Mark Wallice). Did the millionaire die of natural causes, or did the butler do it? Detective Armstrong (Craig Roberts) and his assistant, Miss Walston (Lisa de Leeuw), arrive to get to the bottom of things, which they do, literally, with great alacrity. While Armstrong is screwing the grieving wife, Walston is searching the gardener, Long John (John C. Holmes), and you know what she discovers. Armstrong also takes on the chef, Desiree Ray, and they discover that the night he died Buttons had screwed every female in the house. The butler didn't do it. Buttons committed suicide because after the fourth one he couldn't get an erection. Why did he need another erection? For the butler, of course! It's all so corny and hammily acted you may even laugh.

SWEET SECRETS
CC NN BI
1977 ESSEX

P/D—Saul Weissburg, James Richardson
F/A—Astrid Larson, Robin Luckley, Violet Wilde,
   Rita Lansing
F/A—Jack Benson, Joey Civera

You'll watch this one from beginning to end. With much sex tease and a nice dramatic buildup, the story revolves around Martin Owens (Jack Benson, one of the most handsome guys I've ever seen in adult films). Martin has been released from a long stretch in prison and is picked up by his old buddies, one of whom gets him a job in a big Victorian house in San Francisco run by a homely woman (Miss Phillips) in her 40s who is obviously sexu-ally frustrated. Martin is soon having a love affair with a young female assistant and being spied on by Miss Phillips, who has a safe in her bedroom filled with jewelry and a solid-gold phallus, which she uses. You know that Martin is going to rob the safe, but before he does, in this eerie background, he's seduced by two young women in a nearby park, who steal his billfold and discover where he's living. The plot complications are too detailed to cover, but poor Martin, who never does rob the safe (his buddy does), ends up in Miss Phillips's power and in her bed—like it or not.

TRUE CRIMES OF PASSION
NN BI DS DBD
1983 CABALLERO

P/D—Kim Christy
F/A—Janey Robbins, Carnal Candy
F/A—Johnny Canada

Janey Robbins, as detective B. J. Fondel, tries to "solve" three sex crimes in this Kim Christy sickie quickie. The first case involves a woman who is married to a preacher and is really a dominatrix with a secret apartment filled with chains and leather gadgets and a submissive slave whom she hangs from the ceiling. Next Janey/B.J. is searching for a transsexual killer, who you know right off is the new maid her friend just hired. In the final crime, Janey becomes so horny that she's eventually serviced by the two guys she's chasing.

STRANGER IN TOWN
NN
1975 FANTASY/CABALLERO

P/D—Not given
F/A—Lisa de Leeuw, Maria Tortuga, Candy
   Barbour
F/A—Male actors not listed

There's a plot in this one, I guess, but the director got so involved in the sucky-fucky sequences that it's not very clear. Seems that the stranger in town is a young woman whose sister was raped and murdered prior to her arrival. She's come to ask a gangster for help, and of course, he's the villain, but she doesn't know it yet. She goes to bed with him, and later an informer who screws her tells her the truth, after which the bad guy kills the informer and our heroine pulls a gun on him and forces him to play Russian roulette. You hear the gunshot offscreen. As for the ladies listed above, the only time you see them is naked in the villain's pool, basking or sucking.

Family Sagas

ANTICIPATION
NN   NM   NR   DK
1982   HIFCOA

_____

P/D—Troy Benny
F/A—Sheila Parks, Jesse Adams, Serena, Karo Kamoto
F/A—Allan Todd, Jim Malibu, Jerry Heath

This one has a believable story line and good acting that make it a soap opera with an X rating. Jerry and Julie have just gotten married and have enjoyed some nice sexmaking at a motel. In the meantime, you discover that Jerry has a brother, Stevie, who is in jail for killing his wife's lover. But he's innocent. Wendy, Stevie's wife, proves that the bullet that killed her lover was fired by someone else (not her) and Stevie is released from prison. Julie meets Stevie, and even though she's on her honeymoon, it's love at first sight. Jerry and Wendy are likewise experiencing a mutual attraction. What else can they do but make it a group marriage? But alas, Troy Benny/Carlos Tobalina doesn't get into that.

BLACK JAILBAIT
NN   BI
1984   L.A. VIDEO

_____

P/D—L.M. Burton, Drea
F/A—Silver Satine, Tracy Quartermaine, Sahara
F/A—Tony El'Ay, Marshall Bradley, Alexander James

Drea, a white former porno star, has found a new career making sexvids of black life. The result in this one is what seems like a realistic slice of low-income black life, with an overload of fantasy sex, of course. Ralph Lincoln (Alexander James) is married to Buttercup, who supports him, and has a stepdaughter. Mother and stepdaughter both boss Ralph around. He does the cooking, washing, and housecleaning but gets very little sex from Mama. So he fondles the stepdaughter's girlfriend, who is a babysitter, and she's very cooperative with him. But he doesn't regain masculine power until he discovers Mama and stepdaughter making it in the bedroom, after which he takes indignant charge.

CARNAL FANTASIES
NN   NM   BD   DK
1984   VCX

_____

P/D—Lex Wayne, James Lee
F/A—Jennifer West, Liz Lee Jung, Trish Horne, Laurie Toledo
F/A—Ray Wells, Sam Marsh

As you may have noticed, quite a few sexvids begin in bed in the morning with an unhappy wife waking up with a husband who she knows will want to screw and will probably come before she does. In this one it's Sam and his wife, Joyce (Liz Lee Jung). After their slice-of-life scenario, you can be sure that the little lady won't sit home and sulk. She calls Doctor Albert, and he arrives and massages her back and vulva and fucks her, and now she's contented. Next you're switched to newlyweds who have just arrived in their honeymoon motel and can't wait to jump into the sack. The bride (Jennifer West) is obviously no novice; she has dyed her pussy hair to match her head. Also included are Joyce's sadistic revenge-on-her-husband fantasies in which she's leading a guy around by the collar, shoves a dildo up his ass, and whips him.

CHALLANGE OF DESIRE
NN NM DK
1984 NOW SHOWING

P/D—Lawrence T. Cole
F/A—Becky Savage, Linda Shaw, Lili Marlene
F/A—Jon Martin, Herschel Savage, Grant Lombard

You can't fault Lawrence T. Cole for not coming up with unusual plots. This one could have been a winner, but he blew it and instead created a totally yucky and unbelievable story. The premise is that Dora (Becky Savage), who is married to David (Jon Martin), is in physical competition with him and can do anything better than he can, including outrunning him cross-country and beating him in all sports. The marital challenge soon evolves into weird sexual games. Can David stand by and watch Dora fuck another guy? Can she play the whore and take on a lot of guys? Finally, after an orgy that they both admit was disgusting, they decide to stop playing games like this.

EROTIC HOLIDAY (MRS. SMITH'S)
NN NL (occasionally)
1982 VCX

P/D—Not given
F/A—Becky Savage, Jennifer West, Sally Swift, Maria Tortuga
F/A—Tommy La Roc, Lawrence Rothschild, Ken Starbuck

Captain Nemo (Lawrence Rothschild) runs a weekly cruise ship to Alaska for people who have sexual difficulties. Tommy (Tommy La Roc), who can't get it up with his wife no matter what she does, decides that they should take a "Horny Holiday" on the ship. Aboard they are assigned different cabins, and the hostess tells them that each night they will have a different bed companion. After five nights with five different partners and so many orgasms that they have lost count, Tommy can now get an erection with Jane, and they agree that they are lonesome for the old familiar feel of each other's genitals. No one else on the cruise gets involved, but in between you are treated to nice scenery as the cruise ship motors slowly along the Alaskan coast.

EVERYTHING GOES
NN BI DK
1982 CABALLERO

P/D—Georges Fleury
F/A—Marilyn Gule, Elizabeth Buret, Erica Cool
F/A—Charles Schreiner

Most women will detest Jack DuCray (Charles Schreiner), around whom this French film revolves. Jack has an uncircumsised penis that could compete in size with John Holmes's. Despite the fact that he is married to Annie, he can't help himself. He wants to use it on every available woman, and most of them are readily available. He leaves his wife and goes to live in a rundown hotel. His wife is invited to spend the weekend with her college friend Martine and her husband who are swingers. She is shocked and won't swing at first, but she finally does. Jack is shocked when she gives in to a friend of his whom he sends into their boutique to seduce her. If you're weary of the same old American films, here are some French faces. The genitals are the same, of course, but they "do it" against unfamiliar backgrounds.

FAMILY SECRETS
NN BI
1985 AMBASSADOR

P/D—Jim Travis
F/A—Colleen Brennan, Tamara Longley, Summer Rose, Sheri St. Clair
F/A—Nick Random, Randy West, Scott Irish

Maybe this one should have a CC rating for practically nonstop, soap-opera-style sex. Wealthy Wayne Gregg (Nick Random) is married to Joanna (Colleen Brennan), and they begin the day with a wake-up merger. They have a daughter, Chrissie (Summer Rose), and a chauffeur, Carleton (Randy West) who drives Chrissy to school and at her request gives her a cock-blowing lesson in the back seat of the family's Rolls-Royce. While he's educating the daughter, Mama is entertaining the maid (Sheri St. Clair). Daddy's doing Chrissie's friend. It's all one happy family.

FORBIDDEN FRUIT
NN BI DK
1985   PARADISE VISUALS

P/D—Adam
F/A—Honey Wilder, Candi Shields, Susan Hart, Bunny Bleu, Misty Regan
F/A—Eric Edwards, Tom Byron, Greg Rome

Eric Edwards, unshaved, arrives at his former wife's (Honey Wilder) ranch after 18 years of divorce. He is immediately accosted by one of Honey's daughters (Honey is in town shopping), who asks him if he wants to fuck her. Why not? Before Mama gets home, much to the ranch hands' (Tom Byron, Greg Rome) disgust, he has fucked the other two daughters, too. Honey isn't too happy to see her vagrant husband again, and she tells him that one of the three girls, now in their teens, is his daughter. But she won't tell him which one. Later, at a house party that turns into an orgy, he is shocked to find all three ladies enjoying themselves, and is especially grieved because one of them is his daughter. But later that night, they once again arrive in his bedroom, one at a time, and take care of Daddy. You finally know, even if Eric doesn't, that Candi, who, along with Mama, begs him to stay, is really his daughter. Like Mama, she enjoys forbidden fruit. But Daddy doesn't. He rides off into the sunset.

FRISKY BUSINESS
NN NM BI
1984   VCA

P/D—Albert Berry, Craig Alexander
F/A—Kim Carson, Cara Lott, Honey Wilder
F/A—John Leslie, Randy West

While the title might sound like the 1983 Hollywood film *Risky Business,* the only thing in common in this one is that the parents have gone away and left the house to the kids. Alas, the kids are not in high school, but presumably graduate school. Nicky (Randy West) has two sisters, Monica (Cara Lott) and Jody (Kim Carson), who are in competition for Bryan (John Leslie), and Rachel (Honey Wilder), their former high-school gym teacher, wants Nicky. So do the sisters, who, when they aren't screwing Bryan or Nicky, are masturbating with a shower connector, hairbrushes, and the edges of sofas, or being penetrated with a wiggly vibrator. Run it on fast forward.

HER WICKED WAYS
NN BI DK
1983   CABALLERO

P/D—JoAnne Lewis, Louis Lewis
F/A—Jesie St. James, Joanna Storm, Janey Robbins, Tigr, Shelly Ray
F/A—Paul Thomas, Eric Edwards, Mike Horner, Jon Martin, Dave Cannon

Ruby (Jesie St. James) is the third wife of Oliver Sutton, a San Francisco billionaire who has just kicked the bucket. His daughter Katherine (Joanna Storm) wants to make sure "that bitch" doesn't inherit a penny of the estate. She hires Riff Rafferty, a private eye, to investigate Ruby. Ruby, in the meantime, has Eric Edwards, who is temporarily in charge at Sutton Industries, in the clutch of her crotch. At this point you already know that Ruby is a bad ass. The day Oliver dies she unzips her chauffeur's pants and tells him, "I expect you to drive it home." In the meantime, Katherine has Janey Robbins, who makes love to her while she moans, "Oh Daddy, I love you. Do it to me." Rafferty doesn't reappear until the last scene, when at a board of directors' meeting, Ruby, who is planning to elect herself president, has to give up the idea because, by some miracle, Rafferty has videotaped all the fucking you have previously watched. He will use it to expose her if the board doesn't elect him president of Sutton Industries. If you can stomach the plot, you'll get all the sex you want, including a final orgy in the boardroom.

HOMECOMING
NN DK
1975 FANTASY/CABALLERO

P/D—Not given
F/A—Candy Lane, Lisa de Leeuw, others not
      listed
F/A—John C. Holmes, others not listed

A guy who has presumably been expelled
from college is hitchhiking home and is
picked up by another guy on Van Nuys
Boulevard on his way to downtown Los
Angeles. He entertains the driver with stories of his supposedly wealthy family: There
are cut-ins showing his sister screwing on
satin sheets and the maid and butler enjoying themselves to the music "Born Free."
His brother Winston arrives home, and the
maid, her ass in the air, draws a bath for
him and quickly joins him in the tub, after
which he pops into bed with Lisa de
Leeuw, whose name is not in the credits.
John C. appears. He's the gardener,
cleaning the pool with the assistance of
two ladies who mouth wash his famous
schlong. It all ends up in a poolside orgy,
and then the driver arrives with our storytelling hero. But there's no mansion, only
a small middle-class home. The driver
leaves, grunting, "I'll never believe crap
like that again!" (See notes under *Christy.*)

HOT DREAMS
NN DK BI
1983 CABALLERO

P/D—Warren Evans
F/A—Sharon Mitchell, Tiffany Clark, Anna
      Ventura, Marlene Willoughby, Joanna
      Storm
F/A—Jamie Gillis, George Payne, Michael Bruce,
      Ashley Moore

By mistake Caballero loaned me a cable-
preview version of this one. There are no
erect penises in what is known as "soft
core." Don't worry, your local video store
will have only an X version—complete with
penises and labia, which don't contribute to the story. Sadly, the story isn't much.
Seems that Sharon (all the actors have
screen names) is married to Michael. They
are both yuppies with high-income jobs,
but they have been married 12 years

and Sharon has arrived at a point where
she can't tell her recurrent fantasies (hot
dreams) from reality. They include being
raped by a stranger while she is showering and her husband is shaving but can't
see what is happening, to moments of
bondage and discipline when she's at a
dinner party—with Jamie Gillis, of course.
Followed by four-way bisexual fun that is
happening only in her imagination at an
expensive New York City health club for
females. The only surprise in the film is
a long sequence on an expensive power-
boat with a flying bridge on the Hudson
River. With the New York City skyline in
the background, and with tugboats and
excursion boats passing, Sharon and Michael and another couple (Ashley Moore,
who owns the boat, has locked the wheel
in position) play naked fun and games together. Next time you take a water trip
around Manhattan keep your eyes open!

HOT LIPS
**NN NM BI DK NL (if you're a little
bombed)**
1984 VCA

P/D—Robert Michaels
F/A—Sandi King, Tish Ambrose, Athena Starr,
      Baby Doe, Annette Heinz, Sandi Weinstein
F/A—Bobby Spector, Michael Gaunt

Ricky (Bobby Spector) is a retarded kid
who can't talk. He lives in an affluent
neighborhood with his father, Mr. Frank
(Michael Gaunt), an English teacher. Ricky
spends his time watching his neighbor
across the street, Mrs. Evans (Sandi King),
who has a daughter, Sally (Tish Ambrose),
who practices electric guitar with her female rock group in the house. The noise
drives Ricky's daddy crazy, and he calls
the police to stop the music. Downstairs,
Sally and her girlfriend capture Daddy,
who invades their house and tries to stop
them from playing. When the police arrive, they find Daddy stripped, knocked
out with poppers, and being worked over
by the girls. Before it's all over, Mommy
and Daddy are screwing with each other
and their kids, and so are the police,
along with a female police lieutenant who
has arrived to see who or what is disturbing the peace.

HOT SISTER
NN BI DK
1975 FANTASY/CABALLERO

P/D—Not given
F/A—None are listed

Amy's sister and her husband, Fred, invite Amy and Bob to a swing party at their house. The sister and Fred have been married longer than Amy and Bob, and they believe in playing around to save their marriage. Amy tells Bob that a guy at the party, John, made her give him head. . . . Well, not exactly—she enjoyed it. Bob is more than a little shocked. He's sure that he must remain faithful. But Amy tells him, "Just so long as we love each other, it's all right." Of course, when six couples finally get together in the living room, Bob changes his mind, and he tells Amy, "I'm sorry that I called your sister a whore." Randy West's name appears on the box, but he's not in it. (See notes under *Christy*.)

HOUSE OF LUST
NN BI
1985 VIDCO

P/D—Harold Lime, Jack Remy
F/A—Heather Wayne, Nicole West, Angela Dunlap, Kristara Barrington
F/A—Dan T. Mann, Nick Niter, Peky, Paul Thomas

"My boy Ronnie graduates today, coming home from Harvard Business College," Nelson Broadhurst tells his new young wife, to whom he's making love. But Ronnie has two sisters who aren't happy to see him come back, since they're doing the handyman. The chauffeur is also enjoying Nelson's wife (Heather Wayne), and Nelson is helping himself to the maid. No one really wants Ronnie to come home and screw up this love nest, and they all breathe a sigh of relief when he finally arrives and they discover that he's gay.

INDECENT PLEASURES
NN BI
1984 CABALLERO

P/D—Joe Williams, Philip Jem
F/A—Jesie St. James, Laurie Smith, Bridgitte Monet, Janey Robbins
F/A—Eric Edwards, Jon Martin, Dave Cannon

Kim (Jesie St. James) and Nick (Jon Martin) live in a California dream house overlooking the Pacific. But Nick is not happy in bed with Kim and vice versa. Kim still loves him, but she reluctantly takes a job in a downtown L.A. sex club. Who does she meet in the club but Nick, getting blown by one of the hostesses. That convinces Kim that what's good for the goose is good for the gander, and soon, to Nick's shock, she's doing a live sex show with club owner Eric, whom she later invites home for more romantic fun. Nick telephones to forgive her. But now she's in the driver's seat in more ways than one!

INTIMATE COUPLES
NN BI DK
1984 VCX

P/D—Bill Williams, Scotty Fox
F/A—Rikki Blake, Angel West, Beverly Bliss, Pamela Nimmo, Jacqueline Lorians
F/A—Herschel Savage, Steve Powers, Dino Alexander, Taylor Adams

George and Sue, who are living together, play "Trivia" with their best friends, Jim and Joanne. But George and Sue don't communicate as well as Jim and Joanne and neither knows whether the other is really enjoying him/herself when they screw. George and Sue both seek advice from Jim and Joanne. Soon George, Sue, Jim, and Joanne play switchies, and happiness and communication finally blossom, especially after they invite a third couple and another gal and they all play strip "Trivia" together. So there you are—a new way to pep up your "Trivia" games, with no geniuses allowed!

IT'S MY BODY
NN BI DK
1985 CDI HOME VIDEO

P/D—Jim Reynolds, Jerome Bronson
F/A—Traci Lords, Christy Canyon, Stacey
   Donovan, Honey Wilder, Cara Lott
F/A—Kevin James, Peter North, Randy West,
   Paul Thomas, Tom Byron

Her sister and mother want Maggi (Traci Lords) to stop screwing around, to settle down, get married, and have children. So Mama, (Honey Wilder) tells her. But Maggi refuses to marry. She is well aware that her sister Sue (Christy Canyon), who is married to Howard (Paul Thomas), cheats on him with the delivery boy. So Traci says to hell with marriage. Instead, she takes on three guys at once—sucking them and fucking them to kingdom come.

KISSIN' COUSINS
CC NN BI DK
1984 L.A. VIDEO

P/D—L. Burton, Drea
F/A—Misty Reagan, Heather Wayne, Summer
   Rose, Tara Wine
F/A—Scott Irish, Tony Martin, Herschel Savage,
   James Miles

Marge McCoy, who is recently divorced, moves in with her brother, "Tub" Hatfield. They are both single parents. There is friction and much arguing and turmoil between various members of the two families—hence the play on the surnames Hatfield and McCoy. All ends happily after everyone finds his/her bed partner, including "Tub" and his sister, who delve into a bit of incest without undo moralizing. The CC rating is for (1) the technical quality of the photography, lighting, sound, and sets; (2) the actors and actresses, who are all young and very good-looking and who portray believable characters who seem to be enjoying their sexmaking immensely; and (3) Drea and the editor, who keep the story moving. There are no interminable sex scenes.

LADY LUST
NN BI DK NM
1983 CABALLERO

P/D—Arthur Ben
F/A—Edy Williams, Annette Heinz, Paula
   Meadows, Kimberly Carson, Sharon
   Mitchell
F/A—Paul Thomas, Jerry Butler, George Payne,
   Kenney Dee

Arthur Ben had a great idea for this one, and a very natural average looking American woman (Edy Williams) as the heroine, but he blew it. Nevertheless, while I can't give it a CC rating, it's better than average. The story is about Paul Thomas and his wife (Edy Williams). They enjoy screwing—even in the kitchen while Edy is making breakfast. Then Edy's sister telephones her, and asks Edy if she wants to share the wealth with her. Actually her sister is very well-off, and has a boy friend who no longer "makes mad passionate love to her" and she wonders "why he doesn't want to just plain fuck, anymore." A few scenes later, after Edy leaves Paul to spend a week at her sister's, you quickly discover that both her sister and her husband enjoy orgies, and live in an "anything goes" environment of the idle rich.

THE LAST TABOO
NN BI DK
1985 VISTA VIDEO

P/D—Hector Castenada, Charles De Santos
F/A—Desiree Lane, Cindy Cain, Erica Idol, Rita
   Ricardo
F/A—Blair Harris, Jon Martin, Kirk Wilder

Desiree Lane and Cindy Cain are sisters who enjoy touching and tasting each other. Their brother, Blair Harris, also enjoys a little humping with them as well as with the maid. Mama (Rita Ricardo) passes the time blowing the chauffeur. Daddy (Jon Martin), a new oil millionaire, buys mama a suitcase full of sexy leather underwear and she's delighted and screws with Daddy, too. But afterward Daddy can't sleep and wanders down into the living room, where daughter Desiree is sadly wishing they were back in Oklahoma. Daddy soothes her vagina, which is itching for the guys back home. At the same time, brother Blair is making sister Cindy less horny. They're not only very wealthy, but they never have to leave home. Sex is all in the family.

LET'S GET PHYSICAL
CC NN NR BI
1983   CABALLERO

P/D—Bobbie Deen, Bob Chinn
F/A—Hypatia Lee, Shanna McCullough
F/A—Paul Thomas, Mike Horner, Francois

This low-key story was written by Hypatia and really shows a woman's influence. Maria (Hypatia Lee) is married to Carl (Paul Thomas), and they run a ballet school. Carl used to be a famous ballet star, but, after being caught in the dressing room by Maria with a starlet, he was driving home and trying to convince Maria that it didn't mean anything. But he lost control of the car and was crippled. Now, his career over, the school continues, but his marriage and sex life are on the rocks. They both have affairs with students, but wind up back together. Women will like this one and identify with Hypatia.

LOVE ON TOP
NN DK DS BI
1978   COMPETITIVE VIDEO

P/D—Not given
F/A—Gina Lo
F/A—Not given

Billy is going to marry Betty, and she's spent the night with him in Billy's very nice home. Watching Billy take a shower, you know that he's a kook because he's dreaming of other women and he masturbates instead of servicing Betty, but at breakfast he's very nasty and macho with her when she tells him that she's going to spend the day looking for her wedding gown. When she's gone, Billy telephones a couple of hookers—and it turns out he's a masochist who likes to be tied and played with. Two of them arrive in his living room, and after they have strapped him to a table they proceed to work him over. When Betty returns, she is raped twice by the hookers' male friends. Then she packs her bag, shakes her head, and leaves Billy to his S-and-M games.

LUST IN AMERICA
NN BI
1985   VCX

P/D—S. Williams
F/A—Sheri St. Clare, Summer Rose, Shane Taylor, Karen Summer, Beverly Glen
F/A—Ray Hardin, John Holmes, Jeff Scott

Three couples, Judy and Tom, Bob and Mary, and Lois and Charlie, are friends. Invited over to Judy and Tom's house, the women separate and the guys congregate in the den drinking beer. You soon discover that, despite the fact that their wives are as horny in bed as they are, the men have all managed at least one extracurricular marital escapade, all of them with the local hairdresser and several of them with each others' wives, although they don't identify them. The ladies have also fooled around, one of them with John C. Holmes, who was watering his grass with a hose while they explored his other hose. After a few hours, the spouses recongregate, and believe it or not, they don't have an orgy, but go home to their separate marital beds.

MORTGAGE OF SIN
NN BI DK
1975   FANTASY/CABALLERO

P/D—Alec Reon
F/A—Mona Jenks, Sue Dunn, Jan Wells, Tina Tryon
F/A—Ed Stark, Lee Moore

Frank tells his story in a voice-over: Seems he's married to Marion, who has all the money. They live on a huge estate with stables, but he loves Jennifer. Unfortunately, Jennifer is screwing with the gardener and Marion is making it with the butler. Marion and Jennifer also occasionally hop in the sack together. Frank has joined a monastery, but as he writes to Jennifer he's working in a girls' school, where his genitals never get lonesome. (See notes under *Christy*.)

MY SINFUL LIFE
NN NM BI DK
1983   HIFCOA

P/D—Troy Benny
F/A—Danielle
F/A—Jamie Gillis

A young girl is sent by her foster parents to live with her girlfriend. She tells her how they used her sexually, and in flashbacks you see her screwing with her stepdaddy and stepmommy, and the young brother comes home for further switcheroos. Step-daddy is Jamie Gillis. The young lady, (Danielle) eventually ends up in a bro-thel, where she discovers, mirabile dictu, that the madam is her real mother; soon she is enjoying, with Mommy, a five-way Mulligan stew.

NASTY
CC NN BI DK
1985   NOW SHOWING

P/D—Lawrence T. Cole
F/A—Gail Sterling, Grace West, Lili Marlene
F/A—Jamie Gillis, Mike Horner, Billy Dee, Blair Harris, Lynx Cannon, Jonathon Younger, Ron Jeremy

The CC is for a plot device that is so garbage-pail nasty that you can only laugh or throw up and be happy that Jamie Gillis or Gail Sterling isn't your spouse. It begins with a game that Jamie invented and Gail, his wife, enthusiastically helps him carry out. Lying naked in their bed-room, he plays with himself and listens to her on the intercom while she pretends that she is being fucked by another guy. She describes the action in slimy detail. Later, she asks him if he likes the game they are playing. He sure does! But he'd prefer that the game be for real. So, dur-ing the rest of the film, Gail picks up all the guys and a few of the gals listed above, brings them home, and screws with them while Jamie listens from the bed-room on the intercom, or, in several cases, finally participates in the action. In the things-you've-never-seen-before depart-ment (and you can buy it, if you wish; the manufacturer's name and address are given in the credits) is a coffee table low enough to the floor that a guy can slide under it and stick his cock up through a hole in the center. That's not all! The cir-cular table revolves. To Ron Jeremy's amazement (he's a guy Gail has picked up), Gail spins on it while she flexes on her knees and gives him a weightless fuck. Gail Sterling is a fascinating Brunhild-type woman. Cole should be able to write a better domination story for her.

PRESCRIPTION FOR PASSION
NN NM BI DK
1985   VIDCO

P/D—Di Bacchus, Tony Valentino
F/A—Gina Valentino, Sue Lee, Heather Thomas, Summer Rose
F/A—Sasha Gabor, Nick Niter, Greg Rome, Jimmie Take All

You can lie on Dr. Long's (Sasha Gabor—who looks a little like Burt Reynolds) divan and tell him your sexual fantasies. He's a therapist who hypnotizes his female clients so that they tell him what's really in their subconscious. One lady has always want-ed to suck two guys' cocks at once and be a sandwich. One wants a 16-year-old boy, and one wants Dr. Long and his wife. It all ends up in a four-couple fuckathon.

PRIVATE MOMENTS
NN NL
1983   CAL VISTA

P/D—Sam Norvell, Robert McCallum
F/A—Janey Robins, Laura Lazarre, Honey Wilder
F/A—Eric Edwards, Jon Martin, Herschel Savage, Bill Dee, Jesse Adams, Blair Harris, Tom Byron

Eric is married to Laura. Jon is married to Janey. Honey is married to Herschel. The men are hard-working lawyers who no longer get hard with their wives. So the wives fantasize better sex with each oth-ers' husbands. The ladies are pretty. The dialogue is often amusing and may ap-peal to women whose husbands no long-er are the Romeos they once were.

SECRET DESIRES
DS DK NN (one sequence)
1975   ASTRO

P/D—Joe Serkes
F/A—Peni Burk, Kay Louis
F/A—Joe Kado, Sam Torn

In this one Mama is hung in the attic by Daddy, who fucks her and whips her. When his daughter nearly rescues Mama he captures her, too, strips her, and suspends her from the rafters next to Mama. Then a friend arrives, wondering what has happened to them, and Daddy ties her up. You won't believe it, but he gets one more women before he's captured. The sexvid ends with Daddy in a straitjacket.

SEX SPA USA
NN DK BI
1984 VCA

P/D—James George, Henri Pachard
F/A—Brooke Fields, Annette Heinz, Honey Wilder, Danielle
F/A—Paul Thomas, Joey Silvera, Jerry Butler, George Payne, Bobby Astyr, Stephen Scott

The Sex Spa is a swingers' club. Paul Thomas and his screen wife, Honey Wilder, both of whom, after 12 years of marriage think the other is a dud in bed and lacks sexual imagination, decide to try the place. One the same night so do Jerry Butler and his girlfriend, Annette Heinz. Everyone except Jerry, who loses his gal, go home satisfied—temporarily, at least.

SHACK UP
NN BI DK
1985 VIDEO-X-PIX

P/D—Howard A. Howard, Jeff La Touche
F/A—Rachel Ashley, Gina Carrera, Tiffany Clark, Melissa Scott, Karen Summer, Amber Lynn
F/A—Paul Thomas, Michael Knight, George Payne, Joe Black, Jerry Butler

Walking through Washington Square, in New York City's Greenwich Village, Pam (Rachel Ashley) tells what story there is in this one. "We were four college girls, wild, crazy, horny. We shared each others' men and we shared each other." They still are and they still do.

SHOW YOUR LOVE
NN NM DI DK
1984 VCA

P/D—Edward Bruno, Vince Benedetti
F/A—Sharon Mitchell, Joanna Storm, Kelly Nichols, Alexis Service, Marissa Constantine, Annette Heinz
F/A—Paul Thomas, Joey Silvera, Dave Ruby

Micky (Joey Silvera) is so bored with his sex life, after 12 years of marriage, that he stops on the way home from work, picks up a street prostitute, and pays her $20 to screw him in his car not far from the Hudson River. Later he tells his wife, Kim (Sharon Mitchell), "I think we have a problem, but I don't want to lose you." Unfortunately, she has no answers for him and she masturbates in the bathtub. You've seen this scenario before in adult films, but Mark (Paul Thomas) Micky's partner in an accounting firm who is married to Sara (Joanna Storm), has a solution. He takes Micky to a private club run by April (Kelly Nichols) where there's a lot of live sex shows and where April herself joins her female strippers on stage and makes love with them. Believe it or not, *that* is the solution to Micky's problems. Two girls making it together, or his wife masturbating while he watches, really turns him on. If your lady is strictly heterosexual, she won't like this one, which offers a lot of bisexual action.

SINS OF LUST
CC NN DK
1975 FANTASY/CABALLERO

P/D—Not given
F/A—No actors or actresses listed on credits, but Vanessa Del Rio is identifiable

Bob has been married to Mary for some time. He climaxes but she doesn't. He tells her that it's her fault. She insists that he's to blame. He answers an ad in the *Village Voice* offering the services of surrogates to solve sexual problems. A female surrogate, Carlotta (a plump Vanessa Del Rio), arrives and assures him that she can solve his problem. She does. Soon Bob convinces his wife, who is a bit horrified, that she should try a male surrogate. The bearded guy arrives and comes to the conclusion that it's all Bob's fault. Bob and Mary end up in a happy foursome with Bob's brother and his wife after Bob tells them about their experiences. Seems a change of scenery is all that was required. The sex advice in this one is amusing, and while the concept of surrogates lost favor after Masters and Johnson stopped using them, in case you're interested, in most major cities you'll find them in business under the names of sexual health centers or sex therapists. (See notes under *Christy*.)

SIZZLING SUBURBIA
NN BI
1985 CDI HOME VIDEO

P/D—Jim Reynolds, Will Kelly
F/A—Traci Lords, Cara Lott, Sheri St. Claire,
Pamela Jennings
F/A—Peter North, Starbuck, Francois Papillon

Mike (Peter North) is a well-to-do lawyer married to Vickie (Cara Lott), whom he enjoys in bed. But Vickie is nervous about the way he stares at her sister Sandy (Sheri St. Claire), who has come to stay with them for a few weeks. And Sandy is obviously appraising Mike as a bed companion. Mike is also working out alimony payments for their next-door neighbor, Helen Trent (not the Helen of soap-opera fame but Traci Lords), and Vickie knows that Helen can't be trusted. Karen (Pamela Jennings) tells Vickie that "what's good for the goose is good for the gander," and being a generous soul, she sends her Japanese husband (Starbuck) over to provide her good friend with a little extracurricular loving. It has one thing going for it—no group orgies, only twosomes and one threesome.

SLEEPLESS NIGHTS
NN BI DK
1985 VISTA VIDEO

P/D—Hector Casteneda, Hayes Dupre
F/A—Lili Marlene, Jacqueline Lorians, Rita
Ricardo, Kerri Hart, Helda Holdern
F/A—Jon Martin, Blair Harris, Rocky Baldor

Living in the hills overlooking Los Angeles, wealthy Stevie Farnsworth (Lili Marlene),

who has a classic, square-cut jawline, is overwhelmed by sexual fantasies, which she doesn't dare mention to her husband, Brad (Rocky Baldor). She imagines herself being raped in her bathroom by a masked man. When her husband invites his business associate to dinner, she imagines the guy's wife as a dominatrix forcing her to lap her cunt, and she can see tham all having an orgy. She finally confesses to her husband what is happening, but she thinks she's cured by Sandra (Jacqueline Lorians), a photographer whom she has hired to assist her in her design work. It all ends in a happy orgy. Lili Marlene has a believable acting style. Someone should find a better story for her.

SOUNDS OF SEX
NN BI DK
1985 CABALLERO

P/D—Billy Thornberg
P/D—Tantala Ray, Pamela Jennings, Cara Lott,
Karen Summer
F/A—Tom Byron, Sasha Gabor, Lance Lott,
Francois Papillon, Mark Wallice

Wealthy Mrs Hunnicutt (Tantala Ray, a seamy, curled-mouth lady) tape records all her and her friends' sounds when they are fucking. She has thousands of dollars' worth of equipment, including a sound-collection dish, which she can set up near her swimming pool and pick up the words, moans, and groans of her neighbors.

STRAY CATS
NN BI DK
1985 VIDEO-X-PIX

P/D—Michael De Jou, Eric Anderson
F/A—Blair Castle, Renee Summers, Cody Nicole,
Danielle
F/A—Joey Silvera, Joseph Black, Michael Knight,
George Payne, Johnny Nineteen, Alan
Adrian, David Scott

Mara (Cody Nicole) is married to June's (Blair Castle) old boyfriend, Wilson Ladd (Joey Silvera). June meets Mara jogging and invites her back to her apartment, where they shower and bathe together and renew old acquaintances after many years. After they all have sex with each other and some strangers, Mara agrees with June that the only solution is to share Wilson and live as a threesome. With a video camera and some cooperative friends, you could make a more interesting film.

SUMMER IN HEAT
CC NN NM NR DS (story related)
1979   ESSEX

P/D—Christy and Jerry McCabe
F/A—Desiree Cousteau, Delania Ruffino, Jessie Adams, Juliet Anderson
F/A—Jack Wrangler, Jamie Gillis, John Leslie

Patrick (Jamie Gillis), who has just made love with Liz (Delania Ruffino)—she's not too happy because she hasn't climaxed—offers to take her to Lake Shasta for a romantic weekend. That reminds her of something that took place there a few years ago, when she was married to Senator Jack (Jack Wrangler) and they spent their weekends on a houseboat on the lake with their friends. Liz's story begins with a fun weekend. Alice (Desiree Cousteau) arrives with Jessie (Jessie Adams), Phil (John Leslie), and Judy (Juliet Anderson). They enjoy themselves racing around the lake in high-powered speedboats and screwing in the woods. Up to this point all the sexmaking has been idyllic and beautifully photographed. But now the top blows off and a *Deliverance* plot ensues. Jack is bopped on the head by a surly, tough "cracker." His two girlfriends, who have boarded the houseboat with him, tie the unconscious Jack up, drag him into the woods, hang him between two trees, and damn near rape him to death. At the same time, their male friend, who has been threatening Alice with a knife, ties her up and rapes her viciously. After many hours, they are finally rescued by Liz and Jessie, but the rapists escape after a wild chase around the lake. The story is well told, with believable dialogue and good acting that puts this one high on a list of top sexvids.

UNTHINKABLE
NN NM BI DK
1983   ESSEX

P/D—Mark Corby
F/A—Bunny Bleu, Pamela Mann, Tamara Longley
F/A—Scott Irish, Eric Edwards, Honey Wilder

Silently, younger sister (Bunny Bleu) joins her brother (Scott Irish) in the sunken tub in the bathroom of their affluent suburban home. She opens her bathrobe and kneels to suck his cock, and with no conversation at all, they make love—while downstairs the maid (Tamara Longley) is preparing breakfast. Daddy (Eric Edwards) and Mommy are preparing to leave for the weekend. After they have gone, while brother is eating breakfast, the maid bends over and displays her bare ass to him. He gapes in astonishment, and you know he's going to have a busy weekend. Later, after the maid has helped him with his homework, big sister arrives with her boyfriend and they have a five-way orgy, but big brother really loves little sister, and he's in bed with her when Daddy and Mommy come home and find them. With an amazed "what-the-hell" expression on their faces, Eric and Honey stare into the camera and the film ends. Tamara has a deep, throaty voice, and Bunny really looks a little like a younger sister.

VANESSA, MAID IN MANHATTAN
NN NM BI DK
1984   VCA

P/D—James George, Henri Pachard
F/A—Vanessa Del Rio, Brooke Fields, Danielle, Colleen Brennan
F/A—Eric Edwards, Jerry Butler, George Payne, David Scott, Alan Adrian

The presumption in this one is that porno actresses like Brooke Fields, based on their earnings and residuals, are millionaires. Most female stars are lucky if they gross $50,000 a year. Anyway, along with that daydream you have to swallow another. Colleen Brennan and Chelsea Blake have decided that Brooke Fields is a good catch for their sons. If the sons marry her, they'll become wealthy and can reverse the declining family fortunes that have been lost in the stock market by the likes of Daddy (Eric Edwards). Daddy, at this point in life, would rather fuck with the maid, Juanita (Vanessa Del Rio), than service Mama Colleen. The action concerns the attempts of the two mothers to get their sons engaged to Brooke. As for Vanessa Del Rio, you can see her in a couple of sequences, but most of the time Pachard must have forgotten she was around.

WOMAN IN PINK
NN BI
1985   ESSEX

P/D—Adam
F/A—Christy Canyon, Jessyca Wylde, Donna Derriere
F/A—Tom Byron, Guido Martoni, Peter Pole

Tom (Tom Byron) who it isn't easy to believe is 30 years old, is having a little birthday celebration with his friends. They take him back to their apartment, where they show Tom a porno film on cassette—and lo and behold, the woman on the tube throws her panties at them and they catch them. Back home, Tom is too tired to do his wife. The next day, Tom fantasizes (or actually takes on—you can't tell which) Crystal, an employee in his office.

YOUNG AND RESTLESS
NN NM BI DK
1985   VISTA VIDEO

P/D—Hector Casteneda, Hayes Dupre
F/A—Kimberly Carson, Jennifer Wong, Linda Shaw, Danica Rae, Marie Tortuga, Cristal Lovin
F/A—Paul Thomas, Jack Mason, Mark Wallice, Johnny Stagliano

Somewhere in the Hollywood hills, overlooking Los Angeles, there's a place called the Retreat, which provides guys and gals to service lonely or bored housewives. Laura Hartley (Kimberly Carson), who is married to Bob, isn't getting enough sex, so she visits the place and sees Paul

Thomas, one of the instructors, along with an assistant, make a happy sandwich out of a lady customer, after Paul massages her and beats her ass a little. Laura is intrigued with this sex maniac's delight. After sucking Bob's cock, Laura tells him about the joys of the Retreat. From that point there is no further conversation, just cellar-to-attic sex as they join the club.

Role Playing

BEST LITTLE WHOREHOUSE IN SAN FRANCISCO
NN BI DK
1984   L.A. VIDEO

P/D—Dino Ferrara, Jack Remy
F/A—Candy Samples, Amber Lynn, Taija Rae, Mai Linn, Sondra Stillman, Jenny Goode
F/A—Herschel Savage, Joey Silvera, Jerry Butler, Buck Adams

With a little more interest in character development, this could have been a top sexvid. Fanny Mae (Candy Samples) is the madam of the house. Her best little whore, Lisa LaRue, has gone and gotten herself pregnant and wants to get married. If this concoction had been put together with a more believable actress than Amber Lynn to play the part of Lisa, and if the wall-to-wall sex had been cut back a little, the story could have gotten you involved. As it is, the only thing that holds your interest is Candy Samples's big tits, which seem to have grown and now must approach 50DD-cup size.

BODY SHOP
NN NM BI
1984   VCX

P/D—Not given
F/A—Amber Lynn, Lisa Marie, Tracy Escobar, Christina Lake, Tina Marie, Shaun Michelle, Pam Nino
F/A—R. Bolla, John Holmes, Scott Irish, Claymore Rush

R. Bolla runs an automobile repair business with Scott Irish. Amber Lynn has a string of five hookers who are in trouble with the police. Bolla suggests to Amber that they combine their businesses. Five ladies wind up with their asses on the hoods of cars, and even John C. Holmes, as a customer, arrives to have his main shaft checked. But so does a vice-squad officer, and the venture and the picture end.

BRIAR PATCH DOLLS
CC NN NL BI
1984 VCA

P/D—Barry Dawson, Jerry Edwards, Samantha Hall
F/A—Janet Leigh, Eleanor Taylor, Nancy Ross, and nine other women with English names on the credits who are obviously French, Swedish, or German
F/A—An equal number of European guys whose names aren't given

The American title of this European-made film is a complete misnomer—but don't let that stop you. The story takes place at a college or university and focuses on a biology class presided over by a professor in his late 60s. Three of his female students are flunking, but they stay after class and quickly prove to him that they know more about some aspects of biology than he does. They strip him and give him a loving blow job and you know they have passed biology. What makes the scene laughing and "Continental" is that "the old fart," as they call him, is really a senior citizen—something you rarely see in an American sex film. The rest of the film is filled with the same kind of silliness, with much conversation as the girls shower together after a sex workout in the gymnasium on parallel bars and on a trampoline. That's followed by a class picnic where five naked guys chase five naked women through the woods on a warm summer day and make happy love. There's no plot, but the women are such girlish, cool sexpots and the sex is so natural that you can't help smiling.

BROWN SUGAR
NN BI
1985 VCA

P/D—L. M. Burton, Drea
F/A—Shari Stewart, Linda Morgan, Sahara
F/A—Billy Dee, Bob Wilma, Big Al

Here's a sexvid with five handsome blacks and a white, Billy Dee, who looks as if he needs a suntan. The plot concerns a singing group whose feature song is *Brown Sugar* that is headed up by Sugar (Sahara), with the other two ladies listed above as her backup. The group once made money but is no longer popular. Billy Dee, their agent, tells them that Sugar is washed up, and a slimy character, played by Bob Wilma, claims he can get them making money again, but only if Sugar plays ball with him. She does, but with no results. Never mind, her boyfriend, Jimmy Slick (Big Al), saves the day.

CALIFORNIA SURFER GIRLS
NN BI
1979 ESSEX

P/D—Boot McCoy
F/A—Melba May, Stephanie Young
F/A—Joey Civera, Joe Skeg

The guys who screw in this one don't surf, and neither do the girls, who tie a surfboard to the top of their car to look as if they do. But they do enjoy each others' genitals on the beach and in surfing wagons and at a biker-surfer party, which surprisingly doesn't end in an orgy. Joey Civera, who is still active making films, looks so young in this one you won't believe it, and the occasional scenery intercuts of real surfers and the beaches around La Jolla are pretty.

CHERRY TRUCKERS
NN BI DK
1979 VCX

P/D—R. Owen Tegee, Pik Taziner
F/A—Azure Te
F/A—Dean Gary

You've never seen anyone in this film before. Other than sitting in the cabs of huge trucks, which you never see them drive, the cherry truckers (so named because one of them screwed a guy in the middle of a shipment of cherry pies) spend most of their time in the back of the trucks or in motels. Communicating by CB, they are on their way to San Francisco, where the Mother Truckers of America are holding their convention. Enroute, they have picked up some sad-looking saps, with whom they play B/D games as a feature of the convention. A throwuppy, slurper furker!

COFFEE, TEA OR ME
NN BI
1983   CAL VISTA

P/D—Sam Norvell, Robert McCallum
F/A—Tara Aire, Juliet Anderson, Janey Robbins, Erica Boyer
F/A—Jamie Gillis, Paul Thomas, Herschel Savage

Kathy (Tara Aire) wants to be an airline stewardess. Her sister Julie (Juliet Anderson) is already a senior stewardess but has now qualified for her pilot's license and hopes to be the first woman airline pilot. Hoppy (Jamie Gillis) is a pilot on the Chicago run who sleeps with Julie but doesn't want her to become a pilot because his bed companion will be somewhere else when he comes home. Jason (Paul Thomas) is an airline executive who can hold up Julie's application and does because of his good friend Hoppy. Kathy hears about this and offers Jason "coffee, tea or me."

C.T. (COED TEASER)
NN NM BI DK
1978   VIDEO-X-PIX

P/D—Leon Gucci
F/A—Louise Parsons, Copper Penny, Spring Taylor, Barbara Hawser, Chelsea Manchester, Suzanne Howard, Brooke Bennett, Barbara Samples
F/A—Doug Hamilton, Ron Jeremy, and many other unidentified guys

It would be interesting to know where Gucci picked up the people for this early film. The only ones that I recognized as having survived are Ron Jeremy and Chelsea Manchester (a.k.a. Tigr). As for the story there is none. The Connecticut scenery and lake views are more interesting than the problems of Richard Gordon (Doug Hamilton) and his wife, Gloria (Louise Parsons), who take jobs, as counselors at a summer camp for "wayward guys and gals."

EDUCATING EVA
NN NL BI DK
1985   VCA

P/D—Leon Gucci
F/A—Desiree Lane, Joy Merchant, Karen Summer, China Lee (a.k.a. Kristara Barrington), Lisa Lace
F/A—Nick Niter, Francois Papillon, Doug Bennett

Eva (Desiree Lane) asks her French professor to give her special instructions so that she can communicate better with a French exchange student, Don Phillipe (Francois Papillon). Actually, Don Phillipe communicates better with his prick than with his tongue and doesn't care much about Eva's mind (if she has one). Never mind, Professor Brown (Doug Bennett) has soon invited both Eva and her sexpot girlfriend Belina (Lisa Lake) to his home for special tutoring, which simply amounts to them turning the pages of some books while he daydreams about screwing with Eva. *Educating Rita* it isn't!

FIRST TIME AT CHERRY HIGH
NN NM BI
1984   VCA

P/D—Eve Milan
F/A—Tanya Lawson, Chelsea Blake, Renee Summers, Carol Cross, Mystery Lane
F/A—Jerry Butler, Ron Jeremy, George Payne

Actually it isn't Cherry High School (the title is a misnomer); it's Miss Pepper's School for Girls. Miss Pepper is a frustrated old maid who masturbates in the taxicab on the way to class. The girls all wear the school uniform—black skirts, middy blouses with bows, and saddle shoes—and believe that they have "a lot of serious fucking to do." Invited to a party being given by Senator Weatherman, at which there are many eligible bachelors, they're soon humping and bumping in the cloakroom, on the pool table, in urinals. One lady, Mystery Lane, sets a new Guiness record. In the things-you-can't-believe department, she sucks the cocks of 11 guys wearing masks of famous people and keeps all 11 of them standing and ready for further action. As for Miss Pepper, she marries the senator.

FLASHPANTS
CC NN BI NL DK
1984 VCA

P/D—Eve Milan
F/A—Tanya Lawson, Christie Williams, Alexis X., Athena Star, Michelle Morgan
F/A—George Payne, Jerry Butler

The ambiance of this one is better than that of *Flesh Dance* (see review), and the story, trading on *Flashdance* of course, is more believable. The high-school prom is coming up the same day as a Flashpants contest, and the gals and guys, despite their parents' wishes, plan to attend the contest. Surprisingly, most of the women and the guys, George Payne and Jerry Butler, manage to look and talk like teenagers, and there are some amusing scenes with one girl, Angela, and her boyfriend, who wonders, "Do you think we'll ever live to do it?" Angela finally relents, but prior to that she is constantly examining her vulva in a mirror and playing with herself while Mama yells upstairs, "Angela, do you need any help?" The biscene is also kind of mushy-cute, with two girls exploring their vaginas with stuffed animals, puppets, and the tip of a wine bottle. Throughout, you can sense a woman's directorial touch. The dancing is pretty good, too.

FLESH DANCE
NN BI
1984 ESSEX

P/D—Joanne Jewel, Ken Gibb

F/A—Shanna Evans, Rachel Ashley, Desiree Lane, Tanya Lawson, Kimberly Carson
F/A—John Leslie, Herschel Savage, Ron Jeremy

You want an explicit *Flashdance?* The adult-film producers won't let you down. You can have this version or *Flashpants* (see review). Of course, the stories are not quite the same. In this one, Jennifer (Shanna Evans, who is a black woman) can wiggle her butt pretty well to rock music, and soon she's realizing her desire—appearing at Albert's (Herschel Savage) All-Nude Girl's club. She gets there as one of the ladies in a dance contest, arranged by Albert's pal Brad (John Leslie), which is designed to put new life into the club and make the guys' flesh dance as they take part in sexual fantasies instigated by the female dancers. The winner of the contest is of course Jennifer—after which Brad/John takes her to bed and makes very nice love to her.

FRATERNITY VACATION
R NL
1984 NEW WORLD

P/D—Robert Peters, James Frawley
F/A—Sheree Wilson, Kay Wright, Barbara Crampton
F/A—Stephen Geoffreys, Cameron Dye, Leigh McCloskey, Tim Robbins, Matt McCoy

There's no explicit genital sex on this tape. It's a teenage movie that revolves around fraternity brothers from Iowa State on a week's vacation in Palm Springs who have only one thing on their mind: getting laid. It proves a couple of things. Frank sexual subjects intrigue young and old, and the younger generation enjoy hearing and seeing guys in pursuit of gals and vice versa with no conversational holds barred. The story is familiar, Wendall Tvedt (Stephen Geoffreys) is a nerd. He knows about everything in the world except girls. In a contest between two much more sophisticated fraternity brothers, who bet a thousand bucks which one will be the first to lay Ashley Taylor (Sheree Wilson), a pretty young lady who doesn't know either of them, Wendall is the guy who finally gets to bed with her.

FRENCH POSTCARD GIRLS
NN BI DK
1977 VCA

P/D—Not given
F/A—Jacqueline Bardot, Tina Russell
F/A—Marcel Lettig

This is another VCA release in 1985 of a 1970s film. Most of the top distributors are exploring 1970s films and offering them in 1985 packages, and some of them are superior, as I have noted throughout this book. But this one doesn't add up to much. It supposedly takes place in a French bordello. It's just one humping-in-bed scene after another.

GETTING LUCKY
NN BI DK NR (One tiny sequence)
1985 CABALLERO

P/D—Paul Vatelli
F/A—Tiffany Willis, Ann Whiting, Rose Marie, Misty Dawn, Mary Ann Richard, Janey Robbins, Beth Fix, Lauren Walden, Dushka
F/A—Eric Edwards, Jerry Butler

For the first 20 minutes you can't tell what's really happening. It's the night after a high-school graduation party at one of the girl's homes (her parents are away), but it's so dimly lighted that you have a hard time figuring out what is going on. You know that everyone is screwing someone in the house and/or in cars parked in the driveway. Finally, two guys who aren't making it team up with Eric Edwards (who graduated years before and knows the ropes) and go downtown in search of sure stuff. They all get it somewhere or other. Dushka has white hair cut in a boyish style and very black pubic hair. You may feel lucky if you have a fast-forward button for this one.

GIRLS JUST WANT TO HAVE FUN
NN BI
1984 ESSEX

P/D—Ken Gibbs, Stewart Carter
F/A—Desiree Lane, Liza Breeze, Rachel Free, J. Johnson, Beverly Bliss

F/A—Jim Star, Paul Thomas

From the backgrounds, I think this film was shot around Venice Beach, California, where people watching is a great deal of fun and the girls are just as dopey-looking as Cyndi Lauper. After a boring start, two young women are invited to go sailing for the day. Eventually the guys put up a sail and all four run around the boat naked and are happily screwing. Instead of sailing the boat, they finally end up in the cabin looking at porno movies. Who's steering the boat?

HYPERSEXUALS
NN BI DK
1984 VCA

P/D—James George, Robert Houston
F/A—Brooke Fields, Annette Heinz, Tanya Lawson, Lauri Smith, Carol Cross, Sharon Kane
F/A—Joey Silvera, Bobby Astyr, Herschel Savage, Michael Knight, George Payne, David Christopher

If you have watched many adult films, you realize that the actors are really a repertory company who appear in one after another. The above credits are typical. In this one, Herschel Savage is the leading man and Bobby Astyr, as the house father of fraternity Phi Beta Dappa, allows no girls, no booze, no girlie magazines, no smoking. To the relief of the brothers, who look about 10 years older than college freshmen, Bobby has to leave for the weekend to see his sick mother. In short order the fraternity house is in shambles, with the kitchen on fire and Bobby's 1950s Chevrolet that he has left in their care a total wreck. Herschel, who had been left as second-in-command, is in a state of shock, especially when he finds his girlfriend, Brooke Fields, screwing with another brother. Never mind, she has the solution to raise enough money to restore the fraternity and Bobby's car: turn the frat house into a one-night whorehouse. You may have seen this plot before in the regular Hollywood film *Risky Business*, but here, of course, the humping is explicit.

LONG, HARD NIGHTS
NN BI NL DK
1984 ESSEX

P/D—Henry Pachard
F/A—Taija Rae, Tasha Voux, Spring T., Kristara Barrington
F/A—George Payne, Joey Silvera

Nora (Taija Rae) is a nurse who wears a uniform that shows her behind when she bends over, but she believes in really helping her male patients get better fast by having sex with them. *Adult Film News* gave this one its 1984 award for the "Best Shot on-Video Adult Feature," which isn't saying much.

LOOSE TIMES AT RIDLEY HIGH
NN NL BI
1984 VCX

P/D—William Dancer, Hans Christian
F/A—Kimberly Carson, Renee Summer, Bunny Bleu
F/A—Eric Edwards, Paul Thomas, Tom Byron

William Dancer evidently enjoys producing high-school sexvids (see reviews of *Tomboy* and *Little Girls Blue I and II*). This one is really *Little Girls Black* since the costumes are now black skirts and white blouses instead of blue and white. And if you're looking for a high school, forget it. It's a girls' school, and Dancer uses the same building that was the school in *Little Girls Blue*. In this one, the women look more like teenagers than in most "teenage" sexvids, but they are in greater heat than any female cats you've ever seen.

OUR MAJOR IS SEX
NN NM BI
1984 VIDCO

P/D—Frederic Fox, Jack Remy
F/A—Karen Summer, Bunny Bleu, Dorothy O., Roxanne Holland, Susan Hart
F/A—Mark Wallice, Rocky Rome, Steve Drake

"I'm Horny, I'm Hot" is the theme song of Karen and Susan, who are coeds living in a sorority at a university where they happily suck, and are eaten by, every fraternity brother in sight. The story line is so thin that a flashback is introduced to fill up time, during which one guy reminisces about the great time he had with Bunny Bleu.

PEACH FUZZ
NN BI
1976 DIAMOND COLLECTION/C.D.I. HOME VIDEO

P/D—Not given
F/A—Lisa Thatcher
F/A—Michael Morrison, Billy Dee

Don't confuse this one with *Georgia Peach* (see review), which once had the same title. This one is a 60-minute tape that concentrates, almost wholly (pun intended) on Mary (Lisa Thatcher), who is a nymphomaniac high-school kid, and her older sister, Kathleen (screen name not given). The tape is devoted to either her or Kathleen with the guys above, or each other, in graphic mouth and genital close-ups. Lisa Thatcher was one of the early childish-looking porno stars, but she doesn't seem to be making films anymore.

PLEASURE CHANNEL
NN BI
1984 VCA

P/D—Robert Houston
F/A—Brooke Fields, Laurie Smith, Annette Heinz, Jean Silver, Athena Starr
F/A—Jerry Butler, Michael Knight, Paul Thomas, George Payne

Pleasure Channel is a call-girl service operated by Paul Thomas, who has just hired Brooke Fields. She tells her boyfriend, George Payne, that it's a part-time job. Laurie Smith, her friend, is also hired, and they soon discover that the clients include Brooke's boyfriend. Never mind, she sends Laurie to take her place and eventually they both give George a workout. Brooke Fields, of course, is supposed to look like Brooke Shields—and she goes to college (on film), too. (See review of *Brooke Goes to College*).

PRIVATE SCHOOL GIRLS
NN   DK   NL (occasionally)
1983   CABALLERO

P/D—J. Angel Martine
F/A—Shauna Grant, Sharon Kane, Tara Aire,
   Athena Starr, Veronica Hart
F/A—Michael Knight, Ashley More, Michael
   Bruce, Dan Stephens, Ron Hunter

Shot somewhere in New York State, with lots of snow on the ground, this one begins with Carolyn (Shauna Grant) being told by the high-school principal to stop fooling around with the boys on the football team, immediately after which she ends up in the boys' room blowing one of the guys and sitting on top of a urinal while he eats her. Neither of them seem bothered by what must be a somewhat odoriferous environment. The principal catches her in the act and expels her. In the next scene, her mamma enrolls her in a private school where the young ladies know more about sex than anything else and five of them are determined to raise enough money (about 500 bucks) to get to the Big Apple and hear their favorite group, Johnny and the Waylays, who are going to appear there in a few weeks, but nothing works. (Surprisingly, the very tough-speaking female basketball coach of the school is a very pregnant Veronica Hart. This presumably was her last adult-film appearance. She does not appear naked.) Then, mirabile dictu, Johnny and the Waylays, having lost their way to New York City, stop their van at the school and ask for directions. Soon the group and the groupies are all happily screwing together. (See remarks under *Shauna Grant, Superstar.*)

PUSSYCAT GALORE
NN   DK   BI
1984   VCA

P/D—James George, Jackson St. Louis
F/A—Brooke Fields, Honey Wilder, Danielle,
   Chelsea Blake, Renee Summer, Carol
   Cross, Annette Heinz
F/A—Joey Silvera, Bobby Astyr, Paul Thomas,
   Jerry Butler

Pussy Galore is an escort service run by Joey Silvera and Honey Wilder, and it employs all the ladies listed above as well as a few more. They are former housewives, waitresses, and secretaries who are taught the tricks of dealing with wealthy male (and one female) customers by the owners, who share their commissions for work well done. Maybe someday a more intellectual producer will try to tell the story of a woman in real life who makes a living as an escort lady and who is less promiscuous. At the same time he could develop her character and the "necessities" of her clients.

REVENGE OF THE MOTORCYCLE MAMA
NN   DK   BI   DS
1972   COMPETITIVE VIDEO

P/D—Edward Sams, Balls Stark
F/A—Jo Barry
F/A—Roger Pace

My copy of this one has a very weak soundtrack, but you don't need it because you'll never be able to separate the story from a continuous black-and-white fuck-and-suckathon. One of the Hell's Angels thinks that one of the black girls has squealed to the fuzz about their leader, and he beats her, sodomizes her, slaps her silly, and, holding her back to the wall, eats her, after which she is tied down and given a "hot box" with a cigarete lighter. She escapes, and another guy makes gentle love to her in the woods. As for motorcycles—in case you are looking for them—there aren't any.

SANTA CLAUS COMES TWICE
NN   BI   DK

P/D—Eve, Adam
F/A—Uncle Miltie, Tom Byron, Paul Dirisi, Mr. Shot
   Stud
F/A—Susan Hart

In a red-and-green Christmas package, with the price $39.95 printed right on the box, this one is obviously designed for giving to the man who has everything. Shot on video, it introduces Santa Claus (Uncle Miltie, a man in his 50s with a very big belly). He's wearing his B.V.D.s on Christmas Eve and being blown by Mrs. Claus (Susan Hart). He tells her that he has a letter from a poor young lad of 18 who has yet to know a woman and this is all that the poor boy wants for Christmas.

credit research assignment to explore underwater vessels. All the action takes place on a simulated submarine full of naval lieutenants. The guys' sliding schlongs are soon submerged in the ladies' slippery juices as the submarine slides and shakes in the sea.

SUPER GIRLS DO GENERAL HOSPITAL
NN NM BI DK NL (occasionally)
1985 VCA

P/D—James George, Jackson St. Louis
F/A—Raven, Taija Rae, Kristara Barrington, Kelly Nichols, Carol Cross, Ginger Lynn
F/A—Paul Thomas, Joey Silvera, David Scott, Ron Jeremy, George Payne, Adam Ladd

The super nurses in this one are Kelly Nichols, Taija Rae, and Ginger Lynn. The doctors in General Hospital are Doctor Morecock (Paul Thomas) and Doctor Swazey, his assistant (Joey Silvera). The hospital is failing for lack of funds, but then Raven, a movie star, who appears in an extended B/D sequence at the beginning, collapses and is rushed to the hospital. If Morecock can keep her locked up in the hospital, he can get a lot of publicity for the institution. Raven, as Brenda Brinkley, the actress, spends all her time trying to escape Morecock's clutches, but of course, she has to fuck her way to liberty, and the nurses are all serviced by the doctors as well as the orderlies, which include Ron Jeremy.

SUPER GIRLS DO THE NAVY
NN BI DK NL (occasionally silly)
1985 VCA

P/D—James George, Henri Pachard
F/A—Raven, Taija Rae, Kristara Barrington, Carol Cross, Susan Nero, Kelly Nichols
F/A—Paul Thomas, Joey Civera, Frank Serrone, David Scott, Ron Jeremy, George Payne

The super girls in this one, with the exception of Kelly Nichols, are the same as in *Super Girls Do General Hospital* (see review), but some of them have switched roles. Taija, Raven, and Kristara are now college students who get a summer for-

TEDDY BARE
NN BI
1977 CABALLERO

P/D—David Kahn
F/A—Janet Longs, Connie Coombs
F/A—Bradford Neely, Josh Way

Summer is over. Christopher is going to law school. He gets plenty of sex from two of his young female cousins who live near his country home, but Mother has invited her friend's daughter, Teddy Stewart, to spend a few weeks with them, and Christopher, try as he may, can't convince Teddy that he's the best stud who ever came along. Christopher tells you his ongoing problems in a voice-over, but it's difficult to sympathize with him because one young lady after another is constantly playing with his cock. I have a feeling that the English-dubbed dialogue in this French-made film, which tries to convince you that it is all taking place in California, is entirely different from the original French.

TEENAGE CHEERLEADER
NN BI BK
1978 QUALITY/VIDEO-X-PIX

P/D—Robert A. Taffett, Richard D. Antonini
F/A—Suzie Mitchell, Cindy Travers, Barbara Davies, Marie Botol, Debbie Ranier, Mary Sweeny
F/A—Rick Taylor, Larry Parz, Robert McDowell, Neil Richards, Billy Stavry, Mark Stevens

Mark Stevens is in this one, but he's not identified. Suzie (Suzie Mitchell) is the heroine. You never actually see her cheerleading the basketball team, but before the film is over she's screwed with all the guys on it.

TEENAGE COVER GIRLS
NN BI DK
1975   IVP (Formerly CVX)

P/D—**James Taggert**
F/A—**Annie Sands, Esther Roberts, Susan Presley**
F/A—**Ricky Newman, Jimmy Lawrence,**
      Louis Rupert

Two porno models (one is a very young Annie Sands, a.k.a. Annie Sprinkles) want to upgrade themselves. They meet a handsome black guy who knows everyone in the modeling business and agree that they should try to make him happy. He takes them to Coney Island, and they try all the amusements and then go back to his apartment. In the process, Annie wears a blonde wig, soaps up her pussy, shaves herself, puts lipstick on her labia and nipples, and masturbates with a toothbrush, which she later inserts in her anus, after which she sure enough is ready for the guy! (See notes under *Pleasure Bed.*)

UP IN THE AIR
NN BI DK
1984   VCA

P/D—**Leon Gucci**
F/A—**China Lee (a.k.a. Kristara Barrington),**
      Beverly Bliss, Crystal Blue
F/A—**Nick Niter, Frances Papillon**

If you want to avoid films with no story line and very little character development, get acquainted with the directors. If you enjoy 80 minutes or more of brainless fucking with nothing to even make you laugh, then Leon Gucci is your man. This one takes place on Love Airlines, aboard a plane bound for Jamaica. There's a Cuban woman terrorist aboard, and you have hopes that she might eventually blow the plane up, but she's seduced by a female passenger who convinces her that all her problems stem from a lack of love. This only provides a few minutes' interlude—halfway through. For the rest of the flight, the captain, copilot, stewardesses, and all the passengers are either sucking and fucking in the present or reminiscing in flashbacks about previous encounters. It all ends in an orgy, and you wonder who in hell is flying the plane.

Fetishes

BACK ROAD TO PARADISE
NR NN NM DK
1984   C.D.I. HOME VIDEO

P/D—**Jim Reynolds**
F/A—**Sheri St. Clair, Debbie Green, Dorothy Oh,**
      Fawn Paris
F/A—**Peter North, Mark Wallice, Greg Rome,**
      Tom Byron

This is the adventure of a young husband who, in spite of getting his brains fucked out by his attractive wife, remains unsatisfied. The young man is obsessed with anal sex, but his wife will have none of it. She is willing, however, for him to seek some outside talent. He immediately packs up the family motor home and does exactly that. He encounters two professionals and several amateurs in his quest. As the film draws to a close, after watching one of her husband's performances, the wife relents and gets it in the end!

BARONESS DE NICA
DK DS DB
1972   ASTRO

No producer or actors credits.

This sexvid tears a few pages from Krafft-Ebing and offers all the S&M delights plus, for good measure, some incest, an extended scene of rimming, and white women with strong black lovers. In between their screams, the participants are presumably enjoying themselves.

BETRAYED
DS
1985   CALIFORNIA TRI-STAR

P/D—**Barbara Behr**
F/A—**Georgia Von Helsing, Natasha Cole**
F/A—**Jeremy Whitman, Ted Shaw**

Here's a bondage-and-discipline tape that is more frightening than others reviewed in this book because one victim is *not* willing and is actually quite frightened. Carla, who has a niece Lisa, thinks that she's "spoiled and unruly" and arranges that both she and Lisa will be kidnapped by a male expert in discipline. (Carla's kidnapping is a coverup.) He chains Lisa's wrists and gradually strips her while he whips her lightly with leather thongs. When she's finally naked he pulls her fully erect so that she's dangling on the points of her toes, and he continues to whip her while she sobs and protests. But he keeps telling her how nice it is making her feel. It goes on and on. By the time he releases them, the loving ladies can't wait for the guys to fuck them. Maybe all this is an exciting sexual variation, but I'm afraid to some viewers it looks like *Ilsa the She Wolf* (see review).

BIG BOOB BABES, VOLUME 1 AND 2
BI NM
1984   AMBASSADOR VIDEO

P/D—Not given
F/A—See below

There is only female nudity in Volume 1—no men—and the women are attractively photographed exercising, wandering around a room, lying on a bed, showering, and bathing. They include Candy Samples (44DD), Roxanne Brown (44DD), Roberta Pedon (40DD), Darlene English (42DD), Sza Sza (a sad-looking Polish woman who has a 50DD-cup size and a belly to match, which must bring her in at over 250 pounds), and Rhonda Jo Petty and Marla Monroe, who are a mere 38DD. In Volume 2, the ladies indulge in a lot of sexy conversation, a little bisexuality, and masturbation. They include Keli Stewart (42DD), who is three months pregnant, Angel Cash (36DD), and Carol Miller (44DD), who are lactating.

BIG BUST VIXENS
NM BI
BIG TOP VIDEO

P/D—Not given
F/A—Geri Reeves, Star Murphy, Keli Stewart, Dominique, Brenda, Lori, Raven Delacroix

This one is an 80-minute companion to *Busty Nymphos* (see review). It gives you the mammary dimensions of the ladies, ranging from 42DD to 50DD, with an average of about 46DD. That's about it.

THE BIG E (ENEMA, VOLUME 3)
DK DS
1983   PLATINUM VIDEO

The vinyl box cover on this one warns you: "An hour six-pack of enema tapes." I haven't seen Volumes 1 and 2, but I assume that they're more of the same. This tape offers no genital sex but lots of nudity and every conceivable variety of enema. If you're into enemas, don't miss *Miss Pretty Peaches* (see review) or for a sicky with an enema rapist, try *Water Power* (see review).

BLACK GIRLS IN HEAT
NN BI DK
1985   L.A. VIDEO

P/D—Janet Rainer, David Christopher
F/A—Syreeta Taylor, Satin Summer, Delilah, Marita Ekberg
F/A—David Cristopher, Dick Howard, Joseph James, George Payne, David Ruby

Looking for a job in the suburbs of New York City, Penny (Marita Ekberg, a homely blonde) is interviewed by a heavily built black guy who is really a pimp. After she blows him, Penny is a welcome addition to the stable. If interracial sex intrigues you, you'll find plenty of it in this one. Some of the photography, contrasting white faces on black genitals and vice versa, is interesting. About 20 years ago, Ralph Ginzburg, who published *Eros* magazine, went to jail for similar still photographs.

BONDAGE FANTASIES
BI DB DK
1975   BIZARRE

P/D—Patrick Barnes
F/A—Lady Leather, Sweet Chastity

Compare this one-hour tape to *Bound in Latex*. It's more of the same except that there's a plot of sorts. Miranda is the slave, Silvia the mistress, but Miranda has fantasized reversing their roles and accomplishes this within a few minutes by putting a pill in Silvia's champagne. Thus Sweet Chastity plays the slave (see *Bound in Latex*). If these bondage-and-discipline films were produced with a man as the dominator and a woman as the slave (and I'm sure they must be) they would have to be labeled sadistic—because the rules (and there *are* rules of a sort, which you can discover if you watch them) are that there are limits to the game. A guy pulling a woman around by chains attached to her nipples, or splaying her on a rack and packaging her in leather and latex, is one step further into insanity than a woman doing it to another woman. Moreover, in this one, the ladies finally give up the paraphernalia and finish off in a torrid bisexual scene for guys who like that sort of stuff.

BOTTOMS, BEHINDS & DERRIERES
R DK
1985   NU WEST

P/D—Not given
F/A—Not given

If you are into spanking, or believe that spanking as a sexual stimulus is a British fetish, then you'll be fascinated to know that Nu West, (P.O. Box 1239, San Marcos, CA 92069) offers more than 100 videotapes in full color and with sound featuring female spanking. The women usually end up totally naked, but any actual sexmaking is off camera. Among the many titles are *Mildred Scott, Housemother; Fraulein Ritter; The L. A. Spanking Society; Cult of Discipline; Caning of a Young Lady;* and *Positions of Submission;* as well as the above title. Catalogues are available for $5, and there's a New York City location: Kinematics, 708 Seventh Avenue, New York, NY. Nu West also offers videotapes featuring women who appear partially naked, in pantyhose, girdles, and sexy lingerie.

BOUND
DK DB DS BI
1979   LOVE TV

P/D—None given
F/A—Serena, Judy Carr
F/A—Jamie Gillis

Two masochistic-sadistic sequences shot on videotape for home viewing. Love TV is not aiming at the at-home female market. This sexvid will horrify most women unless they like to watch women being tortured. One slave-and-master sequence, with Serena being whipped and abused by Jamie Gillis as she grovels at his feet, covers most of the B&D scene. There is also an interview with Serena, who says she enjoys pain and sex.

BOUND IN LATEX
BI DK DB
1981   BIZARRE

P/D—Patrick Barnes
F/A—Sweet Chastity

Here's everything you ever wanted to know about bondage and discipline and can't believe—even after you've watched it in a state of semishock. As is necessary, one person is the dominator—in this case a dominatrix—the other is the willing slave, a masochist, and everything that happens to her she wants to have happen, even though she often protests. In this one, which lasts an hour, one woman is dressed by the other first in black skintight latex leaving her breasts, behind, and crotch showing. Then she is gagged with a ball-and-strap gag, and straps are placed around her wrists, which are suspended from ropes attached to pulleys; then a rope is wound around her middle and drawn up through her crotch so that it bites into her vulva, after which she is tied tightly around the knees and ankles. The ensuing action (the dominatrix is dressed in latex, too, wearing four-inch heels, her ass naked) includes continual variations of this, untying and retying the slave in various positions. In between, the slave sucks the dominatrix's pussy and keeps reaffirming to the dominatrix that she is learning to be an obedient person. I'm no expert on the motivations of people who enjoy suffering and pain in the sexual act, but if you're tempted you can send $5 to Centurion Publishing Co., who produces these films (P.O. Box AE, Westminster, CA 92683), and they'll send you catalogues of many other tapes devoted to the subject.

BOX BALLS
NN DK
1983 VIDEO-X-PIX

P/D—Unknown
F/A—Unknown

The only way I know of that you can see this 15-minute tape is to rent or buy *Succulent* (see review), to which it was added as an additional incentive to buy. I've given it a separate listing because, from most males' viewpoint, it's the most godawful sight you've ever seen. You watch in total horror as a woman grasps a guy's prick and starts to twist it like a rope, until she has finally rolled up his balls along with it, literally tying it in knots.

BRA BUSTER, VOLUMES 1 AND 2
Naked females
1982 CABALLERO

P/D—Not given
F/A—See below

These two tapes run for one hour each. But fair warning—don't bring them home to your girlfriend or wife. Never mind her tit size, she won't like what she hears. The tapes are made for horny, female-deprived males. Volume 1 features Candy Samples (44—24—35), Sharon (52—27—38), and Denise (48—27—38), who is black. Smothering you in mountains of mammaries, they talk directly to you. Both volumes offer the viewers four or five other women displaying their charms who don't talk (and with smaller breasts), but in my opinion, Volume 2 is better than Volume 1. It features Uschi Digard (44—26—35),

a Swedish lady who also sells her own tapes direct (see address listing), Keli (42—24—34), and Elaine (50—20—40). This tape also gives a gynecologist's view of several women's vaginas (not Elaine's—you never see hers). If you run the tape in a slow motion, you may see things about the female anatomy (including what looks like a prolapsed uterus) that you've never seen before!

BUSTY NYMPHOS
NN (one sequence) NM BI
1984 BIG TOP VIDEO

P/D—Not given
F/A—Laura Sands, Annie Ample, Cindy Nelson, Salina Fox, Rachel Court, Maryanne, Charlene
F/A—One unidentified male

Some of these ladies look as if they would be more comfortable to lie down on than a water bed. Dimensions are not given, but the women play with their huge mammaries, tweaking and tasting them. For 84 minutes, they talk about themselves, but unlike *Bra Busters* (see review), they don't solicit the viewer or tell him they can't live without him. One black lady has breasts in the 50DD catagory. Anthropologists have deduced that the female mammaries and ass (not present in the same dimensions in four-legged animals) gradually evolved to seduce men, who were losing their sense of smell. They'll find these specimens worth looking at.

CAUGHT
DS DM BI SM
1985 BIZARRE TRI-STAR

P/D—Barbara Behr
F/A—Georgia Von Helsing, Sharon Montgomery, Kate Adams
F/A—Jeremy Whitman, Clyde Loran

Denise Colburn (Georgia Von Helsing) is a tough, rich bitch who enjoys torture and bondage and plays the master to her own "slave," Felicia (Kate Adams). She employs Jeremy Whitman, a photographer, to memorialize the action, during which her husband arrives home and discovers his wife's secret vice. What to do? In B/D films the answer is obvious—punish her. During the remaining hour, the two guys have both Denise and Felicia groaning in despair but really being brought to ecstasy. The women are suspended from Denise's jungle gym with their legs spread-eagled, stretched on a rack, and whipped, with much conversational accompaniment from the men, who tell them what bad girls they are. Eventually, Tammy, a friend of Denise, arrives and is quickly partially stripped and hung upside down by her ankles. When it's all over, the three women totally adore the two guys. *Chacun à son gout*—as the French say.

CURIOSITY EXCITED THE KAT
SM DK
1984 BIZARRE TRI-STAR

P/D—Barbara Behr
F/A—Sharon Montgomery, Jerry Reynolds, Mary Ann Page
F/A—Jeremy Whitman, Don Andrews, T. J. Shaw, Reed Loggerhead

If you don't understand the emotional drives of men and women who enjoy playing sadomasochistic games, then this tape will shock the hell out of you. But if you're interested in the widespread phenomenon of people role playing a master-and-slave relationship with all the paraphernalia that goes with it, you may view this tape from another point of view. This one is a scary amateur production that takes place in some foreign country where the American embassy has been burned down and the general who runs the country has arrested all the prostitutes and is training them in the sex-slave relationship. Kat is Katherine, an American reporter who soon discovers, like the prostitutes, that she has the most exquisite orgasms when she is chained against a wall, or suspended from pipes with her feet scarcely touching the ground, or hung by her legs upside down and has her vulva and ass whipped. Except for an occasional view of a vulva while a woman is spread-eagled on a rack, there is only partial nudity. The whipping with the leather thongs never draws blood, and the bare-breasted women are wearing garters,

stockings, and high heels. The general (Jeremy Whitman), who does most of the indoctrination, never stops talking, and he very easily convinces the women that helplessness enhances their desirability. The paraphernalia includes chains, bridle gags tied in the women's mouths, and nipple clamps. The helplessness of the women, who moan in pleasure and beg the master not to stop, is enhanced by chaining them in such a way that their genitals and anuses are totally exposed and vulnerable. Of course, what keeps this from being sadistic behavior, in the legal sense, is that the victims are wiiling. You're not suppposed to believe it is happening, anyway.

DIVINE ATROCITIES
NN BI DK
1983 CABALLERO

P/D—Kim Christy
F/A—Janey Robbins, Sugar Nicole, Magda Corbitt
F/A—Ric Navarro, Johnny Canada

This is a real stomach turner in two parts. Part I offers Magda Corbitt, a Sulka look-alike, with Sugar Nicole as his/her submissive slave, who on command has to suck his/her cock while he/she plays with her big tits and sucks them.Then Magda decides that Sugar needs a little spanking and beats her ass red with his hand, after which he/she fucks her. Part II offers Janey Robbins,who decides that she's sick of being dominated by her husband or any other man and soon greets her husband and lover wearing nipple clamps, leather stockings, and stilted-heel shoes. Brandishing a whip, she talks constantly and even makes Ric suck Johnny's cock because it really turns her on to watch. You have a feeling in this one and several others (see review of *Loose Ends*) that Janey is not acting but being herself.

DOMINATION BLUE
DS DK
1975 ASTRO

P/D—Joe Davian

F/A—Vanessa Del Rio, Paula Morton, Sharon Mitchell

A sick sexvid that runs about 60 minutes and includes whipping, water sports and a guy led around by a chain around his balls and prick. Supposedly taking place in a women's prison, it covers the gamut of kinky sex.

DOMINATRIX WITHOUT MERCY
DK DS BI
1976   VIDEO-X-HOME LIBRARY

P/D—S. S. Prod, John Stover
F/A—C. J. Laing, Terri Hall, Marlene Willoughby, Vanessa Del Rio
F/A—Jamie Gillis, Mark Stevens, Grover Griffith

Everything, and more, that you ever wanted to know about pain and sexual degradation is packaged in this one. You can watch a woman tied to a rocking chair with a chain around her neck and clamps attached to her nipples while a guy beats her. Or see C. J. Laing's poor, skinny body while she is on her hands and knees, her wrists and ankles tied, as she's penetrated by one penis and sucks another. Or Vanessa Del Rio abused with a banana. Students of abnormal sexuality should put it on their shelf along with Krafft-Ebing.

THE EXPERIMENT
DS DK DBD
1983   BIZARRE TRI-STAR

P/D—Barbara Behr
F/A—Renee Baker, Brandy Martin, Bianco Corjay
F/A—Jeremy Whitman

This one carries bondage and discipline to its almost Nazi-style conclusion (see review of *Curiosity Excited the Kat*). A supposedly sane doctor is in charge of a secret government clinic experimenting with mind control. They have convinced a patient, Max Cole, that he murdered his fiancée and has buried the body somewhere. He believes that only his two nurses know where the body is. He captures them, escapes from the clinic, and soon has them gagged, tied, and splayed, hanging from pipes in the ceiling of a deserted building, where he tortures them to tell him where the body is. As in most of these B&D films, there is no rape, but plenty of whipping on asses, tits, and vulvas, which of course, makes the tortured ladies "all wet" and love their captor. This one carries things too far, and the doctor who has fucked up Max's head in the first place has to reluctantly shoot him.

FEMMES DE SADE
DK DS DB
1976   ASTRO

P/D—Alex de Renzy
F/A—Abigail Clayton
F/A—John Leslie

Best Costumes, 1977 Erotic Film Festival. One thing that Alex de Renzy can do is create a porno film with a story line that goes from A to Z and blends all the porno-film conventions without losing track of the basic plot—no matter how thin it may be. You'll watch this one in horror. It includes rape, nipple burning, and fist fucking. The final scene, a leather bondage party, goes on for 20 minutes and equals anything you've read about the decline and fall of Rome. With what seems like a hundred guests in a San Francisco mansion, it incorporates every kinky sex act you've ever read about.

FOOT LOOSE
DK BI DS (but not seriously)
1983   PLATINUM VIDEO

If you are into fetish sex, check out *The Big Enema* and other Platinum tapes, which offer spanking and foot fetishes along with B&D, all with no explicit male-female sexmaking but lots of nudity. This one offers variations on foot fetishism, with lots of toe sucking and tickling.

FOUR O'CLOCK REPORT
DK
1985   CALIFORNIA TRI-STAR

P/D—Not given
F/A—Not given

This one goes a little further than *Private Lessons* (see review) and involves a lecherous-looking headmaster of a girls' school, who spanks four different young ladies with his bare hand and a cane. The girls sob during the ass twitching and try to protect their bare behinds, but any sexual arousal, whether it is occurring or not, is not seen or discussed.

GETTING OFF
DK   DS   BI
1979   VCX

P/D—Not given
F/A—Desiree Cousteau, Pat Manning, Serena
F/A—John Leslie, Ken Scudder

A sexvid with no story. Poor Desiree, in search of orgasmic ecstasy. Her friends force her to insert a long-stem rose, complete with thorns, into her vagina and squeeze until she bleeds. Then, with a collar around her neck, she is led around naked on her hands and knees, after which she is whipped on the ass and is finally tied in chains to the ceiling, hanging from which she is fucked silly and ends up begging for male cock, which is shoved angrily into her mouth for several minutes. Combined with several sex loops, this one is for the followers of the Marquis.

GIRLS THAT LOVE GIRLS
BI
1984   CABALLERO

P/D—Paul Vatelli
F/A—Bridgitte Monet, Kim Morgan, Cody Nicole, Little Oral Annie, Lisa de Leeuw, Kelly Howe, Lynn Ray, Bunny Bleu

If you enjoy watching women making it with each other, then this one may delight you. There are no guys. Bridgette, Kim, and Cody, on a warm summer afternoon, tell their lesbian experiences to each other. Some of the discussion telling about first encounters with another female are believable, some quite kinky and unbelievable. The cinematography is well done, and all the naked ladies are beautiful.

HEAD
NN   BI   DK
1985   L.A. VIDEO

P/D—Janus Rainier
F/A—Tish Ambrose, Sharon Kane, Sue Nero, Sandy King
F/A—Joey Silvera, George Payne, David Christopher

This is a 60-minute job that won't turn your "head." The box cover states, "For lovers of oral sex." Five sequences include "Paradise Island," "Nurse Sucker," "Body Talk," "Throbbing," and "Rock-and-Roll Appetite."

HOT BUNS
NN   BI   DK   NL (a little)
1984   VCX

P/D—Lee Carroll, Dorothy Oh, Rose Marie, Debra Hopkins
F/A—L. M. Burton, Drea
F/A—Eric Edwards, Dino Alexander, Bobby Bullock

This one gets a prize for assembling the homeliest collection of (with the exception of Eric Edwards) minor adult-film stars. They're really a cross-section of American facial styles. Screwing with his wife, Rose Marie, Eric reminisces about sex in the 1960s and remembers that girls protected their virginity by offering BJs (blow jobs) and BFs (behind fucks). He gets so enamored with his memories that he suggests that Rose Marie, who is a writer, write a book about it called *Bottom Line*. To do the necessary historical research, Rose Marie invites her former college friends, whom she hasn't seen for 15 years, for the weekend. Drea doesn't disappoint you. She offers very clear close-ups of anal sex with pricks and even a dildo inserted into one guy's ass who can only sit down gingerly afterward. At the inevitable group-sex party, Eric discovers that his wife has never experienced "anal-cavity cavorting," so he teaches her how while the others are engaged in tackling all the orifices. He finally decides that the party is such a success that Rose Marie should make it an annual event, with a new title: "Same Time, Next Rear."

HOUSE OF PLEASURE
CC NN BI DBD DK
1984 CABALLERO

P/D—Ted Gorley, Paul Vatelli
F/A—Duscha, Cody Nicole, Jodie Nikko, Cindee Summers
F/A—Mark Wallice, Joseph, Jerry Davis, Herschel Savage

This house of pleasure may not be your idea of fun. It has an aura of back-street San Francisco reality that will keep you watching in horror. Duscha's appearance in a film (she has a silver-blonde masculine haircut) usually means bondage and discipline somewhere in the story. This one gets a CC retch rating for the ugly exaggeration (or reality? I'm not sure which). Duscha owns a mansion and has a chauffeur, a maid, a cook (Cody Nicole), and Jodie Nikko—all of whom do her bidding and are dependent on her although they hate her. She also does outcall work servicing masochistic business executives who like to be whipped and called pigs. Her chauffeur is always nearby to enforce her orders, which she carries out dressed in the requisite leather—her ass and tits showing. The chauffeur collects the semen of her men in a vial. The story of this one finally moves to a rundown bar where two sailors on leave pick up Cody Nicole and Jodie Nikko and soon have persuaded them to spend the night in a sleazy hotel room. One sailor never quite makes it with Jodie until she invites him back to the mansion, where he soon discovers that his beautiful lady has a very big cock. Soon Duscha arrives back home to chastise them all with whippings, after which she drinks the semen her chauffeur has accumulated.

INTERLUDE OF LUST
NN NM NR DK DS BI
1982 HIFCOA

P/D—Troy Benny
F/A—Karen Hall, Liz Renay, Mai Lin
F/A—Leon Marlowe, Andrew Thomas, Freddy Kohn

Many young married couples will identify with Jo Anne (Karen Hall) and Bruce (Leon Marlowe). They still make love but don't really enjoy it, so they decide to get a divorce. Jo Anne ends up in Madame Zoila's whorehouse in Las Vegas, and Bruce, on his own trip, enjoys various sexual encounters. Meanwhile, Jo Anne's sex life is enlarged at Madame Zolia's with rape and bondage fantasies. Then to her dismay, she's kidnapped by some of the shady characters involved with Madame Zolia, who rape her. But when Bruce rescues her, she has learned how to make love again with her old fire.

LADIES WITH BIG BOOBS
NM
1984 AMBASSADOR

P/D—Not given
F/A—See below

Here's another 60-minute tape devoted to voluptuous mammaries and their horny owners. There's Anna Ventura (36D), Tricia Russell (38C), Beth Swenson (40DD), Patty Roesch (40C), Lynn Wilcox (38D), and Tatia Logan (42D). These ladies aren't quite as big as those in *Big Boob Babes* (see review), but most of them play with themselves, offer intimate views of their genitals, and moan about their need to be fucked and eaten.

LESBIAN PASSION
NN BI DK DS
1985 L. A. VIDEO

P/D—Not given
F/A—Sharon Kane, Ann Brown, Leslie Winston
F/A—No guys

Poorly lighted at the beginning, this is a 60-minute pussy lapper, dildo diver, and vibrator levitator that ends up with one lady giving herself a douche and then two of them playing B&D games, tying each other up and clamping their nipples. It ends with one of the women picking up a woman with 40DD tits (or bigger) in a gay bar, bringing her home, and abusing her.

LITTLE ANGELS IN PAIN
DK DS
1975 ASTRO

P/D—Leo Gaylord, Jr.
F/A—Serena Lebec, Leah Muller
F/A—Peter Dauphin

If you want to learn the techniques of discipline and bondage—presumably while game playing because the woman (a sad-looking, skinny wreck with unshaved armpits) tells her lovers how much she enjoys it—then you can find it here. This sexvid includes wearing leather, whipping, nipple clamping, and various instrument insertions.

LUST INFERNO
NN NM BI DK
1983 HIFCOA

P/D—Troy Benny
F/A—Lynx Bannon, Tamara Dwaney, Linda Spencer, Gayle Sperling

This is the story of a fundamentalist, faithhealer, self-ordained minister, Reverend Jerry, who is a sadist. He likes to whip young women before he ejaculates on them. Never mind, he wipes them off with $100 bills, which they happily accept in payment. Despite the fact that he spends a lot of time at a local whorehouse, he has a wife, who is screwing with her psychiatrist, and two daughters, one of whom disguises herself and goes to work at Madame Blanche's (the house of ill repute). Not recognizing her, the reverend must have this new woman. He ends up deflowering his own daughter and then goes beserk.

MY MASTER, MY LOVE
NN NM BI DS DK NR(one sequence)
1975 BLUE VIDEO

P/D—Leon de Leon, Ralph Ell
F/A—Darby Lloyd Raines, Samantha, Annie Sands, Nancy Dare
F/A—Alan Marlo, Don Allen

A lower-class *Punishment of Ann* (see review), this is an ugly weirdie that explores female masochism and submission, not to a man but to another woman. Margaret (Darby Lloyd Raines) is a dominatrix who has totally seduced Roberta (Samantha—who is kind of pathetic with her pockmarked face). She forces Roberta to watch acts of submission. In the last scene Roberta is staring at a candle, perhaps wondering about her horrid compulsions. Like *Punishment of Ann*, it will leave you feeling a little nauseated—and thanking God it isn't you.

NIGHTCALLER
DK BI
1975 ARROW

P/D—Leonard Ashley, Wes Brown
F/A—Monique Starr, Lonna Brooks, Laura Bond
F/A—David Book, Stuart Hemple, Cary Corman

A seamy, squalid, sick, throw-up quickie about an evil-looking, sexually deranged character, Bobby, who makes obscene phone calls and jerks off. It seems that he was seduced once by his mama and sister, and some of his girlfriends know that he's a "phone freak" and play "mommy games" with him while they masturbate and he listens and masturbates. He finally corners a woman who lives in an apartment across the alley who doesn't know that he's the baddy who has been telephoning her. You can't believe this, nor the "rape" that ensues, during which, of course, she gets so aroused that she enjoys herself. You'll need a bath after this one.

NIGHT OF THE SPANISH FLY
NN NL (if you're potted) DK
1981 CAL VISTA

P/D—Bob Mason
F/A—Angel Barrett, Jennifer Jordan
F/A—Jeff Eagle, Beerbohm Tree, Jeffrey Hurst

This one has a 1981 date, but I'd guess it was made in the mid-1970s. The plot, if you can call it that, revolves around a shipment of Go-Go Weiners, into which some dastardly person has put quite a few pounds of Spanish Fly, which is an actual substance that when eaten can seriously irritate your genitals and might even cause death. But here it's an aphrodisiac that turns sheepish guys and passive ladies into nymphomaniacs.

OPEN UP, TRACI
NN NM BI
1985   VIDCO

P/D—Michael Carpenter
F/A—Traci Lords, Candi, Erica Boyer, Crystal Breeze, Cheri Charlene
F/A—Greg Rome, Mark Wallice, Tom Byron, Greg Derek, Steve Drake

Traci adores her beautiful body and her hot pussy, which she can't keep her hands off, and so does her loving girlfriend, Candi, who asks her, "Do you want me to suck your titties and eat you?" which she does while Traci leans up against a tree and pants and moans in sheer delight. But Traci and Candi decide that they need some variety in addition to each other. They find it with various guys in some of the wildest moaning, panting, screaming, wriggling, clutching, slithering, and groaning ("Fuck me, fuck me!") sequences you have ever watched.

PERVERSE DESIRES
NN NM BI DK
1984   CABALLERO

P/D—Caroline Joyce
F/A—Chantal Virapin, Edwige Davis
F/A—Laurence Jarry

The French title of this film translates as *A Perverse Nymphomaniac*, and they weren't kidding. It begins with a wedding in a small country town. A bridegroom, who is obviously wealthy, brings the bride back to his villa, where they have sex, but the bride is not very cooperative. Next morning he goes to Bordeaux for an important meeting and makes a point of locking up a set of keys to various rooms and a garden house, which he tells her that—under no circumstances—must she touch. Of course, the minute he's gone, she prys open the drawer and for the next 48 hours ends up opening doors in the villa, behind which she finds a black woman masturbating (she joins her in a startling color contrast), and then women blowing guys in other rooms, and a whipping orgy of group sex presided over by a black midget whom they stand on a chair so she can fellate him properly. She is indefatigable—and though no one ever talks or introduces him- or herself, they are screwing continuously—much like a scene out of a Hieronymus Bosch painting. You may want to throw up—but the bride doesn't. She wakes up in her husband's arms, a day later, and tells him that she has had a most interesting dream. Yuck.

PLATINUM SPANKING
B&D TAPE #205
DK DS
1983   PLATINUM VIDEO

Here's another weirdo tape from Platinum. See several others reviewed. If they appeal to you, write Platinum for a catalogue. This one, which is several hours long, has quite a few shocking sequences. First is "Roots of Slavery," which focuses on a husband and wife torturing their black maid. Next is "Punished Schoolgirls," a British-made quickie that shows two women being spanked by the school's headmaster. "Whipped Teenagers" is the next twitchingly delectable offering. "Baby Clinic" features a guy dressed in a diaper who talks baby talk while he sucks a pacifier and gets an enema. Then there's "Bar Room" with two women stretched naked on top of a bar with chains around their necks while two guys play with their breasts and pussies, twist their nipples, whip them, and finally pour beer over them, all of which makes the ladies very sexy. Finally, there's "Donna's Dungeon

Ordeal," during which a young lady checks out an apartment for rent and ends up in a dungeon chained to the ceiling.

PRIVATE LESSON
DK
1985   CALIFORNIA TRI-STAR

P/D—Not given
F/A—Not given

With full-color packaging and its own vinyl box, this one (and *Four O'Clock Report;* see review) is a 30-minute British-made spanker. A young female teacher chastises her younger female student for not learning her lessons. She takes her across her knee and spanks her bare bottom barehanded, with the back of a hairbrush, and ultimately with a cane. Ass whacking was a feature of English school life in the 19th and 20th centuries and is the subject of many early pornographic stories. If this one hasn't bored you, California Tri-Star and Platinum Video have many more.

SAMURAI DICK
NN NM BI DK DS
1984   VCA

P/D—Alida Gutter, Kaye Vie
F/A—Kristara Barrington
F/A—Ron Jeremy

Samurai Dick is, of course, Ron Jeremy, whose assistant on the San Francisco police force is Kristara Barrington—also known in other films as China Lee. Seems that a certain nasty Japanese gentleman is involved with an equally nasty old gray-haired American, Mr. Lube, in the female slave traffic, which includes a black female, a white female, and several Japanese ladies (none of whom is identified in the credits). The ladies are tied to chairs and whipped and sadistically raped by a guy who, it turns out at the end, is working for the police, too. You may have more problems than the actors wondering if you can survive to the end.

SEX BUSTERS
NN NM BI BK
1985   PLAYTIME/TARGET

P/D—Not given
F/A—Candi, Karen Summer, Sheri St. Clair
F/A—Steve Drake, Ludwk, Mark Wallice, Blake Palmer

Candi and Karen Summer run a service called Sex Busters. Dressed in shorts and busty T-shirts, they take care of guys whose girls won't service them, or gals whose guys are too busy. This one is for guys who think that two gals adoring them may be better than one.

SEX ON THE SET
NN BI DK
1984   RED LIGHT/VIDEO-X-PIX

P/D—Stuart Allen
F/A—Janey Robbins, Tanya Lawson, Robin Everett, Renee Summer, Taija Rae
F/A—Ron Jeremy, David Scott, Eric Edwards

This tape is supposed to give you some clue as to what some of the porn actors really do when they aren't on camera. Janey Robbins insists that she's into bondage and proves it to Tanya Lawson. Wearing a black bondage outfit, she and Tanya play with dildos and eat each other. Next Eric Edwards is explaining to David Scott how to do it with Robin Everett. You get the feeling that Robin is not acting and is really a little embarrassed by the whole thing. Renee Summer and Taija Rae explore each other's vaginas with dildos, but they also give you the feeling that bisex is not a way of life with them. Whatever else it is, this is not sex on the set, which is a lot more prosaic.

THE SEXPERT
CC NN BI
1975   IVP (formerly CVX)

P/D—Mister Mustard
F/A—Rena Vane, Amy Stone
F/A—Eric Edwards, Jim Crane, Randy West

Rena Vane is actually a young Marlene Willoughby. The professor, listed as Eric

Edwards, isn't, but looks like him. Seems the professor can out-Svengali Svengali with a mind-control system that makes people do things they never expected to do and are unaware afterward that they have done. He has to prove it to a Doctor Fleigle, which he does by making phone calls to Fleigle's patients. Under his control, Marlene picks up a total stranger and fucks him. Randy West, previously a he-man now wearing women's clothes, visits a black dominatrix, and the doctor's female assistant, to his surprise, tackles the doctor. (See notes under *Pleasure Bed.*)

SEX STAR
NN BI DK
1983 CABALLERO

P/D—**Paul G. Vatelli**
F/A—**Kimberly Carson, Danica Ray, Diana Kline**
F/A—**Herschel Savage, Steve Savage, Greg Ruffner**

Danica Ray, a porno actress, tells her director that she can't do "girl-girl stuff." But the truth is she wants to so badly she's afraid that she may be a lesbian. She even fantasizes sex with her best friend. But when she is converted to the joy of loving a woman, she does it with such flair that she becomes a sex star. In between there's an additional 70 minutes of heterosexual sexmaking no different from what you've watched before, except for a long, mind-boggling extended cock-and-vagina-bending sequence that releases Danica's inhibitions for life.

SEX TOYS
NN NM BI DK
1984 CABALLERO

P/D—**Chetley, Paul G. Vatelli**
F/A—**Kimberly Carson, Kristara Barrington, Athena Star, Kelly Green, Bunny Bleu, Pamela Jennings**
F/A—**Greg Ruffner, Tom Byron, Herschel Savage**

Do they still have Tupperware parties? During the early 1980s a new kind of female-oriented house party received a lot of publicity in *Time* and *Newsweek*. Get the guys out of the house, invite a few of your friends, and a woman selling sex gadgets and sexy lingerie will arrive to entertain you and sell you her products. Kimberly Carson is the saleslady in this one. With no guys present, the problem becomes how to demonstrate the sex toys and lingerie. But nothing fazes an adult-film maker. Fantasize the guys, of course. Finally, Kimberly Carson invites you to a second round of parties, soon to come. But you'll have to be pretty hard up to bother.

SHAVE TAIL
NN NM BI DK
1984 AMBASSADOR

P/D—**Bruce Seven**
F/A—**Aurora, Erica Boyer, Cara Lott, Elaine Southern**
F/A—**Dan T. Mann, Jeff Conrad, Steve Powers**

Trying to wake her husband to go to work, Cara Lott pours ice water on his cock. Then when he's suddenly awake, they make love. Later, he decides, while he's shaving himself, that he'd like to shave her pussy. Cara tells her girlfriends of his strange request, and one of them admits that her boyfriend has shaved hers. Soon everybody is doing it, while the camera examines the process in close-up detail. Afterward, they are all so pleased with their naked mounds that they are soon eating and vibrating each other. Their guys like it, too.

SHEER DELIGHT
NN NM BI DK
1984 VCA

P/D—**Rolland Stone, Drea**
F/A—**Drea, Pat Manning, Sharon Mitchell**
F/A—**Jerry Davis, Mark Morris, William Margold**

A few years ago, Drea was a porn actress. Then she met Bill Margold, and now he writes the screenplays and she directs the films. If he'd forget his kinkiness and concentrate on writing and acting his funny dialogue, Margold could probably produce a really funny sexvid. But, alas, he thinks kinky is funny to a point where he often makes it sick. This one has no story except that in the beginning Margold plays twin brothers, one of whom is married to Drea. The brothers hate each other, and after a funny opening you have hopes that this could be a laughing sexvid. But, alas, they never appear again, and most of the rest of the tape is devoted to Drea strapping on a dildo and buggering a guy who is, presumably, her brother. In the meantime, William Bare (Margold) goes to bed with his teddy bear and wears a pair of blue sheer panties that some unknown gal has sent him in the mail. When Drea finds out, she threatens to bugger him, too.

SLAVE MANSION
R DK
BIZARRE

P/D—Richard Christopher
F/A—Countess Angelique, Marc Trevor
F/A—Jason Marks

Note the rating. There is no explicit sex in this one. Don't be misled by the box it comes in. The only reason for purchasing it might be to watch it with a woman or another couple, but only after you are half sloshed. It seems that Janice can't stand her "lazy, macho husband." She calls the Baroness de Sade, who comes right over. They bind Jason to the wall with chains, then to a specially designed table. They stick a leather helmet over his head, and, wearing leather and garter belts, they whip him very unconvincingly while he wears his underpants. Believe it or not, Jason becomes a slave and, wearing a maid's costume after his training, does all the cooking and housework. Pretty silly.

SLAVE OF PLEASURE
NN DK BI DS
1978 BLUE VIDEO

P/D—Russ Carlson
F/A—C. J. Laing, Gloria Todd
F/A—Jamie Gillis, Roger Caine

Sultana (Gloria Todd) is a black woman who lives in New York and can eat two cocks at once. She also likes to be "raped by white men two at a time," and she's in business with Henry Picard (Jamie Gillis), who lives in Paris. They operate a white-slave ring. Abdul, an Arab, wants two women, one "insatiable" and one stupid. Richard is married to Eileen, who is insatiable, and he's having an affair with Barbara (C. J. Laing), who wants to get rid of Eileen, even though she supposedly is Eileen's best friend. How to do it? You guessed! Sultana has the insatiable Eileen kidnapped. When a remorseful Barbara tries to save Eileen, she is captured and tortured. In the things-you've-never-seen-before department, C. J. Laing is suspended from the ceiling, whipped, and brutalized. This is a sicky flicky that will make most women gag. Russ Carlson had a potentially terrifying and erotic story line with plenty of conflict, but alas, he got caught up in the adult-film conventions.

SLIT SKIRTS
NN NM DK DS
1983 VIDEO-X-PIX

P/D—Frank Della, J. D. Marlowe
F/A—Joanna Storm, Rachel O'Rien, Candy Staten, Sharon Kane
F/A—Ron Jeremy, Jim Davey, Joe Santino, Bill Mac, Steve Stud, Joey Silvera

This one begins with a rape scene, during which two unwashed, unshaved guys break into an apartment and strip the maid (she's wearing pantyhose, amazingly, and not a garter belt) and rape her, with some cooperation. A scene later, one of them is being dragged into a mental hospital described by the boss doctor, Joey Silvera, as housing the worst criminals in the state. During the next 70 minutes you meet them in flashbacks. Allison (Joanna Storm), who seduced her brother and was caught in the act by her father; Toby Gardiner (Rachel O'Rien), a nymphomaniac who needs two cocks in her mouth at once. Another lady is obsessed with sodomy, but you see her only masturbating. In the terminal ward, Ron Jeremy is chained by his wrists to the bedposts because he won't leave his cock alone. He rolls over and manages to suck it (a Jeremy specialty) before he's relieved by a nurse who arrives, sits on his dick, and then gives it a thorough workout. Then there's a guy who's a necrophiliac and his girlfriend (Sharon Kane) plays dead to turn him on. Finally, Joey as the doctor and a black lady as a nurse who is supposed to take over the wards he has shown her join the patients and become as looney as they are.

SQUALOR MOTEL
NN   BI   DK
1985   ESSEX

P/D—Kim Christy
F/A—Colleen Brennan, Desiree Lane, Lisa de Leeuw, Cody Nicole
FF/A—Randy West, Nick Random, Herschel Savage, Jamie Gillis

The letter *S* is the key to this one. Take *squalor*, add *sleazy* and *slimy*, and garnish with *surrealist* and *symbolic* cinematography, and maybe you have a cult film like *Cafe Flesh* (see review), and maybe you don't. Miss Clark (Colleen Brennan) is a manager of a motel owned by a pervert, Manny (Nick Random), who spies on the weirdos who rent various bedrooms and a function room called the "Reptile Room." Nancy (Desiree Lane) arrives still wearing her wedding veil. Soon she is in the Reptile Room sucking Jamie Gillis's cock, after which he tosses her into a nightmarish party environment where a half-naked female rock group is providing music for a roomful of creepy-looking people who look as if they just left the makeup room of *Star Wars*. In another room there's a guy making love to inflated dolls that come to life. All the action is watched by the drooling manager, who is now wearing a Miss Piggy costume and enjoying the sight of a blood-covered doctor telling the naked lady on an operating table, "Your battery is dead" —after which, with the help of Lisa de Leeuw, they give her shock therapy and she ecstatically takes care of both the doctor and the nurse.

SWEET CAPTIVE
NN   DS   DK   BI
1979   FREEWAY

P/D—John Le Carde, Leoni Valentino
F/A—Rhonda Jo Petty, Denis O'Brien, Bonita Dyan
F/A—John C. Holmes, Paul Thomas

To save her boyfriend from jail, Rhonda Jo becomes a sexual slave to John C. and Paul. "We want to see your asshole, asshole," they tell her when she arrives at their mansion. And they mean it! Later, with a candle stuck in her vulva and her legs overhead while it drips hot wax on her buttocks, she provides candlelight while they do a double insertion on another lady guest. The big surprise is that their slave doesn't give a damn about her boyfriend but is laughing at her captors and really enjoys being tied up and pussy whipped. If you like nasty people, you'll like this one.

TASTE FOR PASSION
(EMBASSY GIRLS)
NN   NM   BI
1984   AMBASSADOR

P/D—Not given
F/A—Vabess DeLanu, Alexandria, Betty West
F/A—Fred Sutter, Kelly Putz

See notes under *International Intrigue* and *Right Stiff.* This one offers Alexandria, who has a 40DD cup size, plus some other sexually acrobatic, domestically inclined ladies whom you've never seen before, copulating on the kitchen floor and the living-room couch. One of them experiments with a cucumber.

THROAT 12 YEARS AFTER
NN   NR   BI   DK
1984   VCA

P/D—Gerard Damiano
F/A—Sharon Mitchell, Michele Maran, Joanna Storm, Sharon Kane
F/A—George Payne, Eric Edwards, Jerry Butler, Joey Silvera

Throat, is of course, *Deep Throat.* But if you think that Linda Lovelace has been resurrected, forget it. This is Damiano's view of sex in America in 1984, and Linda, who made *Deep Throat* in 1972, has written a book called *Ordeal* in which she claims that she was practically enslaved and forced to perform her oral technique. Damiano tells three separate stories in this one. After the first two, he gets to the reason he probably made the film. Joey Silvera and his wife are in an open marriage. They go to the Sewer, a sex club where anything goes and the waiters even jerk off in the special rum drink, which is served in mugs shaped like tits. This is followed by 15 minutes of throwuppy sex put together with Damiano's very slick editing and cinematography.

TOO MANY PIECES
NN   DK   DS (Jamie Gillis style)
1975   FANTASY/CABALLERO

P/D—Not given
F/A—No credits, but Jamie Gillis and Bobby Astyr are identifiable

The board of directors of the Maypole Museum, all properly attired, have gathered to see whether the museum wants to accept Potter's sex slide show as an addition to the museum. Seems, however, that the slide show (you see it in montages) turns on every one who looks at it, including Jamie Gillis, who is one of the directors. Soon Jamie takes one of the female directors into one of the museum rooms, ties her up, and beats her ass. In another room, another director, with 50DD tits, is being knocked off by another director. Soon all the directors are happily fornicating and are convinced to vote yes. (See notes under *Christy*.)

TOP SECRET
DB   DS   DK
1982   BIZARRE TRI-STAR

P/D—Barbara Behr
F/A—Vanessa Del Rio
F/A—Chris Edwards, and others impossible to identify on the credits

An evil B/D master captures Juanita (Vanessa Del Rio). The master and his male servant gag her, strip her, hang her by her arms from the ceiling, and splay her legs. She twists and turns as she gets her ass and vulva whipped. Next she's bound with leather straps and dressed in six-inch high heels, and is still trying to escape a leather switch being snapped at her.

TRANSVESTITE CASTLE
DK
1980   BIZARRE

P/D—Kern Vore
F/A—Countess Angelique, Lady Heather
F/A—Martin Majors

John's wife, Heather, is in love with Angelique and no longer wants sex with John. How to solve the problem? Simple—transform John into a woman and then they can all love each other. Angelique is a specialist in these matters and has a castle with a dungeon, in which John is subjected to all the armory of bondage and discipline, including chains, handcuffs, and a red mask rather than a black leather one because this is a female symbol. Sixth-graders could act more convincingly—but it qualifies for the things-you've-never-seen-before department.

ULTRA MILKMAIDS
(BEYOND THE VALLEY OF)
NN   BI
1984   FOUR-PLAY

P/D—Loretta Sterling
F/A—Lynn Anne, Angel Cash, Terry Pepper
F/A—Bob Spirey, JoBob

The box this one comes in advises you that these are lactating ladies and are recommended by the American Dairy Association. For many single guys who can't remember Mama's tits, this one could be udder fascination.

VICTIMS OF LOVE
NN   DS
1975   IVP (formerly CVX)

P/D—Not given
F/A—**Vanessa Del Rio, Lea McCloud, Violet Reason, Pamela Brown**
F/A—**Gary Wright, Hans Locke, David Chase**

There's a clinic for rape victims where they can get therapy by talking about their rapes with other victims. This plot device thus gives you three rapes in one film. At the clinic, a woman tells how she was dragged into a deserted building by two guys, forced to undress, and covered with car grease, after which she was raped. Another woman tells how she returned home from the library and found a guy wearing a silk stocking waiting for her in her bedroom. The third victim is a guy who tells about picking up two female hitchhikers who forced him at knifepoint into a deserted building and wore him to a frazzle while he begged for mercy. During the therapy, the guy is attracted to the girl who was raped by the masked bandit, and although she's married, soon they are having sex together. But afterward, he coolly tells her that his story was a fake and that he uses it at the clinic to seduce women like herself. In truth, she discovers to her shock, he was the bandit in her bedroom. (See notes under *Pleasure Bed*.)

WINTER HEAT
DK   DS   BI
1977   ADULT VIDEO

P/D—**Claude Goddard**
F/A—**Sue Rowan, Helen Madigan, Lisa Young**
F/A—**Jamie Gillis, Bob Tucker**

Three rough-looking guys and one woman walking through snow-covered mountains arrive at a mountain cabin. Why are they there? Why, as one guy tells another that his wife (not present) is a hot piece of ass, does the woman calmly suck one of the guys (Jamie Gillis) while the others watch? Cut to the next day. Three women are arriving at a home in another part of the mountains to go skiing. A few hours later they are invaded by the original four. "What do you and your friends want?" one of the young women asks Jamie Gillis. He and his buddies quickly make it obvious. As the worst of the lot, Jamie forces one of the women to undress, smears her with frosting from the refrigerator, and fucks her doggie style while another forces another woman to suck him off. The original female rapes another woman, and Jamie takes on a third with a belt around her. Most women will watch this one in horror. And they will really retch when they finally come to the end and the three victims are no longer victims but are enjoying their rapes and are now in total sexual command of their captors.

WOMEN WITHOUT MEN
BI
1985   VIDEO-X-PIX

P/D—**Stuart Allen**
F/A—**Amber Lynn, Rachel Ashley, Gina Carrera, Karen Summer, Crystal Breeze, Candi**

"Hi, my name is Amber," Amber Lynn tells you in a sultry voice. "I want to tell you about two friends of mine who like to play with each other." Her friends are Karen Summer and Crystal Breeze, who are playing in a big black tub which appears in many porno flicks. Giggling and laughing like six-year-olds playing doctor, the ladies wash each other's ass and pussy, and when they are nice and clean, they happily lick and lap each other from head to foot. Then Amber tells you about two other friends. They're Rachel Ashley and Gina Carrera, who join the other two on a great big bed and spend a lot of time trying on sexy underwear, accompanied by much fake giggling, after which they slither together and become a sighing, sexy sow pile. The tape concludes in the things-you-can't-believe department, as Amber pours oil on her vulva and anus. When she has a thoroughly greasy runway, she slips a two-way dildo into her vagina and asshole while she winks lasciviously at the astonished male viewers. Most women will find this one super boring (unless they prefer dildos and vibrators to live cocks), and it may make men feel a little redundant.

YELLOW FEVER
NN BI
1984 L. A. VIDEO

P/D—L. Burton, Drea
F/A—Mai Lin, Kristara Barrington, Tamara Chang, Amber Lynn
F/A—Paul Thomas, Jay Sterling

Bob (Jay Sterling) has acquired a fetish for Oriental women, to the exclusion of all others—including his beautiful wife, Ellen, played by Amber Lynn. The plot involves Bob getting his friend and neighbor Lance (Paul Thomas) to service Ellen for him while he is off to Chinatown to get his jollies with Mai, Kim, and Sue. Lance does a noble job with Ellen in several very erotic encounters; however, Bob always seems to be struggling to make it with his sexy Oriental friends, but don't worry—he does. The technical quality and clear color are excellent.

YOU'LL LOVE THE FEELING
DB DS DK
1984 BIZARRE TRI-STAR

P/D—Not given
F/A—Zoe Jardine, Paula Meadows, Natasha Pulinakova
F/A—Douglas Dawson

If you are into spanking for sexual pleasure, you may understand this one better than I do. It takes place on the grounds of an English estate with a kidney-shaped swimming pool. The owner, a guy in his 50s, is married to a younger woman who is shocked by the idea, but he has a female friend who is coming for the weekend with her "slave" and will show her all the fun that she's been missing. In the many spanking scenes, you never see any male genitals and only fleeting glimpses of female vulvas, but you see lots of red asses and pink tits. Also you will discover that the spanker never stops talking as he is spanking. And the spankee agrees that she's been terribly naughty and deserves everything that happens to her, including, in this one, being tied to a tree in a nearby forest and whipped very thoroughly. But later they prove how much they all love her by covering her with strawberries and whipped cream and eating dessert off her stretched-out body.

Vignettes

ALL THE SENATOR'S GIRLS
NN NM BI DK
1977 VCX

P/D—En Cognito
F/A—Valerie Parker, Connie Burnett, Lois Parsons, Beverly Hutton
F/A—Glen Swallow, Alan Sterling, Rod Harris

Frank Parsons is so busy running for senator that he hasn't time to bring his live-in girlfriend to a climax, but never mind, when he gets to his law office his secretary is quick to fellate him and keep him comfortable. He needs something to pep up his campaign, so he decides to run on an antiporn platform. But before he has time to make any speeches, a Texas oil millionaire, Gaylord Wheeler, invites him to a campaign party aboard his 65-foot yacht, the SS *Waterbed*. With all the yachts anchored in southern California, you'd think that more sexvids would be shot on them. Anyway, most of this one does take place on the ship, and there's screwing from stem to stern, of course. The big party takes place in the main lounge, with Gaylord, a Burl Ives look-alike weighing a good 275 pounds. But he's rich and has no trouble finding a nubile young lady to blow him and belly bump on his private waterbed. Other than this unlikely sexvid scene, which should give corpulent males more confidence, there isn't anything you haven't seen before.

AMBER AROUSED
NN NM BI DK
1985 CABALLERO

P/D—Vinnie Rossi, Mark Davis
F/A—Amber Lynn, Crystal Breeze, Shaun Michelle, Tracy Duzit, Jan Sterling, Mindy Rae

F/A—**Sasha Gabor, Herschel Savage, Billy Dee, Ron Jeremy**

Terry (Amber Lynn), applying for a job as a live-in maid at the home of Harvey and Magda (Crystal Breeze), picks up Sasha Gabor (a Burt Reynolds look-alike), whose car has broken down and quickly satisfies her early-morning itch with him in her car, thus proving that she's a very horny young lady. You never see Sasha again, but you soon realize why Harvey needs her. He has invented a robot that not only serves drinks but has a penis attachment to serve women. Alas, it can't suck his cock, and neither will his wife, Magda. And so on.

BEACH HOUSE
NN   NM   BI
1981   CABALLERO

P/D—**Robert Norman**
F/A—**Beth Anne, Marlene Willoughby, C.J. Laing, Jennifer Jordan**
F/A—**Wade Nichols, Tony "the Hook" Perez**

Every time I go all out and extol a particular director (see reviews of *Mystique* and *Woman in Torment*), I find a bomb that he or she has made. The story is told, in flashbacks, by the women stars who have rented a house for the summer, and it reveals their various sexual encounters, which are no different from those you have seen in other films—with one major exception—Tony "the Hook" Perez is the star of the film. He doesn't talk much, but all the women want him. His prick is longer than and thicker than John C. Holmes's, and it curves into his stomach in a magnificent hook. Another reason for watching the film is to see Beth Anne and C. J. Laing, who no longer make sexvids.

BEFORE SHE SAYS I DO
NN   BI   DK
1985   MASTERPIECE

P/D—**Jerome Bronson, John Stagliano**
F/A—**Candy, Diane Rochelle, Gina Valentino, Karen Summer, Erica Boyer**
F/A—**Steve Drake, Mark Wallice, Tony Martino, Francois Papillon**

Shawn (Diane Rochelle) is a nice girl who hasn't had too many guys in her life. She's going to get married to a guy who was a friend of her roommate Lonnie (Candy). Lonnie screws everything in sight. Before Shawn marries Ron (Steve Drake) he is invited by his friends to a bachelor party with a couple of hookers. Shawn is left alone with Lonnie and goes to bed with her. Then Lonnie arranges a bachelorette party for Shawn with a couple of male strippers, and Shawn finds strange cock as tasteful as Ron's. But the next day she marries Ron, and presumably they'll live happily ever after, but only if Shawn shares Ron occasionally with Lonnie and whoever else may come along.

BETWEEN THE SHEETS
CC   NN   NL
1984   CABALLERO

P/D—**Michelle Aimes, Anthony Spinelli**
F/A—**Seka, Annette Haven, Chelsea Manchester, Arcadia Lake, Veronica Hart, Vanessa Del Rio**
F/A—**John Leslie, R. J. Reynolds, Randy West, Richard Pacheco, Eric Edwards, Joey Silvera**

Whether this one should have a CC rating depends on your point of view. It's not one story but six short ones. But it's not old loops patched together, either. The stories were created for the film, which, like *Autobiography of a Flea* (see review), uses an independent narrator. This time it's a female mattress and a male brass bed, who talk about their long history with human lovers. The stories include Annette Haven as a Colonial lady trying not to jump into bed with a British soldier; Richard Pacheco being shocked that he's not going to get a big ad-agency job that Veronica Hart, who still wants to screw with him, has denied him; Joey Silvera and Chelsea Manchester as a couple of 1960s flower children; and Eric Edwards as a Yankee soldier in Confederate territory looking for a bed and finding it with Arcadia Lake. The best stories are at the end, with John Leslie as a 1920s gangster and his moll, Seka. Spinelli and Marga Aulbach (Michelle Aimes?) should have made this into a full-length film; and Randy West trying to make out with Vanessa Del Rio and not succeeding until he gives her the engagement ring is happily silly.

BLACK BALLED
NN BI
1984 AMBASSADOR

P/D—Not given
F/A—Reva Wondu, Euone Taylor, Ekalia Swartza
F/A—Guys not listed

Another Ambassador series, this time of "integrated loops" (see review of *International Intrigue*). This one offers all interracial couples.

BLACK BUN BUSTERS
NN NM BI DK
1985 VCA

P/D—Junior Bodden
F/A—Sahara, Steph, Jessica Hunter, Summer Rose
F/A—Jack Baker, Field Marshall, Mark Bradley, Ric Roc

A black therapy group wants to discuss "butts and asses" with their therapist, a moronic-looking character who tells them, "Rectal intimacy is a serious subject for discussion." "Is that some kind of science word for butts?" one guy asks him. Soon, one by one, they are relating their experiences, mostly with white guys and gals, who penetrate each other in all directions. Probably made on a weekend for a few thou. You can live without it!

BLUE RIBBON BLUE
NN BI
1984 CABALLERO

P/D—Many, but not given
F/A—Seka, Annette Haven, Abigail Clayton, Bridgette Monet, Lee Carol, Veronica Hart, Lisa de Leeuw, Serena, Sharon Mitchell, Brooke West
F/A—See below

If you want to see most of the major female adult-film stars on one tape, this offers cuts from various films featuring the above actresses copulating or fellating with Jamie Gillis, Paul Thomas, Herschel Savage, and a few other guys. Eric Edwards is the host, telling (tongue in cheek, I would guess) how excited these ladies make him when he watches them on film.

BOUNCING BUNS
NN NM BI DK
1983 VCA

P/D—John Stag, Bruce Seven
F/A—Tracy Donovan, Renee Summer, Bridgitte Royale, Sadie Mae
F/A—Brian Curtis, Richard Andersen

Two guys who own a new company providing striptease telegrams, Bouncing Buns, interview prospective ladies for the work—on their knees and on their backs. The tape offers a number of sequences during which the living telegrams display their charms and use them on the lucky male recipients. One episode ends up in a group-sex party raided by the cops, who bring along Wesson Oil to facilitate a 10-minute genital slide-around.

CABALLERO COLLECTIONS, VOLUMES 5–8
NN NR NM BI DK
CABALLERO

P/D—Various
F/A—See below

I haven't watched all the volumes in this series of one-hour tapes, but they feature various actors and actresses in six-to-ten-minute cuts, linked by a featured mistress of ceremonies who comments on the action you are about to watch and may or may not appear in one or more of the sequences. The various cuts are from loops or longer films that you may or may not have seen. Volume 5 is hosted by Ginger Lynn and includes Rhonda Jo Petty seducing a TV repairman, Lisa de Leeuw romping in a sports car, Danielle in some back-door sex, and Bridgette Monet in an encounter with David Cannon. Volume 6 is linked together by Cindee Summers and includes in the things-you've-never-seen-before department, a champagne enema and much anal sex. Volume 7 again offers Ginger Lynn ooing and ahing over the various scenes you are about to watch. Volume 8 is more of the same, with Cindee Summers hosting from a bathtub where she is lathering herself. These collections are not for sexvid aficionados but for newcomers who may think they are a way of finding out what adult films are all about. Unfortunately, they only give a raincoat-crowd perspective.

CATHOUSE FEVER
NN BI DK
1984 VCA

P/D—Billy Thornberg
F/A—Becky Savage, Rhonda Jo Petty
F/A—Rick Cassidy, Herschel Savage

Imagine a sexvid with only four actors. Unfortunately, there are a few more than that in this one, but they are not listed in the credits. Becky Savage is the star, and she plays a woman whom guys have never dated or even looked at. She lives on her fantasies. Eating her frozen dinner alone, she imagines herself at a candlelit table with Herschel Savage, indulging in conversation that will either embarrass you or make you laugh. Deciding that her daydreams need the test of reality, she goes to Las Vegas and works in a cathouse run by Rhonda Jo Petty and of course encounters everything you ever watched in a sexvid before.

CENTERFOLD CELEBRITIES #5
NN BI DK
1985 VISUAL ENTERTAINMENT

P/D—Bobby Hollander
F/A—Amber Lynn, Tracy Duzit, Brandy Alexander, Fawn Dell, Karen Summer
F/A—John Leslie, Jamie Gillis, R. Bolla, Ken Starbuck, Gerry David, Ron Jeremy

Centerfold Celebrities #1 was reviewed in the first edition of this book (see review). I haven't seen #2, #3, #4, but except for different guys and dolls I'm sure

they are indistinguishable one from the other. This one, shot on videotape, has fuzzy color. Like the *Reader's Digest*, featuring the same stuff from month to month, it grows deadly to watch.

CHARMING CHEAPIES, VOLUMES 1–6
NN NM BI DK
1985 4-PLAY VIDEO

P/D—Not given
F/A—See below

A collection of glorified 30-minute loops that are packaged in four-color lithographed boxes the same way as longer-running cassettes. They retail for $19.95 each and are available directly from 4-Play in individual volumes. They feature people that for the most part you've never seen before and may not want to again. Volume 1 *Joy's Many Loves,* features Jade Nichols, Devin Caloway, and Shone Tee. Joy's husband doesn't take care of her well in bed. Volume 2, *No Holes Barred,* with Brandy Alexander, Jade Nichols, Shone Tee, and Gary Sheme, features a dominatrix who has a masochist female friend. Volume 3, *Day and Night,* features Tim Knight, George Cox, and Dey Lature in a threesome that you rarely see in a heterosexual film. The guys are bisexual and take turns sucking each other's cocks. Volume 4, *Dueling Dildos,* has Tony Peper and Lisa Savage, two women who play a vibrator-and-dildo symphony on each other's genitals. Volume 5, *Fancy Flesh,* with Ron Jeremy, Lynn Anne, and Mandy James, features two plump ladies, one of whose husband (Ron) has gone away on business for the weekend. Volume 6, *Red Tide,* features Athena Star, Gary Sikes, and Robin Watson. One white girl with a black guy and a white guy.

CHROME WHEEL CIRCUS
NN BI
1975 FANTASY/CABALLERO

P/D—Not given
F/A—Heather Cauley
F/A—Jerry Sales

Mark is a long-distance runner who has run away with a rich girl, Susan, whose father is looking for them and would have him murdered if he dared. Susan is screwing Mark and Debra, a black woman, and a masked male prostitute they hire to join them. Mark doesn't seem to mind, and eventually a guy named Larry arrives. Soon he's making love with Debra. Susan tells Mark that he prefers winning a gold cup to her, and she says good-bye. That's all folks. Where the title came from is a mystery. (See notes under *Christy*.)

C.I.M. PRESENTS
NN NM BI
1985 AMBASSADOR

P/D—Not given

These are six 30-minute tapes packaged individually in the type of four-color packages that usually contain 60 to 90 minute features. All of them could have appeared on one or two Diamond Collection or Swedish Erotica tapes, but in the competitive sexvid market, price is a factor, and these may eventually be sold below 10 bucks. They should have an overall title of *Ladies Loving Themselves and Other Ladies and a Few Guys*. Obviously the series was designed for males who like to watch women enjoying the same indoor sport as they do.

CLASSIC STAG FILMS OF THE PAST VOLUMES 1 AND 2
NN NM BI
1940s and 1950s   GM VIDEO

P/D—Unknown
F/A—Unknown

I wouldn't call these classics. They are typical of the stag films that were available on 8-mm and 16-mm reels in the period of 1940 through the 1950s, when they started to appear in color, as a few of these do. Whoever put together this collection (each tape runs about 70 minutes) offers no comment. The sex is accompanied by a canned musical background, and the films are silent.

COME SOFTLY
NN NM BI DK
1975   IVP (formerly CVX)

P/D—Greg Poupon
F/A—Marlene Willoughby, Sandy Bottom, Jan Pearce
F/A—Eric Edwards, Gary Marion, David Pollack

This is a series of vignettes. It begins with a guy coming all over his wife's face and her shouting angrily at him. "Blow your wad in my ear. Am I supposed to like that?" Followed by a young Marlene Willoughby hanging by her feet spread-legged from a chandelier, blowing her boyfriend while he, standing on the bed, eats her. Followed by two women with a carrot. Followed by Eric Edwards as a freelance porno star who services married ladies for a price. In the things-you've-never-seen department, he shows two of them how to lie back to back on a couch with their legs bent to their heads while he pops first in one exposed vagina and then in the other. (See notes under *Pleasure Bed*.)

COTTON TAIL CLUB
NN BI DK
1985   ESSEX

P/D—Dick Dumont, Charles De Santis
F/A—Amber Lynn, Patti Petit, Mauvais Denoire, Lili Marlene, Magenta
F/A—John Leslie, Jon Martin, Marvin Bates, Don Fernando

Obviously trading on the Hollywood production called *Cotton Club*, this one has no plot and nothing resembling a nightclub that you couldn't fake better in your own living room. One interminable scene after another, and about 10 words of dialogue.

CUMMIN ALIVE
NN BI
1984   VCA

P/D—L. M. Burton, Jack Remy
F/A—Colleen Brennan, Mindy Rae, Britt Nielsen, Crystal Breeze, Sandra Stillman

F/A—Jerry Butler, Billy Dee, Jay Sterling

Wealthy Jessica Van Buren (Colleen Brennan) invites her niece and her niece's college friends to spend the weekend on her estate, and then because she's so busy in the sack with her boyfriend (Jerry Butler), she never arrives to chaperone the girls' activities. Never mind, there's a count living on the estate. He peers out of his windows and takes pictures of the ladies making love to each other, and there's a handyman/chauffeur proficient in soothing all their vaginal itches. The most interesting thing about this tape is the multimillion-dollar home that provides the backdrop. Situated somewhere in the Los Angeles canyons, with manmade waterfalls dropping into a curvaceous pool, the house will make your mouth water more than the ladies do.

DESIRES OF WENDY
NN
1975   FANTASY/CABALLERO

P/D—Not given
F/A—Not given

This is a ho-hummer with a guy you've never seen before watching a porno film that he has just made and midway calling his girlfriend Wendy to come over and watch with him. When Wendy arrives, wearing practically nothing, you know what her desires are. The rest of the film cuts back and forth between the movie they are watching and the fun they are having themselves, thus giving you 60 minutes of nothing you haven't seen before.

DIAL F FOR FANTASY
NN BI DK DBD
1984   L. A. VIDEO

P/D—L. M. Burton, Drea
F/A—Janey Robbins, Pat Manning, Bunny Bleu, Equinette, Debra Lynn
F/A—Tom Byron, Steve Drake, Blake Palmer, Mark Wallice, Randy West, William Margold

Bill Margold insists that porno-film makers are "in the meat business." This one is a nonstop eaty-meaty-beaty. Based on the assumption that you can Dial *F* and get a fantasy service provided by Janey Robbins and Pat Manning, this 90-minute film is really a sneaky way of putting together a number of unrelated loops. The first one involves an older guy (Randy West) who wants to experience sex with two teenagers. Despite their pigtails, they look well over 25. Then there's a guy writing a term paper on Hemingway. He's provided with a female toreador, who lies down with her bull. Margold appears as a macho male who gets his comeuppance from Janey Robbins, who becomes a female dominatrix and drags him around the kitchen making him confess, "I have an insignificant worm between my legs."

DIRTY GIRLS
NN NM BI
1984   MITCHELL BROTHERS

P/D—Alex de Renzy
F/A—Stacey Donovan, Cody Nicole, Jacqueline Lorians, Joanna Storm, Helga Sven, Colleen Brennan
F/A—Francois Papillon, Jamie Gillis, Rocky, Michael Knight

In his later years Alex de Renzy seems incapable of producing a full-length sex-vid. This one is a series of loops that are shown to Jacqueline Lorians by Jamie Gillis. In between the cuts they are gradually feeling each other and are finally making love while the loops are being run.

EBONY BLUE
NM
1985   AMBASSADOR

P/D—Not given
F/A—Women's names not given. No male actors.

The blurb on the box reads, "Luscious black babes masturbating for you." Most of the 10 or so ladies are big-breasted (one must have a 50DD cup size). They play with themselves on the couch, in the bathtub, with their fingers, and with exotic vibrators.

EMPLOYEE BENEFITS
(EMBASSY GIRLS)
NN   NM   BI   DK
1970s   AMBASSADOR

P/D—Not given
F/A—Andrea True, Penny Claire, Becky O'Grady, Heidi ElkWicke
F/A—Mark Stevens, Mike Stans, Manuel Cruz

See reviews of *International Intrigue* and *The Right Stiff*. This one offers a young Andrea True and the famous Mark Stevens (Mr. 10½) for a few minutes, as well as other, less familiar, pussies and cocks—all doing what comes naturally. Some of the guys look as if they had been resurrected from 1940 stag films.

EROTIC INTERLUDES
NN   BI
1984   CABALLERO

P/D—William Reeves, John Reeves, Jeff Winestock
F/A—Seka, Judith Anderson, Bridgitte Monet, Angel Cash
F/A—Kevin James, Mike Kramer, Ron Jeremy, Skip Bennett, Mike Ranger

Five guys rafting on the Colorado River find a place along the shore to camp for the night. Alas, the women are the women in stories the men tell each other. So you soon discover that you are watching four unconnected loops pasted together as stories told over a campfire. The first one is about two cheerleaders after the big game who make final touchdowns with a couple of the team members. The second story is told by Ron Jeremy, who doesn't quite climax with Angel Cash, who leaves him sucking his own cock. Then Judith Anderson (Aunt Peg) arrives looking for a job and quickly demonstrates her athletic abilities. Mike Ranger tells about his encounter with a chick (Bridgitte Monet) who has been after his body from the first day he met her, and Kevin James

tops them all with a story about the day he goes to fix Seka's telephone and she demonstrates in advance her oral technique on a dildo and then on his "screwdriver." Save your money.

FANTASIES UNLTD.
NN   BI   NR
1985   CDI HOME VIDEO

P/D—Jim Reynold, Bob Chinn
F/A—Christy Canyon, Josephine Carrington, Tamara Longley, Bunny Bleu
F/A—Eric Edwards, Harry Reems, Peter North, Greg Derek

Tom (Eric Edwards) and Sue (Josephine Carrington) run a business called Fantasies Unlimited, from whom, with a phone call, you can live out your favorite sexual fantasy, which is put together somehow by a computer. Although they work together, Tom has never had sex with Sue, and he spends much of his time diddling his own dipstick as he thinks about her. Their clients' fantasies make up the bulk of the film.

FANTASY PEEPS, BLACK & WHITE
NN   BI   DK
1985   4-PLAY VIDEO

P/D—Not given
F/A—Not given

Here are six more loops, 10 minutes each, on a 60-minute tape, this time featuring integrated sex.

FANTASY PEEPS, UNTAMED DESIRES
NN   BI
1985   4-PLAY VIDEO

P/D—Not given
F/A—See below

If you're bored by longer, 80-minute-and-up tapes, Fantasy Peeps, like Swedish Erotica and the Diamond Collection, to mention a few of the packaged loops, give you a fast-changing copulating panorama, often with actors and actresses whom you may be able to identify. (There rarely are any credits.) This one, in six segments, features Lisa de Leeuw, Tina Russell, Eric Edwards, Jamie Gillis, and Herschel Savage.

FEELINGS
NN BI
1975   IVP (formerly CVX)

P/D—Bill Hill
F/A—Lisa de Leeuw, Mandy St. John, Diana Larkin
F/A—Guys not listed in credits

Lisa de Leeuw is not listed in the credits, but she appears momentarily as an earlier, skinnier version of herself. (She can still lap her nipples.) It's supposed to be about various women's dreams. With no transition, the scene shifts to four women (count them) making love together in a big bed. None of them is Lisa. Soon they are joined by a guy. Cut to a gal swinging in a swing in a leafy tree. Her legs are wide open, and a guy enjoys a free-floater, after which they change positions. This is followed by a pretty woman sitting on a toilet and being worked over by a black guy. There are several additional sequences involving twosies and threesies. (See notes under *Pleasure Bed*.)

FEMALE SENSATIONS
NN BI
1983   VCA

P/D—Rod McKane, Sam Roberts
F/A—Cherri Roberts, Desiree Lane, Andrea Adams
F/A—Mark Wallice, Greg Direk

If you're bored watching sexmaking indoors, this one is shot almost totally outdoors, which means that with a few blankets, a woodsy environment, plenty of sunlight, and a video camera, the tape could be wrapped up in seven or eight hours on a Sunday. The actors (?) are first two women sleeping in different summer cabins who eventually find each other in bed. Soon a car arrives with two guys and two gals who are their friends. Since there aren't enough guys to go around,

the various scenes that are now recorded on various blankets must involve two ladies. At dusk, they all join in one cabin for a little group groping.

FIREFOXES
NN   NM   BI   DK
1985   PLAYTIME/TARGET

P/D—Giovani Fiolini, Adam Tarasclus
F/A—Josephine Carrington, Sheri Januler, Robin Cannes, Kristara Barrington, Sheri St. Clair, Gina Gianelli, Jessica Longe
F/A—Tony Martino, Mark Wallice, Dan T. Mann, Peter North, Blake Palmer

A series of vignettes evolving from a 10-year reunion of three college girls. Looks like an off-the-cuff production put together on a long weekend.

FOXY BROWN
NN   NM   BI
1984   VCA

P/D—Rod McKnee, Sam Roberts
F/A—Sahara, Sherri, Steffi
F/A—Sweet Lorrian, Tony El'ay, Calif Palm

A happy screwing marathon that includes Foxy (Sahara), who is in love with a white woman, Lydia, and enjoys her in an extended bi sequence as much as she does her black live-in friend, Ralph (Tony El'ay), who enthusiastically services Foxy as well as all the black and white women Foxy is auditioning in her beautiful suburban home (complete with pool) for jobs as dancers. The only plot is when Foxy decides that Ralph must share both her and Lydia. How can he object? The only penises in this one are black and magnificent.

GIRL FRIENDS
NN   BI   DK
1983   MITCHELL BROTHERS

P/D—Alex de Renzy
F/A—Janey Robbins, Lili Marlene, Taire Aire, Genoa
F/A—Jamie Gillis, John Leslie, Ron Jeremy

This is de Renzy's first film in two years, and he still hasn't come up with a plot.

Little more than a series of loops, it begins with two unidentified women, presumably foreign, who sing to each other in German as they have sex together. The next vignette features the Regional Suck-Off Contest, hosted by Jamie Gillis, during which Tara Aire and Genoa compete against each other. And so on.

GIRLS OF PENTHOUSE
R BI
1985 VESTRON

P/D—**Bob Guccione, Vivian R. Moss, Edward Holzman**
F/A—**Penthouse center-spread girls are listed at the end of the tape, if you're interested**

It's surprising that thus far neither *Playboy* nor *Penthouse* has been able to offer anything in the adult field (the exception being *Caligula*—see review—or *Playboy's Girls of Rock & Roll*) but a magazine format in motion. This one is an hour-long tape concentrating almost entirely on women who don't talk. Other than the nudity, the only explicit sex is bisexual, and the end result is boring. There are five or more separate sections, all photographed in a supersophisticated, glossy, MTV style. With titles such as "Back to the Bone," "The Locket," "Ghost Town," and "Tattoo," they feature much "brillo rubbing," which doesn't disqualify an R rating, but you won't remember any of it five minutes after you have watched the tape. The only interesting part is when Guccione finally appears and is shown "arranging" the ladies for *Penthouse* photographic sessions.

GIVE IT TO ME
NN DK NL (Pachard style)
1984 ESSEX

P/D—**Henri Pachard**
F/A—**Taija Rae, Sonia Frye, Carol Cross, Kristara Barrington**
F/A—**Joey Silvera, R. Bolla, Frank Serrone**

In this one, Joey Silvera and Taija Rae offer a live sex show that they have taped of a couple screwing in front of a male audience in some New York City club. While the audience cheers, the lady, who is being screwed doggie style, keeps whispering to her lover, "Think about the weather, or mashed potatoes" so he won't come too soon and spoil the show. Another segment has Carol Cross screwing off camera with a clown (R. Bolla) who is the host of a daytime children's TV show. Then you are taken to Eats, New York City's most risqué restaurant. In the blow-your-mind department, you visit a tony restaurant where the menu features you and your dinner companion. Everyone is eating at the table, under it, and next to it, and they don't stop for 15 minutes. Then there's a sequence with a flaky guy and woman demonstrating sex toys, which include all the gadgets you've ever heard about, including peter pumps, cranked-up dildos, and ben-wa balls. When the show is about to be aired Joey and Taija decide to kick it off with their own live sex demonstration.

GLORIA LEONARD'S PHONE SEX FANTASIES
NN NM BI DK
1978 QUALITY/VIDEO-X-PIX

P/D—**Howard A. Howard, Henri Pachard**
F/A—**Rachel Ashley, Sharon Cain, Gina Carrera, Karen Summer**
F/A—**Joey Silvera, George Payne, Michael Knight, Francois Papilion**

Gloria, who is the publisher of the men's magazine *High Society* (and deals in low society), is the hostess of this one, which tries to make you believe that your phone calls to her explaining your sex dreams can come to life. Gloria says that Volume II of her telephone fantasies are in preparation. I hope they're better than these.

GOLDEN GIRLS
NN DK
1973 SELECT/ESSEX

P/D—**Alan Everett**

F/A—John Leslie, Jamie Gillis
F/A—Rachel Ashley, Callie Aimes, Tina Ronie,
Terry Benoum, Debbie Cole, Beverly Hills

Three very wealthy guys in San Francisco somehow convince ten lovely ladies to appear in a Miss Fantasy Beauty Contest. For this purpose they have rented the Civic Center and a converted tenament house to accommodate the ladies. The film begins with the contestants arriving, and it's obvious that the lady who goes to bed with the most judges will win the contest. Actually, after some ninety minutes of screwing the film finally concludes with John Leslie telling the assembled ladies that they've all been canned: there is no contest.

GOOD-BYE, MY LOVE
NN BI
1975 FANTASY/CABALLERO

P/D—Robert Gold
F/A—Elaine Freeman, Connie Peterson, Sally
Swift, Barbie Turner
F/A—Mike Ranger, Jack Gooding, Chuck Fabrae

Tom (Mike Ranger), an actor, works days. Lynn, his live-in girlfriend, works nights and plays days. A friend wants to drop off a commercial script for Tom. Although she's scarcely out of bed with Tom, Lynn is soon fiddling with the friend's zipper and ignoring his worry: "What if Tom comes home?" In an unrelated sequence, Bobby Astyr is making it with another gal. He's not listed on the credits. Then Lynn goes to Paul's apartment for some afternoon fun in the sack. On the way home Tom sees her car in front of the apartment and is pretty sure what she's doing. She convinces him that she's really his woman and makes love with him again. Her fourth fuck today. But when she wakes up she finds Tom's note. He's had it. Good-bye, my love! (See notes under *Christy*.)

HARD TO SWALLOW
NN DK
1985 PARADISE VISUALS

P/D—Michael Phillips, Adam

F/A—Little Oral Annie, Patti Petite, Erica Boyer,
Kathleen Kelly, Rita Ricard, Justice
Howard
F/A—John Leslie, Joey Silvera, Ron Jeremy, Tom
Byron, Francois Papillon, Jonathon Hill

Women will find this one pretty hard to swallow. John Leslie plays the part of a guy who presumably started the sexual revolution and lives in a mansion surrounded by lovely ladies. Any resemblance to Hugh Hefner is purely coincidental. Joey Silvera is a TV reporter who is interviewing him, along with his cameraman Ron Jeremy. Joey is intent on proving that John is a sleazy character, and John decides to give him some sleazy entertainment. It all quickly becomes an anal-vaginal fuck dance. When it's over, Ron refuses to cooperate with Joey. It wasn't sleazy at all, just good fun!

HOLLYWOOD PINK
NN BI DK
1985 ESSEX

P/D—J. Essex, Jim Travis
F/A—Bunny Bleu, Cheri Jannier, Debra Lynn,
Kathleen Kelly, Robin Cannes
F/A—Studley Doright, Peter North, Ray Hardin,
Rusty Zipper, Greg Derek

Hollywood Pink is a men's magazine with overtones of *Hustler* and with a Larry Flynt look- and sound-alike (Studley Doright) as the publisher. If you've seen the four-color package this one comes in, you know that it has a tiny heart pasted over a rear view of a woman's vulva that you can scratch and sniff. The story revolves around an offer of a $1,000 prize for the best real-life sex story about a celebrity. The problem is that you've never seen most of the people who play the celebrities before, and they all look alike, fucking and sucking. Doright's secretary wins the prize with a story about the leaders of a punk-rock group called the Worst. The tape is not the worst, but almost.

HOME MOVIES LTD., VOLUME 2
NN BI
1985   ESSEX

P/D—See below
F/A—Not given

Once again, despite the opening statement that this presentation is produced, directed, and performed by amateurs, it ain't so! Like Volume 1 (see review), there are separate sections. These have more of an amateur flavor than Volume 1, with the camera being held in one scene, but in the longest segment you'll quickly recognize Karen Summer and Colleen Brennan. If you want to see *real* amateur productions, see reviews of *Sweet Dreams* (Baker Video) and *Susan's Video* tapes.

HOT FUDGE
NN NM BI DK
1984   ESSEX

P/D—Janus Rainier, David Christopher
F/A—Satin Summer, Shareta Taylor, Francine Star, Phaedra Grant, Dolly Daine
F/A—Ron Jeremy, Jose Duval, Dave Ruby

This one opens with Ron Jeremy screwing a black woman, Satin Summer. The phone rings, and it's his daddy, who has just arrived in town with his new wife. Daddy and his new wife arrive, and after a few minutes of faked shock by the new wife, the rest of the film is a fuckfest with Daddy and Mommy both exploring black pussy and Ron Jeremy having a great time with his new stepmother.

HOT GIRLS IN LOVE
NN BI
REDLIGHT/VIDEO-X-PIX

P/D—Howard A. Howard, Alan Stuart
F/A—Crystal Breeze, Gina Carrera, Honey Wilder, Candy
F/A—Joey Silvera, Jose Duvall, Ron Jeremy

Joey Silvera is a photographer shooting lingerie pictures for Honey Wilder in Jose Duvall's mansion. For a few minutes you think a potentially interesting story may develop, as Honey attacks Joey for shooting pictures without class. Honey is obviously older than his model, Gina Carrera, and she stalks out angrily, leaving Joey with Gina. For the next 80 minutes, Joey makes extended, acrobatic love to Gina Carrera, followed by Ron Jeremy, who evidently is Joey's assistant, being propositioned by another model, Crystal Breeze. Later Honey returns, and the possible story about a guy who shoots smutty pictures instead of doing class photographic work disappears as Honey proves to Joey that she's just as good in the sack as any 18-year-old.

HOT LICKS
NN BI DK
1984   ESSEX

P/D—Henri Pachard
F/A—Kelly Nichols, Sharon Kane, Carol Cross, Sara Bernard
F/A—Joey Silvera, Charlie La Tour, George Payne, R. Bolla

A last will and testament left by some wealthy, crusty old codger is a perennial plot device in adult films. In this one, the hopeful heirs of Zachary McVale discover, in his lawyer's (R. Bolla) office, that the rat has videotaped all the sexual activity that's been going on in his mansion over the past years. Now that he's dead, they are forced to sit in the lawyer's office and watch the tapes of their various encounters, after which he'll announce who gets his millions. With one of those video cameras that is omnipresent and omniscient, Zachary has also managed to tape an extended orgy involving all of them, which includes a buttered ass, and anal sex in close-up detail like you've never seen before. Never mind, Zachary is so happy that they all provided him with X-rated excitement, right in his own home, that he leaves them $2 million apiece, and even his lawyer gets $1 million.

HOT PROPERTIES
NN BI DK
1975   FANTASY/CABALLERO

P/D—Not given
F/A—Guys and gals you've never seen before

Christie asks her roommate, "How was your date last night?" Answer: "We fucked all night." The dialogue sets the tone for this one. Forget it. (See notes under *Christy*.)

HOT SPA
NN   NM   BI
1984   CABALLERO

P/D—Bruce Seven, John Stagliano
F/A—Lynn Ray, Karen Summer, Cara Lott,
    Renee Summer, Pamela Jennings
F/A—J.B., Mark Wallice, Greg Dere, Richard
    Anderson, Steve Sanders

What little plot there is in this two-hour tape (you'll count the minutes) involves Gina (Lynn Ray), who has been married so long to Bill that he practically ignores her when she tries to entice him away from his newspaper with an erotic strip-tease. She heads back to her health club, where the ladies and guys listed above are all bending, squatting, flexing their legs, and exercising nude on the various exotic gym equipment that allows them to show and use their genitals in unique positions. You may wonder if the tape will ever end. And you'll wonder how Bruce Seven can continue to make the same film (shot on video) over and over again, unless of course you enjoy watching sweaty cocks and vulvas for two hours.

HUSTLER VIDEO MAGAZINE
VOLUMES 1 AND 2
NN   NL   NM   BI   DK
1984   ESSEX

P/D—Larry Flynt
F/A—Ron Jeremy, Kay Parker (Volume 1)
F/A—Jamie Gillis, Loni Sanders, Brandi,
    Constance Money (Volume 2)

I hadn't seen the first *Hustler Video Magazine* when the first edition went to press, but I mentioned it in the reviews. The first volume is hosted by Jeremy Wells. Each volume contains the standard *Hustler* feature department, such as: mail-order, X-rated reviews, a featured interview with a porn star, and of course, a *Hustler* centerfold. In Volume 1, she is Brandi, and after telling how she got into the porn business, Brandi masturbates to happy or-

gasm. This is followed by a two-gal shower scene that soon turns into a threesome when a handsome guy arrives. Kay Parker is the featured, interviewed adult star, and there are clips from her films. The tape ends with Ron Jeremy joining a brother and sister in a threeway, including making a sandwich of the lady. Volume 2, in addition to the above features, shows film clips from various sexvids, followed by an interesting interview with Loni Sanders, who describes the difficulties that she experienced in her own love life when she began making porn films. The interviewer is still Jeremy Wells. You can say this for *Hustler Video Magazine:* Unlike *Playboy* and *Penthouse*, it pulls no punches. It is strictly hard-core and covers all bases. In Volume 2, a young lady shaves her pussy, then uses an electric toothbrush to masturbate. In addition to regular sexmaking, there are several anal sequences.

INTERNATIONAL INTRIGUE
(EMBASSY GIRLS)
NN   BI
1970s   AMBASSADOR

P/D—Not given
F/A—Candida Royalle, Desiree, Andrea Travis
F/A—Mario Stevens

Someone at Ambassador got the clever idea of taking some early porno-film loops and marketing them under the overall title of *Embassy Girls,* featuring women who supposedly work for various foreign embassies or as undercover agents. A voice-over at the beginning of the tape tries to convey this atmosphere and convince you that the women are actually engaged in espionage. These 60-minutes tapes come in attractively designed boxes and look like more current films. But unlike *Swedish Erotica* and the *Diamond Collection* (see reviews), which make no bones about it, it's difficult to tell that these are really loops that were made many years ago until you actually view them. See also the review of *The Right Stuff*, which will clue you to the other *Embassy Girls* tapes.

INTIMATE REALITIES #1
NN NM BI DK
1983 VCA

P/D—Lucy Diamonds, Richard Wright
F/A—Serena, Cara Lott, Gina La Rosta
F/A—Ron Jeremy and many unidentified studs

Serena wears white tails and a top hat and carries a riding crop in her "cum-back debut," which purports to be an inside view of today's sex stars. Alas, it's just one loop after another. First with Ron Jeremy screwing Gina La Rosta, presumably for the first time, then a B/D sequence with two guys and two women. Then Serena strips and masturbates with her crop. Then two gals enjoy a two-way dildo, followed by a lady in a special chair called "the monster" which elevates her ass for easy penetration.

INTIMATE REALITIES #2
NN BI
1984 VCA

P/D—Alida Gutter, John Christopher
F/A—Kay Parker, Becky Savage, Tara Aire,
    Claudine, Laura Sands, Crystal Lake, Rose
    Marie
F/A—Eric Edwards, Randy West, Greg Derek,
    Blake Palmer

The second tape of this series, with Kay Parker as the interviewer and, finally, one of the performers, is much better than the first one. Kay gives the impression of an unstructured interview, but unfortunately the questions she asks, in short interviews with the ladies listed above, are designed to lead into little sexual vignettes in which they participate and illustrate the theme of their lives. *Example:* Tara Aire is in a dominant scene, Laura Sands is in a bi sequence, and Eric Edwards has sex with Kay.

KATHY'S GRADUATION PRESENT
NN BI DK
1975 FANTASY/CABALLERO

P/D—Not given
F/A—Annie Sprinkles and many others not listed
F/A—Jamie Gillis

Kathy's parents are in Europe and send her a combination graduation birthday present of $500. Her friend Annie hires a caterer/short-order cook, whose wife knows how to pep up a party with her own powdered aphrodisiac, which she sprinkles on the hors d'oeuvres. Annie invites all Kathy's friends, and she knows that the thing Kathy really wants in all the world is two cocks at once in her mouth. Annie proves that if Kathy can't do it, she can. Soon everyone is at the party nibbling the food and each other and poking and sucking every genital and tit in sight. (See notes under *Christy.*)

LET ME TELL YA ABOUT WHITE CHICKS
NN BI DK
1984 VCA

P/D—The Dark Brothers, Walter and Gregory
F/A—Sondra Stillman, Desiree Hopkins, Maria
    Tortuga, Christy, Helen Detroit
F/A—Jack Baker, Doobie Brown, Robby Dee,
    Tony El'ay, Fast Talking Sammy

There is no overall story. Six black guys, all young and very hip, speaking in a black vernacular that may force you to listen again to understand what they are saying, are all sitting around drinking and telling their experiences with white chicks. All the women they've had, whom they met on the job as taxi drivers or telephone repairmen, are very white, and the cameraman delights in the contrast of very black pricks penetrating white vaginas and asses. During 1984, adult-film producers suddenly realized that they were overlooking a potentially big market of black male viewers. But I am sure that their black lady friends would cut their balls off if they caught them watching this one.

LOOSE ENDS
DK DM BI
1984 4-PLAY VIDEO

P/D—Bruce Seven
F/A—Janey Robbins, Erica Boyer, Karen Summer,
    Rikki Blake, Summer Rose
F/A—Harry Reems, Mark Wallice, Tom Byron,
    Steve Drake

Plotless, this one runs an hour and 45 minutes with nonstop fucking and penises, dildos, and fingers entering every female orifice, while the cameraman records close-ups of shaved and unshaved female pubes and anuses. Next to Marilyn Chambers, Janey Robbins probably deserves an Erotica award as a female masochist, and if you believe that the only way to achieve sexual ecstasy is being worked over while you are tied up, you'll love this one.

LOVING FRIENDS
NN BI DK
1975 IVP (FORMERLY CVX)

P/D—Not given
F/A—Alexis Kirby, Carrie Conatfe, Alice Wray, Priscilla Alden
F/A—Names of guys not given

In an unnamed suburb, three ladies who work for an insurance company live together in their own house. They're all in heat, and they tackle the guy delivering pizza and one of the girl's boyfriends. The offended girl is pacified with four naked guys. She happily swallows all their shlongs, after which they all play pig pile. (See notes under *Pleasure Bed*.)

LUSTY LADIES
NN BI
1975 FANTASY/CABALLERO

P/D—Not given
F/A—Not given

An hour of nice-looking people that you've never seen before copulating and fellating with intimate close-ups of the ladies' vulvas. It's linked together by two guys jogging and exercising in the park. They hope to be chosen in the upcoming Olympic trials. They make several deals with the wives of the judges, but the director evidently ran out of film before he could tell what finally happened. (See notes under *Christy*.)

MAKE ME FEEL IT
NN BI DK
1984 ESSEX

P/D—Arthur Ben, Henri Pachard
F/A—Kelly Nichols, Carol Cross, Sharon Kane, Talja Rae, Kristara Barrington
F/A—R. Bolla, Klaus Multia, Jake West

R. Bolla is the publisher of hard-core paperbacks written by hacks, who include most of the people listed above. He advises them that the stuff they write is no longer turning him, or anyone else, on, and he gives them a week to go out and get some real experiences that they can write about. "Make me feel it," he tells them. About all you can say about this icky-sicky is that Pachard kept the lights on. The sexmaking is sharply photographed.

MARATHON
NN NM BI DK
1983 HIFCOA

P/D—Troy Benny
F/A—Suika, Drea, Mai Lin, Jesse Adams, Sharon Mitchell
F/A—John C. Holmes, Ron Jeremy, Jamie Gillis, Herschel Savage

Carlos Tobalina (a.k.a. Troy Benny) rides again! The title tells all, but *Copulation* would be a better name for the costume party given by Jamie Gillis, which lasts the entire 84 minutes of this film. The tape has no story, but as you can see from the credits, it offers many top male stars screwing everything in sight. When their cocks are not in some vagina, they are in some happy female's mouth. When the guests of honor fail to arrive at the party (they've been in a ski accident), the orgy adjourns to the hospital, where it continues unabated.

MICHELLE'S SURRENDER
BI
1980s AMBASSADOR

P/D—Not given
F/A—Michelle Gillis, Dolly Venice, Babs Du, Nina Treat, Alice Enoch
F/A—No guys

Michelle gets rid of her male lover in the first scene because he's too rough with her, and then she calls up all her girlfriends. They end up pussy bumping, sucking dildos, and even enjoying the dick of a rubber doll. Boring.

MID SUMMER NIGHT'S DREAM
NN BI DK
1985 4-PLAY VIDEO

P/D—Loretta Sterling, Bruce Seven, Michael Cates
F/A—Erica Boyer, Nicole West, Cara Lott, Heather Wayne, Christy Canyon
F/A—Steve Drake, Mark Wallice, Tom Byron, Dan T. Mann, Peter North

Here's another Seven come Eleven (or more) dewy, chewy, screwy episodes with insatiably horny women, who are a Bruce Seven trademark. "Do you mean that you cheat on George when he's out of town?" Rochelle (Erica Boyer) and Gloria (Cara Lott) have sex with everyone in sight, from the plumber to a Bible salesman.

MISS PASSION
NN BI
1985 VIDCO

P/D—Suzie Randall
F/A—Ginger Lynn, Traci Lords, Crystal Breeze, Rachel Ashley, Lisa de Leeuw
F/A—Guys are unidentified

The women listed above live somewhere in the future on the planet Eros and are competing in a Miss Passion Contest. Suzie Randall (as Suzie Cooze), who made the film, is mistress of ceremonies. For approximately eight minutes apiece, each lady proves her erotic ability in the arms of a handsome guy or another woman; Ginger Lynn takes on two at once. Males watching this one can choose the gal they prefer. The tape is a "weekender."

NOONER
NN BI NM DK
1985 AMBASSADOR

P/D—Not given
F/A—Bubbles Darling, Della Damage, Joan Leslie
F/A—Rex Hondo, Jonathan X., Goldie, Hard Hat

Like the *Embassy Girls* series (see review of *International Intrigue*), this is a group of loops that have been intercut to show how some people spend their lunch hours. There are two guys picnicking with one woman and eating each other instead of the picnic. There are two guys who take a lunch break from their hard-hat jobs and munch on passing muff, and there are a guy and a gal in a motel enjoying a lunchtime quickie.

OPEN FOR BUSINESS (EMBASSY GIRLS)
NN BI DK
1970s AMBASSADOR

P/D—Not given
F/A—Mimi Morgan, Janis King, Mini Toy, Sharon Mitchell, Andrea True, Brigitte Hill
F/A—John Holmes, Johnny Deyes

See notes under *International Intrigue* and *The Right Stiff*. Sixty minutes of more of the same cuts and loops. Adult-film buffs may be interested in a bi sequence with Andrea True, an old-time porno star, and a short sequence with John Holmes.

ORIENTAL LESBIAN FANTASIES
BI
1984 L.A. VIDEO

P/D—L. Burton, Drea
F/A—Mai Lin, Kristara Barrington, Karen Summer, Bunny Bleu, Tamara Longley, Heather Thomas

The entire film is composed of the lesbian fantasy vignettes of a group of pregnant ladies gathered in an obstetrician's waiting room. The technical quality of this film is excellent, probably indicating the use of the same highly qualified staff that made *Kissin' Cousins* and *Yellow Fever* (see reviews). There are no guys.

PASSIONS
NN NM DK BI DS
1985 MITCHELL BROTHERS

P/D—Alex de Renzy
F/A—Stacey Donovan, Kelly Nichols, Diana Sloan, Mauve, Gail Sterling, Angel, Laura Birch, Toni Brooks
F/A—Kevan Gladstone, John Leslie, Michael Knight, Dan Mann

Once again, Alex de Renzy relies on quantity (12 women) rather than quality. This is a series of fucky-sucky vignettes in which the actors are identified by their screen names. You'll wonder whether Alex could ever watch this film with pride.

PASTRIES
NN BI DK
1975 VCX

P/D—Not given
F/A—Uschi Digart is the only person identified.

This is an incoherent potpourri told by Uschi Digart to a Swedish friend after she returns to Sweden. You watch intercuts of Sweden where nothing happens, intercuts of totally unidentified fucking (perhaps what Uschi is thinking about), intercuts of Uschi's American friends screwing and sucking, and a few sequences where Uschi is supposedly a famous Hollywood star who becomes a nurse. If you like big tits, then you can see more of Uschi in some of Russ Meyer's films (see reviews).

PIPE DREAMS
NN NM BI DK
1985 4-PLAY VIDEO

P/D—Loretta Sterling
F/A—Erica Boyer, Jessica Longe, Helga Sven, Summer Rose, Sahara, Cheri Janivier
F/A—David Watson, Dan T. Mann, Tim Knight, Blake Palmer

The Roto-Rooter Sewer Screwer Company is owned by Helga Sven (a buxom blonde). Her employees include David Watson, a nice-looking black guy who is married to Sahara, a pretty black woman. Dan T.

Mann is married, too, but you see his wife only once. Summer Rose also works for the company as dispatcher. Whoever Loretta Sterling, the director, is, she doesn't make adult films for women. This one is an anal-vaginal plumberthon.

PLAYBOY'S GIRLS OF ROCK AND ROLL
R
1985 CBS FOX

P/D—Hugh Hefner, Carol Rosenstein, David Winters
F/A—Michelle Rohl, Natalie Pace, Celenea Allen, Brenda Holliday, Ava Cherry, Kimberly McArthur, Dagmar Petersen, Debra Raye, Cheryl Rixon, Rainey

If you enjoy MTV, *Playboy* gives it a new, sexy zetz with female nudity and a few brief scenes of sexmaking added. All the young ladies listed above sing songs composed especially for this tape, and they prove that Cyndi Lauper, Madonna, and Tina Turner have plenty of competition. The fast-moving cinematic techniques have yet, despite *New Wave Hookers* (see review), to find their way into adult films. The women in this one not only sing but give you little intimate insights into their lives.

PLEASURE #2
NN DK DS
1985 L.A. VIDEO

P/D—Not given
F/A—Not given

Like *Pleasure #1*, most of this one was shot in Europe, except possibly "The American Way of Love" segment, which supposedly takes place in San Francisco, but could have been filmed in Europe. It has one familiar face, a woman who looks like Jesie St. James who runs a house to teach young American males how to make love. This one is the least interesting vignette and offers nothing you haven't seen before better. Another story, "Smash," also supposedly has an American flavor and involves some high-ranking WAC officers enjoying a wild fuckfest with the men on top of their jeep. While the stories on this one are not as clever as those on *Pleasure #1*, one called "Orient Express" is amusing and takes place mostly at night in the dining car of the famous train headed for Istanbul. Another episode is "The Trick," in which a prostitute, who turns out to be a cop, helps a low-ranking policeman entrap a detective.

PLEASURE ZONES
NN BI
1984 ESSEX

P/D—Billy Thornberg, Harold J. Perkins
F/A—Laura Lazar, Janey Robbins, Mai Lin, Rachel Wells, Cindy Swift, Tara Aire
F/A—John Leslie, Jamie Gillis, Paul Thomas, Herschel Savage, Jon Martin

A male voice introduces this potpourri of unrelated episodes, beginning with a female photographer taking improbable shots of a guy and a gal making love. She finally can't resist the guy's cock and takes a suck or two, and the photographer makes it a threesome. The rest of the stories offer another two-female-one-male threesome and John Leslie enjoying one-to-one sex.

PORNO SCREEN TESTS
NN BI DK
1983 VCA

P/D—Pierre Balakoff (a.k.a. Ted Roter)
F/A—Sissy Pirollena
F/A—John Hollyfield, Ron Jeremy, Jon Martin

Don't confuse this one with any real porno screen tests. Ted Roter's name doesn't appear, and it's obvious that he must have needed a few bucks so he put together this series of loops, which includes a gal who likes to dominate her men and some bisexual couples and ends up on a circular bed that doesn't revolve. John and Sissy introduce the various loops, and you'll be sure that Sissy is totally spaced out on something stronger than pot.

THE RIGHT STIFF (EMBASSY GIRLS)
NN BI
1984 AMBASSADOR VIDEO

P/D—Not given
F/A—Angel Cash, Poppia Lottela, Zenia Damage, Joan Leslie
F/A—Dean Rusten, Jonathan X.

There are five other tapes (that I know of) with the overall title *Embassy Girls* (see reviews of *International Intrigue, Employee Benefits, Urgent Desires, Open for Business,* and *Taste for Passion*). They run 60 minutes each and supposedly take place in various embassies. This one is in the Italian embassy and is a plotless bump-pump-and-rump grinder.

RUB DOWN
NN BI DK
1985 VCX

P/D—Not given
F/A—Kimberly Carson, Amber Lynn, Bunny Bleu, Mindy Rae
F/A—Harry Reems, John C. Holmes, Jerry Butler

In the 1980s some adult-film producers and directors have come full circle. They are not afraid of going to jail like their forebears, but they don't want to put their names on some of the junk they are shooting on video and packaging in fancy boxes. You'll wonder why Harry Reems even agreed to appear in this one. As Mr. Bixby, he hires ladies to work for his company only if they'll go down on their knees first. Three of his employees, Kimberly Carson, Amber Lynn, and Bunny Bleu, finally tell him to go to hell and start their own business, an outcall massage service that includes more sex than massage.

SATISFACTIONS
NN NM BI DK
1983 CABALLERO

P/D—Harold Lime, M. Murray, Robert McCallum
F/A—John Leslie, R. Bolla, Eric Edwards, Ron Jeremy, Herschel Savage, Jon Martin

F/A—Rhonda Jo Petty, Kay Parker, Laura Lazanne, Honey Wilder, Cherry Beauchamp, Cara Lott, Carmel

This one starts out as if there might be a story worth watching. Wealthy contractor, Bud Stone (Frank Holowell) is married to Elaine (Honey Wilder), but is presumably so busy making money he doesn't have time to screw her. After he departs one morning she fires the butler and maid, Carl (John Leslie) and Lauren (Tess Hunter), but Carl quickly subdues Honey, and she becomes his grateful adoring sex slave. Exit all three. You never see them again. Instead you see lots more sex.

SCENES THEY WOULDN'T LET ME SHOOT
Volume One of the Great Director Series
NN BI DK
1983 VCA

P/D—Henri Pachard
F/A—Honey Wilder, Tish Ambrose, Tiffany Clark, Annette Heinz, Sharon Caine, Renee Summer
F/A—Jamie Gillis, Eric Edwards, George Payne, Jerry Butler

The scenes that Henri Pachard (Ron Sullivan) reveals were either too bizarre or didn't fit the story lines of his previous pictures. "They" wouldn't let him shoot them, for good reason. Henri Pachard should be locked in a closet for releasing this mess.

SCREW MAGAZINE #1
NN BI DK
1985 L.A. VIDEO

P/D—L. M. Burton, Jack Remy
F/A—Al Goldstein, host, with Angie and Kay Parker

Here's Big Al putting on weight again and getting so old he can't remember his jokes without prompting from notes that he's holding. After that he introduces Angie, a sexy-looking, fully dressed lady, who will cohost the program with him; she gradually undresses as the various segments proceed. They include film clips from *Go for It* and *Lorelei* (see reviews) and also clips from all-black and interracial mov-

ies, which have sold very well in the past few years. They have names like *Hot Chocolate, Brown Sugar, Black Jailbait,* and *Black Baby Dolls,* some of which are reviewed in this book. *Screw* also offers a couple of original vignettes, one called "The Newlyweds" and another called "Deluxe Service." There's also an interview with Kay Parker. It concludes with Al telling you that this is only the first volume, that the next one is in preparation and will be even better. I hope he's right. The only big laugh in this one is the final scene, when Angie finally takes off her panties and reveals that "she" is a man.

SCREWPLES
NN DK DS BI
1980 SELECT-A-TAPE

P/D—Claire Dia
F/A—Kandi Barbour, Serena, Laurien Dominique
F/A—Jamie Gillis, Paul Thomas

Don't confuse this one with the novel about a boutique on Rodeo Drive. It's a series of loops hung together by Nancy Larson, an investigative reporter whose assignment is to "explore the average guy's sexual fantasies." Things you've never seen before: a female's anus being massaged while the female sucks the masseur's cock; in a threesome, one woman pulling a cock from her friend's cunt, sucking it awhile, and putting it back. But this one's claim to dubious fame is another S&M scene performed by Jamie and Serena (See *Bound*). She whips him, puts lipstick on him, and tells him to suck her dildo. Much anal and vulva whipping. Claire Dia must have forgotten she's a woman.

SILK, SATIN & SEX
NN NM BI NR DK
1985 ESSEX

P/D—Cliff Carter, Lawrence Talbot
F/A—Jesie St. James, Vanessa Del Rio, Joanna Storm, Mai Lin, Tiffany Clark, Veronica Hart
F/A—Paul Thomas, Jerry Butler, David Sandler, Jose Duvall

Jesie St. James runs a company, Intimate Body Wear, that offers at-home parties for women (and guys) where they can try on and purchase her new creations. But right now Jesie is recruiting new saleswomen. At a get-acquainted party, they tell each other how they acquired their husbands or boyfriends and their stories are usually re-created.

SILKY
NN BI DK
1980   VIDEO-X-PIX

F/A—Merle Michaels, Hillary Summers, Robin Byrd, Christine deShaffer, Sandi Suarez, Gloria Leonard
F/A—Bobby Astyr, Ron Jeremy, Dave Ruby, R. Bolla, Wayne Daniels, Rick Iverson, Ron Hudd, George Payne

In between screwing with many of the various guys listed above and explaining that her name is Veronica Carlson (Merle Michaels, who is no longer making sexvids) and that "men call me Silky because my skin is so soft," Silky tells you that she's not the only female in the neighborhood who has hot pants, and then she tells you a series of stories, which of course are graphically depicted. As for Silky/Merle, all she does is plough around in the sack and look a little the worse for wear.

SISSY'S HOT SUMMER
NN BI
1981   CABALLERO

P/D—Not given
F/A—Candida Royalle, Jennifer Walker, Michelle Moore, Laurien Dominique
F/A—Jeremy Harden, John C. Holmes, Tony Bond

A quickie that Candida Royalle, who wasn't then making her own films, would probably like to burn. She appears as the host on a TV show on station WYSEX, which is running a movie of the above title. In between, as hostess, she pushes anal stimulators, cock enlargers, and vibrators, which she doesn't demonstrate in any detail. As for the story—Sissy, Janet, and Jack

are about to be evicted from the apartment they share unless they come up with the overdue rent. The only thing they have to sell is their bodies, and in various sequences you watch them as they become hookers for the night and Jack offers himself as a male escort. All the other women in this film have disappeared, but Candida is now producing her own films aimed at the female audience. (See review of *Femmes*.)

69 PARK AVENUE
NN BI DK
1985   ESSEX

P/D—J. Essex, Mike Handley
F/A—Colleen Brennan, Erica Boyer, Tiffany Duponte, Little Oral Annie, Patti Petite
F/A—Tom Byron, Mike Hoffman, D. T. Mann

Despite the New York skyline, the location is a 19th-century house somewhere in San Francisco. The time is the present, but Tom Byron, a reporter on his first assignment, to get the lowdown on the famous madam who runs the brothel (Colleen Brennan), wears a 1940-style felt hat and has his hair dyed blonde. The action is little more than a series of loops hung together by Colleen, who tells stories about how she and her partner finally became famous madams. A candlelighted orgy scene that appears in dull red, so that you can scarcely tell what is happening (if you give a damn), occupies about 15 minutes of tape time.

SKIN DEEP
NN BI DK
1982   CABALLERO

P/D—Randall Hayes
F/A—Rhonda Jo Petty, Toni Renee, Darling Darla, Debbie Truelove
F/A—Charles Anthony, John Holt, Rick Flick

Did you ever wonder what porno actors and actresses do on their days off? Maybe it's something like this. There's a pool in a middle-class home owned by the director, where the ladies can swim and play together. There's a French exchange student trying to pay for her education by acting in porno movies. She's busy in the kitchen with one of the actors or the director. Pretty soon they're all indoors enjoying each other singly and in a group.

SLIP INTO SILK
NN BI DK
1985 CABALLERO

P/D—Joe William, Mike Stryker
F/A—Kelly Nichols, Janey Robbins, Laurie Smith
F/A—Jamie Gillis, Eric Edwards, Tom Byron

Silky Sullivan (Kelly Nichols) hosts a sexy late-night show on radio WLAY. Her sultry conversation attracts lovers young and old who listen to her while they make love. Station director Eric Edwards is her lover. Harry Monahan (Jamie Gillis) is an egomaniac who is chairman of the board of the station and who tells his girlfriend Sylvia (Janey Robbins) if she doesn't suck him off properly, he'll send her back to the grimy massage parlor where he found her. Sylvia's not worried, she's a master dork washer. What's more, she wants to take over Silky's show. She nearly succeeds, but she's thwarted by Silky's friends Tom Byron and Laurie Smith, who also work at the station. Silky is reinstated. To reward Laurie and Tom, Eric and Kelly switch partners. If all else fails, Kelly Nichols can certainly get a job as a disc jockey. But this one will do nothing for her reputation as a top adult-film star.

SOAKING WET
NN DK
1985 CAL VISTA

P/D—Robert McCallum
F/A—Sheri St. Clair, Swallo, Jacqueline Roget
F/A—Ron Jeremy, Billy Dee, Nick Random, Michael Jefferies, Mark Jennings

After making such an excellent film as *Suzie Superstar* (see review), Robert McCallum must have felt the need to make a fast buck with a potboiler. This one, shot on video, involves the three ladies listed

above, who decide that they are going to create a magazine better than *Playboy*. Their only problem is they have no money and no smarts about publishing. Never mind, they have other assets. The ladies can't act, but they have luscious bodies and compliant vaginas, which they use to convince printers, photographers, and writers to contribute their work and talent with no advance payments.

STAR 84, THE TINA MARIE STORY
NN BI NM DK
1984 VIDEO EXCLUSIVE

P/D—Mark Curtis, Bruce Seven, John Stag
F/A—Tina Marie, Laurie Smith, Cody Nicole, Cara Lott, Erica Boyer
F/A—M. Goldberg, Skip Canasi, Rico Vespa, Rank James, Romeo, Verdi, Mark Wallice

Here's everything you ever wanted to watch in a porno film and probably have seen a thousand times. A two-hour tape that tells you on the box that it has 15 full-length sex scenes and 16 wet orgasms. You get that in spades with a rock-music background and occasionally some pretty interesting sexmaking cinematography. After showing you everything from vibrators to masturbators and twosomes, to sandwiches, anal sex, and two cocks at a time in one mouth, the tape concludes with four guys exploring all the orifices of four willing females. If you want to watch a sequel, see review of *Where the Girls Are*, which is more of the same with a different cast.

STARLETS
NN BI DK
1985 4-PLAY VIDEO

P/D—Loretta Sterling, Bruce Seven
F/A—Amber Lynn, Heather Wayne, Gail Force, Christy Canyon, Lauri Smith, Karen Summer
F/A—Tom Byron, Dan T. Mann, Francois Papillon, Steve Drake, Scott Mallory, Greg Rome, Peter North

A quote from the director, Bruce Seven, that appears on the box ("It's one hell of a fuck film") sums this one up—except for the missing word "nonstop." Bruce even has the chutzpah to appear in his own picture as the director who is looking for starlets. When the starlets are finally approved and arrive at the "studio" (a room equipped with bondage-and-discipline equipment) the starlets are soon dressed in leather and chained for some explicit moviemaking, which Bruce records with a hand-held TV camera.

STEPHANIE'S LUST STORY
NN NM BI DK
1983 VCA

P/D—Michael Wright, Pierre Balakoff, Erica Fox
F/A—Gena Lee, Tigr, Drea
F/A—John Hollyfield, Bill Margold, Wayne Reynolds

Stephanie (Gena Lee) lives with a couple of other women who party with the wrong guys. One of them (John Hollyfield) has kicked her out of his house and has spread the word that she's a cheap whore. Poor Stephanie/Gena. She screws with a producer and gets a porno part, but she is so dejected at what she has done that she goes home, starts to drink, and finishes off with sleeping pills. Had Balakoff (a.k.a. Ted Roter) concentrated on the story, he might have had a good film. Unfortunately, 50 percent of the story involves her friends screwing in an extended orgy, while she's dying of pills and booze.

STRIP TEASE
NN BI
1984 VCA

P/D—Alida Gutter, Phil Hall
F/A—Tara Aire, Tanya Lawson
F/A—John Leslie, Ron Jeremy, Wesley Emerson

If you've never been inside a strip theater of the 1980s, then the strippers in this one will give you a pretty good sample of the modern version of "take it off," which combines "showing it all" and at the same time giving the male a view of their squirming inner sanctums, which are just dripping for him. Other than this, the story of Sylvie (Tara Aire) and Guido (John Leslie) quickly gets lost in the screwing shuffle, which involves the ticket collector, the master of ceremonies (Ron Jeremy), and the house guard who is in love with one of the strippers.

STUD HUNTERS
NN BI DK
1983 CABALLERO

P/D—Suze Randall
F/A—Pippi Anderson, Joanna Storm, Lisa La Roo, Amy Allison, Misty Mallory
F/A—Mark Wallice, Michael Morrison, Randy West

Randy Fox (Misty Mallory) is a photographer for men's magazines who has plenty of women but not enough studs. So she sends her gals out hunting on Muscle Beach (Venice, California). Searching for the "perfect 10," they pick up sailors, surfers, and beach bums. Fifi (Pippi Anderson) ends up in a run-down part of town in a men's gym. When she hands out her business cards, five guys immediately show her their enormous cocks, and she enthusiastically samples them as they stand in a circle around her. They finally give her a jism bath and fall on the floor exhausted. Guys with beer bellies will be fascinated to watch Michael Morrison, the only really plump guy in adult films, happily making out with flat-stomached, big-breasted ladies.

SUPERSTARS (THREE VOLUMES)
NN BI DK NM
1984 CABALLERO

P/D—Various
F/A—Janey Robbins, Seka, and Bridgette Monet as hostesses

I've watched three separate volumes in the *Superstar* series put out by Caballero under the Swedish Erotica label. They are in addition to the regular Swedish Erotica product, which now comprises over 60 separate one-hour tapes with three or four loops on each (see Swedish Erotica reviews.) The Janey Robbins tape opens with a lecture by her on the joys of anal intercourse and quickly adjourns to a beach house, where a young lady takes care of Ron Jeremy and another guy and quickly becomes a sandwich. The rest of the tape is cuts from various films in which Janey has appeared. The Seka *Superstar* tape gives you choice excerpts from various films that she has appeared in, including one with a screwing machine. In between the cuts, Seka tells you a little about herself and why she enjoys making adult films. The Bridgette Monet tape is a little more romantic. Bridgette and her real husband, David Cannon, watch cuts from various films and then prove what every viewer of sexvids knows: It's more fun doing it than watching it!

SUZIE'S TAKE-OUT SERVICE
NN
1975   FANTASY/CABALLERO

P/D—Not given
**F/A—Terri Hall, Hella Mau, Carla Bias, Karen
    Black**
F/A—Alan Grogan, C. R. King

This one is really a 15-minute loop extended to 60 minutes. There's a call-girl service that provides Pacifiers, male or female, to the various callers. One guy gets a black female Pacifier, whom he enjoys so much that he soon calls for a white model. A homely woman keeps calling for a handyman but takes a black deliveryman, thinking he's the one she ordered. Then the right one arrives. All the scenes are interracial. (See notes under *Christy*.)

SWEDISH EROTICA #53, #54, #55, #56
NN BI DK
1975–1985   CABALLERO

P/D—Not given
F/A—Various

For those who like their sex (or whiskey) neat, without too much story, Swedish Erotica now comprises more than 65 one-hour tapes, or approximately 195 slice-of-sex vignettes.

SWINGING SHIFT
NN DK
1984   CDI HOME VIDEO/CINDERELLA

P/D—Jim Reynolds, Tom Morton
**F/A—Kristara Barrington, Raven, Lisa de Leeuw,
    Sheri St. Clair, Lacy Misty Anderson**
F/A—Blake Palmer, Tom Byron, Shone Taylor

It's early morning. A black guy crawls in a suburban window and finds a blonde sleeping. He puts his hand over her mouth and screws her. "Don't worry," she tells him, finally pushing his hand away, "we can make all the noise we want—my brother is down at the employment office getting his check." Blake Palmer and Tom Byron spend the rest of the tape recounting their sexual adventures with various ladies in flashbacks and finally agree that they want to try some "Greek." Blake knows a lady, Sheri St. Clair, who can provide it. Somehow she gets on top of the sandwich instead of in the middle, and the camera examines her two-cock gymnastics with great fidelity.

THE T&A TEAM
NN BI DK
1984   VCA

P/D—Eve Milan
**F/A—Carol Cross, Valerie LeVeau, Renee
    Summer, Joanna Storm, Tanya Lawson,
    Silver Starr, Natasha Ski**
F/A—Jerry Butler, George Payne, Ron Jeremy

This one begins with a great action scene. A group of guys (you guess they are women) wearing masks and camouflage suits and brandishing machine guns, board a helicopter and fly across the New Jersey Meadowlands to an abandoned warehouse where five naked guys are being held captive by a woman who sprays them with "extract of euphoria," which makes them willing to do anything she wishes. You think this is the story? Sorry—it really isn't. While the ladies are waiting for the appropriate moment to rescue the guys, they tell each other stories of their sex lives, which include screwing Santa Claus on the night before Christmas. Was he really Daddy? Another is about a female office manager who is convinced her assistant is a homosexual and makes him prove that he isn't. After an hour and 20 minutes of this stuff, you won't feel sorry for the guys when they are rescued and are still screwing anything in sight—euphorically!

TEENAGE CRUISERS
NN NM NL (occasionally) DK
1975 VCX

P/D—Not given
F/A—Serena, Christine, Schaeffer, Lynn Margulies
F/A—John C. Holmes, Tony Cohn, Jerry Sokorski, William Margold

In the 1970s, when this film was released, it probably was funny, sexy, and shocking. But what you laughed at then may bore you now. Especially because there's no unifying story, just a series of insanities. These include Serena, as a very young-looking redhead, and her girlfriend at a nude bakeoff; J. C. Holmes enjoying an underwater fuck; and Bill Margold, as Professor Flinch, playing masochist to some woman who beats him and makes him eat her. The piece de resistance is a young woman in a barn grooming a donkey and getting so excited that she lies down in the hay. Fortunately, it's left to your imagination as the bleary-eyed donkey approaches her.

TEENAGE DESIRES
NN NL (a little)
1975 IVP (formerly CVX)

P/D—Rik Taziner
F/A—Paula Thomas, Dorothy Holiday, Judy Egon, Sharon Saint
F/A—Jay Seemon, Shel Silas

Although her name isn't in the credits, Seka is here—much younger and long-haired— sitting on a beach, playing with a guy, and telling him a story about her sister and a cowboy. Soon you are watching two different sex actions intercut with each other. The next day, as a housewife, she tries to get two guys to repair a table but ends up getting her own "plumbing" fixed

instead. That night they hire a baby-sitter, who arrives with a poster photograph of John Travolta, which she spends the evening sitting on bare ass and moaning happily until the parents arrive home early and introduce her to real, live flesh. (See notes under *Pleasure Bed*.)

TERMS OF EMPLOYMENT
NN BI DK
1985 L.A. VIDEO

P/D—Phil Prince
F/A—Shone Tee, Sheri St. Clair, Mimi Daniels
F/A—Billy Dee, Randy Alexander, Robert Naska

Shot on video, on a Sunday afternoon probably, this one tells about a dinner party that John's wife must give for the big boss, J.B., to ensure that John will get a promotion. A vagina-ass-mouth-penis-orgy that goes on interminably.

THAT LADY FROM RIO
NN BI DK
1976 QUALITY/VIDEO-X-PIX

P/D—Amanda Barton
F/A—Vanessa Del Rio, Marlene Willoughby, Roxanne Louis, Joanna Hau, Sharon Mitchell
F/A—Bobby Astyr, Jamie Gillis, Roger Caine

For the first 15 minutes of this one, Amanda Barton, who has a good cinema sense (see review of *Midnight Desire*), builds a neat feeling of intrigue with Number One (Vanessa Del Rio). Speaking only Spanish, Vanessa arrives at midnight in a yacht from Rio at some marina near New York City. But then a yucky story defeats the director. Seems that Vanessa is head of a worldwide organization called World Sphincter Control, which runs a female white slave trade and supplies women to brothels and whorehouses. It all ends after much unbelievable sexual action and dialogue with Number One returning to Rio on her yacht and Don Vittorio watching in the background with a big grin as the bomb that he's planted on it blows Number One skyhigh.

THAT'S EROTIC
NN DK
1983 CAL VISTA

P/D—Adele Robbins
F/A—See below

Adele Robbins's contribution to this one was evidently about 25 minutes of some joyous screwing aboard an expensive motorboat circling near Marina Del Rey (probably) while the hosts provide comments about various porno films that they have watched featuring 23 porno stars, many of whom are no longer making adult films. The seagoing sex is more interesting than the cuts, which include scenes from a film with John Holmes and Serena, who happily swallows his jism; John Leslie with an unidentified lady whose anus he's exercising; cuts from the film *A Dirty Western* (see review); Eric Edwards and several others in an orgy scene with Georgina Spelvin; another cut with Annette Haven trying unsuccessfully to deep-throat John C. Holmes; Mike Ranger (identified by our hosts as Eric Edwards) with a very young Georgina Spelvin; Desiree Cousteau and Seka enjoying two anonymous cocks; Mike Ranger (again identified as Eric Edwards) with Serena; a young John Leslie making it with Tina Russell and a woman identified as Janet Beaver; Helen Madigan with an unidentified guy; and Bobby Astyr and John Leslie making a squirming sandwich out of Vanessa Del Rio.

THREE WOMEN
NN NL (wacky dialogue)
1975 IVP (formerly CVX)

P/D—Richard Bontont
F/A—Rita Berlin, Julie Combs, Misty
F/A—Don Silva, Rich Plada, Herb Ivan, Alex Carson

Three gals meet at lunch and compare sexual notes. One had to screw her boss, one does the delivery boy, and one is in love. (See notes under *Pleasure Bed.*)

THUNDER BUNS
NN NR NM
1976 VCX

P/D—Russell Flynn, Thomas Marker
F/A—Jennifer Welles, Linda Wong, Annette Haven, Lesbian Twins
F/A—Bobby Astyr, Joey Silvera

This is a package of sex sequences from three other films. I can identify only one of them, in which Joey Silvera is living with Linda Wong, who isn't at all happy that he earns a living making porno films. This excerpt gives him 10 minutes of screwing with Linda, and because she's unhappy with him, during a second sequence from the same film, she visits her friend Annette Haven and enjoys a threesome with Annette's husband. The tape opens with a very pretty Jennifer Welles, who seduces a young guy who doesn't look over 15 years old. And what follows is a novelist's daydream of how young men should get introduced to sex by an older woman. A third sequence has the lesbian twins, who really do look alike, making love together. And the final cut from another film reveals a young woman in pigtails admiring her naked self in a mirror and later playing with a dildo, during which her daddy walks in, introduces her to the real thing, and when they finish, begs her, "Don't tell Mommy!"

TINA'S PARTY
NN BI DK
1975 FANTASY/CABALLERO

P/D—Not given
F/A—Not given but no one you've ever seen before

For the first 10 minutes there's no sex in this one. Couple after couple are gathering at Tina's home for a party. The reason for the party is not given, and Tina is hard to identify. Never mind, during the evening, at least 10 couples arrive and, after playing feelsies in the living room and drinking wine, soon are all over the house for a 50-minute oral-genital ballet. (See notes under *Christy.*)

TOO GOOD TO BE TRUE
NN BI
1984   MASTERPIECE

P/D—Jerome Bronson, Steve Scott
F/A—Ginger Lynn, Stacey Donovan, Cynthia Brooks, Jade Nichols, Gina Valentino
F/A—Peter North, Tony Savage, Marc Goldberg, Harry Reems, Steve Drake

Tom Hadley (Peter North) a young, hard-working farmer, has a nice young lady friend, who takes care of him in the barn. But he's suddenly informed that his uncle has died and left him a whorehouse in Los Angeles, more than $1 million, a limousine, and his uncle's girlfriend Felicia (Ginger Lynn). All of the ladies can't wait to service their new boss, which they do in the shower, in the pool, and wherever they can loosen his zipper.

THE ULTIMATE Q
NN BI DK
1985   NOW SHOWING

P/D—Lawrence T. Cole
F/A—Stacey Donovan, Nina Hartley, Lili Marlene
F/A—Paul Thomas, Herschel Savage, Billy Dee

Matthew (Paul Thomas) and Rosemary (Stacey Donovan) run a love cult where women can learn to experience the ultimate orgasm in four stages. Really just an excuse for orgies.

UP, UP, AND AWAY
NN BI NM DK
1985   CABALLERO

P/D—Bob Bouchard, Sam Hunter
F/A—Cody Nicole, Laurie Smith, Ginger Lynn, Stacey Donovan, Bridgitte Monet, Colleen Brennan, Shasha Gabor, Gabrielle Behar, Lisa Thomas
F/A—Paul Thomas, Jamie Gillis, Jerry Butler, Craig Roberts

I have listed all the women in this one because they presumably are the *All-American Girls* (see review) who have appeared in two other films together. But sadly, the producer and director threw away what might have been a good story by trying to feature each one of these ladies, bouncing or sulking in sequences that have little to do with the story, which revolves around the financial ups and downs at an airline.

URGENT DESIRES (EMBASSY GIRLS)
NN BI DK
1970s   AMBASSADOR

P/D—Not given
F/A—Bobi Hall, Carlie Zacks, Gail Scott, Alma Maize
F/A—Randy Barstow

More 1970s loops hooked together under the Embassy label (see review of *International Intrigue*). Lots of the same stuff you've seen before, with unfamiliar faces, mouths, and genitals engaged in twosomes, three-ways, foursomes, and frantic masturbation.

VELVET HUSTLE
NN NM BI
1975   FANTASY/CABALLERO

P/D—Joe Serkes, John Banks
F/A—Kay Louis, Penny Burke
F/A—Sam Tom, Joe Kado, Ronny Frey, Sam Falus

"I don't know whether Highway Patrol would like this," the guy tells a young lady who unzips his pants while he's driving a Cadillac toward a models' party. They arrive at a very expensive home, where a guy named Joe is the "pubic"-relations manager. Soon the attractive lady models are withdrawing with the attractive males to snack on each other between drinks. After 60 minutes of this (you could write the dialogue on half a page), the original lovers drive off together. (See notes under *Christy*.)

WE LOVE TO TEASE
NN NM BI (lots of)
1985   VIDCO

P/D—Michael Carpenter
F/A—Traci Lords, Jasmine, Robin Cannes, Dallas Miko, Tanja, Tiffany Gleason, Amy Rogers, Buffy M.

F/A—Mark Wallice, Peter North, Greg Rome, Kevin James, Ron Jeremy

If you don't get enough of Traci and Candi in *Open Up Traci* (see review), here's a sequel, or maybe it came before *Open Up.* Anyway, the subject is just the same—lots of beautiful ladies coming with each other and the guys listed above. There must be a satiation point for these plotless fuck- and suckathons, but apparently it hasn't been reached yet.

WET DREAMS
NN NM BI DK
1985 CABALLERO

P/D—Henri Pachard
F/A—Cody Nicole, Kelly Nichols, Taija Rae, Renee Summer, Carol Cross
F/A—Joey Silvera, George Payne, Billy Dee, Joe Santino, David Scott, Casey Moran, Eric Edwards

Methinks that Henri tried to patch together a few loops for this one and either lost his way or forgot where he began. (See *Swedish Erotica* or *Diamond Collection* tapes for better treatments.)

WET SEX
NN BI DK
1985 CABALLERO

P/D—Paul Vatelli
F/A—Susan Hart, Debbie Amore, Laurie Powell, Fawn Paris
F/A—Ron Jeremy, Greg Ruffner, Greg Rome, Mark Wallice

This one is supposed to have been made at a private hideout in a mountain resort somewhere near New York City, but more likely it was the Caballero back lot. You never leave the living room, bedrooms, swimming pool, or Jacuzzi. Five women and four guys arrive for the weekend and have an 80-minute potpourri of twosomes, threesomes, and girl/girl encounters, which take place over two nights.

WHEN A WOMAN CALLS
NN NR BI DK
1976 QUALITY/VIDEO-X-PIX

P/D—Roberta Prentiss, William Haddinston, Jr.
F/A—Bree Anthony, Helen Madison
F/A—Jamie Gillis, Alex Mario, Bobby Astyr

Despite a romantic start during which Peggy (Bree Anthony) remembers her first year of marriage to Michael (Jamie Gillis), there's scarcely a minute in this 80-minute tape that someone isn't fucking or sucking someone else.

WHERE THE GIRLS ARE
NN NM BI DK
1985 VIDEO EXCLUSIVES

P/D—Mark Curtis
F/A—Raven St. James, Cody Nicole, Laurie Smith, Erica Boyer, Tina Marie, Linda Shaw, Janey Robbins, Cara Lott, Suzy Star, Lynn Ray, Tracey Donovan
F/A—Ron Jeremy, Craig Roberts, Mark Wallice, Greg Rome, Rick Johns, Brock Stevens

Where the girls are isn't Fort Lauderdale, but southern California. Four of the guys listed above tell you about their experiences with them. I can't imagine who could sit through an hour and 45 minutes of this kind of film, or *Stars 84* (see review), which lasts a full two hours. I suspect that most guys and gals stick the cassette in their VCRs and do something else. The box blurb tells you that it contains 12 full-length sex scenes and 14 spectacular orgasms, with everything from oral sex to tit banging, threesomes, fourways, female masturbation, muff munching, all-girl orgies, and juicy, squirting dildos.

THE WHORE'S PORT
NN BI DK
1985 CABALLERO

P/D—Jose Benzaref
F/A—Michele Valentin
F/A—Lawrence Eyemard

Jose Benzaref makes these movies for European consumption. In the Caballero versions, with dubbed English, they run 60 minutes, but I have a feeling that they have been cut from the originals, which often makes the action confusing. This one gives you high hopes in the beginning as it follows three hookers on their rounds of a port town on the Costa del Sol and you watch their realistic encounters with several tricks whom they take to a local hotel room. But the realism is soon lost when they are picked up by a smooth hustler who takes them off to his mansion and prepares them for an orgy that he's setting up that night for his own customers. The young ladies are altogether too-willing participants in an anything-goes orgy similar to the one in *Making of a Porno Movie* (see review).

WIDESPREAD SCANDALS OF LYDIA LACE
NN NM DK BI
1983 CABALLERO

P/D—Michael Dejou, Henri Pachard
F/A—Bolla, Joey Civera, Sean Elliott, Ashley Moore
F/A—Joanna Storm, Lee Carroll, Sharon Mitchell

This is a quickie that Pachard must have flipped off on a rainy Manhattan weekend, and then gave it a zoomie, cryptic title which means nothing.

WORKING FOR LOVE
NN BI
1981 CABALLERO

P/D—Not given
F/A—Not given

Other than beautiful faces and bodies that you've never seen before, this West German–made quickie doesn't offer much. What there is of a story involves an American, Mr. Roberts, who has arrived in Paris to finance a porno film that will cost $1.5 million. Lots of microphones hovering over actors are photographed, along with pricks and vulvas. This one proves that even foreign filmmakers can produce some bombs. Other than a few slowly paced and caring sex sequences, with subdued lighting, this one isn't worth the overnight rental cost.

YOUNG DOCTORS IN LUST
NN BI DK
1982 NOW SHOWING

P/D—Lawrence T. Cole, Darr Michaels
F/A—Sharon Kane, Chris Cassidy, Betsy Ward
F/A—Paul Thomas, John Leslie

The doctor in charge tells you, "This is a sex clinic for women who have serious sex problems. We cure them and have fun curing them, as you will see." Leslie and Thomas appear in one scene each to help solve the ladies' problems. But after that, in several non-sequitur sequences, the screwing moves outdoors. The clinic has plenty of other male helpers, including a handsome black guy who, along with the female nurses, quickly restores the patients' zest for sex. Before it's over, although you may not be able to tell one cock from another, you'll recognize the ladies by their vulvas as well as their faces!

THE YOUNG LIKE IT HOT
NN NM BI DK
1983 CABALLERO

P/D—Gall Palmer, Bob Chinn
F/A—Herschel Savage, Eric Edwards, Bud Lee, Paul Thomas, William Margold, Joey Silvera
F/A—Hypatia Lee, Kay Parker, Callie Aimes

Credits state that Gail Palmer wrote the story and screen play as well as directed this one. She didn't work very hard on the story. Seems that a local telephone switching office in an unidentified town in California is about to be computerized, with the consequent loss of jobs of the boss, Mr. Fishbait (Eric Edwards), the supervisor, Lonnie (Hypatie Lee), and three other ladies, plus one guy named Dave (Bud Lee) who handles the switchboard and an outdoor lineman. How to prove the company needs live personnel? Lonnie suggests to Mr. Fishbait that they provide intimate services that a computer can't. From that point on, under the direction of Lonnie, the ladies offer sexual advice to the telephone company's customers and direct genital servicing for those who arrive at the office. This film presumably introduces Hypatia Lee, who is of Cherokee Indian and Irish ancestry. She's an Annette Haven, Veronica Hart type of woman. Callie is the perfect virginal looking blonde. Watching them is the only reason for buying this tape.

YOU'RE THE BOSS
NN   NM   BI (lots of)
1984   VIDCO

P/D—**Michael Carpenter**
F/A—**Treonna, Jessyca Wylde, Caressa Nature, Tess Ferre, Nicole**
F/A—**Mark Wallice, Tony Martino, Greg Rome, Craig Roberts, Dan T. Mann, Ron Jeremy**

Michelle, Lynn, and Jennifer live together, and Jennifer wins a bet that allows her to do anything she wishes with them. As their "boss," Jennifer gives Michele a dildo and tells her, "Fuck Lynn in the ass with it." Lynn is delighted to comply and Michelle only moans a little. Pretty soon the ladies are slobbering all over each other in ecstasy. You've never seen most of the women before.

Documentaries

AMATEUR LOVERS' EROTIC BEDROOM VIDEOS, #1 AND #2
NN   NM   DK
1985   M. SCHMIDT

Like Baker Video, Susan's Video, and FIV—Voyeurs (see reviews), M. Schmidt buys and sells videotapes of amateurs who get turned on when they perform before their home video cameras. These two tapes (as well as many others) run about two hours and sell for $57 direct from M. Schmidt (573 North Mountain, #284, Upland, CA 91786).

HOME MOVIES LTD.
NN   NM   BI
1983   SELECT/ESSEX

P/D—**Lance Venture**
F/A—**Gina Martel, Frank James, Kimberly Carson, Desiree Lane**
F/A—**Frank James, Tom Byron**

Self-made, home video movies have become a business for several different groups. See the listing for *Susan's Video,* and check classifieds in your video magazines for the many amateurs in the business, and, of course, read the section in the front of this book on how to make your own sexvids. But don't buy this tape and expect to see strictly amateurs. The photography is quite professional. Despite the flamboyant advertising on the box and the suggestion that if you wish to participate in a forthcoming Home Movies Ltd. contest write to them care of Select Essex, P.O. Box 1054, Northridge, CA 91324, you won't be an amateur when you finish. Perhaps Select Essex is trying to develop semi-professionals.

HOW TO DO IT ON TAPE
(THE GUIDE TO AMATEUR VIDSEX)
NN   BI
1984   FIV—VIDEO VOYEUR CLUB

FIV, the Video Voyeur Club, is the only place I know that offers a 70-minute how-to-do-it tape, which you can order directly from them: FIV, P.O. Box 114, Murrysville, PA 15668. They offer suggestions on cameras and lighting, and a female voice-over guides you through the action, which includes two young married women experimenting with their husbands' equipment and ending up in a bi scene, after which they are joined by a black neighbor and her husband, who amusingly can't get it up or come when three women are working on him at once and he is being videotaped. There is an extended husband-and-wife scene, but the entire tape is never a one-couple effort. I still believe that millions of couples will eventually make their own sexvids—but for the most part not in a group or a swinging situation. So a single couple won't learn much about making their own tape from this one, but may be startled that ordinary guys and gals can act just as horny with each other as the professionals do, and may wish to submit their own tape for exchange with other couples', which is a service FIV offers.

MASTER'S DEGREE (IN FEMININE SEXUAL LIBERATION)
NN BI
1973   QUALITY/VIDEO-X-PIX

P/D—Sam Lake Entertainments
F/A—Sheila Ross; no others identified

Back in the 1970s, Sam Lake was the big honcho at Quality pictures and one of the first in the country who dared to challenge New York City law by showing porno films in theaters near Times Square. I would guess this one was made to give the impression of a sex-education film, which it is, but also to offer one of the first films that showed human beings making love. Sheila Ross, who hosts the film, is presumably a doctor of psychology, and her diplomas are shown. She describes some of her cases of sexual problems, which are acted out. Mostly of historical interest. We've come a long way from this film in the intervening years. If you don't think so, watch *Guide to Sexual Positions* and other sex-education films I have reviewed.

MEN'S VIDEO MAGAZINE
R
1984   VCX

P/D—Michael Fitzgerald, Yvonne Wallace, Stan Lipton
F/A—Kay Parker and other models
F/A—Vince Gardner (host)

While I have no statistics on the success of this type of tape (see reviews of *Hustler, Playboy,* and *Penthouse* tapes) I would guess that, even for Playboy, which has now released eight or more volumes, they are not very profitable, and they won't be until they are sold at giveaway prices and sustained by advertising. This one offers several strip sequences, a brief wrestling match (during which the ladies wear bikinis), and an aerobic dance ses-

sion that is photographed using every imaginable camera and cutting technique. The best section is a long, fully clothed interview with Kay Parker, in which she tells about her career and acting in such films as *Taboo* and *Body Talk* (see reviews). Kay believes that adult films in many cases are more sexually honest than the regular Hollywood variety, and she enjoys her work because it has transformed her from a rather inhibited woman into a woman who thoroughly enjoys sex and men.

NIGHT TIMES
NN BI DK
1984   BAKER VIDEO

P/D—Not given
F/A—Not given

This is another 70-minute offering from Baker Video (for details see review of *Amateur Productions* and *Sweet Dreams*). The producers in this one, as well as the guys and gals, are the same people you pass every day on the street and may wonder how they spend their evenings. Here you can learn from four very crisp black-and-white video sequences. You can be sure that right now, all over the United States, many hundreds of young and middle-aged people are playing sex games while their video cameras watch them, thus preserving their sexmaking for posterity and for them to view in their old age.

NUDE BEACHES
R
1982   T. PAGE

P/D—T. Page
F/A—Friends and fellow nudists

If you live in the Northeast and watch this one in the winter, you'll be calling your travel agent for a fast trip to southern California and a directory of nude beaches, many of which still lead a precarious, day-to-day existence. There is no voice-over or credits on this tape, just pleasant music accompanying an almost-two-hour survey of naked human beings enjoying themselves, mostly on Black's Beach, not far from San Diego. Page's tape, which I would guess was made over many weekends, watches women and guys of all shapes, sizes, colors, and ages (there are many kids and babies) playing in the surf, body painting, sunning, playing frisbee, taking pictures of each other, and just enjoying a community of several thousand people happily milling about and appreciating each other and the fact that they are alive. When you are about to give up on adult movies, it's fun to watch one like this where being naked leads to loving laughter instead of sex.

Supplemental Listing of Sexvids

Key to the Abbreviations

R means R-rated or "soft-core"; there is no explicit genital sex. P/D means Producer/Director, in that order. If only one name is given, the individual acted in both capacities. F/A means Featured Actors and Actresses (as many as I've been able to determine from dealers' catalogues and other sources). If information is fragmentary, it means that thus far no one has copied the essential information off the film credits and to get it, it would be necessary to view the particular tape. If *no* date is given, this means the film was produced sometime between 1970 and 1979. An exact date may be impossible to determine since many films were not copyrighted. If no distributor's name is given, it means that the tape is temporarily "out of print" but could be reissued.

Together with the preceding listing of sexvids, to my knowledge, this is the most comprehensive listing of heterosexual adult films available anywhere. But unlike the preceding reviews of more than 1,300 adult films produced between 1970 and 1985, the following listing of more than 2,840 additional sexvids is not rated with my unique rating system, nor does it offer any purchasers' guide with comments on particular films. Finally, it does not identify some of them as Collector's Choice.

I have not watched any of the following films on tape. There are several reasons for this. Some very current films were not yet released on tape when the book went to press.

Wherever possible, I have tried to give the name or names of the exclusive distributor/owner of these tapes, and they have been coded so they are easily identified, and you can order them directly. In the few cases where the particular distributor does not sell directly, I'm sure they will advise where you can purchase their tapes. In any event, your check must accompany an order. Prices range between $19.50 and $89.50 (depending on the length of the tape in most cases), and most distributors will be happy to send you their complete catalogues (often produced in four-color) if you will send them a check for $5.

But you should be aware that most distributor catalogues promote particular tapes as flamboyantly as possible, and do not give you a rating guide or the kind of comments on films that appear in the preceding listing. Also, unfortunately for collectors and aficionados, the catalogue listings of many tapes do not list the actors or producer/directors. Again, many distributors seem unaware that ultimately there will be many collectors of these tapes who will want to search out tapes with actors and actresses such as Harry Reems,* Andrea True, Marc Stevens, Renee Bond, Tina Russell (who is dead) and others who no longer appear in these films. And, in many cases, these earlier films (for reasons I have pointed out in the previous text) are more fun to watch than some current films on tape.

I mentioned in the first edition of this book that there was no central source or library where researchers could view adult films. Late in 1984 I received a letter from the Kinsey Institute for Research in Sex, Gender and Reproduction, affiliated with Indiana University. In an exchange of correspondence, Douglas K. Freeman, head of collections, wrote me: "The Kinsey Institute applauds your intention to make your videotape collection available for scholarly research. As the world's largest archive and research facility relating to sexuality, we certainly would be interested in your materials. Although we have a very comprehensive collection of early stag films, our coverage beginning 1950 is not very complete, and we have only a few videotapes."

I have assured all the key distributors who have loaned me tapes for review (and I hope will continue to keep me on their review lists) that the entire library of tapes reviewed in this book is intact, and either Kinsey or a Boston museum that agrees to set up a viewing room under strict control for filmmakers, sexologists, and historians interested in this vast sidelight on human sexuality will end up with this collection.

In the meantime, as I have mentioned in several places in this book, the costs of developing your own library of sexvids is no longer out of reach. And if you are interested you can also expand this to include hundreds of homosexual and lesbian films that are available from most of the key distributors.

As in the previous edition, here is a very comprehensive listing of adult films that are not reviewed. Again, the reason that particular tapes are not reviewed is that I was unable to get a screening copy, either because the film had not yet been released or because the distributor would not supply me with one. In any event, if you prefer to be an explorer, most of these tapes that I have not reviewed are available for sale or rent somewhere.

Abigail Leslie Is Back in Town	Home Video
Acid Love	Boccaccio 100
Acting Out	R Wonderlust Video
Adultery	Video Station
Adult Movie Bloopers	F/A Candy Samples: Vintage Video, 1983
Adventures in Bondage	Bizarre, 1982
Adventures of a Bad Mama Jama	F/A Bad Mama, a 300-pound black lady: CPLC Video
	1983
Adventures of a Hustler Cover Girl	
Adventures of Flash Beaver	F/A Brandy O'Toole, Chesley Noone: Class X

Adventures of Tracy Dick	P/D Jerome Tanner F/A Traci Lords, Stacey Donovan, Heather Wayne: Western Visuals, 1985
Aerobisex Girls	P/D Bruce Seven F/A Tina Blair, Misty Dawn, Becky Savage, Christina Ray, Kristi Bryant, Bridgette Royale, Lipstick: 1983
Affair	
The Affairs of Miss Roberts	P/D Phil Prince F/A Champagne, Burnt Amber, Tawny Fox, Ron Jeremy, Billy Dee
Afterschool Exams	VIP
Afternoon Tease	VCX
After the Ball	Boccaccio 100
Age of Consent	P/D Bob Chinn F/A Angel West, Gail Force: AVC, 1985
Agent Oosex	F/A Barbara Bourbon, Rick Cassidy: Caravan/4-Play
Agent 69	Silhouette Video
Aggressive Women	F/A Victoria Slick, Mike Horner, Linda Lee, Billy Dee, Danielle: 1983
Agony of Lace, Lace and Love	F/A Fred Lincoln, Sheila Stoar: Astro
Airplane, the Bondage Movie	Janus
Airport Girls	F/A Cindy West, Rita Davis: Video-X-Pix
Alex de Renzy's Dirty Girls	P/D Alex de Renzy F/A Stacey Donovan, Cody Nicole, Jac- queline Lorians, Helga Sven, Jamie Gillis, Kelly Nichols, Joanna Storm: Mitch- ell Bros., 1984
Alice, Ted and Carol	
All About Angel Cash	F/A Angel Cash, Juliet Anderson: Video-X-Pix, 1982
All About Leslie	X-tra Vision
All About Sex	Video Station
All American Hustler	P/D W. L. Kleiger F/A Frank Rhodes, Tracy Scott, Paula Mason
All American Super Bitches	Bizarre
All Around Service	
All Day Sucker	Boccaccio 100
All Her Way	Morning Glory
All in the Family: Home Sweet Home	P/D Kirdy Stevens F/A Erica Boyer, Kristara Barrington
All in the Sex Family	Boccaccio 100
All the Action	P/D B. Ron Elliott F/A Becky Bitter, Donna Jones, Ron Jer- emy, Terri Galko, Michael Starr: Mas- terpiece, 1984
All the Devil's Angels (Formerly titled The Psychiatrist, see review)	F/A Diane Miller, Gena Lee, Tovia Borodyn, Matacha, Nancy Cox: VCA
All the King's Ladies	F/A Serena, Rhonda Jo Petty, Sharon Mitchell, Juliet Anderson, Holly McCall, Michael Morrison: Superior, 1980
All the Loving Neighbors	R

All the Way	F/A Georgina Spelvin, Nicki Ronson: Boccaccio 100, MSI Video
All the Way	F/A Candy Samples, Eric Edwards, Russ Meyer: Cal Vista
Almost Anything Goes	Astro
Alpine Romance	F/A Olinke: 1982
Always Ready	F/A John Holmes, Marlene Monroe: 1981 (Holmes's last film?)
Always Ready for Four	Orchids International, 1985
Amateur Coed Frolics	P/D Gypsy Marr
	F/A Jessica Henner, Dennis Wade, Gypsy Marr: 1985
Amateur Nite	F/A Elizabeth Lynn: Western Visuals, 1983
Amazon Island	Video Home Library, 1984
Amber's Desires	Caballero, 1985
American Tickler	P/D Chuck Vincent: 1983
Amour	F/A Fritzi Ross, George Blue, Gaby Hiller, Siegmar Deubner, Martine Gerrault: VCA
Amorous Adventures of Cissy	Wonderful World
Anal Annie and Her Willing Husband	F/A Richard Pacheco, Karen Summer, Blair Harris: Lipstick Video, 1985
Anal Annie and the Backdoor Housewives	P/D Charles De Santos
	F/A Nina Hartley, Lili Marlene, Alley Cat Anderson: Video Tape Exchange, 1984
Anal Annie Can't Say No	F/A Same actors as above, plus Jamie Gillis: Lipstick Video, 1985
Anal Intruders	Ja-Rae Productions
Anatomy of a Whorehouse	Boccaccio 100
And Now the Cane	Bizarre
And Then Came Eve	VCX
Angel in White	R F/A Yoko Katagiri, Haijimi, Tainmoto, Emi Hrar: 1979
Angel of Heat	R F/A Marilyn Chambers: Vestron, 1982
Angel of the Night	F/A Paul Thomas, Angel, Brittany Stricker: Island Home Video, 1985
Angels	P/D Gary Stevens, Robin Macks
	F/A Jamie Gillis, Amber Hunt, Susan McBain: Blue Video
Angels in Distress	P/D William Hunt, Joseph Scarpelli
	F/A Marlene Willoughby, Mistress Candice, Janice Dupre, Ron Jeremy, George Payne, Dave Rube
Angels of Passion	CDI Home Video
Angel's Revenge	F/A Angel, Harry Reems: Island Home Video, 1985
Anger in Jennie	Video-X-Home Library
Angie	F/A Samantha Fox, Vanessa Del Rio: MSI Video
Animal Lovers	
Animals	
Anita Nymphet	
Anne Randall's "Lies"	P/D Cecil Howard
	F/A Ron Jeremy, Tammy Tigr, Copper Anna Turner, Sharon Mitchell, Marissa Constantine: Command, 1982

Another Love, Another Place		F/A Fritzi Ross: International Home Video
Another Roll in the Hay		F/A Traci Lords, Eric Edwards, Paul Thomas, Elizabeth English, David Dukeham, Clarence Percy: Collector's Video, 1985
Ante Up—Deal Me in Place		Boccaccio 100
Anything Goes		
Ape Over Love		F/A Harry Reems, Annette Haven, Suzi West, Barbara Hughes: Blue Video
The Appointment	R	Cal Vista
Armed Services		Boccaccio 100
Around the World in 60 Minutes		
Around the World with J.W.		PVX
Aroused		F/A Traci Lords, Steve Powers, Sheri St. Clair, Christine Howard, Ali Moore, Tom Byron: Vista Video, 1985
Artful Lover		F/A Ken Scudder: Boccaccio 100
Art School		F/A C. J. Laing: Video-X-Home Library
Ass Busters		Western Visuals
Assault of Innocence		F/A Mark Stevens: Video-X-Home Library
As You Like It		F/A Candy Samples, John Holmes: Boccaccio 100
Auditions	R	P/D Harry Tampa: Modern, Wizard, 1978
Audra's Ordeal		Bizarre, 1983
Auto-Erotic Practices		VCR
Avalon Calling		TGA
The Avengers		F/A Patrick MacNee, Diana Rigg: Bizarre
Avon Calling		Boccaccio 100
The Awakening of Sally		F/A Lorrie Smith, Crystal Lake, Mimi Morgan, Vicki Cedarguest, Blaire Castle, Mona Page, Kyota Kim, Sun Ling, Jane Wan Loo: VCR, 1984
AWOL		Home Entertainment
Babe in the Woods		1982
Baby Blue		VBM
Baby Bubbles		Boccaccio 100
Baby Cakes		Select/Essex 1983
Baby Face		F/A Cuddles Malone, Amber Hunt, Linda Wong
Babylon Gold		P/D Cecil Howard
		F/A Samantha Fox, Kandi Barbour, Veronica Hart, Lisa de Leeuw, Jamie Gillis: Command, 1983
Baby Oil		F/A Jamie Gillis, C. J. Laing: Video-X-Home Library
Baby Sister		F/A Danielle, Rhonda Jo Petty, Tara Aire: Gourmet (shot directly on videotape)
The Babysitter		Gourmet
Bachannale		P/D Amero Brothers
		F/A Uta Erickson: Cal Vista
Bachelorette Party		JVP Video, 1984
Bachelors in Distress		Boccaccio 100
Back Door		Boccaccio 100
Back Door Babes		F/A Dick Rambone (16-inch penis!): Wet Video, 1985

Back Door Girls		F/A Marlene Willoughby: VCR, 1983
Back Door Romance		F/A Sheri St. Clair, John Holmes, Lili Marlene, Yoko Wong, Fawn Paris, Paul Thomas, Blair Harris: Vista Video, 1985
Back Road to Paradise		P/D Jim Reynolds: F/A Sheri St. Clair, Peter North, Debbie Green, Dorothy O: CDI Home Video
Backstreet Alley Cat (see *Alley Cat*)		VCR
Back Street Girl		Boccaccio 100
Back to School		Bizarre, 1985
Bad	R	P/D Andy Warhol F/A Jed Johnson, Carroll Baker, Perry King, Susan Tyrell: 1971
Bad Barbara		F/A Susan McBain, Sharon Mitchell: Blue Video
Bad Black Beulah		P/D Ann Robin F/A Minni White, Patti Dixon: VCX, VIP
Bad Company		P/D Wesley Emerson F/A Traci Butler, Mandy Lane, Dorothy LeMay: Cal Vista
Badge 69		F/A Mark Stevens, Leslie Murray, Lynn Stevens: Blue Video
Bad Girls II		P/D David Frazer F/A Susanna Britton, Blair Castle, Jacqueline Lorians, Herschel Savage, Honey Wilder: Collector's Video, 1983
Bad Girls III		F/A Traci Lords, Crystal Breeze, Rachel Ashley, Jerry Butler, Stacey Donovan: Collector's Video, 1985
Bad Habits		P/D Fred Lincoln F/A Natasha, Anna: Venture
Bad Timing	R	P/D Nicholas Roeg F/A Theresa Russell, Art Garfunkel, Harvey Keitel: 1980
Ball Busters		P/D Alex de Renzy F/A Gina Carrera, Jacqueline Lorians, Nina Hartley, Ginger Lynn, Erica Idol, Kelly Nichols, Joanna Storm, Jamie Gillis, Dan T. Mann: Cal Vista, 1985
Bananas		VIP
Bang Bash		F/A Jamie Gillis, Cindy Grant: 1979
Bang Gang		Video Station
Barbara's Psychiatrist		Select/Essex
Bare Cunty		Boccaccio 100
Barely Legal		F/A Tasha Voux: CDI Home Video, 1985
Bare Mountain		F/A Heather Wayne, Tamara Longley: Gourmet, 1985
Barn Doors		Masterpiece Video, 1985
Battina		Boccaccio 100
Battle of the Stars Championship		P/D Lawrence T. Cole: Now Showing Video, 1985
Bavarian Cream and Other Delights		Paradise Visuals, 1985
Bawd in Bed		
Bawd in Red Caper		VIP
Beauty and the Beast		F/A Jamie Gillis, Loni Sanders

Bedroom Bedlam	Video Home Library
Bedroom Fantasies	F/A Bobby Jackson, Tina Hart: 1983
Bedtime Video, Volumes 1–10	Gourmet (one-hour tapes—five 12-minute loops each)
Beg	P/D Michael Carpenter
	F/A Stacey Donovan, Susan Hart: Video, 1985
Behind the Greek Door	4-Play
Bella	1982
Below the Belt	R. International Home Video
Beneath the Mermaids	P/D Frank Renfroe
	F/A Mike Shea, Darby Lloyd Raines: 1975
Beneath the Valley of Ultra Milkmaids	F/A Angel Cash, Lynne Anne, Terry Pepper: 4-Play
Bent Over the Rent (Spanking)	F/A Gina Valentine, Sheri St. Clair: SKJ Productions, Box 16191, Philadelphia, PA 19115
Best Little Who? In Texas	F/A Margarita, Terri Starr, K. C. Layne: Vegas Video Product
Best of Alex De Renzy, Parts 1 and 2	Mitchell Brothers, 1983
Best of Bizarre, Bondage, Volumes 1, 2, 3, 4	Bizarre Video, 1985
Best of Cecil Howard	Command, 1983
Best of Danielle	F/A Danielle Martin, Marilyn Monroe: Gourmet
Best of Gail Palmer	Wonderful World of Video
Best of John Leslie	Cal Vista
Best of Las Vegas Burlesque	F/A Margarita, Terri Starr, K. C. Layne: Vegas Video Product
Best of Midnight Blue, Parts 1 and 2	
Best of Richard Rank, Volumes 1 and 2	Gourmet
Best of Shauna Grant	Gourmet
Best of the Big Boob Battles	Curtis Dupont, 1983
Best of Ugly George	P/D Ugly George, Ed Asner: Kenyon, 1982
The Bet	
Betrayed Teens	Video-X-Home Library
Betty Blue	F/A Cindy West, Cindy Reems, Bobby Astyr: Blue Video
Between You and Me	Boccaccio 100, Video Station
Beverly Hills Cox	F/A Ginger Lynn, Bridgitte Monet: Caballero, 1985
Beverly Hills Wives	F/A Bridgette Monet, Amber Lynn, Nikki Charm, Herschel Savage, Honey Wilder: L.A. Video, 1985
Beyond Taboo	Velvet Video, 1984
Beyond Taboo	F/A Helga Sven, Desiree Lane, Yoko Wong, Lili Marlene, Jon Martin, Dan T. Mann: Vista Video, 1985
Beyond the Blue	F/A John Franks, Christine Kelly, Becky Ann Thornton
Beyond Your Wildest Dreams	P/D Gerard Damiano
	F/A Jon Martin, Aaron Stuart, Juliet Anderson, Holly McCall, Lysa Thatcher: Visual Entertainment, Video Home Library, 1980

Bibi
Bi, Bi Baby — P/D Dark Brothers, 1985
Big Abner — F/A Sonny Landham, Shirley Cat: Video-X-Pix

Big Bird Cage — R | F/A Pam Grier
Big Black Mamas — Ja-Rae
Big Bust — Boccaccio 100
Big Busted Girls of Ugly George — H&S Sales, 1985
Bi-Coastal (Gays and Lesbians) — F/A Cara Lott, Sheri St. Clair, Troy Ramsey, Tico Patterson, Diedre Hopkins: Catalina Video, 1985

The Big E (ENEMA) Volumes 1–3
The Big E Review — California Star Prod., 1985
Big Rape — Boccaccio 100
The Big Spender — Curtis Dupont Associates, 1985
Big Split — Home Entertainment, Silhouette Video
Big Switch — P/D Paul Norman
F/A Bunny Bleu, Athena Star, Beverly Glen, Tex Anthony, Mark Miller, Michael Vincent: Catalina Video, 1985

Big Thing Linda Can't Stop — P/D Quinton Carr, Peter Higgins
F/A Mark Stevens, Jim Todd, Tina Russell, Teresa Bismark, Jill Pettington: Video-X-Home Library

The Big Thrill — CVX
Big Tits — Bizarre
Bilitis — R | P/D David Hamilton
F/A Patti D'Arbanville, Mona Kirtsen, Bernard Giradeau: 1977

Bimbo, Hot Blood 1 — F/A Linda Chu, Nick Fernaire, Barbie Dahl, Ashley Moore: Video-X-Pix, Red Light, 1985

Birds and the Beads — F/A John Aston, Georgina Spelvin, Tina Russell: VCA, 1974

Birthday Baby — Class Video
Birthday Ball — F/A C. J. Laing, James Gillis, Constance Money: Video-X-Home Library, 1975

Birthday Present — Boccaccio 100
A Bit of Hanky Panky — F/A Jamie Gillis, Ginger Lynn, Jerry Butler, Ashley Britton, Ron Jeremy, Bunny Bleu

A Bit Too Much, Too Soon — VCX, 1983
The Bitch Goddess — F/A Jennifer West, Sylvia Moser, Terri Ritter, Mark Harris: Bizarre

Bittersweet Revenge — Caballero, Creative Video
Bizarre Bondage, Volumes 1–3 — Bizarre
Bizarre Fantasies, Volumes 1–6 — L.A. Video, 1985
Bizarre Fantasies — Bizarre Video, 1982
Bizarre Marriage Counselor — Bizarre
Bizarre Moods — F/A Gloria Leonard, Vanessa Del Rio: Gourmet, Boccaccio 100

Bizarre People — Caballero, 1983
Bizarre Sex — 1979
Bizarre Styles — F/A Vanessa Del Rio: 1981
Bizarre Women — F/A Dominique Caracott: Gourmet, 1982

Bizarre World of Mistress Michelle		F/A Michelle Peters: L.A. Video, 1985
Bizarre Wrestling, Volumes 1–5		Bizarre
Black Angel		VCA, 1985
Black & Blondes, Volumes 1–12		Western Visuals
Black and White Affair		F/A Lisa De Leeuw, Desiree Lane: Video, 1984
Black Baby Dolls		F/A Sahara, Jennie Pepper, Lady Stephanie, Billy Dee: Target Video, 1985
The Black Bunch	R	Astronics
Black Desire		F/A Nicole Black, Kathy Kay: Now Showing
Black Dynasty		P/D Jack Genero
		F/A Linda Thompson, Sahara, Andrew Bolp. F. M. Bradley, Cherry Laine: VIDCO, 1985
Black Garters		Eros
Black Jailbait		Ambassador Video
Black Licorice		C.D.I. Home Video, 1985
Black Lust		VCR
Blackmail for Daddy		P/D Cooper Bros./Bert Cooper
		F/A Henry Conrad, Betty de Muir, Buddy Davis, Fred Greenberg, Marie Gruber: Home Entertainment, VCX, 1976
Black Neighbors		Video City
Black Pearl		Blue Video
Blacks and Blondes, Volumes 1–8		P/D R. Williams
		F/A Ol' King Paul: Western Visuals, 1984 (30-minute tapes)
Blacks Have More Fun		P/D Drea
		F/A Jamilla, Tony El-Lay, Athena Star, David Fox: AVC, 1985
Black Sister, White Brother		F/A Satin Summers, George Payne, Sharon Kane
Blacksnake	R	
Black Taboo		P/D Drea
		F/A Tina Davis, Angel Hall, Tony El-Lay, Marie Lavar: JVP, 1984
Black Throat		P/D Dark Brothers
		F/A Traci Lords, Christy Canyon, Sahara, Mark Wallice, Erica Boyer: VCA, 1985
Black, White, Red All Over		F/A Gina Blair, C. C. Edwards, Jessie Adams, Jamie Gillis: Excalibur, E.T./TGA
Black Widow's Nest		F/A John Holmes, Sharon Thorpe: 1976
Black Workout		4-Play
Blade Runner	R	1982
Blame It on the Blondes		Paradise Visuals, 1985
Blind Date		
Blind Love		Boccaccio 100
Blonde in Black Lace		F/A John Holmes, Barbara Bosquet: Home Entertainment, 1973
Blonde Next Door		P/D Joe Sherman, Roy McBride
		F/A John Leslie, Lisa de Leeuw, Ron Jeremy, and others: Cal Vista, 1982
Blondes on the Run		Paradise Visuals, 1985

Blondie

F/A Gina Carrera, Colleen Brennan, Rikki Blake, Cara Lott, Renee Tiffany: Tara Video, 1985

Bloopers, Outtakes, Embarrassing Moments

P/D Bobby Hollander
F/A Ron Jeremy, Sharon Mitchell, Shauna Grant, Lori Smith, Cody Nicole: Arrow

Blow Dry

P/D Joey Vincent, Laser Sceptre
F/A Warren Peece, Richard Bolla, Helen Madigan, Peonies Young: Home Entertainment

Blow Hard

P/D Allen Morse
F/A Tina Russell, Valerie Marin: Cal Vista

Blowing Your Mind (Video Vixens)

P/D Ron Jeremy
F/A Kelly Nichols, Tanya Lawson: R.S.V.P., 1985

Blow Some My Way

F/A Lara Christie: Video-X-Home Library

The Blue Balloon

P/D Svig Sven, Gunnar Lasberg
F/A Lisbeth Olsen: Video Home Library

Blue Confessions

P/D T. T. Lord
F/A Jesie St. James, Jennifer West, John Leslie, Paul Thomas, Loni Sanders: VCR, 1984

Blue Dream Lover

P/D Peter Vanderbilt
F/A Misty Regan, Beverly Bliss, Summer Rose, Sheri St. Clair, Steve Powers, Blake Palmer: Tara Video, 1985

Blue Ecstasy

F/A Leslie Bovee, Jamie Gillis, Samantha Fox, Candida Royalle

Blue Fantasies

1979

Blue Interview

F/A K. C. Valentine, Mercedes, Jenny Russell

Blue Memories
Blue Memories II

Superior Video

Blue Paradise
Blue Perfume

1983
P/D Charles Vienna
F/A Peter Halcomb, Margo Neal, Rayna Brown, Dawn Starr: 1980

Blue Shorts

F/A Kandi Barbour, Lysa Thatcher, Samantha Fox: Preview Tape Command

Blue Video

P/D Ted Russell
F/A K. C. Valentine, Steve Douglas, Christy Beauchams, Becky Savage: 1983

The Boarding House

F/A Erica Adams: Western Visuals, 1983

Boarding School (Le Pensidnatt)

Visual Entertainment

Boat Girls

Orchids International, 1983

Bob's Lesson

Bizarre, 1984

Bodies by Jack

F/A Amber Lynn, Sheri St. Clair: I.V.R., 1985

Bodily Magic

Select/Essex, 1983

Body Action

F/A Blair Castle, George Payne, Joey Silvera, Lori Smith, Herschel Savage, Cody Nicole, Michael Bruce

Body Candy

F/A John Holmes, Georgia Tech: Masterpiece Video

Body Fender

VIP

Body Love	F/A Lolita Da Nova, Jack Gatteau, Glenda Farrel: Caballero, 1983
Body Lust	F/A Sergio Leonardo, Angela O'Day, Teri Morgan: Video Home Entertainment
Body Talk	F/A Angelique Petty John, Kay Parker, Don Hart: 1982
Bold Fantasies	F/A Susan Kay, Laura Lee, Anne Brime, Mike Horner, Bill John, Tigr, Jesse Adams, Little Red: Now Showing
Bondage and Bliss	Video Vortex, GV
Bondage at Emmitville House	Janus
Bondage Classics, Volumes 1 and 2	Bizarre
Bondage Interludes, Volumes 1 and 2	P/D Bruce Seven
	F/A Mary Tierny, Bridgette Royale, Micki Randall, Beverly Bliss, John Stag: Black & Blue Video/VTE, 1984
Bondage Pleasures, Volumes 1 and 2	F/A Uschi Digard, Laurel Blake, Candy Austin, Jennifer West, Loni Sanders: Harmony/Four-Play
Bootsie	P/D Jack Remy
	F/A Amber Lynn, Jerry Butler, Taija Rae: Coast to Coast Video, 1985
The Bordello Girls R	
Both Ways	International Home Video
Bottoms Up: Volumes 1–5	F/A Eric Edwards, John Holmes, Maria, Phaedra, John Seeman, Kathy and Ric Lutz, Blanca Luz, Polly Perkins: AVC
Bound by Desire	Bizarre, 1983
Bound for Slavery	P/D Bruce Seven
	F/A Bridgette Royal, Joan Stag, Rene Summer, Bunny Bleu: Black & Blue Video
Bound in Love	Bizarre
Bound in Wedlock	Bizarre, 1979
Breakdown	
Breaker Beauties	F/A Susan McBain: International Home Video, Visual Entertainment
Breaking and Entering	F/A Gabrielle Pontello, Lawrence Eyemard: Caballero, 1985
Breaking It, a Story About Virgins	P/D David Frazer, Svetlana
	F/A Paul Thomas, Traci Lords, Rachel Ashley, Jamie Gillis, John Leslie, Margaret Nuit: 1985
Breezy	F/A Crystal Breeze, Raven, Stacey Donovan, Tom Byron, Paul Thomas: Cinema Tech, 1985
Bridal Intrigue	F/A Paula Reison: Video-X-Home Library
Bride's Delight	
Bride's Initiation	F/A Carol Connors: Select/Essex, Visual Entertainment
Bring Your Own Body	F/A Tess Ferre, Sasha Gabor: Video, 1985
Broad Jump	P/D Richard Mailer: Coast to Coast Video, 1985
Broadside	Boccaccio 100
Brother and Sister	
Brute Therapy	F/A Renee Bond

Bun Busters	F/A Ginger Lynn: VCR, 1984
Bunnies	1982
Bunny Hutch	Boccaccio 100
Bunny's Office Fantasies	F/A Sharon Kane, Eric Edwards, Honey Wilder, R. Bolla, Chelsea Blake, Cassandra Leigh, Bobby Astyr
Burning Desires	F/A Jill Hunter, Tony Ellis, Becky Savage, Tara Chang, Cherry Adams, Maria Tortuga, William Margold: Hollywood Video, 1983
Burning Sensation	F/A Glen Joseph, Ginger Franklin: Astro
Burning Snow	P/D Olinka, Gabrielle Pontello
Burning Wild	Silhouette
Business As Usual	F/A Jack Teague: 1979
Butt Bondage	Janus
Butter Me Up	Video Tape Exchange, 1984
B.Y.O.B.	P/D Tony Valentino
	F/A Kristara Barrington, Tesse Feree, Skip Stoke, Sasha Gabor, Gary Sheene: VIDCO, 1985
Cadillac Named Desire	International Home Video
Cafe Flesh II	
Calendar Girls	
California Cowgirls	Caballero, 1983
California Heat	F/A Cindy Fields, Steve Lerner: Blue Video, Silhouette Video (TGA)
California Valley Girls	P/D Hal Freeman
	F/A John Holmes, Becky Savage, Sharon Mitchell: Hollywood Video, 1983
Call Me Angel, Sir	F/A Wade Nichols, Diane Dalton, Ultra Maxine, Annie Sprinkles: Video-X-Home Library
Camp Beaver Lake	P/D Bobby Hollander
	F/A Paul Thomas, Crystal Breeze, Fawn Parris, Billy Dee: Arrow, 1984
Campus Capers	Silhouette Video (TGA)
Campus Pussycats	Video Station
Campus Swingers	Video Station
Campus Teasers	
Canadian Erotica	Sunshine Productions, 1983
Candid Casting	
Candi Girl	F/A Samantha Fox, John Holmes, Serena, Bobby Astyr
Candy Girl	F/A John Holmes, Samantha Fox, Serena: Visual Entertainment
Candy Girls Volumes 1, 2, and 3	Adult Video (includes 12 loops)
Candy Goes to Washington	Wonderful World, 1983
Candy Lips	F/A Suzy Humpfree, Gloria Leonard, Marlene Willoughby, Domitta, April May, Jeanette Sinclair: VCX
Candy's Candy	F/A Candy Samples, John Holmes, Pattie Douglas: Blue Video
Candy's Sweet Interview	F/A Candy Samples
Candy Store	F/A Candy Samples: Gourmet, VIP, Video Audio Electrics

Candy Stripers II		P/D Chuck Vincent
		F/A Kathlyn Moore, Colleen Brennan, Karen Summer, Taija Rae, Ron Jeremy, Michael Gaunt: Arrow Video, 1985
Cane Dane		California Star Prod.
Caned in Wet Pants		Bizarre Tri-Star
Cannonball		F/A Annette Haven: Video Station, 1980
Canterbury Tales	R	P/D Pier Palo Pasolini
		F/A Pier Palo Pasolini, Laura Betti, J. P. VanDyke: 1972
Can't Get Enough		F/A Maria Faluasviet: Corporate Video, Janus Video
Can't Stop Coming		P/D Michael Angelo Finucci
		F/A Lisa de Leeuw, Dorothy LeMay: 1984
Can Wait Until Dark		Orchids International, 1985
The Caper	R	
Captives!		F/A Samantha Fox, Serena, Victoria Slick, Don Fernando, Juliet Anderson, Michael Morrison: Bizarre, 1983
Card Game		F/A Danielle Guequad: Caballero, 1985
Caresses		VIDCO, 1985
Carnal Competition		F/A Jennifer West, Tiffany Clark: Western Visuals, 1985
Carnal Couples		
Carnal Cuties		Silhouette (TGA)—Cinnar Distributors
Carnal Encounters of the Barest Kind		F/A John Holmes, Mike Ranger, Jamie Gillis, Serena, Seka, Lisa de Leeuw
Carnal Games		F/A John Leslie, C. J. Laing, Sharon Mitchell: Blue Video, 1979
Carnal Olympics		F/A Rosie Kay, Herschel Savage: Caballero, 1985
Carole		F/A Vanessa Del Rio, 1983
Carrie, Sex on Wheels		P/D Jack Genero
		F/A Heather Wayne, Greg Ruffner: American Adult Video, 1985
Casino of Lust		P/D Adam
		F/A Crystal Breeze, Eric Edwards, Dorothy Onan, Tom Byron: Atom Video, 1984
Casting Couch		P/D Ron Jeremy
		F/A Ron Jeremy, Susan Nero, Gypsy Lee, Brooke West, Sharon Cane: Collector's Video, 1983
Catnip		Boccaccio 100
Cat Tails		CVX
Caught from Behind		P/D Hal Freeman: Hollywood Video, 1983
Caught from Behind II		P/D Hal Freeman
		F/A Jesse Blue, Paul Thomas, Eric Edwards, Angel Cash, Rosemarie, Ray Sheena, Sue Wadsworth, Ron Jeremy, Rhonda Shantell, Karen Klein, Tom LaRock: Hollywood Video, 1984
Caught from Behind III		P/D Hal Freeman
		F/A Ali Moore, Kristara Barrington, Ron Jeremy, Cheri Garner, Paul Thomas: Hollywood Video, 1985

Caught from Behind IV	Hollywood Video, 1985
Caught in the Act	F/A Juliet Anderson: Masterpiece
Cave Woman	F/A Annette Haven, Abigail Clayton, Amber Hunt, Montana, Tina Orchid: Select-A-Tape (See review in First Edition)
Celebration	F/A Rhonda Jo Petty, Taija Rae, Ron Jeremy, Susan Hart: Gourmet Video, 1984
Celestine	
Cells of Passion	F/A Erica Boyer, John Leslie: VIDCO
Cemetery Girls	
Censored Acts	P/D Roberta Findlay: 1983
Censorship USA	Select-A-Tape
Centerfold Celebrities #2	P/D Bobby Hollander F/A Cody Nicole, Crystal Loving, Blair Castle, Jamie Gillis: Visual Entertainment
Centerfold Celebrities #3	F/A Jamie Gillis, Ron Jeremy, Cody Nicole, Crystal Lake, Becky Savage, Shauna Grant: Visual Entertainment
Centerfold Celebrities #4	P/D Bobby Hollander F/A Amber Lynn, John Leslie, Jamie Gillis, Brandy Alexander, Pamela Jennings: Visual Entertainment, 1984
Ceremony: Ritual of Love	P/D Robert Kinkade, Fred Stand, Andrew Minotti F/A Kathy Collins, Sharon Thorpe, Ken Scudder: Pacific Ocean Film, Moving Video, 1984
Certified	Class X (Time: 47 minutes)
Certified Mail	F/A Lynn Stevens, Mark Stevens, Sandi Fox: Blue Video, 1975
Chained	F/A Michael Morrison, Jamie Gillis, Barbara Leigh, Stephanie Bond, Serena: Bizarre, Erotic, Video Home Library
Chambermaids	F/A Andrea True: Eros
The Champ	F/A John Holmes, Rhonda Jo Petty: Western Visuals, 1984
Champagne Orgy	P/D Troy Benny F/A Carlos Tobalina: HIFCOA
Champagne Party	Boccaccio 100
Chariots for Hire	
Charity Ball	
Charity's Affair	Q.E.L. Quark
Chastity	F/A Taija Rae, John Leslie, Joanna Storm, Tom Byron, Jessyca Wylde, Melissa Christian, William Margold: Rainbow Distributors
Chastity Kidd	F/A Chelsea Manchester, Samantha Fox: Command, 1983
Chatterbox	P/D Tony de Simone F/A Candice Rialson, Larry Gelman, Jane Keane, Perry Bullington: Vestron, 1978
Cheap Thrills	Video-X-Pix, 1985
Cheaters	Boccaccio 100
Cheating Wives	F/A Phaedra, Don Hart, Lili Marlene, Rita Richards, Jan Martin, P. Kalbach: Pacific Ocean Films, Moving Video, 1984

The Cheerleaders	R	P/D Paul Clickler: Harmony Vision
Cheerleaders '85		VIDCO, 1985
Cheri		F/A John Holmes, Renee Bond: VCX
Cherry		Orchids International, 1985
Cherry Blossom		F/A Mark Stevens: Video-X-Pix
Cherry Cheesecake		F/A Rhonda Jo Petty, Melanie Scott, Joey Silvera, Tish Ambrose, R. Bolla, Ron Jeremy, George Payne: Arrow, 1985
Cherry Hustlers		P/D Art Ben
		F/A Roger Caine, Jennifer Jordan, Vanessa Del Rio: Ventura Video
Cheryl Surrenders		F/A Sue Rowan: Video-X-Home Library
Chesty Anderson		Unicorn Video, 1982
China Cat		F/A John C. Holmes, Kyoto: Caballero, 1985
China Doll		F/A Ann Logan, Vanessa Del Rio: Video-X-Home Library
Chinese Fortune Cookies		P/D Alex de Renzy
		F/A Supaeeye Vicht, Marion Boonkoonk, Varee, Pornsavan, Nop Naun: Astro, Video-Vista
Chocolate Candy		P/D Jack Genero
		F/A Ebony Wilson, Lorraine Adams: VIDCO, 1984
Chocolate Cherries		F/A Latice Chevron, Bianca Bradley, Marshall Bradley, Andre Bolla: Coast to Coast Video, 1985
Chocolate Cream		F/A Lisa de Leeuw, Jamie Gillis, Billy Dee: Superior Video, 1984
Chocolate Delights #1, #2		F/A Sahara, Cinnamon Dream, Tina Davis, Marie Lavar, Angel Hall, Tony El'ay, Billy Dee, Ralph Height: Target, 1985
Cinderella		F/A Stacey Donovan: Velvet Video, 1985
Cinderella 2000		
Cinnamon		
City of Sin		Silhouette Video (TGA)
City Woman		F/A Renee Bond: Boccaccio 100
Class of '69		P/D D. Hardon, H. Burton: Boccaccio 100, 1983
Class of '84, Parts I and II		
Class Reunion		P/D Robert Lynn
		F/A Tanya Turner, Tara, Nikko Dolla: Blue Video
Classics—B&D Tapes		Tab Productions, 1983
Classified Sex		C.P.L.C.
Claudia		
Cleopatra's Bondage Revenge		F/A Pia Sands, Victoria Wilde, Nick Random: Bizarre
Climax		F/A Cody Nicole, Rhonda Jo Petty, Rene Summer, Kelly Nichols, Taija Rae, Tish Ambrose: 1985
Climax of Blue Power		P/D R. C. Perl
		F/A Jason Carns, Sally Martin, Linda Harris, Betty Childs: Eros
Closet Casanova		

Close Up — P/D Enrico Stea
F/A Phil Paladin, Debbie James, Mimi Van Aent, Terry Morris

Cloud 9 — Boccaccio 100

Cocktails — P/D Ron Jeremy
F/A Amber Lynn, Tiffany Clark: Atom Video, 1985

Co-ed Fantasy — Diamond Collection—CDI Home Video

Co-ed Teasers — F/A Louise Parsons, Copper Penny, Spring Taylor, Barbara Halser, Tammy, Chelsea Manchester: Video-X-Pix, 1983

Coffee and Cream — P/D Jack Genero
F/A Tracy Austin, Sheri St. Clair, Pam Jennings, Mark Wallice, Jack Baker

Coffee Pot — Boccaccio 100

Collector's Classics — Video-X-Pix, 1985

Collector's Series I

College Girls — F/A Harry Reems, Dolly Sharpe, Darby Lloyd Raines: Video-X-Pix

College Girls in Bondage — Janus Video

College Lesbians — Janus Video

Collegiates — P/D Carter Stevens
F/A Harry Reems: Swan Video

Come Again, Doctor — Blue Video, Visual Entertainment, 1984

Come and Get It — Class X Video

Come As You Are — P/D Bobby Hollander
F/A Tracy Duzit, Mark Wallice, Nicole West, Andrea Britton: Superstar Video, 1985

Come Deadly — Boccaccio 100

Come Get Me — P/D Charles DeSantos
F/A Kandi Barbour, Martina Jon Brazil, Jennifer West, Susan Wild: Pacific Ocean Film

Come Love Me — Video Showtime

Come Ring My Chimes — F/A Bambi Allen, Barbara Mills, Jim Cassidy, Richard Smedly

Come Under My Spell — P/D Troy Benney
F/A Fernando Fortes, Connie Peterson, Marlene Monroe: HIFCOA

Come with Me, My Love — P/D Luigi Manicottale
F/A Ursula Austin, Jeffrey Hurst, Annie Sprinkles, Michael Grant, Mike Jeffries: Wonder World Video

Coming Attractions (Sex Drive) — F/A Desiree West, Sharon Thorpe, John Leslie: Visual Entertainment

Coming of Angels (The Sequel) — Caballero, 1985

Coming of Angie — Gourmet Video

Coming of Joyce — Masterpiece, 1985

Coming Through the Window — F/A Arlana Blue, Michele Magazine: Video-X-Home Library

Commuter Husbands — R — Visual Entertainment

Companions — Gourmet Video, 1983

Computer Girls — P/D Constantine Bisensco
F/A Tantalya Nave, Colleen Brennan,

		Raysheena Mercado Shanteel, B. B. Zarr: Lipstick, 1983
Confessions		P/D Leonard Burke F/A Cindy Johnson, John Leslie, Karen Custick, Ron Rogers: Video Showtime
Confessions of a Candy Striper		F/A Angel West, Beverly Bliss, Nick Niter, Desiree Lane, Karen Summer, Ebony Clark, Joy Merchant: VCA, 1984
Confessions of a Madam		Boccaccio 100
Confessions of a Roman Orgy		P/D Bruno Corbucci, 1979
Confessions of a Young American Housewife		F/A Jennifer Welles, Rebecca Brooke, Eric Edwards
Confessions of Candy		F/A Karen Summer, Desiree Lane, Dan T. Mann, Nick Niter: Island Home Video, 1985
Confessions of Linda Lovelace		Arrow
Confessions of Seka		P/D Leon Gucci F/A Seka, Veronica Hart, Eric Edwards: Select-A-Tape, 1982
Confessions of Sex Slaves		P/D Guy Gilmert F/A Eric Falk, Gina Jansen: 1979
Confidential Apartment		Boccaccio 100
Congressional Playgirls	R	F/A Kathy Richards, Sharon Josephson: Home Entertainment
Consenting Adults		P/D Gerard Damiano F/A Annie Sprinkles, Veronica Hart, Mark Stevens, Ron Hudd, 1982
Contact		F/A Claudia Brooks, Julia Goodyear, Gus Thomas, Lisa Grant, Sandy Bernhardt: VCA
Correction of Julie		California Star (30-minute tape)
Countess Anne in Lashes		Blue Video
Country Club Girls		Select/Essex
Country Club Ladies		Boccaccio 100
Country Cuzzins	R	Channel X Video
Country Doc		
Country Girl		P/D Bob Chinn F/A Traci Lords, Colleen Brennan, Herschel Savage, Tom Byron: AVG, 1985
Country Girl		Video City
Country Hooker		P/D Harry Novak/Lou G Winn F/A Renee Bond, Sandy Dempsey
Country Singer		
Couples in Love		P/D Raffaelli F/A Seka
Cousine Pauline		
Cover Girls		F/A Kimberly Carson, Lana Burner, Bunny Bleu: Video Exclusives, 1985
Cover Girls Fantasies, Volumes 1–3		F/A Jennifer West, Loni Sanders, Lee Carol, Kathy Clark, Crystal Dawn, Jill Morgan, R. J. Reynolds, Kristina Arnold
Cravings		P/D Gerard Damiano
Crazy Holiday in Paris		Caballero, 1985
Creme de Cocoa, Volumes 1–32		Regal Home Video, 1985

Creme de Femme	F/A Rhonda Jo Petty, Maria Tortuga, Susan Nero, Kandi Barbour, Candida Royalle: AVC
Critic's Choice, Volumes 1 and 2	Select/Essex
Cry Rape	P/D Arlo Bettinger
	F/A Bob St. Clair, Sandy Fox: Astro, Silhouette Video
Crystal's Palace	Q.E.L. Quark
Cumshot Review	Hollywood Video
Cunning Coeds	IVP 1985
Cunning Coeds—Girls of Summa Tita	F/A Sheri St. Clair, Renee Summer, Bunny Bleu, Tamara Longley, Jerry Davis, Dean Mortimer: I.V.P., 1985
Cunning Stunt	Boccaccio 100
Cupid's Arrow	P/D Drea
	F/A Lisa de Leeuw, Rosemarie: VCR, 1984
Cynthia's Sister R	P/D Harry Novak
	F/A Paul Kirby, Emmett Henessy, Susan Bowan, Flanagan: Astronics
Daddy	P/D McKenzie
	F/A Tyler Horn, Paul Wain, Sharon Culp: Blue Video
Daddy (Her Heart Belongs To)	F/A Ken Scudder, Sharon Culp: 1978
Daddy Darling R	
Daddy Doesn't Know	Hollywood Video
Daddy's Darling	
Daddy's Girl	Morning Glory
Daddy's Little Girl	F/A Desiree Cousteau: Silhouette Video, Video City
Daddy's Rich	Home Entertainment
Damiano's Fantasies—Whose Fantasy Is This Anyway?	P/D Gerard Damiano
	F/A Sharon Kane, Honey Wilder, Annette Hynes, Janey Robbins, Eric Edwards, Ron Jeremy: AVC, 1984
Damiano's People	P/D Gerard Damiano
	F/A Serena, Samantha Fox, Marlene Willoughby, Jamie Gillis, Richard Bolla
Dance Fever	F/A Ginger Lynn, Misty Regan, John Stagliano: Cinema Tech, 1985
Dance of Love	F/A Leslie Murray, Andrea True: Blue Video
The Dancers, Volume 2: Penetration	F/A Samantha Fox
Dangerous Curves	F/A Sharon Mitchell: Caballero, 1985
Dangerous Passions	P/D Robert Lynn
	F/A Liza Bertini, Wanda Scott, Claudine Zanta, Andre Chenne, Jacques Marboeuf: VCA, 1985
Dangerous Stuff	P/D Cecil Howard
	F/A Angel, Renee Summer, Eric Edwards, Taija Rae, Robin Everett, Tiffany Clark, R. Bolla: Command, 1985
Dangling Berries	1982
Danielle's Girlfriend	F/A Tara Aire, Becky Savage, Annie Owen: Gourmet Video
Danish Erotica, Volumes 1 and 2	
Daring French Tongue	Quality

Dark Angel — F/A Desiree Lane, Jamie Gillis, Blair Harris: VCA, 1985

Dark Passions — VCA, 1983

Dark Side of Danielle — Video City

Daughters of Darkness — F/A Roger Roll, Lil Squeeze, Passion Rose: Astro

Daughters of Emmanuelle — F/A Jeanette James, Jennifer Russell: VXC, 1983

Day Dreams — Wonderful World

A Day of Love — Orchids International, 1985

Deadly Love — P/D Alexander Newman
F/A Heather Leigh, Peter Lane, Don Richie, Jule Martino, D. Kramer, Susan Keiger: Excalibur

Deal Me In — Boccaccio 100

Dear Throat — P/D D. Allen Murphy
F/A Maureen Bradley, Susan Seaforth: Boccaccio 100, 1979

Debbie Does Dallas III — F/A Bambi Woods, Joanna Storm, Jerry Butler, Kristara Barrington, Ron Jeremy: Video Select, 1985

Debbie Does Hawaii

Debbie Does Hollywood

Debbie Does Las Vegas — King of Video

Debbie's Birthday

Debbie's Confessions — Bizarre Video, 1984

Debbie's First Time — Boccaccio 100

Decameron — R | P/D Pier Palo Pasolini
F/A Franco Citti, Ninetto Davoli, Angela Luce: 1970

Deep Chill — F/A Harry Reems, Susan Hart, Kristara Barrington: Atom Home Video, 1985

Deep Encounters — Video City

Deep Ghost — P/D Linda Shaw
F/A Herschel Savage, Lisa de Leeuw, Randy West: Allied Video, 1984

Deep Inside Little Oral Annie — Video-X-Pix

Deep Passage — F/A Dorothy Le May, Davie Blair, Kyoto, Angelo Rivera

Deep Spikes — California Star, 1985

Deep Stroke — Yvonne Ellers, Sandy Warner: MSI Video

Deep Tango — Visual Entertainment

Deep Throat Girls — F/A Ushi Dansk, Joan Holmes, Gloria Shower

Delicious — F/A Veronica Hart, Desiree Cousteau

Deliveries in the Rear — P/D Drea
F/A Kristara Barrington, Buffy Davis, Kevin James, Dan T. Mann: AVC, 1985

Der Big Tits — Ja-Rae Productions

Desert Lesbian — F/A Mindy West, Gina Carrera: Liberty Video, 1985

Desperate Living — R | P/D John Waters
F/A Liz Renay, Mink Stole, Edith Massey: 1977

Desperately Pleasing Debbie — P/D Henri Pachard

Desperately Seeking Susie, Cindy, Lissa, Barbara and Madonna

Deviates in Love

The Determinator

Deviations

Devil in Miss Jones According to the Dark Brother

Devil's Due

Devil's Little Acres

Devil's Mistress

Dial F For Fantasy

Dial P for Pleasure

Diamond Collection Series Volumes 1–70

Diamond Connection

Diamond Double Cross

Diana's Destiny

Diary of a Bed

Diary of a French Tongue

Diary of a Kitty

Diary of a Nymph

Diary of a Schizo

Diary of a Sinner

Diary of a Young Writer

Diary of My Secret Life

Dick of Death

Different Strokes

Dinner with Samantha

Dirt Bike Bangers   R

Dirty Books

Dirty Letters

Dirty Lilly

Dirty Little Filmmaker

Dirty Mary

Dirty Mind of Young Sally

Dirty Movie Maker

Dirty Movies, Volumes A, B, C

F/A Little Oral Annie, Stacey Donovan, Tim Byron: Coast to Coast Video, 1985

P/D Harold Lime

F/A Heather Wayne, Cara Lott, Lara Burner, Jessyca Wylde: VIDCO, 1985

Video Station

Coast to Coast Video, 1985

F/A Mike Horner, Lili Marlene, Billy Dee, Connie Lindstrom, Robin Everett: Select/Essex, 1983

P/D Dark Brothers: VCA, 1985

Video Showtime, VIP

Boccaccio 100

Ambassador Video

F/A Susan Wong, Sharon Mitchell, Rosy Icing: Blue Video

Cinderella Distributors (three loops on each sixty minute tape)

Boccaccio 100

Bizarre, 1984

P/D L. Wilson

F/A Rod Shortener, Ass Pumpin: Home Entertainment, 1979

Boccaccio 100

P/D Anthony Spinelli: Class X Video

Video City

Video City

F/A Isobel Beaumont: Home Entertainment

P/D Sharon Mitchell

F/A Sharon Kane, George Payne, Jerry Butler, Chelsea Blake, Sarah Bernard: Visual Entertainment, 1985

Silhouette

F/A Samantha Fox: TGA, 1983

P/D Earl Anderson

F/A Danielle, Honey Wilder, Carol Cross, Sharon Mitchell

VCX

P/D Michael Carpenter

F/A Christy Canyon, Susan Lion, Josephine Carrington, Kristi Bryant, Mark Wallice, Greg Derek: VIDCO, 1985

P/D Chuck Vincent

C.V.L.C.

P/D Jerry Ware

F/A Victoria Corsault, Deborah Morgan, Peter Andrew: Blue Video

P/D Harry Novak: Caballero

Boccaccio 100

(loops on one-hour cassettes)

Dirty Pictures

P/D Dominic Lubo
F/A Traci Lords, Tom Byron, Ami Rogers, Mark Wallice, Cara Lott: Superior Video, 1985

Dirty Shary

P/D Harold Lime
F/A Christy Canyon, Heather Wayne, Bunny Bleu, Colleen Brennan, Billy Dee, Steve Drake, VIDCO, 1985

Dirty Susan

P/D Russ Carlson: C.P.L.C., 1979

Dirty Words

Disco Madness

R | F/A Mary Mitchell, Cindy Tree, Beth Anne, Luther Whatney: Video Station

Disco Sex

Diving Atrocities

F/A Sulka, Lili Marlene: Caballero, 1983

Diving Atrocities #2

F/A Janey Robbins, Magna Corbitt

Dixie

P/D Steve Brown
F/A Abigail Clayton: Video Home Entertainment

DMJ II

P/D James George, Henri Pachard
F/A Jack Wrangler, Joanna Storm, Jacqueline Lorians, Annette Heinz, Georgina Spelvin: VCA, 1980

Doctor All Come

Boccaccio 100

Dr. Bizzaro

Bizarre 1983

Doctor Cock Love

Video City

Doctor Desire

P/D Harold Lime
F/A Heather Wayne, Christy Canyon, Susan Hart, R. Bolla: VIDCO, 1985

Dr. J's Hang-ups

Boccaccio 100

Doctor's Desires

P/D Harold Lime, Jack Remy
F/A R. Bolla, Susan Hart, Christy Canyon: VIDCO, 1985

Doctor's Disciples

Dr. Strange Sex

F/A Kristara Barrington, Gina Carrera: Caballero, 1985

Dr. Sullivan's Files

1983

Dr. Teen Dilemma

F/A Mark Stevens, Andrea True, Tina Russell: Video-X-Home Library

Dr. Yes

Video City

Do It Again, Sam

Class X Video

Dolls to Dragons

F/A Jamie Gillis, Ron Jeremy

Doma Club

Bizarre Tri-Star, 1985

Dominated by Desire

P/D Sands
F/A Cody Nicole, Marguerite Chaney, Brooks Peterson: 4-Play Video, 1985

Domination in Spiked Heels

Bizarre

The Domination of Anne Pierce

California Star Prod. 1985

Domination of Tammy

Janus Video Productions

Don't Stop

P/D John Christopher: 1982

Don't Tell Mama

VIP

Doogan's Woman

F/A Susan McBain, Eric Edwards, Philip McCann, Eric Bardo, Susan Marlow

Doors to Passion

Dork and Cindy

VCA

Double Agent 73

R | F/A Chesty Morgan: Home Entertainment

Double Down	F/A Bunny Bleu, Cara Lott: Ambassador, 1985
Double Exposure	F/A John Holmes: VCX
Double Header	F/A Andrea True, Sandy King: Blue Video
Double Luck	Class-X-Video
Double Your Pleasure	P/D Carter Stevens
	F/A Bobby Astyr, Roger Caine, Brooke Young, Taylor Young: Cal Vista
Down and Dirty	P/D Charles Santos
	F/A Candy Samples, Janey Robbins, John Holmes: Velvet Video, 1985
Dracula's Bride	
Dream Lovers	F/A Traci Lords, Harry Reems, Pamela Jennings, Tom Byron, Starbuck, Francois Papillon, Sheri St. Clair: C.D.I. Home Video, 1985
Dream Lovers	F/A Sulka, Loni Sanders, Craig Roberts: 1981
Dream Girl	P/D Charles De Santos
	F/A Paul Thomas, Bonnie Holiday, Sandy Penny, John Seeman: AVC, 1974
Dream Girls, Volumes 1 and 2	F/A Angel Cash, Hillary Summer, Nancy Mae: Caballero
Dreamer	Morning Glory
Dreams Are Forever	F/A Bob Dixon, Nick Henning, Laurie Newton, Amber Smythe: Adult Video
Dreams of Natasha	F/A Nina Hartley, Janey Robbins, Jon Martin, Lili Marlene: AAH Video, 1985
Dresden Diary	Bizarre Video, 1984
Drills and Frills	F/A Mark Stevens: Boccaccio 100
Dude Ranch	Home Entertainment
Dungeon of Lust	P/D Roger Hart
	F/A Phillip Childes, Cheryl Blank, Annette Haven, Diane Willis: Adult Video
Dungeon of Pain	Visions of Fantasy
Dust to Dust	Boccaccio 100
Duty and Discipline	California Star, 1985
Dynamite	P/D Amero Brothers
	F/A Monica Rivers, Dolly Sharp, Uta Erickson: Video-X-Pix, 1973
E-3—The Extra Testicle	P/D Ron Jeremy
	F/A Robin Canney, Dan T. Mann, Jessica Longe, Steve Drake, Lana Burner, Bunny Bleu, Francois Papillon: Collector's Video, 1985
Eager Beaver	F/A Mark Haskins, Margo Drake, Elaine Lewis: Adult Video
Eager to Please	Orchids International, 1985
Early Morning Riser	Diverse Maximum
Easy Woman	F/A George McDonald: Mitchell
Ebony Erotica, #1 and #2	F/A Crystal Lake, Tracy Booker, Mark Wallice, Tina Russell: VCR, 1985
Ebony Goddesses	Royal Video
Ebony Lust	Horizon Video
Ebony Lust II	F/A Johnny Keyes, Yuba, Misha

Ecstasy	P/D Billy Thornberg
	F/A John Holmes, Barbara Barton, Jenny
	Sue Logan, Kathy Reilly: Select/Essex
Ecstasy for Two	Action Video
Educating Nina	F/A Juliet Anderson, Nina Hartley, Karen
	Summer, Lili Marlene, Don Hart, Billy
	Dee: Atom Home Video, 1984
Educating Trisha	F/A Christina, Elizabeth Bure, Claudia Loir,
	Gabrielle Pontello: VIDCO, 1984
Education	Morning Glory
Education of Velvet	Bizarre, 1983
Eighteen & Anxious	Diamond Collection—C.D.I. Home Video
Electric Blue, Volumes 1–22	Caballero, 1985
Electro Sex	
The Elevator	T.G.A.
Elizabeth & Her Aunt	Bizarre
El Topo	R P/D Alexander Jodorowsky
	F/A Alexander Jodorowsky, Maria
	Lorenzio, Brontis Jodorowsky: 1971
	F/A John Holmes, Andrea True, Sharon
Embassy Girls	Mitchell: Ambassador, Video
Emmanuelle II	R Paramount
Emmanuelle, The Queen of Sados	
Emmanuelle and Joanna	Xana Home Video, 1983
Emmanuelle on Taboo Island	F/A Laura Gemser: 1983
Endless Summer Love	1983
Erica's Hot Summer	Channel X Video
Erotica (Paul Raymonds)	R Kenyan Video
Erotic Adventres of Cassandra	International Home Video
Erotic Adventures of Cindy	Video Showtime
Erotic Adventures of Dr. Storm	P/D B. D. Smith
	F/A Angel Cash, R. J. Reynolds, Crystal
	Kaye, Cara Davis, Michael Lee, Me-
	lissa duBois, Jay Daniels: X-Travision
Erotic Adventures of Lolita	F/A Tammy, Copper Penny, Ron Jeremy:
	Video-X-Pix, 1982
Erotic Adventures of Peter Pan	P/D Philip Marshak
	F/A Geza X.
Erotic Adventures of Pinocchio	P/D Chris Warfield
	F/A Alex Roman, Diann Thorne, Karen
	Smith: JLT Films, 1983
Erotic Adventures of Zorro	R
Erotica Jones	P/D Jack Giasero
	F/A Christy Canyon, Harry Reems, Paul
	Thomas, Pat Manning, Cheri Janiver,Mark
	Wallice: AVC, 1985
Erotic Aerobics, Volumes 1 and 2	F/A Drea, Crystal Lake, Tamara: VCX,
	1984
Erotic Amateur Video, Volumes 1–10	1981
Erotic Awards Special	P/D Joe DiVincenzio (An 80-minute pre-
	sentation of the Fifth Annual Erotic Film
	Awards, 1981; sixth annual award tape,
	due in late 1982, was never released.)
Erotic City	Caballero, 1985
Erotic Deal	Boccaccio 100

Erotic Dimensions, Volumes 1–8	F/A Nicole Black, Kathy Kay, Kristal Love, Sharon Kane, Tigr, Victoria Slick, and others: Now Showing, 1983
Erotic Dr. Jekyll	F/A Harry Reems, C. J. Laing: Video-X-Pix
Erotic Dream House	Orchids International, 1985
Erotic Express	Cal Vista, 1984
Erotic Family Affair	F/A Linda Shaw, Ron Jeremy, Cody Nicole: AVC, 1984
Erotic Fantasies, Volumes 1–3	Cal Vista (collection of explicit short sex loops)
Erotic Fantasies: The Best of John Leslie	Cal Vista
Erotic Fortune Cookies	Home Entertainment, VCX
Erotic Gold	F/A Seka, Serena, Traci Lords, Juliet Anderson, and nine others: Ventura Video, 1985
Erotic Gold II	F/A Amber Lynn, Seka, Serena: Ventura Video, 1985
Erotic Interlude	Caballero, 1981
Eroticise	P/D Ed Hansen
	F/A Kitten Natividad, Kit Fargo, Gigi Anthony, Ashley St. Jon: Vestron, 1983
The Erotic Lab	
Erotic Mystique	F/A Sandi King, Don Lawrence: Blue Video
Erotic Obsessions	1984
Erotic Radio	F/A Desiree Lane, Renee Summer, Herschel Savage, Kay Parker
The Erotic Seven	Excalibur, 1985
An Erotic Trilogy	P/D Richard Rank: Gourmet
Erotic World of Candy Shields	VCR, 1984
Erotic World of Cody Nicole	F/A Cody Nicole, Gina Martell, Eric Edwards, Frank James, Craig Roberts: VCR
Erotic World of Crystal Dawn	VCR, 1983
Erotic World of Crystal Lake	P/D William Reynolds
	F/A Becky Savage, Lorrie Smith, Jamie Gillis, Michael Morrison, Jesie Adams: VCR, 1984
Erotic World of Linda Wong	P/D Charles De Santos
	F/A Linda Wong, Richard Pacheco, Lili Marlene, Cindy Carver, Jon Martin, Blair Harris: VIDCO, 1985
Erotic World of Nicole	VCR, 1984
Erotic World of Seka	VCR
Erotic World of Sylvia Benedict	Gourmet Video, 1983
Erotic World of Vanessa	VCR
Erotic World Series	VCR
1. Erotic World of Renee Summers	
2. Erotic World of Sunny Day	
Erotic Zones, #1, #2	P/D J. F. Pryor
	F/A Herschel Savage, Don Taylor, Cindee Summers, Steve Taylor, Traci Lords, Paul Thomas, John Leslie: Caballero, 1985
Erotikus	MSI Video
Erotique, Volumes 1–3	American Broadcast Video, 1984

Escape to Ecstasy
Eureka Bound
Eurotica   Goldstripe Video
Everyman's Fantasies   P/D F. J. Lincoln
                                                 F/A Spike Adrian, Joanna, Tifanny Clark,
                                                 Jeane Silver, Chino Kong: Video-X-
                                                 Home Library, 1983
Everyone Is Watching Us   Cal Vista
Everything You Always Wanted   Video Station
Evil Angel   F/A Christy Canyon, Erica Boyer, Tesse
                                                 Terre, Harry Reems: VCR, 1985
Evil Pleasure   VIP
Evil Pleasures   P/D Harry Harper: Astro
Evil Ways of Love   Arrow
Excalibur, Volumes 1–12   TGA, Silhouette
Exchange Student   California Star: 1985 (30-minute tape)
Executive Lady   International Home Video
Exotic French Fantasies   F/A Linda Lovelace, Andrea True: PVX,
                                                 MSI Video, 1975
Experiment I   F/A Sharon Mitchell, Dana Denis
Expressions of Love   F/A Bridgette Monet, Dave Cannon: Car-
                                                 avan Video
Eyes of a Dreamer   F/A Buffy Mast, Steve King
Eyes of Eddie Mars   P/D Fay Ann
                                                 F/A Robin Cannes, Tamara Longley, Cher
                                                 Delight, Renee Tiffany, Jay Sterling,
                                                 Buck Adams: Foxy Video, 1985
Eye Spy   Class-X-Video
"F" (Dream Girl of F)   P/D Svetlana, David Frazer
                                                 F/A Annette Haven, John Leslie, Seka,
                                                 Chris Anderson, Kandi Barbour, Rhonda
                                                 Jo Petty, Becky Bitter, Mary Darling, Laura
                                                 Smith, Piper Smith: Collector's Video,
                                                 PVX
Fade to Rio   P/D Henri Duval
                                                 F/A Bonnie Webb, Cindy James, Sam
                                                 Hodges, Rene Robert, Ron Houston:
                                                 Video Home Entertainment, 1984
Fairy Tales   R P/D Harry Tampa
                                                 F/A Don Sparks, Sy Richardson, Brenda
                                                 Fogarty, Martha Reeves: Media, 1978
Family Affair   F/A Kevin James, Jo Ann Harris, Yolanda
                                                 Clark
Family Fun   F/A Tony Nacivers, Helen Madigan: 1980
The Family Jewels   Gourmet
Famous Tits and Ass   F/A Ursula Andress, Bridgette Bardot, Jac-
                                                 queline Bissett, Sybil Danning, Phyllis
                                                 Davis, Ushi Digart, and many others: Ken-
                                                 yon Video
Fanny   F/A Mindy Wilson, William Osborne, Ali-
                                                 cia Trent
Fanta-Seat   P/D Ron Jeremy: 1985
Fantasies of Jennifer Fay   F/A Margaret Smith, John Leslie, Ron Jer-
                                                 emy, Monique Perry: Gourmet, 1983
Fantasm Comes Again   P/D Tony Ginkane, William Margold

Fantastic Orgy

F/A John Holmes, Iris Medina, Annette Haven, Leslie Bovee

Fantastic Voyeur

P/D Cooper Bros.
F/A Paul Vance, Linda deLove: Adult Video

Fantasy Club

Western Visuals, 1984

Fantasy Club of America

F/A Mark Stevens, Bobby Astyr, Joann Peters: Blue Video

Fantasy Factor

F/A Danielle

Fantasy Fever

F/A Tom Monroe, Marc Rusk, Carla Lange, Debbie Harlow: Adult Video

Fantasy Fever

F/A Mona Jinz, Ed Stark: C.P.L.C. Video

Fantasy Follies

P/D William Margold
F/A Drea, Serena, Becky Savage, Eric Edwards, Carmel, Herschel Savage, Seven Star Productions

Fantasy in Blue

P/D Roger Kramer
F/A John Toland, Sharon Thorpe: Media, International Home Video

Fantasy Peeps
   Sensuous Delights
   Solo Girls
   Three for Love
   Women in Love

4-Play

Fantasy Video, Volumes 1–25

F/A John Holmes, Rhonda Jo Petty, and many others

Fantasy Weekend

VIDCO, 1984

Fantasy World of Nicole

L.A. Video, 1985

Farewell Scarlet

P/D Cecil Howard, Chuck Vincent
F/A J. P. Parradine, Terri Hall, Darby Lloyd Raines, Jennifer Jordan, Kim Pope: Command, 1976

Farmer's Daughters

F/A Gloria Leonard, Zebedy Colt, Bill Core, John Black, Phillip Marlowe, Susan McBain, Marlene Willoughby: VCA

Fashion Fantasy

Gourmet, 1985

Fashion Show

Fast Ball

F/A Harry Reems, Andrea True: Video-X-Pix

Feast of Lust

VCX, 1985

Feel the Heat

P/D Jack Genero
F/A Ashley Wrelles, Ashley Moore, David Morris, Miss De-Hana: AAH Video, 1985

Female Agent

Boccaccio 100

Female Chauvinists

F/A Rick Dillon, Roxanne Brewer: 1975

Female Specimen

Boccaccio 100

Female Trouble   R

P/D John Waters
F/A Divine, David Locary, Mink Stole, Edith Massey: 1974

Femme 2

P/D Candida Royalle: 1985

Fetish Phone Fantasies

TAO Productions, 1985

Fetishes of Monique

F/A Gerry Austin, Peter Andrews: Video-X-Home Library

Feuch

Boccaccio 100

Fever	F/A Rhonda Jo Petty, Toni Renee, Gaylene Marie, Adri Love, Chara Antway, Jerry Davis: Eros
Fighting Femmes	
Filthiest Show in Town R	
Final Blow	F/A Brett Dailey, Samantha Moore: Blue Video
Final Sin	F/A Linda Wong, Ursula Brandywine, Melba Walsh: Command
Final Test	F/A Vanessa Del Rio, Jamie Gillis: Red Hutt Video, 1985
Fine Art of Anal Intercourse (½ hour tape)	P/D John Stagliano
	F/A Erica Boyer, Mark Wallice: VCR, 1985
Finger Lickin' Good	L.A. Video, 1985
Fire in Francesca	F/A John Holmes, Eric Edwards, Sarah Nicholson: Astro, Silhouette Video
Fire Storm II	P/D Cecil Howard
Fireworks Woman	1975
First Convertible	
The First Time I Ever	Arrow—VIP
First Unofficial Porn Starlet Contest	P/D Eric Edwards
	F/A Robin Everett, Renee Summer: Gourmet, 1984
First Week Term	Bizarre Tri-Star, 1985
Five Kittens	P/D Jean Francois, Roger Fellows
	F/A Jean Marie, Clarke Davy, Anne Liebert, Elizabeth Drancourt, Pauline Larrieu, Phillipe Aste, Marie Pascal
Five Loose Women	F/A Richard Adams, Renee Bond, Talie Cochrane: Adult Video, 1975
Flaming Tongues	TGA
Flashtrance	F/A Sheri St. Clair, Ron Jeremy, Jessie Eastern: I.V.P., 1985
Flesh and Blood Show R	P/D Peter Walker
	F/A Ray Brooks, Patrick Barr, Jenny Hanley, Luan Peters: Wizard
Flesh & Ecstasy	P/D Harold Line
	F/A Heather Wayne, Eric Edwards, Christy Canyon, Colleen Brennan, R. Bolla: VIDCO, 1985
Flesh & Fantasy	F/A Sharon Kane, Marita Ekberg, Scarlett Scharean
	P/D Gerard Damiano: 1984
Flesh Dance Fever	P/D Alex Robbins
	F/A Eric Edwards, Pam Anderson, Desiree Lane, Tara Aire, Tanya Lawson, Ron Jeremy, Jesse Adams, Herschel Savage, Cara Lott, Toni Renee
Flesh Factory	F/A Richard Adams, Ruth Blank, Nana Flack, Patti Segal: Adult Video
Flesh for Fantasy	P/D Robert McCallum, Vista Video, 1985
Flesh Grinders	
Flesh of the Lotus	F/A John C. Holmes: VCX, Visual Entertainment
Fleshtones	C.P.L.C.

Flipside		Cal Vista, 1985
Flossie		American Entertainment Network
Flying Sex (Four Star)		Xana, 1983
Flying Sex Man		Orchids International, 1985
Fongaluli	R	P/D Eduardo Cerrano: Home Entertainment
		1982
Forbidden		1982
Forbidden Dreams		Bizarre
Forbidden Entry		Cinema Tech, 1985
Forbidden Fantasies		
Forbidden Loves of Romeo and Juliet		P/D Harry Novak: Channel X Video
Forbidden Ways		F/A Vanessa Del Rio: Gourmet Video
Foreign Affairs		F/A Jacqueline Lorians, Joanna Storm, Scott Baker: 1982
Formula 69		P/D Drea
		F/A Kelly Nichols: Janus Video
Fort Lauderdale		Platinum Pictures
For Love & Lust		P/D Anthony Spinelli
		F/A Nino Hartley, Richard Pacheco, Lili Marlene, Morgan Lee, Rick Savage, Alex Martin, Mariko: AVC 1985
For Love of Money		Home Entertainment, VCX
For Members Only		P/D Gunter Otto, Hans Billian
		F/A Ilona Bach, Barbara Strasberg: VBM, 1980
For Services Rendered		P/D Tim McDonald
		F/A Bridgitte Monet, Maria Tortuga, Rick Cassidy, Cindee Summers: Caballero, 1985
Forth (4th Man)		P/D Paul Verhoeven
		F/A Renee Soutendijk, Jeroen Krabbe, Thom Hoffman: Media, 1984
For Your Thighs Only		F/A Jamie Gillis, Gail Force: Western Visuals, 1985
Foul Play		1982
Four Times That Night	R	
Four Women in Trouble		F/A John Holmes: VCX
Fox Fever		P/D Peter Eastwood
		F/A Drea, William Margold, Tantala, Niki Ming: 1983
Foxy Boxing		P/D Jack Genero
		F/A Samantha Fox: AVC, 1983
Foxy Lady Videos, #1 and #2		F/A Lady Teresa: L.A. Video, 1985 (German loops)
Frankenstein		P/D Philip Marshak
		F/A John Holmes: Creative Video, 1985
Frat House Frolics		F/A Eric Edwards, Rena Vane: C.P.L.C. Video, 1983
Frauleins for Pleasure		Blue Video
Freak Sisters		Boccaccio 100
Freeway Honey		P/D Jack Genero
		F/A Paul Thomas, Honey Wilder: T.G.A., 1984
Freeze Bomb		
French Butler (Les Parisiennes)		Gourmet Video, 1983

French Classmates	F/A Michelle Dumee: PVX Adult Video, 1983
French Fantases	P/D Phillipe Libon
	F/A Michelle Cohn-Bendit, Jacques Devore, Denise Martin: VCA
French Heat	P/D Henri Pierre Duval
	F/A Jacques Sanders, Antoinette, Zoe Lucien, Lilli Darc: Wonderful World
French Kiss	F/A Samantha Fox, John Holmes, Mark Stevens, Darby Lloyd Raines, Lisa Bee, Brooke Bennet: PVX, 1979
French Lessons	F/A Josephine Carrington, Stacey Donovan, Harry Reems: Video Executive, 1985
Frenchmen's Gardens	International Home Video
French Postcard	Tri-Vid Home Video
French Pussycat	
French Romance	P/D Robert Lynn
	F/A Claudia Zante, Andrea Grae, Robert Le Ray, Mina Love, Jacques Marboeuf: VCA, 1974 (A retitling of *Maid in France*, or *Le Chat*; see review.)
French Schoolgirls	F/A Harry Reems, John Holmes, Tina Russell: Cal Vista
French Teens	P/D J. A. Martines
	F/A Bobby Astyr, Pepe, Jacqueline Bardot, Sharon Mitchell: Cal Vista
French Throat	F/A Francoise Germain, Janine Bitosch, Agnes Silver, Lila Coutard, Michele Cohn-Bendit: VCA, 1985
The French Touch	F/A Cassis Poivre: Ja-Rae
French Woman	R F/A Klaus Kinski, Francoise, Fabian
Frenchy and the Stripper	1979
Fresh and Foxy	
Fritz the Cat	P/D Ralph Bakshi (cartoons)
Also Nine Lives of Fritz the Cat	
Frustrated Wives	
F.T.V.	C.P.L.C. Video
Fulfilling Young Cups	P/D Joseph Tarrone
	F/A Serena, Vanessa Del Rio: 1978
Fun Buns	
Funky Cartoons	C.P.L.C.
The Sex Orgy	
Piggy Princess	
The Knight	
Funky World of Adult Cartoons	Arrow
Fury in Alice	F/A Nina Rush: Video-X-Home Library
Future Voyeur	P/D Bobby Hollander
	F/A Traci Lords, Nicole West, Julie Winchester, Craig Roberts, Mark Wallice: Superstar Video, 1985
Fyre	R International Home Video
Gabriella	R
A Game of Love	P/D James Wood
	F/A Shelia Stuart, Fred Lincoln: Blue Video
Games Without Rules	MSI Video

Gang Bang	Video City
Gang-Bangs	P/D John Stagliano
	F/A Christy Canyon, Peter North, Nina Hartley, Erica Boyer, Karen Summer, Susan Hart, Mark Wallice: VCR, 1985
Gas Pump Girls	Wonderlust Video
The Geek	Class-X-Video
Gemini	MSI Video
General Hospital	UCA, 1984
General's Mistress	Orchids International, 1985
Gentlemen Prefer Ginger	Vivid Video, 1985
Getting Ahead	P/D Marc Roberts, Vince Benedetti
	F/A Dave Ruby, Alexis Service, Jim Davey, Michelle Morrison, Angel Cash, Veronica Vera, Annette Heinz: 1983
Getting It Off	Boccaccio 100
Getting Off	F/A John Leslie, Ken Scudder, Desiree Cousteau, Pat Manning, Serena: VCX, 1979
Getting Lucky	Island Home Video, 1985
Getting Personal	P/D Henri Pachard: Caballero, 1985
Ghost Town	Boccaccio 100
Gift of Love	F/A Mari Lewis, Sue Collins: 1979
Gigolo and the Maid	Video City
Gina the Foxy Chick	F/A Simone Valdez, Jack Roven: MSI Video
Ginger Asylum	F/A Ginger Lynn: Vivid Video, 1985
The Ginger Effect	F/A Terri Lynn, Kristara Barrington, Cara Lott, Tom Byron, Jerry Butler: Vivid Video
Ginger Makes History	F/A Ginger Lynn, Amber Lynn, Stacey Donovan: Vivid Video, 1985
Ginger on the Rocks	F/A Ginger Lynn: Vivid Video, 1985
Ginger's Private Party	F/A Ginger Lynn, Tom Byron, Gina Valentino, Beverly Bliss, Blair Powers: Vivid Video, 1985
Girl Friend of Candy Wong	Lipstick
Girl From A.U.N.T.I.E.	F/A Gio Banina, Madame Lee: Class-X-Video
The Girl from S.E.X.	F/A Lisa de Leeuw: Caballero
Girl in a Basket	Video City
Girl in a Penthouse	F/A Harry Reems: Class-X-Video, Video City
Girl Next Door	Boccaccio 100
Girl on Girl	Gourmet
Girl on the Run	F/A Kimberly Carson, Lili Marlene, Jon Martin: Vista Video, 1984
Girl Scout Cookies	F/A John Leslie, Carla Dawn: Video-X-Home Library
Girl Service	Boccaccio 100
Girls and Their Toys	F/A Shannon Sweetwater, Sky Sand, Maria Tortuga, Melanie Scott: VTE, Lipstick Video, 1983
Girls of Cell Block F	Western Visuals, 1985
A Girl's Best Friend	P/D Robert Sumner, Henri Pachard
	F/A Juliet Anderson, Ron Jeremy,

Samantha Fox, Veronica Hart, Merle Michaels, Jody Maxwell, Richard Bolla, Bobby Astyr, Veri Knotty

Girls from Lesbian Orgy		Ja-Rae
Girls from Whambam		
Girls in the Band	R	P/D Chuck Vincent: VBM
Girls of Charlie Company		P/D Bob Augustus: 1982
Girls of 42nd Street	R	Video Station
Girls of Hollywood Hills		F/A Deborah de la Creme: Visions of Fantasy Video
Girls of Klit House		Lipstick Video
Girls of the A Team		F/A Ali Moore, Sahara, Josephine Carrington, Harry Reems, Tamara Longley, Ron Jeremy, Tom Byron: Western Visuals, 1985
Girls of the Night		F/A Amber Lynn, Harry Reems: Caballero, 1985
Girls on Fire		Channel X Video
Girls on Girls		P/D Laurie Smith
		F/A Uschi Digart, Kitten Natividad, Kimberly Carson, Desiree Lane: VCA, 1982
Girls USA		P/D Joe Davian
		F/A Robert Bolla, Marc Valentine, Vanessa Del Rio, Samantha Fox, Merle Michaels: VBM
Girls with the Hungry Eyes		P/D Jonathan Burroughs
		F/A Renee Tiffany, Amber Lynn, Mindy Rae, Dino Alexander, Jimmy Davis: Vista Video, 1984
Gladys and Her All-Girl Band		1979
Glamour Girls		F/A Kimberly Carson, Kristara Barrington: Cinderella Distributors, 1985
Glen or Glenda	R	F/A Bela Lugosi, Lyle Talbot, Dolores Fuller, Edward Woods: Bizarre
Gloria Comes Home		Video City
Glory		F/A Jerry Butler, Blair Castle, Lori Smith, Sharon Mitchell: Command
The Godson	R	Astronic
Go Fly a Kite		F/A Andrea True, D. J. Laing: Video-X-Home Library, 1974
Goin' Down		F/A Summer Rose, Jacqueline Lorians, Jessyca Wylde, Paul Thomas, Peter North, Damon Christian
Going Wild		F/A Jesie St. James, Joan Leslie, Mai Lin: 1982
Gold Diggers		P/D Paul Lyons
		F/A Misty Regan, Bunny Bleu, Gina Valentino, Jessyca Wylde, Mark Wallice: Trivid Home: Video, 1985
Golden Foxes		Command Video
Golden Girls		Golden Girls, 1982–1985 (Wrestling, Boxing, Cat-Fights—19 separate one-hour tapes, mostly R-rated)

Golden Girls, Volumes 1–14 | Caballero
Golden Girls, Volumes 1–17 | Blue Video, VIDCO, 1984
Goldenrod |
Gold or Bust | F/A Lysa Thatcher, Kathy Stein, Eric Edwards, Nancy Spofman: Blue Video
Good-Bye Girls | F/A Hillary Summer, Kandi Barbour, Tiffany Clark: Cinderella Distributors, 1978
Good Girl, Bad Girl | Video-X-Home Library
Good Girls | F/A Elaine Clark: 1982
Good Girls Do | P/D Hal Freeman
| F/A Nikki Charm, Susan Hart, Renee Summer: Hollywood Video, 1984
Good Little Girls | F/A Copper Penny, Tammy, Ron Jeremy, Chelsea Manchester: 1982
Good Morning, Little Schoolgirl | F/A Frank Breed, Candy Bark: Blue Video
The Good, the Bad & the Beautiful | Select/Essex, 1983
The Good, the Bad & the Dirty | 4-Play, 1984
The Good, the Bad & the Horny | F/A Amber Lynn, Bunny Bleu, Billy Dee, Shone Taylor: VCX, 1985
Good Time Girls | F/A Erica Boyer, Lori Smith, Cara Lott, Don Hart, Billy Dee, Misty Regan, William Margold: 1984
Good Times | Boccaccio 100
Go on Your Own Way | F/A Eric Edwards, Robin Bird: Astro
Gourmet Collection, Volumes 1–24 | Gourmet
Gourmet Quickies | Gourmet, 1985 (30-minute tapes)
Gourmet Video Featurettes | Gourmet, 1985
Go Your Own Way | International Home Video—C.D.I. Home Video
Granada Affair |
Grand Ecstasy (Four Star) | P/D Pamicia Rhomm
| F/A Eva Kris, Jeran Brower, Joselyn Claran: Xana, 1983
Grand Opening | F/A Kevin James, Kristara Barrington: Atom Home Video, 1985
Grave Desires |
Great British Striptease | R | Caballero, 1982
Greatest Cathouse in Vegas | Eros, 1983
Greek Lady | P/D Jack Genero
| F/A Ron Jeremy, Sheri St. Clair: T.G.A., 1984
Grocery Boy | R |
Groupies | Ja-Rae
Growing Up | VCX, 1984
G-String Geisha | F/A Yoko Mihara, Megumi Hori: 1978
G-Strings | P/D Henri Pachard
| F/A Susan Nero, Kelly Nichols, Annette Heinz, Sharon Kane: Command Video, 1983
Guess Who's Coming | F/A Eric Edwards, Georgina Spelvin: Video Showtime
Guess Who's Coming This Weekend | Class-X-Video
Gulp | Silhouette Video
Gums | P/D Robert Kaplan
| F/A Brother Theodore, Terri Hall: Adult Video

Gypsy Ball		Cinnabar Distributors
Handful of Diamonds		P/D Martin Campbell
		F/A Elizabeth Aubry, Megan Ross, Niegel Evans, Edmund Searre, Colin Taylor: Command
Handsome		
Handyman and Stepdaughter		International Home Video
Hang-up		
Hanky Panky		F/A Jamie Gillis, Jerry Butler, Ginger Lynn, Bunny Bleu: VCX, 1984
Hanky Panky	R	P/D H. Smithston
		F/A Elene Peterson, Connie Duval: Home Entertainment
Hanky Panky (A Little Bit Of)		P/D David Frazer, Svetlana
		F/A Ginger Lynn, Ashley Britton, Jamie Gillis: Collectors Video, 1984
Happening		Orchids International, 1985
Happy Birthday Bondage Gram		F/A Jennifer West, Melanie Scott, Christina Hill: Bizarre, 1983
Happy Holiday	R	P/D Suzanne Hunt, Jon Sanderson
		F/A Nina Lund, Karl Blake, Karen Karlsson, Stephen Roberts: Caballero, 1982
Happy Hooker	R	F/A Lynn Redgrave, Adam West: International Home Video, Wanderlust
Hard at It		Boccaccio 100
Hard Bargain		VCX
Hard for the Money		F/A Cynthia Brooks, Gina Carrera, Heather Wayne, Peter North: Target Video
Hardly Working		C.P.L.C., 1984
Hard Ride		Video Showtime
Hard Times		F/A Lili Marlene, Goldie Hawk, Kirk Wilder: Boccaccio 100, Western Visuals, 1984
Hard Worker		F/A Angel Cash, Tommy La Rock, Denise Berrison: Adult Video
Hardy Girls		P/D Robert Simon, Allen Ruskin
		F/A Tina Russell, Andrea True, Peaches Hardin, Lydia Burke, Carla Chasen: Video-X-Home Library
A Harlequin Affair		F/A Tom Byron, Traci Lords, Christy Canyon, Sahara, Eric Edwards, Al Brown, Tamara Longley, Mark Wallice' Cinema Trex Corp, 1985
Harlot		P/D Andre Marchan
		F/A Ursula White: Visual Entertainment, 1983
Harmony Burlesque Video		Video (1507 New York Avenue, Huntington Station, NY 11746)
Harry Hard		Boccaccio 100
Hattie's Pleasure Palace		F/A Buddy Jackson, Marie deMuir, Astro
Having Fun		Morning Glory
Having it All		P/D Richard Mailer
		F/A Harry Reems, Tiffany Barnes, Gail Force: Island Home Video, 1985
Hawaiian Sex-O		F/A Julie Neussberg: Adult Video

Hawaiian Summer		F/A John Leslie, Mai Lin, Jesie St. James, Rhondo Jo Petty, Jesie Adams
Hay Country Swingers	R	P/D Alos Brummer
		F/A Peter Muhlen, Eva Karinka, Sandra Reni: Blue Video
Head Games		P/D Bruce Seven
		F/A Amber Lynn, Karen Summer, Heather Vane, Peter North, Miles, Mark Wallice: Western Visuals, 1985
Head Nurse		F/A Mark Stevens, Andrea True, Cindy West: Video-X-Pix
Heads and Tails		F/A Tamara Longley, Ami Roberts, Bunny Bleu, VIDCO, 1985
Heads or Tails	R	F/A Jill Keri, Randi Oliver, Marlene Senick
Headset		F/A Rachel Harris: Video-X-Pix
Heartbreak Girl		F/A Heather Wayne, Paul Thomas, Gina Valentino, Herschel Savage: Gourmet, 1985
Heart Throbs		F/A Gina Valentino, Lurri Smith, Raven, Treonna, Moroan Lane, Suzi Hart, Jade Nichols: Caballero, 1985
Heat		4-Play
The Heat Is On		P/D Jerome Tanner
		F/A Cara Lott, Kim Morgan, Mai Lin: Western Visuals, 1985
Heat of the Moment		VCX F/A Jennifer West, John Holmes
Heat Wave		P/D Cecil Howard
		F/A Gloria Leonard, Sharon Mitchell, Ming Toy, Veri Knotty
Heavenly Desires		Western Visuals
Heavy Load		F/A Jamie Gillis, Andrea True, Darby Lloyd Raines, Samantha McClaren: Command, 1975
The Heist		
Helena		F/A Valerie Boissel, Wonderful World
Helen Bedd		International Home Video
Hellfire West		Bizarre, 1983
Hell's Kittens		Boccaccio 100
Helpful Hanna		Q.E.L. Quark
Her Body		
Here Comes Candy Pants		
Here Comes the Bride		F/A David Morris, Joey Civera, Samantha Fox, Colleen Andersen, Clea Carson: Cal Vista
Here Kitty		Video Station
Here's Lead in Your Pencil		
Her, She and Him		Cinema Concepts
Her Total Response		F/A Jennie Joseph, Vanessa Lombard, Ingrid Johannsen, Carole Hoffman: Video-X-Home Library
He's Porno, She's Erotic		Xana, 1983
Hey, There's Naked Bodies On My TV	R	Media
High Fashion Models		
High School Blow Out		P/D Gerald Wayne
		F/A Kari Foxx, Gale Force, Tracy Adams: C.D.I. Home Video, 1985

High School Bunnies	P/D Angle Martine, John Christopher; F/A Beth Anne, Clea Carson, Roger Caine, Peter Andrews: VCA
High School Honeys	P/D Carter Stevens: Adult Video
High School Picnic	Boccaccio 100
High School Report Card	F/A William Margold, Terri Hannon, Pat Manning: Caballero
High School Reunion	Video City
High Time	Boccaccio 100
Highway Hookers	P/D Carter Stevens
The Hippy Hooker	F/A Ginger Lee Hawkins, Darren Rock
His Master's Touch	MSI Video
The History of Pornography	Class-X-Video
History of the Blue Movie	P/D Alex de Renzy: California Video
Hitchhiker	F/A Ron Jeremy, Velvet Summers: Adult Video, 1983
Hitler's Harlots	F/A Natalie Kane, Jeff Parker
Hole	Orchids International, 1984
Holiday	1982
Holiday Hooker	Video City
Holiday with Ingrid	P/D Erwin Dietrich, Michael Thomas, 1979
Hollywood After Dark	Boccaccio 100
Hollywood Confidential, Volumes 1–5	F/A Mona Page, Melanie Scott, Mark Wallice, and others: Class-X-Video, Producer's Concepts
Hollywood Cowboy	MSI Video
Hollywood Goes Hard	
Hollywood Heart Breakers	F/A Traci Lords, Rick Savage, Amber Lynn, Beverly Buss, Nicole West, Craig Roberts: Video Exclusives, 1985
Hollywood High	International Home Video
Hollywood Honeys, Volumes 1 and 2	Connoisseur Video (loops on 1-hour cassettes)
Hollywood Lesbians	
Hollywood Pink	Essex 1983
Hollywood She Wolves	P/D Peter Balakoff: Select/Essex
Hollywod Vice	VIDCO, 1985
Hollywood Starlets	P/D Bruce Seven
	F/A Amber Lynn, Heather Wayne, Christy Canyon, Laurie Smith, Karen Summer, Tom Byron, D. T. Mann, Steve Drake, Peter North: 4-Play, 1985
Holy Rolling	P/D Harvey
	F/A Cody Nicole, Ron Jeremy, Nicole Black: AVC, 1984
Home From the Sea	F/A Carol Hines, Lynn Rae, Harold Mason
Home Town Girls	F/A Suzie Wong, Suzie May, Janie Lee
Home Video, Volumes 1–12	Marlowe Sales (two or three loops per tape)
Honey Buns	F/A Renee Bond, Ushi Digart: Blue Video
The Honey Cup	F/A Nancy Dare: Video-X-Pix
Honeymoon	Boccaccio 100
Honeymooners	Video Show Time
Honeymooners	P/D Wizard Glick
	F/A Jeff Eagle, John Dupre, Terri Hall, C.J. Laing: Select-A-Tape, Cal Vista

Honeymoon Suite	F/A Mark Stevens, Georgina Spelvin, Tina Russell: Video-X-Home Library, 1974
Honey Pie	P/D Howard Ziem
	F/A Jennifer Welles, Al Goldstein, B. Astyr, and others
Honeysuckle Divine	Mitchell
Honeysuckle Rose	P/D Robert Brivar
	F/A John Holmes, Rikki O'Neal: International Home Video
Honey Suckle Rose	F/A Samantha Fox, John Holmes: Caballero, 1985
Honey, Sweet Honey	F/A Honey Wylder, Gena Valentino, Nicole West: Visual Entertainment, 1985
Honey Throat	P/D John Christopher
	F/A John C. Holmes, Eric Edwards, Arcadia Lake, Samantha Fox: Cal Vista, 1980
Honolulu Hustle	Caballero
Hooked-Up Hooker	Golden Ram, 1985
Hooker's Holiday	TGA
Horny Hobo	Silhouette Video
Horror in the Wax Museum	TAO
Hospitality Suite	Hollywood Video
Hot & Nasty	P/D Kimberly Carson, Desiree Lane, Renee Summer: Playtime Video, 1985
Hot Assets	International Home Video, Visual Entertainment
Hot Babes	P/D Mike Strong
	F/A Gregory, Max Pardos, Sophie Dufluct, Fiore Marlene: VBM
Hot Blooded Newlyweds (Hollywood Honeys)	Caballero, 1983
Hot Bodies	F/A Serena, China Lee, Maria Tortuga: Ventura Video, 1985
Hot Channels	P/D R. G. Benjamin
	F/A Davy Jones, Melanie Daniels, Catherine Warren: Arrow
Hot Child in the City	P/D John Christopher
	F/A John Holmes, L'Oriele, Steven Mitchells, Brenda Lockwood: Wonderful World
Hot Chocolate	P/D Drea
	F/A Cinnamon Dream, Tony El'ay, Silver Satin, Alexander James, Jack Baker: Shotgun Wedding Productions
Hot Circuit	F/A Sally Paradise, Jaci Duquesne, Pris Teen, Simon Fallique: VCA, 1985
Hot Close-Ups	P/D R. Williams
	F/A Helga, Kirk Wilder, Mistress Grace, Patricia Laura, Robert Lee: Western Visuals, 1984
Hot Country	F/A Genoa, Kirk Wilder, Dan Darling, Lola Star, Carrie Malone: Western Visuals, 1984
Hot Dallas Nights	P/D Julian Ornynski, Toni Kendrick
	F/A Alexander Kingsford, R. J. Reynolds,

	Hilary Summer, Raven Turner, Tara Flynn: VCX, 1980
Hotel Flesh	F/A Jamie Gillis, Paul Thomas, Tara: Cal Vista, 1983
Hotel Hooker	F/A Marge Stewart
Hot Girls in Love	F/A Kimberly Carson, Jacqueline Lorians, Danica Rhae, Lili Marlene, Marie Tortuga: Vista Video, 1985
Hot Gypsy Love	F/A Joanna Storm, Mindy Rae, Jay Sterling, Jeannie Pepper, Sheri St. Clair, Buck Adams: Night Owl, C.D.I. Home Video, 1985
Hot Lessons	L.A. Video, 1985
Hot Love	F/A Serena, Jamie Gillis, Maria Tortuga: Select-A-Tape
Hot Merchandise	F/A Mindy Rae, Paul Thomas, Rick Star, Ricky Savage, Greg Rome, Bunny Bleu, Kevin James: AVC, 1985
Hot Monies	
Hot Nazis	Mitchell (See main filmography listing under *Never a Tender Moment*)
Hot Numbers	F/A Lisa Lake, Rose Marie, Larry Hardwood, Greg Rome: Gourmet, 1984
The Hot Ones	F/A Lysa Thatcher, Rhonda Jo Petty, Jamie Gillis, and others: Superior
Hot Oven	VCA, 1985
Hot Pink	F/A Tiffany Clark: VCR, 1985
Hot Pistols	Boccaccio 100
Hot Rackets	Cal Vista, 1982
Hot Rockers	P/D Tiffany Clark
	F/A Sharon Kane, Jose Duval, Taija Rae, Melanie Scott, Heather Wayne, George Payne: JVP, 1985
H.O.T.S.	F/A Susan Kiger, Pamela Bryant, Kimberly Cameron, Lisa London: Select-A-Tape
Hot School Reunion	P/D Jonah Whalin
	F/A Desiree Lane, Mauvais, Crystal Dawn, Sharon Mills, Chelsea Manchester, Jon Martin: Channel X Video
Hot Shots	F/A Jennifer Jordan, Miranda Parks, Alice Holtzer, Valerie Petcher: Command 1983
Hot Skin (3D)	F/A Vanessa Del Rio: Big Top Video, 1984
Hot Spots	P/D Eric Anderson
Hot Stuff	F/A Danielle, Jacqueline Lorians, Joanna Storm, Cody Nicole, Carol Cross: Video-X-Pix, 1984
Hot Summer in the City	P/D Gail Palmer
	F/A Duke Johnson, Shorty Roberts, Lisa Baker: Wonderful World
Hot Summer Night	Video Station
Hot Tacos	Tri-Vid Home Video, 1985
Hot Tails	F/A Amber Lynn, Bunny Bleu, Angel West: Ventura Video, 1985
Hot Teenage Lovers	

Hot Truckin'
Hot Vibrations and Glove Love
Hot Wire

Hot Wives
Housebroken

House of Bondage
House of Christina

House of Delights
House of Desires

House of Green Desire

House of Ill Repute

House of Kinky Pleasures
House of Love

House of Missing Girls
House of Sin

House of the Rising Sun

House of Whores
House Sitter
House Slave Discipline
Housewarming
How Sweet It Is

How to Do It
How to Enlarge Your Penis

How to Lose Weight
How to Make Love to a Woman

Hugh Bras, Volumes 1 and 2
Hungry Coeds
Hungry-Eyed Woman

Hungry Mouth

Hungry Young Women
Husbands, Wives and Other Strangers
Hustler Around Town
Hustler 17

MSI Video
International Home Video
F/A Amber Lynn, Rachel Ashley, Sharon Cain, Jamie Gillis, Michal Knight, Gloria Leonard: Video-X-Pix, 1985
F/A Christa Andersen: Video-X-Pix
F/A Lady Diana, Little Velvet Summers, Jason: Bizarre, 1983

Home Entertainment, VCX, Visual Entertainment

F/A Mimi Morgan, Dorothy LeMay, Marlene Monroe, Lisa Rue: Blue Video
F/A Risa Evans, Bobby Taylor, Dorothy LeMay, Marlene Moore; C.P.L.C. Video, 1983
F/A Michele Valentine, Danielle Guegaud: Caballero, 1985
VCX
F/A Colette Mareril, Denise Fevier, Jacques Marbeuf, Pierret Raymond: VCA
R F/A Anna Gael, Hans Meyer: Video Station
F/A Long Jean Silver, Honey Stevens, Mistress Candice, Richard Bolla, Dave Christopher: 1982
P/D Chuck Vincent
F/A Tish Ambrose, Rachel Ashley, Paul Thomas, Taija Rae, Jerry Butler, Scott Baker: Essex, 1985
Boccaccio 100
Orchids International, 1985
Bizarre
VIP
F/A Jon Roy Jones, Abbie Trevor, Brigette Maier: Select/Essex
Boccaccio 100, Video Station
P/D Scott Taylor, John Stagliano
F/A Scott Taylor, Erica Boyer: VCR, 1985 (half-hour tape)
Boccaccio 100
F/A Cody Nicole, Candy Austin, Marci Damon: Vision Video
Western Visuals
Channel X Video
P/D Saul Cohen
F/A Angela Steiger, Maggie Williams: Adult Video
F/A Peggy Simpson, Linda Southern, Jackie Richards: Video-X-Pix

Select/Essex
P/D Charles De Santos
F/A Camilia, Karen Summer: Velvet Video

Hypatia Lee's Let's Get Physical		1984
Hypnotic Sensations		F/A Ginger Lynn, Christy Canyon, R. Bolla: Gourmet, 1985
Hypnorotica		F/A Tina Russell, Andrea True: Eros/King of Video
I, a Woman	R	
I Am Always Ready		HIFCOA
I Am Curious (Blue)	R	
I Am Curious (Yellow)	R	
I Am No Virgin		World Wide Video
Ice Cream Video		Producer's Concept, 1983
I Do Voodoo		Class-X-Video
The Idol		F/A John Holmes, Jacqueline Lorians, Helga, Jennifer Summers, Summer Rose: Western Visuals, 1984
If Mother Could See Me Now		Video City
If My Mother Only Knew		Caballero, 1985
I Like to Be Watched		F/A Cara Lott, Rikki Blake, Sara Wine, Tom Byron, Tracey Austin, Mark Wallice: VIDCO, 1985
Illegal Entry		Cal Vista
Illusion of Ecstasy		P/D Lawrence Cole
		F/A Jamie Gillis, Ginger Lynn: Now Showing, 1984
Illusions		P/D Gerard Vernier
		F/A Brigitte Lahaye, Jean Louis Vattier, Babette Bure: 1982
Illusions of a Lady		Video Showtime
Illusions of Love		F/A Jamie Gillis, Iris Flouret: Command Video
Illusions Within Girls		P/D Catherine Balough: VEP (French)
I Love My Secretary		Xana
I Love You	R	P/D Walter Clark, Arnaldo Jabor
		F/A Sonia Braga, Paulo Perelp, Vera Fischer, Maria Dahla
I'm Always Ready		P/D Troy Benny
		F/A John Holmes, Fernando Fortes, Barbara Wallace: HIFCOA, 1979
Immoral Tales		International Home Video
In a Week		Orchids International, 1984
Inches		MSI Video
Incredible Sex Ray Machine		
In Love		P/D Larry Revene, Chuck Vincent
		F/A Kelly Nichols, Jerry Butler, Tish Ambrose, Joanna Storm, Samantha Fox, Jack Wranger: 1983
Indecent		Video Station, VIP
Indian Lady		F/A Debbie Truelove, Andrea Martin, Rick Valenzio, Sunny Summers: Masterpiece
I Never Say No		P/D Judy Jason, Miller Kirkson
		F/A Paul Thomas, Desiree Lane, Karen Summer, Lisa Lake, and others: Atom Home Video, 1984
In-Flight Service		F/A Lana Preston, Jay Grant, Denise Robbins: Blue Video

Inhibition | Blue Video
Initiation of Cynthia | F/A John Leslie, Paul Thomas, Colleen Brennan, Katherin Moore, Jerry Butler, Sharon Cain: Video-X-Pix, 1985

In Memory of Connie |
In Praise of Older Women | R | Vid America
In the Realm of Senses | P/D Nagisa Oshima
| F/A Elko Matsua, Tatsuya Fuji: 1979
In the Spring | Boccaccio 100
In Too Deep | P/D Grey Poupon
| F/A Glen Joseph, Erica Johnson: National Video, 1979

The Innocence of Valerie | F/A Katrina Rexford: Blue Video
Innocent Beaver | Boccaccio 100
Innocent Girl | Silhouette Video
Insane Desires | P/D Grey Poupon
| F/A Stacy Blue, Cindy Lou Hammer, Christine Kelly, Jessie Chandler, Becky Ann Thornton

Insane Lovers | Masterpiece, 1985
Inside Andrea True | F/A Andrea True: Blue Video
Inside Babysitter | P/D Owen T. Gee, Riz Taziner
| F/A Tracy O'Neil, Ken Marsh, Kristine Heller: Movies at Midnight
Inside Every Body | P/D Gerard Damiano
| F/A Sally Rose, Jill Morehead, Janey Robbins, Ron Jeremy: AVC, 1984

Inside Ginger Lynn | VIDCO, 1985
Inside Daneille | F/A Danielle, Traci Lords: VCA, 1985
Inside Little Oral Annie | P/D Danielle: Video-X-Pix, 1984
Inside of Me | F/A Judy Samples: National Video
Inside Pussycat | P/D Cooper Bros.
| F/A Linda deLove, Paula Vance: 1979
Inspirations | P/D Harry Novak
| F/A Ron Jeremy, Serena, Lisa de Leeuw, Don Hart, Nicole Black: 1982
Inspirations | R | P/D Joe Sherman, Mutt Jeffrey
| F/A Ron Jeremy, Lisa de Leeuw, Serena, Danielle, Don Hart, Herschel Savage: Channel X Video

Interlude of Lust | F/A Karen Hall, Mai Lin: Caballero, 1985
International Sex Olympics | Select/Essex, 1983
Intimate Action, Volume 2 | F/A Long Jeanne Silver, Annie Sprinkles, Sharon Kane
Intimate Confessions of Stella | P/D Zacarias
| F/A Azucena Hernandez
Intimate Desires | P/D Arlo Shifflin, Gloria Leonard
| F/A John Leslie, Gloria Leonard, Beth Anne: Blue Video
Intimate Illusions | P/D Jack Sloane, Paul Levis
| F/A Desiree Cousteau, John Leslie: Select/Essex
Intimate Lessons | P/D Philip Marshall
| F/A Paul Thomas, Kay Parker, Danielle Martin, K. C. Valentine, Geoff Conrad,

		Maria Tortuga, Becky Savage, William Margold: Collector's Video, 1983
Intimate Playmates	R	F/A Lynn Ross, Carole Parker: Blue Video
Intimate Teenagers		F/A Mark Stevens, Darby Lloyd Raines, Kim Pope
Invasion of the Love Drones		World Wide Video
Island Love		F/A Ambrosia Fox, Licia, Cheri Champagne: Showcase, 1983
Island of Dr. Love		P/D Lawrence Young
		F/A Amanda Farris, John Cassidy, Rebecca Smyth, Al Adams
Islands of Love		P/D James Genevo
		F/A Diana Hunter, Ray Sheena: Cal Vista, 1984
I Spy		Video City
Italian Erotica Family		Ja-Rae (European)
It Happened in Hollywood		P/D Jim Buckley, Peter Locke
		F/A Melissa Hall, Harry Reems, Mark Stevens, Helene Buckley, Susan Harris, Peter Bramley: Wonderful World of Video
It's Incredible		F/A Heather Wayne, Shana McCullough, Bunny Bleu, Rita Ricardo, Rick Savage, Ron Jeremy, Eric Edwards: Essex, 1985
I've Never Done This Before		P/D Lawrence T. Cole: Now Showing, 1985 (Mini-series)
I Wanna Be Teased		P/D Mark Corby, B. Floriana
		F/A Bunny Bleu, Eric Edwards, Marie Tortuga, Melanie Scott, Nicola Baxter, Scott Irish, Mark Harris, Sher Tierney, Jerry Davis: Essex, 1981
I Want It All		P/D Michael Carpenter
		F/A Susan Hart, Ginger Lynn, Janey Robbins, Mark Wallice, Tom Byron, Candye Kane: VIDCO, 1984
I Want to Be a Mistress		Royal Video
I Want You		P/D Michael Baudricot
		F/A John Holmes: Caballero
I Want What I See		P/D Dark Brothers: VCA, 1985
		F/A Richard Lilianne, Charlie Schriener, Lemieuve
Jacquette		F/A Jacquette, Vanessa Del Rio, Cynthia Vee: C.D.I. Home Video
Jail Bait		P/D Kirdy Stevens: Standard Video, 1985
Jail Bait Babysitter	R	Video Station
Jail House Girls		F/A Ginger Lynn, Kelly Nichols, Raven, Kristara Barrington, Taija Rae, Paul Thomas, George Payne: VCA, 1985
Jane Bond		P/D Bob Kirk
		F/A Bob Kirk, Sharon Thorpe: Video City, 1979
Jane Bond		F/A Heather Wayne: VIDCO, 1985
Jane Bonda's Bizarre Workout		P/D John Drake
		F/A Pia Sands, Robert Lakewood, Christina Mill
Januarius		HIFCOA

Jaw Breakers | F/A Seika, Vanessa Del Rio, China Lee: Ventura Video, 1985

Jean Jeni | Caballero, 1985

Jeannie's Magic Box | F/A Tracy Lords: Gina Carrera

Jesie St. James Fantasies | VCR, 1983

Joanna | Xana, 1983

Joanna Storm on Fire | P/D Robert McCallum: Vista Video, 1985

Joe Rock Superstar | F/A Tina Russell, Mark Stevens, Jean Dalton: TGA

John Holmes, Superstar | Adult Video

John Holmes Exposed | F/A John Holmes, Maria Tortuga, Serena: AVC

John Holmes Signature Series | Masterpiece, 1985

Johnny Does Paris | F/A John Holmes, Gloria Leonard, Delania Raffino, Jacques Gatteau: 1982

Johnny Wadd | F/A John Holmes: VCX Astronics

Jokers Are Wild | Boccaccio 100

Josephine | F/A Laurie Whitmore, Sharon Christy, Richard Mason, Maria Peron: VCA, 1984

Journey into Pain | H.O.M. Video, 1984

The Joy of Sex |

Joy Riders | F/A Mark Stevens, Linda Lovelace, Danella Di Orici, Nicole Lowe: Select-A-Tape, Blue Video

Joys of Erotica, 1 and 2 | F/A Vanessa Del Rio, Susan Nero, Phaedra Grant, Serena: VCR/TGA, 1984

Joy Toys | F/A Gina Carrera, Heather Wayne, Sarah Summers, Kevin James, Mark Wallice, Steve Powers: Wet Video, 1985

Jubilee of Eroticism | Collector's Video, 1985

Judge for Yourself | Bizarre

Judy's B&D Slave School | Bizarre, 1980

Juggs | VCR, 1985

Juice | F/A Jolie Poitring, Donna Duke, Marilyn Seyers, Shelly Summers: Command

Juicy Jaws (Hollywood Honeys) | Caballero, 1983

Julia | R | Just Married

The Junkyard | TAO

Just Another Pretty Face | P/D Scotty Fox

| F/A Traci Lords, Stacey Donovan, Jacqueline Lorians, Jessyca Wylde, Paul Thomas: Adult Video, 1985

Just Call Love | Morning Glory

Justine, a Matter of Innocence | Morning Glory

Just Plain Sex | Morning Glory

K-Sex | F/A Serena, Paul Thomas, Joliet Anderson, David Blair, Bonnie Holiday, Michael Morrison

Kama Sutra | Visual Entertainment

Karla | F/A Suzan Thomas, Betty Whitman, Henry Ross, Danielle Leman, Joe Sarno

Keep It All in the Family | Boccaccio 100

Keep on Truckin' | F/A Andrea True, Cindy West, Mark Stevens, Jamie Gillis: Blue Video

Keyholes Are for Peeping | Electric Video

KHOT Radio	1983
Kid from L.A.	MSI Video
Kidnapped	Boccaccio 100
Kid Sister	Cal Vista
Kid Stuff	F/A Richard Bolla, Jake Teague, Lysa Thatcher: 1981
King Karl	Arrow Video, 1985
Kiko's Seduction	Orchids International, 1985
Kinky Couples	Bizarre
Kinky House of Pleasure	
Kinky Korners' Greatest Moments	Select/Essex
Kinky Lesbian Orgy	Ja-Rae
Kinky Tricks	F/A Sharon Lewis, Danny Flynn: Blue Video, 1982
Kissin' Cousins	Ambassador Video
Kiss Me, Lovely	Video Showtime
Kiss My Analyst	Class-X-Video
Kittens	P/D Jean Francois Davy, Roger Fellows F/A Marie-Claire Davy, Elizabeth Drancourt, Pauline Larrieu, Anne Liebert, Marie Georges Pascal, Phillippe Gaste
Kleinhoff Hotel	F/A Corinne Clery, Katya Rupe, Peter Kern, Bruce Robinson, Michelle Placido
Kneel Before Me	F/A Annie Sprinkles, George Payne, Allan Adrian, Ron Jeremy, Tony Mansfield
Knickers Up, Knockers Down	1983 (British)
KOCK-FM 169	
Kowloon Connection	F/A John Holmes, Suzy Chung: VCX
L.A. Babes	1983
Labia from Libya	Ambassador
La Cage Aux Folles	F/A Michel Serrault, Ugo Tognazzi: International Home Video Club
Lacey Bodine	VCX
A Lacy Affair	P/D Hal Freeman F/A K. C. Valentine, Maria Tortuga: Hollywood Video
Ladies' Bed Companion	F/A J. C. Holmes, Boccaccio 100
Ladies' Bed Companion	Home Entertainment
Ladies in Love	1
Ladies' Night	F/A Chelsea McClane, Annette Haven, Lisa de Leeuw, Nicole Noir: Select-A-Tape
Ladies' Night	P/D Lewis Brothers F/A Nicole Noir, Chelsea McClane: VEA
Ladies of the '80s	P/D Mark and Rita Richards F/A Jacqueline Lorians, Tamara Longley, Sheri St. Clair, Lana Burner, Steve Drake, Dan T. Mann: Paradise Visuals, 1985
Ladies Three	P/D Richard Rank
A Lady at Last	Bizarre
Lady Casanova	F/A Robin Cannes, Ray Hardin, Pamela Jennings, Summer Rose, Greg Rome, Steve Powers: AVC, 1985
Lady from Rio	
Lady Luck	F/A John C. Holmes: VCX

Lady Madonna | F/A Stacey Donovan, Ron Hudd, Ashley Wells: Video-X-Pix, 1985

Lady of the House | Bizarre
Lady on a Couch | Video-X-Pix
Lady on Top | F/A Sandy King, Paula Gaines, Larry Kirk: Blue Video

Lascivious Loops | Gold Stripe Video, 1983 (series of tapes)
Lashes One and Countess Anne | Bizarre, 1982
Lashes II | Bizarre
Last Days of Pompeii | P/D William Rotsler
F/A Stan Patt, Uchi Digart, Candy Samples: 1975

Last Foxtrot in Burbank | ETC
Last Sensation |
Last Sex Act | F/A Stacy Blue, John Hyde, Leslie Duncan, Becky Ann Thornton

Last Virgin |
Latex Slaves | R Bizarre
Laura's Desires | F/A Sigurd Theil, Iris Steen: International Home Video
Lay Over | P/D Hal Freeman
F/A Ali Moore, April Maye, Aphrodite, Susan Hart, Paul Thomas, Sandy Reed: Hollywood Video, 1985

Leather Mistress | Bizarre
Leather Revenge | Bizarre, 1983
Le Cabaret | Goldstar Video, 1983
Lecher | P/D Cecil Howard, Marc Ubell
F/A Georgina Spelvin, Robert Bell, Jody Bright, Cherry Grame, Berta Russ: Command

Left at the Altar | F/A Yvonne Rivers, Mary Lou Morris, Patty Sherwood: Adult Video

Legacy of Love | Boccaccio 100
Legacy of Lust | F/A Oral Annie, Tamara, John Leslie, Jerry Butler, Joey Silvera: Caballero, 1985

Leg Lovers & Foot Fetish Fantasy | Video Vortex/GV
Le Lit: Ze Bawdy Bed | R | Blue Video
Lenny's Comeback | C.D.I. Home Video
Lesbian Desires | Bizarre, 1983
Lesbian Foot Lovers | Video Vortex/GV
Lesbian Lingerie Party | Ja-Rae
Lesbian Love | Bizarre
Lesbian Lunatics | Curtis Dupont Associates, 1985
Lesbian Lust | Bizarre
Lesbian Orgy | F/A Victoria Jones, Sharon Ashes: Lambda Video

Lesbians Galore | Ja-Rae
Lesbos | Gold Stripe Video, 1983
Leslie Bovee's Fantasy Films |
Les Parisiennes, Volumes 1–4 | Gourmet (French; English subtitles)
Lesson in Bondage | Bizarre
Lesson in Love | Cal Vista
Le Toy Shoppe | R |
Let Me Count the Lays | F/A John Holmes: King of Video

Let Me Tell Ya About Black Chicks		P/D Dark Brothers
		F/A Cherry Lay-Me, Aphrodite, Black Sapphire, Purple Passion, Lady Stephanie, Mark Wallice: VCA, 1985
Let My Puppets Come		P/D Gerard Damiano: Caballero, 1983
Le Striptease		Goldstar Video, 1983
Let's Make a Dirty Movie		F/A Claude Basseur: 1980
Let's Play House		P/D Ted Roter: 1984 (filmed in Sweden)
Liahleh		F/A Steve Queen: Caballero
The Liars		F/A Dianne Sellars: Action X/TGA
The Libertine	R	F/A Catherine Spark, Jean Louis: Trintignant
Liberty		Cinnar Distributors
Liberty Belles		
Libriana		
Lickety Split	R	P/D Carter Stevens: Vista Video
Licorice Twist		F/A Ingrid Eliot, Stephen Harder, Ernie Steam, William Spam, Linda Thompson: Wet Video, 1985
Life at the Domma Club		California Star, 1985
Life Span		P/D Alexander Whitelaw
		F/A Tina Aumont, 1979
Like a Bat Out of Hell		
Like a Virgin		F/A Christy Canyon, Peter·North, Gail Force, Debra Lynn, Heather Wayne, Mark Wallice, Tony Martin: Atom Video, 1985
Likes of Louise		F/A April Harper, David Kane, Tami Reed: Blue Video
Limo Connection		F/A Danielle Martin, Lori Smith: Silhouette Video (TGA)
Linda and Cheri		Silhouette Video (TGA)
Linda Can't Stop		F/A Tina Russell, Jamie Gillis: MSI Video, VHL
Linda Lovelace for President		F/A Skip Burton, Linda Lovelace, Vaughan Meader: 1975
Linda Lovelace Meets Miss Jones		F/A Harry Reems, Linda Lovelace, Georgina Spelvin: Adult Video, 1975
The Lingerie Party		F/A Traci Lords: Gourmet, 1985
Lip Service		Video-X-Home Library
Lisa Meets Mr. Big		Video-X-Home Library
Little Angel Puss		F/A Sharon Thorpe: Cal Vista
A Little Dynasty		F/A Karen Summer, Francois Papillon, Cheri Garner: Coney Island Fog Productions, 1985
Little French Maid		F/A Connie Peters, John C. Holmes, Mike Ranger, Phil Tobias, Johnny Keys: Collector's Video
Little Gems		C.D.I. Home Video, 1985 (half-hour tapes)
Little Girl Lost		Silhouette Video
Little Girls Blue, Part II		VCX, 1984
Little Kimmi Johnson		F/A Kimmi Johnson, Jesie Adams, Steve Douglas, Colleen Brennan: Visual Entertainment, 1984
A Little More Than Love		P/D Peter Balakoff
		F/A Steve Event, John Hollyfield, Gene Lee, Heather Gordon: Select/Essex, 1980

Little More Than Love	P/D Ted Roter: 1981
Little Muffy Johnson	P/D Sharon Mitchell
	F/A Heather Wayne, Karen Summer, Mark Wallice, Misty Regan, Billy Dee: Visual Extertainment, 1985
Little Oral Annie Takes Manhattan	Video-X-Pix, 1985
Little Sisters	P/D Alex de Renzy: Wonderful World, Visual Entertainment
Live at Hellfire	Corporal Video
Live from Las Vegas	Video Tape Enterprises
Live Show	P/D Lee Young, Kris Kezer
	F/A John Seeman, Sandy Eileen: 1979
Living In	Boccaccio 100
Loads & Other Erotic Films	P/D Curt McDowell, 1985
Lolita Goes to College	
Lollipop	World Wide Video
Lollipop for Judy	Video City
Lonely Lady	Ventura Video
Lonely Lady Collection	F/A Amber Lynn, Angel West, Rick Cassidy, Sheri St. Clair: Late Nite Video Prod., 1985
Lonely Swinger	F/A Dolly Knight: Lambda Video
Lonesome Housewife	Boccaccio 100
The Longest Foot	P/D Gail Palmer
Long Jeanne Silver	P/D Alex de Renzy
	F/A Long Jeanne Silver (amputee): International Home Video
Long Sword of Seigfried Swift	Xana, 1983
Looking for Lust	P/D Charles De Santos
	F/A Desiree Lane, Karen Summer, Lili Marlene, Nick Niter: Velvet Video, 1984 (shot on videotape)
Looking for Mr. Goodsex	F/A John C. Holmes: Coast to Coast Video, 1985
Looking Good	F/A Mary Loup, Cathy Steward, Mary Linn Jess, Stephanie Ricci: AB Video, 1984
Loop Hole	F/A Tiffany Clark, Samantha Fox, Lisa Be
Loose Ends II	P/D Bruce Seven
	F/A Karen Summer, Erica Boyer, Janey Robbins: 4-Play Video, 1985
Loose Threads	F/A Sebrina Taylor, Ralph Galt: Blue Video
Losing Control	F/A Harry Reems, Kristara Barrington: Patti Petite, Eric Edwards, Randy West: C.D.I. Home Video, 1985
Lost in Lust	F/A Misty Dawn, Pam Jennings, Kelly Howell, Blake Palmer, Mark Wallice
Love Airlines	P/D John Fowler
	F/A Georgina Spelvin, John Leslie, Bridgette Graham, Paulene Atkins
Love Bites	F/A Traci Lords, Amber Lynn, Harry Reems, Heather Wayne
Love and Kisses	
Love & Lust	P/D Anthony Spinelli
	F/A Richard Pacheco, Nina Hartley, Lili Marlene: AVC, 1985

Love Boccaccio Style	R	F/A Jason Yukon, John C. Holmes, Candy Samples, B. Verdi: 1977
Love Bondage		4-Play
Bondage 1—Target for Torment		
Bondage 2—Trouble with Tikki		
Love Button		F/A Amber Lynn, Tess Ferre, Herschel Savage, Bunny Bleu: AVC, 1985
Love Champions		F/A Danielle, Roxanne Potts, Tom Byron, Colleen Brennan
Love Couch		F/A Joan Miquel, Teddy Bear, Eric Edwards: Video Home Entertainment, Harmony
Love Explosions		Channel-X-Video
Love Farm		
Love for Sale		VIP
Love from Paris		Silhouette Video
Love Games		F/A Sheila Stewart: Select-A-Tape
Love Hollywood Style		
Love Hotel	R	
Love-in Maid		F/A Cindy West, Joey King, Sue O'Day: Blue Video
Love in Strange Places		F/A John Holmes, Crystal Sync: Caballero
Love in the Dark		Vista Video, 1984
Love Is Not Enough		F/A Jan Jordan: Silhouette
Loveland		F/A Burt Allen, Carla Montgomery, Leslie White: Video Station
Love Lessons		VCA, 1984
Love Letters		F/A Jennifer West, Monica Vicare, Lili Marlene
Love Lies Waiting		Video City
Love Lips		P/D Dale J. Martin
		F/A Judy Hutcheson, Sharlin Alexander, Anne Nevens, Catherine Osborne, John Buchanan, Stephen Bently, John Everson: VCA
Love, Lust and Violence		F/A Anthony Fortunada: 1975
Lovely Intentions		Hollywood Video, 1985
Love Machine USA		
Love Makers USA		Home Entertainment
Lovemaking		Boccaccio 100
Love Me Again		Orchids International, 1985
Love Muscle		
Love Notes		F/A Serena, Rhonda Jo Petty: Twilight Video, Eros (King of Video)
Love Office Style		F/A L. Bailey, Brady T. Scott: Boccaccio 100
Love Retreat		Boccaccio 100
Love Scene		P/D Jerome E. Bronson
		F/A Jacqueline Lorians, Gina Valentino, Gail Force, Randy West: C.D.I. Home Video, 1985
Love Slaves		P/D Dave Goldstein, Robert Hussong
		F/A John Leslie, Sharon Thorpe, Pat Lee, Laura Bourbon, Alexandra Lyon, Desiree West: Wonderful World

Loves of Lolita	VCA, 1984
Love Station WXXX	P/D Bob August: VCA, 1984
Love Strange Love	1985
Love Stimulants	Silhouette Video
A Love Story	F/A Mike Stapp, Seka Scorpio
Love's Vicious Cycle	
Love Swedish Style	R F/A Karen Ciral: Home Entertainment, Video Station
Love Syndrome	P/D Sam Norvell F/A Harry Reems, Bobby Astyr, Samantha Fox, Merle Michaels: Cal Vista, 1982
Love Teachings of the Kama Sutra	ANW Associates, 1983
Love Theatre	P/D Mona, Edith Argentina, Sherri Breyer, Sharon Wolfen, Robert Zellis, Larry Kielbasa; VCA, 1985
Love Thy Neighbor	International Home Video
Love Thy Neighbor's Wife	P/D Yoshio Murai, Masaru Onuma F/A Maiko Kazama, Izuma Shima, Rei Kithaam
Love to Mother	F/A Tantala Nave, Blake Palmer, Maria Tortuga: Vista Video, Ecstasy Video
Love Too	Select/Essex
Love Toy	Cal Vista
Love Tunnel	Boccaccio 100
Love Under 16	F/A Susan Sands, Elaine Darby: PVX, 1983
Love Under 21	F/A Susan Sands, Elaine Darby, Larry Carr: Video Station
Love Victims	
Love Witch	Arrow
Love Ya, Florence Nightingale	F/A Marilyn Chambers: 1983
Love You to Death	P/D Frank Millotti F/A John Corleone, Angel Gionelli, Alan LaCosta, Mario Ferelli: Wonderful World
Lust Bug	P/D Hal Freeman F/A Ali Moore, Kristara Barrington, Sharon Mitchell, Tiffany Blake, Peter North: Hollywood Video, 1985
Lust Fight 2000	F/A Mike Ranger, Ric Lutz, Vicki Glick, Pat Manning: Video Home Library, 1978
Lustful Feelings	Kemal Video, MSI Video
Lust in Old Edo	F/A Machi Takabara, Yuriko Hishimi: 1978
Lust in Space II	F/A Jessica Lange, Lana Burner, Harry Reems, Jerry Butler, Ali Moore, Ron Jeremy, Gina Carrera: Paradise Visuals, 1985
Lust in the Dust	New World
Lust Story (Stephanie's)	P/D Erka Fox, Ted Ruter F/A Gena Lee, John Hollyfield, Drea, Tigr, Nicole Black, William Margold
Lust Weekend	F/A Rhonda Jo Petty, Danielle, Tara Aire: Gourmet Video, 1980
Lusty Adventure	Collector's Video, 1985
Lusty Ladies Volumes 1–6	F/A Juliet Anderson, Mike Staff, Jamie Gillis, Dick Fulton, and others: 4-Play
Lusty Business	Cal Vista, 1985

Lusty Business	F/A Pamela Lynn, Joyce McLay: Caballero, 1985
Lusty Princess	P/D Troy Benny
	F/A John Holmes, Fernando Fortes, Ronnie Ross, Linda Thompson, Denise LaFrance, Gary James: HIFCOA, 1978
Lynde	1983
Loving Daughter	F/A Harry Reems, Gina Fox: Video-X-Home Library
Loving Lesbos	VCR, 1983
Luau Orgy	F/A Elke Stein, Ron Jeremy, Don Fernando, Sue Lee, Lei Dim: Fantasy Club
Lube Job	Boccaccio 100
Lucky Arthur on the Isle of Paradise	P/D Svetlana, David Frazier
	F/A Jerry Butler
Lucky Swingers	Cal Vista
Lumber Jacks	Video Station
Lunch	P/D Cort McDowell
	F/A Velvet Busch, Mark Ellinger, Rick Biacicota, Lucinda: VCA, 1970s
Luscious	P/D Chuck Vincent, Bill Slobodian
	F/A Samantha Fox, Lisa de Leeuw, Champagne, Michael Knight: 1982
Luscious Linda	
Lust	F/A Vanessa Del Rio: Visual Entertainment
Lust American Style	F/A Mark Wallice, Peter North, Ron Jeremy, Nicole West: Western Visuals, 1985
Lust at the Top	F/A Heather Wayne, Stevie Taylor, Taney Robbins, R. Bolla, Nicole, Mark Wallice: Cinderella Distributors, 1985
Lust Boat	F/A Monique Guru: Now Showing
Lust Bug	F/A Ron Jeremy, Cheri Garner, Karen Summer: Hollywood Video, 1985
Machismo	International Home Library
Macho Women	F/A Mai Tai, Laura Lee, Susan Nile, Doris Light, Mike Horner, Danielle, Victoria, Mac Bird: Now Showing
Madame Black Rose	
Madame Kitty	P/D Giovanni Tinto Brass
	F/A Helmut Berger, Ingrid Thulin, Teresa Ann Savoy: 1976
Madame Zenobia	F/A Tina Russell: Home Entertainment
Made to Order	Eros (King of Video)
Mafia Girls	F/A Serena, Claudine Beccaire: Select-A-tape
Magic Ring	Eros (King of Video)
Magnum Griffin	
Maharajah of Bangmore	Video Station
Maid in Manhattan	VCA, 1984
Maidens of Fetish	1983
The Maids	P/D Jack Jackson
	F/A Serena, Uchi Digart: 1975
Main Attraction	R	F/A Samantha Fox: Harmony Vision

Maitresses — R | P/D Barbet Schroeder
F/A Gerard Depardieu, Bulle Ogier, Andre Rovyer: 1976

Make My Night — P/D Gerald Wayne
F/A Mindy Rae, Tiffany Blake, Kari Foxx, Peter North, Blake Palmer

Making of a Star — F/A John Leslie, Lisa de Leuuw

Male Chauvinist Pig — F/A Paul Taylor, Georgina Spelvin, Tina Russell: Quality, 1975

Males in Motion: Beyond Brief — Ambassador Video, 1985

Malibu Beach — R | Malibu High

Malibu Summer — F/A Dominique, Crystal Lake, Ron Jeremy: VIDCO, 1983

Malibu Swingers — P/D Hal Freeman
F/A Sharon Mitchell, Kristara Barrington, Paul Thomas, Tiffany Blake, Tom Byron: Coast to Coast Video, 1985

Malicious — F/A Laura Antonelli: International Home Video

Maltese Dildo — F/A Richard Pacheco, Seka, John Leslie: VCA, 1984

Mama's Boy — F/A Kelanie Klave: Ecstasy Video

Maneaters — P/D Fred Lincoln
F/A Joey Silvera, Sharon Kane, Kelly Nichols, Sharon Mitchell, Tiffany Clark, Jean Silvers: VCA, 1984

Manhattan Mistress — P/D Joe Davian
F/A Richard Bolla, George Payne, Erica Boyer, Merle Michaels, Juliet Anderson: VBM, 1980

Manhunt — Orchids International, 1985

Man to Maiden — F/A Sandy Steel, Lana Cazar, Veronica Moon: Bizarre

The Man Who Came to Dinner — R |

Mardi Gras — VIP

Marilyn and the Senator — HIFCOA

Marilyn, My Love — F/A Olinka (a.k.a. Mary Monroe), Andre Kay, Lisa Anderson, Dominique, Gerald Gregory: Essex, 1985

Marina Heat — L.A. Video, 1985

Marisa — Eros (King of Video), Action X Video

Marital Aids —

Marquise Marie — Bizarre, 1983

Marriage and Other Four-Letter Words — F/A Rainbow Robbins: TVX

Married Woman — Video City

Martin Cane's Cheap, Sleazy Movie —

Mary Ann's Honeymoon Suite —

Mary Flegas, Mary Flegas — Glen Joseph, Victoria Corsaw: Astro

Mary Jane — Blue Video, Video Entertainment

Masked Ball — F/A John Holmes: VCX

Massacre at Central High — R |

Massage Girls — Orchids International, 1983

Massage Parlor — Home Entertainment

Massage Parlor Wife — R | P/D Harry Novak, Barry Spinello
F/A Jen Gillian, Steve Rodgers, Brandy

	Saunders, Susan Snow: International Home Video
Master Control	F/A Sharon Montgomery, Georgia von Helsing, Bianca Corjay, Tony Stern: California Star, 1985
Master, Mistress and Slaves	Bizarre
Masterpiece	F/A Sarah Michelob, Eddie Cannon, Ursula Touche, Ken Scudder, Kathy Carlton: Wonderful World, Visual Entertainment
Masters and McJohnson	P/D Peter Balakoff
	F/A Larry Moore, Haleva, Anthony Richards, Don Perry, Vivi Vallini, Jennifer West: Select-A-Tape
A Matter of Love R	
The Max	
Maximum, Volumes 1–7	F/A Candy Samples: Diverse Maximum, 1983–1984 (one-hour collections of loops)
Meatballs R	F/A Bill Murray: International Home Video
Meet Me in the Park	Boccaccio 100
Meet Rachel Blondin	R. V. Productions (P.O. Box 3282, Nashua, NH 03061)
Melissa's Inside Straight	
Melts in Your Mouth	F/A Raven Royal Video: Moving Video, 1984
Memoirs of a Madam	
Menage a Trois	Command, 1985
Menage a Trois, Volumes 1–3	1985 (previews of 50 or more Caballero tapes)
Merry Go Round R	F/A Maria Schneider, Helmut Berger, Sydney Rome, Senta Berger: Home Entertainment
Miami Spice	Ventura Video, 1985
Miami Vice Girls	Video-X-Pix, Redlights, 1985
Michelle Makes Maui	Paradise Visuals, 1985
Midnight Ecstasy	
Midnight Graduate	
Midnight Hard-On	VIP
Midnight Lady	F/A Kimberly Carson, Jessica Long, Ray Hardin: American Video, 1985
	P/D Harry Novak: Astronics
Midnight Plowboy	P/D Bruce Seven
Mid Slumberi Night Dream	F/A Erika Boyer, Cara Lott, Heather Wayne, Mark Wallice, Tom Byron: 4-Play, 1985
Mile High Club	F/A Crystal Lovin: Cal Vista, 1983
Milk Chocolate	Masterpiece, 1985
Millionairess	F/A Andrea True, Mark Stevens: Blue Video
Million-Dollar Mona	F/A Candy Samples: Video Station, VIP
Mind Blowers	F/A Mary Stuart: Blue Video
Minu: Making a Porno Star	CSVS, Truex
Miss American Dream	P/D Peter Lambe
	F/A Karen Summer, Misty Regan, Sasha

	Gabor, Dawn Adams, Dan Fisher: Coney Island Fog Productions, 1985
Miss Bikini USA Beauty Pageant	Ed Rich Productions
Miss Kinsey's Report	P/D Larry Winsor, Bo Koop
	F/A Eric Edwards, Susan McBain: Blue Video
Miss Laid	
Miss Nude Pageant	Video World Productions
Miss Nude World Contest	Video World Productions
Miss Passion	F/A Traci Lords, Ginger Lynn: VIDCO, 1985
Mr. and Mrs. Nude Texas Pageant, 1983 and 1984	Classic Productions, 1983–1984
Mr. Uptight's Reformation	1979
The Mistress	F/A Kelly Nichols, Richard Pacheco: Cal Vista, 1982
The Mistress	P/D Bernado Spinelli
	F/A Kelly Nichols, Anna Turner, Richard Pacheco, Juliette Anderson, and others: Cal Vista, 1983
Mrs. Barrington	International Home Video
Mistress Candy	Bizarre
Mistress Candy—Shemale	Q.E.L. Quark, Bizarre
Mistress Electra	F/A Long John Silver, Marlene Willoughby: 1983
Mistress Monique	Bizarre
Mistress Mir . . . at Her Best	Bizarre, 1984
Mistress Pamela	Caballero
Mistress Renata and Her Grease Monkey	Video Vortex/GV
The Mistress Speaks	F/A Mistress Antoinette and her Slave: Imperial Video
Misty	
The Mob Job	P/D Godfrey Daniels
	F/A John Alderman, Dennis Drake, Sharon Kelly: 1979
Modern Fantasies	Select/Esex, 1983
Modesty Gold	F/A Drea, Ron Jeremy, Stanford Grossman: Midnight Video
Moments of Love R	P/D Harry Novak, Joe Sherman, H. Hershey
	F/A Ron Jeremy, John C. Holmes, Rhonda Jo Petty, Lisa de Leeuw, Mai Lin, Nicole Black: Channel X Video, 1982
Momma's Boys	P/D Kim Christy
	F/A Tantala, Jerry Butler, Sheri St. Clair, Shannon, Jill Hunter: VIDCO
Mommy Queerest	Janus
Mommy's Panty Boy	Imperial
Mona	
Monda Cane R	P/D Gualtiero Jacopetti, 1961
Mondo Fetish	Janus
Mondo Topless 2	P/D Russ Meyer
	F/A Candy Samples, Lisa de Leeuw
Money Buys Happiness	F/A Tara Aire: VIDCO
Montage	Home Entertainment
Monument to a Madam	Boccaccio 100
Moonshine Girls	F/A Jerry Mills, Mary Martin: Wonderful World

More Games Women Play		TVX, 1982
More Than a Voyeur		F/A Dean Hayes, Linda Lovelips, Jean Jill
More Than Friends		F/A Marsha Hart: Action X Video/TGA
More Ways Than one		Silhouette Video
Most Valuable Pussy		
The Most Willing P———y		VIP
The Motel		
Mother, Brother and I		VIP
Mother's Pride		P/D Steven Pride
		F/A Colleen Brennan, Kimberly Carson,
		Beverly Glen: Diverse Industries, 1985
Mother's Wish		
Movie Buffs	R	
Movie Star (Les Parisiennes)		Gourmet, 1983
Ms. Nude Dancer and Entertainer Contest		Classic Production, 1985
Ms. Nude Galaxy Beauty Contest		Classic Production, 1985
Ms. Woman of the Year		F/A Bill Coney, Naomi Jensen: Blue Video
Mud Madness		F/A Ron Jeremy, Rhonda Jo Petty: Adult
		Video, 1983 (3-D)
Mummy, Daddy & Daughter Jenny		Bizarre
Mustang	R	Media
My Armour		Boccaccio 100
My Bed Is Crowded		Video City
My Brother and I		Video Station, Boccaccio 100
My Father's Wife	R	P/D Enzo Doria
		F/A Adolfo Celi, Carroll Baker, Cesare
		Barro, Gabriella Giorgelli: Movies at
		Midnight
My First Time		F/A Mimi Morgan, Joey Civera, Jack
		Wright, Georgia Ilene, Sonya Spizer:
		Select/Essex
My Gun Is Hard		F/A Desiree Lane, Jamie Gillis, Herschel
		Savage, Alex Gabor, Fred C. Dobbs:
		Allied Video
My Heart Belongs to Daddy		F/A Paula Wain: Blue Video
My Husband the Producer		
My Little Sister		Home Entertainment
My Name is Kala	R	Home Entertainment
My Pretty Go Between		P/D Jonathan Burroughs
		F/A Beverly Glen, Melanie Scott, Leslie
		Winston, Shaun Michele: Video Select,
		1985
My Private Party		F/A Christy Canyon, Bunny Bleu, Lori Smith:
		Vivid Video, 1985
My Secretary I Love	R	P/D Jack Genero: Adult Video, 1983
My Secret Life		
My Sex-Rated Wife		
My Sister Eileen		F/A Patty Ball: Astro, Home Entertainment
My Sister, My Love	R	F/A Carol Kane, Lee Grant: Wizard
My Teenage Daughter		P/D R. Burton, Donald Dillingham
		F/A Marie Exorre, Terry Larsen, Max Horn,
		Brent Warburg: Select/Essex
My Tongue Is Quick		F/A John Holmes: TGA
My Wife the Hooker		Arrow
Naked Bodies on My TV	R	

Naked Eyes		F/A Bunny Bleu, Herschel Savage, Susan Hart: Producer's Concepts, 1985
Naked Glitter		1983
Naked Hunter		Boccaccio 100
Naked Lovers		
Naked Lust		F/A Bunny Bleu, Kimberly Carson, Beverly Bliss, Craig Roberts, Greg Rome: Video Exclusives, 1985
Naked Nights		P/D John Stagliano
		F/A Heather Wayne, Robin Cannes, Steve Drake, Rusty Zipper: VCR, 1985
Naked Paradise	R	F/A Laura Gemser
Naked Scents		F/A Jerry Butler, Taija Rae, Baby Doe, R. Bolla, Tish Ambrose: VCA, 1985
Naked Stewardesses		
Nathalie	R	P/D Ilia Milonko
		F/A Marcella Petri, Grazia deGiorgi, Pauline Tietscher, Andrew Johnson: Media, 1984
Nattie's Pleasure Palace		F/A Buddy Jackson, Marie deMuir, Kathy Davis, Terry Grubber: Adult Video
Naughty Au Pair		Bizarre
Naughty Cheerleaders		F/A Ali Moode, Ron Jeremy, Paul Thomas, Lee Brown, Cecil Deville: Hollywood Video, 1985
Naughty Coeds	R	F/A Jill Peterson, Marianne Crosby: International Home Video
Naughty Freshman		
Naughty Neighbors	R	
Naughty Nostalgia, Volumes 1–8		Class-X-Video
Naughty Nurses		VCR, 1983
Naughty Nymphs		
Naughty Roommates	R	
Nazi Brothel		Boccaccio 100
Neighbors and Friends		Boccaccio 100
Nest of Joy		F/A David and Lesa: Gourmet Video (shot directly on videotape)
Nevada Pleasures		1981
Never Enough		F/A Lisa de Leeuw: Select/Essex, 1984
Never Say No		P/D F. J. Lincoln
		F/A Tiffany Clark, Joey Silvera, Gabrielle: 1983
Never Sleep Alone		F/A John Leslie, Victoria Jackson, Joanna Storm, Joey Silvera, Anna Ventura, Chelsea Manchester: Caballero, 1983
Never So Deep		P/D Gerard Damiano
		F/A Mike Ranger, Paul Thomas, Richard Pacheco, Loni Sanders, Marin Tortuga, Serena: VCX, 1981
Newcomers		F/A John C. Holmes, Tantala, Misty Dawn, Nick Random: VCX, 1985
Newcomers		P/D Lloyd Kaufman
		F/A Harry Reems, Mark Stevens, Georgina Spelvin, Tina Russell: Video Show Time, 1973

New Girl in Town	Home Entertainment, Video Audio Electronics
Newlyweds	Dreamland Video, 1985
New Wave Hustler	LA. Video, 1985
New York City Woman	F/A John Holmes, Jennifer Jordan, Georgina Spelvin, Crystal Sync, C. J. Laing: Blue Video, 1980
New York Erotic Film Festival	Harmony Vision
New York Vice	P/D Henry Pachard
	F/A Stacey Donovan, Gina Carrera, Danielle, Tom Byron: Coast to Coast Video, 1985
The Nibblers	Video Select, 1985
Nice and Naughty	P/D Sventlana: Collector's Video
Nice Girls Do	F/A Jamie Gillis: Blue Video
Night After Night	L.A. Video, 1985
Night at Hellfire	P/D Robert Michaels, Felix Daniels
Night Bird	F/A Roger Caine, Misty Winter, Marsha Valentino: Blue Video
Nightcaller	F/A David Book, Monique Starr: Arrow VCR, 1985
Night Dreams	P/D Phillip Marshak
Night Flight	F/A Jamie Gillis, Tiffany Clark, Serena, Maria Tortuga: Creative Video, 1984
Night for Lovers	Orchids International, 1985
Night Games	P/D Roger Vadim
Night Hunger	P/D Gerard Damiano
	F/A Eric Edwards, Honey Wilder, Sharon Mitchell, Jerry Butler, Sharon Kane: Adult Video, 1983
Night Moods	VCX, 1982
Night Moods	P/D Drea
	F/A Jacqueline Lorians, Chanel Price, Steve Draile, Zend: AVC, 1985
Night Moves	P/D Domingo Lubo
	F/A Lili Marlene, Billy Dee: Superior Video, 1983
Night of Submission	P/D Joseph Davian
	F/A Peter Sutinov, C. J. Laing, Annie Sprinkles, Cheryl White, Vanessa Del Rio, Lee Griffin: Video-X-Home Library
Night of the Head Hunter	F/A Stacey Donovan, Ron Jeremy, Erika Boyer: Western Visuals, 1985
Night of the Voyeur R	
Night of the Warlock R	
Night of the Wild Side	F/A Kay Parker, John Holmes, Janey Robbins: Vista Video, 1984
Night Peeper	Boccaccio 100
Night Pleasures	Wonderful World
Night Porter R	P/D Robert G. Edwards
	F/A Liliana Cavani, Charlotte Rampling, Dirk Bogarde, Philip Le Roy, Gabrielle Ferzetz
Night Prowlers	F/A Harry Reems, Cara Lott, Heather

Older Men with Younger Girls	P/D Jack Remy
	F/A Harry Reems, Joanna Storm, Summer Rose, Bunny Bleu, Nick Random: Coast to Coast Video, 1985
Older Women with Young Boys	F/A Honey Wilder, Pat Manning, Tom Byron: Coast to Coast Video, 1984
Oldest Pleasure	Boccaccio 100
Oldest Profession	R P/D Jean Luc Goddard
	F/A Raquel Welch, Jeanne Moreau, Elsa Martinelli: Boccaccio 100
Old Time Blue	Videocraft Classics
Olé	F/A John Holmes: Eros
Olinka, Grand Priestess of Love	F/A Olinica, Gabrielle Pontello: Caballero, 1985
On a Clear Day	Video Station
Once and for All	Home Entertainment
Once in a Lifetime	F/A Ronnie Michaels, Dave Head, Alice Thatch, Sylvia Daniels: Adult Video
Once Over Nightly	F/A Terri Hall, Annie Sprinkles: Video-X-Pix
Once Upon a Girl	Select-A-Tape (cartoon)
Once upon a Madonna	P/D Adam
	F/A Patti Petite, Erica Boyer, Kathleen Kelly, Little Oral Annie, John Leslie, Joey Silvera, Tom Byron, Ron Jeremy: Paradise Visuals 1985
Once Upon a Secretary	P/D Ron Jeremy
	F/A Alex X, Pamela Louise, R. Bolla, Jerry Butler, Samantha Fox, Kelly Nichols, Veronica Hart
Once Upon a Time	F/A Amber Hunt, Abigail Clayton, Annette Haven: Blue Video
One Hot Night of Passion	P/D David Razer
	F/A Traci Lords, Christy Canyon: Collector's Video, 1985
One Last Fling	F/A Jamie Gillis, Bree Anthony: C.P.L.C. Video, 1984
One Night at a Time	F/A Colleen Brennan, Harry Reems, R. Bolla, Mai Lin, Desiree Lane: Allied Video
One Night of Passion	F/A Paul Thomas, Traci Lords, Christy Canyon, Ron Jeremy, Sasha Gabor: Collector's Video, 1985
One Night Stand	Select Video Productions
One of a Kind	P/D Mike Merino, Troy Benny
	F/A Leslie Bovee, Annette Haven, Sharon Thorpe: HIFCOA
1001 Danish Delights	P/D Svend Mehling
	F/A Axel Strobye, Dirch Passer, Judy Gringer, Lone Hirtz: Arrow
One, Two, Three	P/D Wakefield Poole
	F/A J. D. Slater, Dave Connors, Steve Kaye, Rydar Hanson, Tom Stone: L.A. Video
Only Play with Me	Video City
On the Street	VIP
Opening Night	F/A Heather Thomas, George Payne, Su-

Pain & Pleasure	California Star
Pain by Lana	California Star
Painful Desires	F/A Bobby Astyr: Blue Video
Painful Reunion	Bizarre, 1984
Pajama Party	Caballero
Palm Spring Girls	Liberty Video
Palomino Heat	P/D Drea
	F/A Deidra Hopkins, Olga, Erica Boyer, Kelly Howell, Mimi Daniels: Command, 1985
Pancho's Chickens	J.M. Chevalier, 1985
Panorama Blue	F/A John Holmes, Renee Bond
Panty Party	R
Panty Raid	P/D David Frazer, Svetlana
	F/A Jerry Butler, Raven, Ashley Britton, Sandra Stillman: Collector's Video, 1983
Paradiso	Video Station
Paranoia	
The Paris Connection	Gourmet Video, 1983
Party	F/A Wanda Long, Greg Walters, Mike Mitchell: National Video
Party Girl	F/A Danielle, Jacqueline Brooks, Viva: Gourmet (shot directly on videotape)
Party Stripper	F/A Shauna Grant, Eric Edwards, Kimberly: Gourmet, 1983
Passage to Pleasure	F/A Vanessa Del Rio, Lisa de Leeuw, Kathy Harcourt: Caballero
Passion for Bondage	P/D Bruce Seven
	F/A Erica Boyer, Tantala, Cara Lott, Brian Curtin: Black & Blue Video/VTE
Passion Parlor	Class X Video
Passion Pit	P/D Dick Dumunt
	F/A Traci Lords, Stacey Donovan, Lili Marlene, Little Oral Annie, John Holmes: Essex, 1985
Passion Play	F/A Lisa de Leeuw, John Holmes, Jennifer West: Western Visuals, 1984
Passion Procession	F/A Vanella Astro
Passions	P/D Alex de Renzy
	F/A David Allen, Laura Birch, Toni Brooks, Stacey Donovan, John Leslie, Richard Pacheco, Kelly Nichols: Mitchell Brothers, 1985
The Passion Seekers	Silhouette Video
Passion Toys	F/A Tiffany Clark, Sylvia Benedict, Laurie Smith, Arcacia Lake, Kyoto Sunn, Lisa Bunn: Cinema Tech, 1985
Paula's Punishment	Bizarre, 1983
Paying for It	Silhouette Video
Pay Off	F/A Terri Ruggiero, Rick Laverne: Video Home Library
The Peek-a-Boo Gang	P/D Ron Jeremy
	F/A Traci Lords, Gina Carrera, Heather Wayne: Collector's Video, 1985
Peeking Cameras	Boccaccio 100

Peepholes	P/D Vince Benedetti, Marc Roberts
	F/A Mai Lin, Jeannie Silver, Bobby Astyr:
	1982
Peeping Tom	F/A Callie Aimes: Diverse Maximum, 1983
Peep Shows: Blonde Godesses	F/A Seka, Serena, Carol Connors, Jesie
	St. James, Nancy Suiter, Chris Cassidy,
	Sharon Kane, Lee Carol, Nancy Hoffman,
	Jean Jennings: Wonderful World of Video
Peggy	R Silhouette Video
Penelope	R
Penetration Volumes 1–6	P/D Lasse Braun, Jack Generos
	F/A Lisa de Leeuw, Julie Winchester, Ron
	Jeremy, Dawn Adams, and many oth-
	ers: AVC, 1984
Pen Pals	F/A Andrea True: TGA, 1975
Penthouse Pleasures	F/A Jane Abrams, Shelly Linx: Video
	Station
Pepper	R Vestron, 1982
Perfection	P/D Harold Lime
	F/A R. Bolla, Tish Ambrose, Heather Wayne,
	Karen Summers: VIDCO, 1985
Perfect Position	Silhouette Video
Perfect Weekend	F/A Kimberly Carson, Paul Thomas: AVC
Perils of Payne	Bizarre
Perils of Prunella	Bizarre
Prescription for Passion	VIDCO, 1985
Personal Playmates	1983
Personals	P/D Cecil Howard
	F/A Tina Russell, Darby Lloyd Raines, Joan
	Kerry, Rosalind Nolian: Command
Personal Touch	F/A Sharon Mitchell, Shauna Grant: Ar-
	row, 1982
Personal Touch I and II	P/D Bobby Hollander
	F/A Shauna Grant, Cody Nicole, Joanna
	Storm, Pamela Louise, Paul Thomas: Ar-
	row, 1983
Personal Touch III	F/A Lisa de Leeuw, Jerry Davis, Nikki Ran-
	dall, Jamie Gillis: Arrow, 1984
Perversions	P/D Jack Genero
	F/A Jamie Gillis, Lee Carroll, Ron Jeremy,
	Julie Winchester: AVC, 1984 (shot on
	video)
Peter Galore	F/A Rick Cassidy, Tony Lane, Dalana
	Bisonette, Shari Kay, Lee O'Donnell,
	Cindee Summers: 4-Play, 1985
Peter Sweeper	VIP
Philappetite	P/D I. L. Lifkin
	F/A Mistress Michelle, Becky Savage,
	Lady Rozanne, Dean Richmond
Phone Sex	1983
Photo Flesh	P/D Hal Freeman
	F/A Eric Edwards, Rosemarie, Ginger Lynn,
	Janice Rhae, Susan Hart, Raven: Hol-
	lywood Video, 1984
Physical	F/A Julie Anderson: Select-A-Tape

Physical II	F/A Traci Lords, Tom Byron, Cara Lott, Linda Shaw, Herschel Savage, Jamie Gillis, Juliet Anderson: Superior Video, 1985
Pick-Up	Boccaccio 100
Piece of the Action	
Piercing of Jamie	Bizarre, 1983
Piercing of Laura	Bizarre
The Pigkeeper's Daughter	P/D Harry Novak, Bethel Buckalew F/A Terry Gibson, Patty Smith: International Home Video
Pink Flamingos	R P/D John Waters F/A Divine, David Luchen, Mary Vivan Pearce: Harmony Vision
The Pink Fox	TVX
Pink Lagoon	P/D David Fraser, Svetlana F/A Ginger Lynn, Jerry Butler, Raven, Jay Serling, Sondra Stillman, Ron Jeremy: Collector's Video, 1984
Pink Lips	VCX
Pinocchio	
Pin-up Playmates	
Pitfalls of Bunny	Video-X-Home Library
Pit of Perversion	
Playground Sisters	Boccaccio 100
Playmates	R F/A John Claude Beroq, Donna Michele: Video Station
Play Only with Me	Class-X-Video
Plaything	Visual Entertainment
Plaything of the Devil	
Please Please Me	F/A Erica Straus: Arrow
Pleasure and Company	F/A Mistress Pleasure, Mistress Paula, Jonathon Payne: Video Home Library, Bizarre
Pleasure Beach	P/D Richard Lawrence, Arthur Bressan, Jr. F/A Michael Christopher, Johnny Dawes, Scot Sedgwick, T.J., Stephen Daniels, Beay Mathews: VCA
Pleasure Business	Orchids International, 1985
Pleasure Dome	F/A Maria Tortuga, Ken Starbuck, Drea, Jennifer West, Lee Carroll, Jeff Conrad: Essex
Pleasure Fair	F/A Marsha LaMonte, Jill Shephard: Astro
Pleasure Island	F/A Tish Ambrose, Chelsea Blake, Kelly Nichols, Kimberly Carson, Renee Summer, Dick Howard, Joesy Skuero, R. Bolla: Arrow, 1984
Pleasure Island	F/A Monica Jenks, Ed Stark, Jo Amariz, Tina Hutton: Home Entertainment, VCX 1972
Pleasure Is Our Business	Cal Vista
Pleasure Motel	P/D Hal Freeman
Pleasure Party	F/A Danica Rhae, Josephine Carrington, Kristara Barrington, Paul Thomas, Peter North: Coast to Coast Video, 1985

Pleasure Party	F/A Traci Lords, Barbie Dahl: Gourmet, 1985
Pleasure Productions 1–4	F/A Vanessa Del Rio, Susan Nero, Samantha Fox, Merle Michaels, and others: VCR, TGA, 1984 (6 loops on each 1-hour cassette)
Pleasure Seekers	F/A Heather Wayne: Atom Home Video, 1985
Pleasure Seekers	VEP
Pleasure So Deep	F/A Big Jean-Paul, Laurien St. Germain: Atom Home Video, 1984 (foreign)
Pleasures of Erika Swenson	
Pleasure Zone	F/A Laura Lazare, Tamie Robin, Tara Aire: Select/Essex, 1983
Pledge Sisters	Boccaccio 100
Polyester	P/D John Waters
	F/A Tab Hunter, Edith Massey, Mink Stole, Divine
Pom-Pom Girls	F/A Robert Carradine, Connie Benet, Monique Perry
Pony Girls	F/A Maureen Kelly, Diane Baxter, Susan Critz, Mary Pearson
Pool Party	MSI Video
Pool Service	F/A Rhonda Jo Petty, Connie Benet, Monique Perry: Gourmet Video (shot directly on videotape)
The Poonies	P/D Bruce Seven
	F/A Ginger Lynn, Sharon Mitchell, Heather Wayne, Amber Lynn, Kevin James, Mark Wallice, Peter North, Herschel Savage: Vivio Video 1985
The Porn Birds	P/D Scott Fox
	F/A Jessyca Wylde, Herschel Savage, Andrea Rolland, Mindy Rae, Mark Wallice: AVC, 1985
The Porn Brokers	F/A John Collins, Ilsa Stupp, Elvira Clark, Jamie Gillis, Helen Madigan: Video Audio Electronics
Porno Connection	Boccaccio 100, Video City
Pornography and Prostitution in the U.S.A. R	Astronics
Pornography in Hollywood	Video-X-Pix
Porno Mondo	Boccaccio 100
Porn Stars at Play	F/A Samantha Fox: VCA
Portrait of Desire	F/A Karen Summer, Leslie Winston: IVP, 1985
Portrait of Lust	F/A Traci Lords, Eric Edwards, Gina Valentino, Jessica Wylde, Nicole West, Steve Drake: Coast to Coast Video, 1985
Possessed	VCX
Potpourri	
Power of Nicole	1983
Praised Sister	Video City
Pregnant Baby Sitter	F/A Robert Lee, Brenda Bush: Western Visuals, 1985

Pregnant Mamas | Ambassador, 1985
Preppies | P/D Chuck Vincent: 1983
Prescription for Passion | P/D Di Bachus
| F/A Sasha Gabor, Sue Lee, Jamie Tokall, Heather Thomas, Gina Valentino: VIDCO, 1985
Presidential Peepers | F/A Richard Dixon, Tina Russell: 1975
Pretty As You Feel | F/A Ginger Lynn, Tom Byron, Jerry Butler, Raven, Bunny Bleu, Lynn Ray, Kim Warner, Slip Stokey, Sandy Taylor, Debbie Northrup: Atom Video, 1984
Pretty Baby | Essex, 1985
Pretty Party People |
Prison Babies |
Prisoner of Pleasure | F/A Long Jean Silver, Patrice Trudeau
Prisoners of Love | F/A Liza Bertini, Wanda Scott: Blue Video 1983
Private Ecstasy |
Private Nurse | F/A Vanessa Del Rio, Misty Dawn: Gourmet Video
Private Practice, Come and Be Purified | F/A Jamie Gillis: L. A. Video, 1984
Private Sex Lessons | Orchids International, 1985
Prized Possession |
Probation Officers' Discipline | L.A. Video, 1985
Proficient Profession |
Programmed for Pleasure | F/A Christine Muller, Marilyn Jess, Catherine Marsile, Frederic Carton: VIDCO, 1985
Proposition 8 | VIP
Prostitution and Porn in the Orient |
Prurient Interest | Blue Video
Psyched for Sex | F/A Andrea True, Mark Stevens, Belle North, Rita Weems: Blue Video
Psychodrama | Boccaccio 100
Pulsating Flesh | F/A Tamara Longley
Pumpkin Farm | F/A Jesse Adams and others: Fantasy Club
Punch and Judy | R | Eros, 1975
Punished, Volumes 1–4 | Bizarre, 1984–1985
Punk Rock | P/D Carter Stevens
| F/A Wade Nichols: Wonderful World of Video
Purely Physical | F/A Laura Lazare, Juliet Anderson, Kitty Shane: Select/Essex, 1982
The Pussy Burglar | F/A Cheri Champagne: Showcase, 1983
Pussy Cat Ranch | P/D J. A. Martine, John Christopher
| F/A Wade Nichols, Richard Bolla, Samantha Fox, Colleen Anderson: Cal Vista
Pussy Willow | P/D Bobby Hollander
| F/A Susan Hart, Robin Canne, Mark Wallice, Misty Regan: Andrea Britton, Tom Byron, Cheri Garner: Super Star Video, 1985
Queen of Sex |
Queen of Wresting II | Curtis Dupont Associates, 1985

Quick Turnover	F/A Rachel Harms, Judy Michaels, Ruth Sims: Video-X-Pix
Rabin's Revenge	F/A George MacDonald, Linda Jensen, Cindy Spittler: Mitchell Brothers, 1971
Radio KKum	P/D Hal Freeman
	F/A Susan Hart, Rose Marie, Cindy Carver: Hollywood Video, 1984
Rainbow Jam	F/A Ron Jeremy, Lisa Be, Tiffany Clark, Marissa Constantine: Command, 1982
Rampaging Nurses	F/A Bobby Friedman, Jen Friedman: Mitchell Brothers, 1971
Ranch Hand	Silhouette Video
Randy Stiler	F/A Veronica Hart
Rape	VIP
Rape Victims	Video Showtime
Rated Sex	Essex, 1985
Rated X: The Movie	Select/Essex
Raven	F/A Paul Thomas, Ginger Lynn, Breezy: VCR, Cinema Tech
Ready When You Are, C.B.	F/A Charles "C.B." Bond, Barbara Roberts, John Seeman, Gwen Steward, Paul Orbois, Jane Graham: Blue Video
Real Estate	F/A K. C. Valentine, Linda Shaw, Carrie Evans: Gourmet (shot directly on Videotape)
Rear Action Girls, 1 and 2	F/A Nina Hartley, Little Oral Annie, Lili Marlene, Nikki Blaze: Lipstick, 1984
Rear Ended	Western Visuals, 1985
Rear Entry	F/A Gina Valentino, Sheri St. Clair, Michael Morrison, Taylor Evans, Athena Stara: VCR, 1985
Rebecca	P/D William Hunt
	F/A Sharon Mitchell, Velvet Summers, Stella Steven, Lori Ambrosia, David Christopher, George Payne: 1983
Rebecca's Dreams	F/A Rebecca Heels, Mistress Antoinette, Maid Lisa: Vision of Fantasy, Imperial
Reckless Claudia	F/A George MacDonald, Devin Daugherty: Mitchell Brothers, 1971
Red Heat	Eros, 1975
Red Liners	F/A Brenda Vixen, Rachel Frank, Ruth Sims: Video-X-Pix
Red Tape International, Volume 2	International Home Video
Reefer Madness	Select-A-Tape
Reel People in Denmark	Anthony Spinelli Productions, 1985
Reel People in Sweden	Anthony Spinelli Productions, 1985
Referral Service	F/A Eric Edwards, Darby Lloyd Raines, Sharon Stewart, Jerry Grover; Blue Video
Refinements in Love	F/A Liz Renay: HIFCOA
Regency Home Video, Volumes 1–12	F/A Ilene Wells, Ron Jeremy, Robert Cole, and many others: TGA
Reincarnation of Serena	Gourmet, 1983
Remember Connie	F/A John Holmes: Masterpiece
Rendezvous with Destiny	F/A Mistress Destiny: L. A. Video, 1985
The Rent Collector	Video Station

Return to Alcatraz	Janus Video
Return to Alpha Blue	P/D Gerard Damiano
	F/A Chelsea Blake, Jerry Butler, Sharon Kane: AVC
Return to Sex World	Select/Essex, 1984
Reunion	F/A Bree Anthony, Tony Richards, Taylor Young, Alan Lugin; Blue Video
Revelations	Silhouette Video
Revenge of the Cheerleaders	F/A Jerri Woods, Rainbeaux Smith, Carl Ballantine, Eddra Gale: Select-A-Tape
Revenge of the Rope Masters	P/D Carter Stevens
	F/A John Ashton, Yolanda Sevalas, Susan McBain: 1979
Revolving Teens	F/A Harry Reems, Helen Madigan: Class-X-Video, Video-X-Home Library
Ribald Tales of Canterbury	F/A Hypatia Lee: 1985
Ribald Tales of Robin Hood R	Media, International Home Video
Richard Rank: (The Best of Volumes 1 and 2)	Gourmet Video
Rich Bitch	F/A April, Susan Hart, Ali Moore, Mark Wallice, Paul Thomas: Hollywood Video, 1985
Rich Girls	P/D Hal Freeman
	F/A Susan Hart, Ali Moore, Paul Thomas, April May, Alan Royce: Hollywood Video, 1985
Ride a Cocked Horse	F/A John C. Holmes: 1973
Riding Mistress	F/A Lonnie Harris, Dana Douglas: Bizarre, 1983
Ring My Chimes	Hollywood Video, 1985
Rings of Passion	
Ripoff	P/D Dakota Brothers
	F/A Richard Austin, Susan Dreger
Ripoff of Millie	Video-X-Home Library
Ripples & Wrinkles	F/A Big Mamma Jackson, Pia Amora: TGA, 1984
Rise and Fall of Sparkle	F/A Bill Cody, Belinda Ross, Angela Wells, Carla Thomas: Blue Video
Road Service	F/A Jamie Gillis, Andrea True, Mark Stevens: Video-X-Home Library
The Rocky Porno Picture Show	F/A Kristara Barrington, Tantala, Karen Summer, Francois Papillon, Mark Wallice, Bianca
Rolls-Royce, Volumes 1–6	Silhouette
Romeo and Juliet	International Home Video
Romp Around	TGA
Roommate in Bondage	Bizarre, 1983
Roommates	Boccaccio 100
Room Service	International Home Video
Rope Burns	F/A Cody Nicole, Marguerite Partee, Pia Sands: 4-Play, 1985
Rope of Flesh	P/D Russ Meyers
	F/A Hal Hopper, Lorna Maitland: 1969
The Rose and the Bee	F/A Jimmy George, Wanda Simmons: Video Station

Rough Cut — MSX Video

Round Robin — F/A Rose Stevens, Laura Bently, Judy Michael: Video-X-Pix

Round-up — P/D Henri Pacharo: Caballero, 1986

Rubber Party — California Star, 1985 (30-minute tape)

R.S.V.P. — P/D Ron Jeremy
F/A Jose Duval, Kandi Barbour, Kelly Nichols, Herschel Savage, 1985

Running Wild — F/A Adrienne Bellaire, Jamie Gillis, and others: Superior Video, 1984

Run, Jack, Run — Video Station, 1979

Russians Are Coming — F/A Georgina Spelvin: Video City

Rx for Passion — F/A Candy Samples, Heather Wayne, Jessyca Wylde, Herschel Savage, Treanna: L.A. Video, 1985

Rx for Sex — P/D Caldweld Farmer, P. McDowell
F/A Julia Perrier and others: Atom Video

S&M Party at Midnight — California Star, 1985

Sacrilege — Boccaccio 100

Sadistic Adventures of Maria and Anna — Tao Video (7046 Hollywood Boulevard, Los Angeles, CA 90028), 1983

Saleslady — Morning Glory

Salesman's Hotel — Boccaccio 100

Sally Robert's Bondage, Volumes 1–4 — Royal Video, 4-Play

Sally Sauna — Q.E.L. Quark

Sally's First Lesson — California Tri-Star, 1985

Salo-20 Days of Sodom — R P/D Pier Palo Pasolini
F/A Paolo Bonacelli, Giorgio Cataldi: 1977

Salon d' Amour — F/A Jacques Marboeuf, Denise Fevrier, Colette Marevil, Pierret Raymond: International Home Video

Samantha's Elixir — Boccaccio 100

Same Time Every Year — P/D Fred Lincoln
F/A Paul Thomas, Joel Caine, Tiffany Clark, Holly McCall, China Leigh, Loni Sanders: Blue Video, 1981

San Francisco Erotica — Janus

San Francisco General Hospital — (loops)

San Francisco Original: No. 1–9, A —

Sassy Sue — R Channel X Video

Satan's Cheerleaders — R

Satan Was a Lady — P/D Kenyon Wintel
F/A Bobby Astyr, Tony Rich, Bree Anthony, Annie Sprinkles: Blue Video, 1980

Satin Dolls — P/D Jack Remy
F/A Cindee Summers, Bunny Bleu, Billy Dee, Jerry Butler, Gina Carerra, Andrea Britton, Steve Drake: Coast to Coast Video, 1985

Satin Lust — Boccaccio 100

Satisfaction — Video Station

Satisfaction Guaranteed — Silhouette Video

Saturday Night Special — P/D Robert Petroff, Sam Blotch
F/A Jamie Gillis, Jeffrey Hurst, Georgette Jennings: Cal Vista, Eros

Satyricon	R	P/D Federico Fellini
		F/A Martin Porter, Hiram Keller, Max Born: 1969
Savaged and Ravished		Video Vortex
Savage Fury		P/D Mark Curtis
		F/A Beverly Bliss, Christy Canyon: Video Exclusives, 1985
Savage Lust		Silhouette Video
Savage Roommates		
Savage Sex		
Scandal in Denmark		
The Scavengers	R	
Scent of a Woman		Gourmet, 1985
School Daze		F/A Ambrosia Fox, 1983
School for Sexual Arts		Video Home Library
School for S/M		Adult Video
School for Sex		Boccaccio 100
School for Swingers		
Schoolgirl Reunion		Video-X-Home Library
School Girls		Caballero
School Reports 2		California Star
The School Teachers		F/A Elvira Simpson, Sylvia Conners, Jill Davis, Kathy Williams, Judy Patton, Robert Washington: Hollywood Video
School Teacher's Weekend Vacation		P/D Wallace Merkin
		F/A Priscilla Ponzi, Mannie Harding, Mimi Woodstock: Video-X-Home Library
Scoremobile		Collector's Video, 1982
Screen Play		F/A Jacqueline Roget, Amber Lynn, Tracy Duzit, Mark Goldberg: X-Travision, 1985
Script Tease		F/A John Holmes, Taylor Evans: Western Visuals, 1985
Season of the Witch		P/D George Romero
Secluded Passion		P/D David Christopher
		F/A Kelly Nichols, Sue Nerd, Helen Madigan, Mistress Candice, David Christopher, George Payne
Secret Affair of Cleopatra		Channel X Video
Secret of Stage Five		P/D Paul Lyons
		F/A Karen Summer, Paul Baresi, Cara Lott, Alan Royce
Secrets		P/D Rafelli
		F/A Seka, Seren, Monica (seven loops)
Secret Sex Lives of Romeo and Juliet	R	Astronics
Secret Society		F/A Paul Thomas, Stacey Donovan: Now Showing, 1985
Secrets of a Willing Wife		P/D Mitch Delray, Norman Gerney
		F/A Eric Edwards, Merle Michaels, Rikki O'Neal, Arcadia Lake: Video-X-Pix
The Secrets of Jennifer		F/A Jennifer West: Now Showing
Secrets of Marilyn		F/A Olinka
Secret World of Erotic Art		Vestron Video, 1985
Seduce Me Tonight		P/D Cole Crenshaw, M. L. Hooper;
		F/A Thomas Scintilla, Richard Porter, Travis O'Neill, Les Hansen: Atom Home Video, 1984

Seduction	F/A Andrea True, Jamie Gillis, Terri Hall: Video-X-Pix
The Seduction	R Media, 1982
Seduction From Deep Space	Select-A-Tape
Seduction of Cindy	F/A Veronica Hart, Seka, Lisa de Leeuw, Samantha Fox, Sharon Mitchell, Vanessa Del Rio, Ron Jeremy: 1982
Seduction of Joyce	F/A Peter Andrews, Valerie Adams: Blue Video
Seduction of Lana Shore	F/A Eric Edwards, Sharon Mitchell, Renee Summer, Lori Smith
Seed of Terror	
Seka for Christmas	Caballero
Seka in Tara	F/A Seka, Samantha Fox, Jamie Gillis, Veronica Hart: 1983
Seka's Lacy Affair	F/A Seka: Hollywood Video, 1985
Seka's Teenage Diary	P/D Rafelli
	F/A Seka, Mike Ranger, Herschel Savage: Hollywood Video, 1985
Self-Service Schoolgirls	R F/A Georgette Pope, Margo Younger: Blue Video, 1975
Selling It	Laura Cannon: Blue Video
Seniors	F/A Dennis Quad, Priscilla Barnes: Vestron, 1982
Sensational Janine II	F/A Patricia Rhomberg: Caballero
Sensual Encounters of Eve	International Home Video
Sensuality	HIFCOA, 1982
Sensual Meditation	F/A Eric Edwards, Grey Poupon, Masugana Roy: Astro
Sensuous Caterer	P/D Roy Winnick
	F/A Mark Stevens, Toni Rose, Jill Monro, Serena, Seka: Harmony Vision
Sensuous Delights	F/A Pat Manning, Sally Swift, Tina Russell, Mark Stevens: 4-Play, 1973
The Sensuous Detective	P/D M. M. Dimitri
	F/A John Leslie, Serena, Laurien Dominique: Select-A-Tape
The Sensuous Fly Girls	P/D Nicholas Berland
	F/A Mary Stewart, Bobby Darlin, Lynn Bodica: VHL
Sensuous Housewife	
Sensuous Moments	F/A Danica Rhae, Gina Martell, Loni Sanders, D. J. Laing: Vista Video, 1984
Sensuous Nurse	F/A Ursula Andress: International Home Video, 1975
Sensuous Playgirls	P/D Nicholas Berland
	F/A Mary Stewart, Baby Darlin, Lynn Budice, Mark Stevens, Alan Logan: Video-X-Home Library
Sensuous Vixens	
The Sentimentalist	Video City
Separate Vacations	Boccaccio 100
Serena	P/D Vinnie Rossie, Fred Lincoln
	F/A Jamie Gillis, Paul Thomas, Serena, China Leigh: Wonderful World, 1979

Serena as Sugar	F/A Serena: Ja-Rae Productions
Service with a Smile	F/A Betty Midnight, Robert Marks: VIDCO, 1985
The Session	Class-X-Video
Sessions of Love Therapy	Video Station
Sex Academy, First Assignment	VIDCO, 1985
Sex and the Comics	VCA, 1984
Sex and the Dames	Video City
Sex and the Girl R	
Sex and the Office Girls R	P/D Ron Clark Medy: International Home Video
Sex and the Stars	Select-A-Tape
Sex Academy	Target Video, 1985
Sex Animals	Essex
Sex Appeal	F/A Laurie Smith, Lili Marlene, Tara, Carol Smith, Denise: 1984
Sex As You Like It	F/A John Holmes, Candy Samples, Sandi Dempsey, Sandi Carey: Silhouette Video (T.G.A.)
Sexations	P/D Ned Morehead, Jerry Ross
Sex-a-Vision	F/A Gina Carrera, Joey Silvera, Herschel Savage, Tamara Longley, Sheri St. Clair: Dreamland, 1985
Sex Bloopers	Select/Essex, 1983
Sex Busters	Target, 1985
Sexcapades II	P/D Henri Pachard
	F/A John Leslie: VCA, 1984
Sex Clinic Girls	F/A Renee Bond: Select-A-Tape
Sex Crimes 2084	P/D Chuck Vincent: Essex, 1985
Sex Delivery	Boccaccio 100
Sex Drive	P/D Chuck Vincent
	F/A Taija Rae, Kathlyn Moore, Melissa Christian, Sheri St. Clair, Michael Knight: Video-X-Pix, 1985
Sex Drive	F/A Sharon Thorpe
Sex, Drugs & Rock & Roll	P/D F. J. Lincoln
	F/A Tiffany Clark, Tish Ambrose, Sharon Kane, Susan Nero, Dick Howard, F. J. Lincoln: Video Home Library, 1985
Sexed	F/A Heather Wayne, Bunny Bleu, Blake Palmer, Rick Savage, Heady La Mars, Robin Carnes: Bavana Video, 1985
Sex Education	C.D.I. Home Video
Sexercise Clinic	Caballero, 1983
Sexercise Girls	Video Station
Sexercises	Boccaccio 100
Sex Experiment	
Sex Fifth Avenue	F/A Traci Lords, Christy Canyon, Heather, Wayne, Gail Forrest, Nicole West: Western Visuals, 1985
Sex Goddess	F/A Traci Lords, Christy Canyon, Rikki Blake, Tom T. Hall: Gourmet, 1985
Sex Goddesses, Volumes 1–3	1984
Sex in Marriage	Boccaccio 100
Sex Loose	VCA, 1984

Sex Machine		Boccaccio 100
Sex Madness		International Home Video
Sex Odyssey (2069)		Video Show Time
Sex on the Run	R	
		F/A Tony Curtis, Britt Ekland: Wonderlust Video, 1975
Sexorama		F/A Colleen Brennan, Rita Ricardo, Don Hart, Shayla Grant: 1985
Sexpert		F/A Rena Vance, Eric Edwards, Amy Stone, Jim Crane, Suzy Kaye: Visual Entertainment
Sex Pertease		VIDCO, 1985
Sex Princess		Orchids International, 1985
Sex Problems		Boccaccio 100
Sex Prophets		Boccaccio 100
Sex Pursuit		Boccaccio 100, Video City
Sex Ray Machine		
Sex Recycled		Orchids International
Sex Rink		Video Home Entertainment, 1985
Sex Romance		Orchids International, 1985
Sexsations		P/D Lawrence Cole
		F/A Annette Haven, John Leslie: Now Showing
Sex School for Girls	R	
Sex Shoot		F/A Traci Lords, Heather Wayne, Tom Byron, Cara Lott, Ron Jeremy, Jessica Long, Peter North, Steve Powers: Atom Video, 1985
Sex Sirens		
Sex Stalker		F/A George Payne, Ambrosia Fox, Velvet Summers, David Christopher, Chari Champagne: 1983
Sex Stars		P/D Paul Vatelli
		F/A Herschel Savage, Lynn Z., Kimberly Carson, Danica Ray
Sex Stewardesses		Orchids International, 1985
Sex Stunt		Cal Vista
Sextasy		P/D Radley Metzger
		F/A Marianne Flowers, Patrice Cherone, Diane DuBois: Command, 1985
Sextoons	R	Harmony Vison, Home Entertainment
Sex Tycoon		JVP
Sexual Communication		F/A John Franks, Sheila I. Rossi, George Martin, Rosemary Morlan: HIFCOA
Sexual Ecstasy of the Macumba		F/A John Fox, Nina Fausse: 1975
Sexual Fantasies		P/D Werner Hedman: 1979
Sexual Freedom		F/A Andrea True, Janet Jones
Sexual Freedom in Brooklyn		Video Station
Sexual Freedom in the Ozarks		F/A Andrea True, Janet Jones: Boccaccio 100
Sexual Heights		F/A Jamie Gillis, John Holmes, Serena, Tawny Pearl, Mai Lin: 1981
Sexual Initiation of a Married Woman		VIDCO, 1984
Sexual Odyssey		F/A Mai Lin, Amber Lynn, Jerry Butler, Nick Random, Rachel Ashley, Karen Summer: 1985

Sexual Practices in Sweden R	Video Station
Sexual Therapist	Cinnabar Distributors
Sexual Witchcraft	International Home Video
Sex USA	Arrow
Sexus in Paradise	Boccaccio 100
Sex Wars	F/A Richard Pacheco, Lori Smith, Paul Thomas: Excalibur, 1985
Sex Waves	P/D David Michel
	F/A Eric Edwards, Traci Lords, Angel West, Ken Starbuck, Julie Winchester: Excalibur, 1985
Sex with Stars	P/D Anward Mawardi
	F/A Martin Burrowes, Janie Love
Sex with Lil' Red	F/A Li'l Red Hood, Rhonda Jones, Michael Mench, Desire X.: TGA
Sexy Vibrations	Boccaccio 100
Shades of Ecstasy	F/A Janey Robbins, Ron Jeremy, Misty Dawn, Cara Davis, Michel Lee, Melanie Scott, Mona Page, Desiree Lane, Allen Royce, Tom Byron: Hollywood Video
Shades of Flesh	International Home Video
Shameful Desires of Black & White Girls	F/A Sharon Kane: L.A. Video, 1985
Shameless	F/A Monica Vicare, Lili Marlene, Blaire Harris, Suzanne Silk, Linda Shaw, Joel Jay, Billy Dee, Ken Scudder, Mary Lauree, Mike Horner: 1983
Shame of the Jungle	International Home Video
Shanghai Girls	Horizon Video
Shannon	Caballero, 1983
Shape Up for Sensational Sex	P/D Gail Palmer
	F/A Ginger Lynn, Eric Edwards: Essex, 1985
Sharon	F/A Susan McBain, Jean Jennings: Select-A-Tape
Sharon in the Rough	F/A John Christopher, Richard Bolla, Marlene Willoughby, Angel Martine: Video Show Time, 1979
Sharon In The Rough House	F/A Jamie Gillis: Vidco, 1984
Sharon's Rosebud	F/A Sharon Thorpe: Silhouette Video
Shauna, Every Man's Fantasy	P/D Roberta Findlay: Cabellero, 1985
Shaved	F/A Desiree Lane, K. C. Valentine: VCR, 1984
Shaved Bunnie	P/D Charles De Sangs
	F/A Nina Hartley, Tiffany Dupont, Betty Beaver: Lipstik Video, 1985
Shave Tail II	F/A Cara Lott: Ambassador, 1985
She Couldn't Say No	
She Did It Her Way	VIP
She Did What He Wanted	Video City
She Does What I Ask	Cal Vista, 1985
Sheer Panties	P/D Billy Thornberg
	F/A John Holmes, Linda Wong: Select/Essex
Sheer Rapture	F/A Jerry Nichols, Kelly Nichols, Annette Heinz: 1984

Sheila's Payoff   VCX, Visual Entertainment

She/Male Confidential   P/D Kim Christy
F/A Serna Saunders, Magnificent Margo, Summer St. Cerly: VIDCO, 1985

Sheri & the Bandit   I.V.P. Video, 1985
Sherlick Holmes   F/A Harry Reems, Bobby Astyr: Blue Video
She's No Angel   Astro Silhouette Video
Shoe Store   F/A Craig Roberts, Rikki Blake, Pam Nino, Lee Winston: Bizarre, 185

Shoot or Get Off the Pot
A Short Affair   Orchids International, 1985
Showdown   P/D Winn Thotas: 1976
Showdown at the Erogenous Zone   P/D Regina Jay
F/A Leslie Winston, Gabrielle, Brandy Alexander, Tamara Longley: Seven Star Prod., 1985

Showgirl Fantasies   F/A Phaedre Grant, Holly McCall, Samantha Fox: VCR, 1983

Show Girls   Essex, 1985
Showgirl Superstars, Volumes 1–18   VCR
    Volume 1: Seka's Fantasies
    Volume 2: Leslie Bovee's Fantasies
    Volume 3: Tina Russell's Fantasies
    Volume 5: Crystal Dawn's Fantasies
    Volume 6: Sue Nero's Fantasies
    Volume 7: Arcadia Lake's Fantasies
Show Me   1983
Showtime
Shy House Boy   L.A. Video, 1985
Silhouette
Simply Irresistible   F/A Samantha Fox, Richard Pacheco, Nicole Black: Select Essex, 1983

Sin City
Sinfully Yours   F/A Christy Canyon, Stevie Taylor, Eric Edwards, Pam Jennings: Hollywood Video, 1983

Sinful Pleasures of Reverend Star
Sins of Desdemona   1982
Sins of Johnny   MSI Video
Sins of Sandra   F/A Phil King, Darlene Devone, Sandra Kyoto: Adult Video

Sins of the Flesh   Video Station, Vision of Fantasy
Sip the Wine   Mitchell
Sister Eve
Sister Midnight   F/A Vanessa Del Rio
Sisters Punishment   California Star, 1985
Six Easy Pieces   T.G.A.
Six Faces of Samantha   P/D Jack Tanero
F/A Samantha Fox: Ave, 1984
Six for Sex   Boccaccio 100
Sixty-Nine Minutes
Six Women   P/D Ed de Priest, Mike Bennett
F/A James Sweeney, Marsha Jordan: 1975
Ski Ball   F/A Sue Mitchell: Boccaccio 100

Ski Bunnies		
Ski Hustlers		Silhouette Video, Select Video
Skin Deep		P/D Gail Palmer
		F/A Rhonda Jo Petty: Caballero, 1983
Skinema		P/D Robert Niosi
Sky Pies		F/A Raven, Ron Jeremy, Gina Carrera, R. Bolla, Sasha Gabor, Nichulu, Misty Regan, Tom Byron: Collector's Video, 1985
Slammer Girls		VCA 1984
Slave Exchange		F/A Rikki Blake, Pam Nino, Leslie Winston, Craig Roberts: Bizarre, 1985
Slaves of Love	R	P/D Charles Nizat: Media
Slave Therapy		Bizarre
Slave Training		Bizarre
Slick As Snot		1982
Slip of the Tongue		F/A Alicia Hunt, Helen Futon, Joan Saar: Video-X-Pix
Slippery When Wet		F/A C. J. Laing, Annie Sprinkles: Video-X-Pix
Slumber Party		F/A Ginger Lynn, Eric Edwards, Danica Rhae, Tom Byron: Hollywood Video
Slumber Party '57	R	F/A Debra Winger: Vestron, 1982
Slum Goddess		Boccaccio 100
Sluts in Heat		P/D Richard Aldrich: Gold Medallion, 1985
Small Change		F/A Bobby Astyr, Dave Ruby, Clea Carson: C.D.I. Home Video
Small-Town Girls		P/D William Dancer
		F/A Aaron Stuart, David Morris, Dorothy Le May, Serena: Select-A-Tape
Smartie Pants	R	
		F/A Melissa Greene, Gayle Summer: Blue Video, 1975
Smokers from the Past, Volumes 1–3		F/A Candy Barr (#1), Marilyn Monroe (#2): Wonderful World of Video
Snack Time		P/D Hal Freeman
		F/A Sandy Reed, Tom Byron, Gregory Ruffener, Carrie Stevens, Monica Copeland, Stephen Evans
Snake Eyes		P/D Cecil Howard
		F/A Lori Smith, Cassandra Leigh, Paul Thomas, Brooke Fields, Joanna Storm, Jerry Butler, Rikki Harte: Command, 1985
The Snatch		Boccaccio 100
Snowballing		Boccaccio 100, VIP
Snow Balling		Gourmet, 1985
Snow Honeys		F/A Rhonda Jo Petty, Vanessa Del Rio, 1983
Snow Job		
Snow Man		F/A Marie Savage: Blue Video
So Many Men, So Little Time		F/A Justin Thyme, Ed Stifler, Sven Jensen: Blue Video
Softie		F/A Mike Haven, Robin Williams, Nancy Herbie: Adult Video

Soft Stroke		S&L/VCX
Solo Girls		4-Play
Some Kind of Woman		F/A Ginger Lynn, Joanna Storm, Amber Lynn, Paul Thomas, Herschel Savage: 1985
Sons and Mothers		
Sophie Says No		P/D D. J. Lang
		F/A Mark Stevens, E. Edwards: Video-X-Home Library
Sophisticated Pleasures		F/A Lili Marlene: Western Visuals
The Sorceress		F/A Leslie Murray, Andrea True, Eric Edwards: Blue Video
Sore Throat		Collector's Video, 1985
Souperman		F/A Mark Stevens: International Home Video
Southern Comfort	R	P/D Harry Novak
		F/A Jack Richeson, Jacob Oft, Judy Angel, Wendy Gale: Astronics
South of the Border		F/A Jamie Gillis: Video Home Entertainment
Souzy's House		F/A Renee Bond: Boccaccio 100
The Spanking Salesmen		California Star, 1985
Spanking Scenes		TAO
Spanking Tutor		L. A. Video, 1985 (half-hour tape)
Spare the Rod		Bizarre Tri-Star
Special Order		F/A Leslie Murray, Eric Edwards: Blue Video
Spectators		P/D Anthony Spinelli
		F/A Richard Pacheco, Kay Parker, Herschel Savage, Gaye Sterum: AVC, 1984
Speed Trap		1983
Spiked Heels		Bizarre
Spirit of '76		P/D Ricki Kreimm
		F/A John Holmes, Annette Haven: International Home Video
Splendor in the Sack	R	
Splits		1983
Spread in the Sack	R	
Spread the Action		P/D Jim Reynolds
Stacy's Hot Rod		F/A Raysheena, Eric Edwards, Amy Copeland, Teresa Jones: Cal Vista, 1984
Stage Girls		F/A Brooke Fields, Taija Rae, Danielle, Renee Summers
Stalag 69		F/A Dorothy Le May: Video Home Entertaiment, 1985
Star Cuts, Volumes 1–6		Hollywood Video, 1985
Star 85		Video Exclusives, 1985
Star 84, The Tina Marie Story		F/A Cody Nicole, Tina Marie, Cara Lott, Laurie Smith, Erica Boyer
A Star Is Porn		F/A Bunny Bleu, Heather Wayne, Ron Jeremy, Tamara Longley, Patty Petite, Erik Edwards: Cinematrix, 1985
The Starlets		F/A Amber Lynn, Heather Wayne: 4-Play, 1985
The Starlets		Video Show time, 1979

Starlette Exposed

Starlette Nights — F/A Leslie Bovee, Monique Le Bare, Sandy Nichols, Tyler Horne: X-Tra Vision, 1982

The Starmaker — F/A Cintrice, Kenny Dino, Copper Penny, Ron Feilen, Jamie Gillis: VCA, 1983

Starship Eros — P/D Wesley Emerson, Scott McHaley F/A Mike Ranger, Lori Rogers, Becky Saunders: Select/Essex, 1980

Starved of Affection — P/D Vinnie Rossi, William Margold F/A Joanna Storm, Nikki Charm, Jerry Butler, Tess Ferre, Tami Lee Curtis, Duck Adams, Jay Sterling: AVC, 1985

Starwoman — Target, 1985

Steam Heat — P/D Mittis Gettich, Umber Corleone F/A Jamie Gillis, Tina Rose, Cheryl Collette, Heather de Stahl, Valerie Brand: Command, 1979

Steamin' Hot — F/A Seka, Serena: 1982

Steamy Dreams — F/A Lisa de Leeuw, Tim Fields: C.P.L.C. Video, 1984

Sticky Fingers — International Home Video, Innovative Video

Sticky Situation — F/A Art North, Richard Grant, Darby Lloyd Raines, Cindy West: Video-X-Pix

The Stimulators — F/A Maria Sentry, Ron Jermy, Dave Ruby: Mico Silver Star

Stocks and Bonds — 1979

Stolen Lust — F/A Cara Lott, Summer Rose, Shaun Michele: AAH Video, 1985

Story of Bobby — F/A Countess Angelique, Sandra Steel, Bobby Land, Veronica Moon, Lana Cazar: Bizarre

Story of Eloise — F/A Jean Dalton, Barbara Ames: Video-X-Home Library

Story of O — R — F/A Corrine Clery, Anthony Steel: Bizarre

Story of K — R — Bizarre

Story of the Bizarre

Straight Banana — Boccaccio 100

Strange Bedfellows — Cinematrix, 1985

Strange Diary — Silhouette Video

Strange Family — Gourmet, 1982

Strangers When We Mate — F/A John C. Holmes: VCX

Stray Cuts — Hollywood Video, 1985 (30-minute tapes)

Street Girls of N.Y. — Silhouette

Street Heat — F/A Amber Lynn, Desiree Lane, Mai Linn, Athena Starr

Street of a Thousand Pleasures — R

Strictly for Ladies Only — P/D William Higgins: Laguna Pacific, Catalina

Stripped for Action — Boccaccio 100

The Stud — F/A Joan Collins

The Student Body — R — P/D Ed Carlin, Gus Trizonis F/A Warren Stevens, Jillian Kessner, Janice Hedden, June Fairchild: Video Station

Studio of Lust	P/D Hal Freeman F/A Debbie Shaw, Sally Douglas: Holly-wood Video
Studio Sex	X-Travision
Stud Wars	P/D Lawrence T. Cole F/A Billy Dee, Peter North, Gail Sterling: Now Showing, 1985
Submission of Serena	Video-X-Home Library
Suburban Lust	F/A Sharon Grant, Cody Nicole: Gourmet Video, 1983
Suburban Wives	P/D Derek Ford F/A Eva Whishaw, Barry Linehan, Heather Chasen, Richard Thorpe: Video Station
Suckula	Boccaccio 100
Sue Prentiss, R.N.	F/A Annie Sprinkles: Video-X-Home Library
Sugar in the Rain	F/A Duane Marks, Cindy Lynn, Terri Nelson: Adult Video
Sugar in the Raw	F/A Terri Nelson, Suzi Flynt, Tommy Long, Duane Marks: Adult Video
Sultry Nights	Select Video
Summer Beach House	F/A Danielle, Becky Savage, Laurie Noel: Gourmet Video, 1980 (shot directly on videotape)
Summer Break	F/A Stacey Donovan, Bunny Bleu: Video Exclusives, 1985
Summer Heat	R	1973
Summer Lovers	R	
Summer Lust		International Home Video
Summer of '72		F/A Annette Haven, Loni Sanders, Ginger: 1982
Summer of Suzanne		F/A Jennie Wexler: Video-X-Home Library
Summer Session		F/A Andrea True: Blue Video
Summer's Love		
Summertime Blue		P/D Carl La Blanche F/A John Holmes, Eric Edwards, Samantha Fox, Serena, Jean Jennings: Wonderful World, Visual Entertainment
Summer Vacation		
Sunny Days		Boccaccio 100
Sunset Strip Girls		F/A Tina Russell, Annie Sprinkles, Sandy Fox, Jamie Gillis: Silhouette, TGA
Super Ball		Home Entertainment
Superbowl Bondage		Janus
Super Charger		Boccaccio 100
Super Chic		F/A Joey Silvera, China Lee, Paul Thomas, Ron Jeremy: VCA, 1985
Super Knight, Erotic Adventures of		Home Entertainment, Blue Video
Super Salesman		
Super Star		F/A John Holmes, Amber Hunt, Laurien Dominique: Adult Video, Home Entertainment
Superstar Ladies: The Best of Alex de Renzy, Part 1		P/D Alex de Renzy F/A Abigail Clayton, Desiree Cousteau, Kikko, Linda Wong, Christine Heller, Nicole Black: Mitchell Brothers

Superstars	F/A Bridgette Monet, Shauna Grant, Seka,
Featuring Bridgette Monet	John Holmes, Annette Haven, Dave
Featuring Seka	Cannon: Caballero, 1984
Super Tease	F/A Mindy Rae, Tamara Longley: Video,
	1985
Superware Party	F/A Mike Rogers, William Margold, Seka,
	Jennifer West: Scorpio Arrow, 1979
Surfer Girls	International Home Video
Surrender in Paradise	P/D David Frazer
	F/A Jerry Butler, Ginger Lynn, Crystal Hol-
	land, Rene Tiffany: Collector's Video,
	1984
Suze Centerfold, Volumes 1–9	VIDCO
Suze's Super Girls, Volumes 1 and 2	P/D Suze Randall: New Wave Produc-
	tions, Caballero
Suzie's Birthday Bang	F/A Jo Anna Stephen, Colleen Brennan,
	Jeannie Pepper, Sheri St. Clair, Ron Jer-
	emy: Night Owl Productions, C.D.I. Home
	Video, 1985
Suzie Superstar II	F/A Ginger Lynn, Traci Lords: Caballero,
	1986
Suzie's Sweethearts	International Home Video
Swap	F/A Bobby Astyr, Flo Rivers, Danielle
	Dubre
Swap Meet	F/A Lynn True, Cilla Pink: VIDCO, 1985
Swedish Erotica, Volumes 1–52	F/A John Holmes, Aunt Peg, Johnny Keys,
	and others: Caballero
Swedish Erotica Special Edition #1,	Caballero
Nostalgia Blue	
Swedish Massage	
Swedish Minx	
Sweet As Pie	Silhouette Video
Sweet Dominance	F/A Danielle, Ron Jeremy: Gourmet, 1983
Sweet Dreams	P/D Johnny Rio, Sven Conrad
	F/A Jon Jones, Abbie Trevor, Bridgette
	Maier: Nouveaux Video
Sweet Erotica	Blue Video
Sweet Folds of Flesh	F/A John Seeman, Tracy O'Neil, Linda
	Wong, Ann Sylmar: Astronics
Sweet Georgia	
Sweet Honey	
Sweet Little Sister	F/A Cheri Champagne, Velvet Summers:
	Showcase, 1983
Sweet Little Sisters	International Home Video
Sweet Little Thing	F/A Traci Lords, La Petite, Blake Palmer,
	Ron Jeremy: Collector's Video
Sweet Lust	L.A. Video, 1985
Sweet Movie R	P/D Dusan Makavejev
	F/A Carol Laure, Pierre Clementi, Anna
	Prucnal, 1974
Sweet Nightmares	Bizarre Tri-Star
Sweet Paradise	P/D Mike Strong
	F/A Jean Charlie, Belle Claudet, Chloe
	Gregory, Cat Gerlin: VBM, 1980
Sweet Sister	Silhouette Video

Sweet Sixteen — F/A Carla Young: Video-X-Home Library

Sweet Surrender — P/D Vinni Rosse
F/A Sheri St. Clair, Bunny Bleu, Tess Ferre, Joey Silvera, Bill Margold: AVC, 1985

Sweet, Sweet Freedom — F/A John Holmes, Marlene Willoughby, Jeff Hurst: Blue Video

Sweet Taste of Honey — F/A Holly Chambre: Action X Video/TGA

Sweet Temptations — F/A Randy Dickerson, Cindy Lynn, Debbie Garland, Earl Rawlings, Mike Lewis: Adult Video

Sweet Thing

Sweet Throat — P/D John Christopher
F/A Eric Edwards, Al Lavinsky, Beth Anna, Clea Carson: Cal Vista, 1979

Sweet, Wet Lips

Sweet White Dream — Boccaccio 100

Sweet Young Age — Boccaccio 100

Sweet Young Foxes — P/D Bob Chinn
F/A Cara Lott, Cindy Carver, Kay Parker, Pat Manning, Bud Lee, Ron Jeremy, Hypatia Lee: VCX, 1985

Swinger's Ball — Video City

Swinging Ski Girls — R P/D Don Trendall: Media, X-Tra Vision

Swinging Sorority — VCX

Swinging Sorority Girls — R P/D Don Trendall: Media, International Home Video

Swing Set — Boccaccio 100

The Swing Thing — F/A John Holmes: Action X Video

Switch Blade Sister — R

Switchcraft — F/A Andrea True, Mark Stevens: Video-X-Home Library

Taboo IV — P/D Kirdy Stevens
F/A Ginger Lynn, Jamie Gillis, Karen Summer, John Leslie, Honey Wylde, Cindee Summers, Kevin James, Kay Parker: Standard Video, 1985

Taboo, the Lip and the Single — P/D Curt McDowell

Taboo Video, Volumes 1–4 — TGA, 1984

Tabu, Volumes 1–4 — European: Arrow

Tailenders — F/A Erika Boyer, Kristara Barrington, Sahara, Heather Mansfield, Mark Wallice, Steve Powers: Wet Video, 1985

Tailhouse Rock — F/A Traci Lords, Eric Edwards, John Byron, Stacey Donovan, Josephone Carrington: Western Visuals, 1985

Take Me Now — F/A Erica Boyer, Kristara Barrington, Sahara, Heather Mansfield, Mark Wallice, Steve Powers: Wet Video, 1985

The Takers — P/D Harry Novak

Taking Off — VCA, 1984

Talent Scout — Orchids International, 1985

Tales of a High-Class Hooker — F/A Joy King, Betty Scott, Angie Van: Video-X-Pix

Tales of Seduction — Boccaccio 100

Tales of the Bizarre — F/A Velvet Summers, Ambrosia, Troy Lane, Cheri Champagne: 1983

Talk Dirty to Me (One More Time)		P/D Anthony Spinelli F/A John Leslie, Colleen Brennan, Harry Reems: Spinelli Productions, 1985
The Taming of Rebecca		F/A Cheri Champagne: Buzz Productions, 1982
Tampon Tango		P/D Tamamoto F/A Aya Misawa, Kaori Kawaguchi, and others: Orchids International, 1975
Tanya	R	P/D Harry Novak, Nate Rogers F/A Marie Anderson, Sasha Gibson, Suzi Adams: Video Show Time, 1975
Tara, Tara, Tara		F/A Seka, Veronica Hart, Jamie Gillis, Samantha Fox: 1982
Tarot Temptress		F/A Tiffany Clark, Jessyca Wylde, Greg Rome, Greg Ruffner: American Adult Video
Taste of Betty		Video-X-Home Library
Taste of Cherry		P/D L. M. Burton, Mark Rigney F/A Tish Ambrose, Dan T. Mann, Beverly Glynn, Jerry Butler, Demian Wolf
Taste of Honey		
Taste of Money		F/A Constance Money, Jamie Gillis, Sharon Mitchell, Don Hart, Paul Thomas: Atom Video, 1983
Taste of Paradise		P/D Hal Freeman F/A Stevie Taylor, Peter North, Ron Jeremy, Misty Regan: Hollywood Video, 1985
A Taste of Sugar		F/A China Jade, Eileen Welles, Joey Civera, John Seeman: Select/Essex, Arrow, VCX, Adult Video
Taste Takes a Holiday		VCA, 1985
Tasty		1985
Tattooed Lady		F/A Christine DeShaffer: Twilight
The Tattooed Lady		F/A Greg Walters, Marsha Moore, Sandy Kline: Bizarre, Adult Video
Taxicab for Ladies		Xana (Foreign)
Taxi Girls		Western Visuals, 1985
Taxi Girls II		Video Van, 1985
Teach Me		F/A Lisa Be, Bitou Rivage, Leonard Silver: VIDCO, 1985
Teacher's Pet		P/D Anthony Spinelli F/A Raven, John Leslie, Justine, Rick Savage: AVC, 1985
Teasers		P/D John Stag, Bruce Seven F/A Ginger Lynn, Lynn Ray
Tease Me		F/A Krista Barrington, Misty Regan, Gina Rae, Nicole West, Billy Dee, Rick Savage: Wet Video, 1985
Teenage Beauties		F/A Mark Stevens, Dana Mann, Ruth Vermouth: Class-X-Video
Teenage Bikers		Silhouette Video
Teenage Birthday Ball		Silhouette Video, Cinnabar Distributors
Teenage Bondage Sluts		Janus
Teenage Coeds		F/A Carri Stephens, Barbara Jason: PVX

Teenage Cousins		F/A Dana Andes, Jack Webb, Martha Mitchell: Blue Video
Teenage Cycle Sluts		
Teenage Deviate		F/A Annie Sprinkles: Video-X-Pix
Teenage Fantasies #2		F/A Renee Bond: Home Entertainment, VCX, X-Tra Vision, Arrow
Teenage Games		P/D Hal Freeman
		F/A Kristara Barrington, Steve Taylor, Nicole, Jessyca Wylde: Hollywood Video, 1985
Teenage Goddess		Video Home Entertainment, 1983
Teenage Hustler		F/A Beth Anna, Clea Carson, Roger Caine, Peter Andrews: VCA
Teenage Innocence		
Teenage Love Goddess		World Wide Video
Teenage Lovers		F/A Renee Bond: VBM
Teenage Massage Parlor		Wonderful World
Teenage Masseuse		F/A Annie Sprinkles, Susan Sparkle, Marcy Davis: Blue Video
Teenage Milkmaid	R	International Home Video
Teenage Pajama Party		P/D Jim Clark
		F/A C. J. Laing, Terry Hall, Sharon Mitchell: Wonderful World, Visual Entertainment
Teenage Party People		P/D J/J Films
		F/A Bev Jackson, Elie Sheer, Nancy Lee, Patty Singer
Teenage Playmates		F/A Mike Ranger, Jamie Gillis, Judy Carr, Bonnie Holiday: Love TV
Teenage Pony Girls		P/D Harry Chow, Mary Thomas
		F/A Maureen Kelly, Diane Baxter, Susan Critz, Mary Pearson, Bonnie Mulford: Wonderful World
Teenage Prostitutes		P/D Carlo Lizaani
Teenage Runaway		F/A Howard North, Linda Doyle, Jean Carr, Mary Tyler: Blue Video
Teenage Runaways (shot on Video)		F/A Wade Nichols
Teenage Sex Maid		
Teenage Sorority Girls		X-Tra Vison
Teenage Stepmother		Video-X-Home Library
Teenage Surfer Girls		F/A Melba May, Vicky Lynn: Select/Essex
Teenage Throat		F/A Renee Bond: 1975
Teenage Trouble		
Teenage Twins		P/D Carter Stevens: Wonderful World
Teenage Twins		F/A Brooke and Taylor Young
Teen Ten		1982
Telefantasy		P/D Bob Chinn
		F/A John Leslie, Mimi Morgan, Desiree Cousteau: Arrow
Telesex		Video City
Tell The Doc		Wonderful World
Temptation: Story of a Lustful Bride		Now Showing, 1983
The Temptress		F/A Ron Jeremy, Destiny Duval, Tigr, Cheri Champagne
Tenderloins		F/A Serena, Linda Wong, Anna Karina: VCX

Tender Trap		P/D Mr. Kezar
		F/A John Seeman, Eileen Welles, Jessica Moore: International Home Video
Ten Little Maidens		F/A Harry Reems, Ginger Lynn, Lisa de Leeuw, Eric Edwards, Jamie Gillis: Excalibur, 1985
Teresa, the Woman Who Loves Men		F/A Teresa Oklowski: Caballero, 1985
Terms of Desire		P/D Paul Lyons
		F/A Paul Thomas, Jessica Longe, Erica Boyer, Heather Wayne: Tri-Vid, Home Video, 1985
Teri Gets Her Wish/Memories of Amanda		F/A Jeanne Martel, Marcia Moreno: Tri-Vid, 1985
Terri's Lesson in Bondage		Bizarre
Terri's Revenge		F/A Terri Hall: Blue Video
Thank You for Cummin'		L.A. Video, 1985
That Lucky Stiff		P/D Robert Sumner, Chuck Vincent
		F/A Randi West, Kandi Barbour, and others: Quality, 1979
That's My Daughter	R	F/A Lisa de Leeuw, John Leslie, Sharon Mitchell, Eric Edwards: 1982
Then Came Ecstasy		Channel X Video
Then Came Eve		
Therapist		F/A Connie Beney, Danielle, Amber Rose: Gourmet (shot directly on videotape)
Therese and Isabelle	R	
They Came Together		
They Came to Play		Boccaccio 100
They Deliver		Dreamland Video, 1985
They Shall Overcome		F/A Linda Lovemore, Jennifer Jordan: Video Station
Thigh High		F/A Bobby Jackson: 1983
This Lady Is a Tramp		P/D Chuck Vincent
		F/A Samantha Fox, Gloria Leonard, Veri Knotty, Richard Bola: Cal Vista
Those Young Girls		P/D Miles Kidder
		F/A Ginger Lynn, Traci Lords: Paradise Visuals, 1984
Three Beauties and a Maid		F/A Danica Rhae, Jennifer West, Maria Tortuga, Eleyna: Lipstick Video/VTE
Three Came Running		F/A John Holmes, Aleen May, Cheryl Brit: Adult Video
Three Cheers For B.J.U.		VCX
Three-Day Pass		
Three for Love		Four-Play
Three Little Pennies		Boccaccio 100
Three Phases of Eve		Boccaccio 100
Three Shades of Flesh		F/A John Leslie, Helen Carrol, Leslie Ash: Innovative Video
Three the Hard Way		VIP
Thrilling and Drilling		P/D Stan Cory
		F/A Mark Stevens, Lynn Stevens: Blue Video, 1974
Thrill Street Blues		P/D Jerome Tanner
		F/A Erica Boyer, Ron Jeremy, Stacey Donovan: Western Visuals, 1985

Thunder Track	P/D Curt McDowell: Video Drome, 1985
Thunder Thighs	F/A Molly McGuire, Karen Posey: TGA, 1984
Tickled Pink	P/D Robert Michaels, Jay Paul
	F/A Taija Rae, Eric Edwards, Rhonda Jo Petty, Sharon Kaive
A Tidal Wave Is Coming	VIP
Tied, Trained, Transformed	F/A Jennifer Jordan, Candy Matthews, Mibi Nest, Jerry Kellar: Bizarre
Tiffany Jones	R
Tight and Tender	F/A Gina Carrera, Sheri St. Clair: Caballero, 1985
Tight Delight	Video-X-Pix, 1985
Till Marriage Do Us Part	F/A Laura Antonelli
Time After Time	
Tina Makes a Deal	F/A John Ashton, Mary Stuart: Boccaccio 100
Tobacco Roady	R
Today, Tomorrow and Yesterday	F/A Lisa Be, Leondra Silver, Bijou Ravage: Gold Stripe, 1984
Tokyo Miserable	Orchids International, 1985
To Man From Woman	F/A Loni Sanders, Mai Ling, John Leslie: Blue Video
The Tongue	F/A Brigit Maier, Tastee Freeze, Al Poe: 4-Play Video, 1984
Tongue in Cheek	
Tongues	P/D Niva Buschell
	F/A Al Poe, Bigit Maier: Boccaccio 100, 1975
Tonight I Love You	F/A Lix Renay: HIFCOA
Tonight We Love	1983
Ton of Action	Video Show time
Too Hot to Handle	F/A Kim Garling, Nell Gale, Ella Butler, Archie Flynn: Blue Video
Too Hot to Touch	Cal Vista, 1985
Too Young to Care	F/A Leslie Bovee, Bobby Astyr, Vanessa Del Rio: Boccaccio 100
Too Young to Know	F/A Bunny Bleu, Gina Valentino: Coast to Coast Video, 1984
Top Secret	California Star, 1985
Tortured Women	F/A Helen Haynes, Veri Knotty, Beth Anne, Nadine Russell: Video-X-Home Library, 1979
Totally Awesome	L.A. Video, 1985
The Touch	F/A John Holmes, Lincoln Regan, Jean French, Louise Barnet: Adult Video
A Touch of Blue	P/D William Dancer, Joanna Williams
A Touch of Desire	VCR, 1983
A Touch of Genie	P/D Jason Russell
	F/A Harry Reems, Mark Stevens, Karen Craig, Lynn Stevens: 1974
Touch of Love	Video Home Entertainment
Touch of Mischief	Tri-Vid Home Video
A Touch of Sex	
Tough Cookie	F/A John C. Holmes: Western Visuals, 1985

Tourist Trap		Creative Video/Caballero
Tower of Love		P/D George Drazich
		F/A Jean Pascal, Kitty Lombard: Gourmet, Eros, (shot directly on videotape)
The Toy		
The Toy Box	R	P/D Harry Novak
		F/A Evan Steel, Ann Myers, Deborah Osborne, Lisa Goodman
The Toy Woman		P/D Yoshiaki Yuki, Yoshihisa Nakagawa, Masaru Knouma
		F/A Maiko Kazama, Taksuaki Azuma, Nobutaka Matsutomi, Rumi Tama, Asami Ogawa, Rika Takher (soft X)
Traci Lords		P/D Milton Ingley
		F/A Traci Lords, Paul Thomas, Cindy Lynn, Breezy, Herschel Savage: Cinema Tech, 1984
Traci in Heaven		P/D Jerome Tanner
		F/A Traci Lords, Gina Valentina, Jacqueline Lorians: Western Visuals, 1984
Trading Partners		P/D Peter Vanderbilt
		F/A Deva, Arnaud, Martina Mike, Eric Boyer, Billie Dee: AB Video, PVX
Trading Places		P/D Ned Morehead, Jerry Ross
		F/A Gina Carrera, Herschel Savage, Joey Silvera: Dreamland Video, 1985
The Training		P/D Bruce Kennedy
		F/A Cindee Summers, Cynthia Brooke, Sharar Desiree: Bizarre
Training Academy		L.A. Video, 1985 (half-hour tape)
The Training of Julia		Bizarre Tri-Star (half-hour tape)
The Tramp		P/D Chuck Vincent
		F/A Samantha Fox, Gloria Leonard, Veri Knotty, Richard Bolla: Cal Vista
Transsexual Secretary		F/A Pasha, Jean Langston, Lynn Anne Wilson, Morgan Monroe: Bizarre
The Trap		California Star, 1985
Trash	R	P/D Andy Warhol, Paul Morrissey
		F/A Joe D'Allessandro, Holly Woodlawn, Jane Forth: 1970
Trauma		International Home Video
Travelin'		Video City
Travels of June		Video-X-Home Library
Treasure Chest		F/A Ron Jeremy, Christy Canyon, Heather Wayne: Gourmet, 1985
Triangle of Love		F/A Tom Allen, Trish Cole: Astro
Triangle of Lust		F/A Cody Nicole, K. C. Valentin, Crystal Dawn: VCR, 1983
Trick or Treat		Essex, 1985
Trilogy of the Bizarre		Caballero 1983
Triple Cross		Bizarre
Triple Play		F/A Dorothy LeMay, Kathy Robertson, Ron Jeremy, John Seeman, Vicky Edwards, Jane Allison, Kimberly Warner
Triple Play		F/A Lisa Manning, Rick Lieter, Kimberly

Rule, John Winston, Sara Connelly, Julie Richardson: Video Home Entertainment

Triple Sex Play — Orchids International, 1985

Tripleys — F/A Crystal Breeze, Herschel Savage, Raven, Bonnie Holiday, Michael Morrison: Cinema Tech, 1985

The Trouble with Young Stuff — P/D Odus Hamlin
F/A Richard Bolla, Roger Caine, Christine Williams, Marlene Willoughby: Wonderful World, Blue Video

Truck Stop Women — R | F/A Claudia Jennings

True Confessions & Other Erotic Films — P/D Curt McDowell

The True Way — Silhouette Video

Try It, You'll Like It

Try My Wife

Tuesday's Lover — F/A Kimberly Carson, Herschel Savage: Tri-Vid Home Video

Turkish Delight — P/D Paul Verhoeven
F/A Monique Van de Ven, Rutger Hauer, Tony Hurdemann: 1973 Home Entertainment

Turnabout

Turn Me Around

Turn on Blondie — F/A Danielle: Collector's Video

Tutorial Lessons — Orchids International, 1985

Twelve Years After — P/D Gerard Damiano

2069—A Space Odyssey — Target

Twice a Virgin — F/A Shannon: JVP Video

Twice Is Not Enough — International Home Video

Twilight Cowboy — Boccaccio 100

Twilight Pink — F/A Veronica Hart, Kandi Barbour, Tiffany Clark, Annie Sprinkles: Arrow, 1980

Twilight Zone — F/A Traci Lords, Cindee Summers: Caballero, 1985

Two Days in a Hot Place — MSI Video

Two Hours on Sunday — Video City

Two Lives of Jennifer — F/A Gary Austin, Roseanne Farrow: Video-X-Home Library, 1979

Two Senoritas — F/A Jamie Gillis, Mark Stevens, Sue Lynn, D. J. Lang: Video City, Video-X-Home Library

Two Sisters — P/D Peter Balakoff
F/A Gene Lee, Nancy Hoffman: Select/Essex, 1979

Two Timer — F/A Sue McBain, Eric Edwards, Sharon Mitchell: Blue Video

Two Way Mirror — Caballero, 1985

Tycoon

Tycoon's Daughter — F/A Mark Stevens, Andrea True: Video-X-Home Library

Udderly Fantastic — Excalibur Series, TGA, 1983

Ugly George — R | P/D Ugly George: Kenyon Video, 1982

Ugly George Tape-of-the-Month Club — 1985

Ultimate Perversion — Boccaccio 100

The Ultimate Pleasure — P/D Bruce Van Buren, Merino Fortes

Van Nuys Boulevard	R	
Varsity Plaything	R	F/A Sharon Hall, Eve Landers: Home Entertainment
Veil of Lust		F/A Marie Forsa: Blue Video
Velvet High		P/D Carter Stevens
		F/A Misty Middleton, Christy Ford, Merle Michaels: PVX
Velvet Touch of the Velvet Tongue		P/D Fadik Gaspar, Felix Lomax
		F/A Guita Kobar, Maggie Jones, Anik Larie, Garee Tigan, Greg Allen: International Home Video
Venture into the Bizarre		P/D William Box, Harry Gordon
		F/A Marlene Willoughby, Charlotte McNeal: Video-X-Home Library
Venus Delights		Select Video Productions
Vera		Silhouette Video
Veronica's Kiss		P/D Bruce Wilson
		F/A Mark Stevens, Joanne Barker, Hannah: Video City, 1979
A Very Small Case of Rape		
Vessel Virgins		Western Visuals
Victorian Bondage		Janus Video
Victorian Old-Time Stag		Silhouette, Ja-Rae
Victoria's Secret Desires		S&L Video/VCX
Video Girls		P/D Paul Harmon
		F/A Rita Ricardo, Lili Marlene, Candy Wong, Joy Cummings, Mai Lin: Lipstick Video, 1984
A Video Guide to Sexual Positions		Ambassador Video
Video Kix		Gold Star, 1983 (magazine-style tape)
Video Tramp		P/D Jack Genero
		F/A Christy Canyon, Jessyca Wylde, Tom Byron, Linda Daniel: AVC, 1985
Video Vixens: Blowing Your Mind		P/D Ron Jeremy
A View to a Thrill		Playtime Video, 1985
Violated		F/A Dorothy Brekeu, Anne Small: PVX
Violation of the Bitch		P/D Jose Ramon Larrez
		F/A Monserrat Larrez, Patricia Granada Orchids International, 1984
Virgin		F/A Jennifer Welles: TVX
Virgin and the Lover		P/D Roger Colt, Zebedy Colt
Virgin Dreams		F/A Jean Jennings, Gloria Leonard, Terri Hall, Wade Nichols, Susan McBain, Zebedy Colt: Wonderful World, Visual Entertainment
Virgin Forest		F/A Don Watson, Carol Welk, Jill Felton: Adult Video, Astro
Virgin Hostage		Boccaccio 100
Virgin Rape		Video Show time
Virgins from Outer Space		F/A Paul Thomas, Jerry Butler, Herschel Savage, Kimberly Carson, Sharon Mitchell: 1984
Viscious Virgin		Boccaccio 100
Visions of Lust		Gourmet, 1983
Visual Aids		Boccaccio 100

Vixanna's Revenge	F/A Lana Burover, Harry Reems, Jerry Butler, Ali Moore, Jessica Longe, Ron Jeremy: Paradise Visuals
Vixens	F/A Sally Jordan, Polly Vale: Adult Video
Vixens in Heat	P/D Jonathan Burroughs
	F/A Crystal Breeze, Amber Lynn, John Johnson, Renee Tiffany: Vista Video, 1984
Vixens of Kung Fu	VCA, 1985
Voluptuous Predators	P/D Antonia De Rosa
	F/A Suzanne McBain, Paula Stuart, Steve Tucker, Peter Andrews: Video-X-Home Library
Voluptuous Vera	Home Entertainment, 1976
Voluptuous Vixens '76	VIDCO, 1985
Vote Pink	P/D Chuck Vincent: VCA, 1985
The Voyeur	Boccaccio 100
Voyeurism	Ambassador
Vulger, Volga, Vulva	Boccaccio 100
Waiting for Roxanne	
Wanda R	International Home Video
Wanted, Al Parker Is	International Home Video
The Wanton Nymph	Class-X-Video
Ward Sex	
Watch My Lips	F/A Cara Lott, Shaun Michele, Steve Drake: AAH Video, 1985
Waterfront Honey	F/A Beverly Sirens, Wanda LaPar, Debbie Brooks: X-Tra Vision
Watermelon Babies	VCR
Water People	Video Station
Way Down Deep	Astro, C.D.I. Home Video
Ways of Women	International Home Video
Weekend Girls	World Wide Video
Weekend Lovers	F/A Don Watson, Jill Felton, Carol Welk: Adult Video
Weekend Roulette	Home Entertainment, VCX
Welcome, Home Baby	
Welcome, Strangers	
Welcome to Fantasy Land	F/A Harry Reems, Susan Hart: L.A. Video, 1984
Welcome Wagon	VCX
Wet	VIDCO, 1985
Wet Dreams	F/A Suzy Spazz, Bo Bridget, Diana Straub, Lee Carol, Drea, Mike Ranger: Wonderful World
Wet Lips	Video City
Wet Raindrops	
Wet Rocks	F/A Bree Anthony, Jamie Gillis, Mary Madigan: Blue Video
Wet Shots	VCR, 1983
The Wetter the Better	F/A Andrea True, Jennifer Jordan: Video Station
Wet, Wild and Wooly	Silhouette Video
Wet Wilderness	VCX
Wham Bam	Visions of Fantasy

Wham Bam, Thank You, Spaceman — F/A Jay Rasumny, Diane Thorne: Astro, VBM, PVX

What Are Friends For? — F/A Tamara Longley, Jerry Butler, Sheri St. Clair, Buck Adams: Masterpiece, 1985

What Bottoms Are For — California Star Prod., 1985

Whatever Gets You Through the Night — 1984

What Happened in Bunny's Office — F/A Eric Edwards, Cassandra Leigh, Honey Wilder, Sharon Kane, Joey Civera, Bob Astyr: VCA

What it Was — Boccaccio 100

What Would Your Mother Say — F/A Bill Margold, Tiffany Clark, Maria Tortuga, Jennifer Wren, Drea, Arcadia Lake: Harmony Vision

What's a Nice Girl Like You . . . — F/A Annie Young, Eve St. John: 1981 (documentary on sex shows on San Francisco's North Beach)

What's Behind Love — F/A Alicia Novel, Marlene Willoughby: 1979

What's My Punishment? — F/A Tantala Nava, Missy Morgan, Roy Phipps: Bizarre

When a Lady Dances — 4-Play

When Sex Was Dirty — F/A Georgina Spelvin, John Leslie, Vanessa Del Rio, Chelsea Manchester, Richard Bolla, Ron Jeremy, Joey Silvera

When She Was Bad — MSI Video

Where Joey Lives — F/A Lee Carol, Maria Fause, Tina Marie, Linda Shaw, Janey Robbins, Cody Nicole, Raven, Lauri Smith, Erica Boyer

Where the Girls Are — P/D Mark Curtis

Where the Girls Are — F/A Tina Marie, Cody Nicole, Laurie Smith, Janey Robbins, Cara Lott, Raven St. James: 1984

Whip Me Please — California Tri-Star, 1985

Whipped into Shape — C.P.L.C., 1984

Whistle Blowers — F/A Jason Russell, Kim Pope, Tina Russell

White Hot — P/D Carter Stevens

F/A Charlie Latour, Baby Doe, Michael D'Atrore, George Payne, Michael Gaunt, Peter Johns, Roxanne Reynolds, Crystal Cox, Toni Thomas: Video-X-Pix, 1985

White Slaver — Adult Video

Who Killed Cock Robin? — Silhouette Video

Whore of the Worlds — F/A Jessica Longe, Ali Moore, Lana Burner, Jerry Butler: Paradise Visuals, 1985

Whose Child Am I? — P/D Gerard Damiano

Whose Fantasy Is This Anyway? — F/A Sharon Kane, Honey Wilder, Annette Heinz, Tanya Lawson, and others: AVC

P/D Lewis Brothers

Wicked Ways — F/A Jesie St. James, Joanna Storm, Janey Robbins, Shelley Rey, Tigr: Caballero

P/D Mike Carpenter

Wicked Whispers — F/A Lana Burner, Nicole West: VIDCO, 1985

The Widespread Scandals of Lydia Lace	P/D Henri Pachard, Michael Dejoy F/A Lee Carroll, Joanna Storm, Susan Nero, Sharon Kane, R. Bolla: Caballero, 1983
The Widow	
Wife Next Door	Orchids International, 1985
Wilbur and the Baby Factory R	P/D Harry Novak, Alex Combie F/A Tom Shea, Keith McConnel, Larisa Sherbert, Stuart Lancaster: IHV
Wild Cat Fantasy Club	Western Visual (30-minute tape)
Wildcats of St. Trinian	P/D Frank Launder, Sydney Gilliat F/A Joe Melia, Shelia Hancock: 1979
Wild Cherry	P/D Man Wah F/A Tsang Kong, Lo Wok Kong: Orchids International, 1983
Wild Toga Party	F/A Gabrielle, Mindy Ray, Sheri St. Clair, Summer Rose: VIDCO, 1985
Wings of Passion	P/D Hal Freeman F/A Tom Byron, Susan Hart, M. Goldberg: Hollywood Video
Winnebango	VCX
The Winning Stroke	F/A John Holmes, Ric Lutz, Cindee Summers: King of Video, Home Entertainment, 1975
Winter of 1849	F/A Andrea True, Tony Rittle, Ross Benton, Renee St. Clair: Blue Video
Wish You Were Here (Red Light Series)	F/A Rhonda Jo Petty, Taija Rae, Sharon: Video-X-Pix, 1984
Witchcraft	Adult Video
With Love, Annette	F/A Annette Haven: Caballero, 1985
Without Shame	VCA
Woman in Love	P/D Kemal Korolu F/A Richard Bolla, Phil Tobus, Samantha Fox, Jack Teague, Laurien Dominique, Vanessa Del Rio: Kemal Video
Woman in Torment	Home Entertainment
Woman of the Night	F/A Arlene Ross, Maggie Smith: Mitchell Brothers
A Woman's Dream	P/D A. Stootesbury F/A Jamie Gillis, Randy West, Lysa Thatcher, Suzannah French, Mai Lin: 1980
Woman's Work Is Never Done	Boccaccio 100
Women at Play	F/A Sharon Kane, Tigr, Danielle, Cara Lott, Sharon Mitchell, Jerry Butler, George Payne: Essex, 1984
Women in Heat	VCA
Women in Love	F/A Lisa de Leeuw: 4-Play
Women in Uniform	F/A Mark Stevens: Video-X-Home Library
Women's Desires	Bizarre
Women's Fantasies	F/A K. C. Valentine, Danielle, Annie Owen: Gourmet (shot directly on videotape)
Women's Secret Desires	Lipstick Video, VTE, 1983
Women × 4	F/A Tina Marie and others: Lipstick Video
Women Who Love Women	F/A Rhonda Jo Petty, Monique Perry, K. C. Valentine: Gourmet

Women Who Seduce Men
F/A Cara Lott, Shanna Evans, Ron Jeremy: Gourmet Video, 1982

Wonderful World of Women
Working Girl
Working Girls
Boccaccio 100
P/D Holley McCall, Samantha Fox, Herschel Savage: Blue Marquee Video, 1984

Work Load
Boccaccio 100

The World According to Ginger
F/A Ginger Lynn: Vivid Video, 1985

World of Erotica
Essex, 1983

World of Henry Paris
Essex, 1985

Worlds of Love

W.R.: Mysteries of the Organism
P/D Dusan Makavejev
F/A Milena Dravic Jagoda Kaloper, Ivica Vidovic: 1971

Wrap-A-Round
T.G.H., 1985

Wrecked 'Em
P/D Mark Roberts
F/A Mikki Wright, Barbie Dahl, Tasha Voux, Scarley Scharleau, K. Y. Lee: Coast to Coast Video, 1985

Wrestling-Boxing Tapes
California Supreme-Bellstone, 1983 (all tapes one hour or more)

   Video Wrestling #1
   Girls Wrestling #2
   Girls Boxing #3
   Mixed Matched Classics #4
   Cat Fight Classic #5
   Perilous #6
   TV Boxing Show #7
   Bellstone's Most Erotic #8

Wrestling Cheerleaders

Wrestling Classes Volumes 1–3
F/A Serena, Brooke West, Pussy Cat Jones: TAO, 1984

Wrestling Sluts Volumes 1–8
Video Vortex

Wrestling Women Volumes 1–5
Bizarre

The X-Factor
P/D Hal Freeman
F/A Eric Edwards, Danica Ritae, Pam Anderson, Paul Thomas, Kimberly Carson: Hollywood Video, 1983

X-Rated Highlights
F/A Many top stars: Movietime

X-Rated Love
Xana, 1983

X-Rated Movie Bloopers
F/A Candy Samples: 4-Play

Xrco Awards Show
AVC, 1985

The X Team
P/D Drea
F/A Randy West, Herschel Savage, Melanie Scott

Y'All Come
F/A Betty Lou, Ann Carter, Jack Hays, Richard Long: Adult Video, Home Entertainment

Yamahamma Mamas
Excalibur Series, TGA, 1983

Yankee Seduction
P/D Joe Tanner
F/A Kristara Barrington, Ron Jeremy, Jack Baker, Janey Robbins: Western Visuals, 1984

Yank My Doodle, It's a Dandy
P/D Richard Aldrich: AVC, 1985

Yellow Fever
Ambassador Video

Yellow House of Pinnasberg
R | Home Entertainment

Yes, My Lady	P/D F. J. Lincoln F/A Sharon Kane, Michael Bruce, Tiffany Clark, China Wong
You Make Me Wet	F/A Christy Canyon, Bunny Bleu, Ron Jeremy, Pam Jennings, Janey Robbins: VIDCO, 1985
Young and Abused	Astro
Young and Innocent	P/D J. A. Martine, Beau Janson F/A Tiffany Clark, Brooke Bennet, Ron Jeremy: VCX
Young and Naughty	P/D Hal Freeman F/A Nikki Charm, Renee Summer: Hollywood Video, 1984
Young and the Foolish	International Home Video
The Young and the Restless II	P/D Robert McCallum F/A Traci Lords, Christy Canyon: Vista Video, 1985
Young and Wet	Home Entertainment
The Younger the Better	Image Video
Young Girl	
Young Lady Chatterly	P/D Alan Roberts F/A Harlee McBride: Select-A-Tape
Young Love	VCX, VIP
Young Nymphs	P/D George Steel, Ralph Lander F/A Richard Fellow, Kim Pope, Cindy West: 1973
The Young Seducers	P/D Irwin Dietrich, Michael Thomas F/A Evelyn Traeger, Ingrid Steeger: Blue Video
The Young Students	P/D P. C. Kake F/A Suzie Muffet, Vickie Lindsey, Sandy Stram, Marsha Wolf, David Reisen, Philip Abbot: Wonderful World
Young Working Stiffs	
Your Neighborhood Doctor	Cal Vista
Youthful Lust	
Yummy Nymphs	Excalibur Series, TGA, 1983
Yum Yum Girls R	
Ze Bawdy Bed R	P/D Joseph Green: Video Station
Zodiaction	Boccaccio 100
Zolita	F/A John Holmes: Adult Video

Index